A NEW CENTURY
ENGLISH-CHINESE COMPUTER DICTIONARY
(SECOND EDITION)

新世纪
英汉计算机词典
（第二版）

《新世纪英汉计算机词典》编委会　编

电子工业出版社
Publishing House of Electronics Industry
北京·BEIJING

内 容 简 介

《新世纪英汉计算机词典》(第二版)在第一版的基础之上,删除了多条过时的词汇,新增了一千多条最新词汇,并按照国家自然科学技术名词审定委员会推荐的有关标准给出了准确的中文译名。本词典包括计算机软件、硬件、网络、多媒体、人工智能、过程控制、计算机科学理论等领域的内容,也包括少量与计算机专业密切相关学科的常用术语。考虑到我国计算机使用者主要集中在个人计算机领域,在选择术语时,特别侧重收集当前主流软、硬件方面的内容,并着力于反映计算机与信息处理技术的最新发展。

本词典覆盖面广、词汇量大、编选科学、实用性强,是计算机专业工作者及翻译人员,大专院校师生,各行业计算机用户及业余爱好者必备的工具书。

图书在版编目(CIP)数据

新世纪英汉计算机词典/新世纪英汉计算机词典编委会编.2版.
-北京:电子工业出版社,2001.6
ISBN 7-5053-6762-5

Ⅰ.新… Ⅱ.英… Ⅲ.电子计算机-词典-英、汉 Ⅳ.TP3-61
中国版本图书馆 CIP 数据核字(2001)第 035376 号

书　　　名:	新世纪英汉计算机词典(第二版)
编　著　者:	《新世纪英汉计算机词典》编委会
责任编辑:	寇国华　鄂卫华
印　刷　者:	北京天竺颖华印刷厂
出版发行:	电子工业出版社出版
	北京市海淀区万寿路173信箱　邮编100036
	URL:http://www.phei.com.cn
开　　　本:	787×1092　1/32　印张:30.5　字数:2030千字
版　　　次:	2001年6月第2版　2001年6月第1次印刷
印　　　数:	10000
书　　　号:	ISBN 7-5053-6762-5/TP・3792
定　　　价:	48.00元

凡购买电子工业出版社的图书,如有缺页、倒页、脱页者,请向购买书店调换。
若书店售缺,请与本社发行部联系调换。电话68279077

目　　录

第二版前言
出版前言
编委会名单
序
前言
使用说明
词汇正文 ································· (1～963)
A ···································· (1)
B ···································· (53)
C ···································· (83)
D ···································· (164)
E ···································· (230)
F ···································· (265)
G ···································· (305)
H ···································· (322)
I ···································· (351)
J ···································· (404)
K ···································· (410)
L ···································· (418)
M ···································· (448)
N ···································· (512)
O ···································· (550)

P	(576)
Q	(668)
R	(674)
S	(716)
T	(854)
U	(896)
V	(914)
W	(938)
X	(953)
Y	(959)
Z	(960)

第二版前言

《新世纪英汉计算机词典》出版至今已经一年有余,在这段时间里,计算机技术又有了突飞猛进的发展,一些词汇逐渐被淘汰,一些新词汇涌现出来,为了跟踪计算机词汇的变化,为读者奉献更有实用价值的词典,我们推出了《新世纪英汉计算机词典》的第二版。这一版本的最大变化在于:

1. 经反复筛选,增加了近一千多条新词汇。
2. 经认真审查,删除了二百多条旧词汇。

在此基础上,精心调整了全书的版式。

编撰出版词典是一项极为艰苦的工作,它要求所有参与者必须具备高度的责任心,不辞辛苦的精神和严谨细致的工作作风,想到这本词典为读者带来的帮助,我们所做的一切都是值得的。我们将继续努力,使这本词典越编越好,我们也仍然希望听到读者的意见和建议。

主编　宋文强

2001 年 4 月

出 版 前 言

计算机科学技术和网络技术的迅猛发展,导致相关的英文新词汇、新缩略语的大量涌现。为使广大读者有一本得心应手的工具书,本社组织计算机专家学者编撰了《新世纪英汉计算机词典》。

本词典选编的宗旨是:新、实、准、全。即,所收词汇是1999年底以前正在流行的新词汇,侧重个人计算机领域的主流软硬件及网络方面的词汇,中文释义力求规范准确,在保持合理篇幅的前提下尽量收全。

计算机专家柳克俊教授认真细致地审校了全书,中国工程院陈太一院士特为本书作序。对他们为本词典所付出的劳动,我们深表谢意。

随着信息时代的到来,计算机科学技术必将有更快的发展,计算机新术语、新词汇还会蜂拥而至,我们将继续跟踪,不断推出更新的版本,使本词典能够继续适应读者的需要。

电子工业出版社
http://www.phei.com.cn
2000年4月

《新世纪英汉计算机词典》编委会名单

主　　编：宋文强

副 主 编：王志刚　魏绍康　郭志忠　邓子坚
　　　　　杜振民　孙中臣

编　　委：梁兰华　杨海波　杨　胜　陈　卫
　　　　　郭光春　李爱国　邹金凯　梅　文
　　　　　寇　锦　齐德广　许东民　杨代云
　　　　　周渝霞　王文峡　王　昆　王开发
　　　　　宋海涛　王小民　陆伯雄

主　　审：柳克俊

序

从1946年第一台庞大笨重的电子数字计算机ENIAC到今天功能强大的微型计算机,仅仅经历了半个多世纪。如今,计算机的功能越来越强,速度越来越快,而体积则越来越小。计算机科学技术的飞速发展,计算机应用的日益普及,覆盖全球的因特网的高速增长,使计算机技术已经渗透到经济建设与社会生活的各个领域。计算机技术已经成为知识经济的先导和信息时代的重要标志。

与之相伴,由于新技术的发展、新概念的提出,以及计算机网络文化的不断创新,使相关的新词汇、新术语也大量涌现。特别是在近十年间,新词汇的出现甚至达到日新月异的程度。制造、开发和使用计算机的人们在著书立说和言谈话语之间大量使用普通词典或较老的专业词典上没有的、新奇的"独创"词汇,常常使中国读者在接触英文版计算机图书、文献和资料,以及浏览网站时感到困惑。因此,他们迫切希望能有一本既新又实用的英汉计算机词典摆在案头,作为学习和工作时得心应手的工具书。

收集和整理计算机词汇是一件非常重要的事情,也是一件非常难做的事情。事实上,这种收集和整理总是跟不上发展。这样说不仅仅是因为"后果不可能超越前因",也是因为计算机技术发展太快,应用领域太广,由此导致产生的新词汇太多。

尽管如此,一些同行仍然孜孜不倦、兢兢业业,致力于为大家提供新词汇精确的释义。如果把从事创造发明的人称为"开拓者",那么也可以把总结、归纳和整理新词汇的人称为"铺路人"。他们是同业中的重要成员、专家,以编著词典体现着学识渊博,以成千上万的词典条目体现着涉猎广泛,以一丝不苟、释义规范体现着细密严谨。在"开拓者"之后,"铺路人"拓宽平整出一条条高速路。每当我们顺畅地通过时,应当像对待"开拓者"一样,对"铺路人"表示敬意。

我以为,计算机词典,贵在常新,好在实用。前者旨在能够及时地收录新词汇,后者旨在经过筛选收录有实用价值的词汇且词义准确。《新世纪英汉计算机词典》新且实用,也体现出作者和出版社的水平,谨此作序。

陈太一

中国工程院院士
全国科学技术名词审定委员会信息科技新词审定组组长
电子学名词审定委员会副主任

前　　言

在科学技术领域中,计算机是一个发展速度极快的专业。伴随着计算机软件、硬件、网络、系统集成技术的不断进步,人们用来表达新思想、新概念,描述新技术、新产品的术语也不断地涌现出来。因特网越来越广泛的应用,使一个新术语被创造出来之后,只需几分钟的时间,便可以通过因特网传遍全世界,随之就会在各种报刊杂志和书籍中出现。但当人们在阅读计算机专业文献、浏览网上信息、查看软件联机帮助信息和技术说明书的时候,常常会对那些陌生的新术语困惑不解。

我们编写这本词典,就是想尽量收集反映当代计算机领域中最新思想、最新成就、最新技术和最新产品的词汇,并对它们作出准确的解释,为广大计算机用户提供一个有效、实用的阅读工具。为了实现这个目标,我们通过各种渠道尽力拓展词汇收集的来源,包括研究收集到的专业文献,参加各种学术交流会议、技术讲座和展览会,浏览世界著名计算机与信息产业公司的网站,分析网上发布的一些计算机专业词典;我们还登门访问了许多著名外国公司设在中国的分公司、办事处或联络点,获得他们提供的大量技术资料,试用了数百种系统软件和应用软件。从这些文献、网上信息和技术资料中,我们收集了 1999 年底以前正在流行的大量的新词汇。

在计算机诞生之后的几十年间,与计算机专业有关的词汇(包括词组)层出不穷,数不胜数,其中有许多词汇已成为历史陈迹,现在已基本无用了。为此,我们在筛选、整理本词典的词汇时,本着"厚今薄古、实用新颖"的原则,把重点放在计算机用户可能涉及的内容上,并使词汇条目的总数控制在 72000 条左右,以求保持合理的整书篇幅。对于那些反映新技术、新产品的词汇,以当前的主流产品和系统结构为主;对于已约定俗成、广泛习用的缩略语(如 TCP/IP),则仅在该缩略语的排序位置上以括号注释形式给出它

的英文全称,其余位置上皆以缩略语形式出现;对于由多个单词组成的组合词,如果其译名可以由同一页面上相邻的组合词推知,便予以省略。

大部分新生的计算机术语源自使用英语的人群,为它们赋予准确、恰当的中文译名是颇费功夫的,有些术语至今还没有一个为大家都接受的中文译名。本书中的大部分词汇是按照国家自然科学技术名词审定委员会推荐的标准名称赋予中文译名的。对于那些最近出现,尚未见标准名称公布的术语则按编者的理解,在多方面征求专家意见的基础上确定。还有一些表示专有产品或体系结构的名词,保留原名,不予译出。

为了使本词典的内容尽可能准确,尽量减少文字录入错误,编者利用专门的软件对全书的英文词汇进行了拼写检查。

编者希望这本词典能对广大读者有所帮助,但因水平和阅历有限,舛误难免,敬请读者不吝指正,以便再版时予以改进。

《新世纪英汉计算机词典》编委会
2000 年 1 月

使用说明

一、编辑格式

1. 普通词条由三部分组成：英文词汇、英文缩略语（选项）和中文译名，各部分之间用空格分开。
2. 缩略语词条由三部分组成：英文缩略语、英文词汇全称名和中文译名，各部分之间用空格分开。
3. 词条中出现的英文词汇和缩略语用加粗的 Times New Roman 字体编排，中文译名用宋体编排。
4. 普通词条中作为选项的英文缩略语，以及缩略语词条中的英文词汇全称名用括号括起，并且使用常规的 Times New Roman 正体编排。
5. 若一个英文词汇对应着多个中文译名，则将意义相近、可互相代换使用的不同译名用逗号分开；将意义相差较远、不可互相代换的不同译名用分号分开。
6. 正文中 (或⑬)右面的文字为其上（或下）一行文字的延续。

二、排序规则

1. 所有词条均按英文字母顺序排列，不区分大小写。若组成一个词汇的字母完全相同，且包含不同的大小写字母时，则将含有大写字母的词汇排在前面。
2. 组合词中各单词之间的空格、连线、斜杠等符号在排序时均视为空格。
3. 为了便于读者查找，并且考虑到许多英文缩略语已逐渐成为常规词汇的现实（如 spool），本书中将缩略语词汇与其他词汇统一排序。

三、几种特殊情况的说明

1. 为了说明缩略语的构成,对应的英文词汇全称名中各单词第一个字母的大小写与构成缩略语的字母大小写相一致。
2. 对于数字及希腊字母开头的词汇,在排序时忽略这些数字及希腊字母,而按其后的英文字母排序。若有多个词汇在相同英文单词之前或之后出现数字,则按其阿拉伯数字值的大小排序。
3. 中文译名之前,在圆括号之内,用常规字体编排的部分,通常表示该术语的应用环境,如(Unix)。
4. 中文译名之后,在圆括号之内,用常规字体编排的部分,通常表示该术语为某个团体的专有名词或首创者,如(IBM)、(微软)等;说明企业或组织机构名称的词汇,其后圆括号内的内容为所属的国家,如(美)、(日)等。
5. 中文译名中间,在圆括号之内的部分,通常表示可替换前面部分的选项,读者根据上下文不难理解。

A a

A(Ampere) 安培
A-algorithm A算法
A/B roll （多媒体影像编辑中的）A/B卷
A&C(Arithmetic and Control) 运算控制器
A/D(Analog to Digital) 模拟-数字（转换）
A/D hybrid integrated circuit 模拟-数字混合集成电路
A/D simulator 模拟-数字仿真器
A * graph-search control strategy A*图搜索控制策略
A register A寄存器
A type address constant A型地址常数
AUM language AUM语言
A/UX A/UX操作系统（苹果）
AA(Absolute Address) 绝对地址
AA(Adaptive Amplifier) 自适应放大器
AA(Automatic Answer) 自动应答
AAC(Abort Advisory Channel) 有故障的咨询信道
AAC(Automatic Amplitude Control) 自动振幅控制
AACS(Asynchronous Address Communication System) 异步选址通信系统
AAD(Active Acoustic Device) 有源声器件
AAD(Audio Analog Disc) 模拟音响光盘
AAD(Automatic Architectural Design) 自动结构设计
AAE(American Association of Engineers) 美国工程师协会
AAI(Accumulator Adjust Instruction) 累加器调整指令
AAL(ATM Adaptive Layer) 异步传输模式适配层
AAP(Associative Array Processor) 相联阵列处理机
AAP(Attached Applications Processor) 附加应用程序处理机
AAS(American Academy of Science) 美国科学院
AAS(Automatic Audio Switching) 自动音频交换（技术）
AAT(Availability Analysis Tool) 可利用率分析工具
AB(Address Bus) 地址总线
AB(Automatic Backup) 自动备份
abandon 放弃
abandoned call 放弃呼叫
ABB(Array of Building Block) 积木式阵列
abbreviate 缩写,简略
abbreviated address 短缩地址
abbreviated address calling 短缩地址呼叫
abbreviated addressing 短缩编址
abbreviated calling 缩位呼叫；简略调用
abbreviated combined relation condition 简略组合关系条件
abbreviated dialing 缩位拨号
abbreviated dialing prefix 缩位拨号前缀
abbreviated dialing services 缩位拨号业务
abbreviated form of command 命令的缩写形式
abbreviated head 缩写标题
abbreviated name 缩写名称
abbreviated notation 缩写记法
abbreviated number 缩位号码
abbreviation document 缩略文卷
ABC(Answer-Back Code) 应答码
ABC(Advanced Ballistic Computer) 高级弹道计算机
ABC coding system 初级编码系统
abduction 推断,推测,诱导
abduction mechanism 诱导机制

abductive inference 外延推理
abductive matching 推测匹配
abductive reasoning 反绎[诱导]推理
ABEND(Abnormal END) 异常终止
abend code 异常终止代码
abend dump 异常终止转储
abend exit 异常结束出口
abend recovery program 异常终止恢复程序
aberration 象差,色差;畸变
ABI(Application Binary Interface) 应用程序二进制接口
ABIC(Adaptive Bilevel Image Compression) 自适应二值图像压缩
abilityphone （主要供残疾人使用的）万能电话
ABIOS(Advanced Basic Input/Output System) 先进的基本输入/输出系统
ABL(Automatic Brightness Limiter) 自动亮度限制电路
ABM(Asynchronous Balanced Mode) 异步平衡模式
abnormal condition 异常状况
abnormal distribution 异常分布
abnormal end of task(ABEND) 任务异常结束
abnormal exit 异常出口
abnormal propagation 异常传播
abnormal recognition 异常识别
abnormal return 异常返回
abnormal return address 异常返回地
abnormal statement 异常语句 └址
abnormal termination 异常终结
abort 异常终止,放弃
abort branch 异常结束转向程序
abort cycle 异常终止周期
abort dump 异常终止计时器
abort frame 异常结束帧
abort key 终止键
abort package 异常结束包
abort remirror 终止重镜像
abort sequence 异常终止序列
abort statement 终止语句,放弃语句
abort timer 异常终止计时器
abort transaction 异常终止事务
aborted connection 终止连接
aborting task 终止任务

abortive disconnection 异常断开
abortive release 异常终止释放
About Box 告示框
ABR(Answer Bid Ratio) 应答试占比
ABR(Available Bit Rate) 有效比特率
Abramson code 艾伯拉姆逊码
abrasivity 耐磨性
abridge 缩写,节略
abridged edition 缩编本
ABS(ABSolute value) 绝对值
ABS function 绝对值函数
abscissa 横坐标   「器
absent extension advice 无人分机通报
absent subscriber service 用户缺席服
absolute accuracy 绝对准确度 └务
absolute address 绝对地址
absolute addressing 绝对寻址
absolute assembler 绝对地址汇编程
absolute branch 绝对分支   └序
absolute cell address 绝对单元地址
absolute cell reference 绝对单元引用
absolute code 绝对代码
absolute coding 绝对编码
absolute command 绝对命令
absolute constant 绝对常量
absolute coordinate 绝对坐标
absolute coordinate data 绝对坐标数
absolute data 绝对数据   └据
absolute disk read 直接地址磁盘读出
absolute disk write 直接地址磁盘写
absolute error 绝对误差   └入
absolute expression 绝对表达式
absolute format 绝对格式
absolute indexed mode 绝对索引模式
absolute instruction 绝对指令
absolute language 绝对语言
absolute liveness 绝对活动性
absolute loader(AL) 绝对地址加载程
absolute location 绝对定位   └序
absolute maximum rating 绝对最大额定值
absolute module 绝对模块
absolute moniker 绝对别名
absolute naming 绝对命名法   「序
absolute object program 绝对目标程
absolute operation code 绝对操作码
absolute operator 绝对操作数

absolute order 绝对指令
absolute path name 绝对路径名
absolute plotter control 绝对绘图仪控制
absolute pointing device 绝对定位设备
absolute priority 绝对优先级
absolute program 绝对程序
absolute program loader 绝对程序加载程序
absolute programming 绝对程序设计
absolute reference 绝对引用
absolute resolution 绝对分辨率
absolute section 绝对段
absolute sector 绝对扇区
absolute segment 绝对程序段
absolute shared region 绝对共享区域
absolute signal delay 绝对信号延时
absolute stability 绝对稳定性
absolute term 绝对项
absolute time 绝对时间
absolute value(AV) 绝对值
absolute value computer 绝对值[全值]计算机
absolute-value device 绝对值设备
absolute-value sign 绝对值符号
absolute value transducer 绝对值转换器
absolute vector 绝对向量,绝对矢量
absolute virtual address 绝对虚地址
absolute zero 绝对零度
absolute zero point 绝对零点
absolutely approximate algorithm 绝对近似算法
absorb loss 吸收损耗
absorbency 吸墨性
absorptance 吸收比,吸收率
absorption 吸收
absorption circuit 吸收电路
absorption coefficient 吸收系数
absorption current 吸收电流
absorption law 吸收律
absorption loss 吸收损耗
absorption modulation 吸收调制
absorption peak 吸收峰值
absorption spectroscopy 吸收光谱
abstract 摘要,文摘
abstract algebra 抽象代数学
abstract algorithm 抽象算法
abstract automata theory 抽象自动机理论
abstract class 抽象类
abstract data type 抽象数据类型
abstract database system 抽象数据库系统
abstract family of language(AFL) 抽象语言族
abstract individual 抽象单体[个体]
abstract machine 抽象机
abstract modeling 抽象建模
abstract network 抽象网络
abstract semantics 抽象语义学
abstract signal flow model 抽象信号流模型
abstract software specification 抽象软件规范
abstract symbol 抽象符号
abstract syntax 抽象语法
abstract syntax notation(ASN) 抽象语法表示法
abstract test suite(AST) 成套抽象测试
abstracting 编制文摘
abstracting service 文摘服务
abstraction 抽象概念
abstraction mapping 抽象映射
abstraction utilization 抽象用法
abstraction verification 抽象验证
AC(Access Control) 访问[存取]控制
AC(Alternating Current) 交流(电)
AC-DC(Alternating Current to Direct Current) 交流至直流
AC/DC ringing 交直流振铃
AC dump 交流断电保护
AC erasing 交流消磁
AC indicator 交流信号指示器
AC input module controller 交流输入模块控制器
AC output module 交流输出模块
AC plasma display 交流等离子体显示器
AC signaling 交流信令
ACA(American Communication Association) 美国通信协会
ACA(American Cryptogram Association) 美国密码技术协会
ACA(Associative Content Addressable

memory) 相关内容可寻址存储器
ACA（Asynchronous Communications Adapter) 异步通信适配器
ACAM（Augmented Content-Addressed Memory) 可扩充的内容定址存储器
ACAP(Applications Configuration Access Protocol) 应用程序配置访问协议
ACAS(Automatic Central Alarm System) 中央自动警报系统
ACB(Adapter Control Block) 适配器控制块
ACB(Application Control Block) 应用程序控制块(IBM)
ACB（Asynchronous Communications Base) 异步通信基地址
ACB(Automatic Circuit Breaker) 自动断路器
ACC(Access Control Center) 访问控制中心
ACC(ACCumulator) 累加器
ACC（Automatic Chrominance Control) 自动色度控制
Accelerated Graphics Port(AGP) 图形加速接口
accelerated iterative method 加速迭代法
accelerated life test 加速寿命试验
Accelerated Strategic Computing Initiative(ASCI) 加速战略性计算启动
acceleration factor 加速系数[因子]
acceleration period 加速期
acceleration ratio 加速比
acceleration time 加速时间
accelerator 加速器
accelerator board 加速板
accelerator card 加速卡
accelerator key 加速键,快捷键
accent 强调符号,着重号
accent mark 重音标记
accent type 强调类型
accented character 强调字符
accentuated contrast 强化对比度
accentuation 强调;加重
accentuation rule 强调规则
accept 接受
accept action 接受动作,接受响应
accept any object 响应任何对象

accept for update 更新接收
ACCEPT statement 接受语句
accept with error 有错误仍予接受
accept with warning 有警告仍予接受
acceptability 可接受性
acceptable estimates 可接受估计量
acceptable filename 可接受文件名
acceptable interference 可容许的干扰
acceptable quality level(AQL) 质量合格标准
acceptable quality level test 质量合格标准测试
acceptable reliability level 可接受的可靠性标准
acceptable string 可接受字符串
acceptable use 可接受使用
acceptance angle 容许角;接收角
acceptance by empty stack 栈空接受
acceptance by final state 终态接受
acceptance cone 接收锥角
acceptance criteria 验收准则,接收判据
acceptance data package 验收数据包
acceptance gauging 验收量度
acceptance input 认可输入
acceptance inspection package 验收检查软件包
acceptance output 认可输出
acceptance pattern 接受曲线图;接受模式
acceptance problem 接收问题
acceptance review 验收性评审
acceptance test 接收检验,验收测试
acceptance testing period 验收测试时间
accepted language 接受的语言
accepted signal call 呼叫接收信号
accepted tolerance 可接受容差
accepting computation 接受计算
accepting station 接收站
acceptor 受主
acceptor impurity 受主杂质
acceptor material 受主材料
Access Access 数据库软件(微软)
access 存取,访问
access arm 存取臂
access arrangement 存取安排,存取排列
access attempt 存取尝试,访问企图
access authority 存取授权,访问权限

access barred 存取禁止,访问阻止
access barred signal 阻止存取信号,阻止接入信号
access bits 存取[访问]位
ACCESS. bus 存取[访问]总线
access button 存取按钮
access by record file address 通过记录文件地址访问
access category 访问范围,存取级别
access capability 存取能力,访问能力
access channel control 存取[访问]通道控制
access charge 存取费用,访问收费
access code 存取码,访问代码
access compatibility 存取兼容性
access conflict 存取[访问]冲突
access constraint 存取约束,访问限制
access contention 存取竞争;接入争用
access control 存取[访问]控制
access control bits 存取控制位
access control field(ACF) 访问控制字段
access control key 访问控制键
access control levels 访问控制级
access control list(ACL) 访问控制表
access control lock 存取控制锁
access control matrix 存取控制矩阵
access control matrix basic operations 存取控制矩阵基本操作
access control mechanism 存取控制机制
access control register(ACR) 存取控制寄存器
access control word(ACW) 存取控制字
access cycle 存取周期,访问周期
access date 存取日期
access denial 存取拒绝,访问拒绝
access denial probability 存取拒绝概率
access denial time 存取拒绝时间
access environment 存取环境,访问环境
access expanded memory 访问扩充内存
access failure 存取失败,访问无效
access gap 存取间隙
access guide 访问指南
access hole 存取孔,读写孔
access interrupt mark 存取中断标志
access interval 存取时间间隔

access key 存取键,访问键
access latency 访问等待时间
access level 存取级;存取层
access level structure 访问的层次结构
access light 读写指示灯;访问指示灯
access-limited logic 存取受限逻辑
access list 存取[访问]权限表
access lock 访问锁
access macro 存取宏指令
access mapping 存取映像;存取变换
access mask 访问屏蔽位
access matrix 存取矩阵,访问矩阵
access matrix model 访问矩阵模型
access mechanism 存取机构;访问机制
access method 存取方法
access method interface 存取方法接口
access method routines 存取法例程
access method service 存取方式服务程序
access mode 存取方式,访问模式
access mode clause 存取方式子句
access name 存取名称,访问名字
Access Node(CA) 访问节点路由器
access node 存取节点,访问结点
Access Node Hub(ANH) 访问节点集线器
access number 存取号码,访问号
access object 存取目标,访问对象
access order 访问顺序
access-oriented method 面向存取的方法
access-oriented programming 面向存取的程序设计
access originator 存取源,访问源头
access overhead 访问开销
access panel 存取控制面板
access password 存取口令
access path 存取路径,访问路由
access path independence 访问路径独立性
access path journaling 访问路径日志
access path widening 访问路径展宽
access pattern 访问模式
access period 存取周期
access permission 访问许可
access plan 访问计划
access point(AP) 存取点;线路入口
access policy 访问策略

access priority	访问优先级
access privilege	访问特权
access privilege matrix	访问特权矩阵
access procedure	访问规程
access protection	存取保护
access protocol	访问协议
access provider	因特网访问服务供应商
access queue	存取队列
access rate	访问率
access record	存取记录,访问记录
access request(AR)	存取要求,访问请求
access resolution	存取分辨率
access restriction	存取限制
access right	存取[访问]权限
access routine	存取例程
access scan	存取扫描
access scheme	存取方案
access sequence	存取顺序
access server	访问服务器
access slot	访问时间片
access specifier	存取说明符
access speed	存取速度
Access Stack Node(ASN)	访问堆叠式节点路由器
access stencil	存取模板
access strategyl	访问策略
access switch	存取[访问]开关
access table	存取表
access time	选取时间;存取时间
access time gap	存取时间间隙,访问时隙
access token	访问令牌
access transparency	访问透明性
access type	存取类型,访问类型
access unit	存取单元
access value	存取值,访问值
access view	存取视图
access violation	存取违例
access waiting time	访问等待时间
access window	存取窗口
access zero	零存取
AccessBuilder	远程访问软件(3Com)
accessibility	可存取性,可访问性
accessibility of system	系统可访问性
accessible boundary point	可达边界点
accessible field	可访问字段
accessible point	可到达点
accessible state	可达状态
accessible stationary point	可达稳定点
accessing formula	访问公式
accessing strategy	访问策略
accession designation number	存取注册号
accession number index	登记号索引
accessor	存取者,存取程序
accessor environment element	访问者环境元
accessor function	访问者函数
accessories group windows	附件组窗口
accessory	附件;辅助设备
accessory channel	辅助通道
accessory slot	附件插槽,扩展槽
accessory terminal	辅助终端
accessory word	附属词
ACCF(Area Communications Control Function)	地区通信控制功能
accident	(偶然性)故障
accidental data	非本质数据,偶然数据
accidental destruction	偶然性的破坏
accidental error	偶然性误差
accidental event	意外事件
accidental threat	偶然威胁
accommodation	适应性
accommodation coefficient	适应系数
accommodator	调节器,适配器
accomplish	完成
accordance	一致,协调,匹配
accordion	伸缩接头
accordion seek	往复寻道[定位]
accordion structure	折叠式结构
account	账户,账号
account balance	账号余额
account bill	账单
account current	流水账单
account expires	账号到期日
account file	记账文件,账户文件
account lock	账号锁定
account name	账户名
account number	账号,账户号
account policy	记账策略
account restriction	账号限制
account routine	记账例程
account string	账户字符串
account transaction	记账事务
accountability	责任

accountability information 可记账信息
accountable time 可记账时间
accounting 记账；账目管理
accounting application program 会计应用程序，记账实用程序
accounting check 记账校验
accounting code 记账码
accounting computer 记账计算机
accounting entry 记账表目
accounting exit routine 记账出口例程
accounting format 记账格式
accounting function 会计[记账]功能
accounting information 记账信息
accounting journal 记账日志
accounting language 会计[记账]语言
accounting level 记账级
accounting machine 会计[记账]机
accounting manager 记账管理程序
accounting number 账号
accounting package 记账软件包
accounting period 会计[结账]周期
accounting procedure 记账程序，结账过程
accounting routine 会计[记账]例程
accounting segment 记账时间段
accounting server 记账服务器
accounting service 记账[会计]服务
accounting software 记账[会计]软件
accounting system 会计系统
accounting tabulator 会计制表程序
accounting terms 记账[收费服务]项
Accounts Index(AI) 会计索引目
accredit 委任；鉴定
accreditation 身份鉴定
ACCT(ACCess Time) 存取[访问]时间
accumulate(ACC) 累加，累计
accumulated deviation 累计偏差
accumulated error 累积[累计]误差
accumulated round-off 累计舍入
accumulated value 累加值
accumulating 累加计算
accumulative carry 累加进位
accumulative error 累积误差
accumulative estimation method 累加估计法
accumulative reception 累计接收
accumulative total 累计总和
accumulator(A,ACC) 累加器

accumulator address 累加器地址
accumulator addressing 累加器寻址操作
accumulator jump instruction 累加器跳转指令
accumulator latch 累加器锁存
accumulator register 累加寄存器
accumulator shift instruction 累加器移位指令
accumulator transfer instruction 累加器转移指令
accuracy 准确度
accuracy constraint 准确度约束
accuracy control character 准确度控制字符
accuracy control system 准确度控制系统
accuracy of equalization 均衡准确度
accurate approximation 准确近似
accurate placement 准确布局
ACD(Automatic Call Distributor) 自动呼叫分配器
ACE(ACknowledge Enable) 应答允许
ACE(Advanced Client Environment) 高级客户环境(联想)
ACE(Advanced Computing Environment) 先进计算环境组织，ACE联盟
ACE(Automatic Computing Engine) 自动计算引擎
Acer 宏基公司(台湾省)
ACF(Advanced Communication Function) 高级通信功能
ACF/NCP(Advanced Communications Function for the Network Control Program) 高级通信操作程序中的网络控制程序(IBM)
ACF/SSP(Advanced Communications Function for the System Support Program) 高级通信操作程序中的系统支持程序(IBM)
ACF/TAP(Advanced Communications Function for the Trace Analysis Program) 高级通信操作程序中的跟踪分析程序(IBM)
ACF/TCAM(Advanced Communications Function for TeleCommunica-

tions Access Method) 高级通信操作程序中的远程访问法(IBM)

ACF/VTAM(Advanced Communications Function for VTAM) 高级通信操作程序中的虚拟远程通信访问法(IBM)

ACH(Attempts per Circuit per Hour) 每小时每对线路的呼叫

ACH(Automatic Clearing House) 自动票据交换所

achievable accuracy 可达精度

achieved reliability 实际可靠性

achromatic colors 消色

ACI(Adjacent Channel Interference) 邻道干扰

ACI(Application Communication Interface) 应用程序通信接口

ACI(Asynchronous Communication Interface) 异步通信接口

ACIA(Asynchronous Communications Interface Adapter) 异步通信接口适配器

ACIA interface signals 异步通信适配器接口信号

ACIA interface signals for MPU 微处理机单元异步通信接口配接器接口信号

ACIA microcomputer control 异步通信接口适配器微计算机控制

ACK(ACKnowledgement) 确认,认可

ACK 0(even positive ACKnowledgement) 偶次确认应答(字符)

ACK 1(odd positive ACKnowledgement) 奇次确认应答(字符)

ACK/NAK Transmission "确认/否认"传输方式

ACK packet 确认包,肯定信息包

ACK process 确认进程

ACK queue 确认队列

Ackermann's function 阿克曼函数

acknowledge 确认,应答,认可

acknowledge character(ACK) 确认字符

acknowledge cycle 确认周期,应答周期

acknowledge field 肯定字段

acknowledge interrupt 中断应答

acknowledge signal 应答信号,确认信号

acknowledge timeout 应答超时

acknowledged mail 应答邮件

acknowledged run flag 确认运行标志

acknowledged sequence number 确认顺序号

acknowledgement 确认

acknowledgement indicator 确认指示

acknowledgement of seizing signal 占线确认信号

acknowledgement signal unit(ACU) 确认应答信号单元

acknowledgement window 确认窗口

ACL(Access Control List) 访问控制列表

ACL(Agent Communication Language) 智能通信语言

ACL(Application Control Language) 应用程序控制语言

ACL(Audit Command Language) 审计命令语言

ACM(Association for Computing Machinery) 计算机协会(美国)

ACM(Automatic Coding Machine) 自动编码机

ACM Transaction on Database System 《ACM 数据库系统汇刊》

ACM Transaction on Mathematical Software 《ACM 数学软件汇刊》

ACM Transaction on Programming Language and System 《ACM 程序设计语言与系统汇刊》

CAN(Adjacent Channel Noise) 邻道噪声

acoustic bass (MIDI)低音伴奏

acoustic couple 声耦合

acoustic coupler(AC) 声耦合器

acoustic coupling 声音耦合

acoustic deflector 声音偏转器

acoustic delay line storage 声延迟线存储器

acoustic eavesdropping 声音窃收

acoustic feedback 声音反馈

acoustic filter 声滤波器

acoustic generator 声音发生器

acoustic holography 声全息照相术

acoustic imaging 声成像

acoustic impedance 声阻抗

acoustic input device 声音输入设备

acoustic load 声负载

acoustic memory 声存储器
acoustic microscope 声显微镜
acoustic modem 声调制解调器
acoustic panel 隔音板
acoustic patttern 声模式
acoustic-phonetic recognizer 声学语音识别器
acoustic phonetics 声响语音学
acoustic programming 语音编程
acoustic reading material 有声读物
acoustic shield 声音屏蔽
acoustic spectrograph 声谱仪
acoustic storage 声存储器
acoustic transmittivity 声传输系数
acoustical hologram 声全息图
acoustical holography 声全息照相术
acoustical imaging 声成像
acoustical sound enclosure 隔音箱
acoustical treatment 隔音措施
acoustics 声学
acousto-data coupler 数据声耦合器
acousto-optic deflector 声光偏转器
acousto-optic effect 声光效应
acousto-optic medium 声光介质
acousto-optic modulator 声光调制器
acoustooptics 声光学
ACP(Associate Computer Program) 专业性计算机相关考试
acquire 获取,捕捉
acquire display 获取显示,申请显示
acquisition 获取,采集;探测
acquisition and control system 数据采集与控制系统
acquisition query rule 获取查询规则
acquisition strategy 获取策略
acquisition time 获取时间,采集时间
ACR(Allowed Cell Rate) 允许的信元速率
ACR(Automatic Call and Retry) 自动呼叫与重试
Acrobat 电子图书阅读软件(Adobe)
acronym 缩写词,字首组合词
across tape 交替运用磁带
across-the-board rule 全域规则
across-the-wire migration 跨线转移
across-then-down 先行后列
across worksheets 跨越工作表
ACS(Adaptive Computer System) 自适应计算机系统
ACS(Advanced Connectivity System) 先进布线系统
ACS(Asynchronous Communication Server) 异步通信服务器
ACS(Automatic Coding System) 自动编码系统
ACSE(Association Control Service Element) 联合控制服务元素
ACSL language(Advanced Continuous Simulation Language) 高级连续仿真语言
ACT(Automatic Code Translation) 自动代码翻译
ACT(Automatic Connection Test) 自动连接测试
act fork 决策点分支
actigram 活动图
action 作用,动作
action code 动作码,指令码
action command 动作命令,行动命令
action coordination system 动作协调系统
action current 作用电流
action cycle 作用周期,动作周期
action description 动作描述
action entity 作用-实体
action entries 动作款目
action file 现用文件
action frame 作用帧
action group 指令群,指令组
action icon 作用图标
action list 操作表
action message 动作[作用]消息
action panel 作用面板,指令画面
action paper 压感纸
action paper survey 压感纸鉴定
action path 作用路径
action period 作用周期
action portion 作用部分
action prompt 动作提示符
action schedule 动作调度,动作表
action sequence diagram 动作顺序图
action server 作用服务器
action specification 动作说明
action spot 作用点,激活点(CRT内)
action statement 作用[动作]语句
action stub 作用末段,动作桩

action token 动作信标[令牌]
ActionMedia Ⅱ 多媒体技术(IBM)
activate 激活;启动
activate as 启动类型
activate button 启动键,激活键
activate channel 激活通道,作用信道
activate key 启动[激活]键
activate primitive 激活原语
activate user 启动用户
activating 活化,激活,激励
activating signal 启动[激活]信号
activation 敏化,活化,激励,激活
activation block 赋活分程序
activation cycle 敏化周期
activation environment 赋活环境
activation flag 激活标志
activation fragment 激活段
activation machinery 激活机制,启动机制
activation mechanism 激活机制
activation network 敏化网络
activation pointer 赋活指针,激活指示字
activation processor 激活处理机
activation record 活动记录
activation request 赋动请求
activation stack 激活堆栈
activation table 敏化表
active 活动的;有源的;主动的;当前
active accommodation 主动调节
active address key 当前地址键
active area 活动区域,现用区
active attach 主动攻击
active bank 活动块,可使用数据库
active block 有源组件
active border 活动边框
active button 活动按钮
active card 现用卡,活卡
active caret 活动脱字符(^)
active cell 当前数据单元
Active Channel 活动频道(微软)
active channel 现用通道,活动信道
active color technology 活跃颜色技术
active communication satellite 有源通信卫星
active component 有源组件
active computer 现役[主动]计算机
active configuration 活跃配置
active connector 有源连接器
active control 活动控件
active corrective maintenance time 有效校正维护时间
active data dictionary 有效数据字典
active data set 现用数据集
active database 现用数据库
Active Desktop 活动桌面(微软)
active device 有源装置
active directory 活动目录,当前目录
active drive 活动驱动器,现用驱动器
active DO-loop 现用 DO 循环
active domain 有效值域
active element 有源元件
active files 现用[活动]文件
active filter 有源滤波器
active gateway 有源网关
active grab 主动占取
Active Group Active 组织(ActiveX 技术开发)
active group job 现役成组作业
active help system 主动帮助系统
active high 高电平有效
active hub 有源集线器
active illumination 主动照明
active image 活动图像
active index 工作索引
active infrared detection 主动式红外探测
active interconnection 主动[有源]互连
active intruder 积极干扰者
active item record count 使用中的项目记录数
active job 活动作业
active light 工作灯
active line 活动线路;有效扫描线
active line per frame 每帧有效扫描线数
active line-tap 主动线路窃听
active link 有源链;有效链路
active location 主动定位
active low 低电平有效
active maintenance time 有效维护时间
active master file 现用主文件
active master item 主活动项
active matrix 有源阵列
active matrix LCD 有源阵列液晶显示器
active memory cell 有源存储单元

active message 主动消息
active messaging collection 活动消息集合
active messaging library 活动消息库
active messaging object 活动消息对象
active mixer 有源混频器
active monitor 现用监视(监督程序)
active movie control object 活动影像控制对象
active network 有源网络
active node 现用结点,主动节点
active object 主动对象
active page 活动页,现用页面
active page queue 活动页队列
active partition 现用分区,活动分区
active pipeline 活动流水线
active pixel region 活跃像素区域
active position 当前位置,主动位置
active position addressing(APA) 主动位置寻址
active preventive maintenance time 有效预防性维护时间
active procedure 现时过程,活动过程
active process 活动进程
active processor module 活动处理机模块
active profile 活动轮廓
active program 活动程序
active pull-up 有源提升,有源上拉
active record 有效记录
active redundancy 主动[活动]冗余
active region 活动区
active relay 有源转发器(中继器)
active resource 现用资源
active satellite 有源卫星
active scanning 活动扫描;有源扫描
active screen 当前屏幕画面
active segment table 现用段表
active sensing 启动侦测,激活检测
Active Service Components Server 活动服务部件服务器
active server 活动服务器
Active Server Pages(ASP) 活动服务器网页(微软)
active set method 有效集方法
active sheet 当前表格
active signaling link 主动信令链路
active simulation 主动模拟[仿真]
active site 活动站点;有源位置
active sort table 活动排序表
active stack 活动堆栈
active star 有源星形
active state 活动状态
active station 活动站,主动站
active status bit 活动状态位
active structure network(ASN) 活动结构网络
active subfile 现用子文件
active subfile record 现用子文件记录
active substrate 有源衬底
active suspension 主动挂起
active task list 活动任务列表
active terminal 有源终端
active time 有效活动时间
active tracking 有源跟踪
active transducer 有源换能器
active type 主动类型
active user 现时用户,当前用户
active value 活动值
active virtual terminal 现行虚拟终端
active volume 可用容量;现用卷
active wait 活动等待
active window 活动窗口,现用视窗
active wire tapping 主动(线路)窃收
ActiveX ActiveX 框架(微软)
ActiveX automation ActiveX 自动化
ActiveX Component ActiveX 组件
ActiveX Controls ActiveX 控件
ActiveX Data Object(ADO) ActiveX 数据对象(微软)
ActiveX object ActiveX 对象
ActiveX scripting ActiveX 脚本编写
ActiveX Server Component ActiveX 服务器组件(微软)
ActiveX Server Page(ASP) ActiveX 服务页面(微软)
activity 活动,活动性
activity analysis 活动分析
activity buffer 活动缓冲区
activity content 活动量
activity definition 活动性定义
activity directed simulation 直接活动模拟
activity factor 活动因子,利用系数
activity graph 活动图

activity inventory 活动清单
activity level 活动程度
activity light 活动灯
activity list 活动表
activity loading 活动加载
activity logging 活动日志
activity model 活动模型
activity queue 活动队列
activity ratio 活动比
activity restart cycle 活动重启动周期
activity save area 活动保留区
activity scanning 活动扫描
activity sequence 活动序列
activity set 活动集
activity template 活动模板
activity trace 活动跟踪
activity trail 活动收尾记录
activity vector 活动向量
activity working space 活动工作空间
ACTOR ACTOR语言
actor 角色；动作体
actor computer 动作体计算机
actor language 角色语言
actor model 动作体模型
actual 实际的，实在的，现行的
actual address 实地址
actual argument 实际变元，实际参数
actual block processor(ABP) 实际块处理程序
actual capacity 实际容量
actual coding 实际编码
actual count 实际统计
actual counted quantity 实际计数量
actual data transfer rate 实际数据传输率
actual decimal point 实际十进制小数点
actual declarator 实在说明符
actual entry 实际表项；实际入口
actual filename 实际文件名
actual gain 实际增益
actual job 实际作业
actual key 实际键
actual line 实际行
actual lower bound 实际下界
actual parameter 实际参数，实参数
actual parameter association 实际参数结合
actual parameter list 实在参数表

actual relative level 实际相对电平
actual sound 实声音
actual source 实(资)源
actual start 实际起点
actual start date 实际开始日期
actual storage 实际存储器
actual switching point 实际交换点
actual time 实际时间
actual upper bound 实际上界
actual view 实际观察
actual work time(AWT) 实际工作时间
actuating signal 启动信号
actuator 激励器，致动器，传动机构
ACU(Association of Computer User) 计算机用户协会
ACU(Automatic Calling Unit) 自动呼叫装置
acuity 敏锐度
acutance 锐度
ACV(Access Control Vectors) 存取控制向量
ACW(Access Control Word) 存取控制字
acyclic circuit 非循环电路
acyclic feeding 非周期性馈送
acyclic graph 非循环图
acyclic process 非循环进程，非周期性过程
acyclicity 无环性，非周期性
Ada language Ada语言
Adaline 自适应线性元
ADAPLEX language ADAPLEX语言
ADAPT language ADAPT语言
adaptability 适应性，自适应性
adaptability of software 软件自适应性
adaptable 自适应的
Adaptable Data Base System(ADABAS) 自适应数据库系统
adapter 适配器
adapter blank 适配器空插件
adapter check 适配器校验
adapter control block(ACB) 适配器控制块
adapter port 适配器端口
adapting 适应，调适
adaptive 适应的
adaptive algorithm 自适应算法
adaptive attenuation 自适应衰减

adaptive automatic equalizer 自适应自动均衡器
adaptive autoregressive model 自适应自回归模型
adaptive bilevel image compression 自适应二值图像压缩
adaptive channel action 自适应通道作用
adaptive channel allocation 自适应通道分配
adaptive checking experiment 自适应检查实验
adaptive clustering scheme 自适应群集技术(DEC)
adaptive communication 自适应通信
adaptive compression 自适应压缩技
adaptive control 自适应控制　术
adaptive control of constraint(ACC) 限制式自适应控制
adaptive control system 自适应控制系统
adaptive cushioning 自适应减震
adaptive delta modulation(ADM) 自适应增量调制
adaptive delta pulse code modulation (ADPCM) 自适应增量脉冲编码调制
adaptive differential pulse code modulation(ADPCM) 自适应差分脉冲编码调制
adaptive equalizer 自适应均衡器
adaptive filter 自适应滤波器
adaptive forward differencing 自适应正向差分
adaptive frequency estimator 自适应频率估算器　　　　　　「统
adaptive fuzzy system 自适应模糊系
adaptive grid method 自适应网格法
adaptive histogram adjustment 自适应直方图调整
adaptive hybrid method 自适应混合　「法
adaptive instructional system 适应性教学系统
adaptive integration method 自适应积分方法
adaptive interface 自适应接口(界面)
adaptive manipulator 自适应操纵器
adaptive mesh refinement 自适应网求精法
adaptive mobile access protocol 自适应移动访问协议
adaptive model matching 自适应模型匹配　　　　　　　　　　「器
adaptive multiplexer 自适应多路复用
adaptive neural network 自适应神经网络　　　　　　　　　　「噪
adaptive noise cancellation 自适应消
adaptive organization 自适应结构[组织]
adaptive pacing 自适应调步
adaptive partitioning algorithm 自适应分区算法
adaptive predictive coding(APC) 自适应预测编码
adaptive predictive image coding 自适应预测影像编码
adaptive production system 自适应产生式系统
adaptive quantization 自适应量化
adaptive receiver 自适应接收机
adaptive recognition algorithm 自适应识别算法
adaptive recursive filtering 自适应递归滤波
adaptive refinement strategy 自适应求精策略
adaptive regulator 自适应调节器
adaptive remeshing 自适应重新网格化
adaptive remote control 自适应遥控
adaptive robot 自适应机器人
adaptive routing 自适应路由选择
adaptive session pacing 自适应对话调步
adaptive session-level pacing 自适应话路级调步
adaptive system 自适应系统
adaptive system theory 自适应系统理
adaptive testing 自适应测试　　「论
adaptive threshold control 自适应阈值控制
adaptive time sharing 自适应分时
adaptive tracking 自适应跟踪
adaptive transversal equalizer 自适应横向均衡器
adaptive tree walk protocol 自适应遍

历树协议
adaptive user interface 自适应用户界面
ADB(Apple Desktop Bus) Apple桌面总线
ADC(Adapter for Data Channel) 数据通道适配器
ADC(Analog to Digital Converter) 模数转换器
ADCCP(Advanced Data Communication Control Procedure) 高级数据通信控制规程(IBM)
ADCCP(Advanced Data Communication Control Protocol) 高级数据通信控制协议(IBM)
ADD 加法指令
add 增加,添加
add authority 增加权限
Add Custom AutoFormat 添加自定义套用格式(微软)
add-delete list 附加删除表
add echo 增加回声
add file 添加文件
add fonts 添加字体
add-in 加入,添加,附加
add-in memories 附加内存,内插式扩充存储器
add-in program 外加程序
add list 添加表
add name space 增加名字空间
add-on 追加,提高,扩充
add-on board 扩充卡 「器
add-on memory 增设内存,附加存储
add-on security 追加安全措施
add-on storage 附加[增设]存储器
Add Overlay 添加覆盖图(微软)
Add/Remove Windows Components 添加/删除Windows组件(微软)
Add Routing Slip 添加传递名单(微软)
Add Subtotal to 添加分类汇总(微软)
add-subtract time 加减时间
Add Template 添加模板(微软)
add time 加法运算时间
Add to Spike 添加到图文场(微软)
Add to Template 添加到模板(微软)
Add Watch 添加监视点(微软)
add-without-carry gate 无进位加门,"异"门
added bit 附加位
added block 附加数据块
added block probability 附加数据块概率
added entry 附加入口;附加条目
addend 加数
addend address 加数地址
addend register 加数寄存器
adder 加法器
adder-accumulator 加法器-累加器
adder amplifier 加法放大器
adder circuit 相加电路
adder-subtracter 加减器 「则
adding alternative rule 添加可选项规
adding fields 增加字段
adding files to a catalog 向目录中追加文件
adding information to the database 向数据库增加信息
adding network 加法网络
adding operator 加法算子[运算符]
adding tracks 增加轨道
addition circuit 加法电路
addition item 添加项,补充项
addition of polynomial 多项式加法
addition principle 加法原理
addition record 增添记录,附加记录
addition speed 加法速度
addition table 加法表
addition without carry 无进位加法
additional 增添的,附加的
additional channel 附加信道
additional character 增添[附加]字符
additional detail 增添明细,附加细节
additional form feature 增添形状特征
additional header information 附加报头信息
additional increase rate(AIR) 附加增长速率
additional information 附加信息
additional keys 增添键,额外键
additional license 增加特许
additional memory 附加内存
additional memory module 附加内存模块
additional operation description 增添操作说明

additional record 增添[补充]记录
additional routine operation description 增添例程操作说明
additional storage 外加存储器
additive circuit 加法电路
additive color system 加色系统
additive mixture 加色混合
additive noise 外加噪声
additive process 添加处理,添加法
additive smoothing 相加平滑
additivity 可加性
address(ADDR) 地址
address access time 地址存取时间
address access type 地址存取型
address alignment 地址配准
address allocation 地址分配
address assignment 地址分配
address book 地址簿
address book container 地址簿容器
address book provider 地址簿提供者
address boundary 地址边界
address buffer 地址缓冲器
address bus 地址总线
address bus driver 地址总线驱动器
address calculation 地址计算
address calculation sorting 地址计算排序
address chaining 地址链锁[连接]
address check 地址校验
address code 地址码
address comparator 地址比较器
address compare control 地址比较控制
address complete signal 地址完全信号
address component 地址部分
address computation 地址计算
address constant 地址常数
address conversion 地址转换
address counter 地址计数器
address decoder 地址译码器
address decrement 地址减量　　「器
address demultiplexer 地址多路分配
address descriptor 地址描述符　　「止
address disable 使地址失效,地址禁
address display lights 地址显示灯
address driver 地址驱动器
address fault 地址错误
address field 地址域[字段]

address field extension 地址字段扩充
address format 地址格式　　　「序
address-free program 非绝对地址程
address function unit 地址功能单元
address generation(AG) 地址产生
address head 地址标题
address incomplete signal 地址不完全信号
address increment 地址增量
address independence mode 地址无关模式
address information 地址信息
address interleaving 地址交错
address key 地址键
address label 地址标号
address latch 地址闩锁[锁存]
address latch enable 地址锁存选通
address latching unit 地址锁存部件
address line(AL) 地址线
address list 地址列表,地址清单
address mapping 地址映射[变换]
address mark 地址标志
address mask 地址屏蔽
address match 地址匹配
address message 地址消息
address mode 地址方式,寻址模式
address modification(ADM) 地址修
address modifier 地址修改量　　「改
address out bus 地址输出总线
address out of range 地址越界
address part 地址部分
address permutation 地址交换
address pointer 地址指针
address port 地址端口
address predecessor 先行地址
address prefixing 地址前缀
address priority 地址优先权
address property 地址属性
address reference 地址参考;地址引
address register 地址寄存器　　「用
address relocation 地址重定位
address resolution 地址转换,地址解析
address resolution cache 地址转换高速缓存
Address Resolution Protocol(ARP) 地址转换协议
address selector 地址选择器

address signal complete 地址信号完整
address signals 地址信号
address skew method 地址斜移法
address space 地址空间
address space identifier(ASID) 地址空间标识符
address stop 地址符合停机
address stream 地址流
address strobe 地址选通
address substitution 地址替换
address switch register 地址切换寄存器
address table sorting 地址表排序
address template protection 地址模板保护
Address To 收信者地址
address trace 地址跟踪
address track 地址磁道
address transform instruction 地址变换指令
address translation 地址转换
address translator 地址转换器
address vector 地址向量
address window 地址窗口
address word 地址字
addressability 寻址能力
addressability problem 寻址能力问题
addressable cursor 可寻址光标
addressable horizontal position 可寻址水平位置
addressable horizontal/vertical positions 可按址访问的水平/垂直位置
addressable memory 可寻址存储器
addressable point 可寻址点
addressable register 可寻址寄存器
addressable vertical positions 可寻址垂直位置
addressed direct access 按址直接访问
addressed sequential access 按址顺序存取
addressing 寻址(操作)
addressing abnormal 寻址异常
addressing capability 寻址能力
addressing character 寻址字符
addressing control field 寻址控制字段
addressing error 寻址错误
addressing level 寻址级
addressing mode 寻址模式,寻址方式
addressing object 寻址对象

addressing operation 寻址操作
addressing range 寻址范围
addressing space 寻址空间
addressing structure 编址结构
addressing system 寻址系统
addressing technique 寻址技术
addressing types 寻址类型
addressing violation 寻址违规
addressing warning 寻址告警
Addressing Wizard 寻址向导
addressless format 缺地址格式
addressless instruction format 无地址指令格式
ADE(ADdress Enable) 地址允许
ADE(Application Development Environment) 应用开发环境
adherence 粘附特性;依附力
adherent point 依附点
adhesion 粘着,附着
adhesive face 粘合正面
adhesive reverse 粘合背面
ADI(Autodesk Device Interface) Autodesk 设备接口
adjacency 邻近,邻接
adjacency algorithm 邻接算法
adjacency list 邻接表
adjacency graph 邻接图
adjacency matrix 邻接[连接]矩阵
adjacency multilist 邻接多重表
adjacency vertex 邻接顶点
adjacent 相邻
adjacent basic point 相邻基点
adjacent-bit-dependent code 邻位相关型代码
adjacent channel 相邻信道
adjacent channel attenuation 邻道衰减
adjacent channel interference 邻道干扰
adjacent channel selectivity 邻道选择性
adjacent character 相邻字符
adjacent control point 相邻控制点
adjacent domains 邻域,相邻域
adjacent edge 邻边,邻界
adjacent extreme point 相邻极点
adjacent feasible solution 邻近可行解
adjacent free area 相邻空闲区域
adjacent-group-dependent code 邻组

相关型编码
adjacent identifier 相邻标识符
adjacent layer 相邻层
adjacent level 相邻级
adjacent link storage image 相邻链路存储器影像
adjacent matrix 邻接矩阵
adjacent method 邻接法
adjacent nodes 邻近节点,相邻结点
adjacent signaling points 相邻发信点
adjacent sound carrier 邻道伴音载波
adjacent subarea 邻近子区
adjacent video carrier 邻道视频载波
adjoin 毗连
adjoinment 邻接
adjoint 伴随,毗连,相邻
adjoint equation 伴随方程
adjoint matrix 伴随矩阵
adjoint network 伴随网络
adjoint point 邻点
adjoint process 伴随进程
adjoint system 伴随系统
adjoint variable 伴随变量
adjunct 附加的;附属;附件
adjunct register set 附加寄存器组
adjunctive 附属的
adjust(ADJ) 校准,调整
adjust effect data 调整效果数据
adjust line end 行末调整
adjust skew 调整扭斜
adjust text mode 调整正文模式
adjustable 可调节的
adjustable dimension 可调节尺寸
adjustable extent 可调节范围
adjustable-size aggregate 可变大小聚合体
adjusted decibel(s) 已调整分贝(数)
adjusted ring length 已调整环路长度
adjusted to calendar 调整日期
adjustment 调整
adjustment amount 调整量,调节量
adjustment extension 调整范围
adjustment handle 调整柄
ADM(ADdress Modification) 地址修
admeasurement 测量;尺度　　└正
ADMIN object 管理对象
administration 管理;行政机构
administration category 管理范围
administration decision-making 管理事务决策
administration software 管理软件
administrative data processing 管理数据处理
administrative engineering 管理工程
administrative expenditure 行政管理费
administrative group 系统管理员组
administrative information 管理信息
administrative operator 管理操作员
administrative operator station 管理操作员站
administrative planning system 行政管理规划系统
administrative preventive maintenance 日常预防性维护
administrative processor 管理处理机
administrative science 管理科学
administrative security 管理安全
administrative software 管理软件
administrative support system 管理支持系统
administrative terminal system(ATS) 管理终端系统
administrative time for corrector maintenance 修复性维护的管理时间
administrative utility 管理实用程序
administrator(ADMIN) 管理人员
administrator name 管理员名字
admissibility 可采纳性
admissibility condition 许可条件
admissibility of an algorithm 算法可采纳性
admissibility of heuristic search algorithm 启发式搜索算法的可采纳性
admissible 可容许的,可采用的
admissible action 可容许行为
admissible base 宜取基,容许基
admissible character 容许字符
admissible class of grammars 可容许文法类
admissible control 容许控制
admissible curve 容许曲线
admissible error 可容许误差
admissible function 容许函数
admissible heuristics 可采纳试探
admissible interpolation constraint 可

容许内插约束
admissible mark 容许标志
admissible number 容许数
admissible parameter 容许参数
admissible partial function 允许部分函数
admissible path 容许路径
admissible situation 宜取形势
admissible state semantics 可容许状态语义
admissible transformation 宜取变换
admission delay 容许延迟;进场延迟
admission rule 容许规则
admit 接纳,允许进入
admittance 导纳
admittance matrix 导纳矩阵
ADO(ActiveX Data Object) ActiveX数据对象(微软)
Adobe Acrobat Acrobat 文档阅读软件(Adobe)
Adobe Illustrator Illustrator 绘图软件
Adobe Photoshop Photoshop 图像处理软件
Adobe Premiere Premiere 视频图像编辑软件(Adobe)
Adobe PostScript 页面描述语言(Adobe)
Adobe type manager(ATM) 轮廓字形解释软件
Adonis 电子文献系统
adopted authority 被采用权限
adornment 修饰
ADP(Association of Database Producers) 数据库生产者协会(英)
ADP(Automatic Diagnostic Program) 自动诊断程序
ADPCM(Adaptive Delta Pulse Code Modulation) 自适应增量脉冲编码调制
ADPCM(Adaptive Differential PCM) 自适应差分脉冲编码调制
ADPLL(All Digital Phase-Locked Loop) 全数字锁相环
ADS(Application Data Structure) 应用程序数据结构
ADS(Application Design System) 应用程序设计系统(IBM)
ADSI(Active Directory Service Interface) 活动目录服务界面
ADSL(Asymmetric Digital Subscriber Link) 不对称数字用户线
ADSL(Asynchronous Digital Subscriber Loop) 异步数字用户环路
ADSN(Automatic Dial Switching Network) 自动拨号交换网络
ADSP(Advanced Digital Signal Processor) 高级数字信号处理器
ADT(Active Disk Table) 当前磁盘表
ADT(Application Data Table) 应用程序数据表
ADT(Asynchronous Data Transfer) 异步数据转移
ADT(Attribute Distributed Tree) 属性分布树
ADT(Automatic Data Transfer) 自动数据转移
ADT(Autonomous Data Transfer) 独立数据传送
ADT(Available Device Table) 可用设备表
ADTR(Actual Data Transfer Rate) 实际数据传输率
ADU(Automatic Dialing Unit) 自动拨号单元
adult language 成熟语言
ADV(Adaptive Digital Vocoder) 自适应数字声码器
advance 超前,进展,提前,进步
advance control 先行控制
advance deviation report 偏差先期报告
advance interrupt control transfer 先行中断控制转移
advance item 超前项
Advance net 高级网络
advance read status transfer 先行读状态转移
advance signal processing system 前置信号处理系统
Advanced BASIC 高级 BASIC 语言
advanced calling service(ACS) 预约呼叫服务
advanced chipset setup(ACS) 高级芯片组设置
Advanced CMOS Setup 高级 CMOS 设置

advanced communication function (ACF) 高级通信功能
advanced communication function for the network control program (ACF/NCP) 用于网络控制程序的高级通信功能
advanced communication function for the telecommunication access method (ACF/TCAM) 用于远程通信访问法的高级通信功能
advanced communication system (ACS) 高级通信系统
advanced communications service (ACS) 高级通信服务(AT&T)
advanced computing environment (ACE) 先进计算环境组织,ACE联盟
advanced configuration and power interface (ACPI) 高级配置与电源接口
Advanced Connectivity System (ACS) 先进布线系统
advanced control 超前控制,先行控制
advanced course 高级教程
Advanced Data Communication Control Procedure (ADCCP) 高级数据通信控制规程
Advanced Data Link Controller (ADLC) 高级数据链路控制器
advanced data management system 高级数据管理系统
advanced database 新一代数据库
advanced database management system 高级数据库管理系统
advanced development objective 远景发展目标
advanced early warning system (AEWS) 高级预警系统
Advanced Encryption Standard (AES) 高级加密标准
advanced feed 前置导孔带
advanced fetch 先行取指令
Advanced Filter 高级筛选程序(微软)
advanced freephone service 高级免费电话业务
advanced function for communication 高级通信功能
advanced function printing (AFP) 高级功能打印(IBM)
advanced hybrid computing system 高级混合计算系统
Advanced Information System (AIS) 先进信息系统公司
Advanced Information System Net (AISN) 高级信息系统网络
Advanced Instruction station 先行指令站
Advanced Instruction system 高级指令系统
Advanced Intelligent Network Switch (ASW) 高级智能网交换系统
Advanced Interactive Debugging System (AIDS) 高级交互调试系统
Advanced Interactive Executive (AIX) 高级交互执行程序
Advanced Intercontinental Missile System 先进洲际导弹系统
advanced-level user 高层用户
advanced linear programming system (ALPS) 高级线性规划系统
Advanced Micro Devices Inc. (AMD) AMD公司
Advanced Mobile Phone Service 先进移动电话服务
Advanced Monitor Deflection Control (AMDC) 先进监视器偏转控制(Philips)
Advanced Network System Architecture (ANSA) 先进网络系统体系结构
advanced operating environment (AOE) 先进操作环境
Advanced Operating System (AOS) 先进操作系统(DG)
Advanced Peer-to-Peer Network (APPN) 高级对等网络(软件)
advanced placement program 高级布线程序
advanced project 远景规划
Advanced Program-to-Program Communication (APPC) 高级程序间通信(软件)
advanced query 高级查询
advanced reconfigurable computer system 高级可重配置计算机系统
Advanced Research Project Agency Network (ARPANET) 远景研究

规划局网络
advanced RISC computing 先进精简指令集芯片计算
advanced run-length limited code(ARLL) 改进型游程长度受限码
Advanced Scientific Computer(ASC) 高级科学计算机,ASC计算机
Advanced Script 高级脚本
Advanced SCSI Programming Interface(ASPI) 高级SCSI编程接口
advanced setup 高级设置
advanced signal-processing system 高级信号处理系统
Advanced Solid Logic Technology(ASLT) 先进固体逻辑技术
advanced software(ASLT) 高级软件
advanced software facility(ASLT) 高级软设施
advanced station 先行站
advanced statistical analysis program(ASTAP) 高级统计分析程序,ASTAP语言
advanced system architecture 先进系统体系结构
Advanced System Development Division 高级系统开发部(IBM)
Advanced Systems, Inc.(ASI) 先进系统公司
advanced systems management system(ASLT) 高级系统管理系统
advanced terminal management system(ATMS) 高级终端管理系统
AdvanceNet 先进网络
advancing page 导前页
advancing phrase 前导短语
adverse state 不利状态,逆向状态
advertisement rotator 广告发布轮转程序
advertiser 广告发布者
advertising 广告发布
advice-giving system 咨询系统
advice of change of extension accessibility 分机改号存取建议
advice taking 采纳建议法
advise sink 建议的信宿
advisory 顾问
Advisory Council for Applied Research and Development(ACARD) 应用研究与开发顾问会议
advisory engineer 咨询工程师
advisory holder 咨询保持对象
advisory sink 咨询接收对象
advisory system 咨询系统
AEC(Automatic Error Correction) 自动纠错
AEN(Address ENable) 地址允许
aerial cable 架空电缆
aerial insert 架空接入
aerial photograph 航空拍摄照片
aerospace computer 航天计算机
AES(Advanced Encryption Standard) 高级加密标准
AEWS(Advanced Early Warning System) 高级预警系统
AF(Advanced Function) 高级操作程序(IBM)
AF(Auxiliary-carry Flag) 辅助进位标志
AFAC(Automatic Field Analog Computer) 自动战场模拟计算机
AFC(Automatic Fidelity Control) 自动保真度控制
AFC(Automatic Frequency Control) 自动频率控制
AFC(Available Frame Counter) 有效帧计数器
AFCC(Available Frame Capacity Counter) 有效帧容量计数器
AFE(Analog Front End) 模拟前端
AFE(Apple File Exchange) Apple文件交换
affect analysis 偏差分析
affine block cipher 仿射分组密码
affine control system 仿射控制系统
affine coordinate system 仿射坐标系
affine hull 仿射包
affine mapping 仿射映像
affine ring 仿射环
affine scaling 仿射比例
affine set 仿射集
affine space 仿射空间
affine transformation 仿射变换
affinity analysis 结合性分析
affinity-based routing 相似路由选择,姻亲路由选择 「号
affirmative acknowledge 确认回答信

affix grammar 缀词文法
AFIPS(American Federation of Information Processing Societies) 美国信息处理协会
AFG(Arbitrary Function Generator) 任意函数发生器
AFI(Automatic Fault Isolation) 自动故障隔离
AFL(Automatic Fault Location) 自动故障定位
AFP(Apple Talk Filing Protocol) AppleTalk 文件编制协议
AFP(Automatic Floating Point) 自动浮点
AFQ(Available Frame Queue) 可用帧队列
AFR(Acceptable Failure Rate) 可接受失效率
AFS(Andrew File System) 安德鲁文件系统
AFT(Active File Table) 现用文件表
AFT(Automatic Fine Tuning) 自动微调
AFT(Automatic Funds Transfer) 自动资金转账
after add 新增后
after care 售后服务
after change 变更后
after change by item 依项目变更后
after glow 余辉
after-image 后映像,后影像
after image file 后映像文件
after image journal 后映像日志
after reload 重新装入后
after service 售后服务
after treatment 后处理,补充处理
after update 更新后
aftermarket 售后市场,配件市场
AG(Address Generation) 地址生成
AGE(Attempt to GEneralize) AGE 专家系统工具
agency 代办机构
agenda 待议事件,备忘录
agent 代理者,软件代理
agent case 代理者角色
agent list 代理集合
agent-oriented programming 面向主体的编程

agent server 代理服务器
agent structure 代理结构;主体结构
aggregate 聚合,聚集
aggregate assignment 集合体赋值
aggregate bit rate 总计位速率
aggregate channel 集合信道
aggregate expression 聚合表达式
aggregate function 合计函数,聚合函数
aggregate notation 聚合记法
aggregate object 聚合对象
aggregate operator 合计运算子
aggregate query 聚合查询
aggregate signal 集合信号
aggregate value 总值
aggregation 聚合,集合
aggregation complex-object language 聚合复合对象语言
aggregation hierarchy 聚合分级结构
aggregation method 聚合法
aggregation pipe 聚合管道
aggregation-disaggregation algorithm 聚合-反聚合算法
aggregative closure 综合闭包
aggressive device 主动装置
aging 成熟过程,老化
aging periods 老化周期,衰老周期
agitation error 扰动误差
AGL (Application Generation Language) 应用程序生成语言(Olivetti)
AGP(Accelerated Graphics Port) 图形加速端口
agreed indication 统一表示法
agreement algorithm 一致性算法
agreement protocol 一致性协议
AGS(Advanced Graphic System) 高级图形系统
AH(Accumulator High) 累加器高位字节
AH(Add Halfword) 半字加
AH(Ampere-Hour) 安培-小时
Aho-Corasick algorithm 阿霍-克拉思克算法,AC算法
Aho-Corasick pattern-matching automaton 阿霍-克拉思克模式匹配自动机,AC自动机
AI(Address Incomplete) 地址不完全
AI(Artificial Intelligence) 人工智能

AI-based educational tool 基于人工智能的教育工具
AIDS(Advanced Interactive Debugging System) 高级交互式调试系统
AIM(Advanced Information Manager) 高级信息管理程序(Fujitsu)
AIM(Associative Index Method) 相关索引法
AIMDS AIMDS 语言
AIFF AIFF 文件格式
aiming field 引导字段
aiming symbol 引导符号,瞄准符号
AIPS(Average Instructions Per Second) 平均每秒执行指令数
AIR(Additional Increase Rate) 附加增长速率
air bearing disk 空气承载磁盘
air boundary layer 空气分界层
air bubbles 气泡
air cooling 空气冷却,风冷
air cushion 空气减震垫
air data computer 飞行数据计算机
air duct 通风管道
air filter 空气过滤器
air-floating head 空气浮动(磁)头
air-flow type ink-jet printing head 气流型喷墨打印头
air gap 空气隙,气隙
air lubricated guide 空气润滑导轨
air restrictor board 气流限定板
air-support structure 空气承载结构
air-tight seal 气密垫
air warning system 防空警报系统
airborne computer 机载计算机
airborne early-warning radar(AEW radar) 机载预警雷达
airborne electronic terrain map system 机载电子地形图系统
airborne warning and control system computer 空中预警控制系统计算机
airbrush 喷枪,喷刷
airline reservation system 飞机订位系统
airspeed computer 空速计算机
AIX(Advanced Interactive eXecutive) 高级交互执行程序(IBM)
AIX/ESA(AIX/Enterprise System Architecture) 适用于企业系统体系结构的 AIX 操作系统(IBM)
AIXwindows toolkit AIX 窗口工具箱(IBM)
AL(Absolute Loader) 绝对地址装入程序
AL(Accumulator Low) 累加器低位字节
AL(Activity Logging) 活动日志
AL/X AL/X 语言
alarm 告警,报警
alarm call services 告警呼叫业务
alarm circuit 警报电路
alarm control 闹钟控制,告警控制
alarm device 警报装置
alarm display 警报显示
alarm free 无告警
alarm indication signal 告警指示信号
alarm indicator 告警指示
alarm rate 告警率
alarm-repeated transmission 重复警报传送
alarm return address 告警返回地址
alarm sensor 告警传感器
alarm signal 告警信号
alarm statement 告警语句
alarm system 告警系统
ALAS(Automated Literature Alerting System) 自动化文献提示系统
ALB(Advanced Load Balancing) (交换机)高级负载平衡方法
Albert 爱尔伯特通信机
ALC(Adaptive Logic Circuit) 自适应逻辑电路
ALC(Automatic Level Compensation) 自动电平补偿
ALC(Automatic Level Control) 自动电平控制
ALC(Automatic Locking Circuit) 自动锁定电路
ALCU(Asynchronous Line Control Unit) 异步线路控制单元
Aldus Pagemaker 页面编辑程序(Aldus)
Aldus Persuasion Persuasion 演示程序(Aldus)
ALE(Address Latch Enable) 地址锁存使能
ALE(Application Linking and Embed-

ding) 应用程序链接与嵌入
alert 警告,警示
alert box 警告框,警示框
Alert Legend 警示图例
Alert Popups 弹出式告警
alertable thread 可报警线程
alertor 报警器
ALF(Application Library File) 应用程序库文件
ALF(Automatic Line Feed) 自动换行
algebra 代数
algebra-oriented language 面向代数的语言
algebraic adder 代数加法器
algebraic approach restoration 代数方式复原
algebraic cipher 代数密码
algebraic enciphering 代数加密
algebraic expression 代数表达式
algebraic language 代数语言
algebraic linguistics 代数语言学
algebraic manipulation language 代数操作语言
algebraic precision of quadrature formula 求积公式的代数精度
algebraic semantics 代数语义学
algebraic sign 代数符号
ALGOL(ALGOrithmic Language) 算法语言,ALGOL语言
ALGOL(ALGebraic Oriented Language) 面向代数语言,ALGOL语言
algorithm 算法
algorithm analysis 算法分析
algorithm chart 算法图
algorithm comparison 算法比较
algorithm complexity 算法复杂性
algorithm convergence 演算收敛
algorithm decomposition 算法分解
algorithm flow chart 算法流程图
algorithm generator 算法产生程序
algorithm language 算法语言
algorithm module 算法模块
algorithm routine 算法例程
algorithm stability 算法稳定性
algorithm theory 算法理论
algorithmic approach 算法逼近
algorithmic language (ALGOL) ALGOL语言

algorithmic language program conversion 算法语言程序转换
algorithmic routine 算法例程
algorithmic translation 算法转换
ALI(Asynchronous Line Interface) 异步线路接口
alias 别名;乱真信号,假信号
alias description entry 别名描述项
alias name 别名,替换名
alias network address 别名网址
alias object 别名实体;别名对象
ALIAS option 别名可选项
alias problem 别名问题
aliasing 别名使用;图像失真;混叠,锯齿现象
aliasing distortion 混淆[折叠]失真
aliasing effect 交叠效应
aliasing error 混叠误差
aliasing frequency 假信号频率
aliasing problem 假信号问题
ALICE ALICE语言
alien 外来的,异类的
alien tones 异己音调,杂音
align 对准,校准,对齐
aligned bundle 定位光纤束
aligned words 调整[校准]字组
aligner 调整程序;校准器
alignment 对准,校准;排列
alignment clause 对齐子句
alignment disk 校准磁盘
alignment diskette 校准用软磁盘
alignment error rate monitoring 校准误码率监测
alignment function 对齐功能
alignment indicator 定位指示符
alignment mark 对准标记,调整标志
alignment network 校准网络
alignment of data 数据对齐
alignment pattern 校准图形
alignment rule 对齐[对准]规则
ALL(Application Load List) 应用程序装载表
All at Once 整批传送
all busy circuit 全忙碌线路
all caps 全为大写字母
all-channel CATV amplifier 全通道公用天线电视放大器
all clear 全清除

all correct matched 完全正确匹配
all-digital correlation 全数字相关
all-digital display 全数字显示
all-digital simulation 全数字仿真
"all or no" principle "全或无"原则
all-in-one 全合一,单板组装
all-in-one computer 一体化计算机
all off 全部结束
all-page locking 全页面加锁
all-pair problem 全配对问题
all-parallel A/D converter 全并行模/数转换器
all-pass network 全连通网络
all points addressable(APA) 全部像点可寻址的
all-purpose computer 通用计算机
all-purpose controller 通用控制器
all-purpose language 通用语言
all-purpose robot 通用机器人
all-reference 全引用
all-relay automatic system 全继电器自动控制系统
all resume 全部重新开始;全部恢复
all right reserved 保留全部权利,全权所有
all routes broadcast 全路由广播
all-station address 全部站址
all-suspend 全挂起
all-trunks busy 所有中继线忙
all-zero signal 全零信号
Allegro-MCM Allegro多芯片组件设计软件
Alliant minisupercomputer system Alliant小巨型计算机系统
Alliant Network Supercomputer Resource system Alliant网络巨型机资源系统
ALLOC(Allocation) 配置,分配,定位
Alloc Memory Pool (Netware)分配存储池
allocate 配置,分配,定位
allocate event 指定事件
allocate memory 存储器配置,内存分配
allocate node 分配节点
allocate storage 配置存储区
allocated resource table entry 已分配资源表目
allocated state 已分配状态
allocating 配置,派定
allocating physical file space 分配物理文件空间
allocating system resource 配置系统资源
allocation 配置,分配,定位
allocation matrix 分配矩阵
allocation of data set 数据集地址配置
allocation quantity audit 配置数量审核
allocation records 配置记录
allocation units 分配单元
allocator 配置器,分配符
allow 容许
allowable value 容许值
allowable working speed 容许工作速度
allowance 容差,容许度
allowed cell rate(ACR) 允许的信元速率
alloy belt printer 合金带打印机
alloy diffusion 合金扩散
alloy junction 合金结
ALM(ALarM) 告警,报警
ALM(Asynchronous Line Multiplexer) 异步线路复用器(Sun)
ALOHA access mode ALOHA存取方式
ALOHA protocol 阿洛哈协议
ALOHA System 阿洛哈系统,ALOHA计算机网
alpha 阿尔法(α)
alpha atom α原子
Alpha AXP Alpha AXP体系结构(DEC)
alpha-beta pruning α-β修剪
alpha-beta search α-β搜索
alpha channel α通道
Alpha chip Alpha 64位处理机芯片(DEC)
alpha cutoff α修剪
alpha flux α通量
ALPHA language ALPHA语言
alpha mode α模式
Alpha Only 只允许用字母
alpha-particle sensitivity α粒子灵敏度
alpha particles α粒子
alpha particles analysis system α粒子分析系统
Alpha privileged architecture library

(Alpha PAL) Alpha 特许体系结构库(DEC)
alpha radiation soft error α射线辐射软误差
alpha soft error α 软失效
alpha spectrometer α 能谱仪
alpha test α 测试
alpha value α 值
alphabet 字符,字母表
alphabet field 字符[字母]字段
alphabet length 字母长度
alphabet name 字符表名
alphabet soup 字母"汤"
alphabetic addressing 字符寻址
alphabetic character 字母符号
alphabetic code 字符码
alphabetic coded character set 编码的字母字符集
alphabetic coding 字符[文字]编码
alphabetic command 字符命令
alphabetic data item 字符数据项
alphabetic field 字符字段
alphabetic-numeric 字符数字
alphabetic order 字符顺序
alphabetic shift 字符移位,换字母档
alphabetic string 字母字符串
alphabetic symbol 字母符号
alphabetic tree 字母树
alphabetic word 字符文字
alphabetical list 同义词列表
alphabetizing convention 字符顺序约定
alphageometric graphics 字符几何图形
alphageometrics 字符几何法
alphamosaic 镶嵌法字图显示,字母颗粒图像
alphamosaic graphics 字符镶嵌图形
alphamosaic teletex 代码方式图文电视
alphanumeric character set 文数字符集
alphanumeric coded character set 字母数字编码字符集
alphanumeric data item 字母数字数据项
alphanumeric display device 字母数字显示设备
alphanumeric edited data item 字母数字编辑的数据项
alphanumeric field 字母数字字段
alphanumeric-graphic display 文数图形显示器
alphanumeric instruction 文数指令
alphanumeric keyboard 字母数字键盘
alphanumeric mode 字母数字方式
alphanumeric printer 字母数字打印机
alphanumeric reader 字母数字阅读机
alphanumeric shift 字母数字换档
alphanumeric sort 字母数字排序
alphanumeric visual display 文数视觉显示器
alphanumerical 按字母数字顺序的
alphaphotographic 照像法字图显示
alphascope 字符显示终端
ALPURCOM(ALl PURpose COMmunications system) 通用通信系统(美国军用)
ALR(Automatic Level Recorder) 自动电平记录仪
ALR(Automatic Load Regulator) 自动负荷调节器
ALS(Ada Language System) Ada 语言系统
ALS(Adaptive Learning System) 自适应学习系统
alt key 交替键,选择键
alt-route 更替路由
Altair 8800 Altair 8800 计算机
Altas * Graphics Altas 专题地图图形软件
alter mode 修改模式
Altera Altera 公司
alterable memory 可替用内存
alteration switch 转换[变更]开关
altering 变更,改为
altering error 变更误差
altering search space 变换搜索空间
alternate 替用
alternate buffering 替用缓冲
alternate characters 替用字符
alternate CPU recovery(ACR) 替用 CPU 恢复操作
alternate digit inversion 交替数字的反转
alternate direction 换向
alternate index 替用索引,替换下标

alternate key 替用关键字；交替作用键
alternate mark inversion(AMI) 传号交替反转
alternate mark inversion code 传号交替反转码
alternate mark inversion violation 交替传号反转违例
alternate mode 替用模式，轮流方式
alternate name spaces 可替换名字空间
alternate optima 可选用的最佳解答
alternate path retry(APR) 替用路径重试
alternate recovery(AR) 转换恢复
alternate route 替用路由
alternate routing 替用路由选择法
alternate size 替用量，备用大小
alternate track 替用磁道
alternate triples 替用三元组
alternating current(AC) 交流(电)
alternating current signaling 交流信令
Alternating Direction Edition Next Array(ADENA) ADENA计算机
alternating flashing 交替闪动
alternating logic 交替逻辑
alternating non-return-to-zero(ANRZ) 交替不归零制
alternating operating system 交互式操作系统
alternating points 交错点组
alternating projection neural network(APNN) 交替投影神经网络
alternating Turing machine(ATM) 交替图灵机
alternation 交替；交错
alternative 选择对象，替换目标
alternative attribute 二中选一属性
alternative box 交替框
alternative plan 备用计划
alternative route 候补路由
alternative routing indicator 替用路由指示符
alternative version 选择[替换]版本
Alto Alto个人计算机
Altos-net Altos网络
ALTRAN ALTRAN语言

ALU(Arithmetic-Logic Unit) 算术逻辑单元
ALU architecture 算术逻辑单元体系结构
Alumna ceramic 氧化铝陶瓷
Always on Top 始终在最前面
AM(Amplitude Modulation) 调幅，幅度调制
AM(Animation Metafile) 动画元文件
AM×86 AM×86系列CPU
AM-VSB(Amplitude Modulation-Vestigial SideBand) 残留边带调幅
AMA(Automatic Message Accounting) 自动消息结算
ambience 环境
ambient 周围，环境
ambient conditions 周围[环境]条件
ambient light 环境光线；漫射光
ambient noise level 环境噪声电平
ambient property 环境属性
ambient temperature 环境温度
ambiguity 含糊，多义性，模糊点
ambiguity delay 含糊延迟
ambiguity error 含糊误差，多义性错误
ambiguity of knowledge 知识模糊性
ambiguity problem 含糊问题，二义性问题
ambiguity processor architecture 含糊处理器体系结构
ambiguous data 含糊数据，歧义数据
ambiguous grammar 含糊文法
ambiguous language 含糊语言
ambiguous name resolution 含糊名称解析
ambiguous reference 含糊[二义性]引用
AMCA(Apple Media Control Architecture) Apple多媒体控制体系结构
AMD(Active Matrix Display) 有源矩阵显示器
AMD(Advanced Micro Devices Inc.) AMD公司(美)
AMD Athlon AMD速龙微处理器
AMD Duron AMD毒龙微处理器
AMD K5 AMD K5微处理器
AMD K6 AMD K6微处理器
Amdahl 470V/60 Amdahl 470V/60

计算机
Amdahl's law 阿姆代尔定律
amending plan 修改规划
amendment file 修改文件
amendment language 修改语言
amendment record 修改记录
American Institute of Electrical Engineers(AIEE) 美国电气工程师协会
American National Standard Control Characters 美国国家标准控制字符
American National Standard Institute(ANSI) 美国国家标准学会
American National Standard Labels(ANSL) 美国(国家)标准标号
American Society for Information Science(ASIS) 美国信息科学协会
American Standards Association(ASA) 美国标准协会
American Telephone and Telegraph(AT&T) 美国电话电报公司
Ames Research Center Ames研究中心
AMF(Animation Metafile Format) 动画元文件格式
AMHS(Automatic Message Handling System) 自动消息处理系统
AMI(Alternate Mark Inversion) 传号交替翻转
AMI BIOS AMI基本输入输出系统
Amiga operating system Amiga操作系统
Amiga Vision Amiga多媒体著作工具
AMIGO AMIGO操作系统
amorphous 非晶态的,无定形的
amorphous material 非晶态材料
amorphous memory 无定形存储器
amorphous silicon phototransistor 无定形硅光电晶体管
amorphous substances 无定形物质
AMOS(Associative Memory Organizing System) 相联内存组织系统
AMOS(Avalanche injection type Metal-Oxide Semiconductor) 雪崩注入金属氧化物半导体(器件)
amount 数量,统计
amp-mixer 混响放大器
ampere(A) 安,安培

ampere-turns 安匝
ampersand "&"字符
amphibolous 意义含糊,不明确
amplidyne 直流功率[微场电流]放大器
amplification 放大,放大率
amplification factor 放大系数[因子]
amplifier 放大器
amplifier distortion 放大器失真[畸变]
amplifier noise 放大器噪声
amplify 放大
amplitude 振幅,幅度
amplitude characteristic 振幅特性
amplitude comparator 幅度比较器
amplitude detection 幅度检测
amplitude discriminator 鉴幅器
amplitude frequency characteristic 振幅频率特性
amplitude frequency distortion 幅频失真
amplitude frequency response 幅频响应
amplitude limiter 限幅器
amplitude modulation(AM) 调幅,幅度调制
amplitude quantized control 幅度量化控制
amplitude sensing 幅度感测
amplitude separation data detection(ASDD) 幅度分离型数据检测
amplitude shift keying(ASK) 振幅键控
AMPS(Advanced Mobile Phone Service) 先进的移动式电话服务
AMX(Active MatriX) 活动矩阵
AN(Artificial Network) 仿真网络
AN code AN码
analog 模拟;类推;模拟量
analog adder 模拟加法器
analog approach 模拟途径[求解]
analog audio 模拟音频
analog backup 模拟备份
analog channel 模拟通道[信道]
analog communications 模拟通信
analog comparator 模拟比较器
analog component 模拟分量
analog computer 模拟计算机
analog control 模拟控制
analog data 模拟数据

analog delay line 模拟延迟线
analog-digital adapter 模-数适配器
analog-digital-analog converter system 模-数-模转换器系统
analog-digital computer 模拟-数字计算机
analog display 模拟显示
analog divider 模拟除法器
analog facility terminal(AFT) 模拟设施终端
analog form 模拟形式
analog front end(AFE) 模拟前端
analog function generator 模拟函数发生器
analog indicator 模拟指示器
analog input 模拟输入
analog input card 模拟输入卡
analog input channel 模拟输入通道
analog input expander 模拟输入扩展器
analog input module 模拟输入模块
analog input operation 模拟输入操作
analog integrated circuit 模拟集成电路
analog intelligence test 模拟智能测试
analog-intensity modulation 模拟强度调制
analog line 模拟线路
analog line driver 模拟线路驱动器
analog magnetic head 模拟磁头
analog monitor 模拟监视器
analog multiplexer 模拟多路转换器
analog multiplier 模拟乘法器
analog network 模拟网络
analog output 模拟输出
analog output card 模拟输出卡
analog output channel amplifier 模拟输出通道放大器
analog plot mode 模拟绘图方式
analog processor-controller 模拟处理器控制器
analog recording 模拟记录法
analog repeater 模拟增音机
analog representation 模拟表示法
analog scaling 模拟比例因子
analog signal 模拟信号
analog signaling 模拟发信;模拟信令
analog simulation 模拟仿真
analog standard cell 模拟标准单元
analog switch 模拟开关
analog system 模拟系统
analog-to-digital conversion 模-数转换
analog-to-digital conversion accuracy 模数转换准确度
analog-to-digital conversion precision 模数转换精确度
analog-to-digital conversion rate 模数转换速度
analog-to-digital converter(ADC) 模数转换器
analog-to-digital encoder 模拟数字编码器
analog-to-digital LSI 模拟-数字大规模集成电路
analog-to-frequency converter 模拟频率变换器
analog value 模拟值,模拟量
analog variable 模拟变量
analog variable assignment 模拟变量赋值
analog video 模拟视频
analog video overlay 模拟视频覆盖
analogical control 类推控制
analogical inference 类推[模拟]推理
analogical means-ends analysis 类推分析
analogical problem solving 类推问题求解
analogical problem space 类推问题空间
analogical reasoning 类推论证法
analogical representation 模拟表示法
analogical simulation 相似模拟
analogue 模拟
analogue error detection 模拟检错
analogy 模拟,类比
analogy computing device 模拟计算设备
analogy driven inference 类比驱动推理
analogy induction knowledge acquisition 类比归纳知识获取
analogy intelligence 类推[模拟]智能
analogy intelligence test 类推智能测验
analogy relation representation 相似关系表示
analysis 分析

analysis block 分析块[段]
analysis graphics 分析图
analysis mode 分析模式
analysis model 分析模型
analysis of algorithm 算法分析
analysis pass 分析通过
analysis phase 分析阶段
analysis program 分析程序
analyst 分析员
analytic hierarchy process 分析层次过程
analytic learning 分析学习
analytic model 分析[解析]模型
analytic relationship 分析关系
analytic signal 解析信号
analytical attack 解析攻击
analytical engine 分析机
analytical function generator 解析函数发生器
analytical graphics 分析图
analytical-method mathematic model 解析法数学模型
analytical model 分析模型
analytical modeling 解析建模
analyze 解析
analyzer 分析程序;分析器
anamorphic lens 变形镜头
Anarchy network Anarchy 网络
ANC(All Number Calling) 全号呼叫
ancestor node 源始[先辈]结点
ancestor task 源始[先辈]任务
ancestor window 源始窗口
ancestral task 源始任务
ancestry filter 源始[先辈]过滤器
ancestry filtered form strategy 源始过滤策略
anchor 锚区,位置;锚标志
anchor cell 锚定单元
anchor graphic 锚定图
anchor point 锚点,定位点
anchored graphic 已锁定的图形
anchored scan test 锚式扫描测试
AND "与"
AND gate "与"门
AND node "与"节点
AND NOT "与非"
AND NOT gate "与非"门
AND/OR form "与或"形

AND/OR graph "与或"图
AND/OR tree "与或"树
Andrew file system(AFS) 安德鲁文件系统
android 似人机器人
angiography 脉管绘图法
angle bracket 尖括号
anglicize 符号码英语化
angular brackets 尖括号
angular curve 尖角曲线
angular domain 角域
angular error 角误差
angular momentum 角动量
angular resolution 角分辨率
angular misalignment loss 角偏差损耗,不同心偏差
angular perspective 斜透视
angular resolution 角分辨率
ANI(Automatic Number Identification) 自动号码识别
animate 活动的,动画制作
animated graphics 动画图形
animated screen capture 活动屏幕捕获
animatic 活动的
animation 动画
animation kit 动画制作成套工具
animation language 动画制作语言
animation metafile 动画元文件
animation metafile format(AMF) 动画元文件格式
animation script 动画脚本
animation system 动画制作系统
Animator Animator 动画创作软件
anion 阴离子,负离子
anisochronous signal 非等时[准同步]信号
anisochronous transmission 准同步[非等时]传输
anisotropic 各向异性的
anisotropic composite material 各向异性复合材料
anisotropic sound bearing medium 各向异性传声介质
anisotropy 各向异性
ANL(Automatic New Line) 自动换行
ANL(Automatic Noise Limiter) 自动噪声限制器

ANN (Artificial Neural Network) 人工神经网络
annealing 退火
annex 附录,附件
annex memory 附添内存,相联存储器
annex storage 相联存储器
annotate 注解,注释
annotated predicate calculus 带注释的谓词演算
annotation 注解,评语,批注
annotation file 批注文件
annotation symbol 注释符号
annual conference 年会
annual report 年度报表
annual transmission variations 年传输变动
annual units 全年单位量
annular 环形的
annular tube 套管
annunciator 报警器
anode 阳极
anomalistic 不规则的,异常的
anomalous situation 异常情况
anonym 假名,化名
anonymous 匿名的;无记录的
Anonymous File Transfer Protocol 匿名文件传输协议
Anonymous FTP 匿名文件传输协议
Anonymous Login Convention (FTP)匿名注册约定
anonymous-only logons 只用匿名登录
anonymous pipe 无命名管道
anonymous processor pool 均一处理机群
anonymous remailer 匿名邮件转发器
anonymous server 匿名服务器
anonymous variable 匿名变量
ANS (American National Standard) 美国国家标准
ANSA (Advanced Network System Architecture) 高级网络系统体系结构(东芝-日电)
ANSCII (American National Standard Code for Information Interchange) 美国国家信息交换标准码
ANSI (American National Standards Institute) 美国国家标准学会
ANSI C ANSI C语言

ANSI character set ANSI字符集
ANSI. SYS 标准系统设置文件
ANSI terminal ANSI终端机
answer 回答,应答,答复
answer-back code 响应代码
answer-back drum 自动应答器
answer-back key 应答键
answer-back signal 回覆[应答]信号
answer-back unit simulator 回覆单元仿真器
answer code 回答码,应答码
answer delay 回答延迟
answer extraction 回答摘取
answer list 回答表,应答清单
answer mode 应答方式
answer only modem 只应答调制解调器
answer/originate modem 应答/呼叫型调制解调器
answer process 应答进程
answer schema 应答模式,应答计划
answer seizure ratio(ASR) 回答占用率
answer signal 回答信号
answer statement 应答语句
answer time 应答时间
answerback 回覆,应答
answering 回答,应答
answering circuit 回答电路
answering delay 回答延迟
Answering Machine 应答机
ANSYS ANSYS通用工程分析软件
antagonicity 对抗性
antagonism game 对抗性对策
antecedent 先行的
antecedent goal 先行目标
antecedent rule 先行规则
antenna 天线
antenna gain 天线增益
anthropological 人类学的
anthropomorphic dummy 人形假人
anthropomorphic robots 拟人的机器人
anthropomorphic software agent 拟人化软件代理
anti-clash key 防碰撞键
anti-compiler 反编译程序
anti-moniker 反别名
anti-phase 反相,逆相
anti-phase flashing 反相闪动

anti-saturated logic circuit 抗饱和逻辑电路
anti-shock device 防震装置
anti-virus program 抗病毒程序
antialiasing 抗混叠,消除锯齿
antibuggin 防错法「器
anticipated carry adder 超前进位加法
anticipated demand 预期需求
anticipated fixed cost 预期固定成本
anticipated input 先行输入
anticipation mode 预期模式
anticipatory buffering 预期缓冲
anticipatory paging 先行调页
anticipatory staging 预期移入,先行登台
anticlockwise 反时针方向的
anticoincidence element "异"门
anticoincidence gate 非一致门
anticoincidence operation "异"操作
ANTICPG(ANTICipatory PaGing) 超前调页,先行调页
Antifuse 反熔断技术
antijamming 抗干扰
antijamming margin 抗干扰容限
antilogarithm 反对数
antinode 波谷
antinomy 悖论,自相矛盾
antiphase 反相,逆相
antireflection coating 抗反射涂层,增透膜
antistatic device 防静电设备
antistatic mat 防静电垫子
antistop list 关键词表;非禁用词表
antisymmetric cryptology 非对称密码
antisymmetric law 反对称律
antisymmetric matrix 反对称矩阵
antisymmetric state 反对称态
antitone mapping 反序映射
antivibration 抗振动
antivirus software 防病毒软件
antitrust law 反托拉斯法
ANVIL ANVIL软件系列
ANW(Apollo NetWork) 阿波罗网络
any mode 任何模式
any-sequence queue 任意顺序队列
AOB(Address-Out Bus) 地址输出总线
AOC(Automatic Overload Control) 自动过载控制
AOL(All ON-Line) 全部联机
AOL(America On Line) 美国在线(网站)
AOP(Automatic Overload Protection) 自动过载保护
AOS(Annotation Overlay Symbols) 覆盖标准符号
AP(Access Point) 存取点,访问点
AP(Access Privileges) 存取特权
AP(Application Process) 应用进程
AP(Array Processor) 阵列处理机
AP(Attached Processor) 附加处理机
APA(All-Points-Addressable) 全点可寻址的
APA (Analytical Processing Benchmark) 分析处理基准程序
Apache (Unix/Linux)阿帕奇Web服务器软件
apartment model multi-threading 房间模型多线程化
apartment thread 房间线程
APC(Adaptive Predictive Coding) 自适应预测编码
APC(Asynchronous Procedure Call) 异步过程调用
APCM(Adaptive Pulse Code Modulation) 自适应脉冲编码调制
APCS(Associative Processor Computer System) 相联处理机计算机系统
APE(Adaptive Predictive Encoding) 自适应预测编码
aperture 孔径,窗孔
aperture card 窗孔卡片
aperture distortion 孔径失真
aperture effect 孔径效应
aperture grill 微孔网(SONY)
aperture mask 孔罩
aperture slot 光圈,孔隙
aperture time 孔隙时间
apex 峰,顶点,尖
APG(Automatic Priority Group) 自动优先级分组(IBM)
API(Application Programming Interface) 应用程序编程接口(微软)
API(Automatic Priority Interrupt) 自动优先中断
APIC (Advanced Processor Interrupt

Controller) 高级处理器中断控制器
APL(A Programming Language) APL 语言
APLICOT APLICOT 语言
APOC (Advanced Paging Operator Code) 高级寻呼操作码
apogee 远地点
Apollo II MPEG 压缩卡(DV Studio)
apostrophe character 撇号字符
apostrophe edit 撇号编辑
APP(Associative Parallel Processors) 相联并行处理机
app(APPlication) 应用程序
apparatus 设备,仪器
apparent 明显的;视在的
apparent color 视在颜色
apparent contour 外观轮廓
apparent distance 视距
apparent height 视在高度
APPC(Advanced Program-to-Program Communication) 先进的程序间通信方法
appearance 外部连接;外貌
appearance check 外观检查
append 附加,追加,添加
append blank command 追加空记录命令
append command 附加命令,增添命令
append file 附加文件
append from command 从其他数据库追加数据命令
append lines 追加行
append lines command 追加行命令
append mode 追加模式
append query 追加查询
append record 附加记录
appendage 输入/输出附加控制
appendage task 附加任务,附属任务
appearance 外观
Apple 苹果公司,Apple 公司
Apple II Apple II 计算机
Apple III Apple III 计算机
Apple Desktop Bus(ADB) Apple 桌面总线
Apple Desktop Interface Apple 台式机界面

Apple DOS Apple 磁盘操作系统
Apple extended keyboard Apple 扩充型键盘
Apple File Exchange Apple 文件转换程序
Apple key Apple 键
Apple menu Apple 菜单
Apple Network Assistant Apple 网络助手
Apple PowerBook PowerBook 笔记本计算机(苹果)
Apple QuickTake QuickTake 数码照相机(苹果)
Apple QuickTime QuickTime 图像播放软件(苹果)
Apple Remote Access Apple 远程访问
AppleShare AppleShare 网络操作系统
AppleShare file server Apple 共享文件服务器
AppleShare PC 苹果机的 PC 兼容软件
applet 小应用程序
AppleTalk AppleTalk 网络协议
AppleTalk File Protocol(AFP) AppleTalk 文件协议
AppleTalk Link Access Protocol AppleTalk 链路访问协议
Appleton layer 阿普尔顿层
Appletviewer 小程序浏览器
AppleWorks AppleWorks 综合软件
application(app) 应用;应用程序
application access service 应用软件存取服务
application association 应用联结
application aware networking 应用认知网络连接
application awareness 应用认知
application benchmarks 应用程序基准测试程序
application buffer 应用缓冲器
application context 应用程序上下文
application control file(ACF) 应用控制文件
application control language(ACL) 应用控制语言
application control menu 应用软件控制菜单
application data 应用数据

application Data Protocol (SSL) 应用数据协议
application defined function 应用程序定义函数
application developer 应用程序开发人员
application development language 应用程序开发语言
application development system 应用开发系统
application environment 应用环境
application file 应用文件
application form library 应用程序窗体库
application gateway 应用网关
application generating system 应用程序生成系统
Application generator 应用程序生成器
application group 应用程序群组
application heap 应用软件堆
Application icon 应用程序图标
application layer 应用层
application layer communication protocol 应用层通信协议
application level frame(ALF) 应用层组帧
application level gateway(ALF) 应用层网关
application library 应用程序库
application library file(ALF) 实用程序库文件
Application Manager 应用程序管理器
application manual 应用手册
application media pool 应用程序媒体池
application metering 应用程序计量
application note 应用注释
application oriented language(AOL) 面向应用的语言
application package 应用程序包
application performance explorer 应用程序性能探测程序
application portability 应用程序可移植性
application process(AP) 应用进程
application processor 应用处理机
application program(AP) 应用程序
application program interface(API) 应用程序接口
application program logon request 应用程序注册请求
application program termination 应用程序终止
application programmer 应用程序员
application programs running 应用程序运行
application-required language 应用需求语言
application root 应用程序根目录
application server 应用服务器
application service element 应用服务元素
application shortcut key 应用程序快捷键
application software(ASW) 应用软件
application software engineering 应用软件工程
application software prototyping 应用软件原型化
application specific integrated circuit (ASIC) 专用集成电路
application specific integrated circuit design 专用集成电路设计
application-specific language 特定应用语言
application specific memory 专用内存
application specific standard part(ASSP) 专用标准部件
application specific standard product (ASSP) 专用标准产品
application study 应用研究
application suite 成套应用程序
application supplied video window 应用程序支持的视频窗口
Application System(AS) 应用系统
application system 应用系统
application timer 应用定时器
application window 应用程序窗口
applicative language 应用式语言
applied data bit 附加数据位
applied mathematics 应用数学
applique 附加器
apply style 使用样式
APPN (Advanced Peer-to-Peer Network) 高级对等网络
appointment 约会，预约

appointment mode 预约方式
Approach Approach 数据库(Lotus)
approach 途径
approve recommended for release 建议发行的批准
approver 协议验证程序
approximate calculation 近似计算
approximate combinatorial algorithm 近似组合算法
approximate cycle signal 准周期[近似周期]信号
approximate data 近似数据
approximate match 近似匹配
approximate reasoning 似然推理
approximate solution 近似解
approximate string matching 估计串匹配
approximate value 近似值
approximation 近似值
AppWizard(Application Wizard) 应用程序向导
APR(Active Page Register) 活动页面寄存器
APR(Algorithm for Pattern Recognition) 模式识别算法
April Fool's jokes 愚人节玩笑
apron 附表
APS(Accessory Power Supply) 辅助电源
APT(Application Program Table) 应用程序表
APT(Automatic Programmed Tools language) 自动程控工具语言
Aptiva Aptiva 多媒体计算机(IBM)
AQL(Acceptable Quality Level) 可接受质量水平
aquire display 申请显示
AR(Access Request) 存取请求
AR(Annual Report) 年度报告
AR(Auxiliary Routine) 辅助例程
ARA(AppleTalk Remote Access) AppleTalk 远程访问协议
Arago Arago 数据库管理系统
ARB(ARBitration) 仲裁
Arabic character 阿拉伯字符
Arabization 阿拉伯化
arbiter 仲裁器;判优程序
arbitrary access 任意存取

arbitrary function generator 任意函数发生器
arbitrary input 任意输入
arbitrary object 任意目标,任意对象
arbitrary selection 任意选择
arbitrary sequence computer 任意顺序计算机
arbitrary string 任意字符串
arbitrary value 任意值
arbitrary-write 任意写
arbitrated signature 仲裁签名
arbitration(ARB) 仲裁
arbitration logic 仲裁逻辑
arbitration network 仲裁网络
arbitration system 仲裁系统
arbitration unit 仲裁单元
ARC(Advanced RISC Computing) 高级精简指令芯片计算
ARC(Automatic Ratio Control) 自动比率控制
arc 电弧
arc splines 圆弧样条
arc welding robot 弧焊机器人
arcade game 拱廊游戏机
Archie 网络查询工具
Archie client Archie 客户
Archie gateway Archie 网关
Archie server Archie 服务器
Archie site Archie 网站
architecture 体系结构
architecture characteristics 体系结构特性
architecture comparison 体系结构比较
architecture difference 体系结构差异
architecture for managing data structure 用于管理数据结构的体系结构
architecture for searching 搜索用的体系结构
architecture limit 体系结构限制
architecture neutral 结构中立性
architecture prototyping 体系结构原型
architecture taxonomy 体系结构分类学
archival 归档
archival backup 增量[归档]备份
archival database 存档式数据库
archival location 归档保存位置
archival repository 档案库

archival storage 归档存储器
archive 归档;归档文件;大容量外存
archive attribute 增量[归档]属性
archive bit 归档位
archive diskette 归档[文件]软盘
archive file 存档文件
archive manual page 归档库人工页面
archive site 归档网站,归档库现场
archived file 已归档文件
archiving 存档,归档
ARCnet(Attached Resource Computer network) 连接资源计算机网,ARC网络
Arden's rule 阿登规则
area 区,面
area assignment 区域赋值
area attribute 区域属性
area chart 区域图,分区图
area code 地区代码
area composition 区域合成
area composition machine(ANM) 区域拼图机
area coordinate 区域坐标,面积坐标
area definition 区域定义
area fill 区域填充
area graph 区域图
area identification field 区域识别字段
area in storage 存储器中的区域
area map 区域映射
area navigation computer 区域导航计算机
area of region 区域面积
area sampling 区域取样
area search 区域检索
area shading 区域[面]阴影
area variable 区域变量
areal density 面密度
areal recording density 面记录密度
arg(argument) 变元,自变量
arg list(argument list) 参数表
argonomics 人类工程学
argument 自变量,参数,变元
argument address 参数[变元]地址
argument association 参数结合
argument byte 参数字节
argument list 自变量表,变元表
argument pointer 参数指针
argument separator 参数分隔符号
argument stack 变元堆栈
argument subscript 变元下标
argument transfer instructions 参数转换指令
arithmetic 算术
arithmetic addition 算术加法
arithmetic address 算术地址
arithmetic and logic box 算术逻辑框
arithmetic and logic unit(ALU) 算术逻辑单元
arithmetic assignment statement 算术赋值语句
arithmetic bus 算术总线
arithmetic capability 算术[运算]能力
arithmetic check 算术校验
arithmetic coding 算术编码
arithmetic constant 算术常数
arithmetic conversion 算术转换[变换]
arithmetic data 算术数据
arithmetic delimiters 算术定界符
arithmetic difference 算术差
arithmetic distance 算术间距
arithmetic element 算术元素
arithmetic exception 算术异常
arithmetic expression 算术表达式
arithmetic IF statement 算术条件语句
arithmetic instruction 算术指令
arithmetic logic unit(ALU) 算术逻辑单元
arithmetic mean 算术平均数[中项]
arithmetic operation 算术运算
arithmetic operator 算术算子
arithmetic organization 算术组织机构
arithmetic overflow 算术上溢
arithmetic picture data 算术图像数据
arithmetic pipeline 算术流水线
arithmetic primary 算术初等项
arithmetic product 算术乘积
arithmetic progression 算术[等差]数列
arithmetic register 算术寄存器
arithmetic relation 算术关系
arithmetic scan 算术扫描
arithmetic section 算术部分
arithmetic series 算术级数
arithmetic shift 算术移位
arithmetic shift left 算术左移位

arithmetic shift right 算术右移位
arithmetic statement 算术语句
arithmetic sum 算术和
arithmetic term 算术项
arithmetic trap mask 算术自陷屏蔽
arithmetic underflow 算术下溢
arithmetic unit 运算单元
arithmetic upperflow 算术上溢
arithmetical unit 算术单元
arithmetization of formal system 形式系统算术化
arithmometer 四则运算器
ARM(Asynchronous Response Mode) 异步应答方式
arm 臂,机械臂
armature 衔铁,电枢
armature winding 电枢绕组
armed interrupt 待命中断
armed state 待命状态
around 正文环绕
ARP(Address Resolution Protocol) 地址解析协议(TCP/IP)
ARPA computer network (Advanced Research Projects Agency computer network) 高级研究计划署计算机通信网
ARPA network control program ARPA网络控制程序
ARPA network elements and operation ARPA网络部件与操作
ARPA network message handling ARPA网络消息处理
ARPA network messages ARPA网络消息
ARPA packet switching ARPA网络分组交换
ARPA protocol levels ARPA网络的协议级
ARPAnet(Advanced Research Projects Agency network) 高级研究计划署网络
ARPAnet protocol ARPA网络协议
ARPS(Advanced Real-time Processing System) 先进实时处理系统
ARQ (Automatic Retransmission reQuest) 自动重发请求
ARQ system 自动重发请求系统
Arrange All 全部重新安排

arrange icons 重排图标
arrangement 排列
array 阵列,矩阵,数组
array acceptor 阵列接收机
array algorithm 阵列算法,数组算法
array and vector computer 阵列与向量计算机
array architecture 阵列体系结构
array assignment 阵列[数组]赋值
array attribute 阵列属性,数组属性
array-based computation 基于数组的计算
array bound 阵列界,数组边界
array box 数组块
array compiler 阵列编译程序
array component 阵列编件,数组分量
array computer 阵列[向量]计算机
array coprocessor 阵列协处理器
array copy subroutine 数组复制子例程
array creation 阵列[数组]建立
array declaration 阵列[数组]说明
array declarator 阵列说明符
array define 数组定义
array destruction 阵列撤消
array dimension 数组维数
array element 数组元素
array expression 阵列表达式
array formal parameter 阵列形式参[数
array index 数组下标
array information vector table 数组信息向量表
array initialization 数组初始化
array input statement 数组输入语句
array item 阵列项,数组项
array logic 阵列逻辑;数组处理机
array manipulation 数组处理
array module 阵列[向量]模块
array multiplier 阵列乘法器
array name 阵列名,数组名字
array operation 阵列[数组]运算
array-oriented language 面向阵列的语言
array pipeline 矩阵[数组]流水线
array printer 点阵打印机
array processing 阵列[数组]处理
array processor 阵列处理机
array radar 阵列[相控阵]雷达

array reading statement 阵列[数组]读入语句
array reference 阵列[数组]引用
array selection circuit 阵列选择电路
array subscript 阵列[数组]下标
array type conversion 数组类型变换
array type definition 数组类型定义
array unit 阵列单元,阵列部件
arrival interval 到达间隔
arrival rate 到达率
arrow 箭头符号
arrow button 方向按钮
arrow diagram 简图,矢量图,向量图
arrow head 箭头
arrow keys 箭头键,方向键
arrow tool 取向工具
arrow head 箭头的头部
ARS(Attitude Reference System) 姿态参考系统
ARS(Automatic Route Selection) 自动路由选择
arsenic(As) 砷
ART(Alternate RouTe) 替用[替代]路径
ART(Authorization and Resource Table) 特许资源表
ART(Automated Reasoning Tool) 自动推理工具
ART(Average Retrieval Time) 平均检索时间
ART(Average Run-Time) 平均运行时间
art 样式
Art Bibliographic Modern 现代艺术文献数据库
article 文章;条款
articular 分级的;关节的　　　[引
articulated index 题外关键词相关索
articulated robot 有关节的机器人
articulation 清晰度
articulation index 清晰度指数
articulation point (关节)连接点
articulation reference equivalent 清晰度参考当量
artifact 人为因素
artificial 人工的
artificial antenna 人工[仿真]天线
artificial body parts 人工[仿真]人体部件
artificial cognition 人工识别
artificial constraint 人为约束
artificial continuity 人工邻接
artificial evolution 人工进化,仿真进化
artificial intelligence(AI) 人工智能
artificial intelligence decision support system(AIDSS) 人工智能决策支持系统
artificial intelligence language 人工智能语言
artificial intelligence programming 人工智能程序设计
artificial language 人工语言
artificial life 人工生命
artificial line 仿真线
artificial load 仿真负载,假负荷
artificial network 模拟[仿真]网络
artificial neural nets 人工神经网络
artificial neuron 人工神经元
artificial parallelism 人工并行性
artificial perception 人工知觉
artificial perceptron 人工感知器
artificial reference counting 人工引用计数
artificial syntax 人工语法
artificial texture 人工纹理
artificial vision 人工视觉
artificial voice 合成音响
artword 艺术字
artwork 原图
artwork master 照相原版
ARU(Audio Response Unit) 声音应答器
Arvind Arvind并行计算机(MIT)
ARX(Automatic Retransmission eXchange) 自动转发交换
AS(Adaptable Software) 自适应软件
AS(Address Stream) 地址流
AS(Application System) 应用系统
AS(Automatically Switching) 自动交换
AS/400(Application System/400) AS/400小型计算机(IBM)
ASC(Automatic Synchronized Control) 自动同步控制
ASC function 求ASCII码函数

ascender 上超部分,上升部分
ascending 升序,递升,递增
ascending key 升序键,递增关键字
ascending order 递增排列,升序
ascending phase 升序短语
ascending sequence 递增顺序
ASCII(American Standard Code for Information Interchange) 美国信息交换标准码
ASCII control characters ASCII 控制字符
ASCII extended character set ASCII 扩充字符集
ASCII file ASCII 文件
ASCII keyboard ASCII 键盘
ASCII sort ASCII 排序
ASCII standard character set ASCII 标准字符集
ASCII string ASCII 字符串
ASCII terminal ASCII 终端
ASCII text file ASCII 文本文件
ASCIIZ string ASCIIZ 字符串
ASCIIZ transfer ASCII 传送
ASCS (Active Service Components Server) 活动服务部件服务器
ASCS(Automatic Storage Control System) 自动存储控制系统
ASET (Automated Security Enhancement Tool) 自动安全增强工具(Sun)
ASF (Advanced Streaming Format) 高级(音频/视频)流模式
Ashton-tata Ashton-tata 公司
ASIC (Application Specific Integrated Circuit) 专用集成电路
ASID (Address-Space IDentifier) 地址空间标识符
Asimov's laws of robotics 阿西摩夫机器人法则
ASK (Amplitude Shift Keying) 移幅键控
ASK (Applications Software Kit) 成套应用软件
ask Sam system ask Sam 系统公司
ASM(ASseMbler) 汇编程序
ASM (Association for Systems Management) 系统管理协会
ASN (Abstract Syntax Notation) 抽象语法记号
ASN (Asynchronous Sequential Network) 异步时序网络
ASN.1(Abstract Syntax Notation.1) 抽象语法记法.1
ASP(Active Service Page) 活动服务页面
ASP(ActiveX Server Page) ActiveX 服务页面(微软)
ASP(Advanced Signal Processor) 高级信号处理器
ASP(Associative-data Structure Package) 相联数据结构软件包
ASP(Attached Support Processor) 附属支援处理机
ASPEC (Adaptive Spectral Perceptual Entropy Coding of high quality musical signal) 高质量音乐信息自适应谱熵编码方式
aspect 标记,特征,标号
aspect card 标记卡,特征卡
aspect holding 宽高比保持
aspect indexing 特征索引
aspect keeping 宽高比保持
aspect ratio 宽高比,帧面纵横比
aspiration level 愿望水平
ASQ(Application Software Quality) 应用软件质量
ASS(Automatic Software Synthesis) 自动软件综合
assassin scenario (用计算机病毒攻击敌方信息系统的)"暗杀"方案
assemble 汇编;装配,组装
assemble-and-go 汇编并执行
assemble debugging system 汇编调试系统
assemble duration 汇编持续时间
assemble error 汇编错误
assemble list 汇编列表
assemble time 汇编时间
assemble to order 订单式生产
assemble to stock 存料组合,库存式生产管理
assembled line balancing 装配线平衡
assembled origin 汇编原点
assembled source statement 汇编后的源程序语句
assembler 汇编程序

assembler base　汇编程序库
assembler code　汇编程序代码
assembler commands　汇编命令
assembler control statement　汇编控制语句
assembler directive　汇编程序导向命令
assembler error code　汇编出错码
assembler instruction　汇编指令
assembler language(AL)　汇编程序语言
assembler macrocall　汇编程序宏调用
assembler microprogramming language　汇编微程序设计语言
assembler operators　汇编程序操作码
assembler output list　汇编程序输出列表
assembler pseudo-operations　汇编程序伪操作
assembler routine　汇编例行程序
assembler source code　汇编源码
assembler source file　汇编源文件
assembler source program　汇编源程序
assembling　汇编
assembling jig　装配支架(夹具)
assembling phase　汇编阶段
assembling time　汇编时间
assembly　汇编，装配
assembly automation　装配自动化
assembly control statement　汇编控制语句
assembly debug program　汇编调试程序
assembly drawing　装配图
assembly language　汇编语言
assembly language coding(ALC)　汇编语言编码
assembly language editor　汇编语言编辑程序
assembly language listing　汇编语言列表
assembly language output　汇编语言输出
assembly language processor　汇编语言处理器
assembly level　装配阶段
assembly line　装配线；汇编行
assembly line balancing　装配线平衡
assembly list　汇编列表
assembly manipulation　装配操作
assembly output language　汇编输出语言

assembly robot　装配用机器人
assembly sequence　装配顺序
assembly strategy　装配策略
assembly system　汇系统
assembly testing　组合测试,组装检测
assembly unit　汇编单元,汇编程序单
asserted　宣称的,尚待证实的
assertion　确认,断言
assertion language　断言语言
assertion list　断言表
assertion statement　确证语句,断言语句
assertion system　断言校验系统
assertion table　断言表
assertion trace set　断言迹集合
assessment　评价,评估
assign　指派,赋值
assign macro　(为对象)指定宏
assign network address　指定网址
assigned branch　赋值转移
assigned frequency　指派频率
assigned GO TO statement　赋值转向语句
assigned number　指定号
assigned priority　指派优先权,指定优先级
assignment　赋值
assignment by name　按名赋值
assignment command　赋值命令
assignment compatible type　赋值相容类型
assignment expression　赋值表达式
assignment facilities(executive)　设施指派(执行例程)
assignment for request　按需分配
assignment index　赋值索引
assignment operation　赋值操作
assignment operator　赋值运算符
assignment problem　指派问题
assignment rule　赋值规则
assignment statement　赋值语句
assignment symbol　赋值符号
assignment table　赋值表
assistance call　辅助呼叫
assistance code　辅助码
assistance traffic　辅助话务量
assistant　助手,助理
assisted　辅助的
assisted access　加速存取

assisted call 辅助呼叫(调用)
assisted instruction 辅助指令,加速指令
associated 相关的,结合的,关联的
associated address 相联地址
associated connectors 关联连接符
associated contents table 相关内容表
associated digraph 关联有向图
associated document 关联文件
associated information 相关信息
associated model 结合[伴随]模型
associated signaling 随路信令
associated value 关联值
associated variable 关联变量
associated with 与指定文件关联
associated word 关联词
associating inputting 联想输入法
association 结合,关联
association diagram 关联图
Association for Computing Machinery (ACM) (美国)计算机协会
Association Francaise de Calcul (AFCAL) 法国计算机协会
Association of Computer Programmer and Analysts(ACPA) 计算机程序员和分析员协会
association pattern 关联模式
association retrieval 关联检索
association storage 相关存储器
association table 相关表
associative addressing 相联寻址
associative array processor 相关阵列处理机
associative data 相关数据
associative dedicated circuit 相关专用通路
associative dimensioning 相关度量
associative indexing 结合索引,关联编目
associative induction knowledge acquisition 联想归纳知识获取
associative key 相联关键字
associative language 相联语言
associative list 结合表,关联表
associative memory 相关内存
associative process 联想处理
associative processor 相联处理机
associative pushdown memory 相联下推存储器

associative register 相关寄存器
associative storage 相关存储器
associative structure 相联结构
associative thinking 联想思维
associative transaction 相关事务
associativity 结合性
associatron 联想机
associator 联系文件
assorted 相匹配;分类排列
assortment 分类;种类
assumed decimal point 假设小数点
assumed-size aggregate 假设大小聚合体,假定范围聚合
assumed value 假设值
assumption 假设,假定
assumption-based reasoning 基于假定的推理
assurance 保证
assurance method 保证法
assured pipeline 保险管道
AST(Atlantic Standard Time) 大西洋标准时间
AST Research Inc. (Albert Wang, Safi Qureshey, Thomas Yuen) 虹志(电脑)有限公司
astable multivibrator 多谐振荡器
astatic 非定向的,非稳定的
asterisk 星号
asterisk fill 星号填充
asterisk protection 星号保护
asterisk wildcard 星号通配符
astigmatism 散光,像散现象
astronautics 宇航学
astronomical computing 天文计算
astronomy 天文学
ASVT(Address Space Vector Table) 地址空间向量表
ASW (Advanced Intelligent Network Switch) 高级智能网交换系统
asymmetric application 不对称应用程序
asymmetric devices 不对称设备
asymmetric digital subscriber link(ADSL) 不对称数字用户线
asymmetric distortion 不对称失真
asymmetric I/O 不对称输入/输出
asymmetric key cipher algorithm 非对称密钥号算法

ATA

asymmetric key system 不对称密钥系统
asymmetric multiprocessor 非对称型多处理机
asymmetric multiprocessing 非对称多道处理技术
asymmetric system 非对称系统
asymmetric video compression 非对称视频压缩
asymmetrical compression 不对称压缩
asymmetrical modem 非对称调制解调器
asymmetrical network 不对称网络
asymmetrical sideband transmission 不对称边带传输,残留边带传输［输］
asymmetrical transmission 非对称传输
asymptotic complexity 渐近复杂性
asymptotic convergence rate 渐近收敛速度
asynchronous 异步的
asynchronous algorithm 异步算法
asynchronous attack 异步冲击
asynchronous binding 异步绑定［联编］［统］
asynchronous bus system 异步总线系
asynchronous call 异步调用
asynchronous communication server 异步通信服务器
asynchronous communication system 异步通信系统［信］
asynchronous communications 异步通信
asynchronous communications interface adapter(ACIA) 异步通信接口适配器
asynchronous computation 异步计算
asynchronous computer 异步计算机
asynchronous control 异步控制
asynchronous data transfer 异步数据传输
asynchronous data transmission 异步数据传输
asynchronous device 异步装置
asynchronous flow 异步数据流
asynchronous graph 异步程序图
asynchronous input 异步输入
asynchronous line driver 异步线路驱动器
asynchronous logic 异步逻辑
asynchronous mode 异步模式［器］
asynchronous modem 异步调制解调
asynchronous moniker 异步别名
asynchronous multiplexer 异步多路复用器
asynchronous multiplexer communication system 异步多工通信系统
asynchronous network 异步网络
asynchronous operation 异步操作
asynchronous pipeline 异步流水线
asynchronous procedure 异步过程
asynchronous procedure call(APC) 异步过程调用
asynchronous processing 异步运算
asynchronous record operation 异步记录操作
asynchronous replication 异步复制
asynchronous request 异步请求
asynchronous response mode(ARM) 异步响应模式
asynchronous sequential circuit 异步时序电路
asynchronous serial transmission 异步串行传输
asynchronous signaling 异步信号发送
asynchronous system trap(AST) 异步系统自陷
asynchronous system trap level 异步系统自陷级
asynchronous terminal 异步终端机
asynchronous termination 异步终结
asynchronous time-division multiplexing (ATDM) 异步时分多路复用
asynchronous transmission 异步传输
asynchronous trap 异步自陷
AT(Advanced Technology) AT型个人计算机(IBM)
AT attachment(ATA) AT扩充接口
AT bus AT总线
AT class AT级［集］
AT command set (MODEM)AT命令
AT keyboard AT键盘
at symbol @符号
AT&T(American Telephone & Telegraph company) 美国电话电报公司
ATA (Advanced Technology Attachment) ATA接口(相当于IDE)

ATA interface connector(AT Attachment) ATA接口连接器
ATAPI(Advanced Technology Attachment Packet Interface) AT附加分组接口
ATC(Authority Training Center) 认证培训中心(微软)
ATCON(AppleTalk CONsole) AppleTalk控制台
ATDM(Asynchronous Time-Division Multiplexing) 异步时多路复用
ATDP(Asynchronous Transaction Control Program) 异步事务控制程序
ATDP(ATtention Dial Pulse) 启动脉冲拨号
ATDT(ATtention Dial Tone) 启动双音频拨号
Athlon "速龙"处理器(AMD)
ATL(**Advanced Table Lookup**) 先进查表法
ATLAS ATLAS计算机
ATLAS language(Abbreviated Test Language for All System) ATLAS语言
ATM(Adobe Type Manager) Adobe轮廓字形解释软件
ATM(Asynchronous Transfer Mode) 异步转移(传输)模式
ATM(Automatic Teller Machine) 自动柜员机,自动出纳机
ATM adaptive level(AAL) 异步转移模式适配层
ATM adaptive technology 异步转移模式适配技术
ATM cell 异步转移模式信元
ATM cell head 异步转移模式信元头
ATM downlink 异步转移模式下行链路
ATM Forum ATM论坛
ATM network 异步转移模式网络
ATM network integrated processing ATM网络综合处理
ATM network to network interface(ATM NNI) ATM网络到网络接口
ATM node ATM节点
ATM scalability 异步转移模式可伸缩性
ATM station 异步转移模式工作站
ATM switch 异步转移模式交换机
ATM transparency 异步转移模式透明性
ATM unit 异步转移模式单元,ATM单元
ATM user to network interface(ATM UNI) ATM用户到网络接口
ATM virtual connection 异步转移模式虚连接
ATN(ATtentioN) 注意(信号)
atom 原子
atom action 原子活动
atomic data element 原子数据单元
atomic formula 原子公式
atomic operation 原子操作
atomic proposition 原子命题
atomic transaction 原子事务
atomicity 原子数;原子化
ATTACH 连接实用工具
attach 附加,加上;连接
Attach Table Button 附加表按钮
Attach Text to 将文本文件附加到
Attach Title to 附加标题到指定位置
attached document 附加文档
attached header 附加标题,副标题
attached processing 附加处理
attached processor(AP) 附加处理器
Attached Resource Computer Network(ARCnet) 附加资源计算机网络
attached support processor(ASP) 附加增援处理机
attached table 附加表,添加表
attached vector processor 附加式向量处理机
attachment 附件,附加装置
Attachment Manager 附加管理程序
attachment table 附加表
attachment unit interface(AUI) 附件接口
attack 密码攻击
attack time 攻击时间
attainable accuracy 可得精度
attempts per circuit per hour(ACH) 每小时每对线路的呼叫
attendant 值机人员,维护人员
attendant exclusion 值机互斥,操作禁止
attended device 关注[引起注意]装置

attended operation 值管作业,值班操作
attended time 值管时间
attended trail printer 值管跟踪打印机
attention 关注(信号),引起注意信号
attention code 注释码
attention device 关注装置
attention display 关注[报警]显示
attention field 关注[提示]字段
attention interrupt 关注中断
attention key 关注键
attention symbol 关注符
attenuation 衰减
attenuation coefficient 衰减系数
attenuation compensation 衰减补偿
attenuation constant 衰减常数
attenuation distortion 衰减失真
attenuation equalizer 衰减均衡器
attenuation rate 衰减率
attenuator 衰减器
Attmac Attmac 终端
ATTN(ATTeNtion) 关注,引起注意信号
attribute 属性
attribute access 属性存取
attribute alterable 属性变更性
attribute assignment 属性赋值
attribute byte 属性字节
attribute class 属性类
attribute description 属性描述
attribute domain 属性域
attribute error 属性误差
attribute grammar 属性文法
attribute inheritance 属性继承
attribute integration 属性集成
attribute list 属性表
attribute migration 属性迁移
attribute of discrete type 离散型属性
attribute of entry 入口属性
attribute of fixed-point type 定点类型属性
attribute relationship 属性联系
attribute section 属性段,属性部分
attribute simulation 属性模拟
attribute translation grammar 属性翻译文法
attribute tree 属性树
attribute value 属性值

ATX(AT eXternal) ATX 主板结构(Intel)
auctioneering device 拍卖装置
audibility 可听度
audibility limit 可听度极限
audible alarm 声音报警
audible busy signal 可闻忙音信号
audible cue 可闻提示
audible feedback 声音响应
audible indication 音频指示
audio 音频的
audio amplifier 音频放大器
audio annotation 声音注释
audio attribute control 声音属性控制
audio clip 声音片段
audio coding communication 音频编码通信
audio communication 声频通信
audio communication line 音频通信线路
audio compression 音频压缩
audio cue 声音提示
audio disc 声盘
audio dubbing 配音,灌音
audio file 音频文件
audio frequency 声频,音频
audio frequency oscillator 音频振荡器
audio frequency shift keying(AFSK) 声音频移键控制
audio helper 助听器
audio input device 声音输入设备
audio input level 音频输入电平
audio inquiry 声音询问
Audio Interchange File Format(AIFF) 声音交换文件格式(苹果,SGI)
audio mixer 音频混合器
audio monitor 音频监视器
Audio Object Content Architecture(AOCA) 声音对象内容结构
audio output port 音频输出端口
audio port 音频端口
audio processing 声音处理
audio response 声音应答,音频响应
audio response device 声音应答装置
audio response message 声音应答消息
audio response terminal 声音应答终端
audio response unit(ARU) 声音应答装置

audio segment 声音片段
audio state 声频状态
audio stream 声音流
audio subcarrier 音频信号副载波
audio synthesis 声频合成
audio system 话音系统,语音系统
audio-tape storage unit 音频磁带存储设备
audio taping 磁带录音
audio telecommunication line 音频电信线路
audio terminal 声频终端机
audio typing 声控印字
audio unit 声音装置
Audio Video Connection(AVC) 视听连接
Audio Video Interleaved(AVI) 音频视频交错存放格式(多媒体)
Audio Video Kernel(AVK) 音频视频核心软件
Audio Video Support System(AVSS) 音频视频支持系统
Audio Web 网络声音通信卡
audiogram 听力图,闻阈图
audioslider 有声幻灯片
audiovisual 视听的
audiovisual computer program 视听计算机程序
audiovisual computer system 视听计算机系统
audiovisual synchronization 视听同步
audiovisual system 视听系统
audit 审计
audit log 审计记录
audit program 审计程序
audit-review file 审计复查文件
audit software 审计软件
audit trail 审计追踪
AUDITCON 审计工作台
auditing 审计,监察
audition 听觉
auditor 审计者
augend 被加数
augmentation 扩增,增大
augmented grammar 扩充文法
augmented human intelligence 强化人类智能
augmented matrix 增广矩阵

augmented network 扩展网络
augmented operation code 扩增操作码
augmented transition network 增值传递网络
augmented transition network parsing 扩增转移网络语法分析
augmentor 替身机器人
aural 听力的
AUI(Attachment Unit Interface) 附加设备接口;附件接口
AUI cable 附件连接电缆
AUL(Average Useful Life) 平均使用寿命
AUSINET(AUStralian Information NETwork) 澳大利亚信息网络
Australian Computer Science Network(ACSNET) 澳大利亚计算机科学网络
AUT(Advanced User Terminal) 高级用户终端
authentication 鉴认,确证,证实
authentication algorithm 验证算法
authentication certificate 身份验证证书
Authentication Header (Ipv6)验证选项包头
authentication key 验证密钥
authentication of message 消息鉴定,报文鉴别
authentication of user 用户验证
authentication process 验证过程
authentication system 鉴认系统
authenticator 消息鉴认码,鉴定符
author language 编辑语言
author tool language 编辑者工具语言
authoring 编著
authoring language 创作语言,编辑用语言
authoring platform 创作平台
authoring system 创作系统
authoring tool 创作工具
authority 授权,特许
authority credentials 权限凭证
authority file 规范文件
authority holder 授权拥有者
authorization 授权,特许
authorization code 特许代码
authorization process 授权过程

authorize assistant(AA) 授权判别辅助软件
authorized end node 特许端节点
authorized environment 特许环境
authorized library 特许程序库
authorized operator 特许操作员
authorized path 特许路径
authorized program 特许程序,特权程序
authorized program facility 特许程序设施
authorized state 特许状态
authorized user 特许用户
Authorware 多媒体课件创作软件(Macromedia)
auto abstract 自动抽取
auto-answer 自动回答
auto-answer modem acoustic coupler 自动回答调制解调声耦合器
auto-associative memory 自联想内存
auto bypass 自动旁通
auto-call 自动呼叫
auto-cast 自动投送
auto changer 自动换盘机
auto-diagnosis 自动诊断
auto dial 自动拨号
auto dialer 自动拨号装置
auto document feeder(ADF) 自动文档送纸器
auto-index 自动索引
auto-indexed addressing 自动索引寻址
auto-interactive design 自动-交互设计
auto-kerning 自动靠拢
auto-key 自动键
auto-line-ending 自动行结束
auto logon 自动登录,自动注册
auto-manual 自动手动转换开关
auto-network shutdown 网络自动关闭
auto poll 自动轮询,自动探询
auto redial 自动重拨号
auto-repeat 自动重复
auto resume 自动重续,自动恢复
auto scaling 自动定标,自动缩放
auto start 自动启动
auto stop 自动停机
auto thermal compensation 自动温度补偿
auto-update 自动更新

auto wake 自动唤醒
AutoCAD 自动计算机辅助设计软件(Autodesk)
AutoCaption 自动插入题注
autochart 自动绘流程图程序
Autocircuit 自动电路连接工艺(Autosplice)
autocode 自动码
autocoder 自动编码器
autoconfiguration 自动配置
autoconvergence 自动会聚
AutoCorrect 自动更正
autocorrelation coefficient 自相关系数
autocorrelative function 自相关函数
autocorrelative matrix 自相关矩阵
autocue 自动提示器
autodecrement addressing 自动减量寻址
autodecrement mode 自动递减模式
autodegauss 自动消磁
Autodesk Device Interface(ADI) Autodesk设备接口
Autodesk Inc Autodesk公司
autodial 自动拨号
Autodialer 自动拨号程序
Autodialer Button 自动拨号按钮
AUTODIN(AUTOmatic Digital Information Network) 自动数字信息网络
AUTODIN AUTODIN计算机网络
AUTODIN operation AUTODIN数字网络的操作方式
AUTODOC(AUTOmatic DOCumentation) 自动文档编制
autodraft 自动绘草图
autoepistemic reasoning 自认识推理
autoexcitation 自激励
AUTOEXEC.BAT 自动执行的批处理文件
AUTOEXEC.NCF 自动执行的网络批处理文件(Netware)
autofax 自动传真
autofiling program 自动编档程序
AutoFill 自动填充
AutoFilter 自动筛选
AutoFit Selection 自动宽度选择
autofloating field 自动浮动字段
autofocus 自动聚焦
AutoFont Support Files 自动套用字体

支持文件
AutoForm Wizard 自动制表单向导
AutoFormat 自动套用格式
AutoFormat Table 自动套用数据透视表格式
autogeneration 自动产生[生成]
autogression 自动回归
autohub 自动卡盘
autohyphenation 自动加连字符
autoincrement addressing 自动增量寻址
autoincrement mode 自动递增模式
autoindexing 自动建索引;自动变址
Autolayout 自动布局软件
autolayout 自动布局
AutoLISP AutoLISP语言
autoloading head arm 自动加载磁头臂
AutoMark 自动作标记
automat 自动售货机
automata 自动机,自动学
automata theory 自动机理论
automatch 自动转换[匹配]程序
automate 自动化
automated abstracting 自动摘要
automated assembly 自动装配
automated audit 自动审计
automated bibliography 自动书目,自动文献目录
automated composition 自动排版,自动拼版
automated decision system 自动决策系统
automated design engineering 自动设计工程
automated design tool 自动设计工具
automated dictionary 自动字典
automated documentation 自动文件编制
automated drafting 自动制图
automated fingerprint recognition system 自动指纹识别系统
automated glossary 自动词汇表
automated inventory control system 库存自动控制系统
automated knowledge acquisition 知识自动获取
automated layout program 自动布局程序
automated lexicon 自动词汇
automated logic diagram(ALD) 自动逻辑图
automated management 自动化管理
automated office 自动化办公室
automated operator user-exit routine 自动操作员用户出口程序
automated paper carriage 自动输纸架
automated process planning system (AUTOPROS) 自动过程规划系统
automated production management 自动生产管理
automated retrieval 自动检索
automated software engineering 自动软件工程
automated stock control 自动库存控制
automated system initialization 自动系统初始化
automated teller machine(ATM) 自动柜员机,自动提款机
automated test generator 自动测试生成程序
automated translation 自动翻译
automated verification system 自动验证系统
automated verification tool 自动验证工具
automated warehousing 自动存货
automatic 自动的
automatic adaptive equalizer 自适应均衡器
automatic alarm receiver 自动警报接收机
automatic alignment 自动对准,自动排列
automatic alternate routing 自动替用路由
automatic answer-back code exchange 自动应答交换码
automatic answering 自动回答[应答]
automatic answering device 自动回答设备
automatic answering system 自动应答系统
automatic array scaling(AAS) 自动数组定标
automatic backup 自动备份

automatic bank 自动化仓库
automatic booked call 自动预定呼叫
automatic branch exchange 自动交换分机
automatic brightness control 自动亮度控制
automatic call device 自动呼叫装置
automatic call distribution 自动呼叫分配
automatic call distributor(ACD) 自动呼叫分配器
automatic calling 自动呼叫
automatic calling and answering equipment 自动呼叫回答器
automatic calling equipment(ACE) 自动呼叫设备
automatic calling unit(ACU) 自动呼叫单元
automatic camera/platemaker 自动照排/制版装置
automatic carriage 自动输送架
automatic carriage return 自动回车
automatic carrier landing system 自动舰载降落系统
automatic carry 自动进位
automatic centering 自动对中
automatic check 自动校验,自动检测
automatic check interrupt 自动校验中断
automatic chrome control 自动色度控制
automatic circuit layout 自动线路布局
automatic circuit tester 自动电路测试器
automatic coding language 自动编码语言
automatic collision detection 自动碰撞检测
automatic control 自动控制
automatic control alarm 自动控制报警
automatic control engineering 自动控制工程学
automatic-control stability 自动控制稳定性
automatic control system 自动控制系统
automatic correction 自动校正
automatic credit card service 自动信用卡服务
automatic data migration 自动数据迁移

automatic data-processing auxiliary equipment 自动数据处理辅助设备
automatic data processing equipment (ADPE) 自动数据处理设备
automatic data processing system 自动数据处理系统
automatic data recovery restart operation 自动数据恢复再启动操作
automatic data reduction 自动数据精简
automatic data reduction equipment 自动数据精简设备
automatic data switching center 自动数据交换中心
automatic decimal alignment 自动十进制对准(调整)
automatic decimal tab 自动小数点标记
automatic deduction 自动演绎推理
automatic derivative system 自动推导系统
automatic dialer 自动拨号器
automatic dialing set 自动拨号设备
automatic dialing unit(ADU) 自动拨号装置
automatic dictionary 自动字典
automatic digital message switching center(ADMSC) 自动数字信息交换中心
automatic dimensioning 自动标注尺寸
automatic directory listing 自动目录列表
automatic discover of attribute 属性的自动发现
automatic dispatch system 自动分发系统
automatic document classification 自动文献分类
automatic document clustering 自动文献归类
automatic document retrieval system 自动文献检索系统
automatic drafting 自动制图
automatic drafting machine 自动制图机
automatic dynamic incremental nonlinear analysis(ADINA) 自动动态增量非线性分析程序
automatic electronic data switching center 自动电子数据交换中心

automatic equalization 自动均衡
automatic error correction(AEC) 自动纠错
automatic error detection 自动检错
automatic error detection and correction system 自动检错与校正系统
automatic exchange 自动交换
automatic exposure control 自动曝光控制
automatic extraction 自动摘要
automatic feature negotiation 自动特性协商
automatic feed mechanism 自动馈送机构
automatic field duplication 自动字段复制
automatic file locking 自动文件加锁
automatic file select 自动文件选择
automatic file sort 自动文件排序
automatic flowcharting 自动绘制流程图
automatic flowcharting program 自动绘制流程图程序
automatic focus 自动聚焦
automatic font downloading 自动字形载入
automatic footnote tie-in 自动放置脚注
automatic frequency control(AFC) 自动频率控制
automatic gain control(AGC) 自动增益控制
automatic head parking 自动磁头归位
automatic headers/footers 自动标题/脚注
automatic hold 自动保持
automatic hyphenation 自动加连字符
automatic identification on outward dialing(AIOD) 向外拨号自动识别
automatic indentation 自动缩进
automatic indexing 自动编索引
automatic input underlining 自动输入下划线
automatic insertion(AIC) 自动插入
automatic inspection(AIC) 自动检查
automatic intercept center(AIC) 自动截接中心
automatic intercept system(AIS) 自动截接系统

automatic interlock 自动联锁
automatic interrupt 自动中断
automatic justification 自动对齐
automatic key cipher 自动键号密码
automatic language translation 自动语言翻译
automatic language translator 自动翻译机
automatic lexical code 自动化词典代码
automatic library call 自动库调用
automatic line/paragraph numbering 自动行/段编号
automatic line spacing 自动行间隔
automatic link 自动链接
automatic load balancing 自动负载平衡
automatic loader 自动加载程序
automatic loader diagnostic 自动加载程序诊断
automatic logging 自动登录[注册]
automatic logon 自动进入系统,自动注册
automatic mapping(AM) 自动绘制地图
automatic margin adjust 自动边缘调整
automatic mathematical translator 自动数学解答机
automatic measurement technology 自动测量技术
automatic member 自动型成分
automatic meshing 自动网格化
automatic message accounting system 自动消息记账系统
automatic message routing 自动消息路由
automatic message switching 自动消息交换
automatic message-switching center 自动消息交换中心
automatic mode switching 自动模式切换
automatic modulation control 自动调制控制
automatic modulation limiting(AML) 自动调制限制
automatic monitor 自动监视器
automatic network switching 自动网络切换
automatic new line 自动换行
automatic number analysis 自动号码

分析
automatic number identification 号码自动识别
automatic numbering 自动编号功能
automatic object 自动对象
automatic object template 自动对象模板
automatic observation of the service quality 服务质量的自动观察
automatic open loop control 自动开环控制
automatic operating and scheduling program(AOSP) 自动操作与调度程序
automatic page numbering 自动页编号
automatic pagination 自动加页码,自动分页
automatic paging 自动分页,自动调页
automatic paper carriage 自动托纸架[输送筒]
automatic paper feeder 自动送纸器
automatic partition of letters 信函自动分选
automatic patching system 自动编排系统
automatic path planning 自动路径规划
automatic pattern recognition 自动模式识别
automatic phase control(APC) 自动相位控制
automatic picture transmission(APT) 自动图像传输
automatic placement 自动布置
automatic plotting 自动描图
automatic poll 自动轮询,自动探询
automatic power off 自动断电
automatic priority group(APG) 自动优先权组
automatic program interrupt 自动程序中断
automatic program reusability technique 自动程序重用技术
automatic program verification system 自动程序验证系统
automatic programming 自动程序设计
automatic programming tool(APT) 自动编程工具
automatic proof(APT) 自动证明
automatic protection(APT) 自动保护

automatic quality control 自动质量控制
automatic question modification 问题自动修饰
automatic queue 自动队列
automatic recalculation 自动重算
automatic recall 自动再呼叫
automatic record locking 自动记录锁定
automatic recovery 自动恢复
automatic recovery program(ARP) 自动恢复程序
automatic refreshing 自动更新
automatic repagination 自动加页码
automatic repeat attempt 自动再尝试
automatic repeat key 自动重复键
automatic repeat request(ARQ) 自动重发请求
automatic repetition 自动重复
automatic repetition system 自动重传系统
automatic request for repetition(ARQ) 自动请求重发
automatic restart 自动重始[再启动]
automatic return 自动返回,自动回车
automatic reverse 自动反向
automatic rollback 自动回溯
automatic route management(ARM) 自动路由管理
automatic routing 自动布线,自动寻径
automatic scanner 自动扫描器
automatic schema translation 自动模式翻译
automatic segmentation and control 自动分段和控制
automatic segmentation of Chinese words 汉语词汇的自动划分
automatic sequence control 自动顺序控制
automatic sequencing 自动定序
automatic sequential connection 自动按序连接
automatic sequential operation 自动按序作业
automatic shutoff 自动关闭
automatic simulation 自动仿真
automatic source data 源数据自动化
automatic speech processing 自动话音处理

automatic speech recognition (ASR) 自动话音识别
automatic speed sensing 自动速度检测
automatic SPOOL 自动假脱机
automatic stop 自动停机
automatic stop switch 自动停止开关
automatic storage allocation 自动存储分配
automatic switcher 自动转接器
automatic switching 自动切换
automatic switching center 自动交换中心
automatic switching system 自动交换系统
automatic switchover 自动转接
automatic syntax recognition 自动文法识别
automatic teaching 自动教学
automatic teller machine(ATM) 自动出纳机,自动取款机
automatic terrain recognition and navigation(ATRAN) 自动地形识别与导航
automatic test equipment(ATE) 自动测试设备
automatic test pattern generation system (ATPG) 自动测试模式生成系统
automatic test system 自动测试系统
Automatic Text 自动加入文本
automatic theorem proving 自动定理证明
automatic threading 自动进片
automatic threshold selection 自动阈值选择
automatic tint control 自动色调控制
automatic track-shift 自动磁道移位
automatic tracking 自动跟踪
automatic traffic overload protection 自动流量过载保护
automatic train scheduling 自动列车调度
automatic transaction recorder 自动事务记录程序
automatic transferred speed 自动转移速度
automatic translation 自动翻译
automatic tuning system 自动调谐系统

automatic typesetting 自动排版
automatic variable 自动变量
automatic voltage regulator 自动调压器
automatic volume control(AVC) 自动音量控制
automatic volume recognition(AVR) 自动档卷识别
automatic volume switching 自动档卷切换
automatic wake-up 自动唤醒
automatic widow adjust 自动版面调节
automatic width control oneshot 自动脉宽控制单稳电路
automatic word wraparound 自动字卷绕
automatic zero resetting 自动原点复位
automatically programmed tools(APT) 自动编程工具语言,APT语言
automatically reboot(APT) 自动重启动
automation 自动化
automation object 自动对象
automation of enterprise management 企业管理自动化
automaton 自动机
automaton classification 自动机分类
automechanism 自动机构
AutoMigrate 自动迁移
automonitor 自动监督程序
automorphism 自同构
automorphism group 自同构群
automorphism partitioning 自同构分割法
automotive computer 汽车用计算机
automounter 自动装配程序
autonomous 自治的,独立的
autonomous access control 自主访问控制
autonomous automaton 自律自动机
autonomous channel 独立型通道
autonomous channel operation 独立通道操作
autonomous computer system 独立计算机系统
autonomous decentralized system 独立分散系统
autonomous devices 自律装置,独立装置
autonomous finite automaton 自治有限自动机

autonomous land vehicle 无人驾驶陆战车
autonomous packet switching 独立包交换
autonomous robot vehicle 独立自动车
autonomous sequential circuit 自激时序电路
autonomous switching 自主交换
autonomous system 自治系统
autonomous working 自律[独立]工作
autonomy 自主性
AutoNumber 自动编号
Autopiler 自动编译程序
Autoplacement 自动布局程序
autoplay 自动播放
autoplotter 自动绘图仪
autopolling 自动轮询
autopush mechanism 自动推送机制
autoredialing 自动重复拨号
autoredraw 自动重绘
autorepeat key 自动重复键
AutoReport button 自动报表按钮
AutoReport Wizard 自动报表向导
autorestart 自动重始[再启动]
autorouter 自动寻路由程序
autosave 自动保存
autoscore 自动划线
Autoshade 绘图软件(Autodesk)
autosizing 自动调整尺寸
autostart routine 自动启动例程
AutoSum 自动求和
autotest 自动测试程序
autovon 自动电话网
autotracing 自动跟踪,自动转换
AUX(AUXiliary port) 辅助端口
auxiliary access storage 辅助存取存储器
auxiliary carry bit 辅助进位位
auxiliary console 辅助控制台
auxiliary equipment 辅助设备
auxiliary function 辅助功能
auxiliary input/output statement 辅助输入/输出语句
auxiliary memory 辅助存储器
auxiliary port(AUX) 辅助端口
auxiliary power 辅助电源
auxiliary processor 辅助处理机
auxiliary pushdown automaton(APDA) 辅助下推自动机
auxiliary route 辅助路由
auxiliary routine(AR) 辅助例程
auxiliary-second general processor 辅助二级通用处理器
auxiliary storage 辅助存储器
auxiliary storage management(ASM) 辅助存储器管理
auxiliary storage units 辅助存储单元
auxiliary track 辅助磁道
AV(Absolute Value) 绝对值
AV(Attribute Value) 属性值
AVA(Absolute Virtual Address) 绝对虚拟地址
availability 可用性
availability machine time 机器可用时间
availability of instruction set 指令系统的有效性
availability ratio 可利用率
available bandwidth 可用带宽
available bandwidth ratio 可用带宽比
available bit rate(ABR) 有效位速率,可用比特率
available categories 可用的类别
available file space 可用文件空间
available frame count 可用帧计数
available line 可用线路
available machine time 机器可用时间
available memory 可用内存
available mode 可用模式
available page queue 可用页队列
available partition 可用分区
available performance 可用性能
available point 可用点
available ratio 可用率
available reference 有效引用
available space 可用空间
available space list 可利用空间表
available state 可用状态
available storage list 可用存储区表
available time 可用时间
available topics 可用选项[主题]
available unit queue 可用单元队列
avalanche 雪崩
avalanche breakdown 雪崩击穿
avalanche effect 雪崩效应
avalanche injection type MOS memory (AMOS memory) 雪崩注入型

MOS 存储器
avalanche multiplication 雪崩倍增
avalanche photodiode(APD) 雪崩光电二极管
avalanche photodiode coupler(APC) 雪崩光电二极管耦合器
AVC(Audio Visual Connection) 音视频连接软件
average access time 平均存取时间
average arrival rate 平均到达率
average aspect ratio 平均形态比
average background reflectance 背景平均反射率
average-behavior analysis 平均性态分析
average calculating operation 平均计算操作
average-case complexity 平均情况复杂性
average conditional information content 平均条件信息量,条件熵
average contrast 平均对比度
average cost 平均代价
average data transfer rate 平均数据转移率
average detector 平均值检波器
average edge line 平均边线
average effectiveness level 平均有效电平
average filter 平均过滤器
average gradient 平均梯度
average head positioning time 平均磁头定位时间
average information content 平均信息量,率
average information rate 平均信息速
average interconnection length 平均互连长度
average latency time 平均等待时间
average operation time 平均运算时间
average outgoing quality curve 平均检后质量曲线
average packet delay 平均包延迟
average power 平均功率
average printing speed 平均印出速度
average random access time 平均随机访问时间
average response time 平均响应时间
average running time 平均运行时间

average search time 平均查找时间
average seek time 平均寻道时间
average service rate 平均服务率
average transinformation content 平均转移信息量
average transinformation rate 平均转移信息率
average transmission rate 平均传输率
average value 平均值
averaging of multiple image 多图像平均法
AVI(Audio Video Interleaved) 音视频交插(文件格式)
AViiON series AViiON 计算机系列(DG)
avionic software 航空软件
AVISAM(AVerage Indexed Sequential Access Method) 平均索引顺序存取法
AVK(Audio Video Kernel) 音频视频核心软件
AVL tree AVL 树
AVLINE(Audio Visual on-LINE) 在线视听,联机视听
avoidance 避免法
AVOS(Advisor Virtual memory Operating System) 咨询虚拟存储操作系统
AVR(Automatic Volume Recognition) 自动档卷识别
AVSS(Audio Video Support System) 音频视频支持系统
AVT(Attribute Value Time) 属性值时间
AW(Access Width) 存取宽度
awaiting repair time 等待修复时间
Award BIOS Award 基本输入/输出系统
awareness network 了解[认知]网络
A. W. G. (American Wire Gauge) 美国线规
awk(Aho, Weinberger, Kernighan) awk 实用软件
AWL(Average Word Length) 平均字长
AWT(Abstract Window Toolkit) (Java)抽象窗口工具
axiom 公理

axiomatic complexity 公理复杂性
axiomatic semantics 公理语义学
axis 轴
axisymmetric 轴对称的

azimuth 方位,方位角
azimuth magnetic recording 方位角磁记录
Aztech Systems 爱捷特系统有限公司

B b

B(Binary) 二进制的
B(Byte) 字节
B address 基地址
B adjacent code B 邻接码
B axis 基线轴
B channel B 通道,B 信道
B disk B 驱动器
B language B 语言
B-ISDN(Broadband Integrated Services Digital Network) 宽带综合业务数字网络
B-MAC system B-MAC 系统(制)
B machine B 型机器
B mode ultrasound scan B 型超声波扫描
B picture(Bidirectional picture) 双向图像
B pins "B"形插头
B port B 端口
B register 基址寄存器,B 寄存器
B rule 逆向规则,B 规则
b/s(bit/second) 位/秒,比特/秒
B spline B 样条函数
B spline curve B 样条曲线
B spline surfaces B 样条曲面
B tree B 树
B * tree B * 树
B+ tree B+树
B- tree B-树
B+ tree search B+树查寻
B- tree record searching B-树记录搜寻
B/W (Black forward/White background) 黑字白底
BA(Base Address) 基址,基地址
BA(Byte Address) 字节地址
babble 串音
babble noise 混噪声,多重串音
baby AT case 小型 AT 结构机箱

baby AT motherboard 小型 AT 结构主板
back 回退;反向;背部;上一步
back acknowledge 逆向确认,返回肯定
back annotation 反向注解
back azimuth 逆向角,反方位角
back bone channel 基干通道
back bone network 骨架[中枢]网络
back chained inference 后向链推理
back chained reasoning 后向链推理
back chaining 逆向链锁,反向链
back character 退格字符
back clamping 反向钳位
back clipping plane 后剪取面
back coating 底面涂层
back coupling 反向耦合
back door 后门,活门
back door coupling 后门[活门]耦合
back door data 后门(通过非正常途径获得的)数据
back edge 回边
back electromotive force 反电势,反电动势
back elevation 背视图,后视图
back-enable (队列)后端允许
back end 后端,后期
back-end CASE 后端计算机辅助软件工程
back end computer 后端计算机
back end design 后端设计
back end processor(BEP) 后端处理机
back end system 后端系统
back face 背面
back-face culling 背面隐去[消除]
back face removal 背面排除,背面消
back-facing polygon 背面多边形
back file 后备[后援]文件
back haul 空载传输

back light 逆光,背光
back line feed 退行输送
back link 反向链接
back mark 回溯标志
back matter 附录
back off 补偿;回退
back off protocol 回退协议
back-off time (网络冲突所致)回退时延
back order 返回次序
back panel 底板,后面板
back patching 回插,回填
back plane 底板,母板
back porch 后肩
back projection 背面投影
back propagation 反向传播
back propagation learning algorithm 反向传播学习算法
back propagation model(B-P model) 反向传播模型
back propagation network 反向传播网络
back recovery 反向[返回]恢复
back resistance 反向电阻
back roll 反绕;重算
back strike print 背击式打印
back style 背景样式
back tabulation 反向制表
back trace 向后跟踪
back tracking method 回溯法
back tracking point 回溯点
back-up 备份
back-up value 倒推值
back view 背视图
back wiring 反面布线,背面连线
backbone 中枢,主干,干线
Backbone Concentrator Node(BCN) 主干集中器节点
Backbone Link Node(BLN) 主干链路节点
backbone network 基干网络
backbone ring (校园网)主干环路
backbone route 主干路由
backdrop procedure 背景程序
backfilling 回填
backflashing 倒冲法
background(BG, BKGRD) 底色,背景;后台

background aged write 后台延期写
background application 后台应用程序
background authentication 后台认证
background color 背景色
background color value 背景色值
background communication 后台通信
background control 后台控制;背景控制
background data 背景数据
background database 后台数据库
background display image 背景显示影像
background ink 背景[底色]墨水
background inking 背景着色
background items 背景单元,背景项
background job 后台作业
background knowledge 背景知识
background loop 后台环
background mode 后台方式;背景模式
background music 背景音乐
background noise 背景噪声
background pagination 后台分页
background palette 背景模板
background partition 后台分区
background picture 背景图片
background plate 背景图片
background printing 后台打印
background process 后台进程
background processing(BGP) 后台处理
background processing interrupt 后台处理中断
background processor 后台处理机
background program(BGP) 后台程序
background reader 后台读入程序
background recalculation 后台重算
background reflectance 底色[背景]反射
background region 后台区
background signal 背景信号;本底信号
background storage 后备存储器
background stream 后台作业流
background task 后台任务
background terminal 后台终端
backgrounding 后台处理
backing copy 备用复制品,副本
backing memory 后备存储器
backing out 回退
backing sheet 备份表格

backing store 后备存储器;后台存储
backing track 配声[伴音]磁道
backlash 间隙,齿隙;偏移;退回,反冲
backlash compensation 间隙补偿
backlight 背照,背光
backlink 后链
backlit LCD 背照式液晶显示器
backlog 待办事项
Backman diagram 巴克曼图形
backoff algorithm 回退[后退]算法
backout 回退恢复;逆序操作;取消
backout recovery 回退[逆序]恢复
backout routine 回退例程
backplane 底板
backplane placement 底板布局,底板布线
backplane routing 底板走线,底板路由
backplane testing 底板测试
backplate 背面电极;底板
backroll 重算,重新运行,回滚
backscroll buffer lines 回滚缓冲区行数
backslant 逆斜
backslash 反斜杠
backslip 附签
backspace(BS) 退格,回退
backspace character(BSC) 退格字符
backspace correction 回退修改,退格校正
backspace key 退格键,回退键
backspace mechanism 退格机构
backspace tape 反绕带
backtalk 反述,回送
backtracking 回溯
backtracking algorithm 回溯算法
backtracking control strategy 回溯控制策略
backtracking point 回溯点
backtracking program 回溯程序
backtracking specification language 回溯说明语言
backup 备份,备份装置
backup and recovery 备份与恢复
backup and restore 备份与复原
backup battery 备用电池
backup computer(BUC) 后备计算机
backup copy 副本
backup data set 备份数据集
backup diskette 备份盘
backup domain controller 备份域控制器
backup equipment 后备设备
backup file 备份[后备]文件
backup frequency 备份频度
backup memory 后备内存
backup operation 备份操作
backup path 备用路径
backup procedure 备份程序
backup programmer 后备程序员
backup reference station(BUR) 后备参考站
backup register(BUR) 后备寄存器
backup server 后备服务器
backup system 后备[后援]系统
backup trunk 备用中继线
backup utility 后备实用程序
backup volume 备份卷
Backus-Naur form(BNF) 巴科斯诺尔形式
Backus normal form(BNF) 巴科斯范式
backward busying 反向占线,远端占线
backward chained reasoning 反向链接推理
backward chaining 反向链接,逆向链
backward channel 反向信道
backward channel carrier detector 反向通道载波检测器
backward channel ready 反向通道就绪
backward channel received data(BRD) 反向通道接收数据
backward channel received line signal detector 反向通道接收线路信号检测器
backward channel request to send(BRS) 反向通道请求发送
backward clearing 反向[远端]拆线
backward compatibility 向后兼容性
backward compatible 向后兼容
backward conditional probability 后向条件概率
backward counter 逆向计数器
backward crosstalk 反向串音
backward deduction system 反向演绎系统
backward difference method 后向差分法

backward diode 反向二极管
backward echo 反向回波
backward error recovery 逆向差错恢复
backward file recovery 反向文件恢复
backward finite difference 后向有限差分
backward flow problem 后向流问题
backward-forward chaining 双向链;双向计数器
backward-forward counter 双向计数器,可逆计数器
backward fuzzy reasoning 反向模糊推理
backward impedance 反向阻抗
backward indicator bit(BIB) 逆向指示位
backward inheritance 逆向继承
backward interpolation 反向插值
backward learning 逆向学习;反查法
backward link 反向链接
backward link field 反向链字段
backward path 反向路径
backward processing 反向处理
backward production system 反向产生式系统
backward pruning procedure 反向修剪程序
backward read 反读,倒读
backward reasoning 逆向[反向]推理
backward recovery 向后[反向]恢复
backward recycling 反向循环
backward reference 向后引用
backward rule 反向[逆向]规则
backward search 反向搜索,逆向搜索算法
backward search algorithm 反向搜索算法号
backward sequence number 反向顺序号
backward set up 反向建立
backward supervision 反向监督
backward version management 后向版本管理
backwards attribute 反向属性
backwards learning 向后学习法
BackWeb Channel 后Web通道
Bacon Bacon专家系统
BACP(Bandwidth Allocation Control Protocol) 带宽分配控制协议
bacteria 细菌
bad address 错误地址
bad break 错误换行
bad command 错误命令
bad copy 错误复制件,无效拷贝
bad filename 错误文件名
bad page break 错误换页
bad read 阅读失败
bad sector 坏扇区
bad separator 错误分隔符
bad track 坏磁道
bad track table 坏磁道表
bad type 错误类型
badge 标记,标志卡
badge reader 标记阅读器
badge scanner 标记扫描器
Bag Bag类
BAK file 备份文件
balance 平衡,补偿
balance factor 平衡因子,均衡系数
balance set 平衡集
balance slider 平衡滑块
balanced array 平衡阵列
balanced code 平衡码
balanced configuration 平衡配置
balanced cycle 平衡圈
balanced data link 平衡数据链路
balanced duplexer 平衡双工器
balanced error 平衡[对称]误差
balanced error range 平衡误差范围
balanced factor of node 结点平衡因子
balanced hypergraph 平衡超图
balanced line 平衡传输线
balanced low pass filter 平衡式低通滤波器
balanced merge sort 平衡合并排序
balanced network 平衡[均衡]网络
balanced sort 平衡排序
balanced station 平衡式数据站
balanced to ground 对地平衡
balanced tree 平衡树
balanced twisted pair cable 平衡双绞线电缆
balanced-unbalanced transformer 平衡-不平衡变换器
balanced vertex 平衡顶点
balancing network 平衡网络
bale 打包
ballistic gain 轨迹增益
ballistic tracking 动态跟踪

balloon help 气球状求助窗
BALUN(BALanced to UNbalanced) 平衡/不平衡变换器
balun 平衡/不平衡适配器
BAM(Basic Access Method) 基本存取方法
BAM(Block Access Method) 成块存取方法
banana plug 香蕉插头
band 频带,波段
band compression 频带压缩
band edge absorption 带边吸收
band elimination filter 带阻滤波器
band expansion factor 频带扩展系数
band line printer 带式行印机
band matrix 带状矩阵
band number 段号
band-pass filter 带通滤波器
band printer 链带式打印机
band-reduction encoding 压缩频带编码技术
band-rejection filter 带阻滤波器
band-suppression filter 带阻滤波器
bandgap engineering 带隙工程
banding 聚束,带式生成线
bandwidth(BW) 带宽,频带宽度
bandwidth balancing 带宽平衡
bandwidth compression 带宽压缩
bandwidth limited 带宽受限的
bandwidth limited operation 带宽受限作用
bandwidth on demand (ISDN)按需分配带宽
bandwidth range 带宽范围
bandwidth rule 带宽法则
bandwidth throttling 带宽阀
bang 惊叹号(!),"砰"
bang-bang control 冲击式[继电器]控制
bang-bang robot 冲击式[继电器式]机器人
bang-bang servo 继电器式伺服
bang path 惊叹号路径
bank 体,组,堆,集
bank archive management service 银行档案管理业务
bank bit 存储区位
bank card 银行卡
bank clearing 银行票据交换

bank communication system 银行通信系统
bank conflict 存储体冲突
bank descriptor register 存储区描述符寄存器
bank information system network 银行信息系统网络
bank on-line teller system 银行联机出纳系统
bank POS terminal 银行销售点终端
bank processing central terminal unit 银行业务处理系统的中央终端装置
bank random-access disk file 银行随机存取磁盘文件
bank-switched memory 成组切换内存
bank switching 存储体切换
bank teller terminal 银行出纳机终端
banker's algorithm 银行家算法
banking 倾斜
banner 横幅,标语
banner frame (网页)横幅框
banner page 标题页
banner word 标题字
banyan heap 榕树堆
Banyan multistage network Banyan多级网络
Banyan Systems Inc. Banyan企业网系统公司(美)
Banyan VINES Banyan虚拟网络系统
BAP(Body Animation Parameters) 身体动作参数
BAPC(Business Application Performance Corp.) 商业应用性能合作组织
bar 条,杆;巴(压强单位=10^6达因/厘米2)
bar chart 条形图,直方图
Bar Chart AutoFormat 条形图套用格式
bar code 条码,条形码
bar-code character 条码字符
bar-code charge coupled device scanner 条码电荷耦合器件扫描器
bar-code decoder 条码解码器
bar-code laser scanner 条码激光扫描器
bar-code printer 条码打印机
bar-code reader(BCR) 条码读出器
bar-code scanner 条码扫描仪
bar-code symbol standard 条码符号标

准　　　　　　　　　　　　「准
bar-code usage standard　条码使用标
bar diagram　条形图
bar width reduction　条宽缩减
BARB(Board ARBiter)　板仲裁器
barbarous　(声音)刺耳的;不规范的
bare board　裸板(未装元件)
bare bone　裸机;裸件(只提供基本功能的软件);梗概,框架
bare machine　裸机(未装软件)
bare wire　裸线(无绝缘层)　　　「统
barebone system　裸机系统;最简单系
barge in　(网络系统)闯入
barrel　桶
barrel button　桶形按钮
barrel distortion　(CRT)桶形失真
barrel printer　鼓式打印机
barrel switch　桶形开关
barrier　障碍;势垒;阻挡层
barrier function method　障碍函数法
barrier grid storage cathode ray tube　障栅存储型阴极射线管
barrier layer　阻挡层,势垒层
barrier synchronization　障碍同步
base　基数
Base64　(MIME 标准)电子邮件编码规则
base address(BA)　基址,基地址
base address register(BAR)　基址寄存器
base address relocation　基地址重定位
base alignment　基对准,按基线对齐
base area　基区
base attribute　基属性
base band　基带
base class　基类
base cluster　基群集,基簇
base color　基色
base complement　基数补码,补码
base density　片基密度
base displacement addressing system　基数位移寻址系统
base element　基本元素
base exchange　基台交换
base field　基本字段
base font　基本字型
base form feature　基本形式特征
base group　基群

base I/O port address　输入输出端口基地址
base identifier　基标识符
base item　基本项
base-level synthesizer　(MIDI)基本合成器
base line　基线
base line drift　基线漂移
base location　(URL)基本位置
base machine　基准计算机　　　「码
base minus one complement　基减 1 补
base name　(文件的)基本名
base node　基本节点
base notation　基数记数法
base number　基数址
base operand address　基本操作数地
base page addressing　基页寻址
base parameter　基参数
base permission　基本许可
base point　基点,原点
base pool　基本池
base priority　基本优先级
base priority number　基优先数
base RAM　基本 RAM
base record slot　基本记录槽
base reference potential　基极参考电
base region　基region区　　　　　「位
base register(BR)　基址[变址]寄存器
base relative byte address　基本相对字节地址
base scalar type　基本标量类型
base segment　基本段
base set　基本集
base station　基站,基地电台
base stock　基体
base system　基本系统
100Base-T　100Base-T(以太)网络
base table　基表
base time constant　基时间常数
base type　基类型
base vector　基向量
base volume　基卷
baseband　基带
baseband attenuation　基带衰减
baseband coaxial system　基带同轴电缆系统
baseband data network　基带数据网络
baseband directly intensity modulation

基带直接光强度调制
baseband equalization 基带均衡
baseband LAN 基带局域网络
baseband modem 基带调制解调器
baseband network 基带网络
baseband response 基带响应
baseband signal 基带信号
baseband signaling 基带信令
baseband transmission 基带传输
baseband twisted-pair system 基带双绞线系统
based integer 带基整数
based storage allocation 基本存储区分配
based variable 有基变量
baseline 基线,基准线
baseline alignment 基线对齐
baseline angle 基线角
baseline axis 基线轴
baseline configuration management 基线组态管理
baseline correction 基线校正
baseline direction 基线方向
baseline extent 基线范围
baseline increment 基线增量
baseline network 基线网络
baseline offset 基线位移
baseline process 基准过程
baseline sequential axis 基线顺序轴
baseline sequential codec 基线顺序编解码器
baselined documents 用下划线标出的[重要]文档;超链接文档
BaseTime 基本时间操作函数
BASIC(Beginner's All-purpose Symbolic Instruction Code) 初学者通用符号指令码,BASIC语言
basic access method(BAM) 基本存取法
basic assembler program(BAP) 基本汇编程序
basic authentication 基本验证
basic block protocol 基本块协议
basic building block 基本构件
basic cell 基本单元
basic channel unit 基本信道单元
basic character set 基本字符集
basic clock chain 基准时钟链

BASIC compiler BASIC语言编译程序
basic controller 基本控制器
basic conversation 基本会话
basic data exchange 基本数据交换
basic data type 基本数据类型
basic debugging tool 基本除错工具
basic decision model 基本决策模型
basic device unit(BDU) 基本设备(传送)单位
basic direct access method(BDAM) 基本直接存取法
basic disk operating system(BDOS) 基本磁盘操作系统
basic display format 基本显示格式
basic document 基础文档
basic element 基本元件;基本单元
basic encoding rules 基本编码规则
basic error correction method 基本纠错法
basic exchange format 基本交换格式
basic external function 基本外部函数
basic feasible solution 基本可行解
basic file structure 基本文件结构
basic format 基本格式
basic function of a finite element space 有限元空间的基函数
basic functions 基本函数,基本功能
BASIC graphic extensions BASIC图形扩展
basic graphic system(BGS) 基本图形系统
basic group 基群
basic ideographic character set 基本象形字符集
BASIC in ROM 驻留ROM的BASIC语言
basic indexed sequential access method (BISAM) 基本索引顺序存取法
basic induction variable 基本归纳变量
basic information unit(BIU) 基本信息单元
basic information unit segment 基本信息单元分段
basic input/output system(BIOS) 基本输入/输出系统
basic instruction set 基本指令集
basic interconnection test 基本互连测

试

BASIC language BASIC语言,初学者通用符号指令码语言
basic language 基本语言
basic license 基本特许
basic line space(BLU) 基本行距
basic link unit(BLU) 基本链路单元
basic linkage 基本链结
basic loop 基本循环
basic mastergroup 基本主群,主群
basic MIDI 基本乐器数字接口
basic mode 基本模式
basic mode control procedure(BMCP) 基本型控制规程
Basic Mode Link Control(BMLC) 基本模式链路控制规程
basic network 基本网络
basic network utilities 基本网络实用程序
basic noise 基本噪声
basic object 基本对象
Basic Object Simulation System(BOSS) 基本对象仿真系统
basic operation system(BOS) 基本操作系统
basic optimizable expression 基本可优化表达式
basic overlay 基本覆盖
basic partitioned access method (BPAM) 基本分块访问法
basic path testing 基本路径测试
basic peripheral channel 基本外设通道
basic plan generating system 基本规划产生系统
basic platform 基本平台
basic pulse generator 主脉冲发生器
basic rate interface (ISDN)基本速率接口(2B+D)
basic rate ISDN 基本速率ISDN
basic rate user-network interface 基本速率用户-网络接口
basic real constant 基本实常数
basic resolution unit(BRU) 基本分辨单位
basic route 基本路由
basic sequential access method(BSAM) 基本顺序存取法

basic service 基本服务,基本业务
basic session reference 基本对话参考
basic solution 基本解
basic statement 基本语句
basic storage module 基本存储模块
basic symbol 基本符号
basic telecommunication access method (BTAM) 基本远程访问法
basic term 基本项
basic timestamp method 基本时间戳
basic timing cycle 基本定时周期
basic transmission header(BTH) 基本传输标题
basic transmission unit(BTU) 基本传输单元
basic transport protocol 基本传送协议
basis trunk 基干线路
basic user-network interface 基本用户-网络接口
basic utility 基本实用程序
basic variable 基本变量
basic view 基本视图
basic warranty 基本保修
BASICA(BASIC Advantage) BASICA语言(扩充了图形、声音功能)
basis 基础的
basis matrix 基底矩阵
basis rule 基本规则
basis transformation 基底变换
basis vector 基向量
basis weight 基本重量
BASM(Built-in AsseMbler) 内置汇编语言程序
bass 低音,贝司
bass boost 低音提升
bass compensation 低音补偿
bastard 变形的,非标准的
bastard size 非标准尺寸
bastard 变形的,非标准的
bastion host 堡垒主机
BAT(BATch) 整批,分批;批处理
BAT file(BATch file) 批处理文件
batch(B,BAT) 整批,分批;批处理
batch application 成批处理应用程序
batch checkpoint 批量检查点
batch coding sheets 批量编码表
batch command 批命令
batch compiler 成批编译程序

batch control sampling　整批控制抽样
batch counter　选组计数器
batch data exchange　成批数据交换
batch-entry mode　成批输入模式
batch environment　批处理环境
batch execution　成批执行
batch file　批处理文件
batch file extension　批处理文件扩展
batch file transfer　批量文件传送
batch-header document　整批标题文档
batch initiation　成批初启，批启动
batch input reader　成批输入阅读器
batch input spooler　成批输入假脱机程序
batch insertion　成批插入
batch interface log file　批量接口状态记录文件
batch job　整批处理作业
batch job queue　整批作业队列
batch number　批号
batch output spooler　成批输出假脱机程序
batch printer　批量打印机
batch process system　整批处理系统
batch processing　批处理
batch processing configuration　批量处理配置
batch processing editor　成批处理编辑程序
batch processing information retrieval　整批处理信息检索
batch processing interrupt　整批处理中断
batch processing program　批处理程序
batch processing system(BPS)　批处理系统
batch processing terminal　批处理终端
batch program　批处理程序
batch query　成批查询
batch queue　批队列
batch region　整批处理区
batch request　整批处理申请
batch return status　整批返回状态
batch run　批量运行
batch save/restore　整批处理保存/恢
batch scanning　批扫描
batch scheduler　成批调度程序
batch session　整批对话

batch spool monitor　批量假脱机监督程序
batch stream　整批处理流
batch subsystem　批处理子系统
batch task　整批任务
batch terminal(BT)　整批处理终端机
batch total　整批总计，分批总计
batch trailer　整批尾部
batch transaction file　成批事务文件
batch user　批处理用户
batched communication　成批通信
batched job　批量作业，成批作业
batched task processing　批量事务处理
batched telecommunication　整批远程通信
batching with a control total　总和控制的批量处理
bath effect　浴盆效应
bathtub curve　浴盆曲线
battery　电池，电池组
battery cut-off　电池断开
battery pack　电池组
BAUD(BAUDot code)　博多码
baud(Bd)　波特
baud rate　波特率
baud rate generator(BRG)　波特率发生器
Baudot code　博多码
Baudy language　博迪语言
bay　机架，台，盘，舱
Bay Networks Inc.　贝网络公司
Bayes classifier　贝叶斯分类器
Bayes decision rule　贝叶斯决策规则
Bayes law　贝叶斯定律
Bayes risk　贝叶斯风险
Bayes rule　贝叶斯规则
Bayes decision theory　贝叶斯判定理
Bayesian inference　贝叶斯推理
Bayesian inference network　贝叶斯推理网络
Bayesian logic　贝叶斯逻辑
Bayesian theorem　贝叶斯定理
bayonet coupling　卡口接头
BaySIS(Bay Switching Interconnection System)　BaySIS 交换式互连网络(Bay)
B2B(Business to Bussiness)　企业对

企业
BBAT(Bachelor of Business Administration) 商业管理学士
BBC(Broad Band coaxial Cable) 宽带同轴电缆
BBEST(a development tool for Blackboard-Based Expert SysTem) 基于黑板的专家开发工具
BBIAF(Be Back In A Few minutes) 一会儿就回来
BBL(Be Back Later) 过会儿再来
BBS(Be Back Soon) 下次再来
BBS(Building Block System) 积木式系统
BBS(Bulletin Board System) 布告牌系统
B2C(Bussiness to Customer) 企业对客户
bcc(blind carbon copy) 隐名副本(对收件人隐藏其他收件人姓名的电子邮件)
bcc(blind courtesy copy) 隐名副本
BCD(Binary Coded Decimal) 二进制编码的十进制,BCD 码
BCD system 二-十进制系统,BCD 表示法
BCE(Brightness, Contrast & Exposure Time) 亮度、对比度与曝光时间
BCF(Byte Cipher Feedback) 字节反馈加密法
BCH(Block Control Header) 块控制头标
BCH code BCH 码
BCI(Begin Chain Indicator) 链开始指示符
BCK(BaCK up) 后备,备份
BCN(BeaCoN) 信标,标志
BCP(Byte Control Protocol) 字节控制规程
BCPL(Bootstrap Combined Programming Language) BCPL 语言(C 语言的前身)
BCS(Basic Catalog Structure) 基本目录结构
BCS(Binary Synchronous Communication) 二进制同步通信
BCS(Boston Computer Society) 波士顿计算机学会
BCS(British Computer Society) 英国计算机学会
BD(BauD) 波特
BD(Bus Driver) 总线驱动器
BD-BUS(BiDirectional BUS) 双向总线
BDAM(Basic Direct Access Method) 基本直接存取法
BDC(Binary Decimal Counter) 二-十进制计数器
BDTR(Burst Data Transfer Rate) 突发数据传输率
BE(Below or Equal) 小于或等于
beachball pointer 球形指针
beacon(BCN) 信标
beacon delay 信标延迟
beacon reply processor 信标回答处理机
beacon station 信标站
beacon video processing equipment 信标视频处理设备
beaconing 设信标
beaconing station 信标站,报警站
bead 珠;垫圈
beaded screen 珠子屏幕
beam 束,射束,波束,光束
beam-accessed (光)束存取的
beam-accessible memory 光束可存取存储器
beam alignment 射束校准
beam deflection 电子束偏转
beam deflection flat color picture tube 束偏转平板彩色显像管
beam diversity 波束发散,一束多用
beam-landing screen error 射束着屏幕误差
beam-penetration color display 电子束穿透式彩色显示
beam splitter 光束分离器,分束器,分光器
bearer 单向通路;载体,支座,托架
bearer channel (ISDN)荷载通道,B 通道
bearer identification code 荷载识别码
bearer service (ISDN)荷载服务
bearing 方位,方位角;轴承
bearing distance computer 方位距离计算机
bearing mark 方位标记

bearing resolution 方位分辨力
bearing tracking 方位跟踪
beat 节拍;拍
beat generator 节拍脉冲发生器
beating 差拍
BECN(Backward Explicit Congestion Notation) 反向显式拥塞通告
bed 背景音乐;底座
BEDO RAM(Burst Extended-data-out RAM) 突发式 EDO 内存
beep code 笛音码
beep tone 簧音音调,高频音调
beeper 笛音发生器
before image (数据库)前映像
before image file 前映像文件
before method 前方法
before phrase 前短语
Before Sheet 工作表之前
begin 开始
begin block 开始块[分程序]
begin-end block 开始-结束块
begin outline function 轮廓线开始功能
BEGIN statement 开始语句
beginner 初学者;初级技术人员
beginning of a file label(BOF) 文件起始标志
beginning-of-tape marker(BOT,BTM) 磁带起始标志
beginning-of-volume label 卷开始标志
behavior 行为;性能
behavior analysis 性能分析
behavior learning 行为学习
behavior meaning 行为含义
behavior modeling 行为建模
behavior monitoring 行为监视
behavior of a system 系统行为
behavior science 行为科学
behavior test 行为测试
behavioral description language 行为描述语言
behavioral model 行为模型
behavioral reasoning module 行为推理模块
behavioral simulation 行为模拟
behaviorism 行为主义
behaviour 行为;性能(同 behavior)
Bel 贝尔
Belady anomaly 伯拉弟反常现象

belief 信任度;确信,相信
belief base 信念库
belief function 信任函数
belief introspection 信念内省
belief logic 信念逻辑
belief revision 信任修正
belief-revision system 信念修正系统
belief system 信任系统,信念系统
belief update 信任值更新
bell 响铃
Bell 103 300 bps 异步全双工调制解调器标准(AT&T,以下皆同)
Bell 113 Bell 113 标准
Bell 201 2400 bps 半双工调制解调器标准
Bell 202 1800 bps 异步 4 线全双工,1200 bps 2 线半双工调制解调器标准
Bell 208 4800 bps 调制解调器标准
Bell 209 9600 bps 4 线异步调制解调器标准
Bell 212 300 bps 和 1200 bps 异步全双工调制解调器标准
Bell and Howell newspaper index 比勒-豪威新闻索引
bell character(BEL) 响铃[报警]字符
Bell code 贝尔码,Bell 码
Bell communications standards 贝尔通信标准
Bell compatible 贝尔兼容的
Bell integrated optical device(BIOD) 贝尔集成光学器件
Bell & La Padula model 贝尔-拉帕杜拉模型
Bell Laboratories 贝尔实验室(朗讯)
Bell Operating Company(BOC) 贝尔公司,BOC 公司
Bell system 贝尔系统
Bell system Technical Journal 《贝尔电讯技术杂志》
bellboy 随身电话装置
belt printer 带式打印机
benchmark(BM) 基准(测试)程序
benchmark package 基准程序包
benchmark problem 基准测试问题
benchmark test 基准程序测试
benchmark set 基准程序组
bend 弯曲;弯头

bending element 弯曲元
bending loss 弯曲损耗
bending rigidity 抗弯刚度
beneficiary case 受益者角色
benefit/deficit matrix 赢/亏矩阵
benefit matrix 效益矩阵
benign software 良性软件
Bento Bento 结构化存储
BeOS BeOS 操作系统(BE)「机
BEP(Back-End Processor) 后端处理
BER(Basic Encoding Rules) 基本编码规则 「率
BER(Bit Error Rate) 位误码率,位错
Berger code 伯格码
Berkeley extensions 伯克莱扩展版本
Berkeley Internet Name Domain(BIND) 伯克莱因特网名字域
Berkeley Software Distribution(BSD) 伯克莱软件发行版本 「统
Berkeley UNIX 柏克莱 UNIX 操作系
Bernoulli Box 伯努利盒
Bernoulli distribution 伯努利分布
Bernoulli flexible disk drive 伯努利活动盘驱动器
Bernoulli hard disk drive 伯努利硬磁盘驱动器
BERT(Bit Error Rate Test) 位误码率测试
Bessel interpolating polynomial 贝塞尔插值多项式
best approximation 最佳逼近
best-compromise 最好折衷
best estimation 最佳估计
best-few search 最佳少数搜索
best-first search 最优优先搜索
best fit 最佳适配法
best-fit-decreasing rule(BFD) 最佳适合下降规则
best-fit rule(BF) 最佳适合规则
best-fit strategy 最佳适配策略
best match 最佳匹配,最优配合
BESTeam(Business Enterprise Solution Team Program) 最佳系统集成商计划(IBM)
BET(Bit Enhanced Technology) 位增强技术
beta cutoff β修剪
beta form β格式

beta interconnection network β互连网
beta radiation β辐射 「络
beta particle β粒子
beta release β版本
beta site β测试场地
beta software β软件
beta substitution β替换,β规则
beta system β系统
beta test β测试
beta value β值
beta version β版本,测试版本
betaware β(版本)软件
Between Categories 分类之间
between-line entry 行间插入项
between predicate 范围谓词
BEX(Broadband EXchange) 宽带交换机
BeyondMail 电子邮件应用软件包
Between Tick Marks 分类轴刻度线之
beziel 聚光圈,窗口 「间
Bezier curve 贝齐尔曲线
Bezier patch 贝齐尔修补
Bezier spline curve 贝齐尔样条曲线
Bezier triangle patch 贝齐尔三角形补片
BFS(Bootable File System) 可引导文件系统
BFT(Binary File Transmission) 二进制文件传输
BG(BackGround) 后台,背景;基础
BG(Base Group) 基群
BGC(Back-Ground Communication) 后台通信
BGE(Branch if Greater or Equal) 大于等于转移
BGI(Binary Gateway Interface) 二进制网关接口
BGI(Borland Graphics Interface) Borland 图形界面
BGN(Back-Ground Noise) 背景噪声
BGP(BackGround Processing) 后台处理,背景处理 「序
BGP(BackGround Program) 后台程
BGP(Border Gateway Protocol) 边界网关协议
BHC(Busy Hour Call) 忙时呼叫数
BI(Bus Interface) 总线接口
BI bus BI 总线

Bi-CMOS integrated circuit 双极-CMOS集成电路
bi-cubic convolution method 双三次卷积法
BI-DI(BIDIrectional bus) 双向总线
bi-directional 双向的
bi-directional heuristic 双向试探
bi-duplexed redundancy 双向双工冗余
bi-implication form 双蕴涵式
bi-implication letter 双蕴涵词
bi-language form 双语形式
bi-linear interpolation method 双线性内插法
bi-phase level 双相电平
bi-phase mark 双相标记
bias 偏压,偏流;偏磁;偏差
bias check 边缘检验
bias computation 偏差计算
bias current 偏置电流
bias data 偏移数据
bias distortion 偏置畸变
bias error 偏移误差
bias logic 偏置逻辑
bias off 偏置截止
bias oscillator 偏磁振荡器
bias ratio 偏离率
bias sample 偏差试样[样值]
bias test 偏移测试,临界检验
bias winding 偏置绕组
biased error 有偏误差
biased exponent 增阶码,移阶码
biased partitioning 不均等分区
biased statistic 有偏统计量
biaxial crystal 双轴晶体
BIB(Backward Indicator Bit) 逆向指示位
bibliographer 书目检索程序
bibliographic coupling 书目[引文]耦合
bibliographic database 书目数据库
bibliographic retrieval service 文献索引服务
bibliography 文献目录
bibliometric study 文献计量研究
BIC(Bus Interface Card) 总线接口卡
BIC(Bus Interface Chips) 总线接口芯片
biconditional 双条件,等价
biconditional statement 双条件语句
biconnected component algorithm 双连通支算法
biconnected graph 双连通图
bicovering 双覆盖
bicubic interpolation 双三次方插值
bicubic patch 双三次补片
bicubic spline 双三次样条
bicubic surface 双三次曲面
bid 投标,请求;占线企图
bid indicator 投标指示符
biddelta network 双 △(三角形)网络
bidder 投标者
bidder session 投标者对话期
bidding 投标方式,竞争方式
bidding model 投标模型
bidegreed graph 双维图
bidiagonal matrix 双对角线矩阵
bidiagraph 有向偶图
bidirection triggering 双向触发
bidirectional 双向的
bidirectional associative memory 双向联想记忆
bidirectional bus(BD-BUS) 双向总线
bidirectional bus driver 双向总线驱动器
bidirectional cable 双向光缆
bidirectional cabled distribution system 双向电缆分配系统
bidirectional code 双向码
bidirectional control 双向控制
bidirectional counter 双向计数器
bidirectional coupler 双向耦合器
bidirectional data bus 双向数据总线
bidirectional dot-matrix printer 双向点阵打印机
bidirectional flow 双向流程,双向流
bidirectional gate 双向门
bidirectional I/O buffer 双向输入/输出缓冲器
bidirectional inference 双向推理
bidirectional picture 双向(预测)图像
bidirectional printing 双向打印
bidirectional production system 双向产生式系统
bidirectional pulse 双向脉冲
bidirectional search 双向搜索
bidirectional shift register 双向移位寄存器
bidirectional switch 双向开关

bidirectional transmission 双向传输
bids per circuit per hour(BCH) 每电路小时要求
BIF(Benchmark Interchange Format) 基准程序交换格式
biflar 双股的(导线)
bifocal 双焦点的(透镜)
BIFS(BInary Format for Scene description) 二进制场景描述格式
bifurcation 分叉,双态,分歧
bifurcation point 歧点
bifurcation value 分歧值
big 5 code (台湾省流行的)大五码
Big Blue 蓝色巨人,IBM 公司
big head 大特写
big iron 巨型机
big long shot 大远景
BigBook BigBook 公司
big endian 大尾数法,大序法
big endian byte order 低位置前字节顺序(如 X86 指令系统)
big endian computer 大尾数法计算机
big-M method 大 M 法
big red switch (电源)大红开关
bigraph 偶图
bijection 双映射
bilateral agreement 双向协定
bilateral closed user group 双向封闭的用户组
bilateral control 双边控制
bilateral manipulator 双向操纵器
bilateral network 双向网络
bilateral synchronization 双向同步
Bildschirmtext 信息传视系统
bilevel 双电平的
bilevel image 二值图像
bilinear interpolation 二次线性插值
bilinear patch 二次线性修补
Bilingual 双语的
bilingual keyboard 双语[双模式]键盘
bill 账单;票据
bill printer 票据打印机
billi- 十亿(10^9)的词首
billibit 千兆位(10^9 位)
billicycle 千兆周
billing error probability 通告错误概率
billing machine 票据印制机
billion (美)十亿,即 10^9;(英)万亿,即 10^{12}
bilogical 双逻辑的
bimetallic temperature sensor 双金属片温度传感器
bimodal 双模态的
bimodal Gaussian mixture 双模态高斯混合
bimodal optical communication 双模态光通信
bimodulus material 双模材料
bimorph cell 双压电芯片元件
bimorph memory cell 双压电存储元件
BIN(BInary) 二进制的;双态的;二元的
bin card 卡片箱
binary 二进制;二态的
binary adder 二进制加法器
binary arithmetical operation 二进制算术运算
binary B-tree 二叉 B 树
binary baud rate 二进制波特率
binary cell 二进制存储单元
binary chain 二进制链
binary character 二进制符号
binary chop 对分检索,二分查找
binary code 二进制编码
binary-coded character 二进制编码字符
binary-coded decimal(BCD) 二-十进制,BCD 制
binary-coded format 二进制编码格式
binary comparator 二进制比较器
binary compatible 二进制兼容
binary component 双态元件
binary condition 二态
binary countdown 二进制递减计数
binary counter 二进制计数器
binary digit 二进制数字
binary dump 二进制转储
binary encoder 二进制编码器
binary exponential backoff algorithm 二进制指数回退算法
binary field 二进制字段
binary file 二进制文件
binary file transmission(BFT) 二进制文件传输
binary format 二进制格式
binary hypermesh network 二进制超网格网络

binary image 二值图像；二进制映像
binary incremental representation 二进递增表示法
binary insertion sort 折半插入排序
binary large objects(BLOB) 二进制大型对象
binary loader 二进制装载程序
binary logic 二值逻辑
binary matching 二元匹配法
binary message 二元消息
binary method 折半法，对分法
binary newsgroup 二进制新闻组
binary notation 二进制计数法
binary number system 二进制数
binary operator 二目操作数，二元运算符
binary pair 二进偶，双态对，双稳态触发器
binary pattern 二值模式
binary phase-shift keying(BPSK) 双相频移键控法
binary picture 二值图像
binary picture data 二进制图像数据
binary point 二进制小数点
binary program space(BPS) 二进制程序空间
binary query 对分查询
binary radix 二进制基数
binary relation 二元[二目]关系
binary resolvent 二元消解式
Binary RX 二进制接收器(微软)
binary search 对分查找
binary search tree 二叉查寻树，对分搜索树
binary signaling 双态信令
binary symmetric channel 二进制对称通道
binary synchronous communication protocol(BISYNC) 二元同步通信协议
binary to decade counter 二-十进制计数器
binary-to-decimal conversion 二-十进制变换
binary-to-hexadecimal conversion 二-十六进制变换
binary tree 二叉树
binary tree traversal 二叉树遍历

Binary TX 二进制发送器(微软)
binary unit of information content 信息量的二进制单位
binaural 双耳的；立体声
binaural effect 双耳效应，双耳作用
binaural recorder 双声道录音机
BIND 连接；结合
bind 赋值；约束，连接，绑定
bind command 连接命令
bind context 连接上下文
Bind Failed 绑定失败
bind image table 连接映像表
BIND pacing 绑定调步
bind session 连接会话
binder 绑定程序
binder group 汇集器；连接程序组
bindery 连接库，装订库
Bindery Files 平衡数据库文件
Bindery Security 结合安全性
BINDFIX 连接修复
binding 约束，绑定，联编，结合
binding early 超前绑定
binding item 绑定项
binding late 滞后绑定
binding occurrence 约束出现
binding pattern 绑定模式
binding process 联编过程
binding time 绑定时间
binding variable 约束变量
BINDREST 连接恢复，连接复位
BinHex (Mac)电子邮件编码规则
binit 二进制符号
binocular image 双目影像
binocular imaging 双目成像
binocular parallax 双眼视差
binocular stereo vision 双眼立体视觉
binomial coefficient 二项式系数
binomial distribution 二项式分布
binomial theory 二项式定理
BIO(Buffered Input/Output) 带缓冲器的输入/输出
biochip 生物芯片
Biocodes 生命信息数据库
biocommunication 生物通信
biocomputer 生物计算机
biocontrol 生物电控制
biocybernetics 生物控制论
bioelectric model 生物电模型

bioelectric potential 生物电位
bioelectrical phenomenon 生物电现象
bioelectronics 生物电子学
boilerplate 样板文件
biologic engineering 生物工程学
biological analogy 仿生,生物模拟
biological black-box theory 生物黑箱理论
biological image analysis 生物图像分析
biological information 生物信息
biological neural network 生物神经网络
biological robotics 生物机器人学
biological signal processing 生物信号处理
biological synapse 生物突触
biomathematics 生物数学
biomechanics 生物力学
biomedical 生物医学
bionic computer 仿生学计算机
bionics 仿生学
biopack 生物舱
biorobot 仿生机器人
BIOS (Basic Input/Output System) 基本输入/输出系统
BIOS extensions 扩展 BIOS
BIOS redirection BIOS 重定向
BIOS shadow 基本输入/输出系统映像
biosensor 生物传感器
Biosis Previews 生物预测数据库
biostatistics 生物统计学
biotelemetry 生物遥测技术
bioturbation 生物扰动
biowave 生物波
bipartite graph 偶图,二分图
biped robot 双腿机器人
biphase coding 双相编码
biphase mark 双相传号
biphase modulation 双相调制
biphase recording 双相记录
biphase shift-keying 双移相键控
biphase signal 双相信号
biplexer 双线[双路]转换器
bipolar 双极,双极型的
bipolar bit-slice microcomputer 双极型位片式微型计算机
bipolar code with zero extraction 零提取双极性码
bipolar coding 双极性编码
bipolar converter 双极变换器
bipolar CPU slice 双极型 CPU 位片
bipolar integrated circuit 双极集成电路
bipolar memory cell 双极型内存单元
bipolar pulse 双极性脉冲
bipolar random access memory 双极型随机存取存储器
bipolar slice 双极型位片
bipolar slice IC processor 双极型位片集成电路处理器
bipolar slice system 双极型位片系统
bipolar transistor 双极型晶体管
bipolar transmission 双极性传输
bipolar violation 双极违例[干扰]
biprefix code 双前缀码
biquinary-coded decimal number 二-五码十进数
biquinary notation 二-五记法
bird tweet 鸟鸣声
bird's eye view 鸟瞰图
birdies 尖叫声
birefringence 双折射
biresidue code 双剩余码
birth and death process 增消过程
birth-death system 增消系统
birth-death type 增消类型
birthday paradox 生日判定
bis 补充的
BIS-COBOL 修订版 COBOL 语言
BISAM (Basic Indexed Sequential Access Method) 基本索引顺序存取法
BISC (BInary Synchronous Communication) 二进制同步通信
BISDN (Broadband ISDN) 宽带综合服务数字网络
bisection 对分,折半
bisector 平分线,等分线
bispectral analysis 双谱分析
bispectrum 双谱
bistable circuit 双稳态电路
bistable component 双稳态元件
bistable element 双稳态元件
bistable multivibrator 双稳态多谐振荡器
bistable optical device 光学双稳态装置

bistable phosphor 双稳态磷光体
bistable phosphor cathode ray tube 双稳态磷光阴极射线管
bistable relay 双稳态继电器
bistable trigger circuit 双稳态触发电路
BISYNC(BInary SYNchronous Communication protocol) 二元同步通信协议
bisynchronous communication 双同步通信
bit(B,b) 位,比特
bit alignment 位对准,位同步
bit attribute 位属性
bit-bender 电脑迷,数字技术崇拜者
bit block 位块
bit block transfer 位块转移
bit bucket 位桶
bit bumming 位压缩
bit bus 位总线
bit-by-bit asynchronous operation 逐位异步操作
bit-by-bit control 按位控制
bit-by-bit memory 逐位记忆
bit cell 位单元
bit check 位校验
bit clear 按位清除
bit clock 位时钟
bit combination 位组合
bit comparator 位比较器
bit-count integrity 位计数完整性
bit crowding 位拥挤
bit density 位密度
bit depth 位深度
bit drive 位驱动
bit drop-in 位混入
bit drop-out 位丢失
bit error 位误码,比特错误
bit error rate(BER) 位误码率
bit field 位字段
bit flopping 位翻转
bit gravity (X协议)位重力
bit grinding 位析取
bit image 位映像
bit instruction 位指令
bit integrity 位完整性
bit interleaved 位交插[交错]
bit interval 位间隔
bit inversion 位反转

bit jitter 位抖动
bit line 位线
bit location 位单元
bit manipulation 位操作
bit map 位映像,位映图
bit map protocol 位映像协议
bit-mapped font 位映式[点阵图]字形
bit-mapped graphic 位映像图形
bit mapping 位映像
bit mask 位屏蔽
bit multiplex 位多路传输
bit-order of transmission 位传输次序
bit-oriented procedure 面向比特的规程
bit-oriented protocol 面向位的协议
bit packing 位紧凑,位压缩
bit pair 位偶,码元偶
bit parallel 位并行
bit pattern 位模式
bit permutation 位置换
bit plane 位平面
bit plane coding 位面编码
bit port 位端口
bit pulse crowding 位脉冲拥挤
bit rate 位速率
bit-rate-length product 位速率长度积
bit reduction factor 位缩减因子
bit serial 位串行
bit shift compensation 位移补偿
bit slice architecture 位片式体系结构
bit specifications 位规范
bit stream 位流,比特流
bit stream transmission 位流[比特流]传输
bit string 位串
bit string constant 位串型常数
bit-string operators 位串运算符
bit stuffing 位填充法
bit synchronization 位同步
bit traffic 位流量
bit transfer rate 位转移速率
bit twiddler 电脑玩家
bit vector 位向量[矢量]
BITBLT(BIT Block Transfer) 位块传输
BITC(Burned-In Time Code) (视频图像)摄录时间码
bitenary coding 双三进制编码

bitmap 位映像,位图
bitmap file 位图文件
bitmap resource 位图资源
bitmap stretching mode 位图拉伸模式
bitmap texture 位图纹理
bitmapped font 位映像字型,位图字形
bitmapped graphics 位映像图形
bitmapping 位映像法
BITNET(Because It's Time NETwork) BITNET 网络
bitonic merging 双调归并
bitonic network 双调网络
bitonic selection algorithm 双调选择算法
bitonic sequence 双调序列
bitonic sorting 双调排序
bitreverse scheme 倒位模式
bits per inch(bpi) 每英寸位数
bits per second(bit/s,bps) 每秒位数
bitwise AND operator 按位"与"运算符
bitwise-complement operator 按位求反运算符
bitwise exclusive OR operator 按位"异或"运算符
bitwise operator 按位运算符
bitwise-NOT operator 按位求反运算符
bitwise OR operator 按位"或"运算符
bitwise RAM 位操作随机存取存储器
BIU(Basic Information Unit) 基本信息单元
biunique 双对向的
bivariant function generator 二元函数发生器
bivariate interpolation 双变量内插
bivariate polynomial 双变量多项式
bivariate spline 双变量样条
BIX(Byte Information eXchange) 《Byte》信息交换
BL(Base Line) 基线
Black 黑色的
black and white display 黑白显示(器)
black-and-white pattern 黑白图形
Black Apple 黑苹果计算机(苹果)
black body 黑体
black box 黑盒子,未知框
black box approach 黑匣子求解法

black box characterization 黑箱特征记述
Black Box Corporation Black Box 公司
black box interface specification 黑匣子(程序)模块接口规范
black box method 黑箱法
black box model 黑箱模型
black box testing 黑箱测试
black circuit 黑线路
black designation 黑色标志
black hole (路由器)黑洞
black level (视频信号)黑色电平
black recording 黑记录
black screen 黑屏幕
black signal 黑信号
black text 黑色文本,黑字
black transmission "黑区"传输
black watch tape 黑背磁带
blackboard 黑板
blackboard approach 黑板方法
blackboard architecture 黑板体系结构
blackboard memory organization 黑板记忆组织
blackboard model 黑板模型
blackboard system(BBS) 黑板系统
blade 刀片
blade-fork contact 刀口音叉式簧片
blank(BLK,BLNK) 空白;空位,间隔
blank argument 空变元
blank card 空白卡片
blank cell 空白单元格
blank character 空白字符
blank check 空白核对
blank common block 无名公用块
blank diskette 空白软磁盘
blank field descriptor 空白字段说明
blank fill 空白填充符
blank form 空白格式;空表单
blank instruction 空白指令
blank interpretation descriptor 空格解释描述符
blank line 空行,空白行
blank medium 空白媒体,空白介质
blank or blanking interval 空白间隔
blank record 空记录
blank squash 空白压缩
blank tape 空白磁带

blank transmission test 空传输试验
blanket 覆盖[涂]层;覆盖范围广泛
blanket rule 普适规则   」的
blanking 消除;熄灭;消隐
blanking interval 消隐信号间隔
blanking level 消隐电平
blanking pulse 消隐脉冲
blanking signal 消隐信号
blast 过载;强风;清除,收回
blasting 过载失真
bleeder circuit 泄放电路
bleeder resistor 泄放电阻
blemish 瑕疵,缺陷,污点
blend 交融,混色;过渡曲面
blending 混色,调色
blessed folder 系统文件夹
Blessum compensation 伯勒森补偿
blind alley 死胡同
blind computer 无显示的计算机
blind dialing 盲目拨号
blind folio 隐蔽页码(编有页码但不显示)
blind image restoration 无法辨认图像恢复
blind ink 无法辨认的印刷颜色
blind keyboard 盲键盘
blind machine 盲机器
blind search 盲目搜索[查找]
blind sending 盲目发送
blind spot 盲点,盲区
blind zone 盲区
blinking 闪烁
blinking cursor 闪烁光标
BLK(BLanK) 空白,空格;间隔
bloat (不必要的)扩展
bloatware 膨化件(过度膨胀,对系统资源要求太高的软件)
BLOB(Binary Large OBject) 二进制大对象
blob 斑点
Bloch line memory(BLM) 布洛赫线存储器
block(BL) 块,字组;分程序
block access 按块访问
block-acknowledged counter 块确认计数器
block address 块地址
block allocation 块分配

block boundary 块界
block buffering 块缓冲
block cancel character 块取消字符
block chaining 块链接
block check 块核对,字组校验
block check character(BCC) 块校验符
block check procedure 字组核对过程
block cipher 分组密码
block code(BC) 块码
block compilation 成块编译
block completed counter 完全的块计数器
block control 块控制,字组控制
block control head 块控制首部
block control unit(BCU) 块控制单元
block copy 块拷贝,数据块复制
block count(BLC) 块计数
block cursor 矩形光标
block definition 块定义
block delete 块删除
block device 成组设备,块设备
block diagram 方块图,框图
block-driven data-flow processor 块驱动数据流处理机
block encryption 块加密
block format 块格式
block frame 块帧
block frame address 块帧地址
block gap 块间隔
block graphics 块图形
block handling macro instruction(BH macro) 块处理宏指令
block handling routine(BHR) 块处理例程
block header 块首部,分程序标题
block indexing 块索引
block initial statement 块起始语句
block input 块输入
block length(BL) 块长度
block list 块列表
block lock state 块封锁状态
block mark(BH) 块标志
block move 块移动,成组搬移
block multiplexer 块多路复用器
block multiplexer channel(BMC) 块多路复用通道   「式
block multiplexer mode 块多路复用模

block of parameters 参数块
block operation 块操作
block-oriented associative processor 面向块的相联处理机
block-oriented file mapping 面向块的文件映射
block-oriented memory 面向块的存储器
block output 块输出
block paging 块分页
block parity system 块奇偶校验系统
block prefix 字组前缀
block primitive 阻塞原语
block protection 块保护
block search 块搜索,成块查找
block separation 块分隔
block separator 块分隔符
block sequencing 块定序
block size(BS) 块长度,块大小
block sort 块排序
block special file 块特殊文件
block storage 块存储
block structure 块结构,分程序结构
block-structured language 块结构语言
block suballocation 块细分
block trans 成组传送
block transfer(BT) 块转移
block transmission 块传输
block truncation coding 块截断编码方式
block truncation compression 块截断压缩
block variable 块变量
block world 积木世界
blocked call 受阻呼叫
blocked compiling 分块编译
blocked file 分块文件,成块文件
blocked list 锁定列表
blocked record 成块记录
blocked state 阻塞[封锁]状态
blocked state of process 进程阻塞状态
blockette 细块,小块
blocking 编块,成组,分块
blocking acknowledgement signal 阻塞确认信号
blocking encryption 块加密
blocking factor 编块因数,分组系数
blocking matrix 阻塞矩阵
blocking of records 记录编块

blocking signal 阻塞信号
BLOCKING system 混合交换系统
bloom 光晕
bloom filter 光晕过滤器
blooming 起霜,敷霜
blop 消杂音
blow 熔断,熔固
blow back 再放大
blow up 放大
blowback ratio 回放比,放大比
blower 鼓风机
blowing 熔断,熔固
blown fuse 熔断丝
blowup 破坏
BLS(Base-level Synthesizer) 基本型合成器
BLS(Big Long Shot) 大远景
BLU(Basic Link Unit) 基本链路单元
Blue Book (CD)蓝皮书(1986年)
Blue Express 蓝色快车(IBM)
BLUE language 蓝色语言
Blue Mounain "蓝峰"计算机(SGI, 1998年)
Blue Point 蓝点(Linux)软件公司
blue print 蓝图
blue-ribbon 无错的,第一流的
blue-ribbon connector 矩形接插件
blue ribbon program "蓝带程序",一次通过程序
blue screen (Windows故障)蓝屏
blueprint 蓝图
Bluetooth "蓝牙"短距离无线网络(爱立信,诺基亚,IBM,Intel)
Bluetooth Special Interest Group "蓝牙"专题组
Blum measure 布卢姆测度
Blum's speed-up theorem 布卢姆加速定理
blunder 大错误
blur (图像)模糊,柔化
blurred equality 模糊相等
blurred relation 模糊关系
blurring 影像模糊,图像柔化
blurring effect 模糊效应
BM(Background Motion) 背景运动
BMA(Bean Migration Assistant) ActiveX到Java Bean迁移工具(IBM)
BMC(Block Multiplexer Channel) 块

多路通道
BMLC(Basic Mode Link Control) 基本模式链路控制规程
BMP(BitMaP) 位图格式
BNC connector BNC 连接器
BND(Bundle File) 组成文件
BNF(Backus Normal Form) 巴科斯-诺尔范式
BNPF format BNPF 格式
board computer 板式计算机
board guide 插件导轨
board ID 板标识码
board level 板级
board level maintenance 板级维修
board tester 电路板测试仪
boarder 边框
Bode diagram 波德图
body capacitance 体电容
body face 主体字
body-fitted coordinate 体拟合坐标
body group 主体栏,文件栏
body matter 主体内容,正文内容
body object 主体对象
body placeholder 主体界定框
body resistance 体电阻
body statement 本体语句
body stub 体存根
body type 文本字体
BOF(Beginning Of File) 文件开始
BOF action 遇文件开始标记时的响应
BOF label 文件开始标记
bogus 假的,伪造的
bogus folio 假页号
bogus newsgroup 假新闻组
boiler plate 样板,样本
bold 加粗
bold-italic 粗斜体的
boldface 粗黑体字
boldface attribute 加粗字体属性
boldness 鲜明度,醒目程度
bolt 螺栓
Boltzmann machine 玻尔兹曼机
bomb 出错提示;轰炸
bombardment resistance （网站)抗轰击性
bond 结合,键合,粘合,焊接
bond graph 粘合图
bond space 键空间

bonded connection 加固连接
bonding 键合,焊接
bonding pad 焊接区
bonding plate 焊接片
bonus 奖赏
bonus score 奖分
Bonus Pak for OS/2 Warp OS/2 红包实用程序(IBM)
booboo 错误,故障
Booch method 布驰法
book 源程序清单;大段内存;预约
book keeping 簿记
book message 书式消息,预约报文
booked call 预约呼叫
booklet 手册
bookmark 书签
bookmark list 书签列表
bookmark name 书签名
bookmark property 书签属性
books and documents retrieval system 图书文件检索系统
Bookseller Data system 书商数据系统
Boolean(B,BOOL) 布尔运算;布尔数
Boolean add 布尔加
Boolean algebra(BA) 布尔代数
Boolean calculus 布尔运算
Boolean character 布尔字符
Boolean circuit 布尔电路
Boolean connective 布尔连接
Boolean constant 布尔常数
Boolean cube 布尔立方体
Boolean data type 布尔数据类型
Boolean denotation 布尔标志
Boolean difference method 布尔差分法
Boolean differential 布尔微分法
Boolean element 布尔元素
Boolean expression 布尔表达式
Boolean factor 布尔因子
Boolean function 布尔函数
Boolean group 布尔群
Boolean item 布尔项
Boolean lattice 布尔网格
Boolean literal 布尔文字
Boolean logic 布尔逻辑
Boolean minimization 布尔最小化
Boolean n-cube network 布尔n立方体网络
Boolean network chip compiler 布尔

网络芯片编译器
Boolean object 布尔目标,布尔对象
Boolean operation 布尔运算
Boolean operation table 布尔运算表
Boolean primary 布尔初等量
Boolean product 布尔乘积
Boolean quality 布尔量
Boolean query 布尔查询
Boolean variable 布尔变量
boost circuit 升压电路,自举电路
boost priority 提升优先级
booster 增强器,天线放大级
BOOT(BOOTstrap) 启动程序,引导程序
boot 启动,自举
boot block 引导块
boot drive 引导(自举)驱动器
boot failure 自举失败
boot leg program 自引程序
boot record 引导记录
boot ROM 自举 ROM
boot sector 引导[自举]扇区
boot sector virus 引导区病毒
boot segment 引导段
boot sequence 引导顺序
boot type viruses 自举[引导]型病毒
boot up 自举,启动
bootable disk 可自举盘
BootBus 启动总线(Sun)
BootCD 可自举光盘
BOOTCON.SYS 自举配置文件
booting 引导,自举
bootleg 盗版软件
bootleger 盗版软件制造者
bootstrap(BOOT) 引导程序,自举程序
bootstrap circuit 自举电路
bootstrap image 引导映像
bootstrap loader 引导装载程序
bootstrap memory 引导内存
bootstrap program 引导[自举]程序
bootstrap sweep circuit 自举扫描电路
bootstrapping 自举,引导
bootup 自举,引导
bootup sequence 自举顺序
BOP(Byte-Oriented Protocol) 面向字节的协议
BOPS(Billion Operations Pre Second) 每秒十亿次运算

border 边界,边缘,边框
Border Gateway Protocol(BGP) 边界网关协议
border line 框线
border node 边界节点
border pen 画框线笔
border region 边界区域
border router 边界路由器
border style 边框样式
BorderManager 边界管理器
bore 孔径,内径
Boris 波利斯系统
Borland C++ Borland C++语言
Borland International Inc. Borland 国际公司(1998年4月更名为 Inprise)
Borland Office Borland 办公套件
Borland Pascal Borland Pascal 语言
borrow 借位
borrow digit 借位数字
Bose-Chaudhuri codes BCH 码
BOT(Beginning Of Tape marker) 磁带起始标志
BOT label 磁带开始标号
both way 双向
both way trunk 双向中继线
bottle neck 瓶颈
bottle neck problem of knowledge acquisition 知识获取瓶颈问题
bottom 底
bottom alignment 底边对齐
bottom blank line 底部空白行
bottom border 底部边框
bottom document 底层文档
bottom layer 底层
bottom margin 底部空白
bottom-up approach 自底向上法
bottom-up control structure 自底向上控制结构
bottom-up design 自底向上设计
bottom-up development 自底向上开发法
bottom-up estimation 自底向上估算
bottom-up machine 自底向上机器
bottom-up method 自底向上法
bottom-up parsing 自底向上语法分析
bottom-up reasoning 自底向上推理
bottom-up selective 自底向上选择
bottom-up syntax analysis 自底向上

语法分析
bottom-up testing 自底向上测试
bottom view 底视图
bounce 弹回;弹跳
bounce-free switch 无颤动开关
bounce message 退回邮件
bounceless contact 消震触点,无颤动接点
bouncing 颤动
bound 界限,边界;约束
bound control 绑定型控件
bound control module 约束控制模块
bound integer 有界整数
bound occurrence 约束出现
bound of aggregation 聚集边界
bound pair 界偶
bound pair list 界偶表
bound segment 联编段
bound symbol 界限符
boundary(BDRY) 边界,限界
boundary alignment 边界调整[对准]
boundary chain 边界链
boundary condition 边界条件
boundary-contraction method 边界收缩法
boundary controllability 边界可控性
boundary cost 边界成本
boundary detection 边界检测
boundary determination 边界确定
boundary element 边界元素
boundary error 边界差错
boundary estimation 边界估计
boundary extraction 边界抽取
boundary fill 边界填充
boundary-fitted coordinate system 边界拟合坐标系
boundary following 边界跟随
boundary frequency 边[临]界频率
boundary function(BF) 边界功能
boundary localization 边界定位
boundary morphology 边界形态学
boundary node 边界节点
boundary pair 界偶
boundary pixel 边界像素
boundary register 边界寄存器
boundary representation 边界表示
boundary routing system architecture 边界路径选择系统结构

boundary scan 边界扫描
boundary sharpening 边界锐化
boundary singularity 边界奇异性
boundary tag allocation 边界标志定位
boundary tag method 边界标志法
boundary tracing 边界跟踪
boundary value 边界值
boundary value analysis 边界值分析
boundary value problem 边值问题
boundary violation 越界
bounded buffer problem 有界缓冲区问题
bounded context grammar 限界上下文文法
bounded context recognizer 限界上下文识别程序
bounded delay 受限延迟
bounded degree network 有限度网络
bounded existential quantification 有界[受囿]存在量化
bounded existential quantifier 有界存在量词
bounded lattice 有界网格
bounded nondeterministic machine 有界非确定型机器
bounded occurrence 约束出现
bounded operator 受囿算子
bounded parallelism 有界并行性
bounded precision 受限精度
bounded quantifier 有界量词
bounded region 有界域
bounded regular language 有界正规语言
bounded resolution 受限分解力
bounded sequence 有界序列
bounded set 有界集合
bounded universal quantification 有界[受囿]全称量化
bounded universal quantifier 有界全称量词
bounded user modeling 受约束用户模型化
bounded variable 约束变元
bounding box 有边界框
bounding hyperplane 有界超平面
bounding rectangle 有界框
BOUNDP function 约束检测函数
bounds register 限界寄存器

boundscript 界标
Bourne shell　Bourne 命令解释程序（Unix）
bow 弯曲；弓形
box 盒，框
box-and-arrow notation 盒箭头表示法
box description language 框图描述语言
box diffusion 箱式扩散
box in （将若干对象）框入
box model 框模型
box structure 框结构
box top license 盒顶许可证
Boyce/Codd normal form(BCNF) 巴叶斯/科德范式
Boyer-Moore algorithm 贝叶-摩尔算法，BM 算法
Boyer Moore theorem prover 博耶穆尔定理证明系统
BP(Branch of Prediction) 分支预测
BP(Break Point) 断点
BPAM(Basic Partitioned Access Method) 基本分区存取法
bpi(bits per inch) 每英寸字节数
BPI(Bytes Per Inch) 每英寸字节数
BPICF(Bidirectionally Predicted Interpolative-Coded Frames) 双向预测插值编码帧
BPS(Basic Programming Support) 基本程序设计支持系统
BR(Boot Record) 引导记录
BR(BRanch) 分支指令，转移指令
brace 大括弧，花括号
bracket 括号，括弧；括号通信，括号交换
bracket arithmetic expression 带括号的算术表达式
bracket communication 括号通信
bracket pair 括号对
bracket protocol 括号通信协议，(SNA)报文单位交换协议
bracketed 括号括起的
bracketing 定标试验
braille 盲文
brain damaged 伤脑筋的
brain model 脑模型
brain plasticity 脑可塑性
brain science 脑科学
brainstorming 头脑风暴法

BRAM(Broadcast Recognition Access Method) 广播识别存取法
branch 分支，转移；分支指令，转移指令
branch-and-bound method 分支界限法
branch-and-bound search 分支界限搜索法
branch bound algorithm 分支界限算法
branch cable 分支电缆[光缆]
branch construct 分支结构
branch control structure 分支控制机
branch cutting 分支切割
branch exchange 交换分机
branch filter 分支过滤器
branch-history table 转移历史表
branch instruction 转移[分支]指令
branch line 支线
branch mode 转移[分支]模式
branch network 分支网络
branch name 分支名
branch node 树枝结点；分支网点
branch on equality 相等转移
branch on false 假条件转移
branch on switch setting 预定开关转移
branch on true 真条件转移
branch-on-zero instruction 零转移指令
branch point 分支点，转移点
branch prediction(BP) 分支预测
branch prediction block(BPB) 分支预测模块
branch table(BTAL) 转移表
branch target buffer(BTB) 分支目标缓冲器
branch tracer 转移跟踪程序
branch-unconditional instruction 无条件转移指令
branching 分支处理
branching factor 分支系数
brand 商标
BRAP(Broadcast Recognition with Alternating Priorities) 交替优先权广播识别协议
Braunschweig search processor Braunschweig 搜索处理机
BRCH(BRanCH) 分支，转移
breach 违反，破坏
bread board 试验板，面包板
breadth-first and depth-first search 宽

度优先和深度优先搜索
breadth-first procedure 宽度优先过程
breadth-first search(BFS) 宽度优先搜索
breadth-first strategy(BFS) 宽度优先策略
breadth-first traversal of a graph 图的宽度优先遍历
breadth first tree 广度优先树
break(BR) 中断,断开,暂停
break box 中断盒
BREAK construct BREAK结构
break down 击穿;插入呼叫
break feature 中断特性,断开功能
break in 插入
break-in operate time 插入工作时间
break key 断开键,打断键
break mode 中断模式
break package 断开包
break-point 断点
break-point halt 断点停机
break-point instruction(BPL) 断点指令
break-point switch 断点开关
break-point symbol 断点符号
break pulse 断路脉冲
break sequence 间断序列
break signal 断点信号
break statement 中断语句
break through 断缺;漏过
break up for color 分色
break value 断点值
breakout box 分接盒,测线箱
breakpoint address 断点地址
breakpoint counter 断点计数器
breakpoint register 断点寄存器
breakpoint window 断点窗口
breakthrough point 突破点
breather 通气孔
breathing 胀缩
breed 繁殖
brevity 简短,简洁
Brewster angle 布儒斯特角
Brewster's law 布儒斯特定律
Brewster window 布儒斯特窗
BRF(Benchmark Report Format) 基准程序报表格式
BRG(Baud Rate Generator) 波特率产生器

BRI(Basic Rate Interface) 基本速率接口(2B+D)
brick 砖;程序模块
bridge 桥接器,网桥
bridge circuit 桥式电路
bridge limiter 桥式限幅器
bridge node 桥节点
BRIDGE program 桥牌程序
bridge router 桥路由器
bridge tap 分路抽头,桥式分接头
bridge ware 转换软件,"桥"软件;网桥软件
bridging 桥接,跨接
bridging fault 桥接(短路)故障
bridging-off command 拆桥命令
bridging-on command 搭桥命令
bridging order 连接命令
Brief Brief文本编辑程序
brief 提要,摘要
brief acceleration 短时加速度
briefcase computer 公文包式计算机
bright true logic 亮为"真"逻辑
brightness 亮度,视见度,辉度
brightness channel 亮度通道
brightness conservation 亮度守恒
brightness contrast 亮度对比
brightness control 亮度控制
brightness level 亮度级
brightness range 亮度范围
brightness ratio 亮度比
brightness signal 亮度信号
brightness uniformity 亮度一致性
brightness value 亮度值
brilliant 逼真的;极明亮的
brilliant line 亮线
Bring Forward 置前
British Imperial system 英国法定标准制
brittle component 脆性元件
brittleness 脆度
broadband 宽带
broadband channel 宽带通道
broadband communication network 宽带通信网络
broadband exchange(BEX) 宽带交换
Broadband Exchange Service(BEXS) 宽带交换服务系统
broadband integrated service digital net-

work(BISDN) 宽带综合业务数字网
broadband local network 宽带局域网
broadband network 宽带网络
broadband noise 宽带噪声
broadband transmission 宽带传输
BROADCAST 广播程序
broadcast 广播
broadcast address 广播地址
broadcast box 广播式信箱
broadcast communication method 广播式通信
broadcast communication network 广播通信网络
broadcast conference 广播会议
broadcast data device 广播数据设备
broadcast data set 广播数据集
broadcast message 广播消息
broadcast recognition access method (BRAM) 广播识别存取法
broadcast recognition with alternating priorities(BRAP) 交替优先权广播识别协议
broadcast routing 广播式路由选择
broadcast satellite 广播卫星
broadcast station 广播站[台]
broadcast storm 广播风暴
broadcast subnet 广播子网
broadcast videography 图文广播
broadcast videotex 可视图文广播
broadcasting organization 广播组织
broadcasting storms 广播风暴
broadcatch 广捕
broadsheet 宽幅打印纸
broken hyperlink 断开的超链接
broken line 断开的线路
broken link 断链
broker 中介器
Brooklyn Bridge Brooklyn 桥软件
brother chain 同级链
brother link 同级链路
brother node 同级节点
brother task 同级任务
brother tree 同级树
brouter 桥路器,桥路由器
brown 棕色
brownout 电力不足,电压过低
browse 浏览

browse buttons 浏览按钮
browse display 浏览显示
browse down 向下浏览
browse information file 浏览信息文件
browse member 浏览成员
browse mode 浏览模式
browse path 浏览路径
browse sequence 浏览序列
browse up 向上浏览
BROWSER(Browsing On-line With Selective Retrieval) 带选择检索的线上浏览系统
browser 浏览程序,浏览器
browser request rate 浏览器请求速率
BRP(Bandwidth Reservation Protocol) 带宽保留协议
BRS(Bibliographic Retrieval Services) 书目检索服务「统
BRS information system BRS 信息系
BRU(Basic Resolution Unit) 基本分辨单位
brush 画笔,刷子
brush style 画笔字体
brush set 电刷组
brush trajectory coding 笔画轨迹编码
brushless direct drive monitor 无刷直接驱动马达
brute-force approach 蛮干法,强行攻击法
brute-force filter 平滑滤波器
brute supply 未稳压电源
BS(BackSpace) 退格,退位,回退
BSAM(Basic Sequential Access Method) 基本顺序存取法
BSC(Binary Symmetric Channel) 二进对称通道
BSCMAKE (Microsoft Browse Information File Maintenance Utility) 浏览信息文件维护工具(微软)
BSD UNIX(Berkeley System Distribution UNIX) BSD UNIX 版本
BSDL(Boundary Scan Description Language) 边界扫描描述语言
BSI(British Standard Institution) 英国标准协会
BSP(Bulk Synchronous Parallel) 海量同步并行
BSS(Base Support Subsystem) 基础

支持服务子系统
BT(Balanced Transmission) 平衡传
BT(Batch Terminal) 批处理终端
BTAL(Branch TAbLe) 分支表,转移表
BTAM(Basic Telecommunications Access Method) 基本远程通信访问法
BTH(Basic Transmission Header) 基本传输标题
BTM(Beginning-of Tape Marker) 磁带起始标记
BTM(Benchmark Timing Methodology) 基准程序定时法
Btrieve Btrieve 管理程序
BTU(Basic Transmission Unit) 基本传输单元
bubble 气泡
bubble chart 气泡图
Bubble Jet 热泡喷射
bubble memory 磁泡存储器
bubble memory chip 磁泡存储器芯片
bubble propagation 磁泡传播[传导]
bubble sort 冒泡排序法
bucket 桶,存储桶
bucket fill tool 桶式填充工具
bucket index 桶索引
bucket locking 桶加锁
bucket sort 桶排序
buddy algorithm 伙伴算法
buddy system 伙伴系统
budget 预算,预计分配
BUF(BUFfer) 缓冲器
buffer(BUF) 缓冲器
buffer amplifier 缓冲放大器
buffer and refresh memory 缓冲与刷新内存
buffer area 缓冲区
buffer arm 缓冲臂
buffer channel 缓冲通道
buffer configuration 缓冲器配置
buffer depletion 缓冲器耗尽
buffer device 缓冲设备
buffer empty(BE) 缓冲器空
buffer full(BF) 缓冲器满
buffer gate 缓冲门
buffer group 缓冲器组
buffer input 缓冲输入

buffer management 缓冲器管理程序
buffer memory(BM) 缓冲存储器
buffer output 缓冲输出
buffer overflow 缓冲器溢出
buffer pad characters 缓冲器填充字符
buffer pool(BP) 缓冲池
buffer pooling 缓冲池建立
buffer preallocation 缓冲器预分配
buffer prefix 缓冲器前缀
buffer reservation 缓冲区预约
buffer scheduling 缓冲区调度
buffer sharing 缓冲区共享
buffer size 缓冲区大小
buffer slot 缓冲槽
buffer storage 缓冲存储器
buffer swapping 缓冲区交换
buffer underrun 缓冲器掏空
buffer unit 缓冲单元
buffer unit pool 缓冲单元池
buffer vibration device 减震装置
buffered asynchronous communication 缓冲式异步通信
buffered attribute 缓冲属性
buffered computer 缓冲计算机
buffered concentrator 缓冲式集中器
buffered distributor 缓存分配器
buffered exchange 缓冲交换
buffered gate 缓冲门
buffered input 缓冲输入
buffered input/output(BIO) 缓冲输入输出
buffered input/output channel 缓冲输入/输出通道
buffered keyboard 缓冲键盘
buffered line printer 缓冲行式打印机
buffered repeater 带缓冲的中继器
buffered seek operation 缓冲寻道操作
buffered updates 缓冲更新
buffering 缓冲操作
buffering for synchronous operation 缓冲同步操作
bug 错误,故障
bug fix release 修正版
bug model 故障模型
bug monitor 错误监察程序
bug patch 改错补丁
bug pattern 错误模式
bug seed 错误根源

bug seeding 故障撒播
buggy 错误成堆的
build （C语言中的）编译连接
build-in adapter 内建适配器
build-in attribute 固有属性
build-in check 内建校验
build-in predicate 内部谓词
build-in self test 内建自测试
build slide 嵌套幻灯片
build-to-order manufacture 按订单生产
build-up time 建立时间
build virtual machine program 虚机建立程序
builder 生成器
builder lock 生成器锁定
building algorithm 组合式算法
building application 链接编译应用程序
building block 积木式组件
building block architecture 积木式结构法
building block design 积木式设计方法
building block principle 积木原理
building block system 积木式系统
building expert system 建立专家系统
building model methodology 建模方法学
built-in 内部的
built-in adapter 内插式适配器
built-in automatic check 内部自动校验
built in check 内部校验
built-in command 内部[内建]命令
built-in fault tolerance 内建容错
built-in font 内建字形,内建字体
built-in function 内部函数
built-in group 内部组
built-in logic block observation technique 内建逻辑块观测技术
built-in test 内部测试
built-in tracing structure 内部追踪结构
built-in type 内建类型,内部类型
BUILTIN attribute 内部构造属性
bulk 大量的,成批的,整体的
bulk acoustic wave device 体声波器件
bulk annotation 成批注解
bulk data encryption 大批数据加密
bulk degausser 整体消磁器
bulk effect 体效应
bulk effect delay 体效应延迟

bulk effect device 体效应装置
bulk eraser 整盘磁带消磁器
bulk memory 大容量存储器
bulk message testing 大信息量测试
bulk optical glass 体光学玻璃
bulk redundancy 大量冗余
bulk record field exchange 多记录字段交换
bulk row fetching 多行取数
bulk storage 海量存储器
bulk store 后备存储器
bulk testing 整体测试
bulk transfer protocol 大容量传输协议
bulkmaterial absorption 体材料吸收
Bull HN(Bull HN Information System Inc.) 布尔HN信息系统公司
bullet 项目符号,加重说明号
bullet image option 项目符号图形选项
bullet type 项目符号类型
bulleted list 圆点列表
bulleted list chart 条列表
bulletin board 公告牌,布告板
bulletin board system(BBS) 公告牌[布告板]系统
bulletproof program 防弹[安全]程序
bum 不称职程序员
bump contact 凸缘连接
bump texture 凹凸纹理
bumper 阻尼器;减震器
bumpless transfer 无扰动传送
bunched frame alignment signal 聚束帧对准信号
bunched program 捆绑销售程序
bundle 束,光纤束,捆扎
bundle cable 束光缆
bundle cable assembly 束光缆组合件
bundle file(BND) 组成文件
bundle table 束表
bundled feature 附带特性
bundled program 附随程序
bundled software 捆绑销售软件
bundling 整包装[捆绑]销售
bunny suit 兔装,超净防护服
buried cable 埋设[地下]电缆
buried-channel structure in MOST 嵌入式沟道结构MOS晶体管
buried coaxed cable telecommunications union 埋地同轴电缆电信联盟

buried servo 埋层伺服
buried stripe laser 掩埋条形激光器
buried Zener 隐埋齐纳管
burn 熔断
burn-in 老化
burn out 全部曝光
burn through 烧毁
burning recording 烧灼[电热]记录法
burnishing 抛光,压印
Burroughs Scientific Processor(BSP) Burroughs 科学处理机
burst 脉冲串
burst acquisition 脉冲串采集,成组二进制位收集
burst blanking 色同步消隐
burst error 猝发误差,群发错误
burst gate 色同步选通电路
burst gating pulse 色同步选通脉冲
burst isochronous 猝发等时[等时脉冲串]信号
burst isochronous transmission 猝发[群发]等时传输
burst keying pulse 色同步键控脉冲
burst length 猝发[群发]长度
burst mode 猝发模式,突发方式
burst mode multiplexer 突发模式多工器,猝发式多路转接器
burst modem 成组调制解调器
burst noise 突发噪声
burst-oriented data transmission 猝发式数据传送
burst page 突发页面
burst phase control 猝发[突发]相位控制
burst rate 成组传输速率,猝发速率
burst refresh 突发恢复
burst speed 成组传送速度
burst switch 成组开关
burst traffic 猝发传输量
burst transmission 突发传输
burster 分页器,裁纸器
BUS(BUS-bar) 汇流条,总线
bus 总线,母线,汇流条
bus access conflict 总线访问冲突
bus access latency 总线访问延时
bus acknowledge 总线确认
bus acquisition latency 总线获取等待时间

bus adapter 总线适配器
bus addressing 总线寻址
bus allocator 总线分配器
bus amplifier 总线放大器
bus arbiter 总线仲裁器
bus arbitration system 总线仲裁系统
bus available signal 总线有效信号
bus bridge 总线桥
bus busy 总线忙
bus cable 公用电缆
bus card 总线卡
bus category 总线类别
bus chip 总线芯片
bus compatible 总线兼容的
bus concurrency 总线并发
bus connector 总线接插件
bus contention 总线争用
bus control logic 总线控制逻辑
bus controller 总线控制器
bus conversion interface 总线转换接口
bus coupler 总线耦合器
bus cycles 总线周期
bus disenable signal 总线禁止信号
bus driver(BD) 总线驱动器
bus error traps 总线出错陷阱
bus extender 总线扩展器
bus extender module 总线扩展模块
bus extension card 总线扩展卡
bus extension receiver card 总线扩展接收器卡
bus family 总线族
bus grant 总线允许
bus grant acknowledge 总线允许确认
bus grant input 总线允许输入
bus high enable 总线高电平有效
bus hold acknowledge 总线保持确认
bus hold request 总线保持请求
bus hub 总线中枢
bus idle machine cycle 总线空闲机器周期
bus interconnection 总线互连
bus interface(BI) 总线接口
bus interface unit(BIU) 总线接口单元
bus interfacing 总线接口
bus interlocked communication 总线互锁通信
bus interrupt 总线中断
bus load 总线负载

bus lock 总线封锁
bus master 总线主控器
bus message 总线消息[报文]
bus mode 总线模式
bus monitor 总线监视器
bus motherboard 总线母板[底板]
bus mouse 总线式鼠标
bus multiplexing 总线复用
bus network 总线网络
bus-organized structure 总线式结构
bus parking 总线停泊
bus plane 电源层 「构
bus priority structure 总线优先权结
bus protocol 总线协议
bus quiet signal 总线静止信号
bus request 总线请求
bus resource 总线资源
bus responder 总线响应器
bus segment 总线区段
bus slave 总线受控器[从设备]
bus snooping 总线探察
bus standard 总线标准
bus status bit 总线状态位
bus strobe signal 总线选通信号
bus structure 总线结构
bus termination 总线端接器
bus timing 总线定时
bus topology 总线拓扑
bus transaction 总线事务处理
bus transceiver 总线收发器
bus transfer 总线传输
bus unit 总线装置
bus watcher 总线岗哨
business automation 商务自动化
business data processing 商务数据处理
business data processing language 商务数据处理语言
business description language(BDL) 商用描述语言
Business EDP System Technique (BEST) 商务 EDP(电子数据处理)系统技术
business form 商务表格
business game 商业博弈
business graphics 商用图形
business information system(BIS) 商用信息系统

business machine(BM) 商用机器
business machine clocking 商用机内部定时
business programming 商务程序设计
business security 商务安全
business service 商务服务
business software 商业软件
business statistics 商务统计学
business system 商务系统
business systems analyst 商务系统分析员
business system planning(BSP) 商用系统规划
business terminal equipment 商务终端设备
bussback 回输
bust 误操作
bust this 传输失败,信息作废
busy 忙,占线
busy bit "忙"指示位
busy condition 忙态
busy flag "忙"标志
busy hour 忙时,高峰时间
busy hour calls(BHC) 忙时呼叫数
busy period 忙周期
busy pointer "忙"指针
busy state 忙态
busy test 忙碌[占线]测试
busy time 占用时间
busy token "忙"令牌
busy tone 忙音
butt coupling 对接[衔接]耦合
Butterfly "蝴蝶"笔记本计算机(IBM)
butterfly algorithm 蝶形算法
butterfly network 蝶形网络
butterfly operation 蝶式运算
butterfly permutation 蝶式排列
butterfly processor 蝶式处理机
Butterfly Switch 蝶形开关
Butterworth filter 巴特沃斯滤波器
button 按钮
button assignment 按钮赋值
button control 按钮控制;按钮控件
button cursor 按钮形光标
button device 按钮装置
button face 按钮字体
button grab (X 协议)按钮占取[占

用]
button highlight 按钮突出显示
button shadow 按钮阴影
button text 按钮文字
buy 可用量
buzz 蜂鸣音
buzz word 蜂鸣字
buzzer 蜂鸣器
BW(BandWidth) 频带宽度,带宽
by column 按列
by-hand input 手工输入
by modem 经调制解调器的传输
by pass 旁路,旁通
by-pass capacitor 旁路电容器
by-pass mode 旁路模式,迂回方式
by-product recording 附带记录
bylink 旁链路
bypass block 旁路信息组
bypass plug 旁路插头
bypass procedure 旁路过程
bypassing startup command 旁路启动命令(微软)
byproduct 副产品
BYSYNC 二进制同步传输
byte 字节
byte address 字节地址
byte address load 字节地址装入
byte-addressable 按字节编址的
byte-addressable computer 字节编址计算机
byte-addressable storage 按字节编址存储器
byte board 字节插板
byte boundary addressing 字节边界寻址
byte code (Java程序)字节码
byte collection 字节群
byte computer 字节计算机
byte count-oriented procedure 面向字节的计数规程
byte counter 字节计数器

byte decrement 字节减量
byte displacement 字节位移
byte enable 字节允许
byte erasable 可按字节擦除的
byte error correcting code 字节纠错码
byte format 字节格式
byte increment 字节增量
byte indicator 字节指示器
byte instruction 字节指令
byte interleave 字节交叉
byte machine 字节机器
byte manipulation 字节操作
byte memory 字节内存
byte mode 字节模式
byte multiplexer(BYMUX) 字节多路复用器
byte multiplexer channel 字节多路复用通道
byte multiplexer mode 字节多路复用模式
byte operand 字节操作数
byte operation 字节运算
byte-oriented operand 字节操作数
byte-oriented protocol 面向字节的协议
byte parallel 字节并行
byte read 字节读
byte-serial transmission 字节串行传输
byte slice 字节片
byte socket 字节插座
byte space 字节空间
byte stream protocol(BSP) 字节流协议
byte string 字节串
byte stuffing 字节填充
byte swap 字节交换
byte swapped element 字节交换元素
byte symbol 字节符号
byte synchronization 字节同步
bytecode 字节码
bytes per second(byte/s) 字节/秒
bytes used 已使用字节数

C c

C(Capacitor) 电容器
C: C盘

C++ C++语言
C* C*语言

C1 C1 计算机
C2 C2 安全级
C calling convention C 语言调用约定
C character set C 语言字符集
C constant C 常数
C flag 进位标志
C-ISAM C-ISAM 函数库
C language C 语言
C language application C 语言应用程序
C language standard C 语言标准
C linkage specifier C 语言链接说明符
C preprocessor C 语言预处理程序
C program verifier C 程序检验器
C/S (Client/Server) 客户机/服务器
C shell C 命令解释程序
C shell remote control file C 命令解释程序遥控文件
C source file C 语言源文件
C-testability C-可测试性
C. vmp system (Computer vote multi-processor system) 计算机表决多处理器系统
CABS 复数的绝对值函数
CAC(Clear All Channel) 清除所有通道
CA(Cell Animation) 单元动画制作
CA(Cellular Automaton) 细胞自动机
CA(Certificate Authority) 证书管理机构
CA(Channel Adapter) 通道适配器
CA(Circuit Adapter) 线路适配器
CA(Computer Animation) 计算机动画
CA(Computer Art) 计算机艺术
CAA(Computer Aided Analysis) 计算机辅助分析
cabinet 机柜
cabinet assistance 机箱附件
cabinet file(.CAB) 压缩安装文件
cabinet level electromagnetic interference 机柜级电磁干扰
cabinet projection 斜二侧投影
cable 电缆
cable assembly 电缆[光缆]组件
cable bond 电缆接头
cable cast 有线广播
cable clamp 电缆夹
cable connector 电缆连接器
cable dancing 电缆摇荡
cable delay 电缆延迟
cable interface 电缆接口
cable interface unit(CIU) 电缆接口部件
cable jacket 缆护套
cable joint 电缆接头
cable loss 电缆损耗
cable matcher 电缆匹配器
cable modem 线缆调制解调器
cable television(CATV) 有线电视
cable television service 有线电视服务机构
cable termination 电缆端接法
cable termination network 电缆终端网络
cable test 电缆测试
cable text 有线电视文字广播
cable-to-chassis connector 电缆到机架连接器
cable TV 有线电视
cable vault 电缆地下室
CABS 复数的绝对值函数
CAC(Clear All Channel) 清除所有通道
cache 高速缓冲存储器
cache ability 高速缓存的存取能力
cache access 高速缓存访问
Cache Array Routing Protocol 缓存阵列路由协议(微软)
cache bandwidth 高速缓存器带宽
cache buffer 高速缓存缓冲器
cache buffer pool 高速缓存池
cache capacity 高速缓存容量
cache coherency 高速缓存器相关性
cache conflict 高速缓存冲突
cache consistency 高速缓存一致性
cache controller 高速缓存控制器
cache coordinate 高速缓存坐标
cache cycle 高速缓存周期
cache delay 高速缓存时延
cache design 高速缓存设计
cache directory 高速缓存目录
cache driver 高速缓存驱动器
cache entry 高速缓存入口
cache grouping scheme 高速缓存分组方案
cache hit 高速缓存命中
cache initialization 高速缓存初始化
cache interface 高速缓存接口
cache line 高速缓存界线

cache line fill	高速缓存行填充
cache manager	高速缓存管理器
cache memory	高速缓冲存储器
cache memory hit	高速缓存命中
cache memory look ahead	高速缓存预测
cache memory miss	高速缓存未命中
cache memory sharing	高速缓存共享
cache memory system	高速缓存系统
cache miss	高速缓存未命中
cache miss rate	高速缓存未命中率
cache replacement algorithm	高速缓存替换算法
cache simulator	高速缓存仿真程序
cache storage hit	高速缓存命中
cache storage miss	高速缓存未命中
cache store	高速缓冲存储器
cache store-through	高速缓存直写
cache sweep	高速缓存扫描
cache unit	高速缓存单元
cache update	高速缓存更新
cache write	高速缓存写入
cache write-in	高速缓存写回
cache write-through	高速缓存写直达
Cached DRAM	带高速缓存的动态随机存储器
caching	高速缓存操作
caching controller	带高速缓存的控制器
caching disk	高速缓存磁盘
caching-only server	缓存服务器
CAD(Computer Aided Design)	计算机辅助设计
CAD automatic editing tool	计算机辅助设计自动编辑工具
CAD automatic routing program	计算机辅助设计自动布线程序
CAD/CAM(Computer Aided Design/Computer Aided Manufacturing)	计算机辅助设计与计算机辅助制造
CAD/CAM data base	计算机辅助设计/计算机辅助制造数据库
CAD/CAM graphics program	计算机辅助设计/计算机辅助制造绘图程序
CAD/CAM workstation	计算机辅助设计/计算机辅助制造工作站
CAD framework	计算机辅助设计框架
CAD Framework Initiative (CFI)	CAD框架创始协会
CAD graphic display	CAD图形显示
CAD input device	计算机辅助设计输入设备
CAD output device	计算机辅助设计输出设备
CAD workstation	计算机辅助设计工作站
caddy	(光驱或刻录机的)盘托
CADHELP	CADHELP专家系统
CAE(Computer Aided Education)	计算机辅助教育
CAE(Computer Aided Engineering)	计算机辅助工程
CAE simulation programs	计算机辅助工程仿真程序
Caesar cipher	凯萨密码
CAFS database machine (Content Addressable File Store database machine)	内容寻址文件存储数据库计算机
cage	底板,底盘
CAI(Computer Aided Instruction)	计算机辅助教学
CAI network	计算机辅助教学网络
Cairo	Cairo操作系统软件(微软)
Cakewalk	Cakewalk音乐创作软件
Calcomp (California Computer Product.)	加利福尼亚计算机设备公司(美)
Calcomp DrawingBoard	Calcomp数字化仪
Calcomp DrawingSlate	Calcomp数字化仪
Calcomp EcoGrafix	Calcomp胶片绘图仪
Calcomp TechJET Color GT	Calcomp彩色喷墨绘图仪
calculability	可计算性
calculable	可计算的
calculate	计算,运算
calculate access method	计算式存取方法
calculate address guess addressing	计算地址推测寻址
calculate address structure	计算地址结构
Calculate Now	(电子表格)立即重算
calculated address	计算地址

calculated field 计算结果字段
calculated link loss 计算的链路损耗
calculated member 计算成员
calculated path 计算路径
calculated symbol 计算符号
calculating center 计算中心
calculating device 计算设备
calculating dynamic default values 计算动态默认值
calculating inspection 计算检查
calculating mode 计算模式,算态
calculating space for a foreground job 前台作业计算空间
calculating speed 计算速度
calculating station 计算站
calculating terminal 计算终端
calculation 计算
calculation by iteration 迭代法计算
calculation error 计算误差
calculation location mode 计算定位模式
calculation specification 运算说明书
calculation speed 运算速度
calculation syntax 计算语法
calculative 需要计算的,有计算的
calculator 计算器
calculator chip 计算器芯片
calculator for extensive use 多用途计算器
calculator for occasional use 特定用途计算器
calculator mass memory system 计算器大容量存储系统
calculator-oriented microprocessor 面向计算器的微处理器
calculator with external program input 外部程序输入计算器
calculator with postfix notation 后置记法计算器
calculator with reverse-Polish notation logic 逆波兰表示法计算器
calculator without programmability 无编程能力计算器
λ-calculus λ-演算
calculus of propositions 命题演算
calculus of variations 变分法
calculus program 微积分程序
calendar 日历
calendar chip 日历芯片

calendar description 日历描述
calendar file 日程文件
calendar item 日历项
calendar manager 日历管理程序
calendar time 日历时间
calendar view 日历视图
calibration 校准,定标
calibration accuracy 校准精度
calibration factor(CF) 校正因子
calibration pulse 校准脉冲
call 调用,呼叫
call accepted 接受呼叫
call accepted condition 呼叫接受状况
call accepted message 呼叫接受消息
call accepted packet 呼叫接受包
call accepted signal 呼叫接受信号
call address 调用地址
call admission control 呼叫许可控制
call analyzer 呼叫分析程序
call answering service 呼叫应答服务
call attempt 试呼叫
call back 回叫
call back apparatus 回叫设备
call back function 回调函数
call back modem 回叫式调制解调器
call button 呼叫按钮
call by address 按地址调用
call-by-descriptor 按描述符呼叫
call by far reference 远程引用调用
call by literal 按文字调用
call by location 按地址调用
call by name 按名调用,换名
call by near reference 近程参考调用
call by quantity 按值调用
call by reference 参考调用
call by result 按结果调用
call by value 按值调用
call-by-value parameter 按赋值参数调用
call by value/result 按值/结果调用
call capability 调用权力
call circuit 呼叫线路
call clear-down time 呼叫拆线时间
call clearing delay 呼叫清除延时
call collision 呼叫冲突
call collision at the DTE/DCE interface 数据传输终端/数据电路终端接口处的呼叫冲突

call completing rate 接通率
call confirmation 呼叫证实信号
call congestion ratio 呼叫拥塞率
call connected packet 呼叫接通分组
call connected signal 呼叫接通信号
call control 呼叫控制
call control character 呼叫控制字符
call control procedure 呼叫控制规程
call control signal 呼叫控制信号
call delay 呼叫延迟
call directing code(CDC) 呼叫指向码,直呼码
call distributor 呼叫分配器
call duration 呼叫持续时间
call entry 调用入口
call error 调用错误
call establishment 呼叫建立
call executive 调用执行
call forwarding 呼叫转移
call handling capacity 呼叫处理能力
call identifier 呼叫识别号,呼叫标识符
call in 调入
call indicator 呼叫指示符
call information 呼叫信息,呼叫通知
call inquiry service signal 呼叫查询服务信号
call instruction 调用指令
call intensity 呼叫强度
call intent 呼叫意图
call level interface(CLI) 调用层接口
call lose rate 呼损率
call macroinstruction 调用宏指令
call meter 呼叫计数器
call module 调用模块
call name 调用名称
call not accepted signal 呼叫不能接受信号
call number 调用号码
call option 呼叫任选项
call packet 呼叫信息包
call processing program 呼叫处理程序
call processor(CP) 呼叫处理机
call profile 呼叫轮廓文件
call progress signal 呼叫进行信号
call queue register 呼叫队列寄存器
call redirection 呼叫改向
call redirection notification 呼叫转移通知

call rejected message 呼叫拒绝消息
call release 呼叫解除,呼叫释放
call release time 呼叫释放时间
call request 呼叫请求
call request packet 呼叫请求分组
call request signal 呼叫请求信号
call set-up 呼叫建立
call set-up packet 呼叫建立分组
call set-up time 呼叫建立时间
call sign 呼号
call sign series 呼号序列
call signal 呼叫信号
call stack 调用栈
CALL statement 调用语句
call statement manipulation 调用语句处理
call string 呼叫串
call subroutine 调用子程序
call subscriber 主叫用户
call supervision packet 呼叫管理分组
call through 呼叫接通
call transfer 呼叫转移
call up 打开
Call UPS 远程 UPS 通电
call waiting services 呼叫等待服务
call waiting tone 呼叫等待音
call word 呼叫字
callback 回调
callback function 回叫功能
callback list 回叫表
callback mechanism 回叫机制
callback procedures 回叫过程
callback synchronization 回叫同步
called line 被叫线
called line identify 被叫线识别
called line identify indicator 被叫线识别指示符
called party 被叫方
called party release 被叫方释放,被叫方挂机
called procedure 被调用过程
called process 被调用进程
called program 被调用程序
called routine 被调用例程
called service user 被叫服务用户
called station 被呼叫站
called subscriber 被叫用户
caller 调用程序

callers graph window 调用程序图形窗口
calling argument 调用变元
calling classification 调用分类
calling convention 调用约定
calling library 调用库程序
calling line identification 主叫线识别
calling line identify message 主叫线标识信息
calling module 调用模块
calling party 主叫方,呼叫用户
calling party release 呼叫者释放,主叫方挂机
calling point 调用点
calling procedure 调用过程
calling process 调用进程
calling program 调用程序
calling sequence 调用顺序[序列]
calling service user 调用服务用户
calling state diagram 呼叫状态图
calling statement 调用语句
calling station 呼叫站
calling terminal 主叫终端
callisto 分栏符号
calloc 主内存分配函数
callout 说明文字
CAM(Computer Aided Manufacturing) 计算机辅助制造
CAM(Content Addressable Memory) 内容寻址内存
CAM cache 内容可寻址内存高速缓
CAMAC CAMAC总线
Cambridge Information Technology (CIT) 剑桥信息技术
Cambridge ring 剑桥环网
cameo 浮凸字体
camera 摄像机
camera-ready copy 可照相制版的原稿
camma delimited 逗号定界
camma delimiter 逗号定界符
camp-on 预占
campus-wide information server(CWIS) 校园信息服务器
campuses network 校园网
CAN(CANcel character) 作废[取消]字符
Can't Redo 不能重做
Can't Repeat 不能重复
Can't Undo 不能撤消
Canadian Business Periodicals Index (CBPI) 加拿大商业期刊索引数据库
Canadian On Line Enquiry(CANOLE) 加拿大联机查询系统
cancel(CAN,CANL) 作废,取消;终止
cancel button 取消按钮
cancel call 取消呼叫
cancel character(CAN) 作废[取消]字符
cancel closedown 作废关闭
cancel indicator 作废指示符
cancel key 强拆键,作废键
cancel message 作废消息
cancel statement 作废[取消]语句
cancel status word 作废状态字
cancellable 可取消的
cancellation 取消,注销
cancellation advice 注销通知
cancellation completed signal 注消完成信号差
cancellation error 相消误差,消去误
cancellation law 消去律
cancellation law of addition 加法消去
cancellation mark 删除标志,取消标志
cancellation of record 记录消除
canceling signal 取消信号,废止信号
CANCL(CANCeLling) 取消,作废,删除
candidate 候选者
candidate index 候选索引
candidate key 候选关键字
candidate solution 候选解,预备解
candidate solution graph 候选解图
candidate volume 候选卷
canned cycle 固定循环
canned data 固定数据
canned format 固定格式
canned paragraphs 固定段落
canned program 密封程序
canned routine 固定例程,定型例程
canned software 固定软件,封装软件
cannibalization 同型装配
CANOLE(CANadian On Line Enquiry) 加拿大联机查询系统
canon 规范,准则

canonic generation 正规生成,规范生成
canonic schema 规范模式
canonical block 典型块,正则块
canonical coordinate 规范坐标系
canonical form 规范形式,范式
canonical maxterm 规范最大项
canonical minterm 规范最小项
canonical name (Unix/Linux)主机别名,规范名称
canonical order 规范序
canonical schema 规范模式
canonical synthesis 规范合成
canonical topology 典型拓扑
canonical variable 规范变量
cantilever 悬臂
CAP (Communication Access Processor) 通信访问处理机
CAP (Computer-Aided Programming) 计算机辅助程序设计
cap 大写字母;金属帽
cap height 大写字母高度
cap size 大写字母尺寸
capability 能力,效力
capability-based distributed authorization model 基于能力的分布式授权模型
capability check 能力校验
capability list 授权表,能力表
capability manager 授权管理程序
capability mechanism 授权机构
capability revocation 权力撤除
capability test 能力测试
capacitance 电容,电容量
capacitive coupling 电容耦合
capacitive microphone 电容式传声器
capacitive microtransducer 电容微传感器
capacitive touchscreen 电容式触摸屏
capacitivity 电容率
capacitor 电容器
capacitor activated transducer 电容激发传感器
capacitor memory 电容式存储器
capacity 容量;能力
capacity assignment 容量分配
capacity aware 容量认知
capacity exceeding number 超位数
capacity function 容量函数
capacity of a cut 割的容量
capacity of an edge 边的容量
capacity of cell 电池容量
capacity of protocol 协议有效性
capacity of sector 扇区容量
capital 大写字母
capital letter height 大写字母高度
capital shift 大写字母换档
CAPP (Content Addressable Parallel Processor) 内容可寻址并行处理机
Caps Lock key 大写锁定键
capstan 主导轴,主动轮
capstan servo system 主动轮伺服机构
CAPTAIN system 电话提取字符图形信息网络
caption 解释字幕,插图说明,标题
captions for the deaf (CFD) 聋人字幕
captive user 捕获性用户
capture 抓图,获取,捕捉
capture adapter 数据采集适配器
capture board (视频)获取板
capture cache 数据截获缓存
capture region 捕获区域
capture time 捕捉时间
captured keystroke 捕获按键;获取正文
captured packet 截获的信息包
capturing keyboard events 捕获键盘事件
capturing mouse events 捕获鼠标事件
capturing object current status 捕获对象当前状态
CAR (Computer-Assisted Retrieval) 计算机辅助检索
CAR function CAR 函数
CARAM (Content Addressable Random Access Memory) 内容寻址的随机存取存储器
CARB (Central ARBiter) 中央仲裁器
carbon composition resistor 炭质电阻器
carbon copy 打印副本;转发邮件
carbon film resistor 炭膜电阻器
carbon microphone 炭精传声器
carbon ribbon 碳带,聚酯色带
carbonless paper 无碳复写纸
card 卡片
card address 插件插入位置,插件地址

card address backplane 插件地址底板
card address design 插件地址设计
card assignment 插件分派 「机
card-board computer 插件板式计算
card bus 插件总线
card cage 卡笼,插件框架
card chassis 插件框架,插件底座
card column 卡片列
card-controlled calculator 卡片控制计算器
card deck 卡片叠
card ejector 插件拔出器
card file 卡片文件
card frames 卡框,卡架
card guide 插件导轨
card jam 卡片阻塞
card key 卡式密钥
card-level hard disk 卡式硬盘
card level module 插件级模块
card module 卡式模块
card programmed calculator 卡式可编程计算器
card-programmed computer 卡片编程计算机
card puller 插件板启拔器
card puncher 卡片穿孔机
card reader 读卡机
card reproducer 卡片复制机
card row 卡片行
card services 卡服务程序
card slot 插件槽
card stacker 堆卡器,接卡器
card track 卡片导轨
Cardfile 卡片盒,卡片文件
cardinal number 基数
cardinal spline 基数样条
cardinality 基数
cardinality variation 基数差异
careless mistake 疏忽造成的错误
caret 插入记号(^)
caret mark 补入字符符号,插入符号
CARGUIDE 驾驶导向专家系统
carpal tunnel syndrome 腕管综合症
carpet bomb 地毯式轰炸
carriage 输送架;托架,小车 「符
carriage control character 回车控制字
carriage controller 输送架控制器
carriage guide rail 滑架导轨

carriage lock 托架锁定
carriage overflow 托架溢出
carriage paper width 输送架纸宽
carriage positioning 托架定位
carriage rail 输送架导轨
carriage release 输送架释放
carriage restore key 托架恢复键
carriage return(CR) 回车 「符
carriage return character 回车控制字
carriage return key 回车键
carriage space key 输送架空推键
carrier 载波,载体;载流子;载送板
carrier channel 载波通道,载波信道
carrier-current communication 载波通信
carrier detect(CD) 载波检测,载波侦
carrier extension 载波扩展
carrier frequency 载频
carrier mobility 载流子迁移率
carrier's carrier 基础载体
carrier scale internetworking 电信运营商级网络互联
carrier sense multiple access(CSMA) 载波侦听多路访问
carrier sense multiple access/collision avoidance(CSMA/CA) 载波侦听多路访问/冲突避免
carrier sense multiple access/collision detection(CSMA/CD) 载波侦听多路访问/冲突检测
carrier shift 载频偏移;移频
carrier signal 载波信号
carrier signaling 载波信令
carrier-suppressed transmission 载波抑制传输
carrier-switched routing 电信运营商交换路由
carrier telephone communications 载波电话通信
carrier transmission 载波传输
carrier velocity 载流子速度
carrier wave 载波
carry 进位
carry ahead 先行[超前]进位
carry bit 进位位
carry chain 进位链
carry clear signal 进位清除信号
carry-complete signal 进位完成信号

carry condition 进位条件
carry control 进位控制
carry delay 进位延迟
carry delay time 进位延迟时间
carry-dependent sum adder 进位相关和数加法器
carry detection 进位检测
carry digit 进位数
carry flag 进位标志
carry gate 进位门
carry generator 进位发生器
carry in 进位输入
carry indicator 进位指示符
carry input 进位输入
carry line 进位线
carry/link bit 进位/链接位
carry logic 进位逻辑
carry lookahead 进位预测 「器
carry lookahead adder 超前进位加法
carry lookahead generator 超前进位发生器
carry lookahead logic 先行进位逻辑
carry number 进位数
carry-over 接下页
carry propagation 进位传播
carry pulse 进位脉冲
carry register 进位寄存器
carry reset 进位清除
carry separation 进位分离
carry set 进位组
carry signal 进位信号
carry skip 进位跳跃
carry status 进位状态 「器
carry storage register 进位存储寄存
carry time 进位时间
carry type 进位类型
CARS(Computer-Aided Routing System) 计算机辅助路由选择(布线)系统
Cartesian axis 笛卡儿轴
Cartesian-based control 基于笛卡儿坐标的控制
Cartesian coordinate system 笛卡儿坐标系
Cartesian motion 笛卡儿坐标运动
Cartesian path tracking 笛卡儿坐标的轨迹跟踪
Cartesian product 笛卡儿乘积

cartogram 统计图
cartographic font 制图字体
cartoon 卡通片,动画片
cartridge 盒式磁带
cartridge disk 盒式磁盘
cartridge disk drive 盒式磁盘驱动器
cartridge empty 墨粉盒已空
cartridge font 字盒字体
cartridge hard-disk unit 卡式硬盘
cartridge management system 卡带管理系统
cartridge tape 卡式盒带 「构
cartwheel architecture 车轮形体系结
CAS(Column Address Select) 列地址选择
CAS(Content Addressable Storage) 按内容寻址存储器
CAS(Customer Accounting System) 用户记账系统
cascadable counter 可级联计数器
cascade 级联
cascade analog to Gray code converter 级联模拟-格雷码转换器
cascade canonic form 级联典型形式
cascade carry 串进位
cascade channel 级联通道
cascade code 级联码
cascade connection 级联,串级连结
cascade control 级联控制
cascade decomposition 级联分解
cascade entry 级联表目
cascade function 级联功能
cascade interpretation 级联解释
cascade list 级联表
cascade logic 级联逻辑
cascade network 级联网络
cascade partial sum method 级联部分和方法
cascade replication 瀑布结构复制器
cascade table 级联表
cascade windows 层叠窗口,阶梯式排列的视窗
cascaded analog to pure binary converter 串级模拟纯二进制转换器
cascaded carry 级联进位
cascaded expression 级联表达式
cascaded star 级联星形
cascading menu 级联菜单

cascading style sheets(CSS) 级联样式表
CASE(Computer Aided Software Engineering) 计算机辅助软件工程
case 情况
CASE base 范例库
case-based reasoning(CBR) 基于范例的推理
case block 情况块
case branch 情况分支
case clause 情况子句
case-dependent 与大小写有关的
case frames 格框,格框架
case grammar 格文法
case history 典型事例;病历
case label 情况标号,选择标号
case library 案例库
case-oriented representation 面向案例的表示法
case prefix 情况前缀
case relations 格关系
CASE repository 计算机辅助软件工程中心库
case-sensitive 区分大小写的
case-sensitive search 区分大小写的搜
case statement 情况语句
case stream 情况流
CASE structured hierarchy 计算机辅助软件工程结构层次
CASE system 计算机辅助软件工程系
CASE tools 计算机辅助软件工程工具
CASH(Computer Aided System Hardware) 计算机辅助系统硬件
cash on delivery 货到付款
cashless checkless society 无现金无支票社会
CASNET(China Academy of Science NETwork) 中国科学院网络
cashomat 自动提款机
cassette 卡型盒式磁带机
cassette disk 卡式[盒式]磁盘
cassette drive 盒带机,卡式磁带机
cassette interface 盒带机接口
cassette recorder 卡式带匣记录器
cassette tape 卡型盒式磁带
CASSM(Context Addressed Segment Sequential Memory) 上下文寻址段顺序存储器
cast 类型转换,投影,映射
cast animation 造型动画
cast-based animation 基于造型的动画
casting 投影,类型转换
casting up 合计
CASTOFF 回应关闭
CASTON 回应开启
casual analogy 随机类推,偶然类推
casual connection 偶然连接
casual user 临时用户,偶然用户
casualty 故障,意外事故
CAT(Channel Availability Table) 通道可用性表
CAT(Computer-Aided Teaching) 计算机辅助教学
cat(concatenate) (Unix)连结命令
catalog 目录,编目
catalog agent 目录代理
catalog database 目录数据库
catalog directory 目录字典
catalog file 编目文件
catalog function 目录功能,编目函数
catalog list 目录表
catalog memory 目录存储器
catalog record 编目记录
catalog recovery area(CRA) 目录恢复区
catalog relation 目录关系
catalog view 目录视图
catalog search 目录检索
cataloged data set 编目数据集
cataloged load module file 编目装入模块文件
cataloged permanent file 编目永久文
cataloged procedure 编目过程
cataloging program 编目操作程序
catalogue file 目录文件
Catalyst,网络交换机(Cisco)
catalyst 催化剂
catanet 互连网
catastrophe 大灾难
catastrophic error 灾难性错误
catastrophic failure 严重故障
CATCH(Character Allocated Transfer CHannel) 按字符分配的传送通道
catch block (C语言)异常捕捉块

catch handler (C语言)异常捕捉处理程序
catch of exception 异常捕捉
catch statement 捕捉语句
catch up 监察
catchable types 可捕捉类型
catching exception 捕捉异常
catching range 捕捉范围
categorical 无条件的;范畴的
categorical analysis 范畴分析
categorical data 分类数据
categorical descriptor 类属描述符
categorical model 绝对模型
categorical grammar 范畴文法
categorical relation 范畴关系
categorized view 分类视图
categorization 分类
category 类别,范畴
category 1-5 1-5类电缆
category code 分类代码
category labels 分类标志
category of machine 机器范畴
category set metadata 类别集元数据
category scale 分类轴刻度
Category(X) Axis Scale 分类(X)轴刻度
catena 串体,连锁,链接;丛书
catenate 链接
catenationt closure 连接闭包
caterpillar track 履带
cathode 阴极,负极
cathode bias 阴极偏置
cathode follower 阴极跟随器
cathode ray 阴极射线
cathode-ray oscilloscope 阴极射线示波器
cathode-ray tube(CRT) 阴极射线管
cathode ray tube controller(CRTC) 阴极射线管显示控制器
cathode-ray tube display 阴极射线管显示器
cathode-ray tube terminal 阴极射线管终端
cation 正离子,阳离子
CATV(CAble TeleVision) 电缆电视,有线电视
CATV(Community Antenna TV) 共用天线电视

CAU(Controlled Access Unit) 控制存取单元
Cauchy integral formula 柯西积分公式
Cauchy interpolation 柯西插值
Cauchy Machine(CM) 柯西机
Cauchy machine application 柯西机应用
Cauchy machine implementation 柯西机实现
causal 因果的
causal analysis 因果分析
causal graph model 因果图模型
causal independence 无因果关系
causal logic 因果逻辑
causal model 因果模型
causal network 因果网络
causal reasoning 因果推理法
causal sequence 因果序列
causal semantic model 因果语义模型
causal signal 原因信号
causal system 因果系统
causality 因果性,因果律
causality of automaton 自动机的因果律
cause and effect chain diagram 因果链图
cause code 原因码
cause effect graph 因果图
cause effect graph with constraint condition 带约束条件的因果图
cause field 原因字段
caution 警告,提醒
CAV(Constant Angular Velocity) 恒定角速度
CAVE(Computer-Aided Virtual-reality Environment) 计算机辅助虚拟现实环境
caveman 过时产品
cavitation 空穴作用
cavity 空腔,谐振腔
cavity orientation 中空取向
CAW(Channel Address Word) 通道地址字
CAW(Command Address Word) 命令地址字
Cayleys formula 凯莱公式
CB(Channel Buffer) 通道缓冲区
CB(Character Block) 字符块
CB(Check Bit) 校验位
CB(Conditional Branch) 条件分支
CB(Control Buffer) 控制缓存

CB(Current Bit) 当前位

CBEMA(Computer and Business Equipment Manufacturers Association) 计算机与商业设备制造商协会

CBGA(Ceramic Ball Grid Array) 陶瓷球栅阵列

CBI(Conditional Breakpoint Instruction) 条件断点指令

CBIOS(Customized Basic Input/Output System) 定制的基本输入/输出系统

CBL(Computer-Based Learning) 基于计算机的教学

CBO(Channel Bus Out) 通道总线输出

CBP(Channel Buffer Pointer) 通道缓存器指针

CBR(Constant Bit Rate) 恒定比特率

CBT(Computer-Based Training) 基于计算机的训练,计算机模拟训练

CBT(Computer-Based Video Retrieval) 基于计算机的视频检索

CBW(Channel Band Width) 信道带宽

cc:(Carbon Copy) 有名复本

CC(Computer Communication) 计算机通信

CC(Computer Conference) 计算机会议

CC-DOS 汉字磁盘操作系统

cc:Mail cc:Mail 电子邮件(Lotus)

CCA(Common Cryptographic Architecture) 通用密码体系结构

CCA(Communication Channel Adapter) 通信通道适配器

CCA(Communications Control Architecture) 通信控制体系结构

CCB(Channel Control Block) 通道控制块

CCD(Charge Coupled Device) 电荷耦合器件

CCD camera 电荷耦合器件摄像机

CCD memory 电荷耦合器件存储器

CCD storage time 电荷耦合器件存储时间

CCE(Communication Control Equipment) 通信控制设备

CCED(Chinese Character EDitor) 中文编辑软件

CCI(Computer Communication Interface) 计算机通信接口

CCIR(Committee International de la Radio) 国际无线电委员会

CCIS(Coaxial Cable Information System) 同轴电缆信息系统

CCIS(Common Channel Interoffice Signaling) 共路局间信令

CCITT(Consultative Committee on International Telephone and Telegraph) 国际电话电报咨询委员会

CCITT channel type 国际电话电报咨询委员会建议的通道类型

CCITT I series recommendations 国际电话电报咨询委员会的 I 系列建议

CCITT information types 国际电话电报咨询委员会建议的信息类型

CCITT interface CCITT 接口

CCITT man-machine language(CCITT MML) CCITT 人机语言

CCITT series recommendations 国际电话电报咨询委员会的系列建议

CCITT signaling system No. 6 CCITT 6 号信令系统

CCITT signaling system No. 7 CCITT 7 号信令系统

CCITT standard 国际电话电报咨询委员会标准

CCITT V. series recommendation CCITT V 系列建议

CCITT X. series recommendation CCITT X 系列建议

CCIU(Command Channel Interface Unit) 命令通道接口单元

CCL(CalComp Laser printer) CCL 系列激光打印机

CCP(Certificate in Computer Programming) 计算机程序设计资格证书

CCP(Communication Check Point) 通信检查点

CCP(Communication Control Processor) 通信控制处理机

CCR(Channel Control Reconfiguration) 通道控制重新配置

CCS(CHILL Compiling System) CHILL 语言编译系统

CCST(Chinese Character System Teletext) 中国图文电视广播规范

CCU(Central Control Unit) 中央控制单元
CCU(Command Chain Unit) 命令链单元
CCU(Common Control Unit) 公共控制单元
CCW(Channel Command Word) 通道命令字
CCW(Channel Control Word) 通道控制字
CCW(Counter ClockWise) 反时针方向
CD(Carrier Detection) 载波侦测
CD(Compact Disc) 小型数字音频唱片
CD cutting system CD 唱片刻录系统
CD DA(CD Digital Audio) 数字音频光盘
CD-ETOM(CD-G) 电子捕获光存储器
CD-Graphic(CD-G) CD 图示唱片
CD+Graphics CD 加图像光盘
CD-I(Compact Disc-Interactive) 交互式光盘系统
CD-R(CD-Recordable) 可记录光盘
CD recorder CD 刻录机
CD-ROM(Compact Disk-ROM) 只读光盘存储器
CD-ROM driver 只读光盘驱动器,光驱
CD-ROM driver interface 光驱接口
CD ROM changer CD ROM 换盘机
CD ROM Extensions CD ROM 扩展程序
CD ROM interface CD ROM 接口
CD ROM player 光盘放送机
CD-ROM server CD-ROM 服务器
CD-ROM XA(CD-ROM eXtended Architecture) CD-ROM 扩展结构
CD-RTOS CD-RTOS 操作系统
CD-RW(CD-ReWritable) 可重写光盘
CD-Video(CD-V) CD 电视唱片
CD-WORM(CD-Write Once Read Many times) 一次写入多次读出光盘
CDB(Common Data Bus) 通用数据总线
CDB(Current Data Bit) 现行数据位
CDC(Character Display Control) 字符显示控制器
CDDI(Copper Distributed Data Interface) 铜线分布式数据接口
CDE(Common Desktop Environment) 公共桌面环境(Unix)
CDE(Contents Directory Entry) 目录表入口
cdev(control panel device) 控制面板设备
CDF(Channel Definition Format file) 频道定义格式文件
CDF(Comma-Delimited File) 逗号定界文件
CDi-Online CDi-Online 体系结构
CDK(Console Display Keyboard) 控制台显示器键盘
CDK(Control Development Kit) 控件开发成套工具
CDL(Command Definition Language) 命令定义语言
CDM(Compound Document Mail) 复合文档邮件
CDMA(Code Division Multiple Access) 码分复用多路访问
CDOS CDOS 操作系统
CDP(Certificate in Data Processing) 数据处理专业资格证书
CDP(Correlated Data Processor) 相关数据处理机
CDPD(Cellular Digital Packet Data) 蜂窝式数字信息包数据传送
CDR(Compact Data Recorder) 微型数据记录仪
CDR function CDR 函数
CDRAM(Cached DRAM) 带高速缓存器的动态存储器
CDS(Compressed Data Storage) 压缩数据存储器
CDT(Command Definition Table) 命令定义表
CDTOF(Computer control Data Transmission using Optical Fiber) 计算机光纤数据传输系统
CDTV(Commodore Dynamic Total Vision) Commodore 动态视频系统
CDU(Character Display Unit) 字符显示器
CE(Combinational Explosion) 组合爆炸
CE(Correctable Error) 可校正错误

CE(Customer Engineer) 客户工程师
CE cylinder 客户工程师用柱面
CE track 客户工程师用磁道
CEG(Continuos Edge Graphics) 连续边缘图像
CEGL(Cause-Effect Graph Language) 因果图示语言
CEI(Chip Enable Input) 芯片使能输入
ceil 上舍入函数;最高层节点
ceiling 向上取整运算
cel 单帧画面
Celeron 赛扬处理器(Intel,1998年)
CeleronA 新赛扬处理器(Intel)
cell 单元,信元,单元格;细胞
cell address 单元格地址,单元地址
cell animation 单元式动画
cell array 单元阵列
cell attribute 单元属性
cell block 单元块,单元组
cell call 单元调用
cell communication 细胞通信
cell complex 单元复合体
cell control 存储格控制层
cell cube 单元立方体
cell data 单元数据
cell drag and drop 单元格拖放
cell definition 单元格定义
cell delay variation 相邻码元延迟偏差
Cell Directory Service(CDS) 单元目录服务
cell encoding 信元编码
cell format 单元格式
cell interconnection 单元互连
cell interconnection array 细胞互连阵列
cell interconnection mask 单元互连掩模
cell level 单元级
cell library 单元程序库
Cell Link 单元格链接
cell logic 单元逻辑
cell loss priority(CLP) 信元丢弃优先级
cell matrix 单元阵列
cell multiplexing (ATM)信元复合
cell name 单元名
Cell Note 单元格附注
cell-organized display 单元组织显示
cell padding 表格单元中文字(或图像)与单元边框之间的空白
cell pointer 单元格指针

cell position 单元位置
cell potential 细胞电平传感器
cell protection 单元格保护
cell reference 单元格地址参考,单元引用
cell relay 单元中继
cell spacing 表格单元之间的距离
cell splitting 单元分割
cell stack 单元堆栈
cell value 单元值
cellar 后进先出存储区
CellBuilder 单元构筑件
Cells in Frame(CIF) 帧中信元,CIF协议
cellular array 细胞阵列,单元阵列
cellular array processor 细胞阵列处理机
cellular automaton 细胞自动机
cellular chain 细胞链,单元式链
cellular computation 细胞结构式计算
cellular computer 细胞结构计算机
cellular construction 细胞结构,单元结构
cellular digital packet data 蜂窝式数字包数据
cellular fast processor 细胞快速处理机
cellular inverted list 单元式倒排表
cellular list 单元表,单元列表
cellular logic 细胞逻辑
cellular logic array 细胞逻辑阵列
cellular logic device 细胞逻辑装置
cellular memory 细胞存储器
cellular mobile telephone networks 蜂窝移动电话网
cellular multilist 单元式多目表
cellular network 细胞网络
cellular partition 单元式分区
cellular radio 蜂窝状无线电系统
cellular splitting 细胞式分裂
cellular tree structured computer 细胞树结构计算机
cellular unmanned production 单元式无人生产系统
cellular vector computer 细胞式向量计算机
CELP(Code Excited Linear Predictive coding) 码激励线性预测编码
CEM(Customer Engineers Memoran-

dum) 客户工程师备忘录
census computer 人口普查计算机
center 中心,中央
center alignment tab 中心对准标记
center clipping 中心削波
center finding 中心定位
center frequency 中心频率
center horizontally 水平居中
center management 计算中心管理;集中式管理
center mark 中心标记(符号)
center of perspective 透视中心
center of projection 投影中心
center on page 在页面上居中
center regulation 中心调整
center spot 中心点
center-tapped 中心抽头的
center to center spacing 中心间距
center vertically 垂直居中
centering 对中
centering control 定心控制
centerline 中心线
centi- 百分之一
centigrade temperature 摄氏温度(℃)
centimeter(cm) 厘米
central computer 中央计算机
central console 中央控制台
central control(CC) 集中[中央]控制
central control line 中央控制线路
central control module 中央控制模块
central control panel 中央控制面板
central control room 中央控制室
central data acquisition system 中心数据采集系统
central data bank 中央数据库
central data base 中心数据库
central data display 中心数据显示器
central data file 中央数据文件 「机
central data processor 中央数据处理
Central Data Store 中央数据存储
central difference notation 中心差分记法
central file 中央文件
central flow control precedence network 中心流程控制优先网络
central flow control software 中心流程控制软件
central index file 中央索引文件

central input/output multiplexer 中央输入/输出多路复用器
central interconnection 中央互连
central interface unit 中央接口单元
central key 中央密钥
central line 中心线,中央通信线路
central logic control 中央逻辑控制
central mass storage 中央海量存储器
central memory 中央内存
central memory control 中央内存控制
central module 中央模块
central point 中心点 「统
central processing system 集中处理系
central processing unit(CPU) 中央处理单元
central processor subsystem 中央处理机子系统
central queue 中央队列
central-server queuing network 中心服务例程排队网络
central service model 中央服务模型
central station 中央站
central storage 中央存储器
central strength-member optical cable 中心强化光缆
central switching 中心交换
central terminal unit(CTU) 中央终端设备
centrality 集中性
centralization 集中化
centralization of control 控制集中
centralized adaptive routing 集中式自适应路由选择
centralized adaptive routing algorithm 集中式自适应路由选择算法
centralized administration 集中管理
centralized arbiter 集中仲裁器
centralized buffer pool 集中式缓冲池
centralized bus arbitration 集中式总线仲裁
centralized clock interface 中央时钟接口
centralized computer network 集中式计算机网络
centralized computer system 集中式计算机系统
centralized control 集中控制
centralized control signaling 集中控制

信令
centralized data base 集中式数据库
centralized data integrity 集中式数据完整性
centralized data processing 集中式数据处理
centralized decision making 集中决策
centralized hardware arbiter 集中式硬件仲裁器
centralized I/O data 集中输入/输出数据
centralized intelligence 集中式智能
centralized maintenance 集中维护
centralized management 集中式管理
centralized monitoring system 集中监控系统
centralized network 集中式网络
centralized processing 集中式处理
centralized refresh 集中式刷新
centralized resource management 集中式资源管理
centralized routing 集中式路径选择
centralized switch 集中式开关
centralized system 集中式系统
centralized topology 集中式拓扑结构
centralized traffic control 集中流量控制
centralized update library 集中式更新程序库
centre 中心
centre control 中央控制方式
centre of an area 区域中心
centre of symmetry 对称中心
centre random variable 中心化随机变量
centrex 市话交换分局
centrifugal blower 离心式风机
centrifugal elevator unload mechanism 离心升降式卸荷机构
centroid 形心,质心
Centronics interface standard Centronics 并行接口标准
Centronics printer Centronics 打印机
Century 公元年份,世纪
CEO(Chief Executive Officer) (公司)首席执行官
CEO(Chip Enable Output) 芯片启用输出
cepstrum 倒谱

ceram 陶瓷
ceramet 金属陶瓷
ceramic 陶瓷的
ceramic bond 陶瓷接合剂
ceramic capacitor 陶瓷电容器
ceramic dual in-line package 双列直插式陶瓷封装
ceramic flat packing 陶瓷扁平封装
ceramic magnet 陶瓷磁体
ceramic package 陶瓷封装
CERDIP(CERamic Dual In-line Package) 陶瓷双列直插式封装
CERN(European Laboratory for Particle Physics) 欧洲粒子物理研究所(WWW 创建者)
CERN network 欧洲粒子物理研究所计算机网络
CERNET(Chinese Education and Research NETwork) 中国教育科研网
certain decision 确定性决策
certain event 必然事件
certain reasoning 确定性推理
certainty 确定性
certainty equivalence 确定当量,确定性等价
certainty factor 可信度,确定性因子
certificate 证书
certificate authority 证书授予权;授权机构
certificate request 证明请求
Certificate Revocation List 证书撤消列表
certificate verify 证明检查
certification 认证
Certified Novell Administrator 合格 Novell 网络管理员
Certified Novell Engineering 合格 Novell 网络工程师
Certified Novell Engineering Professional Association 合格 Novell 网络工程师专业协会
Certified Novell Instructor 合格 Novell 网络指导者
certified tape 合格带
certify 核准
CF(Compact Flash) 微型闪速记忆卡
CF(Context Free) 上下文无关的

CF(Compact Flash Association) 微型闪速记忆卡联合会
CFA(Current File Area) 当前文件区
CFAA(Computer Fraud and Abuse Act) 计算机欺骗及滥用法规
CFCS(Chinese Federation of Computer Societies) 中国计算机学会
CFG(Context Free Grammar) 上下文无关文法
CFML(ColdFusion Markup Language) (网页制作)ColdFusion置标语言
CFTV(Coin-Freed TeleVision) 投币式电视
CGA(Color Graphics Adapter) 彩色图形适配器,CGA格式
cgets 从控制台读字符串函数
CGI(Common Gateway Interface) 公共网关界面
CGI(Computer Graphics Interface) 计算机图形接口
CGM(Computer Graphics Metafile) 计算机图形元文件
CGMP(Cisco Group Management Protocol) (交换机)Cisco组管理协议
CGSE(Centimeter-Gram-Second Electrostatic system) 厘米克秒静电制
CGSM(Centimeter-Gram-Second electro-Magnetic system) 厘米克秒电磁制,绝对电磁单位制
CH(CHannel) 通道,信道,沟道
CHA(CHannel Adapter) 通道适配器
chain 链,链接,链路
chain addition program 链式添加程
chain address 链式地址
chain addressing 链式寻址
chain area 链域
chain break 链断开
chain carry 链式进位
chain character area 链式字符区
chain circuit 链式电路
chain code 链码
chain code generator 链式码发生器
chain data 链式数据
chain data address 链式数据地址
chain data flag 链式数据标志
chain effect 链锁效应
chain error 链错误

chain feature 链接特征
chain field 链式字段,链域
chain file 链式文件
chain image 链式图像
chain infection 链锁感染
chain job 链式作业
chain link record 链式连接记录
chain linked to next 前向链
chain linked to next and prior 双向链
chain linked to owner 向主链
chain list 链式表
chain maintenance program 链维护程
chain of a hypergraph 超图的链
chain of command 命令链
chain of controllers 控制器链
chain of data(CD) 数据链
chain printer 链式打印机
chain printing schedule 串链式打印调
chain program 链接程序
chain reaction 链锁反应
chain record 链式记录
chain rule 链式规则
chain scheduling 链式调度
chain search 链式搜索
chain segment 链段
CHAIN statement CHAIN语句
chained addressing 链接编址
chained allocation 链式分配
chained command 链锁命令
chained device 链接设备
chained file 链式文件
chained job 链接作业
chained linear list 线性链表
chained list 链接表
chained list search 链接表搜索,链表查询
chained method 链接法
chained mode 链模式
chained record 链式记录
chained sector 链接扇区
chained stack 链式堆栈
chained structured record 链式结构记
chained sublibraries 链式子程序库
chaining 链锁,链接
chaining backward 逆向推理链
chaining bit 链接位
chaining channel action 链式通道动
chaining command 链接命令

chaining command file 链式命令文件
chaining field 链接字段
chaining forward 正向推理链
chaining of backward reasoning 反向推理链接
chaining of forward reasoning 正向推理链
chaining of I/O commands 输入/输出命令的链接
chaining of rules 规则链
chaining overflow 链溢出
chaining search 链接查找,链式检索
challenge/response authentication 挑战/响应身份验证
chameleon segment 变化无常(程序)段
chance coincidence 偶然重合
chance failure 偶然故障
chance player 幸运玩家
change all 全部变更
change bit 变更位
change case 变更大小写
change cipher spec (SSL)变更密码参数
change control procedures 变更控制过程
change direction command indicator 换向命令指示符
change direction protocol 改向协议,换向协议
change-direction request indicator 换向申请指示符
change directory 改变目录
change dump 改后转储
change file 变更文件
change fonts 改变字体
change frame 变更帧
change icon 变更图标
change link 更改链接
change log 变更登录
change-over arrangement 转接设备
change-over gate 转换门,换向门
change-over switch 转换开关,换向开关
change-over time 转换时间
change-prone module 易于更换的模块
change record 变更记录
change request 更改请求
change step 变更步长
change windows size 改变窗口大小
changeable physical layout 可变物理布局
changeable storage 可更换存储器
changeback 倒回
changeback code 倒回代码
changeback procedure 转回程序
changed record 变更的记录
changeover 倒换,转换
changeover switch 换向开关
changing appearance of cells 改变单元格外形
changing chart type 变更图表类型
changing database ownership 改变数据库所有权
changing dominant control 改变支配控件
changing file name 变更文件名
change file-permission setting 变更文件许可设置
changing link diagram layout 变更链接图外观
changing magnification factor 改变放大系数
changing order point 变序点
changing origin relationship name 改变起始关系名
changing search order 改变搜索顺序
changing tab order 改变制表符顺序
changing user access right 改变用户访问权限
changing window styles 改变窗口样式
channel 通道,信道;频道;沟道
channel access 通道存取[访问]
channel acquisition delay 通道获得延时
channel adapter 通道适配器
channel address 通道地址
channel address register 通道地址寄存器
channel address word(CAW) 通道地址字
channel allocation 通道分配
channel assembly 渠道组装(IBM)
channel assignment 信道分配
channel assignment table 通道分配表
channel associated signaling 随路信令
channel attached 通道连接的
channel attached network control program 通道连接的网络控制程序
channel bandwidth 信道带宽

channel-based share 基于通路的共享
channel browser 频道浏览程序
channel buffer storage 通道缓存
channel burst mode 信道突发传输方式
channel bus 通道总线
channel bus controller 通道总线控制器
channel busy 通道忙碌
channel calculation 通道演算
channel capacity 通道流量,信道容量
channel command word(CCW) 通道命令字
channel compression 通道压缩
channel connector 通道连接器
channel control block 通道控制块
channel control reconfiguration 通道控制重构
channel control unit 通道控制器
channel control vector 通道控制向量
channel control word 通道控制字
channel controller(CC) 通道控制器
channel-data check 通道数据校验
channel data selector 通道数据选择器
channel definition file(CDF) 频道定义文件
channel definition format file(CDF) 频道定义格式文件
Channel Definition Wizard 频道定义向导(微软)
channel demodulator 通道解调器
channel demultiplexer 通道分路器
channel description 频道描述
channel disturbance 信道干扰
channel encoder 通道编码器
channel encoding 通道编码
channel end condition 通道结束状态
channel end interrupt 通道结束中断
channel error model 通道错误模型
channel error type 通道错误类型
channel frequency characteristic 通道频率特性
channel grade 信道等级
channel group 通道组
channel group rate 通道组速率
channel identification 通道标识
channel indicator 通道指示器
channel input/output switching 通道输入/输出转换
channel instruction 通道指令

channel interface 通道接口
channel isolation 信道隔离度
channel item property 频道项目属性
channel map 通道映射
channel manager 通道管理程序
channel mapping 通道映射
channel mask 通道屏蔽
channel mode 通道方式
channel modulation 信道调制
channel monitor 通道监控器
channel multiplexer 通道多路复用器
channel noise 信道噪声
channel number 频道数;通道号
channel operation 通道操作
channel output signal 通道输出信号
channel overload 信道过载
channel pair 通道对
channel pointer 通道指示器
channel pool 通道池
channel processor 通道处理机
channel program 通道程序
Channel Property Table 频道属性表
channel protocol 通道协议,信道规程
channel quality moniter 信道质量监视器
channel queue 通道队列
channel read command 通道读入命令
channel reliability 通道可靠性
channel request 通道请求
channel request priority 通道请求优先权
channel reset 通道复位
channel routing 通道路径选择
channel routing algorithm 通道布线算法
channel scanner 通道扫描器
channel scheduler 通道调度程序
channel-select time 通道选择时间
channel selectivity 通道选择性
channel sense command 通道状态字存储寄存器
channel service unit 通道服务单元
channel set 通道组
channel schedule 通道调度
channel scheduling 频道计划时间安排
channel script 频道脚本
channel size 通路宽度
channel speeds 通道速率

channel state word (CSW) 通道状态
channel status 通道状态
channel status indicator 通道状态指示器
channel status table 通道状态表
channel status word (CSW) 通道状态字
Channel Stream table 频道数据流表
channel switching 通道交换
channel synchronizer 通道同步器
channel throughput 通道吞吐量
channel time 通道工作时间
channel time slot 通路时隙
channel-to-channel adapter (CTCA) 通道-通道配接器
channel-to-channel connection 通道连接
channel traffic control 通道流量控制
channel transfer rate 通道传输速率
channel type 通道类型
channel utilization 通道利用率
channel voice-grade service 音频服务通道
channel waiting queue 通道等候队列
channel width 通道宽度；沟道宽度
channel word 通道字
channel write command 通道写命令
channelize 通道化
channelless gate array 无通道门阵列
channels in use 使用中的通道
chaos 混沌
chaos dynamics 混沌动力学
chaos nonlinear system 混沌非线性系统
CHAP/PAP (CHallenge and Authentication Protocol/Password Authentication Protocol) 握手鉴定协议/密码监视协议
Chapin chart 结构化框图法
chapter 章，段
CHAR (CHARacter) 字符；特性
CHAR type 字符型
character 字符
character address 字符地址
character alignment 字符同步
character arrangement 字符排列
character array 字符数组
character array initialization 字符数组预置值
character assembly 字符装配，字符拼装
character assignment statement 字符赋值语句
character-at-a-time printer 一次一字符打印机
character attribute 字符属性
character-based program 基于字符的程序
character-based terminal 基于字符的终端
character-based user interface (CUI) 基于字符的用户界面
character blank 字符空白
character blink 字符闪烁
character block 字符块
character/block transmission 字符/块传输
character board 字符板
character boundary 字符边界
character box 字符框
character buffer 字符缓冲器
character bus 字符总线
character byte 字符字节
character cell 字符单元
character check 字符校验
character code 字符代码
character code conversion 字符代码转换
character coding 字符编码
character comparison 字符比较
character constant 字符常数
character control block 字符控制块
character conversion 字符转换
character count (CC) 字符计数
character crowding 字符拥挤
character cycle 字符循环，字符周期
character data 字符数据
character data type operation 字符数据类型操作
character definition table 字符定义表
character delete 字符删除
character delimiter 字符定界字符
character density 字符密度
character device 字符设备
character dimension 字符大小
character disassembly 字符拆卸[分解]
character display adapter 字符显示适配器
character display device 字符显示设备
character duration 字符传输时间

character edge 字符边缘
character editing 字符编辑
character element 字符要素
character encoding 字符编码法
character error indication 字符错误指示
character error rate 字符出错率
character expression 字符表达式
character field 字符字段
character field descriptor 字符字段描述符
character file 字符文件
character fill 字符填充
character font 字体,字型
character format 字符格式
character frame 字符帧
character frame bit 字符帧码元
character framing 字符成帧
character frequency 字频
character function 字符函数
character generator 字符发生器
character graphic 字符图形
character graphics 字符图示法
character group 字符组
character identifier 字符标识符
character image 字符图像
character information rate 字符信息率
character index 字符索引
character insert 字符插入
character insert mode 字符插入模式
character-interleaved time frame 字符交错时间帧
character interleaving 字符交错
character interval 字符间隔
character key 字符键
character level 字符级
character-like code 类字符码
character literal 字符字面值,字符文
character machine 字符机
character manipulation 字符操作
character map 字符映射
character matrix 字符矩阵
character mean entropy 字符平均信息熵,字符平均熵
character misregistration 字符不正
character mode 字符模式
character mode application 字符模式应用程序
character mode display 字符方式显示器
character modifier 字符修改量
character multiplexer 字符多路转接器
character object 字符对象,字符对象
character operation 字符运算
character order 字序
character ordinal number 字符序号
character oriented computer 面向字符的计算机
character-oriented procedure 面向字符的规程
character-oriented protocol 面向字符的协议
character outline 字符外形[轮廓]
character packing density 字符记录密度
character-parallel transmission 字符并行传输
character parity check 字符奇偶校验
character pattern 字型,字符点阵
character pattern back color 字型背景色
character pattern color 字型色
character pattern input 字型输入,字符点阵输入
character per inch 每英寸字符数
character per page 每页字符数
character per pica 每皮卡字符数
character per second(CPS) 字符/秒
character pitch 字符间距
character position 字符位置
character printer 字符打印机
character pulse 字符脉冲
character quantity 字量
character reader 字符阅读机
character reading 字符读出
character recognition 字符识别
character recognition criteria 字符识别准则
character recognition machine 字符识别器
character recognition system 字符识别系统
character rectangle 字符框,字符矩形块
character reference point 字符参考点
character register 字符寄存器
character relational expression 字符关系表达式

character repertoire 字符集
character rotation 字符旋转
character row 字符行
character scalar 字符标量
character scaling 文字缩放
character segmentation 文字分割
character sensing field 字符读出区
character sequence 字符序列
character-serial transmission 串行传输字符
character set 字符集
character shape 字符形状
character size 字符大小
character size control 字符大小控制
character skew 字符歪斜
character source 字符源
character spacing 字符间隔
character spacing reference line 字符间隔参考线
character special file 字符特别文件
character status bar 字符状态栏
character stream 字符流
character string 字符串
character string constant 字符串常数
character string descriptor 字符串描述符
character string function 字符串函数
character string instruction 字符串指令
character string manipulation package 字符串处理程序包
character string picture 字符串格式描述
character string variable 字符串变量
character stroke 字符笔划
character structure 字符结构
character stuffing 字符插入,字符填充
character style 字体
character subset 字符子集
character substring 字符子串
character suppression 字符消去[压缩]法
character switching 字符交换
character symbol 字符符号
character synchronization 字符同步
character table 字符表
character terminal 字符终端
character token 字符信标[令牌]

character transfer rate 字符转移率[传输率]
character transliteration 字符直译
character tree 字符树
character type 字符类型　　「句
character type statement 字符类型语
character validating 字符有效性检验
character value 字符值
character variable 字符变量
character view 字符显示
character wheel 字轮
character width 字符宽度
character zone 字符区域
characteristic 指数;阶;特性,特征
characteristic adaptive control 特性自适应控制
characteristic adaptive system 特性自适应系统
characteristic analysis 特征分析
characteristic bit 特征位
characteristic condition 特征条件
characteristic description 特征描述
characteristic distortion 特性失真
characteristic element 特征要素
characteristic equation 特征方程
characteristic factor 特征因素
characteristic function 特征函数
characteristic overflow 指数超限,阶码溢出
characteristic overflow exception 阶码上溢异常
characteristic polynomial 特征多项式
characteristic readout voltage pulse 特征读出电压脉冲
characteristic under 阶码下溢
characteristic value 特征值
characteristic vector 特征向量
characterizing description 特征描述
characters per frame display 每帧显示字符数
characters per line 每行字符数
charge amplifier 电荷放大器
charge-coupled device(CCD) 电荷耦合器件
charge coupled devices digital memory 电荷耦合器件数字存储器
charge-coupled image sensor 电荷耦合图像传感器

charge-coupled memory 电荷耦合存储器
charge coupling 电荷耦合
charge density 电荷密度
charge equalizing A/D converter 电荷均衡模/数转换器
charge equalizing D/A converter 电荷均衡数/模转换器
charge image 电荷图像,像
charge pattern 电荷分布图
charge neutrality 电荷平衡
charge sensitivity of pickup 传感器电荷灵敏度
charge storage cell 电荷存储元件
charge transfer 电荷传送
charge transfer device 电荷转移器件
charge-transition time 电荷渡越时间
charge up 充电
charset(character set) 字符集
charstream 字符流
charstring 字符串
chart 表,图表
chart font 图表字体
Chart Gallery 图库
chart layout 图表格式
chart reader 图表阅读器
chart recorder 图纸记录器
Chart Sample 图表示例
chart sheet 图页
chart speed 图表记录速度
chart title 图表标题
chart type 图表类型
Chart Wizard 图表(创建)向导
charting 制图
chase 跟踪,寻迹　　　　　　「式
chase join expression 寻迹联合表达
chassis 机架,框架
chassis assembly 机架组件
chassis earth 机架接地,机壳接地
chassis-mount construction 机架式结
chat message 非正式消息　　　 「构
chat mode 闲谈模式
chat room (网上)聊天室
chat script 聊天脚本
chatter 颤动
chattering 间歇电震
CHDIR(CHange DIRectory) 改变当前工作目录

CHDL(Computer Hardware Definition Language) 计算机硬件定义语言
cheapernet 便宜网络,细缆网络　「近
Chebyshev approximation 切比雪夫逼
Chebyshev interpolation polynomial 切比雪夫插值多项式　　　　　　「式
Chebyshev polynomial 切比雪夫多项
Chebyshev series method 切比雪夫级数法
check 校验,核对
check addition 检验加法
check bit 校验位,监督位
check box 复选框
check code 校验码
check consistency 检验一致性
check disc 校验光盘
check for overflow 超限[溢出]校验
check formula 验算公式
check group 校验字组
check hyperlink 检验超链接
check indicator 检验指示器
check key 校验关键字
check list 校验表
check list method 按表校验法
check loop 校验环路
check mark 复选标记
check number 检验数
check-out time 校验时间
check plugin 检验插件
check point 校验点
check problem 检验题目
check protect 检验保护
check routine 校验例程
check row 校验行
check solution 检验解答
check spelling 拼写检查
check subroutine 检验子例程
check sum 校验和
check sum code 校验和码
check sum digit 校验和数字
check symbol 校验符号
check total 检验总数
check track 校验磁道
check trunk 检验中继线,检验总线
check word 校验字
checkable 可检验的
checked 已检验的
checker 检验员;检验程序

checker board effect 检测板效应
checking bit 校验位
checking by resubstitution 重新代入检查
checking calculation 验算
checking circuit 校验电路
checking experiment 检查实验
checking feature 校验性能
checking loop 检查回路
checking of access right 存取权限检
checking process 校验过程 [验
checking sequence 检验序列
checking symbol 检验符号
ckecklist 检验表
checkout 检验,检查
checkout compiler 校验编译程序
checkout console 测试操作台
checkout routine 检验用例程
checkpoint 校验点
checkpoint and restart procedures 检查点与再启动程序
checkpoint control 检查点控制
checkpoint dump 检查点转储
checkpoint entry 检查点入口
checkpoint file 检查点文件
checkpoint records 检查点记录
checkpoint restart 检验点重新启动
checksum 校验和
checksum error 校验和错误
chemical computer 化学计算机
chemical deposition 化学淀积
cherry picking 随意选取
chess-playing computer 下棋计算机
chess-playing program 下棋程序
chessboard 棋盘
CHI(CHannel Interface) 通道接口
CHIC(Ceramic Hybrid IC) 陶瓷混合集成电路
Chicago "芝加哥"操作系统(Windows 95)
chif analyst 主分析员
chif engineer 总工程师
Chief Execution Officer(CEO) 首席执行官
Chief Information Officer(CIO) 信息主管人员
chief operator 主操作员
chief programmer 主程序员

chief programmer team 主程序员制小组
child 子,子代,孩子
child class 子类
child control 子控件
child dedicated file 子专有文件
child document 子文档
child level 子层
child menu 子菜单
child node 子节[结]点
child page 子页面 [页
child pages under home 主页下面的子
child parent mapping 子代亲体映像
child pointer 子指针
child process 子进程
child resource 子资源
child segment 子段
child-to-parent linkage 子至父[子代至亲体]连接
child widget 子饰件
child window 子视窗[窗口]
children chain 子女链
children relation 子女关系
chill 冷却,致冷
CHILL language CHILL 语言
CHINADDN(CHINA Digital Data Network) 中国公用数字数据网
CHINANet(China High-speed Information Network) 中国公用计算机互联网
CHINAPAC (CHINA PACket network) 中国公用分组交换网
Chinese analysis 中文分析,汉语分析
Chinese character 汉字字符
Chinese character attribute 汉字属性
Chinese character attribute dictionary 汉字属性字典
Chinese character card 汉卡
Chinese character coded character set 汉字编码字符集
Chinese character coding technique 汉字编码技术
Chinese character components 汉字字根,汉字笔划
Chinese character components encoding 汉字字根编码
Chinese character conversational input 汉字会话输入

Chinese character decomposition 汉字分解
Chinese character direct input 汉字直接输入
Chinese character display 汉字显示器
Chinese character display terminal 汉字显示终端
Chinese character dot matrix font 汉字点阵字形
Chinese character encoding 汉字编码
Chinese character exchange code 汉字交换码
Chinese character extended code 汉字扩充码
Chinese character font 汉字字体
Chinese character font library 汉字字模库
Chinese character frequency map 汉字频度分布
Chinese character generator 汉字发生器
Chinese character indexing 汉字索引
Chinese character indirect input 汉字间接输入
Chinese character information processing 汉字信息处理
Chinese character information system 汉字信息系统
Chinese character input keyboard 汉字输入键盘
Chinese character input method type 汉字输入法类型
Chinese character internal code 汉字内部码
Chinese character keyboard input 汉字键盘输入
Chinese character large keyboard input 汉字大键盘输入法
Chinese character library 汉字库
Chinese character matrix pattern 汉字点阵字型
Chinese character mini-keyboard input 汉字小键盘输入法
Chinese character operating system 汉字操作系统
Chinese character pattern 汉字字形
Chinese character pen touch tablet 汉字笔触字盘
Chinese character phonetic/shape encoding 汉字音形编码
Chinese character phototypesetting system 汉字照排系统
Chinese character printer 汉字打印机
Chinese character pronunciation 汉字发音
Chinese character radical coding 汉字字根编码
Chinese character recognition 汉字识别
Chinese character set capacity 汉字集容量
Chinese character shape-oriented encoding 汉字字形编码
Chinese character speech input 汉字语音输入
Chinese character structure 汉字结构
Chinese character style 汉字字体
Chinese character text editor 汉字文本编辑程序
Chinese character type font compression 汉字字形压缩法
Chinese character vocabulary 汉字
Chinese character word encoding 汉字词组编码
Chinese dictionary 汉字词典
Chinese font library 汉字字模库
Chinese information processing system 汉字信息处理系统
Chinese information retrieval system 中文信息检索系统
Chinese input device 汉字输入设备
Chinese language understanding 汉语理解
Chinese language word segmentation specification 汉语分词规范
Chinese machine-readable catalog 中文机读目录
Chinese man-machine interface 中文人机界面
Chinese natural language understanding 汉语自然语言理解
Chinese page description language (CPDL) 中文页面描述语言
Chinese phonetic 汉语拼音
Chinese phonetic keyboard 汉语拼音键盘
Chinese pinyin 汉语拼音
Chinese platform 中文平台

Chinese printer 汉字打印机
Chinese speech analysis 汉语语音分析
Chinese speech information library 中文语音信息库
Chinese speech recognition 汉字语音识别
Chinese speech synthesis 汉语语音合成
Chinese speech understanding 汉语语音理解
Chinese speech understanding knowledge 汉语语音理解知识
Chinese standard exchange code 汉字标准交换码
Chinese word and phrase library 汉语词语库
CHIO(CHannel I/O) 通道输入/输出
chip 芯片;子码
chip attachment 芯片贴装
chip bonding 芯片接合
chip box 芯片盒
chip bus(C-bus) 芯片总线
chip calculator 单片计算器
chip-card 芯片卡
chip defect 芯片缺陷
chip delay line 组件延迟线
chip enable(CE) 组件选通,芯片使能
chip inspection 芯片检验
chip layout 芯片布设
chip level 芯片级
chip material 芯片材料
chip microprocessor 芯片微处理机
chip modem 芯片调制解调器
chip register architecture 芯片寄存器体系结构
chip resistor 片状电阻器
chip select(CS) 组件选择,片选
chip sets 芯片组
chip size 芯片尺寸
chip testing 芯片测试
chip transistor 片状晶体管
chipcard(COD) 芯片卡
Chipcom Chipcom公司(网络产品)
chipping(COD) 分割成芯片
chips on board(COD) 板上芯片
chipset 芯片组
CHK(CHecK) 检验
chlorophyll solar cell 叶绿素太阳电池
chmod 改变文件存取模式函数

CHNN(Continuous Hopfield Neural Network) 连续Hopfield神经网络
choice 挑选,选择
choice again 再选择
choice box 选择框
choice clause 选择子句
choice device 选择设备
choice entry table 选择输入域
choice-finish 选择完毕
choice-in 选进
choice list 选择列表
choice of data structure 数据结构的选择
choice of default 默认选择,缺省选择
choice of language 语言选择
choice-out 选出
choice situation 选择局势
choice-start 选择开始
choke 扼流,阻流
choke packet 阻塞分组
choking coil 扼流圈,阻流圈
cholesteric liquid crystal 胆甾型液晶
Chomsky hierarchy 乔姆斯基层次结构
Chomsky normal form 乔姆斯基范式
Chomsky's grammar 乔姆斯基文法
choose 选择
choose border 选择边框
Chooser 选择器程序
choosing exception handling mechanism 选择异常处理机制
choosing runtime libraries 选择运行时间库
chopper 斩波器
chopper amplifier 斩波放大器
chopper-stabilized D-C amplifier 斩波稳定直流放大器
chopping 截断
chord 连枝;弦
chord keying 和谐键入法
chosen-ciphertext attack 选择密码文本攻击法
chosen-plaintext attack 选择明文攻击法
CHP(CHannel Processor) 通道处理机
CHPT(CHeck PoinT) 检验点
CHR $ function (BASIC)CHR $ 函数
Christmas tree worm 圣诞树蠕虫
Christofides's algorithm 克里斯托费

兹算法
chromatography 色谱学
chroma 色度,色品
chroma control 色度控制
chroma demodulator 色度解调器
chroma drive 色度激励
chroma filter effect 色度过滤器效果
chroma keying 色键
chroma mask 色掩模
chroma oscillator 色度振荡器
chroma recording current 色度记录电流
chroma signal 色度信号
chromakey 色键
chromatic aberration 色度畸变,色像差
chromatic adaptation 色适应
chromatic distortion 色失真
chromatic edgeweight 色边权
chromatic factorization 色分解
chromatic graph 色图
chromatic number of a hypergraph 超图的色数
chromatic partition 染色划分
chromatic polynomial 染色多项式
chromatic signal 彩色信号
chromatic value 色度值
chromaticity 色度
chromaticity coordinates 色度坐标
chromaticity diagram 色度图
chromaticity sensor 色度传感器
chromatograph 色谱
chrominance 色度,色品
chrominance channel 色度通道
chrominance components 色度分量
chrominance frequency 色度频率
chrominance-luminance crosstalk 色亮串扰
chrominance-luminance delay inequality 色度亮度延时不等
chrominance-luminance gain inequality 色度亮度增益不等
chrominance modulator 色度调制器
chrominance non-linearity 色度非线性
chrominance signal 色度信号
chrominance signal bandwidth 色度信号频带
chrominance signal to noise ratio 色度信噪比
chrominance subcarrier 色度副载波
chrominance video signal 色度视频信号
chromosome 染色体
chronic adaptation 慢速适应
chronological backtracking 按时序回溯
chronological file 流水文件
chronological order 年月日次序
chronological set order 时序的系序
chronometric data 计时数据
CHRP(Common Hardware Reference Platform) 公共硬件参考平台
chrysanthemum flower disc console typewrite 菊花盘型控制台打印机
chsize 改变文件长度函数
chunk 块,信息块
chunk size 信息块长度
chunking 程序分块
Church-Turing thesis 丘奇-图灵论题
Church's thesis 丘奇论题
churning 颠簸
CIA(Communication Interface Adapter) 通信接口适配器
CIA(Computer Industry Association) 计算机工业协会
CICS(Customer Information Communication System) 客户信息通信系统
CICS(Customer Information Control System) 客户信息控制系统(IBM)
CICS/2(CICS for OS/2) OS/2操作系统中的客户信息控制系统(IBM)
CICS/400(CICS for OS/400) OS/400操作系统中的客户信息控制系统(IBM)
CICS/6000(CICS for AIX) AIX操作系统中的客户信息控制系统(IBM)
CICS/ESA(CICS for ESA) ESA操作系统中的客户信息控制系统(IBM)
CICS/ISC(CICS/Inter System Communications) 客户信息控制系统的系统间通信软件包(IBM)
CICS/MVS(CICS for MVS) MVS操作系统中的客户信息控制系统(IBM)
CICS/OLTD(CICS/OnLine Test and Debugger) 客户信息控制系统的联机测试与查错软件(IBM)
CICS/VM(CICS for VM) VM操作

系统中的客户信息控制系统(IBM)
CICS/VS(CICS/Virtual Storage) 带虚拟存储的客户信息控制系统(IBM)
CICS/VSE(CICS for VSE) VSE操作系统中的客户信息控制系统(IBM)
CICSPARS(CICS Performance Analysis Reporting System) 客户信息控制系统性能分析报告系统(IBM)
CID(Communication IDentifier) 通信标识符
CIF(Central Index File) 中央索引文件
CIF(Central Information File) 中央信息文件
CIF(Common Interchange Format) 公共交换格式
CIF(Common Intermediate Form) 通用中间格式
CIF(Common source Intermediate Format) 通用源中间格式
CIF(Customer Information File) 客户信息文件
cifax 密码传真
CIH(Chen Ing Hao) CIH病毒(台湾省陈盈豪编写,危害极大)
CIM(Computer Input from Microfilm) 计算机缩微胶片输入
CIM(Computer Integrated Manufacture) 计算机集成制造商
CIM(Continuous Image Microfilm) 连续影像缩微胶卷
CIMS(Computer Integrated Manufacturing System) 计算机集成制造系统
cinching 松带,磁带松折
Cincom advanced software engineering environment Cincom高级软件工程环境
Cincom advanced software programmed environment Cincom高级软件编程环境
CINT function 取整函数
CINTEL (Computer INterface for TELevision) 计算机电视接口
CIO(Chief Information Officer) 信息主管
CIO(Clear I/O) 清除输入/输出
CIP(Communications Interrupt Program) 通信中断程序
CIP(Console Interface Program) 控制台接口程序
cipher 密码
cipher algorithm 密码算法
cipher attack 密码攻击
cipher block chaining 密码组链接
cipher feedback mode 密码反馈方式
cipher mask 密码隐蔽
cipher message 密码电文
cipher system 密码体制
cipher telegram 密码电报
cipher text 密文
ciphergraph 密码技术
ciphertext-only attack 仅知密文攻击
ciphony 密码电话学
CIR(Committed Information Rate) 承诺信息速率
CIR(Current Instruction Register) 当前指令寄存器
circle 圆,圈
circle function 画圆函数
circle of buffer 环形缓冲区
circuit 电路,线路
circuit alarm 线路报警
circuit analysis 电路分析
circuit analyzer 电路分析器
circuit array 电路阵列
circuit board 电路板
circuit breaker 断路器
circuit CAD 电路的计算机辅助设计
circuit capacity 电路容量
circuit code 线路码
circuit complexity 电路复杂性
circuit connector 电路连接器
circuit constant 电路常数
circuit description table 电路描述表
circuit design 电路设计
circuit diagram 电路图
circuit dropout 线路失灵
circuit element 电路元件
circuit equation 电路方程
circuit grade 电路等级
circuit interface protocol 线路接口协议
circuit kit 成套电路
circuit layout record card 电路版图记录卡
circuit level gateway 电路级网关

circuit level simulation 电路级仿真
circuit limiter 电路限幅器
circuit load 电路负载
circuit malfunction 电路失效
circuit matrix 电路矩阵
circuit media 电路媒体
circuit model 电路模型
circuit noise 电路噪声
circuit noise level 电路噪声电平
circuit optimization 电路优化
circuit parameter 电路参数
circuit protection 电路保护
circuit quality control 电路质量控制
circuit simulation 电路仿真
circuit switch 电路交换　　　「接
circuit switch connection 电路交换连
circuit-switched network 电路交换网
circuit switching 电路交换　　└络
circuit switching center 电路交换中心
circuit switching delays 电路交换延迟
circuit switching scheme 电路交换方
circuit testing 电路测试　　　└案
circuit theory 电路理论
circuit tracing machine 电路寻迹机
circuit usage 电路利用率
circuit wait 循环等待
circuit yield 电路成品率[合格率]
circuitry 整机电路;电路元件
circuitry layer 电路层
circulant matrix 循环矩阵
circulant matrix eigenvalue 循环矩阵特征值
circular autoregression 环形自动回归
circular buffering 环形[循环]缓冲
circular convolution 环形[循环]卷积
circular correlation 循环相关
circular definition 循环[环形]定义
circular execution pipeline 循环执行流水线
circular export 循环导出
circular file 环形文件
circular frequency 圆周频率
circular import 循环导入
circular linkage 环形链接
circular list 循环列表
circular orbit 圆形轨道
circular pipeline 循环流水线
circular r-permutation 圆排列

circular r-permutation of a set 集合的r圆排列
circular reference 循环引用
circular scan 圆形扫描
circular shift 循环移位
circular shifting 圆周移位　　「器
circular shift register 循环移位寄存
circular slide knob 循环滑动钮
circular systolic algorithm 循环脉动算法
circular wait 循环等待
circulating memory 环形存储器
circulation 环流;流通
circulation A/D converter 循环模/数转换器
circulation code 循环码　　　　「统
circulation control system 流通管理系
circulation frequency of Chinese character 汉字流通频度
circulation frequency of the data classification 分类流通频度
circulation time 循环[周转]时间
circum-earth orbit (卫星)环地轨道
circumcircle 外接圆
circumference 圆周,周界
circumscribed cone 外切圆锥
circumscribed rectangular coding 限定矩形编码方式
circumscribing 限定;外接,外切
circumscription 限定论
circumscription reasoning 限定推理
circumstance 情况,环境;事件
circumvention 绕过
CIS(Coded Image Space) 图像编码空间
CIS(Compressed Image Sequence) 压缩图像序列
CIS(Customer Information System) 客户信息
CISC(Complex Instruction Set Computer) 复杂指令系统计算机
Cisco AccessPro PC Card AccessPro PC 接口卡
Cisco LAN 2 LAN 网到网连接器
Cisco Router Cisco 路由器
Cisco Systems, Inc. 思科系统公司 (网络产品)
CiscoFusion CiscoFusion 体系结构

CIT(Cambridge Information Technology) 剑桥信息技术
citation 引文;引证
citation analysis 引证分析
citation index 引用索引
citation network 引用网络
citing statement 引用语句
citizens band 民用(无线电)波段
city block distance 城市街区距离
CIU(Central Interface Unit) 中央接口单元
CIU(Channel Interface Unit) 通道接口单元
CIU(Communication Interface Unit) 通信接口单元
CIV(Component Information View) 部件信息查询工具
CKD(Components Knock Down) 小散件
CKW(ClocKWise) 顺时针方向
CL(CLear) 清除
CL(Closed Loop) 闭环
CL/1 (Connectivity Language/1) CL/1 语言
CL environment variable 编译器/链接器环境变量
clad 包层
cladding 敷层,包层
claim device 请求设备
claim graph 要求图
claimed accuracy 要求的[规定的]精确度
clam 夹具
clamp 箝位;夹子
clamp force 夹紧力
clamp-on 预估,待接
clamper 箝位电路
clamping diode 箝位二极管
clamping ring 定位环
CLARiiON CLARiiON 磁盘阵列(DG)
Clarion Clarion 工具程序
Clarion professional developer Clarion 专业开发程序
Claris CAD Claris 计算机辅助设计软件
Claris Corp. Claris 公司
clarity 明确性
Clark-Wilson model 克拉克-沃森模型

clash 冲突;对撞
clasp 夹紧;铆固
class 类
class A amplifier A类[甲类]放大器
class AB amplifier AB类[甲乙类]放大器
Class A certification A级保证
class B amplifier B类[乙类]放大器
Class B certification B级保证
class C amplifier C类[丙类]放大器
class declaration 类声明
class definition 类别定义
Class Designer 类设计器
Class Developer 类开发者
class discrimination 类区分
class dispatch proxy 类分派代理
Class Extension 类扩充
class factory 类生成对象
class function 类属函数
class generation 类生成
class hierarchy 类层次
class hypothesis 类假设
class identifier 类标识符
class interrupt 类中断
class interval 分类间隔
class library 类库
class lock 类别锁
class member 类成员
class method 类方法
class name 类别名
class NP of problem NP问题类
class number 分类号
class object 类对象
class of channel 通道类型,信道种类
class of service(COS) 服务级
class of vector processor 向量处理机分类
class owner 类拥有者
class P P类
class P of problem P问题类
class probability 分类概率,类别概率
class procedure 类属过程
class restrictions 类限制
class scope 类作用范围
class tree 类树
class variable 类变量
class vector 类别向量
class view 类视图

class wrapping 分类包装
classical approach 经典分析法
classical automaton 经典自动机
classical control theory 经典控制理论
classical Jacobi method 经典雅克比法
classical normalization 经典规范化
classical solution 经典解法
classical syntax 经典语法
classification code 区分码,分类码
classification declaration 分类声明[说明]
classification image 分类映像[影像]
classification of automata 自动机分类
classification rule 分类规则
classification tree induction 分类树归纳
classify 分类
classing engine 分类引擎
classless interdomain routing 无级域间寻径
classroom information system (CIS) 课堂信息系统
ClassWizard file 类向导文件
clause 子句
clause body 子句体
clause form 子句形式
clause pool 子句池
clause predicate 子句谓词
clause set 子句集
clause train 子句序列
claw 爪
claw clutch 爪形离合器
clavier 键盘
CLC (CLear Carry) 清除进位
clean boot 清除引导
clean compiling 清晰[成功]编译
clean copy 原始副本
clean install 干净安装,初始安装
clean out (CO) 清除
clean proof 清样
clean room 超净室[工作间]
clean room apparel 洁净室服装
clean stop 完全停机
clean surface 清洁表面
clean-up 清除
clean-up code 清理代码
clean-up database 清除数据库
clean-up time 清理时间
cleaning 清洗

cleaning device 清洗设备
cleaning disc 清洁光盘
cleaning disk 清洁盘
cleaning diskette 清洁盘
cleaning-up 清除
cleanup code 清除代码
clear 清除
clear 87 清除浮点状态字函数
clear accumulator 清除累加器,累加器清0
clear all 全部清除
clear area 干净区;清除区
clear band 干净带,空白区
Clear Both 清除数据及格式
clear box 空白盒,空白箱
clear breakpoints 清除断点
clear carry (CLC) 清除进位
clear clipboard 清除剪贴板
clear collision 清除冲突
clear condition 清除条件[组
clear confirmation packet 清除确认分
clear confirmation signal 拆线确认信
clear cryptographic key 解密密钥[号
clear display 清除显示
clear entry (CE) 清除输入
clear entry function 清除进行[清除输入]功能
clear flag 清除标志
clear-forward signal 前向清除信号
clear indication packet 清除指示分组
clear indicator 清除指示器
clear input 清除输入
clear key 消除键
clear list 清除表
clear memory 清除存储
clear memory key 清除记忆键
clear message 拆线消息
Clear Outline 清除分级显示
clear output 清除输出
clear page 清页
clear prompt 清除提示符
clear pulse 清除脉冲
clear request (CLR) 拆线[清除]请求
clear request packet 清除请求分组
clear recipients 清除接收者
clear screen (CLS) 清除屏幕
clear session 明码对话
clear stop 完全停机

clear-store instruction 清除存储指令
clear switch 清除开关
clear tape 清洗带
clear text 明码通信报文
clear to send(CTS,CS) 清除发送
clear zone 静区,空白引导区
Clearable Warnings 可清除警告
clearance 权限,许可证
clearance check 权限检查,许可证检验
cleardevice 清除图形屏幕函数
clearerr 复位错误标志函数
clearing 拆线
clearing field 清除字段
clearing interrupt 清除中断
clearing signal 清除[拆线]信号
clearing time 清除时间;通信联络断开时间
clearviewport function 清除当前视区函数
CLF(Cross-Link Files) 交叉链接文件
CLI(Call Level Interface) 调用层接口
CLI(Command Language Interpreter) 命令语言解释程序
CLI(Command Line Interpreter) 命令行解释程序
click 单击,点击
Click and Drags 点击并拖动
Click to Activate 单击激活
clickable Image 可点击图像
client 客户,客户机
client application 客户机应用程序
client area 客户区
client-based application 基于客户机的应用程序
client certificate 客户端证明,客户证书
client component 客户组件
client computer fails 客户计算机失效
client connection 客户端连接
client coordinates 客户坐标
client development tools 客户开发工具
client document item 客户端文档项目
client event handler 客户事件处理程序
client extension development option 客户机扩展开发选项
client failure 客户端失效;客户机故障
client hello 客户端问候

client initialization 客户机初始化
client installation option 客户端安装选项
client item 客户项
client key exchange 客户端密钥交换
Client Licensing Mode 客户授权模式
Client Naming Responsibilities 客户端命名要求
client notification status 客户端通知状态
client object 客户对象
client object reference 客户端对象引用
client poke request 客户端发送请求
client process 客户进程
client query 客户查询
client rectangle (窗口中的)客户区
client script 客户机脚本
client-server application developiemt environment 客户机/服务器应用程序开发环境
client/server architecture 客户机/服务器结构
client/server computing 客户/服务器计算
client-server network 客户机/服务器式网络
client-server open developiemt environment 客户机/服务器开放开发环境
Client-Server Paracdligm 客户/服务器模式
client/server protocol 客户机/服务器协议
client/server structure 客户/服务器结构
client/server system(css) 客户/服务器系统
client-side 客户端
client-side execution 客户端执行
client-side image maps 客户端映像布局
client site 客户站点
client stub 客户机占位程序
client tier 客户层级
climbing generalization tree rule 广义爬树规则
clinical chart processing system 病历表处理系统
clip 接线柱,线夹

clip art 剪贴画,剪辑图,插图
clip boundary 剪裁边界,限幅边界
clip connection 卡夹连接
clip gallery 图片库
clip list 剪贴图列表
clip mask 剪贴块屏蔽
clip path 剪裁路径
clip software package 软件包
clipart 剪贴图
clipboard 剪贴板
clipboard computer 剪贴板计算机
clipboard format 剪贴板格式
clipboard owner 剪贴板拥有者
clipboard viewer 剪贴板浏览程序
clipboard-viewer chain 剪贴板浏览程序链
clipbook 剪贴簿
Clipper Clipper 编译程序
clipper 限幅器
clipping 裁剪
clipping algorithm 裁剪算法
clipping divider 裁剪划分器
clipping hardware 裁剪硬件
clipping path 裁剪路径
clipping plane 剪切面,剖面
clipping precision 裁剪精度
clipping region 裁剪区域
clique of a hypergraph 超图的集团
clique tree 团树
CLK(CLoCK) 时钟
CLNP(ConnectionLess Network Protocol) 无连接网络协议
CLNS(ConnectionLess-mode Network Service) 无连接模式网络服务
cloak 伪装;遮蔽
cloak initialization variable 遮蔽初始化变量
cloaked project 被遮蔽工程
clock(CLK) 时钟;时钟脉冲 「板
clock/calendar board 时钟/日历电路
clock control system 时钟控制系统
clock counter 时钟计数器
clock cycle 时钟周期
clock cycle losses 时钟周期丢失
clock damage 时钟破坏
clock double 时钟加倍
clock driver 时钟驱动
clock frequency 时钟频率

clock generator 时钟发生器
clock in 时钟引入
clock interrupt 时钟中断
clock out 时钟输出
clock period 时钟周期
clock phase 时钟相位
clock pulse 时钟脉冲
clock pulse interval 时钟脉冲间隔
clock rate 时钟速率
clock rate testing 时标速率测试
clock recovery 时钟恢复
clock register 时钟寄存器
clock repetition rate 时钟重复率
clock scheduling 计时调度
clock signal generator 时钟信号产生器
clock skew 时钟相差
clock source 时钟源
clock speed 时钟速率
clock tick 时钟周期
clock timing 时钟计时,时钟定时
clock track 时钟轨,时标道
clock tripled 时钟三倍频
clock window 时钟窗口
clocked logic 定时逻辑电路
clocked signals 计时信号
clocking 定时,计时
clocking fault 时钟信号故障
clockless 无时钟脉冲,无节拍
clockwise(CW) 顺时针方向
clone 仿制机,兼容产品;"克隆"
clone device 克隆设备
clone tool 克隆工具(形成数据无损压缩备份的工具软件)
cloneable 可"克隆"的
CLOS(Common LISP Object System) 公共 LISP 对象系统
close 关闭
Close All 全关闭
close button 关闭按钮
close-coupled network 紧耦合网络
close-cycle control 闭环控制
close-down 停机
close file 关闭文件
close fork 关闭分支
close function 关闭文件句柄函数
close keyboard command 关闭键盘命令
close loop system 闭环系统
close primitive 闭型原语

close program 闭型程序
close socket 关闭套接字
close system call 闭系统呼叫
closed architecture 封闭式体系结构
closed array 闭数组,闭阵列
closed bus system 封闭式总线系统
closed circuit 闭路
closed circuit communication system 闭路通信系统
closed circuit signaling 闭路信号方式
closed circuit TV 闭路电视
closed convex hull 闭凸包
closed convex set 闭凸集
closed default 封闭默认
closed domain 闭域
closed file 关闭的文件
closed flow network 闭型流动网络
closed inference 闭式推理
closed instruction loop 闭指令循环
closed interval 闭区间
closed line 闭合线
closed loop 闭环,闭循环
closed-loop bandwidth 闭环带宽
closed loop control system 闭环控制系统
closed loop instruction 封闭循环指令
closed loop program 闭环程序
closed neighborhood 闭邻域
closed network 闭网络;关闭的网络
closed node 关闭的节点
closed polygon 封闭多边形
closed procedure 封闭过程
closed property 封闭特性
closed routine 封闭例程
closed segment function 封闭线段功
closed semantic tree 封闭语义树
closed shop 封闭式计算站
closed subroutine 封闭子例程
closed system 封闭式系统
closed user group 封闭用户群
closed world 封闭世界
closed world assumption 闭世界假设
closegraph 关闭图形系统
closeness relation 密切关系
closing dialog box 关闭对话框
closing file 关闭文件
closing output file 关闭输出文件
closing view 关闭视图

closing workspace 关闭工作区
closure 闭包
closure alert 关闭报警
closure line 封闭线
closure property 闭包性质
cloth ribbon 布质色带
cloud 云
CLP(Cell Loss Priority) 信元丢失优先权
CLP(Communication Line Processor) 通信线路处理机
CLP(Current Line Pointer) 当前行指针
CLPT language (Computer Language for the Processing of Text) 文本处理计算机语言,CLPT语言
CLR(CLeaR) 清除,消零
CLS(CLear Screen) 清屏幕
CLSID(Class Identifier) 类标识符
CLT(Color Look-up Table) 颜色查看表
CLTP(ConnectionLess Transport Protocol) 无连接传输协议
CLU language CLU语言
clue 线索
clump 丛
clumping 聚丛
cluster 群集器;丛集,簇
Cluster Administrator 群集管理程序
cluster agent 集群代理
cluster analysis 集群分析,聚类分析
cluster assignment function 群赋值函数,聚类指定函数
cluster automation server 集群自动化服务器
cluster-aware client 集群感知客户机
cluster-based naming 基于聚类的命名法
cluster center 聚类中心
cluster command register 群集命令寄存器
cluster computing 群集计算
cluster-connected architecture 群集连接体系结构
cluster connected topology 群集连接拓扑
cluster control codes 群集控制码
cluster control unit 群集控制单元

cluster controller 群集控制器
cluster controller node(CCN) 群集控制器节点
cluster data 聚类数据
cluster entry 从集项目;簇表目
cluster function 群集功能
cluster identification 聚合识别
cluster management application 群集管理应用程序
cluster member 集群成员
cluster network 群集网络
cluster node control 群集节点控制
cluster number 簇号
cluster object 群集对象
cluster-oriented system 面向群集的系统
cluster recovery 簇恢复
cluster resource 群集资源
cluster resource type wizard 聚类资源类型向导
cluster seed 聚类种子
cluster server application 群集服务器应用程序
cluster shape 聚类形态
cluster system 聚类系统;群集系统
cluster-unaware client 集群非感知客户机
clustered file 聚类文件,分类归并文件
clustered index 聚类索引
clustered insertion 成群插入
clustered property 聚类属性
clustered insertion 成群插入
clustering 聚类,分类归并,群集
clustering algorithm 丛集算法,聚类算法
clustering file 聚类文件
clustering index 聚类索引
clustering procedure 聚类过程
clustering shape 聚类形态
clustering technique 聚类技术
clustering tendency 聚类趋向
CLUT(Color Look-Up Table) 颜色查看表
clutch 离合器
CLV(Constant Linear Velocity) 恒定线速度
CM(Concurrent Management) 并行管理
cm(centimeter) 厘米,公分

CMC(Computer Multimedia Communication) 计算机多媒体通信
CMF(Creative Music File) Creative 音乐文件
CMI(Computer Management Instruction) 计算机管理教学
CMIP(Common Management Information Protocol) 公共管理信息协议
CMIS(Common Management Information Services) 公共管理信息服务
CMM (Capability Maturity Model) 能力成熟度模型
CMOS(Complement Metal Oxide Semiconductor) 互补金属氧化物半导体
CMOS gate CMOS门
CMOS memory CMOS存储器
CMOS microprocessor CMOS微处理机
CMOS noise immunity CMOS抗扰度
CMOT(CMIP over TCP/IP) TCP/IP协议网络上的公共管理信息协议
CMS(Conversational Monitor System) 会话式监督系统
CMS batch facility CMS批处理设施
CMS nucleus CMS核心程序
CMS ready message CMS就绪消息
CMX(Customer MultipleXer) 客户多路转换器
CMY color model CMY(青、品红、黄)彩色模型
CMYK(Cyan Magenta Yellow blacK) CMYK(青、品红、黄、黑)模型
CNA(Communications Network Architecture) 通信网络结构
CNC(Communications Network Controller) 通信网络控制器
CNC(Computer Numerical Control) 计算机数值控制
CNF(Chomsky Normal Form) 乔姆斯基范式
CNC(Communications Network Management) 通信网络管理
CNIC(Computer Network Information Center) 计算机网络信息中心
CNP(Communications Network Processor) 通信网络处理机
co-agent case 辅助主动者角色
co-channel 共通道,同波道

co-channel interference 同波道干扰
co-NP problem NP补问题
co-processor operation 协处理器操作
co-resident 同时驻留
co-state vector 共状态向量
coagent 伙伴
coalesce 合并
coalition 联合
coarse adjustment 粗调
coarse control 粗控制
coarse grain 粗粒度
coarse grain task 粗粒度计算任务
coarse grained 粗粒度的
coarse grained parallel computer 粗粒度并行计算机
coarse grained system 粗粒度系统
coarse index 粗索引
coarse knowledge 粗略知识
coarse positioning 粗定位
coarse synchronization 粗同步
coarse tuning 粗调谐
coarseness 粗糙度
coarticulation 协同发音
coated fiber 涂复光纤
coated wire 被覆线
coating 涂覆,涂层
coaxial cable 同轴电缆
coaxial-cable carrier communication system 同轴电缆载波通信系统
coaxial cable information system(CCIS) 同轴电缆信息传输系统
coaxial cable interface 同轴电缆接口
coaxial connector 同轴线接插件
coaxial eccentricity 同轴离心
coaxial line 同轴线
coaxial pair 同轴对电缆
cobegin 同时开始
COBOL (Common Business-Oriented Language) COBOL语言,面向商业的通用语言
COBOL construction COBOL结构
COBOL language COBOL语言,通用商业语言
COBOL procedure division COBOL过程部
COBOL standard COBOL标准
cobs 钟形失真
cochannel 同波道,同信道

cochannel interference 同信道干扰
Cocke-Younger-Kasami algorithm CYK算法
CODASYL (Conference On Data SYstems Languages) 数据系统语言会议
CODASYL set CODASYL系
code 码,代码,编码
code audit 代码审计
code bit 代位,码元
code block 码组,代码块
code book 码本
code capacity 编码容量
code center value 码中心值
code check 编码校对,代码检验
CODE clause 编码子句
code color 编码颜色
code combination 编码组合
code comment option 代码注释选项
code compression 代码压缩
code conversion 代码转换
code converter 代码转换器
code data 代码数据
code-dependent system 代码相关系统
code device 编码器
code discriminator 鉴码器
code distance 代码距离
code distinguishability 编码分辨能力
code distortion 符号畸变[失真]
code division 码分割
code editor 代码编辑器
code editor window 代码编辑器窗口
code efficiency 编码效率
code element 码元
code error 代码错误
code extension 代码扩充
code extension character 代码扩充字符
code fetch cycle 取码周期
code file 代码文件
code format 代码格式
code generation 代码生成
code generation pass 代码生成遍
code generation tool 代码生成工具
code generator 代码生成器
code group 码组;密码字组
code image 代码图像
code image read 代码图像读出
code independent 独立于代码的

code independent data communication 代码独立的数据通信
code independent transmission procedure 码独立传输法
code information 代码信息
code insensitive system 代码不敏感系统
code inspection 代码审查
code inspection and walkthrough 码审查与走查
code interpreter 代码解释程序
code key 代码键
code length 代码长度,码长
code level 代码阶
code line 代码行
code list 码本,码表
code modulation 代码调制
code names dictionary(CND) 代码词典
code number 代码数字系统
code of times 时间代码
code optimization 代码优化
code page 代码页
code pattern 码型
code pattern converter 码型变换器
code polynomial 代码多项式
code position 代码位置
code property 代码属性
code rate 代码率
code reader 代码读出器
code receiver(CR) 代码接收机
code recognition system 代码识别系统
code redundancy 代码冗余度
code regenerator 代码再生器
code register 代码寄存器
code reuse 代码重用
code rewriting 代码重写
code rule 代码规则
code segment 代码段,程序段
code selector 选码器
code sender 发码器
code sequence 代码序列
code set 码集
code snippet (描述对象事件过程的)代码片断
code track 代码轨
code transform 代码变换
code transparent data communication 码透明数据通信
code transparent system 码透明系统

code value 码值
code vector 码向量
code violation 代码违例
code violation pattern 违例编码模式
code walk-through 码审查,码走查
code weight 码权重,码重
code wheel 码盘,码轮
code wheel type angular-digital converter 码盘式角度数字转换器
code wide 码宽
code window 代码窗口
code word(CW) 码字
code word dictionary 码字词典
code word synchronization 码字同步
codeblock 码组
codebuilder 编码程序
CODEC(COder/DECoder) 编解码器
codec 编码译码器,编解码器
coded automatic gain control 编码式自动增益控制
coded character 编码字符
coded character set 编码字符集
coded data conversion 编码数据转换
coded data decoder 编码数据译码器
coded decimal 编码的十进制数
coded decimal number 编码的十进位
coded-dependent system 代码相关系统
coded directing character 代码引导字符
coded disc 编码盘
coded font 编码字型[字体]
coded format 编码格式
coded graphics 编码图形
coded identification 编码识别
coded image 编码图像
coded-light identification 编码光辨别
coded mark inversion(CMI) 编码传号反转
coded message 编码消息
coded point 编码点
coded program 编码程序,上机程序
coded representation 编码表示法
coded ringing 编码铃声
coded string 编码字符串
coded word 码字
codeless input system 无编码输入系统
coden 期刊代码
coder 编码器;编码员

codeterministic system 共确定系统
Codeview （汇编语言）符号调试程序
coding 编码
coding cam 编码凸轮
coding circuit 编码电路
coding clerk 编码员
coding component 编码元素
coding delay 编码延时
coding efficiency 编码效率
coding form 编码纸
coding keyboard 编码键盘
coding line 编码行
coding optimum 编码优化
coding paper 编码纸
coding rule 编码规则
coding scheme 编码法,编码方案
coding sheet 程序纸,编码纸
coding style 编码风格
coding tool 编码工具
coefficient 系数,因数
coefficient matrix 系数矩阵
coefficient multiplier 系数乘法器
coefficient of correlation 相关系数
coefficient of determination 确定系数
coefficient of expansion 展开系数
coefficient quantization error 系数量化误差
coefficient scale 比例因子
coend 同时结束
coerced 强制
coercend 强制子句
coercion 强制
coercion operator 强制算符
coercive field 矫顽场
coercive force 矫顽力
Coex Coex 群软件
coexist 共存
COFF(Common Object File Format) 通用目标文件格式
coffee house 咖啡屋,网上聊天室
cognition 认知
cognition time 认知时间
cognitive modeling 认知模型
cognitive psychology 认知心理学
cognitive science 认知科学
cognitive simulation 认知仿真
cognitive system 认知系统
COGO (COordinated GeOmetry) 坐标几何语言
Cohen-Sutherland algorithm 科恩-苏特兰算法
coherence 相关性;相干性
coherence factor 相干因子
coherence function 相干函数
coherent 相关性,相干性
coherent bundle 相关光纤束,定位光纤束
coherent carrier recover 相干载波恢复
coherent detection 相干检波
coherent light 相干光
coherent network 相干网络
coherent optical communication 相干光通信
coherent phase-shift keying (CPSK) 相关相移键控
coherent rotation 一致转动,相关转动
coherent signals 相干信号
cohesion 内聚
cohesion of module 模块的内聚度
coil 线圈,绕组
coil tab 线圈抽头
coin-changing problem 找硬币问题
coin-flipping 抛硬币法
coincide 重合,符合,一致
coincidence 一致,符合
coincidence counter 符合计数器
coincidence decoding 重合译码
coincidence error 重合误差
coincidence gate (CG) 符合门,关
coincidence matrix switch 重合矩阵开关
coincidence selection 重合选择
coincident code 重码
coincident drive system 重合驱动系统
coincidental cohesion 偶然内聚,巧合内聚
coincidental strength 巧合强度
COL(COLumn) 列
cold boot 冷自举,冷引导
cold cathode 冷阴极
cold circuit 冷电路
cold fault 冷故障
cold joint 虚焊,冷焊
cold link 冷链接
cold restart 冷启动
cold site 冷站;冷网点
cold solder joint 虚焊接

cold start 冷启动
cold type 冷排版
collaboration laboratory 合作实验室
collaborative document production 协作文档产品
collapse 收缩;折叠
Collapse Branch 收缩分支
collapse field 缩灭场
collapsible outline 可折叠[收缩]大纲
collapsing FIND 缩减 FIND 操作
collar 套环;卡圈;凸缘
collar bush 轴环衬套
collate 对并,整理,排序
Collate Copies 自动分页
collate program 整理程序,检验程序
collateral-clause 并列子句
collateral elaboration 并行加工
collating sequence 整理顺序
collating sort 整理分类
collation 整理,排序,检验
collation operation 整理操作
collation pass 整理遍
collection 集合,收集
collection class 集合类
collection object 集合对象
collection of garbage 无用单元收集,废料收集
collection of mathematical function 数学函数集
collection of node 节点集
collection of record 记录集,记录群
collection of related data record 有关数据记录集
collection property 集合属性
collection shapes 集合形
collection station 收集站,采集站
collective language 汇集型语言
collective random sequence 聚合随机函数
collector 集电极
collector node 收集节点
collector region 集极区
collector saturation resistance 集电极饱和电阻
collector saturation voltage 集电极饱和电压
collide 碰撞,冲突
colliding data 碰撞数据

colliding packet 碰撞信包
colliding station 冲突站
collimated light 准直光
collimation 准直,对准,平行校正
collimator 准直仪
collinear 共线
collinearity 共线性
collision 冲突,碰撞
collision avoidance 冲突回避[避免]
collision condition 冲突条件
collision count 冲突计数
collision count field 冲突计数域
collision detect 碰撞侦测,冲突检测
collision domain 冲突域
collision enforcement 冲突强化
collision-free multi-access 无冲突多路存取
collision rate 冲突率
collision-resolution technique 冲突排解技术
collision vector 碰撞向量
collision window 碰撞[冲突]窗口
collocation 搭配
collocation dictionary 搭配词典
collocation method 配置法
Colmerauer grammar 科莫劳尔文法
colon 冒号
colon alignment tab 冒号对齐制表符
colon classification 冒号分类法
colon descriptor 冒号描述符
colon edit descriptor 冒号编辑描述符
colon editing 冒号编辑
colophon （印在书上的）出版者商标
colophony 松香,树脂
color 彩色,色彩
color-bar 彩条
color-bar generator 彩条发生器
color-bar test pattern 彩条测试图形
color bit 色彩位
color burst 彩色副载波群;色码组
color calibration 色彩校正
color cast 色投射
color cell 着色单元
color channel 颜色通道 「器
color character display 彩色字符显示
color coat 彩色涂层(技术)(Tektronix)
color code 色码,彩色码

color cycling 彩色循环
color decoder 彩色解码器
color density slicing 彩色密度分割
color depth 色深度
color difference signal 色差信号
color difference signal driver 色差信号激励
color dilution 色冲淡
color display 彩色显示;彩色显示器
color encoder 彩色编码器
color enhancement 彩色增强
color field contamination 色场污染
color graphics adapter(CGA) 彩色图形适配器
color image 彩色图像
color image restoration 彩色图像恢复
color ink-jet printer 彩色喷墨打印机
color killer 彩色抑制器,消彩色电路
color laser printer 彩色激光打印机
color look-up table 查色表
color map animation 绘色动画
color mapping mechanism 彩色绘图机制
color model 彩色模型
color monitor 彩色监视器
color palette 调色板
Color Palette Toolbar 调色板工作条
color pattern 颜色模式
color picker 彩色拾取器
color primaries 基色,原色
color printer 彩色打印机
color profile 彩色配置文件
color purity 色纯
color purity allowance 色纯余量
color rendering intent 着色方案
color saturation 色饱和度
color scanner 彩色扫描仪
color scheme 颜色表
color separation 彩色分解,分色
color set 颜色集合
color similarity 颜色相近程度
color space 彩色空间
color strip 彩条
color table 彩色表
color tone 色调
color transformation 彩色变换
color triangle 色三角形
color value 颜色值

color wheel 色轮
colorability 可着色性
colorable 可着色的
colorant 着色剂
colorchart 色彩表
colored graph 着色图
colored noise 有色噪声
colored token 有色信标
colorimeter 色度计
colorimetry 色度学
coloring 着色,染色
coloring problem 着色问题
colors 色成分
Colossus 巨人机
colour 颜色,色彩(同 color)
column(CL,COL) 列;栏
column address strobe 列地址选通
column bar 竖条
Column Break 分栏符
Column Chart Autoformat 自动套用柱形图
column click event 列单击事件
column collections 列集合
column coordinate 列坐标
column count 列计算
column data 列数据
column decoder 列译码器
column delimiter 分栏符号
column differences 列内容差异
column dominance 以列为主的
column drive wire 列驱动线
column IV element 四价元素
column footer 列脚注
column format 列格式
column graph 直条图
column heading 栏标题
column input cell 按列输入单元格
column jump 列跳越
column major order 列主顺序
column matrix 列矩阵
column move 列移动
column number 列编号
column pitch 列距
column pivoting 列主元法
column printer 竖式打印机
column skip 列跳过
column split 栏分割
column sweep algorithm 列扫描算法

column vector 列向量
column width 栏宽
column-wise recalculation 列主重算
column wrap 列环绕
columnar structure 柱形结构
columnar transposition 列换位
columninch 列长
COM(COMmand) 命令
COM(COMmunication) 通信
COM(Component Object Model) 部件对象模型
COM file(COMmand file) 命令文件
COM port 通信端口
comb filter 梳状滤波器
comb structure 梳状结构
comb type dot matrix printer 梳状点阵打印机
combat game 格斗游戏
combination 组合
combination forbidden 禁用组合
combination hub 组合插座
combination logic circuit 组合逻辑电路
combination of a set 集合的组合
combination of automata 自动机组合
combination of key 关键字组合,键组合
combination switch 组合开关
combinational circuit 组合电路
combinational logic 组合逻辑
combinational logic circuit 组合逻辑电路
combinational logic element 组合逻辑元件
combinator reduction 组合子归约
combinatorial algorithm 组合算法
combinatorial compression 组合压缩
combinatorial explosion 组合爆炸
combinatorial search 组合搜索
combinatorial mathematics 组合数学
combinatorially implosive algorithm 组合爆炸算法
combinatorics 组合数学
combinatory explosion 组合爆炸
combined addressing path 组合寻址路径
combined attribute 组合属性
combined condition 组合条件
combined head 组合读写头
combined index 组合索引
combined logic function 组合逻辑函数
combined monitor 组合监视器
combined print and read 组合打印读出
combined programming 复合程序设计
combined radical character 合体字
combined read/write head 组合读/写磁头
combined station 复合站,组合站
combined strategy 组合策略
combined type digital voltmeter 复合式数字电压表
combining hardware with software 硬、软件结合
combo box 组合框
combo box builder 组合框构造器
combo box style 组合框样式
COMDAT record(COMmon block DATa record) 公用块数据记录
COMDEX(COMputer Dealers EXposition) 计算机销售博览会(1979年始于美国拉斯维加斯)
comic-strip oriented image 连环画式图像
comm port 公用端口
comma 逗号;千分位符
comma alignment tab 逗号对齐制表
comma delimited 逗号定界
comma-delimited file 逗号分隔的文件
comma-free code 无逗点码
Comma-Style 千分位格式
command(CMD,COM) 命令
command abbreviation 命令缩写
command aliasing 命令别名
command analyzer 命令分析程序
command bit 命令位
command block 命令块
command buffer 命令缓冲区
command button 命令按钮
command button group 命令按钮组
command capacity 命令容量,指令容量
command chained storage 命令链接存储
command chaining 命令链锁
command channel 命令通道
command character 命令字符
command code 命令码
command code group 命令码组
command coding scheme 命令编码方案

COMMAND.COM DOS命令文件
command confirmation 命令确认
command continual sending mode 命令连发模式
command continuation 命令延续
command control block(CCB) 命令控制块
command control program 命令控制程序
command decoder 命令译码器
command definition 命令定义
command definition statement 命令定义语句
command description file 命令描述文件
command description language 命令描述语言
command destruction 命令破坏
command display 命令显示
command display station 命令显示站
command-driven 命令驱动
command-driven program 命令驱动程序
command facility 命令设备
command field 命令栏,命令字段
command file 命令文件
command file application 命令文件应用
command file name 命令文件名
command format 命令格式
command frame 命令帧
command function key 命令功能键
command guidance 指令制导
command group 命令组
command handler 命令处理程序
command help 命令帮助信息
command identifier 命令标识符
command information(COIN) 命令信息
command input 命令输入
command input buffer(CIB) 命令输入缓冲区
command interface 命令界面,命令接口
command interpreter 命令解释程序
command key 命令键
command key indicator 命令键指示器
command language 命令语言
command language control 命令语言控制
command language interpreter 命令语言解释程序
command library 命令库

command line 命令行
command-line argument 命令行参数
command line interface 命令行界面
command line interpreter 命令行解释程序
command-line operating system 命令行操作系统
command-line parameter 命令行参数
command-line switch 命令行开关
command macro 命令宏
command message 命令消息
command menu 命令菜单
command mode 命令模式[状态]
command module 命令模块
command name 命令名称
command panel 命令画面
command phase 命令阶段
command pointer 命令指针
command procedure 命令过程
command processing 命令处理
command processor 命令处理程序
command program 命令程序
command prompt 命令提示符
command prompt window 命令提示窗口
command queuing 命令队列
command quick reference 命令快速引用
command readout 命令读出;命令显示
command reentry 命令重执行[重新进入]
command reference 命令引用
command register 命令寄存器
command rejection 命令拒绝
command remote control 命令遥控
command repetition rate 命令重复率
command response 命令回应
command retry 命令重执
command rollback 命令重新运行
command scan 命令扫描
command script 命令脚本
command shell 命令外壳(解释程序)
command signals 命令信号
command statement 命令语句
command status register 命令状态寄存器
command stream 命令流
command string 命令字符串
command structure 命令结构

command substitution 命令替代
command supporting wildcard 命令支援通配符
command syntax 命令语法
command system 命令系统
command time delay 命令时延
command transmit time out 命令传送超时
command verb 命令动词
commander module 主模块
Commandgroup Builder 命令组生成器
commendatory 褒义
comment 注解,注释
comment card 注释卡
comment code 说明码,注释码
comment column 注释栏
comment convention 注释约定
comment declaration 注释声明
comment delimiter 注释定界符
comment entry 注释项,注释体
comment field 注释字段
comment item 注释项
comment line 注释行
comment out 注释禁止,注释掉
comment phrase 注释短语
comment statement 注释语句
comment symbol 注释符号
comment syntax 注释语法
CommerceNet 商场网络
commercial communication 商用通信
commercial communication satellite 商用通信卫星
commercial computer 商用计算机
commercial environment 商用环境
commercial instruction set 商用指令集
commercial mix 商业混合比例计算法
commercial networks 商用网络
commercial software 商务软件
commercial speech recognizer 商品化的语音识别器
commercial system integration 商用系统集成
commit(CIR) 提交,委托;确认,承诺率
commit and termination protocol(CIR) 承诺与端接协议 改
Commit Changes Now(CIR) 立即更
commit-dependency(CIR) 承诺相关性
commit size 提交长度
commitment concurrency and recovery (CCR) 托付并发和恢复
commitment performance 支持性能
committed information rate(CIR) 承诺信息速率
committed page 提交页面
Commodore Business Machine, Inc. Commodore 商用机器公司
Commodore Dynamic Total Vision (CDTV) Commodore 动态视频系统
common access method 公共访问法
common agent technology 共用代理技术
common application repository and environment(CARE) 公共应用资源及环境
common application service element (CASE) 公共应用服务元素
common area 共用区
common assignment channel 公共分配通道
common block 公用块
common block list 公用块表
common block name 公用块名
common block table 公用块表
common buffer 公共缓冲区
common bus 公用总线
common bus multiprocessor 公用总线多处理器
common bus system 公用总线系统
Common Business Oriented Language (COBOL) COBOL 语言
common carrier 公用载波(公司)
Common Channel Interoffice Signaling (CCIS) 共路局间信令
common channel signaling 共路信令
common channel signaling system 共路信令系统
common collector amplifier 共集极放大器
common command language 通用命令语言
common communication adapter 公用通信适配器
common communication area 公用通

信区
common communication line 公共通信线路
common communications support(CCS) 通用通信支援
common computer software 公共计算机软件
common control connection 公共控制连接
Common Cryptographic Architecture (CCA) 通用密码体系结构
common coupling 公共耦合
common data area 公用数据区
common data base 公用数据库
common data bus 公用数据总线
common data network 公共数据网络
common data record 公用数据记录
common declaration 公共说明
common dialog box 公用对话框
common dialog library 公用对话库
common declaration statement 共用说明语句
common emitter amplifier 共发射极放大器
common-environment coupling 公共环境耦合
common error 公用错误
common event flags 公用事件标志
common expression 公用表达式
common extension set 公用扩充集
common field 公共域
common gateway interface(CGI) 通用网关界面,公共网关接口
common hub 公共插孔
common index 共用索引
common interface 公用接口
common interface language 公共接口语言
common interface software 公用接口软件
common library 公用库
COMMON LISP COMMON LISP 语言
common local optimization 公共局部优化
common logarithm 常用对数
Common Management Information Protocol(CMIP) 公共管理信息协议
common mask 公用掩码

common memory 公用内存
common memory information transfer 公用内存信息传送
common memory port 公用内存端口
common message buffer pool 公共消息缓冲池
common message call 公共消息调用
common mode 共模
common-mode characteristics 共模特性
common-mode gain 共模增益
common-mode input impedance 共模输入阻抗
common-mode interference 共模干扰
common mode noise 共模噪声
common-mode rejection 共模斥拒[抑制]
common-mode resistance 共模阻抗
common-mode voltage 共模电压
common-mode voltage amplification 共模电压放大
common network interface property 公共网络接口属性
common node property 公共节点属性
Common Object File Format(COFF) 通用对象文件格式(微软)
Common Object Model(COM) 通用对象模型
Common Object Request Broker Architecture(CORBA) 通用对象请求代理体系结构
Common Object Services Specification (COSS) 通用对象功能规范
common page 公共页,公用页面
common palette 公共调色板
common peripheral interface 公用外围接口
common pool 共用池
Common Request Broker Architecture (CRBA) 公共请求中介体系结构
common resource 共用资源
common resource type property 共用资源类型属性
common return 公共回线
common section 公用节
common segment 公用段
common segment bit 共用段位
common sense 常识
common-sense reasoning 常识性推理

common service area(CSA) 公共服务区
common software 通用软件,公用软件
COMMON statement 公用语句
common storage 公用存储区
common subexpression elimination 公用子表达式消除
common subroutine module 公用子例程模块
common source 公用源
common system area 公用系统区
Common User Access(CUA) 普通用户访问
common user network 公共用户网络
common-user service 公共用户服务
common variable 公共变量
common view 公共视图
common-write 共同写
CommServer (Communication Server) 通信服务程序
communality 公比,公因子方差
communicate with anyone 全球通讯
communicating module 通信模块
communicating protocol 通信协议
communicating terminal 通信终端机
communication 通信
communication access processor(CAP) 通信访问处理机
communication access method 通信访问法
communication adapter 通信适配器
communication among independent tasks 独立任务之间的通信
communication area 通信区
communication band 通信频带
communication barriers 通信障碍
communication-based system 基于通信的系统
communication buffer 通信缓冲器
communication bus 通信总线
communication cable 通信电缆
communication capacity 通信容量
communication card 通信卡
communication channel 通信通道
communication check 通信检验
communication circuit 通信线路
communication close 关闭通信
communication cohesion 通信内聚
communication computer 通信计算机
communication control center 通信控制中心
communication control character 通信控制字符
communication control devices 通信控制设备
communication control package 通信控制分组
communication control procedure 通信控制协议(规程)
communication control unit(CCU) 通信控制单元
communication controller 通信控制器
communication controller node 通信控制器节点
communication coprocessor 通信协处理器
communication deception 通信欺诈
communication description entry 通信描述项
communication description name 通信描述名
communication element 通信部件
communication emulator 通信模仿器
communication entity 通信实体
communication equipment 通信设备
communication hardware 通信硬件
communication-intensive task 通信密集任务
communication interface adapter 通信接口适配器
communication interface circuit 通信接口电路
communication interface module 通信接口模块
communication interrupt 通信中断
communication interrupt control program 通信中断控制程序
communication line adapter(CLA) 通信线路适配器
communication link 通信链接
communication linkage 通信链路
communication management 通信管理
communication management configuration 通信管理配置
communication management host 通信管理主机

communication management layer 通信管理层
Communication Manager/2 通信管理器/2(IBM)
communication mode 通信方式
communication model 通信模型
communication module 通信模块
communication monitor 通信监视器
communication multiplexer 通信多路器
communication network 通信网
communication network architecture (CNA) 通信网络体系结构
communication network management 通信网络管理
communication network management application 通信网络管理应用程序
communication network processor 通信网络处理机
communication of word processing 文字处理通信
communication-oriented computer 面向通信的计算机
communication overhead 通信开销
communication parameter 通信参数
communication parameter list 通信参数表
communication platform 通信平台
communication port 通信端口
communication preprocessor 通信预处理机
communication primitive 通信原语
communication processor 通信处理机
communication program 通信程序
communication protocol 通信协议
communication queue 通信队列
communication region 通信区
communication routing table 通信路由选择表
communication satellite 通信卫星
communication scanner 通信扫描器
communication security equipment 通信保密设备
communication server 通信服务器
communication software 通信软件
communication subnetwork 通信子网
communication subsystem 通信子系统
communication subsystem control 通信子系统控制
communication switching unit 通信转接单元,通信交换部件
communication system 通信系统
communication terminal 通信终端机
communication timer 通信记时器
communication with realistic sensation 临场感通信
communication within domain 域内通信
Communications Application Specification(CAS) 通信应用规范
communications circuit 通信线路
Communications Control Architecture (CCA) 通信控制体系结构
communications sans-connections (COSAC) 通信连接研究网络,COSAC网
Communications Server for AIX(CS/AIX) 用于AIX的通信服务器网(IBM)
Communications Terminal Protocol (CTERM) 通信终端协议
community antenna television 共用天线电视
community automatic exchange 公用自动交换机
community information system 公用信息系统
community name 团体名称
community view 共同视图
commutation 交换;换向;整流
commutative law 交换律
commutative matrix 可交换矩阵
commutative production system 可交换的产生式系统
commutative sequential executing order 可交换顺序执行次序
commutativity of disjunction 析取可交换性
commutativity of multiplication 乘法可交换性
commutator 整流子;换能器
commute 交换
commuting operator 交换算符
COMP(COMParator) 比较器
COMP(COMPlement) 补码,补数
comp 模拟排版
compact 紧缩,密集

compact cassette 小型盒式磁带
compact code 紧凑码,压缩码
compact compiler 简明编译程序
compact disc(CD) 压缩光盘,小型光盘
compact disc digital audio system(CD) 小型光盘数字音响系统
compact disc-read only memory (CD-ROM) 小型光盘只读存储器
compact executable file 紧凑可执行文件
Compact Flash 微型快擦写存储卡
compact Huffman code 压缩霍夫曼码
compact mode 压缩模式
compact set 紧致集
compact testing 压缩测试
compacting garbage collection 压缩无用信息收集
compaction algorithm 压缩算法
compaction pointer 紧缩指针
compactness theorem 紧致性定理
companding 压缩扩张
compandor 压缩扩张器
compandor communication equipment 压扩通信设备
companion keyboard 配套键盘
companion matrix 伴随矩阵
company networks 公司网络
Compaq Computer Corp. 康柏计算机公司
comparability 可比较性
comparand 比较字,比较数
comparative dumping 比较转储
comparator 比较器
comparator circuit 比较器电路
comparator sensitivity 比较器灵敏度
compare 比较
compare-exchange 比较交换
compare full word 全字比较
compare function 比较功能
compare instruction 比较指令
compare of strings 字符串比较
compare OK 比较无误
compare operation 比较运算
compare test 比较测试
compare zone equal 比较区相等
comparing 比较
comparing unit 比较单元
comparison coder 比较编码器
comparison curve 比较曲线
comparison definition 比较定义
comparison expression 比较表达式
comparison indicator 比较指示器
comparison key 比较键
comparison method 比较法
comparison network 比较器网络
comparison-of-pair sorting 成对比较排序
comparison operation 比较操作
comparison operator 比较操作符
comparison software 比较软件学
comparison test 比较测试
compartment 象限;隔间
compatibility 兼容性
compatibility design 兼容性设计
compatibility feature 兼容性特征
compatibility mode 兼容方式
compatibility of color television system 彩色电视制式的兼容特性
compatibility testing 兼容性测试
compatible 兼容的
compatible access mode 兼容存取方式
Compatible Communications Architecture(CCA) 兼容通信体系结构
compatible computer 兼容计算机
compatible crosspoints 互通交叉点
compatible hardware 兼容硬件
compatible integrated circuit 兼容集成电路
compatible microoperation 兼容性微操作
compatible monolithic integrated circuit 兼容单片集成电路
compatible operating system 兼容操作系统
compatible set of operation 兼容运算
compatible software 兼容软件
compatible storage 兼容存储
Compatible Time-Sharing System (CTSS) 兼容分时系统
compatible type 兼容类型
compatible with vector norm 向量范数的兼容性
compendium 一览表,摘要
compensating delay 补偿延迟
compensating error 补偿误差
compensating feedback 补偿反馈
compensation 补偿

compensation adjust 补偿调整
compensator 补偿器
competent 有竞争力的
competing interruption request 竞争中断请求
competing risk model 竞争冒险模型
competitive disposition(CIS) 竞争倾向
competitive equilibrium(CIS) 竞争均衡
competitive inhibition(CIS) 竞争抑制
competitive information system(CIS) 竞争信息系统
compilation 编译
compilation environment test 编译环境测试
compilation time 编译时间
compilation unit 编译单元
compile 编译
compile and go 编译并运行
compile and run time 编译和执行时间
compile directing statement 编译指示语句
compile duration 编译历时,编译时间
compile link and go 编译连接并运行
compile pass 编译遍
compile phase 编译阶段
compile script 编译脚本
compile step 编译步
compile time binding 编译时绑定
compile-time checking 编译时检验
compile time diagnostics 编译时诊断
compile-time error 编译时错误
compile time message 编译时消息
compile time switch 编译开关
compiled knowledge 编译知识
compiled resource file 编译源文件
compiler 编译程序
compiler-based development system 基于编译程序的开发系统
compiler-compiler 编译程序编译器
compiler control program 编译程序的控制程序
compiler cost 编译代价
compiler debugging 编译程序调试
compiler diagnostics 编译程序的诊断程序
compiler directive 编译程序指示

compiler dynamic test 编译程序动态测试
compiler function test 编译程序功能测试
compiler generator 编译程序的产生程序
compiler interface 编译程序接口
compiler language 编译语言
compiler library support 编译库支持
compiler limit 编译程序限制
compiler listing 编译程序列表
compiler of high level language 高级语言编译程序
compiler optimization 编译程序优化
compiler option 编译程序任选项
compiler rate 编译速率
compiler scanner 编译程序的扫描程序
compiler word 编译词
compiling computer 编译计算机
compiling cost 编译成本
compiling macro definition 编译宏定义
compiling phase 编译阶段
compiling program 编译程序
compiling routine 编译例程
compiling time 编译历时,编译时间
complement 补数,补码
complement adder 补码加法器
complement base 补码底数
complement form 补码形式
complement metal oxide semiconductor (CMOS) 互补金属氧化物半导体
complement notation 补码记数法,补码表示法
complement of set 集合的补集
complement on N-1 N-1 反码
complement on nine 对九的补码
complement on one 补数,对一的补码
complement on ten 对十的补码
complement procedure 求补过程
complement set 余集,补集
complement vector 补向量
complement with respect to 10 10 的补码
complemental code 补码
complementary 求补运算
complementary binary 补码二进制
complementary circuit 互补电路
complementary code 补码

complementary colors 补色
complementary constant current logic 互补恒流逻辑
complementary MOS integrated circuit (CMOS) 互补型 MOS 集成电路
complementary MOS memory 互补 MOS 存储器
complementary network 互补网络
complementary operation 互补运算，反演运算
complementary silicon on sapphire (CSOS) 互补硅蓝宝石(集成电路)
complementary operation 互补运算，反演运算
complete axiom system 完备公理系统
complete binary tree 完全二叉树，完备二叉树
complete carry 完全进位
complete chain 全字符串
complete coloring 完全着色
complete conductivity 全导电性
complete flow (信息)总流量
complete graph 完全图
complete group of connectives 完备联结词组
complete indexing 完备索引
Complete installation 完全安装
complete interconnection architecture 全互连体系结构
complete item 完全项
complete object 完全对象
complete operation 完整操作
complete overhaul 完全拆卸检修
complete problem 完全问题
complete program 完全程序
complete routine 完整例程
complete set 完全集合，全集
complete space 完备空间
complete system 完整系统
complete t-ary tree 完全t进树，完备t进树
complete ternary tree 完全三叉树
complete text 全文
completed state 完成状态
completely blank line 完全空白行
completely connected network 全连接网络
completely nest 完全嵌套
completely-reducible graph 完全可归约图
completeness 完整性；完备性
completeness error 完整性错误
completer 完成符
completion code 完成码
completion percentage 布通率
completion rate/percentage 完成率/百分比
completion signal 完成信号
completion status 完成状态
completion time 完成时间
complex attribute 复数属性
complex condition 复合条件
complex conjugate 复共轭 「数
complex constant 复数型常数，复常
complex data binding 复合数据绑定
complex data-bound component 复合数据绑定部件
complex domain 复合域
complex filter 复合过滤器
complex function 复函数
complex instruction set (CIS) 复杂指令系统
complex instruction set computer (CISC) 复杂指令系统计算机
complex mapping 复杂映像
complex number 复数
complex object model 复杂目标模型
complex plane 复平面
complex plexus structure 复杂丛结构
complex relocatable expression 复合可重定位表达式
complex scenes 复杂场景
complex sensors 复合传感器
complex signal 复信号
complex tone 复音
complex transfer function 复传送函数
complex type 复型
complex value 复值
complex variable 复变量
complexity 复杂性
complexity class 复杂性类
complexity function 复杂性函数
complexity index 复杂性指数 「法
complexity index method 复杂性指数
complexity measure 复杂性度量

complexity measure on a programming system 程序设计系统复杂性度量
complexity of a problem 问题的复杂性
complexity of algorithm 算法复杂性
complexity of computation 计算复杂性
complexity of expert system 专家系统的复杂性
complexity of object x 目标 x 的复杂性
complexity profile 复杂性指标
component 部件,元件,组成部分
component activation property 部件激活属性
component class 部件类
component color 基色,元色
component density 元件密度
component diagram view 部件方框视图
component error 组件错误;元件误差
component failure infect analysis (CFIA) 成分失效影响分析
component installation tab 部件安装标记
component lead 元件引线
component level bus 元件级总线
component library 元件库
component monikers 组件别名
component name 零件名
component network 分支网络
component object model (COM) 构件对象模型
component of a record 记录分量
component palette 组件栏
component side 元件面
component specification 元件规格
component surface temperature 元件表面温度
component video 混合视频
components of photo-electric conversion 光电转换元件
compose 撰写,编发;组成,构成
compose note 撰写附注
compose sequence 合成键入,复合输入序列
composed page 复合页,排版页
composed table 合成表
composed-text data stream 正文排版数据流

composed view 复合视图
composite 复合
composite card 复合卡
composite class 复合类
composite color monitor 复合彩色显示器
composite controls 复合控件
composite curve 合成曲线
composite data item 复合数据项
composite display 复合显示
composite drive (阵列式)组合驱动器
composite filter 组合滤波器
composite key 组合键;复合关键字
composite laminate 复合层压板
Composite Manager 复合管理器
composite map 组合图,合成图
composite mapping 合成映射
composite menu bar 复合菜单条
composite module 组合模块
composite moniker 复合别名
composite monitor 复合监视器
composite move 合成移动
composite neural network 组合神经网络
composite node 复合节点
composite object 复合对象
composite operator 复合[合成]算符
composite reference 复合引用
composite relation 复合[合成]关系
composite shell 复合壳层
composite signal 复合信号
composite statement 复合语句[命题]
composite sync signal 复合同步信号
composite theoretical performance (CTP) 综合理论性能
composite type 组合类型
composite video signal 复合视频信号
composite widget 复合窗口部件
composite window 复合窗口
composition association 组合关联
composition disk head 组合磁盘头
composition language 排版语言
composition of production rules 产生式规则合成
compositive frequency of component 部件组字频度
compositor 排版机
compound assignment operator 复合赋值运算符

compound decision rule 复合判定规则
compound device 合成设备
compound document 复合文档
compound document service 复合文献服务
compound entry identifier 复合项标识符
compound expression 复合表达式
compound file 复合文件
compound file resource group(CGRP) 复合文件资源组
compound file table of contents(CTOC) 复合文件内容表
compound hierarchy 复合分层结构
compound IF statement 复合条件语句
compound index file 复合索引文件
compound instruction 复合指令
compound key 复合键,复合关键字
compound modulation 组合调制,多重调制
compound neuron model 组合神经元模型
compound object 组合对象
compound parameter argument 复合参数变量
compound proposition 复合命题
compound section 组合断面
compound signal 复合信号
compound signal element 复合信号单元
compound statement 复合语句
compound switching 复合交换,混合交换
compound term 复合项
comprehensibility 内容广泛性
comprehension 理解
comprehensive database management system 综合性数据库管理系统
compress 压缩
compress technique 压缩技术
compressed audio 压缩音频
compressed binary file 压缩二进制文件
compressed drive 压缩驱动器
compressed encoding 压缩编码
compressed file 已压缩文件
compressed font 压缩字形
compressed video 压缩视频
compressed volume file(CVF) 压缩的卷文件
compressible 可压缩的
compression 压缩
compression board 压缩板
compression/expansion processor(CEP) 压缩/扩展处理机
compression theorem 压缩定理
compressor 压缩程序
compromise 折衷
compromise decision support 折衷决策支持
compromise recording 折衷记录
compromise solution 折衷解
Compsurf Compsurf格式化程序
compufan(computer fan) 计算机迷
compulsive interrupt 强制中断,强迫中断
compunication 计算机通信
CompuServe CompuServe网络系统
Compu serve 昂贵计算服务
Compuserve Information Manager for OS/2(CIM) 适用于OS/2的Compuserve信息管理程序
computability 可计算性
computability theory 可计算性理论
computable function 可计算函数
computable probability 可计算概率
computalk 计算机通话
computalker 计算机通话设备
computation bound 计算边界,计算上限
computation measure 计算度量
computation migration 计算迁徙
computation tree 计算树
computation tuple 计算元组
computational complexity theory 计算复杂性理论
computational geometry 计算几何
computational intelligence 计算智能
computational linguistics 计算语言学
computational logic 计算逻辑
computational neuroscience 计算神经科学
computational stability 计算稳定性
compute cluster 计算簇
compute-intensive applications 计算密集应用
computed path control 计算路径控制
computed relation 计算关系

computed transfer 计算转移
computer 计算机,电脑
computer abuse 计算机滥用
computer access 计算机存取
computer addiction 计算机迷
computer-aided 计算机辅助
computer aided acquisition and logistic support(CALS) 计算机辅助收取与逻辑支持计划
computer-aided circuit analysis 计算机辅助电路分析
computer-aided circuit design 计算机辅助电路设计
computer aided design(CAD) 计算机辅助设计
computer-aided design / computer-aided manufacturing(CAD/CAM) 计算机辅助设计/计算机辅助制造
computer-aided design integrated circuit 计算机辅助设计集成电路
computer-aided diagnosis 计算机辅助诊断
computer-aided documentation 计算机辅助文档编制
computer-aided drafting system 计算机辅助绘图系统
computer-aided education 计算机辅助教育
computer-aided experiment 计算机辅助试验
computer-aided graphic design 计算机辅助图形设计
computer-aided instruction(CAI) 计算机辅助教学
computer-aided management 计算机辅助管理
computer aided manufacture(CAM) 计算机辅助制造
computer aided modeling 计算机辅助造型[建模]
computer-aided page make-up 计算机辅助排版编辑
computer-aided phototypesetting 计算机辅助照相排版
computer aided prototyping(CAP) 计算机辅助原型设计
computer aided software engineering (CASE) 计算机辅助软件工程

computer aided test 计算机辅助测试
computer-aided translation 计算机辅助翻译
computer-aided typesetting 计算机辅助排版
computer allergy 计算机过敏症
computer analyst 计算机分析员
computer and control abstracts 计算机与控制文摘
computer animation 计算机动画
computer application 计算机应用
computer application analyst 计算机应用分析员
computer application engineer 计算机应用工程师
computer application for measurement and control 计算机测量与控制应用
computer architecture 计算机体系结「构
computer architecture for artificial intelligence applications 人工智能应用的计算机体系结构
computer art 计算机艺术
computer-assisted learning(CAL) 计算机辅助学习
computer assisted management 计算机辅助管理
computer-assisted testing 计算机辅助测试
computer augmented 计算机强化的
computer augmented design 计算机强化设计
computer-augmented instruction 计算机强化教学
computer automated measurement and control(CAMAC) 计算机自动测量和控制标准
computer awareness 计算机意识
computer-based consulting system 计算机咨询系统
computer-based control system 基于计算机的控制系统
computer-based education(CBE) 基于计算机的教育
computer-based training(CBT) 基于计算机的训练 「图
computer block diagram 计算机方块
computer capacity 计算机能力,计算

机容量
computer chess 计算机下棋
computer civilization 计算机文化[文明]
computer classification 计算机分类
computer clinical decision making 计算机临床决策制定
computer clock 计算机时钟
computer close-loop control 计算机闭环控制
computer code 计算机代码
computer communication 计算机通信
computer communication network 计算机通信网络
computer communication network component 计算机通信网络部件
computer conferencing 计算机会议
computer configuration 计算机配置
computer console 计算机控制台
computer control 计算机控制
computer control of production process 生产过程的计算机控制
computer control system 计算机控制系统
computer crime 计算机犯罪
computer culture 计算机文化
computer-dependent language 依赖计算机的语言
computer dependent program 依赖计算机的程序
computer design automation 计算机设计自动化
computer diagnosis 计算机诊断
computer diagram 计算机框图
computer efficiency 计算机效率
computer emergency response team (CERT) 计算机应急行动小组
computer engineering 计算机工程
computer ethics 计算机道德
computer error zone 计算机误区
computer evangelism 计算机启蒙
computer family 计算机系列
computer file 计算机文件
computer for coloring 计算机配色
computer fraud 计算机诈骗
Computer Fraud and Abuse Act (CFAA) 计算机欺骗及滥用法案
computer game 计算机游戏

computer-generated data 计算机产生的数据
computer-generated hologram 计算机产生的全息图像
computer generation 计算机世代
computer genetics 计算机遗传学
computer grade book 计算机评分册
computer graphics 计算机制图学,计算机绘图
computer graphics interface(CGI) 计算机图形界面
computer graphics metafile(CGM) 计算机图形元文件
computer graphics system 计算机图形系统
computer hacker 计算机黑客
computer hardware 计算机硬件
computer hardware description language 计算机硬件描述语言
computer hardware structure 计算机硬件结构
computer history 计算机历史
computer hologram 计算机全息图
computer holography 计算机全息术
computer hospital care 计算机医院护理
computer human interaction 计算机与人的交互作用
computer image generator 计算机图像发生器
computer image processing 计算机图像处理
computer implementation 计算机实现
computer in education 计算机教育
computer independent language 独立于计算机的语言
computer industry 计算机工业
computer industry association 计算机工业协会
computer installation 计算机安装
computer instruction 计算机指令
computer instruction set 计算机指令集,指令系统
computer intelligence 计算机智慧
computer interface types 计算机接口类型
computer language 计算机语言
computer language symbol 计算机语

言符号
computer learning 计算机学习
Computer Library 计算机库
computer limited 计算机限制的
computer limited operation 计算机限制操作
computer literacy 计算机文化素养
computer literacy course 计算机扫盲课程
computer load 计算机负荷
computer manager 计算机管理员
computer name 计算机名字
computer naughty 计算机顽童,年轻的计算机迷
computer network 计算机网络
computer network protocol 计算机网络协议
computer network system 计算机网络系统
computer network terminal 计算机网络终端
computer networking 计算机联网
computer numerical control(CNC) 计算机数值控制
computer on a chip 单个芯片上的计算机
computer on slice 单片式计算机
computer open-loop control 计算机开环控制
computer operator 计算机操作员
computer organization 计算机组成
computer-oriented language 面向计算机的语言
computer output equipment on microfilm 计算机缩微胶片输出设备
computer painter 计算机画家
computer pattern recognition 计算机模式识别
computer performance evaluation 计算机性能评价
computer phobia 计算机恐惧症
computer piracy 计算机侵权
computer plotting system 计算机绘图系统
computer power 计算机效率,计算机性能
computer power supply 计算机电源
computer program 计算机程序
computer program annotation 计算机程序注释
computer program certification 计算机程序认证
computer program verification 计算机程序验证
computer readable 计算机可读的
computer resource 计算机资源
computer revolution 计算机革命
computer sabotage 计算机破坏
computer science 计算机科学
computer scientific network(CSNET) 计算机科学网,CSNET网
Computer Search Service(CSS) 计算机搜索服务
computer security 计算机安全
Computer Security Act 计算机安全法
Computer Select 计算机选择服务
computer self-learning 计算机自学习
computer-sensitive language 计算机敏感语言
computer series 计算机系列
computer server 计算机服务器
computer simulation 计算机仿真
computer simulator 计算机仿真程序
computer software copyright cast 计算机软件版权法
computer stealing 计算机盗窃
computer supervisory control system 计算机监督控制系统
computer supported co-operative work (CSCW) 计算机支持的合作工作
computer system 计算机系统
computer system configuration 计算机系统配置
computer system design 计算机系统设计
computer system fault tolerance 计算机系统容错
computer system security 计算机系统安全性
computer telephone integration(CTI) 计算机电话集成
computer terminal 计算机终端
computer test scoring 计算机测试评
computer thief 计算机盗窃
computer threat 计算机威胁
computer time 计算机时间

computer tomography(CT) 计算机 X 射线断层摄像技术
computer typesetting 计算机排版
computer typesetting system 计算机排版系统
computer user 计算机用户
computer user group 计算机用户群
Computer User's Year Book 计算机用户年鉴
computer utility 计算机实用程序
computer virology 计算机病毒学
computer virus(CV) 计算机病毒
computer virus countermeasure (CVCM) 计算机病毒对抗器
computer virus filter 计算机病毒过滤
computer virus industry association (CVIA) 计算机病毒工业协会
computer virus vaccine(CVV) 计算机病毒疫苗程序
computer vision 计算机视觉
computer world 计算机世界
computerese 计算机术语,计算机行话
computerization 计算机化
computerized branch exchange(CBX) 计算机化交换分机
computerized circulation system 计算机化发行系统
computerized conference 计算机化会议
computerized data 计算机化数据
computerized drill and practice 计算机化练习与作业
computerized lessons 计算机化课程
computerized navigation set 计算机化导航系统
computerized serial system 计算机化期刊编目系统
computerized structural analysis and design 计算机化结构分析与设计
computerized tomography 计算机化断层扫描
computing 计算,运算
computing amplifier 运算放大器
computing complexity 计算复杂性
Computing Fabrics 计算结构(HP,微软)
computing jump 计算转移
computing optimal palette 计算优化调色板

computing power 计算能力
computing speed 运算速度
computing unit 计算单元
computopia 计算机乌托邦
CON(CONsole) 工作台
concatenate 并置,链接
concatenated data set 并置数据集
concatenated field 并置字段
concatenated key 并置关键字,连接键
concatenated tuple 串接元组
concatenating string 连接字符串
concatenation 连接,结合,链接
concatenation character 连锁字符
concatenation of string 字符串连接
concatenation operation 并置[连接]运算
concatenation operator 并置[连接]算符
concave-convex-like game 凹凸似然对策
concave edge 凹边
concave function 凹函数
concave lens 凹透镜
concave mirror 凹镜
concave polygon 凹多边形
concavity tree of region 区域凹树
conceal 隐匿
concealed line 隐蔽线
concentrated message 集中消息
concentration 集中,连接,结合;并置;集线
concentration processor 集中处理机
concentration VS multiplexing 集中方式与多路复用方式的对比
concentrator 集中器
concentrator data ready queue(DRQ) 集中器数据就绪队列
concentrator device ID table(DVCID) 集中器设备标识表
concentrator error control 集中器差错控制
concentric cylinder 同心柱面
concept attainment 概念获得
concept classification 概念分类
concept clustering 概念聚类
concept coordination 概念协调[组配]
concept data base design methodology 概念数据库设计方法学
concept dependence 概念依赖
concept description 概念描述

concept dictionary 概念词典
concept learning from examples 从例子中的概念学习
concept orthonormality principle 概念正交性原则
concept tree 概念树
conceptual clustering 概念聚类
conceptual database 概念数据库
conceptual DDL 概念数据定义语言
conceptual dependency theory 概念相关理论
conceptual design 概念性设计
conceptual design for database 数据库的概念设计
conceptual formation 概念形成
conceptual framework 概念化框架
conceptual/internal mapping 概念模式/内模式映像
conceptual knowledge 概念知识
conceptual model 概念模型
conceptual model design 概念模型设「计
conceptual modeling 概念模型法
conceptual network 概念网络
conceptual schema 概念模式
conceptual schema description language 概念模式描述语言
conceptual schema language 概念模式语言
conceptual structures representation language 概念结构表达语言，CSRL语言
conceptual subschema 概念子模式
conceptual subordinate 概念从属
conceptual system 概念系统
conceptualized Chinese character encoding input 联想式汉字编码输入法
concert architecture 协同型体系结构
concert multiprocessor 协同型多处理
conclusion 结论 「机
concordance 重要语汇索引
concordance file 重要语汇索引文件
concrete design 具体设计
concrete syntax 具体语法
concurrence server 并发服务器
concurrency 并行性，并发性
concurrency C language 并发C语言
concurrency control 并发控制

Concurrency DOS 并发DOS
concurrency management 并发管理
concurrency operation 并行操作
concurrency relation 并行关系
concurrent 同时，并发
concurrent access 并行存取
concurrent activity 并行活动
concurrent computation 并行计算
concurrent computational system 并行计算系统
concurrent computer 并行计算机
concurrent control mechanism 并发控制机制 「统
concurrent control system 并发控制系
concurrent engineering 并行工程
concurrent execution 并发执行
concurrent input/output 并发输入/输
concurrent iteration 并行迭代 「出
concurrent license 并行处理许可证
concurrent microoperation 并发微操作
concurrent object oriented programming language(COOPL) 并发性面向对象编程语言
concurrent operation 并发运算，并行操作
concurrent PASCAL 并发PASCAL语言
concurrent process 并发进程
concurrent processing 并发处理 「计
concurrent programming 并发程序设
concurrent programming language 并发程序设计语言
concurrent real-time processing 并发实时处理
concurrent run unit 并发运行单元
concurrent server 并发服务器
concurrent simulation 并发仿真
concurrent simulation engineering 并发仿真工程
condense 压缩，紧排
condense system 致冷系统
condensed font 紧缩字体
condensed print 紧缩打印
condensed type 压缩打印
condenser 聚光器，冷凝器
condition 条件
condition branch 条件分支[转移]

condition breakpoint instruction 条件断点指令
condition code 条件码
condition code register 条件码寄存器
condition/event system 条件事件系统
condition flag 条件标志
condition handler 条件处理程序
condition-incident log 条件关联记录
condition number 条件数
condition number of eigenvalue problem 特征值问题的条件数
condition prefix 条件前缀
condition values 条件值
conditional assembly 条件汇编
conditional branch instruction 条件转移指令
conditional breakpoint instruction 条件断点指令
conditional capture 条件捕获
conditional compile 条件编译
conditional construction 条件构造
conditional control structure 条件控制结构 「段
conditional critical section 条件临界
conditional detection function 条件检测函数
conditional distribution 条件分布
conditional entropy 条件熵
conditional expression 条件表达式
conditional force 条件强制 「门
conditional implication gate 条件蕴含
conditional implication operation 条件隐含运算
conditional information content 条件信息量
conditional instruction 条件指令
conditional jump 条件转移
conditional jump instruction 条件转移指令
conditional Kolmogorov complexity 条件科莫哥洛夫复杂性
conditional loop 条件循环 「展
conditional macroexpansion 条件宏扩
conditional object 条件对象
conditional operator 条件运算符
conditional probability 条件概率
conditional response 条件响应
conditional return 条件返回

conditional risk 条件风险
conditional stop instruction 条件停止指令
conditional transfer instruction 条件转移指令
conductance 电导
conduction cooling 传导冷却
conductive foil 导电箔
conductive rubber 导电橡胶
conductor 导体,导线
conductor flat cable 导电带形电缆
CONDUIT project "导管"计划
cone of vision 视锥
conference bridge 会议网桥
conference call 会议呼叫
conference connection 会议连接
conference of data system language(CODASYL) 数据系统语言会议
conference server 会议服务器
confidence 可靠性,可信度
confidence assignment problem 信任赋予问题
confidence interval 置信区间[间隔]
confidence level 置信级[水平]
confidence program 可靠性检测程序
confidence test 可靠性测试
confidential document 机密文件
confidentiality 机密性
confidentiality clearance 机密许可
CONFIG(CONFIGuration) 配置
config system file 系统配置文件
configurable software 可配置软件
configurable station 可配置站点
configuration 配置
configuration audit 配置审计
Configuration Control Element(CCE) 配置控制单元
configuration control register 配置控制寄存器
Configuration Element Management(CEM) 配置单元管理
configuration file 配置文件
configuration frame 配置[结构]帧
configuration identification 配置标识
configuration image 配置映像
configuration item 配置项
configuration map 配置映像
configuration management 配置管理

configuration option 配置选项
configuration restart 配置重启动
configuration section 设备配置节
configuration service 配置服务
configuration table 配置表
configuration task 配置任务
configure 配置
configure column 配置栏
configure editor 配置编辑器
configure manager 配置管理器
confinement 防护,监护
confirm 证实,确认
confirm deletion 确认删除
Confirm File Delete 确认文件删除
Confirm Page Break 确认分页
Confirm Password 确认口令
confirmability 可验证性
confirmation 确认,许可
confirmation message 确认消息
confirmation signaling 确认信令
conflation algorithm 归并算法,合成解法
conflation of words 词归并
conflict 冲突
conflict discriminate 冲突鉴别
conflict-free access 无冲突访问
conflict-free memory 无冲突存储器
conflict-free protocol 无冲突协议
conflict prediction 冲突预测
conflict reconcile 冲突排解
conflict resolution 竞争消解
conflict set 竞争集
confluence 汇合,集合
conformable array 一致数组
conformance 一致性
conformance requirement 一致性需求
conformance resolution test 一致性判定测试
conformance testing 一致性测试
conforming finite element method 协调有限元法
conformity 符合度
confrontation 对抗
confusion 含混
congestion 拥塞
congestion control 拥塞控制
congestion indication bit(CI) 拥塞指示位

congestion signal 拥塞信号
congestion theory 拥塞理论
congestion time 拥塞时间
congressional information service(CIS) 国会信息服务
congruence 同余
congruence class 同余类
congruent 符合的;同余的
congruent array 同余阵列
congruent figure 全等图形
congruent line 全等线
congruent mapping 同余映像
congruent modulo r 模 r 同余
congruent matrix 相合矩阵
congruent number 同余数
congruent point 叠合点
congruent segment 叠合线段
congruential generator 同余数产生程序
congruential modulo N check 同余模 N 检验
congruential sequence 同余序列
congruous 一致,全等
conic 二次曲线
conjecture 推测,猜测
conjecture method 猜测法
conjugate function 共轭函数
conjugate gradient 共轭梯度
conjugate point 共轭点
conjugate space 共轭空间
conjugate vector space 共轭向量空间
conjunct 合取式
conjunction 连接词,合取
conjunction generalization description 合取广义化描述
conjunctive clause 合取子句
conjunctive form 合取式
conjunctive normal form 合取范式
conjunctive search 共结查找
conjunctive symbol 合取符号
connect charge 连接费用,上网费用
connect node 联结点
connect signal 连接信号
connect speed 连接速度
connect time 连接时间
connectable object 可连接对象
connected component 连接成分,连通分量
connected component algorithm 连通

支算法
connected digit recognition 连续数字识别
connected directed graph 连通有向图
connected-forms paper 连续格式纸
connected graph 连接图,连通图
connected hypergraph 连通超图
connected operation 连接运算
connected-speech understanding capability 连续语音理解能力 「图
connected undirected graph 连通无向
connected user 已建立连接的用户
connected vertex set 连接顶点集合
connected word recognition 连续单词语音辨别
connectedness 连通性
connecting 正在连接中
connection 连接
connection box 连接盒,接线盒
connection charge 连接费用
connection delay 连接延迟
connection endpoint 连接终点
connection establishment 连接建立
connection graph 连接图 「符
connection identifier(CID) 连接标识
connection learning 联接学习
Connection machine 连接机,Connection并行机(Thinking Machines)
connection machine 连接机
Connection Management(CMT) 连接管理
Connection Manager Administration Kit 连接管理程序管理软件包
connection-mode transmission 连接模式传输
connection number 连接号
connection-oriented protocol 面向连接的协议
connection point manager 连接点管理程序
connection point object 连接点对象
connection pooling 连接池缓冲法
connection release 连接释放
connection string 连接字符串
connection time 连接时间
connection time-out 连接超时
connection trap 连接陷阱
connection word 连接词

connectionism 联结主义,连接机制
connectionless 无连接的
connectionless-mode transmission 无连接模式传送
connectionless network protocol(CLNP) 无连接网络协议
connectionless network relay 无连接网络中继
connectionless protocol 无连接协议
connectionless service 无连接服务
connectionless transmission 无连接传输模式
connectionless transport protocol (CLTP) 无连接传输协议
connective 连接词
connective debugging 联接调试,联调
connectivity 连通性,互连性
connectivity demand 连接性要求
connectivity platform 连通性平台
connector 连接符号;连接器
connector assembly 接插组件
connector flange (印刷电路板)插头部分
connector frame 接插件框
connector insertion loss 连接器插入损耗
connector pin 连接针脚
connector symbol 连接符号
connectout command 连出命令
connotative meaning 内涵
cononical signal 规则信号,正则信号
CONP (Connection-Oriented Network Protocol) 面向连接的网络协议
CONS (Connection- Oriented Network Services) 连接模式网络服务
CONS function CONS 函数
conscious error 可意识错误
consecutive 在序的,相继
consecutive data set organization 连续数据集结构
consecutive error 相继(出现的)错误
consecutive line 相继行
consecutive operation 串行操作,相继操作
consecutive processing 相继处理
consecutive retrieval organization 连续检索结构
consecutive retrieval property 连续检

索特性
consecutive sequence computer 连续顺序计算机
consecutive spilling 连续溢出法
consensus 合意,一致
consequence 结论
consequence finding program 结果寻找程序
consequent 后项;结论
consequent of an implication 蕴涵式后项
conservation condition 守恒条件
conservative life cycle 保守的生命周期法
conserved area 保留区域
consistence of instruction format and data format 指令格式与数据格式的一致性
consistency 相容性,一致性
consistency check 一致性检验
consistency enforcer 一致化集;相容执行器
consistency invalid 一致性无效
consistency of knowledge 知识相容性
consistency operation 一致性操作
consistency read 一致性读
consistency read and invalid 一致性读和无效
consistency routine 一致性检验例程
consistency write and invalid 一致性写和无效
consistent estimation 一致估计
console 控制台
console buffer 控制台缓冲器
console cabinet 控制室
console command processor 控制台命令处理机
console debugging 控制台调试
console display 控制台显示器;控制台显示
console interrupt 控制台中断
console log 控制台登录
console operator 控制台操作员
console printer 控制台打印机
console root 控制台根目录
console spooling 控制台假脱机操作
console stack 控制台堆栈
console startup 控制台启动

console terminal 控制台终端
console trap 控制台陷阱
console typewriter(CTW) 控制台打字机
console window 控制台窗口
ConsoleOne 服务器控制台软件(Novell)
consolette 小型控制台
consolidate 整理,合并
consolidate data set 统一数据集
consolidated compiler 统一编译程序
consolidated computer 联合式计算机
consolidated cryptologic program 统一加密程序
consolidation 合并,联合;统一;固定,固化
consolidator 合并例程;连接编辑程序
consonants 辅音
CONST(CONSTant) 常数,常量
constant 常数,常量
constant acceleration 恒定加速
constant address 恒定地址
constant angular velocity(CAV) 恒定角速度
constant area 常数区
constant bandwidth 恒定带宽
constant bit rate(CBR) 恒定位率,固定比特率
constant broadcast 常数传播
constant current device 恒流器件
constant cyclic code 定循环码
constant declaration 常量说明
constant definition part 常数定义部
constant element 常数元素
constant expression 常量表达式
constant factor space overhead simulation 常因子空间开销仿真
constant failure period 偶然失效期
constant identifier 常数标识符
constant increment 常增量
constant linear velocity(CLV) 恒定线速度
constant multiplier 常数乘法器
constant pool 常数池
constant potential 恒定电势
constant ratio code 定比码,恒比代码
constant section 常数段
constant state 常态,恒态

constant sum game 常和对策,常和博弈
constant table 常数表,常量表
constant temperature 恒温
constant value control 定值控制
constant vector 常数向量
constant voltage 恒定电压
constant wavelength recording 恒波长记录法
constant weakest precondition 常量最弱前置条件
constant weight code 定权码
constant workspace 常数工作区
Constellation Ⅱ 星座Ⅱ网络软件包
constellation 构象
constituent 成分
constituent grammar 构成语法
constituent structure 成分结构
constitutional provision （有关软件权益的）规定条款
constrained allocation 约束分配
constrained finite element 约束有限元
constrained objective 约束目标
constrained restoration 约束恢复
constraint 限制,约束
constraint condition 约束条件
constraint date 限期
constraint equation 约束方程
constraint function 约束函数
constraint matrix 约束矩阵,限制矩「阵
constraint propagation 约束传播,约束扩展
constraint reasoning 约束推理
constraint rule 约束规则
constraint satisfaction 约束补偿
construct 构造,结构
Constructing Input Stream Objects 构造输入流对象
Constructing output Stream Objects 构造输出流对象
construction 结构,构造
construction process 组合进程
construction solution 构造解
construction window 构建窗口,剪辑窗口
constructive code 结构码
constructive induction 构造性归纳
constructive inductive learning 结构性的归纳学习
constructive inference 构造性推理
constructive placement algorithm 构造性布局算法
constructive rule 构造性规则
constructive shell representation(CSR) 结构外壳表示法
constructive solid geometry(CSG) 结构实体几何
constructor 构造函数
consultant system 咨询系统
Consultative Committee for International Telegraph and Telephone (CCITT) 国际电报电话咨询委员会
consultative committee on international radio(CCIR) 国际无线电咨询委员会
consumable resource 消耗性资源
consumables 消耗品
consume time 损耗期
consumer 消费者
consumer electronics 消费品电子技术
Consumer Operating System(COS) 消费者操作系统
consumer process 消费者进程
consumer production 消费品
consumer storage 用户存储器
consumer transaction system 用户事务处理系统
consummate simplex method 完善单纯形法
CONT CONT命令
Cont. Notice 接续注明
Cont. Separator 接续分隔符
contact 触点
contact area 接触面积
contact bounce 接触抖动
contact bounce elimination circuit 接触抖动消除电路
contact clearance 接触点间隙
contact etch 接触点腐蚀
contact fault 接触故障
contact head 接触式磁头
contact image scanner(CIS) 接触式图像扫描仪
contact life 触点寿命
contact magnetic head 接触磁头
contact magnetic recording 接触式磁

记录
Contact Name 联系人姓名
contact noise 接触噪声
contact point 碰面开关
contact recording 接触式记录
contact resistance 接触电阻
contact sense module 接触感测模块
contact sensor 触觉传感器
contact size 插针尺寸
contact start flying-off 接触起动浮动停止
contact start stop 接触起停
contact wear 触点磨损
contactless relay 无触点继电器
contagion 蔓延
contain 包含,包括
contained text 包含的文本
container 容器
container application 容器应用程序
container class 容器类
container event 容器事件
container menu item 容器菜单选项
container object 容器对象
container property 容器属性
container renderer 容器润色程序
container type 容器类型
containment 包容性
containment tree 包容树
contaminate 污染
contemplative model 思考模型
contemporary 流行的,现代的
contemporary style 流行样式
contend 竞争
content 内容
content access 内容存取
content addressable filestore 内容可寻址文件存储器
content addressable memory (CAM) 内容可寻址存储器
content-addressed memory 内容可寻址存储器
content-based access method 基于内容的存取方法
content coupling 内容耦合
content directory 内容目录
content frame (网页)内容框
Content Manager Entry Bundle 内容管理登录软件包(IBM)

content search 内容查找
content type 内容类型
contention 竞争情况,争用
contention control 争用控制
contention-free protocol 无争用协议
contention interval 争用时间间隔
contention logic 竞争逻辑,争用逻辑
contention mode 竞争模式
contention model 争用模型
contention network 争用网络,竞争网络
contention PODA 争用的面向优先权按需分配通道
contention problem 争用问题,竞争问题
contention resolution 争用消解
contention ring 争用环
contention system 竞争系统
contention time 争用时间,竞争时间
contents 内含,内容
contents dictionary 目录字典
contents panel 内容画面
contents retrieval 目录检索
contents view 内容视图
context 上下文
context condition 上下文条件
context dependence 上下文相关性
context dependent access 上下文相关存取
context-dependent compression 上下文相关压缩
context-dependent encoding 上下文相关编码法
context-dependent grammar 上下文相关文法
context-dependent language 上下文相关语言
context-dependent transformation 上下文相关转换
context editor 上下文编辑程序
context estimation 上下文估计
context-free branching rule 上下文无关分支规则
context-free grammar 上下文无关文法
context-free language 上下文无关语言
context-free program 上下文无关程序
context-free text 离散文本
context identifier 上下文标识符
context-independent encoding 上下文

独立编码
context indexing 关联索引
context number 上下文关联号
context object 关联对象
context record 上下文记录
context-sensitive grammar 上下文有关文法
context-sensitive help 上下文相关的帮助
context-sensitive language 上下文相关语言
context-sensitive menu 上下文相关菜单
context-sensitive text 连续文本
context specification 上下文相关的说明
context string 上下文字符串
context switching 上下文切换;关联切换
contextual declaration 上下文相关的说明
contextual search 上下文相关检索
contextual sensitive help 上下文相关帮助
contiguous allocation 邻接分配
contiguous area 邻接区域
contiguous field 相连栏,相连字段
contiguous segmentation 相邻段
contiguous storage allocation 邻接的存储器分配
contiguous virtual address space 相连虚地址空间
contingency interrupt 意外中断,偶然中断
contingency planning 应急计划
contingency procedure 偶发过程
contingent allegiance 相依联系
continual value logic circuit 连续值逻辑电路
continuation engineering 继续工程
continuation frame 连续帧
continuation indicator 续行指示符
continuation line 延续行
continuation line statement 续行语句
continuation page 延续页
Continue from Previous Section 续前
Continue timing 继续定时
continued fraction method 连分式法
continued fractions 连分式
continuity failure signal 连接失败信

continuity index 连续索引
continuous carrier 连续载波
continuous cipher synchronization 密码连续同步
continuous-data-stream mode 连续数据流模式
continuous delta modulation 连续增量调制
continuous digit recognition 连续数字识别
continuous distribution 连续分布
continuous file 连续文件
continuous forms 连续打印纸
continuous forms attachment 连续格式纸输送器
continuous forms paper 连续打印纸
continuous function 连续函数,连续作业
continuous Hopfield neural network (CHNN) 连续 Hopfield 神经网络
continuous image characterization 连续图像特征化
continuous media object 连续媒体对象
continuous mode 连续方式
continuous paper 连续纸
continuous-path control 连续路径控制
continuous path operation 连续轨迹作业
continuous resistive touch panel 持久触摸屏
continuous scroll 连续滚屏
continuous simulation 连续仿真
continuous speech recognition (CSR) 连续语音识别
continuous spectrum (CSR) 连续谱
continuous stationary 连续式用纸
continuous stationary reader 连续固定读取机
continuous system diagnosis 连续系统诊断
continuous tone 连续单音;连续色调
continuous tone image 连续色调图像
continuous transmission 连续传送
continuous variable 连续变量
continuously acting computer 连续动作计算机
contone(continuous tone) 连续色调

contour 轮廓
contour accentuation 轮廓加重，勾边
contour analysis 轮廓分析
contour character 轮廓(空心)字
contour coding 轮廓编码
contour correction 轮廓校正
contour curve 等高线，等值线
contour decomposition 轮廓分解
contour detection 轮廓检测
contour enhancement 轮廓增强
contour extraction 轮廓抽取
contour filling 轮廓填充
contour following 轮廓跟踪
contour line 等值线
contour map 等值线图
contour matching 轮廓匹配
contour plot 轮廓绘图
contour representation 轮廓表示
contour segmentation 轮廓分段
contour shape analysis 轮廓形状分析
contour sharpness 轮廓清晰度
contour smoothing 轮廓平滑
contour topology 轮廓拓扑
contour tracking 轮廓跟踪
contouring 产生轮廓
contract network 合同网络，协同网络
contracted notation 简化符号
contractible graph 可收缩图形
contraction 收缩
contraction rule 压缩规则
contradiction 矛盾，永假式
contradictory information 矛盾信息
contradictory proposition 矛盾命题
contrapositive rule 倒置规则
contrary proposition 相反命题，矛盾命题
contrast 对比度
contrast enhancement 对比度增强
contrast gradient 反差梯度
contrast ratio 反差比，对比度
contrast stretching 对比度扩展
control 控制器；控制
control accuracy 控制精度
control action 控制作用，控制动作
control and monitor console 监程台
control and status logic 控制与状态逻辑
control area 控制区
control-area split 控制区划分

control array 控件数组
control ball 控制球
control bit 控制位
control block 控制块
control break 控制变更，控制中断
control breakpoint instruction 控制断点指令
control box 控制框
control bus 控制总线
control button 控制按钮
control byte 控制字节
control center 控制中心
control chain 控制链
control channel 控制通道
control channel information demodulator 控制通道信息解调器
control character 控制字符
control circuit 控制电路
control classes 控件类
control code 控制代码
control code display 控制代码显示
control command 控制命令
control command program 控制命令程序
control command word 控制命令字
control community （Netware）控制共同体
control component 控制部件
control concurrency 控制并行性
control concurrent operating 并发操作控制
control console 控制台
control container 控件容器
control counter 控制计数器
control coupling 控制耦合
control data 控制数据
control data access 控制数据存取
Control Data Corp.（CDC） 控制数据公司
control data item 控制数据项
control data register 控制数据寄存器
control data set 控制数据集
Control Development Kit（CDK） 控件开发成套工具
control dictionary 控制字典
control element 控制元件
control engineering 控制工程
control field 控制字段

control file 控制文件
control flag 控制标志
control flow 控制流
control flow chart 控制流图
control flow complexity measure 控制流复杂性测度
control flow computer 控制流计算机
control flow keyword 控制流关键字
control flow optimized program 控制流优化程序
control format items 控制格式项
control frame 控制帧
control function 控制功能
control functional unit 控制功能单元
control handle 控制柄
control identifier 控件标识符
control information 控制信息
control information list 控制信息表
control input 控制输入
control input/output module 控制输入/输出模块
control instruction 控制指令
control integration 控制集成
control interface 控制接口
control interval definition field 控制间隔定义字段
control key 控制键, Ctrl 键
control knowledge 控制知识
control language 控制语言
control lever 控制杆
control-level indicator 控制级指示符
control library 控制程序库; 控件库
control logic 控制逻辑
control loop 控制环路, 控制回路
control maximize 控件最大化
control memory 控制存储器
control-menu box 控制菜单框
control message 控制消息
control message illegal error 控制消息非法错误
control microcomputer 控制微型计算机
control manimize 控件最小化 └机
control mode 控制模式
control module 控制模块
control oriented language 面向控制的语言
control output module 控制输出模块
Control Panel 控制面板

control panel 控制面板
control panel device 控制面板设备
control path 控制路径
control pattern 控制模式
control pen 控制笔
control point 控制点
control print character 控制打印字符
control procedure 控制程序
control program(CP) 控制程序
control program for microcomputer (CP/M) CP/M 操作系统
control program generation language 控制程序生成语言
control program generation procedure 控制程序生成过程
control program keys 控制程序键
control program structure 控制程序结构
control property 控件属性
control protocol 控制协议
control range 控制范围
control read-only memory(CROM) 控制只读存储器
control record 控制记录
control region base register(CRBR) 控制区基地址寄存器
control register 控制寄存器
control routine 控制例程
control section 控制段
control sequence 控制顺序[序列]
control signal 控制信号
control site 控制站点
control source 控制源; 控件源
control specification 控制说明
control stack 控制堆栈
control statement 控制语句
control station 控制站
control stick 控制杆, 操纵杆
control storage(CS) 控制存储器
control storage save 控制存储器保存
control strategy 控制策略
control stream 控制流
control structure 控制结构
control supply indicator 控制电源指示符
control switching point 控制交换点
control system 控制系统
control system error 控制系统误差

control terminal 控制终端
control time constant 控制时间常数
control token 控制令牌
control transfer instruction 控制转移指令
control transfer statement 控制转移语句
control-type instruction 控制型指令
control unit 控制单元,控制部件
control variable 控制变量
control with look-ahead capability 有超前能力的控制
control word 控制字
control word error 控制字错误
control word format 控制字格式
control word line 控制字行
controllability 可控制性
controlled access unit(CAU) 控制访问单元
controlled accessibility 受控存取性
controlled-carrier modulation 受控载波调制
controlled not ready signal 受控的未准备就绪信号
controlled object 控制对象
controlled parameter 可控参数
controlled plant 受控对象
controlled rerouting 受控返回原路由
controlled rewriting 受控重写
controlled storage allocation 受控存储区分配
controlled system 受控系统
controlled updating 受控更新
controlled variable 受控变量
controller 控制器;控制员
controller buffer 控制器缓冲器
controller bus 控制器总线
controller function 控制器功能
controller interruption 控制器中断
controller storage save 控制器存储器营救
controlling application program 主控应用程序
controlling index tag 主控索引标识
controlling stream 控制流
controlling system 施控系统
controlling tag names 主控标识名
controlling unit 控制单元

controls 控制项,控件
convection 对流
conventional algorithm 传统算法
conventional cipher 传统密码
conventional equipment 常规设备
conventional memory 常规内存
conventional programming 常规程序设计
conventional routing method 常规路由选择法
convergence 会聚,收敛
convergence connector 会聚连接符,框图连接符
convergence control 聚焦控制,会聚控制
convergence error 会聚误差
convergence forward pruning 收敛正向修剪
convergence of finite element method 有限元法的收敛性
convergence of iteration 迭代的收敛
convergence plane 会聚平面
convergence sublayer(CS) 聚合子层
convergence surface 会聚表面
conversation 会话,对话
conversation-based mail 基于会话的邮件
conversation monitor system(CMS) 会话式监控系统
conversation thread 会话线索[线程]
conversational 对话式,会话
conversational algebraic language (CAL) 会话式代数语言
conversational application program 会话式应用程序
conversational compiler 会话式编译程序
conversational computer 对话式计算机
conversational computing 会话式计算
conversational debug routine 会话式调试程序
conversational device 会话设备
conversational file 会话文件
conversational guidance 会话引导
conversational input/output 会话式输入/输出
conversational language 会话式语言
conversational mode 会话方式

conversational processing 对话式处理,交互式处理
conversational time-sharing 交互式分时,会话式分时
converse 逆,反向
converse diagram 逆有向图
converse theorem 逆定理
conversion 变换,转换
conversion accuracy 转换精度
conversion by assignment 赋值转换
conversion code 转换码
conversion costs 转换费用,转化成本
conversion equipment 转换设备
conversion factor 变换因数,变换因子
conversion function 变换函数
conversion key 转换键
conversion mode 转换模式
conversion program 转换程序
conversion rate 转换速率
conversion resolution 转换分辨率
conversion routine 转换例程
conversion table 转换表
conversion time 转换时间
conversion tools 转换工具
convert 转换,变换
Convert Now 立即开始转换
converter 变换器,转换器
converter stability 变换器稳定性
converting 变换,转换
convex 凸起的
convex closure 凸闭包
convex combination 凸组合
Convex computer corp. Convex 计算机公司
convex cover 凸覆盖
convex domain 凸域
convex function 凸函数
convex fuzzy set 凸模糊集
convex hull 凸包,凸壳
convex lens 凸透镜
convex membership 凸隶属度
Convex minisupercomputers Convex 小巨型计算机
convex polygon 凸多边形
convex polyhedron 凸多面体
convex programming 凸规划
convex set 凸集
convex sublattice 凸子格

convexity closure 凸闭包
conveyance 传送;转让
conveyance case 运输工具角色(格)
conveyer 传送带
convolution 卷积
convolution code 卷积码
convolution filtering 卷积滤波
convolvotron 虚拟三维音像定位系统
Cook-Toom algorithm 库克-图姆算法
Cook's theorem 库克定理
Cook's theorem for 2DPDA 库克双向确定型下推自动机定理
cookbook 烹饪手册
cooked mode 成熟方式
cookie （Web）客户状态信息收集包
cookie class cookie 类
cookie database （Web）客户状态信息数据库
cookie function （Web）客户状态信息收集函数
cookies collection 客户状态信息包收集
cookies filtering tool 客户状态信息包过滤工具
cool site 热门站点,酷站
cool start 冷启动
coolant 冷却剂
coolbar 带区容器控件
cooler 冷却器
cooling 冷却
cooling agent 冷却剂
cooling fan 冷却风扇
cooling fin 冷却片
cooling plate 冷却板
COOP(Custom Order On-line Processing) 客户订单联机处理
Coons surface 康恩曲面
cooperating knowledge source 协同操作知识源
cooperating process 协同进程
cooperating program 协同操作程序
cooperating protocol 协同协议
cooperation index 合作指数
cooperative computing 合作计算
cooperative goal structure 合作型目标结构
cooperative installation 合作设施
cooperative intelligence network system 合作智能网络系统

cooperative learning 协作学习
cooperative multitasking 协同多任务处理
cooperative networks 协作型网络
cooperative processing 协同处理,协作处理
cooperative transactional processing 协作事务处理
coordinate 坐标
coordinate-addressable memory 坐标寻址内存
coordinate-axis 坐标轴
coordinate-based modeling system 基于坐标的建模系统
coordinate conversion computer 坐标转换计算机
coordinate data 坐标数据
coordinate digitizer 坐标数字化仪
coordinate dimensioning 坐标维数
coordinate geometry(COGO) 坐标几何
coordinate graphics 坐标图形;坐标制图技术
coordinate indexing 相关检索
coordinate line 坐标线
coordinate module 协同模块
coordinate plane 坐标平面
coordinate position 坐标位置
coordinate primitive 协调原语
coordinate retrieval 协同检索
coordinate scheme 协调方案
coordinate selector 坐标选择器
coordinate system 坐标系
coordinate transformation 坐标变换
coordinated geometry 坐标几何
coordinated job scheduling 协同作业调度
coordinated universal time 全局通用时间
coordination 协调,配合
coordination center 协调中心
coordination net 协调网络
coordination number 配位数
coordination problem-solution 协调问题求解
coordinator 协调程序
COP(Character-Oriented Protocol) 面向字符的协议
Copeland Copeland 操作系统
copied cell 复制的单元格
copies 复制份数
coplanar tape 共面型匣式磁带
copper chip 铜芯片(IBM)
copper-clad laminate 镀铜箔板
copper foil laminate 铜箔叠层板
copper-plate 镀铜层
copper wire 铜线
coprocessing 协同处理
coprocessor 协处理器
coprocessor board 协处理器板
copy 复制,副本,拷贝
copy back 复录,回录
copy cell 复制件
copy check 复制检查
copy counter 复制计数器
copy descriptor 副本描述符
copy function 拷贝操作
copy guide 复印导向器
copy group 复制组
copy holder 拷贝支架
copy-on-reference 引用时复制
copy operation 复制操作
copy option 副本选项
copy program 拷贝程序
copy-protected disk 防拷贝磁盘
copy-protection 拷贝保护
copy quantity selector 复制数量选择
copy revision 复制修订
copy screen mode 拷贝屏幕方式
copy to clipboard 拷贝到剪贴板
copy volume 复制卷
copying image 拷贝图像
copying program 拷贝程序
copyright 版权,著作权
CORAL(Computer On-line Real-time Application Language) 计算机联机实时应用语言
CORBA(Common Object Request Broker Architecture) 通用对象请求代理体系结构
cord 塞绳,软线
cordless plug 无绳插塞,无线插头
cordless pointing device 无绳定位装置
cordless pressure pen 无绳压力笔
cordless telephone 无绳电话

core 纤芯,线芯,磁芯
core bank 磁芯体
core bus 背板总线
core conformance 核心一致性
core connects 内核连接
core event set 核心事件集
core file 核心文件
core gateway 核心网关
Core graphics system Core 图形系统
core image 核心映像
core image library 核心映像库
core load 核心程序装入
core matrix 磁芯矩阵
core memory 磁芯内存
core network 核心网络
core printing 核心打印
core program 常驻程序
core-resident 常驻内存的
Core System 核心系统
core voltage 核心电压
core war 核心战(游戏)
core wrapping 纤芯缠绕
Corel Corporation Corel 公司(加拿大)
Corel DRAW Corel DRAW 绘图软件
Corel Quattro Pro 电子表格软件
Corel WordPerfect 文字处理软件
coresident 协同驻留的
corner 角
corner mark 角标志
corona 电晕
coroutine linkage 协同例程链接
corporate 联合
corporate database 联合数据库
corporate strategy 联合策略
corpus 语言数据库,语料库
correct and copy 校正及复制
correct rate for input 输入正确率
correct recognition rate 正确识别率
correct response 正确响应
correct route 正确路由
correctable error 可改正错误
corrected maintenance time 校正维护时间
correcting code 纠错码
correcting condition 校正条件
correcting feature 纠错特性
correcting signal 校正信号

correction 校正,纠正,改正
correction action 校正作用
correction character 校正字符
correction element 修正项,纠正因素
correction increment 校正增量
correction key 校正键
correction of error 误差校正
correction program 校正程序
correction routine 校正例程
correction term 校正项
correction time 校正时间
corrective action 校正行动
corrective maintenance 校正性维护
corrective maintenance time 出错维修时间
corrective network 校正网络
corrective replacement 校正性替换
correctness 正确性
correctness of algorithm 算法正确性
correctness proof 正确性证明
correlation 关联,相关
correlation coefficient 相关系数
correlation detector 相关侦测器
correlation technology 相关技术
correlogram 相关图
correspondence 对应
correspondence code 对应码
correspondence problem 对应问题
correspondence school 函授教育
correspondent access method 对应存取法,从属访问法
correspondent entity 对接实体
corresponding 对应
corresponding state 对应态
corrosion 腐蚀
corrosion-proof 防腐蚀
corrupted file 被破坏文件
corruption 讹误,恶化,变质
cortex 表层
cortical neuron 表层神经元
COSE (Common Open Software Environment) 公用开放软件环境,COSE 联盟
Coset 系,集合
coset 陪集
COSINE (Cooperation in Open System Interconnection Network in Europe) 欧洲开放系统互连网络合

作组织
cosine equalizer 余弦均衡器
Cosmic Cube Cosmic超立方体多处理机
COSMO Series COSMO计算机系列
cost 成本,花费,耗费值
cost estimation 耗费估计,费用估算
cost performance 性能价格比
cost problem dynamic programming 成本问题动态规划
cotree 余树;补树
cotree branch 余树分支
coulomb(CNT) 库仑
count(CNT) 计数
count area 计数区
count down 递减计数,倒计数
count down circuit 倒计时电路
count-key-data device 计数键数据设备
count-key-data format 计数键数据格式
count modulo N N模计数
count pulse interrupt 计数脉冲中断
count sort 计数排序
count zero interrupt 计数零中断
countability 可数性
countable function 可计算函数
countable set 可数集合
counted string 计数串
counter 计数器;相反的
counter circuit 计数器电路
counter-clockwise direction 反时针方向
counter-electromotive force 反电动势
counter-example 反例
counter inhibit 计数器抑制位
counter motion 逆向运动
counter object 计数对象
counter operation 计数操作
counter overflow 计数器溢出
counter part 副本;配对物
counter-propagation network(CPN) 反向传播神经网络
counter/shift register 计数器/移位寄存器
counter-timer 计数定时器
counteraction 抵消,反作用,中和
counterforce 对抗能力
countermeasure 干扰,对抗措施

counterpart 对应物,副本
counterplot 对抗策略
counterpropagation network 逆向传播网络
counting circuit 计数电路
counting element 计数单元
counting empty cells 计算空单元格
counting forward 正向计数
counting in reverse 反向计数
counting labeled tree 计数标号树
counting loop 计数循环
counting problem 计数问题
counting-rate curve 计数率曲线
counting sorting 计数排序
counting Turing machine(CTM) 计数图灵机
counting type A/D converter 计数型模拟/数字转换器
counting unlabeled tree 计数非标号树
country code 国家代码
country extended code page 国家扩充代码页
country-specific 国家特定的
couple 电偶;耦合
coupled circuit 耦合电路
coupled computer 耦合计算机,配对计算机
coupled drive 共轭驱动,配合驱动
coupled fiber 耦合光纤
coupled matrix 耦合矩阵
coupled modes 耦合模
coupled noise 耦合噪声
coupled system 复合系统
coupler 耦合器,耦合电路
coupling 耦合,耦合度
coupling bit 耦合位
coupling coefficient 耦合系数
coupling degree 耦合度
coupling capacitance 耦合电容
coupling factor 耦合因子
coupling finite element method 耦合有限元法
coupling function 耦合函数
coupling probe 耦合探头
coupling variable 耦合变量
course-and-distance computer 航向和距离计算机
course-and-speed computer 航向速度

计算机
course computer 航线计算机
course development system(CDS) 课程开发系统
course line computer 航线计算机
course of action 行动方针
course of values recursion 串值递归
course writer 课程编写语言
courseware 课件
courseware authoring tool 课件制作工「具
courseware engineering 课件工程
courseware license 课件特许
courtesy 惯例
courtesy copy 抄送[副本]邮件
covariance 协方差
covariance function 协方差函数
covariance matrix 协方差矩阵
covariance sequences 协方差序列
covariance stationary 协方差平稳的
cover 覆盖
cover channel 隐蔽通道
cover time 隐蔽时间
coverability graph 可覆盖性图
coverage 覆盖域,覆盖率
coverage ratio 覆盖率
covered wire 被复线
covering 覆盖
covering bad block 覆盖坏块
covering curve 覆盖曲线
covering number 覆盖数
covering of a hypergraph 超图的覆盖
covering routine 覆盖程序
covert channel 隐蔽通道
CP(Clock Pulse) 时钟脉冲
CP(Communication Platform) 通信平台
CP8 CP8智能卡
CP/A(Computer Press Assn.) 计算机新闻出版业协会
CP/M(Control Program for Microprocessors) CP/M操作系统
CP/M structure CP/M结构
CP/net CP/net操作系统
CPE(Computer Performance Evaluation) 计算机性能评估
CPE(Customer Premises Equipment) 客户选用设备
CPI(Characters Per Inch) 每英寸字符数
cpi(counts per inch) 每英寸步数
CPIC(Common Programming Interface for Communications) 通用通信程序设计接口
CPL (Conversational Programming Language) 会话式程序设计语言
CPM(Critical Path Method) 关键路径法
CPPS (Critical Path Planning and Scheduling) 关键路径规划与调度
CPU(Central Processing Unit) 中央处理单元
CPU affinity 中央处理机的亲合力
CPU architecture 中央处理单元体系结构
CPU-bound CPU受限的
CPU-bound job CPU密集作业
CPU-bound process CPU密集进程
CPU burst CPU猝发
CPU busy time CPU忙碌时间
CPU card CPU板
CPU clock tick CPU时钟节拍
CPU cycle CPU周期
CPU element 中央处理机部件
CPU execution time CPU执行时间
CPU expander CPU扩充器
CPU handshaking CPU联系交换,CPU握手
CPU headway 处理机进度
CPU-I/O burst cycle CPU与输入/输出猝发周期
CPU idle time 中央处理单元空转时间「令
CPU operate instruction CPU作业指
CPU pins and signals 中央处理机引脚和信号
CPU register CPU寄存器「间
CPU time 中央处理机时间,CPU时
CPU timer CPU计时器
CR(Carriage Return) 回车
CR(Change Request) 更改请求
CR(Command Retry) 命令重试
CR(Conversation Ratio) 换算率
CR(Count Reverse) 反向计数
crack 裂缝,裂纹;解密
cracked 有裂缝的;攻破密钥的
cracker 不速之客,黑客

cracking 非法闯入
crank 曲柄；不稳定的，摇晃的
crank shaft 曲轴
crash 系统性故障；崩溃，失效
Crash Defender 故障保护程序（Quarterdeck）
crash dump 故障转储
crash program 故障应急处理程序
crash recovery 故障恢复
crash simulation 故障模拟
crawl （文字或图像在屏幕上）缓缓移动
crawl speed 滚屏速度
Cray-1 Cray-1 巨型计算机
Cray-2 supercomputer Cray-2 超级计算机
Cray Inc. 克雷公司，Cray 公司
Cray Research, Inc. Cray 研究公司
Cray X-MP supercomputer Cray X-MP 超级计算机
Cray Y-MP supercomputer CRAY Y-MP 巨型计算机
CRC（Cyclic Redundancy Check） 循环冗余校验
create 创建，建立
create directory 创建目录
Create Envelope 创建信封
create file 创建文件
create function 创建文件函数
create hyperlink 创建超链接
create new folder 创建新文件夹
create new project 创建新工程
create only 只创建
create palette 创建调色板
create pattern brush 创建格式刷
create pointer moniker 创建指针别名
Create PivotTable 创建数据透视表
create primitive 创建原语
Create Revision Log 创建版本记录
create rule 创建规则
create session 创建对话
creation date 创建日期
creation time 创建时间
Creative Multimedia Deck 创新多媒体工作台
creative set 创造集
Creative SoundFont 创新音色库标准
Creative SOUNDO'LE 创新声音对象嵌入软件
Creative Technology Ltd. 创新科技有限公司(新加坡)统
Creative TextAssist 创新语音合成系
Creative WaveStudio 创新波形文件编辑系统
creator 创建者
creator type 创建者类型
credit 信用量
credit allocation 信用量分配
credit assignment 信任赋值
credit-based flow control 基于信用的流控制
credit card 信用卡
credit card fraud 信用卡行骗
credit card modem 信用卡式调制解调器
credit-card reader 信用卡阅读器
credit certification 信用验证，信用核实
credit message 信用消息，信用报文
credit number 信用数
credit verification 信用核实
credit verification terminal 信用验证终端
creep 蠕变
creeping featurism 蠕变性
creeping random search 蠕行随机搜索
CRIB CRIB 专家系统
crime 犯罪
crime rate 犯罪率
crime law 刑法
crimp connection 压接
crimping 压接法
crippled leapfrog test 踏步检查，原位检测
crippled mode 踏步模式
crippleware 残缺件
crisping （图像）勾边
criteria 准则，条件
criteria range 判定范围；条件区域
criterion 准则，判据
criterion function 准则函数
criterion mastery testing 准则熟悉程度测试
criterion register 判据寄存器
criterion rule 判定规则
critical activity 关键活动
critical area 临界区

critical branching point 临界分支点
critical condition 临界条件
critical current 临界电流
critical damping 临界阻尼
critical decision point 临界判定点
critical demension 临界尺寸
critical error 临界错误,严重错误
critical error handler 临界错误处理程序
critical event simulation 临界事件仿真
critical factor analysis 关键因素分析
critical field 临界磁场
critical focus 临界焦点
critical fusion frequency(CFF) 临界停闪频率
criticalgraph 临界图
critical level 临界电平
critical line 临界线
critical load 临界负载
critical magnetic field 临界磁场
critical maximum 临界最大值
critical microoperation 临界微作业
critical operation 关键操作
critical path 关键路径,临界路径
critical path analysis 要径分析,关键路径分析
critical path length 关键路径长度
critical path method(CPM) 关键路径法
critical path scheduling 关键路径调度
critical path test 要径测试
critical path test generation 要径测试产生法
critical path time 要径时间,关键路径时间
critical path tracing 要径跟踪,临界路径跟踪法
critical path wiring 关键路径布线法
critical piece first 关键部分优先
critical point 临界点
critical race 临界竞争
critical region 临界区
critical resource 临界资源
critical response time 临界应答时间
critical section 临界段
critical situation notification 紧急状态通知
critical subgraph 关键子图
critical table 判定表
critical task 关键任务
critical temperature 临界温度
critical temperature component 临界温度元件
critical value 临界值
criticality 危急度
criticism 评语
CRITTER CRITTER专家系统
CRLF(Carriage Return & Line Feed) 回车换行
CRM(Customer Relationship Management) 客户关系管理系统(IBM)
cron (精密)计时程序
cronograph (Unix)计时程序
crontab file 定时执行文件
crop 修剪,剪切
crop marks 修剪标记
cropping 修剪,剪裁
cross 交叉;十字准线
cross addition 交叉相加
cross assembler 交叉汇编程序
cross assembler software 交互汇编软件
cross assembly 交叉汇编
cross bar structure 交叉开关结构
cross bar switch 纵横开关,交叉开关
cross bar switch matrix 纵横开关矩阵
cross bar switching system 纵横制交换系统
cross channel switching 交叉通道转接
cross check 交叉检验
cross color 串色
cross compilation 交叉编译
cross compiler 交叉编译程序
cross configuration 交叉配置
cross connection 交叉连接
cross correlation function 互相关函数
cross coupling 交叉耦合
cross covariance function 互协方差函数
cross cursor 十字光标
cross development 交叉开发
cross-device link 交叉设备链接
cross domain 交叉域
cross domain communication 跨域通信
cross-domain keys 跨区域键号,跨域密钥
cross-domain link 跨区域链路
cross-domain LU-LU session 跨区域

逻辑单元间对话
cross-domain network 跨域网络
cross-domain subarea link 跨区域子区链路
cross fade
cross feed 写读互扰
cross fire 互扰
cross footing 交叉合计
cross hair 十字准线
cross hair cursor 十字准线光标
cross hairs 十字线
cross-hatch pattern 交叉线状图案,方格
cross hatching 画剖面线
cross-impact 交叉影响法
cross infection 交叉传染
cross-linked cluster 交叉链接簇
cross-linked files 交叉链接文件
cross linking 交叉连接
cross macroassembler 交叉宏汇编程序
cross mark 十字标记
cross modulation 交叉调制
cross-office time 过局时间
cross-over 交越,跨越
cross over frequency 交叉频率
cross parity check 交叉奇偶校验
cross platform 交叉平台,跨平台
cross platform compatibility 跨平台兼容能力
cross platform component architecture 跨平台部件结构
cross platform transfer 跨平台传输
cross-point array 交叉点阵行
cross point switch system 交叉点开关系统
cross post 交叉投寄
cross program 交互程序
cross reference 交互参考
cross reference dictionary 交互参考字典
cross-reference file 交叉参考文件
cross reference generator 交互引用产生器
cross reference list 交互参考表
cross reference list format 交叉参考表格式
cross reference list generator program 交叉参考表生成程序
cross-reference listing 交叉参考列表
cross-reference utility 交叉参考实用程序
cross-referenced type library 交叉引用类型库
cross-referencing 交叉引用
cross section 断面,截面
cross section chart 剖面图
cross section of array 数组截面
cross section sketch 剖面略图
cross sectional testing 断面测试
cross simulator 交叉仿真程序
cross software 交叉软件
cross-stroke 交叉笔划
cross switch system 纵横交换系统
Cross System Product 交叉系统产品
cross-tab query 跨表查询
cross-tab report 交叉表报表
cross talk 串音,串扰
cross tracking 十字追踪
cross validation 交叉验证
cross zero time method 过零时间法
crossbar 纵横制
crossbar connector 纵横连接器
crossbar interconnection 交叉网络互连
crossbar switch 交叉开关,纵横交换
crossbar switch matrix 交叉开关矩阵
crossbar switching network 纵横制交换网络
crossbar switching system 纵横制(电话)交换系统
crossbar telephone switching system 纵横制电话交换机
crossfade (图像帧之间的)叠化
crossfoot 交叉脚标
crossfooting 交叉验算
crossfooting test 交叉结算测试
crosshatch 剖线
crosshatch generator 交叉阴影线产生器
crosshatched pattern 交叉阴影线图案
crossing counter 差值计数器
crossing sequence 穿越序列
crossover area 跨越区域,过渡区域
crossover point 跨越点
crosspoint 交叉点
crosspoint matrix 交叉点矩阵
Crosstalk 交叉对话程序
crosstalk 串扰,串音
crosstalk attenuation 串音衰减

crosstalk disturbance 串音干扰
crosstalk interference 串音干扰
crosstalk meter 串音测试仪
crosstalk suppression 串音抑制
crowding 拥挤
CRQ(Call ReQuest) 呼叫请求,调用请求
CRS(Configuration Report Server) 配置记录服务器
CRT(Cathode Ray Tube) 阴极射线管
CRT controller CRT 控制器
CRT display 阴极射线管显示器
CRT display interface CRT 显示接口
CRT edit function CRT 编辑功能
CRT electron gun 阴极射线管电子枪
CRT function key CRT 功能键
CRT graphic display 阴极射线管图形显示器
CRT graphic terminals CRT 图形终端
CRT highlighting CRT 加亮
CRT inquiry display CRT 查询显示
CRT interface CRT 接口
CRT performance 阴极射线管性能,CRT 性能
CRT screen 阴极射线管屏幕,CRT 屏幕
CRT terminal CRT 终端
CRTC(Cathode Ray Tube Controller) CRT 控制器
crude knowledge 未加工知识,"生"知识
cruise 漫游
crunch 数字捣弄
crunchier 数字捣弄器
cryoelectronics 超低温电子学
cryogenic element 超低温元件
cryogenic memory 超低温存储器
cryogenics 超低温物理学
cryotron 超导体
cryptanalysis 密码分析
cryptanalysis attack 密码分析攻击
cryptanalytically equivalent 密码分析等效的
crypto 密码机
cryptochannel 密码通道
cryptogram 密码电文
cryptographic algorithm 密码算法
cryptographic communication 密码通信

cryptographic control 密码控制
cryptographic facility 密码设备
cryptographic key 密码键号,密钥
cryptographic key data set 密钥数据集
cryptographic key distribution center 密码键分配中心
cryptographic key translation center 密码键翻译中心
cryptographic master key 密码主键号
cryptographic service message 密码服务消息
cryptographic session 密码对话
cryptographic system 密码体制
cryptography 密码术
cryptology 密码学
cryptosystem 密码体制
crystal 晶体
crystal anisotropy 晶体各向异性
crystal defect 晶体缺陷
crystal diode 晶体二极管
crystal element 晶体元件
crystal growth 晶体生长
crystal lattice 晶体点阵,晶格
crystal microphone 晶体麦克风
crystal plate 晶体片
crystal transducer 晶体传感器
crystal unit humidity sensor 晶体振子式湿度传感器
crystallize 晶化
CS(Channel Status) 通道状态
CS(Chip Select) 芯片选择,片选
CSA(Call Path Services Architecture) 呼叫路径服务体系结构
CSA(China Software Alliance) 中国软件联盟
CSCW(Computer Supported Co-operative Work) 计算机支持的合作工作
CSDL(Conceptual Schema Definition Language) 概念模式定义语言
CSEC(Computer Security Evaluation Center) 计算机安全评估中心
CSEN(CHINA Science and technology Education Network) 中国科技教育网
CSG(Context Sensitive Grammar) 上下文相关文法

CSH(Context-Sensitive Help) 上下文相关帮助
CSIC (Customer Specific Integrated Circuit) 客户专用集成电路
CSLIP(Compressed Serial Line Internet Protocol) 压缩串行线路网际协议
CSMA/CA(Carrier Sense Multiple Access with Collision Avoidance) 具有冲突避免的载波侦听多路访问
CSMA/CD(Carrier Sense Multiple Access with Collision Detection) 具有冲突检测的载波侦听多路访问
CSMA/CD-OB 定序后退法
CSMP language (Continuous Systems siMulation Language) 连续系统模拟语言
CSN(Circuit Switching Network) 电路交换网络
CSO(Computing Services Office) 计算服务局
CSR (Customer Service Representative) 客户服务代表
CSS(cascading style sheets) （网页）级联样式表
CSS(Common Support System) 公共支援系统
CSSH (Client/Server Switching Hub) 客户/服务器交换式集线器
CSSL language (Continuous Systems Simulation Language) 连续系统模拟语言
CSSP simulation program 连续系统模拟程序,CSSP 仿真程序
CSU(Channel Service Unit) 通道服务单元
CT(Cellular Telephone) 蜂窝式移动电话
CT(Computer Tomography) 计算机断层扫描
CTI(Computer Telephone Integration) 计算机电话集成
Ctrl(Control) 控制键
Ctrl-Alt-Del （PC 机）热启动键组合
Ctrl-Break （PC 机）终止控制键
Ctrl-C （PC 机）终止控制键
CTS(Clear To Send) 清除发送
CTS/RTS(Clear To Send/Request To Send) 清除发送/请求发送
CU(Channel Unit) 通道单元
CU(Control Unit) 控制单元
CU(Counting Unit) 计数单元
CU-SeeMe CU-SeeMe 电视会议软件
CUA(Common User Access) 普通用户访问
CUB(Central Unit Buffer) 中央单元缓冲
cube 立方体;三次幂
cube ambiguity 单元体不确定性
cube-connected cycle network 立方体连接环网络
cube network 立方体网络
cube root 立方根
cube table 立方表
cubic 立方的
cubic convergence 三次收敛
cubic convolution 立方卷积
cubic fit 三次拟合
cubic-frame memory 立方体素帧存储器
cubic graph 三次图
cubic interpolation method 三次插值法
cubic meter 立方米
cubic notation 立方表示法
cubic splines 三次样条函数
cue 尾接指令;暗示
cue circuit 线索电路,提示电路
cue mark 提示标记
cue point 关键点
cue-region 提示区
cue-response query 尾接应答询问
cue sheet 插入工作表
cue track 提示磁道;尾接磁道
cueing （视频节目中)插入解释性字幕组
CUG(Close User Group) 封闭用户
CUI (Character-based User Interface) 基于字符的用户界面
CUI(Control Unit Interface) 控制单元界面
CUL(See You Later) （网上聊天用语）再会
CUM (Computer Utilization Monitor) 计算机利用率监视器
cumulant 累积量
cumulated service time 累计服务时间
cumulative absolute frequency 累积绝

对频率
cumulative departure 累积偏差
cumulative distribution 累积分布
cumulative effort function 累积作用函数
cumulative failure probability 累积失效概率
cumulative indexing 累加索引
cumulative relative frequency 累积相对频率
cumulative sum 累加和
CUN(Common User Network) 公共用户网
Curie point 居里点
Curie point writing 居里点写入
Curie temperature 居里温度
Curly brackets 花括号,大括号
currency 目前值
currency indicator 目前状态指示符
currency position 货币符号位置
currency sign 货币符
currency status indicator 当前状态指示符
currency symbol 货币符号
current 电流;当前的
current access mode 当前存取方式
current activity 当前活动
current-activity stack 当前动作栈
current address 当前地址
current allowed cell rate 当前允许的信元速率
current amplification 电流放大
current attenuation 电流衰减
current awareness 最新信息通报
current backup version 当前备份版本
current balance relay 电流平衡继电器
current beam position 当前电子束位置
current block number 当前块数
current buffer area 当前缓冲区
current-carrying capacity 载流容量
current cell 目前单元格
current channel register 当前通道寄存器
current cipher spec 当前密码参数
current command file 当前命令文件
current connect group 当前连接组
current context 当前上下文
current cursor address 当前光标地址
current cursor position 当前光标位置
current data array 当前数据阵列
current data segment 当前数据段
current database file 当前数据库文件
current date 当前日期
current date information 当前日期信息
current default directory 当前缺省目录
current density 电流密度
current detail 当前细节
current device 当前设备
current dictionary 现用辞典
current directory 当前目录
current directory path 当前目录路径
current disk 当前磁盘
current distribution 电流分布
current document 当前文档
current driver 当前驱动器
current event 当前事件
current extra segment 当前附加段
current failure finder 电流故障检寻
current feedback 电流负反馈器
current file 当前文件
current file area 当前文件区
current file disk address 当前文件磁盘地址
current file library 当前文件库
current file user 当前文件用户
current form 当前格式
current gain 电流增益
current goal 当前目标
current graph 当前图形
current-group indicator 当前组指示器
current heap 当前文堆
current hogging logic 抢电流逻辑
current host 当前宿主,当前主机
current indicator 现时指示符
current input stream 当前输入流
current instruction register 当前指令寄存器
current left margin 当前左边界
current-limiting protection 限流保护
current line 当前行
current line pointer 当前行指示器
current loaded class 当前加载类
current location 当前位置
current location counter 当前位置计数器

current location pointer 当前位置指针
current logged disk 当前登录磁盘
current loop 电流环路；当前循环
current loop interface 电流环路接口
current matching class 当前匹配级
current mode controller 电流型控制器
current mode logic(CML) 电流型逻辑
current option 当前选项
current page 当前页
current page number 当前页码
current page register 当前页寄存器
current parent 当前双亲
current partition 当前分区
current pointer 当前指针
current position 当前位置
current print position 当前打印位置
current priority 当前优先级
current priority indicator 当前优先权指示器
current priority level 当前优先权
current processor status 当前处理机状态
current program 当前程序
current program segment 当前程序段
current program status word 当前程序状态字
current read state (SSL)当前读状态
current record 当前记录
current record pointer 当前记录指针
current routine 当前例程
current rush 电流骤增
current sector number 当前扇区号
current security label 当前安全标志
current segment 当前段
current session 当前对话
current software priority level 当前软件优先级
current source 电流源
current source file 当前源文件
current stack pointer 当前栈指针
current state 当前状态
current statement number 当前语句编号
current status indicator 当前状态指示器
current status input 当前状态输入
current status list 当前状态列表
current status register 当前状态寄存器
current steering logic 电流导引逻辑电路
current string 当前字符串
current switch 电流开关
current task table 当前任务表
current time 当前时间
current track number 当前磁道号
current transfer order 当前转移指令
current value 当前值
current view 当前视图
current volume pointer 当前卷指针
current window 当前窗口
current working directory 当前工作目录
current write state (SSL)当前写状态
currently allocated resource 当前已分配资源
currently attached servers 当前连接的服务器
currently available 当前可用量
currently logged disk 当前登记的磁盘
curriculum author language 课程编写语言
curriculum information network 课程信息网络
curriculum net 课程网
cursive handwriting 草写体手书
cursive script 草写体
cursive script character recognition 草写体字符识别
cursor 光标；临时体
cursor addressing 光标寻址
cursor blink rate 光标闪烁速度
cursor buffer memory 光标缓冲存储器
cursor control 光标控制
cursor control key 光标控制键
cursor controller 光标控制器
cursor demo menu 光标演示菜单
cursor editor 光标编辑程序
cursor generator 光标生成程序
cursor glyph 光标图案
cursor home 光标复位
cursor indicator 光标指示符
cursor independent scrolling 光标无关滚屏
cursor key 光标键
cursor location property 光标定位属性

cursor left 光标左移
cursor line 光标行
cursor mark 光标符号
cursor-movement keys 光标移动键
cursor pattern load 光标图案装入
cursor plane 光标平面
cursor position 光标位置
cursor positioning 光标定位
cursor register 光标寄存器
cursor remove 光标移动
cursor resource 光标资源
cursor right 光标右移
cursor stability 游标稳定性
cursor stylus 光标指针
cursor switch 光标开关
cursor tracking 光标跟踪
cursor window 光标窗口
curvature 曲率
curvature invariant 曲率不变量
curvature loss 曲率损耗
curve 曲线
curve and spot detection 曲线和亮点侦测
curve description 曲线描述
curve fitting 曲线拟合
curve fitting compaction 曲线拟合压缩法
curve follower 曲线跟随器
curve generator 曲线发生器
curve pattern compaction 曲线式样压缩法
curve plotter 曲线绘图仪
curve segmentation 曲线分段
curve smoothing 曲线修匀,曲线平滑
curve surface definition 曲面定义
curve tracing 曲线跟踪
curved element 曲边元素
curvilinear 曲线
curvilinear coordinate system 曲线坐标系
curvilinear net 曲线网络
curvilinear regression 曲线回归
curved net 曲线网
cushion 后备区;减震器
cushioning 缓冲,柔化　　　　　「导
Custom AppWizard 定制应用程序向
custom architecture 定制体系结构
custom card 定制插卡

custom chip 定制芯片
custom color 自定义颜色
custom control 自定义控件
custom dictionary 自定义字典
Custom Footnote Mark 自定义脚注标
Custom header 自定义页眉　　　「记
custom IC chip 用户集成电路芯片
custom installation 自定义安装
custom integrated circuit 定制集成电
custom interface 自定义接口　　「路
custom menu 定制菜单
custom message 自定义消息
custom palette 自定义调色盘
custom processor 定制处理器
custom program 定制程序
custom programmable read-only memory module 客户可编程只读存储器模块
custom programming 客户编程
custom recipient 自定义接收者
custom recipient entry identifier 自定义接收者项目标识符　　「表
custom recipient table 自定义接收者
custom recipient template entry identifier 自定义接收者模板项标识符
custom resource 自定义资源
custom service 常规服务
custom software 定制软件
custom sort order 自定义排序方式
Custom Toolbars 自定义工具栏
customary 惯例
customer access area 客户访问区
customer controller 客户控制器
customer engineer(CE) 客户工程师
customer engineer disk 客户工程师磁盘
customer engineering 客户工程部
customer identification number 客户识别号
customer information control system (CICS) 用户信息控制系统
customer information control system of virtual storage 虚拟存储系统中的客户信息控制系统
customer interface 客户界面
customer location code 客户位置代码
customer option key 客户选择键
customer-oriented terminal 面向客户

的终端
customer replaceable unit 客户可换单元
customer service record 客户服务记录
customer service representative 客户服务代理
customer set-up 客户安装
customer set-up products 客户安装产品
customer software 客户软件
customer support 对客户的支持
customer support center(CSC) 客户支持中心
Customer Support Web 客户支持站点
customer terminal equipment 客户终端设备
customer testing time 客户测试时间
customization 用户定制
customize 顾客定制
customized chip 定制芯片
customized database 客户定制数据库
customized pattern 定制模式
customized software 定制软件
customizing mail 定制邮件
cut 切割,剪切
cut and paste 剪切与粘贴
cut buffer 剪切缓冲区
cut capacity 割集容量
cut cell 剪切单元格
cut date 截止日期
cut down 削减;删减
cut form （打印）单页,切开的格式纸
cut form mode 单页方式
cut in 切口索引
cut mark 切割标记
cut off 截止,截止点;修剪
cut-off frequency 截止频率
cut-off voltage 终止电压,截止电压
cut-out 切断,关闭
cut-over 接入;转换,开通
cut plane 剖面
cut set 割集
cut-sheet feeder 单页输纸器
cut-sheet paper 单页纸
cut-through lay n switching 直通式第n层交换技术
cut-through switching 直通式交换
cut tree 割树
cut vertex 割点
cutout 剪切块
cutout tool 切割刀片
cutover 换接,接入
cutset 割集
cutter 刀具
cutter compensation 刀具补偿
cutter offset calculation declaration 刀具补偿计算说明
cutter location file 刀具定位文件
cutter path 刀具轨迹
cutter positioning statement 刀具定位语句
cutting line 切割线
cutting plane method 割平面法
CVF(Compress Volume File) 压缩卷文件
CVT(Communications Vector Table) 通信向量表
CW(ClockWise) 顺时针
CW(Continuous Wave) 连续波
CW(Control Words) 控制字组
CW laser 连续波激光器
CWA(Control Word Address) 控制字地址
CWIS(Campus Wide Information System) 广域校园信息网
CX(Change conteXt) 更改上下文
cyan 青色
Cyber Screen 赛柏屏幕(Philips)
cybercash 网络化货币
cyberchat 虚拟空间对话
cyberculture 网络文化
cyberflame 网上煽情
cybermarketing 网络营销
cybernate 计算机化
cybernation 计算机化控制
CYBERNET CYBER计算机网
cybernetic loop 控制环
cybernetic model 控制论模型
cybernetics 控制论
cybernetics system 控制论系统
cyberphobia 计算机恐惧症
cyberpunk 网上滋事者
cybersex 网上情场
cybersight 计算机视域
cybersoldier 计算机化士兵
cyberspace 赛博空间,网络虚拟空间
cybertron 控制机

cyberwar 计算机战,网络战
cyborganization 人工器官化
cybotactic state 群聚态
cycle 周期,循环,环路
cycle access memory 循环存取存储器
cycle availability 有效周期
cycle-based simulation 节拍式仿真
cycle chained linear list 循环链式线性表
cycle channel 循环通道
cycle code 循环码
cycle control 循环控制
cycle count 循环计数
cycle counter 循环计数器
cycle criterion 循环判定
cycle grandfather 原始期,存档期
cycle in action 作用循环
cycle index 循环次数
cycle index counter 循环执行次数计数器
cycle interrupt 周期中断
cycle inventory 周期性储存量
cycle operation 循环作业
cycle redundancy check(CRC) 循环冗余校验
cycle reset 循环复位
cycle sharing 周期共享
cycle shift 循环移位
cycle slip 循环滑移
cycle space 圈空间
cycle steal 周期挪用
cycle stealing data acquisition 周期挪用数据采集法
cycle stealing memory 周期挪用存储器
cycle stealing unit 周期挪用单元
cycle structure 循环结构
cycle test 周期性测试
cycle time 循环时间
cycle timer 循环定时器
cycle vector 循环向量
cycled interrupt 循环中断
cycler 循环控制设备
cycles per minute 周/分钟,每分钟周数
cyclic binary code 循环二进码
cyclic binary unit-distance code 循环二进制单位距离码
cyclic check 循环检验
cyclic check character 循环检验字符
cyclic code 循环码
cyclic code byte 循环码字节
cyclic code generating polynomial 循环码生成多项式
cyclic control system 循环控制系统
cyclic convolution 旋转周期
cyclic correlation 循环相关
cyclic debugging 复现调试法
cyclic decimal code 循环十进码
cyclic directed graph 循环有向图
cyclic distortion 周期畸变
cyclic feeding 周期性馈送
cyclic first fit 循环首次适配
cyclic group 循环群
cyclic interrupt 周期性中断
cyclic iterative method 循环迭代法
cyclic Jacobi method 循环雅克比法
cyclic lexical insertion 循环词汇插入
cyclic matrix 循环矩阵
cyclic memory 循环存储器
cyclic ordering 循环排序
cyclic path 循环通路
cyclic phonological rule 周期音位规则
cyclic polynimial 循环多项式
cyclic queue mode 循环队列模式
cyclic queue system 循环队列系统
cyclic queuing network 循环排队网络
cyclic query 循环查询
cyclic reduction method 循环归约法
cyclic redundancy check character 循环冗余校验字符
cyclic redundancy check code(CRCC) 循环冗余校验码
cyclic rule 循环规则
cyclic scheduling 循环调度
cyclic search 循环检索
cyclic semigroup 循环半群
cyclic shift 循环移位
cyclic storage 循环存储器
cyclic table 循环表
cyclic test 循环检验
cyclic transfer 循环传送
cycling time 循环时间
cyclogram 循环图表,周期图表
cyclograph 圆弧规
cyclomatic complexity 回路复杂性
cyclomatic number 独立圈数
cyclomatic polynomial 割圆多项式

Cycolor　Cycolor 图印技术
CYL(CYLinder)　柱面
cylinder address　柱面地址
cylinder-cylinder-header-sector　磁柱-磁柱-磁头-扇区
cylinder group map　(Unix)柱面组图
cylinder number　柱面编号
cylinder skew　柱面斜移
cylinder overflow　柱面溢出
cylinder scanning　柱面扫描
cylindrical-coordinate robot　柱坐标机器人
cylindrical-coordinate system　柱坐标系
cylindrical working envelope　柱状工作区
Cyrix　Cyrix 公司(美)
Cyrix 6X86　Cyrix 6X86 处理器
Cyrix MediaGX　Cyrix MediaGX 处理器

D d

D(Data)　数据
D(Deci-)　十分之一，10^{-1} 的前缀
D(Decimal)　十进制
D(Diameter)　直径
D(Diode)　二极管
1D(One Dimensional)　一维(的)
2D(Two Dimensional)　二维(的)
3D(Three Dimensional)　三维(的)
D/A conversion of synapse　突触数/模转换
D-bit modification　D 位修改
D-bus　数据总线
D channel　D 通道，D 信道
D flip-flop　D 型触发器
D-HDTV(Digital-High Definition Television)　数字式高清晰度电视
D-link　友讯科技公司(台湾省)
D-MAC system　D-MAC 制
D2-MAC system　D2-MAC 制
3D Studio　三维动画制作软件(Autodesk)
3D StudioMax　三维动画制作软件(Autodesk)
DA(Data Adapter)　数据适配器
DA(Desk Accessory)　桌面附件
DA(Dot Address)　点分(IP)地址
DAC(Digital to Analog Converter)　数/模转换器
DAC(Dual Access Concentrator)　双连接集中器
DADPCM(Delay Adaptive Differential Pulse Code Modulation system)　延迟自适应微分脉码调制系统
DA-DSI(Demand Assignment - Digital Speech Interpolation)　按需分配数字语音插入
Daemon　守护程序，代理进程
daemon process　守护进程，影子进程
daemon thread　精灵线程
DAF(Destination Address Field)　(SNA)目的地址字段
daily activity report(DAR)　日报表
daily backup volume　日备份卷
daily batch　每日批处理
daily traffic　每日通信量
daisy chain bus　雏菊链总线
daisy chain device priority　雏菊链设备优先级
daisy chain interrupt　雏菊链中断
daisy chained cable　雏菊链式电缆
daisy-wheel printer　雏菊轮打印机
DAM(Direct Access Method)　直接存取法
DAMA(Demand Assigned time division Multiple Access system)　按需分配时分多路访问系统
damage　损坏
damaged database　受损数据库
damaged file　受损文件
damp　阻尼
damped oscillation　阻尼振荡
damper　阻尼器
damping　阻尼，衰减
damping coefficient　阻尼系数

damping diode 阻尼二极管
damping matrix 阻尼矩阵
damping pad 减震托垫
damping pressure roller 加湿压辊
damping ratio 阻尼系数
DAN(Direct Attachment Node) 直接连接节点
dangerous area 危险区
dangerous operation 危险操作
dangling ELSE 不匹配 ELSE 语句
dangling reference 挂起引用
DAO(Data Access Objects) 数据访问对象
dark background brightness 暗背景亮度
dark blue 深蓝色
dark burn 暗灼
dark current 暗电流
dark fiber sensor 暗场光纤传感器
dark satellite 失效卫星
dark trace tube 暗迹阴极射线管
dark truth logic 光暗真值逻辑
dark vision 暗视觉
darkness (颜色)深浅度
darkroom 暗室
Darlington circuit 达林顿电路
Darlington pair 达林顿对
Darlington transistor 达林顿晶体管
DART(Dual Asynchronous Receive / Transmit) 双异步收发
DAS(Direct Access Storage) 直接存取存储器
DAS(Directory Allocation Sector) 目录分配扇区
DAS(Distributed Access System) 分布式访问系统
DAS(Dual Access Station) 双连接站点
DAS(Dual Attached Station) 双连接站
DASD(Direct Access Storage Drive) 直接存取存储设备(IBM)
DASH(Directory Architecture for SHared memory) 共享内存目录结构,DASH 计算机系统
dash mark 破折号
dash-out 删去,涂掉
dashboard 仪表板
dashed line 虚线
DASS(Demand Assignment Signaling and Switching unit) 按需分配信令发送和转接单元
DAT(Device Allocation Table) 设备分配表
DAT(Digital Audio Tape) 数码音频磁带(HP, Sony)
data(D) 数据
data abstract 数据抽象
data abstraction language 数据抽象语言
data abstraction mode 数据抽象模式
data access 数据存取
data access application 数据访问应用程序
data access arrangement(DAA) 数据存取设备
data access method 数据存取方法
data access mode 数据存取模式
data access object(DAO) 数据访问对象
data access protocol(DAP) 数据访问协议
data access strategy 数据存取策略
data acquisition 数据采集
data acquisition and control system (DACS) 数据采集与控制系统
data acquisition and conversion system 数据采集与转换系统
data acquisition circuit 数据采集电路
data acquisition computer 数据获取计算机
data acquisition equipment(DAE) 数据采集设备
data acquisition system 数据采集系统
data adapter unit(DAU) 数据适配器单元
data address 数据地址
data administration 数据管理
data administrator(DA) 数据管理者
data aggregate 数据聚合
data aging 数据老化
data analysis 数据分析
data analysis display unit 数据分析显示器
data analysis method 数据分析方法
data appendix 数据附录
data array 数据阵列
data attribute 数据属性
data authority 数据授权
data automation 数据自动化

data availability 数据有效性
data bank 数据库组
data base(DB) 数据库
data base access language 数据库访问语言
data base administrator(DBA) 数据库管理员
data base components 数据库成分
data base control system(DBCS) 数据库控制系统
data base data model 数据库数据模型
data base design 数据库设计
data base design aid(DBDA) 数据库设计辅助
data base design method 数据库设计方法
data base design mode 数据库设计模式
data base design process 数据库设计过程
data base designer 数据库设计员
data base diagnostics 数据库诊断程序
data base dictionary 数据库字典
data base engine 数据库引擎
data base engineering 数据库工程
data base files 数据库文件
data base implementation 数据库实现
data base key(DBK) 数据库关键字
data base language(DBL) 数据库语言
data base link 数据库链
data base load 数据库加载
data base machine 数据库机
data base machine architecture 数据库计算机体系结构
data base management(DBM) 数据库管理
data base management system(DBMS) 数据库管理系统
data base manager 数据库管理员;数据库管理程序
data base mode 数据库模式
data base organization and maintenance program(DBOMP) 数据库组织与维护程序
data base pages 数据库页面
data base processor 数据库处理机
data base profile 数据库配置
data base query language 数据库查询语言
data base recreation 数据库重建
data base reorganization 数据库重组
data base scheme 数据库模式
data base security control 数据库安全控制
data base server 数据库服务器
data base standardization 数据库标准化
data base system 数据库系统
data base task group(DBTG) 数据库工作组
data base user 数据库用户
data base workload 数据库工作负荷
data binding 数据绑定
data bit 数据位
data bit period 数据位周期
data block 数据块
data block buffering 数据块缓冲册
data book 标准产品手册,参考资料手册
data break transfer 中断式数据传送
data broadcasting 数据广播
data buffer 数据缓冲器
data buffer method 数据缓冲法
data buffer register 数据缓冲寄存器
data buffering 数据缓冲
data bus 数据总线
data bus amplifier 数据总线放大器
data bus cascading 数据总线级联
data bus component 数据总线部件
data bus conflict 数据总线冲突
data bus connector 数据总线连接器
data bus coupler 数据总线耦合器
data bus driver 数据总线驱动器
data bus enable 数据总线使能信号
data bus output driver 数据总线输出驱动器
data bus system 数据总线系统
data cache address 数据高速缓存地址
data calling 数据调用
data capacity 数据容量
data capsule 数据包
data capture 数据获取,数据捕捉
data capturing terminal 数据采集终端
data carrier 数据载体
data carrier detected 数据载波检测
data cartridge 数据盒式磁带
data cell 数据单元
data center 数据中心
data centric 以数据为中心的

data chain 数据链
data chaining 数据链接
data channel 数据通道
data channel controller 数据通道控制器
data channel cycle stealing 数据通道周期窃用
data channel mode 数据通道模式
data channel multiplexer 数据通道多路复用器
data character set 数据字符集
data check 数据检查
data chip 数据芯片
data circuit 数据电路
data circuit equipment(DCE) 数据电路设备
data circuit switching system 数据电路交换系统
data circuit terminal equipment(DCE) 数据电路终端设备
data circuit terminating equipment (DCE) 数据电路终端设备
data circuit transparency 数据电路透明性
data class 数据类
data clause 数据子句
data clustering 数据群集,数据聚类
data code 数据代码
data code conversion 数据代码转换
data code index 数据代码索引
data collection 数据收集
data collection and analysis 数据收集与分析
data collection channel 数据收集通道
data collection station 数据收集站
data collection system 数据收集系统
data collision 数据冲突
data communication 数据通信
data communication buffer 数据通信缓冲器
data communication control unit 数据通信控制器
data communication equipment(DCE) 数据通信设备
data communication exchange 数据通信交换机
data communication interface cards 数据通信接口卡
data communication monitor 数据通信监督程序
data communication network 数据通信网
Data Communication Network Architecture(DCNA) 数据通信网络体系结构
data communication package 数据通信软件包
data communication processor 数据通信处理器
data communication protocol 数据通信协议,数据通信规程
data communication software 数据通信软件
data communication station 数据通信站
data communication structure 数据通信结构
data communication system 数据通信系统
data communication terminal 数据通信终端
data compaction 数据精简
data compatibility 数据相容性
data compilation 数据汇编
data component 数据成分
data compression 数据压缩
data concentration 数据集中
data concentration formatting 数据集中格式化
data concentrator 数据集中器
data conferencing network 数据会议网络
data connection 数据连接
data connector 数据连接器
data constant initialization 数据常量预置
data contamination 数据混淆,数据沾污
data content 数据内容;数据目录
data control 数据控制
data control block(DCB) 数据控制块
data control clerk 数据控制员
data control group 数据控制组
data control unit(DCU) 数据控制单元
data control word 数据控制字
data conversion 数据转换
data conversion characteristic 数据转换特性
data conversion library 数据转换库

data conversion line 数据转换线
data conversion utility 数据变换实用程序
data converter 数据转换器
data coordinator 数据协调程序
data correlation 数据相关
data corruption 数据破坏,数据恶化
data country code 数据国家码
data coupling 数据耦合
data declaration(DD) 数据说明
data decompression library 数据解压缩库
data definition(DD) 数据定义 「令
data definition command 数据定义命
data definition language(DDL) 数据定义语言
data definition name 数据定义名称
data definition statement 数据定义语
data delay 数据延迟 「句
data deletion 数据删除
data delimiter 数据定界符
data density 数据密度
data dependence 数据依赖
data dependence graph 数据相关图
data dependency 数据相关性
data description 数据说明,数据描述
data description entry 数据描述项目
data description language(DDL) 数据描述语言
data descriptors 数据描述符
data design 数据设计
data design layout 数据设计计划 「址
data destination address 数据目标地
data dictionary(DD) 数据字典 「录
data dictionary directory 数据字典目
data dictionary system 数据字典系统
data diddling 数据欺诈
data-directed inference 数据指导推理
data-directed input/output 数据定向输入/输出
data-directed stream 数据定向流 「器
data direction register 数据方向寄存
data directory 数据目录
data disk 数据盘
data display 数据显示
data display equipment 数据显示设备
data display module 数据显示模块
data display unit 数据显示单元

data distribution 数据分配
data distribution component 数据分配部件 「统
data distribution system 数据分布系
data distributor 数据分配器
data divide 数据分割
data division 数据部
data-domain test 数据域测试
data-domain test instrument 数据域测试仪器
data dress 数据服装
data-driven architecture 数据驱动体系结构 「机
data-driven computer 数据驱动计算
data-driven execution 数据驱动执行
data-driven method 数据驱动法
data driven programming 数据驱动的程序设计
data-driven reasoning 数据驱动推理
data driven system 数据驱动系统
data edition 数据编辑
data editing 数据剪辑
data element 数据元素
data element chain 数据元链
data element dictionary(DED) 数据元素字典
data encapsulation 数据封装
data encoding format 数据编码格式
data encoding scheme 数据编码方案
data encrypting 数据加密
data encrypting key 数据加密密钥
data encrypting standard algorithm 数据加密标准算法
data encryption 数据加密
data encryption algorithm 数据加密算法
data encryption key 数据加密密钥
data encryption standard(DES) 数据加密标准
data entry 数据入口;数据项
data entry device 数据输入设备
data entry form 数据输入格式
data entry operator 数据录入员
data entry panel 数据输入显示板
data entry program 数据输入程序
data entry station cluster 数据输入站群集
data entry system 数据输入系统

data entry terminals system 数据输入终端系统
data entry utility 数据录入实用程序
data environment command 数据环境命令
data environment designer 数据环境设计程序
data environment result set 数据环境结果集
data error 数据误差[错误]
data escape character 数据换码[转义]字符
data evaluation 数据评估
data examination clerk 数据检验员
data exchange command 数据交换命令
data exchange system 数据交换系统
data exchange unit 数据交换单元
data expression 数据表示
data extend block(DEB) 数据扩充块
data extract 数据提取
data field(DF) 数据区域[字段]
data field masking 数据字段屏蔽
data file 数据文件
data file format 数据文件格式
data file object 数据文件对象
data file pointer 数据文件指针
data filtering 数据过滤
data fitting 数据拟合
data flow 数据流
data flow analysis 数据流程分析
data flow architecture 数据流体系结构
data flow chart 数据流程图 「构
data flow computer(DFC) 数据流计算机
data flow computing 数据流计算
data flow control layer 数据流控制层
data flow control protocol 数据流控制协议
data flow design 数据流设计
data flow diagram(DFD) 数据流程图
data flow language 数据流语言
data flow model 数据流模型
data flow-oriented design 面向数据流的设计
data flow partition method 数据流分割法
data flow processor 数据流处理机

data flow synchronous response 数据流同步响应
data flowchart 数据流程图
data folder 数据文件夹
data fork (Mac)数据派生
data form wizard 数据窗体向导
data format 数据格式
data format item 数据格式项
data format statement 数据格式语句
data formatter 数据格式化程序
data formatting 数据格式化
data formatting statements 数据格式化语句
data frames 数据帧
data gathering 数据收集
Data General Corp. 数据通用(DG)公司
data generator 数据生成器
data given in tabular form 表列数据
data glossary 数据汇总表
data glove 数据手套
data group(DG) 数据组
data group continuity(DGC) 数据组连续性
data group header(DGH) 数据组头部,数据组标题
data group identifier(DGI) 数据组标识符
data group link(DGL) 数据组链
data group repetition(DGR) 数据组重复
data group size(DGL) 数据组长度
data grouping dialog 数据分组对话框
data handle 数据句柄
data handler shift unit 数据处理移位单元
data handling 数据处理
data handling capacity 数据处理能力
data handling system 数据处理系统
data head 数据磁头
data header 数据头部 「符
data header identifier 数据头部标识
data hiding mode 数据隐藏模式 「构
data hierarchy 数据层次,数据分层结
data highway 数据主通道
data highway distributed control system 高速数据通道分布控制系统
data host 数据宿主

data identifier 数据识别码,数据标识符
data imperfection 数据缺陷
data in voice(DIV) 声音数据
data independence 数据独立性
data independence access model(DIAM) 数据独立存取模型
data information 数据信息
data initialization statement 数据初值语句
data-initiated control 数据启动控制
data input 数据输入
data input bus(DIB) 数据输入总线
data input station 数据输入站
data input strobe 数据输入选通
data insertion 数据插入
data integration 数据集成
data integrity 数据完整性
data interchange 数据交换
data interchange code 数据交换码
data interchange format(DIF) 数据交换格式
data interchange format file 数据交换格式文件
data interchange processor 数据交换处理机
data interface 数据接口,数据界面
data interoperation 数据互操作
data into computer 数据进入计算机
data isolation transmission 数据隔离传输
data item 数据项
data item definition 数据项定义
data item occurrence 数据项值
data item type 数据项类型
data item validation 数据项确认
Data Language/one DL/1语言
data layout 数据布置,数据打印格式
data level 数据级
data-level parallel algorithm 数据级并行算法
data-level parallelism 数据级并行性
data library 数据文件库,在库数据
data line monitor 数据线监视器
data line occupied 数据线被占用
data line terminal 数据线路终端机
data link 数据链路
data link adapter 数据链路适配器
data link connection identifier 数据链路连接标识符
data link control(DLC) 数据链路控制
data link control layer 数据链路控制层
data link encryption 数据链加密
data link escape(DLE) 数据链转义
data link escape character 数据链路转义字符
data link frame format 数据链路帧格式
data link layer 数据链路层
data link protocol 数据链路协议
data link supervisory control 数据链路监视控制
data link switch(DLSW) 数据链路交换(IBM)
data link unnumbered control 数据链路无编号控制
data list 数据列表
data load module 数据装入模块
data locality 数据局部性
data location 数据位置,数据单元
data locking 数据锁定
data logger 数据记录器
data logging 数据登录
data logging equipment 数据登录设备
data logging system 数据登录系统
data loop 数据环路
data management 数据管理
data management index 数据管理索引
data management program 数据管理程序
data management programming system 数据管理程序设计系统
data management reference model(DM-RM) 数据管理参考模型
data management software 数据管理软件
data management system(DMS) 数据管理系统
data manipulation 数据操作
data manipulation language(DML) 数据操纵语言,DML语言
data manipulator 数据变换网络
data map 数据布局
data mapping 数据映像
data mark 数据标志
data mask 数据屏蔽
data materialization 数据具体化
data matrix 数据矩阵

data medium 数据媒体
data member 数据成员
data membership 数据从属度
data merge 数据归并
data message 数据消息,数据报文
data message switching system 数据报文交换系统
data migration 数据迁移
data mile 数据哩
data mining 数据挖掘
data mining processor 数据挖掘处理器,数据挖掘工具
data mode 数据模式
data model 数据模型
data modeling 数据建模
data modem 数据调制解调器
data modification 数据修改
data module 数据模块
data module drive 数据模块驱动器
data module object 数据模块对象
data monitor 数据监控器
data move instruction 数据移动指令
data movement capacity 数据传送能力
data movement instruction 数据传送指令
data multiplexer(DMX) 数据多路复用器
data name 数据名
data network 数据网络
data normalization 数据标准化
data object 数据对象
data occurrence 数据事件
data offset 数据偏移量
data operation mode 数据工作模式
data organization 数据组织
data-oriented design technique 面向数据设计方法
data origination 数据源流,数据初始加工
data output 数据输出
data output register 数据输出寄存器
data output strobe 数据输出选通
data owner 数据拥有者
data ownership 数据所有权
data packet 数据包,数据分组
data packing 数据压缩(去除无用部分)

data page locking 数据页面加锁
data parallel algorithm 数据并行算法
Data-Parallel C 数据并行C语言
data parallelism 数据并行性
data path 数据通路
data pen 数据笔
data phase 数据传输阶段
DATA-PHONE "数据电话"
data phone 数据电话机
data phone digital service(DDS) 数据电话数字服务
data phone digital system 数据电话数字系统
data physician 数据医生
data plotter 数据绘图仪
data point 数据点
data pointer 数据指针
data preparation 数据准备
data preprocessing 数据预处理
data privacy 数据专用性
data processing 数据处理
data processing application 数据处理应用程序
data-processing center 数据处理中心
data processing cycle 数据处理周期
data processing equipment 数据处理设备
data processing for statistics of industry 工业数据统计处理
data processing machine 数据处理机
data processing manager(DPM) 数据处理管理员
data processing node 数据处理节点
data processing security 数据处理安全性
data processing standards 数据处理标准
data processing station 数据处理站
data processing system 数据处理系统
data processing system security 数据处理系统安全性
data processor(DP) 数据处理机
data projector 数据投影器
Data Propagator 数据传播程序
data protection 数据保护
data protection convention 数据保护公约
data protection with multiple threads 多线程数据保护

data provider 数据提供者
data providing system 数据提供系统
data pulse amplitude 数据脉冲幅度
data pulse shape 数据脉冲形状
data pump 数据泵
data purification 数据纯化,数据精炼
data qualifier bit 数据类型位
data rate 数据速率,数据传输率
data reader 数据阅读机
data receiver 数据接收机
data record 数据记录
data recorder 数据记录器
data recording 数据记录「器
data recording control 数据记录控制
data recording equipment 数据记录设备
data recording medium 数据记录媒介
data recording program 数据记录程序
DATA RECORDS clause 数据记录子「句
data recovery 数据恢复
data reduction 数据精简,数据归约
data reduction system 数据归约系统
data redundancy 数据冗余
data region 数据区
data register 数据寄存器
data registers 数据寄存器
data registration 数据定位
data reliability 数据可靠性
data replication tool 数据复制工具
data report 数据报表
data representation 数据表示法
data representation standard 数据表示标准
data resampling 数据重采样
data resource management 数据资源管理
data retrieval 数据检索
data row locking 数据行加锁,数据记录加锁
data rules 数据规则
data safety 数据安全
data scattered strategy 数据分散策略
data scramble 数据置乱,数据加密
data search 数据检索
data security 数据安全
data security erase 数据安全性清洗
data segment 数据段

data select 数据选择
data selection and modification 数据选择与修改
data semantics 数据语义
data sensitive fault 数据敏感性故障
data sensitivity test 数据灵敏度测试
data separator 数据分离器
data sequence number 数据顺序号
data series 数据组,数据序列
data set 数据集;数传机
data set adapter 数传机适配器
data set archive 数据集归档
data set authority credential 数据集授权凭证
data set clocking 数传机时钟
data set control 数据集控制
data-set control block(DSCB) 数据集控制块
data-set coupler 数传机耦合器
data set definition(DSD) 数据集定义
data set definition environment 数据集定义环境
data set definition name(DSD name) 数据集定义名
data set definition table(DSD table) 数据集定义表
data set extension 数据集扩充
data set group(DSG) 数据集组
data-set label(DSL) 数据集标号
data set member 数据集成员
data set name 数据集名
data-set organization(DSORG) 数据集组织
data set profile 数据集概貌
data set ready(DSR) 数据设备就绪
data set ready circuit 数据集就绪电路「号
data set reference number 数据集引用
data set utility programs 数据集公用程序
data share 数据共享
data sharer 数据共享者
data sharing 数据共享
data sheet 数据表单
data sheet window 数据表窗口
data signal 数据信号
data signal quality detection 数据信号质量检测

data signal rate selector 数据信号速率选择
data signal rate transparency 数据信号速率透明性
data signaling rate 数据信令速率
data sink 数据接收器，数据宿
data skew 数据歪斜
data smoothing 数据平滑
data source 数据源
data source name 数据源名称
data source object state 数据源对象状态
data source schema browser 数据源结构浏览程序
data source tier 数据源层
data space 数据空间
data space pointer 数据空间指针
data specification 数据规格；数据说明
data specificator 数据描述符
data speed 数据速度
data spying 数据截样
data stabilized Doppler navigation system 数据稳定多普勒导航系统
data stable platform 数据稳定平台
data staging 数据分级
DATA statement 数据初值语句
data station 数据站
data station console 数据站控制台
data storage 数据存储器
data stream 数据流
data stream cartridge 数据流盒式磁带机
data stream computer 数据流计算机
data stream computer architecture 数据流计算机体系结构
data stream computer instruction 数据流计算机指令
data stream control 数据流控制
data stream encoding 数据流编码
data stream format 数据流格式
data stream interface 数据流接口
data stream language 数据流语言
data strobe 数据选通
data strobe offset 数据选通偏调
data structure 数据结构
data structure concept 数据结构概念
data structure definition 数据结构定义
data structure design method 数据结构设计法
data structure diagram 数据结构图
data structure language 数据结构语言
data structure matrix 数据结构矩阵
data structure-oriented design 面向数据结构设计
data sublanguage 数据子语言
data suit 数据服
data summarization 数据汇总
data surface 数据面，数据表面
data surgery 数据诊治，数据手术
data switch 数据转接
data switchange 数据交换局
data switching 数据交换，数据转接
data switching equipment(DSE) 数据交换设备
data switching exchange(DSE) 数据交换机
data switching system 数据交换系统
data symbol 数据符号
data synchronizer 数据同步器
data system 数据系统
data system interface 数据系统接口
data system transmission 数据系统传输
data table 数据表
data tablet 数据输入板
data tape 数据带
data telephone circuit 数据电话电路
data teleprocessing system 数据远程处理系统
data terminal(DT) 数据终端
data terminal equipment(DTE) 数据终端设备
data terminal equipment controlled not ready 数据终端设备受控未就绪
data terminal ready(DTR) 数据终端机就绪
data test 数据测试
data test set 数据测试设备
data thrashing 数据颠簸
data time 数据时间
data token 数据权标，数据令牌
data token frame 数据令牌帧
data tracks 数据磁道
data transcription 数据转录
data transfer 数据转移
data transfer channel 数据传送通道
data transfer class 数据转移类

data transfer distance 数据转移距离
data transfer instruction 数据转移指令
data transfer object 数据转移对象
data transfer phase 数据转移阶段
data transfer rate 数据转移速度「器
data transfer register 数据转移寄存
data transfer request 数据传送请求
data translation system 数据转换系统
data translator 数据转换器
data transmission 数据传送 「特
data transmission bauds 数据传输波
data transmission channel 数据传输信道
data transmission efficiency 数据传输效率
data-transmission equipment 数据传输设备
data transmission interface 数据传送接口
data transmission line 数据传输线路
data transmission ratio 数据传输比
data transmission set 数据传输设备，数传机 「度
data transmission speed 数据传输速
data transmission system 数据传输系统
data transmission terminal installation 数据传输终端设施
data transmission trap 数据传输陷阱
data transmission video display units 数据传输视频显示器
data transparency 数据透明性
data trend graph 数据趋势图
data truncation 数据截断
data tuple 数据元组
data type 数据类型
data type conversion rule 数据类型转换规则
data type mismatch 数据类型不符
data type specification 数据类型说明
data under voice(DUV) 音频以下的数据
data unit 数据单元
data update system 数据更新系统
data upload 数据上载
data use identifier 数据使用识别号
data validation 数据确认[有效性检验]
data validity 数据适用性[有效性]
data value 数据值
data verification 数据验证
data-vet 数据检查
data-vet program 数据检查程序
data view 数据视图
data view window 数据视图窗口
data visualization 数据可视化
data volatility 数据易变性
data warehouse(DW) 数据仓库
Data Warehouse Alliance(DWA) 数据仓库联盟(微软)
Data Warehouse Framework(DWF) 数据仓库框架(微软)
data warehouse system(DWS) 数据仓库系统
data width 数据宽度
data window 数据窗口
data word 数据字
data word size 数据字长度
database 数据库
database accelerator system 数据库加速系统
database access component 数据库访问部件
database administration 数据库管理
database administrator(DBA) 数据库管理员
database analyst 数据库分析员
database application 数据库应用程序
database class 数据库类
database column value properties 数据库列值属性
database computer 数据库计算机
database consistency 数据库一致性
database constructor 数据库构建程序
database control 数据库控制
database creation 数据库创建
database data model 数据库数据模型
database definition 数据库定义
database description entry 数据库说明入口
database descriptive language(DDL) 数据描述语言
database design 数据库设计
database design aid 数据库设计辅助工具

database design evaluation workstation (DDEW) 数据库设计评价工作站
database design methodology 数据库设计方法学
database designer 数据库设计员［程序］
database diagnostics 数据库诊断
database directory 数据库目录
database driver 数据库驱动程序
database dump 数据库转储,倒库
database engine 数据库引擎
database engineering 数据库工程
database environment 数据库环境
database form 数据库窗体
database handler 数据库处理器
database hierarchy 数据库层次结构
database host 数据库主机,数据库宿主
database identifier 数据库标识符
database implementation 数据库实现
database industry 数据库产业
database inquiry 数据库查询
database integration 数据库集成
database integrity 数据库完整性
database interface 数据库接口
database key 数据库关键字
database key item 数据库关键项
database load 数据库装入
database logging 数据库运行记录
database logical organization 数据库逻辑组织
database machine architecture 数据库机体系结构
database maintenance plan wizard 数据库维护计划向导
database management system (DBMS) 数据库管理系统
database manager 数据库管理程序
database memory file 数据库存储器文件
database metadata 数据库元数据
database model 数据库模型
database object 数据库对象
database option macro 数据库选项宏
database producer 数据库生产者「项
database project option 数据库工程选
database protection 数据库保护
database protocol 数据库协议

database record 数据库记录
database recovery 数据库恢复
database recreation 数据库重建
database region properties 数据库区域属性
database reliability 数据库可靠性
database repair 数据库修补
database resource 数据库资源
database schema 数据库模式
database scope 数据库范围
database security 数据库安全性
database selector 数据库选择器
database semantic 数据库语义
Database Server 数据库服务器(IBM)
database server 数据库服务器
database skeleton 数据库骨架
database specification 数据库说明
database standardization 数据库标准
database state 数据库状态
database status indicator 数据库状态指示器
database structure 数据库结构
database subschema 数据库子模式
database synchronization 数据库同步
database system simulator 数据库系统仿真
database task group (DBTG) 数据库任务组
database teat file (DBTG) 数据库备注文件
database template 数据库模板
database upgrade failure 数据库更新失败
database user 数据库用户
datablade 数据刀片(Informix)
DATABUS language DATABUS语言
datacenter 数据中心
DataEase DataEase数据库
datafax 数据传输,数据传真
DATAFORM DATAFORM软件
dataglove 数据手套
datagram 数据报
datagram socket 数据报套接字
datagram transport protocol (DTP) 数据报传输协议
datagrid control 数据栅格表控件
dataless client 无数据客户机
Datamation 《自动数据处理》杂志

datamation 数据自动化
datanet 数据网络
dataphone 数据电话
dataplex 数据多工,数据多路传输
date conversion 日期格式转换
date field 日期字段
date format 日期格式
date interval 日期间隔
date last activity 上次活动日期
date last use 上次使用日期
date math 日期计算
date modified 被修改日期
date prompt 日期提示
date range 日期范围
date representation 日期表示
date/sequence number override 日期顺序号置换
date span 日期跨度
date-time code 日期-时间代码
date/time type (变量)日期/时间类型
dateline 日期变更性
dating format 日期格式
dating routine 时日例程
dating subroutine 时日子例程
DATRAN DATRAN线路交换网络
datum 单数据项,资料;基准线(点)
datum error 基准线误差
datum limit protection 基准线限界保护
datum line 基准线
datum node 参考节点
datum offset 基准偏移量
datum point 基准点
datum setting 基准设置
datum vertex 参考顶点「元
DAU(Dial Access Unit) 拨号访问单
daughter board 子插件板
daughter card 子卡
daughter-mother PC board 子母式PC机板
DAV(DAta Valid) 数据有效
DAVE DAVE分析系统「据
DAVID(Data Above VIDeo) 视频数
day clock 日时钟
day length 日工作时数
day-of-month 月中日
day-of-year 年中日
day setting 日期设置
daylight operation 白日操作

daylight time 日工作时数
daylight time 白昼视觉
Daytona Daytona窗口软件
DB(Data Base) 数据库
DB(Data Bus) 数据总线
DB(Dialog Box) 对话框
db(decibel) 分贝
DB2(IBM DataBase 2) DB2关系数据库(IBM)
DB-9, DB-15, DB-25, DB-37, DB-50 DB系列接插件
DB connector(Data Bus connector) 数据总线连接器
DBA(Data Base Administrator) 数据库管理员
dBASE dBASE 数据库管理系统(Borland)
dBASE compiler dBASE 编译程序(Borland)
dBASE Mac dBASE数据库Mac版本(Borland)
DBAWG(Data Base Administration Working Group, CODASYL) 数据库管理工作组(数据系统语言会议)
DBB(Data Bus Buffer) 数据总线缓冲器
DBB(Data Byte Buffer) 数据字节缓冲器
DBB(Distributed Bulletin Board) 分布式公告牌
DBCC(DataBase Consistency Checker) 数据库一致性检验程序(Sybase)
DBCL(Data Base Command Language) 数据库命令语言
DBCS(Double Byte character Set) 双字节字符集
DBCTG(Data Base Concepts Task Group) 数据库概念任务组
DBD(Data Base Dictionary) 数据库字典
DBDL(Data Base Definition Language) 数据库定义语言
DBF file(Data Base File) DBF格式文件
DBI(Double Byte Interleaved) 双字节交插
DBIC(Digital Bus Interface Card) 数

字总线接口卡
DBLTG(Data Base Language Task Group, CODASYL) 数据库语言任务组(数据系统语言会议)
DBM(Data Base Management) 数据库管理
dBm(decibel based on one milliwatt) 毫瓦分贝,绝对功率电平
dBm0 绝对(功率)电平
DBML(Data Base Management Language) 数据库管理语言
dBmp 加权噪声功率电平
DBMS(Data Base Management System) 数据库管理系统
dBmv 毫伏分贝
DBQ(Data Base Query) 数据库查询
dBR(Disk Bootstrap Record) 磁盘引导记录
dBr 参考分贝,基准分贝,相对(功率)电平 「贝
dBrnc 使用C消息权重的微微瓦分
DBTG(DataBase Task Group) 数据库任务组 「构
DBTG system structure DBTG 系统结
dBXL dBXL 数据库
DC(Device Control) 设备控制
DC(Direct Current) 直流
DC amplifier 直流放大器
DC bias recording 直流偏磁记录 「真
DC component distortion 直流分量失
DC constant speed motor 直流稳速电动机
dc couple 直流耦合
dc coupled flip-flop 直流耦合触发器
DC/DC converter 直流/直流变换器
DC erase 直流抹除
DC erasing head 直流抹除头 「应
DC Josephson effect 直流约瑟夫逊效
DC motor 直流电动机,直流马达
DC parameter 直流参数
DC plasma display panel(DC-PDP) 直流等离子体显示板
DC restoration 直流恢复
DC signaling 直流信令
DC superconducting quantum interference device 直流超导量子干涉器
DC transducer 直流变换器 「件
DCA(Distributed Communication Architecture) 分布式通信体系结构
DCA(Document Content Architecture) 文档内容体系结构
DCA(Double-Conversion Adapter) 双转换适配器 「块
DCB(Data Control Block) 数据控制
DCB(Device Control Block) 设备控制块 「块
DCB(Disk Control Block) 磁盘控制
DCC(Digital Compact Cassette) 小型数字录音带
DCCP(Data Communication Control Procedure) 数据通信控制程序
DCD(Double Channel Duplex) 双通道双工
DCE(Data Communications Equipment) 数据通信设备
DCE(Distributed Computing Environment) 分布式计算环境
DCE clear indication 数据电路终端设备(DCE)清除指示(信号)
DCED(Distributed Computing Environment Daemon) (Unix)分布式计算环境后台程序
DCMP(Data Communication Message Protocol) 数据通信报文协议
DCN(Distributed Computer Network) 分布式计算机网络
DCOM(Distributed Component Object Model) 分布式构件对象模型(微软)
DCP(Data Compression Protocol) 数据压缩协议
DCP(Distributed Communications Processor) 分布式通信处理机
DCS(Desktop Color Separation) 桌面分色
DCS(Digital Cellular System) 数字式蜂窝系统
DCSN(Distributed Computer System Network) 分布式计算机系统网络
DCT(Device Control Table) 设备控制表
DCT(Discrete Cosine Transform) 离散余弦变换
DCTE(Digital Communication Terminal Equipment) 数字通信终端设
DD(Data Dictionary) 数据字典 「备

DD(Data Directory) 数据目录
DD(Double Density) 双密度
DDA(Digital Differential Analyzer) 数字差分分析仪
DDA(Diskette Drive Adapter) 软盘驱动器适配器
DDB(Data Display Buffer) 数据显示缓冲器
DDC(Display Data Channel) 显示数据通道
DDCMP(Digital Data Communication Message Protocol) 数字数据通信消息协议
DD/DS (Data Dictionary/Directory System) 数据词典/目录系统
DDE(Dynamic Data Exchange) 动态数据交换
DDE message 动态数据交换消息
DDI(Device Drive Interface) 设备驱动接口
DDK(Device Driver Kit) 设备驱动程序开发包(微软)
DDL(Data Definition Language) 数据定义语言
DDL(Data Description Language) 数据描述语言
DDL(Direct Down Load) 直接下载
DDL/DML(Data Definition Language/Data Manipulation Language) 数据定义语言/数据操纵语言
DDM(Distributed Data Management) 分布式数据管理
DDM(Drop Down Menu) 下拉式菜单
DDN(Defense Data Network) 国防数据网
DDN(Digital Data Network) (公用)数字数据网
DDP(Datagram Delivery Protocol) 数据报投递协议
DDR(Dynamic Device Relocation) 动态设备重分配
DDR(Dynamic Dump Routine) 动态转储例程
DDS(Direct Dialing System) 直接拨号系统
DDT(Data Definition Table) 数据定义表
DDT(Digital Data Transceiver) 数字数据收发器
DDT(Dynamic Debugging Technique) 动态调试技术
DDV(Dialog Data Validation) 对话框数据确认
DDX(Dialog Data eXchange) 对话框数据交换
DDX(Digital Data Exchange) 数字数据交换
DDX-1 DDX-1 数据网
DDX-3 DDX-3 公用数据网
DDX-P(Digital Data Exchange-Package) 数字数据交换信息包
DE(Data Element) 数据元素
DE(Data Enable) 数据使能
DE(Data Encoder) 数据编码器
DE(Data Encryption) 数据加密
DE(Data Entry) 数据录入
De-Archive (文档)解封
de-emphasis circuit 去加重电路
de facto standard 事实上的标准
deactive 去激励;停止活动
deactive station 非活动站
dead band 死带,静区
dead channel 寂静信道
dead embrace 抱死;死包围
dead end 死端
dead file 死文件,停用文件
dead halt 完全停机
dead key 死键(非英文键盘上用来产生重音符号的键)
dead letter box 死信信箱
dead letter queue 死信队列
dead line 截止期;空线,静线
dead line effect 截止时间效用
dead line game 截止期对策
dead line scheduling 限期调度
dead load 固定负荷
dead lock 死锁
dead page 无效页面
dead position 静局势,僵局
dead sector (空闲但无法存取数据)无效扇区
dead space 无效区,死区,静区
dead time 空档时间,停滞时间,静寂时间
dead track 失效磁道
dead zone 死区,静区

deadline 截止期限
deadlock 死结,死锁
deadlock absence 死锁消除[解除]
deadlock avoidance 死锁避免
deadlock avoidance algorithm 死锁避免算法
deadlock condition 死锁条件
deadlock decision rule 死锁判定法则
deadlock detection 死锁检测
deadlock embrace 包含死锁的
deadlock-free 无死锁的
deadlock prevention 死锁预防
deadlock recovery 死锁恢复
deadlock representation 死锁表示
deadlock state 死锁状态
deadlock test 死锁检测
deadlock test algorithm 死锁检测算法
deadlock theory 死锁原理
deadly embrace 死结
deallocate 解除配置,重新分配
debatable 有争议的
debatable time 昧损时间
debit card(DC) 结算卡
debit card system 信贷卡系统
deblock 解块,数据块分解
deblocking 解块,块分解
deblur (图像)去模糊
debossed 凹陷的
debossed character 嵌印[下凹]字符
debounce 抑制反弹,去除抖动
debounce circuit 除颤电路
debounce cycle 消抖动周期
debounce logic 消抖动逻辑
debounce time 消抖动时间
debouncing 除颤动,去抖动
debug 调试,除错
debug cycle 调试周期
debug line 调试行
debug macro instruction 调试宏指令
debug monitor 调试监督程序
debug phase 调试阶段
debug privilege 调试权限
debug program 调试程序
debug program patches 调试插接程序,调试程序补片
debug strategy 调试策略
debug support system 调试支持系统
debug switch 调试开关

debug symbol table 调试符号表
debug tab 调试选项卡
debug terminal 调试终端
debug version 调试版本
debug window setting 调试窗口设置
debugger 调试程序
debugging 调试,排除错误
debugging activity 调试活动
debugging-aid routine 辅助调试例行程序
debugging aids 辅助调试程序
debugging client script 调试客户机脚
debugging command 调试命令
debugging component 调试成分
debugging console application 调试控制台应用程序
debugging embedded server script 调试嵌入式服务器脚本
debugging events 调试[查错]事件
debugging examples 调试例子
debugging helper 调试帮助程序
debugging initialization routine 调试初始化例程
debugging line 调试行
debugging mode 调试态
debugging module 调试模块
debugging multi-process application 调试多进程应用程序
debugging multithreaded application 调试多线程应用程序
debugging package 调试程序包
debugging process 调试过程
debugging proxy generation DLLs 调试代理生成动态连接库
debugging routines 调试程序
debugging section 调试节
debugging stage 调试阶段
debugging statements 调试语句
debugging step 调试步
debugging system 调试系统
debugging tool 调试工具
debugging trace option 调试跟踪选项
debugging utility 调试实用程序
deburring 清除毛刺
DEC(Data Exchange Control) 数据交换控制
DEC(DECrement) 减量,减1
DEC(Digital Equipment Corp.) 数字

设备公司(美,1998年被康柏公司收购)
DEC Alpha DEC Alpha 处理器
DEC media DEC 多媒体
DEC OSF/1 DEC OSF/1 操作系统
decade 十进制
decade adder 十进加法器
decade counter 十进制计数器
decade ring 十进制计数环
decade scalar 十进制定标器
decade subtracter 十进制减法器
decay 衰变,衰减
decay constant 衰减常数
decay factor 衰减因子
decay time 衰变时间,衰减时间
decay model 衰变模型
decay ratio 衰减比
deceive 欺骗,伪装
deceleration time 减速时间
decentralization 分散
decentralized computer network 分散式计算机网络
decentralized control 分散控制
decentralized control signal system 分散控制信号系统
decentralized data processing 分散数据处理
decentralized input 分散输入
decentralized multipoint 分散式多点
decentralized optimization 分散优化
decentralized processing 分散式处理
decentralized regulator 分散调整器
decentralized system 分散式系统「构
decentralized topology 分散式拓扑结
DEChub DEC 集线器
deci 表示十分之一的字首
decibel(dB) 分贝
decibel meter 分贝计
decibel milliwatt 毫瓦分贝;绝对功率电平
decidability 可判定性
decidable 可判定的
deciding 决定,判定
decimal(D,DEC) 十进位;十进制的
decimal adder 十进制加法器
decimal adjust accumulator instruction (DAA) 十进调整累加器指令
decimal arithmetic operation 十进制算术操作
decimal arithmetic trap mask 十进制算术运算自陷屏蔽
decimal-binary conversion 十进制-二进制转换
decimal code 十进制码
decimal-coded digit 十进制编码数
decimal counter 十进制计数器
decimal encoder 十进制编码器
decimal fraction 十进制小数
decimal notation 十进制记数法
decimal overflow exception 十进制溢出异常
decimal picture data 十进制格式数据
decimal point 十进制小数点
decimal processor 十进处理机
decimal to binary conversion 十进-二进制转换
decimation-in-frequency FFT algorithm (DIF) 按频率提取快速傅里叶变换算法
decimation-in-time FFT algorithm (DIT) 按时间提取 FFT 算法
decimeter(DM) 公寸,分米
decipher 译码,解密
decipherer 解密器,译码器
deciphering key 解密密钥
decision(DEC) 决定,判定,决策
decision action 决策行为
decision algorithm 判定算法
decision boundary 判定边界
decision box 判定框
decision center 决策中心
decision circuit 判决电路,判读电路
decision criterion 决策准则,判决准
decision content 判定量   └则
decision-directed adaptation 判定导向的自适应
decision element 判定元件,阈元件
decision feedback 决定反馈,判定反馈   「统
decision feedback system 判定反馈系
decision function 判决函数
decision fusion 判定熔合
decision gate 判决门
decision hierarchy 决策层次
decision instant 判定瞬间
decision instruction 判决指令

decision integrator　判决积分器
decision level　判决电平
decision logic　判定逻辑
decision maker　决策者
decision making　决策制定
decision making complex　决策复合体
decision-making control　决策控制
decision-making function　决策功能
decision making support system　决策支持系统
decision-making system　决策系统
decision-making theory　决策论,对策论
decision-making under certainty　一定条件下的决策
decision matrix　决策矩阵
decision mechanism　决策机构,判定机构
decision method　决策方法
decision model　判定模型
decision model base　判定模型库
decision path　决策路径
decision plan　决策计划
decision point　判定点
decision problem　决策问题
decision procedure　决策程序
decision region　判定范围
decision result　决策结果
decision room　决策室
decision rule　决策规则,判决准则
decision situation　决策形势,决策状况
decision space　决策空间
decision style　决策风格
decision support system(DSS)　决策支持系统
decision support system generator (DSSG)　决策支持系统生成器
decision support system tools　决策支持系统工具
decision symbol　判定符号
decision table　判定表,决策表
decision theory　决策论
decision tree　决策树
decision-tree classifier　判定树分类法
decision-tree structure　判定树结构
decision under certainty　确定型决策
decision under conflict　竞争型决策
decision under risk　风险型决策

decision under uncertainty　不确定型决策
decision value　决定值
decision variable　决策变量
decision verification　判定验证
deck　卡片叠;走带机构
deck assembly　甲板组件
declaration　宣告,说明
declaration condition　说明条件
declaration of entry attribute　入口属性说明
declaration prelude　说明序部
declaration section　说明节(段)
declaration statement　说明语句
declaration type tab　说明类型标志
declarative array　说明数组
declarative component　陈述性成份
declarative equivalence　说明等价
declarative equivalence　说明等价
declarative indexing　说明性索引
declarative knowledge　说明性知识
declarative knowledge representation　说明性知识表示
declarative language　说明型语言
declarative macro-instruction　说明性宏指令
declarative markup language　说明性标记语言
declarative modeling　描述造型
declarative operation　说明性操作
declarative part　说明性部分
declarative programming　说明性程序设计
declarative security　声明的安全性
declarative statement　说明性语句
declaratives　说明
declarator　说明符
declare　宣告,说明
declared attribute　说明属性
declaring user defined type　说明用户定义类型
DECmate　DECmate 计算机系列
DECmcc (DEC management control center)　DEC 管理控制中心
DECnet　DECnet 网络
DECnet worm　DECnet 蠕虫
decode　解码,译码
decode card　解码卡

decode-history table 译码历程表
decode line 译码行;译码线
decode logic 译码逻辑
decode map file 译码映像文件
decode stage 译码级
decoded operations 译码操作
decoder(DEC) 解码器,译码器
decoder circuit 解码电路
decoder driver 译码驱动器
decoder enable 译码器启动
decoder matrix 译码器矩阵
decoding 解码,译码
decoding algorithm 译码算法
decoding gate 解码门,译码门
decoding matrix 解码矩阵,译码矩阵
decoding network 解码网络
decoding table 译码表
decollate 解并,分开,拆散
decollator 解并器,分开器
decolor 脱色,褪色
decompaction 压缩还原
decompiler 反编译程序
decomposability 可分解性
decomposability attribute 可分解属性
decomposable 可分解的
decomposable game 可分解对策
decomposable model 可分解模型
decomposable operator 可分解算子
decomposable production system 可分解产生式系统
decomposition 分解
decomposition-aggregation analysis 分解-聚合分析
decomposition chart 分解图
decomposition-coordination 分解-协调
decomposition description 分解描述
decomposition of query 查询分解
decomposition of relation schema 关系模式分解
decomposition preserving dependencies 保持依赖的分解
decomposition techniques 分解策略
decompress 解压缩
decompression failure alert 解压缩失败报警
decompressor 解压缩器
deconcentration 分散
deconcentrator 分散器

deconvolution algorithm 去卷积算法
deconvolution filter 去卷积滤波器
decorated name 修饰名
decoration 修饰,装饰
decorative outline 晕影外廓
decoupling 去耦,退耦
decoupling filter 去耦滤波器
decoy 假目标
DECPSK(Differentially Encoded Coherent PSK) 差动编码相干相移键控
decrease 递减
Decrease Font Size 缩小字体
decrease indent 减小缩进量
decrease volume 减小音量
decreasing order 降序
decrement(DEC) 减量,减1操作
decrement counter 减量计数器
decrement field 减量字段
decrement jump 减量转移
decrement operator 减量运算符
decrement stack register 减量堆栈寄存器
decrescent 渐减的
decrescent function 渐减函数
decrypt 解密,解码
decryption 解密,解码,译码
DECstation DEC工作站
DECsystem DEC系统
DECtalk DECtalk语音合成系统
DECwindows DEC视窗
DED(Data Element Descriptor) 数据元素描述符
DED(Data Element Dictionary) 数据元素字典
DED/D(Data Element Dictionary/Directory) 数据元素字典/目录
dedicated 专用的
dedicated automatic test system(DATS) 专用自动测试系统
dedicated buffering 专用缓冲
dedicated bus 专用总线
dedicated channel 专用通道,专用信道
dedicated circuit 专用电路
dedicated computer 专用计算机
dedicated connection 专用连接
dedicated data set 专用[特定任务]数据集

dedicated device 专用设备
dedicated file(DF) 专有文件
dedicated file server 专用文件服务器
dedicated input/output line 专用I/O线
dedicated line 专用线路
dedicated memory 专用存储器
dedicated microprocessor system 专用微处理机系统
dedicated node 专用节点
dedicated port 专用端口
dedicated register 专用寄存器
dedicated server 专用服务器
dedicated service 专项服务
dedicated storage 专用存储器
dedicated system 专用系统
dedicated terminal 专用终端
dedicated tester 专用测试仪
dedication 专用
deduce 演绎
deducible 可演绎的
deduction inference system 演绎推理系统
deduction logic 演绎逻辑
deduction reasoning 演绎推理
deduction rule 推理规则
deduction theorem 演绎定理，推演定理
deduction tree 演绎树
deductive 演绎的
deductive approach 演绎法
deductive capability 演绎能力
deductive database 演绎数据库
deductive inference 演绎推理
deductive inference rule 演绎推理规则
deductive knowledge acquisition 演绎知识获取
deductive learning 演绎学习法
deductive mathematics 演绎数学
deductive method 演绎法
deductive operation on structured object 结构化对象的演绎运算
deductive planning 演绎规划
deductive simulation 演绎仿真
deemphasis 去加重
deenergize 去激励
deep binding 深约束
Deep Blue "深蓝"计算机(IBM)
deep case 深层格
deep cooling 深度冷却
deep copy 深度拷贝
deep equality 深度相等
deep hack mode 完全连通模式
deep knowledge 深层知识
deep reasoning 深度推理
deep sort algorithm 深度排序算法
deep structure 深层结构
Deep Thought "深思"计算机(IBM)
deeply embedded control 深嵌入控制
DEF(DEFinition) 定义
DEF statement 函数定义语句
defacto standard 事实标准
default 缺省,默认,隐含,系统设定
default argument 默认参数
default attribute 默认属性
default button 默认按钮
default chart format 默认图表格式
default choice 默认选择
default condition 默认[系统设定]条件
default constructor 默认构造程序
default cursor type 默认光标类型
default declaration 默认说明
default directory 默认[缺省]目录
default document 默认文档
default drive 默认驱动器
default editor 默认编辑器
default extension 缺省[默认]扩展名
default file 预置文件
default file attribute 默认文件属性
default font 默认字体
default form 默认格式
default format statement 缺省格式语句
default gateway 默认网关
default hardware cursor 默认的硬件光标
default home page 默认主页
default interpretation 缺省值说明
default label 默认标号
default logic 缺省逻辑
default login script 默认登录脚本
default message processing 默认消息处理
default numeric format 默认数值格式
default object handler 默认对象句柄
default option 缺省[隐含]选项
default page 缺省[默认]页面
default parameter 缺省[隐含]参数
default presentation 默认展示

default printer 默认打印机
default profile 系统预置大纲
default prompt 系统预置提示符
default reasoning 缺值推理
default route 缺省[默认]路由
default rule 默认规则
default screen size 默认屏幕大小
default security level 默认安全级
default setting 系统设定,默认设置
default setup 缺省设置
default strategy 空缺[默认]策略
default target frame 默认的目标框架
default task 预置任务
default user name 缺省[系统设定]用户名
default value 缺省[默认]值
default window 系统设定窗口
default window procedure 默认窗口过程
defect 缺陷
defect density 缺陷密度
defect map 缺陷表
defect skip 缺陷跳越
defective tolerance 缺陷容限
defective track 缺陷磁道
defective word cell 缺陷字单元
defender 防护程序
Defense Data Network(DDN) 国防数据网
Defense Research Internet(DRI) 国防部研究型互连网,DRI网
defensive programming 防错性程序设计
defer 递延
defer execution 推迟执行
defer printing 推迟打印
deferral 推迟
deferred address 延后地址
deferred addressing 延后寻址,间接寻址
deferred class 延迟类
deferred constraint 延迟约束
deferred echo 延迟回声
deferred entry 延迟入口
deferred exit 延迟出口
deferred job 延期作业,延后作业
deferred maintenance 延后维护
deferred procedure call 延迟过程调用
deferred processing 延后[延期]处理
deferred restart 延后重启动
deferred run 延期运行

deferred update 延期更新
deficit matrix 亏损矩阵
define 定义,判定,规定
define channel 定义频道
define constant 定义常数
define custom color 定义自选色
define custom event 定义自选事件
define data command 定义数据命令
define database table 定义数据库表
define event control block 定义事件控制块
define event handler 定义事件处理程序
define function 界定函数
define grid 定义网格
define of signal 信号定义
define point 定义点
define statement 定义语句
defined attribute 定义属性
defined context set 已定义上下文集
defined display area 界定显示区
defined file 定义文件
defined occurrence 定义性出现
defined variable 已定义变量
defining mnemonic key 定义助忆键
defining occurrence 定义性出现
defining outline setting 定义大纲设置
defining range 定义范围
defining scalar 定义标量
defining trap destination 定义自陷目标
defining view 定义视图
definite binomial coefficient 确定的二项式系数
definite clause grammar 限定子句文法
definite-correction action 限量校正作用
definite decoding 不变译码,定译码
definite event 确定事件
definite integral 定积分
definite kernel 确定核
definite response 确定响应
definition 定义;清晰度,分辨率
definition environment 定义环境
definition function complex 定义函数复合
definition module 定义模块
definition of programming language 编程语言的定义
definition of subroutine 子例程定义

definition phase 定义阶段
definition point 定义点
definition status 定义状态
definition table 定义表
definitional occurrence 定义性出现
deflate 压缩存储空间
deflation 收缩
deflected gradient 偏斜梯度
deflection 偏转
deflection angle 偏转角
deflection circuit 偏转电路
deflection coil 偏转线圈
deflection electrode 偏转电极
deflection plate 偏转板
deflection sensitivity 偏转灵敏度
deflection system 偏转系统
deflection yoke 偏转轭
defluxing solvent 去焊剂
defocus 散焦
deform 变形
deformed system 形变系统
deformable medium 变形介质
defragment 整理碎片
defragmenting 碎片合并,取消碎片
defringe 消除毛边
defun(define function) 定义函数
defuzzification 消除模糊
degauss 去磁,退磁
degausser 消磁器
degeneracy 退化
degenerate basic feasible solution 退化基本可行解
degenerate cut 退化割平面
degenerate function 退化函数
degenerate inequality 退化不等式
degenerate matrix 退化矩阵
degenerate network 退化网络
degenerate process 退化过程
degenerate quadratic form 退化二次型
degenerate segment 退化线段,简并段
degenerate tree 退化树
degenerate two-dimension systolic array 二维退化脉动阵列
degenerate variable 退化变量
degeneration 衰减,降级,退化
degeneration factor 衰减因子
deglitched circuit 去毛刺电路
deglitcher 暂态限时电路

degradable system 可降级系统
degradation 降格,降级,退化 「数
degradation factor 退化因数,降级因
degradation failure 退化故障
degradation testing 降格测试,老化试验,退化测试
degrade run 降级运行
degraded copy 降级拷贝
degraded recovery 降级恢复
degraded running 降级运行
degree 度数;次数
degree of approximation 逼近度
degree of belief 可信度
degree of confidence 置信度
degree of confirmation 可确定程度
degree of consistency 一致性程度
degree of convergence 收敛程度
degree of distortion 畸变程度
degree of freedom 自由度
degree of isolation 隔离程度
degree of linearity 线性度
degree of membership 隶属度
degree of multiprogramming 多道程序数
degree of node in tree 树结点的度数
degree of parallelism 并行度
degree of separation 分离度
degree of tree 树的度数
digression 下降,递减
dehumidification 去湿
deinitialize 取消初始设置
deinstall 卸载,(将已安装软件)删除
deionized water 去离子水
dejagging 消除锯齿线
dejitterizer 信号稳定器,消抖动电路
DEK(Data Encrypting Key) 数据加密密钥
DEL(DELete) 删除
delay 延迟,延时
delay allowance 延时容许量
delay branch 延迟转移
delay circuit 延时电路 「路
delay coincidence circuit 延迟符合电
delay compensation 延迟补偿
delay constant 时延常数
delay counter 延迟计数器
delay decision 延迟判定
delay-dialing signal 延时拨号信号

delay digit 延迟数位
delay distortion 延迟失真,延迟畸变
delay element 延迟元件
delay equalizer 延迟均衡器
delay factor 延迟因素
delay fault 延迟故障
delay jitter 延迟抖动
delay line 延迟线
delay line capacity 延迟线容量
delay-line memory 延迟线存储器
delay-line register 延迟线寄存器
delay line storage 延迟线存储器
delay-line time compressor 延迟线时间压缩器
delay-load import 延后加载导入
delay loop store 延时循环存储
delay memory 延时存储器
delay modulation 延迟调制
delay MP model 延迟 MP 模型
delay network 延时网络
delay-output equipment 延迟输出设备
delay programming 延迟程序设计
delay queue 延迟队列
delay routine 延迟例程
delay statement 延迟语句
delay task 延迟任务
delay table 延迟表
delay time 延迟时间
delay-time telemetry 延时遥测
delay unit 延时单元
delay vector 延迟向量
delayed action 延迟作用
delayed branch 延迟分支
delayed broadcast 延时广播
delayed charging circuit 延时充电电路
delayed delivery 延迟提交
delayed evaluation 延迟求值
delayed port 延迟端口
delayed relaying communication satellite 延时转发型通信卫星
delayed rendering 推迟格式定义
delayed-request mode 延迟请求模式
delayed response 延迟应答
delayed start 延迟启动
delayed time system 延迟时间系统
delayed vibrato 延时颤音
delaying sweep 延时扫描
delegate 授权,委托

delegate access 委托访问
delegated commit optimization 受托提交优化
delegation 授权,委派
deletable 可删除的
delete(DEL) 删除
Delete After Current Position 删除当前位置以后内容
delete all 全部删除
Delete Before Current Position 删除当前位置以前内容
delete cell 删除单元格
delete character(DEL) 删除字符
delete code 删除码
delete command 删除命令
delete conversion 删除变换
delete entire column 删除整列
delete inhibit 删除禁止
delete key 删除键
delete list 删除表
DELETE m(DELETE program comment with statement m) 从 m 语句开始删去程序注解
DELETE m,n(DELETE program form statement m to n) 从语句 m 到 n 删去程序
delete method 删除方法
delete overlay 删除覆盖
delete projection 删除工程
delete segment function 删除线段功能
Delete Sentry 删除警卫(Central Point)
delete sheet 删除工作表
Delete Tracker 删除跟踪系统(微软)
delete versus new 删除较新的
deleted data mark 删除数据标志
deleted file mark 删除文件标志
deleted item folder 已删除项目文件夹
deleted record 已删除记录
deleted representation 删除表示法
deleted text 已删除文本
DELETENR(DELETE Network Resource) 删除网络资源
deleting custom menu bar 删除自定义菜单栏
deleting exception object 删除例外对象
deleting object attribute 删除对象属性

deleting outline 删除轮廓,删除大纲
deleting relations between tables 删除表间关系
deleting site diagram 删除站点图表
deleting style 删除样式
deleting toolbox item 删除工具箱项目
deletion bit 删除位
deletion record 删除记录
deletion tracking 删除跟踪
delimit 定界
delimiter 定界符,分界符
delimiter elements 定界元素
delimiter macroinstruction 定界符宏指令
delimiter statement 定界语句
delimiter table 定界符表
delimiter transfer table 定界符转换表
delimiting character 定界字符
delink 解除链接
deliverable 可交付,可投递
delivery 交付,交货,提交
delivery cycle 交付周期
delivery date 交货日期,交付日期
delivery envelope 交付包封
delivery platform 传送平台
delivery report 递交报告
delivery service 投送业务
delivery time 投递时间,交付时间
delivery tray 传送托盘
delivery vehicle 传送工具
delivery wheel 输送轮
Delphi Delphi 应用程序前端开发工具(Borland)
delta "△","δ"(希腊字母);增量
delta clock △时钟,δ时钟
delta file 增量文件
delta frame 增量帧,生成帧
delta function △函数,δ函数
delta modulation 增量调制,δ调制
delta network △网络,增量网络
delta noise △噪声,增量噪声
Delta routing △路由选择法
delta rule 增量学习规则,δ学习规则
delta signal △信号,δ信号
delta-t transport protocol δ-t 传送协议
delta time △时间
delurk 复出
demagnetizer 去磁装置,退磁装置

demand 需求,要求
demand assignment multiple access (DAMA) 按需分配多路存取
demand basis 立时接通制
demand buffering 需求缓冲
demand constraint 需求约束条件
demand correspondence 需求对应
demand-driven architecture 需求驱动体系结构
demand-driven execution 请求驱动的执行
demand-driven machine 需求驱动计算机
demand fetching 需求提取;按需取指
demand flow 需求流
demand forecasting 需求预测
demand function 需求函数
demand multiplexing 按需多路复用
demand paging 请求调页
demand paging scheme 请求分页法
demand poll 请求轮询
demand prediction 需求预测
demand priority 请求优先权
demand processing 需求处理,请求处理
demand processing time sharing 请求式分时处理作
demand reading/writing 请求读/写操
demand staging 需求分级,请求登台
demand zero page 请求零页面
demarcation 定界线
demarcation strip 分界条
demerit 缺点,短处
demo 展示,演示
democratic network 共同控制网络
democratic system 民主系统
DEMOD(DEMODulator) 解调器
demodulation 解调
demodulator 解调器
demogram 人口统计图
demographic model 人口统计模型
DEMON(DEbug MONitor) 调试监督程序
demon 守护程序;(UNIX)端口监督程序
Demoncron-Malgrange-Pertuiset's algorithm DMP 算法
demonstration 演示,示范,验证
demonstration edition (软件)演示版

demonstration program 演示程序
demonstration test 验证性测试
demount 拆下,卸下
demountable device 可拆卸设备
demountable storage 可拆卸存储器
demoware 演示软件
demultiplexer 多路分配器
demultiplexing 多路分配,多路分解
DEMUX(DEMUltipleXer) 多路分配器
dendrites 树突
denial 拒绝
denial of service 拒绝
denominator 分母
denotation 指称物
denotational approach 指称方法
denotational semantics 指称语义学
denotational semantics method 指称语义学方法
denote 标志,表示
dense binary code 紧凑二进制码
dense index 稠密索引
dense list 紧凑表
dense matrix 稠密矩阵
dense set 稠密集
dense subgraph 稠密子图
densitometer 密度计
density 密度
density gradient 密度梯度
density layer 密度分层
density modulation 密度调制
density sensor 密度传感器
density slicing 灰度划分
denumerable 可数的,可列的
denumerable outcome variable 可数结果变量
denumerable set 可列集
depacketize 拆包
depart 出发,离去
department computing 部分计算
department LAN 部门局域网
departure 偏差,偏离
departure process 撤离过程
departure time 撤离时间
dependability 可信性,可依赖性
dependable computing 可信性计算
dependence 相关
dependence arc 依赖弧
dependence-driven 相关驱动

dependence edge 依赖边
dependence graph design 相关图设计
dependence test 相关测试
dependency 相关性,从属性
dependency analysis 从属性分析
dependency-directed back-tracking 相关制导回溯
dependency hazard 相关冒险
dependency line 依赖行
dependency-preservation 保持依赖,从属性保持
dependency-preserving decomposition 保持依赖的分解
dependency relation 依赖关系
dependency rule 相关规则
dependent analysis 从属分析
dependent cells 相关单元格
dependent client (MSMQ)非独立客户
dependent compilation 关联编辑
dependent failure 相关失效
dependent fault 相关故障
dependent file 非独立文件
dependent learning 依赖学习
dependent object 非独立对象
dependent optimization 相关优化,与机器有关的最优化
dependent project 非独立工程
dependent relationship 依赖关系
dependent variable 因变量,相关变量
dependent segment 非独立段
dependent worksheet 相关工作表
depletion mode JFET 耗尽型结型场效应晶体管
depletion region 耗尽区
depletion zone 耗尽区
deposit 沉积;转储
deproceduring 非过程化
DEPSK(Differential Encoding Phase Shift Keying) 差分编码相移键控
depth 深度
depth-bound 深度范围
depth buffer 深度缓冲器
depth clipping 深度剪取
depth cueing 深度暗示
depth-first minimax procedure 深度优先的极小极大过程
depth-first number 深度优先数
depth-first procedure 深度优先过程

depth-first search 深度优先搜索
depth-first tree 深度优先树
depth information 深度信息
depth map 景深图,深度图
depth of discharge 放电深度
depth of field 视野深度
depth of indexing specificity 标引深度
depth perception 深度感知
depth queuing 深度排队
depth range 深度量测;深度范围
depthing tool 深度定位工具
depthkeeping 深度保持
DEQ(DEQueue) 解除队列
DEQUE(Double-Ended QUEue) 双端队列
dequeue 出队列
derandomization method 非随机化方法
derangement 错位排列
dereference 非关联化
derelativized coding 非相对编码
derivation 派生,导出
derivation block 导出块
derivation graph 推导图
derivation history 派生过程
derivation rule 推导规则
derivation tree 派生树,推导树
derivational analogy 派生类比
derived association 派生关联
derived class 导出类,派生类
derived constant 导出常量
derived data 导出数据
derived data term 导出数据项
derived field 导出字段
derived font 导出字体,派生字体
derived graph 导出图
derived horizontal fragmentation 派生水平关系片段
derived recordset class 导出记录集类
derived relation 导出关系
derived rule 导出规则
derived sentential form 导出句型
derived type 派生类型
DES(Data Encryption Standard) 数据加密标准
DES system 数据加密标准,DES体制
Descartes principle 笛卡尔法则
descendance 后继
descendant 子代

descendant action 后继动作,分支动作
descendant class 后代类
descendant node 后继节点,子结点
descendant vertex 后继顶点
descendant window 后继窗口
descenders 下阶线,下超部分
descending key 递降键
descending sequence 递降队列
descending order 降序排列
descending sort 降序排序
descending sorting 降幂排序
descrambler 伪随机序列译码器
descreening 去网纹
describe 描述
describe environment 描述环境
described difficult devices 描述困难器件
describing function 描述函数
description attribute matrix 描述属性矩阵
description block 描述块
description complexity 描述复杂性
description entry 描述项
description information of image 图像描述信息
description template 描述模板
descriptive abstract 说明性摘要
descriptive markup 描述性标记
descriptive procedure 描述性过程
descriptive session 描述对话期
descriptive statement 陈述性语句
descriptive text 描述性文本
descriptive top-level specification 描述性高级设计规范
descriptor 描述符
descriptor attribute 描述符属性
descriptor base register 描述符基址寄存器
descriptor code 描述符代码
descriptor flag 描述符标志
descriptor queue element 描述符队列元素
descriptor table 描述符表
descriptor variable 描述符变量
deselect 取消选择
desensitization 降低灵敏度
deserialize 串到并转换
design 设计,规划,计划

design activity 设计活动
design adequacy 设计完备性
design aids 设计辅助工具
design analysis 设计分析
design analyzer 设计分析器
design automation 设计自动化
design competition 设计竞争
design cycle 设计周期
design diversity 设计多样性
design document 设计文档
design entity 设计实体
design error 设计错误
design file 设计文件
design file interface 设计文件接口
design flow management(DFM) 设计流管理
design for testability(DFT) 可测性设计
design inspection 设计审查
design language 设计语言
design method management(DMM) 设计方法管理
design methodology 设计方法学
design objective 设计目标
design optimization 设计优化
design-oriented system 面向设计的系统
design parameter 设计参数
design phase 设计阶段
design philosophy 设计指导思想
design principle 设计原则
Design Procedure Language(DPL) DPL语言
design procedure model 设计过程模型
design process 设计过程
design prototyping technique 设计原型技术
design representation 设计表示
design requirement 设计需求
design review 设计复查,设计评审
design rule check(DRC) 设计规则检查
design science 设计科学
design simulation 设计模拟
design specification 设计规范
design strategy 设计策略
design support 设计支持
design support tool 设计支持工具
design target 设计指标,设计目标
design time 设计时刻[阶段]
design-time ActiveX controls 设计阶段的 ActiveX 控件
design-time control script 设计阶段的控件脚本
design tool 设计工具
design transaction 设计事务
design verification 设计验证
design version 设计版本
design viewpoint 设计观点
design vocabulary 设计字汇
designate 指称,指定,代称
designated bridge 指定网桥
designated name parameter 指名参数
designated router 指定路由器
designated state 指定状态
designation 标志,名称
designation hole 标志孔
designation integrity 标定完整性
designation number 指定数目,标志数
designation punch 指示孔,标志孔
designation strip 指示条,标志条
designational expression 指定表达式,命名表达式
designator 标志符,指示符
desirability 合意性
desired access right 期望的访问权限
desired explicit rate 期望的显式速率
desired value 期望值
Designer Designer 图形设计软件
desk accessory 桌面附件程序
desk analogy system 桌面模拟系统
desk calculator 台式计算器
desk check 桌面检查
desk checking 桌面检验
DeskPro DeskPro 系列计算机(康柏)
deskside 桌边
DeskStar DeskStar 系列硬盘(IBM)
Desktop 工作台面
desktop accessory 桌面附件
desktop application 桌面应用程序
Desktop Application Director(DAD) 桌面应用程序引导块
Desktop Backup Pack 桌面备份包(Sun 磁带机产品)
desktop color publishing 桌面彩色出版
desktop computer 台式计算机
desktop conference 桌面视频会议
Desktop Disk Pack 桌面磁盘组(Sun 磁盘驱动器产品)

Desktop Management Interface(DMI) 桌面管理接口
Desktop Management Task Force (DMTF) 桌面管理任务协会
desktop media 桌面媒体
desktop object 桌面对象
desktop operating system 台式机操作系统
desktop organizer 桌面组织程序
desktop pattern 桌面样式
desktop presentations 桌面表示
desktop publishing(DTP) 桌面印刷
desktop publishing system 桌面印刷系统
Desktop Storage Module 桌面存储模组(Sun)
Desktop Storage Pack 桌面存储包(Sun外置式存储设备)
Desktop SunCD Pack 桌面光盘组(Sun)
desktop system 台式系统
desktop video 桌面影视系统
desktop virtual reality 桌面虚拟现实
desoldering gun 去焊枪
despeckle 去斑点,去噪声
Despooler 假脱机析取程序(微软)
DESQview DESQview视窗软件
DEST(DESTination) 目的地,目标,终点
destage 离台;降级
destination 目标,目的地
destination address 目标地址
destination bus 目标总线,目的地总线
destination case 目的地角色,目标格
destination category 目的的范畴
destination document 目标文件
destination element field 目标元字段
destination field 目标字段,信宿字段
destination figure 终图
destination file 目标文件
destination host 目标主机
destination logical unit 目标逻辑单元
destination memory 目的存储器
destination name 目标名
destination network 目的网络
destination node 目标节点,终结点
destination option header 目的地选项包头

destination parent 目标双亲
destination queuer 目标列队者
destination rectangle 目标矩形区
destination register 目标寄存器
destination set 终点集
destination station address 目标站地址
destination vertex 终端顶点
destination warning market 终点告警标志
destination window 目标窗口
destination workspace register 目标工作区寄存器
destroy primitive 撤消原语
destructive cursor 破坏性光标
destructive read memory 破坏性读出存储器
destructive test 破坏性试验
destructor 析构函数;解除程序
desynchronizing 去除同步,同步破坏
DET(Data Entry Terminal) 数据录入终端
DET(Device Entry Table) 设备登记表
detach 拆卸,分离
detachable plugboard 活动插头板
detachable power supply cord 可拆卸式电源软线
detached keyboard 分离式键盘
detached process 分派进程
detail calculation 详细计算
detail card 细目卡片
detail data 详细数据
detail drawing 详细图
detail enhancer 细节增强程序
detail file 细目文件
detail flow chart 详细流程图
detail line 详细行
detail record 详细记录
detail table 细目表
detail time 逐一处理时间,细目时间
detailed design 细部设计,详细设计
detailed design phase 详细设计阶段
detailed design tool 细部设计工具
detailed report 详细报告
detailed schedule 明细进度表
detailed tracking 详细跟踪
detect idle time 检测空闲时间
detect modem 检测调制解调器
detectability 可检测性;可检取性

detectable 可检测的
detectable element 可检测像素
detectable error 可检测错误
detectable group 可检测像素组
detectable segment 可检测图段
detected new device 已检测到的新设备
detection 检波;检测
detection and estimation theory 检测与估计理论
detection criteria 检测准则
detection efficiency 检波效率
detection model 检测模型
detection of known signal 确知信号检测
detection probability 检出概率
detection radius 检测半径
detection search 检测搜索
detection threshold 检测阈
detection ultrasonics 检测超声学
detection window width 检读窗宽
detection with fixed samples 固定样本检测
detector 检波器
detector diode 检波二极管
detent 定位凹槽,定位器
deterioration failure 磨损失效,退化失效
determinant 决定因子
determinate fault 确定型故障
determined structure 确定性结构
determiner 限定词
determinism 确定性
deterministic 确定性的
deterministic activity 确定型活动
deterministic algorithm 确定型算法
deterministic attack 确定性攻击
deterministic automaton 确定性自动机
deterministic context-free language(DCFL) 确定性上下文无关语言
deterministic decision process 确定型决策过程
deterministic demand 确定性需求
deterministic diagram 确定性有向图
deterministic dynamic programming 确定型动态规划
deterministic error 确定性误差
deterministic expression 确定性表达式
deterministic fault 确定性故障
deterministic finite automaton 确定型有限自动机
deterministic game 确定性博弈
deterministic interconnection 确定性关联
deterministic inventory model 确定型库存模型
deterministic language 确定性语言
deterministic linear bounded automaton (DLBA) 确定型线性有界自动机
deterministic machine 确定型机器
deterministic model 确定型模型
deterministic program 确定性程序
deterministic pushdown automaton 确定型下推自动机
deterministic retrieval 确定性检索
deterministic routine 确定性路由选择
deterministic scheduling 确定性调度
deterministic simulation 确定性模拟
deterministic stack automaton(DSA) 确定型栈自动机
deterministic Turing machine(DTM) 确定型图灵机
deterministic workload model 确定性工作负载模型
determination 确定,判定
detune 失谐
detour 转向
detour matrix 迂回矩阵
DEU(Data Encryption Unit) 数据加密单元
DEU(Data Exchange Unit) 数据交换单元
developed image 显影图像
developed image stabilizer 显影图像稳定剂
developer 显影器
Developer 2000 Developer 2000 开发工具
developer isolation 开发人员隔离
Developer's Guide 开发者指南
developing 显影
developing agent 显影剂
development 开发,研制;发展;显影
development cost 开发成本
development division 开发部门
development environment 开发环境
development life cycle 开发生存周期

development methodology 开发方法学
development period 开发周期
development phase 开发阶段
development project 开发项目
development suite 开发工具套件
development system 开发系统
development systems interrupts 开发系统中断
development team 软件开发小组「间
development time 开发时间,研制时
development tool 开发工具
deviation 偏差,频率偏移
deviation alarm 偏移告警
deviation binary code 偏移二进制码
device 设备,装置,器件
device adapter 设备适配器
device address 设备地址
device allocation 设备分配
device and media control language (DMCL) 设备与媒体控制语言
device area 器件面积
device augmentation 设备扩充
device availability 设备可用性
device backup 设备备份
device base control block 设备基本控制块
Device Bay 标准设备底板,设备坞
device bay 设备架
device busy 设备忙
device check 设备检验
device classification and testing equipment 器件分类和测试设备
device clear 设备清除
device contention 设备竞争,设备冲突
device context 设备上下文
device control character 设备控制符
device control panel 设备控制面板
device control table 设备控制表
device control unit 设备控制单元
device coordinate system 设备坐标系
device cross call 设备交叉调用
device data block 设备数据块
device definition 设备定义
device dependent 与设备相关的,依赖于设备的
device-dependent bitmap 依赖于设备的位图
device description 设备描述

device descriptor block 设备描述块
device design 器件设计
device driver 设备驱动程序
device driver kit(DDK) 设备驱动程序开发包(微软)
device element 设备元素
device emulation 设备仿真
device failure 设备失效
device field 设备字段
device file 设备文件
device flag 设备标志
device font 设备字体
device handler 设备处理[驱动]程序
device helper 设备帮助程序
device identification 设备标识
device independence 设备独立性,设备无关
device independent 设备独立的[无关的]
device-independent bitmap(DIB) 独立于设备的位图
device-independent program 设备无关程序
device information 设备信息
device initialization 设备初始化
device input format block(DIF) 设备输入格式块
device input queue 设备输入队列「块
device interface module 设备接口模
device interrupt vector table 设备中断向量表
device level protocol 设备级协议
device line 设备信息行
device location 设备位置
device manager 设备管理程序,设备管理器
Device Media Control Language (DMCL) 设备媒体控制语言
device message handler(DMH) 设备消息处理程序
device-mode setting 设备模式设置
device model 设备模型
device name 设备名
device node 设备节点
device not ready 设备未准备好
device number 设备号
device object 设备对象
device object program 设备目标程序

device page 设备页面
device parameter 设备参数
device power supply 设备电源
device polling 设备轮询
device pool management 设备池管理
device priority 设备优先级
device queue 设备队列
device ready 设备准备好
device reserve word 设备保留字
device resolution 设备分辨率
device selection bit 设备选择位
device selection code 设备选择码
device selector 设备选择器
device selector logic 设备选择器逻辑
device service task 设备服务任务
device sharing 设备共享
device simulation 器件模拟
device space 设备空间
device spanning 设备跨越
device specific format 设备特定格式
device status byte(DSB) 设备状态字
device status field 设备状态字段
device status table(DST) 设备状态表
device status word(DSW) 设备状态字
device subclass 设备子类
device support facility 设备支持软件
device support routine 设备支持例程
device support station 设备支持站
device switch table 设备开关表
device token 设备标记,设备令牌
device transparency 设备透明
device type 设备类型
device type code 设备类型码
device type logical unit 设备类型逻辑单元
device unit 设备部件
device vector table 设备向量表
device virtualization 设备虚拟化
device waiting queue 设备等待队列
device work queue 设备工作队列
devloader 设备加载程序
dew point temperature 露点温度
dew point test 露点试验
dewet 去湿
DEX(Data EXchange) 数据交换
DF(Data Flow) 数据流
DF(Data Flowchart) 数据流程图
DF(Decision Feedback) 判定反馈

D/F(Depth of Field) 景深,视野深度
DFD(Data Flow Diagram) 数据流程图
DFS(Depth First Search) 深度优先搜索
DFS(Distributed File System) 分布式文件系统
DFSK(Double Frequency Shift Keying) 双移频键控
DFS(Decision Frontier Solution) 决策前沿解决方案套件(Informix)
DFST(Depth-First Spanning Tree) 深度优先生成树
DFT(Discrete Fourier Transform) 离散傅里叶变换
DFW(Disk File Write) 磁盘文件写
DG(Data General corp.) 数据通用公司,DG公司
DG(DataGram) 数据报
DG/UX DG/UX操作系统(数据通用公司)
3DGA(3D Graphics Accelerator) 三维图形加速器
DGA(Direct Graphics Access) 直接图形存取
DGIS(Direct Graphic Interface Specification) 直接图形接口规范
DG/S(Data General's System programming language) 数据通用公司的系统程序设计语言
DH(Dedicated Hardware) 专用硬件
DHBS(Double Host Backup System) 双主机备份系统
DHCP(Dynamic Host Configuration Protocol) 动态主机配置协议
DHNN(Discrete Hopfield Neural Network) 离散Hopfield神经网络
DHTML(Dynamic HTML) 动态超文本标记语言(微软,Netscape)
Dhrystone Dhrystone基准程序
DI(Data Independence) 数据独立性
DI(Data Integrity) 数据完整性
DI(Dimmed Icon) 暗淡的光标
DIA(Document Interchange Architecture) 文档交换结构
DIA(Dual Interface Adapter) 双接口适配器
diacritic 区别符

diacritical marks 读音符号；区分标记
diacritical sign 区分记号
diad 双项目二进制；双位二进制
diadic operator 双值算子
diadic processor 二元处理机
diadic product 双值乘积
diagnosability 可诊断性
diagnosable 可诊断的
diagnosable system 可诊断系统
diagnose interface 诊断接口
diagnose-source file 诊断用源文件
diagnose-source member 诊断用源成
diagnosing sequence 诊断序列 〔员
diagnosis 诊断
diagnostic and monitoring protocol (DMP) 诊断与监控协议
diagnostic board 诊断板
diagnostic check 诊断核对
diagnostic code 诊断码
diagnostic control manager 诊断控制管理程序
diagnostic dictionary 诊断字典
diagnostic diskette 诊断软盘
diagnostic error processing 诊断错误处理 〔统
diagnostic expert system 诊断专家系
diagnostic function test 诊断功能测试
diagnostic graph 诊断图
diagnostic IC test 集成电路诊断测试
diagnostic instruction 诊断指令
diagnostic loader 诊断装入程序
diagnostic log out 诊断注销
diagnostic memory 诊断存储器
diagnostic message 诊断信息
diagnostic microcode 诊断微码 〔用
diagnostic mode enabled 诊断模式启
diagnostic modeling 诊断模型化
diagnostic package 诊断软件包
diagnostic program 诊断程序
diagnostic routine 诊断例程
diagnostic routine simulator 诊断例程模拟器
diagnostic scan 诊断扫描
diagnostic screen 诊断屏幕
diagnostic software 诊断软件
diagnostic structure 诊断结构
diagnostic system 诊断系统 〔序
diagnostic test program 诊断测试程

diagnostic tool 诊断工具
diagnostic trace 诊断追踪 〔序
diagnostic trace program 诊断跟踪程
diagnostic tree 诊断树
diagonal 对角线
diagonal decomposition 对角线分解
diagonal dominance 对角线优势
diagonal dominant matrix 对角线优势矩阵
diagonal element 对角元素
diagonal function 对角函数
diagonal game 对角线策略
diagonal method 对角线法
diagonal microinstruction 对角线型微指令
diagonal isotone mapping 对角线保序映射
diagonal matrix 对角矩阵
diagonal pattern 对角线图形
diagonal resize 沿对角线调整尺寸
diagonal test 对角测试
diagonally dominant matrix 对角优势矩阵
diagram 图；图解
diagram language 图表语言
diagram method 图解法
diagrammatic representation 图示法
diagramming template 画图模板
dial 拨号盘；拨号
dial attempt 试拨
dial back 回拨
dial exchange 拨号交换机
dial-in/dial-out server 拨入/拨出服务器
dial key 拨号键
dial line 拨号线路
dial modem 拨号调制解调器
dial office 拨号局
dial on demand (DOD) 按需拨号
dial-on demand routing 按需拨号路由选择
dial out protocol 拨出协议
dial pulse 拨号脉冲 〔器
dial-pulse interpreter 拨号脉冲转换
dial tone (DT) 拨号音
dial tone delay 拨号音延迟
dial-up 拨上，拨号
dial-up adapter 拨号网络适配器

dial-up connection 拨号连接
dial-up lines 拨号线
dial-up networking 拨号上网
dial-up networking connection enhancement(DUNCE) 拨号上网连接增强工具
dial-up operation 拨号上网操作
dial-up service 拨号服务
dial-up terminal 拨号上网终端
dialback modem 回拨调制解调器
dialect 方言,专用
dialer 拨号程序
dialing mistake probability 拨号错误概率
dialing tone 拨号音
dialog 交谈,对话
dialog bar 对话栏
dialog-based architecture 基于对话框的结构
dialog box 对话框
dialog box setting 对话框设置
dialog box window 对话框窗口
dialog control 对话控制;对话框控件
dialog data exchange 对话框数据交换
dialog data valcation 对话框数据确认
dialog editor 对话框编辑器
dialog file 对话文件
dialog generator 对话生成器
dialog layer 对话层
dialog popup 对话框弹出
Dialog system 对话系统
dialog template 对话框模板
dialog unit 对话单元
dialogue/enquiry CAI 对话/询问式计算机辅助教学
dialogue generator 对话生成器
dialogue layer 对话层
dialogue management 对话管理
dialogue manager 对话管理程序
dialogue tailobility 对话的特制性
dialorder 联机检索系统的原文订购系统
diameter 直径
diamond array 菱形阵列
diamond key 菱形键
diamond property 钻石性质
diamond-shaped box 菱形框
diamond structure semiconductor 金刚石结构半导体
diamond thin film 金刚石薄膜
DIANE (Direct Information Access Network for Europe) 欧洲直接信息访问网络
DIB(Device Independent Bitmap) 设备无关位图(文件格式)
DIB(Dual Independent Bus) 双独立总线
DIBL(Drain Induced Barrier Lowering effect) DIBL 效应
dibit 双位,两位组
dibit encoding 双位编码
DIBOL language(DIgital coBOL) DIBOL 语言
diceable 可分割的,可切割的
diceable test 可分割的试验
dichotomizing 对分,折半
dichotomizing search 二分法检索
dichotomy 对分,二分法
dichotomy system 对分系统
dichroic mirror 分色镜;分色过滤器
dichroism 双色性
dicode 双脉冲码
DICT(DICTionary) 字典,词典
dictionary(DICT) 字典,词典;程序库
dictionary administrator 字典管理程
dictionary applications 字典应用 序
dictionary catalog 字典目录
dictionary code 字典码
Dictionary Inspector 字典观察程序
dictionary lookup 字典查阅
dictionary machine 字典机
dictionary order 词典顺序
dictionary sort 字典式排序
DID(Direct Inward Dialing) 直接拨入
DIDD(Dynamic Integrated Data Display) 动态综合数据显示
DI/DO(Data Input/Data Output) 数据输入/数据输出
die 芯片;硬模
die bond 芯片粘合
die bonding 芯片粘结
die bonding materials 芯片粘结材料
die casting system 压铸系统
die drawing 模具图
die size 芯片尺寸
die slice 小片,晶粒,芯片

dielectric 电介质
dielectric absorption 介质吸收
dielectric breakdown 介质击穿
dielectric constant 介电常数
dielectric film 介质胶片
dielectric interaction 介质互作用
dielectric isolation 介质隔离
dielectric layer 介质层
dielectric loss 介质损耗
dielectric resonator-stabilizer 介质谐振腔稳频振荡器
dielectric strength 介电强度
DIF(Data Interchange Facility) 数据交换设施
DIF(Data Interchange Format) 数据交换格式
difference(DIFF) 差;差分;差值
difference correction 差分校正
difference engine 差分机
difference equation 差分方程
difference expression 差分表达式
difference frequency distortion 差频失真
difference gate 差门,异门
difference method 差分法
difference metric 差别度量
difference mode voltage 差模电压
difference output port 差分输出端口
difference reduction 差异归约法
difference set code 差集码
difference structure 差分结构
difference table 差分表
different 不同的,有区别的
Different Odd and Even Page 奇偶页不同
different time-scale 不同时标
differential 差分;微分
differential amplifier 微分放大器,差动放大器
differential backup 差动备份
differential comparator 差分比较器
differential compression 差分压缩
differential curve 微分曲线
differential duplex 差接双工
differential equation 微分方程
differential file 勘误文件
differential gain 微分增益
differential gain stage 差分增益级

differential gear 差动齿轮
differential inequality 微分不等式
differential input resistance 差动输入电阻
differential linear error 微分线性误差
differential linear error temperature coefficient 微分线性误差温度系数
differential linearity 微分线性度
differential Manchester encoding 差分曼彻斯特编码
differential mode interference 差模干扰
differential model 差异模型
differential nonlinearity 微分非线性
differential observability 微分可观测性
differential phase-shift keying(DPSK) 差分相移键控
differential phase-shift keying modulation 微分相移键控调制法
differential pulse code modulation (DPCM) 差分脉码调制
differential quantization 差分量化
differential reflectivity 差分反射率
differential transformer 差分变压器
differentiating circuit 微分电路
differentiating phase 微分相位
differentiator 微分器
difficulty of expert system 专家系统困难性
diffraction 衍射
diffraction of light 光的衍射
diffractive inference 演绎推理
diffractive system 演绎系统
diffuse convolutional codes 扩散卷积码
diffuse glow 扩散辉光
diffuse highlight 漫射加亮
diffuse illumination 漫射照明
diffuse replection 漫反射
diffused junction 扩散结
diffused layer 扩散层
diffused light 扩散光
diffused resistor 扩散电阻
diffuser 柔光罩,散射体
diffusing object 扩散物体
diffusion 扩散
diffusion capacitance 扩散电容
diffusion current 扩散电流
diffusion depth 扩散深度

diffusion dither 扩散混色
diffusion index 扩散指数
diffusion screen 扩散屏幕,散射荧光屏
diffusion self-alignment MOS integrated circuit 扩散自对准 MOS 集成电路
diffusion transfer process 扩散传送过程
digicom(digital communication) 数字通信
digiplot(digital plotting) 数字绘图
digit(D,DIG) 数字
digit coded voice 数字编码声音
digit communication 数字通信
digit compression 数字压缩
digit delay 数字延迟
digit delay element 数字延迟元件
digit emitter 数字发送器
digit grouping symbol 数字分组符号
digit on-line network 数字联机网络
digit place 数字位置
digit plane 数字面
digit position 数字位置
digit pulse 数字脉冲
digit rate 数字率
digit rearrangement 数字重排列
digit symbol display generator 数字符号显示发生器
digit time slot 数字时隙
digit transfer bus 数字传送总线
digit transfer trunk 数字传送干线
digital 数字的
digital adder 数字加法器
digital-analog channel 数字-模拟通道
digital-analog compatible microwave system 数模兼容微波系统
digital-analog converter(DAC) 数字/模拟转换器
digital analyzer 数字分析器
digital audio 数字声频
digital audio disc 数字声唱片
digital audio disk(DAD) 数字音频唱片
digital audio interface 数字音频接口
digital audio tape(DAT) 数字录音磁带
digital audio tape-recorder(DAT) 数字磁带录音机
digital backup 数字备份
digital block 数字块

digital camera 数码照相机
digital carrier system 数字载波系统
digital cartridge 数字盒式磁带
digital cassette 数字磁带卡(机)
digital cassette tape recorder 数字盒式磁带录音机
Digital Celebris Digital Celebris 台式机
digital channel 数字通道,数字信道
digital channel link(DCL) 数字通道连接
digital-channel multiplexer 数字通道多路转换器
digital circuit 数字电路
digital circuit test 数字电路测试
digital circuit multiplication system 数字话路扩容系统
digital clock 数字时钟
digital code squelch(DCS) 数字编码静噪制
digital coded voice 数字编码声音
digital coding of television signal 电视信号数字编码
digital coefficient unit 数字式系数单元
digital command 数字命令
digital communications 数字通信
digital communications processor 数字通信处理机
digital companding delta modulation 数字压扩增量调制
digital comparator 数字比较器
digital compensator 数字补偿器
digital component recording system 数字分量录像系统
digital computer 数字计算机
digital computing 数字计算
digital concentrator 数字集中器
digital connection 数字连接
digital control 数字控制
digital control robot 数控机器人
digital control system 数字控制系统
digital control unit 数字控制单元
digital controlled delta modulation 数字控制增量调制
digital converter 数字转换器
digital counter 数字计数器
Digital Darkroom 数字暗室
digital data 数字数据
digital data channel 数字数据通道

digital data communication message protocol(DDCMP) 数据通信报文协议
digital data network(DDN) 数字数据网
digital data recorder 数字数据记录器
digital data separator 数字数据分离器
digital data switching 数字数据交换
digital delay generator 数字时延发生器
digital demultiplexer 数字分接器
digital demultiplexing 数字分接
digital device 数字设备
digital diagnostic diskette(DDD) 数字诊断软磁盘
digital differential analysis(DDA) 数字微分分析法
digital display adapter unit 数字显示适配部件
digital encoding 数字编码
digital envelope 数字封装;数字包络
Digital Equipment Corporation(DEC) 数字设备公司,DEC公司
digital event 数字事件
digital filling 数字填充
digital filter 数字滤波器
digital filtering 数字滤波
digital FM music synthesizer 数字调频音乐合成器
digital format 数字格式
digital frequency division 数字分频
digital frequency meter 数字式频率计
digital group switch 数字群开关
digital image 数字图像
digital image analysis 数字图像分析
digital image processing 数字图像处理
digital image synthesis 数字图像合成
digital incremental plotter 数字增量绘图器
digital information display 数字信息显示
digital input 数字输入
digital input channel 数字输入通道
digital input equipment 数字输入设备
digital inquiry-voice answerback(DIVA) 数字查询声音应答

digital integrated circuit 数字集成电路
digital integrator 数字积分器
digital intercontinental conversion equipment(DICE) 数字洲际转换器
digital interface 数字接口
Digital Internet Exchange Digital 互联网络交换中心(DEC)
digital LCR meter 数字式电感、电容、电阻测量仪
Digital Library 数字图书馆(IBM)
digital line 数字线路
digital link 数字链路
digital logic 数字逻辑
digital logic module 数字逻辑模块
digital logic types 数字逻辑类型
digital loop test 数字环路测试
digital magnetic recording 数字式磁记录
digital map 数字地图
digital mapping 数字制图
digital matched filter 数字匹配滤波器
digital media 数字媒体
digital message entry system 数字报文输入系统
digital microwave communication system 数字微波通信系统
digital mix button(MIX) 数字混合钮,数字混响按钮
digital modem 数字调制解调器
digital modulation 数字调制
digital modulation constellation 数字调制星座图
digital monitor 数字式监视器
Digital Movie Icon Properties 数字电影图标属性表
digital multimeter(DMM) 数字万用表
digital multiple-channel per-carrier system(MCPC) 数字群路单载波制
digital multiplex equipment 数字复用设备
digital multiplex hierarchy 数字复接体系
digital multiplex switching system(DMS) 数字多路转接系统
digital multiplexer 数字多路复用器
digital multiplexing 数字复接法
digital multiscan 数字多频扫描
digital nest 数字嵌套

digital network 数字网络
Digital Network Architecture(DNA) 数字网络体系结构
digital noise 数字噪声
digital noise reducer 数字降噪器
digital oscilloscope 数字式示波器
digital output 数字输出
digital output equipment 数字输出设备
digital output module 数字输出模块
digital overlay 数字覆盖
digital PABX 数字式专用自动交换分机
digital pairing 数字配对
Digital Paper "数字纸"
digital panel meter 数字面板表
digital PBX 数字式专用小交换机
digital phase detector 数字式相位检波器
digital phase-lock loop 数字锁相环
digital phaser 数字式移相器
digital photography 数字照相,数字摄影
digital picture 数字图片
digital plot mode 数字绘图方式
digital plotter 数字绘图仪
digital position transducer 数字位置转换器
digital power supplies 数字式电源
digital printer 数字打印机
digital private automatic branch exchange 数字式专用自动交换分机
Digital Prioris Digital Prioris 服务器
digital process control system 数字过程控制系统
digital processing of radar signal 雷达信号数字处理
digital processing oscilloscope 数字处理示波器
digital production effects(DPE) 数字生产效应
digital programmable oscillator 数字可编程振荡器
digital proof 数字证明,数字校验
digital quantity 数字量
digital quantizer 数字量化器
digital radiography 数字X射线照相术
digital range indicator 数字距离指示器
digital readout 数字读出
digital readout indicator 数字读出指示器

digital recorder 数字记录器
digital recording 数字记录
digital remote control 数字遥控
Digital Reposition(DR) 数字存储库
digital representation 数字表示法
Digital Research Inc. 数字研究公司
digital resolution 数字分辨率
digital reverberator 数字混响器
digital rotary transducer 数字旋转变换器
digital scene 数字景象
digital sensor 数字传感器
digital sequence integrity 数字序列完整性
digital servo system 数字伺服系统
digital signal 数字信号
digital signal processing 数字信号处理
digital signal processor(DSP) 数字信号处理器
digital signal resolution 数字信号分辨率
digital signaling 数字信令
digital signature 数字签名
digital simulation 数字仿真
digital simulation discretization 数字仿真离散化
digital simulation language 数字仿真语言
digital simultaneous voice and data(DSVD) 数字式声音与数据同传
digital sonar 数字式声纳
digital sort 数字排序
digital sound 数字声音
digital sound broadcasting 数字声广播
digital sound processing 数字声音处理
digital sound system 数字伴音系统
digital speech coding 数字话音编码
digital speech communications 数字话音通信
digital speech interpolation(DSI) 数字话音插空
digital storage media(DSM) 数字存储媒体
digital storage oscilloscope 数字存储示波器
digital subscriber line access multiplexer 数字用户线接入复用器
digital subscriber link(DSL) 数字用

户线
digital subscriber link modem 数字用户线调制解调器
digital subscriber loop(DSL) 数字用户环路
digital subtraction angiography(DSA) 数字减影血管造影术
digital sum variation 数字和的偏差
digital switching 数字交换
digital switching node 数字交换节点
digital telemetering 数字遥测
digital telephone network 数字电话网
digital television 数字电视
digital television converter 数字电视转换器
digital television receiver 数字电视接收机
digital television standard 数字电视标准
digital television studio 数字电视演播室
digital terrain model 数字地形模型
digital time base corrector(DTBC) 数字时基校正器
digital time delayer 数字延时器
digital time series analysis 数字时间序列分析
digital-to-analog conversion(DAC) 数/模转换
digital topography model(DTM) 数字地形模型
digital transducer 数字转换器
digital transmission 数字传送
digital transmission group 数字传输组
digital tree search 数字树搜索
digital type measuring instrument 数字式测量仪器
Digital UNIX UNIX 操作系统(DEC)
digital vector generator 数字向量发生器
Digital Venturis Venturis 台式机(DEC)
digital video 数字视频
digital video disc(DVD) 数字视盘
digital video effect(DVE) 数字特技
Digital Video Interactive(DVI) 数字视频交互
digital video recorder(DVR) 数字录像机

digital voltmeter 数字式电压表
digital wipe button(WIPE) 数字划按钮
digitally addressed flat display tube 数字寻址平板显示管
digitally assisted television(DATV) 数字辅助电视
digitally programmed amplifier 数字编程放大器
digitally programmed power supply 数字式程控电源
digitization 数字化
digitization of speech signals 语音信号数字化
digitize 数字化
digitized audio 数字化音频
digitized image 数字化图像
digitized picture 数字化图像
digitized points machining 数字化点加工
digitized sound 数字化声音
digitizer 数字化仪
digitizer stability 数字化仪的稳定度
digitizer tablet 数字化仪书写板
digitizing 数字化
digitizing pad 数字化衬板
digitizing tablet 数字化工作台
digraph 有向图
Dijkstra's algorithm 迪克斯特拉算法
DIL(Dual In-Line) 双列直插式
dilatation 膨胀
dilemma reasoning 二难推理
DILIC (Dual In-Line pin Integrated Circuit) 双列直接插式集成电路
DILP(Dual In-Line Package) 双列直插式封装
dimension 度,维,大小;量纲
dimension attribute 维属性
dimension bound 维界
dimension select 维数选择
dimension sensor 尺度传感器
dimension specification 维说明;尺寸说明
DIMENSION statement 定维语句,数组说明语句
dimension systolic array 边界脉动阵列
dimensional analysis 量纲分析
dimensional stability 尺寸稳定性
dimensionality 度数,维数

dimensioned hole 注尺寸孔
dimensioning 定尺寸,尺寸度量
dimidiate 二分的,对半的
diminished radix complement 基数减1补码,反码
diminishing increment sorting 缩小增量排序
diminishing return 回偿递减
DIMM(Digital Image Memory Module) 数字图像存储模块
dimmed command 暗淡的命令
dimmed icon 暗淡的图标
dimple 凹坑
DIN(Deütsches Institute fur Normung) 德国标准协会
DIN connector(Deutsches Institute für Normung) 德国标准化协会连接器,DIN 连接器
DIN-type connector 德国标准连接器
DINA(Distributed Information processing Network Architecture) 分布式信息处理网络体系结构
Dingbats 装饰符号集,Dingbats 符号
Dinic's algorithm 迪尼克算法
diode 二极管
diode array 二极管阵列
diode burn out 二极管烧毁
diode detector 二极管检波器
diode gate 二极管门
diode isolation 二极管隔离
diode limiter 二极管限幅器
diode logic 二极管逻辑
diode matrix 二极管矩阵
diode transistor logic(DTL) 二极管-晶体管逻辑电路
dioxide 二氧化物
DIP(Draft International standard Proposal) 国标标准草案(ISO)
DIP(Dual In-line Package) 双列直插式封装
dip 浸,沾
dip soldering 浸焊
DIP switch 双列直插式开关
diphthong 双元音,复合元音
diplex operation 同向双工操作
dipole modulation 双极调制,偶极调制
DIR(DIRectory) 目录
direct 直接的

direct access 直接存取;直接访问
direct access deflection 直接存取偏转
direct access device 直接存取设备
direct access display channel 直接存取显示通道
direct access file 直接存取文件
direct access hash 散列直接存取法
direct access inquiry 直接存取查询
direct-access library 直接存取库
direct access memory 直接存取存储器
direct access method 直接存取法
direct access queues 直接存取队列
direct access storage 直接访问存储器
direct access unit 直接存取单元
direct acoustic path 直达声程
direct acting 直接作用
direct acting controller 直接作用控制器
direct activation 直接激活
direct address 直接地址
direct address processing 直接地址处理
direct addressing 直接寻址
direct allocation 直接分配
direct assessment 直接评价
direct attach 直接连接
direct attribute 直接属性
direct broadcast 直播
direct broadcasting satellite(DBS) 直播卫星
direct cable connection 直接电缆连接
direct calculation 直接计算
direct call 直接呼叫
direct code 直接码
direct coding 直接编码
direct color 直接彩色
direct color formation 直接彩色形成法
direct compare method 直接比较法
direct-connect modem 直连调制解调器
direct connection line 直连线
direct control 直接控制
direct control connection 直接控制连接
direct control encode 直接控制编码
direct control microprogram 直接控制微程序
direct controlled system 直接控制系统
direct cooling 直接冷却
direct coordinate mode 直接坐标模式
direct correspondence method 直接对应法

direct coupled amplifier 直接耦合放大器
direct coupled machine 直接耦合机
direct coupled system 直接耦合系统
direct coupled transistor logic(DCTL) 直接耦合晶体管逻辑电路
direct current 直流
direct current amplifier 直流放大器
direct-current component 直流分量
direct-current converter 直流转换器
direct-current transmission 直流传输
direct cylinder addressing 直接柱面寻址
direct data access method 直接数据存取法
direct data capture 直接数据收集
direct data entry(DDE) 直接数据输入 「织
direct data organization 直接数据组
direct data set 直接数据集
direct dead lock 直接死锁
direct delay line 直通延迟行
direct derivation 直接导出
direct detection 直接检测
direct digital color proof(DDCP) 直接数字彩色校验
direct digital control(DDC) 直接数字控制
direct distance dialing(DDD) 直接长途拨号
direct distribution satellite 直接分配卫星
direct drive capstan 直接驱动主导轴
direct drive cylinder 直接驱动磁鼓
direct drive motor 直接驱动电动机
direct-drive torque motor 直接驱动转矩电动机
direct electron beam lithographic system 电子束直接曝光系统
direct encoding 直接编码
direct encoding microinstruction 直接编码微指令
direct energy transfer system 直接能量转移系统
direct entry terminal 直接输入终端机
direct executing high-level language machine 直接执行高级语言的机器
direct file 直接文件

direct file organization 直接文件组织
direct graphic interface specification (DGIS) 直接图形接口规范
Direct Graphics Interface Standard (DGIS) 直接图形接口标准
direct histogram specification 直接直方图规范化
direct image film 直接成像胶片
direct index 直接索引
direct input/output(DIO) 直接输入/输出 「程
direct insert subroutine 直接插入子例
direct instance 直接实例
direct instruction 直接指令
direct intervention 直接干涉
direct inward dialing(DID) 直接入局拨号
direct jump 直接转移
direct keying device 直接键控设备
direct line 直达线
direct link 直接链路
direct location mode 直接定位模式
direct lookup 直接查看
direct magnetic recording 直接磁记录
direct manipulation 直接操纵
direct mail 直接邮件
direct manner 直连方式
direct mapping 直接映像,直接映射
direct mapping cache 直接映像高速缓存
direct measurement 直接测量
direct memory access(DMA) 直接存储器访问
direct memory access controller (DMAC) 直接存储器访问控制器
direct memory access inhibit flag 直接存储器访问禁止标志
direct memory access line 直接存储器存取线
direct memory access mode 直接存储器访问模式
direct method 直接法
direct-microprogrammed execution 直接微程序执行
direct mode 直接模式
direct modulation 直接调制 「接
direct network connection 直接网络连
direct numerical control(DNC) 直接

数值控制
direct operand addressing 直接操作数寻址
direct organization file 直接组织文件
direct output 直接输出
direct outward dialing(DOD) 直接出局拨号
direct overwrite 直接重写
direct page register 直接页面寄存器
direct parent 直接父辈
direct plate exposure 直接印刷版曝光
direct positive 直接正片
direct production 直接产生式
direct program interface 直接程序接口
direct projection large screen display 直接投射式大屏幕显示
direct proof 直接证明
direct read after write(DRAW) 写后直接读出
direct read after write optical disk 直接读后写光盘
direct read during write(DRDW) 写时直接读出
direct reading system 直读系统
direct record 直接记录
direct reference address 直接参考地址
direct representation 直接表示法
direct rewriting 直接重写
direct route 直达路由
direct segmenting encode 直接分段编码
direct selling 直销
direct sequence spread spectrum(DS-SS) 直接序列扩频
direct serial 直接串行
direct sharing 直接共享
direct solution 直接解
direct step on wafer(DSW) 直接分步重复曝光
direct substitution 直接代换
direct symbol recognition 直接符号识别
direct syntax analysis method 直接语法分析法
direct temporal connection 直接临时连接
direct-to-plate 直接出图版
direct-to-press (图像数据)直接到印刷机
direct view storage tube(DVST) 直视存储管
direct view storage tube display 直视存储管显示器
direct voice input 直接声音输入
direct wave 直接波
directed 定向的,直接的
directed activation 定向激活
directed acyclic graph version model 有向无环图版本模型
directed branch 指向分支
directed broadcasting address 定向广播地址
directed edge 有向边
directed Euler circuit 有向欧拉图
directed graph(digraph) 有向图,连曲线图
directed Hamilton circuit 有向哈密尔顿回路
directed line 定向线
directed logical relation 有向逻辑关系
directed matching 定向匹配
directed scan 定向扫描
directed semantic graph 直接语义图
directed set 有向集
directed tracing 定向跟踪
directed tree 有向树
directing character code 指向字符码
direction 方向
direction control 方向控制
direction flow 方向流图
direction finding 测向
direction key 方向键
direction fluctuation 方向起伏
direction representation 方向表示法
directional coupler 定向耦合器
directional derivative 方向导数
directional duality principle 定向对偶性原理
directional filter 方向滤波器
directional hearing 方向听觉
directional light 定向光
directional microphone 单向传声器
directional pattern 方向图
directive command 提示性命令
directive statements 指示性语句
directive storage tube 直视存储管
directivity 指向性,方向性
directivity of an antenna 天线的方向

性系数
directly insertion sort 直接插入排序
directly-interpretable language 直接解释执行语言
Director 多媒体创作软件(Macromedia)
director 指挥仪；导向偶极子
director-type computer 指挥仪计算机
directory(DIR) 目录
directory access protocol 目录访问协议
directory area 目录区
directory assistance call 查号呼叫
directory browsing 目录浏览
directory cache 目录高速缓存
directory caching 目录缓存法
directory control entry 目录控制项
directory data set 目录数据集
directory database 目录数据库
directory devices 目录设备
directory entry 目录项
directory file 目录文件,编目文件
directory hashing 目录散列
directory icon 目录图标
directory key 目录键
directory list box 目录列表框
directory management 目录管理
directory markers 目录标记
directory mask 目录屏蔽
directory menu 目录菜单
directory name 目录名
directory of server 服务器目录
directory path 目录路径
directory path name 目录路径名
directory profile 目录轮廓文件
directory record 目录记录
directory replication 目录复制
directory restriction 目录限制
directory routing 目录路由选择
directory search time 目录查找时间
directory section 目录段
directory server 目录服务器
directory server agent 目录服务器代理
directory service 目录服务
directory shared 目录共享
directory sorting 目录排序
directory space limit 目录空间限制
directory stack (Unix)目录堆栈
directory structure duplication 目录结构复制
Directory System Agent(DSA) 目录系统代理
directory table 目录表
directory tree 目录树
Directory User Agent(DUA) 目录用户代理
directory verification 目录校验
directory window 目录窗口
DirectTalk/2 直谈话音处理系统/2 (IBM)
DirectTalk/6000 直谈话音处理系统/6000(IBM)
dirty bit 修改位,"脏"数位
dirty data "脏"(有错乱)数据
dirty galley 毛样
dirty line "脏"(有错乱)行
dirty manuscript 涂改过的手稿
dirty page "脏"[包含无效数据]页
dirty power "脏"电源,有干扰电源
dirty read 错读
dirty rectangle animation 修改块动画
dirty version 错误修改过的版本
DIS(Distributed Information System) 分布式信息系统
DIS (Draft International Standard (ISO)) 国际标准草案(国际标准化组织)
disability 无能力,无资格
disable 使失效,取消,禁止
disable condition 禁止条件
DISABLE LOGIN 取消登录
DISABLE TTS 取消异动跟踪系统
disabled interrupt 失效中断,禁止中断
disabled module 失效模块,被抑制模块
disabled page fault 禁止页面故障
disabled port 禁用端口
disabled state 不活跃状态
disabled switch 禁用开关
disabled text 失效文字
disabled user 被禁止用户
disabler 功能禁止装置
disabling tone 禁止报告音调
disadvantage 不利的,缺点
disagreement set 不一致集合
disallow 不允许
disallowed external interrupt 不允许

的外部中断
disambiguation 澄清,消除二义性
disarm 阻挡,使失效,禁止
disarmed interrupt 拒绝中断,解除中断
disarmed state 阻挡状态
disassemble 反汇编
disassembler 反汇编程序
disaster cutoff 灾难性修剪
disaster dump 灾难性转储
disaster plan 灾难应对计划
disaster pruning 灾难性修剪
disaster recovery 灾难恢复
disastrous result 灾难性结果
disbelief 不信任度
disc (光)盘;唱片
Disc man 袖珍激光唱片放音机
disc stabilizer 唱片稳定器
discard 放弃,丢弃,不考虑,略去
discard change 放弃更改
discard enable(DE) 舍弃许可
discard packet 丢弃信息包
discard policy 废弃策略
discard stop 放弃式停机
discardable 可放弃的
discharge 放电
discharge characteristic curve 放电特性曲线
discharge rate 放电率
discharge switching 放电开关
discipline 规则,规范,规程
disclaimer 否认声明
disclosure(DE) 泄露;解密
discolor(DE) 褪色
discompiler(DE) 反编译程序
disconnect 断开,脱接,拆线
disconnect command chaining 间断命令链接
disconnect signal 拆接信号
disconnected phase 拆接阶段
disconnected recordset 已断开的记录集
disconnecting link 断开链接
disconnection 拆接
discontinuity 不连续性
discontinuous action 不连续作用
discontinuous control system 断续控制系统
discontinuous detection 间歇性检测
discontinuous segment 不连续段

discontinuous shared segment 非连续共享段
discontinuous solution 间断解
discount rate 折扣率
discourse 论文,论述
discourse domain 论域
discourse generation 篇章生成
discourse model 谈话模型
discovery 发现
discovery distance 发现距离
discovery frame 询问帧
discovery learning 发现学习
discovery mechanism 查明机制
discovery system 发现系统
discrambling 去扰
discrete 离散的
discrete analog 离散模拟
discrete approximation 离散逼近
discrete channel 离散通道
discrete command 离散指令
discrete component 分立元件
discrete consumption stream 离散消费流
discrete control system 离散控制系统
discrete convolution 离散卷积
discrete cosine transform(DCT) 离散余弦变换
discrete data 离散数据
discrete data item 离散数据项
discrete data type 离散数据类型
discrete deterministic process 离散确定性过程
discrete device 分立元件
discrete distribution 离散分布
discrete events simulation 离散事件仿真
discrete false-target 离散伪目标
discrete filter 离散过滤器
discrete Fourier series(DFS) 离散傅里叶级数
discrete Fourier transform(DFT) 离散傅里叶变换
discrete Hilbert transform 离散希尔伯特变换
discrete Hopfield neural network (DHNN) 离散Hopfield神经网络
discrete information source 离散信息源
discrete iteration 离散迭代
discrete linear-quadratic problem 离

散线性二次型问题
discrete logic 离散逻辑
discrete mathematics 离散数学
discrete maximum principle 离散极大值原理
discrete memoryless channel 离散无记忆信道
discrete model 离散模型
discrete module 分立组件
discrete multiplexing technology 离散复线技术,离散多路复用技术
discrete optical head 分离式光学头
discrete optimization 离散优化
discrete parameter Markov chain 离散参数马尔可夫链
discrete problem 离散问题
discrete profile 独立轮廓
discrete programming 离散规划
discrete random processes 离散随机过程
discrete random variable 离散随机变量
discrete relaxation 离散松驰法
discrete representation 离散表示法
discrete sample 离散样值
discrete signal 离散信号
discrete simulation 离散模拟
discrete simulation language 离散仿真语言
discrete solution 离散解
discrete source 离散信源
discrete spectrum 离散(频,光)谱
discrete stochastic process 离散随机过程
discrete system 离散系统
discrete system modeling 离散系统建模
discrete system simulation 离散系统仿真
discrete time control 离散时间控制
discrete-time Markovian motion 离散时间马尔可夫运动
discrete time model 离散时间模型
discrete-time signals sequences 离散时间信号序列
discrete-time system 离散时间系统
discrete tone 离散音调
discrete type 离散类型
discrete value 离散值
discrete valued function 离散值函数
discrete valued objective 离散值目标

discrete variable 离散变量
discrete Walsh transform(DWT) 离散沃尔什变换
discrete white noise 离散白噪声
discretional 任意的,无条件的
discretionary 随意的,自由选择的
discretionary access control 随意存取控制,自主型访问控制
discretionary hyphen 自由选定连字符
discretionary protection 自主型保护
discretionary system 自选系统
discretionary wiring method 自由选择布线法
discretization 离散化
discriminant 判别式
discriminant description 鉴别描述
discriminant function 鉴别[判别]函数
discriminated union 鉴别联合
discrimination 鉴别,判别
discrimination function 判别函数
discrimination-feedback type command system 鉴别反馈型命令系统
discrimination instruction 判别指令
discrimination network 鉴别网络
discrimination rule 判别规则
discrimination tree 判别树
discrimination value 判别值
discriminator 区分符
discriminator output error voltage 鉴相器输出误差电压
discriminator sensitivity 鉴相器灵敏度
Discussion Web Wizard 讨论站点向导
disinfect 消病毒
disinfectant program 消毒程序
disinfector 消毒程序;消病毒设备;消毒者
disintermediate 无中介
disjoint binary tree 不相交二叉树
disjoint cycle 不相交的轮换
disjoint figure 不相交图
disjoint path network 不相交路径网络
disjoint sum 不相交和
disjunction 析取
disjunctive-conjunctive goal tree 析取合取目标树
disjunctive decomposition 析取分解
disjunctive normal form 析取范式
disjunctive search 分离查寻,分离检

disjunctive syllogism 选言三段论
disk 磁盘
disk access 磁盘存取,磁盘访问
disk access time 磁盘存取时间
disk address field 磁盘地址域
disk address marks 磁盘地址标志
disk arm 磁盘存取臂
disk array 磁盘阵列
disk array controller 磁盘阵列控制器
disk array data channel 磁盘阵列数据通道
disk array system software 磁盘阵列系统软件
disk bands 磁盘区带
disk brush 磁盘刷
disk buffer 磁盘缓冲区
disk cache 磁盘高速缓存器
disk capacity 磁盘容量
disk cell 磁盘单元
disk channel 磁盘通道
disk cluster allocation map 盘簇分配［图］
disk controller 磁盘控制器
disk crash 磁盘碰划
disk data band 磁盘数据带
disk defragmenter 磁盘碎片合并
disk drive 磁盘驱动器
disk drive controller 磁盘驱动器控制［器］
disk dump 磁盘转储
disk duplex 磁盘双工
disk duplicator 磁盘复制器
disk emulator 磁盘仿真器
disk envelope 磁盘封套
disk file index 磁盘文件索引
disk file manager 磁盘文件管理器
disk file organization 磁盘文件组织
disk file reference 磁盘文件引用
disk format 磁盘格式
disk formatting 磁盘格式化
disk icon 磁盘图标
disk inner guard band 磁盘内保护带
disk instance （可执行文件的）磁盘实例
disk interface 磁盘接口
disk jacket 磁盘护套
disk management 磁盘管理
disk mirroring 磁盘镜像
disk model 磁盘模型
disk operating system (DOS) 磁盘操作系统
disk optimizer 磁盘优化程序
disk outer guard band 磁盘外保护带
disk overlay 磁盘覆盖
disk pack 磁盘组
disk partition 磁盘分区
disk queue control block 磁盘队列控制块
Disk Quick 磁盘加速程序
disk quotas 磁盘限额
disk record form 磁盘记录格式
disk rotation speed 磁盘转速
disk sector 磁盘扇区
disk server 磁盘服务器
disk sharing 磁盘共享
disk size 磁盘尺寸
disk skew 磁盘失衡［负载不平衡］
disk spindle 磁盘转轴
disk storage 磁盘存储器
disk storage module 磁盘存储模块
disk storage unit 磁盘存储单元
disk striping 多磁盘记录块串操作,磁盘分条
disk striping with parity 带奇偶校验的磁盘分条
disk swapping 磁盘交换
disk system 磁盘系统
disk tolerance 磁盘容错
disk track number 磁盘轨道号
disk type 磁盘类型
disk unit 磁盘机,磁盘单元
disk write protect 磁盘写保护
diskette 磁盘
diskette cartridge 盒式磁盘
diskette centering 软磁盘同心度
diskfull client 满磁盘客户机
diskless client 无盘客户机
diskless workstation 无盘工作站
diskware （软）盘载软件
dislocation array 位错矩阵
dislocation density 位错密度
dislocation-free crystal 无位错晶体
dismiss 解散;解除
dismount 拆卸
disorder 无序的 ［机
disorderly closedown 无序［意外］停
DISOSS (DIStributed Office Support System) 分布式办公支持系统

disown 不认可,驱逐
DISP(DISPatcher) 调度程序
DISP(DISPlacement) 位移
DISP(DISPlay) 显示;显示器 「致
disparity 视差;不均匀性;不等,不一
dispatch 调度,分派
dispatch algorithm 调度算法
dispatch delay 调度延迟
dispatch identifier 调度标识符
dispatch interface 调度接口
dispatch list 调度表
dispatch map 指派图
dispatch network 调度网络
dispatch queue entry 调度队列入口
dispatch table 调度表
dispatcher 调度程序
dispatcher control table 调度程序控制表
dispatcher database 调度程序数据库
dispatcher object 调度程序对象
dispatcher ready queue 调度程序就绪队列
dispatcher task 调度程序任务
dispatching center 调度中心
dispatching priority 配送优先权,调度优先级
dispatching sequence 调度顺序
dispatching system 配送系统
dispenser 分配器;自动售货机
dispersal 分散的;配置,处理,整理
dispersal curve 消散曲线
dispersal records 分散记录
dispersal surface 消散曲面
disperse 分散
dispersed intelligence 分散智能
dispersed type AC electroluminescent 分散型交流电致发光
dispersing agent 分散剂,弥散剂
dispersion 分散,色散;弥散
dispersion gate "与"门
dispersion of knowledge representation 知识表示弥散
dispersion phenomenon 色散现象
dispersive media 色散媒体
displace 置换;位移
displaced page 置换页
displacement angle 位移角
displacement byte 位移字节

displacement finite element method 位移有限元法
displacement fiber sensor 光纤位移传感器
displacement field 位移字段
displacement finite element method 位移有限元法
displacement map 位移映像
displacement mode 位移模式
displacement pulse 位移脉冲
displacement transducer 位移变换器
display 显示;显示器
display adapter 显示适配器
display adapter unit 显示适配单元
display area 显示区
Display as Icon 显示为图标
display attribute 显示属性
display background 显示背景
display board 显示板
display buffer 显示缓冲器
display capacity 显示容量
display card 显示卡
display channel 显示通道
display character 显示字符
display character generator 显示字符发生器
display circuit 显示电路 「器
display code generator 显示代码生成
display control 显示控制
Display Control Interface(DCI) 显示控制接口
display control unit 显示控制器
display console 显示控制台
display cursor 显示光标
display cycle 显示周期
display data channel(DDC) 显示数据通道
display-dependent session 依赖于显示器的对话
display device 显示器件;显示设备
display device context 显示设备上下
display digit 显示数字 「文
display element 显示元素
display emulation 显示仿真
display entity 显示实体
display field 显示字段
display file 显示文件
display file compilers 显示文件编译

程序
display foreground 显示前景
display format 显示格式
display frame 显示帧
display free memory 显示空闲内存
display generating software 显示生成软件
display generation time 显示生成时间
display globle memory 显示全局内存
display group 显示组
display halt 显示暂停
display highlighting 显示醒目
display image 显示图像
display-independent session 不依赖于显示器的对话
display item 显示项
display least recently used 显示最近用过的
display level 显示级
display line 显示行
display list 显示列表
display list processor 显示列表处理器
display local heap 显示本地堆
display lock 显示锁定
display memory 显示内存
display menu 显示菜单
display name (MAPI)显示名
display numeric pad 显示数字键区
display offset 显示偏移
display options 显示选项
display packing 显示压缩
display page 显示页
display paging 显示分页
display panel 显示面板
display point 显示点
display position 显示位置
Display PostScript 页面描述语言显示版
display precision 显示精度
display predicate 显示谓词
display primaries 显示基色
display processing unit(DPU) 显示处理单元
display processor 显示处理器
display power management signaling (DPMS) 显示器电源管理信号
display RAM 显示用随机读写存储器
display recall control 显示再现控制
display refresh rate 显示刷新速率
display register 显示寄存器
display resolution 显示分辨率
display rolling 显示画面翻滚
display screen 显示屏幕
display segment 显示段
display size 显示尺寸
display software 显示软件
display space 显示空间
display storage tube 显示存储管
display subroutines 显示子例程
display surface 显示面
display system 显示系统
display table (MAPI)显示表
display task queues 显示任务队列
display technology 显示技术
display terminal 显示终端
display tube 显示管
display type 显示类型
display usage 显示方式
display window manager 显示窗口管理程序
displayable widget 可显示窗口部件
DisplayWrite 显示书写软件
disposable 可任意处理的
dispose procedure 释放过程
disproving 反驳,反证
disregard 不予处理,不顾
disregard message 搁置报文
disrepair 失修
disruption 击穿
disruptive gradient 击穿梯度
dissector 析像器
dissemination 传染;散布
dissimilarity measure 不相似度量
dissipation factor 损耗因数,耗散因
dissipative network 耗散网络
dissipative scheme 耗散格式
dissipative structure 耗散结构
dissolve 渐隐,渐消
dissuasion tone 劝阻音
distal 末端装置
distance 距离
distance concept 距离概念
distance element 距离元
distance function 距离函数
distance host 远程主机
distance learning 远程教学

distance measure 距离测度
distance-only shading 仅取决于距离的阴影算法
distance-preserving mapping 保持距离的映射
distance signal 距离信号
distance vector algorithm 距离矢量算法
Distance Vector Multicast Routing Protocol 距离向量多投路由选择协议
distant control 遥控
distant early warning 远程预警
distant echo 远端回波
distant station 远端局
distinct 独特的,性质截然不同的
distinct interface 独特接口
distinct location 独特位置;不同单元
distinct truth table 有别真值表
distinction 差别,区别,特性
distinctive ringing 特殊振铃
distinguish 辨别,判别
distinguished element 特异元素
distinguished symbol 特异符号
distinguished vertex 奇异顶点
distinguishing attribute 区分属性
distinguishing sequence 区分序列
distinguishing state 区分状态
distinguishing test 区分测试
distinguishing tree 区分树
distortion 失真,畸变
distortion analyzer 失真分析仪
distortion factor 失真系数,失真度
distortion set 失真仪
distress communication 遇险求救通信
distributable executables 可发布执行程序
distribute 分布,分配
distributed 分布式的,分散的
distributed access system 分布式访问系统
distributed adaptive routing 分布式自适应路由选择法
distributed agent approach 分散模块
distributed algorithm 分布式算法
distributed application 分布式应用程序
distributed arbitration 分布式仲裁
distributed array processor(DAP) 分布型阵列处理机

distributed artificial intelligence(DAI) 分布式人工智能
distributed bulletin board 分布式布告牌
distributed cache array 分布式缓存阵列
distributed capacitance 分布电容
distributed channel assignment 分布式通道分配
distributed clock 分布式时钟
distributed communication architecture 分布型通信体系结构
Distributed Component Object Model (DCOM) 分布式部件对象模型
distributed computation 分布式计算
distributed computer architecture 分布式计算机体系结构
distributed computer control system 分布型计算机控制系统
distributed computer network 分布式计算机网络
distributed computing 分布式计算
distributed computing environment (DCE) 分布式计算环境
distributed computing operating system 分布式计算操作系统
distributed concurrency control 分布型并发控制
distributed control system(DCS) 分布型控制系统
distributed data 分布式数据
distributed data base(DDB) 分布式数据库
distributed data model view 分布式数据模型视图
distributed data processing 分布式数据处理
distributed data-processing network 分布式数据处理网络
distributed data processing system 分布式数据处理系统
distributed data switching 分布式数据交换
distributed database 分布式数据库
distributed database architecture 分布式数据库体系结构
distributed database management 分布式数据库管理
distributed database management system

(DDBMS) 分布式数据库管理系统
distributed deadlock 分布式死锁
distributed debugging 分布式调试
distributed decision support system 分布式决策支持系统
distributed delay model 分布时延模型
Distributed Director 分布式导向器 (Cisco)
distributed discrete-event simulation 分布式离散事件模拟
distributed environment 分布式环境
distributed executive-like system 分布式类执行系统
distributed expert system (DES) 分布型专家系统
distributed fault 分布型故障
distributed fault-tolerant computing system 分布型容错系统
distributed file system (DFS) 分布式文件系统
distributed frame alignment signal 分散型帧对准信号「间
distributed free space 分布型自由空
distributed function 分布函数;分布式功能
distributed function computer 功能分布式计算机系统
distributed graphic network 分布式图形网络
distributed host command facility (DHCF) 分布式主机命令设施
distributed indexed access method 分布式索引存取方法
Distributed Information Processing Network Architecture 分布式信息处理网络体系结构
distributed information services 分布型信息服务
distributed information system 分布式信息系统
distributed INGRES 分布式 INGRES 数据库
distributed integrity assertion 分布完整性断言
distributed intelligence 分布式智能
distributed intelligence system 分布型智能系统

distributed interactive simulation 分布式交互仿真 「连
distributed interconnection 分布式互
distributed knowledge base management system 分布式知识库管理系统
distributed logic computer 分布逻辑计算机
distributed logic memory 分布型逻辑存储器
distributed-logic word processing 分布式逻辑文字处理
distributed-logic word processor 分布式逻辑字处理机
distributed logon security 分布式登录安全性
distributed manage environment (DME) 分布管理环境
distributed media access control 分布式媒体访问控制
distributed message switching system 分布式消息交换系统
distributed memory 分布式内存
distributed message switching system 分布式消息交换系统
distributed model 分布式模型
distributed multimedia application 分布式多媒体应用程序
distributed multiprocessing 分布型多重处理
distributed multiprogrammed operating system 分布式多道程序操作系统
distributed naming service 分布式命名服务
distributed network 分布型网络
distributed network system (DNS) 分布式网络系统
distributed object 分布式实体
distributed object-oriented database 分布式面向对象数据库
distributed office automation 分布式办公自动化系统
distributed operating system 分布式操作系统 「化
distributed optimization 分布型最优
distributed organization 分布式组织
distributed overflow space 分布式溢出空间
distributed overhead 分布式内务操

作,分布开销

distributed packet switching 分布式分组交换

distributed parallel logic theory 分布式并行逻辑理论

distributed parameter 分布参数「试

distributed path testing 分布式通路测

distributed pipeline 分布式流水线

distributed presentation management 分布式表示管理

distributed problem solving 分布型问题求解

distributed processing 分布型处理

distributed processing control executive (DPCX) 分布式处理控制执行程序

distributed processing programming executive(DPPX) 分布式处理程序设计执行程序

distributed processing network 分布型处理网络

distributed processing system 分布式处理系统

distributed programming 分布式程序设计

distributed protocol 分布式协议

distributed protocol interface 分布式协议接口

distributed query processing 分布式查询处理

distributed random access machine (DRAM) 分布式随机访问机「踪

distributed ray tracing 分布式光线跟

distributed refresh 分布式刷新

Distributed Relational Database Architecture(DRDA) 分布式关系数据库体系结构(IBM)

distributed relational DBMS (DRDBMS) 分布式关系型数据库管理系统

distributed reliability protocol 分布式可靠性协议

distributed representation 分布式表示

distributed resource management 分布式资源管理

distributed robot 送货机器人

distributed routing 分布式路由选择

distributed scheduler 分布式调度程序

distributed search 分布式查找

distributed semantics 分布式语义学

distributed server 分布式服务器

distributed sharing memory 分布式共享内存

distributed shortest path algorithm 分布式最短路径算法

distributed simulation 分布式仿真

distributed snapshot 分布式抽点打印;分布截获

distributed software system 分布型软件系统

distributed storage 分布式存储器

distributed structure 分布式结构

distributed switching 分布式交换

distributed synchronizer 分布式同步器

distributed system architecture(DSA) 分布型系统体系结构

distributed system environment 分布式系统环境

distributed system executive 分布式系统执行程序

distributed system license option (DSLO) 分布式系统特许选项

distributed system management 分布式系统管理

distributed system node executive 分布式系统节点执行程序

distributed system object model (DSOM) 分布式系统对象模型

distributed task processing system 分布式事务处理系统 「统

distributed test system 分布型测试系

distributed text and database structure 分布式文本与数据库结构

distributed topology 分布型拓扑结构

distributed transaction processing 分布式事务处理

distributed virtual machine 分布式虚拟机

distributed vision system 分布式视觉系统

distributing frame 配线架

distribution (经因特网)发布;分配,分发

distribution amplifier 分配放大器

distribution box 分线盒;配电箱

distribution cable 配电电缆
distribution coefficient 分配系数
distribution computing 分布计算
distribution console 分发控制台
distribution directory 分发目录
distribution-driven simulation 分布驱动仿真
distribution function 分布功能
distribution kit 配送套件
distribution list 分配表
distribution loss 分配损耗
distribution medium 发行媒体
distribution panel 配线面板
distribution point 分派点
distribution request 分配请求
distribution service 分配型业务;分布服务
distribution service level 分布服务级
distribution switch board 配电板「配
distribution time-impulse 时间脉冲分
distribution table 分布表
distribution transparency 分布透明性
distribution zone 分布区
distributive lattice 分配格
distributive law 分配律
distributor 分配器;配电盘
distributor transmitter 分配发送器
disturb 干扰,扰动
disturbance 干扰,摄动
disturbance decoupling 干扰去耦
disymmetric 双对称
dither 混色,抖色;抖动,颤振
dither matrix 抖动矩阵
dither pattern 混色模式
dither signal 抖动信号;伪随机信号
dithered color 渐变色
dithering 混色,渐变色
DIU(Data Interface Unit) 数据接口单元
DIV(DIVider) 除法器
divergence 发散;(显示器)失会聚
divergent birth process 发散增延过程
divergent branching system 发散分支系统
divergent computation 发散计算
divergent matrix 发散矩阵
divergent sequence 发散序列
divergent series 发散级数

divergent tree 发散树
diverse 不同的,多样化的
diversion 转义命令
diversity 相异性,参差
diversity combiner 分集合并器
diversity condition 特异条件
diversity improvement factor 分集改善系数
diversity reception 分集接收
diversity separation 分集间隔
diversity telemetry 分集遥测
diversity time 分集时间
divide-and-conquer method 分治法
divide-by-10 counter 10分频计数器
divide-by-16 counter 十六分频计数器
divide-by-N counter N分频计数器
divide check 除法校验
divide overflow 除法溢出
divide time 除法时间
divided difference 均差
divided job processing 作业分割处理
divided slit scan 分割式扫描器
dividend 被除数
divider 除法器
divider line 分界线
diving cubes 剖分立方体
divisible 可除尽的
division 部;除法
division abnormal 除法异常
division hashing 除法散列
division header 部标题
division ring 除环
division subroutine 除法子例程
divisor 除数
divisor string 除数串
DIY(Do It Yourself) 自装计算机
DJNR(Dow Jones News Retrieval) 道琼斯新闻检索系统
DKI (Driver-Kernel Interface) (Unix)驱动程序核心界面
DL(Dynamic Linking) 动态链接
DLC(Data Link Controller) 数据链路控制器
DLE(Data Logging Equipment) 数据登录设备
DLL(Dynamic Linking Library) 动态链接库
DLM(Data Link Mapping) 数据链接

映像
DLP(Data-Link Processor)　数据链路处理机
DLP(Data-Link Protocol)　数据链路协议
DLPI(Data Link Provider Interface)　数据链路供应商界面
DLRP(Data Link Reference Point)　数据链路参考点
DLT(Data Link Terminal)　数据链路终端
DLT(Decision Logic Table)　判定逻辑表
DLT(Digital Linear Tape)　数码线型磁带(DEC)
DLW(Double-Length Word)　双倍长度字
DM(Data Medium)　数据记录媒体
DM(Digital Multiplexer)　数字多工器
DM(Disk Management)　磁盘管理
DMA(Direct Memory Access)　直接内存访问
DMA control　直接内存访问控制
DMA controller　直接存储器访问控制器
DMA cycle stealing　DMA 周期挪用
DMA transfer　直接存储器访问传送
DMAC(Direct Memory Access Controller)　直接存储器访问控制器
Dmax　(图像或信息源)最大密度点
DMCL(Device Media Control Language)　设备媒体控制语言
DMD(Directory Management Domain)　目录管理域
DME(Distributed Manage Environment)　分布式管理环境
DMF(Digital Matched Filter)　数字匹配滤波器
DMI(Desktop Management Interface)　桌面管理接口
DMIF(Delivery Multimedia Integration Framework)　传输多媒体集成架构
Dmin　(图像或信息源)最小密度点
DML(Data Manipulation Language)　数据操纵语言
DMPL(Digital Microprocessor Plotter Language)　数字微处理器绘图语言
DMS(Dynamic Mapping System)　动态映像系统
DMS/DPCX(Data Management System/DPCX)　数据管理系统/分型处理控制执行程序　「表
DMT(Debug Map Table)　调试映像
DMT(Dynamic Method Table)　动态方法表
DN(Data Network)　数据网络
DN(Domain Name)　域名
DNA(Destination Node Address)　目标节点地址
DNA(Digital Network Architecture)　数字网络体系结构(DEC)
DNA(Distributed Network Architecture)　分布型网络体系结构(NCR)
DNA computer(Deoxyribo-Nucleic Acid computer)　脱氧核糖核酸计算机
DNCS(Distributed Network Control System)　分布型网络控制系统
DNS(Decentralized data processing Network System)　分散式数据处理网络系统
DNS(Domain Name Service)　域命名服务
DNS(Domain Naming System)　域命名系统
DNS reverse lookup　域命名系统反向查找
DNS spoofing　域命名系统诓骗
DO CASE structure　多情况选择结构
DO group　循环语句组, DO 语句组
Do-implied list　隐循环表
DO loop　DO 循环语句
do-nothing instruction　空操作指令
DO statement　循环语句, DO 语句
DO statement range　DO 语句域,循环
DO variable　DO 变量　　　　　「域
DO while　条件循环
Dobby noise limiter　杜比降噪器
DOC(DOCument)　文档
dockable toolbar　可合并工具栏
docked toolbar　已合并工具栏
docking　入坞(图形用户界面下,指可分离的工具箱放入窗口边界上的正

常位置)
docking station 坞站
Docuflow Docuflow 群件
document 文档
document administrator 文档管理员
document alignment 文档对准
document analysis form 文档分析表
document architecture 文档结构
document area 文档区
document assembly 文档(资料)汇编
document bank 文档存储体
document base font 文档基本字体
document body 文档主体
document browser 文档浏览器
document card 文档卡片
document category 文献类目
document centric computing 文档为中心的计算
document change 文档变更
document class 文档类
document clustering 文献聚类
document comparison utility 文档比较实用程序
document connection matrix 文档连接矩阵
Document Content Architecture (DCA) 文档内容体系结构
document conversion processor 文档转换处理程序[机]
document copying machine 文档复印
document data base 文献数据库
document delivery 文档传送
document description language 文档描述语言
document detail 文档细节
document directory 文献目录
document-document similarity matrix 文献间相似性矩阵
document drawer 文档抽屉
document editor 文档编辑器[录]
document entry record 文档登记项记
document environment group 文档环境组
document facsimile equipment Group 2 二类文件传真机
document file icon 文档文件图标
document flow 文档流
document folder 文档资料夹
document format 文档格式
document formatter 文档格式化程序
document generation 文档生成
document handling 文档处置
document icon 文档图标
document image processing (DIP) 文档图像处理
document imprinter 文档印刷机
document index 文献索引
document interchange architecture (DIA) 文档交换体系结构
document interchange format 文档交换格式
document item 文档项目
document leading edge 文档前沿
document level 文档级
document library 文档库
document library object 文档库对象
document library services 文档库服务
document manager 文档管理程序
document mark 文档标记
document merge 文档合并
document misregistration 文件不正，文档未对准
document name 文档名
document object name 文档对象名
document object server 文档对象服务程序
document overlength 文档过长
document preparation 文档准备
document processing 文档处理
document profile 文档轮廓[概况]
document protocol 文档协议
document reader 文档阅读器
document received date 文档收到日期
document reference edge 文件参考沿，文件基准边
document reject rate 文档拒读率
document-relative path 文档相对路径
document retrieval system 文档检索系统
document root 文档根目录
document site 文档站点
document site object 文档站点对象
document skew 文档摆放歪斜
document sorter 文档排序器，文件分类机[查
document spelling check 文档拼写检

document stack 文档栈
document start command 文档启动命令
document structure conventions(DSC) 文件结构约定
document style 文档样式
document template 文档模板
document-term matrix 文档-检索词矩阵
document transportation 文件传送
document type define(DTD) 文档类型定义
document understanding 文档理解
document vector 文献向量
document view 文档视窗
document view object 文档视窗对象
document view site 文档视窗站点
document windows 文档窗口
document writer 文件书写机,文件打印机
documentation 文档编制;文档资料
documentation book 文档说明书
documentation level 文档级
documentation supervisor 文档处理监督人
documentor 文档编制程序
docuterm 文档标题;检索字,文献检索词
DOD(Department Of Defense) 国防部(美国)
DOD(Direct Outward Dialing) 直接向外拨号
DOD-1 DOD-1语言
doduc doduc基准程序
Dolby noise reduction 杜比降噪
Dolby stereo 杜比立体声
Dolby surround 杜比环绕
dollar mark 美元符号($)
dollar sign 美元符号
DOLT(Dictionary On-Line Transaction) 字典联机事务处理(Oxford软件公司)
domain 域
domain axiom 域公理
domain calculus 域演算
domain circumscription 邻域限定
domain closure 域闭包
domain constraint 域约束
domain controller 域控制器
domain currency 域当前值

domain decomposition 域分解
domain directory services 域目录服务
domain expert 领域专家
domain-independent rule 领域无关规则
domain information gropper 领域信息捕捉程序
domain integrity 域完整性
domain knowledge 领域知识
domain model 领域模型
domain name 域名
domain name server(DNS) 域名服务器
domain name service(DNS) 域命名服务
domain name space 域名空间
domain naming system(DNS) 域命名系统
domain of individuals 个体域
domain of interpretation 解释域
domain of object 客体域
domain-planning 领域规划
domain relational calculus 域关系演算
domain search 域搜索
domain shell 域外壳
domain-specific knowledge 特定领域知识,专业领域知识
domain theory 畴理论;论域理论
domain-tip memory 磁域存储器
domain variable 域变量
domain wall 畴壁
domestic exchange system 国内交换系统
domestic robot 家用机器人
domestic satellite 国内通信卫星
dominance 控制,优势
dominance number 支配数
dominance relation 支配关系
dominant carrier 主承载系统
dominant degree method 主势法
dominant pole 主导极点
dominant set 支配集,控制集
dominate 支配,控制
dominated compatible set 优势相容集
dominated convergence theorem 控制收敛定理
domination property 支配性质
dominator 支配顶点
dominator algorithm 支配者算法
dominator tree 支配节点树
dominion 辖集
Domino Domino群件(IBM/Lotus)

domino game 多米诺博弈
domino problem 多米诺骨牌问题
domino thread 多米诺线索
don't care complex 随意复合形
don't care condition 无关条件
don't care gate 随意门
don't care point 任意点
don't care vertex 随意顶点
don't hyphenate 取消断字
don't know state 未知状态
DONA (Decentralized Open Network Architecture) 分散式开放型网络体系结构
done 完成
dongle 软件保护器
donor 施主
donor impurity 施主杂质,施主掺杂「剂
door 门
door-bucket 门桶存储器
doorway 出入口
dopant 掺杂剂
dope vector 加料向量,数组信息
doping 掺杂 「象
Doppler acoustic imaging 多普勒声成
Doppler effect 多普勒效应
Doppler equation 多普勒方程
Doppler navigation system 多普勒导航系统
Doppler navigator 多普勒导航仪
Doppler radar 多普勒雷达
DOR (Data Output Rate) 数据输出速率
DOR (Data Output Register) 数据输出寄存器
dormant file limit 隐藏的文件限制
dormant processor 待用处理机
dormant state 休止状态
DOS (Disk Operating System) 磁盘操作系统
DOS/370 (Disk Operating System/370 IBM 370) IBM 370 计算机磁盘操作系统
DOS client DOS 客户机
DOS command line DOS 命令行
DOS extender DOS 扩展程序
DOS platform DOS 平台
DOS prompt DOS 提示符号
DOS shell DOS 命令解释程序
DOS simulation DOS 仿真
DOS simulator DOS 仿真器
DOSF (Distributed Office Support Facility) 分布型办公室支持设施
DOSK (Distributed Operating System Kernel) 分布型操作系统核心
DOSKEY (DOS)键记忆命令
DOS/TOS (Disk Operating System/Tape Operating System) 磁盘操作系统/磁带操作系统
DOS/VS (Disk Operating System/Virtual Storage) 磁盘操作系统/虚拟存储器
DOS/VSE (Disk Operating System/Virtual Storage Extended) 磁盘操作系统/虚存扩充
DOSGEN DOS 生成
dot 点,像点
dot address 点地址
dot addressable 像点可寻址的
dot AND 点"与"
dot character printing 点式字符打印
dot chart 像点图形
dot com 商务域名(.com)
dot command 圆点命令
dot count register 点计数寄存器
dot cycle 点周期,点循环
dot dash 点划线
dot density 点密度
dot file 点文件
dot format 点格式
dot frequency 点频率
dot generator 点信号发生器
dot group 点群
dot header 点标题
dot line (由点构成的)虚线
dot matrix 点阵
dot matrix character generator 点阵字符发生器
dot-matrix display 点矩阵显示
dot-matrix font 点阵字体
dot-matrix format 点阵格式
dot matrix of Chinese character font 汉字字形点阵
dot-matrix impact printer 点阵击打式打印机
dot matrix printer 点阵打印机
dot-matrix size 点阵大小

dot notation 点标记
dot pair 点对
dot pattern 点模式,点图案
dot pattern generator 点模式发生器
dot per inch(dpi) 每英寸点数
dot pitch 像点间距
dot product of vectors 向量的点积
dot prompt 点提示符号,圆点提示符
dot size 点大小
dot speed 点速度
dot time 点时间
dot type 点类型
dotted AND 点"与"
dotted decimal notation （因特网网站地址）点分十进制记法
dotted line 虚线
dotted OR 点"或"
dotted quad （因特网）点分四元组
double 加倍的,双重的
double acknowledge 双重确认
double-action 双重作用
double-address 双地址
double balanced mixer 双平衡混频器
double base diode 双基极二极管
double bit error 双位错误
double bucket 双桶存储器
double-buffered data transfer 双缓冲数据转移
double buffering 双缓冲
double byte 双字节
double-byte character set 双字节字符集
double byte coded font 双字节编码字型
double byte instruction 双字节指令
double calculation 复算
double-chained linear list 双链式线性表
double-chained tree 双链树
double channel stereophonic system 双通道立体声系统
double click （鼠标器）双击
double click speed 双击速度
double closing quote （右侧）双引号
double coset 双重陪集
double-curved surface 双曲面
double denial law 双重否认定律
double-dense recording 倍密度记录
double density 倍密度
double density disk 双密度软盘

double-density encoding 倍密度编码
double-density format 倍密度格式
double-dereference 双重解除
double-dictionary 双字典
double dot 双点
double-ended queue 双端队列
double-ended synchronization 双端同步
double-entry card 双登录卡
double exposure 双重曝光
double fallback 双故障低效率运行
double-frequency recording 双频制记录
double frequency-shift keying 双频移键控法
double hashing(DH) 双重散列
double height(DH) 倍高
double host backup system(DHBS) 双主机备份系统
double image 双像,重影
double-inputs receiver 双输入接收机
double integration type A/D converter 双积分型模/数转换器
double interpolation 二重插值
double key 双密钥
double key cipher system 双密钥密码体制
double lattice 双格
double layer perpendicular media 双层垂直磁记录介质
double-layer supertwist nematic (DSTN) 双层超扭曲向列型液晶显示器
double leaded 二倍行距
double leaf 双叶
double-length arithmetic operation 双倍长算术运算法
double-length multiplication 双倍长乘
double-length normalization 双倍长规格化
double-length notation 双倍长表示法
double-length numeral 二倍长数
double length register 倍长寄存器
double-length result 双倍长结果
double length transform 倍长度变换
double letter 双写字母
double level cache 二级高速缓存
double level routing 双层布线
double lined border 双线边框

double linkage 双重链接
double linked list 双向链表
double make contacts 双闭合接点
double modulation 双重调制
double negation 双重否定
double opening quote （左侧）双引号
double operand instruction 双操作数指令
double order traversal 双序遍历
double original size 原始大小加倍
double-pivot gimbals 双轴万向平衡环
double-pole double-throw switch(DPDT) 双刀双掷开关
double-pole single-throw switch(DPST) 双刀单掷开关
double poling 双倍轮询
double-precision arithmetic 双精度算「术
double-precision computation 双精度计算
double-precision constant 双精度常数
double-precision exponent 双精度指数
double-precision function 双精度函数
double-precision number 双精度数
double-precision result 双精度结果
double-precision type 双精度类型
double-precision value 双精度值
double-precision variable 双精度变量
double primary address 双重主地址
double pulse recording 双脉冲记录
double pulse resolution(DPR) 双脉冲分辨率
double quotation marks 双引号
double quotes 双引号
double-rail logic 双轨逻辑
double redundant UPS 双备份不间断电源
double recursion 二元递归
double recursive rule 双递归规则
double sampling 复式抽样,二重取样
double sheet detector 双页纸张检测器
double sheet ejector 双页纸张弹出器
double side floppy disk 双面活动盘
double side printed board 双面印刷电路板
double-sideband mixer 双边带混频器
double-sideband signal 双边带信号
double-sided double-density diskette(DS/DD) 双面倍密度软盘
double-sided single-density diskette(DS/SD) 双面单密度软盘
double-sides rank test 双边秩检验
double-stimulus assessment of television picture quality 电视图像质量双重刺激评价
double size(DS) 倍尺寸
double space 双间隔
double stack 双栈
double star network 双重星形网络
double-step write compensation 双阶跃写入补偿
double striking 双重击打
double supertwisted nematic(DSTN) 双扭曲向列型
double-supertwist nematic LCD(DSTN LCD) 双超扭曲向列型液晶显示器
double-tone signal generator 双音调信号发生器
double tracks tape unit 双轨磁带机
double twist 双扭曲型
double underline(DW) 双下划线
double-wide print 双倍宽度打印
double width(DW) 倍宽
double word 双字
double-word boundary 双字界
double-word external data bus(DX) 双字外部数据总线
double-word register 双字寄存器
doublet 二位字节
doubling-up procedure 双重对折方法
doubly chained tree 双链树
doubly connected domain 双连通域
doubly-coupled linear programming 双联线性规划「表
doubly-linked circular list 双重循环链
doubly-linked linear list 双重线性链
doubly-linked ring 双链接环 「表
doubly periodic function 双周期函数
doubly root graph 双根图
doubly stochastic matrix 双随机矩阵
doubtful word 有疑问的字
doubtless 无疑问的
down 停机
down-hill method 下山法
down-lead 下引线

down line 下行线路
down link 下行链路
down reference 向下引用
down-sampling 欠取样
down size 缩小尺寸
down symbol 下降符号
down time 故障时间, 宕机时间
download 向下装载, 下载
download filter 下载过滤器
download font 下载字体
downloadable font 可下载字体
downloading 下载
downloading utility 下载实用程序
downsizing 缩小化
downstream 下游
downstroke 重写笔划, 着重打印
downtime 宕机时间, 停机时间
downward compatible 向下兼容
downward projection 向下投影
downward reference 向下参考[引用]
DOZ(DOZen) 打(12个)
DP(Draft Proposal) 建议草案
DPBX(Digital Private Branch eXchange) 数字专用小交换机
DPC(Data Packet Communications) 数据包通信
DPCM(Differential Pulse Code Modulation) 差分脉码调制
DPCM(Distributed Processing Communications Module) 分布型处理通信模块
DPCX(Distributed Processing Control eXecutive) 分布型处理的控制执行程序
DPE(Distributed Processing Environment) 分布型处理环境
DPEX(Distributed Processing EXecutive program) 分布型处理执行程序
DPFM(Discrete-time Pulse-Frequency Modulation) 离散时间脉冲调频
DPI(Dots Per Inch) 每英寸点数
DPLL(Digital Phase Locked Loop) 数字锁相环
DPM(Dual-Port Memory) 双端口存储器
DPMA(Data Processing Management Asso.) 数据处理管理协会

DPMI(DOS Protected Mode Interface) DOS 保护模式接口
DPPX(Distributed Processing Program eXecutive) 分布处理程序的执行程序
DPPX/BASE(Distributed Processing Programming eXecutive BASE) 分布处理程序设计执行程序/基本部分
DPPX/DPS(DPPX/Distributed Presentation Services) 分布处理程序设计执行程序/分布表示服务
DPPX/DTMS(DPPX/Data base and Transaction Management System) 分布处理程序设计执行程序/数据库和交易管理系统
DPS(Data Processing Standard) 数据处理标准
DPS(Distributed Processing Support) 分布处理支持
DPSK(Differential Phase Shift Keying) 差分相移键控
DQ(DeQueue) 解除队列, 出队列
DQP(Distributed Query Processing) 分布查询处理
DQPSD(Differentially Encoded, Quadriphase Shift Keying) 差分编码四相相移键控
DR(Data Reduction) 数据精简
DR(Dynamic Reconfiguration) 动态重配置
DR-DOS DR-DOS 操作系统
DRA(Data Resource Administrator) 数据资源管理员
Drafix Drafix 软件包
draft 草稿
draft copy 草稿拷贝
draft editing 草稿编辑
draft font 草稿字体
draft international standard 国际标准草案
draft mode 草稿模式
draft proposal 建议草案
draft proposal of international standardized profiles 国际标准化轮廓文件建议草案「式
draft-quality print mode 草稿打印模
draft script 速成脚本; 脚本草稿

draft tube 通风管道
draft view 草稿视图
drafter 绘图机
drafting algorithm 制图算法
drafting machine 描图机
drag 拖动
drag and drop 拖放
drag copy 拖动复制
drag & drop 拖放
drag function 拖动功能
drag icon 拖放(操作中的指针)图标
drag mode 拖放模式
drag over 拖动经过
drag select 拖动选择
dragging 拖动
dragging generated series 拖动生成序列
drain 漏极
drain cut off current of FET 场效应晶体管漏截止电流
DRAM (Dynamic Random Access Memory) 动态随机存取存储器
draw 画线
draw mode (控件)图形外观样式
draw opaque 不透明绘画
draw program 绘图程序
draw stencil 绘图模板
draw style 绘图线条样式
draw text function 绘制文本功能
draw to function 图形移动功能
draw tool 画线工具
draw width 线条宽度
drawer 抽屉
drawer directory 抽屉目录
drawing 抽签;提存;绘图
drawing interchange format 绘图交换格式
drawing interface 图形接口
drawing list 图纸清单
drawing paper 绘图纸
drawing primitive 绘图原语,绘图元
drawing program 绘图程序
drawing section 绘图片段
drawing stencil 绘图模板
drawing view 绘制视图
DRDA (Distributed Relational Database Architecture) 分布式关系数据库体系结构(IBM)
Dreamweaver 网页设计软件(Macromedia)
dribbleware 细流软件
drift 漂移
drift editing symbols 浮动编辑符号
drift region 漂移区
drift velocity saturation 漂移速度饱和
drill down 穿下
drive 驱动,推动
drive bay 驱动器仓
drive current 驱动电流
drive delimiter colon 驱动器定界冒号
drive designator 驱动器指示符
drive element 驱动元件
drive error pattern 驱动误差样式
drive icon 驱动器图标
drive letter 驱动器字母
drive list box 驱动器列表框
drive mapping 驱动器映射
drive name 驱动器名
drive number 驱动器号
drive selection 驱动器选择
drive source 驱动源
driver 驱动器,推动级;驱动程序
driver diagnostic program (DDP) 驱动器诊断程序
driver dispatch table 驱动程序分派表
driver object 驱动程序对象
driver of modules 模块驱动程序
driving power 驱动功率
driving signal 驱动信号
driving unit 推动级,激励级
driving waveform 驱动波形
DRO (Data Read-Out) 数据读出
droop 顶降,降落
drop 分接;赶出;下拉
drop authority 撤销授权
drop cap 下落大字
drop cable 下线电缆,分支电缆
drop-dead halt 完全停机
drop-down combination box 下拉式组合框
drop-down combo box 下拉式组合框
drop-down list 下拉式列表
drop-down list box 下拉式列表框
drop-down menu 下落式菜单
drop-frame 丢帧
drop-frame time code 减帧时间编码
drop-in 偶入,混入脉冲

drop-line 垂直线；下引线
drop-out 偶出；丢脉冲，漏脉冲
drop-out count 丢失总数
drop out detector 漏码检测器
drop out type 反白字形
drop rate 下降速率
drop repeater 分接中继器
drop shadow 下落阴影
drop source 拖动源
drop shadow 拖放目的地
drop zone 下落区域
droplet （嵌入式）短小程序
dropout 漏失字符
dropped bit 丢失数据位
dropped folio 页底页码
droupie(data groupie) 数据追星族
dropping condition rule 摘除条件规则
DRP (Dynamically Relocatable Program) 动态可重定位程序
DRQ(Data Ready Queue) 数据就绪队列
DRQ(Data ReQuest) 数据请求
drum 鼓
drum assembly 磁鼓组件
drum factor 滚筒因数
drum free speed 磁鼓自由速度
drum motor tachogenerator 鼓式电机测速器
drum phase servo 磁鼓相位伺服
drum plotter 滚筒型绘图仪
drum printer 鼓式打印机
drum scanner 磁鼓扫描器
drum scanning 滚筒扫描
drum servo lock 鼓伺服锁定
drum speed PWM 鼓速度脉宽调制器
drum transmitter 滚筒式（传真）发送机
Drums Drums通信网络
dry cell 干电池
dry-film resists 干膜抗蚀剂
dry ink 干性油墨
dry reed contact 干簧触点
dry run 空运行
DS(Data Strobe) 数据选通
DS(Data Structure) 数据结构
DS/HD(Double Sided/High Density) 双面高密度
DSA (Distributed Systems Architecture) 分布式系统体系结构
DSA(Dynamic Service Architecture) 动态服务结构
DSB(Double SideBand) 双边带
DSB(Double-Sided Board) 双面印制电路板
DSD(Data Set Definition) 数据集定义
DSD(Data Set Dictionary) 数据集字典
DS/DD(Double Side/Double Density) 双面/双密度
DSDL(Data Storage Description Language) 数据存储描述语言，DSDL语言
DSDM(Drop Site Database Manager) 下落点数据库管理程序
DSF(DMS System File) 数据库管理系统文件
DSG(Data Set Group) 数据集组
DSI(Dynamic System Interchange) 动态系统交换
DSIMM(Dynamic random access memory ingle Inline Memory Module) 单列直插式动态内存模组
DSL(Default Security Level) 默认安全级
DSL(Digital Subscriber Link) 数字用户线
DSL(Digital Subscriber Loop) 数字用户环路
DSL language(Digital Simulation Language) 数字仿真语言
DSLAM (Digital Subscriber Line Access Multiplexer) 数字用户线接入复用器
DSM(Digital Storage Media) 数字存储媒体称
DSN(Data Source Name) 数据源名
DSP(Digital Signal Processor) 数字信号处理器
DSS(Data Switching System) 数据交换系统
DSS(Decision Support System) 决策支持系统
DSS(Digital Signal Synchronizer) 数字信号同步器
DS/SD(Dual Surface/Single Density) 双面/单密度

DST(Data Service Task) 数据服务任务

DST(Digital Subscriber Terminal) 数字用户终端

DSU(Data Service Unit) 数据服务单元

DSVD(Digital Simultaneous Voice and Data) 数字式声音与数据同传

DSW(Data Status Word) 数据状态字

DSW(Device Status Word) 设备状态字

DT(Data Terminal) 数据终端机

DT(Decision Table) 判定表

DT(Dial Tone) 拨号音

DTB(Data Transfer Bus) 数据传送总线

DTE(Data Terminal Equipment) 数据终端设备

DTE busy 数据终端装置"忙"

DTE controlled not ready 数据终端设备受控未就绪

DTE/DCE(Data Terminal Equipment/Data Circuit-terminating Equipment) 数据终端设备/数据电路终接设备

DTE/DCE interface 数据终端设备与数据通信路设备接口

DTE uncontrolled not ready 数据终端设备未受控未就绪

DTL(Diode-Transistor Logic) 二极管-晶体管逻辑

DTLS(Descriptive Top Level Specification) 描述顶级规范

DTM(Digital Topography Model) 数字地形模型

DTMF(Dual Tone MultiFrequency signaling) 双音多频信号

DTP(DeskTop Publishing system) 桌面印刷系统

DTR(Data Terminal Ready) 数据终端就绪

DTS(Digital Tuning System) 数字调谐系统

DTV(Digital TeleVision) 数字电视

dual 对偶的,成双的

dual access concentrator(DAC) 双连接集中器

dual address stack 双地址栈

dual arm plotter 双臂式绘图仪

dual attached station(DAS) 双连接站

dual auto-alternate sweep 双自动交替扫描

dual bank RAM 双片内存体

dual bus 双总线

dual boot 双重自举

dual cable 双电缆

dual cable broadband LAN 双电缆宽带局域网络

dual capstan tape unit 双主动轮磁带机

dual cartridge printer (彩/黑)双墨盒打印机

dual channel controller 双通道控制器

dual cluster feature 双群集特性

dual coated fiber 双涂覆光纤

dual codes 对偶码

dual coding 双重编码

dual computer speech system 双计算机语音系统

dual computer system 双机系统

dual control 对偶控制

Dual Damascene 双大马士革工艺方法(IBM铜技术)

dual deflection cathode-ray tube 双重偏转阴极射线管

dual disk drive 双软盘驱动器

dual dynamic beam 双重动态光束(NEC)

dual formula 对偶式

dual frequency jamming 双频干扰

dual function 对偶函数

dual-gap disk head 双隙磁盘磁头

dual-gap read-after-write head 双隙写后读磁带磁头

dual head 双头(工作站)

dual homed gateway 双归宿网关,双穴主机网关

dual homing 双归宿

dual hybrid method 对偶杂交法

dual hypergraph 对偶超图

dual-in-line package(DIP) 双列直插式封装

dual-in-line plastic package(DIP) 双列直插式塑料外壳

Dual Independent Bus(DIB) 双独立总线

dual logging 双日志

dual mesh 对偶网格
dual-modem dialing 双调制解调器拨号上网
dual net 对偶网
dual network 对偶网络
dual nonlinear decomposition 对偶非线性分解
dual operation 对偶运算
dual optional solution 对偶最优解
dual phase generator 双相信号发生器
dual plane video system 双平面视频系统
dual port memory 双端口存储器
dual potentiometer 双重电位器
dual power supplies 双电源
dual processor system 双处理机系统
dual recording 双重记录
dual ring 双环
dual-scan display 双扫描(速率)显示器
dual simplex method 对偶单纯形法
dual slope ADC 双斜率 A/D 转换器
dual slope type digital voltmeter 双斜率数字电压表
dual stack 双堆栈
dual stack system 双堆栈系统
dual state push button 双态按钮
dual structure 对偶结构
dual sweep 双扫描
dual system 双机系统
dual time base 双时基
dual-tone multifrequency(DTMF) (电话)双音多频
dual-tone multifrequency signalling 双音多频信令
dual trace oscilloscope 双踪示波器
dual vector space 对偶向量空间
dual y-axis graph 双 Y 轴图形
duality gap 对偶间隙
duality isomorphic 对偶同构
duality law 对偶律
duality map 对偶映射
duality principle 对偶原理
duality problem of nonlinear programming 非线性规划的对偶问题
duality property 对偶性质
DUART(Dual Universal Asynchronous Receiver Transmitter) 对偶式通用异步接收机发送器

DUAT(Direct User Access Terminal) 直接用户访问终端
dub 配音
DUCK DUCK语言
due date (预定)完成日期
due out 待发
dull 呆滞的;阴暗的
dumb 不灵活的,低智能的,哑的
dumb dot-matrix printer 不灵活(无图形能力)的点阵打印机
dumb frame buffer 哑帧缓冲器
dumb hub 非智能集线器
dumb terminal 哑终端
dumb workstation 哑工作站
dummy 虚设,伪的,假的
dummy activity 虚活动
dummy address 伪地址
dummy argument 虚拟变元,哑元
dummy control section 虚控部分
dummy data set 伪数据集
dummy definition 哑定义
dummy demand 假想的需求量
dummy device assignment 虚拟设备分配
dummy entry 虚拟进入
dummy host system input 虚拟主机系统输入
dummy input 伪输入
dummy instruction 哑指令,空操作指令
dummy load 假负载
dummy message 假报文
dummy module 哑模块
dummy node 虚节点
dummy origin 虚构起始点
dummy packet 伪码群
dummy parameter 虚参数
dummy routine 哑程序,空例程
dummy section 虚拟节
dummy statement 空语句
dummy string 伪串
dummy transfer 伪传送
dummy unit 虚单元
dummy variable 哑变量
dump 转储
dump after update 更新后转储
dump before update 更新前转储
dump central memory 转储中央存储器
dump check 转储校验
dump list 转储列表,转储清单

dump point 转储点
dump routine 转储例程
dump virtual storage 转储虚拟存储器
dumper diving 垃圾挖密
duobinary coding 双二进制编码
duotone 双色调
DUP(DUPlex) 双工,双向的,二重的,双的
DUP(DUPlicate) 复制品,副本
dup killer 重复删除程序
dup loop 重复环
duplex 双工
duplex channel 双向通道,双向信道
duplex circuit 双工线路
duplex communication jamming 双工通信干扰
duplex computer 双工计算机
duplex connector 双工连接器
duplex console 双连控制台
duplex printing 双面打印
duplex system 双工系统
duplexed system 双工系统
duplexer 双工器
duplicate 重复,复制
duplicate addresses 重复地址
duplicate file name 重复文件名
duplicate group name 重复组名
duplicate keys 重复键
duplicate original 复制原版
duplicate record 重复记录
duplicate packet 重复分组
duplicate shortcut key 复件快捷键
duplicate volume 复制卷
duplication 重复,复制
duplication check 重复检验
duplication code 重复码
duplication factor 重复因数
duplication redundancy 双模冗余
duplication station 复制站
duplicator 复制机
durability 耐久性,持久性
duration time 持续时间
duster 除尘器
DUT(Dial-Up Terminal) 拨号终端
duty cycle 工作循环,忙闲度
duty factor 占空因数
duty ratio 占空比
DV(Desktop Video) 桌面视频

DVB(Desktop Video Broadcasting) 数字视频广播
DVC(Desktop Video Conference) 桌面视频会议
DVD(Digital Versatile Disc) 数字通用光盘
DVD(Digital Video Disc) 数字视频光盘
DVD-E(Digital Video Disc Erasable) 可擦除数字视频光盘
DVD-R(Digital Video Disc Recordble) 可刻录数字视频光盘
DVD-RW(Digital Video Disc ReWritdble) 可重写数字视频光盘
DVE(Digital Video Effect) 数字视频特技
DVG(Digital Video Generator) 数字视频信号发生器
DVI(Digital Video Interactive) 数字视频交互
DVN(Duplicate Variable Name) 复制变量名
Dvorak keyboard Dvorak 键盘(Dvorak 于 1936 年发明)
DVP(Data Validation Program) 数据验证程序
DVP(Digital Video Processor) 数字视频处理器
DVMA(Direct Virtual Memory Access) 直接虚存访问
DVMA cycle 直接虚存访问周期
DVMA master 直接虚存访问主控器
DVR(Distributed Virtual Reality) 分布式虚拟现实
DVT(Device Vector Table) 设备向量表
DW(Double Word) 双字
DWB(Data Word Buffer) 数据字缓冲器
dwell 静止,延长
dwell time 停延时间
DX4 (486)DX4 处理器(Intel)
DXC(Digital Cross Connector) 数字交叉连接设备
DXF(Drawing Interchange Format) 绘图交换格式(Macintosh)
DXI(Data eXchange Interface) 数据交换接口

dyadic 二元的,双值的
dyadic array 二元数组,二维数组
dyadic operator 二元算符
dye 染料,颜料
dye diffusion 染料扩散,升华
dye-diffusion printing 染料扩散打印方式
dye polymer recording 染料聚合物记录方式
dye sublimation 染料升华
dynalink(dynamic link) 动态链接
dynaload(dynamic load) 动态加载
dynamic 动态的
dynamic access feature 动态接入特性
dynamic accuracy 动态精度
dynamic adaptive routing 动态自适应路由选择
dynamic address resolution 动态地址解析
dynamic address translation(DAT) 动态地址转换
dynamic address translator 动态地址转换器
dynamic allocation 动态存储器分配
dynamic allocator 动态内存分配程序
dynamic analysis 动态分析
dynamic analysis tool 动态分析工具
dynamic analyzer 动态分析程序
dynamic array 动态数组
dynamic assignment 动态分配
dynamic audio frequency domain 动态声频域
dynamic authorization 动态授权
dynamic backout 动态撤消
dynamic backpropagation algorithm 动态反传算法
dynamic bandwidth allocation 动态带宽分配
dynamic behavior 动态特性
dynamic binding 动态绑定[联编]
dynamic bound 动界
dynamic buffering 动态缓冲
dynamic burn-in system 动态老化系统
dynamic burn-in test 动态老化试验
dynamic bus allocation 动态总线分配
dynamic call 动态调用
dynamic cellular automaton 动态细胞自动机

dynamic checking 动态检查
dynamic cluster parameter 动态聚类参数
dynamic coherence check 动态相关性检验
dynamic color regulation(DCR) 动态色彩校正
dynamic communication 动态通信
dynamic compression 动态压缩
dynamic configuration 动态配置
dynamic connectivity 动态连接性
dynamic creation 动态创建
dynamic cross call 动态交叉调用
Dynamic Data Exchange(DDE) 动态数据交换协议
dynamic data schema 动态数据模式
dynamic data set definition 动态数据集定义
dynamic data stream computer 动态数据流计算机
dynamic data structure 动态数据结构
dynamic debugging 动态调试
dynamic declaration 动态声明
dynamic descendance 动态后裔[后继]
dynamic design review 动态设计检查
dynamic device reconfiguration(DDR) 动态设备重配置
dynamic dictionary 动态辞典
dynamic dispatching 动态调度
dynamic display image 动态显示图像
dynamic document 动态文档
dynamic domain naming system 动态域命名系统
dynamic dump 动态转储
dynamic effect 动态效应
dynamic error 动态错误[误差]
dynamic error-free transmission 动态无差错传输
dynamic execution 动态执行
dynamic fault recovery 动态故障恢复
dynamic fault-tolerance 动态容错
dynamic feedback compensation 动态反馈补偿
dynamic file organization 动态文件组织
dynamic flow diagram 动态流程图
dynamic focusing 动态聚焦
dynamic fractal program 动态分形程

dynamic frame 动态帧
dynamic free-form modeling(DFFM) 动态自由曲线(面)造型
dynamic free variable 动态自由变量
dynamic frequency allocation 动态频率分配
dynamic hash 动态散列
dynamic hazard 动态冒险
dynamic home page 动态主页
Dynamic Host Configuration Protocol (DHCP) 动态主机配置协议
dynamic HTML 动态超文本标记语言
dynamic image analysis 动态图像分析
dynamic imagery 动态成像
dynamic index 动态索引
dynamic indirect addressing 动态间接寻址
dynamic instruction 动态指令
dynamic interconnection network 动态互连网络
dynamic interpreting 动态解释
dynamic invocation interface 动态调用接口
dynamic IP address 动态 IP 地址
dynamic key 动态密钥
dynamic knowledge 动态知识
dynamic lag 动态滞后
dynamic library 动态库
dynamic link 动态链
dynamic link module 动态链接模块
dynamic linking 动态链接
dynamic linking library(DLL) 动态链接库
dynamic load balancing 动态负载平衡
dynamic load library 动态安装库
dynamic loading and linking 动态装入与链接
dynamic log 动态登录;动态日志
dynamic logic hazard 动态逻辑冒险
dynamic loop 动态循环
dynamic magnetic neutralization 动态磁中性化
dynamic mapping 动态映射
dynamic mathematic model 动态数学模型
dynamic memory 动态存储器
dynamic memory allocation 动态内存分配
dynamic memory management 动态内存管理
dynamic memory refresh 动态存储器刷新
dynamic memory relocation 动态存储重定位
dynamic menuing 动态菜单选择
dynamic method table(DMT) 动态方法表
dynamic microprogramming 动态微程序设计
dynamic microprogramming control 动态微程序设计控制
dynamic model 动态模型
dynamic modeling 动态建模
dynamic MOS memory 动态 MOS 存储器
dynamic multifunctional pipeline 动态多功能流水线
dynamic network services 动态网络服务
dynamic node addressing 动态节点寻址
dynamic object 动态对象
dynamic optimization 动态优化
dynamic overlay 动态覆盖
dynamic overload control 动态过载控制
dynamic page 动态页面[网页]
dynamic page relocation 动态页面重定位
dynamic parallelization 动态并行化
dynamic parameters 动态参数
dynamic partition balancing 动态分区平衡
dynamic password 动态口令
dynamic path update 动态路径更新
dynamic physical model 动态物理模型
dynamic pipeline 动态流水线
dynamic pool block 动态页池块
dynamic pressure flying head 动压浮动磁头
dynamic printout 动态打印
dynamic priority 动态优先权
dynamic priority allocation 动态优先权分配
dynamic priority scheduling 动态优先权调度
dynamic probabilistic inventory model 概率型动态库存模型

dynamic process creation 动态进程创建
dynamic process deletion 动态进程撤消
dynamic processor allocation 动态处理器分配
dynamic program loading 动态程序装入
dynamic program relocation 动态程序重定位
dynamic programming 动态规划
dynamic protection 动态保护
dynamic RAM 动态随机存取存储器
dynamic random access memory (DRAM) 动态随机存取存储器
dynamic range 动态范围
dynamic reconfiguration 动态重配置
dynamic reconfiguration data set 动态重配置数据集
dynamic recovery 动态恢复
dynamic redundancy 动态冗余
dynamic refresh 动态刷新
dynamic region 动态区域
dynamic reliable 动态可靠性
dynamic relocation 动态重定位
dynamic relocation program 动态重定位程序
dynamic replication 动态复制
dynamic resistance 动态电阻
dynamic resolution 动态分辨率
dynamic resource allocation 动态资源配置
dynamic resource management 动态资源管理
dynamic response 动态响应
dynamic restructuring 动态重新组合
dynamic routing 动态路由选择
dynamic routing protocol 动态路由选择协议
dynamic scalable architecture 动态可伸缩体系结构
dynamic scattering effect 动态散射效应
dynamic scattering mode liquid crystal display 动态散射式液晶显示
dynamic scheduling 动态调度
dynamic scheduling simulator 动态调度仿真程序
dynamic schema evolution 动态模式演变
dynamic scope 动态作用范围

dynamic sensitivity 动态灵敏度
dynamic search algorithm 动态检索算法
dynamic segment attribute 动态区段属性
dynamic segment relocation 动态区段重定位
dynamic sequential control 动态顺序控制
Dynamic Server 动态服务器(Informix)
dynamic set 动态集合
dynamic sharpness control (DSC) 动态锐度控制
dynamic simulation 动态模拟
dynamic SLIP (Serial Line Internet Protocol) 动态串行线路网间协议
dynamic space reclamation 动态空间回收
dynamic splitter window 动态划分窗口
dynamic SQL 动态结构查询语言
dynamic stop 动态停机
dynamic storage allocation 动态存储器分配
dynamic storage area 动态存储区域
dynamic storage cell 动态存储器单元
dynamic storage model 动态存储器模型
dynamic subroutine 动态子例程
dynamic support system 动态后援系统
dynamic system flowchart 动态系统流程图
dynamic system model 动态系统模型
dynamic system theory 动力系统理论
dynamic table 动态表
dynamic test 动态测试
dynamic tests for IC 集成电路动态测试
dynamic threshold alternation 动态阈值改变
dynamic threshold query 动态阈值查询
dynamic tool display 动态刀具显示
dynamic transaction backout 动态事务复原,动态事项逆序操作
dynamic transient pool management 动态瞬时页池管理
dynamic transient segment register save 动态瞬时段寄存器保存
dynamic translation 动态翻译

dynamic tree table 动态树表
dynamic two-value logic 动态二值逻辑
dynamic user microprogrammable machine 动态用户可编微程序计算机
dynamic variable 动态变量
dynamic vibration absorber 动态消振器
dynamic vision 动态视觉
dynamic volume control 动态音量控制
dynamic web page 动态网页
dynamical skew 动态扭斜
dynamical tree 动态树

dynamically redefinable character set (DRCS) 动态可重新定义字符集
DYNAMO language (Dynamic Models) 动态模型语言
dynaset 动态(记录)集
dynastic order 朝代次序
dynaturtle 动态龟标
DYNET (DYNamic NETwork planning technique) 动态网络规划技术
DYNIX operating system DYNIX 操作系统

E e

E (Efficiency) 有效系数;效率
E (Exponent) 指数
E-book 电子图书
E-business 电子商务,电子业务
E-commerce 电子商务
E-consumer 电子消费者
e-disk (emulated-disk) 仿真盘
E-E (End to End) 端对端,终点到终点
E-mail 电子函件,电子邮件
E-mail address 电子邮箱地址
E-money 电子货币
E notation E 表示法
e. p. d (earth potential difference) 对地电位差
E-R (Entity-Relationship) 实体-关系
E-string 实体串
E-time (Execution-time) 执行时间
E-type compensation "E"型补偿
E-unsatisfiability E-不可满足性
E-World 电子化世界(HP)
E-zone E 区域
EA (Effective Address) 有效地址
each other (版面)左右对齐
Eagle "鹰"计划(IBM)
Eagle language Eagle 语言
EAM (Electrical Accounting Machine) 电子记账机
EAN (Electronic Audio Recognition) 电子声音识别
EAR (Electronic Aural Responder) 电子听觉应答器

EAR (External Access Network) 外部访问网络
earcon 有声图标
earlier transmitted bits 先前传送的比特
earlier version 先前的(软件)版本
earliest node time 最早节点(到达)时间
early binding 前期绑定,早期联编
early date 最早日期
early distortion 早期失真,前期畸变
Early effect 厄雷效应
early failure period 早期故障期
early lose efficiency 早期失效
early packet discard 早期分组丢弃
early processing 早期处理
early relay status 继电器初态
early start date 最早起始日期
early token release 早期令牌释放
early warning 预警
early warning computer 预警计算机
early warning net 预警网络
earphone 耳机
earth 接地;地面
earth based station 地面站,陆基站
earth bulging 地面障碍
earth clamp 接地夹子
earth connection 接地
earth coverage 地面覆盖区域
earth current 接地电流
earth fault 接地故障
earth-fixed station 地面固定站

earth plate(EP)　接地板
earth potential　地电位,地电势
earth potential compensation　地电势补偿
earth return　接地回线;地回路
earth segment　地面段,地面部分
earth-stabilized vehicle　地球稳定飞行器
earth station　地球站
earth synchronous satellite　地球同步卫星
earth terminal　接地端
earth-to-satellite communication link　地球-卫星通信链路
East Asian character codes(EA-CC)　东亚字符代码
East Asian character sets(EACS)　东亚字符集
easy axis　易磁化轴
Easy Pay system(EPS)　简便付款系统
easy to read　易读性
easy to use computer card　易用计算机卡
easy to use data base　易用数据库软件
EasyCAD 2　EasyCAD 2辅助设计软件
EasyCD　EasyCD光盘刻录软件
Easynet　简易网,Easynet网
eavesdropping　偷听,窃听
EAX(Electronic Automatic eXchange)　电子自动交换机
EBAM(Electronic Beam Addressable Memory)　电子束可寻址存储器
EBCDIC(Extended Binary Coded Decimal Interchange Code)　扩充的二-十进制交换码(IBM)
Ebers-Moll model　E-M模型
EBR(Electronic Beam Recorder)　电子束记录器
EBS(Electronic Beam Scanning)　电子束扫描
EC(Embedded Computer)　嵌入式计算机
EC(Error correct)　错误纠正
ECC(Error Checking and Correction)　错误检验与改正
eccentric　离心的,偏心的
eccentricity　偏心率
ECF(ECho Frame)　回应帧
ECF(Enhanced Connectivity Facilities)　增强型连接设施
ECF(Externally Caused Failure)　外因导致的故障
echo　反应;回波
echo acknowledgement　回声应答
echo attenuation　回波衰减
echo cancellation　回声消除
echo chancellor　回波消除器
echo check　回送检验
echo effect　回波效应
echo frame(ECF)　回应帧
echo input attribute　回应输入属性
echo noise　回波噪声
echo off　回送关闭
echo on　回送开放
echo program　回送程序
echo protocol　回送协议
echo reply　回送答复
echo request packet　回送请求包
echo suppressor　回波抑制器
echo test　回波测试
echoed signal　回波信号
echolocating　回声探测,回声定位
echoplex　回声复核
echoplex mode　回送模式
ECL(Emitter Coupled Logic)　射极耦合逻辑
ECL microprocessor　射极耦合逻辑微处理器
ECLIPSE MV series　ECLIPSE MV系列计算机
ECM(Electronic Cipher Machine)　电子加密机
ECM(Electronic CounterMeasures)　电子对抗
ECMA(European Computer Manufacture Assn.)　欧洲计算机制造厂商协会
Econet(UK communications network)　UK通信网络
econo-mathematical method　经济数学法
econometrics　计量经济学
economic cybernetics　经济控制论
economic dispatch　经济调度
economic feasibility　经济可行性
economic forecast　经济预测
economic lot-size　经济批量
economic mode　经济模式
economic pattern　经济模式

economic service life 经济使用寿命
economical accuracy of machining 经济加工精度
economization 缩减,节约
ecosystem 生态系统
ECP (Expandable Communications Processor) 可扩展的通信处理机
ECR(Electronic Cash Register) 电子现金出纳机,电子收款机
ECR(Error Card Rejection) 错误卡拒收
ECS(Electronic Countermeasures System) 电子对抗系统
ECS(Embedded Computer System) 嵌入式计算机系统
ECT(Estimated Completion Time) 预计完成时间
ED(Emergency Device) 应急设备
ED(Encryption Device) 密码设备
EDA(Electronic Design Automation) 电子设计自动化
EDA(Electronic Digital Analyzer) 电子数字分析器
EDC(Emergency Digital Computer) 应急数字计算机
EDD(Envelope Delay Distortion) 包络延迟失真
eddy current 涡流
eddy current killed oscillator (ECKO) 涡流衰减振荡器
EDE(Event-Driven Environment) 事件驱动环境
edge 边缘,界限
Edge Binding 装订边
edge-board connector 板边连接器
edge character 字符边界
edge condition 边界条件
edge connectivity algorithm 边连通度算法
edge connector 边缘连接器
edge covering number 边覆盖数
edge crisping 勾边处理
edge definition 边缘清晰度
edge description 边缘描述
edge detection 边缘检测
edge disjoint circuit union 边不相接回路的并集
edge disjoint cut-set union 边不相接割集的并集
edge effect 边缘效应
edge enhancement 边缘增强
edge estimation 边缘估计
edge extraction 边缘提取
edge feature 边缘特征
edge filling 边缘填充
edge fitting 边缘拟合
edge fog 边缘模糊
edge gradient 边缘梯度
edge graph 边图
edge independent number 边独立数
edge independent set of hypergraph 超图的边独立集
edge-induced subhypergraph 边导出的子超图
edge-lighted readout 边缘照明读出
edge matching 边缘匹配
edge operator 边缘算符
edge picture 边缘图像
edge quantization 边缘量化
edge recognition 边缘识别
edge reconstruction 边缘重构
edge response 边缘响应
edge sharpness 边缘锐度
edge spacing 边距
edge-to-edge printing 边缘到边缘打印
edge tracing 边缘跟踪
edge-triggered flip-flop 边沿触发式触发器
edge wave 边缘皱,边缘波纹
edgeboard connector 印刷电路板边缘连接器
edging 镶边
EDI(Electronic Data Interchange) 电子数据交换
EDI service 电子数据交换业务
EDI system 电子数据交换系统
EDIF (Electronic Design Interchange Format) 电子设计交换格式
EDIFACT(Electronic Data Interchange For Administration Commerce and Transport) 商贸运输管理的电子数据交换
Edison Edison 语言
edit 编辑
edit bit 编辑位
edit box 编辑框

edit buffer 编辑缓冲区
edit button 编辑按钮
edit capabilities 编辑能力
edit code 编辑码
edit command 编辑命令
edit control 编辑控制
edit control character 编辑控制字符
edit cost 编辑成本
edit decision list(EDL) 编辑决定表
edit description 编辑描述
edit descriptor 编辑描述符
edit-directed input/output 编辑式输入/输出
edit-directed stream 编辑定向流
edit-directed transmission 编辑式传输
edit display 编辑显示
edit distance 编辑距离
edit dump 编辑转储
edit facility 编辑软件
edit filter 编辑筛选程序,编辑过滤器
edit function 编辑功能
edit functions with APPEND 追加方式的编辑功能
edit hyperlink 编辑超链接
edit insert 编辑插入
edit instruction 编辑指令
edit login script 编辑登录原稿
edit keys 编辑键
edit lines command 编辑行命令
edit list 编辑表
edit macro 编辑宏指令
edit mask 编辑掩码
edit master 编辑原版
edit memory 编辑存储器
edit mode 编辑方式
edit mode command 编辑方式命令
edit object 编辑对象
edit output 编辑输出
Edit Palette 编辑调色板
edit parameters 编辑参数
edit pattern 编辑模式
edit point 编辑点
edit program 编辑程序
edit pulse 编辑脉冲
edit routine 编辑例程
Edit scenario 编辑场景
Edit Series 编辑数据系列
edit session 编辑会话期
edit statements 编辑语句
edit style sheet 编辑样式表
edit symbol 编辑符号
edit text 编辑文本
edit validation 编辑有效权限
edit window 编辑窗口
editable PostScript 可编辑的 Post-Script
edited copy 编辑拷贝
editing 编辑
editing area 编辑区
editing capacity 编辑容量,编辑能力
editing character 编辑字符
editing clause 编辑子句
editing command 编辑命令
editing controller 编辑控制器
editing information 编辑信息
editing key 编辑键
editing keys used with word processor 文字处理软件所用的编辑键
editing operating 编辑作业
editing pattern 编辑图样,编辑模式
editing routine 编辑例程
editing rule 编辑规则
editing run 编辑运行
editing script 编辑底稿,编辑脚本
editing session 编辑对话
editing sign 编辑记号
editing specification 编辑规格说明
editing statement 编辑语句
editing subroutine 编辑子例程
editing symbol 编辑符号
editing terminal 编辑终端
editing text file 编辑文本文件
editing transformation 编辑转换
editing type 编辑类型
editor 编辑程序
editor command 编辑程序命令
editor program 编辑程序
editor store file 编辑程序存储文件
editor work file 编辑程序工作文件
editorial system 编辑系统
EDITRAM model 文本编辑机器模型
EDL(Edit Decision List) 编辑决定表
EDL(Event Definition Language) 事件定义语言
EDL(Event-Driven Language) 事件驱动语言

EDLIN (DOS下的)行编辑程序
EDM(Event Driven Monitor) 事件驱动监督程序
Edmonds' algorithm 埃德蒙斯算法
Edmonds-Karp's algorithm 艾德蒙-卡普算法
EDO(Extended Data Out) 扩展数据输出(RAM)
EDP(Event-Driven Program) 事件驱动程序
EDP capability(Electronic Data Processing Capability) 电子数据处理能力
EDP Center(Electronic Data Processing Center) 电子数据处理中心
EDS(Exchangeable Disk Storage) 可更换磁盘存储器
EDS(Extended Data Set) 扩展数据集
EDSAC(Electronic Discrete Sequential Automatic Computer) 电子离散时序自动计算机,EDSAC计算机
EDTV(Enhanced Definition TV) 增强清晰度电视
education channel 教育频道
education software 教育软件
education support system 教育支持系统
educational groupware system 教育群件系统
educational robot 教育机器人
educational technology 教育技术
educational television 教育电视
educe 推断,演绎
edulcorate 纯化,消除
EDUCOM Planning Council 计算机教育计划委员会
edulcorate 纯化
edutainment 教育娱乐
EDVAC(Electronic Discrete Variable Automatic Computer) 电子离散变量自动计算机,EDVAC计算机
EDX(Event Driven Executive) 事件驱动执行程序
EEMS(Enhanced Expanded Memory Specification) 增强型扩充内存规范
EEPROM(Electrically Erasable Programmable Read Only Memory) 电可擦除可编程只读存储器
EEXT(Exception EXiT) 例外出口,异常退出
EFCI(Explicit Forward Congestion Notification) 显式前向拥塞指示
EFF(Electronic Frontier Foundation) 电子前沿基金会
effect 效果,结果,作用
effect band 效应带
effect-cause analysis 因果分析
effective 有效的
effective access time 有效存取时间
effective acoustic center 有效声中心
effective actuation time 有效动作时间
effective address 有效地址
effective algorithm 有效算法
effective ampere 有效安培
effective area 有效面积
effective bandwidth 有效带宽
effective byte 有效字节
effective byte location 有效字节位置
effective call 有效呼叫
effective capacity 有效电容;有效容量
effective character rate 有效字符速率
effective closure property 有效闭包性质
effective conductivity 有效电导率
effective confusion area 有效干扰面积
effective constant 有效常数
effective current 有效电流
effective cutoff frequency 有效截止频率
effective data transfer rate 有效数据传输速率
effective date 有效日期
effective date to 有效日期至…
effective data transfer rate 有效数据传送速率
effective dead time 有效静止时间
effective deadline scheduling 有效期限调度法
effective delay 有效延迟
effective density 有效密度
effective domain 有效域
effective double-word 有效双字
effective double-word location 有效双字单元
effective duration 有效时间间隔
effective facsimile band 有效传真频带

effective field intensity 有效场强
effective frame 有效帧
effective frequency 有效频率
effective gap 有效缝隙
effective ground 有效接地
effective half-word 有效半字
effective height 有效高度
effective instant 有效瞬间
effective instruction 有效指令
effective interval 有效间隔
effective jamming 有效干扰
effective life 有效寿命
effective machine time 有效机器时间
effective margin 有效富裕度,有效余量
effective memory address 有效内存地址
effective memory band width 有效内存带宽
effective monopole radiated power(EMRP) 有效单极辐射功率
effective noise bandwidth(ENB) 等效噪声带宽
effective operand address 操作数有效地址
effective operation address 有效作业地址
effective output 有效输出
effective percentage modulation 有效调制率,有效调制度
effective picture size 有效画面尺寸
effective printing rate 有效打印速度
effective quality factor 有效品质因数
effective radiation power(ERP) 等效辐射功率
effective radius of the earth 有效地球半径
effective range 有效范围
effective recording width 有效记录宽度
effective reduction 有效缩小值
effective resistance 有效电阻,等效电阻
effective resolution 有效分辨率
effective rights 有效权限
effective root directory 有效根目录
effective search speed 有效查找速度
effective self-reconfiguration capability 有效自重构能力
effective sound pressure 有效声压
effective speed 有效速度
effective speed of transmission 有效发信速度
effective thermal resistance 等效热阻
effective time 有效时间
effective track width 有效磁道宽度
effective traffic 有效业务量
effective transmission rate 有效传输率
effective transmission speed 有效传输速率
effective user ID 有效用户标识符
effective value 有效值
effective value detector 有效值检波器
effective virtual address 有效虚地址
effective word 有效字
effective word location 有效的字单元
effector 格式控制符
efficiency 效率;有效性
efficiency analysis 有效性分析
efficiency factor 效率因数
efficiency factor in time 时间有效因数
efficiency measure 有效性测度
efficiency of an estimation 估计的效率
efficiency of transducer 换能器效率
efficient algorithm 有效算法
efficient estimation 有效估计
efficient solution 有效解
EFT(Electronic Funds Transfer) 电子资金转账,电子汇兑
EFTP(Ethernet File Transfer Protocol) 以太网文件传送协议
EGA(Enhanced Graphics Adapter) 增强型图形适配器
EGCR(Extended Group Coded Recording) 扩展组编码记录
egoless programming 非自我程序设计
egoless programming team 无自我程序设计小组
EGP(Exterior Gateway Protocol) 外部网关协议
EHD(External Hard Disk) 外置式硬盘
EHOG (European Host Operator Group) 欧洲主机操作员小组
EI(Enable Interrupt) 中断允许
EI(External Interrupt) 外部中断
EIA(Electronic Industries Association of USA) (美国)电子工业协会
EIA(Error In Address) 地址错误
EIA color code EIA 色码

EIA interface 电子工业协会接口，EIA接口
EIA-RS-232-C EIA-RS-232-C接口标准
EIA RS-449 EIA RS-449通信接口标准
EIA standard code 电子工业协会标准代码
EIA/TIA 586 EIA/TIA 586通信标准
EIAD(End Item Allocation Document) 最终产品分配文件
EIC(Equipment Identification Code) 设备标识码
eidetic 逼真
Eidophor system 油膜光阀投影电视系统
EIES(Electronic Information Exchange System) 电子信息交换系统
Eiffel Eiffel语言
eigen variable 指导变元
eigenfunction 本征函数
eigenstructure 本征结构
eigentone 本征音
eigenvalue 本征值,特征值
eigenvector 本征向量
eight-bit byte 八位字节
eight-bit data path 八位数据通路
eight level code 八单位码
eight nine modified non-return to-zero change on one(8/9 MNRZ1) 8位变9位的改进型逢"1"变化不归零制
eight queen problem 八皇后问题
EIN(European Information Network) 欧洲信息网络
EISA(Extended Industry Standard Architecture) 扩展型工业标准体系结构
either-or operation "异"操作
either symbol 抉择符号
either-way 半双工
EJ(Electronic Jamming) 电子干扰
eject key 退出键,弹出键
Eject Page Before Report 打印报表前先输出当前页
eject tape 弹出磁带
ejected 跳出,弹出,退出
elaboration 确立
elapsed time 经过(已占用)的时间
elapsed timer 已用时间计时器

elastomeric contact switching 弹性接触交换
elastic buffer 弹性缓存
elastic-joint robot 弹性关节机器人
elastic matching 弹性匹配
elastically-jointed structure 弹性接合结构
elasticity buffering 弹性缓冲
Elbow 机械肘,弯头
electret 驻极体
electret microphone 驻极体麦克风
electret recorder 驻极体记录器
electric aging 电老化
electric breakdown voltage 电击穿电压
electric brush 电刷
electric charge 电荷
electric control 电气控制
electric current 电流
electric delay line 电延迟线
electric dipole 电偶极子
electric-discharge machining 放电金属加工机
electric discharge printer 放电式打印机
electric displacement 电位移
electric doublet 电偶极子
electric energy 电能
electric eye 电眼
electric field 电场
electric field line 电场力线
electric field strength 电场强度
electric field vector 电场向量
electric flux 电通量
electric flux density 电通量密度
electric hysteresis 电滞
electric image 电像
electric line of force 电力线
electric medium constant 电介质常数
electric moment 电矩
electric motor 电动机,马达
electric network 电气网络
electric noise 电噪声
electric potential 电位
electric power 电力
electric shielding 电屏蔽
electric signal 电信号
electric spark 电火花
electric strength 耐电强度,抗电强度
electric substation 变电站

electric tuning 电调谐
electric typewriter 电动打字机
electric vector 电向量,电矢量
electric velocity sensor 电子式速度传感器
electric wave 电波
electrical accounting machine(EAM) 电动计算机
electrical alterable memory 电可改写存储器
Electrical and Electronics Abstracts 《电气和电子文摘》(英国)
electrical angle 电角度
electrical axis 电轴
electrical breakdown 电击穿
electrical brush 电刷
electrical charge 电荷
electrical contact 电触点
electrical distance 电距离
electrical element 电学要素 「度
electrical engagement length 电接合长
electrical erasable read only memory (EEROM) 可擦除只读存储器
electrical generator 发电机
electrical impulses 电脉冲
electrical inertia 电惯量
electrical interference 电干扰
electrical length 电长度
electrical measurement 电测量
electrical network 电网
electrical-optical isolation 光电隔离
Electrical Patents Index(EPI) 《电气专利索引》(英国)
electrical protection 电气保护 「器
electrical quantity sensor 电学量传感
electrical radian 电弧度
electrical relay 电气继电器
electrical resistivity 电阻率
electrical rule checking(ERC) 电气规则检查
electrical scanning 电扫描
electrical safety 电气安全
electrical schematic 电路图
electrical wave 电波
electrical zero 电零点
electrically alterable ROM(EAROM) 电可改写只读存储器
electrically erasable programmable read-only memory(EEPROM) 电擦除可编程只读存储器
electrically short dipole 电短偶极子
electrically variable inductor 电可变电感器
electricity 电
electrify 充电
electro-chromic display(ECD) 电致变色显示
electro-functional polymer 电功能聚合物 「扰
electro-magnetic interference 电磁干
electro-servomechanism 电动执行机构
electroacoustic coupling 电声耦合
electroacoustic effect 电声效应
electroacoustic transducer 电声换能器
electroacoustics 电声学
electrochemical power source 电化学电源 「法
electrochemical recording 电化学记录
electrochemichrominant phenomenon 电化学着色现象
electrochemistry 电化学
electrochromic display 电致变色显示
electrode 电极
electrode capacitance 极间电容
electrodynamic braking 电动制动
electrodynamic loudspeaker 电动式扬声器
electrodynamics 电动力学
electroelectret 电驻极体
electroencephalogram imaging 脑电图
electrofluorescent device 电荧光器件
electroforming 电成形
electrography 电记录术
electroluminescence 电致发光
electroluminescent 场致发光
electroluminescent display device(ELD) 电致发光显示器
electroluminescent display panel 电致发光显示板
electrolysis 电解
electrolytic capacitor 电解电容器
electromagnetic compatibility 电磁兼容性
electromagnetic constant 电磁常数
electromagnetic coupling 电磁耦合

electromagnetic deflection 电磁偏转
electromagnetic energy 电磁能
electromagnetic environment 电磁环境
electromagnetic field 电磁场
electromagnetic force 电磁力
electromagnetic induction 电磁感应
electromagnetic interference(EMI) 电磁干扰
electromagnetic lens 电磁透镜
electromagnetic radiation 电磁辐射
electromagnetic relay 电磁继电器
electromagnetic sensor 电磁式传感器
electromagnetic shielding 电磁屏蔽
electromagnetic unit(EMU) 电磁单位
electromagnetic wave 电磁波
electromagnetics 电磁学
electromatic pollution 电磁污染
electromatic stealth 电磁隐身
electromechanical coupling 机电耦合
electromechanical transducer 机电换能器
electromechanics 机电学
electromigration 电徙动
electromotive force(EMF) 电动势
electromotive series 电动势序
electron 电子
electron amplification 电子倍增
electron art 电子艺术
electron avalanche 电子雪崩
electron beam 电子束
electron beam bonding 电子束焊接
electron beam deflection 电子束偏转
electron beam lithography machine 电子束曝光机
electron beam machining(EBM) 电子束加工
electron beam printing 电子束曝光
electron-beam writing equipment 电子束书写设备
electron gun 电子枪
electron image 电子图像
electron optics 电子光学
electron pair annihiation 电子对湮灭
electronegative 负电性的
electronic 电子学
electronic accounting machine 电子记账机
electronic advertisement 电子广告
electronic animation 电子动画
electronic automatic exchange(EAX) 自动电子交换机
electronic automatic tuning 电子自动调谐
electronic bank 电子银行
electronic blackboard 电子黑板
electronic boardroom 电子会议室
electronic book 电子图书
electronic bookmark 电子书签
electronic bulleting board 电子布告牌
electronic calendar 电子日程表
electronic camera 电子照相机
electronic cash register 电子收银机
Electronic Communications Privacy Act 电子通信保密法案
electronic component 电子元件
electronic composition 电子排版
electronic computer 电子计算机
electronic counter 电子计数器
electronic countermeasure 电子对抗
electronic data interchange(EDI) 电子数据交换
electronic data processing(EDP) 电子数据处理
electronic data-processing system (EDPS) 电子数据处理系统
electronic design automation(EDA) 电子设计自动化
electronic design interchange format (EDIF) 电子设计交换格式
electronic desktop display system 电子桌面显示系统
electronic diary 电子日志
electronic dictionary(ED) 电子词典
electronic distribution 电子分发
electronic document communication system(EDCS) 电子文件通信系统
electronic document delivery system 电子文献提供系统
electronic editing 电子编辑
electronic encyclopedia 电子百科全书
Electronic Engineering 《电子工程》
electronic event logger 电子事件记录仪
electronic field production(EFP) 电子现场节目制作
electronic file 电子文件

electronic filing 电子文件生成
Electronic Frontier Foundation(EFF) 电子前沿基金会
electronic funds transfer(EFT) 电子汇兑
electronic funds transfer-point of sale (EFT-POS) 销售点电子资金转账系统
electronic funds transfer system(EFTS) 电子资金汇兑系统
electronic glass 电子玻璃
Electronic Industries Association(EIA) 电子工业协会
Electronic Industry Association interface 电子工业协会接口,EIA接口
electronic information exchange system (EIES) 电子信息交换系统
electronic information service(EIS) 电子信息服务
electronic intelligence 电子情报
electronic intelligence reconnaissance 电子情报侦察
electronic jamming 电子干扰
electronic journal 电子杂志,电子期刊
electronic library 电子图书馆
electronic mail 电子邮件,电子信箱
Electronic Mail Assn. 电子邮政协会
electronic mail network 电子邮件网络
electronic mail system 电子邮件系统
electronic maildrop(EM) 电子信箱
electronic mailing 电子邮政
electronic map 电子地图
electronic media 电子媒体
electronic message service(EMS) 电子消息服务
electronic message system 电子消息系统
electronic money 电子货币
electronic music 电子音乐
electronic music synthesizer 电子音乐合成器
electronic musical instrument 电子乐器
electronic neuron network simulation 电子神经元网络模拟
electronic news gathering(ENG) 电子新闻采编
electronic noticeboard 电子布告牌
electronic numeric integrator and calculator(ENIAC) 电子数字积分计算机
electronic office 电子办公室
electronic overlay 电子覆盖
electronic packaging 电子电路组装
electronic page make-up 电子页面安排
electronic passport 电子护照
electronic payment 电子支付
electronic pen 电子笔
electronic photograph recording 电子照相记录法
electronic point of sale(EPOS) 电子销售点系统
electronic post 电子邮政,电子邮局
electronic power supply 电子电源
electronic printer 电子印刷机
electronic private automatic branch exchange(EPABX) 专用电子自动交换分机
electronic proof 电子凭据
electronic publication 电子出版物
electronic publishing 电子出版
electronic publishing system(EPS) 电子出版系统
electronic reconnaissance 电子侦察
electronic reconnaissance satellite 电子侦察卫星
electronic relay 电子继电器
electronic reverberator 电子混响器
electronic route map 电子道路图
electronic scale 电子秤
electronic scanning 电子扫描
electronic scanning antenna 电扫描天线
electronic shield 静电屏蔽
electronic shutter 电子快门
electronic speech recognition 电子语音识别
electronic spread sheet package 电子表格软件包
electronic statistical machine 电子统计机
electronic stylus 电子笔,电子记录针
electronic switch 电子开关
electronic token 电子钥匙牌
electronic tone generator 电子音阶发生器
Electronic Trade Opportunity System (ETO) 电子贸易机会系统

electronic translator 电子译码器
electronic tuning 电子调谐
electronic tutor 电子教学装置
Electronic University Network (EUN) 电子大学网络
electronic video recording 电子录像
electronic volt 电子伏特
electronics 电子学
electronics computer aided design (ECAD) 电子线路计算机辅助设计
electronics system design automation (ESDA) 电子系统设计自动化
Electronics Workbench 电子学仿真软件
electrophotographic printer 电子照排印刷机
electrophotography 电子照相术
electroplated film disk 电镀薄膜磁盘
electroplating 电镀
electropositive 正电
electroradiography 电子X射线摄影
electrosensitive printing 电灼式印刷
electrosensitive processor 电火花刻蚀处理机
electrosensitive recording 电火花刻蚀记录
electrostatic 静电
electrostatic absorption 静电吸附
electrostatic actuator 静电激励器
electrostatic deflection 静电偏转
electrostatic deflection plate 静电偏转板
electrostatic discharge 静电放电
electrostatic field 静电场
electrostatic focus 静电聚焦
electrostatic induction 静电感应
electrostatic photography 静电摄影术
electrostatic plotter 静电绘图仪
electrostatic printer 静电式打印机
electrostatic printing (reproduction) 静电印刷
electrostatic printing head 静电打印头
electrostatic protection 静电防护
electrostatic recording paper 静电记录纸
electrostatic shield 静电屏蔽
electrostatic storage 静电存储器
electrostatic storage tube 静电存储管
electrostatic writing head 静电记录头
electrostriction 电致伸缩
electrostrictive effect 电致伸缩效应
elegance 简洁,典雅
elegant program 精致的程序
element 元素,单元,部分
element address 单元地址
element class 元类
element count 单元计数
element descriptor 元素描述符
element entry 元素项
element error rate 码元差错率
element expression 单元表达式
element gain in array 阵列中单元增益
element group 元素组
element ID 单元标识符
element interleaving 码元插入
element list 元素表
element number 单元编号
element occurrence 元素出现
element pattern in array 阵中单元方向图
element size 元素大小
element stiffness matrix 单元刚度矩阵
element string 单元串
element synchronism 码元同步
element variable 元变量
element with distributed parameters 分布参数元件
element with lumped parameters 集中参数元件
elemental contamination 自然损坏
elementary action 基本动作
elementary arithmetic function 初等算术函数
elementary chain 初级链
elementary combinatorial circuit 基本组合电路
elementary component 基本分量
elementary diagram 接线原理图
elementary event 基本事件
elementary file (EF) 元文件
elementary formal system 初等形式系统
elementary function 初等函数
elementary Hermitian matrix 初等埃尔米特矩阵
elementary homomorphism 基本同态
elementary item 基本项,初等项
elementary matrix 初等矩阵

elementary object 基本对象
elementary path 基本通路
elementary predicate 初等谓词
elementary regenerated section 基本再生段
elementary repeated section 基本中继段
elementary sentence 基本命题
elementary symmetrical polynomial 初等对称多项式
elementary transformation 初等变换
elevated floor 活动地板
elevator 滚动条;升降式电梯
elevator seeking 电梯式寻道法
ELF(ElectroLuninescent Film) 电致发光薄膜
ELF(Executable and Linkage Format) 可执行和链接格式(UNIX)
ELF(Extensible Linking Format) 可扩充链接格式(UNIX)
ELF(Extremely Low Frequency) 极低频
ELHILL ELHILL信息检索软件
ELI (Extensible Language) ELI语言,可扩充语言
eliciation 引导,启发
elidible 可删除(取消)的
eligible 入选者
eligible list 入选者列表
eligible process 入选进程
eligible queue of tasks 入选任务队列
elimination 消除,消去
elimination algorithm 消元算法
elimination major-element method 主元素消元法
elimination method 消元法
elimination of common subexpression 公共子表达式的消除
elimination of tautologies 重言式消除
elimination of unknown 未知数消去法
eliminator 抑制器,限制器,消除器
elite elite(一种打字机)字母尺寸
ellipse 椭圆
ellipsis 省略号
ellipsoid 椭球
ellipsoid algorithm 椭球算法
ellipsoidal model 椭球模型
ellipsometry 椭偏法

elliptic 椭圆的
elliptic equation 椭圆方程
elliptic integral 椭圆积分
elliptic problem 椭圆问题
elliptic type 椭圆类型
elliptical 椭圆的
elongation 延伸率
ELR(Electronic Label Reader) 电子标签阅读器
ELP(Electronic Line Printer) 电子行式打印机
ELS(Extended-Level Synthesizer) 扩充型合成器
ELSE 否则语句
ELSE clause 否则子句
EM(Electronic Mailbox) 电子信箱
EM(Electronic Music) 电子音乐
em dash 长破折号;双点线
EM element (印刷排版中的)EM单位
em fraction 斜式分数
em space 双倍间距,全字空格
EMA(Enterprise Management Architecture) 企业管理体系结构
EMA(Extended Memory Area) 扩充存储区
EMACS(Editor MACroS) 编辑宏命令
Emancipatory CAI 解放式计算机辅助教学
embed linked object 内嵌的链接对象
embeddability 嵌入性
embeddable 可嵌入的
embedded 嵌入的,内嵌的
embedded array 嵌入式门阵列
embedded blank 嵌入空白
embedded chain 嵌入链
embedded chart 嵌入图表
embedded chip 嵌入式芯片
embedded code 嵌入代码
embedded command 嵌入式命令
embedded computer 嵌入式计算机
embedded computing 嵌入式计算
embedded controller 嵌入式控制器
embedded font 嵌入字体
embedded formatting command 嵌入式排版命令
embedded hyphen 嵌入连字符
embedded Linux 嵌入式Linux操作系统

embedded Markov chain 嵌入马尔可夫链
embedded object 嵌入对象
embedded pointer 嵌入式指针
embedded rule-based system 基于规则的嵌入式系统,ERS语言
embedded servo 嵌入式伺服
embedded software 嵌入式软件
embedded SQL 嵌入式结构查询语言
embedded style option 嵌入样式选项
embedded style sheet 嵌入式样式表
embedded system 嵌入式系统
embedded text control 嵌入的文本控
embedded tool kit(ETK) 嵌入式工具箱
embedding mapping 嵌入映像
embedding of partial order into linear order 偏序嵌入线性序中
embedding of tree 树的嵌入
Embedix Embedix嵌入式Linux操作系统(Caldera)
embodied virtually 潜在实体
embodiment 具体化,体现
embody 具体化;包括有,收录;补充
emboldening 增亮,加深,加强
embossed card 凸形卡
embossed character 浮雕字符
embossing 压花
embossment 凸出
embracing 包围
Emerald Bay database machine Emerald Bay数据库机
emergency boot disk 应急启动盘
emergency button 应急按钮
emergency call 紧急呼叫
emergency exit 应急出口
emergency light source 应急光源
emergency maintenance time 应急维修时间
Emergency Management Port(EMP) 紧急管理端口(Intel)
emergency mode 应急运行模式
emergency power off 紧急断电
emergency restart 应急重启动
emergency route 应急路由
emergency shutdown 紧急关机
emergency switch 应急开关
emergency unload 紧急卸载
emergent behavior 灵现行为
emerging field 新兴领域
emerging technology 新兴技术,雏形技术
emery 金刚砂
EMI(End of Message Indicator) 报文结束指示符
EMI(External Modem Interface) 外接式调制解调器接口
emission 发射
emission bandwidth 发射带宽
emission current 发射电流
emission efficiency 发射效率
emission power 发射功率
emitron 光电摄像管
emitter 发射极
emitter bias 发射极偏置电压
emitter coupled logic(ECL) circuit 射极耦合逻辑电路
emitter follower 射极跟随器
EMM(Expanded Memory Manager) 扩充内存管理程序
EMM386.EXE (DOS)EMM386内存管理程序
emoticon 情感符号,情感图标
EMP(Emergency Management Port) 紧急管理端(Intel)
emphasis 加重字体,强调字体
emphasized 强调的,加重的
emphasizer 加重电话
empirical 经验的,实验的
empirical data 经验数据
empirical discovery 经验发现
empirical distribution 经验分布
empirical documentation 经验性文档
empirical model 经验模型
empirical formula 经验公式
empirical law 经验法则
empirical learning 经验学习
empirical probability 经验概率
empty argument 空变元
empty binary tree 空二叉树
empty class 空类
empty entry 空登记项
empty function 空函数
empty medium 空白媒体
empty page 空页面
empty position 空位置
empty queue 空队列

empty relation 空关系
empty stack 空栈
empty set 空系,空集
empty string 空串
empty substitution 空置换
empty symbol 空符号
empty template 空样板
empty time slot 空时间槽
empty Web 空站点
EMS(Electronic Mail System) 电子邮政系统
EMS(Expanded memory specification) 扩充内存规范
EMS(Extended Main Store) 扩展主内存
EMS(Expanded Memory Specification) page frame 扩充内存规范页帧
EMT(Electronic Message Terminal) 电子消息终端
emulate 模仿,仿真
emulate text mode 仿真文本模式
emulated disk 仿真盘
emulation bus 仿真总线
emulation bus trace 仿真总线跟踪
emulation code 仿真代码
emulation command 仿真命令
emulation group 仿真群
emulation job 仿真作业
emulation memory 仿真存储器
emulation mode 仿真模式
emulation processor 仿真处理器
emulation program(EP) 模拟程序
emulation system organization 仿真系统组织
emulation terminal 仿真终端
emulation testing 仿真测试
emulator 模拟器,仿真器,仿真程序
emulator binary data file 仿真二元数据文件
emulator circuit 仿真器电路
emulator control 仿真器控制
emulator debug 仿真器调试
emulator document 仿真程序文档
emulator generation 仿真程序生成
emulator library 仿真程序库
emulator memory 仿真程序存储器
emulator mode 仿真模式
emulator program 仿真器程序

emulator section 仿真器部分
emulator station 仿真站
emulator version 仿真程序版本
emulsion 感光乳胶
emulsion laser storage 乳胶激光存储器
emulsion layer 乳胶层
emulsion sheet 乳胶片
EMYCIN(Empty-MYCIN) MYCIN专家系统骨架
EMYCIN(Essential MYCIN) 基本MYCIN推理系统
EMYCIN language EMYCIN语言
En （印刷排版中的）En单位
en dash 中长度破折号
en fraction 横式分数
en space 中长度空格
ENA(Extended Network Addressing) 扩展的网络编址
ENA bar-code 欧洲物品编码
ENA-8 bar-code ENA-8(条)码
ENA-13 bar-code ENA-13(条)码
enable(EN) 启动,允许,使能
enable gateway 启用网关
enable interrupt(EI) 允许中断
enable logic 允许逻辑
ENABLE LOGIN 允许登录
enable position 启动位置
ENABLE TTS 允许事务处理跟踪系统
enable signal 使能信号,允许信号
enabled 允许的,使能的
enabled condition 允许条件
enabled instruction 启动指令
enabled interruption 允许的中断
enabled module 使能模块
enabled page fault 允许的页面故障
enabled state 允许状态
enabling signal 允许信号,使能信号
enamel covered wire 漆包线
enamel insulated wire 漆包(绝缘)线
ENB(ENaBle) 允许,启动,使能
encapsulated data type 压缩数据类型
Encapsulated PostScript file(EPS) 压缩的页面描述语言文件
encapsulated type 节络型,封装型
encapsulating 密封,包封
Encapsulating Security Payload Header (Ipv6) 数据加密选项包头
encapsulation 封装,密封

encapsulation test 密封性试验
encipher 加密,译成密码
encipher algorithm 加密算法
enciphered data 加密数据
enciphering 加密
enciphering key 加密密钥
encipherment protection 加密保护
encipherment scheme 加密方案
enclosure 外壳
encode 编码
encode by group 按组编码
encoded abstract 代码化文摘
encoded keyboard 编码键盘
encoded point 编码点
encoded question 编码问题
encoded Turing machine 编码图灵机
encoder 编码器
encoder matrix 编码器矩阵
encoder overall operating time 编码器总工作时间
encoding 编码
encoding by bit 按位编码
encoding by group 按组编码
encoding law 编码律,编码法则
encoding matrix 编码矩阵
encoding of Chinese font 汉字字形编码
encoding of Chinese stroke 汉字笔划编码
encoding of Chinese word group 汉字词组编码
encoding scheme 编码方案
encoding strip 编码条
ENCOMPASS ENCOMPASS数据库
encrypt 加密
encryption algorithm 加密算法
encryption channel 加密信道
encryption enable 允许加密
encryption standard 加密标准
encyclopedic knowledge system 百科知识系统
END 结束
end-around borrow 循环借位
end-around carry 循环进位
end-around shift 循环移位
end block 末端块,尾块,结束块
end block underline 尾块下划线
end bracket 结束括号,右括号
end branch 末端分支

end cells 附加电池
end column 末列,结束栏
end crosstalk 终端串音
end-cycle time 循环时间
end delay 末端延迟
end distortion 末端失真
end equipment 终端装置
END instruction 结束指令
end file condition 结束文件条件
end frame 末帧
end instrument 末端仪器
End key 结束键
END line 结束行
END mark 结束标志
end network address 端点网络地址
end node 末端结点,端节点
end of address(EOA) 地址结束符
end of block(EOB) 块结束符
end of block mark 字块结束标志
end-of-chain(EOC) 链结束符
end of dialing signal 拨号结束信号
end of field marker 字段结束标志
end-of-file(EOF) 文件结束
end of job(EOJ) 作业结束
end of line(EOL) 行结束
end-of-medium character(EM) 媒体结束符
end-of-message code 报文结束代码
end of page indicator 页面结束指示
end of paragraph(EOP) 段结束符
end of program 程序结束
end of record(EOR) 记录终止符
end of reel 磁带卷尾
end of run 运行结束
end of sequence set indicator 顺序集结束指示符
end of shift 移位终止
end of tape marker(EOT) 磁带结束标志
end-of-text character(ETX) 文本结束符
end of transmission(EOT) 传输结束,传输终止符
end of transmission block character(ETB) 码组传输结束符
end of volume 卷结束
end-of-work-session indicator 工作对话期结束指示符

end office(EO) 端局
end or identification(EOI) 结束或识别线
end outline function 轮廓线结束功能
end packet 结束信息包
end pages 目的页面
end paragraph name 结束段名
end parameter 终值参数,结尾参数
end point control(EPC) 末端控制,终点控制
end point determination 终点确定
end point matching 端点匹配
end point node 末端节点
end point rigidity 末端刚度
end-point sensitivity 端点灵敏度
end-point voltage 终止点电压
end readout 最终读出
end scale value 满刻度值
end sensor 末端传感器
end signal 结束信号
END statement 终止语句
end station 末端站
end symbol 结束符号
end time 结束时间
end to end encipherment 端-端用户加「密
end-to-end encryption 端-端加密
end-to-end mode 端到端方式
end-to-end protocol 端-端协议
end-to-end responsibility 端到端响应
end-to-end search time 从头到尾检索时间
end-to-end session 端到端对话
end-to-end test 端到端测试
end-to-end transfer 端到端传送
end-use device 末端使用设备
end user 最终用户,终端用户
end-user computing 最终用户计算
end-user device 最终用户设备
end user language 最终用户语言
end-user to end-user session 终端用户之间对话
end-user verification 终端用户验证
end value 终值,结果值
end view 侧视图
end voltage 终止电压
ending at 终止于…
Ending Kinsoku Characters 避尾字符
ENDFILE statement 文件结束语句

endless loop 无结尾循环
endnote 文末注解,尾注
endnote separator 尾注分隔符
endurance 耐久,持久性
endurance limit 疲劳极限
endurance test 耐久性试验
endwise feed 末端向前馈送
energetic 高能的
energize 激励,赋能
energized network 受激励网络
energizer 激励器
energizing circuit 激励电路
energy 能,能量
energy band 能带
energy beam 能量射束
energy conversion device 能量转换装「置
energy density 能量密度
energy dispersal 能量扩散
energy efficiency 能量效率
energy engineering 能源工程
energy function 能量函数
energy gap 能隙,禁带
energy gap model 能隙模型
energy gradient 能量梯度
energy level 能级
energy level diagram 能级图
energy loss 能耗
energy model 能量模型
energy-related parameter 能量相关参「数
energy resource system 能源系统
energy spectrum 能量谱
Energy Star "能源之星"
energy state 能态
energy utility system 能量利用系统
Energyline 能源数据库(美国)
ENF(Event Notification Facility) 事件提示设施
enforce 实施
enforced 强制的
enforced circularity 强制循环
enforced idle time 强制空闲时间
enforced lock 强化锁;强制锁定
enforcing reflection 强迫反射
ENG(Electronic News Gathering) 电子新闻采编
engaged condition 占线状态
engaged line 忙线
engaged signal 占线信号

engaged tone 忙音
engine 引擎;核心程序;发动机
engine file 驱动程序文件
engineer of computer maintenance 计算机维护工程师
Engineering and Administration Data Acquisition System(EADAS) 工程管理数据采集系统
engineering anthropology 工程人类学
engineering approximation 工程近似
engineering change log 工程更改记录
engineering compromise 工程折衷方案
engineering computing 工程计算
engineering cybernetics 工程控制论
engineering cylinder 工程柱面
engineering data 工程数据
engineering drawing sizes 工程绘图尺寸
Engineering Index(EI) 《美国工程索引》
Engineering Index, Annual 《工程索引》年卷本
Engineering Index Monthly 《工程索引月刊》
engineering inspection specification 工程检查规范
engineering mechanics 工程力学
engineering radiator 工程辐射源
engineering sample 工程试样
engineering specification 工程标准
engineering workstation 工程设计工作站
English Font Selection 英文字体选择
English mode plotting 英制绘图模式
English Query 英语查询
English word processor 英语单词处理程序
enhance 增强,提高
enhance level 提升电平
enhanced expanded memory specification(EEMS) 增强型扩充内存规范
enhanced graphics adapter(EGA) 增强型图形适配器
enhanced IDE 增强型IDE接口
enhanced keyboard 增强型键盘
enhanced logic link control 增强逻辑链路控制
enhanced MAC system 增强MAC制
enhanced metafile 增强型元文件
enhanced non-return-to-zero(ENRZ) 增强型不归零制
enhanced nonreturn-to-zero change on one 增强型逢"1"变化不归零制
enhanced parallel Port(EPP) 增强型并行端口
enhanced photomultiplier 增强式光电倍增管
enhanced quality television(EQTV) 增强质量电视
enhanced private switched communications service 增强型专用交换通信服务
enhanced small disk interface(ESDI) 增强型小磁盘接口
Enhanced System Device Interface(ESDI) 增强型系统设备接口
enhanced TV(ETV) 增强型电视
enhancement 增强
enhancement/depletion MOS integrated circuit(E/D MOS) 增强型/耗尽型MOS集成电路
enhancement/enhancement MOS integrated circuit(E/E MOS IC) 增强型/增强型MOS集成电路
enhancement mode of JFET 增强型结型场效应晶体管
enhancer 增强器
ENIAC(Electronic Numerical Integrator and Calculator) 电子数字积分计算机(世界上第一台通用电子数字计算机)
enlarge 放大,增大
enlarge font 放大字体
enlargement 放大
ENN(Expand Nonstop Network) 无休止扩展网络
enqueue 入队列
enquiry(ENQ) 询问
enquiry character(ENQ) 询问字符
enrollment 登记,开设
ENRZ(Enhanced Non-Return-to-Zero) 增强不归零制
ENRZ1(Enhanced Non-Return-to-Zero 1) 增强逢1翻转不归零制
ensemble 总体
ensemble average 总体均值

Enter key 回车键
enter line number 输入行号
enter old password 输入旧口令
entering variable 插入变量
enterprise 企业
Enterprise Communication Server (ECS) 企业通信服务器
enterprise computing 企业计算
enterprise management 企业管理
enterprise model 管理模型
enterprise modeling 企业建模
enterprise network 企业网络
Enterprise Network Service(ENS) 企业网络服务
enterprise server 企业服务器
Enterprise Storage Networks(ESN) 企业存储网络(EMC)
Enterprise System Architecture(ESA) 企业系统体系结构(IBM)
Enterprise System Connection Architecture(ESCON) 企业系统连接体系结构(IBM)
entire 整个
entire chart 整个图表
entire column 整列
entire disk 整个磁盘
entire file 整个文件
entire row 整行
entire subtree 整个子树
entire variable 整体变量
Entire Workbook 整个工作簿(微软)
entity 实体
entity activity 实体活动
entity attribute 实体属性
Entity Coordination Management (ECM) 实体协调管理
entity declaration 实体说明
entity function 实体功能
entity identification 实体标识
entity identifier 实体标识符
entity instance 实体事例
entity integrity 实体完整性
entity interface 实体接口
entity metadata 实体元数据
entity model 实体模型
entity occurrence 实体出现
entity record 实体记录
entity reference 实体引用

entity-relationship 实体-关系
entity-relationship approach(E-R) 实体关系方法,E-R方法
entity-relationship data model 实体-关系数据模型
entity-relationship design 实体-关系设计
entity-relationship diagram 实体联系图,E-R图
entity relationship model 实体-关系模型
entity security 实体安全
entity set 实体集
entity type 实体类型
entity system 实体系统
entity use 实体用途
entity world 实体世界
entrance 入口
entrance cable 入局电缆
entrance point 入口点
entropy 熵;平均信息量
entropy coding 熵编码
entropy filter 熵过滤器
entropy of binary source 二元信源熵
entropy of joint event 联合事件熵
entropy of zero order 零阶熵
Entrust Entrust 加密产品
entry 项目,款目;入口
entry address 入口地址
entry attribute 项目属性
entry block 项目块
entry conditions 入口条件
entry data item 表目数据项
entry deletion 项目删除
entry descriptor 项目描述符;入口描述符
entry field 入口域
entry instruction 入口指令
entry label 入口标号
entry-level system 基本系统,入门级系统
entry mask 输入屏蔽码
entry line 输入行
entry name 项目名称
entry page 转入页面
entry platform 转入平台
entry point 入口点
entry point access method 入口点存取法
entry point vector 入口点向量

entry position　登记项位置；入口位置
entry recognition　入口识别
entry screen　输入屏幕
entry-sequenced data set　输入定序数据集
entry system　馈入系统，进入系统
entry-to-exit flow control　入口至出口流量控制
entry variable　入口变量
enum　枚举类型
enum all fonts　列举所有字体
enumerability　可枚举性，可数性
enumerable directed set　可数有向集
enumerate subkeys　计数子项
enumerated data type　枚举数据类型
enumerated scalar type　枚举标量类型
enumerating all paths　列举所有路径
enumeration　枚举
enumeration algorithm　枚举算法
enumeration of binary trees　二叉树枚举
enumeration of graph　图枚举
enumeration of labeled structure　标号结构枚举
enumeration of labeled tree　标号树枚举
enumeration of oriented tree　有向树枚举
enumeration sorting　枚举排序
enumeration sorting network　枚举排序网络
enumeration tag　枚举标志
enumerative classification　枚举分类
envelope　包络；信封
envelope address font　信封地址字体
envelope cursor　包络线光标
envelope delay distortion　包络延时失真
envelope feeder　信封输纸器
envelope printer　信封打印机
envelope return　回信地址
Enviroline　(美国)环保数据库
ENVIRON (ENVironmental Information Retrieval ON-line)　环境信息联机检索
environment　环境；运行环境
environment analysis　环境分析
environment attribute　环境属性
environment control table　环境控制表
environment data base　环境数据库
environment description　环境描述
environment division　(COBOL 语言)环境部
environment erection and protection　环境建立与保护
environment impact analysis　环境影响分析
environment information library technique　环境信息库技术
environment inquiry　环境调查
environment integration technique　环境集成化技术
environment list　环境列表
environment map　环境映像
environment model　环境模型
environment module　环境模块
environment pointer　环境指针
environment record　环境记录
environment simulator　环境仿真器
environment symbol　环境标号
environment temperature　环境温度
environment test chambers　环境试验箱
environment variable　环境变量
environmental condition　环境条件
environmental loss time　环境损失时间
environmental perturbation　环境扰动
environmental protection of electronic equipment　电子设备环境保护
environmental requirement　环境需求
environmental screen　环境筛选
environmental stability　环境稳定性
environmental test　环境试验
EO(End Office)　端局，终点站
EOA(End Of Address code)　地址码结束
EOB(End Of Block)　字组结束，块结束
EOC(End Of Conversion)　转换结束
EOD(End Of Data)　数据结束
EOEM(Electronic Original Equipment Manufactory)　电子初始设备制造厂家，电子产品委托加工
EOF(End Of File)　文件结束
EOF(End Of Forms)　纸尽
EOF mark　文件结束标志
EOI(End Of Inquiry)　询问结束
EOJ(End Of Job)　作业结束
EOL(End Of Line)　行结束
E0L system(Extended Zero-Sided Lindenmayer System)　广义林氏无关

系统,E0L 系统
EOM(End Of Medium) 媒体结束
EOM(End Of Message) 消息结束
EOM indicator 消息结束指示器
EOP(End Of Polling) 轮询结束
EOQ(End Of Query) 询问结束
EOR(End Of Record) 记录结束
EOS(End Of Segment) 段结束
EOT(End Of Tape) 磁带结束
EOT(End Of Test) 测试结束
EOT(End Of Text) 文本结束
EOT(End Of Transmission) 传输结束
EOV(End Of Volume) 卷结束
EPBX(Electronic Private Branch eXchange) 专用电子交换分机
EPCB(Extended Process Control Block) 扩充的进程控制块
Epcot(Experimental Prototype Community of Tomorrow) 明日社会实验模型
ephemeris time(ET) 历书时
EPIC(Explicit Parallel Instruction Computing) 显式指令并行计算(Intel)
epilogue 收尾程序
epimorphism 满射,满同态
episodic knowledge 事件性知识
epistemological analysis 认识论分析
epistemology 认识论
epitaxial growth 外延生长
epitaxial isolation 外延隔离
epitaxial layer 外延层
epitaxial layer isolation 外延层隔离
epitaxial thin film 外延薄膜
epitaxy 外延
EPLA(Erasable Programmable Logic Array) 可擦除可编程逻辑阵列
epoch date 纪元日期
epoxy resin 环氧树脂
EPP(Enhanced Parallel Port) 增强型并行端口
EPRCA(Enhanced Propotional Rate Control Algorithm) 增强型均衡速率控制算法
EPROM(Erasable Programmable Read Only Memory) 可擦除可编程只读存储器
E2PROM(Electrically Erasable Programmable Read Only Memory) 电可擦除可编程只读存储器
EPROM Tunnel Oxide(ETOX) 隧道氧化物 EPROM
EPS(Electronic Publishing System) 电子出版系统
EPS(Encapsulated PostScript file) 压缩的页面描述语言文件(Adobe)
EPS(External Page Storage) 外部页面存储器
epsilon-free homomorphism ε 无关同态
epsilon-free substitution ε 无关置换
epsilon-move ε 动作
epsilon production ε 产生式
epsilon-rule ε 规则
Epson 爱普生公司(日本打印机生产厂商)
Epson emulation Epson 仿真
EPSS(Experimental Packet Switched Service) 实验分组交换服务(英国邮政总局)
EQ(EnQuiry) 询问
eqntott eqntott 基准程序
equal 等于;等号
equal element 相等元素
equal-increment solution 等增量解
equal length code 等长度编码
equal-loudness contours 等响度曲线
equal precision measurement 等精度测量
equal-ripple approximation 等波纹逼近
equal sign 等号
equality 等同性;等式
equality axioms 相等性公理
equality constrained problems 等式约束问题
equalization 均衡
equalized assignment 均衡任务分配
equalized scheduling algorithm 均衡调度算法
equalizer 均衡器
equally probable event 等概率事件
equation 等式;方程
equation of reversible power law 逆幂律方程
equation set 方程组
equation typesetting 方程式排版
equalizer 均衡器

equation 等式,方程式
equation of state 状态方程
equational logic 等式逻辑
equidistance curve 等距离曲线
equilibration 平衡
equilibrium 平衡的
equilibrium consumption 平衡消费
equilibrium distribution coefficient 平衡分布系数
equilibrium model 平衡模型
equilibrium point 平衡点
equilibrium solution 平衡解
equilibrium stability 平衡稳定性
equipment 设备,设施
equipment augmentation 设备扩充
equipment clock 设备时钟
equipment compatibility 设备兼容性
equipment complex 设备复合体
equipment inspection 设备检查
equipment interface 设备接口
equipment maintenance 设备维护
equipment misuse error 设备使用不当错误
equipment mobility 设备可移动性
equipment-oriented data format 面向设备的数据格式
equipment replacement 设备更新
equipotence 等势
equipotent set 等价集合
equipotential bonding 等电位接地
equipotential surface 等位面
equiprobable 等概率
equitable sharing 公平共享
equivalence 等价
equivalence class 等价类
equivalence declaration 等价说明
equivalence gate 等价门,同门
equivalence group 等价群
equivalence name 等价名
equivalence operation 等价运算
equivalence partitioning 等价类划分
equivalence problem of flowchart 流程图的等价问题
equivalence queue 等价队列
equivalence relation 等价关系
equivalence statement 等价语句
equivalence theorem 等价性定理
equivalence transformation 等价变换
equivalent 等价的,等效的;等价值,当量
equivalent background illumination 等效背景照度
equivalent binary content 等效二进制位数
equivalent binary digits 等效二进制数字
equivalent binary weight 等值二进制加权
equivalent bit rate 等效位率
equivalent circuit 等效电路
equivalent earth radius 等效地球半径
equivalent fault 等效故障
equivalent impedance 等效阻抗
equivalent instruction speed 等效指令速度　　　　　　　　　　「阻
equivalent internal resistance 等效内
equivalent noise bandwidth 等效噪声通带
equivalent noise resistance 等效噪声电阻
equivalent noise temperature 等效噪声温度
equivalent normal form method 等价范式法
equivalent object program 等价目标程序
equivalent sampling 等效取样
equivalent scale code 等比码
equivalent tree 等价树
equivalent value 等值
equivalent weight code 等权重码
equivocation 暧昧度,疑义度,条件信息量总平均值
ER(Environment Recording) 环境记录,现场记录
ER(Explicit Route) 显式路由
ER(Exponent Register) 阶码寄存器
eradicate 消除,根除
erasability of storage 存储器可擦性
erasable and programmable ROM 可擦除可编程只读存储器
erasable area 可清除区
erasable CD 可擦写光盘
erasable optical disk 可擦式光盘　「体
erasable optical medium 可擦除光媒
erasable programmable read only memo-

ry(EPROM) 可擦除可改写只读存储器
erasable read-only memory(EROM) 可擦只读存储器
erasable storage 可擦除存储器
erase 清除,删除
erase all 全部清除
erase all unprotected 清除所有未保护的
erase character 删除符,取消符
erase contents 清除内容
erase end-of-line 擦除行结束符
erase head 擦除磁头,清洗磁头
erase previous content 清除先前内容
erase residual 清洗残余
erase tape 清洗磁带
erase width 抹除宽度
eraser 擦除器;橡皮擦
erasing head 抹除头,消磁头
erasing production 删除产生式
ERD(Entity-Relationship Diagram) 实体-关系图
ergod 遍历
ergodic 各态经历的,遍历的
ergodic condition 遍历条件
ergodic hypothesis 遍历假说
ergodic process 遍历过程
ergodic random process 遍历性随机过程
ergodicity 遍历性
ergonomics 人类工程学
ergonomics keyboard 人类工程学键盘
ergonomy 人类工程学,工效学
ERIC(Educational Resource Information Center) 教育资源信息中心
Erlang "爱尔朗",占线小时
erosion 侵蚀
erratum 勘误表
erroneous block 差错块
error 误差,差错,错误
error alert 错误报警
error ambiguity 错误含糊,误差含糊
error analysis 误差分析;错误分析
error bit 出错比特
error bound 偏差界限
error budget 误差预估算
error burst 错误群,误码群,错误猝发
error burst correction code 突发错误校正码
error call 错误调用
error character 错误字符
error checking and correction(ECC) 错误校验纠正
error checking and recovery 错误检测与恢复
error checking code 错误检验码
error class 错误类
error code 出错代码,错误码
error command 错误指令
error comment 错误注释
error compensation 误差补偿
error condition 错误状态
error-condition statement 错误条件语句,错误状态语句
error control 误差控制,差错控制
error-control character 差错控制字符
error control code 错误控制码
error-control decoder 差错控制解码器
error control encoder 差错控制编码器
error control equipment 差错控制设备
error control loop 差错控制环
error control procedure 差错控制过程
error-correcting capacity 纠错能力
error-correcting code 错误校正码,纠错码
error-correcting encoding 纠错编码
error-correcting parser 纠错语法分析程序
error-correcting routine 纠错例程
error-correcting rule 纠错规则
error-correcting system 错误校正系统
error correction 错误校正
error correction by detection and repetition 检测和重复纠错
error correction rule 纠错规则
error-correction submode 错误校正子模式
error counter 错误计数器
error data 错误数据
error density 错误密度
error detecting and feedback system 错误检测与反馈系统
error-detecting capacity 检错能力
error-detecting code 检错码
error detecting routine 错误检测程序
error detecting system 错误检测系统

error detection 检错
error detection routine 错误检测程序
error detection treatment 错误检测处理
error diagnostics 错误诊断
error disappearance 错误消失
error distribution 误差分布
error dump 错误转储
error emphasis 错误强调提示
error equation 误差方程
error estimation 误差估计
error evaluation 误差评估
error exit 错误出口
error explanation 错误说明
error extension 误码扩散
error file 错误登记文件
error-free data transmission 无差错数据传输
error-free message 无差错消息
error freezing 错误冻结
error function 误差函数
error-generation model 错误生成模型
error guessing 错误猜测
error halting state 出错停机状态
error handling 出错处理
error inreading 读数错误
error indicator(EI) 错误指示符
error information table 出错信息表
error interrupt 错误中断
error interrupt processing 出错中断处理
error items 误差项,错误项
error latency 错误潜伏期,错误延迟时间
error list 错误列表
error lock 出错封锁
error log manager(ELM) 差错登录管理程序
error logger 差错登记程序
error mark 错误标志
error message 错误消息
error model 错误模式,错误模型
error multiplication 差错增殖,误码增殖
error multiplication factor 差错增殖系数,误码增殖因子
error of approximation 近似误差
error of estimation 估计误差
error of measurement 测量误差
error of the first kind 第Ⅰ类错误

error of the second kind 第Ⅱ类错误
error of transmission 传输错误
error of truncation 截断误差
error pattern 错误式样,错误模式
error prediction 错误预测
error processing 错误处理
error propagation 错误扩散,差错传播
error propagation limiting code 错误传播受限码
error protection procedure 差错防护规程
error range 误差范围
error rate 误码率,差错率
error rate monitor 差错率监视器
error rate of keying 键控差错率
error rate of translation 译码差错率
error ratio 出错率,错误率
error recognition rate 错误识别率
error recovery 错误校正,差错恢复
error-recovery procedures(ERP) 错误校正过程
error report 错误报告
error retransmission 出错重传
error return 出错返回
error routine 错误处理程序
error second 误差秒
error sensing element 误差敏感元件
error signal 误差信号;出错信号
error size 误差大小
error span 误差跨度
error spread 差错扩展,误码扩散
error status word 错误状态字
error summary counter 错误摘要计数器
error tape 错误记录磁带
error trapping 错误陷入
error trapping decoding 扑错译码
error trapping routine 错误陷阱程序
error transparency 出错透明
error type 错误类型
error value 错误值
errors of chrominance signal demodulation 色度信号解调误差
ERS language ERS语言
Er's parallel topological sorting 艾尔并行拓扑排序
ERTS(Embedded Real Time System) 嵌入式实时系统
ES(Error Status) 出错状态

ES/3090(Enterprise System / 3090) ES/3090 计算机(IBM)
ES/9000 ES/9000 计算机(IBM)
ESA/370(Enterprise System Architecture/370) ESA/370 部件
ESA/390(Enterprise System Architecture/390) ESA/390 部件
ESA/IRS(European Space Agency-Information Retrieval Service) 欧洲空间组织信息检索服务
ESANET(European Space Agency NETwork) 欧洲空间组织网络
ESC(ESCape character) 换码字符
Esc key 转义键,换码键;退出键
escape(ESC) 换码字符,转义字符
Escape Button "脱离按钮"软件(IBM)
escape character(ESC) 换码字符,转义字符;扩展字符
escape code 转义码,逸出码
escape instruction 逸出指令
escape key 换码键
escape sequence 换码序列,转义序列
ESCON(Enterprise System CONnection) 管理系统连接(IBM)
ESCON director ESCON 定向器
ESD(Emergency ShutDown) 事故停机,紧急停机
ESD(External Symbol Dictionary) 外部符号字典
ESDI(Enhanced Small Device Interface) 增强的小型设备接口
ESDS(Entry Sequence DataSet) 输入顺序数据集
ESF(Extended Service Frame) 扩展服务帧
ESG(English Standard Gauge) 英国标准线规
E-SHELL(Expert SHELL) 专家外壳系统
ESI(External Specified Index) 外部规定的索引
ESI communications 外定索引通信
ESP(Executive and Scheduling Program) 执行与调度程序
espresso espresso 基准程序
ESS(Electronic Switching System) 电子交换系统
ESS1(No. 1 Electronic Switching System) 电子交换机系统 1
essence of computer security 计算机系统安全的本质
essential 基本的,实质的,本质的
essential association 基本联结
essential attribute 基本属性
essential general game 本质一般对策
essential hazard 本质冒险
essential maximum 本质最大项 「涵
essential prime implicant 实质本原蕴
essential strategy 本质策略
essential supremum 本质上确界
essential term 本质项,基本项 「性
essentiality 本质,本性;必要性,实质
essentially complete class of decision rule 决策规则的本质完全类
essentially equivalent 实质等价
essentially minimal complete class of decision rule 决策规则的本质极小完全类
essentially non-negative matrix 本性非负矩阵
essentially periodic sequence 本性周期序列 「阵
essentially positive matrix 本性正矩
essentially real-time system 本质实时系统
essentially maximum 本质最大值
established connection 确立连接
establishing clause 建立子句
establishing shot 建立镜头
establishment 建立,确立,制定
estimate 估计
estimate variance 估计方差
estimated program behavior 预计程序性能 「间
estimated time of arrival 预计到达时
estimator 估计值
estimation 估计
estimation criterion 估计准则 「性
estimation invariance 估计量的不变
estimation of motion 运动估计
estimation of reliability parameter 可靠性参量估计
estimation of state 状态估计
estimation of variance of noise 噪声方差估计

estimation operator 估计算子
estimation rule 估计策略
estimation theory 估算理论
estimation with fixed samples 固定样本量估计
estimator 估计量
ET(Exchange Terminal) 交换终端
ETC(Excess Three Code) 余三码
etch 刻蚀,腐蚀
etch cutting 腐蚀切割
etched V-grove silicon chip ribbon fiber connector 硅片刻蚀 V 槽带状光纤连接器
ETEP(Electronic Trading Efficiency Program) 电子贸易效率系统
Ether 3270 software 以太 3270 终端仿真软件
Ether Series 以太系列软件(3Com)
EtherCell EtherCell 交换器(Bay)
Ethermail 以太邮件
Ethernet "以太"网
Ethernet address 以太网地址
Ethernet cable 以太网电缆
Ethernet controller 以太网控制器
Ethernet hardware address 以太网物理地址
Ethernet interface 以太网接口
Ethernet-like net 类以太网
Ethernet meltdown 以太网崩溃
Ethernet packet 以太网络信息包
Ethernet protocol 以太网络协议
Ethernet segment 以太网段
Ethernet Workgroup Switch 以太网工作组交换器(Bay)
Etherprint 以太网打印软件
Ethershare 以太网共享软件
EtherTalk EtherTalk 软件(苹果)
EtherTalk Link Access Protocol EtherTalk 链路访问协议(苹果)
Etherterm software Etherterm 仿真软件
ETI(Extended Terminal Interface) 扩展终端接口(UNIX)
etiquette 礼节
ETK(Embedded Tool Kit) 嵌入式工具箱(微软)
ETO(Electronic Trade Opportunity System) 电子贸易机会系统
ETR(Expected Time of Response) 期待响应时间
ETV(Education TeleVision station) 教育电视台
ETX(End of TeXt character) 正文结束字符
EU(End User) 最终用户,终端用户
Euclid 欧几里德语言,Euclid 语言
Euclid-IS Euclid-IS 辅助设计软件
Euclidean distance 欧几里德距离
Euclidean domain 欧几里德域
Euclidean geometry codes 欧几里德几何码
Euclidean norm 欧几里德范数
Euclidean space 欧几里德空间
EUF(End User Facility) 最终用户设
EULER EULER 语言
Euler constant 欧拉常数
Euler cycle 欧拉圈,欧拉循环
Euler function 欧拉函数
Euler graph 欧拉图
Euler-Maclaurin summation formula 欧拉-马克劳林求和公式
Euler mesh formula 欧拉网孔数公式
Euler method 欧拉方法
Euler number 欧拉数
Euler path 欧拉路径
Euler's rule 欧拉法
Euler summation formula 欧拉求和公式
EUREKA(European Research Coordination Agency) 尤里卡计划(法)
Eurocard 欧式卡
EURODICAUTOM 欧洲自动化辞典
Eurolex 欧洲法律联机检索服务处
Euronet(European Packet Switching Network) 欧洲科技信息联机检索网络,欧洲包交换网络
European Academic Research Network(EARN) 欧洲学术研究网
European Automated Dictionary(EURODICAUTOM) 欧洲自动化词典
European Communication Satellite(ECS) 欧洲通信卫星
European Information Network(EIN) 欧洲信息网
European Patent Office(EPO) 欧洲专利局

European Unix network(EUnet) 欧洲 UNIX 网
EUSIDIC(EUropean association of Scientific Information DIssemination Centers) 欧洲科学信息传播中心联合会
EUSIDIC Guide 欧洲科学信息传播中心联合会指南
eutectic bonding 共晶焊
Eutelsat 欧洲通信卫星用户组织
evacuation 抽真空,排气
evaluate 求值
evaluate tree function 求值树函数
evaluated price 评估价格
evaluation 鉴定;求值
evaluation criterion 评价准则
evaluation function 评价函数,评估函
evaluation model 评估模型
evaluation of Chinese character coding input method 汉字编码输入方法评估
evaluation order 求值顺序
evaluation report 评价报告
evaluation unit 估算单元
evaluation 鉴定;求值
evaluator 计算多项式;鉴别程序
evaporated alloying technology 蒸发合金工艺
evaporated film disk 蒸发薄膜磁盘
evaporation cooling 蒸发冷却
even 偶数的;均匀的
even check 偶校验
even check code 偶校验码
even component 偶分支
even field 偶数域
even function 偶函数
even location 偶数单元
even number 偶数
even-odd check 奇偶校验
even of instruction operation 指令操作匀齐性
even parity check 偶校验
even permutation 偶排列,偶置换
even positive acknowledgement 偶确认
even subgraph 偶子图
even substitution 偶代换
even symmetric 偶对称
event 事件

event attribute 事件属性
event based debugging 基于事件的调
event break 事件中断
event builder 事件建立
event calculus 事件演算
event chain(ECB) 事件链
event class 事件类
event control block(ECB) 事件控制
event counter(ECB) 事件计数器
event description 事件描述
event-driven 事件驱动
event-driven environment 事件驱动式环境
event-driven executive(EDX) 事件驱动执行程序
event-driven language 事件驱动式语
event-driven program 事件驱动程序
event-driven simulation 事件驱动仿真
event-driven task scheduling 事件驱动任务调度
event filter 事件过滤器
event filtering 事件过滤
event flag 事件标志
event generator 事件发生器
event handle 事件句柄
event handler 事件处理程序
event handling 事件处理
event history 事件历史
event hold-off 事件拖延
event list 事件列表
event log wrapping 事件日志滚动覆
event manager 事件管理器
event mask 事件屏蔽
event message 事件消息
event mode 事件模式
event model 事件模型
event name 事件名称
event notice table 事件标志表
event numbering 事件编号
event option 事件选项
event-oriented programming 面向事件的程序设计
event processing 事件处理
event queue 事件队列
event report 事件报告
event scheduling approach 事件调度
event semaphore 事件信号量

event sequence 事件顺序
event sink 事件宿
event source 事件源
event space 事件空间
event synchronization 事件同步,事件同时性
event tag 事件标签
event tracer 事件跟踪程序
event trapping 事件俘获
event tree 事件树
event variable 事件变量
event viewer 事件查看程序
events table 事件表
everyman's database 公众数据库
everywhere computing 随处计算
everywhere convergent 处处收敛
everywhere dense 处处稠密
EVI(Extensible Video Interface) 可扩充视频接口
evidence 证据,迹象
evidence combination 证据组合
evident code 明码
evidential reasoning 证据推理
EVM(Extended Virtual Machine) 扩充虚拟机器
evoke 唤醒
evoke module control 唤醒模块控制
evoked potential 诱发电位
evolute 渐屈线
evolution 进化,演化
evolution program 演化程序
evolution programming 演化规划
evolution strategy 演化策略
evolutionary computing 演化计算
evolutionary development 演化发展,演变性开发
evolutionary development approach 渐近开发法
evolutionary hardware(EHW) 演化硬件
evolutionary optimization(EVOP) 进化调优
evolutionary prototyping method 进化式原型法
evolutionary strategy 进化策略
evolutionism 进化主义
evolvable prototype 进化原型
evolving object 衍生物

EWS(Early Warning System) 预警系统
EX(EXchange) 交换;交换机
Exabyte Corp. Exabyte 公司
exact 精确的
exact breaking method 精确断点法
exact end position 精确结束位置
exact image 精确图解
exact penalty functions 恰当惩罚函数
exactly equal 全等
examination 考试,检查
examination mechanism 验证机制
examine 验证,检查
example 实例,样本
example-based approach 基于样本的方法
example-driven system 实例驱动系统
example program 示例程序
EXAPT(EXtended APT) 扩充 APT 程序
exceed capacity 超容量
Excel 电子表格软件(微软)
excellence 优点
excellent diagnostics 最佳诊断
exception 异常,例外
exception condition 异常条件
exception dictionary 异常字典
exception dispatcher 异常调度程序
exception exit 异常出口
exception gate 禁止门
exception handler 异常处理程序
exception handling 异常处理
exception item 例外项
exception message 异常消息,异常报文
exception operation 排它运算,除外运算
exception principle system 例外原则系统
exception report 异常报告,例外报告
exception request 异常请求
exception response 异常应答
exception scheduling routine 异常调度程序
exception service routine 异常服务例程
exception word dictionary 异常字典
exceptional code 例外码
exceptional condition 异常条件
excerpt 摘录

excess-three code 余三码
excessive subscript 多余下标
exchange 交换
exchange administrator （电子邮件）交换管理员
exchange area 交换区
exchange area facilities 交换区设备
exchange buffering 交换缓冲
exchange call-release delay 局内呼叫释放时延
exchange call set-up delay 局内呼叫建立时延
Exchange Chat Service 在线讨论服务软件（微软）
exchange code of Chinese character 汉字交换码
exchange concentrator 交换局集中器
exchange control system 交换局控制系统
Exchange Directory 邮件目录（微软）
exchange energy 交换能量
Exchange Information Store 邮件信息存储（微软）
exchange instruction 交换指令
exchange memory 交换内存
Exchange Message Transfer Agent 邮件信息传输代理（微软）
Exchange Network Facilities for Interstate Access(ENFIA) 洲际通路交换网络设备　　　　　「务
exchange network service 交换网络服
exchange package 交换包
exchange radio interface 交换机无线接口
Exchange Server 邮件服务器
exchange service 交换服务,交换业务
exchange sort 交换排序
exchange sorting 交换排序
exchange system 交换系统
Exchange System Attendant 邮件系统服务程序
exchange-text string 替换文本字符串
exchangeable disk storage 可更换盘存储器
exchanger 交换器
excimer laser 准分子激光器
excitation 激发;激励
excitation matrix 激励矩阵

excitation 激发;激励
excitation spectrum 激发光谱
excitation table 激励表
excited state atomic laser 激态原子激光器
exclamation mark 感叹号　　　「找
exclude text from search 摒除文字查
excluded range 被排除范围
exclusion 排斥运算符,"异"操作符
exclusion operation 排它运算
exclusion principle 不相容原理
exclusive 排它,独占
exclusive access 排它性访问
exclusive attribute 互斥属性
exclusive branch 排斥转移
exclusive control 排它控制
exclusive event 互斥事件
exclusive in foreground 前台独占
exclusive intent 互斥意图,排它意向
exclusive key 互斥键
exclusive lock 排它型锁
exclusive message 互斥消息
exclusive mode 排它方式　　　　「门
exclusive NOR gate "异或非"门,"同"
exclusive OR gate "异或"门
exclusive - read - exclusive - write PRAM(EREW PRAM) 互斥读写随机存取机器
exclusive reference 互斥引用
exclusive segments 互斥段
exclusive usage mode 互斥使用状态
exclusive-write 互斥写
EXE files 可执行文件（扩展名为.EXE）
EXE loader 可执行文件装入程序
EXEC(EXECution) 执行　　　「能
EXEC built-in function EXEC 内部功
EXEC control statement EXEC 控制语句
EXEC statement EXEC 语句
EXEC user-defined variable EXEC 用户定义变量
EXECUNET(EXECute NETwork) 执行网络
executable 可执行的
executable file 可执行文件
executable form 可执行的形式
executable image 可执行的映像

executable instruction 可执行指令
executable program 可执行程序
executable specification 可执行规格说明
executable statement 可执行语句
execute(EXEC) 执行,运行
execute cycle 执行周期
execute in place(EIP) 就地执行
execute key 执行键,启动键
execute phase 执行阶段
execute protection 执行保护
execute statement 执行语句
execute time 执行时间
executing phase 执行阶段
executing script remotely 远程执行脚本
execution character 执行字符
execution code 执行码
execution command 执行指令,执行命令
execution control function 执行控制功能
execution cycle 执行周期
execution element 执行单元,执行元件
execution-error detection 执行错误检测
execution exception 执行异常
execution file 执行文件
execution key 执行键
execution level 执行级
execution mechanism 执行机制
execution mode 执行模式
execution of an instruction 指令的执行
execution order 执行顺序
execution path 执行路径
execution phrase 执行短语
execution priority 执行优先级
execution profile 执行轮廓文件
execution replay 执行重放
execution request block(ERB) 执行请求块
execution sequence 执行顺序
execution speed 执行速度
execution stack 执行栈
execution statement 执行语句
execution step 执行步骤
execution stream 执行流
execution time(E-time) 执行时间
execution traces 执行跟踪
execution transparency 执行透明
executive 执行程序

executive box 执行盒
executive command 执行指令
executive communication 执行通信
executive communication system 执行通信系统
executive communications 执行通信
executive control 执行控制
executive control language 执行控制语言
executive control system 执行控制系统
executive control utility routine 执行控制实用例程
executive cycle 执行周期
executive diagnostic system 执行诊断系统
executive diagnostics 执行系统中的诊断系统
executive facilities assignment 执行设备分配
executive guard mode 执行保护状态
executive I/O device control 执行例程输入/输出设备控制
executive information system(EIS) 商务信息系统
executive instruction 执行指令
executive job scheduling 执行作业调度
executive language 执行程序语言
executive logging 执行登录
executive mode 执行状态
executive module 执行模块
executive object 执行对象
executive overhead 执行总开销
executive program 执行程序
executive right-of-way service 执行随机服务
executive routine 执行例程
executive routine support 执行例程支持
executive schedule maintenance 执行调度维护
executive state 执行态
executive supervisor 执行管理程序
executive system 执行系统
executive system routine 执行系统例程
executive terminal 执行终端
executive termination 执行终止,执行结束
exegetical model 解释模型
exerciser 操作器;练习程序

exhaust algorithm 穷举法
exhaustion 耗尽
exhaustive index 穷举索引
exhaustive search 穷举搜索「法
exhaustive search algorithm 穷举搜索
exhaustive test 穷举测试
exhaustive testing 穷举调试
exhaustivity 概全性;详尽性
existential closure 存在闭包
existential quantifier 存在量词
existentially quantified variable 存在量词化变元
existing quantifier 存在量词
existing server 现有的服务器
existing system 现存系统
exit 出口;退出
exit framework 退出框架
exit interaction 退出交互
exit macroinstruction 退出宏指令
exit point 出口点,转出点
exit routine 出口例程
exit setup 结束安装,退出安装
exit statement 退出语句,出口语言
exjunction gate "异"门
EXORciser development system EXORciser 开发系统
EXP(EXchange Processor) 交换处理器
expand 展开,扩充
expand branch 展开分支
expand escapement 扩充换码机构
expandability 可扩充性
expandable 可扩充的
expanded ASCII code 扩充的 ASCII 代码
expanded memory 扩展内存
expanded memory board 内存扩充板
expanded memory emulator 扩展内存仿真程序
expanded memory manager(EMM) 扩展内存管理程序
expanded memory specification(EMS) 扩展内存规范
expanded session reference 扩充对话引证
expanded storage 扩充存储器
expanded type 扩充类形
expanded view 延伸观察;扩展视图
expanded virtual toolbox(XVT) 扩展拟虚工具箱
expander 扩展器
expanding node 扩展节点
expander 扩展器
expansible 可扩充的
expansion 放大,扩展
expansion adapter 扩展适配器
expansion-angle variable capacitor 扩展角可变电容器
expansion board 扩充板
expansion bus 扩展总线「颈
expansion bus bottleneck 扩充总线瓶
expansion card 扩展卡
expansion coefficient 扩展系数
expansion interface 扩展接口
expansion of node 节点扩展
expansion of the luminance range 亮度范围的扩展
expansion slots 扩展槽
expansion unit 扩展单元
expect statement 期望语句
expectation-driven 期望驱动
expectation-driven reasoning 期望驱动推理
expected complexity 期望复杂性
expected cost 预期成本
expected run-time 预期运行时间
expected service-time 预期服务时间
expected value 期望值
expedient state 权宜状态
expedited data negotiation 加快数据协商
expedited flow 加急数据流
expedited message handling(EMH) 快速信息处理
expenditure 经费,消费额
experience curve 经验曲线
experiential evidence 实验根据
experiential learning 经验学习
expecrintial packet switching service 实验性包交换业务
Experimental System for Data Driven Processor Array(EDDY) 数据驱动处理器阵列实验系统,EDDY 计算机
ExperLogo ExperLogo 语言
Expert Choice software pack 专家选择软件包

expert knowledge 专家知识
expert opinion method 专家意见法
expert problem solver 专家问题求解
expert programs 专家程序系统
expert report 专家报告
expert system 专家系统
expert system shell 专家系统外壳
expert system tool 专家系统工具
expert system tools for building 专家系统建造工具
expertise 专业知识
expiration check 有效期测试;阶段测试
expiration date 失效日期,有效期截止日期
expire 期满
expiration data 到期失效数据
expireware 超过有效期的软件
explanation 解释
explanation-based learning 解释学习
explicit 明晰的,显式的
explicit address 显式地址
explicit attribute 显式属性
explicit declaration 显式说明
explicit definition 显式定义
explicit dimensioning 显式定界
explicit identification 显式标识
explicit-implicit scheme 显-隐方案
explicit item for inquiry 供查询的显式项目
explicit knowledge 显式知识
explicit literal 显式文字的
explicit method 显式方法
explicit parallel instruction computing (EPIC) 显式指令并行计算(Intel)
explicit partition 显式分区
explicit reference 显式引用
explicit relaxation 显式松弛
explicit route(ER) 显式路由
explicit route length 显式路由长度
explicit specification statement 显式定义语句
explode 分解;爆炸
exploded chart 切开的图表
exploded file 爆炸性文件
exploded pie graph 分离的圆饼图
exploded slice 切出的块
exploded view 分解视图
exploding 扩展,分解

exploit 开拓,开发
exploitable channel 可拓通道
exploratory programming 探索性程序设计
exploratory scenario 探索性方案
Explorer "探索者"浏览器(微软)
explorer 探测器;资源管理器
exploring spot 探测点
explosion command 扩展命令
explosion-proof component 防爆元件
exponent(EX) 指数,阶
exponent characters 指数符号
exponent frame 阶框架
exponent notation 指数表示法
exponent overflow exception 阶上溢异常
exponent part 指数部分
exponent signal 指数信号
exponent underflow 阶下溢
exponential complexity 指数复杂性
exponential decay model 指数衰减模型
exponential dichotomies 指数二分性
exponential distribution 指数分布
exponential filter 指数滤波器
exponential fitting 指数拟合
exponential function 指数函数
exponential growth model 指数增长模型
exponential interpolation 指数插值
exponential lag 指数滞后
exponential law 指数律
exponential notation 指数记数法
exponential order 指数阶
exponential random variable 指数分布随机变量
exponential smoothing 指数平滑法
exponential stability 指数稳定性
exponential transform 指数变换
exponentiation 求幂
export 输出,导出
export file name 导出文件名
exposed zone 暴露区
exposure 曝光;暴露;暴露性
exposure area 曝光区
exposure control 曝光控制
exposure counter 曝光计数器
exposure event 曝光事件
exposure index 曝光指数
exposure latitude 曝光宽容度

EXPR(EXPRession) 表达式
EXPRESS(data EXtraction Processing and REStruction System) 数据抽取、处理与重构系统
Express Express 并行化支援系统
express 表示,表达;明确的
express order wire 专线
Express Publisher Express Publisher 桌面排版软件
express warranty 明确保证
expression 表达式;表语
expression dictionary 惯用语词典
expression parsing 表达式分析
expression read 快读
EXT(EXTernal) 外部的,外接的
extend address 扩充地址
Extend Industry Standard Architecture bus(EISA) 扩展工业标准结构总线
Extend Pack 功能扩展的套装软件
extended addressing 扩展寻址
extended application 扩展应用程序
extended architecture(XA) 扩充体系结构
extended area service(EAS) 扩大服务范围
extended arithmetic element(EAE) 扩充运算单元
extended ASCII 扩展 ASCII 码
extended attribute 扩展属性
extended BASIC 扩展 BASIC 语言
extended binary-coded decimal interchange code(EBCDIC) 扩充二-十进制交换码(IBM)
extended binary tree 扩充二叉树
extended BIOS data area(EBDA) 扩展 BIOS 数据区域
extended BNF(EBNF) 扩展巴科斯范式
extended board 扩展电路板
extended boundary condition method 扩展边界条件法
Extended Capabilities Port(ECP) 扩充容量端口
extended checkpoint/restart 扩充检验点/重启动
extended class 扩充类
extended color 扩充颜色
extended common object file format (XCOFF) 扩充公共对象文件格式
extended control mode 扩充控制方式
extended control program support (ECPS:VSE) 扩展的控制程序支持
extended cost 提高成本
extended D-algorithm 扩展 D 算法
extended data management system (EDMS) 扩展数据管理系统
extended data out(EDO) 扩展数据输出,EDO 存储器(Micron)
extended database system 扩展数据库系统
extended definition TV(EDTV) 扩展清晰度电视
Extended Edition 扩展编辑
extended-entry decision table 扩充型项目判定表
extended Fire code 扩展 Fire 码
extended floating-point numbers 扩展浮点数
extended font 扩充字体
extended format diskette 扩展格式化盘
Extended Graphics Array(XGA) 扩展图形阵列
extended group coded recording(EGCR) 扩展组编码记录
extended Hanmming code 扩展海明码
Extended Industry Standard Architecture(EISA) 扩展工业标准体系结构(总线)
extended interface 扩充接口
extended keyboard 扩充键盘
extended LAN 扩充局域网
extended-level synthesizer 扩充级合成器
extended memory 扩展内存
extended memory adapter emulation (XMEAM) 扩展内存适配板模拟
extended memory manager 扩展内存管理程序
extended memory specification(XMS) 扩充内存规范
extended MIDI format 扩展乐器数字接口格式
extended mnemonic 扩展助记操作符
extended mode 扩展状态
extended name 扩展名
extended networking 扩展组网

extended operation control SSP 扩展的操作员控制系统服务程序
extended operator control station 扩展的操作员控制站
extended partition specification table 扩展的分区说明表
extended-precision floating point 浮点数扩展精度
extended query language 扩展查询语言
extended range of a DO statement DO语句的扩展部分
extended response byte 扩充的应答字节
extended response field 扩充的应答字段
extended-result output 溢出结果输出
extended route 扩充路径
extended selection 扩展选择
extended service frame(ESF) 扩展服务帧
extended source 扩展辐射源
extended-time scale 扩展时标
Extended UNIX Codes(EUC) 扩充的UNIX代码
extended VGA 增强型视频图形阵列
extender 扩充部件；扩张器
extending reference rule 扩充基准规则
extensibility 可扩充性，可扩展性
extensible hashing 可扩充散列法
extensible metalanguage 可扩充元语言
extensible language 可扩充语言
extension 扩充；辅助设备；扩展名
extension against rule 扩展反例规则
extension memory 扩展内存
extension name 扩展名
extension register 扩充寄存器
extension station 扩充站
extensional 外延模拟
extensionality axiom 外延公理
extent 范围，程度
exterior gateway protocol(EGP) 外部网关协议
exterior hash function expression 外散列函数表达式
exterior label 外部标号
exterior node 外部节点
external 外部的
external arithmetic 外部运算
external blocking 外部阻断

external buffer 外部缓冲器
external bus 外部总线，外总线
external call 外部呼叫
external cavity semiconductor laser 外腔半导体激光器
external clocking 外部定时；外部时钟
external command 外部命令
external coupling 外部耦合
external data definition 外部数据定义
external data file 外部数据文件
external data representation(XDR) 外部数据表示
external defined symbol 外部定义符号
external delay 外部延迟
external description 外部描述
external device 外部设备
external device address 外部设备地址
external device code 外部设备码
external device communication 外部设备通信
external device control 外部设备控制
external device data flow 外部设备数据流
external device instruction 外部设备指令
external device interrupt 外部设备中断
external device operand 外部设备操作数
external disk drive 外置式磁盘驱动器
external disturbance 外部扰动
external domain 外部域
external down time 外部停机时间
external elements 外部元素
external efficiency 外部效率，牵引效率
external environment 外部环境
external equipment 外部设备
external error 外部错误
external event detection module 外部事件检测模块
external event module 外部事件模块
external file connector 外部文件连接符
external file name 外部文件名
external flag 外部标记
external fragment 外部碎片
external frequency 外部频率
external function(EXF) 外部函数
External Gateway Protocol(EGP) 外

部网关协议
external hard disk 外置式硬盘
external hardware 外置硬件
external idle time 外部空闲时间
external inhibit interrupt 外部禁止中断
external interrupt enable 外部中断允许
external interrupt inhibit 外部中断禁止
external interrupt line 外部中断线
external interrupt status word 外部中断状态字
external label 外部标签,外部标号
external library member 外部库成员
external line 外线
external lines interrupt 外线中断
external link 外部链接
external loading head assembly 外加载磁头组件
external loss time 外部损失时间
external medium 外部媒体
external memory 外部存储器
external merge 外归并
external message queue 外部消息队列
external model 外部模型
external modem 外置式调制解调器
external modulation 外调制
external name 外部名称
external names definition record 外部名定义记录
external node 外部节点
external noise 外噪声
external number 外部数
external-number repetition 外部数重复
external numbering plan 外部记数法
external observation 外部观测
external optical modulation 外部光调制
external page address 外部页地址
external page table 外部页表
external path length 外部路径长度
external photoeffect 外光电效应
external priority 外部优先顺序
external procedure 外部过程
external program parameter 外部程序参数
external read 外部读
external reference 外部引用
external reference formula 外部引用公式

external registers 外部寄存器
external request 外部请求
external reset 外部复位
external resource 外部资源
external routine 外部例程
external run unit 外部运行部件
external schema 外部模式,库外模式
external searching 外部查找
external security audit 外部安全审计
external security control 外部安全控制
external segment name 外部段名
external self-locking flag 外部自锁标志
external shared page table 外部共享页表
external signal 外部信号
external signal interrupt 外部信号中断
external signal line 外部信号线
external sort 外排序
external source 外部源程序
EXTERNAL statement 外部语句
external status words interrupt 外部状态字中断
external storage 外部存储器
external style sheet 外部样式表
external subroutine 外部子例程
external switch 外部开关
external symbol 外部符号
external symbol dictionary 外部符号字典
external table 外部表格
external text 外部文本
external thermal resistance 外热阻
external timing 外部定时
external transmit clock 外部传输时钟
external trigger 外触发器
external-unit identifier 外部设备标识符
external variables 外部变量
external view 外形
external viewer (WWW)外部阅读器
external visual display equipment 外部直观显示设备
externality 外形,外在性
externally caused failure 外因导致的故障
externally compiled subprogram identifier 外部编译子程序标识符
externally defined symbol 外部定义符

externally driven type DC/DC converter 外驱动型直流/直流变换器
externally specified index 外部专用索引
externally specified index operation 外部特定索引作业序
externally stored program 外部存储程
extinction 退化；熄灭；废弃
extra 额外的，附加的
extra address 附加地址
extra bit 附加位
extra block probability 附加块概率
extra buffer 附加缓冲器
extra byte 附加字节
extra cell 附加单元格
extra code 附加码
extra control lead 附加控制线
extra data model 附加数据模型
extra error 额外误差
extra front-end computer 附加前端机
extra gate 附加门
extra high density(ED) 甚高密度
extra input terminal 附加输入终端
extra key 附加关键码
extra large 特大的
extra limiter 附加限幅器
extra logic element 附加逻辑元件
extra message 附加消息
extra output order 外加输出指令
extra pass 附加遍
extra parallelism 附加并行性
extra pointer 附加指示字
extra pseudo order 外加伪指令
extra pulse 冒脉冲，多余脉冲
extra segment 附加段
extra setting 附加设置
extra symbol 外加符号
extrabold 大黑体字印件
extracode 附加代码，附加程序
extract 抽出，析取，摘录，选取
extract data 节录数据
extract file 节录文件
extract instruction 抽取命令
extracting 抽取，析取
extracting attribute 析取属性
extracting figure 析取图
extraction 取出，抽取，摘录
extraction accuracy 抽取精度
extraction algorithm 析取算法
extraction design method 析取设计方法
extraction display 录取显示器
extraction indexing 摘录索引
extraction instruction 抽取指令，析出指令
extraction marker 录取标志
extraction tool 启拔工具
extractor 析取字，抽取字
extraneous response 额外响应
extrapolate 外推
extrapolated mean 外推平均
extrapolation 外插，外推法器
extrashort pulsed laser 超短脉冲激光
extraterrestrial noise 宇宙噪声
extratext 报文选录系统
extremal 极值
extremal field 极值域
extremal graph 极值图
extremal vector 极值向量
extreme 极限值
extreme close-up 超近景，大特写
extreme long shot 长焦距
extreme direction 极方向
extreme optimal strategy 极优策略
extreme point 极点
extreme value 极值
extreme vector 极向量
extremely high frequency 极高频频
extremely low frequency(ELF) 极低
extremely low frequency communication 极低频通信
extremely low-frequency emission 极低频辐射
extremity of interval 区间末端
extremity routine 末端例程
extremum 极值
extremum principle 极值原理
extremum search 极值搜索法
extremum seeking method 极值寻找
extrinsic 非本征的，非固有的
extrinsic evolutionary hardware 外部演化硬件
extrinsic gain 非本征增益
extrinsic properties 非本征性质体
extrinsic semiconductor 非本征半导
EXTRN(EXTeRNal reference) 外部引用
extrude 挤压，模压

extrusion 拉伸
extrusion pressing 挤压成型
eye ball character 可见性
eye-brain-hand machine 眼脑手机械
eye-brain system 眼脑系统
eye coordinate system 人眼坐标系统
eye diagram 可见图形
eye-hand machine 眼手机器
eye-legible copy(image) 可见拷贝(影像)
eye level 视平线
eye pattern 眼图
Eye Phone 视听屏
eye space 目视空间
eye test 目测
eyeball control 目视控制
eyedropper 吸管
eyelet 空心铆钉

F f

F(False) 假的；错误的，有故障的
F(Frequency) 频率
F connector F 型连接器
F/M(Frame per Minute) 每分钟帧「数
F-rule F 规则，正向推理规则
FA(Finite Automata) 有限自动机
FA(Full Adder) 全加器
fabric ribbon 纺织色带，织造色带
fabricate 制作，加工
fabricated language 人造语言
fabrication 制备，制造
fabrication patterning 结构图案化
fabrication tolerance 装配公差[容差]
FAC(File Access Control) 文件存取控制
FACE (Field Alterable Control Element) 现场可更换控制元件
face 字型，字体；表面
face bonding 面向下键合，表面接着
face-change character 变更字体控制符
face character nonimpact printing technique 表面字符非击打式印刷技术
face classification 面貌分类法
face colorable plane 表面可着色平面
face coloring 表面着色
face-down bonding 俯式[面朝下]结合法
face in frame 帧侧面
face list 面列表
face name 封面名称
face recognition 面貌识别
face shield 前屏蔽
face structure 面结构
face-to-face 面对面
face-up bonding 仰式接合法
face value 视在值
facet 侧面，小平面；琢面
facet analysis 侧面分析法
facet name 侧面名
faceted classification 侧面分类法
faceted shading 侧面阴影
facial expression 面部表情
facilities library 设备程序库
facility 设施，装备；程序；便利；能力
facility allocation 设备分配
facility assignment 设备指派
facility comparison 设施比较
facility inventory 设备目录
facility management 设施[设备]管理
facility record 设备记录 「册
facility registration 设施登记，设备注
facility request 设施请求
facility request separator 设施请求分隔符
facility utilization 设备利用率
facility work order 设备工作顺序
FACOM(FUJITSU Automatic COMputer) 富士通自动计算机 「列
FACOM 230 FACOM 230 计算机系
facsimile(FAX) 传真；精确复制
facsimile baseband 传真基频带
facsimile call creating mode 传真呼叫建立模式
facsimile coding and decoding circuit 传真编码与解码电路

facsimile communication procedure 传真通信过程
facsimile converter 传真转换器
facsimile density 传真密度
facsimile document system 文件传真系统
facsimile laser platemaker 传真激光制版机
facsimile mail 传真信函
facsimile modulation 传真调制
facsimile network control unit 传真机网络控制部件
facsimile picture signal processing circuit 传真图像信号处理电路
facsimile posting 传真邮送
facsimile printer 传真打印机
facsimile protocol 传真协议
facsimile recording mode 传真记录方式
facsimile scan pick-up unit 传真扫描拾取部件
facsimile scanning 传真扫描
facsimile signal simulator 传真信号仿真器
facsimile station 传真站
facsimile synchronizing 传真同步
FACT (Full Automatic Cataloging Technique) 全自动编目技术
FACT (Full Automatic Compiler Translator) 全自动编译转换程序
fact 事实
fact bank 事实库
fact clause 事实子句
fact correlation 事实相关性
fact database 事实数据库
fact-directed function invocation 事实指导的功能调用
fact-directed reasoning 事实指导推理
fact expression 事实表达式
fact-file 事实文件
fact retrieval 事实检索
factographic 罗列事实的
factor 因子,系数,因素,因式
factor analysis 因素分析
factor clause 因子子句
factor comparison method 要素比较法
factor of cooperation 合作系数
factor out 析出因数
factor total 因子累计

factorable 可因子分解的
factorable function 因子分解函数
factorable graph 因子分解图
factored knowledge structure 因式化知识结构
factorial 阶乘
factorial sign 阶乘符号
factoring 分解属性;分解因子
factoring file specification 分解属性文件说明
factoring of attributes 属性提出公因子
factoring polynomial 因子分解多项式
factorization theorem 分解定理
facula 光斑
fade 减弱,渐隐;衰落
fade area 衰落区
fade chart 盲区图,衰落区图
fade down 自上而下淡出
fade in 淡入,信号渐强
fade indicator 衰落指示器
fade out 淡出,信号渐弱
fade up 自下而上淡出
fade zone 消失区,静区,盲区
fading 衰落
fading depth 衰落深度
fading margin 衰落边际
fading period 衰落周期
fading rise 衰落上升,衰落增长
fading signal 衰落信号
Fahrenheit temperature 华氏温度
fail 失效;失败
fail bit 失效位
fail category 失效类别,故障类型
fail-cut method 失败-截断法
fail data 失效数据
fail-frost 故障冻结
fail hardcover 零信满输出故障
fail mask mode 失效屏蔽模式
fail memory 失效内存
fail safe 故障安全,故障不间断
fail safe control 失效安全控制
fail safe default 失效安全默认值
fail-safe disconnect 故障安全切离
fail-safe facility 故障保险设施
fail-safe nature 失效安全性
fail-safe operation 故障安全操作
fail-safe program 故障安全程序
fail-safe sequential machine 故障安全

时序机
fail-safe software 故障安全软件
fail-safe system 故障安全系统
fail-soft 故障弱化
fail-soft behavior 故障弱化特性
fail-soft capability 故障弱化能力
fail-soft function 故障弱化功能
fail-soft mode 故障弱化模式
fail-soft operation 故障弱化操作
fail-soft system 故障弱化系统
fail-softness 故障弱化
fail store mode 失效存储模式
failback 失效恢复
failed to revoke server 撤消服务器失「败
failover 失效接替(单台计算机失效后,由其他连网计算机接替其任务)
failsafe 故障[失效]保险
failure 故障,失效
failure analysis 故障[失效]分析
failure bit 失效位,故障位
failure category 故障分类
failure correction time 故障矫正时间
failure criterion 故障判定标准
failure data calculation 失效数据计算
failure detection 故障探测
failure diagnosis 故障诊断
failure diagnosis time 故障诊断时间
failure distribution 故障分布 「习
failure-driven learning 失败驱动的学
failure effect analysis 故障影响分析
failure exception mode 故障异常模式
failure-free operation 无故障运行
failure function 无效操作,失败功能
failure identification 无效标记,障标识
failure in 10^9 component hours(FIT) 10^9 元件小时一次故障
failure in time(FIT) 时间失效率
failure isolation(FIT) 故障隔离
failure level 故障级,失效层次
failure logging 故障登记[记录]
failure mechanism 故障机制,失效机理
failure mode 故障模式,失效模式
failure mode effect and criticality analysis 失效模式效应及后果分析
failure model 故障模型
failure modeling 失效建模

failure modes and mechanisms 失效模式和机理
failure node 故障节点,失效结点
failure occurrence 失效出现,故障发生
failure prediction 故障[失效]预测
failure rate 故障率,失效率
failure rate function 故障率函数
failure-rate models 失效率模型
failure recognition 故障识别
failure recovery 故障复原,差错恢复
failure state 故障状态
failure testing 故障检测
failure time 失效时间
failure-tolerant control 容错控制
failure-tolerant parallel programming 容错并行程序设计
failure trace 故障踪迹
failure tree analysis 故障树分析
failure unit 故障单位
fair 公正的,合理的
fair distribution 合理分布
fair termination 正常终止
fairly similar 极为相似
fairness control algorithm 合理性控制算法
fairness doctrine 公正准则
fake host 伪主机
fake host communication 伪主机通信
fake root 假根
fall back 退守,撤退,后退
fall in 同步,进入同步
fall out 失去同步,失步
fall out of step 失同步
fall out rate 错检率
fall out ratio 错检比率
fall time 下降时间,下沿时间
fallacious derivation 谬误推理
fallback 退守,预备;低效率运行
fallback data rate 退守数据速率
fallback mode 退守模式
fallback procedure 退守措施
fallback recover 复原退守,保守运行结束
fallback state 后退状态
falling factorial 递降阶乘
fallout 筛出;失同步
fallout ratio 错检率

false 假的,伪的
false add 无进位加,假加
false alarm 误报警
false call 误呼叫
false code 伪码
false code check 假码校验
false color 伪彩色
false color density slicing 伪彩色密度分割
false combination 假组合,无效组合
false contour remove 假轮廓消除
false contouring 假轮廓
false coordinate 假坐标
false dismissal 误解除
false drop 漏检
false error 假误差
false exit 假出口
false floor 活动地板
false key 伪键码
false line lock 行同步假锁定
false operation 误操作
false output 假输出
false proposition 假命题
false retrieval 伪检索,误检
false sharing 伪共享
false signal 假信号,伪信号
false start 假启动,误起动
false statement 假语句
false symbol 假符号
false synchronization 假同步
false target generator 假目标发生器
false-zero test 虚零检验
family 族,系列
family bank service 家庭银行服务
family chip 系列芯片
family computer 系列计算机
family of characteristics 特性曲线族
family of parts 零件族,零件组
family-of-parts programming 零件族的程序设计
family program 程序族,系列程序
family tree 族树
FAMOS(FAst Multitasking Operating System) 快速多任务操作系统
FAMOS (Floating-gate Avalanche-injection Metal-Oxide-Semiconductor) 浮栅雪崩注入金属氧化物半导体
FAMT (Full Automatic Machine Translation) 全自动机器翻译
fan 风扇;扇图
fan-fold 折叠
fan-fold paper 折叠式记录纸
fan-in 扇入
fan-in determined fan-out registered network 扇入测定扇出登记网络
fan-in index 扇入系数
fan-in ratio 扇入比
fan-out 扇出
fan-out capability 扇出能力
fan-out circuit 扇出电路
fan-out index 扇出系数
fan-out node 扇出节点
fan-out source 扇出源
fan-out stem 扇出干线
fancy 幻想;爱好;流行的
fanfold paper 折叠式纸
fanout-free circuit 无扇出电路
fanout-oriented test generation algorithm(FAN) 扇出定向测试生成算法
FAP(Floating-point Arithmetic Package) 浮点运算软件包
FAQ(Frequently Asked Questions) 常见问题,经常问到的问题
far 远的,段间的
far call 远调用
far-end cross-talk 远端串音[串扰]
far infrared 远红外线
far jump 远转移,段间跳转
far pointer 远指针
far return 远返回
far-to-near rotation 由远到近旋转
Farad 法拉
Faraday magneto-optical effect 法拉第磁光效应
Faraday rotation effect 法拉第旋转效应
Faraday shield 法拉第屏蔽
Faradic current 法拉第电流
FARNET(Federation of American Research NETworks) 美国研究网联盟
FAS(Fast Access Storage) 快速存取存储器
fashion 式样,风格,方式
fashionable 流行的
Fast Fast 协议

fast access memory　快速访问内存
fast access retrieval system　快速访问检索系统
fast-access storage　快速访问存储器
fast access to system technical information　系统技术信息的快速访问
fast acting channel　快反应信道
fast acting fuse　快响应保险丝
fast algorithm　快速算法　「序
fast-back parser　快返回语法分析程
fast backward　快速倒带
fast blink　快速闪烁
fast bus　高速总线
fast circuit switching(FCS)　快速电路交换
fast coding　快速编码
fast coincidence circuit　快速符合电路
fast comprehensive recovery　快速全面恢复
fast connect circuit switching　快速连接电路切换
fast connect dial circuit　快速连接拨号电路
fast database access　快速数据库访问
Fast disk　快速磁盘操作软件
Fast Eddy　"急旋涡"CD-ROM(苹果)
Fast Ethernet　快速以太网
fast fading　快衰落
fast forward　快进
fast forward control　快速向前控制
fast Fourier transform(FFT)　快速傅立叶变换
fast Fourier transform analyzer　快速傅立叶变换分析器
fast hub　快速集线器
fast inference　快速推理
fast lens　快速镜头
fast load　快速装入
fast mode　快速模式
fast multiplier　快速乘法器
fast multitasking operating system(FAMOS)　快速多道作业系统　「换
fast packet switch(FPS)　快速分组交
fast page mode　(内存)快速页面模式
fast parallel arithmetic　快速并行运算
fast path　快速通路,快速路径
fast path exclusive transaction　快速路径互斥事务处理
fast path potential transaction　快速路径潜在事务处理
fast path protocol　快速路径协议
fast polynomial transformation　快速多项式变换
Fast Printing Direct to Port　直接到端口的快速打印
fast program loading　快速程序装入
fast recognition　快速识别
fast recovery　快速恢复
fast recovery rectifier　快速恢复整流元件
fast register　快速寄存器
fast response　快速响应
fast retransmit　快速重传
fast return control　快速返回控制
fast rewind　快速反绕
fast rewind control　快速反绕控制
fast save　快速保存
fast scratchpad memory　高速便笺式内存
fast select　快速选择
fast select acceptance　快速选择接受
fast state　快态
fast storage　快速存储器
fast switch over　快速切换
fast sync extend　快速同步扩充
fast threads　快速线程
fast time scale　快时标
fast tip　快速提示
fast turnaround(FTA)　快速周转[换向]
Fastback Plus　快速备份程序
Fastbus　快速总线
FastCAD　FastCAD辅助设计软件
fastener　紧固件,夹具
FAT(File Allocation Table)　文件分配表
fat channel　宽通道
fat client model　肥客户机模型
fat line　粗线
fat link　宽链路,粗线
fat server model　肥服务器模型
fat tree　胖树
fat vector　宽向量
fatal abort code　严重异常结束码
fatal error　致命错误
fatal flag　致命故障标志

FatBits （图像中的）肥点
father 父；起源
father chain 父链
father field 父域
father file 父文件
father link 父链接
father node 父节点
father process 父进程
father tape 父带
father vertex 父顶点，前代顶点
fatigue analysis 疲劳分析
fatigue resistance 抗疲劳性
fatware "肥胖"软件
fault 故障
fault active state 故障活动状态
fault-avoidance 故障避免
fault clearance 故障排除，错误清除
fault code 出错[故障]代码
fault collapsing 故障压缩
fault confinement area 故障界限区
fault correct 故障校正
fault coverage 故障覆盖范围
fault current 故障电流
fault desk 故障记录台
fault detection 故障检测
fault diagnosis 故障诊断
fault diagnosis algorithm 故障诊断算法
fault diagnosis program 故障诊断程序
fault dictionary 故障辞典
fault distinguish 故障区分
fault domain 出错范围
fault dominance 故障支配
fault equivalence 故障等效
fault finding 故障寻找
fault flag 故障标志
fault finder 故障寻迹器
fault folding method 故障折合法
fault-free 无故障的
fault freedom 容错性能
fault grading 故障等级
fault inactive state 故障非活动状态
fault indication device 故障指示装置
fault indicator 故障指示器
fault isolation 故障隔离
fault latency 故障潜伏期
fault localization 故障局部化
fault location 故障定位
fault location program 故障定位程序

fault location testing(FLT) 故障定位测试
fault locator 故障定位器
fault management 故障管理
fault masking 故障屏蔽
fault matrix 故障矩阵
fault model 故障模型
fault persistence time 故障持续时间
fault point 故障点
fault potential 故障电位
fault prevention 故障预防
fault probability 故障概率
fault propagation 故障传播
fault rate 故障率，错误率
fault-rate threshold 故障临限，故障率阈值
fault recording 故障记录
fault report point network 故障报告点网络
fault section 故障段，故障节
fault secure circuit 故障安全电路
fault signal 故障信号
fault signature 故障表征
fault simulation 故障模拟
fault tag 故障标记
fault test generation 故障测试生成
fault testing 故障测试
fault threshold 故障阈值[门限值]
fault time 故障时间
fault tolerance 容错
fault tolerance technique 容错技术
fault-tolerant 容错
fault-tolerant computer 容错计算机
fault tolerant computer system conception 容错计算机系统概念
fault-tolerant computing 容错计算
fault-tolerant concept 容错概念
fault-tolerant design 容错设计
fault-tolerant distributed processing 容错分布式处理
fault-tolerant environment 容错环境
fault-tolerant hardware 容错硬件
fault-tolerant hypercube 容错超立方
fault-tolerant operating system 容错操作系统
fault-tolerant routing algorithm 容错路由选择算法
fault-tolerant software 容错软件

fault-tolerant system modeling 容错系统模型化
fault-tolerant technique 容错技术
fault trace 故障跟踪
fault tree 故障树
fault tree analysis 故障树分析
faulty coverage ratio 故障覆盖率
faulty line 故障线路
faulty link information 故障链路信息
favored execution option 优惠执行选件
Favorites folders 收藏夹
Favorites list 收藏夹列表
FAX(FAcsimile equipment) 传真设备
fax(facsimile) 传真
fax adapter 传真适配器
fax board 传真板
fax/modem 传真/调制解调器
fax server 传真服务器
fax switch 传真切换开关
Fax Works for OS/2 用于 OS/2 操作系统之下的传真服务
FAXCOM(FAcsimile COMmunication service) 传真通信业务
Faxcom 传真通信
FAXDIN(FAcsimile transmission over autoDIN) 自动数字通信网的传真传输
FBA(Fixed Block Architecture) 固定块结构
FBC(Fully Buffered Channel) 全缓冲通道
FBRAM(Frame Buffer RAM) 帧缓冲存储器
FC(Fiber Channel) 光纤通道
FC(Forward Chaining) 正向链接
FC(Forward Channel) 正向信道
FC(Frame Controller) 帧控制器
FC(Front end Computer) 前端计算机
FC-PGA(Flip Chip-Pin Grid Array) 反转芯片针状矩阵
FCB(File Control Block) 文件控制块
FCC (Federal Communications Commission) (美国)联邦通信委员会
FCC(Frame Check Character) 帧校验字符
FCC certification 联邦通信委员会认证
FCFS(First Come, First Serve(d)) 先到先服务
FCL(Full Custom Logic) 全定制逻辑
FCN(Full Connected Network) 全连通网络
FCONSOLE 文件工作台(Novell)
FCS(Fast Circuit Switching) 快速电路交换
FCS(Frame Checking Sequence) 帧校验序列
FCT(File Control Table) 文件控制表
FCT(Frame Creation Terminal) 帧创建终端
FCW(Format Control Word) 格式控制字
FD(Floppy Disk) 软盘,活动盘
FD(Full Duplex) 全双工
FDB(Fiber Distribution Box) 光纤配线盒
FDB(File Descriptor Block) 文件描述符块
FDC(Field Data Computer) 现场数据计算机
FDC(Floppy Disc Controller) 软盘控制器
FDCT(Forward Discrete Cosine Transform) 正向离散余弦变换器
FDD(Flexible Disc Drive) 软盘驱动
FDDI (Fiber Distributed Data Interface) 光纤分布式数据接口
FDDL (File Data Description Language) 文件数据描述语言
FDIC(Facsimile Data Interchange Continuance) 传真数据交换接续设备
FDL (Forms Description Language) 窗体描述语言
FDM(Finite-Difference Method) 有限差分法
FDMA (Frequency Division Multiple Access) 频分多路存取
FDP(Field Developed Program) 现场开发程序(IBM)
FDS(Facsimile Document System) 文档传真系统
FDT(Field Diagnostic Test) 现场诊断测试
FDT(File Description Table) 文件描述表
FDT(Full Duplex Terminal) 全双工

FDT(Function Decision Table) 功能判定表
FE(Field Engineer) 现场工程师
FE(Framing Error) 成帧误差
FE(Front End) 前端
FEA(Finite Element Analysis) 有限元分析法
feasibility 可行性
feasibility analysis 可行性分析
feasibility study 可行性研究
feasible 可行的
feasible computability 可行可计算性,易计算性
feasible constraint 可行约束
feasible decomposition 可行分解
feasible direction 可行方向
feasible direction method 可行方向法
feasible flow 可行流
feasible network 可行网络
feasible path 可行路径[通路]
feasible point 可行点
feasible region 可行域
feasible sequence 可行序列
feasible set 可行集
feasible solution 可行解
feasible structure 可行结构
feasible system 可行系统
feasible vertex labeling function 可行顶点标记函数
feasible zone 可行域
feathering 均齐;羽化
feature 特征,特点
feature analysis 特征分析
feature argument 特征变元
feature-based modeling 特征造型[建模]
feature-based representation 基于特征的表示法
feature close-up shot 特写
feature code 特征代码
feature concentration 特征集中
feature data extraction 特征数据抽取
feature deduction 特征推演
feature detection 特征检测
feature detector 特征检测器
feature extraction 特征提取
feature extraction method 特征抽取法
feature for attaching communication 附属通信性能
feature grouping 特征分组
feature identification 特征标识
feature labeling 特征标记
feature matching 特征匹配
feature modeling 特征建模[造型]
feature pattern 特征模型
feature recognition 特征识别
feature selection 特征选择
feature sensitivity 特征敏感性
feature size 特征尺寸
feature space 特征空间
feature vector 特征向量
feature vector extraction 特征向量抽取
featuring 抽取主题
FEC(Fast Ethernet Channel) 高速以太网通道
FEC(Forward Error Correcting) 前向纠错
FEC(Front End Computer) 前端计算机
FECB(File Extended Control Block) 文件扩展控制块
FECN (Forward Explicit Congestion Notification) 前向显式拥塞通告
FECP (Front End Communications Processor) 前端通信处理机
Federal Communications Commission (FCC) 美国联邦通信委员会
Federal Information Exchange List of WWW servers 万维网上的美国联邦信息交换列表
Federal Information Processing Standards(FIPS) 美国联邦信息处理标准
federated 联邦式数据库
feed 馈送
feed back amplifier 反馈放大器
feed back bridging 反馈桥
feed circuit 反馈电路
feed form 进纸
feed-forward 前向馈送
feed forward control 前馈控制
feed forward connection 前向连接
feed-forward network model 前馈网络模型
feed forward pattern classification 前

馈模式分类
feed forward principle 前馈原则
feed-forward shift register 前馈移位寄存器
feed holes 中导孔,馈送孔
feed in 馈入
feed network 馈送网络
feed pitch 馈孔间距
feed rate 馈送率,进给率
feed rate coding 进给速率编码
feed rate number 馈送率数
feed rate override 进给速率控制
feed reel 馈入卷盘,供带盘
feed roller 送纸轮
feed spool 馈送轴
feed-through 馈通孔,导孔;馈通
feed-through connector 馈通连接器
feed through signal 馈通信号
feed track 馈送轨
feed tractor 牵引送纸
feed tray 馈送托盘,装载架
feedback 反馈
feedback adjustment 反馈调整
feedback bridging fault 反馈桥接故障
feedback amplifier 反馈放大器
feedback channel 反馈通道
feedback circuit 反馈电路
feedback coefficient 反馈系数
feedback control 反馈控制
feedback control action 反馈控制作用
feedback control loop 反馈控制回路
feedback control signal 反馈控制信号
feedback control system 反馈控制系统
feedback controller 反馈控制器
feedback elements 反馈元件
feedback encoding 反馈编码
feedback flow control(FFC) 反馈流控制
feedback-forward network model 反馈-前馈网络模型
feedback free network 无反馈网络
feedback function 反馈函数
feedback gain 反馈增益
feedback impedance 反馈阻抗
feedback loop 反馈环路
feedback path 反馈通路[路径]
feedback queue 反馈序列
feedback ratio 反馈比
feedback register 反馈寄存器
feedback search 反馈搜索
feedback shift register 反馈移位寄存器
feedback system 反馈系统
feedback variable 反馈变量
feeder 馈电线
feeder cable 馈电电缆
feeder line 馈线
feeder route 馈电通路
feeder section 馈电路段
feedover 前馈
feedover condition 前馈条件
feedover processor 前馈处理器
feedrate bypass 进给旁路
feedrate override 进给速率超控
FEFO(First End First Out) 先结束先出
FEM(Finite Element Method) 有限元法
FEM(Finite Element Modeling) 有限元建模
female connector 阴性连接器
fembot (仿)女性机器人
femto 毫微微
femtosecond 毫微微秒,尘秒
fence 警戒图;电子篱笆
FEP(Front End Processor) 前端处理机
Fermat's principle 费尔马原理
Fermi level 费米能级
Ferranti Cetec Graphics Ltd Ferranti Cetec 图形公司
ferric oxide 三氧化二铁
ferrite 陶铁磁体,铁氧体
ferrite core 铁氧体磁芯
ferrite core memory 铁氧体磁芯内存
ferrite film disk 铁氧体薄膜磁盘
ferroacoustic storage 铁声存储器
ferrod 铁氧体棒
ferroelectric 强磁介质,铁电体
ferroelectric display 铁电显示器
ferroelectric memory 铁电存储器
ferromagnetic 铁磁性
ferromagnetic material 铁磁材料
ferromagnetics 铁磁学
ferromagnetography 铁磁性记录法
ferrous oxide spots 氧化亚铁斑点
ferrule 箍,环圈,支持件
fertility (病毒)繁殖能力

ferrule 箍,环圈,支持件
FET(Field Effect Transistor) 场效应晶体管
fetch 取指令
fetch and execute cycle 取指令与执行循环
fetch cycle 取指令周期
fetch instruction 提取指令
fetch/load trace 提取/馈入踪迹
fetch phase 取指令阶段
fetch process 提取过程
fetch protection 取指令保护
fetch routine 提取例程
fetch sequence 取指令顺序
fetch strategy 取用策略
fetch time 取指令时间
fetch unit 取指令单元
fetch violation 读取非法
fetcher 访问程序,访问者
FF(Fast Forward) 快进,快速走带
FF(Flip Flop) 触发器
FF(Form Feed) 输纸
FFL(Free-Form Language) 自由形式语言
FFM(Fixed Format Message) 固定格式报文
FFM(Fixed-Frequency Monitor) 固定频率监视器
FFN(Full Function Node) 全功能节点
FFOL(FDDI Follow On LAN) FDDI 局域网改进标准
FFS(Formatted File System) 格式化文件系统
FFSK(Fast Frequency-Shift Keying) 快速频移键控
FFT(Fast Fourier Transform) 快速傅立叶变换
FFT(Final Form Text) 最终形式文本
FFT maximum process sampling-point number 快速傅立叶变换处理最大取样点数
FFTC(Free-Form Text Chart) 自由形式文本图
FFW(Free Format Write) 自由格式写
FGCS(Fifth Generation Computer System) 第五代计算机系统
FGCS(Future Generations Computer System) 未来计算机系统
FGKL(Fifth Generation Kernel Language) 第五代计算机核心语言
FGKRL(Fifth Generation Knowledge Representation Language) 第五代知识表示语言
FGN(File Generation Number) 文件世代号
FGSC(Fifth Generation and Super Computers) 第五代超级计算机
FH(File Handler) 文件处理程序
FH(Fixed Head) 固定(磁)头
FHMA(Frequency Hopping Multiple Access) 跳频多重访问
FHP(Fixed Header Prefix) 固定标题前缀
FI(Format Identifier) 格式标识符
FI(Front end processor Interface) 前端处理机接口
FIB(File Information Block) 文件信息块
fiber 光纤
fiber buffer 光纤缓冲材料
fiber bundle 光纤束
fiber bundle transfer function 光纤束传输函数
fiber cable 光缆
fiber cable assembly 光缆组件
Fiber Channel 光纤通道
fiber circuit 光纤线路
fiber cladding 光纤包层
fiber coating 光纤被覆层
fiber concentrator 光纤集中器
fiber core 光纤芯
fiber core diameter 光纤芯径
fiber count 光纤数
fiber coupled power 光纤耦合功率
fiber cross-talk 光纤串音
fiber-cutting tool 光纤切割刀具
fiber dispersion 光纤色散
fiber distributed data interface(FDDI) 光纤分布式数据接口
fiber distribution box 光纤配线盒
fiber distribution frame 光纤配线架
fiber drawing 光纤拉制
fiber faceplate 光纤截面
fiber HSLN 光纤高速局域网
fiber jacket 光纤二次被覆层

fiber junction 光纤接合点
fiber light-guide 光纤波导
fiber link 光纤链路
fiber loss 光纤损耗
fiber merit figure 光纤性能系数
fiber optic acceptance angle 纤维光接受角
fiber-optic cable 光缆
fiber optic data link 光纤数据链路
fiber optic emitter 光纤发射机
fiber-optic interface device 纤维光学接口装置
fiber optic local network 光纤局域网
fiber optic modem 光纤调制解调器
fiber optic multiplexer 光纤多路转换器
fiber optic processor 光纤处理机
fiber optic splice 光纤接续
fiber-optic telecommunication cable 长途通信光缆
fiber optic terminus 光纤端接组件
fiber optic transmission system(FOTS) 光纤维传输系统
fiber-optic waveguide 光纤波导
fiber-optical communication(FOC) 光纤通信
fiber optics 纤维光学
fiber optics butting connector 光纤对接连接器
fiber optics cladding 光学纤维包层
fiber optics components 光纤组成成分
fiber optics connector 光纤连接器
fiber optics connector interface 光纤连接器接口
fiber optics system light sources 光学纤维系统光源
fiber scattering 光纤散射
fiber sensor 光纤传感器
fiber strain 光纤应变,光纤变形
fiber to the home(FTTH) 光纤到家
Fiberguide 光纤波导
fiberoptronics 纤维光电子学
fiberscope 光纤显示器
Fibonacci function 菲波那契函数
Fibonacci method 菲波那契法
Fibonacci number 菲波那契数
Fibonacci search 菲波那契检索

Fibonacci sequence 菲波那契数列
Fibonacci series 菲波那契数列
Fibonacci sort 菲波那契排序
Fibonacci string 菲波那契串
fibre 光纤(同 fiber)
fibrous composite material 光纤复合材料
FIC(Film Integrated Circuit) 薄膜集成电路
fiche 卡片;缩微胶片
fiction 假定;虚构
fictitious carry 假进位
fictitious load 假负载
fictitious variable 虚构变量
fidelity 保真度
fidelity criteria 保真度准则
FidoNet Fido 网络
fiduciary object 参照物,参照目标
field 字段,域,栏;场
field-alterable control element(FACE) 现场可变控制元件
field-alterable ROM 现场可变更只读存储器
field attribute 字段属性
field blanking 场消隐
field checking 字段检验
field coil 激磁线圈
field data 现场数据
field decelerator 字段说明符
field definition 字段定义
field delimiter 字段定界符
field descriptor 字段描述符
field descriptor group 字段描述符组
field development program 现场开发程序
field distortion sensing 区域扰动感应
field effect 场效应
field-effect display 场效应显示器
field effect semiconductor laser 场效应半导体激光器
field effect transistor(FET) 场效应晶体管
field engineer 现场工程师
field filter 字段筛选
field format 字段格式
field frequency 场频
field indirect encoding 字段间接编码
field intensity 场强,电磁场强度

field layout 字段布局
field length 字段长度
field length indicator 字段长度指示
field level sensitivity 字段级灵敏度
field list 字段列表
field location 字段位置
field maintenance 现场维护
field mark 字段标志
field name 字段名
field object 域对象
field observation 现场观测
field of constant 常数域
field of knowledge 知识范围
field real numbers 实数域
field of view 视场
field overlapping 字段覆盖
field patch 现场修补
field pitcher 字段选择器
field privilege 字段授权
field programmable gate array(FPGA) 现场可编程门阵列
field programmable logic array(FPLA) 现场可编程序逻辑阵列
field prompt 域提示
field propagation of bubble 磁泡场传
field properties 字段属性
field protect 字段保护
field reliability test 现场可靠性测试
field replaceable unit 现场可替换单
field running test 现场运行试验 元
field selection 字段选择
field separator 字段分隔符 员
field service technician 现场服务技术
field shifty 字段位移
field squeeze 字段挤压,字段紧缩
field strength 场强
field sync pulse 场同步脉冲
field tag 字段标记
field template 字段样板,字段模板
field terminator 域结束符
field test 现场测试
field tester 现场测试器
field-upgrade 现场升级
field upgrading 现场升级
field utilization 字段利用
field value 字段值
field width 字段宽度
fielddata 野战数据

Fieldata code 军用数据码
fieldata family 野战数据集
Fieldata process system 军用数据处理系统
Fieldata system 野战数据系统
Fieldbus 现场总线
FIF(Fractal Image Format) 分形图像格式
FIFO(First In, First Out) 先进先出
FIFO abnormally 先进先出异常
FIFO buffer 先进先出缓冲器
FIFO management 先进先出管理方式
FIFO memory 先进先出内存
FIFO page replacement 先进先出页替换
FIFO queue 先进先出队列
FIFO special file 先进先出专用文件
FIFO stack register 先进先出堆栈寄存器
FIFO storage 先进先出存储器
fifteen puzzle 十五迷宫
fifteen-supergroup assembly link 15超群组合链路
fifteen-supergroup assembly section 15超群组合段
fifth generation computer system (FGCS) 第五代计算机系统
fifth-generation language 第五代语言
FIG(FIGure) 图,图形;数字
figurative constant 象征常量
figure decomposition 图形分解
figure description language 图形描述语言
figure-ground articulation 过图形背景清晰度
figure interpretation function 图形解释函数
figure out 计算出;领会到
figure recognition 图形识别
figure shift 换数字档
filament 灯丝
file 文件
file access 文件存取
file access attribute 文件存取属性
file access auditing 文件存取审计
file access block 文件存取块
file access component 文件访问组件
file access control 文件存取控制
file access error 文件存取错误

file access keys 文件访问关键字
file access listener 文件访问监听程序
file access method 文件存取法
file access mode 文件存取模式
file access protocol 文件存取协议
file access time 文件存取时间
file activity 文件活动性
file activity ratio 文件活动率
file-address checking program 文件地址的检验程序
file-address checking system 文件地址核对系统
file addressing 文件寻址
file allocation 文件分配,文件定位
file allocation table(FAT) 文件分配表
file allocation time 文件定位时间
file amendment 文件修正
file analysis 文件分析
file and record locking 文件与记录锁定
file appending 文件追加
file area 文件区
file assignment 文件指定,文件指派
file attribute 文件属性
file availability 文件可用性[有效性]
file backup 文件备份
file buffer 文件缓冲器
file bus in 文件输入总线
file bus out 文件输出总线
file caching 文件高速缓冲
file catalog 文件目录
file check 文件检验
file class 文件类
file clause 文件子句
file clean-up 文件清理
file close 文件关闭
file compaction 文件紧凑
file components 文件组件
file composition 文件组成
file compression ratio 文件压缩比
file compression utility 文件压缩实用程序
file concatenation 文件并置[连接]
file condensation 文件紧凑,文件压缩
file condition 文件存取条件
file consistency 文件一致性
file constant 文件常量
file contention 文件争用

file control 文件控制
file control block(FCB) 文件控制块
file control system 文件控制系统
file conversion 文件转换
file conversion utility 文件转换实用程序
file copy 文件拷贝;文件复本
file creation 文件创建[建立]
file declaration 文件说明
file definition 文件定义
file definition entry 文件定义项
file definition name 文件定义名
file defragment 文件碎片消除
file deletion 文件删除
file description(FD) 文件说明,文件描述项
file description entry 文件说明[描述]项
file description statement 文件描述语句
file descriptor 文件说明文摘;文件描述块
file devices 文件装置
file-difference problem 文件差异问题
file directory 文件目录
file disposition 文件安排
file dumping 文件转储
file duplication 文件复制
file editor 文件编辑程序
file element 文件元素
file end flag 文件结束标志
file ending label 文件结束标记
file event 文件事件
file exchange program 文件交换程序
file expression 文件表达式
file extended control block 文件扩充控制块
file extension 文件扩展名
file extension specification 文件附加说明
file extent 文件范围
file flattener 文件压平器
file format 文件格式
file format compatibility 文件格式兼容性
file format conversion 文件格式转换
file fragmentation 文件分段
file function 文件操作
file gap 文件间隙

file generation 文件生成
file generation number 文件世代号
file generation utility 文件生成实用程序
file handle 文件句柄
file handler 文件处理程序
file handling routine 文件处理程序
file header 文件标题,文件首部
file icon 文件图标
file ID 文件标识
file identification 文件标识
file identifier 文件标识符
file index 文件索引
file insertion 文件插入
file interrogation program 文件查询程序
file inversion 文件倒置
file label 文件标号
file label beginning 文件标号开始点
file layout 文件布置,文件格式设计
file length 文件长度
file librarian 文件库管理者
file line length 文件行长度
file list 文件列表
file loading 文件载入,文件装入
file locking 文件加锁
file log 文件日志
file maintenance 文件维护
file maintenance program 文件维护程序
file management 文件管理
file management program 文件管理程序
file management subsystem 文件管理子系统
file management system 文件管理系
file manager 文件管理程序
file manipulation command 文件操作命令
file map 文件映像
file mapping object 文件映射对象
file mark 文件标志
file merging 文件合并
file model 文件模型
file moniker 文件别名
file name 文件名
file name extension 文件名扩展
file name extension mapping 文件扩展名映射
file name table 文件名表

file object 文件对象
file of direct access 直接存取文件
file of index access 索引存取文件
file of sequential access 顺序存取文件
file open 文件打开
file operation program 文件操作程序
file organization 文件组织
file option 文件选项
file-organization routine 文件组织例程
file-oriented programming 面向文件的程序设计
file-oriented system 面向文件的系统
file overflow areas 文件超限[溢出]区
file packing density 文件装填密度
file permission bits 文件允许位
file placement 文件配置
file pocket 文件袋
file pointer 文件指针
file preparation 文件准备
file print 文件打印
file privilege 文件使用权,文件授权
file processing 文件处理
file protection 文件保护
file protection ring 文件保护环
file purging 文件净化
file reconstitution 文件重建
file record compaction 文件记录压缩
file record specification 文件记录说明
file recovery 文件恢复
file recovery program 文件恢复程序
file reel 文件卷
file reference 文件引用
file refuse 文件拒收
file renewal 文件更新
file reorganization 文件重组织
file restore 文件恢复
file retention period 文件保留周期
file rotation 文件更迭
file safety 文件安全
file save 文件保存
file save as 文件另存为
file scan 文件扫描
file search 文件检索
file section 文件节
file security 文件保密
file separator(FS) 文件分隔符
file separator character(FSC) 文件分隔字符

file server 文件服务器
file service time 文件服务时间
file set 文件集
file sharing 文件共享
file sharing protocol 文件共享协议
file sharing service 文件共享服务
file size 文件大小,文件长度
file skeleton 文件梗概
file space 文件空间
file space allocation map 文件空间分配图
file space management 文件空间管理
file space usage 文件空间用法
file specification 文件规范;文件说明
file status table(FST) 文件状态表
file storage 文件存储器
file stream 文件流
file structure 文件结构
file structured devices 文件结构性设备
file swapping 文件调换,文件对换
file system 文件系统
file system control block(FSCB) 文件系统控制块
file system hierarchy 文件系统层次
file system object 文件系统对象
file system transparency 文件系统透明
file tidying 文件净化
file title 文件标题
file transfer 文件转移
File Transfer Protocol(FTP) 文件传输协议
file transfer utility 文件传送实用程序
file tree 文件树
file type 文件类型
file update 文件更新
file updating 文件更新
file variable 文件变量
file version number 文件版本号
file view 文件视图
file viewer 文件视读器
file volatility 文件易变性
file volume 文件卷
FileMaker Ⅱ FileMaker Ⅱ 软件
FileMan FileMan 软件
filespec(file specification) 文件描述
filing 编档,文件编辑
filing area 编档区,存档区
filing criteria 编档准则

filing date 编档日期
filing entry 编档款目
filing hierarchy 编档层次,存档等级
filing rule 编档规则
filing section 编档段
filing system 文件编辑系统,存档系统
filing unit 编档单位
fill 填充
Fill Across Worksheets 跨工作表填入
fill algorithm 填充算法
fill area 填充区
fill bucket 填充桶
fill character 填充字符
fill color 填充颜色
fill down 向下填充
fill factor 填充因数
fill-in signal unit 填充信号单元
fill pattern 填充样式[图案]
fill style 填充样式,填充图案
fill tool 填充工具
fill up 向上填充
filled ellipse 填色椭圆
filled freeform 填色手绘多边形
filler 填充符,填充项
filler function 填充函数
filler panel 装填面板
fillet 圆角,凹面
filling algorithm 填充算法
film 膜,胶片
film circuits 薄膜电路
film clip 胶片剪辑
film conductor 膜导体
film frame 软片框
film head 薄膜磁头
film integrated circuit 膜集成电路
film microcircuit 膜微型电路
film network 膜网络
film optical modulation 薄膜光调制
film optical multiplexer 薄膜光多路复用器
film optical sensing device 软片光感器
film optical switch 薄膜光开关
film optical waveguide 薄膜光波导
film reader 胶片阅读机
film record 胶片记录
film recorder 胶片记录器
film scanner 胶片扫描仪
film storage 软片存储体

film strip 幻灯软片
film supertwist nematic(FSTN) 薄膜式超级扭曲向列型液晶显示屏幕
FILO(First In, Last Out) 先进后出
FILTCFG 过滤器配置
filter 过滤器;滤波器;滤镜
filter command 过滤器命令
filter light 取景器光
filter out 筛选出
filter primitive 过滤原语
filter response 滤波器响应
filtered accumulation 筛选累加
filtering 过滤;滤波
filtering algorithm 过滤[筛选]算法
filtering expression 筛选表达式
filtering model 过滤模型
filtering rate 过滤率
filtering rule 过滤规则
filtering schedule compiling 过滤调度编译
FINA(Following Items Not Available) 下列各项现在不可用
final 最后,最终
final address 最终地址,终结地址
final amplifier 末级放大器
final bit 终位,末位
final circuit group 最终电路群
final control element 终端控制元件
final controlling element 最终控制部件
final copy 最后拷贝,最后复本
final demand 最终需求
final electrical test 最终电气测试
final exchange line 终端交换线
final form text 最终形式文本
final form text DCA 最终格式文本文档内容结构
final group 最终组
final image status 最终映像状态
final link 最终链路
final merge phase 最后归并阶段
final model 终结模型
final optimization pass 最终优化遍历
final phase 最后阶段
final result 最终结果
final route 最终路径
final script 最后稿本
final selector 终端选择器
final signal unit 最终信号单位
final state 终态
final station 终站
final termination message 最后终止消息
final test 最终测试
final traffic route 最终信息通路
final trunk 末级中继线
final value 终值
finance communication 金融通信
finance image processor 财务图像处理程序
finance model 财务模型
finance support 金融支持
financial accounting 财务会计学
Financial Accounting Standards Board 财务会计标准委员会
financial EDI 金融业电子数据交换
financial management workstation 财务管理工作站
financial planning language 财务计划语言
financial planning system 财务计划系统
financial point-of-sale system(POS) 销售点财务系统
financial service organization(FSO) 金融服务机构
financial terminal system 金融终端系统
financial utility 财务实用程序
find 寻找,查找
find text string 寻找文本字符串
Find What 查找内容
Find Whole Words Only 全字匹配
Finder (Mac OS)Finder 软件
finder 寻迹器;定位程序
finding 寻找,查找,定位
fine 细微的,精细的
fine adjustment 微调,细调
fine control 微调控制
fine grain 细粒度
fine-grain parallel processing 细粒度并行处理
fine grained 细粒度
fine-grained parallel computer 细粒度并行计算机
fine-grained parallel computer system 细粒度并行计算机系统
fine index 细索引
fine leak 微细泄露
fine line 细线,细实线

fine pattern 精细图案	热分析
fine pitch device(FPD) 细间距器件	finite field 有限域
fine pitch technology(FPT) 细间距技术	finite function 有限函数
fine positioning 精定位	finite game 有限博弈,有限对策
fine sort 细排序	finite goal 有限目标
fine tune 细调谐	finite group 有限群
fineness 光洁度,细度	finite impulse response 有限脉冲响应
fineness of scanning 扫描线密度	finite impulse response digital filter (FIRF) 有限冲激响应数字滤波器
FINGER (Unix)显示登录到本地或远程系统用户信息的程序	finite interval 有限区间
finger 手指;指状接头	finite iteration 有限迭代
finger board 键盘	finite length string 有限长度串
finger control 手动控制	finite matrix 有穷矩阵
finger-tip control 手动按钮控制	finite memory 有限内存
fingerprint 指纹	finite nonempty set 有限非空集
fingerprint analysis 指纹分析	finite population 有限总体
fingerprint reader 指纹阅读器	finite precision number 有限精度数
finish condition 终结条件	finite sequence 有限序列
finish node 最终节点	finite set 有限集
finish time 完成时间	finite-state automaton(FSA) 有限态自动机
finite 有限的	
finite aggregate 有限聚合	finite state grammar 有限态文法
finite automata 有限自动机(单数)	finite-state machine(FSM) 有限状态机
finite automaton 有限自动机,有穷自动机	finite-state sequential machine 有限状态时序机
finite automaton module 有穷自动机模型	finite subset 有限子集
finite automaton with ε-moves 带ε动作的有限自动机	finite substitution 有限置换
	finite table 有限表
finite chain 有限链	finite time average 有限时间均值
finite controller 有限控制器	finite topology 有限拓扑
finite difference 有限差分	finite transducer 有限转换器,有限翻译机
finite difference method 有限差分法	
finite difference solution 有限差分解	finite turn pushdown automaton 有限转折下推自动机
finite difference thermal analysis 有限差分热分析	
	FIPS (Federal Information Processing Standards) 联邦信息处理标准(美)
finite dimensional space 有限维空间	
finite element 有限元	Fire code 法尔码
finite element analysis(FEA) 有限元分析法	fire control computer 射击控制计算机
finite element equation 有限元方程	fire control system 炮火控制系统
finite element mesh generation 有限元网格生成	fire proof 防火
	Fireball "火球"硬盘(昆腾)
finite element method 有限元法	Firewall 防火墙
finite element model 有限元模型	FireWire FireWire 总线规范(IEEE 1394)
finite element modeling 有限元建模	
finite element space 有限元空间	firing 点火;引发
finite element thermal analysis 有限元	firing game 射击对策
	firing rule 点火规则

firm core 固核
firmware 固件,固化软件
firmware building block 固件积木块
firmware circuitry 固件电路
firmware code 固件代码
firmware compatibility 固件兼容性
firmware engineering 固件工程
firmware instructions 固件指令
firmware limitation 固件限制
firmware monitor 固件监控程序
firmware option 固件选项
firmware package 固件程序包
firmware program 固件程序
firmware ROM 固件只读存储器
firmware support 固件支持
firmware testing 固件测试
first approximation 首次近似
first boot 第一引导,首先启动
first bounded interval measure 首次有界区界度量
first capital 句首字母大写
first carrier 第一载波
first-choice route 主选[首选]路径
first column(FCFS) 首列
first-come first-serve(FCFS) 先到先服务
first connected port(FCFS) 首先连接的端口
first data multiplexer 第一级数据多路复用器
first draft 初稿
first element of chain 链中第一元素
first-ended first-out(FEFO) 先结束先送
first entry table 初始输入表
first fit algorithm 首次适合算法
first-fit-decreasing rule(FFD) 首次适合下降规则
first fit method 首次满足法
first-fit strategy 最先适合策略
first generation computer 第一代计算机
first-in-chain 链中首单元
first-in first-out(FIFO) 先进先出
first-in first-out buffering 先进先出缓冲法
first-in first-out memory 先进先出内存
first-in first-out page replacement 先进先出页替换

first-in last-out(FILO) 先进后出
first item inspection 首件检验
first item list 首项表
first jitter 初始抖动
first level address 第一级地址
first-level memory 第一级内存
first-level message member 一级消息成员
first-level of packaging 一级组装
first-level storage 一级存储器
first line 首行
first-line form advance 首行进纸
first-line indent 首行缩进
first loop feature 主环路特制适配件
first moment 一阶矩
first normal form 第一范式
first-of-chain 链中首元素
first operand 第一操作数
first order condition 一阶条件
first order goal 一阶目标
first order logic axiom system 一阶逻辑公理系统
first order model logic system 一阶模式逻辑系统
first-order modeling 一阶模型创建
first order predicate calculus 一阶谓词演算
first order predicate calculus formal system 一阶谓词演算形式系统
first order predicate logic 一阶谓词逻辑
first-order servo system 一阶伺服系统
first-order subroutine 一级子程序
first-out page replacement policy 先进先出页面替换策略
first page indicator 首页指示器
first party release 主叫方拆线
first passage time 首次通过时间
first read rate(FRR) 首次识别率
first ready first execute(FRFE) 先就绪先执行
first recursion theorem 第一递归定理
first remove subroutine 第一级转移子例程,直接引入子程序
first selecting 初次选择
first-serve scheduling policy 先来先服务调度策略
first speaker 发话端

first symbol 开头符号
first term 首项
first variable 第一变量
fish-eye lens image 鱼眼透镜图像
FIT(Failure InTensity) 失效强度
FIT(First Indication of Trouble) 首次故障指示
FIT FIT语言
fit 固定;调整;拟合
fit in windows 装满窗口
fit to page 装满页面
fit wave in windows 使波形满窗口
fitness 适合度
fitted model 拟合模型
fitting 拟合法
fitting criterion 拟合准则
fitting surface 拟合曲面
five-bit byte 五位字节
five-bit code 五单位码
five-in-a-row 五子棋
five-layer four-beterojunction diode 五层四异质结二极管
five-level code 五单位码
five-unit code 五单位码
fix 固定,校正;定影
fix level 固定级
fix point theory 不动点理论
fixed 固定的
fixed-active tooling 固定式主动装置
fixed address 固定地址
fixed allocation 固定分配
fixed area 固定区域,常驻区域
fixed aspect ratio 固定宽高比
fixed attribute 固定属性
fixed beacon guidance 固定光源式导引
fixed beam 固定杆件
fixed beam scanner 固定光束扫描器
fixed bias 固定偏置
fixed binary 定点二进制
fixed bit rate 固定位速率
fixed block 固定块
fixed-block-architecture(FBA) 固定块结构
fixed-block architecture device 固定块结构设备
fixed block format 固定字块格式
fixed block length 固定块长度
fixed block length transmission 固定块长度传输
fixed block transmission 定长块传输
fixed box 固定框
fixed class 固定类
fixed command control 定值控制
fixed connector 固定连接器
fixed control computer 固定控制计算机
fixed coordinate system 固定坐标系
fixed cost 固定成本;固定开销
fixed currency symbol 固定位置货币符号
fixed cycle 固定循环;固定周期
fixed cycle operation 固定周期操作
fixed data 固定数据
fixed data name 固定数据名
fixed decimal 固定十进制数
fixed disk 固定磁盘
fixed disk drive 固定磁盘驱动器
fixed disk setup program(FDISK) 硬盘设置程序
fixed-disk storage(FDS) 固定磁盘存储器
fixed expense 固定费用[开销]
fixed fault 固定性故障
fixed fiber-optic connector 光纤固定连接器
fixed field 固定字段,固定区域
fixed form 固定形式;固定表单
fixed form coding 固定格式编码
fixed format 固定格式
fixed format input 固定格式输入
fixed format language 固定格式语言
fixed format menu 固定格式菜单
fixed-format message 固定格式消息
fixed-frequency monitor 固定频率监视器
fixed head 固定磁头
fixed-head disk 固定磁头磁盘
fixed head disk drive 固定头磁盘驱动器
fixed header prefix 固定标题前缀
fixed-image graphics 固定图像显示
fixed increment rule 固定增量规则
fixed information 固定信息
fixed insertion 固定插入
fixed instruction set graphic controller 固定指令集图形控制器
fixed interconnection matrix 固定互联矩阵

fixed-length 固定长度
fixed-length block 定长块
fixed length code(FLC) 定长码
fixed length data 定长数据
fixed length field 定长字段
fixed length instruction 定长指令
fixed-length record 定长记录
fixed length record file 定长记录文件
fixed-length record format 固定长度记录格式
fixed length word 定长字
fixed-line number 固定行号
fixed linkage mechanism 固定联结机构
fixed mask type ROM 固定掩膜只读存储器
fixed member 固定成员
fixed membership class 固定属藉类
fixed memory 固定内存
fixed name 固定名称
fixed network 固定网络
fixed numeric format 固定数字格式
fixed optical attenuator 固定光学衰减器
fixed optical fiber connection 固定光纤连接
fixed ordering procedure 固定排序过程
fixed overflow 定点溢出
fixed overlayable segment 固定可覆盖段
fixed page 固定页
fixed partitioning 固定分区
fixed-passive tooling 固定式受动装置
fixed permanent segment 固定永久段
fixed pin 固定插销
fixed pitch 固定间距
fixed placement file 固定配置文件
fixed-plus-variable structure 固定加可变结构
fixed-point 定点
fixed point arithmetic 定点算术
fixed-point binary 定点二进数
fixed point calculation 定点计算
fixed point computer 定点计算机
fixed point computing rule 不动点计算规则
fixed-point data representation 定点数据表示法
fixed point division exception 定点除法异常
fixed-point notation 定点表示法
fixed-point number 定点数
fixed point operation 定点运算
fixed-point part 定点部分
fixed-point representation 定点表示法
fixed point theorem 不动点定理
fixed point value 定点数值
fixed portion 定点部分
fixed position addressing 固定位置寻址
fixed program computer 固定程序计算机
fixed radix notation 固定基数记数法
fixed-radix numeration system 固定基数记数系统
fixed radix scale 固定基数记数法
fixed routine 固定例程
fixed routing 固定路由选择
fixed-sequence robot 固定顺序机器人
fixed sequential format 固定顺序格式
fixed set order 固定集次序
fixed single 固定单独的
fixed size record 定长记录
fixed source entropy 固定源熵
fixed space 固定空格
fixed-stop robot 端止机器人,定点机器人
fixed storage 固定存储器
fixed thresholding 固定阈值
fixed time increment 固定时间增量
fixed value 固定值
fixed width font 定宽字体
fixed word length 固定字长
fixed-word length computer 固定字长计算机
fixer 定影剂
fixing 定影
fixpoint theory 不动点理论,定点理论
fixture 夹具
Fkey 功能键程序
FL(File Lockout) 文件锁定
flag 标志,标记,特征位
flag bit 标志位
flag byte 标志字节
flag check 标志检验
flag code 标志码,特征码
flag condition 标志条件
flag control 标志控制

flag data 标志数据
flag event 标志事件
flag indicator 标志指示符
flag lines 标志线
flag of frame 帧标志
flag operand 标志操作数
flag register 标志寄存器
flag sequence 标志顺序,标志序列
flag setting peripheral 设置标志的外围设备
flag status register 标志状态寄存器
flag tests 标志测试
flagged term index 标记词索引
flagging preposition 标志介词
flame （网上）煽情,激怒
flame bait （网上）激怒诱饵
flame war （网上）论战
flare 光斑
Flash 网页动画制作软件(Macromedia)
flash BIOS 快擦写基本输入/输出系统
flash button （网页上的）动感按钮
flash call 特急呼叫
flash card 闪存卡;快擦写存储卡
flash E2PROM 快擦写存储器
flash exposure 闪烁曝光
flash information service 特快信息服务
flash item 快速产品项目;简短项目
flash mass memory 大容量闪存
flash memory 快速擦写存储器,闪存
flash memory writer 闪存写入程序
flash movie file 闪烁动感影像文件
flash override 特级
flash ROM 快擦写只读存储器
flashback 回溯
flashing 闪动
flat 平面,平板
flat address space 平直(线性)地址空间
flat bed plotter 平板式绘图仪
flat-bed scanner 平板扫描仪
flat-bed scanning 平板扫描
flat-bed transmitter 平面传真发送机
flat cable 扁平电缆
flat comb binder 扁平梳状装订器
flat fading 等比[平坦]衰落
flat file 平面文件
flat file database 平面文件数据库
flat-file database management program 平面文件式数据库管理程序
flat file directory 平面[线性]文件目录
flat file system 平面文件系统
flat flexible cable 带状柔性电缆
flat grid structure 平面网格结构
flat leads 共平面引线
flat loss 平坦损耗
flat memory model 平面内存模型
flat namespace 无层次命名空间
flat naming 无层次命名机制
flat optical cable 扁平[带状]光缆
flat order 平坦序
flat organization 平面型组织
flat pack 扁平封装
flat package 扁平封装组件
flat panel display 平板显示器
flat-pattern generation 展开图的生成
flat pyramid structure 扁平式金字塔结构
flat response 平坦响应
flat ribbon connector 扁平带状连接器
flat screen 平面屏幕
flat shading 平坦阴影设置,均匀阴影
flat television receiver 平板电视接收机
flat top response 平顶响应
flat zone 平坦区
flatbed plotter 平板绘图仪
flatness 平坦性,平直度
flatpack 扁平封装组件
flatten 平面化
flattener （纸张）压平器
FLAVORS FLAVORS语言
flaw 裂缝,缺陷
flaw detector 探伤仪
flexboot 多选择启动
flexibility 伸缩性,灵活性,适应性
Flexible Algebraic Scientific Translator (FAST) 弹性代数科学翻译例程
flexible array 灵活阵列
flexible assembly cell 柔性装配单元
flexible asynchronous communication support 柔性异步通信支持
flexible automation 灵活自动化
flexible box 柔性框
flexible bus 软总线
flexible cell 灵活单元
flexible circuit 软电路

flexible compiler 灵活编译程序
flexible connect 柔性连接
flexible disk 软磁盘,可替换磁盘
flexible disk cartridge 盒式可更换磁盘[器]
flexible disk drive 活动盘[软盘]驱动
flexible distributed numerical control 灵活分布式数值控制
flexible disk pack 软磁盘组[构]
flexible header structure 柔性标题结
flexible information transport capability 柔性信息传输能力
flexible joint 软[挠性]连接[手]
flexible joint manipulator 软关节机械
flexible machining cell(FMC) 弹性加工单元
flexible machining module(FMM) 弹性加工模块,灵活加工模块
flexible machining system 弹性加工系统
flexible manufacturing 柔性制造
flexible manufacturing center 柔性加工中心
flexible manufacturing system(FMS) 弹性制造系统,灵活加工系统
flexible network 柔性网络
flexible object manipulation 灵活对象操纵
flexible package 灵活组件[统]
flexible placement system 灵活布局系
flexible print circuit 柔性印刷电路
flexible robot 柔性机器人
flexible service 柔性服务
flexible symbol 可变符号
flexible tolerance algorithm 可伸缩容限算法
flexible tool 灵活工具
flexible topology 灵活拓扑
flexible tracing 灵活跟踪
flexible waveguide 柔性波导管
flexible wire 软线
flexowriter 电传打字机
flexural modulus 挠曲模量
flexural vibration 挠曲振动
flexure 挠曲,弯曲
FLFT(Full Load Frame Time) 满负荷帧时间
FLG(FLaG) 标记,标志

flicker 闪烁
flicker bit 闪烁位
flicker effect 闪烁效应
flicker free capacity 无闪烁容量
flicker-free frequency 无闪烁频率
flicker-free image 无闪烁图像
flicker frequency 闪烁频率
flicker image display 闪示图像
flicker rate 闪烁率
flickering 闪烁
flight environment simulation 飞行环境仿真
flight path computer 航线计算机
flight simulator 飞行仿真器
flight simulator software 飞行仿真器软件
flip 交换;翻转
flip all 全部翻转
flip boot virus 倒转引导病毒
flip-chip 倒装芯片
flip-chip bonding 倒装芯片结合法
flip-flop 触发器
flip horizontal 水平翻转
flip network 交换网络
flip over 翻页
flip vertical 垂直翻转
flippy 双面软盘
flippy board 跳接板
float 浮动
float area 浮动区域
float attribute 浮动属性
float constant 浮点常数
float control 浮动控制
float dollar sign 浮动美元符号
float factor 浮动因子
float head 浮动头,浮动磁头
float palette 浮动调色板
floating action 无静差作用
floating add 浮点加
floating address 浮动地址
floating address register 浮动地址寄存器
floating area 浮动区
floating buffer 浮动缓冲区
floating buses 浮动总线
floating character 浮动字符
floating command line 浮动命令行
floating control 浮动控制

floating controller 无定位控制器
floating currency sign 浮动货币符号
floating-decimal abstract coding system (FACS) 浮点十进制压缩编码系统
floating-decimal accumulator 浮点十进制数累加器
floating-decimal arithmetic 浮点十进制数算法
floating-decimal subroutine 浮点十进制数运算子例程
floating display 浮动显示器
floating executive 浮动执行程序
floating-gate avalanche-injection metal-oxide-semiconductor 浮栅雪崩注入金属氧化物半导体
floating head 浮动磁头
floating image 浮动图像
floating insertion character 浮动插入字符
floating insertion editing 浮动插入编辑
floating interpretive program 浮点解释程序
floating master 浮动主控设备
floating multiply 浮点乘法
floating neutral 浮动中心,浮置中线
floating normalized control 浮点规格化控制
floating object code 浮动目标码
floating overflow trap 浮点溢出自陷
floating pattern 浮动样式
floating point 浮点
floating-point arithmetic 浮点运算
floating-point arithmetic hardware 浮点算术运算硬件
floating-point arithmetic library 浮点算术程序库
floating-point arithmetic operation 浮点算术运算
floating point array processor 浮点阵列处理机
floating-point base 浮点基数
floating-point calculation 浮点计算
floating-point coefficient 浮点尾数,浮点系数
floating-point compaction 浮点简缩
floating-point computer 浮点计算机
floating-point co-processor (FPCP) 浮点协处理机
floating-point constant 浮点常数
floating-point data representation 浮点数据表示法
floating point divide exception 浮点除法异常
floating-point double word 浮点双字
floating-point exponent 浮点阶
floating-point format 浮点格式
floating-point feature 浮点特性
floating-point functional unit 浮点功能单元
floating-point hardware 浮点硬件
floating-point input format 浮点输入格式
floating-point instruction group 浮点指令组
floating-point instruction system 浮点指令系统
floating-point literal 浮点文字[直接量]
floating-point notation 浮点记数法
floating-point number 浮点数
floating-point operation 浮点运算
floating-point overflow 浮点溢出
floating-point package (FPP) 浮点软件包
floating-point precision 浮点精度
floating point processor 浮点处理器
floating-point radix 浮点基数
floating-point register 浮点寄存器
floating-point representation 浮点表示法
floating-point routine 浮点例程
floating-point single word 浮点单字
floating-point subroutines 浮点子例程
floating-point system 浮点制,浮点系统
floating point transformation 浮点转换
floating point underflow 浮点下溢
floating symbolic address 浮动符号地址
floating zero 浮动零点
flood filling algorithm 洪泛填充算法
flood gun 泛射电子枪
flooding 满屏幕;泛滥
flooding method 洪泛法,漫溢法
flooding routing 洪泛式路由选择
floor 基底

floor function 向下取整函数
floor layout 芯片布局设计图
floor of number 向下取整数
floor plan 芯片结构平面布置图
floor planning 芯片布局
floor space (设备)占地面积
floor time 停机时间
floor-to-floor time 在机时间
floppy 软磁盘
floppy data entry system 软磁盘数据输入系统
floppy disc(FD) 活动盘(通常指光盘)
floppy disk(FD) 软磁盘,活动盘
floppy disk controller(FDC) 软盘控制器
floppy disk drives 软盘驱动器
floppy disk format 活动盘格式化
floppy-disk interface 软盘接口
floppy-disk loader 软盘载入器
floppy disk material 软磁盘材料
floppy disk operating system 软磁盘操作系统
floppy disk reference point 软磁盘参考点
floppy-disk sector format 软盘扇区格式
floppy disk tracks 软盘磁道
floppy-disk types 软磁盘类型
floppy drive swap 软盘驱动器对换
floppy interface connector 软盘接口连接器
floppy stringy 活动磁带
FLOPS(FLoating point Operations Per Second) 每秒浮点运算次数
flops 每秒浮点运算次数
Floptical 磁光盘
floptical disk 光磁软盘
floptical disk drive 光磁盘驱动器
flow 流量,流动,流程
flow analysis 流程分析
flow-augmenting path 流-增广路径
flow chart 流程图
flow comment 信息流注释
flow conservation condition 流守恒条件
flow control 流控制
flow-control algorithm 流控制算法
flow-control mechanism 流控制机构
flow-control scheme 流控制方案

flow-control unit 流控制单位
flow diagram 流程图
flow direction 流向
flow line 流程线
flow of control 控制流
flow of information 信息流
flow of logical control 逻辑控制流
flow of work 工作流程
flow potential 流势
flow prediction 流量预测
flow process chart 工作流程图
flow-process diagram 流程图
flow register 流程寄存器
flow relation 流关系
flow shop 流水式车间
flow specification 处理过程明细
flow table 流程表
flow trace 流程踪迹
flow tracing 流程追踪
flowchart 流程图
flowchart connector 流程图连接符
flowchart convention 流程图惯则
flowchart microprogramming language 流程图微程序设计语言
flowchart package 流程图组件
flowchart schema 流程图模式
flowchart symbol 流程图符号
flowchart technique 流程图技巧
flowchart template 流程图模板
flowchart text 流程图文本
flowcharter 流程图绘制器
flowcharting 流程图编制
Floyd-Warshall algorithm 弗洛依德-瓦歇尔算法
Floyd's algorithm 弗洛依德算法
Floyed-Evans production language (FPL) 费洛伊德-伊万斯产生式语言
Floyed production 费洛伊德产生式
fluctuation 波动,起伏
fluent computers 流畅计算机
fluid computer 射流计算机
fluid container 减震箱
fluid logic 流体逻辑
fluid network 流体网络
fluidic sensor 射流传感器
fluidics 射流学
fluorescent display 荧光显示器

fluorescent paint 荧光涂料
fluorescent radiation 荧光辐射
fluorescent screen 荧光屏,屏幕
flush 整版,对齐;清仓
flush closedown 清仓关闭
flush left 左边排齐
flush out 内容清除
flush printed board 齐平印刷电路板
flush right 右边排齐
flush stop 清除停机
flushing 冲洗;(流水线)排空
flushing time (流水线)排空时间
flutter 颤动,抖动
flutter and wow 速度不均匀性,抖动
flutter echo 颤动回波
flux 助焊剂;磁力线,磁通
flux coating 助焊剂涂敷
flux density 通量[磁通]密度
flux leakage 漏磁
flux meter 磁通量计
flux reversal 磁通翻转
flux rise time 辐射流上升时间
flux sensor 流量传感器
flux transition 磁通转变点
flux waveform compensation 磁通波形补偿
fly 浮动,飞驰
fly-by 飞过
fly-by-wire system 电操纵飞行系统
fly-in 飞入
fly lens 蝇眼透镜
flyback 回扫,回程扫描
flyback time 回扫时间
flying head 浮动头
flying height 飞驰高度,浮动高度
flying optical head 飞行光记录头
flying printer 飞击式打印机
flying speed 飞速,浮动速度
flying spot 飞点
flying-spot scanner 飞点扫描器
flying spot scanning 飞点扫描
flying spot scanning digitizer 飞点扫描数字化仪
flying squadron 机动工作组
flying zone 磁头飞行区域
Flynn classification schema 弗林分类法
flywheeling 飞轮技术
FM(Flash Memory) 快擦写存储器,闪存
FM(Frequency Modulation) 调频
FM(Frequency Multiplexing) 频分多路复用
FM recording 调频记录方式
FM-TOWNS FM-TOWNS 多媒体计算机(富士通)
FMS(Forms Management System) 格式管理系统(DEC)
FMVA(Full-Motion Video Adapter) 全动态视频适配器
FN(Functional Network) 功能型网络
FNA(Fujitsu Network Architecture) 富士通网络体系结构
FNC(Federal Networking Council) 联邦网络建设委员会(美)
FNP(Front end Network Processor) 前端网络处理机
focal distance 焦距
focal length 焦距
focal plane 聚焦平面
focal spot 焦点
FOCUS FOCUS 数据库管理系统
focus jump 焦点跳步
focus servo 聚焦伺服
focus window 关注窗口
focused addressing 瞄准寻址
focused ion beam (FIB) 聚焦离子束
focusing 聚焦
focusing coil 聚焦线圈
fog 雾状效果
FOID(Fiber-Optic Interface Device) 光纤接口设备
foil 箔,薄片
FOIRL(Fiber Optic Inter Repeater Link) 光纤中继链路
fold 折叠,合并
fold-over distortion 重叠失真
foldable operation 可折叠运算
folded binary code 对称[折叠]二进制码
folded-over noise 迭加[重叠]噪声
folder 文件夹
folder path 文件夹路径
folder properties 文件夹特性
folding 折叠,合并
folding hashing method 折叠散列法
folding ratio 折合比
folio 页码

follow 跟随
follow copy 跟随复制
follow hyperlink 跟踪超链接
follow margins 紧贴版心边界
follow-on 继续
follow-on bus cycle 继续总线周期
follow symbol 后继符号
follow up control 跟踪[随动]控制
follow-up file 跟踪文件
follow-up servo 随动伺服
follow-up signal 跟踪[随动]信号
follower 跟踪器,读图器;随动机构
following error 随动误差
font 字体,字模,铅字
font card 字模插卡
font cartridge 字模扩充盒
font change(FC) 字体改换
font-change character 字体变换字符
font-change control character 字体更换控制符
font compiler 字模编译器
Font/DA Mover 字型/桌面附件转移程序
font data 字模数据
font data set 字模数据集
font disk 字模盘
font downloader 字型载入程序
font editor 字型编辑器
font face 字体显示样式
font family 字模系列
font file 字模[字体]文件
font generator 字模发生器
font ID conflict 字型识别码冲突
font installer 字体安装程序
font library 字库
font membership 字体组,字模集
font memory 字体存储器
font metric 字型量测
font number 字型编号
font object 字体对象
font on-line 联机字体
font outline 字体外形,字模轮廓
font page 字体页
font pattern 字型,字体样式
font resource 字体资源
font reticle 字型格
font scalar 字型转换器
font size 字型大小,字体尺寸
font smoothing 字型平滑化
font store 字型库
font styles 字体式样
font substitution 字型替换
font type 字体类型
font utility 字模实用程序
FONTAC FONTAC计算机
Fontographer Fontographer排版软件
Fontware Fontware字模软件
footage 尺码
footer 页脚;页小计
footer boilerplate 页脚样板文件
footing area 合计区域
footnote 脚注
footpedal 脚踏开关
footprint 映罩表面,涵盖表面;占地面积
FOR clause 循环子句
FOR list 循环元素表
FOR local 转市话网
FOR long distance 转长途电信网
FOR loop 条件循环
FOR loop optimization 循环优化
FOR/NEXT loop FOR/NEXT循环语句
FOR part 循环参数部分
FOR tablet binding 用于标签装订
for your information(FYI) 供参考
forbidden cell 禁用单元格
forbidden character 禁用字符
forbidden code 禁用代码
forbidden combination 禁用组合
forbidden combination check 禁用组合校验
forbidden-digit check 禁用数字核对
forbidden list 禁用表
forbidden-pulse combination check 非法脉冲组合校验
forbidden value 禁用值
Force Force编译程序
force 人工转移,强制
force administration data system (FADS) 强制管理数据系统
force autosave 强制自动保存
force brute 强行攻击,蛮攻技术
force control 力控制
force-controlled motion commands 力控制运动指令

force disconnect 强制断开
force feedback 力反馈
force finite element method 力有限元法
force placement method 力向布局法
force quit 强制退出
force revert 强制回复
force sense 力觉
force sensor 力传感器
forced air cooling 强制风冷
forced coding program 强制编码程序
forced convection cooling 强迫对流冷却
forced cooling 强制冷却
forced display 强制显示
forced interrupt 强制中断
forced load 强制装入
forced page break 强制换页
forced-path testing 强制性路径测试
forced priority 强制优先权
forced quarantine scenario 强制隔离方案
forced release 强行拆线
forced rerouting 强制迁回
forced response 强迫响应
forced start 强制启动
forced termination 强行终止
forced ventilation 强制通风
forced vibration 强迫振荡
Ford-Fulkerson's algorithm 福特-福克森算法
forearm 前臂
forecast error 预测误差
forecast horizon 预测界限
forecast period 预测期
forecasting 预测,预报
forecasting function 预报函数
forecasting model 预测模型
foreground 前台;前景
foreground-background communication 前-后台通信
foreground/background processing 前后台作业
foreground-background scheduling 前后台调度
foreground color 前景颜色
foreground display 前景显示
foreground image 前景图像
foreground-initiated background job 前台引发的后台作业

foreground initiation 前台初始化
foreground initiator 前台启动程序
foreground job 前台作业
foreground message processing program 前台消息处理程序
foreground mode 前台操作方式
foreground monitor 前台监控程序
foreground partition 前台分区
foreground process 前台进程
foreground process group 前台进程组
foreground processing 前台处理
foreground processor 前台处理机
foreground program 前台程序
foreground region 前景区域;前台区域
foreground scheduler 前台调度程序
foreground task 前台任务
foreign area translation 局外域译码
foreign attachment 局外连接
foreign document 外来文献
foreign exchange line 跨区交换电路
foreign exchange service 跨区交换服务
foreign host 外来主机
foreign key 外关键字
foreign medium 外部媒体
foreign numbering plan area 外部编号平面域
foreseeable fault 可预见故障
forest 森林
forest coding 数据树编码
Forest & Tree "森林与树"程序
forged detach requests 伪造脱离请求
forgetfulness 遗忘
forgetting factor 遗忘因数
forgiving system 宽容系统
FORK 派生指令;分岔,衍生
fork dispatcher 附加分派程序
fork instruction 衍生[分岔]指令
fork primitive 派生元语,衍生原语
fork process 派生进程
forked working 分叉工作方式
form 窗体;表格;格式,形式
form activation 窗体激活
form advance 进页,换页
form analysis 形式分析
form-based icon-aided pictorial query language 基于窗体的图示化图像查询语言
form builder 窗体构造程序

form configuration file 窗体配置文件
form container 窗体容器
form control buffer 格式控制缓冲器
form controls toolbar 窗体控件工具
form definition 窗体定义 ⌊条
form delimiter option 窗体定界符选项
form factor 格式参数,形态系数
form feed(FF) 表格馈送;换页
form feed character(FF) 换页字符
form feed out 格式馈送
form feeding 表格馈送
form filling dialogs 填表对话
form flash 图像生成
form flash negative 格式投影底片
form flash unit 格式投影器
form group 窗体组
form letter 格式化信件
form library provider 窗体库提供者
form management 格式管理
form map 格式映像
form name 格式名;窗体名称
form of subscript 下标格式
form overlay 格式覆盖
form page 窗体页
form parameter 形式参数
form processing 窗体处理
form receiving tray 落纸架,收纸架
form representation 窗体表示法
form resize 窗体改变大小
form resolution 窗体解析[映射]
form server 窗体服务器[程序]
form set 窗体集
form sheet 格式表
form skip 跳页
form stop 纸完停印
form stopper 纸完停印装置
form system 表格系统
form template 窗体模板
form type 窗体类型
form view 窗体视图;形式观察
form viewer 窗体观察程序
form wizard 窗体向导
Formac language Formac 语言
formal 形式的,正式的
formal address 形式地址
formal adjoint 形式伴随
formal analogy 正规类推
formal argument 形式参数,形式变元
formal calculus 形式演算
formal check 形式检验
formal communication 形式通信
formal construction 形式构造
formal control 形式控制
formal declarator 形式说明符
formal deduction 形式演绎
formal definition 形式定义
formal discretization error 形式离散误差
formal grammar 形式文法
formal language 形式语言
formal language and automaton 形式语言与自动机
formal language theory 形式语言理论
formal logic 形式逻辑
formal lower bound 形式下界 ⌈述
formal model description 形式模型描
formal notation 形式标记,形式记号
formal parameter 形式参数
formal parameter list 形式参数表
formal parameter part 形式参数部分
formal parameter table 形式参数表
formal proof 形式证明
formal push-down automaton 形式下推自动机
formal reasoning 形式推理
formal row 形式行
formal rule 形式规则
formal security policy model 形式化安全策略模型
formal semantic 形式语义
formal semantics 形式语义学
formal specification 形式规格说明
formal specification of protocol 协议的形式规范,协议形式说明
formal syntax 形式语法
formal system 形式系统
formal test 形式检验
formal theorem 形式定理
formal top-level specification 形式化高级设计规范
formal variable 形式变量
formal verification 形式化验证
formalization 形式化
formant 共振峰,构形
formant vocoder 共振峰声码器

FORMAT 格式化命令
format 格式;格式化
format 0 MIDI file 0型MIDI文件
format 1 MIDI file 1型MIDI文件
format analyzer 格式分析器
Format Axis Scale 坐标轴刻度格式
Format Callout 标注格式
Format Category Labels 坐标轴刻度线格式
format character 格式字符
format character set 格式字符集
format check 格式校验
format control 格式控制
format conversion 格式转换
format conversion language 格式转换语言
Format Corners 坐标轴刻度格式
Format Data Labels 数据标志格式
Format Data Series 数据系列格式
format definition 格式定义
format description statement 格式说明语句
format display 格式显示
format effector(FE) 格式控制字符
format effector character 格式控制字符
format error 格式错误
format field descriptor 格式域描述符
format file 格式文件
format grammar 格式文法
Format Gridlines 格式化网格线
format identification field 格式识别字段
format implicit address instruction 格式隐地址指令
format item 格式元素,格式项
format label 格式标号
Format Legend Entry 图例项格式
format line 格式行
format list 格式表
format loop 格式环
format macro 格式宏
format member 格式成员
Format Object 对象格式
format output 格式输出
Format Overlay 覆盖图表格式
Format Painter 格式刷(微软)
format parameter entry sequence 格式参数输入项序列
format parameter input 格式参数输入
format pattern 格式图像
Format Plot Area 图形区格式
format primary 格式初等量
format program 格式化程序
format recognition 格式识别
format selection 格式选择
format specification 格式说明
FORMAT statement 格式语句
format string 格式串
Format Trendline 趋势线格式
formatless information 未格式化信息
formatless input 无格式输入
formatted capacity 格式化容量
formatted data model 格式化数据模型
formatted diskette 已格式化软盘
formatted display 格式化显示
formatted dump 格式化转储
formatted field 格式化字段
formatted file 格式化文件
formatted image 格式化图像
formatted input/output 格式化输入输出
formatted logic record 格式化逻辑记录
formatted log on 格式化注册
formatted mass storage 格式化海量存储器
formatted message 格式化报文
formatted program interface 格式化程序界面
formatted read statement 格式读语句
formatted record 格式化记录
formatted request 格式化请求
formatted storage capacity 格式化存储容量
formatted systems services 系统格式化功能
formatted text 格式化文本
formatted volume 格式化卷
formatted write statement 格式化写语句
formatter 格式器;格式化程序
formatting 格式编辑;格式化
formatting layout table 布局表格式化
formed 成形的,有格式的
formed language 有格式语言
formed wire contact 线簧式插头
former 前者;成形设备

former surrounding case　前环境角色
forming process　成形过程
forms control buffer(FCB)　格式控制用缓冲器
formula　公式
formula ALGOL　公式 ALGOL 语言
formula-as-type embedding　作为类型的公式嵌入
formula bar　公式横条
formula extrapolation　公式外推
formula language　公式语言
formula manipulation　公式处理
formula manipulation compiler　公式处理编译程序
formula manipulation language　公式处理语言
formula manipulation system　公式处理系统
formula model　公式模型
formula recognition　公式识别
formula translator　公式翻译程序
formula translator language　公式翻译语言,FORTRAN语言
formulary　准则集
formulate　写成公式,用公式表达
formulation　公式化,系统阐述;模式
formulator　公式化程序
formwork　样板,模板
FORTH language　FORTH 语言
FORTH machine　FORTH 计算机
FORTH microprocessor　FORTH 微处理器
FORTRAN(FORmula TRANslator)　公式翻译语言,FORTRAN 语言
FORTRAN-77 cross compiler　FORTRAN-77 交叉编译程序
FORTRAN 90　FORTRAN 90 语言
FORTRAN Ⅳ　FORTRAN Ⅳ语言
FORTRAN Ⅳ cross assembler　FORTRAN Ⅳ交叉汇编程序
FORTRAN Ⅳ simulator　FORTRAN Ⅳ仿真程序
FORTRAN D　FORTRAN D语言
fortuitous　意外[偶发]失真
fortuitous conductor　意外导体
fortuitous distortion　偶然[偶发]失真
fortuitous jitter　偶发颤动
FORTUNE　《幸福》杂志(美)

forums　论坛
forward　前向,正向
forward-acting code　正向作用码,前向纠错码
forward and store　存储转发
forward-backward counter　双向计数器,可逆计数器
forward bias　正向偏压
forward busying　正向占线
forward chained reasoning　正向链推
forward chaining　正向链接
forward channel(FOCH)　前向通道,正向信道
forward clearing　正向拆线
forward compatible　向前兼容
forward counter　正向计数器
forward current　正向电流
forward difference　前向差分
forward dynamic programming　前向动态规划
forward echo　正向回波
forward error correction(FEC)　前向纠错
forward error protection　前向差错防护
forward explicit congestion notification (FECN)　前向显式拥塞通告
forward error recovery　前向纠错
forward file recovery　前向文件恢复
forward hold　正向保持
forward indicator bit　前向指示位
forward inheritance　正向继承
forward kernel　正向核
forward link　正向连接,前向链接
forward path　正向通路
forward point　正向指针
forward production system　正向产生式系统
forward pruning　正向修剪
forward reading　正向读出
forward reasoning　正向推理
forward recall signal　正向重呼信号
forward recovery　向前恢复
forward reduction　前向递归
forward reference　正向引用
forward robot problem-solving system　正向机器人问题求解系统
forward rule based deduction system　基于规则的正向演绎系统

forward scan 正向扫描
forward scatter 前向[正向]散射
forward scheduling 向前调度
forward search 向前[正向]搜索
forward seizure 正向占线
forward sequence number 前向流水号
forward set-up 正向建立,正向电路接通
forward shift operator 前移算子
forward signal 前向信号
forward slash 正斜杠(/)
forward substitution 前向替换
forward supervision 前向监督,正向监控
forward trace 正向跟踪
forward transfer 正向转移
forward version management 前向版本管理
forwarding 转发
FOTS(Fiber-Optic Transmission System) 光纤传输系统
foundation detail 基础样图
foundation software 基础软件
founding robot 铸造机器人
four address 四址
four-address code 四地址指令
four-address instruction 四地址指令
four-bit byte 四位字节,半字节
four-bit slice system 四位位片系统
Four-color conjecture 四色猜想
Four-color theorem 四色定理
Four corner coding 四角号码
four dimension 四维
four-frequency duplex telegraphy 四频双工电报
four-headed arrow 双向箭头
four-phase modulation 四相调制
Four Russians' algorithm 四个俄国人算法
four-tape sort 四磁带排序
four-wire chain 四线链路
four-wire circuit 四线电路
four-wire repeater 四线中继器
four-wire switching 四线制交换
four-wire system 四线制
four-wire terminating set 四线端接装
four-wire type circuit 四线型电路
Fourier analysis 傅立叶分析

Fourier inverse transform 傅立叶反变换
Fourier series 傅立叶级数
Fourier stability analysis 傅里叶稳定性分析
Fourier transform 傅立叶变换
Fourier transform lens 傅立叶变换透镜
fourth generation computer 第四代计算机
fourth generation language 第四代语言
fourth normal form(FNF) 第四范式
FOX-GEN FOX 应用程序生成器
fox message 狐讯,电传打字机检查报文
Foxbase Foxbase 数据库软件
FoxBASE＋ FoxBASE＋数据库软件
FoxPro FoxPro 数据库软件(微软)
FP(Floating Point) 浮点
FPA(Floating-Point Accelerator) 浮点加速器
FPCF (Forward Predictive-Coded Frames) 前向预测编码帧
FPGA(Field Programmable Gate Array) 现场可编程门阵列
FPLA(Field Programmable Logic Array) 现场可编程逻辑阵列
FPM(Fast Page Mode) 快速页面模式
FPM(Feet Per Minute) 英尺/分钟
FPP(Fixed Path Protocol) 固定路径协议
FPP(Floating-Point Package) 浮点软件包
fpppp fpppp 基准程序
FPS(Feet Per Second) 英尺/秒
FPS(Fixed Program Send) 固定程序发送
FPS(Frames Per Second) 帧/秒
FPU(Floating Point Unit) 浮点单元
FQDN(Fully Qualified Domain Name) 全限定域名
FQHN(Fully Qualified Host Name) 全限定主机名
FR(Failure Rate) 失效率
FR(Floating-point Register) 浮点寄存器
FR(Frame Relay) 帧中继
fractal 分形,分数维
fractal curve 分形曲线
fractal dimension 分形维数
fractal interpolation 分形插值

fractal model 分形模型
fractal pattern 分形图案
fractal pen 分形笔
fractile 分位数
fraction 小数,分数
fraction defect 废品率
fractional arithmetic unit 小数运算部件
fractional fixed point 分数定点
fractional iteration 分数迭代
fractional order 分数阶
fractional part 分数部分,小数部分
fractional programming 分数规划
fractional steps method 分数步长法
fractional T1 T1分线
FRAD(Frame Relay Access Device) 帧中继访问设备
fragile 易碎的
fragment 段落,片段
Fragment Header (Ipv6)分割选项包头
fragment query 关系片段查询
fragment reducer 关系片段简化器
fragment schema 片段模式
fragmentation 分段;碎片,存储残片
fragmentation index 碎片索引
fragmentation transparency 分段透明性
fragmented disk 碎片化磁盘
fragmenting 分割
FRAM(Ferroelectronic RAM) 铁电随机存取存储器
frame 帧,框架
frame(type A) A型机架
frame(type B) B型机架
frame accurate search 帧级精确搜索
frame alignment 帧同步
frame alignment circuit 帧同步电路
frame alignment recovery time 帧同步恢复时间
frame alignment signal 帧同步信号
frame alignment time slot 帧定位时间槽,帧同步时隙
frame anchor 图文框定位处
frame animation 帧动画
frame axiom 画面公理
frame-based language 基于框架的语言
frame-based method 基于框架法
frame blanking 帧消隐
frame boundary 帧分界
frame buffer 帧缓冲器

frame chaining(FCC) 帧链接
frame check character(FCC) 帧校验字符
frame check sequence(FCS) 帧校验序列
frame connector 框架连接器
frame control field 帧控制字段
frame control window 帧控制窗口
frame counting(FCC) 帧计数
frame-creation terminal 成帧终端
frame default 帧缺省值
frame dependent control mode 帧相关控制模式
frame description(FCC) 框架描述
frame differencing 帧差异
frame encapsulation 帧封装
frame end delimiter 帧尾定界符
frame format 帧格式
frame frequency 帧频
frame grabber 帧获取器
frame grabbing 帧获取
frame grammar 框架文法
frame ground 机架地
frame group 帧组
frame head 帧标题
frame in 画面切入
frame inheritance 帧继承
frame level interface 帧级接口
frame lock 帧锁定,帧同步
frame marker 帧标识器
frame member 框架构件
frame memory 帧存储器
frame modeling 框架建模,线框造型
frame number 帧号
frame object 框架对象
frame page 帧页
frame period 帧周期
frame pitch 框距
frame pointer 帧指针
frame problem 框架问题
frame rate 帧速率
frame recognition 帧识别
frame reject 帧拒绝
frame relay(FR) 帧中继
frame relay network 帧中继网络
frame relay segment set 帧中继段集
frame relay switch equipment 帧中继交换设备

frame replenishment 帧补充
frame representation 框架表示
frame representation language 框架表示语言
frame set 帧组
frame size 帧大小,帧长度
frame slip 帧滑移量
frame snatch 帧获取
frame start delimiter 帧首定界符
frame-step recording 帧步进记录
frame-store 帧存储
frame structure 帧结构
frame synchronization 帧同步
frame synchronizer 帧同步器
frame synchronizing 帧同步
frame synchronizing pulse 帧同步脉冲
frame table entry 页帧表目
frame theory 框架原理
frame timing 帧定时
frame type 帧类型
frame window 帧窗口
framebase computer-assisted instruction 帧基型计算机辅助教学
framed 加外框的
frameless 无框架的
FrameMaker FrameMaker 排版软件
frames received 已接收帧数
framework 框架
framework expression 框架表示
framing 成帧,帧形成
framing bit 成帧位
framing code(FC) 成帧码
framing error 成帧错误
framing mask 取景框
framing signal 帧同步信号
fraud 欺骗
free 自由,空闲
free access floor 活地板
Free Agent 自由代理
free area routine 自由区例程
free block list 自由(空闲)块列表
free cell 空闲单元格
free chain 自由链
free choice net 自由选择网
free clusters 空闲(可用)簇数
free component 自由元素
free control interval 自由控制间隔
free convection cooling 自然对流冷却

free curve 自由[任意形状]曲线
free disposal 自由使用权,自由支配
free electron 自由电子
free entry 自由输入
free fiber-optic connector 光纤活动连接器
free fiber optic connector plug 活动光纤连接器插头
free field 自由字段[区域]
free file map 自由文件映像
free float 自由浮动
free form 自由型,自由格式
free-form database 自由格式数据库
free-form language 自由格式语言
free-form text chart 自由格式的文字
free format field 自由格式字段
free format input 自由格式输入
free format menu 自由格式菜单
free function 自由(格式)函数
ε-free grammar 无ε文法
free fuzzy function 自由模糊函数
free fuzzy set 自由模糊集
free garbage 自由无用单元
free joint 自由关节
free lattice 自由格
free line 空闲线
free list 自由表
free memory 空闲内存
free monoid 自由类群,自由独异点
free occurrence 自由出现
free of charge 免费
free page reserve 自由页后备
free path 自由路径
free pool 空闲池,自由池
free reference 自由参照
free resize 随意重定尺寸
free routing 自由路由选择
free running mode 自由运行方式
free schema 自由模式
free semigroup 自由半群
free sketch 手绘草图
free software 自由软件
Free Software Foundation 自由软件基金会
free space 自由[空闲]空间
free space anchor point 自由空间锚点
free-space list 自由空间表
free-space optical communication 自由

空间光通信
free-storage list 自由存储区表
free substitution 自由代换
free surface 自由面
free symbol sequence 自由符号序列
free system resource(FSR) 自由系统资源
free term 自由项
free text searching 自由原文查找
free thread 自由线程
free time 空闲时间
free token 自由令牌,空闲权标
free token frame 自由[空闲]令牌帧
free toner 中性墨粉
free tree 自由树
free union 自由联合
free variable 自由变元
freedom 自由度
Freedomnet 自由交互网络软件
freeform 徒手画多边形
freeform tool 徒手画多边形工具
FreeHand 徒手画软件(Aldus)
freehand selection 徒手画线选择
freehand sketch 徒手画草图
Freelance Graphics Freelance 图形简报软件(Lotus)
freely programmable word-processing equipment 自由可编程字处理设备
Freeman's chain code 弗利曼链码
freephone 被叫方付费电话
freerunning multivibrator 自激多谐振荡器
freeware 免费软件
freeze dump area 冻结转储区域
freeze frame 冻结帧
freeze mode 冻结模式
freeze panes 冻结分割区域
freeze-point 冻结点
freeze point specification 冻结点规范
freeze state 冻结状态
freezing 凝固
freezing time 凝固时间
frequency 频率
frequency agile modems 柔性频率调制解调器
frequency aliasing 频率混叠
frequency analysis compaction 频率分析精简法

frequency analyzer 频率分析仪
frequency band 频带,波段
frequency bandwidth 频带宽度
frequency change signaling 改频信令
frequency changer 变频器
frequency changing 频率变换,变频
frequency channel 频道
frequency characteristic 频率特性
frequency conversion 频率变换
frequency converter 变频器
frequency counter 频率计
frequency departure 频率漂移
frequency-derived channel 频率分割信道
frequency deviation 频偏,频率漂移
frequency dictionary 频率字典
frequency discriminator 鉴频器
frequency distortion 频率失真
frequency diversity 频率分集
frequency diversity reception 频率分集接收
frequency divider 分频器
frequency-division data link 频分数据链路
frequency division multiple access 频分多址连接
frequency division multiplexing(FDM) 频分多路复用
frequency division switching system 频分制交换机系统
frequency domain equalizer 频域均衡器
frequency domain method 频域法
frequency doubler 倍频器
frequency estimator 频率估计值
frequency exchange signaling 换频信令
frequency frogging 频率跳变
frequency generator 频率发生器
frequency histogram 频率直方图
frequency mark 频率标记,频标
frequency-modulated laser 调频激光器
frequency modulation(FM) 调频
frequency-modulation recording 调频记录方式
frequency monitor 频监视器法
frequency multiplexing 频率多路复用
frequency of access 存取频率
frequency of using instruction 指令使

用频率
frequency offset 频率偏差
frequency offset transponder 频偏转发器
frequency pulling 频率牵引
frequency pushing 频率推移
frequency range 频率范围
frequency response 频率响应
frequency response masking 频响屏蔽
frequency reuse 频率重用,频率复用
frequency reuse satellite networks 频率复用卫星通信网
frequency-sampling filter 频率抽样滤波器
frequency shift 频率移位 「控
frequency shift keying(FSK) 移频键
frequency shift modulation 移频调制
frequency spectrum 频谱
frequency sweep 扫频
frequency swing 最大频偏,频率摆动
frequency synthesizer 频率合成器
frequency tolerance 频率容限
frequency transient response 频率瞬时响应
frequency translation 频率变换
frequency uncertainty 频率不稳定度
frequency weighting function 频率加权函数
frequent term 常用词
Frequently Asked Question(FAQ) 频繁查询的问题
frequently-used data 常用数据
fresh approach 最新方法
fresh copy 最新副本
FRF(Frame Repetition Frequency) 帧重复频率
FRFE(First Ready First Execute) 先就绪先执行
friability 脆性
friable 易碎的,脆的
fricative 摩擦音
friction 摩擦
friction clutch 摩擦离合器
friction feed 摩擦输纸
friction feeder 摩擦输纸器
friend function 友元函数
Frieden maximum entropy restoration 费里登最大熵复原

friendliness 友善性,友好性 「序
Friendly Finder Program 友好查找程
friendly name 友好名称
fringe (图像)毛边
fringing (图像)镶边
FRMR(FRaMe Reject) 帧拒收
from 发件人;发自
from template 来自模板
from-to 端点
front-back connection 正反面连接
front-back logic 前后级逻辑
front clipping plane 前截割面,前剪取面
front connection 正面连接
front distance 前距离
front-door coupling 前门耦合
front edge (脉冲)前沿
front elevation 正视图
front end 前端;前端处理机
front end analysis 前端分析
front end application 前端应用程序
front-end CASE 前端计算机辅助软件工程
front-end computer 前端计算机
front end concentrator 前端集中器
front-end design 前端设计
front-end edit 前期编辑
front-end engineering 前期工程
front-end input method 前端输入法
front-end machine 前端机器
front-end network processor(FNP) 前端网络处理机
front-end preprocessor systems 前端预处理系统
front-end processing 前端处理
front-end processing control system 前端处理控制系统 「机
front-end processor(FEP) 前端处理
front end processor advantages 前端处理机的优点
front-end software 前端软件
front-end system 前端系统
front loading 正面装载
front matter 正文前内容
front mounted connector 正面安装的连接器
front panel 前面板
front porch 前沿

front side 前面
front side bus 前边总线
front view 正视(图)
front wire 明线布线
frontier 末梢；前沿
frontier area 前沿领域
frontier node 末梢节点
frontier set 边界集合
FrontPage 网页制作工具(微软)
FrontPage Server Administrator FrontPage 服务器管理程序(微软)
FrontPage Server Extensions FrontPage 服务器扩展(微软)
Frost & Sullivan Computer Graphics Conference Frost 计算机制图会议
frozen coefficient method 冻结系数法
FRU(Field-Replaceable Unit) 现场可替换部件
frustum 平截头体
FS(Field Separator) 字段分隔符
FS(Full Scale) 满刻度
FSA(Finite State Automaton) 有限状态自动机
FSG(Finite State Grammar) 有限状态文法
FSK(Frequency Shift Keying) 移频键控
FTA(Floptical Technology Association) 光磁盘技术协会
FTAM(File Transfer Access and Management) 文件传送存取与管理
FTBBC computer (Fault-Tolerant Building Block Computer) 容错积木式计算机
FTI(Fixed Time Interval) 固定时间间隔
FTMP system (Fault-Tolerant Multi-Processor system) 容错多处理器系统
FTP(File Transfer Protocol) 文件传输协议
FTP(Fixed Term Plan) 固定项目计划(IBM)
FTP user session(File Transfer Protocol) 文件传输协议用户对话
FTR(File Transfer Request) 文件传输请求
FTS(Federal Telecommunications System) 联邦电信系统
FTSC system (Fault-Tolerant Shuttle Computer system) 容错宇航计算机系统
FTTH(Fiber To The Home) 光纤到家庭
FUD(Floating UnDerflow) 浮点下溢
FUJIC(FUJI Computer) 富士通计算
Fujitsu Co. 富士通公司(日本) 机
Fujitsu network architecture(FNA) 富士通网络体系结构
Fujitsu VP supercomputer 富士通 VP 巨型机
full abstract family of language (full AFL) 完全抽象语言类
full access 完全访问
full add 全加,带进位加
full-adder 全加器
full-address 全地址
full-addressing 全地址寻址方式
full ASCII keyboard 全 ASCII 键盘
full assembly 完全汇编
full backup 完全备份
full binary tree 满二叉树
full bootstrap 全引导程序
full capacity 最大容量
full color 全彩色
full computation 完整计算
full conversion 全转换
full custom integrated circuit 全定制集成电路
full data set authority 全数据集特许
full decode address 全译码地址
full demand paging 全请求式页面调度
full drag 全窗口拖动
full DST authority 完全 DST 授权
full dump 全转储
full-duplex 全双工
full-duplex line 全双工线路
full-duplex transmission 全双工传输
full-electronic switching system 全电子交换机系统
full-featured 全特性的
full file protection functionality 全文件保护功能性
full-frame time code 全帧时间编码
full-functional dependency 全函数相关性

full group name 用户组名全称
full handshape authentication 完全握手式认证
full height drive bay 全高驱动器架
full install 完全安装
full justification 双边对齐
full-language 完全语言
full line 整行;实线
full load current 满负荷电流
full-matrix method 满矩阵法
full-motion video 全动感视频
full-motion video adapter 全动感视频适配器,电影卡
full optical communication 全光通信
full-page display 全页显示器
full path name 全路径名
full picture fixed display 全画面固定显示
full picture scroll display 全画面纵滚显示
full populated board 满载电路板
full procedural file 全过程文件
full-range 满量程
full-rank decomposition 满秩分解
full-recovery 完全恢复
full scale 满刻度
full scan 满扫描
full-screen 全屏幕
full-screen application 全屏幕应用程序
full-screen editing 全屏幕编辑
full-screen editor 全屏幕编辑程序
full-screen image 全屏幕显示图像
full-screen processing(FSP) 全屏幕处理
full-screen view(FSP) 满屏观察
Full Service Intranet(FSN) 全服务内联网络
Full Service Network(FSN) 全方位服务网络
full shift capability 全移位能力
full sized pulse 实际大小,实物尺寸
full sized pulse 全幅度脉冲
full-span drift 满量程漂移
full speed 全速率
full spelling 完整拼写
full-subtracter 全减器
full symbolic name 全符号名
full-text database 全文数据库
full text retrieval 全文检索

full-text searching 全文检索
full-time service 全日服务
full tone original 全色调原版
full transparent text mode 全透明文本模式
full trio 完全三元闭合语言类
full vector offering 全向量插入
full wafer LSI 整片大规模集成电路
full wave rectify 全波整流
full-width ellipsis 全角省略号
full-width erase head 全宽度清洗磁头
full word 全字
full-word boundary 全字界
fully-associative buffer storage 全结合缓冲存储器,全相联缓存
fully associative cache 全相联高速缓存
fully-associative mapping 全相联映射
fully automated cataloging technique 全自动编目技术
fully automatic compiling technique (FACT) 全自动编译技术
fully automatic switching system (FACT) 全自动交换系统
fully concatenated key 全联关键字
fully connected network 全互连网络
fully dissociated mode of operation 完全不相联的操作方式
fully dissociated signaling 完全不相联的信号方式
fully formed characters 全成形字符
fully inverted database 全倒式数据库
fully-inverted file 全倒排文件
fully militarized computer 全军用计算机
fully-parenthesized notation 全括号记法
fully populated "满员",插满元件的
fully qualified domain name(FQDN) 全限定域名
fully qualified name 全限定名
fully space constructable function 完全可构造空间函数
fully time constructable function 完全可构造时间函数
function 功能;函数;函词
function allocation 功能分配
function analysis technique 功能分析技术
function argument 泛函自变量

function authority credentials 功能授权使用凭证
function block 功能块
function body 函数体
function button 功能按钮
function call 函数调用
function character 功能字符
function code 功能码
function control block(FCB) 功能控制块
function control signal 功能控制信号
function definition 函数定义
function degrading maintenance 损伤功能的维护
function description table 功能描述表
function design 功能设计
function designator 函数命名符
function diagram 功能图
function element 功能元件
function evaluation routine 函数求值例程
function field 功能字段,功能域
function flowchart 功能流程图
function generator 函数发生器
function hazard 函数冒险
function hole 功能孔
function identification 功能标识
function independent testing 功能无关检测
function interpreter 功能解释程序
function key 功能键
function keyboard 功能键盘
function language 函数型语言
function level simulation 功能级模拟
function level transformation 函数级变换
function library 函数库
function logic 功能逻辑
function management 功能管理
function management data serves 功能管理数据服务
function mapping 函数映射
function mode 功能模式
function model 功能模型
function multiplier 函数乘法器
function name 函数名
function node 功能结点
function optimization 功能优化
function oriented architecture 面向函数的体系结构
function overloading 函数重载
function part 作用部分,功能部分
function permitting failure 功能容忍的故障
function permitting maintenance 功能无损伤维护
function plotter 函数型绘图仪
function point 功能点数
function pointer 函数指针
function preselection 功能预选
function preventing failure 阻碍功能的故障
function preventing maintenance 妨碍功能的维护
function procedure 函数过程
function punch 功能孔,指示孔
function reference 函数引用,函数调[用]
function representation 功能表示法
function request 功能请求
function return value 函数返回值
function sequencer 函数序列发生器
function space 函数空间
function specification 功能说明
FUNCTION statement 函数定义语句
function subprogram 函数子程序
function switch 函数开关;功能开关
function table 函数表
function table tabulation 函数表列表
function test 功能测试
function unit 功能单元[部件]
function value 函数值
function verification 功能验证
Function Wizard 函数向导
function words 功能字
functional address instruction format 功能地址指令格式
functional approximation 函数逼近
functional assembly 功能组件
functional availability 功能有效性
functional block 功能块
functional block boundary 功能块边界图形元素 「述
functional block description 功能块描
functional block specification 功能块说明
functional board tester 功能板测试器

functional burn-in test 功能老化试验
functional character 功能字符
functional characterization 功能特征
functional cohesion 功能内聚
functional command 功能指令
functional completeness 功能完整性
functional decomposition 功能分解
functional dependency 函数相依性
functional description(FD) 功能描述
functional design 功能设计
functional device 功能器件
functional diagram 功能图
functional electronic block 功能电子块
functional element 功能元件
functional enhancement package 功能增强程序包
functional grammar 功能语法,功能文法
functional interchangeability 功能互换性
functional interface 功能接口
functional interleaving 功能交插
functional language 函数型语言
functional layer 功能层
functional level modeling 功能级建模
functional macro instructions 功能宏指令
functional memory 功能存储器
functional mode 功能模式
functional modularity 功能模块化
functional multiplier 函数乘法器
functional multiprocessing(FMP) 功能型多重处理(体系结构)
functional parallelism 功能并行性
functional partition 功能划分,功能分割
functional partition method 功能分割法
functional partitioning microprocessor 按功能划分的微处理器
functional primitive 功能元,功能原语
functional programming 函数型程序设计
functional programming language 函数型程序设计语言
functional - programming - oriented architecture 面向函数程序设计的体系结构
functional prototyping 功能性原型开发

functional query 函数查询
functional recovery routine(FRR) 功能恢复例程
functional redundancy 功能冗余
functional reproducibility 功能复现性
functional requirement 功能需求
functional shell 功能外壳
functional simulator 功能仿真程序
functional software 函数软件;功能软件
functional specialization 功能专用化
functional specification 功能说明
functional subsystem(FSS) 功能子系统
functional symbols 功能符号
functional testing 功能测试
functional trimming 功能整修
functional unit collision 功能部件冲突
functional verification 功能验证
functionality 功能性
functionally accurate cooperative system 功能准确协作系统
functionally distributed computer system 功能分布式计算机系统
functor 函子;功能元件
fundamental circuit algorithm 基本回路算法
fundamental constant 基础常量
fundamental cut-set algorithm 基本割集算法
fundamental cycle 基本周期
fundamental digraph 基本有向图
fundamental extract circuit 基频提取电路
fundamental form 基本形
fundamental frequency 基频
fundamental frequency of voice 浊音基频
fundamental group 基群
fundamental interconnection matrix 基本关联矩阵
fundamental mode 基本工作方式
fundamental noise detection circuit 基噪检测电路
fundamental renewal equation 基本更新方程
fundamental set 基本集
fundamental simplex 基本单纯形
fundamental solution 基本解

fundamental vector 基本向量
funds transfer system 汇兑系统
funginert 防霉性
further function 进退函数
further normalization 逐步规范化
fuse 熔丝,保险丝
fuse cell 熔丝单元
fuse-on toner 熔态墨粉
fuse time computer 引信时间计算机
fused deposition modeling(FDM) 热蜡沉积成形术
fuser 热融器
fusible link 可熔性链,熔丝连接
fusible-link-readout memory 熔断链读出存储器
fusible ROM(FROM) 可熔断只读存储器
fusion point 熔点
fusion splicing 熔接
FUT(Form UTility) 表格实用程序
futility cutoff 无价值修剪
future-activity stack 未来动作栈
future event 未来事件
future generation computer system 新一代计算机系统,未来计算机系统（日）
future surrounding case 将来环境角色,未来环境格
future value 未来价值
FutureBus 未来总线
FutureBus+ 增强型 FutureBus
FutureBus+ arbitration FutureBus+仲裁
FutureBus+ profile FutureBus+概要
fuzzification 模糊性,模糊化
fuzzification function 模糊化函数
fuzzification process 模糊化过程
fuzzify 模糊化
fuzzifying extremum 模糊极值
fuzziness 模糊性
fuzzy algorithm 模糊算法
fuzzy associative memory 模糊联想记忆
fuzzy category 模糊范畴
fuzzy center number representation 模糊中心数表示法
fuzzy clause 模糊子句
fuzzy closed set 模糊闭集
fuzzy clustering 模糊聚类分析
fuzzy continuity 模糊连续
fuzzy control system 模糊控制系统
fuzzy correlation 模糊相关
fuzzy covariance 模糊协方差
fuzzy data dictionary 模糊数据字典
fuzzy data representation method 模糊数据表示法
fuzzy database 模糊数据库
fuzzy decision 模糊决策
fuzzy deductive database 模糊演绎数据库
fuzzy degree 模糊度
fuzzy distance 模糊距离
fuzzy dynamic system 模糊动态系统
fuzzy entropy 模糊熵
fuzzy event 模糊事件
fuzzy extension 模糊外延
fuzzy feature 模糊特征
fuzzy find 模糊搜索
fuzzy finite state automaton 模糊有限状态自动机
fuzzy formula 模糊公式
fuzzy frame 模糊框架
fuzzy function 模糊函数
fuzzy goal 模糊目标
fuzzy grammar 模糊文法
fuzzy graph 模糊图
fuzzy graphic theory 模糊图论
fuzzy identity morphism 模糊恒等映照
fuzzy image recognition 模糊图像识别
fuzzy inference rule 模糊推理规则
fuzzy interval number representation 模糊区间数表示法
fuzzy language 模糊语言
fuzzy level 模糊级
fuzzy linear ordering 模糊线性序
fuzzy linear programming 模糊线性规划
fuzzy logic control 模糊逻辑控制
fuzzy mapping 模糊映射
fuzzy mathematics 模糊数学
fuzzy matrix 模糊矩阵
fuzzy measure 模糊量度
fuzzy membership function 模糊隶属函数
fuzzy model 模糊模型
fuzzy multicriteria modeling 模糊多判

据建模 模糊简单析取分解
fuzzy neural network 模糊神经网络
fuzzy noise 模糊噪声
fuzzy object 模糊目标
fuzzy optimal control 模糊最佳控制
fuzzy output map 模糊输出映射
fuzzy probability 模糊概率
fuzzy production 模糊产生式
fuzzy programming 模糊规划
fuzzy proposition 模糊命题
fuzzy prototype 模糊原型
fuzzy quantity 模糊量
fuzzy random variable 模糊随机变量
fuzzy reasoning 模糊推理
fuzzy recognition 模糊识别
fuzzy relation 模糊关系
fuzzy relaxation 模糊松驰法
fuzzy resolution 模糊归结
fuzzy response 模糊响应
fuzzy restriction 模糊约束
fuzzy rule 模糊规则
fuzzy scheduling 模糊调度[规划]
fuzzy search 模糊查找
fuzzy semantic network 模糊语义网络
fuzzy set theory 模糊集合论
fuzzy simple disjunctive decomposition

fuzzy state-transition matrix 模糊状态转移矩阵
fuzzy state-transition tree 模糊状态转移树
fuzzy statistics 模糊统计
fuzzy structure 模糊结构
fuzzy subset 模糊子集 「数
fuzzy switching function 模糊开关函
fuzzy system mapping 模糊系统映射
fuzzy topological space 模糊拓扑空间
fuzzy topology 模糊拓扑
fuzzy trajectory 模糊轨道 「数
fuzzy transition function 模糊转移函
fuzzy transition matrix 模糊转移矩阵
fuzzy transition vector 模糊转移向量
fuzzy upperbound 模糊上界
fuzzy variable 模糊变量
fuzzy vector 模糊向量
fuzzy volume model 模糊体模型
fuzzy voice recognition card 模糊声音识别卡
FWC(Four-Wire Circuit) 四线电路
FX！32 FX！32仿真软件(DEC)
FYA(For Your Amusement) 供娱乐
FYI(For Your Information) 供参考

G g

G(Gate) 门；栅极
G(Ground) 地，接地
G-64 G-64 总线
G-96 G-96 总线
g-file(get file) （Unix)恢复文件
GA(Generic Algorithm) 遗传算法
GA(Global Address) 全局[全程]地
Gabor code 盖博码 「址
Gabow's algorithm 盖伯算法
gain 增益
gain-bandwidth product 增益带宽积
gain control 增益控制
gain factor 增益系数
gain-frequency characteristic 增益频率特性
gain margin 增益边际[容限]

gain scheduling 增益定序
GAL(Gate Array Logic) 门阵列逻辑
gallery 图库
galley proof 排字校样
gallium(Ga) 镓
gallium arsenide(GaAs) 砷化镓
gallium arsenide devices 砷化镓器件
gallium arsenide diode 砷化镓二极管
gallium arsenide wafer 砷化镓圆片
galloping "1"s and "0"s 跃步"1"和"0"
Galois field 伽罗华域，有限域
gamble 冒险，投机，赌博
game 博弈；游戏
game buster 游戏秘笈，游戏攻略
game chip 游戏芯片

game graph 博弈图
game of chance 机会对策
game over 游戏结束
game paddle 游戏操纵杆
game port 游戏端口
game theory 博弈论,对策论
game tree 博弈树
game tree search 博弈树搜索
game with misperception 有错误感觉的对策
game without saddle point 无鞍点博
Games Group 游戏组　　　　　「弈
gaming courseware 游戏型课件
gaming simulation 博弈模拟,对策仿
gamiest 对策论专家　　　　　　「真
gamma 伽玛,γ
gamma correction 伽玛[γ]校正
gamma distribution 伽玛分布
gamma factor 伽玛[γ]系数
gamma ferric oxide 伽玛氧化铁
gamma function Γ函数,伽玛函数
gamma ray 伽玛射线,γ射线
GAMS (General Algebraic Modeling System) 通用代数模型系统
gamut 音阶,全音域;色域
gamut warning 超色域警告
gang 成群,成组
gang switch 联动开关
gang tuning 统调,联调
ganged control 联动控制
Gantt chart 甘特图,作业进度图
GAP(General Accounting Package) 通用记账软件包
gap 间隙,间隔,空隙
gap azimuth 隙方位角,间隔方位
gap depth 隙深,前隙深度
gap digit 间隔数字
gap length 隙长,间隔长度
gap loss 隙损耗
gap scatter 缝隙离散
gap test 空隙检验,间隙检测
gap width 缝隙[栅缝]宽度
gapless structure 无隙结构
gapless tape 无隙磁带
gapped 有间隙的,有空隙的
gapped tape 间隔带
garbage 无用信息,废料
garbage area 无用区,废料区

garbage collection 无用存储单元收集
garbage collection algorithm 废料收集算法
garbage collector 废料收集程序
garbage-in/garbage-out(GIGO) 废料入/废料出
garbageware 无用软件
garble 错乱收发
garbled message 错乱消息
garbled-statement 错用语句
GARP(Generic Attributes Registration Protocol) 普通属性注册协议 (IEEE 802.1Q)
Garsia-Wachs' algorithm 盖西亚-沃茨算法
gas discharge display 气体放电显示
gas dopants 气体掺杂剂
gas-filled arrester 充气避雷器
gas laser 气体激光器
gas panel 气体放电平面显示板
gas plasma display 气体等离子体显示器
gate 门;栅
gate array 门阵列
gate array logic(GAL) 门阵列逻辑
gate buffer 门控缓冲器
gate capacitance 栅电容
gate circuit 门电路
gate contact 栅极接点
gate controlled switch 门控开关
gate-drain overlap 栅漏覆盖面
gate electrode 栅电极
gate equivalent circuit 门等效电路
gate inverter 门反相器
gate leads 门引线
gate level logic simulation 门级逻辑仿
gate level simulation 门级仿真　「真
gate multivibrator 门控多谐振荡器
gate overlap 栅覆盖层
gate oxide 栅氧化层
gate-pin ratio 门引脚比
gate pulse 选通脉冲
gate region 栅(极)区
gate signal 选通信号
gate-silicon insulator 栅硅绝缘层
gate structure 栅极结构
gate switch 门开关
gate through 通过

gate voltage 栅压
gate yield 门成品率
gated amplifier 选通脉冲放大器
gated buffer 门控缓冲器
gated crossover detection 门控过零检测
gated sweep 门控扫描
gateway 网关,信关
gateway-capable host 可作网关的主机
gateway control function 网关控制函数
gateway daemon(GATED) 网关事务处理软件
gateway exchange 网关交换机
gateway host 网关主机
gateway interface 网关接口
gateway network control program 网关网络控制程序
gateway node 网关节点
gateway of application layer 应用层网关
gateway of network layer 网络层网关
gateway processor 网关处理机
gateway server 网关服务器
gateway switching system 网关交换系统
gateway to gateway protocol(GGP) 网关-网关协议
gateway VTAM 网关虚拟远程通信访问法
gather 收集,集中
gather write 集中写
gather write/scatter read 集中写/分散读
gating 门控,选通
gating element 选通元件
gating matrix 门控阵列
gating pulse 门控脉冲,选通脉冲
gauge 量规;标准尺寸
Gauss 高斯
Gauss distribution 高斯分布
Gauss elimination with total pivoting 全主元高斯消去法
Gauss-Jordan elimination method 高斯-约当消去法
Gaussian beam 高斯光束
Gaussian curve 高斯曲线
Gaussian distribution 高斯分布
Gaussian elimination 高斯消去法
Gaussian filter 高斯滤波器
Gaussian noise 高斯噪声

Gaussian number 高斯数
Gaussian random process 高斯随机过程
Gaussian random vector 高斯随机向量
Gaussian-shaped pulse 高斯型脉冲
GB(GigaByte) 吉字节,千兆字节(10^9 字节)
GB 2312(Guo Biao 2312) 国家标准2312(汉字编码字符集)
Gb(Gigabit) 吉比特,千兆位(10^9 位)
GBIT(GigaBIT) 十亿位,千兆位
GC(Graphics Context) 图形前后关系
GC/S(GigaCycles Per Second) 十亿周/秒,10^9周/秒
gcc gcc基准程序
GCG(Grey Component Replacement) 灰度分量替换
GCI(Generalized Communication Interface) 通用通信接口
GCR(Group Coded Recording) 分组编码记录
GCS(Gate Controlled Switch) 门控开关
GDDL(Graphical Data Definition Language) 图形数据定义语言
GDS(Group Display System) 群显示系统
GDSS(Group Decision Support System) 群体决策支持系统
GDT(Global Descriptor Table) 全局描述符表
GE(General Electric Co.) 通用电气公司(美国)
GE information services 通用电气公司信息服务
GE interproccessing 通用电气公司网络交互处理
GE remote concentrators 通用电气公司远程集讯器
gear 齿轮
Gear's algorithm 吉尔算法
Gelerkin method 伽辽金法
gencode 通用代码
gender changer 同性对接转换器
gene structure 基因结构
general 通用的,广义的,普通的
general accounting system 通用记账系统

general activity simulation program 一般活动仿真程序
general agent 总代理
general arrangement 总装配图
general assembly program(GAP) 通用汇编程序
general broadcast 普通广播
general Chinese report system 通用汉字报表系统
general comment 通用注解,一般注释
general comparator 通用比较器
general computer 通用计算机
general data register 通用数据寄存器
General Electric Co.(GE) 通用电气公司
general escape 广义换码
general file 通用文件
general file translator 通用文件翻译程序
general flowchart 综合流程图
general format 通用格式
general game 一般对策
general graphic controller 通用图形控制器
general instruction set graphic controller 通用指令集图形控制器芯片
general integrating tactics 总体集成策略
general interface 通用接口
general interpretive program 通用解释程序
general knowledge system 通用知识系统
general loader 通用装入程序
general linear group 一般线性群
general member 一般成员
general MIDI(GM) 通用乐器数字界面
general MIDI format 通用乐器数字界面格式
general migration 常规迁移
general NC language processor 通用数值控制语言处理机
general net theory 广义网络理论
general numerical control language processor 通用数值控制语言处理机
general optimal value function 一般最优值函数
general parallel language 通用并行语言
general parameter 通用参数

general parsing 一般语法分析
general pattern 通用样式
general plane theorem 广义平面定理
general pool 通用池
general problem solver 通用问题求解程序
general processor 通用处理机
general program 通用程序
general protect false(GPF) 一般保护性错误
General-Public License 通用公共许可证
general-purpose 通用的,广义的
general purpose application program 通用应用程序
general-purpose calculator 通用计算器
general-purpose compiler 通用编译程序
general purpose computer 通用计算机
general-purpose controller 通用控制器
general-purpose digital computer 通用数字计算机
general purpose function generator 通用函数发生器
general-purpose interface 通用接口
general-purpose interface adapter (GPIA) 通用接口适配器
general-purpose interface bus(GPIB) 通用接口总线
general-purpose language 通用语言
general-purpose macrogenerator 通用宏功能生成程序
general-purpose memory 通用内存
general purpose network 公用网
general purpose operating system 通用操作系统
general-purpose optimizing compiler 通用优化编译程序
general-purpose processor 通用处理机
general purpose program 通用程序
general-purpose register 通用寄存器
general-purpose register file 通用寄存器文件
general purpose robot 通用机器人
general purpose routine 通用例程
general purpose simulation program 通用仿真程序
general-purpose simulation system

(GPSS) 通用仿真系统
general-purpose simulation system/PC (GPSS/PC) 通用仿真系统/PC 版
general purpose software engineering environment 通用软件工程环境
general purpose systems simulator (GPSS) 通用系统仿真语言
general purpose tester 通用测试仪
general quantifier 一般量词,普通性量词
general quiz options 常规测验选项
general recursive function 一般递归函数
general register(GR) 通用寄存器
general register address 通用寄存器地址
general register unit 通用寄存器单元
general remark 通用标志,一般说明
general repair 一般修理
general resource profile 通用资源轮廓文件
general routine 通用例程
general rule 一般规则
general setting 常规设置
general solution 通解
general stability criterion 广义稳定判「据
general telephone network 通用电话网络
general translation program 通用翻译程序
general use open subroutine 通用开型子例程
generality 通用性,相关率
generalization 广义化,通用化
generalization rule 广义化规则
generalize 概括,通用化
generalized 通用的,广义的,一般的
generalized algebraic translator(GAT) 通用代数翻译程序
generalized algorithm 广义算法,通用算「数
generalized convex function 广义凸函
generalized coordinate 广义坐标
generalized correlation 广义相关
generalized database management system(GDBMS) 通用数据库管理系统
generalized data manipulation 通用数据处理
generalized dependency 广义依赖「索
generalized direct search 广义直接搜
generalized drawing primitive 广义绘图原语
generalized eigenvalue problem 广义本征值问题
generalized elimination method 广义消元法
generalized Fourier analysis 广义傅里叶分析
generalized Fourier transform 广义傅里叶变换
Generalized Information System(GIS) 通用信息处理系统
generalized information system 通用信息系统
generalized instruction 广义指令
generalized inverse 广义逆
generalized least squares method 广义最小二乘法
generalized linear programming 推广的线性规划
generalized list 广义链表,广义表
Generalized Mark-up Language tag (GML tag) 通用置标语言标签
generalized matched filter(GMF) 广义匹配滤波器
generalized model 广义模型「理
generalized modus ponens 广义假言推
generalized phrase structure grammar 广义短语结构文法
generalized Poisson distribution 广义泊松分布
generalized polynomial 广义多项式
generalized queue realization(GQR) 广义队列实现
generalized reduced gradient method 广义既约梯度法
generalized routine 广义例程
generalized sequential access method (GSAM) 广义顺序访问法
generalized sequential machine 广义顺序机
generalized sequential machine mapping (GSM mapping) 广义串行机器映射
generalized simplex method 推广的单

纯形法
Generalized Simulation Language(GSL) 通用仿真语言
generalized solution 广义解,通解
generalized sort 通用排序[分类]
generalized sort/merge program 通用排序/合并程序
generalized sort program 通用排序程序
generalized splines 广义样条
generalized stochastic Petri nets(GSPN) 广义随机 Petri 网
generalized subroutine 通用子例程
generalized supervisor calls trace 通用管理程序调用跟踪程序
generalized trace facility(GTF) 通用跟踪程序
generalized variable 广义变量
generate 产生,生成
generate and test 生成与测试
generated address 生成地址
generated code 合成码;生成代码
generated error 生成误差
generated matrix 生成矩阵
generated name 生成的名称
generated sort 生成排序
generated statement 生成语句
generated symbol 生成符号
generating 生成,产生
generating alternatives 生成备选方案
generating code 生成代码
generating element 生成元
generating function 生成函数
generating polynomial 生成多项式
generating raster image 生成光栅图像
generating rule 生成规则,导出规则
generating scheme 生成模式
generating set 生成集
generating system 生成系统
generating tree 生成树
generation 世代;发生,形成
generation data group(GDG) 世承数据群
generation data set 世承数据集
generation file group 世代文件组
generation number 世代号
generation occurrence 生成出现,定值性出现

generation of block 字组形成,字块生成
generation of random number 随机数的产生
generation systems 产生系统
generation technique 世代技术
generative action grammar 生成作用文法
generative capacity 生成能力
generative computer-assisted instruction 生成式计算机辅助教学
generative function 母函数
generative graphics 衍生制图法
generative semantic grammar 生成语义文法
generative transformational grammar 生成转换文法
generator 发生器;发电机
generator polynomial 生成多项式
generator program 产生器程序
generic 类属;通用的,普通的
generic access 类属存取
generic algorithm(GA) 遗传算法
generic application infector 应用程序传染型病毒
generic attribute 类属性
generic block cipher 类属块密码
Generic CADD Generic CADD 软件
generic class 普通类(C 语言)
generic composite moniker 一般复合别名
generic entry name 总入口名
generic function 类函数
generic instance 一般示例
generic key 类键,总键
generic name 类属名
generic package 类属封装
generic program unit 类属程序单位
generic programming 遗传程序设计
generic PROMS 类属 PROMS
generic relation 类属关系
generic set 类集
generic stream cipher 类属流密码
generic unit 类属单位
genesis 创始,起源
genetic 遗传的
genetic algorithm 遗传算法
genetic code 遗传密码

genetic engineering 遗传工程
genetic graph 发展图；遗传图
genetic learning 遗传学习
genetics 遗传学
genial 用户友好的
GEnie(General Electric network for information exchange) 通用信息交换电子网
genlock 发生锁定器　　　　　　「机
genuine computer 真计算机，实计算
genuine solution 真解
genus 示性数,(种)类
geocoding 地理编码
geodesic 短程线
geodesic circle 短程线圆
geodesic method 短程线法
geodesic normal coordinates 短程法线坐标
geodesic system 测地系统
geographic information system(GIS) 地理信息系统
geographic mapping 地图绘制
geographical addressing 地理定址
geometric 几何的,几何学的
geometric algorithm 几何算法
geometric analogy 几何图形模拟
geometric code mode 几何编码模式
geometric computation 几何计算
geometric convergence 几何收敛
geometric correction 几何校正
geometric correlation 几何相关
geometric criterion 几何判据
geometric distortion 几何失真[畸变]
geometric distortion correction 几何失真校正
geometric dual 几何对偶
geometric editor 几何编辑程序
geometric graph 几何图形
geometric growth 几何增长
geometric interpretation 几何解释
geometric mean(GM) 几何平均数；等比中项
geometric model 几何模型
geometric model hierarchy 几何模型层次
geometric modeling 几何模型法,形状表示法
geometric optics 几何光学

geometric pattern 几何图案
geometric primitive 几何原语　「数
geometric progression 几何[等比]级
geometric reasoning 几何推理
geometric series 几何级数
geometric solution 几何解法
geometric splines 几何样条
geometric transformation 几何变换
geometrical mean filter 几何平均滤波
geometrical model 几何模型　　「器
geometry 几何学
geometry-based design support system (GDSS) 基于几何的设计支持系统
geometry engines 几何引擎
geophysics 地球物理学
geostationary 与地球同步的
geostationary orbit 静止轨道
geostationary satellite 静止卫星
geosynchronous satellite 地球同步卫
Germanium(Ge) 锗　　　　　　「星
germanium diode 锗二极管
germanium transistor 锗晶体管
germanium wafer 锗圆片
gesture 手势
gesture mode 手势模式
get 取,得
get area 占用区
Get Color 获取颜色
Get Data 获取数据
Get Focus 获得焦点
Get Palette 选择调色板
get procedure 取得过程
get signal 取得信号
GET statement 取得语句,GET语句
get thread context 取得线程上下文
Get Zone 获得区域
getable virtual storage(GETVIS) 可得到的虚存储区
GetRight GetRight断点续传软件
gettering system 吸杂系统
gettering treatment 除气处理
getting start 入门
getting statistics 正在取得统计资料
getting systime 正在获取系统时间
GFC(General Flow Control) 基本流量控制
GFP(Generalized File Processor) 通用文件处理器

GGP(Gateway to Gateway Protocol) 网关-网关协议(TCP/IP)
GGS(Graphic Generator System) 图形发生系统
Ghost 数据克隆程序(Symantec)
ghost 幻像,重影
ghost canceller 幻像消除器
ghost effect 幻像效应
ghost image 重影
ghost signal 假信号
GHz(GigaHertz) 千兆赫,吉赫兹
giant computer 巨型计算机
gibberish 凌乱信息,无用信息
gibberish total 凌乱总计,无用数据总「和
Gibson mix 吉布逊混合法
GID(Group Identification Number) 组标识号
GIF(Graphics Interchange Format) 图形交换格式
Giga(G) 千兆,吉
gigabit(Gb) 千兆位
gigabit LAN 千兆位局域网
gigabyte(GB) 千兆字节
gigacycle 千兆周
gigacycle computer 十亿次计算机
gigaflops(Gflops) 每秒10亿次浮点运算
gigahertz(GHz) 千兆赫,吉赫兹
gigahertz circuit 千兆赫电路
gigahertz computer 千兆赫计算机
GIGO(Garbage In/Garbage Out) 废料入/废料出
GII(Global Information Infrastructure) 全球信息基础设施
Gilbert(Gb) 吉尔伯特(磁学单位)
Gilbert code 吉尔伯特码
Gildemeister coding system 吉氏编码系统
gill 基尔(完成一次给定操作的时间单位)
Gillbert-Moore's algorithm 吉尔伯特-摩尔算法
GIM(Generalized Information Management) 通用化信息管理
gimbal 万向节
GINO(Graphical INput Output) 图形输入/输出
girth 围长,周长

Giro 银行同业自动财务转账系统
GIS(Geographic Information System) 地理信息系统
GIS(Graphics Input System) 图形输入系统
giveback 归还
given accuracy 给定精度
GKS(Graphics Kernel System) 图形核心系统
GKS language 图形核心系统语言
glare filter 滤光器
glass base 玻璃衬底
glass delay-line memory 石英玻璃延迟线存储器
glass fiber 玻璃纤维
glass laser 玻璃激光器
glass materials 玻璃材料
glass package 玻璃封装
glass seal type transistor 玻璃密封式晶体管
glass semiconductor 玻璃半导体
glass semiconductor device 玻璃半导体元件
glass semiconductor read-only memory 玻璃半导体只读存储器
glass shell 玻璃外壳
glass substrate 玻璃衬底
glass-to-metal seal 玻璃-金属封接
glass transition temperature(Tg) 玻璃临界温度
glass window 玻璃窗口
glassivation 玻璃钝化
glitch 毛刺,瞬变波动;活动故障
global 全局的,全程的,整体的
global account 全局账号
global address 全局地址,全程地址
global address list 共用地址列表
global address vector 全局地址向量
global addressing scheme 全程寻址方
global administration 全局管理 「案
global association 全程相关
global asymptotic stability 整体渐近稳定
global backup 总体备份
global binding 全局结合
global buffer 全局缓冲器
global clock 全局时钟
global code 整体码,全程码

global command 全局命令,全程命令
global common subexpression 全程公用子表达式
global compact 全体压缩
global concept schema 全局概念模式
global constant 全局常量
global control bus 全局控制总线
global controllability 整体可控性
global convergence 全程收敛,整体收敛
global copy operation 整体拷贝操作
global criterion 全局性准则
global data base 全局数据库
global data flow analysis 全程数据流分析
global database of production system 产生式系统的综合数据库
global descriptor table(GDT) 全局描述符表
global directory service 全局目录服务
global discard policy 整体废弃策略
global distributed schema 全局分布模式
global entity 全局实体
global error 全局误差,整体性误差
global fault 全局性故障
global file store 全局文件存储
global find and replace 全程查找与替换
global format 总体格式,全局格式
global function 全功能,总体功能
global group 全局组
Global Information Infrastructure(GII) 全球信息基础设施
global information system 全球信息系统
global instability 全局不稳定性
global kill file 全局性删除文件
global knowledge 全局知识
global label 全局标号
global location 全局位置,全程单元
global lock 全程锁
global login 全局登入
global macro 共用宏
global main process 全局主过程
global manufacture 全球制造
global maximum 全局极大值,整体极大
global member 全局成员
global memory 全局内存
global microcode compaction 全局微码压缩
global minimizing point 全局极小值点,整体极小值点
global minimum 全程最小值
global mode 全程模式
global module 全程模块
global name 全程名
global naming scheme 全程命名方案
global network 全球网络;全局网络
global non-broadcast transfer 全局非广播式传送
global object 全局对象;总体目标
global operation 全局操作
global optimization 全局优化
global optimum 全局最佳值,整体最优值
global optimum first search 全局最佳优先搜索
global output 全局输出
global page table 全局页表
global parameter 全程参数
global partition schema 全局分区模式
global PIN 全局个人识别码
Global Positioning System(GPS) 全球定位系统
global processor 全局处理机
global program 全局程序
global protection 总体保护
global query 全局查询
global reference 全程引用
global register 全局寄存器
global reliability 整体可靠性
global restriction 全局约束
global routing table 全程路由选择表
global satellite communication system 全球卫星通信系统
global search 全程搜索
global search and replace 全程查找与代换
global section 全局区段,全程分区
global segment 全局段
global semaphore 公用信号量
global sequence 全局序列
global service 全局服务
global session identifier 全程对话标识符
global setting 整体设置
global shared resources(GSR) 全局共享资源

global solution 整体解
global stability 整体稳定性
global stack top location 全局栈顶单元
Global Star System "环球之星"低轨道通信系统(Qualcomm)
global stiffness matrix 总刚度矩阵
global step multiplication 全局步进乘法
global storage 全局存储器
global structure 总体结构
global switch 整体开关,总开关
global symbol 全局符号
global symbol table 全局符号表
global task 全局性事务
global template 全局模板
global test 全局测试,全程测试
global title 全局标题,总标题
global tracking network (GLOTRAC) 全程跟踪网络
global transfer command 全局传送命令
global value 全局值
global variable 全程变量,全局变量
global variable reference 全局变量引用
global variable symbol 全程变量符号
global vector table 全程向量表
global view 全局观点
global wiring 全局布线法
globally-addressed header 全程编址标题
Globally Unique Identifier(GUID) 全球惟一确认号码
Globalstar "环球之星"低轨道卫星通信系统(美)
glossary 词汇表,术语词典
glossary function 词汇表功能
glow discharge 辉光放电
glyph 字形;象形
GM(General MIDI) 通用乐器数字接口
GMIS(General Multimedia Information System) 通用多媒体信息系统
GML(Generalized Markup Language) 通用标记(IBM)
GMR(Giant Magneto Resistive Head) 超磁阻磁头(Quantum)
GND(GrouND) 地
GNOME(GNU's Network Object Model Environment) GNU 网络对象模型环境
gnomon 折磬形,磬折形

GNU Public Licence GNU 公众许可证
GNU software 免费软件,GNU 软件
GNS(Global Network Service) 全球网络服务
go 启动,执行;转向命令
go ahead 前进信号,前向信号
go-ahead polling 前向轮询
go-ahead sequence 先行序列,向导序列
go back 后退
go channel 去程通路
go cipher 转到密码
go down 停止作业
go-list 关键词表
go-on symbol 继续符号
go path 去程路径
go plain 转到明码
GO TO 转移语句
go to annotation 定位到批注
GO TO assignment statement GO TO 赋值语句
go to bookmark 定位到书签
go to page 定位到页面
go to special 定位到特定条件
Go To statement 转移语句
go to what 定位到内容
go-word 有用词
goal 目标
goal analysis 目标分析
goal clause 目标子句
goal coordination 目标协调
goal determination 目标确定
goal-directed function invocation 目标制导功能调用
goal-directed inference 目标引导的推理
goal-directed reasoning 目标导向推理
goal drive 目标驱动
goal driven reasoning 目标驱动推理
goal object 目标对象
goal-oriented inference 面向目标的推理
goal regression 目标回归
goal seeking approach 目标搜索法
goal set 目标集合
goal-setting 目标设定
goal stack 目标堆栈
goal state 目标状态
goal track 目标磁道
goal tree 目标树

goal-type-driven method 目标类型驱动法式
goal well-formed formula 目标合式公式
goal wff 目标合式公式
Godel incompleteness theorem 哥德尔不完备性定理
Godel number 哥德尔数
Golay code 格雷码
gold bond type diode 金键二极管
Gold code 哥德码
gold-doped diode 金键二极管
gold-doped TTL process 掺金TTL工艺
gold doping 掺金工艺
gold for plating 镀金
gold plated contact 镀金触点
gold plating 镀金层
gold ratio 黄金比例
gold substitute 黄金替换技术(IBM)
golden common LISP (GCLISP) GCLISP语言
golden ratio 黄金比率
golden section 黄金分割
golden section method 黄金分割法
golding 镀金
Gomory-Hu tree 哥莫利-胡树
Gomory-Hu's algorithm 哥莫利-胡算法
gone west 归西,升天
good algorithm 良算法,好算法
good place 合适的位置
good time 正常工作时间
goodness 优势
Gopher (因特网)地鼠,信息查询服务器
Gopher space Gopher空间
Goppa code 戈帕码
GOSIP(Government OSI Profile) 政府开放系统互连大纲
GOSUB statement 转向子程序语句
got focus 获得焦点
GOTO statement 转移语句,GOTO语句
GOTO-less programming 无GOTO程序设计法
Gouraud shading Gouraud阴影形成
governing 调节,控制
governor 调节器
GPF(General Protection Fault) 通用保护性错误
GPIA (General Purpose Interface Adapter) 通用接口适配器
GPIB(General Purpose Interface Bus) 通用接口总线
GPIB interface adapter GPIB接口适配器
GPL(General Purpose Language) 通用语言
GPOS(General Purpose Operating System) 通用操作系统
gppm(graphics pages per minute) 每分钟图形页数
GPS(Global Positioning System) 全球定位系统
GPS receiver 全球定位系统接收机
GPSS (General Purpose Simulation System) 通用仿真系统
GPSS(General Purpose System Simulator) 通用系统仿真程序
GPSS language 通用仿真系统程序语言
GPSS/PC(General Purpose Simulation System/PC) 通用仿真系统PC版
grab handles 抓取控制柄
grabber 捕获器;抓取钩
grabber hand 抓取手掌
grabber tool 抓取工具
GRACE GRACE数据库机
grace login 优惠(宽限)登录
graceful degradation 适度退化,弱化故障
graceful exit 从容退出
graceful preemption 适度预占
gradation 分级过渡;灰度
grade 等级,程序,分类
grade of channel 通道级
grade of service 服务等级
graded base 缓变基区
graded distribution 梯度分布
graded-index fiber 渐变折射率光纤
graded-index profile 渐变[梯度]折射率分布
graded junction 缓变结
gradient 梯度;斜率
gradient constant 梯度常数
gradient fill tool 梯度填充工具
gradient filter 梯度滤波器
gradient-index fiber 渐变折射率光纤,梯度折射率光纤
gradient line 梯度线

gradient method 梯度法
gradient operator 梯度算子 「法
gradient projection method 梯度投影
gradient related 梯度相关
gradient search 梯度搜索
gradient shading 渐变阴影设置
gradient tool 渐变工具
gradient vector 梯度向量
gradual change 缓变
gradual degradation 性能退化[衰退]
gradual exhaustion 渐次消耗
gradual failure 逐渐失效
gradual switching regression method 逐渐转换回归模型
graduate 分度,刻度;校准;毕业生
graduated symbol 分级符号图
grafport 图形端口
graftal 分形图
grain 粒度
grain classification 粒度分类
grain size 粒度大小
gram 克
Gram determinant 格拉姆行列式
Gram matrix 格拉姆矩阵
Gram polynomial 格拉姆多项式
Gramer rule 克兰姆法则
grammar 文法
grammar category 文法分类
grammar checker 文法检验程序
grammar design 文法设计
grammar explanation 文法解释
grammar graph 文法图
grammar inference by enumeration 枚举式文法推理
grammar isomorphism problem 文法同构问题
grammar rule 文法规则
grammar testing 文法检查
grammatical constraint 文法约束
grammatical formative 文法构成成分
grammatical homonym 文法同音异义
grammatical inference 文法推论
grammatical mistake 文法错误
grammatical rule 文法规则
grammatical synthesis 文法综合
Grammatik 语法检查程序
grand clause 基子句
grand literal 基文字

grand state 大状态
grand substitution instance 基本代换实例
grand total 总值,总计
grandfather 原始数据集,祖父数据集
grandfather cycle 原始周期,存档期
grandfather file 原始文件
grandfather process 祖父进程
grandfather tape 原始带,存档带
grant 授权,授予资格
grant-aid 资助
grant to 授予…资格
grantee 被授权者
granularity 粒度
granularity noise 散粒噪声
granule 区组
graph 图;曲线图
graph algorithm 图解算法 「法
graph-based algorithm 基于图形的算
graph browser 图形浏览器
graph command 图解命令
graph data 图形数据
graph follower 读图器,图形跟随器
graph information retrieval language (GIRL) 图形信息检索语言
graph key 图形键
graph matching 图匹配
graph merge 图形合并
graph method 图解法
graph model 图解模型
graph of function 功能图
graph optimal isomorphism 图形优化同构
graph order 图序
graph recognition 图形识别
graph reduction 图归约 「机
graph reduction computer 图归约计算
graph representation 图表示法
graph-search control strategy 图搜索控制策略
graph structure representation 图形结构表示
graph table 图表
graph table entry 图表项目
graph text 图表正文
graph theory 图论
graph theory model 图论模型
graph title 图标题

graph tool 图表工具
grapheme 语意图示
graphic 图形的;图形
graphic access method 图形存取法
graphic alphanumeric display 图形文数显示器
graphic alphanumeric generator 图形文数产生器
graphic and combinatorial algorithm 图与组合算法
graphic arts 形象艺术;图版工艺
graphic character 图形字符
graphic co-processor 图形协处理器
graphic code extension 图形码扩展
graphic console 图形控制台
graphic controller 图形控制器
graphic cursor 图示光标 「理
graphic data processing 图形数据处
graphic data reduction 图形数据精简
graphic data structure 图形数据结构
graphic description language 图形描述语言
graphic design system 图形设计系统
graphic digitizer 图形数字化仪
graphic display 图形显示器
graphic display controller(GDC) 图形显示控制器
graphic display device 图形显示设备
graphic display program 图形显示程序
graphic display resolution 图形显示分辨率
Graphic Display Systems(GDS) 图形显示系统 「端
graphic display terminal 图形显示终
Graphic Display Unit(GDU) 图形显示装置
graphic distortion correction 图形失真校正
graphic documentation 图形文档处理
graphic editor 图形编辑程序
graphic entity 图解实体 「符
graphic escape character 图形转义字
graphic file maintenance 图形文件维
graphic form 图形表示方式 └护
graphic homeomorphism 图的同胚
graphic image system 图形图像系统
graphic input language 图形输入语言

graphic input/output system(GIOS) 图形输入/输出系统
graphic interface 图形接口
graphic isomorphism 图的同构
Graphic Job Processor(GJP) 图形作业处理程序
graphic kernel system(GKS) 图形核心系统
graphic language 图形语言
graphic limit 图形界限
graphic mark 图形标记,图解符号
graphic metaphor 图形隐喻
graphic method 图形法
graphic object 图形对象
graphic object content architecture(GOCA) 图形对象内容结构
Graphic Operating System(GOS) 图形操作系统
graphic package 图形软件包
graphic panel 图板,图示面板
graphic plotter 绘图仪
graphic primitives 图形原语
graphic printer 图形打印机
graphic processor 图形处理机
graphic report generator 图形报告生成程序
graphic resolution 图形分辨率
graphic software 图形软件
graphic solution 图解
graphic stability 图形稳定度
graphic symbol 图形符号
graphic tablet 绘图板
graphic terminal 图形终端机
Graphic Text Management System(GTMS) 图形文本管理系统
graphic transmission 图形传输
graphic user interface(GUI) 图形用户界面
graphic utility 图形应用程序
graphic visual attribute(GUI) 图形可见属性
graphic workstation(GUI) 图形工作站界面
graphical analysis 图形[图解]分析
graphical calculation 图解计算
graphical cellular automaton 图形细胞自动机
graphical character-based user interface

基于字符的图形用户界面　　「理
graphical-data operation　图形数据处
graphical data space(GDS)　图形数据空间
graphical database(GDS)　图形数据库
graphical display　图形显示[显示器]
graphical elements　图形元素
graphical illustration　图解说明,图例
graphical input device　图形输入装置
graphical input output(GIO)　图形输入/输出
Graphical Interactive Language(GRIL)　图形交互语言
graphical interface　图形界面
graphical interpreter　图形解释程序
Graphical Kernel System(GKS)　图形核心系统
graphical library　图形库
graphical method　图解法
graphical optimization　图解最优化
graphical overlay　图形覆盖
graphical paint box　图形绘制框
graphical pattern　图形样式,图案
graphical primitive　图元,图形元语
graphical primitive elements　图形原语元素
graphical representation　图形表示
graphical user interface(GUI)　图形用户界面
graphical Web browser　图形 Web 浏览器
graphics　图形学
graphics acceleration board　图形加速
graphics adapter　图形适配器
Graphics and Text Editing System (GATES)　图文编辑系统
graphics applications　图形学应用
graphics-based　基于图形的
graphics-based FEA software　基于图形的有限元分析软件
graphics board　图形板
graphics character　制图字符
graphics controller　图形控制器
graphics coprocessor　图形协处理器
graphics CRT display　图形 CRT 显示器　　　　　　　　　　　　「口
graphics device interface　图形设备接
graphics digitizer　图形数字化仪

graphics file format　图形文件格式
graphics input devices　图形输入装置
graphics insertion　图形插入
Graphics Interchange Format(GIF)　图形交换格式(CompuServe)
graphics interface　图形界面[接口]
graphics kernel system(GKS)　图形核心系统
graphics light pen　图形光笔
graphics manipulation　图形操作
graphics mode　图形模式
graphics monitor　图形监视器
graphics overlay　图形覆盖
graphics package　图形软件包
graphics pad　图形板
graphics peripheral　图形外围设备
graphics pipeline　图形流水线
graphics pixel　图素,图元,像素
graphics plotter　绘图仪
graphics plotting　图形绘制
graphics primitive　图形处理原语
graphics processor　图形处理器
graphics resolution　图形分辨率
graphics routines　图形例程
graphics software　图形软件
graphics software packages　图形处理软件包
graphics spreadsheet　图形式电子数据表格
Graphics Station Gold Adapter　图形工作站金卡
graphics subroutine package　图形子程序包
graphics tablet　图形输入板
graphics terminal　图形终端
graphics utilities　图形实用程序
graphics view　图形显示
graphics workstation　图形工作站
graphite material　石墨材料
graphoid　拟图
graphology　笔迹学
graphite material　石墨材料
grasp　夹持,抓取
grating　栅,格子,光栅
grating space　光栅间距
graunch　意外事故;(硬盘)头盘干扰
gravitation　重力,万有引力
gravity　(X 协议)重力控件

gray 灰度;灰色
gray balance 灰度平衡
Gray code 格雷码
Gray-coded excess-3 BCD 格雷余3二
十进码
gray image 灰度图像
gray level 灰度级
gray level histogram 灰度级直方图
gray level transformation 灰度级转换
gray scale 灰度等级
gray-scale image 灰度图像
gray-scale manipulation 灰度处理
gray-scale monitor 灰度显示器
gray-scale picture 灰度图
gray scaling 灰度调整
gray tone 灰色调
grayed command 灰色命令
grayed out 变成灰色
GRE (Graduate Record Examination)
研究生入学考试(美)
GRE advanced test in computer science
计算机科学研究生入学考试
greater-than match 大于符合,大于匹
greater-than-equal match 大于等于符
合,大于等于匹配
greatest common factor 最大公因子
greatest element 最大元素
greatest lower bound 最大下界
greatest member 最大成员
greedy algorithm 贪心算法
greedy matching 贪婪匹配
greedy method 贪心法
greedy parsing algorithm 贪心分析算
greedy strategy 贪婪策略
greedy tree 贪心树
Greek alphabet 希腊字母表
Greek letter representation 希腊字母
表示法
greeked page 不可阅读页面
greeking 概略排版,版面预览
green computer 绿色(节能)计算机
green hands 新手
green machine 绿色机器
green monitor 绿色显示器
Greenwich Mean Time 格林威治标准
时间
Gregorian calendar 格里高里日历
Greibach normal form 格里巴赫范式

grey 灰色,灰度
grey balance 灰色平衡
grey component replacement (GCR)
灰度分量替换
grey level 灰度级
grey level vision system 灰度级视觉系统
grey-scale morphology 灰度标度形态学
grid 栅格,表格;栅极
grid adaptive method 网格自适应方法
grid area 网格区域
grid azimuth 网格方位图
grid builder 表格生成器
grid cell 网格单元
grid chart 栅格图,网格图
grid cipher 网格式密码
grid column 表格列
grid design mode 表格设计方式
grid line 网格线;暗格线
grid method 网格法
grid node 网格节点
grid optimization 网格优化
grid pattern 网格图案,网格式样
grid point 网格点
grid size 格网尺寸
grid-spaced contacts 栅状间隔接点,
等距离触点
GRIL (GRaphical Interactive Language) 图形交互语言
grind 研磨
grip 夹持
gripper 握爪
gripper mechanism 夹紧机构
grommet 绝缘环,橡胶密封圈
groove 槽,凹槽,沟
grooved fiber-alignment connector V
槽光纤对准连接器
grooved waveguide 槽型波导
Grosch's law 格劳希定律
gross 全部的,总量的
gross clipping 粗裁剪
gross error 人为误差,过失误差
gross grain 粗粒度
gross hypothesis 粗略假设
gross index 粗索引
gross information contents 总信息内
容,粗信息量
gross minus 负数总计

gross plus 正数总计
gross requirement 总需求量
gross weight 毛重
ground(GND) 地,接地
ground absorption 地面吸收
ground circuit 接地电路
ground clamp 接地线夹
ground clause 基子句
ground fault 接地故障
ground instance 基例
ground loop 接地回路
ground plane 接地层,地线层;地平面
ground potential 地电位
ground-return circuit 接地返回电路
ground start 接地起动
ground state 基态
ground strap 接地母线
ground stud 地线接线柱
ground switch 接地开关
ground term 基本项
ground wave 地波
grounded 接地的,通地的
grounding 接地
group 组,群;组合
group acknowledgement signal 群确认信号
group address 群地址,组地址
group-address message 群地址消息
group addressing 群寻址
group advance receive 组提前接收
group advance send 组提前发送
group alerting and dispatching system 群示警及调度系统
group alerting system 群告警系统
group analysis 群组分析
group assembly 群组装配
group attribute 群组属性
group box 组合框
group buffering 成组缓冲
group carry 成组进位,分组进位
group carry look ahead 成组超前进位
group channel 群通道,群信道
group check 成组校验
group chuck 群组夹头
group code 群码,组码
group-code entry 群码入口
Group Coded Recording(GCR) 分组编码记录

Group conference 组会议
group control 群控,组控
group counting method 群计数法
group decision support system(GDSS) 群体决策支持系统
group delay 群时延
group delay characteristic 群延迟特性
group delay distortion 群延迟失真
group delay frequency characteristics 群延迟频率特性
group design 群组设计
group digital check 成组数字校验
group distribution frame 群配线架
group drawing 群组图法
group edit 群组编辑
group element 组元素
group entry 组表目 「机
group 1 facsimile equipment 一类传真
group 2 facsimile equipment 二类传真机
group 3 document facsimile equipment 三类文件传真机 「机
group 4 facsimile equipment 四类传真
group field 群栏,群域
group fixture 群组夹具
group frequency 群频率
group hub 工作组集线器
group icon 群图标
group identification 群识别
group index 群折射率
group indicate 群标志
group indication 组指示装置
group information 用户组信息
group inspection 成组检验
group inverse 群逆
group item 群项,组合项
group iterative method 成组迭代法
group layout 群组布置
group length 组长度
group link 群链路
group list 用户组列表
group machines 群组机器
group manufacturing 群组加工
group mark(GM) 组标志 「运
group material handling 群组物料搬
group material planning 群组物料规
group member 用户组成员 「划
group method 群组法

group modulation 群调制
group name 组名
group network 群网络
group number 群号,组号
group object 组实体;群组对象
group occurrence 成组出现
group of isomorphism 同构群
group organization for manufacture 群组制造组织
group output 成组输出
group poll 组轮询
group printing 成组打印
group procedure 成组工艺规程
group product design 群组产品设计
group production 群组生产
group production control 群组加工控制
group production operation 群组生产作业
group production planning 群组生产规划
group records 组记录
group relaxation 成组松驰,群松驰
group repeat count 组重复计数
group resource record 组资源记录
group sampling 分组抽样,分组取样
group section 基群段
group select slave 群选择从属
group selective dissemination of information(GSDI) 团体定题服务
group selector 群选择器,群选线器
group separator(GS) 群分隔号,组分隔符
group set of data 数据的群集
group support system 群组支持系统
group switching 组交换
group synchronization 群同步
group technology 群组技术,成组法
group theory 群论
group translating equipment 群转换设
group value function 群体值函数
group velocity 群速度
group window 成组窗口
grouped object 成组对象
grouped records 成组记录
grouping 分组,归族
grouping data 分组数据
grouping records 成组记录
grouping of records 记录成组

groupware 群件
groupware server 群件服务器
GroupWise GroupWise群件(Novell)
growth 等比级数;生长,增长
growth curve 增长曲线
growth factor 增长因子
growth power 升级能力
growth simulation 生长模拟
GSM(Group Special Mobile) 群组专用移动通信体制,GSM体制
GSR(Global Shared Resource) 全局共享资源
GSS(Graphics Symbol Set) 图形符号集
GST(Graphics Structure Transformation) 图形结构变换
GTK(GNU's Tool Kit) GNU工具箱
GTMS(Graphic Text Management System) 图形文本管理系统
GTS(Graphics Terminal System) 图形终端系统
guaranteed 保证,担保
guaranteed bandwidth traffic 保用带宽通信量
guaranteed cycle 保证周期,保用寿命
guaranteed time 保用时间,保证时间
guard 防护,保护
guard band 防护频带,防护间隔
guard bit 防护位
guard block 保护存储块
guard digit 保护数字
guard disc 防护盘
guard enable 允许保护
guard gap 防护间隙
guard mode 保护模式
guard position 保护位置
guard rail 防护轨
guard ring 防护环
guard signal 防护信号
guard time 保护时间
guard zone 防护区
guarded command 受保护命令
guardian 管理人,保护人
guardian process 监护进程
guarding 保护
GUESS/1 GUESS/1语言
guest 宾客,贵宾
guest group 宾客组
guest-host effect 宾-主效应

guest privilege　宾客特权
guest virtual storage　宾客虚拟存储器
GUI(Graphics User Interface)　图形用户界面
GUID(Globally Unique IDentifier)　全球惟一确认号码;全局惟一标识符
GUID variables　全局惟一标识符变量
guidance　制导
guidance computer　制导计算机
guidance groove　引导槽
guidance radar　制导雷达
guidance system　制导系统,引导系统
guidance tape　制导带
GUIDE(Guidance of Users of Integrated Data processing Equ　GUIDE用户协会
guide　引导;导轨
guide bar　导向条
guide book　指导书
guide card　引导卡片
guide edge　导向边
guide holes　引导孔,中导孔
guide-in window　导入窗口
guide line　导行线
guide line program　导向程序
Guide Media Extensions(GME)　指导媒体扩展
guide pin　导柱
guide position　制导位置
guide roller　导向轮
guided cell scheduling　引导单元调度
guided discovery learning　引导发现学习
guidelines for the definition of managed objects(GDMO)　管理对象定义标准
guiding hole　导向孔,中导孔
gulp　字节组
gun　电子枪;喷枪
gutter　装订线;沟,槽
gutter position　装订位置
GVRP(GARP VLAN Registration Protocol)　普通属性注册协议虚拟局域网注册协议(IEEE 802.1Q)
GWBASIC　GWBASIC语言
GWS(Graphical Windowing System)　图形窗口系统
gyroscope　陀螺仪

H h

H(Hexadecimal)　16进位的
H(Horizontal)　水平的,横向的
H.261　H.261标准(视频编码,CCITT)
H.263　H.263标准(视频编码,CCITT)
H.324　H.324标准(多媒体可视电话,ITU)
H-floating datum　H型浮点数
H&J(Hyphenation and Justification)　连字与调版
HA(Half Adder)　半加器
HA(Home Address)　起始地址,内部地址
HAB(Home Address Block)　内部地址块
HAC(Hierarchical Abstract Computer)　分级抽象计算机
hack　粗糙产品
hacker　黑客
hacking　非法用机
Hadamard inequality　哈达玛不等式
Hadamard transform　哈达玛变换
Hadamard transform encoding　哈达玛变换编码
Hadamard transform matrix　哈达玛变换矩阵
hadron　强子
HAF(Host Access Facility)　主机访问软件
HAG(Home Address Gap)　内部地址间隙
HAI(Hardware Advisory Instruction)　硬件咨询说明书

hair space 最小空白
hairline 细线条
HAISAM (Hashed Index Sequential Access Method) 散列变址顺序访问法
HAIT (Hash Algorithm Information Table) 散列算法信息表
HAL (Hardware Abstraction Layer) 硬件抽象层
HAL (Harwell Automated Loans) 哈威尔自动化外借系统
HAL (Hash Algorithm Library) 散列算法库
halation 晕影
half 一半,半
half-add 半加
half-adder (HA) 半加器
half-adder-subtracter circuit 半加减电路
half adjust 舍入
half amplitude 半幅度
half-amplitude basic pulse width 基本脉冲半幅宽
half amplitude duration 半振幅脉宽
half-angle 半角
half bootstrap 半自展法,半自举法
half bridge 半桥
half-byte 半字节
half-carry 半进位
half current 半电流
half cycle 半周期
half cycle transmission 半周传输
half-duplex (HD, HDX) 半双工
half-duplex contention 半双工争用
half-duplex equipment 半双工设备
half duplex error protocol 半双工差错规程
half-duplex facilities 半双工设备
half-duplex mode 半双工方式
half-duplex operation 半双工操作
half duplex repeater 半双工转发器
half-duplex service 半双工服务
half-duplex system 半双工系统
half duplex transmission 半双工传输
half echo suppressor 半回波抑制器
half-filled entry 半填满项目
half-fixed length record 半固定长度记录

half gateway 半网关
half-height drives 半高式驱动器
half-height micro-Winchester disk drive 半高式微型温彻斯特磁盘驱动器
half-height mini-floppy disk drive 半高式小型软盘驱动器
half-height window 对分窗口;半高窗
half-inch tape 半英寸磁带
half-inch tape drive 半英寸磁带机
half intensity 半亮度
half-interval search 折半查找
half length 半字长
half-life 半衰期
half LSB 二分之一最低有效位
half-ordered set 半序集
half page printer (HPP) 半页打印机
half path (HPP) 半通路
half physical model 半物理模型
half plane filter 半平面滤波器
half router 半路由器
half screen 网膜屏幕
half-session 半对话期
half size 半尺寸
half space 半格
half space key 半空格键
half-speed 半速
half-splitting 折半法,对分法
half title 副标题
half-tone 半色调,中间色调
half-tone original 半色调原版文件
half-tone picture 中间色调图像
half-tone plotting 半色调图形输出
half-tone printing 铜版印刷
half-tone process 半色调处理
half-tone screen 网版
half-wave rectifier 半波整流器
half-word (HW) 半字
half-word boundary 半字界
halfbyte 半字节
halftone image 半色调图像
halftone pattern 半色调图案
halftone representation 半色调表示法
halftone screen 网线板,网目板
Hall activity matrix for systems engineering 霍尔系统工程活动矩阵
Hall coefficient 霍尔系数
Hall effect 霍尔效应
Hall effect device 霍尔效应元件

Hall effect gyrator 霍尔效应回转器
Hall effect isolator 霍尔效应隔离器
Hall effect keyswitches 霍尔效应键开关
Hall effect sensor 霍尔效应传感器
Hall mobility 霍尔迁移率
Hall plate 霍尔片
Hall sensor 霍尔传感器
Hall voltage 霍尔电压
Halo 光环,晕影
halo effect 光圈效应,光环效应
haloed line effect 晕圈线效应
Halstead's software science 霍尔斯特德软件科学
halt 停机
halt burst mode(HBM) 暂停成组传输模式
halt condition 停机条件
halt cycle 暂停周期,停止周期
halt indicator 停机指示符;停机指示器
halt instruction 停机指令
halt mode 停机模式
halt on all errors 遇到所有错误都停机
halt problem 停机问题
halt processor mode 暂停处理机模式
halt state 停机状态,暂停状态
halt statement 停机语句
halt switch 暂停开关,停机开关
halting execution 停止执行
halting problem 停机问题
halting problem of flowchart schema 流程图模式停机问题
halting problem of Turing machine 图灵机停机问题
halting processing state 暂停处理状态
halve 二等分,对分;减半
halving circuit 平分电路
halving register 平分寄存器
HAM(Hardware Associative Memory) 硬件相关存储器
Hamilton function 汉弥尔顿函数
Hamilton ring 汉弥尔顿回路
Hamilton's canonical equations 汉弥尔顿正则方程
Hamiltonian cycle 汉弥尔顿圈
Hamiltonian graph 汉弥尔顿图
Hamiltonian path 汉弥尔顿路径
hammer(HMR) 字锤

hammer bank 字锤组,击打部件
hammer lever 字锤杆
hammer machine 字锤式打印机
hammer magnet 字锤电磁铁
Hamming bound 汉明边界
Hamming check 汉明校验
Hamming code 汉明码
Hamming code assignment 汉明码分配
Hamming distance 汉明距离
Hamming weight 汉明权
Hamming window 汉明窗口
Hamming window function 汉明窗函数
hand annotation 手写批注
hand assemble 手工汇编
hand calculator 手动计算器;手持计算器
hand capacitance 人手电容
hand composition 手工排版
hand computation 手工计算
hand coordinate system 手部坐标系统
hand drawing picture 手绘图形
hand-eye calibration 手眼校准
hand-eye machine 手眼机器
hand feeder 手动馈送器;手动输纸器
hand flag communication 手旗通信
hand free 免手提
hand-free telephone 免手提电话
hand held calculator 手持式计算器
hand held computer 手持式计算机
hand-held data entry device 手持式数据输入设备
hand-held equipment 手持式设备
hand-held scanner 手持式扫描器
hand-off 跨区转接
hand-on background 工作经验
hand operation 手工操作
hand pointer 手形指针
hand-print character recognition 手写体字符识别
hand-print data entry terminal 手写数据输入终端
hand scanner 人工扫描器
hand tool 手形工具度
hand-wand reading speed 光笔阅读速率
hand written character 手写字符
hand written character recognition 手写字符识别
hand written numeral recognition 手

写数字识别
handbook 手册
handheld computer 手持式计算机
handheld PC(HPC) 手持式个人计算机
handing figures 老式数字体
handing indent 悬行
handing time 人工操作时间
handkeys 手动开关,手动键
handle 句柄;图柄;控制器
handle-based function 基于句柄的函数
handle type 控制柄类型
handler 处理程序
Handler classification schema 汉德勒分类法
handling capacity 处理容量,处理能力
handling CCD bar-code scanner 手持式电荷耦合器件条码扫描器
handling time 处理时间
handmarking 人工标记
handover 转移,交班
handprint 手写印刷体
handprint data-entry terminal 手写数据输入终端
hands-off operation 脱机操作,站外操作
hands-off state 脱机状态,脱离状态
hands-on 实际训练;内行
hands-on background 机上操作资历,实际工作经验
hands-on operation 机上操作,实际操作
handset 手持式送受话器,手机
handset mounting 手机架
handshake 联络,反馈检验
handshaking 信号交换,握手
handshaking modem 握手联络式调制解调器
handshaking procedure 接续过程
handshaking protocol 握手协议
handshaking sequence 联络序列
handshaking signal 握手信号,联络信号
handwriting 手写体
handwriting reader 手写字阅读器
handwritten Arabic character recognition 手写阿拉伯字符识别
handwritten Chinese character recognition 手写汉字识别
handwritten number 手写数字
handwritten stroke 手写笔划
handy-type computer 便携式计算机

handyman 灵巧机器人
hang 意外停机,暂停,挂起
hang detect 暂停检测
hang-over delay 释放延迟
hang-up 意外停机;挂断
hang-up key 停机键
hang-up prevention 意外停机保护
hanging indent 悬挂式缩排
hanging cursor position 暂停光标位置
hanging node 悬挂节点
hanging paragraph 悬段
hangover 图像拖尾
hangover delay 释放延迟
hangover time 释放延迟时间
Hankel matrix 汉克尔矩阵
Hankel transform 汉克尔变换
Hanning window 汉宁窗,余弦平方窗
Hanoi tower problem 汉诺塔问题
Hanzi 汉字
Hanzi coding 汉字编码
Hanzi generator 汉字发生器
happened-before relation 先期发生关系
haptic 触觉的
hard 硬的,实体的
hard adder 硬加法器
hard array logic 硬逻辑阵列
hard automation 硬自动化
hard axis 难磁化轴
hard boot 硬自举
hard card 硬插件板
hard coded 硬编码的
hard copy 硬拷贝
hard copy facility 硬拷贝设备
hard copy interface 硬拷贝接口
hard copy interpretation 硬拷贝解释
hard copy/live copy 硬拷贝和实用拷贝
hard copy log 硬拷贝日志
hard copy numeric input 硬拷贝数字输入
hard copy of display image 显示图像的硬拷贝
hard copy output 硬拷贝输出
hard copy terminal 硬拷贝终端
hard copy video interface 硬拷贝视频接口
hard core 硬核
hard decision decoding 硬判决译码
hard disk 硬盘

hard disk array 硬盘阵列
hard-disk cartridge 硬盘盒
hard disk controller 硬盘控制器
hard disk drive 硬盘驱动器
hard disk drive adapter 硬盘驱动适配器
hard disk error 硬盘出错
hard disk interface 硬盘接口
hard disk mode 硬盘模式
hard disk parameter 硬盘参数
hard disk partition 硬盘分区
hard disk partition table 硬盘分区表
hard disk type 硬盘类型
hard edge 硬边
hard error 硬错误
hard-error rate 硬故障率
hard error status 硬错误状态
hard failure 硬失效
hard fault 硬故障
hard ferromagnetic material 硬铁磁材料
hard firing 硬点火
hard format 硬格式
hard hole 硬穿孔
hard hyphen 硬连字符
hard image 硬图像
hard interrupt 硬中断
hard light 硬光
hard macro 硬宏元
hard magnetic material 硬磁性材料
hard metal superconductor 硬金属超导体
hard permalloy 硬坡莫合金
hard problem 困难问题
hard pulse 硬脉冲,强脉冲
hard reset 硬复位
hard return 硬回车
hard sectored disk 硬分区磁盘
hard solder 硬焊料
hard space 硬间隔
hard stop 强迫终止,硬停机
hard superconductor 硬超导体
hard-switch modulator 刚性开关调制器
hard-wire numerical control 硬布线数值控制
hard-wired 硬连线的
hard-wired circuit 硬连线电路
hard-wired communication adapter 固定连接通信适配器
hard-wired controller 硬连线控制器
hard-wired instruction 硬连线指令
hard-wired interconnection 硬布线互连
hard-wired logic 硬布线逻辑
hard-wired numerical control 硬连线数值控制
HardCard 硬盘卡
hardcore 硬核
hardened memory system 固化存储器系统
hardener 硬化剂,固化剂
hardest-first strategy 最难优先策略
hardness 硬度
hardware(H,HDW) 硬件
hardware abstraction layer 硬件抽象层
hardware accelerator 硬件加速器
hardware address 硬件地址
hardware aid to software 软件的硬件辅助
hardware algorithm 硬件算法
hardware arbiter 硬件仲裁器
hardware architecture 硬件体系结构
hardware assembler 硬件汇编程序
hardware association method 硬件结合法
hardware associative memory 硬件结合内存
hardware augmented technique 硬件增强技术
hardware availability ratio 硬件有效率
hardware bootstrap 硬件自举引导
hardware breakpoint 硬件中断点
hardware cell 硬件单元
hardware character generator 硬件字符发生器
hardware check 硬件检验
hardware check routine 硬件检验例程
hardware checksum 硬件校验和
hardware clock 硬件时钟
hardware combination 硬件组合
hardware compatibility 硬件兼容性
hardware compiler 硬件编译程序
hardware configuration 硬件配置
hardware configuration definition 硬件配置定义
hardware console 硬件控制台
hardware construction 硬件构成
hardware context 硬件关联
hardware control 硬件控制

hardware cost 硬件成本
hardware data control 硬件数据控制
hardware data extraction 硬件数据抽取
hardware debug 硬件调试
hardware deficiency 硬件缺陷
hardware dependent 硬件相关的
hardware description language(HDL) 硬件描述语言
hardware development 硬件开发
hardware diagnostic 硬件诊断
hardware digital processing 硬件数字处理
hardware dump 硬件转储
hardware emulator 硬件仿真程序
hardware encrypting 硬件加密法
hardware enhancement 硬件增强
hardware environment 硬件环境
hardware evaluation 硬件评估,硬件评价
hardware event 硬件事件
hardware failure 硬件失效
hardware feature 可选硬件
hardware firmware software trade-off 硬件固件软件权衡
hardware ground 硬件地
hardware implemented fault tolerance (HIFT) 硬件实现的容错技术
hardware implemented sharing virtual memory 硬件实现的共享虚拟存储器
hardware-in-the-loop simulation 硬件在回路中的仿真
hardware independent 硬件无关的,独立于硬件的
hardware instruction 硬件指令
hardware interface 硬件接口
hardware interface module 硬件接口模块
hardware interpreter 硬件解释程序
hardware interrupt 硬件中断
hardware inventory 硬件总量
hardware key 硬件密钥
hardware language 硬件语言
hardware layer 硬件层
hardware level 硬件级
hardware logic diagram 硬件逻辑图
hardware logic simulation 硬件逻辑仿真

hardware measurement tool 硬件测量工具
hardware memory system 硬件存储系统
hardware model 硬件模型
hardware modeling 硬件建模
hardware module 硬件模块
hardware monitor 硬件监视器
hardware monitor interface 硬件显示器接口
hardware multiplier 硬件乘法器
hardware multiply module(HMM) 硬件乘法模块
hardware optimization 硬件优化
hardware option 硬件选件
hardware-oriented algorithm 面向硬件的算法
hardware origin 硬件原点
hardware package 硬件封装
hardware performance 硬件性能
hardware platform 硬件平台
hardware primitive 硬件原语
hardware priority interrupts 硬件优先权中断
hardware process control block 硬件进程控制块
hardware raster image processor (HRIP) 硬件光栅图像处理器
hardware realization of operating system 操作系统的硬件实现
hardware receive mismatch count 硬件接收失配次数
hardware redundancy 硬件冗余法
hardware reliability 硬件可靠性
hardware requirement 硬件需求
hardware reset 硬件复位
hardware resident 硬件驻留
hardware resident built-in test 驻留硬件测试法
hardware resource 硬件资源
hardware resource management 硬件资源管理
hardware security 硬件安全性
hardware serviceability ratio 硬件服务时间比
hardware simulator 硬件仿真程序
hardware-software changeover 硬件-软件转换
hardware-software interface 硬件-软

件接口
hardware-software trade-off 硬件-软件折衷
hardware speedup 硬件加速
hardware spending 硬件开销(花费)
hardware stack 硬件堆栈
hardware structure 硬件结构
hardware support 硬件支持
hardware support device 硬件支持设备
hardware support kit 硬件支持成套设备
hardware support vector operation 硬件支持的向量运算
hardware system command 硬件系统命令
hardware tariffs 硬件价目表
hardware test 硬件测试
hardware timer 硬件计时器
hardware tree 硬件树
hardware trouble interrupt 硬件故障中断
hardware upgrade 硬件升级
hardware virtual memory 硬件虚拟存储器
hardware voter 硬件表决器
hardware windowing 硬件开窗口
hardware word size 硬件字长
hardware work package 硬件工作标准组件
hardwire logic 硬布线逻辑
hardwired 硬布线的
hardwired connection 硬布线连接
hardwired device 硬布线设备
hardwired numerical control 硬布线数控器
hardwiring 硬布线
Hargelbarger code 群发纠错码,哈格尔巴格码
harmful interference 有害干扰
harmful out-of-band components 有害带外成分
harmonic 谐波
harmonic analysis 谐波分析
harmonic characteristic 谐波特性
harmonic component 谐波分量
harmonic distortion 谐波失真
harmonic drive 谐波传动
harmonic function 调和函数

harmonic generator 谐波发生器
harmonic interference 谐波干扰
harmonic oscillator 谐波振荡器
harmonic output power 谐波输出功率
harmonic suppressor 谐波抑制器
harmonic vocoder 谐波声码器
harmony 协调;和谐的
harness 线束,电缆
harness drawing 线束图,线扎图
Harol transform 哈尔变换
Hartley 哈特来(信息量单位)
Hartley's law 哈特来定律
Hartley-Shannon law 哈特来-香农定律
Hartley transform 哈特来变换
Harvard architecture 哈佛体系结构
Harvard Graphics 哈佛图形软件
Hash 散列,杂凑;无用信息
Hash addressing 散列寻址
Hash algorithm 哈希算法,散列算法,杂凑算法
Hash algorithm information table (HAIT) 散列算法信息表
Hash algorithm library(HAL) 散列算法库
Hash code 散列码
Hash coding 散列编码
Hash conflict 散列[杂凑]冲突
Hash file 散列文件
Hash function 哈希[散列]函数
Hash index 散列索引
Hash key 散列键,杂凑关键字
Hash method 杂乱法,散列法
Hash partitioning 散列划分
Hash searching 散列查找
Hash table 散列表
Hash table bucket 散列表元
Hash total 散列总计
Hash transformation 哈希变换,散列变换
Hash vector 哈希向量,散列向量
hashed bit array 散列化位阵列
hashed random file 散列随机文件
hashed value 哈希值,散列值
hashing 哈希法,散列法
hashnet interconnection system 散列网络互连方式
Hasse graph 哈斯图
hat 随机编码

hatch 阴影线
hatch style 阴影线式样
hatching pattern 阴影图案
hatching time 策划时间
hatted code 随机码
haul 通信距离;中继站跳距
Hayes command set 贺氏命令集
Hayes compatible 贺氏兼容的
Hayes Smartmodem 贺氏智能调制解调器
haywire 临时连线
hazard 冒险;相关冒险
hazard elimination 冒险消除
hazard-free circuit 无冒险电路
hazard-free test 无冒险测试
hazard rate 冒险率
hazardless network 无冒险网络
hazardous transition 冒险变换
hazardous voltage 危险电压
haze 模糊
Hazmat(Hazard Material Management system) 有害材料管理系统 (LG&G)
HB(High Byte) 高位字节
HBR(High Bit Rate) 高比特率
HBS(Holographic Based System) 全息照相系统
HC(Hard Copy) 硬拷贝
HC(Home Computer) 家用计算机
HC(Host Computer) 主机
HCB(Highest Control Buffer) 最高层控制缓冲器
HCG(Hardware Character Generator) 硬件字符产生器
HCI(Host Computer Interface) 主机接口
HCMOS(High-density Complementary Metal Oxide Semiconductor) 高密度互补金属氧化物半导体器件
HCN(Heterogeneous Computer Network) 异构计算机网络
HCP(Hard Copy Printer) 硬拷贝打印机
HCS(Hundred Call Seconds) 百秒呼
HCWP(Human-Centric Word Processor) 人性化文字处理器
HD(Hard Disk) 硬盘
HD(High Definition) 高分辨率,高清晰度
HD(Horizontal Drive) 水平驱动
HD-MAC system HD-MAC 制
HDA(Head Disk Assembly) 磁头磁盘组合件
HDB(High Density Bipolar code) 高密度双极性码
HDB3 code (High Density Bipolar 3 code) HDB3 码
HDD(Hard Disk Drive) 硬盘驱动器
HDML(Handheld Device Markup Language) 手持设备标记语言
HDL(HanDLe) 句柄,控制柄
HDL (Hardware Description Language) 硬件描述语言
HDLC(High-level Data-Link Control procedure) 高级数据链路控制规程
HDSL(High-bit-rate Digital Subscriber Link) 高位速率数字用户线
HDTS(Half-Duplex Transmission System) 半双工传输系统
HDTV(High Definition TV) 高清晰度电视
He-Ne laser 氦氖激光器
head 磁头;冲头;打印头;标题,报头
head access window 磁头读写窗口
head address register 磁头地址寄存
head alignment 磁头校准　　　└器
head arm 磁头臂
head assembly 磁头组件
head azimuth deviation loss 磁头方位偏差损失
head carriage 磁头托架
head cleaning device 磁头清洗设备
head clogging 磁头堵塞
head core 磁头心
head crash 磁头碰撞
head degausser 磁头消磁器
head demagnetizer 磁头消磁器
head disk assembly 磁头磁盘组件
head-disk interference 磁头磁盘干扰
head driver 磁头驱动部件
head field 磁头场
head flag 起始标志;磁头标记
head gap 磁头缝隙,磁头间隙
head gap width 磁头缝宽
head gimbaled spring 磁头万向弹簧

head hang mechanism 磁头悬挂机构
head house 磁头罩
head information 磁头信息
head landing zone 磁头着陆区
head-level 标题级别
head life 磁头寿命
head load 磁头加载
head load band 磁头加载区
head load instruction 磁头加载指令
head load pad 磁头加载垫
head load solenoid 磁头加载螺线管
head loader 磁头加载器
head loading mechanism 磁头加载机构
head loading time 磁头加载时间
head lock mechanism 磁头锁定机构
head marker 磁头标志
head message 头部消息
head mounted display 头盔式显示器
head movement 磁头移动
head number 磁头号
head of form 表格头
head of format 打印纸首行
head of list 表头
head of packet 讯包头,分组头
head of queue 队列首
head of string 字符串头
head of the queue 队列头
head-on collision 线路冲突
head-per-track 每道一头
head-per-track disk drive 每道一头磁盘驱动器
head phone 头戴式送受话器
head pointer 头指针,首部指示符
head position 头位置;磁头位置
head position actuator 磁头定位调节器
head positioner 磁头定位器
head-positioning cartridge 磁头定位式盒式磁带机
head positioning mechanism 磁头定位机构
head-positioning time 磁头定位时间
head pressure solenoid 磁头压力螺线管
head record 标题记录
head rotor 磁头转子
head scatter 磁头分散
head search controller 磁头查找控制器
head seek error 磁头寻道错误
head segment 标题段

head select 磁头选择
head select signal 磁头选择信号
head settling time 磁头稳定时间
head skew 磁头斜移
head slider 磁头浮动块
head slot 磁头读写槽
head stack 磁头组
head step settling time 磁头步进稳定时间
head support arm 磁头支撑臂
head switching 磁头切换
head symbol 头部符号,首部符号
head-to-foot 从顶到底
head to head 头到头
head-to-tape contact 头带接触
head-to-tape speed 磁头磁带相对速度
head unification 磁头合一
head unloading 磁头卸载
head-up display 平视显示器
head winding 磁头绕组
headed clause 有头子句
headend 前端,头端
headender 数据转发器
header 标题,报头
header address 磁头地址
header area 标题区
header block 标题字组
header buffer 标题缓冲器
header byte 标题字节
header card 标题卡片
header cell 标题单元
header checking 标题[报头]校验
header element 首元素;标题元素
header entry 标题项,首标项
header field 标题字段
header file 标题文件,头文件
header folder 标题文件夹
header format 标题[报头]格式
header label 首标记,首部标签
header label of file 文件首标号
header label of volume 文卷首标
header leader 引带
header line 标题行
header message 标题消息
header part 标题部分
header positioning system 头定位系统
header record 标题记录
header record format 标题记录格式

header row 有标题行,页眉行
header section 标题节
header segment 标题段
header sheet 标题数据记录纸;标题页
header statement 标题语句
header table 标题表
header translation 报头翻译
headers and trailers 首部与尾部
heading 消息首部,标题
heading and footing 加标题和页码;加标题与合计
heading area 首部区,标题区
heading boilerplate 标题样板
heading block 起始字组,标题字块
heading character 标题字符
heading control 标题控制
heading frame 标题[报头]帧
heading group 标题[报头]分组
heading information 标题信息
heading record 标题记录
heading statement 标题语句
heading syntax 标题语法
headless clause 无头子句
headless format 无标题格式
headphone 头戴式受话器
headplate 磁头板
headset 磁头组;头戴式耳机
health check 正常检查
healthiness conditions 健康条件
heap 堆,堆垒
heap allocation 堆式分配,堆垒分配
heap construction 堆构建,堆垒建造
heap element 堆元素
heap file 堆文件
heap sort 堆排序
heap sort program 堆排序程序
heap storage space requirement 堆存储器空间要求
hearing threshold 听觉阈
heat capacity 热容量
heat conduction 热传导
heat convection 热对流
heat diffusion 热扩散
heat dissipation 热散失
heat drift 热漂移
heat exchanger 热交换器
heat fixing 热定影
heat fusing 热熔断;热熔化

heat gun reflow 加热枪再流
heat insulator 隔热材料
heat loss 热损耗
heat pipe 热管
heat printer 热敏打印机
heat-proof 热防护
heat-seal 热封,熔焊
heat-sensitive printer 热敏打印机
heat set ink 热凝固油墨
heat shield 热屏蔽
heat-shrinkable plastic 热收缩型塑料
heat-shrinkable sleeve 热收缩套管
heat sink 散热片
heat sink compound 散热器填料
heat sink cooling 散热片冷却
heat sink strip 散热条
heat sinking 散热
heat-sinking capability 散热能力
heat-spot 过热点
heat subject 热门话题
heat test 加热试验,耐热试验
heat treat 热处理
heat-writing recorder 热写记录仪
heating-up time 加热时间,预热时间
heatseeker 热寻的器
Heaviside function 海维赛函数
heavy 繁重的
heavy base layer 重掺杂基区层
heavy-duty 重载
heavy-duty industrial robot 重载工业机器人
heavy duty load 重负载
heavy-duty software 广泛适用的软件
heavy hour 忙时
heavy load 重载,重负荷
heavy-loaded circuit 单独用户线电路;重负载电路
heavy-loaded station 单独用户端局;重载站
heavy route 重路由,重路径
heavy route station 重路由站
heavy traffic 通信业务繁忙
hecto(H) 百
hectometer(HM) 百米
hectovolt(HV) 百伏,百伏特
hectowatt(HW) 百瓦,百瓦特
hedging 包围,妨碍
height 高度

height balanced binary tree 高度平衡二叉树
height balanced tree 高度平衡树
height of a node 结点高度
height of a tree 树的高度
heir 后继
heir pointer 后继指针
Heisenberg inequality 海森伯不等式
held over 滞留;加强;保持
held terminal 挂起终端
helical 螺线
helical angle 螺旋角
helical line 螺旋线
helical scan 螺旋式扫描
helium cadmium laser 氦镉激光器
helium neon laser 氦氖激光器
helix 螺旋扫描滚筒
helix joint 螺旋关节
helix printer 螺旋打印机
hello 呼叫信号;问候
hello program 试用程序,介绍性程序
hello request 问候请求
hello screen 介绍画面,友好屏幕
hello software 试用性软件
helmet monitoring device(HMD) 头盔显示装置
helmet wireless telephone set 盔式无线电话机
HELP 求助程序,帮助程序
help command 求助命令
help compiler 求助编译程序
help context 帮助上下文
help facility 帮助信息
help function 帮助功能
help index 帮助信息索引
help information 帮助信息
help key 求助键,帮助键
help menu 帮助选单,求助菜单
help message 帮助信息
help panel 帮助画面;帮助面板
help pop-up 弹出式帮助信息
HELP program 帮助程序
help screen 帮助屏幕
help support 求助配套
help system 求助系统
help text 帮助文本
help window 帮助窗口
help word 帮助字

helper 帮助程序
helper function 助手功能
helpful tips 帮助性提示
Helvetica Helvetica 字形
hemeostasis 自动调节动态平衡
hemicontinuous 半连续
hemivariate 半变量
hemstitching 花边现象
Henry (电感量单位)亨利
heptagon 七边形
Herbrand base 海尔勃朗基 「释
Herbrand interpretation 海尔勃朗解
Herbrand's domain 海尔勃朗域
Herbrand theorem 海尔勃朗定理
Herbrand universe 海尔勃朗全域
hereditary optimal control 遗传最佳控制
hereditary property 传递的性质
hermaphroditic connector 同性接插件
hermaphroditic contact 单一型插头
Hermes system 赫尔姆斯系统
hermetic 密封的,气密的
hermetic chip carrier(HCC) 密封芯片载体
hermetic package 气密封装
hermetic sealing 气密封装
hermetic test 气密性试验
hermetically sealed 全密封的
Hermite curve 埃尔米特曲线 「元
Hermite finite element 埃尔米特有限
Hermite interpolation 埃尔米特插值
Hermite polynomial 埃尔米特多项式
Hermitian function 埃尔米特函数
Hermitian matrix 埃尔米特矩阵
Hertz(Hz) 赫兹
hesitation 暂停
Hessenberg matrix 海森堡矩阵
heterochronous 异步的;异质的
heterochronous digital signals 异步数字信号
heterodyne 外差
heterogeneity 异构
heterogeneous computer 异构计算机
heterogeneous computer network 异构计算机网络
heterogeneous computer system 异构计算机系统
heterogeneous database 异构数据库

heterogeneous database integration 异构数据库集成
heterogeneous database management 异构数据库管理
heterogeneous distributed database system 异构分布式数据库系统
heterogeneous environment 异构环境
heterogeneous LAN-LAN interconnection 异种局域网互连
heterogeneous light 杂散光
heterogeneous multiplex 非均匀多路复用,异构型多路转换
heterogeneous multiplexing 非均匀多路复用
heterogeneous multiprocessor 异构型多处理机
heterogeneous network 异构型网络
heterogeneous parallel simulation computer 异构型并行仿真计算机
heterogeneous structure 异类结构,异构
heterogeneous switching network 非均匀交换网络
heterogeneous system 异构系统
heterogeneous transaction 异构事务
heterojunction 异质结
heterojunction diode laser 异质结二极管激光器
heterostructure 异质结构,异构
heterostructure laser 异质结构激光器
heterostructure tree 异型结构树
heuristic 探索的,启发式的
heuristic algorithm 试探式算法,启发式算法
heuristic approach 试探法,启发法
heuristic binary file index 启发二进制文件索引
heuristic for learning 学习用启发式
heuristic function 探试函数,启发函数
heuristic information 启发信息,探试信息
heuristic knowledge 启发性知识
heuristic method 试探法
heuristic power 启发能力
heuristic problem solution 试探问题解法
heuristic problem solving 启发式问题求解
heuristic program 启发性程序,探索程序
heuristic programming 试探程序设计
heuristic pruning of game tree 博弈树的启发式修剪
heuristic routine 探试例程
heuristic routing 探试性路由选择
heuristic rule 启发式规则 「索
heuristic search 探试搜索,启发式搜
heuristic search method 启发式搜索法 「论
heuristic search theory 启发性探索理
heuristic self-organization 启发式自组织
heuristic stability 启发式稳定性
heuristic technique 探试法
heuristic tuning 探试性调谐
Hewlett Packard(HP) 惠普公司(美)
Hewlett-Packard Graphics Language 惠普图形语言
Hewlett Packard Interface Bus 惠普接口总线
Hewlett-Packard Printer Control Language(HPPCL) 惠普打印机控制语言
HEX(HEXadecimal) 十六进制
hex buffer 六缓冲器
hex head screw 六角螺钉
hex inverter 六反相器
hex pad 16进制键盘
hexadecimal(HEX) 16进制的
hexadecimal addition 16进制加法
hexadecimal address 16进制地址
hexadecimal base 16进制基数
hexadecimal calculator 16进制计算器
hexadecimal code 16进制代码
hexadecimal constant 16进制常数
hexadecimal conversion 16进制转换
hexadecimal format 16进制格式
hexadecimal keyboard 16进制键盘
hexadecimal notation 16进制表示法
hexadecimal number system 16进制数系
hexagon 六边形
HF bias 高频偏置,高频偏磁
HFC(Hybrid Fiberoptic/Coaxial) 混合光纤同轴电缆

HFS(Hierarchical File System) 分层文件系统
HGC(Hercules Graphics Card) 大力神(单色)图形适配卡
HGL(Hierarchical Graph Language) 分层图形语言
HH(Hour Holding) 暂停
Hi address byte 高位地址字节
Hi-Call Hi-Call 交互式音频平台
Hi-Fi(High Fidelity) 高保真度
hi-fi earphone 高保真耳机
hi-fi stereo 高保真立体声
Hi-REL lid 高可靠管帽
hi-tech 高技术
hibernate state 冬眠[休眠]状态
hibernation 休止
hiccup 打嗝
HiColor 增强彩色
HIDAM(Hierarchical Indexed Direct Access Method) 分级索引直接存取法
hidden attribute 隐含属性
hidden buffer 隐含缓冲器
hidden bus arbitration 隐含总线仲裁
hidden codes 隐藏码
hidden computer 隐藏式计算机
hidden data 隐含数据
hidden edge 隐藏边
hidden field 隐式字段
hidden file 隐文件
hidden form field 隐藏窗体域
hidden function 隐含功能;隐函数
hidden line 隐线
hidden line algorithm 隐线算法
hidden line elimination 隐线消除
hidden line plot 隐线式绘图
hidden line removal 隐线消除
hidden memory 内藏式内存
hidden objects 隐藏目标[对象]
hidden refresh logic 隐含刷新逻辑
hidden register 隐含寄存器
hidden routine 隐匿例程
hidden stack 隐式堆栈
hidden surface 隐面
hidden surface elimination 隐面消除
hidden-surface removal 隐面消除
hidden system file 隐含系统文件
hidden text 隐藏文本
hidden unit 隐藏单元
hidden variable 隐变量
hide 隐藏,隐匿
HIDE command 隐命令
hide detail 隐藏细节
hide option 隐藏选项
hide trace 隐藏跟踪
hiding invisible element 隐藏不可见元素
hiding strategy 隐藏策略
hierarchical abstract computer 分级抽象计算机
hierarchical access method(HAM) 分层存取法
hierarchical and compact description chart 层次和紧凑的描述图
hierarchical arrangement 电话分级分区制
hierarchical binary search 分层对分检索
hierarchical cache 分级高速缓存
hierarchical caching 分层缓存机制
hierarchical classification 等级分类
hierarchical clustering 分层群集
hierarchical coding 层次编码
hierarchical common bus 分级公用总线
hierarchical communications 分层通信
hierarchical computer network 分层计算机网络
hierarchical control 多级递阶控制;分级控制
hierarchical control system 层次控制系统
hierarchical cut 层次分割
hierarchical data base 层次数据库
hierarchical data description 分层数据描述
hierarchical data model 分层数据模型
hierarchical data structure 分级数据结构
hierarchical database 层次数据库
hierarchical decomposition 层次结构分解
hierarchical design 分层设计
hierarchical design method 分层设计法
hierarchical development methodology (HDM) 分层开发方法论

hierarchical diagram 分层图,谱系图
hierarchical dialogue structure 分层对话结构
hierarchical direct access method (HDAM) 分层直接访问法
hierarchical direct organization 分层直接组织结构
hierarchical directed graph 分层有向图
hierarchical distributed decision support system(HDDSS) 层次分布式决策支持系统
hierarchical distributed multiprocessor technology 分层分布式多处理机技术
hierarchical file 层次文件,分级文件
hierarchical file structure 层次文件结构
Hierarchical File System(HFS) 层次型文件系统
hierarchical file system 分级文件系统
hierarchical graph 层次图
hierarchical holographic modeling (HHM) 分层全息摄影造型法
hierarchical image understanding model 分级图像理解模型
hierarchical indexed direct access method(HIDAM) 分级索引直接访问法
hierarchical indexed sequential access method(HISAM) 分层索引顺序存取法
hierarchical intelligent control system 层次智能控制系统
hierarchical interrupt 分级中断
hierarchical key group 层次关键码组
hierarchical layout 分级中断
hierarchical memory system 分层存储器系统
hierarchical menu 分层菜单
hierarchical model 分层模型,层次模型
hierarchical-multilevel approach 分层多阶法,层次多级法
hierarchical - multiobjective approach (HMO) 分层多目标法
hierarchical multiobjective system 分层多目标系统
hierarchical multiprocessor system (HMPS) 分层结构多处理机系统
hierarchical network 分层网络
hierarchical ordering 分层的顺序
hierarchical overlapping coordination (HOC) 分层重叠协调法
hierarchical path 分层路径,层次路径
hierarchical planning 分层计划,分级规划
hierarchical pointer 分层指示字;层次指示字
hierarchical process 层级进程
hierarchical routing 分层路径选择法
hierarchical sequence 分层[层次]顺序
hierarchical sequence key 分层顺序关键码
hierarchical sequential access method (HSAM) 分层顺序存取法
hierarchical sequential organization 分层顺序结构
hierarchical serial ordering 分层串行排序
hierarchical storage manager 分层存储器管理程序
hierarchical structure 层次结构
hierarchical structured diagram(HSD) 分层结构线图
hierarchical structured query 分层结构查询
hierarchical system 分层系统,层次系统
hierarchical system control theory 分层系统控制理论
hierarchical team 分层式小组
hierarchical topological design of large computer network 大型计算机网络的分层拓扑设计
hierarchical tree-structure 分层树形结构
hierarchical virtual machine 分层虚拟机
hierarchically synchronized network 分层同步网络
hierarching planning 分层规划
hierarchy 分层[层次]结构
hierarchy access time 分级访问时间
hierarchy chart 层次图
hierarchy computer control system 分层计算机控制系统
hierarchy control 分层控制
hierarchy cost 分层价格

hierarchy data structure 分层数据结构
hierarchy input-process-output 输入-加工-输出分层结构
hierarchy manager 分层管理程序
hierarchy naming 分层命名机制
hierarchy nesting 层次嵌套
hierarchy number 分层数
hierarchy objective 阶层目标
hierarchy of information storage 信息存储层次
hierarchy of interpretive modules 解释模块的分层结构
hierarchy of mask 屏蔽层次
hierarchy of memory 分级存储器
hierarchy of operations 运算层次
hierarchy plus input - process - output (HIPO) 分层结构加输入处理输出
hierarchy segment theorem 层次片段定理
hierarchy sharing memory 分层共享内存
hierarchy table 层次表
HIF(Human-Initiated Failure) 人为故障
HiFD(High capacity Floppy Disk) 大容量活动盘(Sony)
HIFO(Highest-In First-Out) 先进先出
HIFT (Hardware Implemented Fault Tolerance) 硬件实现的容错
Higashi Ikoma Optical Visual Information System 西依光学可视信息系统
high 高的;高度
high accuracy 高精度
high accuracy data 高精度数据
high accuracy position system 高精度定位系统
high address 高端地址
high and dry 暂停,搁置
high bit rate 高比特率,高位速率
high-bit-rate digital subscriber link (HDSL) 高位速率数字用户线
high boost 高频提升
high bound 上界
high brightness X-ray source 高亮度X射线源
high byte 高字节

high byte enable(HBEN) 高字节使能
high byte strobe(HBS) 高字节选通
high capacity 大容量,高容量
high capacity communication 大容量通信
high-capacity mobile telecommunication system(HCMTS) 大容量移动通信系统
high capacity satellite digital service 大容量卫星数字业务
high capacity storage system 高容量存储系统
high capacity terrestrial digital service 大容量地面数字业务
high color 高保真度彩色
high compliance 高顺应性
high compliance loud speaker 高顺性扬声器
high conductivity 高导电性
high-confidence countermeasure 高可靠防范措施
high continuity finite element 高连续性有限元
high contrast 高反差,高对比度
high-contrast image 高对比度图像
high correlation 高度相关
high current density 大电流密度
high definition 高分辨率[清晰度]
high definition television(HDTV) 高清晰度电视
high density(HD) 高密度
high density assembly 高密度封装[装配]
high-density bipolar code(HDB) 高密度双极性码
high density carrier 高密度载波
high density data record(HDDR) 高密度数据记录
high density disk 高密度磁盘
high density electronic packaging 高密度电子组装
high density encode model 高密度编码模式
high-density packaging 高密度封装
high density recording 高密度记录
high density signal carrier 高密度信号负载芯片
high density soft ferrite 高密度软铁氧

high density storage 高密度存储器
high dimensional pattern grammar 高维模式文法
high DOS memory 高端DOS内存
high electron mobility 高电子迁移率
high-end 高端,高档
high-end application 高档应用
high-end product 高端[高档]产品
high energy physics 高能物理学
high-energy tape 高能磁带
high fidelity(Hi-Fi) 高保真度
high frequency carrier 高频载波
high frequency channel 高频信道
high-frequency compensation 高频补偿
high function terminal 高功能终端
high-gain amplifier 高增益放大器
high-gain antenna 高增益天线
high-grade cryptographic system 高等级密码系统
high impact 高冲击强度
high impedance 高阻抗
high impedance relay 高阻抗继电器
high impedance state 高阻态
high impedance state output current 高阻态输出电流
high-integration density 高集成度
high intensity noise 高强度噪声
high-key lighting 浓色调照明
high-key value 高键值
high-layer protocols 高层协议
high-level 高水平的,高级的;高电平
high-level artificial intelligence language 高级人工智能语言
high-level compiler 高级编译程序
high-level control 高层控制
high-level data link control(HDLC) 高级数据链路控制
high-level data link control adapter (HDLCA) 高级数据链路控制规程适配器
high-level data-link control procedure (HDLC) 高级数据链路控制规程
high-level data-link control protocol 高级数据链路控制协议
high level data link control station 高级数据链路控制站
high level debugging 高级调试

high-level format 高级格式化
high-level goal 高级目标
high-level graphics programming instruction 高级图形编程指令
high-level industrial robot 高级工业机器人
high-level job control language 高级作业控制语言
high-level language 高级语言
high level language application program interface(HLLAPI) 高级语言应用程序接口
high-level language architecture 高级语言体系结构
high-level language computer 高级语言计算机
high-level language oriented computer 面向高级语言的计算机
high-level language programming 高级语言程序设计
high-level language programming environment 高级语言程序设计环境
high-level message 高层消息
high-level microprogramming language (HML, HLML) 高级微程序设计语言
high-level network service 高层网络服务
high-level noise margin 高电平噪声容限
high-level nonprocedural language 高级非过程语言
high-level output current 高电平输出电流
high-level output voltage 高电平输出电压
high-level primitive 高级原语
high level process control language 高级过程控制语言
high-level programmer interface 高级程序员接口
high-level programming language 高级程序设计语言
high level protocol 高层协议,高级规程
high-level recovery 高级恢复;高电平恢复
high level representation 高电平表示法
high-level resource scheduler 高级资源调度程序

high-level scheduler 高级调度程序
high-level scheduling 高层调度
high-level software 高层软件
high-level source code 高层源码
high-level structured programming language 高级结构化程序设计语言
high-level synthesis 高级综合
high level system parallel input/output 高级系统并行输入/输出
high-level vector language 高级向量语言
high light 加亮点
high-lighting 突出性,醒目性
high-limiting control action 高限度控制作用
high logic level 高逻辑电平
high-low bias check 高低边缘检验
high-low bias test 高低边缘测试
high-low limit 高低界限
High Memory Area(HMA) 高端内存区域
high-noise immunity logic(HNIL) 高抗扰度逻辑
high-order bit 高序位
high-order byte 高位字节
high-order character 高位字符
high-order digit 高位数字
high-order end 高位端
high-order language 高级语言
high-order mode 高次模
high-order position 高位数字
high pass filter 高通滤波器
high performance communication equipment 高性能通信装置
high performance computer(HPC) 高性能计算机
high performance data compression 高性能数据压缩
high-performance equipment 高性能设备
High Performance File System(HPFS) 高性能文件系统
High Performance FORTRAN(HPF) 高性能 FORTRAN 语言
high performance line printer 高性能行式打印机
high performance MOS(HMOS) 高性能金属氧化物半导体
high performance parallel interface(HIPPI) 高性能并行接口
high performance parallel processor 高性能并行处理机
high persistence phosphor 高持久性荧光粉
high portion 高端部分,上部
high-priority 高优先权
high-priority interrupt 高优先权中断
high-priority record queue 高优先权记录队列
high Q circuit 高品质因数电路,高 Q 电路
high quality graphic 高质量图像
high range 高值域
high-rate discharge 高速放电
high reduction 高缩小率
high reflective coating 高反射膜
high reliability 高可靠性
high reliability transmission system 高可靠性通信方式
high resolution 高分辨率,高清晰度
high resolution graphic 高分辨率图形,高清晰度图像
high resolution graphic terminal 高清晰度图像终端
high segment 高区段
high selectivity 高选择性
high sensitive recorder 高灵敏记录器
high sensitive relay 高灵敏继电器
high sensitivity demodulator 高灵敏解调器
high sensitivity receiver 高灵敏度接收机
high sensitivity tester 高灵敏度检测器,高灵敏度探头
High Sierra 高层 Sierra 标准
high-speed 高速
high-speed A/D converter 高速模-数转换器
high speed arithmetic 高速运算
high speed automatic circuit breaker 快速自动断路开关
high-speed buffer 高速缓冲器
high-speed bus 高速总线
high speed carry 高速进位
high speed channel 高速通道
high speed channel processor 高速通道处理机

high speed circuit-breaker 高速断路器
high speed CMOS integrated circuit 高速 CMOS 集成电路
high-speed comparator 高速比较器
high-speed computer 高速计算机
high speed controller 高速控制器
high-speed data acquisition system 高速数据采集系统
high speed data buffer 高速数据缓冲器
high speed data transmission 高速数据传送
high-speed decision 快速决策
high-speed die bounder 高速芯片粘结机
high speed digital integrated circuit 高速数字集成电路
high speed dump 高速转储
high speed duplication 高速复制
high-speed emulation memory 高速仿真存储器
high speed facsimile 高速传真
high-speed facsimile transmission 高速传真传输方式
high-speed line 高速线路
high-speed line adapter 高速线路适配器
high-speed line printer 高速行式打印机
high speed local network 高速局域网
high-speed look ahead carry generator 高速超前进位发生器
high-speed loop 高速环路
high-speed memory 高速内存
high speed modem 高速调制解调器
high-speed multiplier 高速乘法器
High-speed National Project Computer System(HNPCS) 超高性能国家工程计算机系统(日)
high-speed oscilloscope 高速示波器
high-speed peripheral 高速外围设备
high-speed pipeline computer 高速流水线计算机
high-speed plotter 高速绘图仪
high-speed printer(HSP) 高速打印机
high speed random access 高速随机存取
high-speed reader(HSR) 高速读出机
high-speed register 高速寄存器
high-speed relay 高速继电器

high speed rewind 高速反绕
high speed scan 高速扫描
high speed scanner 高速扫描仪
high-speed scroll 高速翻卷[滚屏]
high-speed seek 高速寻道,高速查找
high speed selector channel 高速选择器通道
high-speed skip 高速跳越,高速跳过
high-speed storage 高速存储器
high-speed storage loading 高速存储器载入
high-speed symbol generator 高速符号发生器
High Speed Technology(HST) 高速技术
high speed TTL circuit(HTTL) 高速 TTL 电路
high-speed type 高速打印
high speed walking robot 高速步行机器人
high technology 高技术
high technology industry 高技术产业
high temperature test 高温试验
high tension 高压
high than high-level language 超高级语言
high thermal conduction module 高热导组件
high-threshold logic 高阈值逻辑
high threshold logic circuit 高阈值逻辑电路
high throughput 高吞吐量
high-torque low-inertia motor 高转矩低惯量马达
high transaction throughput 高事务处理吞吐量
high usage circuit group 高效电路群
high usage intertoll trunk 高利用率长途台间直达通路
high-usage group 高利用率群路
high-usage route 高利用率路由
high-usage trunk 高效直通干线
high-usage trunk group 高利用率线路群
high-velocity scanning 高速扫描
high voltage alarm 高压告警器
high voltage circuit breaker 高压断路器
high-voltage direct current(HVDC) 高压直流电
high voltage IC 高压集成电路

high voltage state 高电压状态
high-voltage test 高压试验
high volume time-sharing(HVTS) 大容量分时
high yield 高成品率
higher layer function 高层功能
higher layer protocol 高层协议
higher mode 高次模
higher-order logic 高阶逻辑
higher-order predicate calculus 高阶谓词演算
higher-order routine 高层例程序
higher priority 较高优先权
higher priority job 较高优先权作业
highest index level 最高索引级
highest order 最高位［值］
highest possible key value 最高可能键
highest priority 最高优先权［优先级］
highest priority-first 最高优先级优先法
highest priority number 最高优先数
highest significant position 最高有效位
highlight 增亮，加亮；高光
highlight bar 加亮条
highlighted text 加亮文本
highlighting 加亮，增亮
highlighting character 高亮度［加亮］字符
highlighting display 高亮度［加亮］显示
highly congested network 高度拥挤的网络
highly modular operating system 高度模块化操作系统
highly overlapped pipeline computer 高度重叠流水线计算机
highly parallel arithmetic 高度并行算法
highly parallel computer 高度并行计算机
highly reflective coating 高反射涂覆
highly reliable system 高可靠性系统
highway 高速通道
highway frame 干线数据帧，高速数据总线帧
highway protocol 干线［高速数据总线］协议
highway switching network 干线［公共通路］交换网络
highway width 总线［干线］宽度

HiJaak HiJaak 图形处理程序
Hilbert cube 希尔伯特立方体
Hilbert-Schmitt theory 希尔伯特-施密特理论
Hilbert space 希尔伯特空间
Hilbert transform 希尔伯特变换
Hilbert transform technique 希尔伯特变换技术
Hilbert's tenth problem 希尔伯特第十问题
hill-and-dale 峰谷
hill bandwidth 峰形带宽，垂直带宽
hill climbing 爬山法
HIMEM.SYS 高端内存管理程序
hinting 微量压缩
hints 提示操作
HIPO(Hierarchy plus Input-Process-Output) 分层结构加输入处理输出，HIPO图
HiPPI(High Performance Parallel Interface channel) 高性能并行接口信道
HIPS(Hybrid Image Processing System) 混合图像处理系统
Hiragana （日文）平假名
HIRS(Holographic Information Retrieval System) 全息照相信息检索系统
Hirschberg's bucket sorting 赫斯彻伯格桶排序
HIS(Hardware Interrupt System) 硬件中断系统
HISAM(Hierarchical Indexed Sequential Access Method) 层次索引顺序存取法
hiss 啸叫声
histogram 梯级频布图，直方图
histogram equalization 直方图均衡
histogram flattening 直方图平坦化
histogram linearization 直方图线性化
histogram modification 直方图修正
histogram normalize 直方图正态化
histogram of differences 差值直方图
histogram specification 直方图规范
histogram thresholding 直方图门限化
historical analogy 历史类推
historical data 历史性数据
historical data device 历史数据设备

historical database 历史数据库
historical file 历史文件
historical reference 历史参考,历史引用
historical trend panel 历史趋势画面
historical version 历史版本
History Brush 历史刷(Adobe)
history command 历史命令
history data set 历史数据集
history dependent control 历史相关控制
history file 历史文件
history list 历史表,经历表
history log 历史运行登录
history memory 历史存储器
history panel 历史面板
history register 经历寄存器
history run 历史数据处理
hit 命中,找到
hit-and-miss 时隐时现;漫无目的
hit counter 点击次数计数器
hit detect function 拾取功能
hit file 命中文件
hit indicator 选中指示器,接通指示器
hit noise 击打噪声
hit-on-the-fly printer 飞击式打印机
hit-on-the-line 线路瞬间干扰
hit probability 命中概率
hit rate 命中率
hit ratio 命中率;激活率
hit record 命中记录
hit timing 偶断时limitado
Hitachi 日立公司(日)
Hitachi Network Architecture 日立网络体系结构
hits 瞬时打扰,瞬态干扰
HLI(Host Language Interface) 主机语言接口
HLP(High-Level Protocol) 高层协议
HLS(High Level Scheduler) 高级调度程序
HLS(Hue, Luminance and Saturation) 色度,亮度与饱和度
HLS/BIT(High Level Synthesis/BIT) HLS/BIT 高级综合系统
HLSI(Hybrid LSI) 混合大规模集成电路
HLT(HaLT) 停机
HMA(High Memory Area) 高端内存区域

HMD(Helmet Monitoring Device) 头盔式监视装置
HMOS(High-performance MOS) 高性能 MOS
HMOS(High-speed MOS) 高速 MOS
HMPL(High level MicroProgramming Language) 高级微程序设计语言
HMS(Hardened Memory System) 固化内存系统
HMS(Home Multimedia System) 家用多媒体系统
Hoare system 霍尔系统
hobby computer 业余计算机
hobby programming 业余编程
hobbyist (计算机)业余爱好者
hog 侈奢程序
hogging 扰乱
hold 保持,维持
hold acknowledge 保持应答
hold button 保持按钮
hold circuit 保持电路
hold coil 保持线圈,维持绕组
hold control 同步调整,保持控制
hold current 保持电流,维持电流
hold delivery 保持传送
hold-down tabulator key 保持按下制表键
hold facility 保持能力;保持设施
hold for delivery on request 保持到请求时发送
hold for enquiry 查询保持
hold graphics 保持图形
hold in range 同步保持范围;同步带
hold input 保持输入
hold instruction 保持指令
hold list 保持信息表
hold mark 保持标志
hold mode 保持状态
hold off 释放
hold-off circuit 释抑电路
hold page queue 保持页面队列
hold queue 保持队列
hold request 保持请求
hold state 保持状态
hold time 保持时间
holder 支持架;夹具
holding action 保持作用
holding beam 维持电子束

holding circuit 保持[维持]电路
holding coil 保持线圈
holding cost 维持费用
holding current 保持[维持]电流
holding gun 保持电子枪
holding line 保持线
holding power 保持[维持]功率
holding register 保持寄存器
holding screen status 保持屏幕状态
holding time 占用时间;保持时间
holding tone 保持音
holding torque 保持力矩,保持转矩
hole 空穴;孔,洞
hole conduction 空穴导电
hole current 空穴电流
hole-electron pair 空穴电子对
hole location 孔位
hole mobility 空穴迁移率
holistic 完整,整体
holistic simulator 整体仿真器
Hollerith card 何勒内斯卡片
Hollerith code 何勒内斯代码
Hollerith machine 何勒内斯机器
hollow ellipse 空心椭圆
hollow PC "空壳"个人计算机
hollow rectangle 空心矩形
holocoder 全息编码器
holoframe 全息图帧
hologram 全息照相
hologram page memory 全息图页寄存
holograph 手稿文献 └器
Holographic Data Store System (HDSS) 全息数据存储系统
holographic display 全息显示
holographic filter 全息照相滤光器
holographic image reconstruction 全息图像重构
holographic input 全息照相输入
holographic lens 全息照相镜头
holographic mask technology 全息掩模技术
holographic memory 全息存储器
holographic optical element 全息光学元件
holographic printer 全息打印机
holographic readout system 全息读出系统
holographic stereo display 全息立体显示
holographic storage 全息照相存储器
holographical display 全息显示
holography 全息照相术
hololens 全息透镜
holomicrography 全息显微照相术
Holonic function 霍洛尼柯功能
holophonics 三维录音
HOLWG(High Order Language Working Group) 高级语言工作组
home 起始位,出发点
home address 起始地址
home-area toll 当地电话,国内长途电话
home automation 家庭自动化
home banking 家用银行业务终端
home block 标识块,起始块
home button 原位按钮
home cell 起始单元
home computer 家庭计算机
home cursor position 起始光标位置
home directory 起始目录,主目录
home environment 本地环境
home information center 家庭信息中心
home information system 家庭信息系统
Home key 归位键
home location 标识位置
home location area 原地方区
home loop 本地回路
home mobile services switching center (HMSC) 原地移动交换中心
home mobile subscriber 原地移动用户
home music center 家庭音乐中心
home numbering plan area 国内编号计划区
home office 家庭办公
home on 直接连线
home optical transceiver 家用光收发机
home optical transmitter-receiver 家用光收发信机
home page 主页,起始页
Home Page Reader 主页阅读器 (IBM)
home position 原始[起始]位置
home record 引导[起始]记录
home robots 家庭机器人
home server 本地服务器
home study 函授教育
home terminal 家庭终端

home window 初始窗口
homebrew 家庭制造的
homegrown software 家庭生产的软件
homelink 标识网
homenet 家庭网络；本地网
homeomorphic 同胚
homeomorphically-irreducible tree 同胚不可约树
homeostasis 动态静止，动态平衡
homeostatic mechanism 自动平衡机构，同态调节机构
homepage wizard 主页向导
homepitaxy 同外延，等外延
homeware 家庭软件
homework software 家庭事务软件
homing 归位，复位；导航
homing beacon 归航信标
homing receiver 自动寻的接收机
homing sequence 引导序列
homing tree 自寻树，引导树
homochromatic 同色的，均色的
homochronous 类同步的，恒步的
homochronous digital signals 类同步数字信号
homogeneity 齐次性，均匀性；同构
homogeneity test 同构性检验
homogeneous boundary condition 齐次边界条件
homogeneous computer 同构计算机
homogeneous computer network 同构计算机网络
homogeneous computer system 同类计算机系统
homogeneous coordinate representation 齐次坐标表示法
homogeneous distributed database system 同构分布式数据库系统
homogeneous environment 同质环境
homogeneous equation 齐次方程
homogeneous function 齐次函数
homogeneous graph 单色图形
homogeneous group 同类组
homogeneous light 单色光
homogeneous linear equations 齐次线性方程组
homogeneous Markov chain 均匀马尔可夫链
homogeneous Markov process 均匀马尔可夫过程
homogeneous medium 均匀媒体[介质]
homogeneous multiplex 同构多路复用
homogeneous multiplexed circuit 均匀复用线路
homogeneous multiprocessor 同构型多处理机
homogeneous multistate system(HM) 齐次多状态系统
homogeneous network 同构网络
homogeneous parallel simulation computer 同构型并行仿真计算机「构
homogeneous plex structure 同类丛结
homogeneous Poisson process 均匀泊松过程
homogeneous program 齐次规划
homogeneous S-coherent multistate system 齐次S相干多状态系统
homogeneous section 均匀段 「构
homogeneous structure 同类结构，同
homogeneous switching network 同类交换网
homogeneous uncertainty vector 齐次不定态向量
homojunction 同质结
homologous design 保型设计
homomorphic convolution 同态卷积
homomorphic filter restoration 同态滤波复原
homomorphic filtering 同态滤波
homomorphic filtering restoration 同态滤波复原
homomorphic image processing 同态图像处理
homomorphic mapping 同态映射
homomorphic processing 同态处理
homomorphic signal processing 同态信号处理
homomorphic speech processing 同态语言处理
homomorphic system 同态系统
homomorphic system for convolution 卷积同态系统
homomorphic system for multiplication 乘法同态系统
homomorphic vocoder 同态声码器
homomorphism 同构，同态

homomorphism equivalence 同态等价
homomorphism interpolation theorem 同态内插定理
homonym character 同音字
homonymy 同音异义
homophone 同音异义词
homophone error 同音异义[别字]错误
homophonic filtering 同音滤波法
homophonic substitution cipher 多名码代替密码
homotopy 同伦
homotype 同型
honesty function 诚实函数
honesty theorem 诚实定理
honeycomb domain structure 蜂房式磁畴结构
honeycomb pattern 蜂房图案
honeycomb network 蜂窝状网络
hood 防护罩,盖,套
hook 挂钩;异常分支
hook chain 钩链
hook controls 挂钩控件
hook ID 挂钩标识符
hook provider 连接提供者
hook-up 搭电路,钩连电路
hook-up wire 安装线
hooked vector 异常分支[陷阱]向量
hookemware "钓鱼"软件,诱饵软件
hooking 挂钩;拍键
hop 过渡段;跳线
hop by hop 逐跳法,逐段法
hop by hop header (IPv6)站至站包头
hop count 跳跃总数,段数
hop count limit 跳跃数[过桥数]限制
hop flow control 段阶流量控制
hop limit (IPv6)跳数限制
hopcheck 跳站检验工具
Hopcroft-Karp's algorithm 霍普克罗夫特-卡普算法
Hopcroft-Tarjan's algorithm 霍普克罗夫特-塔金算法
Hopfield network 霍普费尔德网络
Hopfield neural network 霍普费尔德神经网络
Hopkinson effect 霍普金斯效应
HORIZON "北极星"计算机
horizon 前景,视界,水平线
horizon angle 视角,水平角

horizon distance 视距,水平线距离
horizon range 视界范围
horizon transmission 直接视距传输
horizontal advance 水平移进
horizontal amplifier 水平放大器
horizontal and vertical parity check code 纵横奇偶检验码
horizontal automatic frequency control 水平自动频率控制
horizontal blanking 水平消隐
horizontal blanking pulse 水平回扫消隐脉冲
horizontal blanking signal 水平回扫消隐信号
horizontal centering control 行中心控制
horizontal character 横向字符
horizontal check 水平校验,横向校验
horizontal check parity 水平校验奇偶性
horizontal control 水平控制
horizontal convergence control 水平会聚控制
horizontal definition 水平清晰度
horizontal deflecting circuit 水平偏转电路
horizontal deflecting electrode 水平偏转电极
horizontal deflecting oscillator 水平偏转振荡器
horizontal deflection 水平偏转
horizontal deflection multivibrator 水平偏转多谐振荡器
horizontal deflection output amplifier 水平偏转输出放大器
horizontal display 水平显示
horizontal distributed processing system 水平分布处理系统
horizontal distributed system 水平分布式系统
horizontal distribution 水平分布控制
horizontal drive control 水平驱动控制
horizontal dynamic convergence 水平动态会聚
horizontal flow chart 水平流程图
horizontal flyback 水平回扫
horizontal fragmentation 水平分段
horizontal hold 水平同步
horizontal hold control 水平同步调整
horizontal implication 水平隐含

horizontal instruction 水平指令
horizontal interlaced transmission 水平隔行传送
horizontal jitter 水平晃动[抖动]
horizontal justification 水平调整
horizontal line property 水平分隔线属性
horizontal linearity control 水平线性控制
horizontal lock 水平锁定
horizontal microinstruction 水平微指令
horizontal microprogramming 水平微程序设计
horizontal mode 横向排列方式
horizontal motion index 水平移动位标
horizontal oscillator 水平振荡器
horizontal output stage 水平输出级
horizontal output transformer 行输出变压器
horizontal parallelism 水平并行处理
horizontal parity 水平[横向]奇偶校验
horizontal pointer 水平[横向]指针
horizontal polarized wave 水平极化波
horizontal positions 水平[横向]位置
horizontal raster count 水平光栅计数
horizontal recording 水平记录
horizontal redundancy check (HRC) 水平冗余校验率
horizontal repetition rate 水平扫描频率
horizontal resolution 水平分辨率
horizontal retrace 水平回扫
horizontal retrace ratio 水平回扫时间比
horizontal return 水平[横向]返回
horizontal rule 水平标尺
horizontal scanning 水平扫描
horizontal scanning circuit 水平扫描电路
horizontal scanning frequency 水平扫描频率
horizontal scroll 水平滚动,水平卷动
horizontal shift 水平位移
horizontal spacing 水平间距,横向间隔
horizontal sweep 水平扫描
horizontal sweep transformer 水平扫描变压器
horizontal sync pulse 水平同步脉冲
horizontal synchronization signal 水平同步信号
horizontal synchronizing pulse 水平同步脉冲
horizontal system 水平系统
horizontal tab 水平制表符
horizontal table 横向表
horizontal tabulation 水平制表
horizontal tabulation character (HT) 横向制表字符
horizontal tabulator key 横向制表键
horizontal-vertical check 水平垂直校验法
horizontal-vertical redundancy check (HVRC) 纵横冗余校验
horizontal wraparound 水平卷动,横向移动
horizontally-deflecting coils 水平偏转线圈
horizontally-deflecting plates 水平偏转板
horizontally displayed records 水平分组显示记录
Horn clause 霍恩子句
Horn clause theorem prover (HCPRVR) 霍恩子句定理证明程序
Horner's rule 霍纳法则
Horspool algorithm 豪斯普尔算法
host 宿主;主机,宿主机
host adapter 主机适配器
host address 主机地址
host application program 主机应用程序
host assembler 主机汇编程序
host attachment facility 主机连接设备
host-based support program 基于主机的支持程序
host-based system 宿主系统
host bus adapter 主机总线适配器
host command processor 主命令处理器
host computer 主机,宿主机
host computer interface 主计算机接口
host computer processing 主计算机处理
host configuration 主配置
host control block 主控制块
host conversational function 主机会话功能
host data language 宿主数据语言

host data manipulation language (HDML) 宿主型数据操纵语言
host dependent 与主机有关的
host file 宿主文件
host file transceiver 宿主文件收发程序
host-host protocol 主机-主机协议
HOST-IMP protocol 主机-接口机协议
host independent 与主机无关的
host-initialed program 主机初始化程序
host interconnection 主机互连
host interface 主机接口
host interface module 主机接口模块
host language 宿主语言,主机语言
host language system 宿主语言系统
host link 主链路
host logical unit 主机逻辑单元
host machine 宿主机
host master key 主机主关键字
host master key variant 主机主关键字变量
host module 主模块
host monitoring protocol (HMP) 主机监督协议
host name 主机名
host node 主机节点,主节点
host node cycle 主节点周期
host node locking 主节点封锁法
host-node transmission procedures 主机节点传输程序
host number 主机号
host object 主机对象
host operating system 主操作系统
host-parasite model 主机-寄生物模型
host processor (HP) 宿主处理机,主机处理器
host program 宿主程序
Host Proximity Service (HOPS) 邻近主机服务
host raster image processor 主机栅格式图像处理器
host real storage 主机实存储器
host-resident 常驻主机的
host resource 主机资源
host-satellite system 主机卫星机系统
host scalar processor 宿主标量处理机
host simulation 宿主机仿真
host-slave architecture 主从结构
host software 宿主软件

host subarea 主机子区
host support 主机支持程序
host system 主系统
host system message blocks 主机系统消息块
host system responses 主机系统响应
host table 主机表
host/target relationship 主机/目标机关系
host text 主文本
host-to-host protocol 主机到主机协议
host-to-IMP interface 主机到接口消息处理机接口
host transfer file 主机传送文件
host transit time 宿主转变时间
host virtual storage 主机虚拟存储器
hostel 站
hostel-like process 类站进程
hostile user 不友好用户
hostless system 无主机系统
hot backup 热备份
hot carrier 热载流子
hot cathode 热阴极
hot chassis 带电底盘,带电机架
hot editing 热编辑
hot electron 热电子
hot electron noise 热电子噪声
hot fix 热修复
hot frame 热机架
hot I/O 热输入/输出
hot key 热(快捷)键
hot line circuit 热线电路
hot line service 热线业务
hot link 热链
hot list 热单,热列表
hot object 热物,热对象
hot object response 热物响应
hot pluggability 带电插拔能力
hot point 热点
hot potato routing "热土豆"式路由选择
hot pressed ferrite (HPF) 热压铁氧体
hot side 热点,热边
hot sink 散热片,热沉
hot site 热站点
hot spot 热点
hot stand by 热备份
hot start 热启动
hot swap 热调换

hot topic 热门题目
hot weld 热焊
hot zone 齐行区域,断字区域 「统
hotel management system 酒店管理系
Hotelling transform 霍特林变换
HotJava "热咖啡"(SUN)
HotMetal HotMetal 标记语言
HotSynch 热同步
Hough transformation 霍夫变换
hour format 时间格式
hour holding 计时暂停
hourglass cursor 沙漏光标
hourly rate 小时率
HOUSE 建筑设计通用软件包
house cable 室内电缆
house drop 室内下线
Householder transformation 豪斯霍尔德变换
Householder's method 豪斯霍尔德法
housekeeping 内务处理
housekeeping information 内务信息
housekeeping instruction 内务指令
housekeeping program 内务处理程序
housekeeping routine 内务处理例程
housekeeping run 内务操作
howl-back 啸叫
howler tone 嗥鸣音
HP-compatible printer HP 兼容打印
HP-GL 惠普图形语言 「机
HP-IB (Hewlett-Packard Interface Bus) HP 接口总线
HP-IB standard HP-IB 标准
HP language HPL 语言
HP Open View 惠普开放型网络管理软件
HP Precision Architecture 惠普精密体系结构
HP SureStore 惠普万全存储器
HP-UX 惠普-UNIX 操作系统
HP workstation 惠普工作站
HPC(Handheld PC) 手持式个人计算机
HPC(High Performance Computer) 高性能计算机
HPC Modernization Program 高性能计算机现代化计划
HPCC(High Performance Chip Carry) 高性能芯片载体(IBM)
HPF(High Performance FORTRAN) 高性能 FORTRAN 语言
HPFS(High Performance File System) 高性能文件系统
HPGL(Hewlett Packard Graphics Language) 惠普图形语言
HPM(Hyper-Page-Mode) 超页模式
HPPCL (HP Printer Control Language) 惠普打印机控制语言
HPPI(High Performance Parallel Interface) 高性能并行接口
HPRL (Heuristic Programming and Representation Language) 启发式编程与表示语言,HPRL 语言
HR algorithm HR 算法
HRC(Horizontal Redundancy Check) 横向冗余校验
HRC(Hypothetical Reference Circuit) 假想参考电路
HRDC(Hypothetical Reference Digital Circuit) 假定参考数字电路
HRDP(Hypothetical Reference Digital Path) 假想参考数字路径
HRS(High Resolution System) 高分辨率系统
HS(High Speed) 高速
HSAM(Hierarchical Sequential Access Method) 层次顺序访问方法
HSAP (Hitachi Statistical Analysis Program) 日立统计分析程序
HSB(Hue-Saturation-Brightness) 色调-饱和度-亮度
HSH(High Speed Holography) 高速全息照相
HSI(Horizontal Situation Indicator) 水平位置指示器
HSI(Hue-Saturation-Intensity) 色调-饱和度-强度
HSM (Hierarchical Storage Manager) 分级存储管理程序
HSM (Hierarchical Synchronized Network) 分级同步网络 「议
HSP(HandShaking Protocol) 握手协
HSYNC (Horizontal SYNChronization signal) 水平同步信号
HT (Horizontal Tabulation character) 横向制表字符
HTML(HyperText Markup Language)

超文本标记语言
HTML+ HTML+技术规范
HTML 1.0 HTML 1.0标准
HTML 2.0 HTML 2.0标准
HTML 3.0 HTML 3.0标准
HTML Assistance HTML助手
HTML editor HTML编辑程序
HTML file 超文本标记语言文件
HTML mark 超文本标记语言标注符
HTTP(HyperText Transport Protocol) 超文本传输协议
HTTP server HTTP服务器
httpd(HyperText Transport Protocol Daemony) 超文本传送协议守护程序
Hu-Tucker algorithm 胡-图克算法
hub 集线器
hub board 集线器板
hub card 集线器卡
hub go-ahead 向内探询,向中心探询
hub layout 集线器布局
Hub Management Interface(HMI) 集线器管理接口
hub polling 向内探询,向中心探询
hub ring 定位环
hub server 集线服务器
Hubble image 哈勃图
hue 色调
hue component 色彩成份
hue control 色调控制
hue-saturation-brightness(HSB) 色调-饱和度-亮度
hue-saturation-intensity(HSI) 色调-饱和度-亮度
Hueckel edge fitting 休埃克尔边缘拟合法
Huffman algorithm 霍夫曼算法
Huffman code 霍夫曼码
Huffman encoding 霍夫曼编码
Huffman model 霍夫曼模型
Huffman tree 霍夫曼树
huge memory model 巨量内存模型
huge structure 巨型结构
hull maintenance robot 船体维修机器人
hum 交流声,嗡嗡声
hum bars 交流声条
hum polling 轴心轮询
human-activity system 人类活动(模拟)系统
human-aided machine translation (HAMT) 人工辅助机器翻译
human anatomy 人体解剖学
human brain system 人脑系统
human-caused error 人为错误
human-centric word processor(HCWP) 人性化文字处理器
human characteristics 人的特性
human chromosome 人类染色体
human computer interaction(HCI) 人机交互,人机对话
human control system 仿人控制系统
human engineering 人类工程学
human engineering system simulation 人类工程系统仿真
human error 人为错误
human factor 人的因素
human factor design 人的因素设计
human factor engineering 人类因素工程
human factor in reliability 可靠性中的人为因素
human failure 人为故障
human friendly 人类友好的
human frequency range 人类频率范围
human initiated error 人为差错
human-initiated failure(HIF) 人为故障
human intelligence 人类智能
human interface 人类界面
human judgement 人类判断
human language 人类语言
human learning 人类学习
human operator model 操作者模型
human operator simulator 操作人员仿真器
human-oriented language 面向人类的语言
human performance assurance 人的性能保证
human problem-solving task analysis 人的问题求解任务分析
human reliability 人的可靠性
human resources engineering 人类资源工程学
human resources information system 人类资源信息系统
human-simulated high-level generating

system 仿人智能高级产生式系统
human simulation 人类仿真
human translation 人工翻译
human user interface (HUI) 拟人化用户界面
human vision 人类视觉
human window 运行窗口
humanization 人格化
humanware 人件,人类参与活动因素
humid heat test 湿热试验
humid test 湿度试验
humidity 湿度
humidity control 湿度控制
humidity-dependent semiconductive ceramics 湿敏半导电陶瓷
humidity detector 湿度检测器
humidity-non-operating 非运行湿度
humidity-operating 运行湿度
humidity sensitive capacitor 湿敏电容
humidity sensitive resistor 湿敏电阻
humidity sensor 湿度传感器
humidity transducer 湿度传感器
hundred call seconds (HCS) 百秒呼
hung session 挂起对话
hung system 挂起,死机
hung system 悬浮系统,挂起系统
hung terminal 挂起终端
hung up 挂断
Hunt-Szymanski algorithm 亨特-西曼斯基算法
hunt 寻找,寻线
hunt group 查寻组
hunt phase 查寻阶段
hunt report 查寻报告
hunting 寻找,寻找平衡;寻线;摆动
hunting circuit 寻线电路
hunting period 寻线期间
hunting service 搜索服务,寻线服务
hunting time 寻线时间
hunting zone 搜索范围
HW (Half Wave) 半波
HWI (HardWare Interpreter) 硬件解释程序
hybrid 混合网络
hybrid access method 混合存取法
hybrid analog-digital simulation 模数混合仿真
hybrid ARQ 混合自动反馈重发方式
hybrid assembly and placement equipment 混合电路组装和安放设备
hybrid coil 混合线圈,差动线圈
hybrid computer simulation 混合计算机仿真
hybrid control 混合控制
hybrid diagnostic program 混合诊断程序
hybrid digital analog computer 混合式数字模拟计算机
hybrid distributed processing system 复合分布式处理系统
Hybrid Document Reproduction Apparatus 混合文件复制设备
hybrid encoding 混合编码
hybrid error control 混合差错控制
hybrid error correction 混合纠错方式
hybrid finite element method 杂交有限元法
hybrid hardware control 混合硬件控制
hybrid integrated circuit 混合集成电路
hybrid interface 混合接口
hybrid language programming 混合语言编程
hybrid library 混合程序库
hybrid local network 混合区域网络
hybrid logic simulation with real chip 含有实际芯片的混合逻辑模拟
hybrid microcircuit 混合微电路
hybrid microwave integrated circuit 混合微波集成电路
hybrid mode 混合模
hybrid model 混合模型
hybrid modular redundant 混合模块冗余
hybrid (N, S) modular redundant system 混合(N,S)模块冗余系统
hybrid modulation 复合调制
hybrid monitor 混合监视器
hybrid network 混合网络
hybrid position/force control 位置和力混合控制
hybrid programming 混合程序设计
hybrid RAM 混合RAM
hybrid redundancy 混合冗余
hybrid relational-hierarchical model 关系-层次混合(数据库)模型
hybrid relational-network model 关系-

网络混合(数据库)模型
hybrid routing 混合式路由选择
hybrid simulation method 混合模拟方法
hybrid software 混合软件
hybrid structure 混合式结构
hybrid substrates 混合电路衬底
hybrid switching network 混合交换网络
hybrid switching technique 混合交换技术
hybrid teletex 混合方式图文电视
hybrid thin film circuit 混合薄膜电路
hybrid transmission system 混合传输方式
hybrid virus 混合型病毒
Hydra 测试软件
hydraulic robot 液压机器人
Hyper Card 超级卡
Hyper cart 超级文本卡
hyper channel 超级通道
Hyper Document 超级文卷
hyper link 超链接
Hyperaccess 超媒体存取
hyperacoustic zone 超声区
hyperbola 双曲线
hyperbolic paraboloid 双曲抛物面
hyperbolic waveform 双曲波形
HyperCard 超媒体卡系统
hyperchannel 超级通道
Hyperchannel network 超级通道网络
hypercube(HC) 超立方体结构
hypercube database 超立方体数据库
hypercube emulator 超立方体仿真程序
hypercube ensemble 超立方总体
hypercube interconnection network 超立方体互连网络
hypercube multiprocessor 超立方体多处理机
hypercube system 超立方系统
hyperdisk 超级磁盘
hyperexponential random variable 超指数随机变量
hyperfine structure 超精细结构
hyperfinite set 超有限集
hypergraph 超图
hypergraphic based data structure 基于超图的数据结构
hypergroup 超群
hyperlink 超级链接

hyperlink browse context 超链接浏览上下文
hyperlink container 超链接容器
hyperlink frame object 超链接框架对象
hyperlink object 超链接对象
hyperlink rollover effect 超链接翻转效果
hyperlink site object 超链接站点对象
hyperlink target object 超链接目标对象
hypermedia 超媒体
hypermedia application 超媒体应用程序
hypermedia galaxy 超媒体多道程序批处理操作系统
hypermesh topology 超网格拓扑
hypernet 超级网络
hyperobject 超目标
HyperPAD HyperPAD 系统
hyperplane method 超平面法
hyperpure Germanium detector 超纯锗检波器
hyperrectangular 超矩形网络
hyperresolution 超消解法
hyperresolvent 超预解式
hyperrule 超规则
HyperScript HyperScript 命令语言
hypersonic flow 超声速流
hyperspace 超空间
hypersynchronous 超同步
HyperTalk 超级对话语言
hypertape unit 快速磁带部件
HyperTerminal 超级终端
HyperText 超文本软件
hypertext 超文本
hypertext abstract machine 超文本抽象机
hypertext database 超文本数据库
hypertext link 超文本链接
HyperText Markup Language(HTML) 超文本标记语言
HyperText Transport Protocol(http) 超文本传输协议
HyperText Transfer Protocol Daemon (httpd) 超文本传输协议守护程序
HyperText Transport Protocol Server (https) 超文本传输协议服务器
hypertexture 超纹理结构

HyperTransport （提高芯片间连接速度的）超级传输技术（AMD）
hypervisor 管理程序
hyperware 超媒体制品
hyperzine 超媒体杂志
hyphen 连字符
hyphen drop 连字符去除
hyphen ladder 连字符阶梯
hyphenate 连字符连接
hyphenation 连字技术
hyphenless justification 无连字符行对齐
hyphentes justification 空格调整
hypothesize-and-test 假设与测试
hypothetical algorithm 假想算法
hypothetical instruction 假想指令
hypothetical loop 假想环路
hypothetical memory 假想内存, 虚拟存储器
hypothetical reference circuit 假设参考电路
hypothetical reference circuit for telephony 电话假设参考电路
hypothetical reference connection 假设参考连接
hypothetical reference digital path 假想参考数字通路
hypothetical reference digital path at 64 kbit/s 64 千比特/秒的假设参考数字信道
hypothetical syllogism 假言三段论
hypothetical world 假设世界
hysteresis 滞后现象
hysteresis gap 滞后间隙
hysteresis loop 滞后回线
hysteresis loss 迟滞损耗
HYTEL(HYbrid TELecommunication) 混合远程通信

I i

I 电流有效值
i286 Intel 80286 处理器芯片
i386 Intel 80386 处理器芯片
i486 Intel 80486 处理器芯片
I-beam pointer 插入指针, I 形指针
I-button 信息按钮(Dallas)
I-CASE(Integrated CASE) 综合性计算机辅助软件工程
I-conversion 整数转换, 定点数转换
I-F-R(Image-to-Frame Ratio) 像帧率
I-field 信息字段, 信息域
I-node (UNIX)信息节点
I/O(Input/Output) 输入/输出
I/O-bound job 输入/输出密集作业
I/O-bound process 输入/输出密集型进程
I/O buffer(Input/Output buffer) 输入/输出缓冲器
I/O burst I/O 猝发
I/O bus structures 输入/输出总线结构
I/O cable 输入/输出电缆
I/O channel 输入/输出通道
I/O command 输入/输出命令
I/O communication modes 输入/输出通信模式
I/O concurrent 输入/输出并行操作
I/O control 输入/输出控制
I/O device assignment 输入/输出设备分配
I/O exchange buffering 输入/输出交换缓冲
I/O executive 输入/输出执行程序
I/O housekeeping system 输入/输出内务处理系统
I/O interface 输入/输出接口
I/O interrupt 输入/输出中断
I/O interrupt indicator 输入/输出中断指示器
I/O interrupt mask 输入/输出中断屏蔽
I/O limited 输入/输出受限
I/O lockdown 输入/输出锁定
I/O management 输入/输出管理
I/O map 输入/输出映像
I/O medium 输入/输出媒体
I/O mode 输入/输出模式
I/O pack 输入/输出组件

I/O parity interrupt 输入/输出奇偶中断

I/O port 输入/输出端口

I/O port address 输入/输出端口地址

I/O privileged instruction 输入/输出特权指令

I/O queue 输入/输出队列

I/O request 输入/输出请求

I/O spooling 假脱机输入/输出

I/O table 输入/输出表

I/O task queue 输入/输出任务队列

I/O traffic control 输入/输出流量控制

I/O trunk 输入/输出中继线

I picture(Intra picture) I图像,帧内图像

I series recommendations of CCITT 国际电话电报咨询委员会I系列推荐标准

I-shape cursor 插入光标,I字形光标

I-WAY I-WAY实验网络

IA(Immediate Access) 立即存取

IA(Immediate Address) 立即地址

IA(Instruction Address) 指令地址

IA(Interface Adapter) 接口适配器

IAB(Internet Architecture Board) 因特网体系结构研究会

IAC (InterApplication Communications) 应用程序间通信

IAF(InterActive Facility) 交互工具

IANA(Internet Assigned Numbers Authority) 因特网编号管理局

IAP(Industry Application Program) 产业应用程序(IBM)

IAR(Image Annotation Record) 图像注释记录

IAU(Interface Adapter Unit) 接口适配器单元

IAW(Indirect Addressing Word) 间接寻址字

IAW(Interrupt Address Word) 中断地址字

IB(Identification Beacon) 识别信标

IBC(Internet Business Center) 因特网商务中心

IBD(Instrument Bus Data) 仪器总线数据

IBF(Input Buffer Full) 输入缓冲器满

IBM(International Business Machines Corp.) 国际商用机器公司,IBM公司

IBM 386SLC 386SLC处理器芯片

IBM 3740 floppy disk format IBM 3740软盘格式

IBM 8514/A display adapter IBM 8514/A显示卡

IBM asynchronous communications adapter IBM异步通信适配器

IBM binary synchronous communications adapter IBM二进制同步通信适配器

IBM cabling system IBM电缆线路系统

IBM card IBM(标准)卡

IBM-compatible PC IBM兼容个人计算机

IBM compensation IBM补偿

IBM Database Server IBM数据库服务器

IBM Digital Library IBM数字图书馆

IBM Directory and Security Server 目录与安全服务器

IBM Global Network(IGN) 全球网络

IBM Internet Connection Server 因特网连接服务器

IBM mainframes IBM大型计算机

IBM minicomputers IBM小型计算机

IBM NetworkStation IBM网络工作站

IBM Open Blueprint IBM开放蓝图

IBM operating system IBM操作系统

IBM PC IBM个人计算机

IBM PC/AT IBM PC/AT个人计算机

IBM PC/XT IBM PC/XT个人计算机

IBM personal computer IBM个人计算机

IBM Personal Dictation System(IPDS) IBM个人听写系统

IBM personal system/2 IBM个人计算机系统

IBM PS/2 IBM个人计算机系统

IBM RS/6000 IBM RS/6000计算机

IBM Software Servers IBM软件服务器

IBM Stretch(IBM 7030) IBM Stretch计算机

IBM ThinkPad ThinkPad笔记本计

算机
IBM virtual machine facility IBM 虚拟机器设施
IBU(Instruction Buffer Unit) 指令缓冲单元
IC(Input Context) 输入上下文
IC(Integrated Circuit) 集成电路
I2C bus(Internal Integrated Circuit bus) 内部集成电路总线
IC card(ICC) 集成电路卡
IC card operating system IC 卡操作系统
IC card standardization IC 卡标准
IC density 集成电路密度
IC design system 集成电路设计系统
IC DIP package 集成电路双列直插式封装
IC doping 集成电路掺杂法
IC electrical contact 集成电路电接触
IC electrical isolation 集成电路电气隔离
IC etching 集成电路蚀刻法
IC layout 集成电路布局
IC logic design 集成电路逻辑设计
IC lithography 集成电路光刻
IC module compiler 集成电路模块编译器
IC multimedia coder 集成电路多媒体编码器
IC pattern generation equipment 集成电路图型发生器
IC socket standard 集成电路插座标准
IC tester 集成电路测试仪
ICA(Integrated Communications Adapter) 集成通信适配器
ICAM(Integrated Communications Access Method) 集成通信访问法
icand 被乘数
icand register 被乘数寄存器
ICB(International Computer Bibliography) 国际计算机书目
ICB(Interrupt Control Block) 中断控制块
ICC(IC Card) 集成电路卡
ICCC(International Conference on Computer Communication) 国际计算机通信会议
ICCCM(Inter-Client Communication Conventions Manual) 客户间通信约定手册
ICCP(Institute for Certification of Computer Professional) 计算机专业资格审批机构
ICDL(Integrated Circuit Description Language) 集成电路描述语言
iceberg principle 冰山原则
ICES language(Integrated Civil Engineering System) 综合民用工程设计系统语言
ICIC(UNESCO)(International Copyright InformationCenter) 联合国教科文组织国际版权信息中心
ICIP(International Conference on Information Processing) 国际信息处理会议
ICL(International Computers Limited) 国际计算机有限公司(英)
ICM(Image Compression Manager) 图像压缩管理程序
ICM(Institution for Computer Management) 计算机管理协会
ICMP(Internet Control Message Protocol) 因特网控制消息协议
iCOMP index(Intel COmparative Microprocessor Performance index) 微处理器性能比较指数(Intel)
icon 图符,图标
Icon Author 图标编辑器
icon box 图标框
icon class definition language 图标类定义语言
icon file 图标文件
icon gadget 图标小配件
icon layout policy 图标布局策略
icon menu 图标菜单
icon pattern 图标样式[图案]
icon representation 图标式表示方法
icon resource 图标资源
icon system 图标系统
iconedit 图标编辑程序
iconic interface 图标式界面
iconic level 图像电平
iconic model 缩比模型
iconic programming 图标程序设计
iconic representation 图标表示法
iconographic model 图示[图解]模型
iconography 插图,图解学

iconoscope 光电摄像管
ICOT(Institute for new generation COmputer Technology) 新一代计算机技术研究所(日本)
ICP(Image Cosmetic Processing) 图像整饰处理
ICP(Initial Connection Protocol) 初始连接协议
ICP(Interface Communication Processor) 接口通信处理机
ICP(International Computer Programs Incorporated) 国际计算机程序公司
ICPL(Initial Connection Program Load) 初始控制程序加载
ICQ(I seek you) 网上寻呼软件
ICS(Interactive Computing System) 交互式计算系统
ICS(International Computer Software Corporation) 国际计算机软件公司
ICS(International Computer Symposium) 国际计算机专题讨论会
ICS(International telephone and telegraph Communications System) 国际电话电报通信系统
ICSE(International Conference on Software Engineering) 软件工程国际会议
ICSI(International Conference on Scientific Information) 国际科学信息会议
ICSL(Interactive Continuous Simulation Language) 交互式连续仿真语言
ICSTI(International Center for Scientific and Technical Information) 国际科技信息中心(设在莫斯科)
ICT(Intelligent Communications Terminal) 智能通信终端
ICT(Interactive Control Table) 交互控制表
ICT(International Computers and Tabulators Ltd.) 国际计算机与制表机有限公司(英)
ICU(Interface Control Unit) 接口控制单元
ICW(Initial Condition Word) 初始条件字
ICW(Initialization Control Word) 预置控制字
ICW(Interface Control Word) 接口控制字
ID(IDentifier) 标识符
ID-Card(IDentification Card) 识别卡
ID language 标识符语言
ID number(IDentification number) 产品识别号;身份标识号
ID PROM (Sun 工作站上)标识用可编程只读存储器
IDA(Integrated Disc Adapter) 集成磁盘适配器
IDA(Intelligent Drive Array) 智能型驱动器阵列
IDAL(Indirect Data Address List) 间接数据地址表
IDAM(Indexed Direct Access Method) 索引直接访问法
IDAPI(Integrated Database Application Programming Interface) 集成数据库应用编程接口
IDB(Integrated Data Base) 集成数据库
IDB(Internal Data Bus) 内部数据总线
IDBMS(Integrated Data Base Management System) 综合数据库管理系统
IDC(Integrated Disk Controller) 集成磁盘控制器
IDC(Internal Device Communication) 内部设备通信机制
IDC(Internet Database Connector) 因特网数据库连接程序
IDD(Integrated Data Dictionary) 综合数据字典
IDD(International Direct Dialing) 国际直接拨号
IDDE(Integrated Development Debug Environment) 集成开发调试环境
IDDS(International Digital Data Service) 国际数字数据业务
IDE(Integrated Development Environment) 集成开发环境
IDE(Integrated Drive Electronics) 集成驱动电子设备
IDE(Intelligent Drive Electronics) 智

能化驱动电子设备
IDE connector IDE 连接器
IDE controller IDE 控制器
IDE drive IDE 接口磁盘驱动器
IDE Flash Drive IDE 接口快擦写盘
IDE interface IDE 接口
idea database 观念数据库
idea processor 概念处理程序
idea sketch 观念简图
ideal 理想
ideal benchmark characteristic 理想基准程序特性
ideal blackbody 理想黑体
ideal capacity 理想能力,理想容量;理想生产能力
ideal code 理想码
ideal communication channel 理想信道
ideal conversion characteristic curve 理想转换特性曲线
ideal filter 理想滤波器
ideal instant of modulation 理想调制时刻
ideal orientation 理想取向
ideal receiver 理想接收机
ideal solution 理想解
ideal value 理想值
idealized pattern 理想化模式
idealized system 理想化系统
idealized value 理想化值
idempotence 幂等
idempotent element 幂等元
idempotent law 幂等律
idempotent transformation 幂等变换
iDEN (integrated Digital Enhanced Network) 数字集群系统
identical 同一;恒等
identical argument list 恒等变元表
identical distribution 恒等分布
identical entry 恒等项
identical function reference 恒等函数引用
identical operation 恒等运算
identical permutation group 恒等置换群
identical sensor 恒等检测器
identical sublist 恒等子表
identical subtree 恒等子树
identically false 恒假,永假
identically true 恒真,永真

identifiable target 可识别恒等目标
identification(ID) 标识符
identification address mark 标识地址记号
identification burst 标识组,识别段
identification card 标识卡
identification character(ID) 标识字符
identification condition 标识条件
identification division 标识部
identification field 标识字段
identification item 标识项
identification mark 标识符号,识别标记
identification number 标识号
identification on outward dialing 向外拨号标识
identification point 标识点,识别位置
identification problem 标识问题
identification recovery 标识恢复
identification system 识别系统
identifier 标识符
identifier attribute 标识符属性
identifier declaration 标识符说明
identifier length 标识符长度
identifier list 标识符表
identifier name 标识符名
identifier pointer 标识符指示字
identifier table 标识符表
identifier word 标识字
identify 标识,识别
identify alternatives 标识备选方案
identify control section 标识控制段
identify dummy section 标识空段
identify unmarked device 识别不知型号设备
identifying 识别,标识
identifying code 标识码
identities for combinations 组合恒等式
identity 一致,恒等;单位
identity authentication 身份验证
identity-based access control 基于身份验证的访问控制
identity card 身分识别卡
identity cipher 恒等密码
identity element 单位元素
identity endomorphism 恒等自同态
identity gate 恒等门,符合门
identity graph 么图
identity law 恒等律,同一律

identity mapping 恒等映像
identity matrix 单位矩阵
identity matrix statement 单位矩阵语句
identity of operation 等同运算
identity operation 全同运算
Identity Palette 对等调色板
identity relator 等同关系符
identity sign 恒等记数，等同符号
identity token 标识令牌
identity unit 恒等单位，全同单元
ideogram 表意文字，像形文字，表意符号
ideogram spacing 字间距
ideographic 修饰表意文字的
ideographic laser printer 表意文字激光打印机
ideographic session 表意符号对话
ideographic symbol 表意符号
IDF(Image Description File) 图像描述文件
IDF(Integrated Data File) 综合数据文件
IDFT(Inverse Discrete Fourier Transform) 离散傅立叶反转换
IDG(International Data Group) 国际数据集团(美)
IDI(Intelligent Dual Interface) 智能双接口
IDL(Interface Definition Language) 接口定义语言
idle block 空闲块
idle call 空调用
idle channel state 空闲通道状态
idle character 空闲字符，空转字符
idle communication mode 空闲通信模式
idle hour 空闲时间
idle indication signal 空线指示信号
idle instruction 空闲指令
idle interrupt 空闲中断
idle line 空闲线路
idle line indicator 空线指示器
idle link 空闲链路
idle list 空闲表
idle loop 空载回路
idle pattern 空组合，空闲图样
idle request 空闲重发校正
idle resource 空闲资源

idle routine 空闲例程
idle search 空闲搜索
idle signal 空闲信号
idle signal unit 空闲信号单元
idle state 空闲状态
idle thread 空闲线程
idle time 空闲时间
idle trunk 空闲中继线
idle wire 空线
IDN(Integrated Data Network) 综合数据网络
IDN(Integrated Digital Network) 综合数字网
IDN(Intelligent Data Network) 智能数据网络
IDOM(Isolated Digital Output Module) 隔离数字输出模块
IDP(Iterative Development Process) 叠代开发过程
IDS(Integrated Display System) 综合显示系统
IDS(Interactive Digital System) 交互式数据系统公司
IDSS(Intelligent Decision Support System) 智能决策支持系统
IDT(Intelligent Data Terminal) 智能数据终端
IDT(Item Description Table) 项目描述表
IDT IDT 专家系统
IDU(IDle signal Unit) 空闲信号单元
IDU(Interface Data Unit) 接口数据单元
IE(Index Error) 索引错误
IE(Interrupt Enable) 中断允许
IEC(International Electrotechnical Commission) 国际电子技术委员会
IECC(Informix Enterprise Command Center) Informix 企业管理中心
IEE(Institute of Electrical Engineers) 电气工程师学会(英国)
IEEE(Institute of Electrical and Electronic Engineers) 电气电子工程师学会
IEEE-488 IEEE-488 可编程测试仪器用标准总线接口
IEEE-488 bus controller IEEE-488 总

线控制器
IEEE-488 bus coupler functions IEEE-488 总线耦合器功能
IEEE 583 IEEE 583 模块化仪器与数字接口系统标准
IEEE 583/CAMAC IEEE 583/计算机自动化测量与控制
IEEE-696 bus IEEE 696 总线(UNIX)
IEEE 802 committee IEEE 802 委员会(1980 年 2 月成立)
IEEE 802 standards IEEE 802 标准(局域网)
IEEE 802.1 standards 局域网标准总论
IEEE 802.2 standards 逻辑链路控制标准
IEEE 802.3 standards 基于以太网的局域网标准
IEEE 802.4 standards 基于令牌总线网的局域网标准
IEEE 802.5 standards 基于令牌环网的局域网标准
IEEE 802.6 standards 城域网标准
IEEE 802.7 standards 宽带网标准
IEEE 802.8 standards 光纤局域网标准
IEEE 802.9 standards 多媒体局域网与 ISDN 标准
IEEE 802.10 standards 局域网安全模型标准
IEEE 802.11 standards 无线局域网标准
IEEE 802.12 standards 高速局域网标准
IEEE 1394 IEEE 1394 总线
IEEE floating point standard IEEE 浮点标准
IEEE standard bus interface IEEE 标准总线接口
IEF(Information Engineering Facility) 信息工程设施
IEI(Interrupt Enable Input) 中断允许输入,中断使能输入
IEN(master Interrupt ENable) 主中断允许,主中断使能
IEN(Internet Experiment Note) 因特网实验备忘录
IEO(Interrupt Enable Output) 中断允许输出
ier 乘数;乘法器
ier register 乘数寄存器
IESG(Internet Engineering Steering Group) 因特网工程指导组
IETF(Internet Engineering Task Force) 因特网工程部
IEU(Instruction Execution Unit) 指令执行部件
IF(Instruction Field) 指令字段
if-and-only-if 当且仅当
IF block 条件块
if clause 条件子句
if-else statement 如果-否则语句
if statement 如果语句,IF 语句
IF-THEN-ELSE 如果…则…否则
IFC(Inter-Frame Codecs) 帧间编解码器
IFC(InterFace Clear) 接口清除
IFCS(International Federation of Computer Science) 国际计算机科学联合会
IFF(Identification Friend-or-Foe) 敌友识别
IFIP(International Federation of Information Processing) 国际信息处理联盟
IFR(InterFace Register) 接口寄存器
IFS(Information Flow Standard) 信息流标准
IFS(Installable File System) 可安装文件系统
iFS(Internet File System) 因特网文件系统(Oracle)
IFS(InterFace Specification) 接口规范
IFT(Inverse Fourier Transform) 傅立叶反变换
IFU(Instruction Fetch Unit) 取指令单元
IFU(InterFace Unit) 接口部件
IGES(Initial Graphics Exchange Specification) 原始图形交换规范(ANSI)
IGL(Interactive Graphics Library) 交互式图形库(Tektronix)
IGMP(Internet Group Management Protocol) 因特网组管理协议
igniter 点火器

ignition system 点火系统
ignore 忽略
ignore all 全部忽略
ignore bit 忽略位,无用位
ignore block character 无用块字符
ignore character 忽略字符
ignore character block 无用字符块
ignore class 忽略类
ignore gate 忽略门
ignore if inactive 非活动时忽略
ignore instruction 忽略[舍弃]指令
ignore mouse 忽略鼠标
ignore other application 忽略其他应用程序
ignore remote requests 忽略远程请求
ignore specification 忽略说明,舍弃说明
IGP(Interior Gateway Protocol) 内部网关协议
IGRP(Interior Gateway Routing Protocol) 内部网关路由协议
IGS(Interactive Graphics System) 交互式制图系统
IHV(Independent Hardware Vendor) 独立硬件供应商
IIA(Information Industry Assn.) 信息工业协会
IID(Implicit IDentification) 隐式标识
IIL(Integrated Injection Logic) 集成注入逻辑
IIR(Internal Interrupt Register) 内部中断寄存器
IIS(Interactive Instructional System) 交互式教学系统
IIS(Internet Information Server) 因特网信息服务器(微软)
IIT(Illinois Institute of Technology) 美国伊利诺依斯理工学院(该学院研制了 ILLIAC Ⅳ 计算机)
IK(Information Kiosks) 信息亭
ikon 图符,图标,肖像(同 icon)
IL(Intermediate Language) 中间语言
IL(Interpretive Language) 解释语言
I2L(Integrated Injection Logic) 集成注入逻辑
I2L microprocessor 集成注入逻辑微处理器
I3L (Isoplanar Integrated Injection Logic) 等幅集成注入逻辑电路
ill-conditioned 病态的
ill-conditioned equation 病态方程
ill-conditioned linear equations 病态线性方程组
ill-conditioned matrix 病态矩阵
ill-conditioned polynomial 病态多项式
ill-conditioned problem 病态问题
ill-conditioned system of equations 病态方程组
ill-conditioning 病态的,病态条件
ill coupling 病态耦合
ill-posed 提法不适当的
ill-posed problem 不适定问题
illegal 非法的,禁用的
illegal access 非法存取
illegal address 非法地址
illegal addressing mode 非法寻址模式
illegal blank field 非法空白字段
illegal character 非法[禁用]字符
illegal code 非法码,禁用代码
illegal command 非法命令
illegal command check 非法命令校验
illegal element name 非法元素名
illegal entry count 非法入口计数
illegal field width 非法字段宽度
illegal file name 非法文件名
illegal function name 非法函数名
illegal guard mode 非法防护方式
illegal host connection 非法主机连接
illegal instruction 非法[禁用]指令
illegal interrupt 非法中断
illegal load address 非法装入地址
illegal memory access 非法存储器存取
illegal operation 非法操作
illegal packet 非法信息包
illegal punctuation 非法标点
illegal request 非法请求
illegal state 非法状态
illegal user 非法用户
illegal variable name 非法变量名
ILLIAC(ILLinois Integrator and Automatic Computer) 伊利诺斯理工大学积分仪和自动计算机
ILLIAC network ILLIAC 网络
ILLIAC Ⅳ computer ILLIAC Ⅳ 计算机
illuminance 照度
illuminant 发光体

illuminated plane 照射板
illuminating engineering 照明工程
illumination model 光照模型
illuminator 照明设备
illuminometer 照度计
illusion 幻影,幻觉,假象
Illustra Information Technology Illustra 信息技术公司
Illustra Server Illustra 服务器
illustrated parts catalog 插图部分目录
Illustration program 演示程序
Illustrator 88 Illustrator 88 绘图程序
IM(Imaging Model) 成像模型
IM(Index Marker) 索引标志
IM(Intelligence Multimedia) 智能多媒体
IM(Input Method) 输入方法
iMac(Internet Macintosh) iMac 计算机(苹果)
image(IM) 图像,影像,映像
image activator 映像激活程序
image algebraic operation 图像代数运算
image amplifier 图像放大器
image analysis 图像分析
image AND operation 图像"与"运算
image annotation record 图像注释记录
image archive 图像归档
image area 图像区域
image arrangement 图像编排
image aspect 图像宽高比
image attribute 图像属性
image averaging 图像取平均值,图像均值法
image base 图像库
image binaryzation 图像二值化
image binaryzation processing 图像二值化处理
image bitsperpel 图像每点位数
image block 图像块
image brightness 图像亮度[辉度]
image buffer 图像缓冲区
image cache 图像高速缓存
image capture device 图像获取设备
image cell 图像单元,像元
image channel 图像通道
image channel noise limited sensitivity 图像通道噪声限制的灵敏度

image channel synchronizing sensitivity 图像通道的同步灵敏度
image charge 影像电荷
image coding 图像编码
image communication 图像通信
image comparison 图像比较
image compression 图像压缩
image computing 图像计算
image contour 图像轮廓
image contract 图像压缩,图像抽取
image contrast 图像对比度
image conversion 图像转印,图像变换
image converter 显像管;光电图像变换器
image converting 图像变换
image copies 图像副本
image correction logic 图像校正逻辑
image cosmetic processing 图像修饰处理
image creation system 图像建立系统
image crosstalk suppression 图像串扰抑制
image cut 图像切割
image data 图像数据
image data base 图像数据库
image data base management system 图像数据库管理系统
image data compression 图像数据压缩
image data format 图像数据格式
image data structure 图像数据结构
image decomposition 图像分解
image defect 图像缺陷
image degradation 图像质量下降,图像退化
image description 图像描述
image diagnostic system 图像诊断系统
image digital filter 图像数字滤波器
image digitizer 图像数字化仪
image directory 图像目录
image disparity 图像不均等性
image display 图像显示器;图像显示
image dissection 析像,图像剖析
image dissector 析像管,图像分析器
image distortion 图像失真[畸变]
image drop-out 图像信号失落
image editing software 图像编辑软件
image editor command 图像编辑指令
image edge detection 图像边缘检测

image element 像元,像素
image encoding 图像编码
image enhancement 图像增强
image enhancing equipment 图像增强设备
image estimation 图像估计
image evaluation 图像评价
image exclusive OR operation 图像异或运算
image field 像场
image file 图像文件
image file format 图像文件格式
image filtering 图像滤波
image frame grabber board 图像帧获取板
image frequency 图像频率
image function 图像函数
image geometric distortion 图像几何失真
image graphics 图像图形
image gray levels 图像灰度级
image injury 图像受损
image illumination uniformity 像面照度均匀性
image input device 图像输入设备
image intensifier 图像增强器
image intensity 图像亮度
image interference 图像干涉,镜像干涉
image interpolation 图像插值
image inverter 图像反相器
image library 图像库
image lock 图像锁定,图像同步
image master 图像原版[底片]
image magnification 图像放大
image match 图像匹配
image-matching algorithm 图像匹配算法
image memory 图像内存
image mixing 图像混合
image mode 图像模式
image mosaic 图像镶嵌
image motion 图像运动
image name 映像名
image object content architecture (IO-CA) 图像对象内容结构
image OR operation 图像"或"运算
image output device 图像输出设备
image overlay 图像覆盖

image parameter 镜像参数
image pattern recognition 图像模式识别
image plane 图像平面
image point 像点
image prediction coding 图像预测编码
image preprocessing 图像预处理
image primitive 图像原语
image privilege 映像特许级
image processing 图像处理
image processing operating system 图像处理操作系统
image processor 图像处理机
image properties dialog box 图像属性对话框
image quality 图像质量
image quantization 图像量化
image random distortion 图像随机畸变
image read interface 图像读出接口
image recognition 图像识别
image reconstruction 图像重建
image recovery 图像恢复
image refresh database 映像刷新数据库
image registration 图像配准[对齐]
image rejection mixer 镜像抑制混频器
image repetition 图像再现
image resolution 图像分辨率
image restoration 图像还原[复原]
image reversal 图像反转
image reversing film 图像反转片
image roam 图像漫游
image rotation 图像旋转
image rotator 图像旋转器
image sampling 图像取样
image scale 图像缩放比
image scanning 图像扫描
image scrolling 图像卷起,图像滚动
image section descriptor 映像段描述符
image segmentation 图像分段[分割]
image select 图像选择器
image sensor 图像传感器,像感器
image sequence 图像序列
image sequence understanding 图像序列理解
image sharpening 图像锐化
image shrink 图像收缩
image sketch 图像简图
image smoothing 图像平滑

image space 图像空间
image stack 图像堆栈
image storage space 图像存储空间
image-storage tube 图像存储管
image symbol set(ISS) 图像符号集
image template matching 图像模板匹配
image thought 形象思维
image thresholding 图像阈值
image transformation 图像变换
image transmission 图像传输
image tube 图像管
image type 图像类型
image understanding 图像理解
image variance 图像方差
image warping 图像扭曲
image workstation 图像工作站
image zoom 图像变焦
ImageLink 图像链系统
imagemap 图像映射
imagery 制像,成像
imagesetter 图像排版机,照排机
ImageWriter 图像打印机
imaginary 虚数的;假想的
imaginary axis 虚轴
imaginary line 虚线
imaginary number 虚数
imaginary part of symbol 符号虚部
imaginary part operation 虚部运算
imaginary terminal 虚终端
imaginary test 假想检验
imagination 想象
imaging 图像形成,成像
imaging device 成像设备
imaging item 图像项目
imaging model 成像模型
imaging system 图像系统,成像系统
imaging transformation 映像变换
IMAP(Internet Mail Access Protocol) 因特网邮件存取协议
imbalance 不平衡
IMDL(Information Model Description Language) 信息模型描述语言
IMHO(In My Humble Opinion) 依本人愚见
IMIS(Integrated Management Information System) 综合管理信息系统
imitate 仿效,模仿
imitation 模拟

imitation game 模拟博弈
imitator 模拟器
IML(Initial Machine load) 初始机器装入;初始机器荷载
IML(Initial Microprogram Load) 初始微程序装入
IMM(Intelligent Memory Manager) 智能内存管理程序
immediate 立即的,直接的
immediate access 立即存取
immediate add 立即加
immediate address 立即地址
immediate address instruction 立即地址指令
immediate addressing 立即寻址
immediate cancel 立即取消
immediate control mode 立即控制模式
immediate data 立即[现场]数据
immediate direct execution mode 立即直接执行模式
immediate dominator 直接支配点
immediate error 突发错误
immediate execution mode 立即执行模式
immediate extended addressing 立即扩展寻址
immediate instruction 立即指令
immediate mode 立即模式
immediate printing 立即打印
immediate request mode 立即请求方式
immediate response mode 立即响应模式,实时应答方式
immediate successor 直接后继
immediate symbol 立即符号
immediate task 立即任务
immediated address 立即地址
immersion 浸入;临境感
immersion cooling 浸泡冷却
Immersive 临境的,具有现场感的
immersive virtual reality 临境虚拟现实
immobile 固定的,不动的
immovable 不可移动的,固定的
immunize 免疫
IMP(Interface Message Processor) 接口消息处理器
IMP computer(Interface Message Processors computer) 接口消息处理器计算机

IMP-IMP protocol 接口机-接口机协议
IMP software 接口消息处理机软件
IMP throughput 接口消息处理机吞吐量
IMP-to-host interface 接口消息处理机与主计算机的接口
IMP-to-IMP protocol 接口消息处理机间协议
impact 冲击,打击;影响
impact dot matrix printer 击打式点阵打印机
impact force 击打力
impact line printer 击打式行式打印机
impact paper 压敏纸
impact printer 击打式打印机
impact resistance 抗冲击性
impact strength 冲击强度
impact test 冲击试验
impact wear 击打磨损
impairment 减损
impedance 阻抗
impedance characteristic 特性阻抗
impedance compensation network 阻抗补偿网络
impedance matching 阻抗匹配
impedance matching network 阻抗匹配网络
impedance mismatch 阻抗失配
imperative 强制的,命令的
imperative macroinstruction 强制宏指令
imperative operations 强制作业
imperative statement 强制语句
imperfect 不完善的,有缺陷的
imperfect contact 不良接触
imperfect earth 接地不良
imperfect field 不完全域
impersonate 顶替,模仿
impersonation 冒名顶替
impersonation token 顶替令牌
implant 插入,注入
implantation 注入,移植
implementater 实现程序
implementation 实现,安装步骤
implementation architecture 实现体系结构
implementation correctness 实现正确性
implementation dependency 实现相关性
implementation environment 实现环境
implementation expert 执行专家
implementation grammar 实现文法
implementation language 实现语言
implementation mandatory 实现必备
implementation module 实现性模块
implementation_only attribute 仅执行属性
implementation phase 实现阶段
implementation plan 实现计划
implementation process 实现进程
implementation requirement 实现要求
implementation restriction 实现限制
implementation rule 实现规则
implementation strategy 实现策略
implementation tool 实现工具
implementation verification 实现验证
implementor name 设备名;完成者姓名
implicant 蕴涵项,蕴涵
implication 蕴涵,蕴涵式
implication dependency 蕴涵依赖
implication graph 蕴涵图
implication relation 蕴涵关系
implication table 蕴涵表
implicature 蕴含
implicit action 隐含动作
implicit address 隐含[蕴涵]地址
implicit address instruction format 隐含地址指令格式
implicit attribute 隐含属性
implicit computation 蕴涵[隐含]计算
implicit connection 隐含连接
implicit decision 隐判定
implicit declaration 隐含说明
implicit difference scheme 隐式差分格式
implicit differentiation 蕴涵微分,隐微分
implicit enumeration 隐含枚举
implicit estimation 隐含估计
implicit event 隐式事件
implicit-explicit scheme 隐-显格式
implicit function 隐函数
implicit identification 隐式识别[标识]
implicit instruction format 隐含指令格式

implicit interrupt instruction 中断隐指令
implicit knowledge 隐式知识
implicit method 隐式方法
implicit modeling 隐含造型
implicit parallel 隐式并行
implicit parameter 隐含参数
implicit partition state 隐分区状态
implicit pointer 隐式指针
implicit reference 隐含引用
implicit representation 隐含表达
implicit scope terminator 隐含范围终止符
implicit solution 隐含求解
implicit statement 隐含语句
implicit storage 隐含存储器
implicit variable 隐含变量
implicit type 隐含类型
implicit word order 隐含字序
implicity 隐含性
implied addressing 隐含寻址
implied AND 蕴涵"与"
implied DO 隐循环,隐 DO
implied expression 隐式表达「束
implied linear constraint 隐式线性约
implied memory addressing 隐式存储器寻址
implied OR 蕴涵"或"
implode 拼装,组装
IMPLODE function 合并函数
imply 蕴涵,隐涵
import 导入,引入
import custom lists 导入自定义序列
import folder 导入文件夹
import library 导入库
import picture 导入图片
import print device 导入打印设备
Import Web Wizard 导入站点向导
import wizard 导入向导
importance 重要性
importance sampling 重要性抽样
importance test 重要性检验
imported signal 导入信号
imposition 装版
impossibility 不可能性
impossible event 不可能事件
impractical 不切实际的
imprecise 不精确的
imprecise information risk 不精确信息风险
imprecise interrupt 不精确中断
impression 印压,字迹
impression control 字迹轻重控制
impression cylinder 压印滚筒
impressionist 印象派
imprimitive matrix 非本原矩阵
imprint position 印刷[打印]位置
imprinter 压印机
imprinting 加印记
improper 非正常的 「符
improper character 不当[非正常]字
improper code 非正常码,非法码
improper command 不当[异常]命令
improper command check 不当命令校
improper update 不当更新 」验
improved 改进的
improved D-algorithm 改进的 D 算法
improved spool file recovery 改进的假脱机文件恢复
impulse 脉冲
impulse coding 脉冲编码
impulse dialing 脉冲拨号
impulse function 脉冲函数
impulse noise 脉冲噪声
impulse response 脉冲响应
impulse train 脉冲群
impulsive control problem 冲击控制问题
impure code 不纯码
impure vector 不纯向量
impurity 杂质
impurity absorption 杂质吸收
impurity compensation degree in semiconductor 半导体杂质补偿度
imputation 超值向量;归因于
imputed cost vector 归属价值向量
IMR(Interruption Mask Register) 中断屏蔽寄存器
IMS(Information Management System) 信息管理系统
IMS(Integrated Manufacturing System) 综合生产系统
IMS/2 IMS/2 系统
IMS/VS(Information Management System/Virtual Storage) 虚拟存储信息管理系统(IBM)

in-band 带内信号传输
in-band signaling 带内信令
in-channel interference 同通道干扰
in-circuit emulation 电路内模拟
in-circuit emulation bus 电路内模拟总线
in-circuit emulator (ICE) 内部电路仿真器
in circuit functional test (ICFT) 在线功能测试
in-circuit post assembler testing 组装后电路内测试
in-circuit tester 电路内测试器
in-circuit testing 电路内测试
in-connection 内连接,输入连接
in-connector 内连接符
in-core compiler 内存编译程序
in-depth analysis 深入分析
in-depth audit 彻底审计
in-doubt message 有疑问消息
in-flight task 正在处理中的任务
in hardware 以硬件方式
in-house 自用,内部
in-house line 自由线路,内部线路
in-house network 自用网络,内部网络
in-house system 自用系统,内部系统
in-junction gate 抑制门,禁止门
in-line 线内,内部,直接插入
in-line checks 线内检验,内部校验
in-line code 直接插入码
in-line coding 线内[直接插入]编码
in-line control statement 直接插入控制语句
in-line data processing 线内数据处理
in-line diagnosis 直接插入诊断
in-line equipment 在线[联机]设备
in-line execute 在线[联机]执行
in-line expansion 直接插入展开
in-line function 直接插入函数
in-line image 联机图像
in-line macro 直接插入宏指令
in-line package 直插封装
in-line printer 在线打印机
in-line procedure 线内过程,内部过程
in-line processing 直接插入处理
in-line recovery 线内复原
in-line subroutine 直接插入子程序
in-list 内目录

in-phase 同相
in-place activation 原位激活
in-place computation 现场计算
in-place migration 原位迁移
in-plant system 室内系统
in-process 进程内
in-process analysis 实时处理过程分析
in-process component 正在执行的部件
in-process server 进程内服务程序
in-processing 在线[联机]处理
in-service training 在职学习
in site 现场,就地
In-slot signaling 时间槽内信令
in software 以软件方式
in-station test 站内测试
in-stream procedure 流内过程[步骤]
in-sync 同步
inaccessible page 不可存取页面
inaccuracy 不准确度
inactive 非活,非现用
inactive age 待用期限
inactive block 非活动块,静态分程序
inactive character 无效字符
inactive constraint 不起作用的约束
inactive DO-loop 非活 DO 循环,非现用 DO 循环
inactive entry 非活动入口
inactive event variable 非活动事件变量
inactive file 非活文件,非现用文件
inactive line 非活[待用]线路
inactive link 待用[非活]链路
inactive mass storage volume 待用海量存储器卷
inactive node 非活节点
inactive page 非活页面,不活动页
inactive program 非活[非现用]程序
inactive queue 待用队列
inactive signaling link 非活动信令链路
inactive state 非活动状态
inactive station 不活动站
inactive time 非活动时间,无效时间
inactive title bar 不活动标题栏
inactive volume 待用卷
inactive window 不活动窗口
inadequate 不够的,不完全的
inadmissible automatic character checking 自动非法字符检验
inadmissible-character check 禁用字

符检验
inadmissible strategy 不宜采用策略
inadvertent disclosure 无意泄密
inband signaling 带内信令
inbetweening 插画；中间运动
inblock 整块，整体
inblock subgroup 按块分组
inboard channel 内侧信道
inbound 接收的，入站的
inbound link 入站链路
inbound pacing 入站调步，入站整速
inbound path 入站通路
inbound signaling 入站信令
inbox 收件箱
inbranch 入站支路
INC(INCreased) 递增的
INCA(INformation Council of the American) 美国信息委员会
incandescent lamp 白炽灯泡
incessancy 不间断性
inching switch 微动开关
incidence 关联，入射
incidence cut-set 关联割集
incidence edge 关联边
incidence function 关联函数
incidence matrix 关联矩阵
incidence relation 关联关系
incident angle 送入角，入射角
incident light 入射光
incident rate 呼唤率，事件率
incident record 送入记录，事件记录
incidental amplitude modulation 寄生调幅
incidental frequency modulation 寄生调频
incidental phase modulation 寄生调相
incidental time 额外时间，非主要工作时间
incipient failure 早期失效，初发故障
include 包含
include file 包含文件
include library 包含文件库
include member 内含[可包括]成员
include set 包含集合
include statement 包含语句
inclusion 包含；内含物
inclusion method 包含法
inclusion principle 包含原理

inclusion relation 包含关系
inclusive 包括在内的，内容丰富的
inclusive reference 包含参考，蕴涵引用
inclusive segment 包含段，相容段
incoherent 不相干的
incoherent bundle 非相干光纤束
incoherent light 非相干光
incoherent reception 非相干接收
incoherent wave 非相干波
INCOMEX (INternational COMputer EXhibition) 国际计算机博览会
incoming 进入的，引入的
incoming call 入局呼叫
incoming call packet 呼入包
incoming circuit 进入电路，入局电路
incoming degree 入度
incoming event 外来事件
incoming frame 入局机架
incoming group 进入群，输入消息组
incoming line 引入线，入局线
incoming message 进入消息
incoming register(ICT) 来话记发器
incoming selector 入局选择器
incoming source document 输入源文档
incoming task 输入任务
incoming traffic 入局通信量
incoming trunk(ICT) 入局中继线
incomparability 不可比性
incomparable 不可比的
incompatibility 不相容性
incompatible 不相容的，不兼容的
incompatible action 不相容动作
incompatible data 不相容数据
incompatible version 不兼容版本
incompatibility 不相容性，不兼容性
incomplete 不完全的，未完成的
incomplete decomposition 不完全分解，带余分解
incomplete information description 不完全信息描述
incomplete model 不完全模型
incomplete parameter checking 不完全参数检验
incomplete program 不完全程序
incomplete relation 不完全关系
incomplete routine 不完全例程
incomplete syntax description 不完全的语法描述

incompletely specified function 不完全确定函数
incompletely specified unicode assignment 非完全指定的通用码赋值
incompleteness theorem 不完全性定理
incompressible 不可压缩的
incomputebility 不可计算性
inconnector 流线内接符
inconsistent 不相容的,不一致的
inconsistent estimator 不相容估计量
inconsistent formula 全假公式
inconsistent knowledge 不一致知识
inconsistent order 非一致序
inconsistent statement 不相容语句
inconstant 易变的
inconvenience 不方便,不适合
inconvertible 不可变换的
incorporate 采用,吸收,合并
incorrect 不正确的
incorrect bit 不正确位
incorrectness 不正确性
INCR(INCrement Register) 增量寄存器
increase(INC) 递增;增量
increase indent 增加缩进量
increment(INC, INCR, INCRE) 递增;增量
increment factor 增量因子
increment list 增量表
increment operator 递增算子,增量运算符
increment pointer 增量指针
increment size 递增大小,增量尺寸
incremental after write 增量后写入
incremental allocation 增量分派
incremental backup 增量备份
incremental compaction 增量精简法
incremental compiler 递增编译例程,逐句编译程序
incremental computer 增量型计算机
incremental control 递增控制,增量控制
incremental coordinate 增量坐标
incremental data 增量数据
incremental development 递增式开发
incremental dimension 递增维,增量维数
incremental display 增量显示
incremental dump 增量转储
incremental execution 增量执行
incremental feed 递增馈给,增量馈送
incremental implementation 递增实现
incremental integrator 增量积分器
incremental model 递增模型
incremental packet writing 增量包刻录技术(Philips)
incremental parameter 递增参数,增量参数
incremental parser 递增式语法分析器
incremental plotter 增量式绘图仪
incremental plotter control 增量式绘图仪控制
incremental program constructor 递增型程序构造器
incremental quantum efficiency 递增量子效率
incremental record 递增记录
incremental recording 递增记录法
incremental representation 增量表示
incremental sign 递增符号,增量符号
incremental size 增距
incremental spacing 递增间隔
incremental system 递增系统,增量系统
incremental tape 递增磁带
incremental tape drive 递增[增量]磁带机
incremental tape units 递增磁带机
incremental transducer 增量变换器
incremental update 递增式更新
incremental vector 递增向量
incubation 潜伏性
incubation period 潜伏期
indecomposability 不可分解性
indefinite blocking 非确定性阻塞
indefinite form 不定型
indefinite matrix 不定矩阵
indefinite postponement 无限期延迟
indent 缩进编排,锯齿状书写
indent from left 从左边缩进
indent tag character 缩排制表符
indentation 缩进编排,锯齿状书写
indented paragraph 缩进编排段落
independence 独立性
independent compilation 独立编译
independent control point 独立控制点
independent equations 独立方程式
independent events 独立事件

independent failure 独立故障
independent manufacturer support program(IMSP) 独立制造商支持计划
independent modularity 独立模块性
independent operation 独立作业
independent optimization 独立[与机器无关的]优化
independent overflow area 独立溢出区
independent process 独立进程
independent program loader 独立程序装入程序
independent request control 独立请求控制
independent resource 独立资源
independent routine 独立例程
independent sector 独立段;独立扇区
independent segment 独立段
independent set of a hypergraph 超图的独立集
independent sideband communication system 独立边带通信制
independent sideband modulation 独立边带调制
independent sideband transmission 独立边带传输
independent software vendor(ISV) 独立软件供应商
independent utility programs 独立实用程序
independent variable 独立变量;自变量
independent verification and validation 独立验证和确认
independent workstation 独立工作站
indeterminacy 不确定性
indeterminate fault 不确定性故障
indeterminate(X) state 不确定状态
index 索引[址]
index absolute addressing 变址绝对寻址
index access file 索引存取文件
index array 索引阵列
index block chaining 索引块链锁
index build 索引建立
index constraint 指针[下标]约束
index counter 索引计数器
index data item 下标数据项
index data name 下标数据名
index detector 索引检测器

index entry 索引项目
index field 索引字段
index file 索引文件
index frame 索引帧
index gap 索引隙
index hole 索引孔
index identifier 索引标识符
index input 索引输入
index key 索引键
index level 索引级
index maker 索引生成器
index mapping 索引映像
index marker 索引标志
index mechanism 索引机制[机构]
index memory 变址存储器
index mode 索引模式[方式]
index modification 索引修正,变址修改
index name 索引[下标]名
index notation 索引表示法
index number 索引号
index of cooperation 合作索引
index of sorted mode 索引或排序模式
index order 索引排序
index page 索引页面
index point 索引点
index position 索引位置
index pulse 索引脉冲
index record header 索引记录标题
index register(IR) 变址寄存器
index return character 索引返回字符
index search 索引查找
index segment 索引段
index sensing 索引感测
index sensor 索引传感器
index sequential file 索引顺序文件
index servo 索引伺服
index slot 索引槽
index sort 索引排序
index source segment 索引源段
index stack 索引栈
index storage 索引[变址]存储器
index structure 索引结构
index tag 索引标签
index target segment 索引目标段
index term 索引词,索引字
index track 索引磁道
index transducer 索引转换器
index update flag 索引更新标志

index validity flag 索引有效标志
index value 索引值
index variable 下标变量,索引变量
index vector 变址向量
index word 索引字,变址字
index word register 索引字寄存器
indexable 可加索引的,可变址的
indexed 索引的
indexed access 索引存取
indexed address 索引地址
indexed addressing 索引寻址
indexed color 索引颜色
indexed component 索引分量,下标成「分
indexed data set 索引型数据集
indexed file 被索引文件「织
indexed file organization 索引文件组
indexed file structure 定位文件结构
indexed grammar 索引文法
indexed I/O 索引输入/输出
indexed indirect addressing 变址间接寻址
indexed language 索引语言
indexed list 索引表
indexed non-sequential file 索引非顺序文件
indexed organization 索引组织
indexed random file 索引随机文件
indexed search 索引搜索
indexed sequential access method (ISAM) 索引顺序存取法
indexed sequential data set 索引顺序数据集
indexed sequential file 索引顺序文件
indexed sequential organization 索引顺序组织
indexed set type 索引集类型
indexed structure 索引结构
indexed variable 下标变量
indexed zero page addressing 变址零页寻址
indexing 索引法
indexing language 索引语言
indexing slot 标引槽
Indian parallel ETOL system 印度并行 ETOL 系统「法
Indian parallel grammar 印度并行文
indicate abstract 指示性摘要
indicated color system 表色系统

indicated resource 指示的资源
indicating instrument 指示仪器
indicating recorder 指示记录器
indicative abstract 指示性文摘
indication error 指示误差
indication primitive 指示原语
indicative abstract 指示性摘要
indicative function 示性函数
indicator 指示器;指示符
indicator area 指示符域
indicator chart 指针图表
indicator diagram 示功图
indicator term 指示语句
indicator variable 指示变量
indicatrix 指标线
indifference class 无差异类
indifference curve 无差异曲线
indifference relation 无差别关系,中性关系
indifferent 中性的,不偏的
indigenous fault 固有[内在]故障
indirect 间接的
indirect A/D converter 间接模/数转换器
indirect activation 间接激活
indirect address 间接地址
indirect address computation 间接地址计算
indirect address register 间接地址寄存器
indirect addressing 间接寻址
indirect assignment 间接赋值
indirect binary n-cube network 间接二进 n 立方体网络
indirect branch 间接转移
indirect call 间接调用
indirect command file 间接命令文件
indirect control 间接控制「统
indirect controlled system 间接受控系
indirect controlled variable 间接受控变量
indirect coupling 间接耦合
indirect deactivation 间接撤消
indirect encoding microinstruction 间接编码微指令
indirect execution 间接执行
indirect index 间接索引
indirect indexed addressing 间接变址

寻址
indirect instruction 间接指令
indirect method of variational problem 变分问题的间接解法
indirect network 间接网络
indirect operator 间接运算符
indirect output 间接输出
indirect pointer 间接指针
indirect probability 间接概率
indirect recursion 间接递归
indirect reference address 间接引用地址
indirect relative address 间接相对地址
indirect searching optimization 间接查找优化
indirect segmenting encode 间接分段编码
indirect sharing 间接共享
indirect threaded coding 间接串线编码法
indirect user 间接用户
indirect utility 间接效用
indirect wave 间接波
indirectly controlled system 间接受控系统
indirectly controlled variable 间接受控变量
indirectly-coupled system 间接耦合系统
indistinguishable 不可区分的
individual 个体;个别的;单独的
individual address 单个地址
individual call sign 个人呼号
individual constant 个体常元
individual control 个别[单独]控制
individual debugging 个别调试,分调
individual decision making 个体决策
individual distortion 个别畸变
individual effect 单独效应
individual gap azimuth 个别间隙方位
individual line 独用线,专用线路
individual loop 个体常元
individual polling 个别探询
individual rationality 个体合理性
individual task 单项任务
individual variable 个体变元
indivisible 不可除尽的
indivisible operation 不可分操作
induced anisotropy 感生各向异性

induced failure 诱发故障
induced interference 感应干扰
induced jitter 感应抖动
induced noise 诱发噪声,感应噪声
induced norm 导出范数
induced optical conductor loss 诱发光导体损失,感应光导体损耗
inductance 电感,感应系数
induction 归纳法;感应现象
induction algorithm 归纳算法
induction axiom 归纳公理
induction coil 感应线圈
induction hypothesis 归纳假设
induction inference 归纳推理
induction learning 归纳学习
induction parameter 归纳参数
induction principle 归纳原理
induction reasoning 归纳推理
induction synchronizer 感应同步器
induction variable 归纳变量
inductionless 无感应的
inductive assertion 归纳断言
inductive coupling 电感耦合
inductive head 感应式磁头
inductive inference 归纳推论
inductive interference 诱发性[感应干扰]
inductive knowledge acquisition 归纳式知识获取
inductive learning 归纳式学习
inductive proof method 归纳证明法
inductive proposition 归纳命题
inductive read/write head 感应式读写头
inductive reasoning 归纳推理
inductive statistics 归纳统计学
inductive switch 感应开关
inductive tool 归纳工具
inductive transducer 电感性传感器
inductively-derived decision rule 归纳导出的决策规则
inductor 电感器
industrial control 工业控制
industrial control modules 工业控制模块
industrial data processing 工业数据处理
industrial interference 工业干扰
industrial PC(IPC) 工业用个人计算机

industrial process control 工业过程控制
industrial robot 工业机器人
industries process control system 工业生产过程控制系统
industry standard architecture (ISA) 工业标准体系结构(总线)
industry-standard user interface 工业标准用户界面
inediting 中间编辑
ineffective call 无效呼叫
ineffective time 无效时间
inefficiency 低效率
inefficient algorithm 非有效算法
inefficient serial algorithm 低效串行算法
inequality 不等式;不等
inequality constraint 不等式约束
inequality operator 不等于算子
inequivalence 不对等,异或
inequavalence gate 不对等门,异或门
inert gas 惰性气体
inertial delay 惯性延迟
inertial guidance integrating gyro 惯性制导积分陀螺[统
inertial guidance system 惯性制导系
inertial matrix 惯性矩阵
inertial navigation computer 惯性导航计算机
inertial profilometer 惯性轮廓测定仪
inertialess deflection 无惯性偏转
inessential cooperative game 非本质合作对策
inessential general game 非本质一般对策
inexact 不精确的,不确切的 「法
inexact breaking method 不精确断点
inexact concept 不确切概念
inexact data 不准确数据
inexact environment 不确切环境
inexact function 不确切函数
inexact reasoning 不精确推理
inexact regression analysis 不确切回归分析
inexact statement 不确切命题
inexpensive disk 廉价磁盘
infant 初期的,新建的
infant mortality 初期[早期]失效
infeasible path 不可行路径

infection 传染
infection carrier 传染载体
infection condition 传染条件
infection density 传染密度
infection mode 传染模式
infection of computer virus 计算机病毒的传染
infection range 传染范围
infection routes 传染途径
infection source 传染源
infection success rate 传染成功率
infection vector 传染媒介
infection velocity 传染速度
infection way 传染方式
inference 推断,推理
inference chain 推理链
inference clause 推论子句
inference data-directed 数据引导推理
inference engine 推理引擎[机构]
inference hierarchy 推理层次
inference knowledge 推理知识
inference machine 推理机
inference method 推理方法
inference mode-directed 面向模式的推理
inference network 推理网络
inference node 推理节点,推论节点
inference procedure 推理过程
inference program 推论程序
inference programming 推理编程
inference rule 推理规则
inference step 推理步
inference strategy 推理策略
inferior 低等的;下部的;下标,脚注
inferior figure 下标,脚注;下角数字
inferior window 下层[下级]窗口
inferiors 下层子窗口
infiltrator 渗入者
infimum 下确界
infinite 无穷大;无限
infinite antagonistic game 无限对抗对策
infinite goal 无穷目标
infinite graph 无限图
infinite impulse response digital filter (IIRF) 无限冲激响应数字滤波器
infinite integral 无穷积分
infinite light 无穷远光源
infinite loop 无限循环

infinite matrix 无穷矩阵
infinite memory filter 无限记忆滤波器
infinite-pad method 无限衬垫法
infinite-period Markovian decision process 无限周期马尔可夫决策过程
infinite point 无穷远点
infinite programming 无限规划
infinite sequence 无穷序列
infinite series 无穷级数
infinite set 无穷集
infinite state automaton 无穷状态自动机
infinite symmetric group 无限对称群
infinite tree 无穷树
infinite wait 无限期等待
infinite word 无限字
infinitely great 无穷大
infinitely small 无穷小
infinitesimal 极小量
infinity 无限,无穷
infinity lemma 无穷性引理
infix expression 中缀表达式
infix form 中置式,中缀式
infix notation 中置记法,中缀表示法
infix operator 中置算子,中缀运算符
inflection 词尾变化;转折
inflection point 拐点
inflexible 不灵活的;硬性的
influence diagram 影响图
influence function 影响函数
influence line 影响线
influence number 影响数
info categories 信息分类
info field 信息字段
info window 信息窗口
InfoLine InfoLine信息服务
Infonet Infonet网络
infoport 信息港
infopreneur 信息前端工作者
inforcosm 信息社会
inform 通知,通告
informacial 信息商业
informal 非正式的
informal coalition 非正式联盟
informal design review 非正式设计评审
informal programming language 非正式程序设计语言
informal proof 非形式证明
informal syntax tree 非形式语法树
informat 信息提供者
informatics 信息学;信息控制论
information 信息
information abstract 信息摘要
information acquisition 信息获取
information age 信息时代
information analysis 信息分析
information and data 信息与数据
information appliance 信息电器
information area 信息区域
information availability 信息可用性
information bank system 信息库系统
information bearer channel 信息载运信道
information behavioral pattern 信息行为模式
information bits 信息位
information broadcast 信息广播
information bulletin 信息公告
information capacity 信息容量
information carrier 信息载体
information carrying capacity 信息承载能力
information center 信息中心
information channel 信息通道
information character 信息字符
information code 信息代码
information compaction 信息压缩
information compression 信息压缩
information conditional 条件信息含量
information content 信息量,信息内容
information content binary unit 信息内容二进单位
information content decimal unit 十进制单位的信息量
information content natural unit 信息量自然单位
information content of program 程序信息量
information conversion 信息转换
information cost 信息成本
information density 信息密度
information economics 信息经济学
information efficiency 信息效率
information encoding 信息编码
information engineering 信息工程

Information Engineering Facility(IEF) 信息工程设施
Information Engineering Workbench(IEW) 信息工程工作平台
information entropy coding 信息熵编码
information environment 信息环境
information environment science 信息环境学
information explosion 信息爆炸
information feedback 信息反馈
information feedback system 信息反馈系统
information field 信息字段[域]
information filtering 信息过滤
information float 信息浮动
information flow 信息流程,信息流
information flow analysis 信息流程分析
information flow chart 信息流程图
information flow control 信息流控制
information flow model 信息流模型
information format 信息格式
information frame 信息帧
information freeway 信息高速公路
information function 信息函数
information gate 信息门
information group 信息组
information handling center 信息处理中心
information heading 信息标题
information hiding 信息隐藏
information highway 信息高速公路
information industry 信息产业
information infrastructure 信息基础设施
information input device 信息输入设备
information integrity 信息完整性
information interchange 信息交换
information island 信息孤岛
information item 信息项
information language 信息语言
information link 信息链
information loss 信息损失
information magnitude 信息量级
information management system(IMS) 信息管理系统
information management system for virtual storage(IMS/VS) 虚拟存储信息管理系统
information measure 信息计量
information message 信息消息
information modeling 信息模型化
information network 信息网络
information obsolescence 信息废弃
information on demand 信息点播服务
Information on your finger 信息在您指端(Bill Gates)
information-oriented language 面向信息的语言
information packet 信息包,分组
information parameter 信息参数
information path 信息路径[通路]
information pattern 信息模式
information pollution 信息污染
information privacy 信息保密性
information process 信息处理
information processing 信息处理
information processing center 信息处理中心
information processing language(IPL) 信息处理语言
information processing language-V(IPL-V) 数据处理语言V
information processing management 信息处理管理
information processing psychology 信息处理心理学
information processing system 信息处理系统
information processor 信息处理机
information professional 信息专业人
information property 信息财富
information protection 信息保护
information provider 信息供应者
information quality 信息质量
information rate 信息传输率;信息率
information redundancy 信息冗余
information representation 信息表示
information requirement 信息要求
information resource dictionary(IRD) 信息资源辞典
information resource dictionary system(IRDS) 信息资源辞典系统
information resource sharing 信息资源共享
information resources management

(IRM) 信息资源管理
information retrievable(IR) 信息检索
information retrieval system 信息检索系统
information retrieval technique 信息检索技术
information revolution 信息革命
information science 信息科学
information security 信息安全
information selection systems 信息选择系统
information separator(IS) 信息分隔符
information separator character 信息分隔字符
information sharing 信息共享
information sink 信宿,信息接收者
information society 信息社会
information society science 信息社会学
information source 信息源
information source coding 信息源编码
information space 信息空间
Information Stop 信息亭
information strength 信息强度
information structure 信息结构
information super-highway 信息高速公路
information symbol 信息符号
information system(IS) 信息系统
information system analyst 信息系统分析师
information system base language(IS-BL) 信息系统基础语言
information system development methodology 信息系统开发方法学
information system engineering 信息系统工程
information system factories(ISF) 信息系统加工线
information system flowchart 信息系统流程图
information system master 信息系统设计管理者
information technology(IT) 信息技术
information theory(IT) 信息论
information throughput 信息吞吐量
information trading 信息交易
information transfer channel 信息转移通道
information transfer module 信息传送模块
information transfer phase 信息传送阶段
information transfer rate(ITR) 信息转移率
information transmission 信息传输
information transmission system 信息传输系统
information tree 信息树
information trunk 信息主干线
information uncertainty 信息不确定性
information unit 信息单位
information utility 信息公用事业
information value 信息价值
information vendor 信息供应商
information word 信息字
information world 信息世界
informational cluster 信息簇
informational message 信息性消息
informative abstract 信息性文摘
INFORMIX INFORMIX 数据库
Informix-4GL Informix 第四代语言
Informix-DCE/NET Informix-DCE/NET 连接工具
Informix Dynamic Scalable Architecture(DSA) Informix 动态可缩放体系结构
Informix-Enterprise Gateway Informix 企业网关
Informix Gateway with DRDA 用于分布式关系数据库体系结构的 Informix 网关
Informix-NewEra NewEra 开发环境
Informix-OnLine Dynamic Server Informix 联机动态服务器
Informix-OnLine Extended Parallel Server(OnLineXPS) Informix 联机扩展并行服务器
Informix-OnLine Workgroup Server(OnLine XPS) Informix 联机工作组服务器
Informix Software Cor. 英孚美软件公司(美)
Informix-SQL Informix 结构查询语言
Informix Universal Server Informix 通用服务器
informosome 信息体

inforswitch network 信息交换网络
infortainment 信息娱乐
Infoscope(Information Scope) 信息透镜〔站
InfoSeek Guide InfoSeek 搜索引擎网
InfoSoft 信息软件公司
infostructure 信息资源设施
infoware 信息体
InfoWindow 信息窗
infrared 红外线
infrared guidance 红外制导
infrared high output optical fiber 红外高强度输出光纤
infrared image 红外图像
infrared interface 红外接口
infrared light 红外光
infrared port 红外端口
infrared remote control 红外遥控
infrared sensor 红外传感器
infrared tracking system 红外跟踪系统
infrared transmission 红外传输
infrared viewer 红外观察器
infrastructure 信息基础设施
INGRES(INteractive Graphics and REtrieval System) 交互式图形与检索系统
INGRES system 交互制图检索系统
inherent ambiguity 固有二义性
inherent error 固有误差
inherent priority 固有优先权
inherent stability 固有稳定性
inherent system rationality 内在的系统合理性
inherent transparency 固有透明性
inherent weakness failure 固有弱点造成的失效
inherently ambiguous language 固有多义语言
inheritability 可继承性
inheritance 继承
inheritance attribute 继承属性
inheritance code 继承码
inheritance hierarchies 继承体系
inheritance logic 继承逻辑
inheritance preemption principle 继承占先原则
inheritance reasoning 继承推理
inherited 继承的,承袭的

Inherited Rights Filter(IRF) 继承权过滤器
Inherited Rights Mask(IRM) 继承权屏蔽
inhibit 抑制,禁止
inhibit circuit 抑制电路,禁止电路
inhibit counter 计数器抑制[禁止]
inhibit gate 抑制门,禁止门电路
inhibit input 禁止输入
inhibit line 抑制线,禁止线
inhibit pulse 抑制[禁止]脉冲
inhibit signal 抑制[禁止]信号
inhibit wire 抑制线,禁止线
inhibiting input 禁止输入
inhibiting signal 禁止[抑制]信号
inhibition 抑制,禁止
inhibition gate 抑制门,"禁"门
inhibition rule 抑制[禁止]规则
inhibitor 抑制门
inhomogeneous 不均匀的;非齐次的
inhomogeneous boundary condition 非齐次边界条件
inhomogeneous fiber 不均匀光纤
inhomogeneous problem 不同质问题
INIT(INITiator) 初始化程序
init graphics function 图形初始化功能
init process 初始进程(Unix)
init states 初始状态(Unix)
initial 启始字符,开头字符
initial access time 初始访问时间
initial address 起始地址
initial alias file 初始协同文件
initial alignment 初始调整
initial appearance 初始出现
initial attribute 初始属性
initial bias 初始偏差
initial boundary value problem 初边值问题
initial cap 起始大写,开头大写
initial chaining value(ICV) 初始链接值
initial condition 初始条件
initial condition adjustment 初始条件调整
initial condition mode 起始条件模式
initial configuration 初始配置
initial connection protocol 初始连接协议
initial control word 初始控制字

initial cycle error 初始周期误差
initial data 原始数据
initial database description 初始数据库描述
initial definition 初始定义
initial design 初始设计
initial diagnostics 初始诊断
initial disturbance 初始扰动
initial edge 出发边
initial error 初始误差
initial examination and measurement 初始检测「程
initial external procedure 初始外部过
initial failure 早期故障,初期失效
initial flow data 初始流程数据
initial function 初始函数
initial gap 初始间隔
initial graphics exchange specification (IGES) 基本图形交换规范
initial information 初始信息
initial instruction 起始指令,初始指
initial interval 初始间隔 「令
initial license 初始特许
initial line 起始行
initial loading 起始加载,初始装入
initial model 初始模型
initial node 初始节点,起始结点
initial order 起始命令;初始顺序
initial outcome variable 原始结果变
initial parameter 初值参数 「量
initial period 起算时间
initial point 起始点,初始点
initial position 起始位置
initial print 初始打印
initial problem 起始[初始]问题
initial procedure 初始过程
initial program 初始程序
initial program load (IPL) 初始程序装入
initial program loader (IPL) 初始程序加载程序
initial program loading 起始程序加载
initial replication 初始复制
initial request 初始请求
initial reset 初始复位
initial row 初始行,起始行
initial seed 初始种籽,起始种子数
initial segment 起始段

initial set data 原始给定数据
initial setting 初始设置
initial signal unit 起始信号单位
initial snapshot 初始瞬像
initial solution 初始解
initial start 初始起动
initial state 初始状态
initial strain 初始应变
initial sum 初始和
initial symbol 初始符号
initial table 初始表
initial task index 初始任务指标
initial term 初始项,初项
initial tree 起始树
initial uncertainty 初始不定态
initial upper bound solution 初始上界
initial value 初始值 「解
initial value estimation 初值估计
initial value parameter 初值参数
initial - value problem 初值问题
initial velocity 初速度
initial vertex 初始顶点
initialization 初始化
initialization file (Unix)初始化文件
initialization string 初始化串
initialize 初设,预置
initialize routine 初设例程,预置程序
initializing 起始,初设
initializing declaration 初始化说明
initializing modem 初始化调制解调
initiate 启动 「器
initiate button 启动按钮
initiate control word 启动控制字
initiate key 启动键
initiate mode 起始模式
initiate scavenging 开始清除
initiate statement 初始化语句
initiate - transaction - sequence indicator 初启事务序列指示符
Initiating LU 初始逻辑单元
initiating signal 启动信号
initiating station 起始站
initiating task 起始任务,启动任务
initiation area discriminator 初域鉴别
initiation sequence 起始顺序 「器
initiator 初始化程序;启动站
initiator task 启动任务
initiator/terminator 启动终止例程

inject_statement attribute 插入语句属性
injection 注射,喷射
injection laser 注入式激光器
injection logic 注入逻辑
injection nozzle 墨水喷嘴
injector 注射器,注入器
ink 墨水,油墨
ink bleed 墨水渗漏
ink cartridge 墨水盒
ink cartridge low 墨水盒液位过低
ink density 墨水浓度
ink distributor roller 油墨滚筒
ink droplet 墨滴
ink duck 储墨槽,油墨槽
ink fog printer 墨雾打印机
ink jet 喷墨
ink jet method 喷墨法
ink jet plotter 喷墨绘图机
ink jet printer 喷墨打印机
ink-jet printing head 喷墨打印头
ink mist printer 墨雾打印机
ink mist recording 墨雾记录
ink nozzle 喷墨嘴
ink pump 墨水泵
ink recorder 墨水记录器
ink recording 印墨记录
ink reflectance 印墨反射比
ink ribbon 油墨色带
ink screen 油墨滤网
ink selector 油墨选择器
ink smudge 墨水污染
ink squeezeout 墨水渲染
ink stylus 墨水笔
ink surface tension 墨水表面张力
ink tank 储墨水罐
ink trouble 记录故障
ink uniformity 墨迹均匀性
ink-vapor recording 墨水蒸汽记录
ink viscosity 墨水粘性
inking 墨迹式画图
inking up 上墨
inkless recording 无墨水记录
inlay 镶嵌
inlead 引入线
inlet 引入线　　　　　　　　　　「装
inline assembly 线内装配,插入式组
inline code 直接插入代码
inline coding 线内编码,序列式编码
inline comment 内部注释
inline compiler 内编译程序
inline data file 直接插入数据文件
inline data processing 成簇联机数据处理
inline direction 行方向
inline extent 联机范围;行方向范围
inline function 内函数,直接插入函数
inline images 内含图像,插入图像
inline macro 直接插入宏指令
inline margin 行方向边界
inline package 直插封装
inline processing 线内处理,直接处理
inline recovery 直接插入恢复,联机恢复
inline subroutine 直接插入子例程
inline system 直接处理系统
inline template 内联模板
inner face 内面
inner flag register 内标记寄存器
inner join 内联
inner linearization 内线性化
inner loop 内循环,内层循环
inner macroinstruction 内部宏指令
inner point method 内点法
inner stop 内停止区
inner track 内磁道
innermost cylinder 最内柱面
innermost loop 最内层循环
innovation process 革新过程
Innov schema 雅诺夫模式
inoculate 无害计算;嫁接
inoculating 登记,接种
inode(information node) 信息节点(Unix)
inoperable 不可操作的
inoperable time 不可操作时间
inorder 中序
inorder traversal 中序遍历
Innovatron Group Innovatron(IC卡)集团
INP(Intelligent Network Processor) 智能网络处理机
inplace algorithm 原地置换算法
inplant computer network system 近距离计算机网络系统
input(I,IN) 输入

input aperture 输入窗孔
input area 输入区
input attribute 输入属性
input axis 输入轴
input block 输入块
input blocking factor 输入编块因数
input bound 受输入约束的
input box 输入框
input buffer 输入缓冲器
input buffer register 输入缓冲寄存器
input bus 输入总线
input capacitance 输入电容
input channel 输入通道
input characteristic 输入特性
input common-mode range 输入共模范围
input compatible 输入相容的
input connection matrix 输入联结矩阵
input converter 输入转换器
input cursor 输入光标
input data 输入数据
input data error 输入数据错误
input data validation 输入数据确认
input dependence 输入相关
input destination message handler (IDMH) 输入信宿报文处理机
input device 输入设备
input device simulation 输入设备模拟
input document 输入文件
input driver 输入驱动器
input editing 输入编辑
input element 输入元素,输入单元
input equipment 输入设备
input error voltage 输入误差电压
input field 输入字段,输入区域
input file 输入文件
input focus 输入焦点(input area 的旧称)
input form 输入窗体
input frame 输入帧
input function 输入函数
input guard 输入保护
input handler 输入处理程序
input image 输入图像
input impedance 输入阻抗
input information 输入信息
input inhibit 输入禁止
input instruction code 输入指令码

input job 输入作业
input job queue 输入作业队列
input job stream 输入作业流
input level 输入电平
input limited 受输入限制的
input-limiter 输入限幅器
input line 输入线;输入行
input list 输入列表
input loading 输入加载
input loading factor 输入加载因数
input locking mask 输入锁定掩码
input magazine 送卡箱
input mask 输入掩码
input media 输入媒介
input medium 输入媒体
input method server 输入法服务程序
input method status 输入法状态
input mode 输入模式
input module 输入模块
input number 输入数
input offset current 输入补偿电流
input offset voltage 输入失调电压
input option 输入选项
input order 输入次序
input/output (I/O) 输入/输出
input/output adapter 输入输出适配器
input/output addressing mode 输入/输出寻址模式
input/output-bounded 受输入/输出限制的
input/output buffer 输入/输出缓冲器
input/output bus 输入/输出总线
input/output cable 输入/输出电缆
input/output channel 输入/输出通道
input/output channel controller 输入/输出通道控制器
input/output chart 输入/输出表
input/output condition 输入/输出条件
input/output connector 输入/输出连接器
input/output control (IOC) 输入/输出控制
input/output device 输入/输出设备
input/output device driver 输入/输出设备驱动器
input/output interface 输入/输出接口
input/output interrupt 输入/输出中断

input/output interrupt indicator 输入/输出中断指示器
input/output interrupt inhibit 输入/输出中断禁止
input/output-limited 受输入/输出限制的
input/output line 输入/输出线
input/output list 输入/输出表
input/output macro 输入/输出宏指令
input/output module 输入/输出模块
input/output multiplexer(IOM) 输入/输出多路转换器
input/output parity interrupt 输入/输出奇偶性中断
input/output port 输入/输出端口
input/output port control 输入/输出端口控制
input/output processor (IOP) 输入/输出处理机
input/output queue(IOQ) 输入/输出队列
input/output request 输入/输出请求
input/output section 输入/输出节
input/output sequence 输入/输出顺序
input/output simultaneity 输入/输出同时性
input/output standard interface 输入/输出标准接口
input/output switching 输入/输出转接
input/output table 投入产出表
input/output traffic control 输入/输出流量控制
input/output traffic table 输入/输出流量表
input/output transfer block 输入/输出传送块
input/output trunk 输入/输出总线
input panel 输入屏幕画面
input parameter 输入参数
input pattern 输入格式
input phase 输入阶段
input port 输入端口
input predicate 输入谓词
input primitive 输入原语
input problem 输入问题
input procedure 输入过程
input process 输入过程

input prompt 输入提示符
input protection 输入保护
input queue 输入队列
input range 输入范围
input rank 输入等级,输入顺次
input recorder 输入记录器
input redirection 输入重定向
input reference 输入参考值
input reference axis 输入基准轴
input register 输入寄存器
input request 输入请求
input resolution 输入消解
input-restricted dequeue 输入受限的双端队列
input routine 输入例程
input section 输入节
input semantics 输入语义
input sheet 输入表单
input side 输入边
input signal 输入信号
input source 输入源
input state 输入状态
input station 输入站
input storage 输入存储器
input stream 输入流
input stream control 输入流控制器
input string 输入串
input style 输入风格
input subsystem 输入子系统
input symbiont 输入共存程序
input tape test 输入带测试
input terminal 输入终端
input text type 输入文本类型
input-to-output approach 输入至输出途径
input transaction 输入事务
input translator 输入翻译程序
input tray 进纸匣
input unit 输入单元
input validation 输入确认
input variable 输入变量
input vector 输入向量
input well 输入井
input wire 输入线
input work queue 输入工作队列
INQ(INQuire) 查询
inquire answer 查询回答
inquire by file 按文件查询

inquire by unit 按单元查询
inquire property item 查询特性项
inquire response 查询应答
INQUIRE statement 查询语句
inquiry 查询
inquiry and answer system 查询回答系统
inquiry and communication system 查询与通信系统
inquiry and subscriber display 查询与客户显示器
inquiry and transaction processing 查询与事务处理
inquiry answer 查询应答
inquiry application 查询应用
inquiry character 查询字符
inquiry clause 查询子句
inquiry display terminal 查询显示终端
inquiry job 查询作业
inquiry message 查询报文
inquiry mode 查询模式
inquiry reply 查询回答
inquiry-response 查询与应答
inquiry/response communication 查询/响应通信
inquiry/response operation 查询/响应操作
inquiry/response processing 查询/应答处理
inquiry session 查询对话
inquiry specifier 查询说明符
inquiry station 查询站
inquiry system 查询系统
inquiry terminal 查询终端
inquiry unit 查询单元
inquiry-with-update 查询与更新
inrush current 浪涌电流
inscribe 读写作用,登记
inscriber 记录器
inscribing 写印字符
inscription 记入,注册
inscroll 记录,登入
insecurity 不稳定,不安全
insensitive code 不敏感码
insensitive time 不敏感时间,静寂时
inseparable 不可分的
inseparable action 不可分动作
insequence 按序

insert 插入
insert acknowledgement 插入确认字
insert annotation 插入批注
insert cell 插入单元格
insert chart 插入图表
insert clip art 插入剪贴图
insert command 插入命令
insert dialog 插入对话框
insert footnote 插入脚注
Insert key 插入键
insert line 插入行
insert mode 插入模式
insert icon 插入图标
insert object 插入对象
insert spike 插入图文框
insert title 插入标题
insert trendline 插入趋势线
insert with automatically justify 自动整版插入
insert worksheet 插入工作表
insetability 可插入性
inserted subroutine 插入子例程
insertion 插入
insertion character 插入字符
insertion class 插入类
insertion criterion 插入准则
insertion editing 插入编辑
insertion gain 插入增益
insertion loss 插入损耗
insertion mass sequential 大量顺序插
insertion method 插入法
insertion picture character 插入格式描述符
insertion point 插入点
insertion sort 插入法分类
insertion switch 插入开关
insertion symbol 嵌入符号
inside border 内部框线
inside plant 内站
insight 见识;洞察力
insignificant digit 无效数位
inspect statement 检测语句
inspection 检验;审查
inspector 检验员;检验程序
inspiration thought 灵感思维
INST(INSTalation) 安装,配置
instability 不稳定度
instability condition 不稳定条件

instable algorithm 不稳定算法
install 安装
install driver 安装驱动程序
install program 安装程序
installable device drive 可安装设备驱动程序
Installable File System(IFS) 可安装文件系统
Installable I/O procedure 可安装输入输出过程
installation 计算站,设施,装备;装设,安装
installation and checkout phase 安装验收阶段
installation charge 安装费用
installation date 装设日期,装就日期
installation diskette 安装软盘
installation exercise 安装作业
installation exit routine 安装出口程序
installation license 安装特许
installation performance specification 安装性能说明
installation process 安装过程
installation processing control 装设处理控制
installation profile 安装概要,安装预置文件
installation program 安装程序
installation script 安装脚本
installation series number 安装序列号
installation spec 安装说明
installation tape number 装设带号码
installation time 装设时间,安装时间
installation verification procedure 安装验证过程
installation wizard 安装向导
installed drivers 已安装驱动程序
installed fonts 已安装字体
installed printer 已安装打印机
installed user program 已安装用户程序
installer 安装程序
InstallShield Wizard 安装向导
instance 示例
instance attribute 示例属性
instance-based learning 基于实例的学习
instance generation 示例生成
instance graph 实例图
instance inheritance 实例继承性

instance method 示例法
instance modification 示例修改
instance object 示例目标;实例对象
instance space 示例空间
instance transformation 图例变换,实例变换
instance variable 实例变量
instancing 建立实例
instant 瞬时的
instant distortion 瞬时失真
instant insanity 瞬时错乱
instant messaging 消息即送
instant print 即刻印出,立即打印
instant replay 即时重放
instant watch 即时监视
instantaneous 瞬时的
instantaneous access 瞬时存取,立即存取
instantaneous availability 瞬时有效性
instantaneous code 瞬时码,立即码
instantaneous communications 瞬时通信
instantaneous companding 瞬时压扩技术
instantaneous data transfer rate 瞬时数据传输率
instantaneous description(ID) 瞬时描述
instantaneous failure rate 瞬时失败率
instantaneous frequency 瞬时频率
instantaneous impact prediction 瞬时命中点预测
instantaneous overload 瞬时过载,瞬时过压
instantaneous sound pressure 瞬时声压
instantaneous storage 瞬时存储器,立即存取存储器
instantaneous transmission rate 瞬时传输速率
instantaneous unavailability 瞬时不可用性
instantaneous value 瞬时值
instantaneous velocity 瞬时速度
instantaneous voltage 瞬时电压
instantiate 实例化
instantiated 例示,以例说明
instantiation 实例化,例示
institute 协会,学会,研究所
Institute for Certification of Computer Professionals(ICCP) 计算机专业

证书学会
Institute of Electrical and Electronic Engineers(IEEE) 电气和电子工程师学会(美)
instructable production system 可示教产生式系统
instruction 指令
instruction address 指令地址
instruction address register(IAR) 指令地址寄存器
instruction address stop 指令停止地「址
instruction analysis and execute control 指令分析与执行控制
instruction area 指令区
instruction block 指令块
instruction book 说明书,指导书
instruction box 指令盒
instruction break point 指令断点
instruction buffer 指令缓冲器
instruction cache 指令高速缓存
instruction catalog 指令表
instruction character 指令字符
instruction check 指令检验
instruction check indicator 指令检验指示器
instruction code 指令码
instruction constant 指令常数
instruction control circuits 指令控制电路
instruction control unit(ICU) 指令控制单元
instruction counter 指令计数器
instruction cycle 指令周期
instruction deck 指令卡片组
instruction decode and control 指令解码与控制
instruction decoder 指令译码器
instruction delay 指令延迟
instruction dependent control unit 指令相关控制设备
instruction dependency 指令相关性
instruction diagnostic 指令诊断
instruction execution logic 指令执行逻辑
instruction execution sequence 指令执行顺序
instruction execution time 指令执行时间

instruction external devices 指令外部设备
instruction fetch microoperation 取指令微操作
instruction fetch phase 取指令阶段
instruction field 指令字段
instruction flowchart 指令流程图
instruction format 指令格式
instruction group 指令组
instruction length 指令长度
instruction level multiprogram 指令级多道程序「真
instruction level simulation 指令级仿
instruction list 指令表
instruction location register 指令位置寄存器
instruction look ahead unit 指令超前控制单元
instruction manual 指令手册
instruction mix 指令混合
instruction mnemonic 指令助记符
instruction modification 指令修饰,指令修改
instruction modifier 指令修改量
instruction operating 作业指令,操作指令
instruction operation time table 指令操作时间表
instruction pack 指令压缩
instruction packet 指令包
instruction pipeline 指令流水线
instruction pointer 指令指针
instruction prefetch 指令预取
instruction processor 指令处理器
instruction processing unit 指令处理单元
instruction queue 指令队列
instruction register(IR) 指令寄存器
instruction repertoire 指令表,指令系统
instruction repertory 指令清单,指令目录
instruction rescue 指令援救
instruction retry 指令重执
instruction scheduler 指令调度程序
instruction scheduling 指令调度
instruction semantic 指令语义
instruction sequencing 指令定序

instruction set 指令集,指令系统
instruction set expandability 指令系统可扩展性
instruction short 指令短语
instruction space 指令空间
instruction stack 指令堆栈
instruction statement 指令语句
instruction storage 指令存储器
instruction stream 指令流
instruction stream control 指令流控制
instruction stream direction control 指令流向控制
instruction stream out control 指令流出控制
instruction table 指令表
instruction time 指令时间
instruction trace 指令跟踪
instruction type 指令类型
instruction unit 指令单元
instruction word 指令字
instructional CAI 指导式计算机辅助教学
instructional constant 指令常数
instructional cycle 指令周期
instructional database system (IDBS) 教学数据库系统
instructional dialogue 教学式对话
instructional expert syste 教学专家系统
instructional software 教学软件
instrument 仪器,设备
instrument case 工具角色,工具格
instrument error 仪表错误
instrumentation 检测仪表,测试设备
instrumentation application 仪表应用
instrumentation bus 仪表总线
instrumentation calibrate 仪表标定
instrumentation correction 仪表设备校正
instrumentation tool 检测工具
insufficient disk space 磁盘空间不足
insufficient memory 内存不足
insufficient privilege 权限不够
insulated gate field effect transistor (IGFET) 绝缘栅场效应管
insulation film 绝缘薄膜
insulation paper 绝缘纸
insulation resistance 绝缘电阻
insulator 绝缘体

insulator layer 绝缘层
insurance 保险,保证
intact of instruction set 指令系统规整性
intaglio 凹版印刷
intake 入口;纳入
intake roller 进纸辊
intangible benefit 无形效益
INTAP (Interoperability Technology Association for Information Processing) 信息处理协同技术联合会(日)
integer 整数;整型;整体
integer attribute 整数属性
integer BASIC 整数 BASIC 语言
integer constant 整型常量
integer data type 整数类型
integer descriptor 整型描述符
integer double variable 整型双字变量
integer expression 整型表达式
integer function 取整函数
integer linear programming 整数线性规划
integer modulus m 整模数 m
integer numbering system 整数编号系统
integer overflow trap 整数溢出自陷
integer part 整数部分
integer performance 整数性能
integer programming 整数规划
integer solution 整数解
integer type 整数类型
integer variable 整型变量
integer vector 整型向量
integral 整数的,整个的;积分
integral action limiter 积分作用限制
integral boundary 完整边界
integral choice pattern 整选择模式
integral control 积分控制
integral control action 积分控制作用
integral control programming 积分控制程序设计
integral disc 整磁盘
integral domain 整环,整区
integral keyboard 整体键盘
integral modem 内置式调制解调器
integral number 完整数目,整数
integral pattern 整模式
integral point 整数点
integral reset controller 积分重设控

制器
integral symbol 积分符号
integralization 整化
integrand 被积函数
integrated 集成的,整体的,综合的
integrated accounting package 集成会计软件包
integrated adapter 集成式适配器
integrated adaptive routing system 综合自适应路由选择系统
integrated analog/digital converter 集成模/数转换器
integrated application 集成应用软件
integrated approach 综合解决办法
integrated attachment 整体附件
integrated automatic test system 综合自动测试系统
integrated CASE 综合计算机辅助软件工程
integrated catalog facility 综合目录功能程序
integrated catalog facility catalog 综合目录功能程序目录
integrated circuit(IC) 集成电路
integrated-circuit diode-matrix memory 集成电路二极管矩阵存储器
integrated circuit fabrication 集成电路制作
integrated civil engineering system(ICES) 综合土木工程系统语言
integrated communication network 综合通信网
integrated communications adapter(ICA) 综合(内置式)通信适配器
integrated component 集成组件
integrated composition and production software(IC PS) 集成组版生产软件
integrated concept 集成概念
integrated console 综合控制台
integrated data base(IDB) 集成数据库
integrated data dictionary 集成数据词典
integrated data file 综合数据文件
Integrated Data Object Control Architecture(IDOCA) 合成数据对象控制结构
integrated data processing(IDP) 集成数据处理
integrated data processing system(IDPS) 集成数据处理系统
integrated data retrieval system(IDRS) 综合数据检索系统
integrated data store(IDS) 统一数据存储
integrated database management system(IDMS) 集中数据库管理系统
integrated design 综合设计
integrated development environment(IDE) 集成开发环境
integrated diagnosis model 综合诊断模型
integrated digital/analog converter 集成数/模转换器
integrated digital network(IDN) 综合数字网络
integrated disk 一体化磁盘
Integrated Drive Electronics(IDE) 集成驱动器电子电路
integrated emulation 整体仿真
integrated emulator 整体仿真程序
integrated engineering database(IEDB) 整体性工程数据库
integrated environment 集成化环境
integrated expert system 综合性专家系统
integrated file adapter 集中文件适配器
integrated filter 集成滤波器
integrated force method 综合强制法
integrated fuse logic 集成熔丝逻辑
integrated head 集成磁头
integrated injunction logic(IIL, I2L) 集成注入逻辑电路
integrated level 集成度
integrated library system 图书馆综合应用系统
integrated manufacturing software system 综合生产软件系统
integrated manufacturing system(IMS) 综合制造系统
integrated mass storage 整体式大容量存储器
integrated model 组合模型
integrated modeling 综合造型(建模)
integrated modem 综合(内置式)调制解调器
integrated monitor panel 综合监控台
integrated monolithic circuit 集成单

片电路
integrated motor 积分电动机
integrated multivendor network system 复合多售主网络系统
integrated network management 集成网络管理
integrated network processor 综合网络处理机
integrated office system 综合办公系
Integrated On-demand Network(ION) 综合点播网络(Sprint)
integrated open hypermedia 集成开放超媒体
integrated operating system(IOS) 综合操作系统
integrated operational amplifier 集成运算放大器
integrated optical channel 集成光通道
integrated optical circuit 集成光路
integrated optical device 集成光学器件
integrated optical fiber system 综合光纤系统
integrated optics 集成光学
integrated power supply 集成电源
integrated printer adapter 集成式打印机适配器
integrated process 综合过程
integrated production line 综合生产线
integrated program 集成软件
integrated programming support environment(IPSE) 综合型程序设计支持环境
integrated project support environment(IPSE) 集成化工程支持环境
integrated representation 综合表示法
integrated resister 集成电阻
integrated sensor 集成传感器
integrated service digital network(ISDN) 综合业务数字网
Integrated Service Hub(ISH) 综合业务集线器
integrated service local network(ISLN) 综合服务局域网
integrated software 集成软件
integrated software development environment 集成软件开发环境
integrated software engineering environment 集成软件工程环境
integrated software engineering support environment(ISESE) 集成化软件支撑环境
integrated software package 集成软件
integrated solid modeling 综合实体造型(建模)
integrated structure 整体结构
integrated structured design philosophy 总体结构化设计原理
integrated system 集成化系统
integrated system development strategy 整体型系统开发策略
integrated task index 综合任务指标
integrated terminal equipment(TTE) 综合终端设备
integrated test 综合测试
integrated test system 综合测试系统
integrated traffic 综合信息流量
integrated user interface 综合用户界
integrated vector processor 一体化向量处理机
integrated video terminal 一体化视频终端
integrated vision system 综合视觉系
integrated visualization environment 综合目视环境
integrated voice data system 综合语音数据系统
integrated voltage regulator 集成稳压
integrated word processing system 综合文字处理系统
integrating amplifier 积分放大器
integrating circuit 积分电路
integrating factor 积分因子
integrating mechanism 积分机构
integrating motor 积分电动机
integrating network 积分网络
integration 积分;综合;集成,一体化
integration degree 集成度
integration level 集成度
integration stage 通信网集成度
integration test 集成测试,综合检验
integrator 积分器
integrator capacitors 积分器电容器
integrator computing unit(ICU) 积分器计算单元
integrator drift 积分器漂移

Intelligent Database Machine(IDM)

integrity 完整性 「序
integrity check routine 完整性核对过程
integrity constraint 完整性约束
integrity control 完整性控制
integrity detection 完整性检测
integrity management system 完整性管理系统
integrity of knowledge 知识完整性
integrity subsystem 完整性子系统
Intel 386 Intel 386 处理器
Intel 386DX 386DX 处理器
Intel 386SL 386SL 处理器芯片
Intel 386SX 386SX 处理器芯片
Intel 387 387 协处理器芯片
Intel 486 486 处理器芯片
Intel 486DX 486DX 处理器芯片
Intel 486DX2 内部时钟速率加倍的 486 处理器芯片
Intel 486DX4 486DX4 芯片
Intel 486SX 486SX 处理器芯片
Intel 586 586 处理器芯片(正式名称为 Pentium)
Intel 4004 4004 微处理器(1971)
Intel 8080 8080 微处理器
Intel 8085 8085 微处理器
Intel 8086 8086 微处理器
Intel 8088 8088 处理器
Intel 80186 80186 处理器
Intel 80286 80286 处理器
Intel 80287 80287 数学协处理器
Intel 80386 80386 处理器
Intel 82385 82385 芯片
Intel Co. 英特尔公司(美)
Intel communications application specification(ICAS) Intel 通信应用规范
Intel Hex Format(IHF) IHF 磁带记录格式
Intel network Intel 网络
Intel overdrive Intel 加速驱动器
Intel Pentium 奔腾微处理器
Intel Socket Intel 插座规范
Intel X86 Intel 公司 86 系列芯片
intellect 智能,智力
intellection 智力活动
intellectronics 智能电子学
intellectualized programming environment 智能化程序设计环境

Intellifont Intellifont 字模库
intelligence 智能;信息
intelligence agent architecture 智能代理体系结构
intelligence amplifier 增智机
intelligence base 智能库
intelligence communication 智能通信
intelligence control 智能控制
intelligence instrument 智能仪表
intelligence interface 智能接口
intelligence quotient(IQ) 智商
intelligence robot 智能机器人
intelligence sample 智能样本
intelligence simulation 智能仿真
intelligent 智能的
intelligent agent 智能代理
intelligent artifact 智能产品
intelligent assistant 智能助理
intelligent authoring system 智能写作系统
intelligent automaton 智能自动机
intelligent backtracking 智能回溯
intelligent building 智能建筑
intelligent cable 智能电缆 「能
intelligent cable feature 智能电缆性
intelligent cable interfacing 智能电缆接口
intelligent cable processor 智能电缆处理器 「统
intelligent CAD system 智能 CAD 系
intelligent coach 智能教练
Intelligent Communication Adapter(ICA) 智能通信卡
intelligent communications terminals 智能通信终端
intelligent computer 智能计算机
intelligent congestion control techniques(ICCT) 智能拥塞控制技术(算法)
intelligent consumer product 智能型消费品
intelligent control 智能控制
intelligent controller 智能控制器
intelligent copier 智能复印机
intelligent courseware 智能课件
intelligent data entry terminal 智能数据录入终端
intelligent database 智能数据库
Intelligent Database Machine(IDM)

智能数据库机
intelligent decision support system 智能决策支持系统
intelligent device 智能设备
intelligent digitizer 智能数字化仪
intelligent disk array 智能磁盘阵列
intelligent disk controller 智能磁盘控制器
intelligent disk storage 智能磁盘存储器
intelligent display device 智能显示器
intelligent draft system 智能绘图系统
Intelligent Drive Array(IDA) 智能磁盘机阵列
Intelligent Drive Electronics(IDE) 智能驱动器电路
intelligent editor 智能编辑程序
intelligent electronic mail system 智能电子邮件系统
intelligent gateway 智能网关
intelligent gripper 智能机械爪
intelligent guidance system 智能制导系统
intelligent hub 智能集线器
intelligent inference machine 智能推理机
intelligent instructional device 智能教学设备
intelligent instrument 智能仪器
intelligent interface 智能接口
intelligent keyboard system 智能键盘系统
intelligent knowledge base system 智能知识库系统
intelligent layer 智能层
intelligent learning system 智能学习系统
intelligent mail 智能邮件
intelligent management agent 智能管理代理
intelligent modem 智能调制解调器
Intelligent Network(IN) 智能网
intelligent paper 智能表格
Intelligent Peripheral Interface(IPI) 智能外设接口
intelligent plotter 智能绘图仪
intelligent printer 智能打印机
Intelligent Printer Data Stream(IPDS) 智能打印数据流
intelligent question-answer system 智能问题解答系统
intelligent real time product(IRTP) 智能实时控制机
intelligent remote multiplexer 智能远程多路转换器
intelligent retrieval 智能检索
intelligent robot 智能机器人
intelligent science 智能科学
intelligent sensor 智能传感器
intelligent signal processing 智能信号处理
intelligent simulation 智能仿真
intelligent telephone 智能电话
intelligent terminal 智能终端
intelligent tutor 智能导师端
intelligent voice terminal 智能语音终端
intelligent workstation 智能工作站
intelligentize 智能化
intelligibility 了解度,清晰度
intellivision 电视游戏机
intensified 增强,强化
intensified field 增亮字段
intensifier 增强器
intension 内涵;内包
intensional 内涵类别
intensional data 实质性数据
intensity 强度,亮度
intensity level 反差等级
intensity modulation 强度调制
intensity of traffic 话务强度,话务量密度
intent 意向
intent lock 意向封锁
intent propagation 意向传播
intent scheduling 意向调度
intention 意向,意图
intention list 意向表
intention logic 内省逻辑
intentional system 意向系统
Inter-Application Communication(IAC) 应用程序间通信规范
inter-arrival time 到达之间的时间
inter-board connection 板间连接
inter-block gap 块间隙,块间隔
inter-editing 中间编辑道
inter-exchange channel(IXC) 互换通
inter-frame time fill 帧间时间填充

inter net 互联网络
inter-office signaling 局间信令
inter-process communication 进程间通信
inter-program communication module 程序间通信模块
inter-track crosstalk 道间串扰
interacting activity 交互活动
interacting goal 相制目标
interacting simulator 交互仿真器
interaction 交互
interaction among individuals 个体间交互作用
interaction association 交互关联
interaction balance 关联平衡
interaction crosstalk 交互串音
interaction fault 交互故障
interaction model 交互作用模型
interaction point 交互作用点
interaction prediction 交互预测
interaction region 交互作用区
interaction time 交互时间
interaction wizard 交互式向导
interactive 交互式的,对话式的
interactive application 交互式应用程序
interactive assembler 交互汇编程序
interactive audio system 交互式话音系统
interactive batch processing 交互式成批处理
interactive boot 交互式引导
interactive cable TV 交互式电缆电视
interactive computer graphics 交互式计算机制图
interactive computing 交互式计算
interactive conference 交互式会议
interactive consistency 交互一致性
interactive console uses 交互控制台使用
interactive control 交互式控制
interactive data definition utility 交互式数据定义实用程序
interactive debugging system 交互调试系统
interactive design 交互式设计
interactive development environment 交互式开发环境
interactive device 交互式设备
interactive diagnosis 交互式诊断

interactive dialog 人机对话
interactive editor 交互式编辑程序
interactive environment 交互式环境
interactive formatting system 人机对话格式形成系统
interactive geometric design system 交互式几何设计系统
interactive graphical input 交互图形输入
interactive graphics 交互式绘图
interactive graphics display technology 交互式图形显示技术
interactive graphics system 交互式绘图系统
Interactive Graphics and Retrieval System(INGRES) 交互式图形与检索系统
interactive image processing 交互式图像处理
interactive information processing system 交互式信息处理系统
interactive information retrieval 交互信息检索
interactive input 交互式输入
interactive interface 交互式接口
interactive keyboard printer 交互式键盘打印机
interactive knowledge acquisition 交互式知识获取
interactive language 交互语言
interactive light pen 交互式光笔
interactive mode 交互方式
interactive multimedia system(IMS) 交互式多媒体系统
interactive multiprocessor systems 交互式多处理机系统
interactive operation 交互式操作
interactive placement 交互式布局
interactive problem control system 交互式问题控制系统
interactive processing 交互式处理
interactive processing mode 交互处理模式
interactive program editing 交互程序编辑
interactive proof checker 交互式证明检验程序
interactive proof system 交互式证明

系统
interactive protocol 交互式协议
interactive rendering system 交互式着色系统
interactive restoration 交互式复原
interactive router 交互式布线程序
interactive searching 交互式检索
interactive service 交互型业务
interactive session 交互式对话
interactive simulation language 交互式仿真语言
interactive system 交互式系统
interactive task 交互式任务
interactive television 交互式电视
interactive terminal 交互式终端
interactive terminal interface 交互式终端接口
interactive terminal processing 交互式终端机处理
interactive time sharing 交互分时
interactive time simulator 交互式定时模拟程序
interactive tracing 交互式跟踪
interactive traffic 交互式通信量
Interactive UNIX 交互式 UNIX 操作系统
Interactive UNIX Base Solution 交互式 UNIX 基本方案
Interactive UNIX Graphical Solution 交互式 UNIX 图形方案
Interactive UNIX Network Solution 交互式 UNIX 网络方案
interactive user profile 交互式用户轮廓文件
interactive video 交互式视频
interactive zero-knowledge proof 交互式零知识证明
interactivity 交互性
interairline network 航线间网络
interarrival time 到达间的时间
interassembler 交互式汇编程序
InterBase InterBase 数据库
interblock 内阻隔
interblock gap (IBG) 块间隙
interblock space 组间间隔
intercalate 内插,插入
intercalation 内插
intercarrier signal 内载波信号

intercept 截取,窃听
intercept operator 截听操作员
intercept receiver 截收机
intercept trunk 居间干线,暂用中继
intercepted station 被窃听站点 └线
intercepting 截取
interchange 交换,互换
interchange address 互换地址
interchange box 交换箱
interchange code 交换码
interchange format 交换格式
interchange graph 交换图
interchange group separator 交换图分隔符
interchange node 交换节点
interchange point 交换点
interchange record separator 交换记录分隔符
interchange trunk 互换中继线
interchangeability 互换性
interchangeable connector 可互换连接器
interchangeable disk 可互换磁盘
interchangeable manufacturing 可互换性制造
interchangeable parts 可互换部件
interchangeable variable length block format 可互换变长块格式
interchannel interference 信道间干扰
interchannel time displacement (skew) (ICTD) 通道间时间偏移
intercharacter space 字符间间隔
intercipher gap 密码间隔
intercity communication 城市间通信
intercluster bus 群集间总线
intercom 内部通信
intercom service 内部通信服务
intercompilation 内部编译 「统
intercommunication system 互通信系
intercomputer communication 计算机间通信
interconnect 互连的
interconnect architecture of neural network 神经网络互连体系结构
interconnect delay 互连延迟
interconnect line width 互连线宽
interconnect materials 互连材料
interconnected business system 互连商

用系统
interconnecting device 互连设备,转接器
interconnecting line 互连线路
interconnecting main 互连干线
interconnection 互连,互通
interconnection constraint 关联约束
interconnection cost 互连费用
interconnection diagram 接线图
interconnection function 互连函数
interconnection line 互连线路
interconnection matrix 关联矩阵
interconnection network 互连网络
interconnection network with cache cluster 带高速缓冲器簇的互连网络
interconnection pattern 互连模式
interconnection rule 互连规则
interconnection section 互连部件
interconnection vector 关联向量
interconnector 互接符号
interconsole message program 控制台间消息程序
intercontinental circuit 洲际线路
intercontinental connection 洲际连接
interconversion 相互转换
interdeducible 可相互推导的
interdependency 相互依赖性
interdependency of instruction 指令相依性
interdependent node 内部相关节点
interdisciplinary 交叉学科的,跨学科的
interdisciplinary approach 跨学科方法
interdisciplinary document 交叉学科文献
interdisciplinary simulation 跨学科模拟
interdiction 封锁
interdigital transducer 叉指式换能器
interdynamic factor 互动因素
interface 界面,接口
interface adapter 接口适配器
interface address decoder 接口地址译码器
interface bus 接口总线
interface card 接口卡
interface channels 接口信道
interface chip 接口芯片
interface circuit 接口电路

interface circuitry 接口电路元件
interface clear(IFC) 接口清除线
interface computer 接口计算机
interface configuration 接口配置
interface condition 接口条件
interface control 接口控制电路
interface control information 接口控制信息
interface control unit(ICU) 接口控制单元
interface controller 接口控制器
interface data 接口数据
interface data unit(IDU) 接口数据单元
Interface Definition Language(IDL) 接口定义语言
Interface Definition Language Stub (IDL) 接口定义语言承接块
interface device 接口设备
interface equipment 接口设备
interface flexibility 接口灵活性
interface function 接口功能
interface hardware 接口硬件
interface identifier 接口标识符
interface information 接口信息
interface latch 接口锁存器
interface latch chip 接口锁存器芯片
interface logic 接口逻辑
interface message interchange mode 接口信息交换模式
interface message processor(IMP) 接口消息处理机
interface message processor computer 接口消息处理计算机
interface message processor throughput 接口消息处理机吞吐量
interface message processor-to-host protocol 接口消息处理机与主机协议
interface message processor (IMP-to-IMP protocol) 接口消息处理机之间的协议
interface microprocessor 接口微处理机
interface module 接口模块
interface primitive 接口原语,接口基元
interface processor 接口处理机
interface repository(IR) 接口储存库
interface requirement 接口需求
interface routine 接口例程
interface signal format 接口信号格式

interface software 接口软件
interface specification 接口规范说明
interface standard 接口标准
interface starting program 接口启动程序
interface status conversion diagram 接口状态转换图
interface supervisory program 接口监控程序
interface supervisory subroutine 接口监控子例程
interface surface 接面
interface system communication 接口系统通信
interface terminal 接口终端
interface testing 接口测试
interface unit 接口单元
interference 干扰
interference analyzer 干扰分析仪
interference checking 干扰检测
interference filter 抗干扰滤波器
interference source 干扰源
interference source suppression 干扰源抑制
interference threshold 干扰阈值
interfield validity check 字段内有效性校验
interfix 交接
interflow 混流
interframe coding 帧间编码
interframe compression 帧间压缩
interframe spacing 帧间间隔
interframe time fill 帧间时间填充
interim report 临时报告
interim system 过渡系统
interior communication (国家)内部通信
interior element 内元素
interior gateway protocol(IGP) 内部网关协议
interior label 内标记,内部标号
interior penalty function 内部惩罚函数
interior surface 内表面
interitem relationship 项间关系
interlace 交错;隔行扫描
interlace mode 交错模式
interlace operation 交叉操作
interlace scanning 隔行扫描
interlace sync 交织同步法
interlaced memory 交播内存
interlanguage 内语言
interlayer connection 层间连接
Interleaf Interleaf排版软件
interleave 交插,交错
interleave code 交错码
interleave factor 交错系数
interleaved 2 of 5 交替五取二码
interleaved bar code 交替条码「码
interleaved 2-5 bar-code 交叉2-5条
interleaved code 交插码,交错代码
interleaved memory 交叉访问内存
interleaved subscript 交错下标
interleaving access 交错存取
interleaving memory 交插内存
interline space 行间距
interlingua 中间语言
interlinkage 相互链接
INTERLISP language 交互式表处理语言
INTERLISP-D INTERLISP-D语言
INTERLNK 互连命令
interlock 联锁,互锁,相关
interlock bypass 联锁旁路
interlock circuit 联锁电路,相关线路
interlock code 互锁码,联锁码
interlock sheet 联锁图表
interlock switch 联锁开关
interlocked communication 联锁通信
interlocked operation 互锁操作
interlocked time 互锁时间
interlocked update 互锁更新
interlocking signal 联锁信号
interlude 内间程序,插算
intermediary language 中间语言
intermediate assignment 中间赋值
intermediate block check 中间块检验
intermediate buffer 中间缓冲器
intermediate code 中间代码
intermediate continuous motion statement 连续运动中间语句「环
intermediate cycle 过渡循环,中间循
intermediate dialing center 中转拨号中心局
intermediate distribution frame 中间配线架
intermediate document 中间文档

intermediate host node 中间主机节点
intermediate language 中间语言
intermediate line link 中间线路连接
intermediate loop 中间环路
intermediate memory 中间内存
intermediate node 中间节点
intermediate node routing 中间节点寻径
intermediate object program 中间目标程序
intermediate pass(sorting) 排序中间通过
intermediate quatity 中间量
intermediate reduction 中间归约
intermediate result 中间结果
intermediate routing node (SNA)中间路由选择节点
intermediate session routing 中间对话路由选择
intermediate storage 中间存储器
intermediate system 中间系统
intermediate text block 中间文本块
intermediate text language(ITL) 中间文本语言
intermediate total 中间合计,中间和
intermediate vertices 中间点
intermediate zones 中间区
intermessage delay 消息间延迟
intermessage fluctuation 消息长短不一
intermittency 间歇现象
intermittent 间歇的,断续的
intermittent control 间歇控制,断续控制
intermittent errors 断续错误,间发错误
intermittent failure 间歇失效
intermittent service 间歇工作
intermittent signal 断续信号
intermittent timing transmission 间歇定时传输
intermodulation(IM) 互调
intermodulation crosstalk 互调串音
intermodulation distortion 互调失真
internal absorptance 内部吸收比
internal analog transmission 内部模拟传输
internal arithmetic 内部运算
internal attribute 内部属性
internal auditor 内部审查员
internal block 内程序块

internal boundary condition 内边界条件
internal bracket 内层括号
internal buffer 内缓冲器
internal bus 内总线
internal call 内部调用
internal checking 内部校验
internal clock 内时钟
internal clock frequency 内时钟频率
internal code 内码
internal commands 内部命令
internal congestion 内拥塞
internal conjunction 内部共结,内部合取
internal constant 内部常数
internal control system 内控系统
internal coupling 内部耦合
internal cycle time 内部周期时间
internal data 内部数据
internal data bus 内部数据总线
internal data definition 内部数据定义
internal data path 内部数据通道
internal data transfer 内部数据转移
internal data type 内部数据类型
internal data way 内部数据通道
internal decimal 紧缩十进制
internal diagnostics 内部诊断
internal disjunction 内部析取
internal file 内部文件
internal file name 内部文件名
internal firmware 内置固件
internal flag 内部标志
internal float point 内浮点
internal font 内部字模
internal format 内部格式
internal fragment 内部碎片
internal fragmentation 内存储残片
internal function register(IFR) 内部功能寄存器
internal hard disk 内置式硬盘
internal hemorrhage 内"出血"
internal home network 室内网络
internal hyperlink 内部超链接
internal idle time 内空闲时间
internal information 内部信息
internal interrupt 内中断
internal knowledge 内部知识
internal knowledge base 内部知识库
internal label 内标记

internal layer 内层
internal library defomotopm 内部库定义
internal manipulation instruction 内部操纵指令
internal memory 内部存储器,内存
internal model 内部模型
internal modem 内置式调制解调器
internal modulation 内调制
Internal Multimedia Network Infrastructure(IMNI) 多媒体网络内部基础设施
internal name 内部名字
internal navigation aid 内部导航辅助
internal node 内部结点
internal number 内部编号
internal object 内部对象
internal photoeffect 内光电效应
internal pointing device （笔记本计算机中的)内置式定位装置
internal priority 内部优化级
internal procedure 内过程
internal processing unit 内处理单元
internal reference 内部引用
internal reflection angle 内反射角
internal schema 内模式
internal searching 内部查找
internal secret file(ISF) 内部保密文件
internal security 内部安全
internal sequence number 内部顺序号
internal setup 内部安装
internal sort 内部排序
internal sorting 内排序,内分类
internal stability 内部稳定性
internal storage 内存储器「量
internal storage capacity 内存储器容
internal storage code 内存储码「置
internal storage location 内存储器位
internal stored program 内存储程序
internal subprogram 内部子程序
internal subroutine 内部子例程
internal table 内表
internal timer 内定时器
internal trace 内部跟踪
internal traffic 网络内部通信量
internal transmittance 内透射比
internal trap 内自陷
internal unit 内部单元

internal view 内部形态
internally initiated trap 内启动陷阱
internally stored program 内储程序
international algebraic language(IAL) 国际代数语言
international alphabet No. 5 国际5号字母表
International Association of Teachers of English as a Foreign Language(IATEFL) 国际非英语国家英语教师协会
International Business Machines Cor. (IBM) 国际商用机器公司,IBM公司
international character 国际字符
international code 国际码
International Computation Center(ICC) 国际计算中心
International Computer Center(ICC) 国际计算机中心
international digital data service(IDDS) 国际数字数据业务
International Directory of Software 国际软件目录
International Electrotechnical Commission(IEC) 国际电工技术委员会
International Federation for Information Processing(IFIP) 国际信息处理联合总会
International Organization for Standardization(ISO) 国际标准化组织
International Packet Switching Service (IPSS) 国际分组交换服务
International Radio Consultative Committee(CCIR) 国际无线电咨询委员会
international standard 国际标准
International Standard Book Number (ISBN) 国际标准书号
International Standard Series Number (ISSN) 国际标准连续出版物号码
International Standardized Profile(ISP) 国际标准化轮廓文件
International Telecommunication Satellite Organization(INTELSAT) 国际(商业)电信卫星组织
International Telecommunication Union (ITU) 国际电信联盟

International Telecommunications Satellite Consortium(INTELSAT) 国际卫星电信协定
internationalization 国际化
Internet(INTERactive NETwork) 交互式网络
Internet(Information trash over every network) 网上信息垃圾(对因特网的一种讥讽提法)
Internet(Interesting new toy) 有趣的新玩具(对因特网的一种讥讽提法)
Internet 因特网,互联网络
internet 互联网络
Internet Access Board 因特网活动委员会
Internet Access Kit 因特网访问工具
Internet Access Provider(IAP) 因特网访问供应商
Internet Activity Board(IAB) 国际网络执行委员会
internet address 互联网地址
Internet Architecture Board(IAB) 因特网体系结构研究会
Internet Assigned Numbers Authority(IANA) 因特网编号管理局
Internet Business Center(IBC) 因特网商业中心
Internet control message protocol 因特网控制信息协议
Internet Connection for OS/2 用于OS/2的因特网连接程序
Internet Connection Provider 因特网连接供应商
Internet Connection Service 因特网连接服务
Internet Control Message Protocol 因特网控制消息协议
Internet Draft 因特网草案
Internet Engineering Note(IEN) 因特网工程备忘录
Internet Engineering Task Force(IETF) 因特网工程部
Internet Eye 因特网慧眼(图像采集系统)
Internet Information Server(IIS) 因特网信息服务器
Internet Locator Server(ILS) 因特网定位服务程序(微软)

Internet Mail Server(IMS) 因特网邮件服务器(Sun)
Internet Movie Database Browser(IMDB) 因特网电影数据库浏览器
Internet Packet Controllers(IPCS) 因特网信息包控制器
Internet Packet eXchange(IPX) 因特网分组交换
Internet phone(IP) 因特网电话
Internet Protocol(IP) 网间协议,网际协议
Internet Protocol suite 因特网协议组
Internet Relay Chart(IRC) 因特网上聊天
Internet Research Task Force(IRTF) 因特网研究部
InterNet Router 因特网路由器
Internet Service Manager 因特网服务管理程序
Internet Service Provider(ISP) 因特网服务供应商
Internet Shopping Network(ISN) 因特网购物网络
Internet Society(ISOC) 因特网协会
Internet Spider 因特网蜘蛛(搜索程序)
internet support package 网间支援包
Internet TV 因特网电视
Internet worm 因特网蠕虫(病毒)
internetwork control message protocol(ICMP) 网际控制消息协议
Internetworking 网络连接
Internetworking Operating System(IOS) 网间互联操作系统(Cisco)
Internetworking Switch Links 因特网交换链路
internodal awareness 节点间状态监视
internodal awareness system service program 节点互识系统服务程序
internodal coordination 节点间状态监视
internodal destination queue 节点间目的地队列
internodal message handler 节点间消息处理程序
internodal sequence number synchronization system service program 节点间顺序号同步系统服务程序

internodal sequence prefix　节点间顺序号前缀
internode routing　节点间路由选择
interoffice communication　局间通信
interoffice trunk　局间中继线
interoperability　互操作性,互通性
interoperable　可互操作的
interpedia　因特网百科全书
interpersonal messaging (IPM)　个人间消息传送
interpersonal messaging service　个人间消息传送服务
interpolate　插值
interpolated resolution　插值分辨率
interpolated subroutine call　内插式子例程调用
interpolating function　插值函数
interpolation　内插法,插值法
interpolation digital speech　数字话音内插法
interpolation error　插值误差
interpolation formula　插值公式
interpolation method　插值法,内插法
interpolation polynomial　插值多项式
interpolation spline　插值样条
interpolator　插补器
Interpress　Interpress 语言
interpret　解释;译码
interpretation　解释
interpretation execution　解释执行
interpretation procedure　解释程序
interpretation rule　解释规则
interpretation time　解释时间
interpreted language　解释语言
interpreter　解释程序;解释器
interpreter code　解释程序代码
interpreter definition　解释程序定义
interpreter language　解释语
interpreter operation　解释操作
interpreter-oriented instruction　面向解释程序的指令
interpreter pointer　解释指示字
interpreter programming　解释程序设计
interpreter semantic model　解释程序语义模型
interpreting　解释,翻译
interpreting line　解释行
interpreting system　解释系统
interpretive execution　解释执行
interpretive language　解释语言
interpretive mode　解释模式
interpretive program　解释程序
interpretive simulation　解释模拟
interpretive trace program　解释性跟踪程序
interpretive translation program　解释翻译程序
interprocess communication　进程间通信
interprocessor communication　处理机间通信
interprocessor interference　处理机间干扰
interprocessor interrupt　处理机间中断
interprocedural analysis　过程间分析
interprocedural data flow analysis　过程间数据流分析
interprogram communication　程序间通信
interrecord gap (IRG)　记录间隙
interrecord gap length　记录间隙长度
interrecord structure　记录间结构
interreflection　相互反射
interrelated databank　相关数据库
interrelated items　相关项目
interrelationship　相互关系
interreversal time (IRT)　翻转间隔时间
interrogate　查询
interrogating　查询
interrogation pulse　查询脉冲
interrogator control terminal　查询控制终端
interrupt (INT)　中断
interrupt analysis　中断分析
interrupt assignment strategy　中断指派策略
interrupt bit　中断位
interrupt capability　中断能力
interrupt class　中断类
interrupt clearing routine　中断清除例程
interrupt code　中断码
interrupt code checking　中断码检验
interrupt condition　中断条件
interrupt confirmation packet　中断确认分组
interrupt control and reset logic　中断控制与复位逻辑

interrupt control routine 中断控制例程
interrupt device 中断设备
interrupt dispatch block(IDB) 中断分派块,中断配送块
interrupt driven 中断驱动的
interrupt driven system 中断驱动系统
interrupt driven transfer 中断驱动转移
interrupt enable and interrupt disable 中断使能与中断失效
interrupt event 中断事件
interrupt exchange area 中断交换区
interrupt flag bit 中断标志位
interrupt flexibility 中断灵活性
interrupt freeze mode 中断冻结模式
interrupt handler(IH) 中断处理程序
interrupt handling capacity 中断处理能力
interrupt handling logic 中断处理逻辑
interrupt handling routine 中断处理程序
interrupt I/O 中断输入/输出
interrupt identification 中断识别
interrupt information 中断信息
interrupt inhibit 中断抑制,中断禁止
interrupt input line 中断输入线
interrupt inquiry 中断查询
interrupt interface 中断接口
interrupt isochronous 等时中断
interrupt latency 中断等待时间
interrupt level 中断级
interrupt level branch table 中断级分支表
interrupt level status table 中断级状态表
interrupt line 中断线
interrupt linkage 中断链接
interrupt lockout time 中断封锁时间
interrupt log word 中断标志字
interrupt logging 中断标志,中断记录
interrupt manipulation instruction 中断处理指令
interrupt mask(IM) 中断屏蔽
interrupt mask bit 中断屏蔽位
interrupt mask word 中断屏蔽字
interrupt mode 中断模式
interrupt nesting 中断嵌套
interrupt object 中断对象

interrupt-oriented 面向中断的
interrupt packet 中断信息包
interrupt phase 中断阶段
interrupt priority 中断优先权
interrupt priority logic 中断优先权逻辑
interrupt priority system 中断优先权系统
interrupt priority table 中断优先权表
interrupt procedure 中断过程
interrupt processing 中断处理
interrupt program time-out 中断程序超时
interrupt queue 中断队列
interrupt recognition 中断识别
interrupt recovery routines 中断恢复例程
interrupt register 中断寄存器
interrupt request(IRQ) 中断请求
interrupt request clearing 中断请求清除
interrupt request lines 中断请求线
interrupt request priority 中断请求优先权
interrupt request priority threshold 中断请求优先阈
interrupt request signal 中断请求信号
interrupt response 中断响应
interrupt response time 中断响应时间
interrupt response vector 中断响应向量
interrupt return 中断返回
interrupt return address 中断返回地址
interrupt return check 中断返回校验
interrupt return instruction 中断返回指令
interrupt routine 中断例程
interrupt scanner 中断扫描程序
interrupt sensing 中断识别
interrupt service routine 中断服务例程
interrupt servicing 中断服务
interrupt signal 中断信号
interrupt signal feedback 中断信号反馈
interrupt-signal switch 中断信号交换
interrupt source 中断源
interrupt spot 中断现场
interrupt stack 中断堆栈
interrupt stack pointer 中断堆栈指针

interrupt starting address 中断起始地址
interrupt strategy 中断策略
interrupt system 中断系统
interrupt time-out 中断超时
interrupt transfer vector 中断传送向量
interrupt trap 中断陷阱,中断捕获
interrupt vector 中断向量
interrupt vector address 中断向量地址
interrupt vector decoder 中断向量译码器
interrupt vector generator 中断向量产生器
interrupt vector status word 中断向量状态字
interrupt vector table 中断向量表
interrupt vector trap 中断向量捕获
interrupt vectoring 中断向量法
interrupt waiting time 中断等待时间
interrupt word 中断字
interrupt word register 中断字寄存器
interrupted isochronous transmission 有间断等时传输
interrupted system call 中断系统调用
interruptible 可中断的
interruptible instruction 可中断指令
interruption attention 引起注意的中断
interruption determinated microaddress 中断确定型微地址
interruption masked status 中断屏蔽式状态
interruption network 中断网络
interruptive event 中断事件
intersatellite link 卫星间链路
intersatellite service 星际通信业务
intersect 相交,逻辑乘
intersecting chain 相交链
intersecting subgroup 相子群
intersecting trim curves 相交截剪曲线
intersection 交集,交叉,相交;逻辑乘,"与"
intersection data 交叉数据
intersection function 交集函数
intersection gate 交叉门,"与"门
intersection graph 交图

intersection number 相交数
intersection search 交叉搜索
intersection set 交集
intersegment linking 段间链接
intersegment reference 段间引用
interspace 空间,间隙
interstage 级间的
interstate 间态
interstation 站间,台间
interstress interval 重音间隔
intersymbol dependence 码间相关性
intersymbol interference 符号间干扰
intersymbol interference equalizer 符号间干扰均衡器
intersync mode 互同步模式
intersystem communication 系统间通信
intertask communication 任务间通信
intertoll trunk 长途局间中继线
intertrack crosstalk 轨道间串扰
interval 间隔,区间
interval clock 间隔时钟
interval contraction 区间收缩
interval counter 间隔计数器
interval estimation 区间估计
interval halving 区间折半
interval linear programming 区间线性规划
interval migration 区间迁移
interval modulation 间隔调制
interval partition 区间划分
interval polling timer 间隔轮询定时程序
interval query 区间查询
interval resolution 间隔分解度
interval temporal logic 区间时态逻辑
interval timer 间隔定时器
intervention 干预,介入
intervention button 防毁钮,应急按钮
intervention-required check 请求干预校验
intervention-required message 请求干预消息
intervention schedule 紧急干预按钮
intervention switch 应急手动开关
interview 探询
interview mode 交互模式
Interwave Interwave 音频处理器
interword gap 字间间隔

interwork 互工作
interworking 网络互通
interzone call 区域间呼叫,跨区呼叫
intimate 关系密切软件;功能相似的,联系密切的
intolerance 无法容忍的
intonation 语调
intra-area communication 区域内通信
intra-domain call 域内调用
intra-media file transfer 媒体文件传送
intra-office connection 局内连接
intra picture 帧内图像
intra-process sharing 进程内共享
intra-query parallelism 查询内并行度
IntraBuilder IntraBuilder开发工具
intraclass variance 组合方差
intraconnection 内连,互连
intractable problem 难解问题
intraframe coding 帧内编码
intraframe compression 帧内压缩
intralayer communication 层内通信
intramemory communication 存储器内通信
intraprogram documentation 程序内文档处理
Intranet 内联网,企业网,内部因特网
intranode routing 节点内路由选择
intransitive 非传递的
intrarecord data structure 记录内数据结构
intrasite communication 现场内通信
intrastate 状态内的
Intraware 企业网件
intricate 错综复杂的,交叉的
intrinsic 本质的,内在的,固有的
intrinsic absorption 本质吸收,本征吸收
intrinsic call 内部调用
intrinsic charge 本征电荷
intrinsic command 内部命令
intrinsic conductivity 本征导电性
intrinsic error 固有误差
intrinsic evolutionary hardware 内部演化硬件
intrinsic font 本征字体,固有字体
intrinsic function 本质函数,内部函数
intrinsic impedance 固有阻抗
intrinsic instability 固有不稳定性

intrinsic internal photoeffect 固有内部光电效应
intrinsic noise 固有噪声
intrinsic optical communication 纯光通信,全光通信
intrinsic procedure 固有过程,内部过程
intrinsic semiconductor 本征半导体
intrinsic statement 内部语句
intrinsic value 固有值
intro play 简介播放
introduction review 介绍性评审
introductory 简介,引言
introductory screen 介绍性画面
introspection 自省,自我训练
introspective program 内省程序
intruder 入侵者
intrusion tone 侵入音,打扰音
intrusive virus 入侵型病毒
intuition 直觉,直观;直觉知识
intuitionistic logic 直观逻辑
intuitionistic prepositional logic 直观命题逻辑
intuitive forecasting 直觉预测
intuitive imagery 形象源
intuitively-built recognizer 靠直觉建立的识别程序
invalid 无效的
invalid abort request 无效异常中止请求
invalid access 无效存取
invalid address 无效地址
invalid argument 无效参数
invalid bit 无效位
invalid character 无效字符
invalid cluster 无效簇
invalid code 无效码
invalid command 非法命令
invalid condition detection 无效条件检测
invalid data 无效数据
invalid destination 无效目的地
invalid digit 无效数位
invalid exclusive reference 无效互斥引用
invalid file name 无效文件名
invalid function argument 无效的函数参数
invalid frame 无效帧
invalid instruction 无效指令

invalid interrupt level 无效中断级
invalid key condition 无效键条件
invalid line number 无效行号
invalid operation 无效作业
invalid page 无效页面
invalid password 无效口令
invalid priority 无效优先级
invalid property 非法属性
invalid punch 无效穿孔
invalid received frame 无效接收帧
invalid request 无效请求
invalid scaling factor 无效缩放比例
invalid sequence 无效顺序,无效序列
invalid trap vector address 无效陷阱向量地址
invalid unit number 无效单元号
invalid window identifier 无效窗口标识符
invariance theorem 不变性定理
invariant 不变式,不变量
invariant assertion method 不变断言法
invariant assignment optimization 不变量赋值优化
invariant computation 不变量计算
invariant embedding 不变嵌入
invariant factor 不变因子
invariant feature extraction 不变特征析取
invariant field 固定长字段
invariant function 不变量函数
invariant imbedding 不变嵌入法
invariant integer 不变整数
invariant object recognition 不变目标识别
invariant pattern recognition 不变式,不变量
invariant permutation 不变模式识别
invariant point 不变点
invariant region 不变量置换法
invariant representation 不变量表示
invariant routing 固定路由选择法
invariant scalar 不变标量
invariant subspace 不变子空间
invariant testing 不变量测试
inventory 库存,存货清单
inventory analysis 库存分析
inventory control 库存控制统
inventory control system 存货控制系

inventory data control 库存数据控制
inventory detail 库存清单细目
inventory file 库存文件,清单文件
inventory master file 库存主文件
inventory real-time processing 库存实时处理
inventory records 库存记录
inventory stock report 库存材料报表
inverse adjacency list 逆邻接表
inverse assembler 反汇编程序
inverse association 反向结合
inverse channel 倒置信道
inverse checksum code 校验和反码
inverse color 补色,反转色
inverse conversion 逆转换
inverse discrete cosine transform 离散余弦反变换
inverse dynamics 逆向动力学
inverse eigenvalue problem 反特征值问题
inverse element 逆元素原
inverse filter restoration 反向滤波复
inverse Fourier transform 傅里叶逆变
inverse full shuffle 逆全混洗换
inverse function 反函数
inverse gate 反相门
inverse homomorphism 逆同态
inverse hyperbolic function 反双曲函
inverse interpolation 逆插值数
inverse isoparametric mapping 逆等参数映像
inverse iteration 反迭代,逆迭代
inverse kernel 逆核
inverse kinematics 逆向运动学
inverse Laplace transformation 拉普拉斯反变换
inverse magnetostriction effect 逆磁致伸缩效应
inverse mapping 逆映射
inverse matrix 逆矩阵
inverse move 逆移动
inverse network 倒置网络
inverse operator 逆(反)算子
inverse point 反演点
inverse probability 逆概率
inverse proportionality 反比例
inverse proposition 逆命题
inverse residue code 反剩余码

inverse substitution 反代换
inverse video 反视频图像
inversion 反转,倒序,反演,倒频
inversion charge model 反转电荷模型
inversion constant 反演常数
inversion current 反向电流
inversion layer capacitance 反型层电容
inversion mode 倒转模式
inversion problem 反演问题
inversion sequence 逆序数列
inversion signal 反相信号
inversor 反演器,倒置器
invert 倒置;逆选
inverted access 反向访问
inverted alignment zone 对齐区颠倒
inverted backbone 倒置主干
inverted directory 倒置目录
inverted file 倒排文件
inverted index 倒排索引
inverted input 反相输入
inverted list 倒排表
inverted list database 倒排表数据库
inverted output 反相输出
inverted sequence 逆序,反序
inverted structure 倒置结构
inverted tree 倒置树
inverter 反相器;逆变器
inverter buffer 反相缓冲器
inverter gate 倒相门
invertibility 可逆性
invertible element 可逆元
invertible finite automaton 可逆有限自动机
invertible function 可逆函数
invertible grammar 可逆文法
invertible law 可逆律
invertible matrix 可逆矩阵
inverting amplifier 反相放大器
Inverting buffer 反相缓冲器
inverter 反相器
investigation data processing 调研数据处理
invigilator 监督器
invisible 不可见的,隐形的
invisible break 不可见分隔符
invisible elements preferences 不可见元素参数选择
invisible file 不可见文件

invitation 邀请
invitation delay 邀请延迟
invitation list 邀请单,邀请列表
invitation to send(ITS) 请求发送
invocatable 不可挽回的
invocatable control strategy 不可挽回式控制策略
invocation 调用,启用,引用
invocation of sub-schema 子模式启用
invoice 清单,发货单
invoke 调用,请求
invoked block 被调用程序块
invoked procedure 被调用过程
invoking block 调用块,请求块
involuntary interrupt program 偶然中断程序
involute 渐开线,渐伸线
involution 乘方
involution law 双重否定律
involve 包含,涉及
inward correspondence 内向对应
inward dialing 入局拨号
inward wide-area telephone service 局内广域电话服务
IO(Input-Output) 输入输出
ioctl(I/O control) (Unix系统调用)输入输出控制
Iomega (活动盘驱动器生产厂商)艾美加公司(美)
ION(Integrated On-demand Network) 综合点播网络(Sprint)
ion 离子
ion beam cleaning 离子束清洗
ion beam implantation 离子束注入
ion beam machining 离子束加工
ion deposition 离子沉积
ion deposition printer 离子沉积型打印机
ion gun 离子枪
ion implantation 离子注入
ion implantation apparatus 离子注入装置
ionic accelerator 离子加速器
ionization 电离作用,电离化
ionization process 电离过程
ionized cluster-beam deposition 离子聚束沉积
IONL(Internal Organization of the

Network Layer) 网络层内部组织(ISO)
ionized gas readout 离子化气体显示
ionosphere 电离层;显示空格字符(微软)
ionospheric forecast 电离层预报
ionospheric reflection 电离层反射
IOP(Input/Output Processor) 输入/输出处理器
IOP multiplexer 输入/输出处理机多路转换器
IOS(Internetworking Operating System) 网间互联操作系统(Cisco)
IP(Information Provider) 信息供应商
IP(Interface Processor) 接口处理机
IP(Internet Protocol) 互联网协议
IP address IP 地址
IP network number IP 网络编号
IPC(Inter-Process Communication) 进程间通信
IPI(Intelligent Peripheral Interface) 智能外围设备接口
IPM(InterPersonal Message) 个人间消息
IPM subtree 个人间消息子树
IPng(IP next generation) 下一代 IP 协议
IPP(Internet Platform Provider) 因特网平台服务商
IPSC/1 IPSC/1 并行计算机系统
IPSJ(Information Processing Society of Japan) 日本信息处理协会「本
IPv6(IP version 6.0) IP 协议 6.0 版
IPX(Internet Packet eXchange) 因特网包交换
IPX external network number IPX 外部网号
IPX internal network number IPX 内部网号
IPX/SPX(Internet Packet eXchange / Sequenced Packet eXchange) 网际包交换/顺序包交换协议(Novell)
IPXCON IPX 控制台
IPXODI (Internet Packet Exchange Open Datalink Interface) IPX 开放式数据链路接口
IPXPING IPX 探询模块

IPXS IPXS 模块
IQ(Intelligence Quotient) 智商
IQ(Inverse Quantizer) 反量化器
IR(Icon Representation) 图标表示法
IR(Information Retrieval) 信息检索
IR(Instruction Register) 指令寄存器
IR(Interrupt Request) 中断请求
IRC(Internet Relay Chart) 因特网中继聊天
IrDA(Infrared Data Association) 红外线数据协会
IRIS station IRIS 图形工作站
IRIX operating system IRIX 操作系统
IRMA board IRMA 板
IRMALAN IRMA 局域网产品
iron-cobalt-nickel alloy 铁钴镍合金
iron core 铁心
iron-dust core 铁粉心
iron-nickel alloy 铁镍合金
iron-oxide 氧化铁
iron powder 铁粉
IRONMAN language requirement "铁人"语言要求(美)
IRQ(Interrupt ReQuest) 中断请求
irradiance 辐照度
irrational 无理的,不合理的
irrational function 无理函数
irrational number 无理数
irrational root 无理根
irrecoverable error 不能恢复的错误
irreducibility 不可约性
irreducible 不可约的
irreducible element 不可约元
irreducible factor 不可约因子
irreducible graph 不可约图
irreducible image 不可约映像
irreducible matrix 不可约矩阵
irreducible polynomial 不可约多项式
irreducible tree 不可约树
irreducible unit 不可化简单元
irredundant circuit 无冗余电路
irredundant cover 无冗余覆盖
irredundant set 无冗余集
irregular 不规则的
irregular collective 无规则集合
irregular domain 不规则域
irregular interior node 不规则内节点
irregular shaped region 不规则形状区

域
irregular topology 不规则拓扑
irregular variation 不规则偏差
irregular working envelope 不规则工作区域
irregularity 不规则性
irrelevance 不恰当组合
irreversibility 不可逆性
irreversible 不可逆的
irreversible code 不可逆代码
irreversible element 不可逆元件
irreversible encryption 不可逆加密
irreversible magnetic process 不可逆磁化过程
irreversible process 不可逆过程
irreversible rotation 不可逆旋转
irreversible state 不可逆状态
irreversible transformation 不可逆变
irrevocable 不可撤回的　　└换
irrevocable control strategy 不可撤回控制策略
IRS(Information Retrieval System) 信息检索系统
IRTF(Internet Research Task Force) 因特网研究部
IS(International Standards) 国际标
IS pipeline 智能印刷机缓冲器　└准
IS-ISP(Intermediate-System to Intermediate-System Protocol) 中间系统间协议(ISO)
ISA(Industry Standard Architecture) 工业标准体系结构
ISAAC(Information System for Advanced Academic Computing) 高级科学计算信息系统
ISAM(Indexed Sequential Access Method) 索引顺序存取法
ISAM files 索引顺序访问法文件
ISAPI(Internet Server Application Program Interface) 因特网服务器应用程序界面(微软)
isarithmic control 有节奏控制
isarithmic network 有节奏网络
ISBC(Intel Single Board Computer) Intel单板微型计算机
ISBD (International Standard Bibliographic Description) 国际标准书目说明(美国图书馆协会建立的国际通用文件著录规则)
ISBN (Integrated Service Broadcast Network) 综合业务广播网
ISC(Item Status Coding) 项目状态编码
ISCI(International Standard Commercial code for Indexing) 国际标准商用索引码
ISD(IBM Standard Data) IBM标准数据
ISDN(Integrated Service Digital Network) 综合业务数字网
ISDN address ISDN地址　　　┌构
ISDN channel structure ISDN通道结
ISDN numbering plan 综合服务数字网编号计划
ISDN point-to-multipoint ISDN一点对多点通信　　　　　　　┌信
ISDN point-to-point ISDN点对点通
ISDN reference configuration ISDN参考配置　　　　　　　　　┌道
ISDN standard channel ISDN标准通
ISDN terminal ISDN终端
ISDN user-network interface 综合业务数字网络用户-网络接口
ISDS (Integrated Software Development System) 集成软件开发系统
ISH(Integrated Service Hub) 综合业务集线器
ISI manufacturing ISI制造公司
ISIS(Intel Systems Implementation Supervisor) 系统执行管理程序(Intel)
island driving 孤岛驱动
island network 岛网络
island of automation 自动化岛
ISN(Internet Shopping Network) 因特网购物网
ISO(International Standards Organization) 国际标准化组织
ISO (International Organization for Standardization) 国际标准化组织
ISO-7 国际标准化组织字符码
ISO 8802/7 standards 时间片环形局域网的物理层与媒体存取控制子层标准
ISO 9000 国际质量标准
ISO 9660 国际CD ROM数据编码格

式标准
ISO network management model 国际标准化组织网络管理模型
ISO OCR-A A套光学字符识别字形
ISO OCR-B B套光学字符识别字形
ISO/OSI model 国际标准化组织的开放系统互连模型
ISO reference mode ISO参考模型
ISO/TC(ISO/Technical Committee) 国际标准化组织技术委员会
isoarithmic 均匀算法
isobar 等压线,等权数
isobits 等值位,等值比特
ISOC(Internet Society) 因特网协会
isochromation 等色的
isochronous 等时的;异步的,非同期
isochronous burst 丛发等时信号,突发等时信号
isochronous digital signal 等时数字信号
isochronous distortion 等时性失真
isochronous modulation 等时调制
isochronous service 即时服务
isochronous signal 等时信号
isochronous transmission 等时传输,同步传输
ISODE(ISO Development Environment) 国际标准化组织开发环境
isogram 等值线
isograph 等值线图
isolate 隔离的,绝缘的,孤立的
isolated adaptive routing 孤立自适应路由选择
isolated amplifier 隔离放大器
isolated digit recognition 孤立数字识别
isolated digital input/output module 隔离数字输入/输出模块
isolated gate field effect transistor 绝缘栅场效应管
isolated I/O module 隔离输入/输出模块
isolated locations 隔离位置
isolated network 孤立网络
isolated node 孤立节点
isolated pacing response 隔离调步响应
isolated point 孤立点
isolated pulse half width 孤立脉冲半幅宽
isolated solution 孤立解
isolated subsystem 孤立子系统
isolated vertex 孤立顶点
isolated word recognition 孤立字(单词)识别
isolated workstation 分立式工作站
isolation 隔离
isolation diffusion 隔离扩散
isolation level 隔离级别
isolation loss 隔离损耗
isolation network 隔离网络
isolation region 隔离区
isolation test routine(ITR) 隔离测试例程
isolator 隔离器
isoline 等值线
isometric 等角投影图,等距画法
isometric embedding 等距嵌入
isometric mapping 等距映像
isometric projection 等角投影
isometric surface coordinates 等距曲面坐标
isometric view 等轴测图,平行立体视图
isomorphic 同构,同态
isomorphic cooperative game 同构合作对策
isomorphic graph 同构图
isomorphic iterative method 同构迭代法
isomorphic mapping 同构映射
isomorphic representation 同构表达
isomorphism algorithm 同构算法
isomorphism problem 同构问题
isoparametric finite element 等参数有限元
isoplaner integrated injection logic(I3L) 等平面注入逻辑电路
isoplaner isolation 等平面隔离
isoplaner oxide-isolation 等平面氧化隔离
isopleth curve 等值曲线
isopleth map 等值线图
isopotential 等位势线
ISOR(ISO Recommendation) 国际标准化组织推荐标准
ISOS(InSecure Operating System) 不安全操作系统
isosynchronous serial I/O 等同步串行输入输出
isotherm 等温线

isothermal region 等温区
isotone mapping 保序映像法,保角映射
isotonicity 保序性
isotope 同位素
isotropic 各向同性
isotropic dielectric 各向同性电介质
isotropic displacement 各向同性的位移
isotropic mapping 各向同性映射
isotropic material 各向同性材料
isotropic source 各向同性源
ISP(Internet Service Provider) 因特网服务供应商
ISP(Inside System Programmable) 系统内可编程的
ISPF(InterACTIVE System Productivity Facility) 交互式系统生产程序
ISR(Interrupt Service Routine) 中断服务例程
ISS(Industrial Standard Specification) 工业标准规格
ISS(Internet Security Scanner) 因特网安全扫描程序
ISSN(International Standard Series Number) 国际标准(出版物)序列号
issue 课目,问题;发行,发布,发表
issue and example paradigm 课目与示例法
issue evaluator 课目评估器
issue recognizer 课目识别器
issuer 发行者
IST(Internal STandard) 内部标准
ISU(Interface-Sharing Unit) 接口共享部件
ISV(Independent Software Vendor) 独立软件供应商
IT(Information Technology) 信息技术
italic font 斜体字
item 项目,项
item advance 项目前移,按项进行
item advance technique 项目迁移技术
item-by-item sequential inspection 逐项顺序检查
item count 项目计数
item description 项目描述
item design 项目设计
item file 项目文件
item mark 项目标志[记号]

item moniker 项目别名
item name 项目名称
item-on-term file 检索词记录文件
item quotation 项目保价单
item separation symbol 项目分隔符号
item size 项目大小
item terminator 项目结束符
iterate 反覆,迭代
iterate game 迭代对策
iterate logic array testing method 迭代逻辑阵列测试法
iterated algorithm 反覆,迭代
iterated interpolation method 迭代插值法
iterated line graph 迭线图
iterated morphism 迭代形态
iterated network 累接网络,链接网络
iterated shuffle 迭代混洗
iterate 反覆,迭代
iteration 反覆,迭代
iteration algorithm 迭代算法
iteration control structure 重复控制结构
iteration count 迭代计数
iteration cycle 迭代周期
iteration diagram 迭代图
iteration factor 迭代因子
iteration form 迭代形式
iteration grouping 迭代群
iteration method 迭代法
iteration number 迭代数
iteration operator 迭代运算符
iteration per second 每秒迭代次数
iteration process 迭代过程
iteration statement 迭代语句
iteration time 迭代时间
iteration tree 迭代树
iterations 迭代次数
iterative 迭代,反覆
iterative array 迭代阵列,迭代数组
iterative computing 迭代计算
iterative constrained restoration 迭代约束复原
iterative formula 迭代公式
iterative impedance 累接阻抗
iterative instruction 重复执行指令
iterative least square method 迭代最小二乘法

iterative loop 迭代循环
iterative network 累接网络,级联网络
iterative operation 迭代运算
iterative optimization 迭代优化法
iterative placement algorithm 迭代布局算法
iterative process 迭代过程
iterative refinement 迭代求精
iterative routine 迭代程序
iterative search method 迭代搜索法
iterative solution 迭代解
iterative test generator 迭代测试生成程序
ITS(Integrated Transaction Service) 集成事务处理
ITS(Intelligent Terminal Systems) 智能终端系统
ITU(International Telecommunication Union Geneva) 国际电信联盟
ITV(Interactive Television) 交互式电视
IU(International Unit) 国际单位
IUP(Independent Utility Program) 独立实用程序
IUS(Interchange Unit Separator) (EBCDIC码)互换单元分隔符
IV(Initialization Vector) 初始向量
IV(Interactive Video) 交互式视频
IVI(Indeo Video Interactive) Indeo 视频交互系统(Intel)
iWARP iWARP阵列处理器
IWS(Intelligent Work Station) 智能工作站
IZE IZE系统

J j

J(Junction) 结;连接
JA(Job Analysis) 作业分析
JA(Jump Address) 转换地址
jabber 颤音;超时传输
jabber control 超时控制
jack 插口,插孔,插座
jack box 插孔箱,插孔盒
jack-ended 插接线
jack in 登录
jack panel 插口板
jack part 插口部分
jack plug 插头
jack screw 插座启拔器
jack socket 插口,插座
jack strip 插口簧片排
jacket 罩,盖,外壳,护套
Jackson method 杰克逊法
Jackson structured programming(JSP) 杰克逊结构化程序设计法
Jacobi algorithm 雅克比算法
Jacobi iteration 雅克比迭代
Jacobi method 雅克比法
Jacobi polynomial 雅克比多项式
Jacobian matrix 雅克比矩阵
Jacobian symmetry 雅克比对称
Jacquard loom Jacquard织布机
JAD(Joint Application Design) 联合应用程序设计
JAF(Job Accounting Facility) 作业记账程序
jaff 复式干扰
jag 锯齿状缺口,V字形缺口
jagged 锯齿状的,有缺口的
jaggy 有缺口的
jam 堵塞,卡纸
jam input 阻塞输入
jam nut 锁紧螺母
jam recovery 卡纸恢复
jam sensor 压紧传感器
jam signal 阻塞信号;卡纸信号
jammer 干扰机,人为干扰台
jamming 扰乱,人为干扰
jamming effectiveness 干扰有效性;干扰信号比
JANET(Joint Academic Network) 联合学术网(英)
Japan Information Center of Science and Technology(JICST) 日本科技信息中心
Japan Patent Information Center(JA-

PATIC) 日本专利信息中心
Japanese Industrial Robot Association(JIRA) 日本工业机器人协会
Japanese Industrial Standard(JIS) 日本工业标准
Japanese Industrial Standard Committee 日本工业标准委员会
Japanese Information Processing Network(JIPNET) 日本信息处理网络
Japanese Online Information System(JOIS) 日本联机信息系统
JAPATIC(Japan Patent Information Center) 日本专利信息中心
jargon 术语,行话
JAS(Job Accounting System) 作业记账系统
JAS(Job Analysis System) 作业分析系统
Jasmine Jasmine 数据库系统(CA)
Java Java 语言(SUN)
Java API(Java Application Programming Interface) Java 应用程序设计界面
Java applet Java 小应用程序
Java application Java 应用程序
Java Camp Java 培训(SUN)
Java chip Java 芯片(SUN)
Java compiler Java 编译器(SUN)
Java Database Connectivity(JDBC) Java 数据库连接
Java Generic Library(JGL) Java 生成库(Sun)
Java Flash Compiler Java 快速编译器
Java interface definition language Java 界面定义语言
Java interpreter Java 解释程序
Java Native Interface(JNI) Java 本机界面
Java Network Package Java 网络软件
Java platform Java 平台「包
Java Script Java 脚本语言(Sun)
Java Studio Java 开发环境
Java virtual machine Java 虚拟机(SUN)
Java WorkShop Java 开发环境(Sun)
JavaBeans Java 豆(完全用 Java 编写开放性应用程序界面的计划)
JavaOS JavaOS 操作系统(SUN)
JavaStation JavaStation 网络计算机
Javelin Plus Javelin+电子表格
jaw 爪
Jaz Jaz 活动盘驱动器(Iomaga)
Jazz 爵士乐创作软件
JBIG(Joint Bi-level Image coding experts Group) 联合二值图像编码专家组标准
Jbuilder Java 开发工具(Borland)
JCB(Job Control Block) 作业控制块
JCL(Job Control Language) 作业控制语言「言
JCL language 作业控制语言,JCL 语
JCT1(Joint Technology Committee 1) 联合技术委员会
JCP(Job Control Program) 作业控制程序
JDBC(Java DataBase Connectivity) Java 数据库连接(规范)
JDK(Java Development Kits) Java 开发工具
JDS(Job Development System) 作业开发系统
JEIDA(Japanese Electronic Industry Development Assn.) 日本电子工业发展协会
JEN(Junctor Equipment Number) 级间链路设备号
JES(Job Entry Subsystem) 作业输入子系统
jet nozzle 喷嘴
jet pump 喷射泵
jewel bearing 宝石轴承
JF(Journal File) 日志文件
JFC(Java Foundation Class) Java 基础类
JICST(Japan Information Center of Science and Technology) 日本科技信息中心
jig 夹具
jig-bore 坐标镗床
Jini Jini 软件技术(SUN)
JIRA(Japanese Industrial Robot Association) 日本工业机器人协会
JIS(Japanese Industrial Standard) 日本工业标准「码
JIS 7-bit code 日本工业标准 7 单位

JIS 8-bit code 日本工业标准8单位码
JIS code 日本工业标准代码
jitter 颤动,抖动
jitter noise 颤动噪声,抖动噪声
jitter reduce 颤动抑制
jitter reducer 抖动抑制器
JK flip flop JK触发器
JMF(Java Media Frame) Java媒体框架
JMP(JuMP) 转移,跳转
JMP instruction 转移指令
JNDI(Java Name Directory Interface) Java目录接口
JNI(Java Native Interface) Java本机接口
JMPR(JuMPeR) 跳线
job 作业
job accounting interface(JAI) 作业记账接口
job accounting table(JAT) 作业记账表
job action command 作业处理命令
job analysis(JA) 作业分析
job and skill analysis 作业技能分析
job average turnaround time 作业平均周转时间
job batch 作业批
job block 作业块,作业控制分程序
job body 作业体
job card 作业卡片
job card deck 作业卡片叠
job catalog 作业目录
job characteristics model 作业特征模型
job class 作业分类
job class queue 作业分类队列
job classification 作业分类
job cluster 作业群,作业簇
job communication block 作业通信区
job content 作业内容
job control 作业控制
job control authority 作业控制授权
job control block(JCB) 作业控制块
job control card 作业控制卡
job control communication 作业控制通信
job control language(JCL) 作业控制语言
job control macro 作业控制宏
job control processor 作业控制处理程序
job control program(JCP) 作业控制程序
job control statement 作业控制语句
job control table(JCT) 作业控制表
job controller 作业控制程序
job cycle 作业周期
job cylinder map 作业柱面映像
job data program 作业数据程序
job date 作业日期
job deck 作业卡片叠
job definition 作业定义
job definition language 作业定义语言
job description(JD) 作业说明
job design 作业设计
job dilution 作业细分;工作稀释
job dividing 作业划分
job docket 作业记事
job end control card 作业结束控制卡
job end statement 任务结束语句
job enlargement 作业扩展
job enrichment 作业充实
job entry central services(JECS) 作业输入中枢服务
job entry date 作业进入队列的日期
job entry peripheral services(JEPS) 作业输入外围业务机构
job entry subsystem(JES) 作业输入子系统
job entry system 作业输入系统
job entry time 作业进入队列的时间
job evaluation 作业评估
job factor 作业要素
job families 作业系列
job file 作业文件
job file control block 作业文件控制块
job flow 作业流
job flow control 作业流程控制
job grading 作业分级
job header 作业标题
job identification 作业标识
job identification card 作业标识卡
job information block 作业信息块
job initiation 作业初始化
job input 作业输入
job input device 作业输入设备
job input file 作业输入文件
job input queue 作业输入队列

job input stream 作业输入流	job queue management 作业队列管理
job instruction training 工作指导训练	job range 作业范围
job journal 作业日志	job ranking 作业分级
job library(JOBLIB) 作业库	job recovery control file 作业恢复控制文件
job load 作业载入	job region 作业区域
job log 作业运行记录	job related output 作业相关的输出
job login 作业登录	job relation 作业关系
job logout 作业注销	job request selection 作业请求选择
job management 作业管理	job rotation 作业轮换
job management procedure 作业管理过程	job run 作业运行
job management program 作业管理程序	job schedule 作业调度
job message queue 作业消息队列	job scheduler 作业调度程序
job migration 作业迁徙	job scheduling algorithm 作业调度算法
job mix 作业混合	job scope 作业范围
job mixing 作业混合态	job security 作业安全
job monitor 作业监督程序	job selection 作业选择
job networking 作业联网处理	job separator pages 作业分隔页
job name 作业名	job separation 作业分隔
job offset 作业交叠	job sequence 作业序列
job-oriented language 面向作业的语言	job-sequencing module 作业定序模块
job-oriented terminal 面向作业的终端	job sequencing system 作业定序系统
job output device 作业输出设备	job shop simulation 作业安排模拟
job output file 作业输出文件	job specification 作业描述
job output queue 作业输出队列	job stabilization 作业稳定性
job output stream 作业输出流	job table(JT) 作业表
job pack area(JPA) 作业装配区	job stack 作业堆栈
job parameter 作业参数	job-stack system 作业堆栈系统
job performance standards 作业性能标准	job stacking 作业堆积
job preparation 作业准备	job standardization 作业标准化
job priority 作业优先权,作业优先级	job statement 作业语句
job processing 作业处理	job status 作业状态
job processing control 作业处理控制	job step 作业步
job processing master file 作业处理主文件	job step control 作业步控制
job processing monitor 作业处理监督程序	job step control block 作业步控制块
	job step initiation 作业步初始化
job processing monitor system 作业处理监督系统	job step restart 作业步重起动
job processing monitor termination 作业处理监督终止	job step task 作业步事务
	job stick 操纵杆
job processing system 作业处理系统	job stream 作业流
job processing unit 作业处理单元	job stream input 作业流输入
job program 作业程序	job stream processor 作业流处理程序
job program mode 作业程序模式	job support task 作业支持事务
job queue 作业队列	job table 作业表
job queue entry 作业队列表项	job task 作业任务
	job throughput 作业吞吐量
	job timeout 作业超时
	job-to-job transition 作业间转换

job transfer and manipulation(JTM) 作业传送与操纵
job turnaround time 作业周转时间
job weighted average turnaround time 作业加权平均周转时间
JOBLIB(JOB LIBrary) 作业库
jog 慢进,慢移,逐帧移动
join 连接,关连;逻辑"和"运算
join an existing site 加入现有站点
join class 连接类
join dependency 连接相关
join field 连接字段
join graph 连接图
join level specification 连接级说明
join line 连接线
join logical file 连接逻辑文件
join operator 求并运算符,连接运算符
join query 连接查询
join rule 连接规则
join strategy 连接策略
join style 结合风格
join topology 连接布局,连接拓扑结构
joint 接头,接合,焊接,连接,关节
joint account 联合账户
joint action 联合作用
joint actuator 关节驱动器
joint agreement 联合协议
joint application design(JAD) 联合应用程序设计
Joint Application Development(JAD) 联合应用程序开发
joint arm 关节臂
joint assembly 连接汇编
joint-based control 基于关节的控制
Joint Bi-level Image Coding Experts Group(JBIG) 联合二值图像编码专家组标准
joint cost 共同成本,联合成本
joint denial 联合拒绝,"或非"
joint denial gate "或非"门
joint dependency 连接相关
joint distribution 联合分布
joint ergodic random process 联合遍历随机过程
joint estimation 联合估计
joint gate "或"门
joint index 联合索引
joint information content 联合信息量
joint level control 关节级控制
joint mark 连接标记
joint mode 关节模式
joint motion 关节运动
joint parameter 关节参数
Joint Photographic Expert Group (JPEG) 联合图像专家组规范
joint probability 联合概率
joint random variable 联合随机变量
joint rate control 关节速率控制
joint requirements planning(JRP) 联合需求计划
joint sheet 接合垫片
joint space 关节空间
joint stationary random process 联合随机过程
joint style 联接方式
joint use 共用,联合使用
Joint Users Group(JUG) 用户组联合会
jointed-arm configuration 关节臂式结构
jointed-arm robot 关节臂式机器人
jointed fiber 接续光纤,连接光纤
jointed-spherical robot 有球面关节的机器人
jointer 接线器
jointly development 联合开发
jointly stationary random process 联合平稳随机过程
JOIS (Japanese Online Information System) 日本联机信息系统
Jordan canonical form 约当标准型
Jordan decomposition 约当分解
Jordan form 约当形式
Josephson device 约瑟夫逊器件
Josephson memory 约瑟夫逊存储器
Josephson storage 约瑟夫逊存储器
Josephson tunneling logic device 约瑟夫逊隧道逻辑器件
joule(J) (能量单位)焦耳
journal 日志;杂志,期刊
journal analyzer 日志分析程序
journal buffer 日志缓存器
journal control command 日志控制命令
journal dump 日志转储
journal entry 日志登录项
journal file 日志文件
journal number 日志编号

journal output 日志输出
journal reader 日志阅读器
journal record 日志记录
journal roll-back 日志卷后翻
journal roll-forward 日志卷前翻
journal sheet 日志表单
journal tape 会计记录带
journal volume 日志卷
journaling 日志报表,记流水账
JOVIAL language (Jules' Own Version of the International Algebraic Language) JOVIAL语言
joybox 操纵盒
joystick 游戏杆
joystick interface 游戏杆接口
joystick pointer 操纵杆指针
JP(JumP) 跳转
JP(JumPer) 跳线,跨接片
JPA(Job Pack Area) 作业装配区
JPEG (Joint Photographic Experts Group) 联合图像专家组标准
JPEG Optimizer 静态压缩图像优化程序
JTAG(Joint Test Action Group) 联合测试行动组
judder 振动,颤动,抖动
judgement 判断,鉴定
jukebox 光盘库
Jules' Own Version of the International Algebraic Language (JOVIAL) JOVIAL语言,Jules版本国际代数语
Julian date 儒略日期(记法) 「言
jumbo chip 大型芯片
jumbo fiber 大号光纤
jumbo group 巨群
jumbo size 大尺寸
jump 转移,跳转 「址
jump address(JA) 跳转地址,转移地
jump condition 跳转条件
jump cut 跳格剪辑
jump forward 向前跳转
jump function 跳跃函数
jump if not 若非则跳转
jump instruction 跳转指令
jump lock 转移封锁
jump menu 转移菜单
jump on carry(JC) 进位跳转
jump on minus(JM) 遇负转移

jump on no carry(JNC) 非进位跳转
jump on nonzero(JNZ) 非零跳转
jump on positive(JP) 遇正值转换
jump on zero(JZ) 遇零转移
jump operation 跳转运算
jump prediction 转移预测
jump program 跳转程序
jump reverse 回跳
jump routine 跳转例程
jump statement 跳转语句,转向语句
jump subroutine 跳转子例程
jump table 跳转地址表
jump trace 转移跟踪
jump vector 转移向量
jumper 跳线
jumper block 跳线插塞
jumper cable 跳接线,跨线
jumper list 跳线选择列表
jumper selectable 可用跳线选择的
jumper selectable interrupt requests 跳线可选择中断请求
jumper switch 跳线开关
jumper wiring 跳线,跨接线
jumping trace routine 转移跟踪例程
JumpStart 直接跳转到开始(一种较少用户交互的软件安装方法)
junction 接面,结
junction at equilibrium 平衡结
junction box 分线盒,配线箱
junction capacitance 结电容
junction circuit 连接电路
junction diode 结型二极管
junction hole 中导孔
junction line 中继线
junction point 结点,连接点
junction return loss 连接中间回损
junction station 汇接站
junction summing 接合和
junction table 纽带表
junctor 连接器
junctor equipment number(JEN) 级间链路设备号码
junctor pattern 级间链路方案
juncture rule 连音规则
jungle 蛙鸣(提示音)
junior computer operator 初级计算机操作员
junior keypunch operator 初级穿孔员

junior operator 初级操作员
junior programmer 初级程序员
junior system analyst 初级系统分析员
junk 无用数据;退役卫星
junk fact 无价值事实
junk ring 密封环,衬圈
just 对准
just-in-time activation(JIT) 及时激活
just-in-time manufacturing(JIT) 适时制造方式,间隙
justifiable digit time slot 可调数字时隙
justification 整版,对齐;调整,调节
justification control signal 位速调整控制信号
justification function 证明操作;调节功能
justification range 调节范围
justification rate 调位率,填充系数
justification ratio 调整率
justification routine 调整例程
justification service digit 调整服务数字
justified clause 对齐从句,对齐子句
justified margin 边缘调整
justified right-hand 右边齐
justify 调整;段落重排;证明正确
justify align （段落）两边对齐
justify inhibit 禁止对齐
justifying digit 调整数字
juxtaposition 并置,并列

K k

K(Key) 键,关键字,密钥
K 千(1024)
k 千(10^3)
K5 K5 微处理器芯片(AMD)
K6 K6 微处理器芯片(AMD)
K7 K7 微处理器芯片(AMD)
K-convex function K-凸函数
K-density K 稠密性
k-limited erasing k 有限删除
K-means clustering procedure K 均值聚类过程
K-nearest neighbor rule K 最近邻规则
k-out-of-n code n 中取 k 码
k-out-of-n system 表决系统,n 中取 k 判决系统
K-parallelism K 并行性
K pattern K 图
K-PRAM K 并行随机存取机器
K-rating K 评价指数
K shell K 外壳程序
K shell script 外壳文摘程序
kA(kiloAmpere) 千安培
Kalman filter 卡尔曼滤波器
Kana （日文）假名
Kana key 假名键
Kanji （日语当用）汉字
Kanji character 汉字字符
Kanji display 汉字显示器
Kanji printer 汉字打印机
Kanji selecting board 汉字选字键盘
Kanji utility 汉化实用程序
KAPSE (Kernel Ada Programming Support Environment) 核心 Ada 程序设计支持环境
Karaoke CD 卡拉 OK 激光唱盘
Karhunen-Loeve transformation K-L 变换
Karnaugh map 卡诺图
Karp-Rabin algorithm 卡普-罗宾算法
Karzanov's algorithm 卡兹诺夫算法
Kasami code 卡沙米码
KAT(Key-to-Address Transformation) 键地址变换
Katakana （日文）片假名
Katakana character recognition 片假名字符识别
Katmai Katmai 处理器(Intel,即奔腾 Ⅲ)
KB(KiloByte) 1024 字节
kb(kilobit) 千位
kB/s(kiloByte per second) 每秒千字节
kb/s(kilobit per second) 每秒千位
KBD(KeyBoarD) 键盘
KBMS(Knowledge Base Management

System) 知识库管理系统
KC-regularity lemma KC 正则引理
KCU(Keyboard Control Unit) 键盘控制单元
KDC(Key Distribution Center) 密钥分配中心
KDE(K Desktop Environment) K 桌面环境
KDL (Knowledge Description Language) 知识描述语言
keep 排版；保持
keep aspect ratio 保持宽高比
keep connection 保持连接
keep-in （版面）紧排
keep lines together 段中不分页
keep-out （版面）疏排
keep-out areas 禁止区
keeper 保持器
keeping priority 保持优先
keeplist 标识符列表
keisen 自由表格
Kell factor 克尔系数
Kelvin(K) 开尔文（绝对温度）
kent 绘图纸
Kerberos Kerberos 安全系统
Kermit Kermit 协议（美国哥伦比亚大学）
Kermit PC-VAX PC-VAX 计算机接口软件
kern 字母紧排
kern at 字距调整
kerned character 出格字符
kerned font 出格字模
kernel 核心程序
Kernel Ada Programming Support Environment(KAPSE) 核心 Ada 程序设计支持环境
kernel architecture 核心体系结构
kernel-based system 基于核心的系统
kernel benchmarks 核心程序段基准程序
kernel code 内核码
kernel data structure 核心数据结构
kernel design 核心设计
kernel diagnosis 核心诊断
kernel driver 核心驱动程序
kernel function 核函数
kernel instruction set 核心指令集
kernel interprocesses communication 核心进程间通信
kernel language 内核语言
kernel layer 核心层
kernel-level interface 内核级界面
kernel level thread model 内核级线程模型
kernel mode 内核模式
kernel module 核心模块
kernel object 核心对象
kernel of homomorphism 同态的核
kernel of multiprocessor operating system 多处理机操作系统内核
kernel of the Ada run-time environment Ada 运行时环境的核心
kernel polynomial 核多项式
kernel primitive 核心原语
kernel process (Unix)核心进程
kernel process object 核心进程对象
kernel program 核心程序
kernel program method 核心程序法
kernel service 核心服务,内核业务
kernel size 内核大小
kernel software 核心软件
kernel stack 内核堆栈
kernel statement 核心语句
kernel status 核心态
kernel test program 核心测试程序
kernel thread object 核心线程对象
kernel window manager 核心窗口管理程序
kerning 出格法；字母紧排,压缩字距
Kerr cell 克尔盒
Kerr constant 克尔常数
Kerr effect 克尔（磁光）效应
Kerr magneto-optical effect 克尔磁光效应
ket language 无用语言
kev(kilo Electron Volts) 千电子伏特
key 键,关键字,密钥
key access 键存取
key activity 关键活动
key address 键地址；关键字地址
key amount 密钥量
key architecture 密钥体系结构
key argument 键变元,关键字变量
key assignments 功能键设定
key autokey mode 密钥自密钥型

key binding 键操作联编
key breakthrough 关键突破
key buffer 键缓冲区
key change 键变换
key characteristics 关键字的特征
key class 键种类
key code 键代码
key code table 键码表
key coder 键编码器
key coding element location 关键字编码元定位
key coding element sort program 关键字编码元排序程序
key color 关键色,主色
key column 键列;关键列
key compare technique 关键字比较法
key component 关键字成分
key compression 关键字压缩
key condition 关键条件
key conversion 键转换;关键字转换
key data entry device 键数据输入设备
key data item 关键字数据项
key data station 键控数据站
key data terminal 键控数据终端
key data type 键数据类型
key descriptor block 关键字描述符块
key descriptors 关键字描述符
key display call indicator 键显示呼叫指示器
key distribution center 密钥分配中心
key down 键按下
key driven 键驱动
key driver 键驱动器;键驱动程序
key element set 键元集
key encode 键编码
key encoder 键编码器
key-encrypting key 密钥加密密钥
key entropy 密钥熵
key-entry 键入
key-entry area 键入区
key event 关键事件
key factor 关键要素
key field 关键字段
key field level specifications 关键字段级说明
key fill gun 密钥注入枪
key folding 关键字折合法
key frame 关键帧
key frame animation 关键帧动画
key generation 关键字生成
key generator 密钥产生器,密钥生成程序
key hole table 键孔表
key in 键入
key in flag 键输入标志
key information 键信息;关键信息
key input-checking visual-display unit 键输入检查显示单元
key instruction 键指令
key interlock 键联锁
key joint 键接
key label 键标记
key length 键长度
key letter 键盘字母
key letter in context 上下文内关键字
key loader 键载入程序
key loader module 键载入模块
key lock 键锁定
key lock switch 键锁开关
key management 密钥管理
key management facility 密钥管理设施
key management system 密钥管理系统
key mapping table 键位映射表
key mat 键垫
key match 键匹配
key matching 键匹配
key name 键名
key of reference 参考关键字
key off 键断开
key on 键接通
key operation 关键操作
key option 键选项
key organization 关键字组织
key pad 小键盘,键台
key pair 密钥对
key panel 键盘面
key path 关键路径
key phrase 关键字短语;密钥词组
key phrase cipher 密钥词组密码
key pitch 键距
key position 键位置;关键字位置
key press 键按动
key process 键处理,关键字处理
key prototype 关键原型
key pulse 键控脉冲
key punch machine 键控穿孔机

key puncher 打孔员
key range 关键字范围
key row 键行
key scan 键扫描
key search 关键字检索
key sender 键发送器
key sequence 键顺序
key-sequenced data set 键控顺序数据集
key-sequenced file 键控顺序文件
key set 密钥集
key-set tabulator 键设置制表机构
key sorting 键分类,键排序
key space 关键字空间
key state 关键状态
key station 主站
key status indicator 键盘状态指示器
key stream generator 密钥序列发生器
key stroke 击键,敲键
key stroke verification 击键验证
key structure 密钥结构
key switch 按键开关
key symbol 关键符号
key table 键表,键标表
key term 关键词组
key-to-address-transformation(KAT) 键地址变换
key top 键顶,键帽
key touch selector 触键选择器
key transformation 关键码变换
key transformation table 键码变换表
key transformer 关键码变换程序
key tree 关键字树
key up 键抬起
key value 键值
key value radix technique 键值基数法
key variable 关键变量
key version method 关键版本法
key window 键窗口
key word 关键字
key word identifier 关键字标识符
keyboard 键盘
keyboard accelerator 键盘加速器
keyboard adapter unit 键盘适配器
keyboard and display control 键盘与显示控制
keyboard buffer 键盘缓冲器
keyboard buffer overflow 键盘缓冲区溢出

keyboard checking circuit 键盘检验电路
keyboard classes 键盘种类
keyboard clear pushswitch 键盘清除按钮开关
keyboard command 键盘命令
keyboard command prompt 键盘命令提示符
keyboard common contact 键盘公共接点
keyboard components layout 键盘组件布置
keyboard computer 键盘式计算机
keyboard computer printer 键盘计算机打印机
keyboard connector 键盘连接器
keyboard console 键盘控制台
keyboard constant table 键盘常量表
keyboard contact 键盘触点
keyboard contact bounce 键盘接触颤动
keyboard control key 键盘控制键
keyboard controller 键盘控制器
keyboard edit keys 键盘编辑键
keyboard encoder 键盘编码器
keyboard enhancer 键盘增强程序
keyboard entry 键盘输入
keyboard entry and inquiry 键盘输入与查询
keyboard equivalent 键盘等价点
keyboard features 键盘性能,键盘特点
keyboard function definition 键盘功能定义
keyboard function key 键盘功能键
keyboard grabbing 键盘占用
keyboard hardware interrupt 键盘硬件中断
keyboard input 键盘输入
keyboard input flag 键盘输入标志
keyboard input IC tester 键盘输入集成电路测试器
keyboard input matrix 键盘输入矩阵
keyboard inquiry 键盘查询
keyboard interaction 键盘交互作用
keyboard interface 键盘接口
keyboard labels 键标号,关键字标号
keyboard layout 键盘布局
keyboard lock flag 键盘锁定标志
keyboard lockout 键盘锁定
keyboard macro 键盘宏

keyboard mapping 键盘映射
keyboard monitor 键盘监控程序
keyboard overlay 键盘覆盖板
keyboard processor 键盘处理器
keyboard program 键盘程序
keyboard repeat 键盘重复
keyboard scan 键盘扫描
keyboard scanning code 键盘扫描码
keyboard selection 键盘选择
keyboard shift 键盘换(上下)档
keyboard software interrupt 键盘软件中断
keyboard switch 键盘开关
keyboard template 键帽贴片
keyboard time-out 键盘超时
keyboard types 键盘类型
keycap 键帽
keycoder 键编码器
keyed access 键控存取
keyed access method 键控存取法
keyed attribute 键属性
keyed clamping 键控钳位
keyed direct access 键控直接存取
keyed file 键控文件
keyed interval 键控间隔
keyed sequence 键控顺序
keyed sequence access path 键控顺序访问路径
keyed sequential access 键控顺序存取
keyed sequential access method 键控顺序存取法
keyed sequential file 按关键字排序的文件
keyed serial file 键式串联文件
keyframe 关键帧,关键画面
keying 键控
keying circuit 键控电路
keying relationship 键控关系
keying wave 键控波
keylock feature 键锁特制件
keymat 键标套
keypad 键台,小键盘
keypad application mode 小键盘应用模式
keypad numeric mode 小键盘数字模式
keystroke 击键
keystroke counter 击键计数器
keystroke macro 击键宏指令
keystroke message 击键消息
keyswitch 键控开关
keytop symbol 键顶符号
keyword 关键词
keyword and context index 关键词和上下文索引
keyword and UDC index 关键词和国际十进分类法索引
keyword-from-title index 标题关键词索引
keyword identifier 关键词标识符
keyword in context 上下文内关键词
keyword-in-context index 上下文内关键词索引
keyword index 关键词索引
keyword item 关键词项
keyword macro 关键词宏调用
keyword macro argument 关键词宏参
keyword macro instruction 关键词宏指令
keyword out of context 上下文外关键词
keyword out-of-context index 上下文外关键词索引
keyword parameter 关键词参数
keyword recognition 关键词识别
keyword root 关键词根
keyword spotting 关键词定位
keyword table 关键词表
KFA(Key Frame Animation) 关键帧动画
KG(Key Generator) 密钥发生器
Khornerstones Khornerstones 基准程
kHz(kilo Hertz) 千赫兹
kick 突跳,急冲
kick off 脱离,离开
kick out 分离,断开
kickback 快速回程
kickoff meeting 首次会议
kill 取消；注销；删除
kill character 消行字符
kill server 取消服务器
killer 断路器；删除程序
killer app "杀手"应用程序
killer program 计算机病毒清除程序
kilo 千
kilobaud 千波特
kilobit(kb) 千位,千比特
kilobit per second(kb/s) 每秒千位

Kilobyte(KB) 千字节
kilobyte per second(KB/s) 每秒千字节
kilocycle per second(kc/sec) 每秒千周,千赫兹
kilohertz(kHz) 千赫,千赫兹
kilomega 千兆
kiloohm 千欧姆
kilovolt 千伏
kilovolt-ampere 千伏安
kilowatt 千瓦
kilowatt hour 千瓦小时,度
kiloword 千字
kinematic chain 运动链系
kinematic data 动态数据
kinematic equation 动态方程
kinematic function 动态函数
kinematic model 运动模型
kinematic modeling 动态建模
kinematic nonlinearity 动态非线性
kinematic parameter 动态参数
kinematic path control 动态路径控制
kinematic redundancy 动态冗余
kinematic system 动态系统
kinematic variable 动态变量
kinematics 计算机辅助运动分析
Kinesis ergonomic keyboard 人类工程学键盘
kinetic control system 动态控制系统
kinetic 动态的,运动的
kinetic control system 动态控制系统
kinetic filter 动态滤波器
Kinetics FastPath Kinetics 快速路径
kineto-angle transducer 运动角度传感器
kinsoku character 避头尾字符
kiosk 信息亭；公用电话间
Kirchhoff's laws 基尔霍夫定律
Kirchhoff's laws of electric circuit 基尔霍夫电路定律
kiss pressure 接触压力
kit 成套组件
kit assembler 成套汇编程序
kit hardware and software system 成套硬件和软件系统
kit processor card 成套处理器插件板
kit reliability 整套可靠性措施
kit size 套件尺寸
kit software 套装软件

kit processor card 成套处理器插卡
kit utility 套件
Klamath Klamath 处理器
Kleene closure 克林闭包
Kleene's theorem on regular set 克林正则集定理
KLIC(Key Letter In Context) 上下文关键字母
klirr factor 失真系数
kludge 不成熟产品
kMC/S(kiloMegaCycle per Second) 千兆赫/秒
knapsack algorithm 渐缩算法,背包算法
knapsack problem 渐缩问题,背包问题
knapsack vector 渐缩向量
knee 拐点
knee of characteristic 特性曲线拐点
KNI(Katmai New Instructions) Katmai 新指令集(Intel)
knife switch 闸刀开关
knob 按钮,调节旋钮
knock-knee layout 笨拙设计
Knockout Knockout 交换结构
knockout 剔除
knot 纽结点,僵局
knot complexity 结点复杂性
knotted list 错综复杂的列表
know-how 技术诀窍
knowledge 知识
knowledge abstraction 知识抽象
knowledge accommodation 知识调节
knowledge acquisition 知识获取
knowledge acquisition tool 知识获取工具
knowledge application 知识应用
knowledge assimilation 知识同化
knowledge atom 知识原子
knowledge attribute 知识属性
knowledge base 知识库
knowledge base compiler 知识库编译器
knowledge base debugger 知识库调试程序
knowledge base machine 知识库机
knowledge base management 知识库管理系统
knowledge base system 知识库系统
knowledge base update 知识库更新
knowledge-based approach 基于知识

的方法
knowledge - based computer - assisted instruction 基于知识的计算机辅助教学
knowledge-based consultation program 基于知识的咨询程序
knowledge-based consultation system 基于知识的咨询系统
knowledge-based editor 基于知识的编辑程序
knowledge-based expert system 基于知识的专家系统
knowledge-based inference 基于知识的推理
knowledge-based integrity constraint 基于知识的完整性约束
knowledge-based interface 基于知识的界面
knowledge-based modeling 基于知识的建模,基于知识的造型
knowledge-based perspective 基于知识的观点
knowledge - based programming environment 基于知识的程序设计环境
knowledge-based report generation 基于知识的报表生成
knowledge-based simulation system (KBS) 基于知识的模拟系统语言
knowledge-based software development 基于知识的软件开发
knowledge-based solution 基于知识的解答
knowledge-based system 基于知识的系统
knowledge-based task 基于知识的任务
knowledge-based tool 基于知识的工具
knowledge-based understanding 基于知识的理解
knowledge-based vision 基于知识的视觉
knowledge compilation 知识编译
knowledge compiler rapid prototype (KCRP) 知识编译快速原型
knowledge completeness 知识完备性
knowledge complexity 知识复杂性
knowledge concentrated industry 知识密集型产业

knowledge construct 知识构造
knowledge creation 知识创建
knowledge-directed data base 知识引导的数据库
knowledge-dictionary 知识字典
knowledge discovery 知识发现
knowledge editor 知识编辑器
knowledge elicitation 知识引出,知识提取
knowledge engineer 知识工程师
knowledge engineering 知识工程
knowledge engineering environment 知识工程环境系统
knowledge evolution 知识进化
knowledge expression 知识表达式
knowledge extraction 知识析取
knowledge factor 知识因子
knowledge flow 知识流
knowledge frame 知识框架
knowledge fuzzy representation 知识模糊表示法
knowledge graph 知识图
knowledge heuristic 知识启发
knowledge image coding 知识图像编码
knowledge implementation 知识实现
knowledge incompleteness 知识不完备性
knowledge industry 知识产业
knowledge information processing 知识信息处理
knowledge information processing system(KIPS) 知识信息处理系统
knowledge integration 知识集成
knowledge intensive industry 知识密集型产业
knowledge intensive learning 知识密集型学习
knowledge interchange format 知识交换格式
knowledge interpretation 知识解释
knowledge item 知识术语,知识项
knowledge layer 知识层
knowledge level modeling 知识水平建模
knowledge library expert system 知识库专家系统
knowledge logic 知识逻辑
knowledge maintenance 知识维护
knowledge management 知识管理

knowledge manipulation system 知识处理系统
knowledge migration 知识迁徙
knowledge model 知识模型
knowledge modeling 知识模型化
knowledge object 知识对象
knowledge-object transformation 知识-对象变换
knowledge of programming 程序设计知识
knowledge operationalization 知识操作化
knowledge organization 知识组织
knowledge-oriented architecture 面向知识的体系结构
knowledge paradigm 知识范例
knowledge presentation 知识表示
knowledge preservation 知识保存
knowledge processing 知识处理
knowledge production 知识产生
knowledge query 知识查询
knowledge reasoning 知识推理
knowledge refinement 知识提炼
knowledge reliability 知识可靠性
knowledge reorganization 知识重构
knowledge representation 知识表示
knowledge representation language (KRL) 知识表示语言
knowledge representation mode 知识表示模式
knowledge representation system 知识表示系统
knowledge resource 知识资源
knowledge retrieval 知识检索
knowledge reusability 知识可重用性
knowledge reuse 知识重用
knowledge schema 知识模式
knowledge sharing system 知识共享系统
knowledge source 知识源
knowledge space 知识空间
knowledge structure 知识结构
knowledge substrate 知识根基
knowledge subsystem 知识子系统
knowledge support system 知识支持系统
knowledge transfer 知识传送
knowledge transformation 知识变换
knowledge understand 知识理解

knowledge utilization system 知识运用系统
knowledge validation 知识确认
knowledge verification 知识验证
knowledgeable dialogue 有知识对话
knowledgeware 智件
known address 已知地址
known ciphertext only attack 仅知密文攻击
known component 已知组件
known error condition 已知错误条件
known-how 技术决窍
known information 已知信息
known lines 已知线路
known plaintext attack 已知明文攻击
known segment 已知段
known state 已知状态
known universe 已知整体
Knuth-Morris-Pratt algorithm KMP算法
Kodaliths 柯达反转片
Kolmogorov complexity 科莫哥洛夫复杂性
Konigsberg bridge problem 哥尼斯堡桥问题
KOPS (Thousands of Operations Per Second) 千次运算/秒
Kordic algorithm 科迪克算法
Korn shell K外壳程序,K外围程序
KP signal 开始发码信号
Kruskal's algorithm 克鲁斯卡算法
Krylov sequence 克雷洛夫序列
Krylov subspace 克雷洛夫子空间
KSA forum KSA论坛
KSAM (Keyed Sequential Access Method) 键控顺序访问法
KSDS (Key Sequenced Data Set) 键控顺序数据集
KSH (Key Strokes per Hour) 每小时击键次数
KSR1 KSR1计算机
KTU (Keyword Transformation Unit) 关键字变换单元
Kuck classification schema 库克(计算机)分类法
Kuhn-Munkres' algorithm 库恩-蒙克鲁斯算法
Kuhn-Tucker condition 库恩-塔克条

件
kurtosis 陡峭度
KUIPNET 京都大学信息处理网(日)
KW(KeyWord) 关键字
KW(KiloWatt) 千瓦

KWIC(Key Word In Context) 上下文中关键字
kymogram 记录图
kymograph 波形记录

L l

L(Length) 长度；持续时间
L-1 approximation L-1 逼近
L-∞ approximation L-∞逼近
L-Edit L-Edit 设计软件
0L-grammar 0L 文法
0L-system 0L 系统
L-system L 系统
LA(Line Adapter) 线路适配器
label 标记,标号
label address 标号地址
label alignment 标记对齐
label area 标记[标号]区域
label attribute 标号属性
label constant 标号常数
label cylinder 标记柱面
label data 标号数据
label definition file 标号定义文件
label expression 标号表达式
label field 标号字段
label file 标签文件
label format record 标号格式记录
label group 标号组
label histogram 标号直方图
label index mode 标号变址方式
label information area 标号信息区
label information cylinder 标记信息柱面
label layout 标签布局
label key 标号键
label list of a label variable declaration 标号变量说明标号表
label list of a statement 语句标号表
label location 标号位置
label notation 标号标记
label parameter 标号参数
label prefix 标记前置符,标号前缀
label printer 标签印制机

label record 标号记录
label save area 标号保存区
label set 标号集
label subscript 标号下标
label symbol 标记符号
label table 标号表
label terminator 标号终结符
label trace 标号跟踪
label updating 标号更新
label variable 标号变量
label verification 标号验证
labeled tree 标号树
labeled common 有标号的公共部分
labeled common block 有标号公用块
labeled data stream 有标号数据流
labeled field 有标号字段,标号域
labeled graph matching 标定图匹配法
labeled image 有标号图像
labeled input file 有标号输入文件
labeled instruction 有标号指令
labeled picture 带标号图片
labeled statement 有标号语句
labeled transitive digraph 标定可迁徙有向图
labeled tree 标号树
labeling algorithm 标记算法
labeling function 标记函数　　「记
labeling of speech signal 语音信号标
labeling procedure 标记过程
labeling range picture 标号范围图
Labolink 实验室链路计算机网(日本京都大学)
labor productivity 劳动生产率
laboratory automation system 实验室自动化系统
laboratory environment 实验室环境
laboratory instrument computer(LINC)

实验室仪器计算机
LABORDOC 劳工文献数据库
labware 实验设备
ladder adder 梯形加法器
ladder code 梯形码
ladder diagram 梯形图
ladder network 梯形网络
lag 延迟,滞后
lag covariance 滞后协方差
lag network 滞后网络
lag regression 滞后回归
lag time 滞后时间
lag window 滞后窗 「理
lagged product theorem 滞后乘积定
lagging current 滞后电流
Lagrange expression 拉格朗日表达式
Lagrange finite element 拉格朗日有限元
Lagrange interpolation polynomial 拉格朗日插值多项式
Lagrange inversion formula 拉格朗日反演公式
Lagrangian coordinate 拉格朗日坐标
Lagrangian functional 拉格朗日泛函
LALR(1) method LALR(1)分析法
lambda binding λ约束
lambda calculus λ演算
lambda expression λ表达式
lambda lifting λ提升
lambda list λ表
lambda notation λ记法
lambda parameter λ参数
lambda variable λ变量
Lamber (亮度单位)朗伯
laminar combined convection 分层混合对流 「成
laminar elastic composite 分层弹性合
laminar flow heat transfer 分层对流热传导
laminate 层压,叠片,叠层板
laminated anisotropic stiffener 分层非均质加强构件
laminated board 层压板
laminated bus plate 层压汇流条
laminated resin material 叠层树脂材
lamp 指示灯 「料
LAN(Local Area Network) 局域网
LAN analyzer 局域网分析仪 「络

LAN analyzer for Windows 局域网分析器 Windows 版本
LAN aware 局域网件
LAN-aware program 网络版程序 「件
LAN backup program 网络版备份软
LAN broadcast 局域网络广播通信
LAN Desk Manager 局域网桌面管理程序
LAN Distance 网络远程访问软件
LAN driver 网络驱动程序
LAN gateway 局域网络网关
LAN-ignorant program 单机版软件
LAN Lord 局域网监控软件
LAN Manager 局域网管理程序
LAN memory management program 网络内存管理程序
LAN multicast 局域网络组播通信
LAN network manager 局域网网络管理软件
LAN Patrol 局域网巡查程序
LAN requester 局域网请求者
LAN Server 局域网服务软件
LAN server 局域网服务器
LAN station 局域网工作站
LAN Station Manager 局域网工作站管理软件
LAN-WAN interconnection 局域网-广域网互连
LAN WorkGroup 局域网工作组
LAN Workplace 局域网工作场
land 连接盘,焊盘
land station 地面站
landing 连接
landless hole 无连接盘孔
Landmark rating Landmark 速率测试
LANDP(Local Area Network Distributed Platform) 局域网分布平台(IBM)
LANDP/2 PS/2 局域网分布平台(IBM)
LANDP/400 AS/400 局域网分布平台(IBM)
LANDP/6000 RS/6000 局域网分布平台(IBM) 「式
landscape 风景画方式,横宽幅打印格
landscape left 横向偏左版面
landscape monitor 宽幅显示器
landscape orientation 横式取向

landscape page 横向页面
landscape right 横向偏右版面
landscape sample (打印模拟显示)宽幅示例
LANE(LAN Emulation) (ATM)局域网仿真
LANGUAGE 语言支持软件
language 语言
language analysis 语言分析
language binding 语言绑定
language board 语言板
language complexity 语言复杂性
language construct 语言构成
language convention 语言约定(惯例)
language conversion program 语言转换程序
language converter 语言转换器
language definition 语言定义
language-dependent parameter 与语言有关的参数
language description 语言描述
language editor 语言编辑程序
language engineering 语言工程
language extensibility 语言可扩充性
language features 语言特征
language formalization 语言形式化
language generated by grammar G 由文法G产生的语言
language inference 语言推理
language information 语言信息
language information processing 语言信息处理
language interface 语言接口
language interpreter 语言解释程序
language knowledge base 语言知识库
language media format 语言媒体格式
language model 语言模型
language of production system 产生式系统语言
language or discriminating digit signaling system R2 语言或鉴别数字(R2信号系统)
language pair 语言对
language pattern 语言模式
language primitive 语言原语
language processor 语言处理器
language reliability 语言可靠性
language rules 语言规则

language script property 语言脚本属性
language selection 语言选择
language shift 语言切换
language size 语言规模
language space 语言空间
language specification 语言规范
language statement 语言语句
language structure 语言结构
language subset 语言子集
language support environment 语言支援环境
language tool 语言工具
language transformation 语言转换
language transition 语言过渡
language translation(LT) 语言翻译
language translator(TRANSLAN) 语言翻译器
language understanding system 语言理解系统
LanguageAccess 语言存取软件
LANtastic LANtastic操作系统
LAP(Link Access Procedure) 链路访问过程
LAP(Logical Access Path) 逻辑存取路径
lap 抛光,研磨
LAP-B(Link Access Procedure-Balanced) 平衡链路访问过程
LAP-D(LAP-D channel) 平衡链路访问过程D通道
LAP-M(LAP-Modem) 平衡链路访问过程M通道
lap splice 搭接
LAP-X(LAP-half-dupleX) 平衡链路访问过程半双工-全双工
LAPB(Link Access Procedure Balanced) 平衡型链路接入规程
LAPD(Link Access Procedure on the D channel) D通道链路接入规程
lapel microphone 佩戴式麦克风
Laplace operator 拉普拉斯算子
Laplace transform(LT) 拉普拉斯变换
Laplacian mask 拉普拉斯掩模
LapLink LapLink文件转换程序
lapping 搭接,重叠
laptop computer 膝上型计算机
LAR(Local Address Register) 局部地址寄存器

large button (图形用户界面上的)大按钮	large step method 大步长法
large capacity disk 大容量磁盘	large syntactic mark 大语法标记
large complex dynamic system(LCDS) 大规模复杂的动力学系统	large value capacitor 大容量电容器
large deformation 大形变	largest integral equivalent 整体最大等效
large displacement perturbation 大位移扰动	largest known prime 最大已知素数
large format 大号	largest observation 最大观测值
large geometry control 大几何尺寸控制	largest syntactic mark 最大语法标记
large grain data flow 大粒度数据流	laser(light amplification by stimulation of emitted radiation) 激光器
large icon 大图标	laser addressing liquid crystal light valve 激光寻址液晶光阀
large internet packet 大型互联网络信息包	laser alignment telescope 激光导向仪
large injection 大量注入	laser array 激光器阵列
large join query 大型联合查询	laser audio disc 激光唱片
large memory model 大内存模型	laser audio player 激光唱机
LARGE mode 大模式	laser beam focusing 激光束聚焦
large object(LOB) 大对象	laser beam machining 激光束加工
large-order descretized system control 高次离散化系统控制	laser beam printer 激光束打印机
large planar frame 大型平面框架	laser beam recorder(LBR) 激光束记录器
large plastic plane strain 大塑性平面应变	laser Chinese character composition system 激光汉字排版系统
large sample theory 大样本理论	laser clock 激光钟
large scale distributed control system 大型分布式控制系统	laser communication 激光通信
large scale integrated circuit(LSI) 大规模集成电路	laser connector 激光连接器
large-scale mathematical programming 大规模数理规划法	laser cutting 激光切割
large scale nonlinear programming 大规模非线性规划法	laser deposition of conductor pattern 激光布线
large scale system 大规模系统	laser display 激光显示
large-scale system methodology 大规模系统方法论	laser drilling 激光打孔
large-scale system network problem 大规模系统网络问题	laser grooving 激光刻槽
large-scale system theory 大规模系统理论	laser guidance 激光制导
large scale unconstrained non-linear optimization problem 无大规模约束条件的非线性最优化问题	laser heat-treatment 激光热处理
	laser holography 激光全息术
	laser holographic nondestructive testing 激光全息无损检验
large screen projector 大屏幕投影仪	laser line follower 激光线跟随器
large size redundant structure 大规模冗余结构	laser lithography system 激光光刻系统
	laser localized heating 激光局部加热
	laser location 激光定位
large sparse linear system 大型稀疏线性系统	laser marking 激光标记
	laser marking equipment 激光印记设备
	laser memory 激光存储器
	laser modulation 激光调制
	laser optical videodisc 激光视盘
	laser phototelegraph 激光传真电报

laser platemaker 激光制版机	last term 末项
laser plotter 激光绘图仪	last terminal 最末终结符
laser printer 激光打印机	last test step 最后测试步
laser processing 激光加工	last write time 最近写入时间
laser recorder 激光记录仪	latch 闩锁,锁存
laser scanner 激光扫描仪	latch circuit 闩锁电路
laser scriber 激光划片器	latch-down key 锁停键
laser scribing 激光划片	latch enable 锁存允许
laser storage 激光存储	latch logic 闩锁逻辑
laser telecine 激光影视	latch register 闩锁寄存器
laser television 激光电视	latch-up 闩上,闭锁,锁定
laser typesetter 激光照排机	latching 锁定,锁存
laser TV system 激光电视系统	latching circuit 锁定电路
laser videodisk 激光视盘	latching current 锁定[自锁]电流
laser welding 激光焊接	late binding 后期联编
laserdisc 激光盘	latency 等待[潜伏]时间;暂留时间
LaserJet 激光打印机(HP)	latency time 尚需等待时间,反应时间
LaserWriter LaserWriter打印机(苹果)	latency tolerance 延时容限
	latent heat 潜热
lasso tool 套绳工具	latent image 潜像
last cell 右下角单元格	latent-image fade 潜像退色
last change 上次修改	latent period 潜周期
last column 末列	latent root 特征根
last current state 最近当前状态	latent vector 本征向量,特征向量
last date used 上次使用日期	lateral 横向的,侧向的
last driver 最后驱动器	lateral diffusion 横向扩散
last element 最末元素	lateral parity 横向奇偶校验
last executed instruction 最后执行指令	lateral redundancy check 横向冗余校验
last in chain 链中最末(元素)	lateral reversal 横向翻转,横向回转
last-in first-out(LIFO) 后进先出	latest 最迟的
last-in first-out stack 后进先出堆栈	latest allowable time 最迟允许时间
last-in last-out(LILO) 后进后出	latest finishing time 最迟完成时间
last item 末项	latest node time 最迟节点时间
last location 最后位置,最后单元	latest starting time 最迟开始时间
last mile 最后一英里,(网络)末端分支用户线	Latin alphabet 拉丁字母表
	Latin letter 拉丁字母
last number 最后编号	latitude 曝光宽容度
last of chain 链尾	LATRIX(Light Accessible Transistor Matrix) 光可存取的晶体管矩阵
last operation 最后操作	
last pass phase 最后通过阶段	lattice 格,点阵,晶格
last place 最底层	lattice defect 晶格缺陷
last printed 上次打印时间	lattice digital filter 网格数字滤波器
last priority level 最低优先级	lattice-like structure 网状结构,格状结构
last row 末行	
last saved 上次保存时间	lattice model 格模型
last sector 最末扇区	lattice point 网格点
last significant figure 最低有效数字	lattice search 格点探索法
last subscript 最末下标	lattice structure 晶格结构

lattice vibration 晶格振动
LattisCell LattisCell 交换器
LattisSwitch System Lattis 交换系统
launch 开始,启动;发射
launch default browser 启动默认浏览器
Launch Pad (OS/2)快速启动板
launching fiber 发射光纤
LAURA LAURA 功能分析系统
lavaliere microphone 颈挂式麦克风
law of absorption 吸收律
law of association 结合律
law of causality 因果律
law of commutation 交换律
law of contradiction 矛盾律
law of distribution 分配律
law of excluded middle 排中律
law of idempotence 幂等律
law of identity 同一律
law of large number 大数法则
law of reciprocity 互反律
law of sufficient reason 充足理由律
LAWN(Local Area Wireless Network) 局域无线电网络
Lawrence Radiation Laboratory Translator(LRLTRAN) 劳伦斯射线实验室的翻译程序语言
lay down 敷设,安装
lay in 导入
layer 层
layer discrimination 层次识别
layer independence 层独立性
layer management 层管理
layer protocol 分层协议
layer-to-layer signal transfer 层间信号传送
layer-to-layer spacing 层间距
layered dictionary 分层字典
layered interface 分层接口
layered interrupt priority 分层中断优先权
layered medium 分层介质
layered network 分层网络
layered protocols 分层[层次]协议
layered structure 分层[层次]结构
layered structure of teletext system 图文电视系统的分层结构
layering 分层
laying 敷设

laying apparatus 敷设设备
layout 布局,布线;布线图,装配图
layout algorithm 布局算法
layout button 布局按钮
layout character 格式符,布局控制字
layout check 布局检验
layout description language 版面描述语言
layout design 草图[概略]设计
layout editor 版图编辑程序
layout file interface 布设文件接口
layout guideline 布局准则
layout matching 版面匹配
layout parameter extraction(LPE) 布设参数提取
layout pattern extrapolation 版面模式外推
layout rule 布线规则
layout setting 格式设置,轮廓设置
layout simulation 布局模拟
layout synthesis 版图合成
layout tool 版面设计工具
layout versus schematic(LVS) 布设与原理图对照
layout view 版面[布局]视图
lazy evaluation 迟缓计算
LB(Local Buses) 本地[局部]总线
LBA(Linear Bounded Automation) 线性有界自动机
LBA(Logical Block Access) 逻辑块存取
LBA-problem LBA 问题
LBC(Local Bus Controller) 局部总线控制器
LBR(Laser Beam Recorder) 激光束记录器
LBR(Librarian) 库管理程序
LC(Leased Channel) 租用信道
LC(Line Concentrator) 线路集中器
LC(Lossy Compression) 有损压缩
LCB(Line Control Block) 线路控制块
LCC(LAN Client Control) 局域网客户机控制
LCC(Leadless Chip Carrier) 无引线芯片载体
LCD(Liquid Crystal Display) 液晶显示
LCD camera 液晶显示放映机

LCD display 液晶显示
LCD panel 液晶显示透射屏
LCD printer 液晶打印机
LCN(Logical Channel Number) 逻辑通道号
LCN(Loosely Coupled Network) 松耦合网络
Lcon language Lcon 语言
LCP(Link-Control Protocol) 链路控制协议
LCP(Local Check Point) 局部检验点
LCR(Least Cost routing) 最小代价路由选择
LCU(Loop Control Unit) 环路控制部件
LD(Laser Disc) 激光唱盘
LD(Line Driver) 线路驱动器
LD(LoaD) 负载;装入;取数
LDAP(Lightweight Directory Access Protocol) 轻载目录访问协议
LDB(Large Data Base) 大型数据库
LDB(Logical Data Base) 逻辑数据库
LDM(Limited Distance Modem) 有限距离调制解调器
LDT(Logical Device Table) 逻辑设备表
LDU decomposition LDU 分解
LE(Logical Element) 逻辑元件
lead 引线,引脚
lead frames 引线框架
lead-in 引入;段首
lead-in page 引入页面
lead-lag network 超前滞后网络
lead-out 引出;段结尾
lead pitch 引线间距
lead processing equipment 引线处理设备
lead programmer 主程序员
lead screw 丝杠
lead time 研制周期,交付周期
leaded chip carrier 带引线芯片载体
leader 头标,标题,引导段
leader label 前导标记,引导标记
leader record 首记录,引导记录
leader tape 带头,磁带引导部分
leaderless chip carrier(LCC) 无引线芯片载体
leaders 指引线

leading 行距,空行;前导,开始
leading blank 前导空格
leading character 前导字符
leading control 前导控制,超前控制
leading decision 超前判断,前导判定
leading diagonal 主对角线
leading edge 前缘,前沿
leading end 前端
leading flag 开始标志
leading graphic 标题图形
leading page 前导页
leading principal minor 前主子式
leading punct 前置标点
leading space 前导空格
leading time 提前时间
leading zero 前导零,先行零
leading zero suppress 前导零删除
leadless chip carrier(LCC) 无引线芯片载体
leadless device 无引线器件
leadless inverted device(LID) 无引线转换装置
leaf 叶,叶子
leaf class 叶类
leaf node 叶节点
leaf object 叶实体
leaf procedure (Unix)叶过程
leaf site 叶位置
League for Programming Freedom 编程自由同盟
leakage 泄漏,泄密
leakage current 泄漏电流
leakage fault 泄漏故障
leaky bucket (信元速率)"漏斗"算法
leapfrog test 跳位测试,跳步检查
learn mode 学习模式
learner-based coach 基于学员的教练
learner-computer interface 学习者计算机接口
learner-computer interface device 学习者计算机接口设备
learner-computer interface language 学习者计算机接口语言
learning 学习,训练
learning automation 学习自动机
learning bridge 学习桥
learning by analogy 类推学习,类比学
learning by being told 传授学习,讲

授学习
learning by doing 通过实作的学习
learning by experimentation 实验学习
learning by independent exploration 独立探索式学习
learning by observation 观察学习
learning control 学习控制
learning control system 学习控制系统
learning controller 学习控制器
learning curve 学习曲线
learning from example 示例学习
learning from instruction 示教学习
learning from observation 从观察中学习
learning from observation and discovery 观察与发现学习
learning from solution paths 从解题路径中学习
learning in heuristic problem solving 启发式问题求解学习
learning in problem solving 在问题求解中学习
learning machine 学习机
learning outcomes 学习收益
learning program 学习程序
learning simple conception 学习简单概念
learning strategy 学习策略
learning theory 学习理论
learning without teacher 无教师学习
lease duration 租用时间
lease expires 租约到期
leased channel 租用信道
leased circuit 租用线路　　　「接
leased circuit connection 租用电路连
leased circuit data transmission service 租用电路数据传输业务
leased line 租用线路　　　「器
leased line modem 租用线路调制解调
leased-line network 租用线路网络
least action 最小作用量
least-commitment principle 最小约束法;最小承诺原则
least-commitment rule 至少约定规则
least core 最小内核
least cost estimating 最低成本估计
least element 最小元素
least energy principle 最小能量原理

least favorable distribution 最不利分
least fixpoint 最小不动点　　「布
least frequently used memory 最不经常使用内存
least-frequently-used page replacement 不常使用页替换
least input increment 最小输入增量
least member 最小成员
least model 最小模型
least privilege 最低许可,最低特权
least recently used 最近最少使用的
least recently used memory(LRU) 最近最少使用的内存
least-recently-used page replacement 最近很少使用页替换
least significant bit(LSB) 最低有效位　　　　　　　「符
least significant character 最低有效字
least significant digit 最低有效数字
least spanning tree 最小生成树
least square approximation 最小二乘逼近
least square curve fitting 最小二乘曲线拟合
least square data fitting 最小二乘数据拟合
least square estimation 最小二乘估计
least square linear regression 最小二乘方线性回归
least square method 最小二乘法
least square multiple regression 最小二乘方多重回归
least square solution 最小二乘解
least square straight-line fitting 最小二乘直线拟合
least upper bound(LUB) 最小上界
least-weight route 最小权路由
leave at destination 放在终点
LEAVE construct LEAVE 结构
leave voice message 语音留言
lecture call 演讲式呼叫
LED(Light Emitting Diode) 发光二极管
LED printer 发光二极管打印机
Lee's algorithm 李氏(印刷电路板布线)算法
left adjust 左调节
left align 左对齐

left arrow 左箭头
left bracket 左括号
left-cancellable 左可约的
left column 左列
left continuous function 左连续函数
left coset 左陪集
left end marker 左端点标志
left-hand margin indent 左边缘缩排
left-hand mouse 左手鼠标器
left-handed subtree 左侧子树
left-handed coordinate system 左手坐标系
left ideal 左理想
left identity 左幺元
left indent 左边缩进
left justified 左边对齐,左整版
left-justify 左整版,向左对齐
left leaf 左叶子
left-linear grammar 左线性文法
left list layout 左表布局
left mean-square estimate 最小均方估
left nibble 左尼(半字节)
left parenthesis 左括号
left part list 左部表
left recursion rule 左递归规则
left-right parsing 由左至右分析
left-sentential form 左句型
left shift 左移位
left-sided derivative 左侧导数
left truncation 左截断
leftist tree 左高树
leftmost bit 最左位
leftmost cell 最左单元
leftmost derivation 最左派生
leftmost nonterminal 最左非终结符
leftmost prime phrase 最左素短语
leftmost sequence 最左序列
leftmost simple phrase 最左简单短语
leftmost string 最左串
leftmost terminal set 最左端终止集
leftmost tree 最左树
leg 支线,支路,引线
legacy hardware 遗留硬件
legacy system 遗留系统
legacy to ISA (PC)保留给 ISA 总线
legacy wire 遗留线路
legal analysis system 法律分析系统
legal engineering 法律工程学

legal file name 合法文件名
legal offset range 合法偏移量范围
legal move 合理走步
legal pattern 合法模式
legal retrieval 合法检索
legal size (纸张的)法定尺寸,规定尺
legal trademark 合法商标
legal unit 法定单位
legend 图例,图标符号,图注
legend entry 图例项
legend key 图例标示
legend text 图例文字
legged walking robot 有腿行走机器人
legibility 清晰度
legible 清晰的,易读的
lemma 引理
LEN(Low Entry Networking) 低级入口联网
Lengauer-Tarjan's algorithm 伦高-塔金算法
length 长度,字长,记录长度,块长
length indicator 长度标志
length specification 长度说明
lengthen label 加长标号
lens 透镜,镜头
lens system 聚焦系统
LEP(Low-End Product) 低端产品
less-than 小于
less-than match 小于匹配
lesson authoring system 课程编写系
LET statement (早期版本 BASIC 语言)赋值语句
letter 字母
letter code 字母码
letter descriptor 文字描述符
letter generator 字母发生器
letter hash 字母散列
letter key 字母键
letter out 字符清除
letter-quality print mode 铅字质量打印模式
letter quality printer 铅字质量打印机
letter recognition 字母识别
letter row 字母行
letter shift 字母移位,换字母档
letter string 字母串
letterphone 书写电话机
letterpress 凸版印刷,铅字印刷

letters shift signal 字母键位信号
letterset 胶印
letterspacing 字母间隔
level 层次;电平
level 0 dump 零级转储(完全转储)
level 2 cache 二级高速缓存
level 3 dump 三级转储(增量转储)
level 7 dump 七级转储(例行增量转储)
level adjustment 电平调整;色阶调整
level alignment 电平校准
level-by-level adaption 逐层适配
level check 电平检验
level compensator 电平补偿器
level control table 分级控制表
level crossing 平面交叉法
level date 层次日期
level diagram 电平图
level displacement table 层位移表
level-enable flip-flop 电平启动触发器
level-enable signal 电平使能信号
level fluctuation 电平波动,电平起伏
level indicator 电平指示器;层指示符
level number 层号,级号
level of addressing 寻址级别
level of confidence 置信水平
level of maintenance 维护等级
level of nesting 嵌套层次
level one variables 一阶变量
level saturation method 级饱和法
level sensitive circuit 电平敏感电路
level-sensitive scan design(LSSD) 电平相关扫描设计法
level sensor 电平传感器
level shift diode 电平转移二极管
level shifting 电平移位
level surface 水平面
level translation buffer 电平转换缓冲器
level translator 电平转换器
level-triggered flip-flop 电平触发的触发器
leveling zone 均匀分布区,调整区
levels 层次,级
Levenshtein distance 李文施坦距离
lever 杠杆
leverage 杠杆作用
levitation 悬浮
lexeme 语辞元素,语义

lexemic alternation pattern 词位交替模式
lexical 词法的,词典的
lexical ambiguity 词汇多义性
lexical analysis 词法分析
lexical analyzer 词法分析程序
lexical attachment 词项附加
lexical category 词汇范围
lexical characteristic 词法特征
lexical closure 词法闭包
lexical concatenation 词汇连结
lexical conversion 词法转换
lexical entry 词条
lexical feature 词汇特征
lexical form 词汇形式
lexical-free variables 词法自由变量
lexical information base 词语信息库
lexical insertion 词汇插入
lexical item 词项
lexical level 词法级
lexical matrix 词法矩阵
lexical meaning 词汇意义
lexical node 词汇节点
lexical object 词法对象
lexical redundancy rule 词汇冗余规则
lexical representation 词汇表示
lexical scan mean 词汇扫描手段
lexical scoping 词法域
lexical substitution 词汇替换
lexical token 词法标记
lexical transformation 词汇转换
lexical unit 词法单位
lexicographic 字典式的
lexicographic algorithm 字典式算法
lexicographic enumeration 字典式枚举
lexicographic length-increasing order 辞典长度递增顺序
lexicographic order 辞典序,字典序
lexicographic scan 词典方式扫描
lexicographic sort 词典排序
lexicographic tree 字典树
lexicography information service 辞书编辑信息服务系统
lexicon 专门字典
lexics 词汇学
lexon 词子
lexonic alternation pattern 词子交替

模式
lexotatics 词子结构学
LF(Line Feed Character) 换行字符
LF(Line Frequency) 水平扫描频率,行频
LFSR(Linear Feedback Shift Register) 线性反馈移位寄存器
LFU(Least Frequently Used memory) 最近最少使用内存
LHA LHA压缩软件
LHARC LHARC压缩软件
LHN(Long-Haul Network) 远程输送网络
li li基准程序
Liapunov's direct method 李雅普诺夫直接法
libname 库名
librarian 程序库生成程序
librarian program 库管理程序
library 库
library allocation 库分配
library and information science abstracts 图书馆与信息学文摘数据库
library automation 图书馆自动化
library automation system 图书馆自动化系统
library call 库调用
library catalogs 图书目录
library command 库命令
library data base 图书馆数据库
library data processing 图书馆数据处
library directory 库目录
library facilities 库存设施
library file 库文件
library file editor 库文件编辑程序
library function 库函数
library item 库项
library link 库存链
library list 库表
library macro definition 库宏定义
library member 库成员
library migration table 库迁徙表
library module 库存模块,库模块
library name 库名
library network 图书馆网络
library object 库对象
library of congress machine readable catalog 国会图书馆机器可读目录数据库(美)
library of data 数据库存
library of lessons 课程程序库
library package 库软件包
library postlude 库尾部
library prelude 库序部
library program 库程序
library programming 库存规划
library public 公用程序库
library reference programming 引用库程序设计
library routine 库存例程
library subroutine 库存子程序
library tape 库存带
library template 库模板
library terminal 库终端
library text 库文本,库正文
library track 库存记录轨,目录磁道
library unit (Ada语言)库单位
library work area 库工作区
librious 库存的,文件管理程序库
license 许可证
License Option (NetWare)许可选项
licensed application program 特许应用程序
licensed documentation 特许文档
licensed material 特许资料
licensed program 特许程序
licensed publication 特许出版物
licensed purchased 已购买许可证
LIDE(LED InDirect Exposure) 发光二极管间接曝光(扫描仪技术)
lie detector 测谎器
life 寿命
life aging 寿命老化
life cycle 生存周期,生命期
life cycle cost analysis 生命周期成本分析
life cycle of database system 数据库系统生命周期
life cycle of information 信息生命周
life drift 寿命漂移
life expectancy 估计寿命
life profile 寿命轮廓
life science 生命科学
life span 生存期
life test 寿命试验

life type software 生命型软件
lifeline game 生命线对策
lifetime 生存期,寿命
lifetime curve 寿命曲线
lifetime prediction 寿命预测
LIFN(LANanalyzer for Netware) Netware 局域网分析程序(Novell)
LIFO(Last-In, First-Out) 后进先出
LIFO stack 后进先出堆栈
ligature 连字,连接
light 光;轻的,淡的
light-A A 指示灯
light absorption 光吸收
light accessible transistor matrix 光可存取的晶体管矩阵
light activated element 光敏元件
light beam deflector 光束偏转器
light beam stiffening 光束增强
light button 光钮
light conduit 光纤导管
light coupled device 光耦合器件
light deflection 光偏转
light detector 光检波器,光电控测器
light emitting diode(LED) 发光二极管
light-emitting diode display 发光二极管显示器
light face 轻体字,淡体字
light fatigue 光疲乏
light flux 光通量
light frequency modulation 光频率调制
light gray 淡灰色
light guide 光导
light guide communication 光导通信
light guide fiber 光导纤维
light gun 光枪,光笔
light measurement 光测量
light modulator 光调制器
light memory 光存储器
light object 光对象
light path 光程
light pen 光笔
light pen attention 光笔中断
light pen detection 光笔检测
light pen hit 光笔命中
light pen strike 光笔触击
light pen stroke 光笔选通
light pen tracking 光笔追踪

light pipe 光导管,光纤
light pulse compression technique 光脉冲压缩技术
light pulse modulation 光脉冲调制
light pulse repetition rate 光脉冲重复频率
light pulse width 光脉冲宽度
light quantum 光子
light ray 光线
light sensitive 光敏的
light sensor 光传感器
light source 光源
light spectrum 光谱
light stylus 光笔
light traffic link 低通信量链路
light valve 光阀,光调制器
light valve array 光阀阵列
light wave 光波
light wave communication 光波通信
light weight typewriter 轻便打印机
lighting model 光照模型
Lightweight Directory Access Protocol (LDAP) 轻型目录访问协议
lightweight process 轻量进程
Lightyear software pack Lightyear 软件包
like 类似的,相似的
like attribute 相似属性
like parity 同奇偶性
likelihood 似然性
likelihood criterion 似然准则
likelihood equation 似然方程
likelihood function 似然函数
likelihood ratio method 似然比法
likelihood-product vector 似然积向量
likeness 相似性
LILO(Last-In Last-Out) 后进后出
LILO(Linux LOader) Linux 加载程序
LIM EMS (Lotus-Intel-Microsoft Expanded Memory Specification) LIM 扩充内存规范
limit 极限,限界
limit address 界址
limit check 极限检查,极限测试
limit current circuit 限流电路
limit depth 极限深度
limit height 极限高度

limit in mean 平均极限
limit line spacing 极限行距
limit physical parallelism 有限物理并行性
limit priority 极限优先级,极限优先权
limit priority or range limit 限制优先权或范围限制
limit register 限界寄存器
limit superior 上极限
limit switch 限位开关
limit test 极限测试
limit value 极限值
limitation 界限
limited 限制的,有限
limited-access data 限制访问数据
limited acuity 有限敏锐度
limited aperture problem 有限孔径问题
limited availability 有限利用率
limited broadcasting address 有限广播地址
limited compute 有限计算
limited degree-of-freedom robot 有限自由度机器人
limited distance adapter 有限距离适配器
limited distance modem 有限距离调制解调器
limited distribution 有限分布
limited entry decision table 限定项判定表
limited fault 有限故障
limited feedback sensing 有限反馈传感
limited generic formal part 有限类属形式部分
limited infrared detector 有限红外检测器
limited integrator 受限积分器
limited page allocation 有限页面分配
limited private type 有限专用类型
limited prepositional reasoning 有限命题推理
limited purpose computer 有限功能计算机
limited reachability 有限可达性
limited recursion 有限递归
limited-resource link 有限资源链接
limited round-robin scheduling 有限轮转调度法

limited scanning 有限扫描
limited state model 有限状态模型
limited vocabulary comparison 有限词表比较
limited word index 有限词索引
limiter 限制器,限幅器
limiter circuit 限幅电路
limiting 限幅,削波
limiting control 极限控制,限界控制
limiting resolution 极限分辨率,极限清晰度
limits file 限界文卷,界限文件
linage 行数
linage counter 行计数器
Linda Linda 编程环境
line 行;线,线路
line access point 线路访问点,线路入口点
line adapter 线路适配器
line adapter unit 线路适配单元
line advance 换行
line amplifier 线路放大器
line analyzer 线路分析仪
line art 线画稿,线条图
line-at-a-time printer 行式打印机
line-at-a-time printing 行印
line balance 线路平衡
line balancing problem 生产线平衡问题
line blanking interval 行消隐期间
line buffer 线路缓冲器
line buffer control program 线路缓冲器控制程序
line buffer pool 线路缓冲池
line buffering 行缓冲
line cap 线端头
line character 换行字符
line chart 折线图
line chart autoformat 折线图自动套用格式
line clipping 线段剪取
line code 线路码
line coloring 线条着色
line command 行命令
line concentrator 线路集中器
line conditioning 线路制约,线路调节
line connectivity 边连通度
line control unit 线路控制单元
line control block 线路控制块

line control discipline 线路控制规程
line control procedures 线路控制过程
line controller 线路控制器
line copy 轮廓图副本
line counter 线计数器,行计数器
line coupler 线路耦合器
line covering number 边覆盖数
line data set 行式数据集
line delay 线路延迟
line delay register 延迟线寄存器
line delete character 删行字符
line delete symbol 删行符
line density 线密度
line discipline 线路规程
line display generator 线段显示发生器
line distortion 线路失真,线路畸变
line drawing 线提取,绘线图形
line drawing algorithms 绘图算法
line drawing display 绘线显示
line drive signal 行驱动信号
line driver 线路驱动器
line drop 行丢失;线缺失
line editing 行编辑
line editor 行编辑程序
line editor program 行编辑程序
line-end adjustment 行尾调整
line-end lock 行尾锁定
line-end zone 行尾区
line-ending zone 行结束区
line equalization 线路均衡
line equalizer 线路均衡器
line error 传输线路误差
line escapement 行操纵器
line feed 换行
line feed character 换行字符
line feed code 换行码
line feed time 换行时间
line finder 寻线器
line fitting 直线拟合
line flyback 线路回扫
line folding 行折返
line follower 线条跟踪器
line format item 行格式项
line frequency 行频
line graph 折线图;线绘图
line graphics 线划图形
line group 线群
line handshake 线路信号交换

line height 行高
line hit 线路干扰,传输线瞬断
line identification number 行识别号
line impedance 线路阻抗
line-in 线路输入
line-in use 线路占用
line independence number 边独立数
line index 行索引
line input 线路输入
line interface 线路接口
line interface base 线路接口基座
line interface hardware 线路接口硬件
line interlace 隔行扫描
line inversion 线反演
line item 行项,同行项
line iteration 线迭代
line justification 线合理性
line key 行键
line label 行标号
line length estimate 线长估算
line level 线路电平
line link 链路,线路
line load 线路负荷,线路负载
line logical fault 线路逻辑故障
line loss 线路损耗
line mask 线框模
line merge 行合并;线合并
line misregistration 行不重合,行位不正
line mode terminal 行式终端
line mute 线路静音
line noise 线路噪声
line number 行号,行编号;线数
line number editing 行号编辑
line of sight 视线
line of sight link 视线链路
line option 行任选项
line output 线路输出
line overrelaxation 行超松驰
line overrun 行超限
line pad 线路衰减器
line pairing 双线
line pattern 线条模式图案,线型
line pattern object 线型对象
line per inch 每英寸行数,行/英寸
line pitch 线间距
line printer 行式打印机
line printer controller 行式打印机控制器

line printing 行印
line private buffer 线路专用缓冲器
line procedure specification 线路操作过程说明
line protocol 线路协议,线路规程
line rate 线路速率
line receiver 线路接收器
line recovery 线路恢复
line receiver 线路接收器
line reference 线路标记
line relay 线路中继
line renumbering 重编行号
line replace command 行替换命令
line response mode 线路响应方式
line retry parameter 线路重执参数
line routine algorithm 线段布线算法
line ruler 行标尺,行标尺装置
line scanning 行扫描
line security 线路安全性
line segment 线段
line seizure 线路占用
line selector 线路选择器
line set 线组,线路集
line sharing device 线路共享设备
line sharing system 线路共享系统
line signaling 线路信令
line size option 行尺寸选项
line skew 线歪斜
line smoothing 线平滑
line space 行距
line space mechanism 行距调整机构
line space ratchet 行距束轮
line space selector 行距选择器,行距选择算子
line speed 线路速率,通道速率
line squeeze 空行挤压,空行压缩
line statement 行语句
line status 线路状态
line structure language 行结构语言
line style 线型样,行图形
line style or type 线条类型
line surge 线路浪涌电流
line switching 线路交换,线路转接
line sync pulse 行同步脉冲
line template 线模板 「器
line terminal controller 线路终端控制
line termination unit 线路终端单元
line tool 直线工具

line traffic 线路通信量
line transient 线路瞬变
line transmission 按行发送
line turnaround 线路换向
line turnaround delay 线路换向延迟
line type 线型,线条类型
line voltage 线路电压
line width 线条宽度；行宽
line zero pointer 第零行指针
linear 线性,线性的
linear acceleration ratio 线性加速比
linear actuator 线性执行机构
linear addressing 线性寻址
linear addressing architecture 线性寻址结构
linear analogue control 线性模拟控制
linear approximation 线性逼近
linear audio 线性音频
linear bit density 线性位密度
linear black box 线性黑箱
linear block code 线性分组码 「归
linear Boolean recursion 线性布尔递
linear bounded automaton(LBA) 线性有界自动机
linear bus(LBA) 直接总线
linear carriage head-positioning actuator 车载直线移动式磁头定位驱动器
linear cipher system 线性密码体制
linear classification 线性分类
linear classifier 线性分类器
linear code 线性码
linear combination 线性组合
linear complexity 线性复杂度 「法
linear congruential method 线性同余
linear context-free language 线性上下文无关语言
linear control 线性控制
linear control system 线性控制系统
linear convergence 线性收敛
linear damping 线性阻尼
linear deduction 线性演绎
linear dependence 线性相关
linear descriptor 线性描述符
linear detection 线性检测
linear discriminant function 线性判别函数
linear distortion 线性失真,线性畸变
linear equation 线性方程式

linear estimation 线性估计
linear extrapolation method 线性外推法
linear feature extraction 线性特征抽取
linear feedback shift register 线性反馈移位寄存器
linear filtering theory 线性滤波理论
linear finite automaton 线性有限自动机
linear function 线性函数
linear grammar 线性文法
linear growth process 线性增长过程
linear hashing 线性散列
linear hypothesis model 线性假设模型
linear increase backoff algorithm 线性增长回退算法
linear independence 线性独立,线性无关
linear inferences per second 每秒线性推理次数
linear insertion sort 线性插入排序
linear integer programming 线性整数规划
linear integrated circuit 线性集成电路
linear interpolation 线性插值
linear language 线性语言
linear least squares problem 线性最小二乘问题
linear list 线性表
linear-logarithmic intermediate-frequency amplifier 线性-对数中频放大器
linear machine 线性机
linear magnetostriction 线性磁致伸缩
linear mapping 线性映射
linear matching 线性匹配
linear model-following control system (LMFC) 线性模型跟踪控制系统
linear modulation 线性调制
linear modulator 线性调制器
linear motor 直线电机,直线马达
linear multistep method 线性多步法
linear network 线性网络
linear operational element 线性运算元件
linear optimal control 线性最优控制
linear optimization 线性最佳化,线性优化
linear order 线性序,全序
linear ordered relation 线性有序关系

linear ordered set 线性有序集
linear organization 线性组织方式
linear-phase 线性相位
linear pipeline 线性流水线
linear planning 线性规划
linear positioner 直线定位机构
linear prediction analysis 线性预测分析
linear predictive coding(LPC) 线性预测编码
linear probing 线性探查
linear processing technique 线性处理技术
linear program 线性程序
linear programming 线性规划
linear programming dual problem 线性规划的对偶问题
linear programming inequalities 线性规划不等式
linear quadratic regulator 线性二次型调节器
linear query 线性查询
linear quotient method 线性商法
linear recording 线性记录
linear recurrence 线性递归
linear regression 线性回归
linear regulator 线性稳压电源
linear rehash method 线性再散列法
linear representation 线性表示法
linear residue code 线性剩余码
linear resolution 线性消解
linear retrieval 线性检索
linear rule 线性规则
linear scale 线性标度
linear scanning 线性扫描
linear search 线性检索,线性查找
linear selection 线性选择
linear separable function 线性可分函数
linear separator 线性分离器
linear sequential circuit 线性时序电路
linear sequential machine 线性顺序机
linear smoothing 线性平滑
linear space 线性空间
linear speed-up theorem 线性加速定理
linear state feedback control law 线性状态反馈控制定律
linear structure 线性结构
linear subgraph 线性子图
linear subspace 线性子空间

linear substitution 线性代换
linear sweep 直线扫描
linear system 线性系统
linear system reduction method 线性系统简化法
linear system theory 线性系统理论
linear threshold 线性阈值
linear time algorithm 线性时间算法
linear time base 线性时基
linear time-lag system 线性时滞系统
linear-time simulation 线性时间模拟
linear transducer 线性传感器,线性换能器
linear transformation 线性变换
linear tree 线性树
linear unit 线性单元,线性器件
linear variety 线性变化
linear velocity transducer 线性速度传感器
linear version model 线性版本模型
linear voltage regulator 线性稳压器
linear weighted cell model 线性加权细胞模型
linearise 线性化
linearity 直线性,线性
linearity control 线性调态
linearity curve 线性曲线
linearity error 线性误差
linearization 线性化,直线化
linearizing ratio 线性化率,线性比
linefeed 换行「数
lines per inch 每英寸线数,每英寸行
lines per minute 每分钟行数
linguistic approximation 语言近似
linguistic model 语言模型
linguistic object 语言学对象
linguistic possibility 语言的可能性
linguistic truth value 语言的真理值
linguistic variable 语言变量
linguistics 语言学
linguistics knowledge representation 语言学知识表示
lining 划线
link 链接;链路
link access attribute 链路访问属性
Link Access Procedure(LAP) 链路访问过程
Link Access Protocol for Modems (LAPM) 调制解调器链路访问协议
link attribute 链路属性
link bit 链接位
link bit register 链接位寄存器
link button 链接按钮
link-by-link transfer 逐链转发方式
link checksum 链路校验和
link connection 链路连接
link control 链路控制
link data set 链式数据集
link downward 向下链接
link edit 链路编辑
link editor 连接编辑程序
link encryption 链路加密
link entry 链接项
link establishment 链路建立
LINK. EXE 链接执行程序
link failure 链路失效
link fault 链路故障
link field 连接字段
link fuse 线路保险丝
link group 链群,连接组
link header 链路头,链路标题
link in programming 程序设计中的连接程序
link indicator 连接指示器
link integrity verification test 链路一致性检验测试
link level 链路级
link library 链接库
link list 链表
link loader 链接装配程序
link loss 链路损耗
link management 链路管理
Link Manager Protocol(LMP) 链接管理协议
link map 链接映像
link name 链接名
link negotiation 链接协商
link object 链接对象
link overflow 链接溢出
link pack area 链接装配区
link pack area directory 链接装配区域目录
link pack area extension 链接装配区域扩展
link pack area library 链接装配区域程序库

link pack area queue 链接装配区域队列
link pack update area 链接装配更新区域
link pair 链路对
link pointer 链接指针
link primitive 链接原语
link problem determination aid 链路故障检测工具
link protocol 链路协议
link protocol converter 链路协议转换器
link protocol data unit 链路协议数据单位
link queue 链路排队
link redundancy level 链路冗余级
link rename 链路重命名
link repeater 链路转发器
link scheduler 链路调度程序
link segment 链接段
link sort 链接分类
link source 链接源
link state routing algorithm 链路状态路由算法
link station 链路站
link status signal unit 链路状态信号单元
link support layer 链路支持层
Link-Switch 链路交换器(3Com)
link test 链路测试
link time 链接时间,联编时间
link to link encipherment 线路加密
link to node 链接到节点
link to template 链接到模板
link topic 链接主题
link trace 链路跟踪
link trailer 链路尾标
link variable 链路变量
link word 链接字
linkable editor 可连接编辑器
linkable image 可连接映像
linkable program 可连接程序
linkage 链结,连接;联动
linkage computer 联动计算机
linkage convention 连接约定
linkage coroutine 连接共行例程
linkage editing 联动编辑,链接编辑
linkage editor 连接编辑程序
linkage fault 链接故障,联动故障

linkage instruction 链接指令
linkage interrupt 链接中断
linkage name 连接名,可行程序名称
linkage operation optimization 链接运算优化
linkage register 链接寄存器
linkage section 链接节
linkage segment 链接段
linked allocation 链接分配
linked file 链接的文件
linked list 链接表
linked list insertion sort 链表插入排序
linked object 链结对象
linked page 链页
linked pie/column graph 链结的圆饼/直条图
linked queue 链式队列
linked sequential file 链接顺序文件
linked set 链式集
linked stack 链式栈
linked subroutine 闭type子例程
linked to owner 链接到主文件
linker 链接程序
linking 连接过程
linking loader 连接装配程序
linking loader executive 链式装载器执行程序
Linotronic Linotronic 排版机
LINPACK benchmark LINPACK 基准程序
lint(Long Integer) 长整数
Linux Linux 操作系统(芬兰,Linus Torvalds,1991 年)
Liondop committee Liondop 委员会
LIP(Large Internet Packet) 大型互联网络信息包
lip 凸缘
lip-synch (动画中人物的)嘴唇同步
LIPS(Logical Inferences Per Second) 每秒逻辑推理次数
LIPS(Logical Instructions Per Second) 每秒逻辑指令数
liquid cooling 液体冷却
liquid core fiber 液芯光纤
liquid crystal 液晶
liquid crystal display 液晶显示器
liquid crystal printer 液晶打印机
liquid crystal shutters 液晶遮光板

liquid crystal switching printer(LCSP) 液晶光闸打印机
liquid phase epitaxial method 液相外延法
liquid source diffusion 液体源扩散
LIS(Log-In Security) 登录安全检查
Lisa 利沙计算机；利沙数据库
LISP(List Processing) 表处理；编目处理
LISP(List Processor) 表处理语言
LISP language 表处理语言，LISP语言
LISP machine LISP机器
LISP Object-Oriented Programming System LOOPS语言
LISP symbol LISP符号
LIST(LISTing) 列表
list 列表
list area 列表区
list box 列表框
list bullet 列表项目符号
list cell 表元，表目
list compacting 表紧缩
list count 列表内项目数
list cursor 编目光标
list-directed input 表式输入
list-directed input/output 表式输入输出
LIST DEVICES (NetWare)设备列表
list driven 表驱动的
list element 列表元素
list entry 输入序列
list event scheduling 列表事件调度
list handling statement 表处理语句
list index 列表索引
list inserting 表插入法
list name 名称列表
list notation 表记法
list of fonts 字体列表
list-oriented architecture 面向列表的体系结构
list parameter 列表参数
list pattern 列表模式
list price warranty 标价保修
list priority 列表优先级
list processing 列表处理
list processing language 表处理语言
list processing program 表处理程序
List Processor(LISP) 表处理语言，LISP语言
List recent pages 列出已浏览页
list scheduling 表格调度
list sorting 表排序
list structure 表结构
listbox 列表框
LISTDIR 目录列表
listed database files 已列表数据库文件
listen only 只听
listen while talk(LWT) 边讲边听
listener 收听站
listener address 收听站地址，收听者地址
listening mode 监听方式
listing 列表，列清单
Listserver 电子论坛
lit. (liter) 升
LIT(LITeral) 文字的
liter 升
literal 文字，字面量，基本式，句节
literal atom 文字原子
literal character string 原文字符串
literal constant 基本式常量，字面常量
literal data 文字型数据
literal meaning 字面意义
literal mode 文字方式
literal node 基本式节点，文字结点
literal order 文字指令
literal operands 文字操作数
literal pool 文字池
literal reference 文字引用
literal register 文字寄存器，常数寄存器
literal string 文字串
literal table 文字表
literal term 文字项
literal translation 直译，硬译
literary and linguistic index 文学与语言索引
literature search 文献查寻，文献检索
lithium battery 锂电池
lithography 平版印刷
litre 升
little endian 小尾数法，小序法
live chassis 带电机壳
live copy/paste 活的拷贝/剪贴
live data 活数据
live keyboard 活键盘
live load 工作负载，有用负载
live net 活网

live operation 有效操作
live program 正在运行的程序
live system 活系统
live window 活动窗口
live wire 负荷,负载;装入
liveboard 活板,电子黑板
livenet 活网
Livermore FORTRAN kernels Livermore FORTRAN 内核
liveware 人件,活件
living 生物的,活性的,起作用的
living clock 生物钟
living computer system 运行中的计算机系统
living model 生物模型
living system 活动系统
living system cybernetics 活动系统控制论
LL(Leased Line) 租用线,专线
LL(Local Line) 局部线路,本地线路
LL(1) method LL(1)分析法
LL(k) grammar LL(k)文法
LL(K) method LL(K)分析法
LLA(Leased Line Adapter) 租用线路适配器
LLC(Logical Link Control) 逻辑链路控制
LMA(Logic Machine Architecture) 逻辑机器体系结构
LME(Layer Management Entry) 层管理项
LMF(Language Media Format) 语言媒体格式
LMP(Link Manager Protocol) 链接管理协议
LN(Link Number) 链路编号
LNE(Local Network Emulator) 局域网络仿真器
load 加载;负载,负荷
load-and-go 程序加载且立即执行
load-and-go compiler 加载并执行编译程序
load balancing 负载均衡;加载平衡
load bind routine 加载联编程序
Load BIOS Defaults 加载 BIOS 默认
load capacity 负载容量 └值
load cell 负载传感器
load clear key 馈入清除键

load chart 负载分布图
load control 负载控制
load curve 负载曲线
load facility 馈入设备
load factor 馈入因子,装填因子,负载系数
load fault 加载故障
load image 负载映像图
load impedance 负载阻抗
load indicator 馈入指示器
load initial table 初始装入表
load key 加载键
load leveling 负载均衡
load life 负载生命期
load life 加载寿命
load line 加载线
load map 馈入图,加载映像
load matching 负载匹配
load mode 加载模式,装载方式
load module 装配模块
load module library 装配模块库
load normal key 馈入正常键
load on call 调用馈入
load origin 加载起始地址
load overlay segment 加载重叠段
load point 加载点,开始读写点
load program block(LPB) 馈入程序
load regulation 负载调节 └块
load request block 加载请求块
load routine 馈入程序
load rule 加载规则
load segment 加载段
Load Setup Defaults 加载预设默认值
load sharing 负载分担
load sharing facility(LSF) 负载分担系统
load test 加载试验
load time 加载时间,装载时间
load transfer 负载转移
load-transfer-acknowledgement signal 负载转移证实信号
load transfer signal 负载转移信号
loadable kernel module 可加载核心模
loadable module 可加载模块 └块
loaded line 加感线路,负载线路
loaded origin 加载起点,加载起始地
loaded state 加载状态 └址
loader 加载程序

loader routine 加载例程
loaders and linkage editors 加载链接编辑程序
loading 加载,加感
loading coil 加感线圈
loading error 加载错误,馈入错误
loading-location misuse errors 馈入位置滥用差错,加载定位误用说明
loading pattern 装填模式
loading procedure 装载过程
loading scatter 分散馈入
loading state 加载状态
loading user profile 加载用户配置文件
lobe 波瓣;环瓣
lobe attaching unit 环瓣连接单元
lobe bypass 环瓣旁路
local 局部的,本地的
local access network 局部存取网络
local account 本地账号
local acknowledgement 本地应答,局部响应
local address 本地[局部]地址
local address table configuration 本地[局部]地址表设置
local alias 本地别名
local application 局部应用程序
local area decision network 局域决策网络
local area network(LAN) 本地[局域]网络
local area network interconnection 局域网互连
local area network on bus topology 总线型局域网络
local area network on ring topology 环形拓扑局域网络
Local Area Transport(LAT) 局域传送协议
local assistance 本地支援
local association 局部相关
local autonomy 局部自主性
local batch job 本地成批作业
local batch processing 本地成批处理
local battery 局部电源
local buffer 局部缓存,本地缓存
local burst mode 局部突发模式
Local Bus 局部总线,本地总线
local bypass 局部旁路

local call 本地呼叫;局部调用
local central office 地区中心局,本地中心局
local channel 局部通道,本地信道
local cipher 局部(本地)加密
local clipboard 局部剪贴板
local clock 局部时钟
local code 局部代码
local computer network(LCN) 局部计算机网络
local concept subschema 局部概念子模式
local connectivity 局部连通度
local control 局部控制方式
local convergence 局部收敛
local coordinate 局部坐标
local criterion 局部判据
local data base 局部数据库,本地数据库
local data base management system(LDBMS) 局部数据库管理系统
local destination 局部终点
local diagnosis 局部诊断
local discard policy 局部废弃策略
local distributed data interface(LDDI) 局域分布式数据接口
local distribution service 近程分配服务
local domain name 局部域名
local drive 本地磁盘驱动器
local echo 本地回应
local entity 局部实体
local environment 局部环境
local equalize 局部均衡
local exchange center 本地交换中心
local extremum 局部极值
local fault 局部故障
local file 本地文件
local flag 局部标记
local format control buffer(LFCB) 局部格式控制缓冲器
local format storage 局部格式存储
local forms control 局部格式控制
local gray-level operation 局部灰度处理
local group 本地组,局部组
local histogram 局部直方图
local host 本地主机
local identifier 局部标识符
local improvement 局部改进
local index 本地索引

local key 局部键
local knowledge 局部知识
local line 局部线路,市内线路
local-local link 局部-局部链,本地-本地链路
local lock 局部封锁,局部锁
local loop 局部回路,市内回路
Local Management Interface(LMI) 本地管理界面
local manual power off 本地手工断电
local mapping transparency 局部映射透明性
local maximum 局部最大值
local memory 局部内存,本机内存
local mesh refinement 局部网格细化
local microcode compaction 局部微码压缩
local minimum 局部最小值
local minimizing point 局部极小值点
local mode 局部方式,本地方式
local modem 本地调制解调器
local NCP(local network control program) 局域网络控制程序
local network control program 局域网络控制程序
local network reference model 局域网络参考模型
local node 本地节点
local non-SNA major node 局部非SNA大节点
local number 本地号码
local office 市内电话局
local operation 局部运算
local optimal solution 局部最优解
local optimization 局部优化
local or own type 局部或固有类型
local output 本地输出
local PIN 局部个人识别码
local power on 本地手工加电
local printer 本地打印机
local processor 局部处理器
local recovery 局部恢复
local redundancy 局部冗余
local-remote link 本地远程链路
local replacement 局部置换
local replication mechanism 本地复制机制
local resource 本地资源

local result 局部结果
local root foldert 本地根文件夹
local search 局部搜索
local security 本地安全性
local segment 局部段
local server 本地服务器
local service area 本地服务区;市话服务区
local session identification(LSID) 本地会话识别
local shared resources 局部[本地]共享资源
local site 本地网站 「点
local SNA major node 本地SNA大节
local solution 局部解
local specification 局部说明
local stability 局部稳定性
local stack 本机堆栈,局部栈
local station 本地站
local storage 局部存储器
local symbol 局部符号
local system 本地系统,局部系统
local system queue area(LSQA) 本地系统队列区域
local terminal 本地[局部]终端
local title 本地标题 「库
local topology database 局部拓扑数据
local transaction 本地事务处理
local update procedure 本地更新过程
local variable 局部变量 「明
local variable declaration 局部变量说
local variable symbol 局部变量符号
local view 局部[本地]视图
local virtual protocol 本地虚拟协议
local workstation 本地工作站
locale 本地术语集
localhost 本地主机
locality 局部性
locality predication 局部推算
localization 本地化
localization of faults 故障定位
locally optimal plan 局部最优方案
LocalTalk 局部会话
locate 定位
locate chain 定位链
locate directory 确定目录位置
locate mode 定位方式
locate search 定位搜索

locate setup file 查找安装文件
location 存储单元
location accuracy 定位精度
location case 地点角色,地点格
location constants 单元常数
location counter 位置计数器
location delimiter 存储区定界符
location-free procedure 与位置无关的程序
location holes 定位孔
location identifier 存储区[位置]标识符
location independent 与位置无关的
location license 场地特许
location life 存储单元[位置]寿命
location mode 定位方式
location mode data item 定位方式数据项
location name 位置名
location of zeros of polynomial 多项式根界
location pin 定位销
location transparency 地点透明性
locational analysis 配置分析
locational model 配置模型
locator 定位器
locator device 定位输入装置
locator qualification 定位器限定
locator variable 定位[位置]变量
lock 锁,锁定
lock ashore 锁定点
lock and key protection 锁和钥匙的保护
lock cell 锁定单元格
lock hierarchy 锁的分层结构
lock image 封锁图像
lock-in synchronism 锁定同步
lock key 锁定键
lock mode 锁定方式
lock-on 锁住
lock-out 封锁,切断
lock queue 锁定队列
lock register 锁定寄存器
lock resolution 锁归结,锁消解
lock step 锁步
lock text 锁定正文
lock up 锁住,锁死
lock value block 锁值块
lock workstation 锁定工作站
locked field 封锁字段
locked file 上锁[加锁]文件
locked keyboard 被锁键盘
locked name 被锁名字,锁定名
locked page 锁定页
locked record 锁定记录
locked region 被锁定区域
locked resource 被锁资源
locked volume 被锁卷
locking 同步,锁定
locking a page in memory 锁定内存页面
locking a page in working set 锁定工作集页面
locking device 锁定装置
locking escape 锁定换码[转义]符
locking-shift character 封锁换码字符
lockout 封锁
lockout switch 闭锁开关
LOFS(LOopback File System) 回送文件系统
LOG(Logging) 登录
log 注册
log control table 记录控制表
log data set 登录数据集
log detailed events 记录详细事件
log-down 注销,取消注册
log file 日志文件
log-in 注册,登记
log in/off 连通/结束注册
log-in script 登录脚本,入网底稿
log-in security 登录保密
log-off 注销
log-on 注册,登录
log-on file 登录文件
log-out 注销,退出系统
log sequence number 记录序号
log setting 日志设置
log sum algorithm 对数和算法
log tape write head 对数磁带写头
logarithmic axis 对数轴
logarithmic complexity 对数复杂性
logarithmic contrast 对数反差
logarithmic graph 对数图
logarithmic measure 对数度量
logarithmic scale 对数刻度
logarithmic search method 对数查找法
logarithmic transformation 对数变换
logged resource 已登录资源
logger 登录器,注册器

logger task 登录任务
logging 登录,日志
logging list 登录列表,填表
logging service facility 登录服务功能
LOGIC LOGIC语言
logic add 逻辑加
logic address 逻辑地址
logic algebra 逻辑代数
logic analysis 逻辑分析
logic analyzer 逻辑分析仪
logic array 逻辑阵列
logic-based data language 基于逻辑的数据语言
logic-based language 基于逻辑的语言
logic-based method 基于逻辑的方法
logic behavior 逻辑特性
logic bomb 逻辑炸弹
logic box 逻辑框
logic calculus 逻辑演算
logic cell array 逻辑单元阵列
logic chart 逻辑流程图
logic chip 逻辑芯片
logic circuit 逻辑电路
logic comparator 逻辑比较器
logic comparison 逻辑比较
logic-controlled sequential computer 逻辑控制时序计算机
logic convention 逻辑约定
logic coordination method 逻辑组配法
logic decision table 逻辑判定表
logic decoder 逻辑译码器
logic design 逻辑设计
logic design automation 逻辑设计自动化
logic device 逻辑设备
logic diagram 逻辑图
logic difference 逻辑差
logic element 逻辑元件
logic entity 逻辑实体
logic equation simulation 逻辑方程模拟
logic error 逻辑错误
logic event 逻辑事件
logic expression 逻辑表达式
logic fault 逻辑故障
logic file 逻辑文件
logic flexibility 逻辑灵活性,逻辑柔性
logic flow 逻辑流
logic flowchart 逻辑流程图
logic function 逻辑函数,逻辑功能
logic gate 逻辑门
logic hazard 逻辑冒险
logic high 逻辑高电平
logic inference machine 逻辑推理机
logic instruction 逻辑指令
logic interface 逻辑接口
logic inverter 逻辑反相器
logic level 逻辑电平
logic level simulation 逻辑级仿真
logic light 逻辑指示灯
logic line group 逻辑线路组
logic link layer 逻辑链路层
logic low 逻辑低电平
logic machine architecture 逻辑机器体系结构
logic map 逻辑图;逻辑映像
logic model 逻辑模型
logic multiply 逻辑乘
logic operation 逻辑运算,逻辑操作
logic-oriented architecture 面向逻辑的体系结构
logic-oriented design system (LODS) 与逻辑有关的设计系统
logic oscilloscope 逻辑示波器
logic partitioning 逻辑划分
logic polarity 逻辑极性
logic primitive 逻辑基元
logic probe 逻辑探头,逻辑探针
logic probe indicator 逻辑探头指示器
logic product 逻辑乘积
logic product gate 逻辑乘门
logic programming 逻辑程序设计
logic record 逻辑记录
logic seeking printer 逻辑搜索打印机
logic sequence 逻辑序列
logic shift 逻辑移位
logic short fault 逻辑短路故障
logic simulation 逻辑模拟
logic state analyzer 逻辑状态分析器
logic sum 逻辑和
logic sum gate 逻辑和门
logic swing 逻辑摆幅
logic symbol 逻辑符号
logic synthesis 逻辑综合
logic testing 逻辑测试
Logic Theorist LT学习程序
logic thought 逻辑思维

logic timing analyzer 逻辑时序分析仪
logic track address register 逻辑磁道地址寄存器
logic unit 逻辑单元
logic verification system 逻辑检验系统
logic zero 逻辑零
logical 逻辑的
logical access control 逻辑访问控制
logical access level 逻辑存取级,逻辑访问层
logical access path 逻辑存取路径
logical access path network 逻辑存取路径网络
logical access path structure 逻辑存取路径结构
logical action 逻辑动作,逻辑作用
logical address 逻辑地址
logical algebra 逻辑代数
logical analysis 逻辑分析
logical axiom 逻辑公理
logical block 逻辑块,逻辑单元
logical block access(LBA) 逻辑块存取
logical block address(LBA) 逻辑块地址
logical block number 逻辑块号
logical channel 逻辑信道
logical channel group number(LCGN) 逻辑信道组号
logical channel identifier 逻辑通道标识
logical channel number(LCN) 逻辑信道号
logical character delete symbol 逻辑字符删除符号
logical chart 逻辑流程图
logical child segment 逻辑子女段
logical circuit 逻辑电路,逻辑线路
logical cohesion 逻辑内聚
logical combination 逻辑组合
logical comparison 逻辑比较
logical compatibility 逻辑兼容性
logical compression 逻辑压缩
logical connection terminal 逻辑连接终端
logical connective 逻辑连接
logical consequence 逻辑结果
logical constant 逻辑常数
logical construction 逻辑构造
logical conversion 逻辑转换
logical data 逻辑型数据
logical data base 逻辑数据库
logical data base record 逻辑数据库记录
logical data independence 逻辑数据独立性
logical data structure 逻辑数据结构
logical data transmission 逻辑数据传输
logical decision 逻辑判断,逻辑决策
logical design 逻辑设计
logical design for database 数据库逻辑设计
logical device 逻辑设备
logical device address 逻辑设备地址
logical device list 逻辑设备表
logical device name 逻辑设备名
logical device order 逻辑装置指令
logical device table 逻辑设备表
logical diagram 逻辑图
logical difference 逻辑差
logical drive 逻辑驱动器
logical edit 逻辑编辑
logical element 逻辑元素,逻辑元件
logical element symbol 逻辑元件符号
logical equivalence 逻辑等价
logical escape symbol 逻辑转义符号
logical expression 逻辑表达式
logical factor 逻辑因子
logical fault 逻辑故障,逻辑错误
logical field descriptor 逻辑字段说明符
logical file 逻辑文件
logical flowchart 逻辑流程图
logical format 逻辑格式化
logical frame 逻辑框架
logical function 逻辑函数
logical group 逻辑组
logical group instruction 逻辑指令集
logical group number 逻辑组号
logical image 逻辑图像
logical implication 逻辑隐含,逻辑蕴含
logical inclusion 逻辑包含
logical indicator 逻辑指示符
logical inference per second(LIPS) 每秒逻辑思维步数,每秒逻辑推理次数
logical input device 逻辑输入设备
logical input/output 逻辑输入/输出
logical input/output control system 逻

辑输入/输出控制系统
logical instruction 逻辑指令
logical join 逻辑联结
logical leading end 逻辑前端
logical level of a structure member 结构成员的逻辑层次
logical line 逻辑行
logical line delete symbol 逻辑行删除符号
logical line end symbol 逻辑行结束符
logical line group 逻辑线路组
logical link 逻辑连接
logical link control(LLC) 逻辑链路控制
logical link control and adaptation protocol(L2CAP) 逻辑链路控制与自适应协议
logical link control protocol 逻辑链路控制协议
logical link control sublayer 逻辑链路控制子层
logical link path 逻辑连接路径
logical logging 逻辑登录
logical message 逻辑消息,逻辑报文
logical mistake 逻辑错误
logical model 逻辑模型
logical module 逻辑模块
logical monotonicity 逻辑单调性
logical name 逻辑名
logical network 逻辑网络
logical number 逻辑编号
logical operation 逻辑运算
logical operators 逻辑操作符,逻辑算子
logical output device 逻辑输出设备
logical overlap coefficient 逻辑重叠系数
logical overlay 逻辑覆盖
logical page 逻辑页面
logical page identifier 逻辑页标识符
logical page number 逻辑页号
logical paging 逻辑分页
logical palette 逻辑调色板
logical parallelism 逻辑并行性
logical parent 逻辑亲体,逻辑双亲
logical parent segment 逻辑双亲段
logical partition 逻辑分区
logical pointer 逻辑指示字
logical primary 逻辑初等量
logical product 逻辑乘积

logical programming language 逻辑编程语言
logical race 逻辑竞态
logical reasoning 逻辑推理
logical record 逻辑记录
logical relation 逻辑关系
logical relationship 逻辑联系
logical representation 逻辑表示
logical resource 逻辑资源
logical schema 逻辑模式
logical segment 逻辑段
logical semantic term relation 逻辑语义项关系
logical sequence method 逻辑顺序法
logical shift 逻辑移位
logical shift left 逻辑左移
logical shift right 逻辑右移
logical space 逻辑空间
logical statement 逻辑语句
logical storage 逻辑存储器
logical storage address 逻辑存储器地址
logical storage structure 逻辑存储结构
logical structure 逻辑结构
logical stuck-fault model 逻辑固定型故障模型
logical sum 逻辑和
logical swapping 逻辑对换,逻辑换出换入
logical switch 逻辑开关
logical symbol 逻辑符号
logical system 逻辑系统
logical term 逻辑项
logical terminal 逻辑终端
logical terminal subpool 逻辑终端子池
logical theorem 逻辑定理
logical thinking 逻辑思维
logical thread 逻辑威胁
logical tracing 逻辑跟踪
logical track 逻辑磁道
logical truth 逻辑永真式,逻辑真
logical type 逻辑型
logical unit 逻辑单元
logical unit connection test 逻辑单元连接测试
logical unit services 逻辑单元服务
logical unit type 6.2(LU 6.2) 6.2型逻辑单元
logical value 逻辑值

logical variable 逻辑变量
logical view 逻辑视图
logical volume 逻辑卷
logical work station 逻辑工作站
logically connected terminal 逻辑连接终端
logically structured query 逻辑结构查询
login 注册,进入系统
login command 登录命令
login directory 注册目录
login information 注册信息
login name 注册名
login prompt 注册提示符
login request 注册请求
login script 入网底稿,登录原稿
login session 登录对话
login setup 登录设置
login shell 登录界面
login string 记入字串
login time 登录时间
logistic support system 后期保障系统
logistic time 保障时间
LOGLISP LOGLISP语言
LOGO LOGO教学语言
logo screen 问候画面
logoff 注销,退出系统
logon 注册,登录
logon data 注册数据
logon domain 登录域
logon hours 登录时间
logon interpret routine 登录解释例程
logon message 注册信息
logon mode 注册模式
logon mode table 注册模式表
logon procedure 登录过程
logon request 登录请求
logon restriction 登录限制
logon script 注册稿本,登录脚本
logon security 注册安全
logon server 登录服务器
LOGOS 控制中心型设计法
logout 注销,退出,撤消登记
long card 长卡
long citation 长引文
long comment 长注释
Long Date Format 日期长格式
long-distance copying 远程拷贝
long-distance local 本地长距离站

long-distance loop 长途环路
long-distance xerography 远距离复印技术
long-distance Xerox(LDX) 远距离静电印刷术
long filename 长文件名
long-haul modem 远程调制解调器
long-haul network 远程网络
long instruction computer 长指令计算机
long integer 长整数
long line effect 长线效应
long message 长消息,长报文
long name 长名称
long offset addressing 长偏移量寻址
long persistence phosphor 长余辉荧光体
long persistence screen 长余辉屏幕
long precision 长精度
long range forecast 长期预报
long short 广角拍摄
long span transmission 大跨度传输
long string 长串
long-term bit error rate 长期位码误率
long-term entry identifier 长期项目标识符
long term fix area 长期固定区域
long term memory 长期记忆
long-term scheduler 长期调度程序
long transaction 长事务
long vector 长向量
long word 长字
longest common subsequence 最长公共子序列
longest path 最长路径
longitudinal check 纵向校验
longitudinal judder 纵向抖动
longitudinal lines 纵向线条
longitudinal magnetic recording 纵向磁记录
longitudinal parity check 纵向奇偶校验
longitudinal redundancy 纵向冗余
longitudinal redundancy check character 纵向冗余校验字符
longitudinal scan 纵向扫描
longitudinal transmission check 纵向传输校验
look ahead 预测先行,超前
look-ahead analysis 先行分析

look-ahead carry generator 超前进位产生器
look-ahead control 预测控制,超前控制
look-ahead field 先行字段
look-ahead slice 超前控制片
look-and-feel 外视感觉
look-aside buffer 旁视缓冲区
look-aside register 旁视寄存器
look-through 通阅,浏览
look-up 查表
look-up choice region 查看选择区
look-up choice representation 查看选择展示(项)
look-up list 查看表
look up table 查用表
loop 循环;回路,环路
loop actuating signal 回路启动信号
loop adapter 回路适配器
loop animation 循环动画制作
loop body 循环体
loop check 环路校验,回送校验
loop clause 循环子句
loop compilation 循环编译
loop computing 循环计算
loop construct 循环结构
loop control 循环控制
loop control instruction 循环控制指令
loop control statement 循环控制语句
loop control structure 循环控制结构
loop control variable 循环控制变量
loop counter 循环计数器
loop end 循环结束
loop feed-back signal 回路反馈信号
loop-free microprogram 无循环微程序
loop gain 环路增益
loop index 循环变址
loop initialization 循环预置,循环初始化
loop input signal 回路输入信号
loop invariant 循环不变量
loop inversion 循环反演,循环逆程
loop jack switch board 回路插座板
loop nesting 循环嵌套
loop operation 循环操作
loop optimization 循环优化
loop output signal 循环输出信号
loop parameter 循环参数
loop restriction 循环约束
loop restructuring technique 循环重构技术
loop reversal 循环倒换
loop statement 循环语句
loop start 回路起动
loop station connector(LSC) 回路站连接器
loop stop 循环停机
loop structure 循环结构
loop termination 循环结束
loop testing 循环检查
loop topology 循环拓扑结构
loop transfer frame 回路传输结构
loop transfer function 回路传递函数
loop transmission 回路传输,环形传输
loop transmission frame 环路传输帧
loop unrolling 循环展开
loop update 回路更新
loop wiring concentrator(LWC) 环形线路集中器
loopback 回归,回送
loopback address 回送地址
loopback checking 回送校验
loopback checking system 回送校验系统
loopback plug 回送连接头
loopback point 环回点,回送点
loopback test 回送检查
looped outlet 回路引出线
loophole 漏洞
looping 循环
looping execution 循环执行
loose consistency 松散一致性
loose constraint 松驰约束
loose-coupled parallel computer 松耦合并行计算机
loose line 稀疏行
loose list 松驰表
loose replicatable complex frame 松散可重复的复数框架
loose replicatable digit frame 松散可重复的数字框架
loose replicatable exponent frame 松散可重复的指数框架
loose replicatable point frame 松散可重复的小数点框架
loose replicatable suppressible character frame 松散可重复的可删除字符

框架
loose synchronization 松散同步
looseleaf 活页
loosely-coupled 松散耦合的
loosely coupled computer 松耦合计算机
loosely coupled multiprocessing 松耦合多元处理系统
loosely organized system(LOS) 松散组织的系统
loosely related 松散关联的
LOP(Line-Oriented Protocol) 线路专用协议
loss 损耗,衰减
loss failure period 老化失效期
loss function 损失函数
loss matrix 损失矩阵
loss of control 失去控制
loss of frame alignment detector 帧失位检测器
loss of significance 有效数字损失
lossless channel 无损耗信道
lossless compression 无损压缩
lossless join 无损连接
lossless line 无损耗线
lossy compression 有损压缩
lost call 呼损,未接通呼叫
lost chain 漏失串链
lost cluster 丢失簇
lost focus 失去焦点
lost time 损失时间
lost traffic 损失业务量
lot number 批号
lot size 批量
lot size scheduling 批量问题
Lotus 1-2-3 Lotus 1-2-3 多功能软件
LOTUS 1-2-3-4-5 LOTUS 1-2-3-4-5 组合软件
Lotus 1-2-3 for Windows 窗口环境下的 Lotus 表格软件
Lotus Add-in Toolkit 功能添加工具
Lotus cc:Mail cc:Mail 电子邮件系统
Lotus Development Corp. Lotus 公司
Lotus-Intel-Microsoft Expanded Memory Specification(LIM EMS) LIM 扩充内存规范
Lotus menu Lotus 菜单
Lotus Notes Notes 群件
Lotus SmartSuite SmartSuite 套件

loudness 音量
loudspeaker 扬声器
louver 百叶窗
low activity data processing 低活动率数据处理
low address protection 低端地址保护
low-asserted 低电平表示的
low body cabinet 卧式机箱
low cost code 低成本码
low disparity code(LDC) 低差别编码
low end MPU 低档微型计算机装置
low end products 低价位产品,低档产品
low entry networking(LEN) 低级入口联网
low-frequency 低频
low function terminal 低性能终端
low impedance path 低阻抗通路
low level 低电平;低水平的;低级的
low-level code continuity check 低级码/连续性检查
low level exclusive 低级互斥
low level firmware 低级固件
low level format 低级格式化
low level language 低级语言
low level logic 低电平逻辑
low level protocol 低级规程
low-level scheduling 低级调度
low-level software 低级软件
low operand 下界操作数
low-order bit 低序位,低位
low order character 低位字符
low order digit 低位数
low order end 低位端
low order position 低位位置
low overhead time-sharing system 低开销分时系统
low pass filter 低通滤波器
low point 低点
low-priority ready queue 低优先级就绪队列
low resolution 低分辨率
low resolution self-scan pattern recognition 低分辨率自扫描模式识别
low speed 低速
low speed printer 低速打印机
low speed storage 低速存储器
low speed transmission 低速传输

low temperature shutdown 低温断电
low temperature warning 低温报警
low threshold 低阈值
low toner indicator "墨粉(水)不足"指示器
low voltage indicator 低电压指示器
low watermark 浅淡水印
lower acceptance value 下限接受值
lower binding 下层绑定,下层联编
lower bound 下界
lower broadcast state 下播状态
lower CASE 下端计算机辅助软件工程
lower case 小写
lower envelope 下部包络
lower layer protocol 下层协议
lower level interrupt 较低级中断
lower level node 下层网点
lower level problem 较低级问题
lower limit register 下界寄存器
lower node 下层节点
lower paper tray 下层纸匣
lower priority group 低优先权组
lower priority job 低优先级作业
lower real-time simulation 欠实时仿真
lower sideband 下边带
lower stack bound pointer 堆栈下限指针
lower stack limit 堆栈下界
lower stream 下层流
lower triangular matrix 下三角矩阵
lower window edge 窗口下界
lowercase 小写字母
lowering the typing line 下移打印行
lowest common denominator 最小公分母
lowest common multiple 最小公倍数
lowest level routine 最低级程序
lowest order 最低位
lowest point 最低点
lowest priority 最低优先权
lowest term 最小项
lozenge 棱形
LP(Line Printer) 行式打印机
LP(Line Protocol) 线路规程
LP(List Processing) 表处理
LPA(Link Pack Area) 链接装配区
LPA(Logical Pack Area) 逻辑装配区
LPC(Linear Predictive Coding) 线性预测编码
LPN(Logical Page Number) 逻辑页号
LPT(Line Print Terminal) 行式打印机终端
LQP(Letter Quality Printer) 铅字质量打印机
LR(Line Receiver) 线路接收器
LR(Logical Record) 逻辑记录
LR algorithm LR算法
LR method LR分析法
LR(0) grammar LR(0)文法
LRC(Longitudinal Redundancy Check Character) 纵向冗余校验字符
LR(k) grammar LR(k)文法
LRS LRS专家系统
LRU(Least Recently Used) 最近最少使用的
LSB(Least Significant Bit) 最低有效位
LSCN(Load Sharing Computer Network) 负载均衡计算机网络
LSF(Load Sharing Facility) 负载共享系统软件
LSI-11 microprocessor LSI-11微处理器
LSPIT(Laser Shot Photographic & Imaging Technology) 激光点射成像技术(佳能)
LSR(Local-Shared Resources) 局部共享资源
LTM(Local Transactions Manager) 局部事物管理程序
LTU(Line Termination Unit) 线路终端装置
LU(Logical Unit) 逻辑单元
LU connection test 逻辑单元连接测试
LU decomposition 逻辑单元分解
LU factorization 逻辑单元分解法
LU-LU session initiation 逻辑单元间对话开始
LU-LU session termination 逻辑单元间对话终止
LU-LU session type 逻辑单元对话类型
LU-LU session type 0 0型逻辑单元间会话
LU-LU session type 1 1型逻辑单元间会话
LU-LU session type 2 2型逻辑单元

LU-LU session type 3 3型逻辑单元间会话
LU-LU session type 4 4型逻辑单元间会话
LU-LU session type 6 6型逻辑单元间会话
LU-LU session type 7 7型逻辑单元间会话
LU services manager 逻辑单元服务管理程序
LUB(Least Upper Board) 最小上界
lubricated magnetic disk 润滑磁盘
Lucifer 罗斯福密码
LUE(Link Utilization Efficiency) 链路利用效率
lug 接线柱;柄,把手
luggable computer 便携式计算机
Lukasiewicz notation 路卡兹维克记法
lumen (光通量单位)流明
Lumena Lumena绘画程序
luminance 发光率,亮度
luminance compensation 亮度补偿
luminosity 光亮度
luminous flux 光通量
luminous intensity 发光强度
lumped element 集总参数元件
lumped loading 集总加载
lumped model 集总模型
lumped network 集总网络
lumped parameter approximation 集总参数近似
lumped parameter delay line 集总参数延迟线
lumped parameter system 集总参数系统
LUN(Logical Unit Number) 逻辑单元号
LUS(Language Understanding System) 语言理解系统
LUS(Logical Units) 逻辑单元
LUS(Logical Unit Services) 逻辑单元服务
LUT(Look-Up tables) 查看表
lux 勒克斯(照度单位)
luxmeter 照度计
luxurious version 豪华版本
LV(Laser Video) 激光视盘
LV(Linear Velocity) 线性速度
LVA(Local Virtual Address) 本地虚地址
lvalue(left value) 左值
LVF(Linear Vector Function) 线性向量函数
LVT(Linear Velocity Transducer) 线性速度传感器
LVM(Logical Volume Manager) 逻辑卷管理程序
LWB(LoWer Bound) 下界
LWP(LightWeight Process) 轻载过程
LX-7400 LX-7400网络系统(东芝)
Lycos Lycos网点
LZW encoding(Lempel-Ziv-Welch encoding) LZW编码方法
LZW decoding(Lempel-Ziv-Welch decoding) LZW译码方法

M m

M(Mega) 兆,10^6,2^{20}
m(meter) 米
M(Micro) 微,百万分之一
m(milli) 毫
M(Million) 兆,百万
M2 M2微处理器(Cyrix)
M3 M3微处理器(Cyrix,1999年)
m-ary information element m项信息
m-ary signaling m元信号传输
m-derived filter m分支滤波器
M-matrix M矩阵
M-motion M-motion平台
M-O effect 磁-光效应
M out of N code N中取M代码
M-S(Master-Slave) 主-从
mA(milliAmpere) 毫安
MA(Multiple Access) 多路存取
Mac(Macintosh) 麦金塔计算机(苹

果)
MAC(Machine Aided Cognition) 机器辅助识别
MAC(Media Access Control) 媒体访问控制子层
MAC(Multi Application Computer) 多用途计算机
MAC(Multiplexed Analog Component) 多重模拟分量
MAC bridge algorithm(Media Access Control driver) 媒体访问控制桥路算法
MAC driver(Media Access Control driver) 媒体访问控制驱动程序
MAC layer bridge(Media Access Control driver) 媒体访问控制层桥路
MAC protocol(Media Access Control driver) 媒体访问控制协议
Mac to midrange Macintosh机到中型机连接
MacAPPC Macintosh程序间通信软件(苹果)
MacBinary MacBinary文件传送协议(苹果)
MacDFT(Macintosh Distributed Function Terminal) Macintosh分布式功能终端软件(苹果)
MacDraw Pro MacDraw Pro绘画程序(苹果)
Mach Mach操作系统
Mach band 马赫带
machinable 机器可读的,机器可用的
machinable medium 机器可用媒体
machine 机器
machine address 机器地址
machine address instruction 机器地址指令
machine aided retrieval(MAR) 机器辅助检索
machine-aided translation(MAT) 计算机辅助翻译
machine architecture 机器体系结构
machine available time 机器可用时间
machine charge 机器负荷
machine check handler(MCH) 机器故障检查处理程序
machine-check indicator 机器检验指示器

machine check interruption(MCI) 机器检查中断
machine check masking 机器检查屏蔽
machine check record 机器检查记录
machine class 机器类
machine code 机器码
machine code instruction 机器码指令
machine code programming 机器码编程
machine cognition 机器认知,机器识别
machine-collating sequence 机器归并顺序
machine composition 机器排字,机器拼版
machine computation 机器计算
machine configuration 计算机配置
machine configuration record 机器配置记录
machine control unit 机器控制单元
machine cycle(MC) 机器周期
machine cycle time 机器周期时间
machine datum 机器基点
machine dependent 与机器相关的
machine-dependent language 机器相关语言
machine-dependent optimization 与机器相关的优化
machine dictionary 机器词典
machine discovery 机器发现
machine equation 机器方程
machine equivalence 机器等价
machine error 机器误差
machine failure 机器失效,机器故障
machine-independent operating system 与机器无关的操作系统
machine independent programming 与机器无关的程序设计
machine-independent solution 机器无关解
machine learning rule 机器学习规则
machine malfunction 机器故障
machine notation 机器表示法
machine-oriented language 面向机器的语言
machine-processible media 机器可处理媒体
machine-proof 机器证明
machine-readable information 机器可

读信息
machine reasoning 机器推理
machine recognizable 机器可识别的
machine run 机器运行
machine script 机器字迹,机器可读数据
machine searchable information 机器可检索信息
machine sensible 机器可感测的,机器可读的
machine sensible information 机器可读信息
machine shorthand 机器速记
machine-spoiled time 机器浪费时间
machine spoiled work-time 机器工时损失
machine storage pool 机器存储池
machine time 机器时间
machine-tool control 机床控制
machine translation(MT) 机器翻译
machine translation support system 机器翻译支持系统
machine translation system 机器翻译系统
machine-usable form 机器可用形式
machine vision 机器视觉
machine vision inspection system 机器视觉检测系统
machine word 机器字
machineability 可加工性
machinery isolation 机械隔离
machinery mount 机械支架(底座)
machining （机械）加工
machining accuracy 加工精度
machining center 加工中心
machining complex 加工系统
machining cost 机械加工成本
machining data bank 加工数据库
machining data bank system 加工数据库系统
machining error 加工误差
Macintosh 麦金塔个人计算机(苹果)
MacintoshⅡ 麦金塔Ⅱ计算机
Macintosh Classic 麦金塔 Classic 计算机
Macintosh Client 麦金塔客户机
Macintosh File System Macintosh 文件系统
Macintosh user interface Macintosh 用户界面
MacIRAM MacIRAM通信板
MACLIB(MACroLIBrary) 宏程序库
MacLink Plus Maclink＋程序
MacOS MacOS操作系统(苹果)
MacPaintⅡ MacPaintⅡ绘画程序
MacPC MacPC仿真软件
Macpppp Macpppp驱动程序
MACRO(MACROassembler) 宏汇编程序
macro 宏
macro architecture design 宏体系结构设计
macro argument 宏变元,宏参量
macro assembler 宏汇编程序
macro assembly processor 宏汇编处理程序
macro assembly program(MAP) 宏汇编程序
macro block 宏模块
macro body 宏体
macro call 宏调用
macro cell 宏单元
macro cell library 宏单元库
macro cell redundancy 宏单元冗余
macro chip 宏芯片
macro code 宏代码
macro coding 宏编码
macro command 宏命令
macro control statement 宏控制语句
macro cross reference 宏交叉引用
macro dataflow graph 宏数据流图
macro declaration 宏指令说明
macro definition 宏定义
macro definition library 宏定义库
macro definition exit 宏定义出口
macro directory 宏目录
macro editor 宏编辑器
macro element 宏元件,宏组件
macro expansion 宏扩展
macro expression 宏表达式
macro facility 宏功能
macro feature 宏功能特性
macro flag 宏状态标志
macro flowchart 宏流程图
macro generating program 宏生成程序
macro generation 宏生成
macro generation program 宏指令生

成程序
macro generator 宏生成程序
macro instruction 宏指令
macro instruction link 宏指令链
macro instruction linkage 宏指令链接
macro instruction operand 宏指令操作数
macro instruction sorts 宏指令排序
macro language 宏语言
macro layout system 宏布局设计系统
macro library 宏程序库
macro LISP 宏 LISP 语言
macro logic 宏逻辑
macro model statistical optimization 宏模型统计优化
macro-modular computer 宏模块计算机
macro name 宏名
macro nest 宏嵌套
macro null statement 宏空语句
macro operator 宏算子
macro options 宏选项
macro-parallelization 宏并行化
macro parameter 宏参数
macro paused 宏暂停
macro pipeline 宏流水线
macro pipeline parallel algorithm 宏流水线并行算法
macro plus 宏扩充
macro preprocessor 宏预处理程序
macro processing instruction 宏处理指令
macro processor 宏处理程序
macro program library 宏程序库
macro programming 宏程序设计
macro prototype statement 宏原型语句
macro recorder 宏记录程序
macro recursion 宏递归
macro sheet 宏表
macro skeleton structure 宏骨架结构
macro skeleton table 宏骨架表
macro statement 宏语句
macro statement number 宏语句编号
macro substitution 宏代换
macro successor 宏后继
macro symbol table 宏符号表
macro system 宏系统
macro-tasking 宏任务化
macro-time event list 大延迟时间事件表
macro-time variable 宏时间变量
macro trace 宏跟踪
macro transformation 宏变换
macroeconomic model 宏经济模型
macroelement 宏组件
macroencapsulation material 宏封装材料
macroexpander 宏扩展程序
macroflow graph 宏流程图
macrograph 宏观检查图,低倍照相图
macrologic 宏逻辑
MacroMind Director MacroMind 指导程序
macromodeling 宏建模,宏造型
macropipeling algorithm 宏流水线算法
macroprototype 宏原型
macroscale particle simulation 宏规模粒子仿真
macroscheme 宏模式
macroscopic concept 宏观概念
macrosubstitution 宏代换
macrosuccessor 宏后继(符号)
macrotask graph 宏任务图
macrotasking 宏任务处理
macrotime event list 宏时间事件列表
macrotrace 宏跟踪
MACS (MultiAccess Computer Switching) 多路访问计算机交换
MACS (Multiproject Automated Control System) 多元自控系统
MACSYMA language 数学符号处理语言
MacTCP MacTCP 协议(苹果)
MacTerminal Mac 终端仿真程序(苹果)
MacTwin MacTwin 连接系统(苹果)
MacWeb MacWeb 浏览器(苹果)
MacWrite II MacWrite II 文字处理程序(苹果)
Mad Dog "疯狗"集成软件(Lotus)
MADA (Multiple Access Discrete Address) 多路访问离散地址(方式)
MADS (Machine-Aided Drafting System) 计算机辅助绘图系统
MADS (Multiple Access Digital System) 多路访问数字系统
MAE (Mean Absolute Error) 平均绝

对误差
MAE(Memory Address Extension) 存储器地址扩充
MAFLOS(MAterial FLOw Simulator) 物流仿真程序
mag head 磁头
mag tape 磁带
magazine 卡片槽;暗片盒;杂志
Magazine Index 杂志索引数据库
magazine slot 媒体储存槽
Magellan Magellan 盘管理软件
magenta 品红,洋红
MAGIC(Master Group Information System) 主群信息系统
MAGIC(Machine for Automated Graphics Interface to a Computations) 自动绘图计算接口用机
MAGIC(Matrix Algebra General Interpretive Coding) 矩阵代数通用解释编码
magic box 幻箱
magic cookie 幻饼(网络安全跟踪程序)
magic dictionary 幻像目录
magic number 幻数
magic-set technique 魔集技术
magic square 幻方
magic wand 魔棒
magnet 磁铁
magnetic after effect 磁后(剩磁)效应
magnetic anisotropy 磁各向异性
magnetic axis 磁轴
magnetic bias 磁偏,磁偏置
magnetic biasing 磁偏法
magnetic bubble 磁泡
magnetic card 磁卡
magnetic card file(MCF) 磁卡文件
magnetic card reader 磁卡阅读机
magnetic-card unit 磁卡机
magnetic cell 磁格,磁存储单元
magnetic character 磁性字符
magnetic character reader 磁字符阅读机
magnetic circuit 磁路
magnetic coating 磁涂层
magnetic coercivity 磁矫顽力
magnetic core(MC) 磁芯
magnetic core memory(MCM) 磁芯内存
magnetic coupling 磁耦合
magnetic damping 磁阻尼
magnetic delay line 磁性延迟线
magnetic disc 磁盘
magnetic disk 磁盘
magnetic disk adapter 磁盘适配器
magnetic disk controller 磁盘控制器
magnetic disk drive 磁盘驱动器
magnetic disk file 磁盘文件
magnetic disk pack 磁盘组
magnetic disk storage 磁盘存储器
magnetic dispersion 磁性扩散,磁漏
magnetic document sorter-reader 磁性文档分类阅读机
magnetic drum(MD) 磁鼓
magnetic effect proximity sense 磁效应邻近感
magnetic eraser(MD) 消磁器
magnetic field gradient 磁场梯度
magnetic field sensor 磁场传感器
magnetic figure 磁场图
magnetic film 磁膜
magnetic film memory 磁膜存储器
magnetic flux 磁通量
magnetic flux density 磁通密度
magnetic focusing 磁聚焦
magnetic gap 磁隙
magnetic gripper 磁力抓取器
magnetic head(MH) 磁头
magnetic-head positioning construction 磁头定位机构
magnetic head unload mechanism 磁头卸载机构
magnetic hologram 磁全息照相
magnetic hysteresis loop 磁滞回线
magnetic hysteresis loss 磁滞损耗
magnetic induction 磁感应
magnetic ink 磁性墨水
magnetic ink character 磁墨字符
magnetic ink character reader(MICR) 磁墨字符阅读器
magnetic ink character recognition(MICR) 磁墨字符识别
magnetic ink character recognition code (MICR code) 磁墨字符识别码
magnetic ink character sorter 磁墨字符分类机

magnetic ink scanner 磁墨扫描器
magnetic isotropic 磁各向异性
magnetic layer 磁层
magnetic leakage 磁漏
magnetic loss 磁损耗
magnetic mark reader 磁性标志阅读器
magnetic master 磁性主盘,原版磁带
magnetic matrix 磁性存储矩阵
magnetic media 磁性媒体
magnetic memory 磁存储器
magnetic needle 磁针
magnetic optic effect 磁光效应
magnetic original 原(声/像)磁带
magnetic oxides 磁氧化层
magnetic path 磁路
magnetic pen 磁(记录)笔
magnetic permeability 磁导率
magnetic plate wire memory 磁镀线存储器
magnetic playback head 磁回放头
magnetic potential 磁势
magnetic read/write head 读写磁头
magnetic record file 磁记录文件
magnetic recording 磁记录
magnetic recording head 记录磁头
magnetic recording medium 磁记录媒体
magnetic recording mode 磁记录模式
magnetic relaxation effect 磁驰张效应
magnetic reproduce head 再生磁头
magnetic resistance(MRI) 核阻
magnetic resonance imaging(MRI) 核磁共振成像
magnetic rigid disk 硬磁盘,固定盘
magnetic saturation 磁饱和
magnetic separation 磁分选
magnetic shield 磁屏蔽
magnetic strength 磁场强度
magnetic storm 磁暴
magnetic stripe 磁条
magnetic strip credit card 磁条信用卡
magnetic strip file 磁条文件
magnetic strip reader 磁条阅读机
magnetic strip system 磁条系统
magnetic surface recording 磁表面记录
magnetic surface storage 磁表面存储器
magnetic tape 磁带

magnetic tape adapter 磁带适配器
magnetic tape back-up station 磁带后备站
magnetic tape buffer 磁带缓冲器
magnetic tape cartridge 磁带盒,磁带匣
magnetic tape clear 磁带清洁器
magnetic tape density 磁带密度
magnetic tape drive 磁带驱动
magnetic tape driver 磁带机驱动器
magnetic tape driving system 磁带驱动系统
magnetic tape durability index 磁带持久性指标
magnetic tape file 磁带文件
magnetic tape file label 磁带文件标号
magnetic tape file operation 磁带文件操作
magnetic tape format 磁带文件格式
magnetic tape group 磁带组
magnetic tape handler(MTH) 磁带处理机
magnetic tape head 磁带头,磁带机磁头
magnetic tape label 磁带标记
magnetic tape leader 磁带引导段,磁带首部
magnetic-tape librarian 磁带库存例程
magnetic tape loader 磁带装载器
magnetic tape operation system (MTOS) 磁带操作系统
magnetic tape parity 磁带奇偶校验
magnetic tape reel 磁带卷盘
magnetic tape sorting 磁带排序
magnetic tape start-stop time 磁带启停时间
magnetic tape station 磁带站
magnetic tape storage 磁带存储器
magnetic tape strip 磁带条
magnetic tape transport mechanism 磁带传送机构
magnetic thin film 磁性薄膜
magnetic thin film storage 磁薄膜存储器
magnetic track 磁道,磁轨;磁性声带
magnetic transfer 磁转印
magnetic wire 磁线,录音钢丝
magnetic wire storage 磁线存储器
magnetics(MRI) 磁学
magnetism(MRI) 磁性

magnetizable medium 可磁化介质
magnetized spot 磁化点
magnetizerm 导磁体
magneto-crystalline anisotropy 磁晶各向异性
magneto-crystalline anisotropy energy 磁晶各向异性能量
magneto-holographic memory type 磁全息存储类型
magneto-optic disc 磁光盘
magneto-optic display 磁光显示
magneto-optic driver 磁光驱动器
magneto-optic effect 磁光效应
magneto-optic rewritable optical disc 磁光型可擦写光盘
magneto-optical memory material 磁光存储材料
magneto-resistive head (MR) 磁阻磁头(IBM)
magneto-striction 磁致伸缩
magneto-striction transducer 磁致伸缩转换器
magneto-strictive delay line 磁致伸缩延迟线
magneto-strictive effect 磁致伸缩效应
magneto-strictive sensor 磁致伸缩传感器
magneton 磁子
magnetooptics 磁光学
magnetoresistance 磁阻
magnetoresistive head 磁阻记录头
magnetoresonic wave 磁声波
magnetorestriction transducer 磁致伸缩传感器
magnifiable preview 可放大预览
magnification factor 放大因数,放大倍数
magnification lens 放大透镜
magnifier 放大镜,缩放工具
magnify 放大
magnifying power 放大倍数
magnitude (MAG) 量,数值;大小,刻度
magnitude accuracy 量值精确度
magnitude portion 尾数部分
Mahalanobis distance 马哈朗诺比斯距离
MAHT (Machine Aided Human Translation) 机器辅助人类翻译
MAI (Motorola Active Interface Diagnosis) 摩托罗拉有效接口诊断程序
mail-aware application 邮件识别应用程序
mail bomb 邮件炸弹
mail bombing 邮件轰炸
mail box 邮箱
mail box buffer 邮箱缓冲区
mail box database 邮箱数据库
mail box fashion 邮箱方式
mail bridge 邮件网桥
mail client 邮件客户
mail directory 邮件目录
mail-driven response 邮件驱动响应
mail drop 邮件缓存文件
mail exploder 邮件分发器
mail folder 邮件夹
mail gateway 邮件网关
mail host 邮件主机
mail log 邮件登录
mail merge 邮件合并
mail ordering 邮购
mail path 邮件路径
mail queue 邮件排队
mail reflector 邮件反射器
mail relay 邮件中继
mail server 邮件服务器
mail survey 信件查询
mailbox 邮箱,信箱区
mailbox memory 邮箱式存储器
mailbox service 邮箱区业务,电子信箱服务
mailbox system 邮箱系统
mailer (Solaris)"邮寄者"协议(Sun)
mailer daemon 邮件收发后台程序
mailing labile 邮件标签
Mailing List 邮件投送专题组
mailing list program 信址列表程序
mailing merge 信址合并
mailslot buffer 信箱缓冲区
main beam 主波束
main board 主板
main body 主体
main cable 主电缆
main chart 主要图表
main clock 主时钟

main command 主命令	main operation control program 主操作控制程序
main communication center 主通信中心	main operation house-keeping routine 主操作内务程序
main constraint 主要约束	
main control panel 主控面板	main page pool 主页池
main control unit 主控单元	main path 主通路
main cycle 大周期	main performance 主要性能
main data area 主数据区	main procedure 主过程
main diagonal 主对角线	main program 主程序
main display area 主显示区	main relay center 主转发中心
main distribution frame 主配线架	main ring path 主环路径
main document 主文档	main scheduling routine 主调度程序
main entry 主入口,主表目	main segment 主程序段
main executive module 主执行程序模块	main sequence 主序列
main file 主文件	main station 总站,主台
main flux 主磁通	main storage 主存储器
main folder 主文件夹	main storage partition 主存储区划分
main frame 巨型计算机	main storage region 主存储区
main frame caption 主框架标题	main switch 总开关,主开关
main frequency 主频	main system 主系统
main function 主函数	main task 主任务
main gating pulse 主选通脉冲	main text buffer 主文本缓冲器
main group 主群组	main thread 主线程
main group windows 主群组窗口	main traffic station 主通信站
main index 主索引	main tray (打印机)主纸盒
main internal memory 主内存	main trunk 主干线
main lens 主透镜	main unit 主单元,主要部件
main line 主线	main window 主窗口
main line code 主线程序代码	mainboard 主板
main line module 主线模块	mainframe 巨型机;主机柜,主机机架
main line section 主干线部分	mainframe augmentation 巨型主机扩容
main lobe 主波瓣	mainframe era 巨型主机时代
main loop 主循环;主环路	mainframe memory system 巨型主计算机存储器系统
main machine interface(MMI) 主机接口	mainframe on-line test system 巨型主机联机测试系统
main machine system 主机系统	mainline program 主线程序
main memory 主内存	maintain 维护;保持
main memory address space 主内存地址空间	maintainability 可维护性
main-memory mapping 主内存映射	maintainability design criteria 可维护性设计准则
main memory module(MMM) 主内存模块	maintainability prediction 可维护性预测
main memory stack 主内存堆栈	maintained switch 保持开关
main memory unit(MMU) 主内存单元	maintenance 维护,维修
main menu 主菜单	maintenance control panel 维护控制面板
main module 主模块	
main network address 主网络地址	maintenance credits 维护信用卡
main objective 主目标	
main operation 主操作	

maintenance engineering 维护工程
maintenance-free 免维护的
maintenance mechanism 保持机制
maintenance panel 维护面板
maintenance plan 维护计划
maintenance process 维护过程
maintenance program(MP) 维护程序
maintenance program chain 维护程序链
maintenance program procedures 维护程序步骤
maintenance programmer 维护程序员
maintenance release 修订版
maintenance service 维修业务,维护服务
maintenance standby time 维修待命时间
maintenance time 维护时间,维修时间
major axes 主轴
major class field 一级栏目;一级字段
major conjunctive normal form 主合取范式
major control change 主要控制变化
major control cycle 大控制周期
major control data 主控数据
major control field 主控字段
major cycle 主循环;主周期
major device number 主设备号
major disjunctive normal form 主析取范式
major event code 主事件代码
major failure 重大失效
major gate 多数逻辑门
major gridlines 主要网格线
major key 主关键字
major loop 主循环
major/minor device numbers 主/次设备号
major module 主模块
major motions 主轴运动
major node (VTAM)大节点
major overhaul 大修
major path 主通道
major relay center 大转发中心
major sorting field 主排序字段
major state 主状态,主控状态
major-state generator 主状态发生器
major state logic generator 主状态逻辑发生器
major structure 主结构
major synchronization point 主同步点
major synchronization point service 主同步点服务
major system kit 主系统套件
major task 主任务
major time slice 主时间片
major total 合计,总计
major track 主磁道
major unit 主要单元
major utility 大型公用程序
majority 多数,多数逻辑
majority carrier 多数载流子
majority circuit 多数逻辑电路
majority consensus algorithm 多数一致算法
majority decision gate 多数决定门
majority element 多数逻辑元件
majority logic 择多逻辑,多数决定逻辑
majority organ 多数符合元件
majority principle 多数原则
majority unknown elimination 多数逻辑未知数消元法
majority voting 多数表决
make busy 闭塞
make connection 接通
make directory 创建目录
make busy 闭塞
make percent 接通率
make pulse 接通脉冲
make system disk 制作系统盘
make-up 追补,拼版
make-up time 追补时间
makefile (Unix)make命令描述文件
makeup time 追补时间,补算时间
MAKEUSER 用户维护
MAL(Meta Assembly Language) 元汇编语言
MAL(Monolithic Array Logic) 单片阵列逻辑
mal-rule 出错规则
male connector 阳性(插针式)连接器
male contact 阳性接触件
malfunction 失灵,故障,出错,误动作
malfunction alert 事故报警,故障报警
malfunction detection system(MDS)

故障检测系统
malfunction interrupt 故障中断,出错中断
malfunction routine 查错程序
malicious software 恶性软件
malicious virus 恶性病毒
maloperation 不正确操作
malposition 位置不正,错位
Maltron keyboard Maltron 键盘
MAN(Metropolitan Area Network) 城域网
man-in-loop simulation 人在回路中的仿真
man-machine communication 人机通信
man-machine dialogue 人机对话
man-machine digital system 人-机数字系统
man-machine engineering 人-机工程
man-machine interaction(MMI) 人机交互,人机对话
man machine interface 人机联系,人机接口
man-machine simulation 人机仿真
man-machine system 人-机系统
man-made device 人造设备
man-made fault 人为故障
man made noise 人为噪声
man-year 人年(工作量计算单位)
managed agent 受控代理,被管代理
managed children 受控子节点
managed information tree(MIT) 管理信息树
managed object(MO) 管理对象
managed object modeling 管理对象建模
managed window 受控窗口
management(MGMT) 管理
management access time 管理存取时间
management accounting 管理会计学
management agent 管理代理
management audit 管理审计
management automation 管理自动化
management by objectives(MBO) 目标管理
management class 管理类别
management consulting 管理咨询
Management Contents 管理内容数据库
management control level 管理控制级

management data 管理数据
management decision support system 管理决策支持系统
management development 管理开发
management environment 管理环境
management file 管理文件
management functions 管理职能
management game 管理对策
management information 管理信息
management information retrieval(MIR) 管理信息检索
management information system(MIS) 管理信息系统
management model 管理模型
management object 管理对象
management operating system(MOS) 管理操作系统
management of package 管理软件包
management policy 管理策略,管理政策
management psychology 管理心理学
management reports 管理报表
management science 管理科学
management services 管理服务
management software 管理软件
management tool 管理工具
management training 管理训练
manager 管理者;管理程序
manager of systems analysis 系统分析管理员
manager widgets 管理程序小配件
managerial roles 管理角色
managing packets in the network 网络中的信息包管理
managing replicating data 管理复制数据
Manca Manca 公司
Manchester code 曼彻斯特码
Manchester dynamic data stream computer 曼彻斯特动态数据流计算机
Manchester encoding(ME) 曼彻斯特编码
mandatory 强制性的;必须遵循的
mandatory access control 强制存取控制
mandatory cryptographic session 强制保密会话

mandatory member 指定成员
mandatory membership class 强制属藉类别
mandatory procedure 强制性过程
mandatory retention 强制保持
mandatory service 强制性(必备)服务
Manhattan distance 曼哈顿距离
manifold paper 复写纸
manifolding 复写,复印
manipulated directly controlled variable 直接受控变量
manipulated variable 受控变量
manipulating key 操纵键
manipulation 操纵,操作
manipulative index 操纵索引
manipulator 机械手
manipulator level control 机械手级控制
manipulator-type robot 机械手型机器人
manpower loading curve 人力负荷曲线
manpower scheduling 人力调配
MANTIS MANTIS语言
mantissa 尾数
manual 人工的,手动的;手册
manual address switches 手动地址开关
manual air traffic control system 人工空中交通管制系统
manual analysis 人工分析
manual back-up 人工后备,人工替换
manual calling 人工呼叫
manual computation 手工计算,笔算
manual control(M/C) 人工控制,手控
manual cut 手工切割
manual data access arrangement 人工数据存取设备
manual data entry module 人工数据录入模块
manual data input(MDI) 人工数据输入
manual data processing 手工数据处理
manual device backup 手动设备备份
manual driven duplicator 手动复印机
manual driver 手动传动装置,手动驱动器
manual entry 人工录入
manual equalizer 手动均衡器
manual exchange 人工交换,手动交换
manual exchanger 人工交换机
manual feeder 手动输纸器

manual function 手动功能
manual hyphenation 人工加入连字符
manual indicator 人工指示器,手动指示器
manual information management system 手工式信息管理系统
manual input(MANIP) 人工输入
manual-input unit 人工输入单元
manual insertion 人工干预
manual line break 人工插入分行符
manual link 人工链接
manual manipulator 手工纵机械手
manual membership class 人工藉属类别
manual mode 手动模式
manual number generator 手工数字发生器
manual operation 手动操作,人工操作
manual override 手动超驰控制
manual part programming 手工编程零件加工程序
manual programming 手工编程,示教式编程
manual read 人工读入
manual recalculation 手重算
manual record locking 人工记录加锁
manual robot 手动式机器人
manual skill 手工技巧
manual storage switch 手动存储控制开关
manual switch 手动开关
manual switch storage 手动开关存储
manual teaching 人工示教器
manual toning control 手动色调控制
manual wire embedding 人工嵌线
manually-controlled input device 手动控制输入设备
manually-operated plotting board 手工操作绘图板
manufacturability 工艺性,可制造性
manufacturer's customer engineer 制造厂家的用户工程师
manufacturing 制造,生产
Manufacturing Automation Protocol (MAP) 加工自动化协议
manufacturing control language(MCL) MCL语言,加工控制语言
manufacturing drawing 加工图
manufacturing engineers 制造工程师

manufacturing management 生产管理
manufacturing management workstation 生产管理工作站
manufacturing message specification (MMS) 加工业消息规范
manufacturing resource planning-Ⅱ (MRP-Ⅱ) 制造资源计划系统
manuscript 原始信息,手稿,原稿
many body simulation 多体仿真
many-for-one language 多对一语言
many-sorted logic 多分类逻辑
many-to-many medium 多对多媒体
many-to-many relationship 多对多关系
many-to-one 多对一
many-valued logic 多值逻辑
many-variable system 多变量系统
many-way selection 多路选择
MAP MAP 程序分析工具
MAP(Manufacturing Automation Protocol) 制造自动化协议
MAP(Matrix Algorithmic Processor) 矩阵算法处理机
MAP(Multi-Associative Processor) 多相关处理机
MAP(Multiple Array Processor) 多重阵列处理机
MAP 映射命令
map 映射,映像,变换;地图
map address 变换地址
map digitization 地图(图像)数字化
map editor 映像编辑程序
map feature 地图项
map file 映像文件
map generalization 地图概括
map generation 图的生成
map-guided approach 映像导向法
map information processing 地图信息处理
map list 地图列表;映像表
map matching 地图匹配
map overlay 地图覆盖
map representation 地图表示
map request 映射请求
map section 映射区域
map specification library 地图规格库
MAPI(Mail API) 邮件应用程序接口
MAPI(Messaging API) 通信应用程序接口
MAPI configuration file 通信应用程序接口配置文件
MAPI message store object 通信应用程序接口消息存储对象
MAPI session 通信应用程序接口对话
MAPI spooler 通信应用程序接口假脱机程序
MapLand MapLand 地图绘制软件
Maple Maple 机器人语言
mapped buffer 映像缓冲区,变换缓冲器
mapped drive 映像驱动器
mapped file 映射文件
mapped memory 映像内存
mapped physical storage 映像物理存储器
mapped system 映射系统
MAPPER MAPPER 语言
MAPPER language(MAintaining, Preparing and Processing Executive Reports) MAPPER 语言
mapper 映射程序
mapping 映像,映射
mapping address 映像地址
mapping cache 映像高速缓存
mapping device 映像设备
mapping field 映像字段
mapping function 映射功能
mapping language 映像语言,映射语言
mapping logic 映射逻辑
mapping mode 映像模式,变换方式
mapping-oriented language 基于映像的语言
mapping pipeline 映射流水线
mapping problem 映像问题
mapping rule 映射规则
mapping type 映射类型
mapping vertex 映射顶点
mapping window 映像窗口,变换窗口
MARC format MARC 磁带书目记录格式(美国国家图书馆)
marching ants 行军蚂蚁(活动点线)
marching cube 行进立方体
marching cube shading 渐进立方体明暗绘制
marching display 跨步显示器
marching "1"s and "0"s test 跨步"1"和"0"测试

margin 边缘;边际,改正力
margin-adjust 边缘调整
margin capacity 备用容量
margin control 边际控制
margin error 边缘错误
margin for page 页边
margin height 分栏边缘与栏中文本的垂直距离
margin justify 边界调整
margin-release key 极限释放键
margin-release mechanism 边界释放机构
margin sample 边距示例
margin scale 极限刻度
margin stop indicator 边限停止指示器
margin stop mechanism 边限停止机构
margin stop setting control 边限停机设置控制
margin text 页边文本
margin width 分栏边缘与栏中文本的横向距离
marginal 边缘的,边缘的
marginal analysis 边际分析
marginal check 边际校验
marginal check components 边际校验成分
marginal checking 边际检验
marginal control 界限控制器,界限控制
marginal error 边际误差
marginal forward pruning 限界正向修剪
marginal operation 边际操作
marginal probability 边缘概率
marginal profit 边际利益
marginal stability 临界稳定性
marginal testing 边际测试法
marginal utility 边际效用
marginal value 边际值
marginal value vector 边际值向量
MARK Ⅰ MARK Ⅰ 计算机
MARK Ⅱ MARK Ⅱ 计算机
MARK Ⅲ MARK Ⅲ 计算机
MARK Ⅳ MARK Ⅳ 计算机;MARK Ⅳ 信息处理系统
MARK Ⅴ MARK Ⅴ 程序
MARK Ⅸ MARK Ⅸ 程序
mark 标记;传号

mark active 标记为活动
mark and space 传号和空号
mark bit 标记位
mark character 标记字符
mark citation 引文标记
mark detection 标志检测
mark edge recording 光斑坑缘记录
mark entry 标记项
mark field 标记字段,标记域
mark form sequence 标记形成序列
mark frequency 传号频率
mark function 标记功能
mark-hold 传号保持
mark index entry 标记索引项
mark matching 标志匹配,标志符合
mark pen 标记笔
mark position 标记位置
mark pulse 传号脉冲,标记脉冲
mark reading 读标记
mark revision 标记修订
mark scan 标记扫描
mark scanning 标记扫描
mark scraper 标记擦除器
mark sense 标感,读出标记
mark sense cards 标记读出卡片
mark sensing 标记读出
mark-sensing column 标记感读列
mark-sensing row 标记感读行
mark space 传号间隔
mark-space multiplier 传号-空号放大器
mark-space ratio 标间比,传号-空号比
mark symbol 标记符号
mark-to-space ratio 标间比,占空比
mark to space transition 传号到空号的过渡
mark track error 标记磁道错误
mark up 标注排版要求
mark zone 标记区
marked graph 加标记图
marked index 标记索引
marked nonterminal 标记非终结符
marked page reader 标记页面阅读器
marker 标识器;标记,标志
marker bubble 标志泡
marker object 标志对象
marker-passing system 标记传送系统
marker primitive 标志原语
Market Advisor 市场顾问

marketing model 营销模型
marketing on line 网络营销
marking 传号
marking bias 传号偏移
marking class 标记类
marking condition 传号状态
marking-end distortion 传号末端失真
marking interval 标记间隔
marking-off 划线
Markov algorithm 马尔可夫算法
Markov chain 马尔可夫链
Markov filter 马尔可夫过滤器
Markov process 马尔可夫过程
markup 标高;记账
maroon 暗红色
marquee 罩框,选框
marquee setup 选取框设置
marquee tool 选框工具
marriage 匹配
marriage adjustment 匹配调整
marriage chain 结合链
marriage problem 匹配问题
marriage relation 结合关系
marriage theorem 配偶定理
married chain 配对链
married document 配对文档
married print 合成拷贝
married problem （运筹学中的）配对问题
married relation 结合关系
marshal 编组,调度;引导
marshaling 调度;编组
martians 意外信息包,"火星人"分组
mask 掩模,掩码;蒙版;屏蔽
mask art 掩模原图
mask alignment 掩模对齐
mask bit 屏蔽位
mask bus 屏蔽总线
mask byte 屏蔽字节
mask creation 掩码生成
mask design 掩膜设计
mask field 屏蔽字段
mask frame 掩模框
mask interrupt enable flag 允许屏蔽中断标志
mask level 屏蔽级
mask making 掩模制备
mask matching 掩码匹配,屏蔽符合

mask off code 屏蔽码,掩码
mask opening 掩模开窗孔
mask-programmable logic array 掩膜可编程逻辑阵列
mask programmable read-only memory 掩膜可编程只读存储器
mask register 屏蔽寄存器
mask ROM 掩膜型只读存储器
mask set 掩码字组
mask supplier option 掩码提供者选项
mask value 屏蔽值
mask words 屏蔽字
maskable interrupt(MI) 可屏蔽中断
maskant 保护层
masked 屏蔽的
masked off 屏蔽掉
masked ROM 掩膜只读存储器
masked state 屏蔽状态
masking 屏蔽,遮蔽,遮掩
masking redundancy 屏蔽冗余
masking sheet 蒙片,蒙版
maskless 无屏蔽
MASM(Macro ASseMbler) 宏汇编程序
masquerader 冒充程序
masquerading 冒充访问
MASS(Multiple Access Sequential Selection) 多路访问顺序选择法
mass 海量的,大容量的
mass cache memory 大容量高速缓冲存储器
mass data 大量数据,海量数据
mass-data multiprocessing 大量数据多重处理
mass device 海量存储设备
Mass Downloader (Multiple Aceess Switching System Downloader) 多路访问交换系统下载程序
mass executive storage 大量执行存储器
mass file 大存储量文件
mass library 大容量程序库
mass matrix 质量矩阵
mass media 大众传播媒介
mass memory(MM) 海量存储器
mass-producted 大批量生产的
mass properties 质量特性
mass-properties calculation 多种参数计算

mass sequential insertion 大量顺序插
mass spectrograph 质谱仪
mass spectrum 质谱
mass storage(MS) 大容量存储器
mass storage device 海量存储设备
mass storage dump 海量存储器转储
mass storage dump/verify program 大容量存储器转储/校检程序
mass storage file 海量存储器文件
mass storage file segment 海量存储文卷段
mass storage system(MSS) 大容量存储系统
mass storage volume(MSV) 海量存储
mass storage volume control(MSVC) 海量存储卷控制程序
mass storage volume control journal 海量存储卷控制日志
mass storage volume group 海量存储卷组
mass storage volume inventory 海量存储卷目录
massaging 版面调整;数据精处理
massive dump 巨量信息转储
massively parallel 大规模并行
massively parallel architecture 大规模并行体系结构
massively parallel processors(MPP) 大规模并行处理机
massive parallel system 大规模并行系
masstone 多色调
master(MSTR) 主文件;原本;总声
master abort 主设备中止;原版放弃
master-active file 主现用文件
master address 主地址
master address space 主地址空间
master alignment control 原版定位对齐控制器
master arm 主臂
master attachment control 原版固定控制
master back-end controller 主后端控制器
master bass level 主低音电平
master board 主板,母板
master body(MBR) 主体
master boot record(MBR) 主引导记
master card(MC) 主卡片

master catalog 主目录
master chip 主芯片
master clamp 原版夹具
master clear 主清除开关
master clock(MCLK) 主时钟
master clock frequency 主时钟频率
Master CNE(Master Certified Novell Engineer) 高级 Novell 工程师
master configurational record 主配置记录
master console 主控制台
master control(MC) 主控制;主控程
master control code 主控制代码
master control interrupt 主控中断
master control program(MCP) 主控程序
master control routine 主控制例程
master cryptography key 主密码密钥
master cylinder 母版滚筒
master data 主数据,基本数据
master delivery 原版递送
master document 主文档
master driver 主驱动器
master ejection 原版送出
master environment 主环境
master file 主文件
master file directory block 主文件目录块
master file job processing 主文件作业处理
master-file-up-date program 主文件更新程序
master file utility routines 主文件实用例程
master frequency 主频率
master frequency generator 主频发生器
master frequency oscillator 主频振荡
master gate control block(MGCB) 主门控制块
master group 主群
master heading 原版导进器;主标题
master history file 主历史文件
master index 主索引
master index tag 主索引标签
master interrupt control 主中断控制
master key concept 主密钥概念
master key data set(MKDS) 主密钥

数据集
master library tape　主程序库带
master loading　原版装入
master map　原图
master mask　主屏蔽；母掩膜
master mode　主模式
master monitor　主监视器
master mute　主音量静音
master negative film　阴图底片，主底片
master node control　主节点控制
master oscillator(MO)　主振荡器
master password　主口令
master positive　原稿翻正片
master process　主进程
master processor　主处理器
master production schedule(MPS)　主生产计划
master program　主程序
master program file　主程序文件
master program file update　主程序文件更新
master properties　主属性
master pulse　主脉冲
master record　主记录
master resident core　主驻留核心程序
master reticle　掩膜原版
master scheduler(MS)　主调度程序
master scheduler task　主调度任务
master segment　主段
master sequencer　主定序器
master server　主服务器
master-slave(M-S)　主-从
master-slave computer system　主从计算机系统
master-slave control　主从控制
master-slave manipulator　主从机器人
master/slave mode　主从模式
master/slave multiprocessor organization　主/从式多元处理机组织
master/slave multiprogramming　主从多道作业
master/slave operating system　主/从式操作系统
master/slaver relationship　主/从关系
master/slaver replication　主/从结构复制器
master/slave scheduling　主/从调度
master-slave system　主从系统

master-slave timing system　主从定时方式
master slewing device　原版定位调整装置
master slice　母片
master source program　主源程序
master state　主状态
master station(MST)　主站
master stream handler　主流管理器
master switch　主控开关
master synchronizer　主同步器
master tag　主标识
master terminal　主终端
master timer control block(MTRCB)　主定时器控制块
master title(MBR)　主标题
master treble level　主高音电平
master unit　主单元，主部件
master user　主用户
master volume　主音量；主卷
master volume control　主音量控制
master workstation　工作总站
masterboard　母板，主板
mastering　原版唱片制作
mastermind　策划者
masterplate　模板
masterwork　杰作
masthead　发行人栏
MAT(Machine Aided Translation)　机器辅助翻译
match　匹配
match case　区分大小写
match-merge　匹配合并，符合归并
match phrase　匹配短语
match stop　符合停机
match whole word only　全字匹配
match words　逐字匹配
matched filter　匹配滤波器
matched impedance　匹配阻抗
matched junction　匹配接头
matched load　匹配负载
matched pattern　匹配模式
matched power gain　匹配功率增益
matched termination　匹配终端
matched transmission line　匹配传输线
matching　匹配
matching algorithm　匹配算法
matching criterion　匹配准则

matching error 匹配误差
matching literal 匹配文字
matching materials 匹配材料
matching of a hypergraph 超图的匹配,超图的对集
matching phrases 匹配词组
matching section 匹配段
matching template 匹配模板
matching threshold 匹配阈值
matching transformer 匹配变压器
matching with don't cares 无关匹配
matching word 匹配字
material dispersion 材料色散,物质弥散
material-handling robot 物料搬运机器人
material-processing robot 材料处理机器人
material requirements planning(PRM) 物料需求计划
materials handling 物料搬运,物料传送
math CAD 数学计算机辅助设计(软件包)
math chips 数学芯片
math coprocessor 数学协处理器
mathematic discovery 数学发现
mathematic induction 数学归纳法
mathematic model 数学模型
mathematic-physical model 数学-物理模型
mathematic-physical simulation 数学-物理仿真
mathematic simulation system 数学仿真系统
mathematical approximation 数值逼近法
mathematical check 数学检验
mathematical chip 数学运算芯片
mathematical compiler 数值编译程序
mathematical control mode 数学控制模式
mathematical decomposition 数学分解
mathematical definition 数学定义
mathematical expectation 数学期望
mathematical expression 数学表达式
mathematical function 数学函数
mathematical function library 数学函数库
mathematical function program 数学函数程序
mathematical induction 数学归纳法
mathematical isomorphism 数学同构
mathematical linguistics 数学语言学
mathematical lofting 数学放样
mathematical logic 数理逻辑
mathematical model 数学模型
mathematical operator 数学算符
mathematical optimization 数值优化
mathematical parameter 数学参数
mathematical programming(MP) 数学规划
mathematical programming system (MPS) 数学程序规划系统
mathematical relation 数学关系
mathematical routine 数值程序
mathematical simulation 数学仿真
mathematical software 数学计算软件
mathematical software library 数学软件库
mathematical statistics 数理统计
mathematical subroutine 数学子例程
mathematical treatment 数学处理
mathematics 数学
Mathfile 数学文献数据库
MATHLIB 数学库
matrix 矩阵;浮雕片
matrix-addressed storage device 矩阵选址存储设备
matrix algebra table 矩阵代数表
matrix band width 矩阵带宽
matrix calculation 矩阵计算
matrix character generator 点阵式字符发生器
matrix encoder 矩阵编码
matrix generator 矩阵生成元
matrix inversion 矩阵求逆
matrix iteration 矩阵迭代
matrix matching 矩阵匹配
matrix model 矩阵模型
matrix norm subordinate to vector norm 从属向量范数的矩阵范数
matrix notation 矩阵记法
matrix of consequence 结果矩阵
matrix of relation 关系矩阵
matrix organization 矩阵式组织
matrix parity check 阵列奇偶校验
matrix printer 矩阵式打印机,点阵打

印机
matrix printing 点阵式打印
matrix representation 矩阵表示法
matrix storage 矩阵存储器
matrix switch 矩阵开关
matrix table 矩阵表
matrix tree theorem 矩阵树理论
matrix300 matrix300 基准程序
matroid 拟阵
MATS(Multiple Answering Teaching System) 多路应答教学系统
Matsushita Matsushita 机器人制造公司(日)
matte volume 暗淡体
mature 成熟的
maturity date 成熟日期
maturity stage 成熟阶段
MAU(Multi-station Access Unit) 多站存取单元
MAVC MAVC 多媒体应用程序
Mavica 马维卡数码照相机(索尼)
MAVIX(Multimedia Audio Video Information Exchange) 多媒体音视频信息交换系统
max architecture 最大结构
max-flow-min-cut theorem 最大流最小割定理
max/median filter 最大/中项过滤器
max-min controllability 最大最小可控性
max-min criterion 最大最小判据
MAX node 最大节点
max pipelining 最大流水线方法
maximal characteristic description 最大特征描述
maximal compatible set 最大相容集
maximal conjunctive generalization 最大合取概括
maximal discovery rate 最大发现率
maximal edge 极大边
maximal element 极大元素
maximal flow 最大流量
maximal length null sequence 最大长度空时序
maximal linearly independent set 极大线性无关组
maximal matching 极大匹配,极大对集

maximal member 极大成员,最大成员
maximal outplanar graph 最大外部可平面图
maximal parallelization 最大并行化
maximal planar graph 最大可平面图
maximal-ratio combiner 最大速率组合器
maximal shortest-distance tree 最大的最短距离树
maximal tree 最大树
maximal utility independent chain 最大效用的独立链
maximal value 最大值
maximax criterion 最大最大准则
maximax utility 最大最大效用
MaxiMem technology (打印机)内存扩容技术(EPSON)
maximin criterion 最大最小判据
maximin strategy 最大最小策略
maximin utility 最大最小效用
maximization 最大化
maximize button 窗口最大化按钮
maximize icon 最大化图标
maximize top pane 最大化顶部窗格
maximizing 达到最大值
maximum acceptance angle(MAA) 最大接收角
maximum active power dissipation 最大有用功消耗
maximum allowable link loss 最大允许链路损耗
maximum ascender 最大上行高度
maximum available gain 最大有效增益
maximum byte count 最大字节计数
maximum common mode voltage 最高共模电压
maximum contrast 最大对比度 「元
maximum decision element 最大判定
maximum decision set 最大判定集
maximum descender 最大下行深度
maximum element 最大元素
maximum entropy spectral analysis 最大熵谱分析
maximum entropy spectrum estimation 最大熵谱估计
maximum expected value 最大期望值

maximum flow 最大流
maximum flow minimum set theorem 最大流量最小割集定理
maximum frequency operation 最高工作频率
maximum history state 最多历史状态
maximum hops 最多允许的中继站数目
maximum image area 最大图像面积
maximum inventory 最大库存量
maximum justification rate 最大调整率
maximum latency 最大等待时间
maximum length sequence 最长序列
maximum likelihood 最大似然
maximum likelihood criterion 最大似然率准则
maximum likelihood decoding 最大似然率译码
maximum likelihood detection theory 最大似然率检测理论
maximum likelihood error-correction parser 最大似然率误差校正分析程序
maximum likelihood estimate 最大似然率估计
maximum likelihood estimator 最大似然率估计值
maximum likelihood extraction 最大似然率提取
maximum likelihood membership function 最大似然率类属函数
maximum likelihood principle 最大似然率原理
maximum likelihood stochastic language 最大似然率随机语言
maximum line length 最大行长
maximum link utilization 最大链路利用率
maximum matching 最大匹配, 最大对集
maximum memory expansion 最大存储器扩展
maximum modulus theory 最大模定理
maximum norm 最大范数
maximum normal mode voltage 最高常模电压
maximum operating frequency 最高工作频率

maximum packet lifetime 最长包寿命, 最长分组保存期
maximum password age 最长口令有效期
maximum path flow 最大通路流量
maximum percent overshoot 最大百分比超调量
maximum picking out 最大值检出
maximum principle 极大值原理
maximum print position 最大打印宽度
maximum printer lines 最大打印行数
maximum probability search 最大概率搜索
maximum pulse rate 最大脉冲速率
maximum queue length 最大排队长度
maximum region 最大区域
maximum reset time 最长复位时间
maximum segment lifetime 最长段寿命
maximum sheet size 最大纸张尺寸
maximum storage time 最大存储时间
maximum stuffing rate 最大填充率
maximum supported configuration 最大支持的配置
maximum transfer rate 最高传送率
maximum transfer unit 最大传输单位
maximum tries 最多尝试次数
maximum usable frequency 最大可用频率
maximum usable viewing time 最大可用观察时间
maximum value 最大值, 极大值
maximum vertex 最大顶点
maxint 最大整数值
maxmini algorithm 最大最小算法
maxterm 全或项, 最大项
maxterm expression 最大项表达式
maxterm form 最大项形式
Maxwell 麦克斯韦
Maxwell bridge 麦克斯韦电桥
Maxwell's equations 麦克斯韦方程
Maxwell's law 麦克斯韦定律
MAYBE compiler MAYBE 编译程序
maybe language "可能"语言
maze decision stack 迷宫判定栈
maze routing 迷路路由选择
maze search operation 迷路探索
maze type 迷宫类型

MB(MegaByte) 兆(2^{20})字节
MBR(Megabit) 兆(2^{20})位
MBR(Master Boot Record) 主引导记录
MBone(Multicast Backbone) 多向广播主干网
MC(Model Coordinates) 模型座标
MC 6800 microprocessor MC 6800 微处理器(Motorola)
MC 68000 microprocessor MC 68000 微处理器(Motorola)
MCA(Micro Channel Architecture) 微通道体系结构(IBM)
MCAD (Mechanical Computer-Aided Design) 计算机辅助机械设计
MCAI(Multimedia Computer Assisted Instruction) 多媒体计算机辅助教学
MCD(Media Control Driver) 媒体控制驱动程序
MCDBA(Microsoft Certified Database Administrator) 微软认证数据库管理员(计划)
MCG(MultiColor Graphics Array) 多色图形阵列
MCI(Media Control Interface) 媒体控制接口
MCI device 媒体控制接口设备
MCI file 媒体控制接口文件 「块
MCM(Multi-Chip Module) 多芯片模
MCM Station 多芯片模块设计软件
McOS(Mechitosh Operating System) 麦金塔操作系统(苹果)
MCP(Message Control Program) 消息控制程序
MCP(Multi-stream Conversation Protocol) 多流对话协议 「站
MCS(Master Control Station) 主控
MCS(Message Control System) 消息控制系统
MCSPG continuous simulation language MCSPG 连续仿真语言
MCU(Moving Compensation Unit) 运动补偿单元
MD(Macro Directory) 宏目录
MDA(Monochrome Display Adapter) 单色显示器适配器
MDAC(Microsoft Data Access Components) 微软数据访问部件
MDB(Multiple-Device Boot) 多设备启动
MDI(Multiple Document Interface) 多文档界面
MDM(Media Device Manager) 媒体设备管理程序
Mealy machine 米立机器
mean 平均的,中间的;中项;手段
mean access time 平均访问时间
mean accuracy 平均准确度,平均精度
mean allowed cell rate(MACR) 平均允许信元速率
mean arrival rate 平均到达时间
mean available time 平均有用时间
mean availability 平均有效度
mean busy hour 平均忙时
mean center difference 平均中心差分
mean conditional information content 平均条件信息量
mean deviation 平均偏差,平均偏移
mean downtime(MDT) 平均停机时
mean effective value 平均有效值 「间
mean-end analysis 手段-目标分析
mean-end method 手段-目标方法
mean entropy 平均信息熵
mean error 平均误差
mean free error time 平均无故障时间
mean grade 平均级
mean information content 平均信息量
mean line 平分线,中线
mean microinstruction cycle 平均微指令周期
mean packet delay 平均包延迟
mean pulse time 平均跳变时间
mean recurrence time 平均循环时间
mean sort 平均分类法
mean-square 均方
mean-square deviation 均方偏移
mean-square error 均方误差
mean-square error criteria 均方误差判据 「数
mean-square error norm 均方误差范
mean-square regression 均方回归
mean-square continuity 均方连续性
mean-squared error 均方误差
mean-squared error optimization 均方差的最优化

mean-time between arrivals 两次到达间的平均间隔时间
mean-time-between-failures(MTBF) 平均无故障时间,平均故障间隔时间
mean-time between replacement 两次更换之间的平均间隔时间
mean time to detection(MTTD) 平均故障检测时间
mean time to failures(MTFF) 平均故障时间
mean time to first failure 首次故障平均时间
mean-time-to-repair(MTR) 平均修复时间,平均修理间隔时间
mean transinformation content 平均转移信息量
mean up time(MUT) 平均操作时间
mean value function 均值函数
mean value theorem 中值定理
mean-variance criterion 均方差判据
meaning domain 意义域
meaningful information 有意义信息
meaningless message 无意义消息(报文)
means-end chain 手段-目标链
means-ends analysis 手段目的分析,中间结局分析
means-goal staircase 手段-目标阶
measurability 可量性,可测性
measurable function 可测函数
measurable stochastic process 可测随机过程
measurand 被测量值
measure of effectiveness 有效性量度
measure of fuzziness 模糊性量度
measure of goodness 优度的量度
measure of information 信息量度
measure of relative value 相对值的量
measure space 量度空间 ⌊度
measured 被测参数
measured backspace 可测度回退,精确回退
measured value 测量值
measured variable 被测变量
measurement 测量
measurement category 测量范畴
measurement error 测量误差

measurement range 测量范围
measurement reproducibility 测量再现性
measuring point 测量点
mechanical 机械的
mechanical analog computer 机械式模拟计算机
mechanical calculator 机械计算器
mechanical data processing 机械数据处理
mechanical dictionary 机器词典
mechanical differential 机械微分
mechanical differential analyzer 机械微分分析器
mechanical engineering 机械工程
mechanical fuse 机械保险装置
mechanical grip devices 机械式夹持装置
mechanical gripper 机械式夹持器
mechanical interface 机械接口
mechanical man 机械人
mechanical mouse 机械鼠标器
mechanical noise 机械噪声
mechanical optical switch 机动光开关
mechanical recognition system 机器识别系统
mechanical reference surface 机械参考表面
mechanical scanner 机械式扫描器
mechanical synchronization 硬性同步
mechanical tints 机械色调图样 「译
mechanical translation(MT) 机械翻
mechanical variable measurement 机械变量测量
mechanical verification 机械核对
mechanicals 定格式稿件
mechanism 机制
mechanized data processing system 机械式数据处理系统
mechanized housekeeping 机械化内务处理
mechanotronics 机械电子学
media 媒介,媒体
Media Access Control(MAC) 媒体访问控制子层
media access method 媒体存取方法
media access unit(MAU) 媒体存取设
media bank 媒体存储器 ⌊备

media clip 媒体剪辑
media compatibility 媒体兼容性
media component 媒体组件
media component capability 媒体组件能力
media component type 媒体组件类型
media control driver 媒体控制驱动程序
Media Control Interface(MCI) 媒体控制接口
media conversion 媒体转换
media conversion buffer 媒体转换缓冲器
media converter 媒体转换器
media device 媒体设备
media device capability 媒体设备能力
media device connection 媒体设备连接
media device connector 媒体设备连接器
media device connector index 媒体设备连接器索引
media device ID 媒体设备标识符
media device instance 媒体设备实例
media device manager 媒体设备管理器
media drive selector 媒体驱动选择器
media driver 媒体驱动器
media element manager 媒体元素管理器
media eraser 媒体擦除器
media failure 媒体失效
media file 媒体文件
media independent interface 介质独立接口
media initialization 媒体初始化
media integration 媒体集成
media interface connector(MIC) 媒体接口连接器
media model 媒体模型
Media Player 媒体播放器
media programming interface(MPI) 媒体编程接口
media-resident software 媒体常驻软件
media room 媒体间
media segment 媒体片段
Media Server 媒体服务器
media service 媒体服务
media sharing network 媒体共享网络
media stability 媒体稳定性
media technology 媒介技术
media type 媒体类型
media unit 媒体单元
media volume 媒体卷
media volume file 媒体卷文件
MediaGX MediaGX 微处理器(Cyrix)
median 中值,中位数
median error norm 中值误差范数
median filter 中值滤波器
median filtered image 中值滤波处理的图像
mediated instruction 媒介教学
mediation device 传达装置
mediator language 中介语言
medical CAI (Computer-Assisted Instruction) system 医学计算机辅助教学系统
medical database 医学数据库
medical diagnostic system 医学诊断系统
medical image recognition 医学图像识别
medical information system 医疗信息系统
medical literature database 医学文献数据库
medical record database 医疗记录数据库
medicine nomenclature 医学术语
medicine prescription 医疗处方
medium(M) 媒体,介质;中等的,中间的,一般的
medium access control frame 媒体存取控制帧
medium access control protocol 媒体存取控制协议
medium access control sublayer(MAC) 媒体存取控制子层
medium access memory 中速读写存储器
medium attachment unit(MAC) 媒体连接单元
medium close-up 中近景
medium contrast 中等对比度
medium data rate 中等数据传输速率
medium dependent interface(MDI) 专用媒体接口
medium distance modem 中距离调制

解调器
medium-grained parallel 中粒度并行
medium interface connector(MIC) 媒体接口连接器
medium map 媒体图
medium memory mode 中型内存模式
medium-mini computer 中小型计算机
medium model 中间模型
medium overlay 媒体覆盖
medium priority 中等优先级
medium range forecast 中期预报
medium reduction 中度约简
medium-scale integration(MSI) 中规模集成电路
medium shot 中距离镜头
medium size 半角(字)
medium size network 中等规模网络
medium speed 中速
medium speed printer 中速打印机
medium-technology robots 中级技术机器人
medium-term scheduling 中期调度
meet 交汇
meet me conference 会议会晤设备
meet operation "与"操作
meeting timetable 会议时间表
meetingware 会(议)件
mega(M) 百万(10^6);兆(2^{20})
mega macro 巨宏元
megabit(Mb) 兆比特,兆位
megabit chip 兆位芯片
megabit per second(Mb/s) 每秒兆比特
megabus 兆位速率总线
megabyte(MB) 兆字节
megabyte per second(MB/s) 每秒兆字节
megacell 巨型单元
megacycle(MC) 兆周
Megadoc System 兆级文献系统
megaflops 每秒百万次浮点运算
megahertz(MHz) 兆赫兹
megapixel display 兆像素显示器
megassembly system 大件组装系统
Megastream 兆级数据流(英国数据通信网)
megatrends 大趋势
megavolt 兆伏特
megaohm 兆欧

melody 旋律,曲调
member(M) 成员,成分,构件
member array 成员数组
member condition 成员条件;成分条件
member function 成员函数
member ID 成员标识符
member list display 成员列表显示
member name 成员名
member number 成员编号
member object 成员对象
member pointer 成员指针
member record 成员记录
member server 成员服务器
member type 成员类型
membership 成员资格;从属关系
membership class 成员类,属藉类别
membership function 隶属函数
membership grade 隶属度
membership operator 隶属运算符
membership problem 成员资格问题
membership table 成员表
membrane 膜
membrane eigenvalue 膜本征值
membrane eigenvalue problem 膜本征值问题
membrane element 膜元
membrane keyboard 薄膜式键盘
membrane switch 膜片开关
memex 假想存储器
memistor 非磁性存储器
MemMaker (DOS)内存优化程序
memo 备忘录
memo field 备注字段
memo file 备注文件
memo posting 记录的记入;便笺记入
memomotion 控时摄影(长时间间隔)
memorability 可记忆性
memorable 可记忆的
memorize 记忆,存储
memory(M,MEM) 存储器,内存
memory access 内存访问,存储器存取
memory access conflict 内存访问冲突
memory access fault 内存访问故障
memory access protection 内存访问保护
memory across access 内存交叉存取
memory accumulator 存储累加器
memory activity 存储器活动

memory address 内存地址
memory address assignment 内存地址分配
memory address bus(MAB) 内存地址总线
memory-address counter 内存地址计数器
memory address driver 内存地址驱动器
memory address pointer 内存地址指针
memory address register(MAR) 内存地址寄存器
memory address selector 内存地址选择器
memory address space 内存地址空间
memory addressing 内存寻址
memory addressing mode 内存寻址模式
memory allocation 内存分配
memory allocation overlay 内存分配覆盖
memory and device control 内存与设备控制
memory and device control unit 内存与外围设备控制器
memory and I/O address 内存及输入/输出地址
memory annex 内存附属装置
memory area 内存区域
memory array organization 存储器阵列组织
memory assignment map 内存分配图
memory bandwidth 内存带宽
memory bandwidth-limited computer 内存带宽限制计算机
memory bank 存储器组,存储体
memory bank select 存储体选择
memory based address 内存基地址
memory-based reasoning 基于记忆的推理
memory block table(MBT) 内存分块表
memory board 存储器板
memory bottleneck 存储器瓶颈
memory bounded 受内存限制的
memory-bounds register 内存界限寄存器
memory buffer 存储器缓冲区
memory buffer register(MBR) 存储缓冲寄存器

memory bus(MB) 存储器总线
memory byte format 内存字节格式
memory cache 内存高速缓冲
memory capacity 内存容量
memory card chassis 内存插卡底板
memory cell 存储单元
memory character format 存储字符格式
memory chip 存储器芯片
memory clear 内存清除
memory coherence 存储相关性
memory collision 内存冲突
memory compaction 内存压缩
memory configuration 内存配置
memory conflict 内存冲突
memory conflict-free access 内存无冲突存取
memory contention 内存争用
memory contents dump 内存内容转储
memory control block(MCB) 内存控制块
memory control logic 内存控制逻辑
memory controller 存储控制器
memory controller gate array 内存控制器门阵列
memory cube 存储立方体
memory cycle 存储周期
memory cycle time 存储周期时间
memory data bus 内存数据总线
memory data register(MDR) 存储数据寄存器
memory deallocation 内存释放
memory decoder 内存译码器
memory density 存储密度
memory depth 存储器深度
memory descriptor 存储描述符
memory diagnostic 内存诊断
memory dump 内存转储
memory effect 记忆效应
memory element 存储元件
memory enhancement technology 内存增强技术(HP)
memory enter 内存入口
memory error 存储器错误
memory exchange 内存交换；存储器转接设备
memory expansion modules 内存扩充模块
memory expansion motherboard 内存

扩充母板
memory expansion option 内存扩充选件
memory fault 内存故障
memory fetch 从内存取指令
memory field 内存区域
memory file 内存文件
memory fill 内存填充
memory guard 存储保护
memory hazard 存储器冒险
memory hierarchy 存储器分层体系结构
memory hole 内存"空洞"
memory idle 内存闲置
memory immediate instruction 内存立即指令
memory in use 已占用内存空间
memory indication 内存指示
memory integrated vector processor 内存一体化向量处理机
memory interface protocol 内存接口约定
memory interleaving 内存交错存取
memory latency time 内存等待时间
memory light 内存指示灯
memory limit register 内存界限寄存器
memory load and record operation 存储器装入和记录操作
memory load index 内存加载索引
memory location 存储单元
memory lock write 内存写入封锁
memory lockout 内存锁定
memory lockout register 内存封锁寄存器
memory management 内存管理
memory management exception 内存管理异常
memory-management program 内存管理程序
memory management unit(MMU) 内存管理单元
memory map 内存分配图,内存映像
memory map list 内存映像表
memory-mapped device 内存映像设备
memory-mapped display 内存映像显示
memory-mapped graphics 内存映像制图法
memory mapped I/O 内存映像的输入/输出
memory-mapped I/O bus 内存变换输入/输出总线
memory-mapped interface 内存映像接口
memory mapped video 内存映像显示
memory mapping 内存映像,内存布局
memory matrix 存储矩阵
memory model 内存模型;记忆模型
memory module(MM) 内存模块,存储体
memory multiplexer(MM) 存储器多路转换器
memory node 存储节点
memory operation 存储器操作
memory organization 存储器组织
memory overlay 内存覆盖操作
memory package interface 内存部件接口
memory page 内存页面
memory parity 内存奇偶校验
memory parity and protect option (MPP) 内存奇偶校验与保护选择
memory parity generator 内存奇偶性发生器
memory parity interrupt 内存奇偶性中断
memory partitioning 内存分区
memory plane 存储平面
memory playlist 内存演播表
memory pointer register 内存指针寄存器
memory port 内存端口
memory power 存储能力
memory print-on-alarm 存储器报警打印
memory print-out 存储信息转储
memory priority 存储优先级
memory property 内存性能
memory protect 存储保护
memory protect privileged instruction 存储保护特权指令
memory protect violation program 内存防护程序
memory protecting 内存保护
memory protection key 存储保护键
memory protection option 存储保护任选

memory protection scheme 存储保护方案
memory protection violation error 存储保护违规错误
memory random access 内存随机存取
memory raster 内存光栅
memory read cycle 内存读周期
memory read enable 内存读允许
memory ready 内存准备就绪
memory reduce technology(MRT) 内存减少技术(佳能)
memory reference instruction(MRI) 内存引用指令
memory refresh 内存刷新
memory register(MR) 存储器寄存器
memory reliability 存储器可靠性
memory relocation 内存重定位
memory request 存储器请求
memory requirement 内存需求量
memory resident 内存驻留的,常驻内存的
memory-resident program 内存驻留程序
memory-resident virus 内存驻留病毒
memory resource sharing 内存资源共享
memory response 内存响应
memory retention 存储器保存
memory scan 内存扫描
memory-segmentation control 存储分段控制
memory sharing multiprocessor system 内存共享多处理机系统
memory size 内存大小
memory sniffing 内存嗅察
memory space 内存空间
memory stack 内存堆栈;存储体
memory status indicator 内存状态指示器
memory structural units 存储器结构件
memory swapping 内存交换
memory test software 内存测试软件
memory time-slice method 内存时间片法
memory timer 存储器定时器
memory timing generator 存储器定时发生器
memory tracking 记忆跟踪
memory transfer 内存转储
memory transfer rate 内存传送速率
memory transparency 内存透明性
memory trap condition 内存自陷条件
memory types 存储器类型
memory typewriter 记忆打字机
memory unit(MU) 存储单元
memory variable table 内存变量表
memory violation 存储违规
memory windows 存储窗口
memory word length 内存字长
memory workspace 内存工作区
memory write cycle 内存写周期
Memphis Memphis 操作系统(即 Windows 98)
MEMTEST 内存测试操作
mental context 思维环境
mental imagery 心像,表像
mental model 思维模型
mental representation 思维表示
mentality 智力,思维方法
Mentor Graphics Mentor 图形公司
menu 菜单,选单
menu bar 菜单条
menu builder 菜单生成程序
menu command 菜单命令
menu-driven 菜单驱动
menu-driven use interface 菜单驱动用户界面
menu editor 菜单编辑器
menu file 菜单文件
menu interface 菜单接口
menu item 菜单项
menu layout window 菜单布局窗口
menu operation 菜单操作
menu parameter 菜单参数
menu program 菜单程序
menu popup 菜单弹出
menu prompt 菜单提示
menu screen 菜单屏幕
menu script 菜单脚本
menu security 菜单安全保护
menu selection 菜单选择
menu selector 菜单选择器
menu sheet 菜单项目表
menu shell 菜单命令解释程序
menu text 菜单文本,菜单内容
menu title 菜单标题
menu window 菜单窗口

menuing software 菜单式软件
Mercury 墨克利网格
mercury delay line 水银(汞)延迟线
mercury memory 水银(汞)存储器
merely positive subdefinite 仅次正定
merely pseudoconvex 仅伪凸
merely quasiconvex 仅拟凸
merge 合并,归并;(图像)拼接
merge cell 合并单元格
merge conflict 合并冲突
merge exchange sorting 归并交换排序
merge file 合并文件
merge input file 合并输入文件
merge-match 合并匹配,合并比较
merge network 归并网络
merge node 合并节点
merge order 归并阶,合并次序
merge output coding 合并输出编码
merge pass 合并趟,归并遍
merge point 交汇点
merge purge 合并清除
merge scenario 合并方案
merge sort 归并分类,合并排序
merge-sorting 合并排序,合并分类
merge-splitting sorting 归并-分拆排序
merge statement 归并语句
merge subdocument 合并子文档
merged flow table 归并流表
merged global symbol table 合并全程符号表
merging 合并,归并
merging algorithm 合并算法
merging of data item and frequency 数据项与频度归并法
merging of data item and functional dependency 数据项与函数相关归并法
merging pattern 合并模式
merging routine 合并例程
merging scan 归并扫描
merging sort 合并排序,合并分类
meridional rays 子午光线
merit 优点
Merkle-Hellman Merkle-Hellman 背包体制
MESFET(MEtal Semiconductor Field-Effect Transistor) 金属半导体场效应晶体管
mesh 网格,网孔

mesh analysis 网孔分析
mesh architecture 网格体系结构
mesh array 网格阵列
mesh boundary 网格边界
mesh configuration 网格型配置
mesh connected multicomputer 网状连接多计算机
mesh data 网格数据
mesh equation 网孔方程
mesh generation 网格生成
mesh generator 网格生成程序
mesh network 网状网络,多通路网络
mesh refinement 网格求精
mesh region 网格区域
mesh spacing 网格间隔
mesh structure 网格结构,格栅结构
meshed ring structure 网孔环状结构
meshsort algorithm 网格排序算法
mesochronous 平均同步
mesoscale model 中间比例模型
mesosphere 文件名
message(MSG) 消息,报文
message accuracy 消息准确性
message acknowledgement 消息证实(确认)
message alignment indicator 消息定位符
message analysis 消息分析
message audit 消息审查
message authentication code 消息鉴定码
message backlog 信息积压
message beginning character 消息开始字符
message bit 消息位
message block 消息块
message blocking 报文组块传输
message body 消息体
message box 消息框
message buffer 消息缓冲区
message buffering 消息缓冲
message buffering facility 消息缓冲设施
message buffering synchronization 消息缓冲同步
message catalog 消息目录
message center 消息中心
message channel 消息通道
message circuit 消息电路
message circuit noise 通话线路噪声
message class 消息等级

message class identifier 消息等级标识符
message concentrator 消息集中器
message content 消息内容
message control block 消息控制块
message control flag 消息控制标记
message control program(MCP) 消息控制程序
message data(MD) 消息数据
message data set 消息数据集
message decoding 消息[报文]译码
message delete option 消息删除选件
message description 消息说明
message display console 消息显示控制台
message drain 消息泄露
message-driven program 消息驱动程序
message editing 消息编辑
message editor procedure 消息编辑器过程
message-ending character 消息结束字符
message envelope 报文包封
message error record 消息差错记录
message exchange 消息交换器
message feedback 信息反馈
message field(MFLD) 消息字段
message file time 消息文件交付处理时间
message filter 消息过滤器
message filtering 消息过滤
message filtering gateway 消息过滤网关
message finder 消息查找程序
message format 消息格式,报文格式
message format conversion 消息格式转换
message format service(MFS) 消息格式服务
message forwarding queue 消息转发队列
message fragment 报文分段
message handler(MH) 消息操作程序
message handling 消息处理
message handling protocol 消息处理协议
Message Handling Service(MHS) 消息处理服务
Message Handling System(MHS) 消息处理系统

message header(MH) 报头,消息标题
message header interpretation 信息标题解释
message help 消息求助信息
message identification 报文标识
message identifier 报文标识符
message indicator 消息指示符
message input descriptor(MID) 消息输入描述符
message intercept processing 信息截收处理
message intercept table 消息截取表
message interchange format 消息交换格式
message interface 消息接口
message interpolation 消息插入
message journaling function 消息日志记录功能
message key 报文密钥
message level 消息级
message line 消息行
message lock mode 消息锁定模式
message log 消息日志
message loop 消息循环
message member 消息成员
message metering service 报文计费服务
message mode 报文方式
message model 消息模型
message network 信息网络
message numbering 消息编号,报文编号
message oriented middleware 面向消息的中间件
message output descriptor(MOD) 消息输出描述符
message passing 消息传递
message passing interface 消息传递接口
message-passing system 消息传递系统
message pattern 消息式样
message pending 消息待决
message polling 消息轮询
message preamble 报头
message precedence 消息优先级
message preprocessor 消息预处理程序
message priority 消息优先级
message processing 消息处理
message processing directives 信息处理指令
message processing program(MPP) 消

息处理程序
message queue 消息队列
message queue client 消息队列客户端
message queue data set 消息队列数据集
message queue server 消息队列服务器
message queuing 消息排队
message rate 报文速率
message reassembly 消息重新组装
message recipient 收件人
message-record-log data set 消息-记录-登录数据集
message recovery point 消息恢复点
message redundancy 消息冗余度
message reference block 消息引用块
message reference key 消息引用键
message release time 消息释放时间
message-response time 消息响应时间
message restoring 消息重存
message resynchronization 消息再同步,报文恢复同步
message retention area 消息保留区,报文存留区
message retransmission 消息重传
message retrieval 消息检索,报文检索
message router 消息路由选择器
message routing 消息路由选择
message sample 消息取样(样本)
message segment 消息段,报文段
message selector 消息选择器
message sender 消息传播者
message service table 消息服务表
message sink 信宿,报文接收器
message site 消息站点
message slot 消息槽,报文页槽
message source 消息源
Message Store 消息库,报文库
message store provider 消息库提供者
message structure 消息结构
message subject 消息主题
message switch 消息交换
message switching 消息交换操作
message switching applications 消息转接应用
message switching center 消息交换中心
message switching computer 信息转接计算机
message switching computer access 消息交换计算机存取
message switching concentration (MSC) 信息集中转发
message switching concentration advantage 消息集中转发的优点
message switching network 消息交换网络
message switching procedures 信息转接过程
message switching processor 消息转接处理机
message switching system 消息交换系统
message switching system components 报文交换系统部件
message telecommunication service (MTS) 消息远程通信业务
message telephone service 长途电话服务
message text 消息正文[文本]
message traffic 消息流量
message transfer agent(MTA) 消息传输代理
message transfer envelope(MTE) (X.400)消息传输包封
message transfer part 消息传送部分
message transfer system (X.400)消息传输系统
message transfer time 消息传输时间
message transliteration 报文直译
message transmitting hyper-parallel computer 消息传输型超级并行计算机
message type 消息类型
message type pipe 消息型管道
message unit 消息单位
Message Watch 手表式寻呼机
messaging (直接)消息传送
messaging API 消息型应用程序界面
messaging application 消息传输应用程序
messaging domain 消息传送域,站点
messaging hook provider 消息传输连接提供者
Messenger Messenger 软件包
META 5 META5 语言
meta- 元
meta assembler 元汇编程序
meta-authoring environment 原创环境
meta character 元字符,超越字符

meta class 元类
meta-computer 元计算机
meta control 元控制
meta data 元数据
meta-expression 元表达式,M表达式
meta file 元文件
meta-heuristics 元试探,元启发式
meta-implementation 元实现
meta inference 元级推理
meta-interpreter 元解释程序
meta key 元键(Sun)
meta knowledge 元知识
meta knowledge system 元知识系统
meta language 元语言
meta-level reasoning 元级推理
meta-logic 元逻辑
meta modeling technique 元建模技术
meta name 元名称
meta planning 元规划
meta-rule 元规则
meta-schema 元模式
meta-theorem 元定理
meta-theory 元理论
metabase 元库
metabit 元位
metacall 元调用
metacharacter 元字符
metaclass 元类
metacode 元码
metacognition 元认识
metacompilation 元编译
metacompiler 元编译程序
MetaCube MetaCube 软件包(Informix)
metadata 元数据
metadatabase 元数据库
metafile 元文件
metafile descriptor 元文件描述符
metafile element 元文件元素
metafile generator 元文件生成程序
metafile interpreter 元文件解释程序
metafile palette 元文件调色板
metafile record 元文件记录
Metafile System 元文件系统程序
metafile translator 元文件翻译软件
metafont 元字体
metagame 亚对策
metagame theory 变化博弈论

metainference 元级推理
metainference mechanism 元推理机构
metainterpreter 元解释程序
metaknowledge 元知识
metal base 金属衬底
metal ceramic 金属陶瓷
metal core printed board 金属芯印刷「板
metal cutting 金属切削
metal-film resistron 金属膜光阻摄像管
metal-forming operation 金属成型工「艺
metal-insulator-silicon(MIS) 金属-绝缘体-硅
metal-nitride-oxide semiconductor (MNOS) 金属-氮化物-氧化物半导体
metal oxide semiconductor(MOS) 金属氧化物半导体
metal-oxide semiconductor field-effect transistor(MOSFET) 金属氧化物半导体场效应晶体管
metal-oxide-semiconductor memory 金属氧化物半导体存储器
metal-oxide-semiconductor random access memory(MOS RAM) 金属氧化物半导体随机存取存储器
metal oxide silicon 金属氧化硅
metalanguage 元语言
metalevel communication 元级通信
metalevel reasoning 元级推理
metalinguastic bracket 元语言括号
metalinguastic connective 元语言连接词
metalinguastic formula 元语言公式
metalinguastic variable 元语言变量
metalinear language 元线性语言
Metalist Metalist 系列硬盘(希捷)
metallization 金属喷镀
metallization pattern 金属喷镀式样
metallized ceramic module 金属喷镀陶瓷模块
metallography 金相学
metalog system 元记录系统
metalogic 元逻辑
metamedia 元媒体
metamember 元成员
metanotion 元概念
metaobject protocol 元目标协议

metaphor comprehension 隐喻理解
metaphoric language 隐喻语言
metaplanning 元规划
metapredicate 元谓词
metaprimitive 基元
metaproblem 元问题
metaproduction rule 元产生式规则
metaprogramming 元程序设计
metareasoning 元推理
metarelation 元关系
metaroutine 元例程
metarule 元规则
metascience 元科学
metaschema 总体模式
metaservice 元服务
metastable state 亚稳态
metastructure 亚结构
metasymbol 元符号
metasystem 元系统
metatask 元任务
metatheorem 元定理
metavariable 元变量
metaview architecture 元视图体系结构
meteor scatter communication 流星散射通信
meteorological phenomena database 气象数据库
meteorology 气象学
meter 仪表,计;米
metering pulse 计数脉冲
metering technique 测量技术
method 方法
method analysis 方法研究
method base 方法库
method caching 方法存储
method code 方法代码
method descriptor 方法描述符
method drive 方法驱动
method driver 方法驱动器
method for arbitration 判优方法
method for choosing representation 选择表示法
method name 方法名
method of agreement 契合法
method of approximation 近似法
method of assumed states 假设状态法
method of bisection 对分法「法
method of clustering center 聚合中心

method of difference 差分法「法
method of equal coefficient 等系数方
method of exhaustion 穷举法
method of false position 试位法「法
method of finite difference 有限差分
method of fractional steps 分步法
method of induction 归纳法
method of iteration 迭代法「法
method of leading variable 引入变量
method of least squares 最小二乘法
method of moving average 移动平均
method of order reducing 降阶法「法
method of regression 回归法
method of relaxation 松驰法
method of revolution surface 旋转曲面法
method of simultaneous displacement 同时置换法
method of statistical testing 统计实验法「法
method of steepest descent 最陡下降
method of successive approximation 逐步逼近法
method of successive displacement 逐次置换法
method of superposition 叠合法
method of three bending moments 三弯矩法「法
method of three turning angles 三转角
method of transition matrices 转移矩阵法
method of trial 试探法
method of unconstrained optimization 非约束最优化方法
methodology 方法论
Methodology for Unmanned Manufacturing(MUM) 无人制造方法计划
methodology of system engineering 系统工程方法论
metonymy 转喻
metric 公制;度量,尺度
metric attribute 度量属性
metric mapping mode 度量单位对应模式
metric mode plotting 公制绘图模式
metrical information 计量信息
metropolitan area network(MAN) 城域网

MF(Medium Frequency) 中频
MFC(Microsoft Foundation Class Library) 微软基类库
MFC(MultiFunction Computer) 多功能计算机
MFD(MultiFunction Device) 多功能设备
MFF(MIDI File Format) MIDI 文件格式
MFlops(Million Floating point operations per second) 每秒兆次浮点运算
MFM(Modified Frequency Modulation) 改进型频率调制法
MFP(MultiForm Printer) 多格式打印机
MFR(MultiFrequency Receiver) 多频接收机
MFS(Macintosh File System) 麦金塔文件系统(苹果)
MFSK(Multiple Frequency Shift keying) 多频移键控
MFSTEST(Message Format Service TEST) 消息格式服务测试
MFT(Multiprogramming with a Fixed number of Tasks) 固定任务数多道作业(IBM)
MFT with subtasking 带有子任务的固定任务数多道程序作业
MG(Main Group) 主群
MGA(Monochrome Graphics Adapter) 单色图形适配器
MHEG(Multimedia and Hypermedia information coding Expert Group) 多媒体与超媒体信息编码专家组(标准)
MHL(Microprocessor Host Loader) 微处理器主加载程序
MHP(Message Handling Processor) 消息处理程序
MHP(My Home Page) 我的主页
MHS(Message Handling Service) 消息处理服务
MHS(Message Handling System) 消息处理系统
MHz(MegaHertz) 兆赫
MIB(Machine-Independent) 与机器无关的
MIB(Management Information Base) 管理信息库
MIB(Motif Interface Builder) (Unix)图形界面构造程序
MIC(Media Interface Connector) 媒体界面连接器
MIC(MICrophone) 传声器,麦克风
MIC(Missing Interruption Checker) 丢失中断检测程序
MIC(Monolithic Integrated Circuit) 单片式集成电路
mic mute 麦克风静音
mica 云母
MICR(Magnetic Ink Character Reader) 磁墨字符阅读机
MICR code 磁墨字符识别码
MICR scan 磁墨字符识别扫描
micro 百万分之一,微
Micro Channel Architecture(MCA) 微通道体系结构(IBM)
micro code 微码
micro coding 微码程序设计
micro copy 缩微复制件
Micro DOS(Deposition On Silicon) head 微硅淀积打印头(Penrod)
Micro Dry Process(MDP) 微干处理技术(Penrod)
Micro EC(Energy Controller) 微能量控制器(Penrod)
micro film reader 缩微胶片阅读器
micro instruction 微指令
micro kernel 微内核
micro manager 微型管理者
micro-parallelization 微并行化
MICRO-PROLOG 微 PROLOG 语言
micro rollback 微重算
micro to mainframe 微型机到大型机
micro virtual circuit service 微虚电路服务
micro Winchester disk 微型温彻斯特磁盘驱动器
microampere 微安培
microarchitecture 微结构,微体系「构
microassembler 微汇编程序
microbending loss (光纤)微弯损耗
microbiological cell 微生物电池
microbotics 微机器人学
microbus 微总线

microcard 缩微卡片
microcassette 微型盒式录音机
microcell 微单元;微型电池
microchip 微芯片
microcircuit 微电路
microcircuit isolation 微电路隔离
microcircuit wafer 微电路芯片
microcircuitry 微复合电路
Microcobol 微型 COBOL 语言
microcode 微码
microcode analyzer 微码分析器
microcode compaction 微码压缩
microcode engine 微码引擎
microcode instruction set 微码指令集
microcode translation 微指令转换
microcode width 微指令宽度
microcoded high-level language 微代码高级语言
microcoded read-only memory 微编码只读存储器
microcoding 微程序设计,微编码
microcoding device 微程序设计部件
Microcom Networking Protocol(MNP) Microcom 组网协议
Microcom Protocol Microcom 协议
microcommand 微命令
microcomponents 微元件
microcomputer 微型计算机
microcomputer addressing modes 微型计算机寻址模式
microcomputer analyzers 微型计算机分析器
microcomputer architecture 微型计算机体系结构
microcomputer bus 微型计算机总线
microcomputer bus system 微型计算机总线系统
microcomputer card 微型计算机插件
microcomputer cards versus a CPU chip 微型计算机卡对 CPU 芯片
microcomputer components 微型计算机组件
microcomputer control panel 微型计算机控制板
microcomputer-controlled terminal 微型计算机控制的终端机
microcomputer CPU 微型计算机中央处理器

microcomputer data base system 微型计算机数据库系统
microcomputer development hardware 微型计算机开发硬件
microcomputer development kit 微型计算机开发配套元件
microcomputer development system (MDS) 微型计算机开发系统
microcomputer disk operating system (MDOS) 微型计算机磁盘操作系统
microcomputer execution cycle 微型计算机执行周期
microcomputer I/O architecture 微型计算机输入/输出结构
Microcomputer Index 微型计算机索引数据库
microcomputer instrument 微型计算机仪器
microcomputer interfacing kit 微型计算机接口配套元件
microcomputer interrupt 微型计算机中断
microcomputer local bus 微型计算机局部总线
microprocessor master clock 微处理机主时钟
microcomputer master/slave operation 微型计算机主/从操作
microcomputer performance criteria 微型计算机性能标准
microcomputer POS systems 微型计算机销售点系统
microcomputer prototype system 微型计算机原型系统
microcomputer S-100 bus 微型计算机 S-100 总线
microcomputer storage 微型计算机存储器
microcomputer support devices 微型计算机支持设备
microcomputer system(MCS) 微型计算机系统
microcomputer system basic components 微型计算机系统基本组件
microcomputer system monitor 微型计算机系统监控程序;微机监视器
microcomputer terminal 微型计算机

终端
microcomputer timing modules 微型计算机定时模块
microcomputer word processing 微型计算机文字处理
microconsole 微控制台
microcontext 最小上下文
microcontrol microprogramming 微控制微编程
microcontroller 微控制器
microcontroller characteristics 微控制器特性
microcontroller external input signals 微控制器外部输入信号
microcontroller functional components 微控制器功能组件
microcontroller I/O system 微控制器输入/输出系统
microcontroller register 微控制器寄存器
microcontroller simulator 微控制器仿真器
microcontroller working registers 微控制器工作寄存器
microcontroller working storage 微控制器工作存储器
microcrack 微裂痕,微疵点
microcycle 微周期
microcylindrical lens 微圆柱形透镜
microdevice 微型器件
microdiagnosis 微诊断
microdiagnosis loader 微诊断装入器
microdiagnostics 微诊断程序,微诊断法
microdisk drive 微型(磁)盘驱动器
microelectronic circuit 微电子电路
microelectronic device 微电子器件
microelectronic packaging 微电子组装
microelectronics(ME) 微电子学
microelement 微元件
microelement wafer 微元件芯片
microemulator 微仿真器
microenergy logic circuit 微能耗逻辑电路
microenvironment 微环境
microetch 微刻蚀
microevent 微事件
microfabrication 微制造,微型装配

microfarad （电容计量单位）微法拉,微法
microfiche 缩微平片,缩微胶片
microfiche book 缩微胶片图书
microfiche management system 缩微胶片管理系统
microfiche reader 缩微胶片阅读器
microfiche viewer 缩微胶片观察器
microfile 缩微文件
microfilm(MF) 缩微胶卷
Microfilm Association of Great Britain 英国缩微胶片协会
microfilm flow camera 缩微胶卷自动照相机
microfilm image 缩微胶卷图像
microfilm reader 缩微胶卷阅读器
microfilm reader-printer 缩微胶卷阅读打印机
microfilm recorder 缩微胶卷记录器
microfilmer 缩微胶卷记录器
microfloppy 微型活动盘
microfloppy-diskette drive 微型活动盘驱动器
microflowchart 微流程图
microfolio 缩微品护封
microfont 缩微大写字体
microform 缩微印刷品
microform in color 彩色缩微品
microform reader 缩微图片阅读器
microform reader-copier 缩微印刷品阅读复印机
microform reader-printer 缩微品阅读复印两用机
microformat 缩微格式
microframe computer 微型结构计算机
microfreeze 微冻结
microfunction decoder 微功能译码器
microgram mapping 微程序地址变换
micrographics 缩微图形学
microgrid 微细网格
microgroove 密纹唱片
microhologram 显微全息照片
microholography 显微全息技术
microimage 缩微图像
microinstruction 微指令
microinstruction cycle 微指令周期
microinstruction debug 微指令调试
microinstruction decoder 微指令解码

器
microinstruction encode 微指令编码
microinstruction field 微指令字段
microinstruction flexibility 微指令灵活性
microinstruction input 微指令输入
microinstruction interrupt service routine 微指令中断服务程序
microinstruction length 微指令长度
microinstructionmemory 微指令存储器
microinstruction register 微指令寄存器
microinstruction sequence 微指令序列
microinstruction simulation 微指令模拟
microinstruction storage 微指令存储器
microinterpreter 微指令解释程序
microinterrupt 微中断
microjacket 微封套
microJAVA 微型JAVA语言
microjustification 微调整
microkernel 微内核
microkit 微型计算机套件
microlanguage 微型语言
microlens 微型透镜
microlink interface 微型连接接口
micrologger 微型记录器
micrologic 微逻辑
micrologic card 微逻辑插件
micrologic elements 微逻辑元件
micromainframe 微巨型机
micromainframe microcomputer 微巨型微型计算机
micromanipulator 微型机器人
micromation 微胶片自动化
micromatrix 微矩阵
micromechanics analysis 微力学分析
micrometer(μM) 微米
micrometrics 微测量学
micromini 微型化小型机
microminiature 超小型,微小型
microminiature discrete modules 微型化分立组件
microminiaturization 微型化,超小型
micromodel 微模型
micromodule(MM) 微模块;微程序模块
micron(μM) 微米

micron pitch 微米间距
Micronet 微机网
microoperation 微操作
microoperation exclusive 微操作互斥
microoperation sequence 微操作序列
microorder 微命令
micropackage 微封装
microperipheral interface 微外设接口
microphone 传声器,麦克风
micropipeline 微流水线
microphonics 颤噪效应;微音扩大
microphotography 缩微照相
microplasma effect 微等离子效应
micropower 微功率
microprint 缩微印刷品
microprobe 微探针
microprocessing systems 微处理系统
microprocessing unit(MPU) 微处理单元
microprocessor 微处理器,微处理机
microprocessor architecture 微处理机体系结构
microprocessor assembler simulator 微处理器汇编程序仿真器
microprocessor cache memory 微处理器高速缓存
microprocessor cards 微处理机卡,微处理机插件
microprocessor chip 微处理器芯片
microprocessor chipset 微处理机芯片组
microprocessor compiler 微处理机编译程序
microprocessor components 微处理器元件
microprocessor controller 微处理机控制器
microprocessor cross-assembler 微处理机交叉汇编程序
microprocessor debugging program 微处理机调试程序
microprocessor design 微处理机设计
microprocessor development system 微处理机开发系统
microprocessor educator system 微处理机教育系统
microprocessor emulation 微处理机仿真

microprocessor I/O 微处理机输入/输出
microprocessor I/O categories 微处理机输入/输出类别
microprocessor instruction set 微处理机指令系统
microprocessor intelligence 微处理机智能
microprocessor language assembler(MLA) 微处理机语言汇编程序
microprocessor language editor(MLE) 微处理机语言编辑程序
microprocessor life cycles 微处理机寿命周期
microprocessor maintenance console 微处理机维护控制器
microprocessor master / master operation 微处理机主/主作业
microprocessor master/slave system 微处理机主/从系统
microprocessor memory interface 微处理机内存接口
microprocessor modem 微处理机调制解调器
microprocessor monitor 微处理机监督程序
microprocessor read-only memory programmer 微处理机只读存储器编程器
microprocessor series(MPS) 微处理机系列
microprocessor slice 微处理器位片
microprocessor system(MPS) 微处理机系统
microprocessor system analyzer 微处理机系统分析仪
microprocessor system organization 微处理机系统组织
microprocessor terminal 微处理机终端
microprocessor training aid 微处理机训练用辅助设备
microprogram(MP) 微程序
microprogram addressing 微程序寻址
microprogram assembly language 微程序汇编语言
microprogram branching 微程序分支,微程序转移
microprogram control(MPC) 微程序控制
microprogram control functions 微程序控制功能
microprogram control logic(MCL) 微程序控制逻辑
microprogram control section 微程序控制节
microprogram control unit(MCU) 微程序控制器
microprogram counter 微程序计数器
microprogram debugging 微程序调试
microprogram description 微程序描述
microprogram development 微程序开发
microprogram diagnosis 微程序诊断
microprogram display 微程序显示
microprogram efficiency 微程序效率
microprogram emulation 微程序仿真
microprogram fetch phase 微程序提取阶段
microprogram field 微程序字段
microprogram firmware 微程序固件
microprogram implementation 微程序实现
microprogram indexing 微程序索引法
microprogram instruction set 微程序指令系统
microprogram load 微程序装入
microprogram looping 微程序循环
microprogram machine instructions 微程序机器指令
microprogram mapping 微程序地址变换
microprogram memory 微程序存储器
microprogram microassembler 微程序微汇编程序
microprogram microcode 微程序微码
microprogram optimization 微程序优化
microprogram parameterization 微程序参数化
microprogram routine 微例程
microprogram sequencing control 微程序顺序控制
microprogram specification 微程序说明书
microprogram subroutine 微子例程
microprogrammable 可编微程序的

microprogrammable computer 可编微程序计算机
microprogrammable instruction 可编微程序指令
microprogrammable processor 可编微程序处理机
microprogrammable ROM 可编微程序的只读存储器
microprogrammed 微程序控制的
microprogrammed diagnostics 微程序诊断程序
microprogrammed interface 微程序控制接口
microprogrammed microprocessor 微程序控制处理机
microprogrammed processor 可编微程序处理机
microprogrammed subroutines 微程序设计子例程
microprogramming 微程序设计
microprogramming/fixed instruction 固定指令微程序设计
microprogramming language 微程序设计语言
microprogramming parameterization 微程序设计参数化
microprogramming simulation 微程序设计仿真
microprogramming support software 微程序设计支持软件
microprogramming techniques(MPT) 微程序设计技术
microrobotics 微机器人学
microscope check up 微观检查
microscopic image processing system 显微图像处理系统
microsecond(μS) 微秒
microsignal processing 微信号处理
Microsoft BookShelf 微软书库
Microsoft C 微软C语言
Microsoft Corp. 微软公司(美)
Microsoft Data Access Components (MDAC) 微软数据访问部件
Microsoft Encarta World Atlas 微软Encarta世界百科全书
Microsoft Excel 微软Excel表格软件
Microsoft Exchange 微软Exchange群件
Microsoft Explorer 微软浏览器
Microsoft Internet Assistant 微软因特网助手
Microsoft Mail 微软邮件程序
Microsoft mouse 微软规格鼠标器
Microsoft Network 微软网络
Microsoft Office 微软办公套件
Microsoft Solution Provider 微软方案提供者
Microsoft Windows 微软视窗软件
Microsoft Word 微软Word文字处理软件
Microsoft Works 微软Works综合软件包
microspace adjusting 微小空间调整
microspacing 微空间调整
microstatement 微语句
MicroStation 微工作站
microstep 微(程序)步
microstrip line 微带线
microstructure 微结构
microswitch 微动开关
microsyn 精密自动同步机
microtasking 微任务化
Microtek 全友公司(台湾省扫描仪生产商)
microtext 缩微原文
microtool 微工具
microtron 电子回旋加速器
microtronics 微电子学
MicroVAX 微VAX计算机(DEC)
microvolt (电压单位)微伏(10^{-6}伏特)
microwave(M/W) 微波
microwave communication 微波通信
microwelding 微元件焊接
microworld 微观世界
Microwriter Microwriter微型打字机
mid-batch recovery 成批数据中的错误校正
mid 中间的
mid-level manager 中级管理器
mid-level network 中间层网络
mid-model 中间模型
mid-shot 中距离镜头,中景
mid-split 中间分裂;平分
mid user 中间用户
mid-value select 中值选择

mid-value splitting technique 中值分割法
midcareer plateau 中年平坦期
middle alignment 中间对齐
middle element 中间单元
middle in chain(MIC) 链中部
middle infrared 中红外区
middle letter row 中排字母键行
middle management 中层管理
middle RU of chain 链中间请求应答单元
middle-square method 平方取中法
middle tier 中间层
middle tray (打印机)中层纸匣
middleware 中间件
MIDI(Musical Instrument Digital Interface) 乐器数字界面
MIDI cuing 乐器数字界面演奏指示符
MIDI file MIDI 文件
MIDI mapper MIDI 映射
MIDI port MIDI 端口
MIDI Sequencer MIDI 音序器
MIDI synthesizer MIDI 合成器
midman architecture 夹层体系结构
midpoint 中间点
midrange computer 中程计算机
midtone 中间色调
migration 迁移
migration cleaning 迁移清除
migration data host 迁移数据宿主
migration evaluation 转移评估
migration imaging 转移成像
migration methodology 转移方法学
migration path 迁移路径
Migration Toolkit 转移工具(Informix)
migration volume 迁移卷
MIH(Missing Interruption Handler) 丢失中断处理程序
MII(Media Independent Interface) 与媒体无关接口(Sun,40引脚)
mil (英制长度计量单位)密尔
milestone 里程碑
milestone scheduling 里程碑式计划方法
milestone state 里程碑状态
military computer 军用计算机
military decision analysis 军事决策分时器
Miller code 米勒码
milli 毫,千分之一,10^{-3}
milliampere(mA) 毫安
milliliter(ml) 毫升
millimeter(mm) 毫米
millimicron 毫微米,纳米
millimicrosecond 毫微秒,纳秒
million floating-point operations per second(MFLOPS) 每秒百万次浮点运算
million instructions per second(mips) 百万条指令/秒
million operations per second(MOPS) 每秒百万次操作
millisecond(ms) 毫秒
millivolt(mV) 毫伏
milliwatt(mW) 毫瓦
MIMD(Multiple - Instruction stream Multiple - Data stream) 多指令流多数据流
MIMD architecture 多指令流多数据流结构,MIMD 结构
MIMD-RAM 多指令流多数据流随机存取机器
MIME (Multipurpose Internet Mail Extensions) 通用因特网邮件扩充服务
mimesis 模仿,模拟
mimetic 模仿的
mimic 仿造品;伪造品
mimic program 模仿程序
mimicking 模仿
MIMO(Manuel In - Machine Out) 手工输入-机器输出
MIN(Multistage Interconnection Network) 多级互连网络
min-cut 最小割
min-cut placement method 最小切割布局法
min-max heap 极小极大堆
min-max linear estimation 极小极大线性估算
mind 智力,智能
mind bus 共识总线
mind system 智能系统
mini-block coloring 微区着色
mini floppy 小型软磁盘

mini-floppy disk 小型软磁盘 「法
mini-max dual method 极小极大对偶
mini-supercomputer 小巨型机
MINI-UNIX 小型 UNIX 操作系统
miniassembler program 小型汇编程序
miniature diskette drive 小型软盘驱动器
miniature hand-held scanner 小型手持式扫描仪
miniature rectangular connector 小型矩形连接器
miniature title bar 小标题栏
miniaturization 小型化
Minicard 小型卡;缩微胶片
minicartridge 小型盒式磁带
minicomposite head 小型组合磁头
minicomputer(MINI) 小型计算机
minicomputer communication processor 小型计算机通信处理机
minicomputer concentrator 小型计算机集中器
minicomputer cross compilation 小型计算机交叉编译
minicomputer device controller 小型计算机设备控制器
minicomputer message switching 小型计算机信息转接
minicomputer node 小型计算机节点
minicomputer remote concentrators 小型计算机远程集中器 「端
minicomputer terminal 小型计算机终端
minicomputer terminal controller 小型计算机终端控制器
minicomputers message switching 小型计算机消息交换
minidiskette 小型软磁盘
minihost 小型主机
minilot 小型电磁旋转开关
minimal 最小的,极小的
minimal access coding 最快存取编码
minimal automaton 最小自动机
minimal bar width 最窄条符宽度
minimal BASIC 最小 BASIC 语言
minimal close form 最小闭覆盖
minimal coding access 最短编码存取
minimal complete class 最小完备类
minimal cost path 最小代价路径

minimal cover 最小覆盖
minimal cut 最小割
minimal dominant set 极小支配集
minimal element 最小元素,极小元
minimal entropy coding 最小熵编码
minimal form 最小形式
minimal functionally complete set 最小全功能集合
minimal latency programming 最短等待时间编程 「程
minimal latency routine 最短潜时例
minimal least square 最小极小二乘方
minimal machine 最小机器
minimal-model semantics 最小模型语义学
minimal network 最小网络
minimal norm generalized inverse 最小范数广义逆
minimal-path problem 最短路径问题
minimal perfect hashing 最小完全散列法
minimal perturbation 极小扰动
minimal polynomial 极小多项式
minimal realization 最小实现
minimal segment 最小片段
minimal state-space realization 最小状态空间实现
minimal tree 最小树
minimal upper bound 最小上界
minimal value 极小值
minimal variation 最小变分,最小偏
minimal vector 极小向量 「差
minimality 极小性
minimalization 极小化;取极小值
minimax 极小极大法,最大最小法
minimax approximation 极小极大逼
minimax criterion 极小极大准则 「近
minimax decision rule 极小极大决策规则
minimax design 极小极大设计方法
minimax error norm 极小极大误差范
minimax estimation 极小极大估计
「数
minimax loss 最小最大损失
minimax negative utility 最小最大负效用
minimax principle 极小极大原则
minimax risk criterion 最小最大风险

判据
minimax roboustness 极小极大坚固性
minimax search 极小极大搜索
minimax search algorithm 极小极大搜索算法
minimax solution 极小极大解
minimax strategy 极小极大策略
minimax system 极小极大系统
minimization 最小化；极小化
minimization of redundancy 冗余度最小化
minimize 最小化
minimized button （视窗）最小化按钮
minimizing set 最小集合
minimum 最小，最快；最小(极小)值
minimum access code 最快存取码
minimum-access coding 最短访问时间编码
minimum-access programming 最快存取编程
minimum-access routine 最快访问例
minimum cell rate 最小信元速率
minimum-cost flow algorithm 最小代价流算法
minimum cut 最小割
minimum delay programming 最小延迟程序设计
minimum description length principle (MDLP) 最小描述长度原理
minimum dimension 最小维数，最小尺寸
minimum discriminable signal 最小可识别信号
minimum distance 最小距离
minimum distance classification 最小距离分类法
minimum distance classifier 最小距离分类器
minimum distance code 最小距离码
minimum dominant set 最小支配集
minimum entropy 最小熵
minimum feature size 最小特征尺寸
minimum gap 最小间隙
minimum implementation model 最小实现模型
minimum interval 最小时间间隔「码
minimum-latency code 最小等待时间
minimum-latency programming 最小等待时间程序设计 「程
minimum latency routine 最快存取例
minimum-matching algorithm 最小权匹配算法
minimum mean square error restoration 最小均方误差恢复
minimum partition problem 最小划分问题
minimum password 最短口令长度
minimum path 最小路径覆盖
minimum period 最小周期
minimum projection 最小投影
minimum redundancy 最小冗余
minimum required configuration 最小需求配置 「声
minimum round-off noise 最小舍入噪
minimum size executive routines 最短执行程序
minimum spanning tree 最小生成树
minimum square error 最小方差
minimum timeslice 最小时间片
minimum truncation 最短截取
minimum variance criterion 最小方差判据
minimum weight routing 最小加权路径选择
minimum weighted path length tree 最小赋权路径长度树
miniplug 小型插头
miniprinter 小型打印机
minisupercomputer 小巨型计算机
minitower case 小立式机箱
Minnesota Mining Manufacturer data cartridge 3M数据盒式磁带机
minor 次要的；局部的；小型的
minor axes 短轴
minor control 细控制，次要控制
minor control change 细控变化
minor control data 细控数据
minor control field 细控字段
minor cycle 副周期，小循环
minor determinant 子行列式
minor diagonal 次对角线
minor failure 轻度失效
minor function 下函数
minor gridlines 次要网格线
minor key 次键，辅助键
minor lobe 副瓣，旁瓣

minor loop feedback 局部反馈
minor node 小节点
minor relay center 小转报中心
minor sorting field 辅助排序字段
minor structure 子结构
minor synchronization point service 次同步点服务
minor tick 次节拍,次间隔
minor time slice 小时间片
minor total 小计
minor utility 小型公用程序
minority carrier 少数载流子
Minsky's conjecture 明斯基猜想
minterm 最小项
minterm expression 最小项表达式
minuend 被减数,被减量
minus 减号,负标记
minus flag 负标记
minus lens 负透镜
minus letter spacing 缩小字母间隔
minus sign 负号
minus zone 负数区,负区
minutia 细节特征
MIP(Mixed Integer Programming) 混合整数规划
MIPS(Microprocessor without Interlocked Pile Stages) 无互锁流水线级微处理器
MIPS(Million Instruction Per Second) 每秒百万条指令
MIPS chip MIPS处理器芯片(SGI)
miracle 奇迹
miracle chip 超大规模集成电路芯片
mirror 镜像;对称;反射
mirror drive 镜像驱动器
mirror image 镜像
mirror-image programming 镜像编程
mirror-image switch 镜像开关
mirror language 镜像语言
mirror margins 对称页边距
mirror plot 镜像绘图
mirror processor 镜像处理器
mirror set 镜像集
mirror status 镜像状态
mirror transaction 镜像事务处理程
Mirror Ⅱ MirrorⅡ通信程序
mirrored declustering 镜像反聚类法
mirrored pair 镜像对
mirrored protection 镜像保护
mirroring 映射,反射
Mirrors Mirrors转换软件
MIRS(Motorola Integrated Radio System) 摩托罗拉集群通信系统
MIS(Management Information System) 管理信息系统
MIS display program 管理信息系统显示程序
misaddress 错误地址
misalignment 未对准,未重合;失调
misc 杂项
miscalculation 错误计算
miscellaneous 杂项的,其他的
miscellaneous clipart 杂项剪贴图
miscellaneous data 杂项数据
miscellaneous function 杂类函数
miscellaneous intercept 杂项截除
miscellaneous time 杂项服务时间
mischif 故障
misclassification 错误分类
misconception 错误概念
misconnection 错误连接
miscount 错误计数
MISD(Multiple-Instruction steam - Single Data stream) 多指令流单数据流
misdata 错误数据
MISE(Mean Integrated Square Error) 积分均方差
misentry 错误输入
misfeed 误传送,传送失效
misfit 错配
mishit 错误命中
misidentification 错误标识
misinput 错误输入
misinterpretation 错误判断
misjudgement failure 从属故障
mislead 误导
mismark 错误标志
mismatch 失配
mismatch indicator 失配指示器
mismatch-of-core-radius loss 芯径不匹配损耗
mismatch sensitivity 失配灵敏度
mismatched domain 失配域
mismatched Guassian channel 失配高斯通道

mismatched uncertain system 失配不确定系统
misoperation 误操作
misprint 错误打印
misread 读错误
misrecognition 误识
misregistration 不重合,位置不正
misrepresentation 错误表示
misroute 错误路由选择
miss 故障,失误,差错
miss ratio 未命中率
missed synchronization 漏同步
missequence 失序
missile guidance computer 导弹制导计算机
missing address marker 漏地址标志
missing argument 缺失变元
missing bit 缺失位
mission code 漏码
missing data 遗漏数据
missing dots 漏点
missing error 漏失错误
missing interruption handler(MIH) 丢失中断处理程序
missing page interruption 缺页中断
missing parameter 遗漏参数
mission pulse 漏脉冲,丢脉冲
missing segment interrupt 缺段中断
missing variable 缺变量
mission 任务,使命
mission control center 任务控制中心
mission critical 关键使命
mission-dependent interface 任务相关界面
mission effectiveness assessment 任务有效性评价
mission factor 使用因数,任务因子
mission flow diagram 任务流程图
mission profile 任务概述
mission sequence 任务序列
misspecified model 错定的模型
misspelling correction 拼写错误纠正
mist 墨雾
mistake 错误,过失
Mistel Mistel 可视数据系统
mistermination 端接失配
misunderstanding 错误理解
misuse failure 误用失效,误操作故障

MIT (Massachusetts Institutes of Technology) 麻省理工学院(美)
MIT-MAGIC-COOKIE-1 (X11)"幻饼"协议(麻省理工学院)
mitre 斜面接合
Mitrenet Mitre 网
Mitsubishi electric Co. 三菱电气公司(日)
mix 混合
mix gate "或"门
mix instruction 混合指令
mix with file 与文件混合
mixed action 混合作用
mixed-base notation 混合基记数法
mixed calculation 混合计算
mixed cell reference 混合式单元格寻址法
mixed column/line chart 直条折线混合图
mixed continuous group 混合连续群
mixed data set 混合数据集
mixed dominance 混合支配
mixed environment 混合环境
mixed file 混合文件
mixed finite element method 混合有限元法
mixed format print data set 混合格式打印数据集
mixed hiding strategy 混合隐藏策略
mixed highs 混合高频
mixed-initiative tutoring system 混合启动型教学系统
mixed instruction 混合命令
mixed interconnection 混合互联
mixed job stream 混合作业流
mixed language programming 混合语言编程
mixed layer 混合层
mixed linear programming 混合线性规划
mixed list 混合表
mixed-media system 混合媒体系统
mixed-mode arithmetic 混合运算
mixed-mode expression 混合方式表达
mixed network 混合网络
mixed penalty method 混合惩罚函数
mixed pixel 混合像素
mixed processing on-line access 混合

处理联机存取
mixed radix 混合数基
mixed-radix numeration system 混合数基记数制
mixed search strategy 混合搜索策略
mixed strategy precedence grammar 混合策略优先文法
mixed-type expression 混合型表达式
mixed-unit representation 混合单位表示
mixed variational method 混合变分法
mixed-vendor environment 不同厂家的设备配置
mixer 混音器,混响器
mixing 混合,混录
mixing network 混合网络
mixing sound 混声
mixing studio 混录演播室
MKS system 米-千克-秒制
MKS unit 米-千克-秒单位
mkuser(make user) (Unix)创建用户命令
ML(Machine Language) 机器语言
ML(Macro Library) 宏程序库
ML series CNC robot ML系列计算机数字控制机器人
MLA Bibliography 美国现代语言协会文献数据库
MLP(Multiple Line printing) 多行打印
MLU(Majority Logic Unit) 多数逻辑单元
MMB(Multiport Memory Bank) 多端口存储体
MMC(Microsoft Management Console) 微软管理控制台
MMC(Multi Media Communication) 多媒体通信
MMCodec 多媒体编码解码器(Sun)
MME(Multi Media Extensions) 多媒体扩展
MMI(Man Machine Interface) 人-机接口
MMIO(MultiMedia Input/Output) 多媒体输入输出
MMIO file services 多媒体输入输出文件服务
MMIO manager 多媒体输入输出管理器
MMM(Main Memory Module) 主内存模块
MMP(Multiplex Message Processor) 多路转换消息处理机
MMS(Mass Memory System) 海量存储系统
MMS(Multi-Modular Storage) 多模块存储器
MMS(Multiport Memory System) 多端口存储器系统
MMU(Memory Management Unit) 内存管理单元
MMU(Memory Mapping Unit) 内存变换部件
MMX(MultiMedia eXtensions) 多媒体扩充技术(Intel)
MMX data type MMX数据类型(Intel)
MMX instruction set MMX指令集(Intel)
MMX register MMX寄存器(Intel)
mnemonic(MNE) 助记符号
mnemonic address 助记地址
mnemonic address code 助记地址码
mnemonic code 助记码
mnemonic instruction code 助记指令码
mnemonic key 助记键
mnemonic language 助记语言
mnemonic name 助记名
mnemonic operation code 助记操作码
mnemonic symbol 助记符号
mnemonic table 助记符号表
MNP(MicroCom Networking Protocol) Microcom网络协议
MO(Magneto-Optic disk) 磁光盘
MO(Manual Output) 手工输出
MO:DCA(Mixed Object:Document Content Architecture) 混合目标文献内容体系结构
mobile 移动的,便携的;活动体
mobile communication 移动通信
mobile computing 移动计算;易变计
mobile database 易变数据库
mobile messaging gateway 移动信息处理网关
mobile phone service 移动电话服务
mobile robot 移动式机器人
mobile sensor 移动式传感器

mobile switching center (MSC) 移动交换中心
mobile systems 移动式系统
mobile telephone services 移动电话服务
mobility 迁移率;移动性;易变性
mobility model 移动性模型
MOD(MODification) 修改,改进
MOD(MODdule) 模块
MOD(MODdulo) 模数;求模运算
mod 修饰号;求模
mod function 求模函数
mod operation 求模运算
modal 模态的,形式的
modal analysis 模式分析
modal deduction 模态演绎
modal dialog box 模态对话框
modal dispersion 模式色散
model distortion bandwidth 模畸变带宽
modal logic 模式逻辑
modal logic retrieval system 模式逻辑检索系统
model matrix 模态矩阵
modal number 原型数
modal parameter 模态参数
modal superposition 模式叠加
model transform 模型变换
modal window 模式窗口
mode(MOD) 方式,模式;模
mode bit 模式位
mode conversion 模式变换
mode dispersion 模式色散
mode fiber 模式光纤
mode field 模式字段
mode indicator 模式指示符
mode inspector 模式检验程序
mode mixer 搅模器,模式混合器
mode name 方式名
mode request register 方式请求寄存器
mode scrambler 搅模器,混模器
mode select 模式选择
mode setting command 模式设置命令
mode shift key 工作方式转换键
mode specifier 方式说明符
mode switching 方式转换
mode transformer 模式变换器
model(M, MOD) 模型,样机
model adjustment technique 模型调整法
model analysis 模型分析

model base 模型库
model-based expert system 基于模型的专家系统
model-based reasoning 基于模型的推理
model-based vision 基于模型的视觉
model building 模型建立
model calibration 模型校准
model-decomposition 模型分解
model-dependent logout 模型相关运行记录
model design 模型设计
model-directed inference 模型指导推理
model-driven method 模型驱动法
model extraction 模型析取
model file 模型文件
model fitting 模型拟合
model generator 模型生成程序
model library 模型库
model machine 样机
model matching 模型匹配
model loading 模型加载
model of endorsement 认可模型
model-oriented software 面向模型的软件
model base 模型库
model parts 样机部件
model-preference default 模型自定义默认值
model reduction 模型归约
model reference system 模型参考系统
model selection criteria 模型选择准则
model representation 模型表示
model space 模型空间
model statement 模型语句,样板语句
model symbols 模型符号
model transferring 模型变换
model view 模型视图
modeler 模型处理程序
modeless dialog box 无模式对话框
modeless editor 无模式编辑程序
modeling 建模,造型
modeling algorithm 建模算法
modeling control strategy 建模控制策略
modeling database 造型数据库
modeling framework 建模模架
modeling language 建模语言
modeling measurement 建模测试
modeling production management sys-

tem 模拟生产管理系统
modeling proportion 造型比例
modeling rendering 模型绘制,建模润色
modeling tool 建模工具
modeling transformation 造型变换
modelization 模型化
modem 调制解调器
modem check control 调制解调器校验控制
modem chip 调制解调器芯片
modem command 调制解调器命令
modem connect-line control 调制解调器连接线控制
modem diagnostics 调制解调器诊断
modem digital loopback control 调制解调器数字回路控制
modem eliminator 调制解调器消除器(连接电缆)
modem-encryption devices 调制解调器密码设备
modem equalization 调制解调器均衡
modem functions 调制解调器功能
modem operation 调制解调器操作
modem packaging 调制解调器的组装
modem pool 调制解调器池
modem receive-only control 调制解调器只接收控制
modem server(MSU) 调制解调服务器
modem sharing unit(MSU) 调制解调器共用单元
modem standards 调制解调器标准
modem synchronization 调制解调器同步
modem tester 调制解调器测试器
moder 脉冲编码装置
moderate rotation 适度旋转
moderated mailing list 仲裁邮递表
moderately-coupled system 适度耦合系统
moderator 仲裁人
modern algebra 近世代数
modern control engineering 现代控制工程
modern face 现代字体
modern typeface 现代字体
modest capacity memory 适度容量存储器
modest-size program 适度规模程序

modifiability 可修改性
modifiable alternate program communication block 可修改替换程序通信块
modifiable parameter 可修改参数
modification 修改,改变,改进
modification by program-self 程序自修改
modification cycle 修改周期
modification level 修改级
modification loop 数据改变循环指令
modified 修改的,改进的
modified chemical vapor deposition process(MCVD) 改进型化学气相淀积过程法
modified Euler method 修正的欧拉方法
modified frequency modulation(MFM) 改进调频法
modified frequency modulation recording 改进型调频记录
modified least square method 改进型最小二乘法
modified page zero addressing 改进的零页寻址法
modified top-down testing 改进型自顶向下测试法
modifier 修改量
modifier command 变址命令
modifier formula 修正公式
modifier key 修正键
modifier register 变址寄存器
modify 修饰,修改
modify file type 修改文件类型
modify structure 修改结构
modify ticket 修改标签
modify view setting 修改视图设计
Modula-2 (Modular Language-2) Modula-2 语言
modular 模块化的,积木式的
modular accounting package 模块化会计套装软件
modular adaptive signal sorter 模块化自适应信号排序程序
modular algebra 模代数结构
modular architecture 模块化体系结构
modular concurrent program 模块化并发程序
modular connector 模块连接器

modular constraint 模约束
modular construction 模块化结构,积木式结构
modular decomposition 模块分解
modular design 模块化设计
modular expansion 模块扩充
modular jack 模块化插孔
modular language 模块语言
modular microcomputer component 模块化微型计算机部件
modular microprogramming 模块化程序设计
modular multiaxis system 模块式多轴系统
modular neural network 模块神经网络
modular organization 模块化组织
modular programming 模块化程序设计
modular redundancy 模数冗余度
modular robot 积木式机器人
modular self-synchronizing 模块化自同步
modular software 模块化软件
modular supercomputer architecture 模块化巨型计算机体系结构
modular system 模块化系统,积木式系统
Modular TV System(MTS) 标准型电视系统
modular unit 模块式组合件
modularity 模块性
modularity design 模块性设计
modularity software 模块化软件
modularization 模块化
modularization structure 模块化结构
modularized hardware 模块式硬件
modularized program 模块化程序
modulate 调制
modulated carrier 已调载波
modulated light 被调制光
modulating and demodulating unit 调制解调单元
modulating index 调制指数
modulating signal 调制信号
modulation 调制
modulation capability 调制能力
modulation code 调制码
modulation distortion 调制失真
modulation envelope 调制包络线

modulation factor 调制系数,调制度
modulation index 调制指数
modulation noise 调制噪声
modulation parameters 调制参数
modulation rate 调制速率
modulation suppression 调制抑制
modulation transfer function 调制传递函数
modulation types 调制类型
modulator 调制器
modulator-demodulator 调制器-解调器
module 模块,组件
module attribute 模块属性
module block time 模块阻塞时间
module body 模块体
module checking routine 模块检验例程
module cohesion 模块内聚性
module coupling 模块耦合
module declaration 模块说明
module definition file 模块定义文件
module descriptor 模块描述段
module downtime 模块失效时间
module external design 模块外部设计
module frame 模帧
module generator 模块生成器
module homomorphism 模同态
module idle time 机组空闲时间
module independence 模块独立性
module input 模块输入
module interface 模块接口
module isomorphism 模同构
module library 模块库
module logical design 模块逻辑设计
module masking 模屏蔽
module microcircuit 模块微电路
module name 模块名
module operation 模块工序
module operation time 模块工序时间
module output 模块输出
module pin 组件引脚
module 3 redundancy system 模3冗余系统
module's cohesion 模块内聚性
module strength 模块强度
module testing 组件测试
module uptime 模块可用时间
module utilization 模块利用率
modulo 求模运算

modulo check 模数检验
modulo level 模级
modulo-N arithmetic 模 N 运算
modulo-N check 模 N 校验
modulo-N counter 模 N 计数器
modulo symbol 模符号
modulo-two adder 模 2 加法器
modulus 模数,模量
modulus of continuity 连续模
modus ponens 假言推理
modus tollendo ponens 拒取式
moire 云纹,龟纹
moire enlargement 波纹放大
moire strain analysis 波纹应变分析
moisture 潮湿,湿气
moisture-proof 防潮
moisture sensor 湿度传感器
mold design 模板(模具)设计
molded circuit board 模压电路板
molded substrate 模压衬底
molded thermoplastics 模压热塑性
molecular 分子
molecular beam epitaxy 分子束外延
molecular bonding 分子焊接
molecular electronic device(MED) 分子型电子元件
molecular integrated circuit 分子集成电路
molecular intelligence 分子智能
molecular laser 分子激光器
molecular modeling 分子建模
molecular statement 分子命题
molecule model program 分子模型程序
molecule structure 分子结构
MOM(Mass Optical Memory) 海量光存储器
MOM(Merger Overview Model) 合并综览模式
moment 矩;时刻
moment restriction 矩量限制
moment sensor 力矩传感器
moment value estimation 力矩估值
momentary connection 瞬时接通
momentary position 瞬时位置
momentum 动量
momentum conservation 动量守恒
monad 一元
monadic 单体,孤立项;一元的

monadic Boolean operator 一元布尔运算符
monadic formula 单值公式
monadic indicator 一元指示符
monadic operation 一元运算,单值操作
Mondex Mondex 智能卡
moniker 别名
moniker class 别名类
moniker client 别名客户机
moniker server 别名服务器
moniputer 监视/计算一体机
monitor(MON) 监视,监听;监控程序;监视器
monitor call 监督程序调用
monitor command description 监控命令描述
monitor community (Netware)监督程序共同体
monitor console 监控台
monitor desk 监控台
monitor event simulation system 监控事件仿真系统
monitor mode 监控状态
monitor program 监控程序
monitor scheduler 监督调度程序
monitor task 监督任务程序
monitor unit 监督单元
monitor window 监视窗口
monitored instructions 受监视指令
monitored local job 受监视本地作业
monitoring 监测
monitoring agent 监控代理
monitoring console 监控台
monitoring dynamic process 监控动态进程
monitoring key 监视键,监听键
monitoring network 监控网络
monkey and banana problem "猴子与香蕉"问题
monoalphabetic substitution cipher 单表代替密码
monoblock 单体的,整块的
monoboard microcomputer 单板微机
monobrids 单片混合微电路
monobus 单总线
monochip 单芯片
monochrolaser printer 单色激光打印机
monochromatic 单色的

monochromatic bitmap 单色位图
monochromatic light 单色光
monochromatic radiation 单色辐射
monochrome 单色,单色的
monochrome adapter 单色适配器
monochrome bitmap 单色位图
monochrome display adapter(MDA) 单色显示器适配器
monochrome graphics adapter(MGA) 单色图形适配器
monochrome graphics printer port (MGP) 单色图形打印端口
monochrome image 单色图像
monochrome monitor 单色显示器
monochrome supertwist nematic LCD 单色超扭曲向列型液晶显示器
monocode 单代码,树式结构码
monocular vision 单眼视觉
monofiber cable 单纤光缆
monofiber connector 单纤维连接器
monofile monovolume 单文件单卷
monofile multivolume 单文件多卷
monoid 独异点,类群
monoid-closure 独异点闭包
monoline 单线
monoline digital filter 单线数字滤波器
monolithic 单片的
monolithic A/D converter 单片模/数转换器
monolithic head 单体(整体结构)磁头
monolithic integrated circuit(MIC) 单片集成电路
monolithic magnetic head 整体式磁头
monolithic memory 单片存储器
monolithic microprocessor 单片微处理器
monolithic processors 单片处理机
monolithic storage 单片存储器
monomial 单项的
monomode fiber 单模光纤
monomode optical fiber 单模光纤
monophase microinstruction 单步微指令
monophonic 单声的
monoprogram 单道程序
monosemantic 单语义的
monospaced character 等宽字符
monospacing 单间隔,固定宽度
monostable 单稳态的

monostable circuit 单稳态电路
monostable multivibrator 单稳态多谐振荡器
monostable trigger circuit 单稳态触发电路
monosyllabic word recognition 单音节词识别
monotone 单调的
monotone context-sensitive syntax 单调上下文相关语法
monotone control functional 单调控制函数
monotone convergence 单调收敛
monotone data-flow problem 单调数据流问题
monotone decreasing 单调递减
monotone functional 单调泛函
monotone hull 单调壳体
monotone increating 单调递增
monotone multiple decision function 单调多维决策函数
monotone order 单调的次序
monotone restriction 单调限制
monotone variable 单调变量
monotone variational inequality 单调变分不等式
monotonic abduction 单调诱导
monotonic Boolean function 单调布尔函数
monotonic convergence 单调收敛
monotonic filtering 单调滤波
monotonic logic 单调逻辑
monotonic reasoning 单调推理
monotonic transformation 单调变换
monotonicity 单一性
monotonicity constraint 单一性约束
monotropic function 单值函数
montage grammar 画面文法,蒙太奇文法
Monte-Carlo algorithm 蒙特-卡罗算法
Monte-Carlo generator 蒙特-卡罗发生器,随机数产生程序
Monte-Carlo method 蒙特-卡罗法
month leading zero 月份前置零
Mopier(Multiple Original Printer) 多源打印机
Moore machine 摩尔机器
Moore-Penrose generalized inverse 莫

尔-宾洛斯广义逆
Moore's law （关于计算机硬件技术的）摩尔定律(Intel)
MOP(Multiple Online Programming) 多道联机程序设计
MORE Ⅱ MORE Ⅱ桌面表现程序
more 其余的;更多的
more than 大于
morph 变形;形态
morph fitting 形态拟合
morpheme 语素,词素
morpheme extraction 语素抽取
morpher 变形软件
morphic function 形态函数
morphism 同型,同形
morphological analysis 词法分析
morphology 语源学,词态学
morphology parsing 词法分析
morphometric cytology 形态度量细胞学
Morse code 莫尔斯码
Morse key 莫尔斯键
Morse simplex 莫尔斯单工机
MOS(Mean Opinion Score) 主观平均判分法
MOS(Metal Oxide Semiconductor) 金属氧化物半导体
MOS character generator MOS字符发生器
MOS dynamic random access memory 金属氧化物半导体动态随机读写存储器
MOS memory 金属氧化物半导体存储器
MOS transistor MOS晶体管
Mosaic （因特网）Mosaic界面软件
mosaic 镶嵌块,马赛克
mosaic character set 镶嵌字符集
mosaic effect （图像显示）马赛克效果
mosaic mapping 镶嵌成像
mosaic mode 镶嵌模式
mosaic printer 点阵打印机
mosaic printing 镶嵌式印出
mosaic set 镶嵌集
mosaic structure 镶嵌结构
MOSFET(Metal Oxide Semiconductor Field-Effect Transistor) 金属氧化物半导体场效应晶体管
most-closely-nested rule 最近嵌套原则

most-frequently-used index 最常使用索引
most general unification 最一般合一
most probable distribution 最大可能分布
most significant bit(MSB) 最高有效位
most significant character(MSC) 最高有效字符
most significant digit(MSD) 最高有效数字
most significant slice 最高有效位片
motd(message of the day) (Unix)日常问候报文
mother block 主程序块
mother block 主程序段
mother board 母板
mother file 母文件,原文件
mother system of MIS 管理信息系统的母系统
Motif Motif图形界面(开放软件基金会)
motion 运动;移动
motion-adaptive interpolation 运动自适应插值
motion blurred image 运动模糊图像
motion compensated predictive coding 运动补偿预测编码
motion compensation 运动补偿
motion control 运动控制
motion control photography 运动控制照相
motion estimation 运动估计
motion field 运动场
motion hold 运动保持
motion-image encoding 运动图像编码
motion image recognition 运动图像识别
motion parallax 运动视差
motion path 移动路径
motion picture 运动画面
Motion Picture coding Expert Group (MPEG) 运动图像编码专家组规范
motion register 控制运动寄存器
motion sensing 运动传感
motion-sequence programming 运动顺序程序设计
motion study 动作研究
motion video capture adapter 动态视频捕获卡

Motion Video Content Architecture (MVOCA) 动态视频对象内容结构
motion vision 运动视觉
motor(MOT) 马达,电动机
motor advance 马达正转
motor control 电机控制,马达控制
motor controller 马达控制器
motor drive 电机驱动
motor on-off switch 马达启停开关
motor protector 电动机保护装置
motor starter 电动机启动器
Motorola 68000 68000 处理器
Motorola 68020 68020 处理器
Motorola 68030 68030 处理器
Motorola 68040 68040 处理器
Motorola 68881 68881 协处理器
Motorola Inc. 摩托罗拉公司(美)
mould design 铸模设计
mount 安装
mount attribute 安装属性
mount point 安装点
mounted volume table address 安装卷表地址
mounting hole 安装孔
mousable interface 可用鼠标的界面
mouse 鼠标器;窥探器
mouse action 鼠标动作
mouse algorithm 窥探算法
mouse-based interface 基于鼠标的界面
mouse button 鼠标按钮
mouse control panel 鼠标控制面板
mouse driver 鼠标驱动程序
mouse event 鼠标事件
mouse grab (X 协议)鼠标占取
mouse icon 鼠标图标
mouse motion counter 鼠标移动计数器
mouse pad 鼠标垫
mouse pointer 鼠标指针
mouse port 鼠标器端口
mouse scaling 鼠标器标度变换
mouse sensitivity 鼠标器灵敏度
mouse threshold 鼠标阈值
mouse tracking speed 鼠标跟踪速度
mouse trail 鼠标踪迹
MOV(MOVe) 数据传送指令
movable 可移动的
movable-active tooling 移动式主动装置
movable head 可动磁头
movable head disk 移动头磁盘
movable-passive tooling 移动式受动装置
movable random access memory 可更换式随机存取存储器
move 移动;传送
move capture 动画面获取
move instruction 传送指令
move into folder 移入文件夹
move mode 移动模式
move operation 移动操作
move page 移动页
move pen 移动笔
move place 活动余地
move statement 传送语句
move to chart 移到图表
move to overlay 移到覆盖图
move up/move down 上下移动
movement 移动;传送
mover 移动按钮
movie controller 影像播放控制器
movies on demand(MOD) 点播电影
movies on PC 个人计算机上播放的电影
moving arm disk 移动臂磁盘
moving average filter 滑动平均滤波器
moving bar menu 移动条形菜单
moving border 流动边框
moving coordinate system 移动坐标系
moving cursor 移动光标
moving equilibrium 运动平衡
moving-head disk system 移动头磁盘系统
moving object 活动目标(对象)
moving paper carrier 走纸小车
moving platen document copying machine 移动台板式文档复印机
moving singularity 可去奇点
moving target indicator(MTI) 运动目标指示器
moving target search plan 活动目标搜索方案
moving type box printer 活动字盒式打印机
moving window 移动窗口,活动窗口
MP(Major Path) 主路径
MP(Memory Pointer) 内存指针
MP(Multi-Processing) 多道作业
MP(Multi-Processor) 多处理机

MP/M (MultiProgramming Monitor) 多道程序监督程序，CP/M 操作系统

MP recovery 多道作业恢复

MPA (Multi-Pass Automaton) 多遍自动机

MPA (Multi-Peripheral Adapter) 多外设转接器

MPC (Massively Parallel Computer) 大规模并行计算机

MPC (Multimedia PC) 多媒体个人计算机

MPCI (Multiport Programmable Communication Interface) 多端口可编程通信接口

MPE (MultiProgramming Executive) 多道作业执行系统

MPEG (Moving Picture Experts Group) 运动图像专家组标准

MPEG-1 MPEG-1 压缩标准

MPEG-2 MPEG-2 压缩标准

MPEG-3 MPEG-3 压缩标准

MPEG-4 MPEG-4 压缩标准

MPEG chip MPEG 芯片

MPEG compressor MPEG 压缩器

MPEG decompressor MPEG 解压器

MPEG Movies MPEG 电影卡

MPI (Media Programming Interface) 媒体编程接口

MPI application services 媒体编程接口应用程序服务

MPL (Macro Procedure Language) 宏过程语言

MPL (Message Processing Language) 消息处理语言

MPLS (MultiProtocol Label Switching) 多协议标记交换

MPM algorithm (Malhotra, Pramodh Kamar, Maheshwari) MPM 算法

MPOA (MultiProtocol Over ATM) 异步传输模式上的多协议

MPP (Massively Parallel Processor) 大规模并行处理器

MPP (MicroProgrammable Processor) 可微编程处理机

MPPE (Microsoft Point-to-Point Encryption protocol) 微软点对点加密协议

MPROLOG language MPROLOG 语言

MPR Ⅱ (瑞典有关视频终端辐射强度的) MPR Ⅱ 标准

MPROM (Mask Programmed Read Only Memory) 掩膜程序只读存储器

MPRouter MPRouter 路由器 (Motorola)

MPS (MicroProcessor System) 微处理机系统

MPS (MultiProcessing System) 多道作业系统

MPS software tools 微处理机系统软件工具

MPSK (Multiple Phase Shift Keying) 多相移频键控

MPSS (MultiPurpose System Simulation) 多功能系统仿真程序

MPSX language (Mathematical Programming System eXtended) 数学规划系统扩展语言，MPSX 语言

MPU (MicroProcessor Unit) 微处理器单元

MPU control 微处理机控制

MPU hardware 微处理机硬件「片

MPU support chips 微处理机支持芯

MQH (Memory Queue Handler) 存储器队列管理器 (Sun)

MR (Magneto Resistive head) 磁阻磁头 (IBM)

MR (Mail Reflector) 邮件反射器

MR (Modem Ready) 调制解调器准备好

MR (Multiple Requesting) 多重请求

MRAD (Mass Random Access Disk) 海量随机存取(磁)盘

MRC (Master Resident Core) 主常驻核心程序

MRCI (Microsoft Real-time Compression Interface) 实时压缩界面 (微软)

MRCX (MultiRate Circuit Switching) 多速率电路交换

MRDOS (Mapped Real-time Disk Operating System) 存储映像实时磁盘操作系统

MRI (Magnetic Resonance Image) 核磁共振影像

MRP Ⅱ(Manufacturing Resource Planing) 制造资源计划Ⅱ
MS(Master Scheduler) 主调度程序
MS(Master Sequencer) 主定序器
MS(Master Switch) 主开关,总开关
MS-DOS(MicroSoft-Disk Operating System) MS-DOS 操作系统(微软)
MS-Net(MicroSoft Network) 微软网络
MS-Windows 微软窗口软件
MSA(Mass Storage Adapter) 大容量存储器适配器
MSAM(Multiple Sequential Access Method) 多路顺序存取方法
MSB(Most Significant Bit) 最高有效位
MSC(Main Studio Center) 主演播中心
MSC(Message Switching Center) 消息交换中心
MSC(Mobile Switching Center) 移动交换中心
MSC(Most Significant Character) 最高有效字符
MSCDEX(Microsoft CD EXtensions) 微软 CD 扩充程序
MSCS(Master of Science in Computer Science) 计算机科学理科硕士
MSD(Most Significant Digit) 最高有效数位
MSDN(**MicroSoft Developer Network**) 微软开发者网络
MSI(Medium Scale Integration) 中规模集成电路
MSK(Minimum Shift keying) 最小位移键控
MSL(Map Specification library) 映像说明库
MSM(Message Switching Multiplexer) 消息交换多路转换器
MSMC(MicroSoft Management Console) 微软管理控制台
MSMQ(MicroSoft Message Queue) 微软消息队列
MSN(Message Switching Network) 消息交换网络
MSP(Multiprocessing Server Pack) 多重处理服务器程序包
MSP(Multitasking System Program) 多任务系统程序
MSP format MSP(图形文件)格式(微软)
MSP operating system MSP 操作系统(富士通)
MSS(Massive Storage System) 海量存储系统
MTA(Message Transfer Agent) 消息转移代理
MTBF(Mean Time Between Failure) 平均故障间隔时间
MTC(Main Trunk Circuit) 主干线
MTC(Master Table of Contents) 总目录
MTC(Message Transmission Controller) 报文传输控制器
MTC(Multimedia Telephone Communication) 多媒体电话通信
MTEX(MultiThreading EXecutive) 多线程执行程序
MTFF(Mean Time to First Failure) 平均首次故障时间
MTI(MIPS Technologies Inc.) MTI 公司
MTL(Message Transfer Layer) 消息传输层
MTM(MultiTerminal Monitor) 多终端监控程序
MTS(Microsoft Transaction Server) 微软事务服务器
MTS(Modular TV System) 标准型电视系统
MTS(Multiterminal Time-sharing System) 多终端分时系统
MTS System Corp. MTS 系统公司
MTT(Message Transfer Time) 消息传送时间
MTTR(Mean Time To Repair) 平均修理间隔时间
MTU(Magnetic Tape Unit) 磁带机
mu(multiple unit) 复合单元
MUA(Multi-Unit Addressing) 多台设备寻址
MUD(Master User Directory) 主用户目录
MUD(Multiple User Dialog) 多人对话(游戏)
MUD(Multiple User Dimension) 多

MUD(Multiple User Dungeon) 人世界(游戏)

MUD(Multiple User Dungeon) 多用户游戏

muddy 混乱,杂乱

muddy water pixel 混水像素,模糊像素

muddymedia software 混乱媒体软件

MUK(Multimedia Upgrade Kits) 多媒体计算机升级套件

muldem 多路解调器

muldex 多路调制解调器

mulfunction 误动作

Muller's method 米勒法

multi-access 多路存取,多路访问

multi-access communication system 多路卫星通信方式算

multi-access computing 多用户存取计算

multi-access controller(MAC) 多路访问控制器

multi-access memory 多路存取存储器

multi-access network 多路存取网络

multi-access online programming 多路存取联机程序设计

multi-access system 多用户存取系统

multi-address 多地址

multi-address calling 多地址调用

multi-address code 多地址码

multi-address instruction 多址指令

multi-address message 多地址消息

multi-agent plan 多节点规划

multi-agent reasoning 多主体推理

multi-arm robot 多臂机器人

multi-aspect search 多方面查寻

multi-associative processor(MAP) 多相联处理器

multi-band antenna 多波段天线

multibit raster 多位光栅

multi-branch 多支路,多分支

multi-block method 多体法,多分程序法

multi bus 多总线

multi-channel 多通道传输方式

multi-channel I/O 多通道输入/输出

multi-chip-rate system 多子码速率系统

multi-chips ceramic package 多芯片陶瓷封装器件块

multi-chips module(MCM) 多芯片模块

multi-connection domain 多连通域

multi-connection switching network 多连接开关网络

multi-context processing 多语境处理

multi-criteria basis 多判据基

multi-cursor display 多光标显示

multi-dimensional search algorithm 多维搜索算法

multi-directional gradient code 多向梯度码器

multi-display adapter 多重显示适配

multi-domain 多域,多畴

multi-drop channel 多点通道

multi-element control system 多元素控制系统

multi-exposure 多次曝光

multi-environment real-time operating system 多环境实时操作系统

multi-expert architecture 多专家体系结构

multi-file tape 多文件磁带

multi-frame alignment signal 多帧定位信号

multi-frame capturing 多帧捕获

multi-grid method 多网格法

multi homed host 多穴主机络

multi hop packet network 多转发包网

multi host configuration 多主机配置

multi-image 多重图像

multi-inheritance 多重继承

multi-instruction single-data stream system 多指令流单数据流系统

multi-interpreter system 多解释器系统译

multi-language translation 多语种翻

multi-layer actuator head(MECH) 多层压电打印头(EPSON)

multi-layer microfiche 多层缩微平片

multi-layer wiring 多层布线

multi-leaving remote job entry 多点传送远程作业输入

multi-leaving support 多流支持

multi-length working 多倍长度工作

multi-level address 多级地址

multi-level expert control system 多级专家控制系统

multi-level feedback queues 多级反馈队列

multi-level hierarchy 多级层次结构

multi-level multi-access 多级多路存取
multi-level interconnection network 多级互连网络
multi-level interrupt structure 多级中断结构
multi-level management information system 多层次管理信息系统
multi-level pipelining 多级流水线作业
multi-line control 多线控制
multi-line inference 多路推理
multi-lingual information processing 多语种信息处理
Multi-link Interface Driver (MLID) 多链路接口驱动程序
multi-linked list structures 多链表结构
multi-load case 多负载情况
multi-loop network system 多环网络系统
multi-media 多媒体
multi-mode latch buffer 多模式锁存缓冲器
multi-module access unit 多模块存取部件
multi-monitor system 多监视器系统
multi network environment 多网络环境
multi-objective linear programming 多对象线性规划
multi-level feedback queues 多级反馈队列
multi-operand 多操作数
multi-packet transmission 多分组传输
multi-part 多联复写纸
multi-passes compiler 多遍扫描编译程序
multi-path branch 多路径分支
multi-port memory 多端口存储器
multi-position controller 多位置控制器
multi processor (MP) 多处理机
multi-programming monitor control program (MP/M) 多元规划监控程序的控制程序
multi-protocol over ATM (MPOA) 异步传输模式上的多协议
multi-punching 复打孔
multi-queue scheduling algorithm 多队列调度算法

multi-record bucket 多记录桶
multi-reel 多卷的
multi-region operation (MRO) 多区域操作
multi replace 多(文本)替换
multi-resolution matcher 多分辨率匹配器
multi-response parameter estimation 多响应参数估算
multi-segment structure 多段结构
multi-select 多重选择
multi-sensation 多感知性
multi-shadow assist 多阴影辅助
multi-sound character 多音字
multi-specification source map 多规范源图
multi-station access unit (MAU, MSAU) 多站存取单元
multi-step error detection 多步错误检测
multi-stream batch processing 多流成批处理
multi-subnet architecture 多子网结构
multi-substitution cipher 多重置换密码
multi-table query 多表查询
multi-target compiler 多目标编译程序
multi-target tracking 多目标跟踪
multi-tasking 多任务
multi-threading 多线程方法
multi-tier architecture 多层结构
multi-tiered view 多级视图
multi-track error 多道错误
multi-unit message 多元消息
multi-user database management system 多用户数据库管理系统
multi-variable statistic reasoning 多元统计推理
multi-variant stochastic reasoning 多元随机推理
multi-version programming 多版本程序设计
multiaccess computer (MAC) 多路存取计算机
multiaddress 多重地址
multiaddress calling facility 多重寻址设备
multiaddress instruction 多地址指令
multiagent 多求解器;多主体
multiagent planning 多求解器规划

multiagent reasoning 多主体推理
multiagent structure 多主体结构
multiarchitecture machine 多体系结构计算机
multiaspect 多方面,多方位
multiaspect indexing 多信息组索引
multiassociative processor 多关联处理机
multiattribute retrieval 多属性检索
multibanking parallel memory 多体并行存储器
multibatch processing 多批处理
multibeam switched system 多波束转换系统
multibit latch 多位锁存器
multibody dynamic system 多体动态系统
multibranch 多分支
multiburst signal 多波群信号
MULTIBUS MULTIBUS总线标准
Multibus Ⅰ Multibus Ⅰ 总线标准
Multibus Ⅱ Multibus Ⅱ 总线标准
multibus 多总线
multibus multiprocessor 多总线多处理机
multibus network 多总线网络
multibus system architecture 多总线体系结构
multibyte 多字节
multibyte character 多字节字符
multicache consistency 多高速缓存一致性
multicast 复播,多点传送
Multicast Backbone 多点广播式骨干网
Multicast group 多点组播
multicast-oriented service 面向多点的通信服务
multicast packet 多播包
multicast routing 多点广播式路径选择
multicast server 多点传送服务器
multicast wormhole routing 复播虫孔路径选择法
multicategory system 多畴系统
multichannel 多通道,多信道
multichannel access 多通道存取
multichannel bundle cable 多束光缆
multichannel cable 多通道光缆
multichannel disk 多通道磁盘

multichannel image 多通道图像
multichannel imagery 多通道成像
multichannel recording head 多通道记录头
multichannel single-fiber cable 多通道单纤光缆
multichip 多芯片电路
multichip circuit(MCC) 多片电路
multichip IC 多片集成电路
multichip integrated circuit 多芯片集成电路
multichip microcircuit 多芯片微电路
multichip module 多芯片模块
multiclass estimation 多类估计
multiclick 多次点击
multiclient system 多客户系统
multicode state assignment 多码状态分配
multicolor drawing 多色绘图
MultiColor Graphics Array(MCGA) 多色图形阵列
multicolor image 多色图像
multicomponent architecture 多组件体系结构
multicomputer system 多计算机系统
multicomputer system functions 多计算机系统功能
multiconnection network 多芯连接网
multiconstrainet optimization 多约束优化
multicopy 多拷贝,多复本
multicore cable 多芯电缆
multicriteria optimization 多判据优化
MULTICS(MULTiplexed Information and Computing Service) 多路信息传送与计算服务
multicycle data entry 多周期数据输入
multicycle feeding 多周期馈送
multicycle sort 多周期排序
multidatabase transaction 多数据库事务处理
multidecision game 多步判定对策
multideclared label 多重说明标号
multidestination protocol 多目的地通信协议
multidigit shifting 多数位移位
multidimensional access memory 多维存取存储器

multidimensional advective 多维平流
multidimensional array access 多维数组存取
multidimensional binary search tree 多维二叉搜索树
multidimensional cluster 多维聚类
multidimensional consequence 多维结果
multidimensional cyclic convolution 多维循环卷积
multidimensional data structure 多维数据结构
multidimensional digital filter 多维数字滤波器
multidimensional filtering 多维过滤
multidimensional key 多维密钥
multidimensional language 多维语言
multidimensional normal distribution 多维正态分布
multidimensional optimal control 多维最优控制
multidimensional outcome variable 多维输出变量
multidimensional search algorithm 多维搜索算法
multidimensional subscript 多维下标
multidimensional texture 多维纹理
multidimensional tree 多维树
multidimensional Turing machine 多维图灵机
multidimensional utility 多维效用
multidimensional voting 多维表决
multidimensioned array 多维数组
multidirected search 多定向搜索
multidisplay terminal 多显示器终端
multidomain adaptive parameter 多域自适应参数
multidomain boundary element 多域边界元
multidomain network 多域网络,多畴网络
multidomain structure 多域结构
multidrop 多点,多分支 「路
multidrop circuit 多站线路,多分支线
multidrop connection 多点连接
multidrop line 多站线路
multidrop network 多点网络
multidrop station 多点站

multidrop topology 多点拓扑 「接
multiend point connection 多端点连
multiextremal optimization 多极值优
multifiber cable 多纤光缆 └化
multifiber connector 多纤连接器
multifield index 多字段索引
multifilament cable 多纤光缆
multifile search 多文件查寻
multifile sorting 多文件排序
multifile volume 多文件卷
MultiFinder 多任务 Finder 软件
multifont optical reader 多字体光学字符读取设备
multifont reader 多字体阅读器
multiform printer 多格式打印机
multiframe 多帧
multifrequency 多频传输法
multifrequency monitor 多频监视器
multifrequency pulsing 多频率脉冲
multifrequency push-button set 多频按钮式电话机
multifrequency receiver (MFR) 多频接收机
multifrequency signal 多频信号
multifrequency terminal 多频终端
multifunction computer 多功能计算
multifunction device 多功能设备 「机
multifunction peripheral 多功能外围设备
multifunction pipeline 多功能流水线
multifunction system 多功能系统
multigap head 多隙磁头
multihead Turing machine 多头图灵
multihomed 多起始地址的 └机
multihomogeneous model 多同质模型
multihop access environment 多转发器存取环境
multihop network 多中继站网络
multihost network 多主机网络
multihost operation 多主机操作
multijob operation 多作业操作
multijobbing 多作业执行 「式
multikey hashing scheme 多键散列模
multikey retrieval 多键检索
multikey searching 多关键词查找
multilanguage code page 多语言代码页面
multilanguage operating system 多语

言操作系统
multilateral 多边的
multilayer 多层
multilayer board 多层电路板
multilayer control structure 多层控制结构
multilayer interconnection 多层导电箔互连
multilayer printed board 多层印刷电路板
multilayer structure 多层结构
multilayered database 多层数据库
multilayered knowledge base 多层知识库
multilead 多引线
multileaving 多点传送
multilength arithmetic 多倍长度运算
multilevel address 多级地址
multilevel addressing 多阶寻址法
multilevel control system 多级控制系统
multilevel feedback queue 多级反馈队列
multilevel index 多级索引
multilevel indirect addressing 多级间接寻址
multilevel interrupt 多级中断
multilevel multiaccess (MLMA) 多级多处存取
multilevel plexus structure 多级丛结构
multilevel priority interrupts 多级优先权中断
multilevel reasoning system 多级推理系统
multilevel security 多级安全
multilevel signal 多电平信号
multilevel software 多层软件
multilevel sort 多字段排序,多级排序
multilevel subroutine 多级子例程
multilevel syllogistic 多级演绎推理
multilevel vectored interrupt logic 多级向量中断逻辑
multiline 多线;多行
multiline edit 多行编辑
multiline controller 多元线路控制器
multilink 多链路
multilingual information processing 多语种信息处理
multilingual database system 多语种数据库系统
multilingual word processor 多语种文字处理程序
multilink 多链路的;多重链接的
multilink channel interface 多链路通道接口
multilink frame 多重链接帧
multilink procedure 多链路规程
multilink window 多重链路窗口
multilinked structure 多重链接结构
multilist 多目表
multilist chain 多目表链
multilist file 多重表文件
multilist organization 多表组织
multiloop control 多环控制,多回路控制
multiloop feedback system 多环反馈系统
MultiMan MultiMan 管理软件包
multimaster system bus 多主控系统总线
multimastering 多主控模式
MultiMate 多伙伴程序
multimarker 多标志
multimedia 多媒体
multimedia authorware 多媒体创作工具
multimedia clips 多媒体剪辑
multimedia communication 多媒体通信
multimedia communication environment 多媒体通信环境
multimedia communication network 多媒体通信网络
multimedia computer 多媒体计算机
multimedia computing 多媒体计算
multimedia conference system 多媒体会议系统
Multimedia Content Description Interface 多媒体内容描述接口(MPEG-7)
Multimedia Control Interface (MCI) 多媒体控制接口
multimedia courseware 多媒体课件
multimedia data object 多媒体数据对象
multimedia data processing 多媒体数据处理
multimedia database 多媒体数据库
multimedia database system 多媒体数据库系统

multimedia document 多媒体文档
multimedia editing tool 多媒体编辑工具
multimedia editor 多媒体编辑程序
multimedia environment for remote multiple attended interactive decision making(MERMAID) 远程多参加者交互决策多媒体环境
multimedia extension 多媒体扩充
Multimedia Extensions(MMX) 多媒体扩展指令集(Intel)
multimedia file I/O services 多媒体文件输入输出服务
multimedia information 多媒体信息
multimedia information system 多媒体信息系统
multimedia input/output(MMIO) 多媒体输入输出
multimedia navigation system 多媒体导航系统
multimedia operating system 多媒体计算机操作系统
multimedia personal computer(MPC) 多媒体个人计算机
multimedia platform 多媒体平台
multimedia presentation system 多媒体演示系统
multimedia simulation 多媒体仿真
multimedia standardization 多媒体标准
multimedia technology 多媒体技术
multimedia terminal 多媒体终端
Multimedia Tool Book 多媒体工具手册
multimedia traffic 多媒体通信
multimedia user interface 多媒体用户界面
multimedia video 多媒体视频
multimedia windows 多媒体窗口软件
multimeter 万用表,多用途测量工具
multimicroprocessor 多微处理器
multimode communication 多模式通信
multimode component 多模元件
multimode dispersion 多模色散
multimode fiber 多模光纤
multimode group-delay spread 多模群延迟扩展
multimode interface 多模式接口
multimode international data acquisition service(MIDAS) 多方式国际数据搜集业务
multimode laser 多模激光器
multimode optical fiber 多模光纤
multimode stepped-index optical fiber 多模突变型折射率光纤
multinest 多重嵌套
multinode broadcast 多节点广播
multinomial coefficient 多项式系数
multinomial theorem 多项式定理
multiobjective decision-making 多目标决策法
multiobjective programming 多对象程序设计
multioperand 多操作数
multioperation distribution 多重操作分配
multioutlet assembler 多出口汇编程序
multipacket message 多分组报文
multipage node 多页面节点
multiparallel processor 多重并行处理机
multiparameter adjustment algorithm 多参数调整算法
multiparameter flow cytometry 多参数流细胞测定学
multipart document 多部份文档
multipart forms 多份格式
multiparticle system 多粒子系统
multipartition 多分区
multiparty communication 多同线通信
multiparty interaction 多方交互作用
multipass merging sort 多遍归并排序
multipass overlapping 多遍重印
multipass sort 多遍排序
multipass translation 多遍翻译
multipath 多路径
multipath effect 多径效应
multiphase charge-coupled device 多相电荷耦合器件
multiphase clock 多相时钟
multiphase compiler 多相编译程序
multiphase program 多相程序
multiphase sampling 多阶段抽样
multiphase switched-capacitor 多相开关电容
multipipeline vector processor 多流水线向量处理机
Multiplan Multiplan 电子表格软件

(微软)
multiplatform 多平台
multiple 复接,多重
multiple access(MA) 多路访问
multiple access device 多路存取设备
multiple access discrete address(MA-DA) 多路存取离散地址
multiple access protocol 多路存取协
multiple-access virtual machine 多路访问虚拟机
multiple address 多地址
multiple-address instruction 多地址指令
multiple-address message 多地址消息
multiple-address space 多地址空间
multiple-address space partition 多地址空间分区
multiple agent planning 多主体规划
multiple alternative decision 多择一判定
multiple argument routine 多变元例程
multiple array processor(MAP) 多重阵列处理机
multiple aspect searching 多方位搜索
multiple association list 多向连接表
multiple-attachment support 多连接支持
multiple attribute decision making 多属性决策,多因素决策
multiple attribute retrieval 多属性检索
multiple attribute tree database organization 多属性树型数据库组织
multiple axis chart 多轴图
multiple backend database system 多后端数据库系统
multiple backtrace 多回溯
multiple blank suppression 多空格抑制
multiple branching construction 多分支结构
multiple broadband local network 多重宽带局域网
multiple broadcasting 多向广播
multiple bus architecture 多总线体系结构
multiple byte instruction 多字节指令
multiple call processing unit 多路呼叫处理单元
multiple case 多重情况

multiple camera technique 多摄影机技术
multiple channel control circuit 多通道控制电路
multiple check 多重检验
multiple child pointer 多子女指针
multiple chip hybrid circuit 多片混合电路
multiple-choice knapsack problem 多选择背包问题
multiple cluster control 多群集控制
multiple coincidence 多重符合
multiple computer operation 多计算机作业
multiple computer system 多计算机系统
multiple concept learning 复合概念学习
multiple connected polygon 多连通多面体
multiple connector 多行连接符
multiple console support(MCS) 多控制台支持程序
multiple consolidation 多重汇总数据
multiple context 多重文本
multiple coordination 多重协调
multiple copy control 多种厚度拷贝纸调整
multiple correlation coefficient 多重相关系数
multiple criteria 多判据,多准则
multiple crossbar network 多交叉点网络
multiple data stream 多数据流
multiple declaration 多重说明
multiple dedicated bus 多专用总线
multiple definition global symbol 多重定义全局符号
multiple delay logic simulator 多延迟逻辑仿真器
multiple devices 复接装置
multiple directory 多重目录表
Multiple Document Interface(MDI) 多文档界面
multiple-domain network 多域网络
multiple-DOS configuration 多种操作系统配置
multiple echo 多重回波
multiple end user 多端用户

multiple entrance 多入口点
multiple error stochastic model 复合误差随机模型
multiple evaluation 多重计值
multiple exit 多出口点
multiple explicit routes 多显式路由
multiple extension 多重扩展
multiple faults testing 多故障测试法
multiple feature pattern 多特征样式
multiple field editing 多字段编辑
multiple frequency constraint 多频率约束
multiple gateway 多网关
multiple grid method 多重网格法
multiple host support 多主机支持
multiple-in-line package(MIP) 复接线内封装
multiple indexing 多重索引
multiple indirect addressing 多重间接寻址
multiple indirect file 多重间接文件
multiple induction loop 多重归约循环
multiple inheritance 多继承性
multiple instance 多实例
multiple instruction multiple data stream(MIMO) 多指令多数据流
multiple instruction stream 多指令流
multiple instruction stream-single data stream 多指令流单数据流
multiple integration 多重积分 「线
multiple interleaved bus 多重交错总
multiple interpolation 多重插值
multiple interrupt 多重中断 「线
multiple-interleaved bus 多重交叉总
multiple-job processing 多道作业处理
multiple join attribute 多重连接属性
multiple key hashing 多键散列
multiple key organization 多键组织
multiple key retrieval 多关键词检索
multiple label 多重标号
multiple large file transfer 多个大文件传送
multiple layer architecture 多层结构
multiple-length arithmetic 多倍长度算术
multiple-length number 多倍长数
multiple-length working 多倍字长工作

multiple level combinational network 多级组合网络
multiple linear recursion 多重线性递归
multiple linear regression 多重线性回归
multiple lines of reasoning 多线推理,多重推理
multiple lines printing 多行打印
multiple lines structure 多线结构
multiple list 多重表
multiple load module processing 多装入模块处理
multiple load system 多负载系统
Multiple Master "多面手"软件(Adobe)
multiple match 多重匹配,多重符合
multiple match resolution 多重符合分
multiple meaning 多义性   「解
multiple meaning association 多重含义结合   「序
multiple merge program 多重归并程
multiple message mode 多消息方式
multiple midstop 多点停止器
multiple mission sequential decoder 多任务顺序译码器
multiple model-based control 基于多模型的控制
multiple modulation 多重调制
multiple module access(MMA) 多模块存取
multiple monitor system 多重监视系统,多监视器系统
multiple names 复名称
multiple normal correlation 多重正态相关
multiple objectives optimization 多目标函数优化
multiple operations 多操作
multiple order derivation 多级派生,多级推导
multiple original printer 多源打印机
multiple output system 多输出系统
multiple packet transmission 多分组传输
multiple-page microcode 多页微码
multiple parallel link 多重并行链路
multiple-parameter reduced base 多参数简化库

multiple part form 多联表格
multiple partition support (MPS) 多分区支持
multiple pass printing 多遍打印
multiple path 多路径
multiple pen plotter 多笔绘图仪
multiple peripheral adapter 多外设转接器
multiple phase frame buffer 多相帧缓冲器
multiple pipeline processor 多流水线处理机
multiple port 多端口
multiple-port cell 多端口元件
multiple precision 多倍精度
multiple precision arithmetic (MPA) 多倍精度运算
multiple precision number 多倍精度数
multiple-process operation system 多重处理操作系统
multiple processing 多重处理
multiple program loading 多重程序装入
multiple programming 多重程序设计
multiple protocol layer 多协议层
multiple provider router (MPR) 多供应者路由器
multiple record format 多记录格式
multiple record locking 多记录锁定
multiple recording medium word processing equipment 多记录媒体文字处理设备
multiple regression analysis 多重回归分析
multiple request 多重请求
multiple response 多重响应
multiple revisions 多次修订
multiple ring interconnection 多环互连
multiple root 多重根
multiple routing 多路由选择
multiple segment query 多段查询
multiple selection 多重选择
multiple sequence operation 多序操作
multiple sequential list 多顺序列表
multiple session 多次对话;多会话期
multiple session remote job entry 多次对话远程作业输入
multiple sources of knowledge 多重知识源

multiple-speed floating controller 多速浮点控制器
multiple spindle disk memory 多轴磁盘存储器
multiple stack manipulation procedure 多栈操作过程
multiple stage joint 多级关节
multiple state representation 多状态表示
multiple statement line 多语句行
multiple step task 多步任务
multiple-string processing 多串处理
multiple-stylus recorder 多针记录器
multiple substitution enciphering system 多次代换加密体制
multiple system coupling feature (MSC) 多系统耦合特制件
multiple systems networking 多系统联网
multiple table cipher 多表密码
multiple tag 多标记
multiple target tracking 多目标跟踪
multiple-task management 多任务管理
multiple tense programming 多时态编程
multiple terminal access (MTA) 多终端访问
multiple terminal access feature 多终端访问功能
multiple terminal interface 多终端界面
multiple thread 多线程
multiple time-sharing bus 多重分时总线
multiple tracks operation 多磁道操作
multiple transition time decomposition 多次跃迁时间分调法
multiple transmission medium token-ring 多传输媒体令牌环
multiple user control 多用户控制
multiple utility 多用设备
multiple value logic 多值逻辑
multiple version protocol 多版本协议
multiple view model 多视图模型
multiple virtual space 多重虚拟空间
multiple virtual storage (MVS) 多重虚拟存储器
multiple window 多窗口
multiple word template 多字模板
multiple x-y recorder 复X-Y记录器
multiplex 多工,多路复用,多路转换

multiplex adapter 多路转换适配器
multiplex communication system 多路通信方式
multiplex data terminal 多工数据终端
multiplex interface 多路转换接口
multiplex link 多路复用链路,复接链路
multiplex mode 多工方式
multiplex operation 多工操作,多路复用操作
multiplex transmission 多工传输,多路传输
multiplexed bus 多路复用总线
multiplexed line 多路复用线路
multiplexed operation 多路操作
multiplexed sequence 复合序列
multiplexer 多路复用器,多路转接器
multiplexer and bus interface 多工器与总线接口
multiplexer channel 多路复用通道
multiplexer channel operations 多路转换通道操作
multiplexer interface 多路转换器接口
multiplexer IOP 多工器输入/输出处理机
multiplexer mode channel 多路复用通道
multiplexer polling 多路转换器轮询
multiplexer simulation 多路转换器仿真
multiplexing 多路复用,多路转换
multiplexing broadcasting 多工广播
multiplexing techniques 多路复用技术
multiplexor 多路复用器
multiplexor channel 多工通道
multiplicand(MLPC) 被乘数
multiplication(MP) 乘法
multiplication circuit 乘法电路
multiplication cross 叉乘,矢量乘
multiplication-cycle time 乘法周期时间
multiplication principle 乘法原理
multiplication table 乘数表,乘法表
multiplication time 乘法时间
multiplication transformation cipher 乘法密码
multiplier(MUL) 乘法器;乘数
multiplier-accumulator 乘法-累加器
multiply connected component 多重连通成分
multiplier factor 乘式因数,乘数

multiplier-quotient register(MQR) 乘数商数寄存器
multiplier register 乘数寄存器
multiplier unit 乘法单元
multiply-add fused 乘-加熔合单元
multiply-divide instruction 乘除指令
multiply field 乘法字段
multiply operation 乘法运算
multiplying punch 多功能打孔机
multipoint channel 多点通道
multipoint circuit 多点线路
multipoint configuration 多点配置
multipoint connection 多点连接
multipoint data link 多点数据链路
multipoint iteration scheme 多点迭代格式
multipoint link 多点链路
multipoint network 多点网络
multipoint restriction 多点约束
multipole switch 多接点开关
multiport memory 多端口内存
multiport memory multiplexer 多端口内存多路转换器
multiport memory structure 多端口内存结构
multiport modem 多端口调制解调器
multiport register 多端口寄存器
multiport storage 多端口存储器
multiported memory 多端口内存
multiprecision arithmetic 多倍精度算术
multipriority 多优先级
multipriority queue 多优先级队列
multiprocess communication 多进程通信
multiprocess executive 多进程执行程序
multiprocessing(MP) 多道处理
multiprocessing efficiency 多道处理效率
multiprocessing environment 多元处理环境,多重处理环境
multiprocessing operation 多重处理操作
multiprocessing organization 多元处理组织
multiprocessing recovery 多道处理恢复
multiprocessing server pack(MSP) 多重处理服务器程序包
multiprocessing system(MPS) 多元处

理系统
multiprocessor(MP) 多处理机
multiprocessor allocation 多处理机分配
multiprocessor configuration 多处理机配置
multiprocessor control 多处理机控制
multiprocessor interleaving 多处理机交错工作
multiprocessor performance analysis 多处理机性能分析
multiprocessor scheduling 多处理机调度
multiprocessor system 多处理机系统
multiprocessor-system types 多元处理机系统类型
multiprogrammed repeatable robot 多道作业重复式机器人
multiprogrammed time-sharing system 多道程序分时系统
multiprogramming(MP) 多道作业
multiprogramming dispatching 多程序调度
multiprogramming environment 多道程序环境
multiprogramming executive 多道作业执行例程
multiprogramming interrupts 多道程序中断
multiprogramming memory protect 多道程序存储保护
multiprogramming requirements 多道作业要求
multiprogramming sequencing 多道程序定序
multiprogramming system(MPS) 多道作业系统
multiprogramming with a fixed number of tasks(MFT) 固定任务数多道作业
multiprogramming with a variable number of tasks(MVT) 可变任务数多道作业;MVT操作系统
multiprogramming with fixed tasks 固定任务数多道作业
multiprogramming with variable tasks 可变任务数多道作业
multiproject automated control system 多元自控系统
multiprotocol communication chips 多协议通信芯片
multipurpose assembly language(MAL) 多功能装配语言,MAL语言
multipurpose key 多用途键盘
multipurpose universally programmable intelligent decoder(MUPID) 多用途通用可编程智能解码器
multiqueue dispatching 多队列调度法
multirate circuit switching(MRCS) 多速率电路交换
multirecord block 多记录块
multireel file 多卷(磁带)文件
multireel sorting 多卷排序
multirefracting crystal 多折射晶体
multiresource arbiter 多资源仲裁器
multisatellite link 多卫星链路
multiscalar 多标量
multiscanning monitor 多扫描监视器
multischedule private line 多种价格专用线路
multisegment integration 多分段积分
multisensor fusion 多传感器汇合
multisequencing 多重序列定序
multisequential process 多时序进程
multisequential system 多时序系统
multiserver network 多服务器网络
multiservice network 多种服务网络
multisession 多次会话;多节段
multishare network architecture 多重共享网络体系结构
multishift operation 多次移位运算
multisource 多源
multispectral image 多光谱图像
multispectral scanner(MSS) 多光谱扫描器
multispeed broadcast 多速率广播
multispeed clock feature 多速时钟特制件
multisplitting 多次划分
multistack machine 多栈机
multistage classifier 多级分类器
multistage cube network 多级立方体网络
multistage decision process 多阶段决策过程
multistage game 多阶段对策
multistage interconnection network structure 多级互连网络结构

multistage network 多节网络,多级网络
multistage sampling 多阶段取样
multistation 多站
multistation access unit(MAU) 多站访问单元
multistep backward difference 多级后向差分
multistep control 多步控制
multistep decision 多步判定
multistep formula 多步公式
multistep task 多步任务
multistream system 多流系统
MultiSync monitor 多速率同步监视器
multisystem 多元系统
multisystem network 多系统网络
multisystem networking facility (MSNF) 多系统联网设施
multitap connection 多端连接
multitap transformer 多抽头变压器
multitape Turing machine 多带图灵机
multitask management 多任务管理程序
multitask monitor 多任务监督程序
multitask operation 多任务作业
multitasking 多任务处理
multitasking executive 多任务执行程序
multitasking/multiprogramming 多任务操作/多重程序设计
multitasking operation 多任务操作
multitasking overhead 多任务开销(内务操作)
multitemplate 多模板
multithread 多线索,多线程
multithread application program 多线索应用程序
multithread operation 多线程操作
multithread processing 多线程处理
multithread test 多线索测试
multithreaded demo 多线程示例
multithreaded operating system 多线程操作系统
multithreading 多线程的
multithreading executive 多线程执行程序
multithreshold circuit 多阈值电路
multithreshold function 多阈值函数
multithrow switch 多掷开关
multitime step algorithm 多时间步算法

multitone 多音调的;多色调的
multitrack parallel recording 多轨并行记录法
multitrack Turing machine 多轨图灵机
multiturn film head 多匝薄膜磁头
multiunit message 多单元消息
multiuser 多用户
Multiuser DOS 多用户磁盘操作系统
multiuser executive 多用户执行程序
multiuser system 多用户系统
multivalue decision 多值决策
multivalue logic simulation 多值逻辑仿真
multivalued dependency 多值相关性
multivalued logic device 多值逻辑器件
multivalued property 多值属性
multivariable 多变元的,多变量
multivariable adaptive control 多变量自适应控制
multivariable decision situation 多变量决策形势
multivariable root-locus 多变元根轨迹
multivariable stability margin 多变量稳定性容限
multivariable stochastic reasoning 多变量随机推理
multivariate 多变元,多变量
multivariate analysis 多元分析
multivariate approximation 多元近似
multivariate distribution 多元分布
multivariate interpolation 多元插值法
multivariate normal distribution 多元正态分布
multivariate polynomial 多元多项式
multivariate sample 多元样本
multivariate spline 多元样条
multivariate stepwise regressing 多元步进式回归
multivendor network 多供应商网络
multiversion 多版本
multiversioned software 多版本软件
multivibrator(MV) 多谐振荡器
multivolume disk file 多卷磁盘文件
multiway classification 多路分类
multiway decision 多路判定
multiway direct access 多路直接存取
multiway gateway 多向网关
multiwire channel 多线制通道

multiword record 多字记录
mumps language 流行性语言
Munsell color system 芒塞尔色度系
Murphy's Law 莫菲定律 └统
MUSE(Multi-User Simulated Environment) 多用户仿真环境
muse 沉思默想
music code mode 音乐编码方式
musical asterisk 提示音乐
Musical Instrument Digital Interface (MIDI) 乐器数字接口
musical signification 音乐表示，音乐含意
mutant 变异体
mutation （计算机病毒）变种
mutator 变种程序，变形程序
mute 静音
mute control 静音控制
mutex 人工干预 └致
mutual consistency 互相兼容，互相一
mutual dependency 互相依赖，互连相关
mutual exclusion mechanism 互斥机
mutual information 互传信息量
mutual isolation 相互隔离
mutual near neighbor 相互近邻
mutual neighborhood graph 相互邻域
mutually exclusive 互斥 └图
mutually protection 互防
mutually synchronized network 交互同步网络
MUX(MUltipleX) 多路复用
mV(milli-volt) 毫伏

MVGA(Monochrome VGA) 单色 VGA 显示器
MVII(Multimedia Video Input Interface) 多媒体视频输入接口
MVM(Minimum Virtual Memory) 最小虚拟存储器
MVOCA(Motion Video Object Content Architecture) 动态视频对象内容结构
MVP(Multimedia Video Processor) 多媒体影像处理器(TI)
MVS(Multiple Virtual Storage) 多重虚拟存储器系统(IBM)
MVS/ESA(MVS/Enterprise Systems Architecture) MVS 企业系统体系结构(IBM)
MVS/XA (MVS/eXtended Architecture) MVS 扩展体系结构(IBM)
Mwave DSP Mwave 数字信号处理器 (IBM) └区
MXA(Main eXchange Area) 主交换
MXCC(Module XBus Cache Controller) 模块化 Xbus 高速缓存控制器(Sun)
My Briefcase 我的公文包(微软)
My compact operating system 自用紧缩操作系统
My Computer 我的电脑(微软)
Myrinet Myrinet 局域网络(Myricom)
mystery 诀窍
mystify 变幻线，旋转多边形
mystique 秘诀

N n

N(Nano) 纳，毫微(词头，意为 10^{-9})
N(Negative) 负的，反的
N(Number) 数，号码，编号
n-address instruction n 地址指令
n-adic predicate n 位谓词
n-ary code n 元码
n-ary digital signal n 元数字信号
n-ary relation n 元关系
n-ary signaling n 元信令

n-best forward pruning n 最佳正向修
N/C machines 数控机 └剪
N-channel N 沟道
N-channel charge-coupled device N 沟道电荷耦合器件
N-channel metal oxide semiconductor (NMOS) N 沟道金属氧化物半导体
N-channel MOS(NMOS) N 沟道金属

氧化物半导体
N-channel sapphire on silicon(NSOS) N沟道硅蓝宝石
N-COCSG(Non-Commutative One-sided Context-Sensitive Grammar) 不可交换单侧上下文有关文法
n-colorable 可n着色的
n-connection n元连接
n-cube n维立方体
n-cycle enciphering system n圈加密系统
N-density N稠密性
n-dimensional cube n维立方体,超立方体
N-entity N层实体
N-ISDN 窄带综合业务数字网络
n,k code n中取k码
N-P-N transistor NPN型晶体管
n-place function n位函词
n-place predicate n位谓词
N-S diagram N-S图
n-th-order group 高次群,n次群
n-th-order harmonic distortion n次谐波失真
N-tuple length register N倍长寄存器
N-type semiconductor N型半导体
N-unit code N单位码
n-valued logic 多值逻辑,n值逻辑
N version programming N版本编程
N-way branch N路分支 「法
NA(Network Address) 网络地址
NA(Numerical Aperture) 数值孔径
NACK(Negative ACKnowledgment) 否认,否定应答
NACT(Network Account Table) 网络记账表
NAD(Network Access Device) 网络访问设备
NAEC(Novell Authorized Education Center) Novell授权教育培训中心
nagware 催款软件
naive user 初级用户,非专业用户
NAK(Negative AcKnowledgement) 否认,否定回答
NAK only 只作否定回答
naked 无壳的
NAM(Navigational Access Method) 导航访问法

NAM(Network Access Machine) 网络存取机
NAM(Network Access Method) 网络访问法
name 名称,名字
name address assignment 名字地址分配 「射
name-address mapping 名字-地址映
Name Binding Protocol(NBP) 名称绑定协议
name block(NAM) 名称字块
name call 按名调用
name code 名称代码
name condition 名称条件
name conflict 名称冲突,命名矛盾
name constant(NCON) 名字常量
name entry 名称项
name equivalence 按名字等价
name expression 名称表达式
name field 名称字段
name identification 名称识别
name-identifier mapping 名称-标识符映射
name key 名称关键字
name label 名称标记;铭牌
name look-up rule 名称查找规则
name management protocol(NMP) 名称管理协议
name of an object 对象名,客体名
name of variable 变量名
name parameter 名称参数
name part 名称部分
name plate 标牌,铭牌
name precedence 名称优先权
name qualification 名称合理性,名字限定法
name recognizer 名称识别
name register 名称寄存器
name replacement 名称替换
name resolution 名称转换,名字解析
name server 命名服务器
name space 名称空间,命名空间 「序
namespace manager 命名空间管理程
name space modification 名称空间修
namespace table 命名空间表 「改
name-stamp protocol 名字标记协议
name substitution 名称替换
name table 名称表

name tag 名签
name transparency 名称透明
named actual parameter 命名实参数
named anchor 命名锚点
named argument 命名参数
named association 命名关联
named common 命名公用块
named common area 命名公用区
named common block 命名公用块
named component 命名分量
named connection 命名连接
named constant 命名常数
named destination 命名目的地
named file 命名文件
named_guids attribute 命名全球惟一标识符属性
named parameter 命名参数
named parameter association 命名参数结合
named pipe 命名管道
named program module 命名程序模块
named property 命名属性
named record type 命名记录类型
named space NLM 命名空间可装入模块
named stream 命名流
named system 命名系统
named target 命名目标
named user file 命名用户文件
named variable 命名变量
namespace 命名空间,名称空间
namespace extension interface 命名空间扩展接口
naming 命名,定名
naming conflict 命名冲突
naming convention 命名约定[惯例]
naming operation 命名操作
naming program 命名程序
naming rule 命名规则
naming variable 命名变量
NAMPS (Narrowband Analog Mobile Phone Service) 窄带模拟移动电话业务
NAN(Network Application Node) 网络应用节点
NAND(Not AND) "与非"
NAND gate "与非"门
NAND operation "与非"运算

nano 纳,毫微(10^{-9})
nano-architecture 纳结构
nanobus 纳秒级总线;纳米级总线
nanocircuit 纳电路,超微电路
nanoinstruction 纳指令
nanoinstruction statement 纳指令语句
nanometer(nm) 纳米,毫微米
nanoprogram 纳程序
nanoprogram level 纳程序级
nanoprogram memory 纳程序存储器
nanoprogramming 纳程序设计
nanoscope 纳秒示波器,超高频示波器
nanosecond(ns) 纳秒,毫微秒
nanosecond circuit 纳秒电路
nanostore 纳程序存储器
nanowatt circuit 纳瓦电路
nanowatt integrated circuit 纳瓦集成电路
NAP(Network Access Processor) 网络访问处理机
NAP(Network Access Protocol) 网络访问协议
Napier 约翰·奈培
napier 奈培(=8.686分贝)
Napier's bones 纳氏骨牌
Napierian logarithm 自然对数
NAPLOG(NAPierian LOGarithm) 自然对数
NAPSS(Numerical Analysis Problem Solving System) 数值分析解题系统
NAR(Network Accounting Record) 网络统计数据记录
NAR(Numerical Analysis Research) 数值分析研究
narrative 解说词,语句式
narrative address 叙述性地址
narrative convention 注解语句规范
narrative message 叙述性消息
narrow band(NB) 窄带
narrow band channel 窄带通道
narrow band filter 窄带滤波器
narrow band interference 窄带干扰
narrow band-ISDN 窄带综合业务数字网络
narrow band line 窄带传输线
narrow band modem 窄带调制解调器
narrow band signal 窄带信号

narrow band time division multiple access(NBDTMA) 窄频带时分多路存取
narrow beam antenna 窄波束天线
narrow channel effect 窄沟道效应
narrow frequency-shift keying 窄频段移频键控
narrowcast 窄带电视广播
NAS(National Academy of Sciences) (美)国家科学院
NAS(Network Accounting Server) 网络记账服务器
NAS(Network Administration System) 网络管理系统
NASA(National Aeronautics and Space Administration) (美)宇航及太空总署
nasa7 nasa7 基准程序
NASAP(Network Analysis for System APplication) 系统应用程序的网络分析
nastygram 恶作剧报文
nation area network 国家范围网络
nation association 全国性协会
National Center for Supercomputing Applications(NCSA) 超级计算应用国家中心
national character 国家字符
national circuit 国内电路
national circuit-group-congestion signal 国内电路群拥塞信号
National Computer Conference (美国)国家计算机会议
National Computer Security Center(NCSC) (美)国家计算机安全中心
National Crime Information System (NCIS) (美)国家犯罪数据系统
National Data Processing Service (NDPS) (英)数据处理服务中心
National Information Infrastructure (NII) 国家信息基础建设,信息高速公路
national language support 民族语言支持能力
National Library of Medicine (美)国家医学图书馆
nation network 国内网络
national numbering plan 全国编号方案
national requirement feature 国家特别要求的特性
National requirements (美)国家要求
National Research and Education Network(NREN) 国家研究与教育网
National Science Foundation Network (NSFnet) 国家科学基金会网
national significant number 本国有效号码
national standard 国家标准
National Technical Information Service (美)全国技术信息服务处
National Telecommunications and Information Administration (NTIA) (美)全国电信和信息管理局
National Telephone Cooperative Association(NTCA) (全美)国家电话合作协会
national television center(NTC) 国内电视中心
National Television System Committee (NTSC) (美)全国电视系统委员会规定制式
national use graphic character 国家用图形符号
National Yellow Pages Service 全国黄页服务
nationwide dialing 全国范围拨号
nationwide service network 全国范围服务网络
native 本机的;本国的;本民族的
native application 本机应用程序
native assembly language 本机汇编语言
native attachment 本机附件
native call 本机调用
native character set 本机字符集
native code 本机码
native code translator 本机代码翻译程序
native collating sequence 先天排列顺序
native command name 本机命令名
native compiler 本机编译程序
native data 本机数据
native file format 专属文件格式
native image 自然影像;本机映像
native language 本机语言
native mode 本机模式,主体模式
native network 本机网络

native service 本机服务
Native Signal Processing(NSP) 主体信号处理,本机信号处理
NATO Codification system 北大西洋公约组织编码系统
natural 自然的;天然的
natural air cooling 自然空气冷却
natural barrier 自然屏蔽,自然障碍
natural basis 自然基
natural binary code 自然二进制码
natural binary-coded decimal(NBCD) 自然二进制编码的十进制
natural boundary 自然边界
natural boundary condition 自然边界条件
natural constraint 自然约束
natural convection cool 自然对流冷却
natural cooling 自然冷却
natural deduction 自然演绎
natural deduction system 自然推理系
natural dialogue 自然交谈
natural extension 自然延拓
natural frequency 自然频率,固有频率
natural frequency of vibration 自然振荡频率
natural function generator 自然函数产生器,解析函数发生器
natural homomorphism 自然同态
natural image 自然图像
natural inference 自然推理
natural join 自然连接
natural language 自然语言
natural language analysis 自然语言分析
natural language application 自然语言应用
natural language communication 自然语言通信
natural language computer 自然语言计算机
natural language explanation 自然语言说明,自然语言解释
natural language information system 自然语言信息系统
natural language input 自然语言输入
natural language interface 自然语言界面
natural language interface to data base 数据库自然语言界面

natural language processing 自然语言处理
natural language programming 自然语言编程
natural language query system 自然语言查询系统
natural language system 自然语言系统
natural language text 自然语言文本
natural language translation 自然语言翻译
natural language understanding 自然语言理解
natural logarithm 自然对数
natural loop 自然循环
natural merging 自然归并
natural noise 自然噪声
natural number 自然数
natural order 自然次序
natural parallelism 自然并行性
Natural Pen (模仿)手持笔(Corel)
natural period 自然周期
natural recalculation 自然重算
natural structure 自然结构
natural texture 自然纹理
natural unit of information content (NAT) 信息内涵的自然单位
natural wavelength 固有波长,自然波长
NAU(Network Access Unit) 网络可存取单元
NAU(Network Addressable Unit) 网络可寻址单元
NAU services 网络可存取单元的服务
NAU services manager layer 网络可寻址单元服务管理层
naught 零,无
navigate icons set 导航图标集
navigation 导航
navigation bar 导航栏
navigation button 导航按钮
navigation computer(NC) 导航计算机
navigation key 导航键,定位键
navigation map computer 导航地图计算机
navigation planning 导航规划
navigation route database 导航路由选择数据库
navigation satellite 导航卫星

navigation screen 导航屏幕
navigation setup 导航设置
navigation tools 导航工具〔法
navigational access method 导航存取
Navigator "领航员"浏览器(Netscape)
NAVSAT(NAVigation-communication SATellite) 导航通信卫星
navy 深蓝色
Navy Electronics Laboratory International Algol Compiler(NELIAC) 海军电子实验室代数编译器(美)
Navy Tactical Data System(NTDS) 海军战术数据系统(美)
NB(Narrow band) 窄带,窄频带
NB(Network Board) 网络板
NB(Number) 数字;号码;序数
NBACKUP(Network Backup) 网络备份命令
NBCD(Natural Binary-Coded Decimal) 自然二进制编码的十进制
NBCH(Natural Binary-Coded Hexadecimal) 自然二进制编码的十六进制
NBFM(Narrow Band Frequency Modulation) 窄带调频
NBM(Non Book Materials) 非书面材料
NBMB balanced-disparity coding 基数N的二进制M元平衡式差异编码
NBS(Numeric Backspace Character) 数值退格字符
NBX(**Networked Branch exchanger**) 网络交换机(3Com)〔机
NC(Navigation Computer) 导航计算
NC(Network Computer) 网络计算机
NC(Network Congestion) 网络阻塞
NC(Network Controller) 网络控制器
NC(No-Connection) 不连接,无关
NC(Numeric Control system) 数值控制系统
NC reduction NC 归约
NC signal 通信网络阻塞信号
NCAM(Network Communication Access Method) 网络通信访问法
NCB(Network Control Block) 网络控制块

NCBA(Nucleus Control Block Area) 核心程序控制块区
NCC(National Computer Center) 全国计算中心
NCC(Network Control Center) 网络控制中心
NCCF(Network Communications Control Facility) 网络通信控制设施
NCCF-CP(NCCF Customization Command Processors) 网络通信控制设施定制命令处理器
NCCF-OP(NCCF Operation) 网络通信控制设施操作
NCD(Network Cryptographic Device) 网络加密装置
NCE(Network Connection Element) 网络连接设备
NCF(Network Configuration Facility) 网络配置设施
NCH(Network Connection Handler) 网络连接处理器
NCL(Network Control Language) 网络控制语言
NCM(Network Coordination Message) 网络协调消息
NCN(Network Control Node) 网控节点
NCOPY(Network COPY) 网络拷贝
NCOS(Non-Concurrent Operating System) 非并发操作系统
NCP(Network Control Processor) 网络控制处理机
NCP(Network Control Program) 网络控制程序
NCP(NetWare Core Protocol) NetWare 核心协议
NCP connectionless SNA transport(NCST) NCP 无连接 SNA 传输
NCP-to-NCP protocol 网络控制程序间通信协议
NCR(National Cash Register Corp.) 国家收银机公司(美)
NCR(No Carbon Required) 无碳复写纸
NCR 7880 NCR 7880 工作站
nCr code 给定符号 n 中取 r 代码
NCS(Network Coordinating Station) 网络协调站点

NCSA(National Center for Supercomputing Application) 国家超级计算应用中心(美)

NCSA(National Computer Security Association) 全国计算机安全协会(美)

NCSC (National Computer Security Center) 国家计算机安全中心(美)

NCT(Network Control Terminal) 网控终端

NCU(Network Control Unit) 网控单元

ncu (network connection utility) (Unix)网络连接公用程序

nCUBE 2E nCUBE 2E计算机

nCUBE 2S nCUBE 2S计算机

ND(Needle Drop) 音乐片段选取

NDBMS(Network Data Base Management System) 网络数据库管理系统

NDC(Network Diagnostic Control) 网络诊断控制

NDC(Normalized Device Coordinates) 规格化设备坐标

NDD(Non-Delivery Diagnostic) 不投送诊断

NDF(No Defect Found) 未发现错误

NDI(Non-Destructive Inspection) 非破坏性检查

NDIR(Network DIRectory) 网络列目录命令

NDIS(Network Driver Interface Specification) 网络驱动程序接口规范(微软)

NDL(Network Description Language) 网络描述语言

NDMS(NetWare Distributed Management System) NetWare分布式管理系统

NDP(Numeric Data Processor) 数值数据处理器

NDPA(Nippon Data Processing Association) 日本数据处理协会

NDR(Network Data Reduction) 网络数据精简

NDRW (NonDestructive Data Read-Write) 非破坏性数据读写

NDS (NetWare Directory Service) NetWare目录服务

NDS(Network Distribution System) 网络分布专家系统

NDT(Network Description Table) 网络描述表

NDT(Network Diagnostic Tool) 网络诊断工具

NE(Not Equal to) 不等于

NEAC(Nippon Electronic Automatic Computer) 日本电子自动计算机系列

NEAP(NetWare Educational Academic Partner) NetWare教育合作者

near 近的,近距离的

near call 近调用

near end crosstalk 近端串扰

near end operated terminal 近端操作终端机

near end signal 近端信号

near fading 近距离衰落

near-feasibility 近可行性

near-feasible point 近可行点

near-infrared 近红外

near jump 近跳越,近转移

near label 近标记

near letter quality printing(NLQ) 接近铅字质量打印

near miss 似是而非

near operation 近操作

near-optimization 接近最优,近似最优

near-optimum solution 接近最优解

near procedure 近过程

near real-time signal processing 接近实时信号处理

near region 近区

near sample 近似样品

near space 近地空间

near video on demand(NVOD) 准点播电视

near zone 近区

nearby pages 相邻页面

nearby telephone number 毗邻户电话号码

nearest distance 最近距离

nearest neighbor algorithm 最近邻法

nearest neighbor classifier 最近邻分类器

nearest-neighbor interpolation 最近邻

插补
nearest neighborhood 最近邻法
NEAT system 尼特系统(全美电子自动编码技术系统)
NEC(Nippon Electric Co.) 日本电气公司
necessary and sufficient condition 充分必要条件
necessary bandwidth 必需带宽
necessary condition 必要条件
necessary environment 必须环境
neck 颈,管颈
need to know 须知
need-to-know policy 需者方知策略
need-to-know principle 需者仅知原则
needle 探针;打印针
needle drop 现成乐段
needle pen 绘图笔
NEG(NEGative) 负的,反的;否定的
negate 反,非;求反
negated combined condition 组合条件求反
negation 反,负,否定;求反运算,"非"运算
negative 负,非;负向,负极
negative acknowledge character (NAC) 否定应答符
negative acknowledgement (NAK) 否认,否定的回答
negative acknowledgement character (NAK) 否定字符
negative AND gate 与非门
negative balance 负平衡
negative carry 负进位
negative charge 负电荷
negative clause 负子句
negative conditional element 否定条件元
negative cycle 负循环
negative definite function 负定函数
negative definite matrix 负定矩阵
negative dictionary 非用词词典
negative direction 反方向,逆向
negative disclosure 否认泄密,反推窃密
negative distortion 负向失真
negative edge 负向边沿,下降沿
negative electrode 负电极
negative entry 负值进入,负输入
negative example 反例

negative feedback 负反馈
negative feedback amplifier 负反馈放大器
negative film 负片
negative flag 负标记
negative frequency deviation 负频偏
negative ghost image 负向重像
negative image 负像
negative impedance 负阻抗
negative indication tone 否认指示音
negative indicator 负指示符
negative input-positive output (NIPO) 负输入-正输出
negative justification 负码速调整
negative logic 负逻辑
negative magnetostriction 负磁致伸缩
negative margin 负边界,压缩边界
negative modulation 负极性调制
negative number 负数
negative number representation 负数表示法
negative OR gate 或非门
negative output 反向输出
negative pattern 负片图案
negative polling limit 否认轮询限制
negative power 负乘方,负幂
negative pressure slider (NPS) 负压磁头浮动块
negative pulse 负脉冲
negative pulse stuffing 负脉冲填充
negative resistance 负电阻
negative-resistance oscillator 负阻振荡器
negative response 否认响应
negative sign 负号
negative temperature coefficient 负温度系数
negative terminal 负端
negative transpose 负转置
negative-true logic 负真逻辑
negative value 负值
negative zero 负零
negator 反相器,非门
negentropy 负熵,负平均信息量
negotiable BIND 可协商连通请求
negotiate line type 协商线路类型
negotiate menu 可(与窗体菜单)合并的对象菜单

negotiation 协商,谈判
negotiation support system 协商支持系统
neighbor 邻域 「波
neighbor average filtering 邻域均值滤
neighbor finding 邻域元素查找
neighbor information frame(NIF) 相邻站点信息帧
neighbor node 相邻节点,邻近结点
neighbor notification transmitter (NNT) 邻近站点信息传递
neighbor preserving contiguous 保持相邻的连接集
neighborhood averaging 邻域平均法
neighborhood classification rule 邻域分类规则
neighborhood effect 邻域影响
neighboring entry 相邻项
neighboring vertices 相邻顶点
neighbour 邻域(=neighbor)
neither-nor operation "或非"
nematic phase (液晶)向列相
neo-modern 最新式的
neocognition 认知机
neocognition algorithm 认知机算法
neocognitron 神经认知机
neogenesis 再生
neon lamp 氖灯
neper(NP) 奈培
neper decibel 纳分贝
NEQ(Not EQual to) 不等于
nerval net 神经网络
nerve 神经
nerve cell 神经细胞
NES(Non Elsewhere Specified) 不另行规定的
nest 嵌套
nest cell 嵌套单元
nest of subroutines 子例程嵌套
nest relation 嵌套关系
nested 嵌套的
nested address space 嵌套地址空间
nested assignment statement 嵌套赋值语句
nested binding 嵌套绑定,嵌套结合
nested block 嵌套块,嵌套分程序
nested block IF 嵌套条件块
nested cell 嵌套单元
nested command 嵌套命令
nested command list 嵌套命令表
nested condition statement 嵌套条件语句
nested conditional directive 嵌套条件指令
nested critical section 嵌套关键节
nested DO 嵌套 DO(循环)
nested ELSE clause 嵌套否则子句
nested format specification 嵌套格式说明
nested function 嵌套函数
nested if structure 嵌套 IF 结构
nested interrupt 嵌套中断
nested loop 嵌套循环
nested loop structure 嵌套循环结构
nested macro call 嵌套宏指令调用
nested macro definition 嵌套宏指令定义
nested macros 嵌套宏指令
nested multiplication method 嵌套相乘法
nested operation 嵌套运算
nested order 嵌套次序
nested parenthesis 嵌套圆括号
nested phrase index 嵌套短语索引
nested polynomial evaluation 嵌套多项式求值
nested procedure 嵌套过程
nested program 嵌套程序
nested relational model 嵌套相关模型
nested rhombic antenna 嵌套菱形天
nested scope 嵌套作用域 「线
nested set of queries 嵌套查询集
nested sign-on 嵌套联机
nested statement structure 嵌套语句结构
nested structure 嵌套结构
nested subroutine 嵌套子例程
nested transaction 嵌套事务处理
nested variant 嵌套变体
nested vias 嵌套通路
nestification 嵌套,叠加
nesting 嵌套法
nesting DO loop 嵌套 DO 循环
nesting level 嵌套层,嵌套级
nesting loop 嵌套循环
nesting storage types 嵌套存储器类型

nesting structure 嵌套结构
NET(NETwork) 网络,网
net 网络;净的,纯的
Net 1000 网络1000(贝尔)
net. abuse 网络滥用
net call sign 网络呼号
net card detection 网卡检测
NET. CFG 网络配置
net change 净变化
net. citizen 网上公民
net control station(NCS) 通信网络控制站
net. cop 网上警察
net distributed decision support system 网状分布式决策支持系统
net elapsed time 净耗时
net extraction 净析取
net gain 净增益
net. god 网络大帝
net information content 净信息内容
net lines 最后完成的打字文档,清样
net list 网表 [稿
net loss 净损,纯损耗
net morphism 网络同型,网同态
net name 网名
net number 网号
net operation 网络作业
net point 网格点
net radio interface 网状无线电接口
net service test 网络业务项目试验
net structure 网状结构
Net Vampire 网络"吸血鬼"(下载断点续传软件)
net watcher 网络监视程序
NETADMIN NetWare 目录管理命令
NETAP(NETwork Analysis Program) 网络分析程序
NetBEUI(NetBIOS Extended User Interface) 网络基本输入/输出系统扩展用户接口
NetBIOS(Network Basic Input-Output System) 网络基本输入/输出系统(协议)
NETBIOS. EXE 网络基本输入/输出系统仿真
NETBIOS protocol 网络基本输入/输出系统协议
NetFind 网上查找程序

netcard detection 网卡检测
netcomputer 网络计算机
NETGEN(Network GENeration) 网络生成
netgroup 网组
NETID(NETwork IDentifier) 网络识别号
netiquette 网络礼仪,网上礼节
netizen 网络公民
NETL NETL 语言
netlist 网络列表;连线表
netlist partition 连线表分块
netlogo service 网络登录服务
netman 上网者,网人
NETNORTH NETNORTH 网络
netprotocol model 网络协议模型
Netscape Commerce Server 网景商业服务器
Netscape Communication Cor. 网景通讯公司(美)
Netscape Navigator 网景"航海者"浏览器
Netscape News Server 网景新闻服务器
NETSET(NETwork Synthesis & Evaluation Technique) 网络综合与评价技术
NETSP(NETwork Security Program) 网络安全程序
NetSync 网络同步软件
Netron Netron 调试工具
NETUSER(NETwork USER) 网络用户
NetView 网络检视软件(IBM)
NetWare NetWare 网络操作系统(Novell)
NetWare access server(NAS) NetWare 访问服务器
NetWare asynchronous communication server(NACS) NetWare 异步通信服务器
NetWare asynchronous remote router NetWare 异步远程路由软件
NetWare command files NetWare 命令文件
NetWare communication channel NetWare 通信通道
NetWare communication interface NetWare 通信接口

NetWare core protocol (NCP)　NetWare 核心协议
NetWare Directory Database (NDD)　NetWare 目录数据库
NetWare Directory Service (NDS)　NetWare 目录服务
NetWare DOS Requester　NetWare DOS 请求
NetWare Express　NetWare 专线服务
NetWare for MVS　NetWare 网络操作系统的 MVS 版本
NetWare for SAA　支持 SAA 的 NetWare
NetWare hard disk channel technology　NetWare 硬盘通道技术
NetWare hub service　NetWare 集线器服务
NetWare interconnection package exchange protocol (IPX)　NetWare 互连分组交换协议
NetWare/IP　NetWare 互联协议模块
NetWare link/64　NetWare 64Kb/s 链路软件
NetWare link/T1　NetWare T1 链路软件
NetWare Link Service Protocol (NLSP)　NetWare 链路服务协议
NetWare link/X.25　NetWare X.25 链路软件
NetWare Lite　NetWare 普及版本
NetWare loadable module (NLM)　网络可加载模块
NetWare Management System (NMS)　NetWare 管理系统
NetWare Multiprotocol Router　NetWare 多协议路由器
NetWare network application access interface　NetWare 网络应用访问接口
NetWare NFS gateway　NetWare 网络文件系统网关
NetWare operating system　NetWare 网络操作系统
NetWare requester for OS/2　支持 OS/2 操作系统的 NetWare
NetWare route selector　NetWare 路径选择算法
NetWare sequential package exchange protocol (SPX)　NetWare 顺序分组交换协议
NetWare service　NetWare 服务
NetWare Shell　NetWare 外壳(命令解释程序)
NetWare SNA gateway　NetWare 系统网络体系结构网关
NetWare SQL　NetWare 结构查询语言
NetWare system fault tolerance　NetWare 系统容错技术
NetWare tools　NetWare 工具
NetWare transaction trace system (TTS)　NetWare 事务跟踪系统
NetWare UPS monitoring　NetWare 不间断电源监控功能
NetWare User International (NUI)　NetWare 国际用户协议
NetWare value added processing (VAP)　NetWare 增值处理
NetWare Video　NetWare 视频模块
NetWare VMS　NetWare 的支持 VMS 版本
NetWare X.25 gateway　NetWare X.25 网关软件
NetWatcher　网络监视器
NetWire　网络在线服务
network (NET)　网络
network abort　网络异常中止
network access control　网络访问控制
network access controller　网络访问控制器
network access device　网络访问设备
network access facility　网络访问设施
network access flow control　网络访问流量控制
network access line　网络访问线
network access machine　网络访问机
network access method (NAM)　网络存取法
network access pricing　网络访问计费
network access processor (NAP)　网络访问服务器
network access protocol (NAP)　网络存取协议
network access unit (NAU)　网络存取单元
network accounting record (NAR)　网络统计数据记录

network accounting server(NAS) 网络记账服务器
network adapter 网络适配器
network address(NA) 网络地址
network address block(NAB) 网络地址块
network address format 网络地址格式
network address translation 网络地址转换
network addressable unit(NAU) 网络可寻址单元
network administration 网络管理
network administrator 网络管理员
network admission delay 网络许可延迟
network alert 网络报警
network algorithm 网络算法
network analog 网络模拟
network analysis 网络分析
network analysis model 网络分析模型
network analysis point 网络分析点
network analysis program 网络分析程序
network analyzer 网络分析器;网络分析程序
network and trunk control 网络与干线控制器
network application 网络应用
network application environment 网络应用环境
network application environment creation 网络应用环境建立
network application maintenance program 网络应用维护程序
network application node(NAN) 网络应用节点
network application support(NAS) 网络应用支持
network approximation 网络近似法
network architecture 网络体系结构
network augmented pyramid 网络增强型金字塔结构
network automatic identification 网络自动标识
network availability 网络利用率,网络有效性
network awareness 网络意识,网络认知
network backbone 网络干线
network bandwidth 网络带宽

Network Basic Input/Output System(NetBIOS) 网络基本输入/输出系统
network board 网络板
network buffer 网络缓冲器
network busy hour 网络忙时
network calculator 网络计算器
network capability 网络能力
network capacity 网络容量
network card 网卡
Network Centric Computing 网络中心计算
network CD server 网络 CD 服务器
network channel access controlling 网络通道存取控制法
network channel access protocol 网络通道存取协议
network channel termination equipment 网络通道终端设备
network chart 网络图
network circuit 网络线路
network class 网络类别,网络分类
network client 网络客户
network cluster 网络群集,网络簇
network communication 网络通信
network communication circuit 网络通信线路
network communication control facility(NCCF) 网络通信控制设施
network communication processor 网络通信处理机
network communication protocol 网络通信协议
network communications circuits 网络通信电路
network complexity 网络复杂性
network components 网络构成要素
network compromise 网络折衷处理
network computer(NC) 网络计算机(Informix)
network computer interfaces 网络计算机界面
network computer program functions 网络计算机程序功能
network computing environment 网络计算环境
network computing system(NCS) 网络计算系统
network concept 网络概念

network configuration 网络布局,网络配置
network configuration tables 网络配置表
network configurator 网络配置程序
network congestion 网络拥塞
network congestion control 网络拥塞控制
network congestion signal 网络拥塞信号
network connect 网络连结
network connection handler 网络连接处理器
network connectivity 网络连通性
network constant 网络常数
network contention 网络争用,网络冲突
network control 网络控制
network control algorithm 网络控制算法
network control block 网络控制块
network control center 网络控制中心
network control channel 网络控制通道
network control function 网络控制功能
network control language 网络控制语言
network control language standards 网络控制语言标准
network control layer 网络控制层
network control message 网络控制消息
network control mode 网络控制模式
network control node 网络控制节点
network control phase 网络控制阶段
network control processor 网络控制处理机
network control program(NCP) 网络控制程序
network control program BSC or SS session 网络控制程序的二元同步通信或起止对话
network control program generation 网络控制程序生成
network control program major node 网络控制程序主节点
network control program node 网络控制程序节点
network control program station 网络控制程序站
network control program/virtual storage 虚拟存储网络控制程序
network control protocol 网络控制协议
network control signaling unit 网络控制信号单元
network control station 网络控制站
network control unit(NCU) 网络控制单元
network controller 网络控制器
network convention 网络约定
network coordinating center 网络协调中心
network coordinating station 网络协调站
network creation 网络创建
network cryptographic device(NCD) 网络加密设备
network data base management system (NDBMS) 网络数据库管理系统
network data dictionary(NDD) 网络数据字典
network data link control(NDLC) 网络数据链路控制
network data manager 网络数据管理器程序
network data model 网络数据模型;网状数据模型
network data reduction(NDR) 网络数据精简
network data translator 网络数据翻译
network database 网络数据库,网状数据库
network definition 网络定义
network delay 网络时延,网络延迟
network description table(NDT) 网络描述表
network design center 网络设计中心
network-design criteria 网络设计准则
network diagnosis 网络诊断
network device driver 网络设备驱动程序
network diagnostic control 网络诊断控制
network diagnostic controller(NDC) 网络诊断控制器
network diagnostic tool(NDT) 网络诊断工具
network diagram 网络图

network digit(ND) 网号码
network directory 网络目录
network disaster recovery 网络故障恢复
network disconnect command 网络拆线命令
network distributed control system 网络分布式控制系统
network distribution equipment 网络分配设备
network distributor 网络分配器
network domain 网络定域
network drills 网络演试
network driver 网络磁盘驱动器
Network Driver Interface Specification(NDIS) 网络驱动程序接口规范
network efficientibility 网络高效性
network element 网络元素;网络单元
network encryption 网络加密
network end-point 网络终结点
network environment 网络环境
network equivalent analysis(NEA) 网络等价分析
network expansion option 网络扩充选件
network failure 网络故障,网络失效
network failure signal 网络故障信号
network fault in local loop signal 局部环网络故障信号
network file access method 网络文件存取法
network file access protocol 网络文件存取协议
Network File System(NFS) 网络文件系统
network flow 网络流量
network flow control 网络流量控制
network flow graph 网络流图
network function 网络函数
network graphics protocol(NGP) 网络图形协议
network harms 网络损害
network host 网络主机
network identifier 网络标识符
network-in-dialing 网络的连通性
network independence 网络独立性
network independent file transfer protocol 网络独立的文件转移协议
Network Information Center(NIC) 网络信息中心

network information management 网络信息管理
network information management system(NIMS) 网络信息管理系统
Network Information Services(NIS) 网络信息服务
network information system 网络信息系统
network initial condition 网络初始条件
network input/output service 网络输入/输出服务
network integration 网络集成
network integrity 网络完整性
network interconnection 网络互连
network interface 网络接口
network interface adapter(NIA) 网络接口适配器
network interface card(NIC) 网络接口卡
network interface control(NIC) 网络接口控制
network interface machine(NIM) 网络接口机
network interface module 网络接口模块
network interface monitor 网络接口监督程序
network interface program 网络接口程序
network interface system 网络接口系统
network interface task 网络接口事务
network interface unit 网络接口单元
network interoperability 网络可互操作性
network isolation circuit 网络隔离电路
network job identifier(NJID) 网络作业标识符
network layer 网络层
network level 网络级
network like structure 类网结构
network line 网络线路
network link 网络链路
network load analysis 网络负载分析
network lock-up 网络死锁
network log 网络运行日志
network logical address 网络逻辑地址
network mail server 网络邮件服务器
network maintenance 网络维护
network maintenance signals 网络维

护信号

network management 网络管理
network management agent 网络管理代理
network management point 网络管理点
Network Management Protocol(NMP) 网络管理协议
network-management signals 网络管理信号
network manager 网络管理员
network map 网络布局图
network mask 网络屏蔽
network message 网络消息
network model 网络模型,网状模型
network modes 网络模式
network monitor 网络监控器
network monitoring 网络监督
network multiple-selection signal code 网络多重选择信号码
network multiprocessors 网络型多处理机
network name 网络名称
Network Neighborhood 网上邻居
Network News Transfer Protocol(NNTP) 网络新闻传输协议
network node 网络节点
network node administration 网络节点管理
network node interface 网络节点接口
network node unit 网络节点单元
network noise 网络噪声
network number 网络编号
network objectives 网络目标
network operating system(NOS) 网络操作系统
network operation center(NOC) 网络操作中心
network operation console 网络操作控制台
network operation interface 网络操作接口
network operator 网络操作员
network operator/administrator 网络操作管理员
network operator command 网络操作员命令
network operator console 网络操作员控制台

network operator log on 网络操作员登录
network operator services 网络操作员服务程序
network optimization 网络优化
network-oriented operating system 面向网络的操作系统
network out-dialing 网络拨入,网外拨号
Network Package 网络包揽(IBM 网络布线解决方案)
network parameter 网络参数
network path 网络路径
network partition 网络分区
network peer service 网络对等服务
network performance analyzer 网络性能分析程序
network performance monitor 网络性能监察器
network physical unit 网络物理单元
network planning 网络规划,网络计划
network port 网络端口
network printer 网络打印机
network problem determination application(NPDA) 网络故障确诊实用程序
network processing unit(NPU) 网络处理单元
network processor 网络处理机
network programming 网络程序设计
network protocol 网络协议
network protocol software 网络协议软件
network provider 网络供应商
network qualified name 网络限定名
network radio interface 网络无线电接口
network recovery 网络恢复
network redirector 网络转发程序
network redundancy 网络冗余
network registry 网络登录,网络登记
network relay 网络中继器
network reliability 网络可靠度
network resource 网络资源
network resource access 网络资源存取
network resource directory 网络资源目录
network resource manager 网络资源管理程序

network role 网络角色
network route 网络路由
network routing center 网络路由选择中心
network scheduling 网络调度
network security 网络安全性
network security center 网络安全中心
network segment 网络段
network selection signals 网络选择信号
network server 网络服务器
network service 网络服务
network service header 网络服务标头
network service procedure error(NSPE) 网络服务程序错误
network service program 网络服务程序
network service protocol 网络服务协议
network setting 网络设置
network setup 网络安装程序
network shared resource 网络共享资源
network site 网络位置
network size 网络规模
network slowdown 网络减速
network sniffer 网络解密工具
network software 网络软件
network stabilization 网络稳定性
network stand-alone system 网络独立系统
Network Station Manager 网站管理器
network status display system 网络状态显示系统
network status initialization 网络状态初始化
network structure 网状结构;网络结构
network supervisor software 网络监控软件
Network Support Encyclopedia(NSE) 网络支持百科全书
network support infrastructure 网络支持机构
network support processor system 网络支持处理器系统
network synchronization 网络同步
network synchronization plan 网络同步方案
network synthesis 网络综合
network terminal 网络终端
network terminal option(NTO) 网络终端选用程序
network terminal protocol 网络终端协议
network terminal system 网络终端系统
network terminating unit(NTU) 网络终端单元
network termination(NT) 网络终端
network termination 1(NT1) 网络终端1型
network termination 2(NT2) 网络终端2型
network termination processor 网络终端处理机
network theory 网络理论
network throughput 网络吞吐量
Network Time Protocol(NTP) 网络时间协议
network timing 网络定时
network topology 网络拓扑
network traffic 网络业务量
network transfer delay 网络传输时延
network transfer function 网络传输函数
network transparency 网络透明性
network trills 网络操演,网络演习
network universality 网络通用性
network user 网络用户
network user access procedure 网络用户访问过程
network user identity 网络用户标识
network user language 网络用户语言
network utility 网络公用信令,网间业务
network utility field 网络公用信令字段,网间业务字段
network virtual terminal 网络虚拟终端
network viruses 网络型病毒
Network Vision 网络电视机
network visualization 网络可视性
network-wide coordination entity 网络范围协调实体
networked computing 网络计算
networked computing data server 网络计算数据服务器
networked session 连网对话
networked telephony 网络电话
networking 网络连接,连网
networking feature 连网功能部件
networking products 连网产品

networking protocol 连网协议
networking support 连网支持
neural architecture 神经元体系结构
neural cell 神经细胞
neural chip 神经元芯片
neural computer 神经计算机
neural computing 神经计算
neural connection 神经元连接
neural emulation processor 神经元仿真处理器
neural expert system 神经专家系统
neural fuzzy inference system 神经模糊推理系统
neural fuzzy logic 神经模糊逻辑
neural logic system 神经逻辑系统
neural net 神经网络
neural network 神经网络
neural network model 神经网络模型
neural network cooperative processor 神经网络协处理机
neural unit 神经单元
neurocomputer 神经计算机
neurocomputing 神经计算
neurodynamics 神经信息学
neurofuzzy controller 神经模糊控制器
neuromodulation 神经调制
neuron 神经元
neuron chip 神经元芯片
neuron function 神经元的功能
neuron model 神经元模型
neuron simulation 神经元仿真
neuropile 神经堆
neutral 中性的;中线;中和
neutral bus 中性公共线
neutral circuit 中性电路,单流回路
neutral ground 中性接地
neutral-ion interaction 中性离子交互作用
neutral relay 中性继电器
neutral state (完全退磁的)中性状态
neutral zone 中性区
neutralization 中和,平衡,抵消
neutron 中子
neutron-irradiated silicon 中子辐照硅
never 从不
never warn 从不告警
new 新的
New Bullet 新项目符号

New Chart 新建图表
new class 新类
New Control Panel 新控制面板
new domain name 新域名
new entry 新项目,新产品
new file 新文件
New File Manager 新文件管理器
new folder 新文件夹
new game 重新开始游戏
new generation computer(NGC) 新一代计算机
new information technology 新信息技术
new input queue 新输入队列
new installation 新安装
new line character(NL) 新行字符
new lower bound 新下界
new media 新型媒体
New Orleans database design frame 新奥尔良数据库设计框架
new pack 新组合件,新拼合
new permanent file 新建永久文件
new production development 新产品开发
new program status word 新程序状态字
new route 新路由
new sink 新信宿,新汇接点
new sync 新同步
new synch 新同步传输
New Technology(NT) 视窗操作系统新技术版本(微软)
new type 新类型
New York Times Information Bank 《纽约时报》信息库
new zone 新区域
newbie 网上新手
NewEra NewEra 开发环境(Informix)
NewEra ViewPoint 新时代视点(Informix)
NewEra ViewPoint Pro 新时代视点专业版(Informix)
newest bound rule 最新界法测
newfig 新图形
Newhall ring 纽霍尔环
News Administrator 新闻管理员
News Articles 新闻稿件
News Group 新闻组
news feed 新闻供应站

news information 新闻资料
news on demand(NOD) 点播新闻
News proxy 新闻代理
News Reader 新闻阅读器
news release 新闻发布
News Server 新闻服务器
NeWS system (Network Extensible Window System) 网络可扩展窗口系统(Sun)
NEWSCOMP (NEWspaper COMposition Program) 报纸组版程序
Newsgroup (USENET)新闻组
newspaper style column 报纸样式分栏
Newspapers On Microfilm 报纸微胶片
NeWSprint package NeWS 打印软件包(Sun)
NewsWatcher 新闻阅读器
newsweeding 新闻剔除
Newton 牛顿掌上型计算机(苹果)
Newton communication architecture 牛顿通信体系结构(苹果)
Newton information architecture 牛顿信息体系结构(苹果)
Newton interpolation 牛顿插值法
Newton iteration 牛顿迭代法
Newton message pad 牛顿消息簿
Newton-Raphson iteration 牛顿拉富松迭代
Newton recognition architecture 牛顿识别体系结构
Newton's binomial theorem 牛顿二项式定理
Newton's tangent line method 牛顿切线法
Newton technology 牛顿技术
NewWave 新浪潮软件(HP)
NexGen NexGen公司
NEXIS 新闻全文数据库
NEXT(Near-End Cross Talk) 近端串音
next 下一个,下一步
next address 下一地址
next-available-register block 下一可用寄存器块
next consecutive bucket 下一相继存储桶
next entry table 顺次输入表
next-event synchronous simulation 下一事件同步仿真
next-executable statement 下一可执行语句
next field 下一字段；转栏
next-fit algorithm 下次适合算法
next-fit rule 下次适合规则
next generation computer 下一代计算机
next higher priority group 较高优先级群
next-in 下一信息进入位置
next instruction 下一指令
next instruction address 下一指令地址
next instruction buffer 下一指令缓存器
next logical page 下一逻辑页
next move mapping 下一动作映射
next-out 下一信息取出位置
next page number 下页页号
next physical page 下一物理页
next-record 下一记录
next-record pointer 下一记录指针
next-state simulation 第二状态仿真
NEXT statement NEXT 语句
next station addressing(NSA) 下一站点寻址
next to axis 轴旁
next transmitted bit (scrambling process) 下一发送位(扰码过程)
next-used information 下一使用信息
NEXTLP(NEXT Logical Page) 下一逻辑页
NEXTPP(NEXT Physical Page) 下一物理页
NeXTStep Developer NeXTStep 开发程序
NeXTStep for Intel Processor 用于Intel 处理器的 NeXTStep 操作系统
nexus 关节,网络节点
NF(Negative Feedback) 负反馈
NF(Normal Form) 标准化形式,范式
1NF(First Normal Form) 第一范式
2NF(Second Normal Form) 第二范式
3NF(Third Normal Form) 第三范式
4NF(Fourth Normal Form) 第四范式
NFA(Normalized Floating Add) 规格化浮点加法
NFAM(Network File Access Method)

网络文件访问方法
NFAP(Network File Access Protocol) 网络文件访问协议
NFC(Negative Feedback Circuit) 负反馈电路
NFA(Normalized Floating Divide) 规格化浮点除法
NFE(Network Front End) 网络前端
NFM(Normalized Floating Multiply) 规格化浮点乘法
NFS(Network File System) 网络文件系统(Sun)
NFS(Normalized Floating Subtract) 规格化浮点减法
NFS(Network File Transfer) 网络文件传送
NGC(New Generation Computer) 新一代计算机
NGP(Network Graphics Protocol) 网络图形协议
NHK(Nippon Hoso Kyokai) 日本广播协会
NHP(Network Host Protocol) 网络主机协议
NHRP(Next Hop Resolution Protocol) 邻站点辨识协议
NI(NonInhibitable) 不可禁止的
NI interrupts 不可抑制中断
NIA(Network Interface Adapter) 网络接口适配器
NIAL(Nested Interactive Array Language) 嵌套交互式数组语言
NIAT(Non-Indexable Address Tag) 非索引址标记
NIB(Negative Impedance Boosting) 负阻自举法
NIB(Node Initialization Block) 节点初始化信息块
nib 笔尖
NIB list 节点初始化块表
nibble 半字节
nibble mode 半字节方式
NIBL(National Industrial BASIC Language) 全国工业用BASIC语言
NIC(Network Information Center) 网络信息中心
NIC(Network Interface Card) 网络接口卡

NIC(Network Interface Control) 网络接口控制
Nicad battery 镍镉电池
niceness value (Unix进程优化级的)优值
nickel-cadmium cell 镍镉电池
nickel-iron cell 镍铁电池
NICS(Network Integrity Control System) 网络完整性控制系统 「识
NID(Network IDentification) 网络
NIF(Network Information File) 网络信息文件
NIFTP (Network Independent File Transfer Protocol) 独立于网络的文件传送协议
night frequency (短波无线电通信)夜间频率,夜频
NII (National Information Infrastructure) 国家信息基础建设
NIL (Network Implementation Language) 网络实现语言
nil 零,无;虚名;引用常量值
nil interference 无干扰
nil link 零链接,空链接
nil pointer 指零指针,空指针
nil string 空串
nil symbol 零符号
niladic 尼拉蒂克操作
nilpotent approximation 幂零逼近
NIM(Network Interface Machine) 网络接口机
NIO(Network Input/Output service) 网络输入/输出服务
nine's complement representation 十进制反码表示 「性
nine-track compatibility 9磁道兼容
ninety column card 90列穿孔卡片
NIP(Nucleus Initialization Program) 核心初始化程序
NIPPAHDR (Nucleus Initializatior Program Parameter Area HeaDeR) 核心初始化程序参数区标头
NIPPAREA(Nucleus Initialization Program Parameter AREA) 核心初始化程序参数区
NIPPATE(Nucleus Initialization Program Parameter Address Table Entry) 核心初始化程序参数地址表

登录
NIPSCHDL(Nucleus Initialization Program SCHeDule parameter List) 核心初始化程序调度参数表
NIS(Network Information Service) 网络信息服务(SunOS 4.x)
NIS＋(Network Information Service) 网络信息服务(SunOS 5.x)
NIS(Network Information System) 网络信息系统
NIS(Network Interface System) 网络接口系统
NIS domain 网络信息服务域(Sun)
NIS maps 网络信息服务图
NIST(National Institute of Standards and Technology) 国家标准技术研究所(美)
NIT(Network Interface Task) 网络接口任务
NIT(Node Initialization Table) 节点初始化表
nit 尼特;尼
nitride-barrier 氮化物阻挡层
nitrogen(N2) 氮气
nitroxide film 氧化氮薄膜
NIU(Network Interface Unit) 网络接口单元
Nixdorf Communication Network(NCN) Nixdorf通信网络(德国)
nixie decoder 数码管译码器
nixie light 辉光数码管
nixie tube 辉光数码管
NL(Native Language) 本机语言
NL(Natural Language) 自然语言
NL(New Line) 换行
NLA(Network Logical Address) 网络逻辑地址
NLA(Normalized Local Address) 规格化局部地址
NLC(Natural Language Computer) 自然语言计算机
NLFSR(Non-Linear Feedback Shift Register) 非线性反馈移位寄存器
NLI(Natural Language Interface) 自然语言接口
NLIST 网络列表
NLM(NetWare Loadable Module) NetWare可装载模块

NLM(Network Loadable Module) 网络可装载模块
NLQ(Near Letter Quality) 接近铅印质量
NLS(National Language Support) 国际语言支持(IBM)
NLSP(NetWare Link Services Protocol) NetWare链路服务协议
NLU(Natural Language Understanding) 自然语言理解
NM(Network Manager) 网络管理者
nm(nanometer) 纳米,10^{-9}米
NMD(Non-Message Driven) 非消息驱动
NMENU(Network MENU) 网络菜单
NMF(New Master File) 新主文件
NMI(NonMaskable Interrupt) 不可屏蔽中断
NMIRQ(NonMaskable Interrupt ReQuest) 非屏蔽中断请求
NMO(Normal Manual Operation) 正常人工操作
NMOS(N-channel Metal Oxide Semiconductor) N沟道金属氧化物半导体器件
NMP(Network Management Processor) 网络管理处理机
NMP(Network Management Protocol) 网络管理协议
NMR-CT(Nuclear Magnetic Resonance-Computer Tomography) 核磁共振计算机断层扫描
NMRR(Normal Mode Rejection Ration) 常模抑制比
NMS(Network Management Services) 网络管理服务
NMSS(Network Maximum Segment Size) 网络最大段长度
nn nn新闻阅读器
NN-1(Nervous Network chip 1) 神经网络芯片(日立)
NNI(Network-to-Network Interface) 网络到网络接口
NNIA(Nearest Neighbor Interpolation Algorithm) 最近邻内插算法
NNP(Network Node Processor) 网络节点处理机
NNS(Neutral Network Simulator) 中

性网络仿真
NNTP(Network News Transport Protocol) 网络新闻传输协议
NO(Normally Open) 常开的,原位断开的
NO.(Number) 数;编号,号码
No. 4 A crossbar system 4号信令A纵横制系统
No. 5 crossbar system 5号信令纵横制系统
No. 6 exchange 6号信令交换机
No. 7 exchange 7号信令交换机
no access 拒绝访问
no-address instruction 无地址指令
no border 无边框
no-buffer queue 无缓冲器队列
no-charge machine-fault time 机器故障免费时间
no-charge not-machine-fault time 非机器故障免费时间
no code 无代码
no connection(NC) 未连接
no-consoles condition 无控制台状况
no control print 无控制字打印
no correction 无须更正
no custom format 无自定义格式
no data 无数据
no detect 未经检测
no-encoding microinstruction 非编码微指令
no error print 无错误打印
no error report 无错报告,未报告差
no first error 非初次错误
no-flux gate head 无磁通门磁头
no fonts installed 未安装字体
no global optimization 非全局优化
no GOTO statement 无GOTO语句
no-guard band recording 无保护带记录法
no header row 没有标题行
no home record 无引导记录
no_implementation attribute 非执行属性
no job definition error 无作业定义错误
no kerning 未调整字距
no load 无负载,空载
no load ratio 无载率,空载率
no load running 空载运行

no load test 空载测试
no logging 未登录,未注册
no manual intervention 无人工干预
no memory 无内存
no_namespace attribute 无命名空间属性
NO OP 无作业,无操作指令
no-operand instruction 无操作数指令
no operation 空操作
no operation instruction(NOP) 无操作指令
no parity 无奇偶校验
no-print key 不打印键
no programming language 非编程语言
no remote 非远程的
no reply 无回答,无应答
no response 无响应,无应答
no return point 无返回点
no-scribble state 非改写状态
no signal 无信号
no space before 此前无空格
no spurious interrupt 非伪中断
no station address 无站址
no such number tone 无此号码音
no test loop 无测试回路
no-test trunk 无测试干线,强行插入干线
no-toner 无墨粉,墨粉用完
no-valid reference 无效引用
no virus found 未发现病毒
no wait mode 无等待模式
no-width non-break 无宽不间断符
no wrap 不自动换行
noagent 无主体;无代理
NOC(Network Operation Center) 网络操作中心
NOD(Network Out-Dialing) 网外拨号,网外拨入
nodal 节点的;枢纽的;波节的
nodal aggregation algorithm 节点聚合算法
nodal analysis method 节点分析法
nodal coarse-mesh method 节点粗网格法
nodal computer 节点计算机
nodal degree-of-freedom 节点自由度
nodal dispersion 波节色散
nodal displacement 节点位移

nodal function 节点功能
nodal operation 节点操作
nodal plane 节点平面
nodal processor 节点处理机
nodal surface 节面
nodal switching center 节点交换中心
node(N) 节点,结点,波节
node address 节点地址
node administration 节点管理
node base 节点基
node branch 节点分支
node-by-node correction 逐节点校正
node-coloring 节点着色法
node cluster 节点群集
node computer 节点计算机
node concentration 节点集讯
node database 节点数据库
node deletion 节点删除
node diagram 节点图
node disjoint path 节点不相交通路
node/edge connectivity 节点边缘连通
node encryption 节点加密性
node failure 节点故障
node identifier 节点标识符
node initialization block(NIB) 节点初始化块
node initialization table 节点初始化表
node insertion 节点插入
node-label controlled graph grammar 受节点标号控制的图形文法
node layering language 节点分层语言
node level 节点层数
node link 节点链路
node list 节点列表
node location 节点位置,节点定位
node matrix equation 节点矩阵方程
node name 节点名
node name table 节点名称表
node number 节点号
node of a finite element 有限元结点
node of tree 树节点
node operator 节点操作员,网点操作程序
node pair 节点对
node partition 网点划分
node queue 节点队列
node record 节点记录
node repair 节点修复

node routing 节点路由选择
node shuffle exchange 节点混洗交换
node space 节点空间
node splitting 节点分割
node structure 网点结构
node subgraph 网点子图
node switching 节点交换
node table 节点表
node traffic 节点信息流量
node transition description 节点转移描述
node type 节点类型
node-weighed graph 节点加权图
noetic science 思维科学
noise 噪声
noise analyzer 噪声分析仪
noise attenuation 噪声衰减
noise bandwidth 噪声带宽
noise canceler 消噪电路
noise-canceling transmitter 噪声消除发送器
noise characteristics 噪声特性
noise covariance matrix 噪声协方差矩阵
noise criteria curve 噪声判据曲线
noise digit 噪声数字
noise diode 噪声二极管
noise distribution 噪声分布
noise-equivalent power(NEP) 噪声等效功率
noise factor(NF) 噪声系数
noise filter 噪声滤波器
noise free printer 无噪声打印机
noise generator 噪声发生器
noise immunity 抗干扰度
noise induction 噪声感应
noise killer 消噪器
noise level 噪声电平
noise limiter 噪声限制器,静噪器
noise load ratio 噪声负载比
noise loading test set 噪声加载测试设备
noise margin 噪声边际,噪声容限
noise measuring set 噪声测量仪
noise mode 噪声模式
noise-operated gain-adjusting device 噪声控制增益调整设备
noise peak 噪声峰值
noise power ratio 噪声功率比

noise ratio 噪声比
noise reducer 噪声减弱器
noise silencer 静噪器
noise smoothing 噪声平滑
noise source 噪声源
noise suppression circuit 噪声抑制电路
noise suppressor 噪声抑制器
noise temperature 噪声温度
noise threshold 噪声阈值[门限]
noise to ground 对地噪声
noise type 噪声类型
noise weighting 噪声加权
noise window 噪声窗口
noise word 干扰字(检索时被忽略的字)
noiseless channel 无噪声信道
noiseless coding 无噪声编码
noiseless pulse 无噪声脉冲
noisy blacks 噪声黑区
noisy deformed tree 噪声畸变树
noisy environment 有噪声环境
noisy mode 杂乱模式,噪声状态
noisy sample 噪声取样
noisy white 噪声白区
noisy work space 噪声工作空间
NOL(Normal OverLoad) 正常超载
nomenclature 名称,术语,目录,命名
nominal 标称的,额定的,名义上的
nominal band 正常频带,标称频带
nominal bandwidth 标称带宽
nominal bit stuffing rate 标称位填充率
nominal black 标称黑信号
nominal delay 标称延迟
nominal impedance 标称阻抗
nominal justification rate 标称调整率
nominal key 名义键
nominal linewidth 正常行宽,标称行宽
nominal margin 正常容限,标称边际
nominal path 标称路径
nominal relative level 标称相对电平
nominal speed 标称速度
nominal stuffing rate 标称填充率
nominal transformation ratio 额定变换比
nominal transmission loss 额定传输损耗
nominal value 标称值
nominal velocity of propagation 名义传播速度

nominal voltage 额定电压,标称电压
nominal white 标称白信号
nomination sample 标称样品,指定取样
nominative testing 按规定进行的测试
nomogram 列线图
nomograph 列线图
non-accountable time 不计量时间
non-action message 非活动消息,不要干预信息
non-add 非增加的,不增加的
non-addressable memory(NAM) 不可寻址内存,非编址内存
non-adjacent area 非邻接区域
non-adjacent selection 非邻接选择
non-algebraic adder 非代数加法器
non-alphanumeric sign 非文数符号
non-analytic complex function 非解析复值函数
non-arithmetic shift 非算术移位
non-arithmetic statement 非算术语句
non-arithmetic uses 非算术应用
non-associated CCIS 非结合(直联)公用通道局间信号传输
non-associated mode of operation 非直联操作模式
non-associated mode of signaling 非直联信令模式
non-associated signal 非直联信号
non-associated signaling 非结合信令
non-atomic data 非原子数据
non-automatic relay center 非自动化转报中心
non-based variable attribute 无基变量属性,非基变量表征
non-binary code 非二进制代码
non-blank input column 非空输入栏
non-blocking 无阻塞的
non-blocking voice/data switching 无阻塞语音-数据切换
non-book materials(NBM) 非书面材料
non-breaking hyphen 不可分连字符
non-busy waiting strategy 非忙等待策略
non-captive user 非受控用户
non-centralized control system 非集中控制系统
non-centralized operation 非集中式操作
non-chronological backtracking 非时序回溯

non-classical damping 非经典阻尼
non-code information 未编码信息
non-coded graphics 非编码图形学
non-coherent bundle 非相干线束
non-coherent modulation system 非相干调制系统
non-coherent optical signal processing 非相干光信号处理
non-coloring contradiction 非着色的矛盾
non-command terminal 非命令终端机
non-commutative setting 非交换排列
non-compact single-entry index 非压缩单项索引
non-compatibility 不兼容性
non-conditional branch 无条件分支,无条件转移
non-conductive pattern 非导电图形
non-conductor 非导体
non-conjunction 非共结,"与非"
non-conjunction gate 非共结门,"与非"门
non-connected storage 非连接存储
non-conservative stability 非保守稳定性
non-contact head 非接触式头
non-contact magnetic recording 非接触式磁记录
non-contact recording 非接触式记录
non-contiguous field 非邻接字段
non-contiguous item 非邻接数据项,孤立项
non-contiguous storage allocation 不邻接的存储器分配
non-conversational mode 非对话方式
non-corrosive flux 无腐蚀性焊剂
non-critical activity 非关键活动
non-critical microoperation 非临界微操作
non-critical path 非关键路径
non-critical value 非临界值
non-data I/O operation control 非数据输入/输出操作控制
non-decreasing order 非递减次序
non-deductive problem solving approach 非演绎问题求解方法
non-deletable file 不可删除文件
non-delimiter 非定界标
non-demand paging 非需求调页

non-dense index 非稠密索引
non-destructive cursor 非破坏性光标
non-destructive inspection(NDI) 非破坏性检查
non-destructive read(NDR) 非破坏性读出
non-determinacy 不确定性
non-deterministic algorithm 不确定算法
non-deterministic automaton(NDA) 不确定性自动机
non-deterministic finite automaton 不确定性有限自动机
non-deterministic finite state recognizer 非确定性有限状态识别机
non-deterministic flow chart 非确定型流程图
non-deterministic model 非确定性模型
non-deterministic processing 不确定序处理
non-deterministic program 不确定程序
non-dialed connection 非拨号连接
non-direct coupling 非直接耦合
non-disclosure 保密,不透露
non-discriminating number 无鉴别号码
non-document 非文档型文件
non-dynamic collection buffer 非动态收集缓冲器
non-empty binary tree 非空二叉树
non-empty finite set 非空有限集
non-empty finite string 非空有限串
non-empty sequence 非空序列
non-empty set 非空集合
non-encode recording mode 不编码记录模式
non-equilibrium mode distribution 非均衡模式分布,非稳态模式分布
non-equivalence element 非对等元件,"异"元件
non-equivalence operation 非等价运算,"异"运算
non-erasable medium 不可抹除媒体
non-erasable storage 不可擦除存储器
non-escaping key 非逸出键,非换码键
non-executable statement 非执行语句
non-existent code 不存在码验
non-existent code check 不存在码校
non-extended logical address space 非扩充逻辑地址空间

non-fade memory 无衰变存储器
non-fatal error 非致命错误
non-feasible solution 不可行解
non-feasible state 不可行状态
non-file structure device 非文件结构设备
non-file structure lookup 非文件结构查找
non-finite state model 非有限状态模型
non-full functional dependency 非完全函数相关性
non-functional instruction 非功能型指令
non-fuzzy event 非模糊事件
non-generic form of intrinsic function 内在函数的非类属形式
non-graphic/video terminal 非图形/视频终端机
non-graphical data 非图示数据
non-hang-up base 立即服务方式
non held output 非保持输出
non-hierarchical communication 非分级通信
non-homing switch 不归位开关
non homogeneous distribution system 非齐次分布系统
non-I/D split 不分离指令/数据
non-identity operation "非全同"运算,非一致运算
non-impact printer(NIP) 非击打式打印机
non-implication 非蕴涵
non-information bit 非信息位
non-inhibit interrupt 非禁止中断
non-inhibitable 不可禁止的
non-integral quantity 非整数量
non-intelligent 非智能的
non-intelligible cross talk 不可懂串音
non-interacting control system 非交互式控制系统
non-interactive 非交互的
non-interactive system 非交互式系统
non-interactive zero-knowledge proof 非交互零知识证明
non-interfering process 无干扰进程
non-interlaced monitor 非隔行显示器
non-interpersonal message 非个人间消息

non-invert 不反相的,同相的
non-inverting bidirectional bus 非反相双向总线
non-isolated amplifier 非隔离放大器
non-key attribute 非键码属性
non-labeled tapes 无标号磁带
non-laser marking equipment 非激光打印机
non-leaf node 非叶节点
non-leak memory 无泄露存储器,永久性存储器
non-linear 非线性的
non-linear code 非线性码
non-linear coupling 非线性耦合
non-linear deduction 非线性演绎
non-linear degree 非线性度
non-linear discriminant 非线性判别
non-linear distortion 非线性失真
non-linear edge enhancement 非线性边缘增强
non-linear editing 非线性编辑
non-linear element 非线性元件
non-linear feedback control system 非线性反馈控制系统
non-linear feedback shift register 非线性移位寄存器
non-linear history 非线性历史记录(Adobe)
non-linear impedance 非线性阻抗
non-linear integrated circuit 非线性集成电路
non-linear network 非线性网络
non linear network simulation and analysis program 非线性网络模拟与分析程序
non-linear optimization 非线性优化
non-linear pipeline 非线性流水线
non-linear programming(NLP) 非线性规划
non-linear regression analysis 非线性回归分析
non-linear system 非线性系统
non-linearity 非线性
non-linearity distortion 非线性失真
non-literal language 非文字语言,非直接量语言
non-loadable character set 不可装载字符集

non-loaded cable 无载电缆,非加感电缆
non-loaded Q 空载品质因数,空载 Q 值
non-local 非局部的
non-local entry 非本地输入
non-local identifier 非局部标识符
non-local variable 非局部变量
non-locking 非锁定性
non-locking code extension character 非锁定代码扩充字符
non-locking escape 非锁定换码,非锁定转义
non-locking key 非锁定键
non-locking shift character 非锁定转义字符
non-magnetic 非磁性的
non-magnetic recording medium 非磁性记录介质
non-manifold geometric modeling 非流形几何造型
non-mapping mode 非映像模式
non-maskable interrupt(NMI) 非屏蔽中断
non-matched data 不匹配数据
non-mathematical program 非数学程
non-maximum suppression 非最大抑制
non-message driven program 非消息驱动程序
non-microprogrammed machine 非微程序控制的计算机
non-modulation system 非调制系统
non-monotonic logic 非单调逻辑
non-monotonic reasoning 非单调推理
non-moved module 不可移动模块
non-NCP station 非网络控制程序站
non-negative integer 非负整数
non-negative matrix 非负矩阵
non-negative number 非负数
non-negative vector 非负向量
non-neighbor node 非相邻节点
non-nested family 非成套类
non-nested hypothesis 非成套假设
non-nested information pattern 非嵌套信息样式
non-network control program station 非网络控制程序站
non-normality 非正态性

non-null class 非空类
non-numeric 非数字
non-numeric application 非数值应用
non-numeric character 非数值字符
non-numeric coding 非数字编码
non-numeric item 非数值项
non-numeric literal 非数值文字
non-numerical 无号的
non-numerical algorithm 非数值算法
non-numerical data processing 非数值数据处理
non-numerical information 非数值信息
non-numerical operation 非数值操作
non-occupied terminal 未占用终端机,空闲终端
non-operable instruction 非操作指令
non-operate current 非工作电流
non-operating time 无操作时间
non-operational load 非工作负载
non-optimal path 非最佳路径
non-orientable 不可定向的
non-oriented graph 无定向图
non-original BCH code 非本原 BCH 码
non-orthogonal data 非正交数据
non-overlap mode 非交叠模式,非并列模式
non-packet mode terminal(NPT) 非分组模式终端
non-pageable dynamic area 不可换页动态区
non-pageable partition 不可换页动态分区
non-paged computer system 非页面式计算机系统
non-parameter model 非参数模型
non-parametric classification 非参数分类
non-parametric classifier 非参数分类器
non-performance instruction 无表现指令
non-permissible code 不允许码,禁用代码
non-persistent unslotted CSMA 非坚持型非时分 CSMA
non-physical device 非物理设备
non-polarized return-to-zero 非极化归零制
non-polarized return-to-zero recording

(NPRZ) 非极化归零制记录
non-precedence call 非居先呼叫
non-preemptive multitasking 非抢占式多任务
non-preemptive scheduling 非预占式调度；非抢占式调度
non-primary path 非主要路径
non-primitive code 非本原码
non-print 不能打印，禁止打印
non-print code 非打印代码
non-print format character 非打印格式定义符
non-print instruction 免印指令
non-printable 不可打印的
non-printing character 非印出字符
non-privileged mode 非特权模式
non-procedural language 非过程语言
non-procedure oriented language 非面向过程语言
non-productive poll 非生产轮询
non-productive task 非生产性任务，辅助性任务
non-programmed halt 非计划停机
non-programming user 非编程用户
non-read 无效阅读
non-ready program 未就绪程序
non-real time processing 非实时处理
non-real-time simulation 非实时仿真
non-reciprocal network 非互易网络
non-recording surface 非记录表面
non-recoverable error 不可恢复错误
non-recursion rule 非递归规则
non-recursive algorithm 非递归算法
non-redundant logic 非冗余逻辑
non-reflective 非自反的；非反射的
non-reflective coatings 非反射涂层
non-reflective ink 无反射墨水
non-reflective star coupler 无反射星形耦合器
non-reflectivity 非自反性
non-regular character 非常规字符
non-regular set 非正规集
non-relevant failure 非关联失效
non-repeatable edit descriptor 不可重复的编辑描述符
non-repetitive sequence 非重复序列
non-replaceable unit 不可更换的部件
non-resident micro diagnostics 非驻留微诊断程序
non-resident partition of a control program 控制程序的非驻留部分
non-resident overlay 非驻存覆盖
non-resident routine 非驻存例程
non-resolution theorem proving 非归结定理证明
non-resonant feeder 非谐振馈线
non-restoring method 不恢复法
non-return policy 不返回策略
non-return-to-reference 不归位制
non-return-to-reference recording 不归基准制记录法
non-return-to-zero(NRZ) 不归零制
non-return-to-zero change(NRZC) 不归零变更制
non-return-to-zero change modulation 变更调制不归零制
non-return-to-zero change on ones modulation 逢"1"变更调制不归零制
non-return-to-zero change recording (NRZC) 不归零制变更记录法
non-return-to-zero code(NRZ code) 不归零码
non-return-to-zero coding 不归零制编码
non-return-to-zero inverted code(NRZI code) 不归零翻转代码
non-return-to-zero level(NRZL) 电平不归零制
non-return-to-zero mark(NRZM) 传号不归零制
non-return-to-zero signal 不归零信号
non-return-to-zero space 非归零空号
non-reusable 不可重用
non-reusable disk queuing 不可重用磁盘排队
non-reusable medium 不可重用记录媒体
non-reusable routine 不可重用例程
non-rigid motion 非刚体运动
non-sales mode 非销售模式
non-saturation magnetic recording 非饱和磁记录
non-scalable font 不可缩放字体
non-scan field 非扫描域
non-scheduled maintenance time 非预定维修时间
non-searchable information 不可查信息

non-segment program 不分段程序
non-segmented mode 不分段模式
non-self-adjoint system 非自毗邻系统
non-self-embedding grammar 非自嵌套文法
non-separated code 非分离码
non-sequence access 乱序存取
non-sequence computer 非顺序计算机
non-sequential computer 非时序计算机
non-sequential stochastic control 非顺序随机控制
non-set-up job 非准备作业
non-shared memory 非共享存储器
non-shared task address space 非共享地址空间
non-simultaneous transmission 非同时传输,半双工传输
non-smooth optimization 非平滑优化
non-SNA station 非 SNA 工作站
non-SNA terminal 非 SNA 终端
non-shared memory 非共享存储器
non-solvability 不可解性
non-standard facilities equipment 非标准化业务设备
non-standard labels 非标准标号
non-stationary stochastic signal 非平稳随机信号
non-stop operation protection 无休止操作保护
non-storage device 非存储装置
non-store through cache 通过高速缓冲器但不存储
non-stream device 非流式设备
non-structural decision problem 非结构化决策问题
non-supervised inference procedure 无监督推理过程
non-suspendable subsystem 不可中断子系统
non-switched connection 非交换连接
non-switched line 非交换线
non-switched point to point line 非交换点对点线路
non-symbolic address debugging 非符号地址调试
non-symmetric relation 非对称关系
non-synchronized network 非同步网络
non-synchronous 非同步
non-synchronous data transmission channel 非同步数据传输通道
non-synchronous network 非同步网络
non-system disk 非系统盘
non-system job 非系统作业
non-systematic code 非系统码
non-technical load 非技术负载
non-temporary data set 非暂时数据集
non-terminal character 非终结字符
non-terminal node 非终端结点,非终节点
non-terminal related main storage data base 与终端无关的主存数据库
non-terminal symbol 未结束符 「件
non-terminating controls 非终止型控
non-textual representation 非文本表示法
non-threshold logic circuit(NTL) 无阈值逻辑电路
non-transitive dependency 非传递相关性
non-transparent mode 非透明模式
non-tree subgraph 非树子图
non-uniform encoding 非均匀编码
non-uniform quantization 非均匀量化
non-uniform quantizing 不均匀量化
non-uniform rational B-splines (NURBS) 非均匀有理 B 样条
non-uniform sampling 非均匀采样
non-uniform scale 非成比例缩放
non-uniformity 非一致性
non-uniformrational B-spline(NURBS) 非一致推理 B 样条法
non-unique alternate key 非惟一替用关键字
non-vector interrupt 非向量中断 「信
non-verbal communication 非语言通
non-visual 不可视的
non-volatile RAM 非易失性随机存取存储器
non-volatile storage 非易失性存储器
non Von Neumann architecture 非冯·诺依曼体系结构
non Von Neumann machine 非冯·诺依曼型计算机
Non-Windows application 非 Win-

dows 应用程序
nonadjacent selection 非相邻区域选择
nonautonomous system 非自主系统
nonaxisymmetric structure 非轴对称结构
nonbatched file 非成批文件
nonbinary cyclic code 非二进制循环码
nonblank character 非空白字符
nonblocking commit protocol 无阻塞提交协议
nonblocking switching network 无阻塞交换网络
nonboundary line 非边界线
nonbreaking hyphen 不间断连字符
nonbreaking space 不间断空格
nonbusy-hour load 非忙时负荷
noncarbon paper 非碳素纸
noncausal estimation 非因果估计
noncentralized control 非集中式控制
noncircular symbol 非循环符号
nonclient area 非客户区
noncoherent modulation system 非相干调制系统
noncommand-language input 非命令语言输入
noncompatible run-time library 非兼容运行时间库
noncomplete independence 不完全独立性
nonconforming finite element 非相容有限元
noncontact longitudinal recording 无接触纵向记录方法
noncontiguous file 不连续文件
noncontiguous item 不连续数据项
noncontiguous page 非邻接页面
nonconvex programming 非凸规划
nondata input 非数据输入
nondecidability 不可判定性
nondedicated server 非专用服务器
nondegenerate basic feasible solution 非退化基本可行解
nondemand paging 非请求调页
nondependence relation 非相关性关系
nondestructive cursor 非破坏性光标
nondestructive testing 非破坏性测试
nondeterminism 不确定性
nondeterministic algorithm 非确定性算法
nondeterministic function 不确定函数
nondeterministic nested stack automata 非确定性嵌套堆栈自动机
nondeterministic polynomial 非确定性多项式
nondeterministic program 非确定性程序
nondeterministic stack automaton (NSA) 非确定型栈自动机
nondeterministic syntax analyzer 非确定性语法分析程序
nondeterministic Turing machine 非确定型图灵机
nondial trunks 不拨号干线
nondisclosure agreement 不泄密协议
nondisjoint codes 非分离码
nondominated solution 非受控解
nondrop-frame timecode 非丢帧时间代码
none 无
none indicator 失配指示字
nondelivery report 未送达报告
nonempty binary tree 非空二叉树
nonempty entry 非空项
nonempty finite set 非空有限类
nonempty sequence 非空序列
nonequivalence operation "异"运算
nonerasable medium 不可擦除媒体
nonerasing stack automaton (NESA) 非删除型栈自动机
nonexecutable statement label 非执行语句标号
nonexistent block 不存在程序块
nonexistent logic device number 不存在逻辑设备号
nonfailure node 非失效节点
nonfatal error 非致命错误
nonfeasible method 不可行方法
nonfunction requirement 非功能需求
nonhierarchical file 不分级文件
nonholonomic transformation 非完整变换
noninhibit interrupt 非禁止中断
nonink stylus 非墨水笔
noninteractive program 非交互式程序
nonisolated solution 非孤立解
nonisomorphic graph 非同构图

nonisomorphic substructure 非同构子结构
noniterative algorithm 非迭代算法
nonlabeled tape 无标号磁带
nonleaf node 无叶结点
nonleaf tree 无叶树
nonleak memory 无泄漏存储器
nonlinear approximation 非线性逼近
nonlinear autonomous system 非线性自治系统
nonlinear boundary condition 非线性边界条件
nonlinear canonical form 非线性标准型
nonlinear controllability 非线性可控性
nonlinear data fusion 非线性数据合并
nonlinear data structure 非线性数据结构
nonlinear deconvolution 非线性去卷积
nonlinear discretization 非线性离散化
nonlinear distortion 非线性失真
nonlinear distributed parameter 非线性分布参数
nonlinear dynamic response 非线性动态响应
nonlinear elastic contact mode 非线性弹性接触方式
nonlinear equalizer 非线性均衡器
nonlinear feedback network 非线性反馈网络
nonlinear filter 非线性滤波器
nonlinear finite element 非线性有限元
nonlinear flexible connection 非线性柔性连接
nonlinear Fourier equation 非线性傅里叶方程
nonlinear functional expansion 非线性函数展开
nonlinear grammar 非线性文法
nonlinear hyperbolic equation 非线性双曲线方程
nonlinear instability 非线性不稳定性
nonlinear least squares problem 非线性最小二乘问题
nonlinear magnetic head 非线性磁头
nonlinear method 非线性方法
nonlinear model 非线性模型
nonlinear multibody system 非线性多体系统
nonlinear network 非线性网络
nonlinear neural network 非线性神经网络
nonlinear observer 非线性观测器
nonlinear operational element 非线性运算部件
nonlinear optimization 非线性优化
nonlinear parabolic equation 非线性抛物线方程
nonlinear passive damping 非线性无源阻尼
nonlinear predictive control 非线性预测控制
nonlinear programming approach 非线性规划方法
nonlinear proximal point algorithm 非线性邻近点算法
nonlinear recursion 非线性递归
nonlinear regression 非线性回归
nonlinear response analysis 非线性响应分析
nonlinear singular problem 非线性奇异问题
nonlinear smoothing filter 非线性平滑滤波器
nonlinear stiffness matrix 非线性刚度矩阵
nonlinear stochastic system 非线性随机系统
nonlinear structural instability 非线性结构不稳定性
nonlinear superposition principle 非线性叠加原理
nonlinear supersonic flutter 非线性超声波抖动
nonlinear system approximation 非线性系统近似
nonlinear term 非线性项
nonlinear time-lag system 非线性迟滞系统
nonlinear transformation 非线性变换
nonlinear transient analysis 非线性暂态分析
nonlinear transmission line 非线性传输线
nonlinear vibration 非线性振动
nonlinear voltage regulator 非线性稳

压器
nonlinearity 非线性
nonlinearly continuous time model 非线性连续时间模型
nonlinking format 非链接格式
nonloadable character set 非装入字符集
nonlocal environment 非局部环境
nonlocking shift character 不锁定换档字符
nonlogical fault 非逻辑故障
nonmagnetic material 非磁性材料
nonmaskable interrupt capability 不可屏蔽中断功能
nonmetric 非公制的
nonmonotonic inference rule 非单调推理规则
nonmonotonic uncertainty reasoning 非单调不确定性推理
nonnegtive number 非负数
nonnested multigrid method 非嵌套多网格法
nonnumeric calculation 非数值计算
nonnumeric literal (COBOL 语言中的)非数值文字
nonoptimal path 非最佳路径
nonorthogonal analysis 非正交分析
nonoverflow entry 非溢出项
overlayed main program link 非覆盖主程序链接
nonpacket mode 非分组方式
nonpageable partition 不可调页分区
nonpageable region 不可调页区
nonparatetric feature 非参数特征
nonparatetric regression 非参数回归
nonparatetric statistics 非参量性统计
nonpath-dependent record 非通路相关记录
nonperiodic forced overflow 非周期性记录溢出
nonpermanent foreground 非永久前台
nonpermissible code block 禁用代码组
nonpersistent CSMA protocol 非坚持型 CSMA 协议
nonpipelined processor 非流水线式处理机
nonprecise interrupt 不精确中断
nonprocedural language 非过程语言

nonredundant circuit 无冗余电路
nonpreemptive multitasking 非抢占式多任务处理
nonpreemptive scheduling 非抢占式调度
nonremovable disk 不可移动盘
nonprimary data structure 非初等数据结构
nonprime attribute 非主属性
nonprint character 非打印字符
nonpriority interrupt 非优先中断
nonprivileged instruction 非特许指令
nonprocedural representation 非过程性表示
nonprogrammed decision 非程序判定
nonprogrammed halt 非程序预定停机
nonprogramming application 非编程应用程序
nonprogramming user 非编程用户
nonqueued message 非排队消息
nonread notification 不可读通知
nonread report 不可读报告
nonreciprocal 不可逆的,非互逆的
nonrecoverable program error 不可恢复程序错误
nonrecoverable transaction 不可恢复事务
nonredundant inequality 非冗余不等式
nonreentrant 非重入
nonrelevant document 非关联文档
nonrelocatable phase 不可重定位执行程序
nonreproducing code 不可复制代码
nonrequesting terminal program 非请求终止程序
nonresident micro diagnostics 非驻留微诊断程序
nonreusable disk queuing 不可重复使用磁盘排队法
nonreusable medium 不可重复使用媒体
nonsap 灵活的,方便的
nonscrolling region 非滚动区域
nonstaturation magnetic recording 非饱和磁记录方式
nonscheduled down-time 非计划停机时间
nonsequenced chain 非顺序链
nonsequential list 非顺序列表
nonsequential operation 非时序操作

nonsequential reasoning 无序推理
nonsequential stochastic programming 无顺序随机规划
nonshared control unit 非共享控制单元
nonsimilar boundary layer 不相似边界层
nonsimultaneous transmission 非同时传输
nonsingular 非奇异的，满秩的
nonsolid color 非纯色
nonspecific 非特定的,非专用的
nonspecific information 不明确信息
nonstandard label 非标准标号
nonstandard syntax 非标准语法
nonstationary random disturbance 非平稳随机扰动
nonstiff 非刚性体
NonStop Cluster 不停机集群（康柏）
nonstop computer 不停止计算机
nonstop computing 无休止计算
nonstop operation protection 无休止操作保护
nonstop processing 不停止处理
nonstop system 不停机系统
nonstructural data type 非结构数据类型
nonsubscripted integer variable 无下标整型变量
nonsupervisor mode 非管态
nonswappable storage 不可交换存储器
nonsymmetric linear system 非对称线性系统
nonsynchronous multiplex system 非同步多路复用体制
nonsynchronous network 非同步网络
nonsynchronous transmission 非同步传输
nonsystematic code 非系统码
nonterminal 非终结符
nonterminal node 非终结点
nontransmittable property 不可发送属性
nontransparent mode 非透明方式
nontrivial 不平凡的
nontrivial condition 非平凡条件
nontrivial grammar 非平凡文法
nonuniform distribution 非均匀分布
nonuniform grid 非均匀网格
nonuniform interconnection scheme 非一致互连方案
nonuniform line 非均匀行
nonuniform mapping 非一致变换
nonuniform sampling 非均匀取样
nonuniform transmission line 非均匀传输线
nonuniqueness 非惟一性
nonurgent batch task 非紧急成批处理任务
nonvector mathematic operation 非向量数学运算
nonvirtual-memory execution time 无虚存执行时间
nonvisibility 不可见性
nonvisual 不可视的,不可见的
nonvisual class 不可视类
nonvisual part 不可视部件
nonvolatile memory 非挥发性存储器
nonzero mask 非零屏蔽
nonzero value 非零值
NOP（No OPeration instruction） 空操作指令
NOP（NO Paper） 无纸,缺纸
NOR "或非"
NOR gate "或非"门
norm 范数
norm optimization 范数优化
norm reducing method 范数化约法,减模法
normal 标准的,常规的,普通的,正常的
normal address 正常地址
normal algorithm 正规算法
normal approximation 正规近似法
normal assignment statement 正常赋值语句
normal attribute 正常属性
normal binary 常规二进制
normal call 正常调用
normal channel 正常通道
normal character 标准字符
normal closing hours 正常关闭时
normal condition 正常条件
normal connection 正常连接
normal contact 正常接触
normal context-switch operation 正规上下文转接操作
normal coordinate 常规坐标
normal correlation function 正态相关

函数
normal cycle 正常循环,正规周期
normal data 正常数据
normal data flow 正常数据流
normal-direction flow 正向流程
normal disk pack 常用盘组
normal distribution 正态分布
normal entry 正常入口
normal equations 正规方程组
normal error integral 正规误差积分
normal exit 正常出口
normal flow 常规数据流
normal font 普通字体
normal form 范式,规范形式
normal form of DPDA 确定型下推自动机的标准形式 「法
normal fuzzy algorithm 正规模糊算
normal grammar 正则文法
normal high 正常高度
normal hyphen 正规连字符
normal identifier 正常标识符
normal indent 普通文字缩进,正文缩
normal index 正常索引 「进
normal initial status 正常起始状态
normal inspection 常规检验
normal install 常规安装
normal language 正则语言,标准语言
normal line sync 正常行同步
normal load 正常负载
normal logic 正逻辑
normal memory 常规内存
normal mode 正常模式,正规模式
normal mode flow table 正常模式流程表
normal mode rejection 简正抑制,共模抑制
normal mode voltage 简正电压,共模电压
normal name call 正常名称调用
normal network traffic 正常网络通信
normal number 正态数(IEEE) 「量
normal operating condition 正常操作条件
normal orientation 正常取向
normal output 正常输出
normal pattern 正常模式
normal priority 正常优先权
normal process 正态过程

normal procedure call 正常过程调用
normal program termination 正常程序终止
normal random number 正态随机数
normal random variable 正态随机变
normal range 正常范围 「量
normal requirement 常规需求
normal response 正常响应,正常应答
normal restart 正常重新启动
normal return 正常返回
normal return address 正常返回地址
normal return point 正常返回点
normal routing of signaling 正常发信路由
normal sample 正常抽样,正常样值
normal script 常规原稿
normal size 标准尺寸
normal sort 正常排序 「制
normal stack mechanism 正规堆栈机
normal state 正常状态,标准状态
normal stochastic process 正态随机过
normal style 普通样式 「程
normal subgroup 正规子群
normal term 范式项
normal termination 正常终结
normal toolbar 常用工具栏
normal traffic 正常通信量
normal variable 正态向量
normal vector 法向量
normal view 普通视图
normal width 正常宽度
normalization 规格化,规范化,归一化
normalization coordinate 规格化坐标系 「化
normalization of speaker 说话人归一
normalization routine 规范化例程
normalization signal 归一化信号
normalize 规范化,标准化
normalized device coordinates(NDC) 归一化设备坐标
normalized floating control 规格化浮点控制
normalized floating-point number 规格化浮点数
normalized floating subtract 规格化浮点减法
normalized form 规范形式

normalized generalized inverse 正规广义逆
normalized offset 归一化偏移量
normalized schema 归范化模式
normalized space 归范化空间
normalizer 标准化部件,信号修正器
normally closed 常闭的
normally closed contacts 常闭触点
normally opened 常开的
normally opened contact 常开触点
normative testing 标准测试,规范测试
normatron 典型计算机
normed space 赋范空间
North American Presentation-Level Protocol Syntax(NAPLPS) 北美表示层协议语法
north bridge （芯片组）北桥
north pole 北极
Nortel 北方电讯公司(加拿大)
Norton Administrator for Networks 诺顿网络管理程序(Symantec)
Norton AntiVirus 诺顿防病毒软件(Symantec)
Norton Internet Security 诺顿因特网安全防护软件(Symantec)
Norton Personal Firewall 诺顿个人防火墙(Symantec)
Norton Utilities 诺顿成套工具软件(Symantec)
NOS(Network Operation System) 网络操作系统
NOS(Network-oriented Operating System) 面向网络的操作系统
NOS/BE(Network Operating System/Batch Environment) 网络操作系统/整批环境
NOS/VE(Network Operating System/Virtual Environment) 网络操作系统/虚拟环境
NOSP (Network Operation Support Program) 网络操作支持程序
NOSS(NEAS Online Software System) 日本电气公司计算机在线软件系统
NOT "非",否定
NOT ACCEPTED screen status "不接受"屏幕状态
not-busy interrupt 非忙中断
not equal to 不等于
NOT logic "非"逻辑
NOT majority "非"多数
not obtainable signal 不能接入信号
NOT operation "非"运算
not ready 未就绪
not-ready condition 未就绪状态
not reusable 不可重用的
not-used-recently page replacement 最近未用页替换
notation 记数法
notch filter 陷波滤波器
notched noise 陷波噪声
note 注释,注解,附注
note command 注释命令
note indicator 附注记号
notebook computer 笔记本式计算机
Notepad 记事本,便笺
Notes Notes 群件(Lotus)
Notes Global Designer Notes 环球设计者(Lotus)
Notes seats Notes 座席(Lotus)
notice 通告,通知,注意
notification 通知,报告
notifier 通告程序
notify 通知
notify call 通知呼叫
notify delivery 通知传递
notify link 交互式链接
notify lock 加锁通知
notify message 通知消息
notify object 通知对象
notify when done 结束时发出通知
notion 概念
nought state 零状态
noun 名词
noun group case 名词组角色,名词组格
noun phrase 名词短语
NOVA 诺瓦计算机
Novell AppWare Novell 成套软件
Novell Authorized Education Center Novell 授权培训中心
Novell DOS Novell 操作系统
Novell Education Academic Partner Novell 教育合作者
Novell UnixWare UnixWare 操作系统
Novell UnixWare application server UnixWare 应用程序服务器
Novell UnixWare personal Edition

UnixWare 单用户版本
Novell Web Server 万维网服务器软件
novice 初学者,无经验者
novice user 无经验用户
NOVRAM(NOn Volatile Random Access Memory) 非易失性随机读写存储器
nozzle 喷嘴
NP(No Parity) 无奇偶校验
NP(Non Print) 不打印
NP-complete problem NP 完全问题
NP-completeness NP 完全性
NP-easy problem NP 容易问题
NP-equivalent problem NP 等价问题
NP-hard problem NP 难题
NPC(Non-Printing Character) 非打印字符
NPL(New Programming Language) NPL 语言
NPL(No Programming Language) 非编程语言
NPL Network NPL 计算机网
NPP(Network Protocol Processor) 网络协议处理器
NPRINT (NetWare)网络打印
NPRINTER(Network Printer) 网络打印机
NPSI(Network control program Packet Switching Interface) 网络控制分组交换接口
NPSI(X.25 NCP Packet Switching Interface) X.25 网络控制分组交换接口
NPT(Network Planning Tool) 网络规划工具
NPT(NonPacket mode Terminal) 非分组模式终端机
NPU(Network Processing Unit) 网络处理部件
NRC(Network Routing Center) 网络路由选择中心
NRC (Network Reliability Coordinator) 网络可靠性协调程序
NRC(Network Routing Center) 网络路由选择中心
NRC (Non-Return-to-zero Change recording) 不归零变更记录
NRDF(NonRecursive Digital Filter) 非递归数字滤波器
NRI(Network Radio Interface) 无线电网络接口
NRL(Network Restructing Language) 网络重构语言
NRM(Normal Response Mode) 正常响应模式
NRM(NoRMalize) 标准化,规格化
nrt-VBR(Non-real-time Variable Rate) 非实时可变比特率
NRTZ(NonReTurn to Zero) 不归零
NRU(Network Resource Unit) 网络资源单元
NRZ(Non-Return-to-Zero) 不归零制
NRZ/C (Non-Return-to-Zero/Change recording) 不归零变更记录
NRZ-L(NonReturn to Zero-Level) 电平不归零制
NRZ-M(Non-Return-to-Zero-Mark) 标号 不归零制
NRZ-S(NonReturn to Zero-Space) 空号不归零制
NRZ1(Non-Return-to-Zero change on 1) 不归零按 1 变更制
NRZ1(NonReturn-to Zero on 1 system) 按 1 不归零制
NRZI(Non-Return to Zero Inverted) 不归零反转
NS(National Standard) 国家标准
NS(Network Services) 网络服务
ns(nano second) 纳秒(10^{-9}秒)
NSA(Next Station Addressing) 下一站点寻址
NSA(No Such Addressing) 无此地址
NSAP(Network Service Access Point) 网络服务访问点
NSC(Network Security Center) 网络安全中心
NSC(Network Switching Center) 网络交换中心
NSC BLA NSC BLA 微计算机
NSCP(National Super speed Computer Project) 国家超高速计算机规划(日本)
NSE(Network Services Engine) 网络服务引擎
NSF(National Science Foundation) 国家科学基金会

NSFnet(National Science Foundation network) (美国)国家科学基金会网络
NSI(Non-SNA Interconnect) 非SNA互连
NSM(Networking Security Module) 网络安全模块
NSM(Networking System Management) 网络化系统管理
NSP(Native Signal Processing) 主体信号处理,本机信号处理(Intel)
NSP(Network Services Protocol) 网络服务协议
NSP(Network Signal Processor) 网络信号处理机
NSR(Non Shared Resources) 非共享资源
NSR(Non Stop Recovery) 不停机恢复
NSR(Normal Service Request) 正常服务申请
NSS(Novell Storage Serbvice) (Netware5)Novell 存储服务
NSU(Network Support Utility) (Unix)网络支持公用程序
NT(Network Terminal) 网络终端
NT1(Network Termination 1) 网络终端1型
NT(Windows NT) 新技术操作系统(微软,1991年)
NT file system(NTFS) NTFS 文件系统(微软)
NT&T(Nippon Telegraph and Telephone public corp.) 日本电报电话(国营)公司
NTAS(NT Advanced Server) NT高级服务器版本
NTC(Network Terminal Circuit) 网络终端线路
NTC thermistor 负温度系数电阻
NTDS(Windows NT Directory Service) NT 目录服务(微软)
NTEL(Non-TELephone terminal) 非电话终端
NTFS(Windows NT File System) NT 文件系统(微软)
nth harmonic 第 n 次谐波
Nth-level address N 级间接地址
NTO device(Network Terminal Options device) 网络终端任选设备
NTP(Network Terminal Protocol) 网络终端协议
NTP(Network Transaction Processing) 网络事务处理
NTR(Next Task Register) 下次任务寄存器
NTR(Nothing To Report) 无事可报
NTSC(National Television Standards Committee) 国家电视标准委员会(美国)
NTT(Nippon Telegraph and Telephone company) 日本电报电话公司
NTTF(Network Test and Training Facility) 网络测试与训练设备
NTU(Network Terminating Unit) 网络终端单元
NTV(Network TV) 网络电视
NuBus 网络用户总线
NUC(resident NUCleus) 常驻核心程序
nuclear battery 原子能电池
nuclear magnetic resonance(NMR) 核磁共振
nucleus 核心程序
nucleus generation 核心生成
nucleus initialization program(NIP) 核心初始化程序
nucleus module 核心模块
NUI(NetWare User International) NetWare 国际用户协会
NUI(Network User Identifier) 网络用户标识
nuisance call 烦扰性呼叫
NUL(Null Character) 空字符
null 空,零
null address 空地址
null argument 空参数,空变元
null array 空阵列,空数组
null bit string 空位串
null character(NUL) 空字符
null character string 空字符串
null command 空命令
null cycle 空周期,无效循环
null data area 空数据区
null data set 空数据集
null delimiter 空定界标
null descriptor 空描述符
null directory 空目录

null element 零元,空元
null event 空事件
null field 空字段
null file 空文件
null filter 空值滤波器
null folder 空文件夹
NULL gate 零位门
null hypothesis 零假设
null indicator 零指示器,空指示符
null instruction 零指令,空指令
null line 空行,零行
null link 空链接;空链
null list 空表
null locator value 零定位符值
null matrix 零矩阵
null modem 虚拟调制解调器
null modem cable 虚拟调制解调器电缆
null output message 空输出的消息
null parameter list 空参数表
null pointer 空指针
null process 空进程,零进程
null record 空记录
null representation 空表示
null set 零集合,空集合
null state 零状态
null statement 空语句
null stream 空流
null string 空串
null suppression 空字符抑制,零抑制
null symbol 空符号
null term 空项,无效项
null terminated string 空字符结尾的字符串
null value 空值
null vector 空向量,零矢量
null-zone detection 零区检错法,间隔检错法
nullable 可空的
NUM(NUMber) 数,数值,编号
NumLock key 数字锁定键(PC)
number 数,数目,数值
number across row 按行编号
number base 数基
number busy signal 号码忙碌(占线)信号
number call 号码呼叫
number column (程序语句的)编号列
number control 数值控制

number cruncher 数字揭弄器,数值运算密集计算机
number crunching 数字揭弄,复杂的数值计算
number discrimination 号码鉴别
number down column 按列编号
number field 数值域,数值字段
number generator 数字发生器
number group 数字组
number identifier connector (NIDC) 号码识别装置连接器
number line 编号行
number lock (Num Lock) 数字锁定(键)
number network 号码识别网
number normalization 数字规范化
number of character per row 每行字符数
number of inverted sequences 逆序数
number of r-combinations r组合数
number of significant conditions 有效状态数
number of tracks 轨数,磁道数
number pad 数字键区
number range 数值范围
number-received signal "号码收到"信号
number line 编号行
number range 数值范围,号码范围
number received 号码收到
number recognition 数值识别
number recorder 号码记录器
number repetition service 号码重复服务
number representation 数表示法
number representation system 数值表示系统,计数制
number sequence 数字顺序,数序
number series 数码序列
number series group 组合号码序列
number service 号码服务
number service operator 号码服务员
number system 数字系统,数制
number type 编号类型
number-unobtainable tone 空号音,NU音
numberal 数字符号,数字
numbered card 已编号卡片
numbered list 已编号列表
numbered node 已编号节点

numbering plan 编号计划
numbering plan area(NPA) 编号计划区
numbering prefix 编号前缀
numbering scheme 编码方案
numbering system 计数系统
numbering zone 编号区
numeral(NU) 数字的,数值的
numeral row 数字行
numeral system 数制
numeralization 数字化,数值化
numeration 命数法
numeration system 命数系统
numeric(N,NUM) 数字的,数值的
numeric arrangement 数字排列,数值排列
numeric atomic symbol 数字原子符号
numeric backspace character(NBC) 数字退格字符
numeric character 数值字符
numeric character data 数值字符数据
numeric character set 数值字符集
numeric character subset 数字字符子集
numeric coded character set 数字编码字符集
numeric comparison 数字比较
numeric constant 数字常数
numeric constraint processing 数值约束处理
numeric control 数值控制
numeric coprocessor 算术协处理器
numeric data 数值型数据
numeric edited character 数字编辑字符
numeric field 数值字段
numeric field descriptor 数值字段说明符
numeric format 数值格式
numeric function 数值函数
numeric item 数值项
numeric keypad 数字键区
numeric literal 数值字串,数值文字
numeric move 数字移动
numeric operand 数值操作数
numeric pad 数字键盘
numeric pad keyboard 数字小键盘
numeric printer 数字打印机
numeric read-out 数字读出
numeric representation 数字表示
numeric shift 数字换档
numeric sort 数字排序
numeric space character(NSP) 数字间隔字符
numeric string 数字串
numeric value 数字值
numeric word 数值字
numerical algorithm 数值算法
numerical analysis 数值分析
numerical aperture(N.A) 数值孔径
numerical approximation 数值近似
numerical argument 数值变元
numerical conformal mapping 数值保角映射
numerical control(NC) 数值控制
numerical control APT APT 语言数值控制
numerical control distribution system (NCDS) 数控分配系统
numerical-control machines 数值控制机器
numerical-control programming 数控程序设计
numerical-control system 数值控制系统
numerical-control tapes 数值控制带
numerical data 数值数据
numerical data processing 数值数据处理
numerical differentiation 数值微分
numerical differentiation with splines 样条数值微分法
numerical display 数值显示
numerical error 数值误差
numerical expression 数值表达式
numerical flow simulation system 数字流仿真系统
numerical grid generation 数字网格生成
numerical integration 数值积分
numerical inversion 数值反演
numerical keyboard 数字键盘
numerical mathematics 数值计算
numerical-method mathematic model 数值法数学模型
numerical methods of ordinary differential equations 常微分方程的数值解法
numerical noise analysis 数值噪声分析
numerical optimization 数值优化

numerical precision 数值精度
numerical recognition 数字识别
numerical semantics 数值语义学
numerical science 数值科学
numerical sequence 数字
numerical shape modeling 数值形式建模
numerical signal 数字信号
numerical simulation language 数字仿真语言
numerical solution 数值解
numerical stability 数值稳定性
numerical thermal analysis 数值解热分析
numerical word 数值字
NURBS (NonUniform Rational B-Spline) 非一致有理B样条
NUS(Network Unit-Switch) 网络转换装置
NUT 网络用户工具
NVDRV (Network Virtual terminal DRiVer) 网络虚拟终端驱动程序
NVER 网络版本号
NVOD(Near Video On Demand) 准点播电视
NVR(Nonspecific Volume Request) 非特定卷请求
NVRAM(NonVolatile Random Access Memory) 非易失性随机读写存储器
NVT(Network Virtual Terminal) 网络虚拟终端
NWADMIN 网络管理
NWEXTRACT 网络解压缩
NWG(Network Work Group) 网络工作组
NWH(Normal Working Hours) 标准工作小时
NWLink(NetWare Link) NWLink协议(微软)
NWSNUT 网络用户工具
NWUSER 网络用户
nybble 尼,半字节
Nyquist interval 奈奎斯特间隔
Nyquist limit 奈奎斯特极限
Nyquist rate 奈奎斯特速率
Nyquist rate sampling 奈奎斯特速率抽样
Nyquist sampling theorem 奈奎斯特采样定理

O o

O(Output) 输出;输出端
OA(Object Authoring) 对象创作
OA(Office Automation) 办公自动化
OA workstation 办公自动化工作站
OAA(Open Application Architecture) 开放应用体系结构
OAA development & maintenance environment 开放应用体系结构开发与维护环境
OAA operating environment 开放应用体系结构操作环境
OAC(Optimal Automatic Control) 最佳自动控制
OADG (Open Architecture Development Group) 开放体系结构开发小组
OAF(Origin Address Field) 初始地址字段
OAI(Open Application Interface) 开放应用程序接口
OAM(Object Access Method) 对象访问方法
OAO(On-line Analog Output) 联机模拟输出
OAR(Output Address Register) 输出地址寄存器
OB(Output Bus) 输出总线
OBC(One Board Computer) 单板计算机
OBE(Output Buffer Empty) 输出缓冲器空
obey 服从,执行

object 对象,目标,物件,客体
object access 对象访问;目标存取
object action paradigm 对象范例
object affine 物体仿射
object attribute 对象属性
object authentication 实体验证
object authority 对象授权
object-based language 基于对象的语言
object-cache scavenger 对象缓存清理程序
object case 对象格
object-centered representation 对象为中心的表示方法
object class 对象类
object code 目标代码
object code compatibility 目标码兼容性
object code program 目标码程序
Object Components Framework(OCF) 对象组件框架
object computer 目标计算机
object concept 目标概念,对象概念
object configuration 对象配置
object connection 对象连接
object content architecture(OCA) 对象内容系统结构
object content envelope 对象内容封装
object converter 目标转换器
object database 对象数据库
object database query language(ODQL) 对象数据库查询语言
object decomposition 对象解体
object definition 对象定义
object definition table(ODT) 实体定义表
object delineation 目标示意图
object descriptor 对象描述符
object diagram 对象图
object design 对象设计
object dictionary 对象辞典
object directory 对象目录
object distribution 对象分配
object domain 对象领域
object embedding 对象嵌入
object encapsulation 对象封装[包装]
object-event model 对象-事件模型
Object Exchange 对象交换软件
object exchange(OBEX) 对象交换
object existence authority 对象存在授权机构
object existence right 实体生存权
object expert 对象专用单元
object extraction 对象析取
object file 目标文件
object format 目标格式
object function 目标函数
object handle 对象控制柄
object history model 对象历史模型
object identity 对象标识
object-image transform 物-镜变换
object implementation 对象实现
object inheritance 对象继承
Object Inspector 对象观察器
object interface 对象界面
object invocation 对象调用
object language 目标语言
object-language program 目标语言程序
object language programming 目标语言编程
object layout 对象布局
object-level clause 对象级子句
object level program 目标级程序
object library 目标库
object line 外形线,可见轮廓线
object linking 对象链接
object linking and embedding(OLE) 对象链接与嵌入
object listing 对象列表
object machine 目标机器
Object Management Architecture Reference Model(OMARM) 对象管理体系参考模型
Object Management Group(OMG) 对象管理组
object manager 对象管理程序
object map 目标映射图
object map compiler 对象图编译器
object modeler 对象模型处理程序
object middleware 对象中间件
object model 对象模型
object modeling technique(OMT) 对象建模技术
object module 目标模块
object module data set 目标模块数据集
object module library 目标模块库
object name 对象名,实体名
object node 目标节点

object of entry 客体,客体部分
object order 对象次序
object-oriented 面向对象的
object-oriented analysis(OOA) 面向对象的分析
object-oriented application 面向对象的应用程序
object-oriented architecture 面向对象的体系结构
object-oriented computing 面向对象计算
object-oriented conception 面向对象概念
object-oriented data base(OODB) 面向对象的数据库
object-oriented data model(OODM) 面向对象数据模型
object-oriented data base system 面向对象的数据库系统
object-oriented DBMS 面向对象的数据库管理系统
object-oriented design 面向对象的设计
object-oriented design methodology 面向对象的设计方法学
object-oriented distributed simulation (OODS) 面向对象的分布式仿真
object-oriented graphics 面向对象图形
object-oriented interface 面向对象的界面
object-oriented language 面向对象的语言
object-oriented method 面向对象的方法
object-oriented operating system 面向对象的操作系统
object-oriented program(OOP) 面向对象的程序
object-oriented programming 面向对象编程
object-oriented programming language (OOPL) 面向对象的程序设计语言
object-oriented programming methodology(OOPM) 面向对象的程序设计方法学
object-oriented technology(OOT) 面向对象技术
object-oriented user interface 面向对象的用户界面
object owner 对象拥有者
object pack 对象群
Object Packager 对象包装程序
Object panel 对象面板
Object Pascal 对象Pascal语言
object persistency 对象持久性
object phase 目标阶段
object phrase 目标短语
object plane 物面
object pool 目标池
object program 目标程序
object program library 目标程序库
object program loader 目标程序馈入程序
object program module 目标程序模块
object-program preparation 目标程序准备
object protection 对象保护
object protocol model 对象协议模型
object prototype 对象原型
object question 对象询问
object realistic rendering 对象真实感着色
object-recognition 对象识别
object-regeneration 对象再生
object-relational DBMS 对象关系型数据库管理系统
object representation 对象表示法
object request broker(ORB) 对象请求代理程序
object retention 对象保留,对象保持
object rights 对象权限
object routine 目标例程
object run 目标运行
object schema 目标模式
object segment 目标段
object server 对象服务器
object service 对象服务
object shape image 物体形状图像
object size 目标大小
object space 客体空间,对象空间
object space shadow generation 对象空间阴影生成
object space tree 对象空间树
object store model 对象存储模型
object subschema 对象子模式
object surface structure 对象表面结

object template 对象模板
object time 目标时间
object tracking 目标跟踪
object transformation 对象变换
object type 对象类型
object user 对象用户
object variable 目标变量
object view 物镜
object window 目标窗口;对象窗口
objective 客观的,目标的;结果
objective analysis 对象分析
objective analysis of information system 信息系统对象分析
objective analysis of organization 组织对象分析
Objective-C language 目标C语言
objective fidelity criteria 客观保真度判定标准
objective function 目标函数
objective interpolation search 目标插值搜索
objective qualification 目标鉴定;客观鉴定
objective rating 客观评价
objective system 目标系统
objectivism 客观性
objectization 对象化,目标化
ObjectVision ObjectVision 系统
ObjectWindows ObjectWindows 类库
oblique 斜体字
oblique parallel projection 斜平行投影
oblique projection 斜投影
oblique view 斜视图
obliteration 丢失
obscure 遮掩;朦胧的
observability 可观察性
observability index 可观察性指数
observable 可观察的,可观测的
observation point 观察点
observational error 可观测误差
observational statement 观察的语句
observed availability 观测值的有效度
observed cumulative failure probability 累积失效概率的观测值
observed failure rate 失效率的观测值
observed mean failure rate 平均失效率的观测值
observed mean life 观测平均寿命
observed mean time between failures 平均寿命的观测值
observed reliability 观测可靠性
observer 观察者;观察器(程序)
observing pattern 观察模式
obsolescence 设备更新
obsolete 废弃,舍弃
obstacle 障碍
obstacle avoidance 障碍避开
obstacle processing program 障碍处理程序
obstruction 遮断;障碍物
OCA (Object Content Architecture) 对象内容体系结构
OCA (Open Communication Architecture) 开放通信体系结构
Occam 奥卡姆语言
Occam channel 奥卡姆通道
occasion 机会;时机;诱因
occluded 封闭的,隔断的
occluded object 被隐匿对象
occluded window 被遮挡窗口
occluding boundary 封闭边界
occluding contour 封闭轮廓线
occlusion 封闭,闭锁
occlusion algorithm 封闭式算法
occupation 占用,占有
occupation probability 占有概率
occupied bandwidth 占有带宽
occupy 占用
occur 出现,发生
occurrence 出现值
occurrence check 出现检查
occurrence frequency 出现频率
occurrence sequence 出现序列
occurrence time 发生时间
occurs (重新)出现
occurs clause 重复子句
OCD (On-line Communication Driver) 联机通信驱动程序
OCF (Object Components Framework) 对象组件框架
OCP (Object Connection Program) 对象连接程序(IBM)
OCR (Optical Character Recognition) 光学字符识别
OCR-A code A型光学字符识别码
OCR-B code B型光学字符识别码

OCR background reflectance 光学字符识别背景反射性能
OCR character 光学字符识别的字符
OCR mark matching 光学字符识别标记匹配法
octal 八进制
octave 倍频程,八度音程
octet 八位长字节
octet alignment 八位长字节对准
octet timing signal 八位长字节定时信号
octonary 八进制的
octree 八叉树
octual sequence 八进制序列
ocular 视觉的
ocular estimate 目测
OCX(OLE Customer Control) 对象链接与嵌入客户控制程序
ODA(Open Document Architecture) 开放文档结构
ODBC(Open Data Base Connectivity) 开放数据库互连
odd 奇数的
odd check code 奇校验码
odd cycle 奇圈
odd-even check 奇偶校验
odd-even merging 奇偶归并
odd-even merging network 奇偶归并网络
odd-even sorting 奇偶排序
odd-even sorting network 奇偶排序网络
odd field 奇数场
odd function 奇函数
odd generation 奇数代
odd loop 奇数环
odd parity 奇校验
odd-parity check 奇数校验
odd permutation 奇排列,奇置换
odd substitution 奇代换
odd symmetric 奇对称
odds ratio 优势率
odevity 奇偶性
odex 六腿机器人
ODF(Optimal Decision Function) 最佳判决函数
ODH(Operation Directive Handbook) 操作指导手册
ODI(Open Data link Interface) 开放数据链路接口
ODI/NDIS support(Open Data link Interface/Network Driver Interface Specification Support) 开放数据链路接口及网络驱动程序接口规范支持
ODJ(Optical Disk Jukebox) 光盘库
ODQL(Object Database Query Language) 对象数据库查询语言
ODP(Original Document Processing) 原始文档处理
ODR(Original Data Record) 原始数据记录
ODS(Optical Docking System) 光学对接系统
ODSI(Open Directory Services Interface) 开放目录服务界面
ODT(Object Definition Table) 目标定义表
ODT(Open DeskTop) 开放桌面(操作系统)
OEM(Original Equipment Manufacture) 初始设备制造厂家,委托加工
Oersted 奥斯特(磁矫顽力单位)
OFC(Objective Fidelity Criteria) 客观保真度标准
OFC(Optical Fiber Connector) 光纤连接器
off 断开,关断
off-axis hologram 离轴全息照片
off-chip communication 芯片外通信
off-contact process 非接触工艺过程
off-design 偏离设计规范
off-diagonal 对角线外的
off-duty (设备)未工作
off emergency 紧急断开
off-gauge 不合标准的,非标准的
off-hand 立即的,自动的
off hook (电话)摘机
off-hook service 热线业务
off-hook signal 摘机信号
off-line 脱机
off-line algorithm 脱机算法
off-line application 脱机应用
off line batch processing system 脱机批处理系统
off-line browser 离线浏览器
off-line cipher 脱机密码
off-line computation 脱机计算

off-line computer 离线计算机
off-line computer system 离线计算机系统
off-line conversion 脱机转换
off line crypt-operation 脱机密码操作
off-line data processing 脱机数据处理
off-line device 脱机设备
off-line diagnostics 脱机诊断
off-line edit 脱机编辑
off-line equipment 脱机设备
off-line fault detection 脱机故障检测
off-line input 脱机输入
off-line job control 脱机作业控制
off-line memory 脱机存储器
off-line mode 脱机方式
off-line operation 脱机操作
off-line optimization 脱机优化
off-line or indirect system 脱机或间接系统
off-line output 脱机输出
off-line peripheral operation 脱机外围操作
off-line printing 脱机打印
off-line processing 脱机处理
off-line reader 脱机阅读器
off-line recovery 脱机恢复
off-line retrieval 脱机检索
off-line seek 脱机查找
off-line state 脱机状态
off-line storage 脱机存储器
off-line system 脱机系统
off-line terms code 脱机检索码
off-line test 脱机测试
off-line Turing machine 脱机图灵机
off-line unit 脱机单元
off-line UPS 离线式不间断电源
off-line working 脱机工作
off-lining 线外,脱机
off-load dump 卸载转储
off-loading 卸载
off-normal 不正常的,偏位的,越界的
off-normal lower 下限越界
off-normal upper 上限越界
off-peak hour 非高峰期
off premise equipment 备用设备
off premise extension 备用分话机
off premise line 备用线路
off premise standby equipment 备用闲置设备
off-screen formatting 幕后排版
off-screen memory 屏外内存
off-the-air monitoring 停播监视
off-the-rack 现成的
off-the-shelf 离架现货,成品,现有的
off-the-shelf hardware 现成硬件
off-the-shelf item 现有项目
off time 空闲时间
off track 偏离磁道
off tune 走调
offered load 提供负载
Office 95 办公自动化套件(微软,1995年)
Office 97 办公自动化套件(微软,1997年)
Office 2000 办公自动化套件(微软,1999年)
office automation(OA) 办公自动化
office automation system(OAS) 办公自动化系统
office communication system 办公通信系统
office computer 办公室计算机
Office Connect Remote Dual Analog 双模拟通道远程办公室连接(3Com)
office document retrieval system 办公文件检索系统
office electronic mail 办公室电子邮件
office electronic mailbox 办公室电子邮箱
office information system(OIS) 办公室信息系统
office manager(OM) 办公室管理软件
office model 办公模型
office procedures 办公过程
office products 办公事务处理产品
office revolution 办公室革命
office typewriter 办公用打印机
Office XP 办公自动化套件(微软,2001年)
OfficeConnect 系列网络产品(3Com)
OfficeVision 办公可视系列软件(IBM)
offline 脱机
offline editing 脱机编辑
offline newsreader 脱机新闻阅读器

offload 卸载
offnet calling 网外呼叫
offprint 单行本;选刊
offset 偏置,偏移量;印墨偏移
offset address 偏移地址
offset binary code 偏置二进制代码
offset bit 偏移位
offset branch 偏移分支
offset correction 偏差校正
offset data 偏移数据;补偿数据
offset error 偏移误差
offset lithography 胶印
offset position 偏移位置
offset sampling 偏移取样
offset variable 位移变量
offset voltage 偏压,补偿电压
offspring 后代,支系
offstandard 非标准的
OFT(Optical Fiber Tube) 光导纤维
Ogden's lemma 奥格敦引理
OGF(OutGoing Trunk) 出局中继线
OGSP (Open Group's Security Program) 开放群组安全访问策略
OH(Off Hook) 摘机,准备拨号
ohm 欧姆(电阻单位)
Ohm's law 欧姆定律
Ohmmeter 欧姆表
OIC(Optical Integrated Circuit) 光学集成电路
OIP(Optical Image Processor) 光学图像处理机
OK button 确认按键,认可按钮
OLAP(On-Line Analytical Processing) 联机分析处理
OLCA (On-Line Communication Adapter) 联机通信适配器
OLDB(On-Line Data Base) 联机数据库
old file name 旧文件名
oldbie 网上老手
older file 较旧的文件
oldest first 先进先出
OLE(Object Linking and Embedding) 对象链接与嵌入(微软)
OLE client 对象链接与嵌入客户
OLE/COM(Object Linking Embedding / Component Object Model) 对象链接与嵌入/组合对象模型
OLE object 对象链接与嵌入对象
OLE server 对象链接与嵌入服务器
OLERT(On-Line Executive for Realtime) 实时联机执行例程
OLF(On-Line File) 联机文件,在线文件
OLIE 供电布线设计系统
oligarchic(synchronized) network 集中(同步)网络
OLIT (OPEN LOOK Intrinsics Toolkit) OPEN LOOK 自有工具箱
Olivatti Corporation Olivatti 公司(意大利)
OLM(On-Line Monitor) 联机监督程序
OLP(On-Line Programming) 联机程序设计
OLQ(On-Line Query) 联机查询
OLRTP(On-Line Real Time Processing) 联机实时处理
OLS(On-Line System) 联机系统
OLTP (On-Line Transaction Processing) 联机事务处理
OLTT(On-Line Terminal Test) 联机终端测试
OLX(On-Line eXecutive) 联机执行程序
OMAP(Object Module Assembly Program) 目标模块汇编程序
Omega-finite automata Ω有限自动机
Omega-graph Ω图
OMFI(Open Media Framework Interchange) 开放媒体交换框架(协议)
OMG(Object Management Group) 对象管理组
OMI(Open Message Interface) 开放信息接口
OMI (Operational Maintenance Instruction) 操作维护说明书
Omininet Omininet 网络
omission 省略,删节,遗漏
omission factor 遗漏因数,漏检率
omit 省略
omit function 省略功能
omitting type 省略类型
omni light 泛光灯
omni-sort 全向排序
omnidirectional antenna 全向辐射天
omnidirectional microphone 全向麦克

风

omnidirectional reading system 全向阅读系统

omnidirectional signaling system 全向信令系统

omnidirectional viewing 全方位观测

omnifont 全字体

omnifont reader 全字体阅读器

OmniPage 全页扫描文字识别软件

OMP(Open Migration Program) 开放迁移方案

OMR(Optical Mark Recognition) 光学标记识别

OMS(Open Management System) 开放管理系统(北方电讯)

OMS (Optoelectronic Multiplex Switch) 光电多路开关

OMS(Output Multiplex Synchronizer) 输出多路同步器

OMT(Object Modeling Technique) 对象建模技术

on 接通,闭合

on-board computer 机载计算机

on-board modem 单板调制解调器

on-board regulation 板上电压调整器

on-board sound card 主板上声卡

on-board video card 主板上视频卡

on-call circuit 通知线路

on-chip cache 片上高速缓存

on-chip control logic 片上控制逻辑

ON condition 根据条件转移语句「踪

on-demand call tracing 请求式呼叫跟

on-demand ink gun 按需式喷墨头「页

on-demand paging 按需调页,请求调

on-demand processing 请求式处理

on-demand system 按需式系统

on drop (对象)放下后的响应设置

on-gauge 符合公差的,标准的,合格

on-hook 挂机 └的

On Item help 项目帮助

on-line 线上,在线,联机 「度

on-line access scheduling 联机访问调

on-line adapter 联机适配器

on-line administrative information system 联机管理信息系统 「法

on-line algorithm 在线算法,联机算

on-line analytical processing(OLAP) 联机分析处理

on-line analog input 联机模拟输入

on-line analog output 联机模拟输出

on-line analysis 联机分析

on-line application 联机应用程序

on-line banking system 联机银行业务系统

on-line bar-code decoder 联机条码解码器

on-line batch processing 联机批处理

on-line central file 联机中央文件

on-line command language 联机命令语言

on-line communication 联机通信

on-line computation 联机计算

on-line computer 联机计算机,在线计算机

on-line computer system 联机计算机系统

on-line control and off-line control 联机控制与脱机控制

on-line courseware 联机课件

on-line crypt-operation 联机密码操作

on-line data processing 联机数据处理

on-line data reduction 联机数据精简

on-line database 联机数据库,在线数据库

on-line debugging 联机调试

on-line detection 联机检测

on-line device 联机设备

on-line diagnostics 联机诊断

on-line direct control 联机直接控制

on-line disk file 联机磁盘文件

on-line equipment 联机设备

on-line file 联机文件,在线文件

on-line help 在线帮助,联机求助

on-line implicit calculation 联机隐式计算

on-line information retrieval 联机信息检索

on-line information service 联机信息服务

on-line input 联机输入

on-line interactive system 联机交互系统

on-line interrogation 联机咨询

on-line job control 联机作业控制

on-line journal 联机杂志

on-line mass storage 联机海量存储器

on-line media 联机媒体

on-line memory 联机存储器
on-line mode 联机模式
on-line operation 联机作业
on-line optimization 在线优化
on-line or direct system 联机或直接系统
on-line order entry system 联机定座登录系统
on-line plotter 联机绘图仪
on-line printer 联机打印机
on-line processing optimization 在线处理优化
on-line program development 联机程序开发
on-line query language 联机查询语言
on-line real-time processing 联机实时处理
on-line real-time system 联机实时系统
on-line reconfiguration 联机重配置
on-line retrieval 联机检索
on-line search 联机检索
on-line secured communications system 联机保密通信系统
on-line service system 在线服务系统
on-line state 联机状态
on-line storage 联机存储器
on-line system environment 联机系统环境
on-line task processing(OLTP) 联机事务处理
on-line teller system 联机出纳系统
on-line terminal 联机终端
on-line terminal test 联机终端测试
on-line test executive program(OLTEP) 联机测试执行程序
on-line test system(OLTS) 联机测试系统
on-line testing 联机测试[测验]
on-line tracking 联机跟踪
on-line transaction 联机事务处理
on-line tutorial text 联机指导文本
on-line unit 联机单元
on-line UPS 在线式不间断电源
on-line user 联机用户
on-line working 联机作业
on-line workload 联机工作负荷
on now 即开
on-off control 开闭控制
on-off element 开闭元件
on-off keying 开闭键控
on-off time ratio 开关时间比
on-premise standby equipment 应急备用设备
on-scene care 现场维护
on-screen data 屏面数据
on-screen editing 屏幕编辑
on-screen instruction 屏上说明信息
on-screen memory 联屏内存
on-site processing 现场处理
on-state 接通状态
on-the-fly error 传输中的错误
on-the-fly printer 飞击式印字机
ON unit 接通单元
ONA(Open Network Architecture) 开放性网络体系结构
ONA(Origin Node Address) 始端节点地址
onboard IDE 主板上IDE接口
onboard SCSI controller 主板上SCSI控制器
onboard simulation 机载模拟
ONE(Open Network Environment) 开放网络环境
one action 单次动作
one-address 单地址
one-address code 单地址码
one-address instruction 单地址指令
one-after-another 逐个进行的
one-ahead addressing 先行寻址
one-cell switching 一单元选通
one-chip microcomputer 单片微型机
one-chip CPU 单片中央处理单元
one-cycle instruction 单周期指令
one-digit adder 一位加法器,半加器
one-digit subtracter 一位减法器,半减器
one-dimension optimization problem 一维最优化问题
one dimensional array 一维数组
one dimensional path sensitization 一维路径敏化
one direct fault 单向故障
one flavor assumption 殊途同归假定
one-for-one 一对一,一一对应
one-for-one translation 一对一翻译
one-key cryptosystem 单一密钥加密

系统
one-key system 单一密钥系统
one-level address 一级地址
one-level code 一级代码
one-level interrupt 单级中断
one-level storage 一级存储器
one-level subroutine 一级子例程
one-line inference 单路推理
one-line operation 单线操作
one-line scanner 单行扫描仪
one-literal rule 单句节规则
one-off (英国习语)一次性的
one-off address 一次性地址
one-off entry identifier 一次性项目标识符
one-off table 一次性表
one-off template 一次性模板
one-off template entry identifier 一次性模板项目标识符
One Page Web 单网页站点
one output "1"输出
one output signal "1"输出信号
one-output terminal "1"输出端点
one overlap 一次重叠
one pass compiler 一遍扫描的编译程序
one-pass operation 一遍扫描作业
one-phase algorithm 单相算法
one-pivot gimbals 单轴万向平衡环
one-plus-one address instruction 一加一址指令
one-point perspective 单点透视
one point theorem 单点定理
one-port network 单端口网络
one-quadrant multiplier 一象限乘法
one's complement 1补数,对一的补码
one-sample test 单样本检验
one-shot program 一次性程序
one-shot request 单发请求
one-sided deadline game 单侧截止期对策
one-sided distribution 单侧分布
one-sided error 单侧错误
one-state pushdown machine 单态下推机
one-step logical design method 单步逻辑设计法
one-step method 一步法
one-step operation 单步操作
one-step t-fault diagnosable t故障一步可诊断的
one step t fault diagnosable system 单步t故障诊断系统
one-tape Turing machine 单带图灵机
one time pad 一次一密
one time programmable(OTP) 可一次性编程的
one-to-many 一对多
"one-to-many" medium 一对多媒体
one-to-one 一对一
one-to-one assembler 一对一汇编程序
one-to-one function 一一对应函数
one-to-one mapping 一对一映射
one-to-one translator 一对一翻译器
one-touch control 单触控制
one-touch key 单触键
one-way cipher 单向密码
one-way deterministic automata 单向确定性自动机
one-way function 单向函数
one-way interaction 单向交互作用
one-way linkage 单向链接
one-way logical relationship 单向逻辑联系
one-way message delay 单向消息延迟
one-way nondeterministic stack 单向不确定栈
one-way only channel 单向通道
one-way only operation 单向工作,单向
one-way propagation time 单向传播时间
one-way ring 单向环
one-way stack automaton 单向栈自动机
one-way tape 单向带
one-way transmission 单向传输
one-way trip 单向路程
one-way trunk 单向干线
onion skin architecture "洋葱皮"结构
ONLINE 在线指示,联机指示
online 联机,在线
online automatic power off 在线自动断电
Online Career Center 联机职业介绍中心
online community(OLCP) 联机团体
online complex processing(OLCP) 在线复杂处理
online documentation 联机文档

online editing(OLCP) 联机编辑
online searching 联机搜索
online service 联机服务
online vendor 联机信息销售商
ONLP (ON-Line Program development) 联机程序开发
only element 惟一元素
only-element-of-chain 链中惟一元素
only field 惟一字段
only-in-chain 链中惟一单元
only RU chain 链中惟一请求应答单元
onomasticon 专有名词表
OO(Object-Oriented) 面向对象的
OODBMS (Object-Oriented DataBase Management System) 面向对象数据库管理系统
OODS (Object-Oriented Distributed Simulation) 面向对象的分布式仿真
OOP(Object-Oriented Program) 面向对象程序
OOPS (Object-Oriented Programming System) 面向对象的程序设计系统
OOSE(Object-Oriented Software Engineering) 面向对象的软件工程
OP(OPeration) 操作,运算
op code(operation code) 操作码
op code microcoding 操作码微编码
op register 操作数寄存器
opacity 不透明度
opaque 不透明的;白底的
opaque area 不透明区域
opaque mask 不透明屏罩[蒙版]
opaque projector 不透明投影器
opaque screen 不透明反光屏
opcode 操作码
open 打开,开放
open addressing 开型寻址
open addressing overflow technique 开型寻址溢出技术
open applications architecture(OAA) 开放式应用软件体系结构
open architecture 开放性体系结构
open as read-only 以只读方式打开
open bus system 开放式总线系统
open capture file 打开获取(图像)文件
open circuit fault 开路故障

open circuit jack 开路插孔
open circuit voltage 开路电压
open client 开放的客户机
open code 开式码
Open Collaboration Environment(OCE) 开放协作环境
open collector 集电极开路
open CSCW 开放型计算机支持的合作工作
Open Data link Interface(ODI) 开放性数据链路接口
open data path 开放式数据通路
open database connectivity(ODBC) 开放式数据库连接性
open database management system 开放式数据库管理系统
Open DeskTop 2.0(ODT) ODT 2.0 操作系统
open discrete modules 敞开式分立组件
open disk drive 开放式磁盘机
open distributed system 开放式分布系统
open domain 开域
open drain 漏极开路
open embedded system 开放式嵌入系统
open ended 开端式,可扩充的
open ended system 开端式系统
open field 开放域
open file 打开文件
Open Graphics Library 开放式图形库
open hash method 开式散列法
open hash table 开式散列表
OPEN/IMAGE 开放式图像系统
open inbox 打开收件箱
open interval 开区间
open line 明线
open linked page 打开链接页面
open list 开型表
open log file 打开日志文件
Open Look Open Look 图形接口软件
open loop 开环
open loop control 开环控制
open loop control system 开环控制系统
open loop gain 开环增益
open loop NC system 开环数控系统
open loop optimal feedback 开环最优化反馈

open loop policy 开环策略
open loop robot 开环机器人
open loop system 开环系统
open loop transfer function 开环传输函数
open loop voltage gain 开环电压增益
open macro 开式宏
Open Management System(OMS) 开放管理系统(北方电讯)
open memory location 开放式存储单元
Open Message Interface(OMI) 开放消息接口
open mode 打开模式
Open Network Architecture(ONA) 开放性网络体系结构
Open Network Provision(ONP) 开放网络服务部
open node 开式结点,开型节点
open numbering 开放编号
open object 开放目标
open operating system 开放式操作系统
open path 开型通路
open plug 开路插头
open policy 公开策略
Open PrePress Interface(OPI) 开放预排版接口
open quadrature formula 开求积公式
open question 待研究的问题
open reel tape transport 开卷式磁带机
open routine 开式例程
Open Scripting Architecture(OSA) 开放稿本体系结构
open security environment 开放式安全环境
open server 开放的服务器
open set 开集
open shop 开放型计算站
open shortest path first(OSPF) 开放最短路径优先
open software 开放型软件
Open Software Foundation(OSF) 开放软件基金会
open source 打开源文件;开放源代码
open source software 开放源代码软件
open statement 开语句
open subprogram 开式子程序
open subroutine 开式子例程

open supercomputing environment 开放超级计算环境
open system 开放系统
open systems architecture 开放系统体系结构
open systems environment(OSE) 开放系统环境
open system interconnection(OSI) 开放系统互连
open systems interconnection architecture 开放型系统互连体系结构
open systems interconnection reference model 开放系统互连参考模型
open system interconnection standard protocol 开放系统互连标准协议
open systems interworking 开放系统交互工作
open task processing monitor 开放的事务进程监控器
open texture 开型纹理
open topology 开放拓扑结构
open transport 开放传输
Open University 开放大学
open window 打开窗口
open wire 明线,架空明线
open wire carrier system 明线载波系统
open wire line 明线线路
OpenDoc 开放文档规范
opened inference 开式推理
OpenEdition 开放编辑软件
OpenFrame 开放框架软件
OpenHub 开放集线器计划
opening linked document 正在打开链接文档
OpenLinux 开放 Linux 操作系统(Caldera)
OpenMail 开放式邮件
OpenSource 开放源代码
OpenView OpenView 软件包
openness 开放度
operability 可操作性
operable 可工作时间,运行时间
operand 操作数
operand address register 操作数地址寄存器
operand call 操作数调用
operand control 运算对象控制
operand delay 操作数延迟

operand effective address 操作数有效地址
operand entry 操作数进入
operand error 操作数错误
operand fetch cycle 取操作数周期
operand fetch instruction 取操作数指令
operand field 操作数域
operand format 操作数格式
operand identification 操作数标识
operand interface 操作数接口
operand page 操作数页面
operand pair 操作数对流
operand precision register 操作数精度寄存器
operand register 操作数寄存器
operand specifier 操作数说明符
operand stack 操作数堆栈
operand table 操作数表
operand type 操作数类型
operand word-length 操作数字长
operate 操作,运算
operate class instruction 操作类指令
operate memory 运算存储器
operate mode 运算方式
operate time 运算时间
operated digit 被操作数位
operating ambient temperature 运行环境温度
operating characteristic curve 工作特性曲线
operating class 操作类别
operating command 操作命令
operating cost 运行费用
operating delay 作业延迟
operating discipline 操作规则
operating distance (机器人的)动作距离
operating environment 作业(运行)环境
operating error 操作误差
operating guide 操作指南
operating index 运行指标
operating knowledge 作业知识
operating lever 操纵杆
operating life 工作寿命
operating load 工作负载
operating log 运行记录
operating mode 工作模式
operating platform 操作平台
operating platform conversion 操作平台转换
operating position 工作位置
operating power 工作时功耗
operating ratio 作业比
operating range 运算范围,工作范围
operating record 操作记录
operating sign 运算符号
operating specification 操作说明书
operating space 作业[操作]空间
operating status 操作状态
operating system(OS) 操作系统
Operating System/2(OS/2) OS/2 操作系统(IBM)
operating system/360 IBM 360 操作系统
operating system component 操作系统成分
operating system functions 操作系统功能
operating system kernel 操作系统核心
operating system monitor 操作系统监控程序
operating system nucleus 操作系统内核
operating system processor(OSP) 操作系统处理器
operating system scheduling 操作系统调度
operating system supervisor 操作系统监督程序
operating system viruses 操作系统型病毒
operating temperature 工作温度
operation 运算,操作
operation acknowledge 操作应答
operation and maintenance center processor 运行与维护中央处理机
operation and maintenance phase 运行和维护阶段
operation and support process 运行支持进程
operation area 作业区域
operation arithmetical 算术运算
operation box 操作框
operation chart 操作[作业]图
operation code 操作码
operation code field 操作码字段
operation code register 操作码寄存器

operation control 运算控制
operation control panel 作业控制面板
operation control statement 作业控制语句
operation control switch 作业控制开关
operation control unit 运算控制器
operation cycle 操作周期
operation decoder 运算解码器
operation exception 运算异常
operation expression 运算表达式
operation independent 独立运算
operation manual 操作手册
operation mistake 操作错误
operation number 运算号码,作业号码
operation overhead 操作开销
operation panel 操作面板
operation part 操作码部分
operation pipeline 运算流水线
operation protection 操作保护
operation ratio 作业比
operation record 操作记录
operation research 运筹学
operation sheet 运算表,操作表
operation simulation analysis(OSA) 操作模拟分析
operation specifications 作业说明书
operation state 操作状态
operation supervisor 操作管理程序
operation symbol 运算符号
operation system 运行系统;业务系统
operation table 作业表
operation testing 运行测试
operation time 运算时间
operation token 运算标志
operation use time 作业使用时间
operational address instruction 作业地址指令
operational address register 作业地址寄存器
operational amplifier 运算放大器
operational approach 操作方法
operational attribute 操作属性
operational character 作业字符
operational circuit 运算电路
operational data 操作型数据
operational data store(ODS) 操作数据存储
operational environment 作业环境,操作环境
operational environment software 操作环境软件
operational feasibility 运行可行性
operational flowchart 作业流程图
operational halt instruction 作业暂停指令
operational information system(OIS) 业务信息系统
operational insulation 工作绝缘
operational knowledge 运算的知识
operational network control 作业中的网络控制
operational object 运算对象
operational program 操作程序
operational reliability 运算可靠性
operational security 作业安全
operational semantics 操作语义学
operational specification 操作功能描述
operational speed of a computer 计算机的运算速度
operational standby program 作业备用程序
operational stop instruction 作业停止指令
operational unit 作业单元
operational use time 作业使用时间
operational word 作业字
operationalization of knowledge 知识操作化
operations control 操作控制
operations manager 操作管理员
operations research(OR) 运筹学
operations research dynamic programming 运筹学动态规划
operator(OP) 运算符;操作员;操作
operator associatively 运算符的结合性
operator class 操作员级别;运算符分类
operator command 操作员命令
operator communication manager 操作员通信管理程序
operator complementary 互补算子
operator console 操作员控制台
operator console facility(OCF) 操作员控制台程序
operator control 操作控制
operator control panel 操作员控制面板

operator control station 操作员控制台(站)
operator control table 操作员控制表
operator delay 操作员延迟
operator difference table 操作差别表
operator domain 算子域
operator equation 算子方程
operator errors 操作员错误;运算符错误
operator grammar 算子文法
operator guidance code 操作员引导码
operator indicator lights 操作员指示灯
operator information area 操作员信息区
operator inquiry 操作员询问
operator interface control block 操作员接口控制块
operator interrupt 操作员中断
operator intervention section 操作员干预部分
operator log 操作员日志
operator logical paging 操作员逻辑分页
operator message 操作员消息
operator monitor 操作员监控程序
operator operand length 算子运算数长度
operator's override 操作员的超越
operator part 算子部分,操作码部分
operator precedence 运算符优先序
operator precedence grammar 算子居先文法
operator precedence language 算子优先语言
operator priority 运算符优先级
operator priority method 算子优先权法
operator register 操作码寄存器
operator response field 操作员响应字段
operator schema 算子模式
operator service 操作员服务
operator stack 操作栈
operator station 操作员站
operator token 运算符信标
operator unit console 操作单元控制台
opposed 对立的;不同极性的
opposite 互相对立的
opposite phase 反相位
opposite sequence 逆序列
opposite-sign template 反号模板
opposite spin 反方向旋转
opposite-type region 反型区域
OPR(Optical Page Reader) 光学页面阅读器
OPR(Optical Pattern Recognition) 光学模式识别
opsearch(operations research) 运筹学
OPT(OPTimization) 最佳化,优化
opt 选取,选择
opt out 退出
optic 光学的
optic bundle 光束
optic communication 光通信
optic connector 光连接器
optic data link 光学数据链路
optic fiber delay line 光导纤维延迟线
optic flow 光流
optic interface device 光接口设备
optic link 光链路
optic modulator 光调制器
optic multiport coupler 多端口光耦合器
optic probe 光探头,光探针
optic reflective sensor 光反射传感器
optic rod coupler 光棒耦合器
optic scrambler 光扰频器
optic splice 光接头
optic telecommunication cable 光远程通信电缆
optic transmission system 光传输系统
optic waveguide 光波导
optical 光学的
optical axis 光轴
optical bar-code reader 光学条码阅读器
optical beam waveguide 光束波导
optical bistability 光双稳度
optical bypass relay 光旁路中继器
optical cable 光缆
optical cable driver 光缆驱动器
optical cable transmission system 光缆传输系统
optical cavity 光谐振腔
optical channel 光通道
optical character background reflectance 光学字符背景反射
optical character mark matching 光学字符标记匹配
optical character photocell matrix 光

学字符光电池矩阵
optical character reader(OCR) 光学字符阅读器
optical character recognition(OCR) 光学字符识别
optical chopper 光斩波器
optical circuit 光电路
optical coincidence index 光符合比索引
optical communication(OPCOM) 光通信
optical comparator 光学比较器
optical computer 光计算机
optical conductor 光导体
optical conductor loss 光导损耗
optical cone 光锥
optical connector 光连接器
optical coupler 光耦合器
optical crosstalk 光串扰
optical data bus 光数据总线
optical data processing 光数据处理
optical deflector 光偏转器
optical demodulation 光解调
optical demultiplexer 光学信号分离器,光学多路分解器
optical density 光密度
optical detector 光检测器
optical detector, video 视频光检测器
optical device bistable 光学双稳态设备
optical directional coupler 光定向耦合器
optical disc 光盘
optical disc autochanger 光盘自动换盘机
optical disc drive 光盘驱动器
optical disc library 光盘库
optical disc servo control system 光盘伺服控制系统
optical disc storage 光盘存储器
optical dispersion attenuation 光色散衰减
optical distortion 光学失真
optical document reader 光学文件阅读器
optical drive 光驱动器,光驱
optical element 光学元件
optical encoder 光学编码器
optical energy density 光能量密度

optical expose 曝光
optical fiber 光导纤维,光纤
optical-fiber acoustic sensor 光纤声传感器
optical-fiber active connector 光纤有源连接器
optical fiber bundle 光学纤维束,光纤束
optical fiber cable 光缆
optical fiber channel 光纤通道
optical-fiber circuit 光纤线路
optical fiber cladding 光纤包层
optical fiber classification 光纤分类
optical-fiber coating 光纤涂层,光纤覆盖层
optical fiber communications 光纤通信
optical fiber concentrator 光纤集讯器
optical-fiber connector 光纤连接器
optical-fiber cord 光纤软线
optical-fiber delay line 光纤时延线
optical-fiber distribution box 光纤分线箱
optical-fiber junction 光纤接面
optical fiber link 光纤链路
optical-fiber merit figure 光纤品质因数
optical fiber preform 光纤预制件
optical fiber pulse compression 光纤脉冲压缩
optical fiber ribbon 光纤带
optical-fiber ringer 光纤振铃器
optical-fiber sensor 光纤传感器
optical-fiber source 光纤光源
optical-fiber splice 光纤分接头
optical-fiber system 光纤系统
optical-fiber transfer function(OFTF) 光纤传递函数
optical-fiber trap 光纤陷阱
optical-fiber video trunk 光纤视频干线
optical waveguide 光纤波导
optical filter 滤光器,光学过滤器
optical finder 光学取景器
optical flow 光流
optical font 光符识别用字体
optical font sensing 光学字体读出
optical frequency division multiplex 光频分多工
optical gain 光增益
optical gain saturation 光增益饱和
optical gate 光闸

optical grating 光学栅格,光栅
optical guided wave transmission system 光波导传输系统
optical harness 组装光缆束
optical harness assembly 组装光缆束组合件
optical head 光记录头,光学头
optical hologram 光全息图
optical hypergraph 光超图
optical illusion 光幻觉
optical imaging path 光成像路径
optical impedance discontinuity 光阻抗不连续性
optical incremental display 光学增量显示
optical information processing 光学信息处理
optical injector 光注入器
optical integrated circuit 光集成电路
optical interference 光干涉
optical interference analogue computer 相干光学模拟计算机
optical isolation 光学隔离,光隔离
optical isolator 光隔离器件
optical journal reader 光期刊阅读机
optical jukebox 光盘库
optical link 光链路
optical link loss 光链路损耗
optical link segment 光链路段
optical logic element 光逻辑元件
optical loss characteristic 光损耗特性
optical mark encoding 光标记编码
optical mark page reader 光学标记页式阅读器
optical mark reader(OMR) 光电标志阅读机
optical mark recognition(OMR) 光学标记识别
optical marked-page reader 光学标记页面阅读器
optical mass storage 光学大容量存储器
optical matched filter 光学匹配过滤
optical memory 光存储器
optical microscope 光学显微镜
optical mixing rod 光混合柱
optical modulator 光调制器
optical mouse 光电鼠标器
optical multichannel analyzer(OMA) 多通道光分析仪
optical multimode dispersion 多光模色散
optical multiplexer 光多路复用器
optical network 光网络
optical neurocomputer 光神经计算机
optical oscillation condition 光振荡条件
optical parametric oscillator 光参数振荡器
optical path length 光通路长度
optical pattern recognition 光模式识别
optical pickup 光学头
optical polariser 光偏振器
optical position assemble 光栅定位组
optical power budget 光功率分配件
optical processing 光处理器
optical profile sensor 光学表面传感
optical projection lithography system 光学投影曝光系统
optical protective coating 光学保护膜
optical read/write head 光学读写头,光头
optical reader 光学阅读器
optical reader input device 感光阅读机输入设备
optical receiver 光接收机
optical recognition 光学识别
optical recording disk 光记录盘
optical recording media 光记录媒体
optical relay 光继电器
optical repeater 光转发器[中继器]
optical resolution 光学分辨率
optical resonator 光学谐振腔
optical scanner 光学扫描器
optical scanning 光学扫描
optical sensor 光传感器
optical signal distortion 光信号畸变(失真)
optical source video 视频光源
optical space-division multiplexing(OSDM) 光空分多工
optical spectrum analysis 光学频谱分析
optical storage 光学存储
optical-storage subsystem 光学存储子系统
optical switch 光开关
optical system 光学系统

optical tactile sensor 光触觉传感器
optical tap off 光分接,光分出
optical taper 光锥
optical terminal 光终端,光端机
optical track 光道(轨) 「数
optical transfer function 光学传递函
optical transmission line 光传输线
optical transmitter 光发射机
optical type font 光型字体
optical video disk(OVD) 光视盘
optical wand 光棒
optical waveguide 光波导 「器
optical waveguide coupler 光波导耦合
optically-captured 视觉捕获的 「离
optically-coupled isolation 光耦合隔
器
optically scanned character automatic reader 光扫描字符自动阅读机
optimal 最佳,最优
optimal adaptive control 最佳自适应控制
optimal algorithm 最佳算法
optimal approximation 最佳逼近
optimal aspect ratio 最佳长宽比
optimal basic feasible solution 最优基本可行解
optimal basic solution 最优基本解
optimal binary search tree 最佳二叉搜索树
optimal control 最佳控制
optimal convergence rate 最佳收敛率
optimal decision rule 最优决策规则
optimal default 最佳默认值
optimal deterministic schedule 最优判定调度
optimal direction of thrust 最佳推进方向
optimal distributed parameter 最佳分布参数
optimal dynamic routing 最优动态路由选择
optimal edge enhancement filter 最佳边缘增强过滤器
optimal error bound 最佳误差界
optimal estimation algorithm 最优估计算法
optimal finish time scheduling 最优完成时间调度方法

optimal fixed-point semantics 最佳定点语义学
optimal filtering 最优滤波
optimal finish time schedule 最佳完成时间调度
optimal granularity 最佳粒度
optimal interpolation 最佳插值
optimal inventory 最佳存货量
optimal join order 最佳连接次序「配
optimal layer assignment 最佳层次分
optimal layout 最佳布局[安排] 「布
optimal load distribution 最优负载分
optimal mapping 最佳映射,最佳变换
optimal match 最佳匹配
optimal merge tree 最佳归并树
optimal mesh decomposition 最佳网格分解
optimal message size 最佳消息长度
optimal observation times 最佳观察次数
optimal operation area 最佳操作区
optimal parallel algorithm 最佳并行算法
optimal parallelization 最佳并行化
optimal partition 最佳分割
optimal path length vector 最优路径长度向量
optimal probabilistic strategy 最佳概率策略
optimal quantizer 最佳量化器
optimal recalculation 最佳重算
optimal reduction path 最优简约路径
optimal remodeling 最佳重建模[重塑]
optimal retrieval 最佳检索
optimal return function 最优返回函
optimal root 最优根 「数
optimal route 最佳路由
optimal routing 最佳路由选择
optimal sample point 最佳取样点
optimal scheduling 最优调度
optimal schema 最佳方案
optimal search tree 最佳搜索树
optimal solution graph 最佳解图
optimal stochastic control 最佳随机控
optimal strategy 最佳策略 「制
optimal trajectory 最佳轨道
optimal third normal form 最佳第三

范式
optimal tour 最优环游
optimal tree 优化树
optimal uniform approximation 最佳一致逼近
optimal window size 最合适窗口大小
optimality criterion 最优程度判据
optimistic 优化的,乐观的
optimistic buffering 优化缓冲
optimistic concurrent control 优化并发控制
optimistic estimate 乐观估计
optimistic-pessimistic forward pruning 乐观-悲观正向修剪
optimizable 可优化的
optimizable loop 可优化循环
optimization 最佳化,优化
optimization algorithm 最优化算法,最佳算法
optimization cost 优化代价
optimization criteria 优化判定标准
optimization of computer series 计算机系列的优化
optimization of microprogram 微程序优化
optimization of system design 系统设计的最优化
optimization problem 最优化问题
optimization procedure 优化过程
optimize 最佳化,优化
optimize control 最佳控制
optimized processing element 优化的处理单元
optimized production timetable 最佳生产时间表
optimizer 最佳化[优化]程序
optimizing compiler 优化编译程序
optimizing configuration 优化配置
optimizing control action 最佳控制动作
optimum alphabetic tree 最优字母树
optimum behavior 最佳行为
optimum binary tree 最优二叉树
optimum branching 最优分枝
optimum code 最佳码
optimum coding 最佳编码
optimum decision strategy 最佳判定策略

optimum duration 最佳工期
optimum-interval interpolation 最优选点插值
optimum merging patterns 最佳归并模式
optimum network 最佳网络
optimum overrelaxation parameter 最佳超松驰参数
optimum programming 最佳规划;最佳程序设计
optimum quantizer 最佳量化器
optimum receiver 最佳接收机
optimum reception 最佳接收
optimum solution 最佳解
optimum stepsize 最佳步长
optimum support warranty 优化支持保修
optimum thresholding 最佳阈值
optimum topology 最佳拓扑
optimum traffic frequency (OTF) 最佳通信频率
OPTINET(OPTIcal NETwork) 光纤网络
option 任选;可选项
option attribute 任选属性
option board 选件板
option button 可选项按钮
option character 任选字符
option explicit (变量)显式说明
option field 任选字段
option group 选项组
option list 选项列表
option negotiation 选项磋商
option pack 选件包
option package 任选软件包
option set 可选集
option switch 选项开关
option table 选择表
optional 任选的
optional break 任选分隔符
optional equipment 任选设备
optional function 可选功能
optional halt 选择停机 「令
optional halt instruction 选择停机指
optional hyphen 可选连字符
optional interrupts 选择中断
optional member 任选成员
optional-membership class 随选属藉

类别
optional network facilities 选用的网络设施
optional parameter 可选参数
optional pause instruction 随停指令
optional point 任选点
optional priority 任选优先权
optional resident routine 可选驻留程[序]
optional retention 可选保留
optional stop instruction 随停指令
optional switched channel 任选交换通[道]
optional word 取舍字,可选字
Optivity Network Management (ONM) Optivity 网络管理系统(北方电讯)
Optivity Service Accounting (OSA) Optivity 服务统计(北方电讯)
optoacoustic transducer 光声转换器
optocoupler 光耦合器
optoelectronic device 光电设备
optoelectronic directional coupler 光电定向耦合器
optoelectronic scanner 光电扫描器
optoelectronic technology 光电子技术
optoisolator 光隔离器
optomagnetics 光磁学
optomechanical mouse 光学机械鼠标[器]
optosensor 光传感器
optron 光导发光元件
OPTS (On-line Peripheral Test System) 联机外围设备测试系统
OR "或"
OR node "或"节点
Oracle Oracle 数据库
oracle 例示,提示;启示程序
Oracle Co. Oracle 公司(美)
Oracle distributed database management system Oracle 分布式数据库管理系统
oracle tape 提示带
oracle Turing machine 提示图灵机
Orange book 桔皮书,橙皮书
orange peel 桔皮缺陷
ORB(Object Request Broker) 对象请求代理程序
ORB(Operation Request Block) 操作申请模块

orbit 轨道
orbit closure 轨道闭包
orbit control 轨道控制
ORBIT information system ORBIT 信息系统
orbit velocity 轨道速度
ORDER (On-Line Order Entry System) 联机登录定座系统
order 次序;阶;指令
order block 命令块,序组
order-by-merging 合并排序
order code 命令码
order field 排序字段
order filtering 命令筛选
order format 命令格式
order item 排序项
order number 凭单编号
order of merge 归并序数
order options box 排序选项框
order pickup robot 按单拣货机器人
order rate spectrum 阶比谱
order register 命令寄存器
order structure 命令结构
order wire 传令线,联络线
ordered clause 有序子句
ordered domain 有序域
ordered enumerated type 有序枚举类[型]
ordered list 顺序表,有序表
ordered retrieval 有序检索
ordered search 有序搜索
ordered search algorithm 有序搜索算[法]
ordered stroke 有序笔划
ordered tree 有序树
ordered word 有序字
ordering 定序,排序,排列次序
ordering bias 定序偏移
ordering by merge 合并定序
ordering criteria box 排序条件框
ordering specification 排序规范说明
ordering statement 定序语句
ordering strategy 定序策略
orderly close-down 有序停机,顺序关[闭]
orderly start 顺序启动
ordinal 按序的,序数
ordinal number 序号,序数
ordinal position 顺序位置
ordinal preference field 顺序自选方式域

ordinal relation 顺序关系
ordinary binary 普通[标准]二进制
ordinary file (Unix)普通文件
ordinary privileged slave program 常规特许从属程序
ordinary symbol 常规符号,标准符号
ordinary token 普通筹码
ordinate 纵坐标
organic 有机的,有组织的
organization chart 组织结构图
organization definition 组织结构定义
organization model 组织模型
organization name 组织名称
organization object 组织实体
organizational decision making 集体决策
organizational knowledge system 组织知识系统
Organizer "组织者"系统管理软件（微软）
orientation 定向
orientation coating disk 定向涂覆磁盘
orientation parameter 定位参数；方向参数
orientation ratio 定向比；校准比
orientation tool 定向工具,定位工具
oriented binary tree 有向二叉树
oriented communication network 有向通信网络
oriented edge weighted network 有向边加权网络
oriented graph 有向图
oriented path 有向路径
oriented texture 有向纹理
oriented tree 有向树
oriented vertex 有向顶点
origin 原点；起始地址；数据源
origin node address 起始节点地址
origin port address 起始端口地址
original 初始的,本原的
original BCH code 本原BCH码
original block 初始块
original board situation 初始棋局状态
original calendar file 原始的日历文件
original character form 原始字符形式
original command string 初始命令串
original configuration 原始配置
original data 原始数据

original default 初始默认值
original document 原始文件
original e-mail 原创电子邮件
original equipment manufacture(OEM) 原始设备生产厂家,委托加工
original footage 初始长度；原始脚注
original hash address 初始散列地址
original language 原始语言,源语言
original master 原装母带(盘)
original pattern 原稿
original problem 初始问题
original signal 原信号
original size 原始大小
original symbol 原始符号
original symbolic language 原始符号语言
originating call 发起呼叫
originating connection 发起连接
originating network 发端网络
originating office 发发局
originating packet 源端分组
originating point 发源点
originating system 源系统
originating UA 始发用户代理模块
originating user 始发用户
origination 起源,起点
originator 发送方；创始者
orphan 孤儿(孤立行)
orphan detection 孤立行检测
orphan killing 孤立行删除
orphan process (Unix)孤儿进程
orthochromatic film 正色胶片
orthocode 正交码,垂向码
orthocorrection digit 垂向校正位
orthofilm 正片
orthogonal code 正交码
orthogonal error control 正交误差控制
orthogonal fast channel 正交快速道
orthogonal linked list 正交链表
orthogonal organization 正交组织
orthogonal polynomial 正交多项式
orthogonal processor 正交处理机
orthogonal triangulation decompositio 正交三角分解
orthogonal vector 正交向量
orthogonality 正交性
orthogonalization 正交化
orthogonally-persistent 正交持久性

orthographic projection 正交投影
orthonormal 标准正交,规范化正交
orthonormal basis 规范正交基
orthonormal function 规范正交函数
orthonormality 规范正交性
orthonormalization 规范化正交
orthoscanner 垂向扫描仪
orthotropic 正交的,垂直的
orthotropic control 正交控制
Orwell ring Orwell 环形网
OS(Operating System) 操作系统
OS/2 OS/2 操作系统(IBM,以下皆同)
OS/2 2.0 OS/2 2.0 版本
OS/2 2.1 OS/2 2.1 版本
OS/2 Client OS/2 客户机
OS/2 Developer OS/2 开发者软件
OS/2 Enterprise Client OS/2 企业客户版本
OS/2 Enterprise Server OS/2 企业服务器版本
OS/2 Entry Client OS/2 Entry Client 操作系统
OS/2 for PowerPC OS/2 的 PowerPC 版本
OS/2 Mobile OS/2 Mobile 版本
OS/2 Presentation Manager(OS/2 PM) OS/2 演示管理程序
OS/2 Symmetric Multiprocessing OS/2 对称多处理版本
OS/2 Warp OS/2 Warp 操作系统
OS/2 Warp 3 Full Pack OS/2 Warp 全套
OS/2 Warp Connect OS/2 Warp 网络版本
OS/390 OS/390 操作系统(IBM)
OS/400 OS/400 操作系统(IBM)
OS/VS(Operating System/Virtual Storage) 操作系统/虚拟存储
OSA(Open Systems Architecture) 开放系统体系结构
OSCAR(Optically Scanned Character Automatic Reader) 光扫描字符自动阅读机
OSCAR 奥斯卡(三维绘画)系统
oscillating circuit 振荡电路
oscillating sort 交替分类
oscillation frequency 振荡频率
oscillator 振荡器
oscillogram 示波图
oscilloprobe 示波器探头
oscilloscope 示波器
oscilloscope tube 示波管
OSD(Optical Scanning Device) 光学扫描器件
OSDM(Optical Space-Division Multiplexing) 光空间分割多路转换
OSDP(On-Site Data Processing) 现场数据处理
OSE(Open System Environment) 开放系统环境
OSE(Operational Support Equipment) 运算(操作)支持设备
OSF(On-Screen Formatting) 可视排版
OSF(Open Software Foundation) 开放软件基金会
OSF(Operating System Firmware) 操作系统固件
OSI(Open System Interconnection) 开放系统互连
OSI base standards OSI 基本标准
OSI general standard OSI 总体标准
OSI level OSI 层
OSI overall standard OSI 总体标准
OSI reference model standard OSI 参考模型标准(ISO)
OSI/RM(Open System Interconnection/Reference Model) 开放系统互连参考模型
OSI service OSI 服务
OSI service conventions OSI 服务约定
OSN(Operating System Nucleus) 操作系统核心
OSPF(Open Shortest Path First) 最短开放路径优先
OSS(Operation System Supervisor) 操作系统管理程序
OSSF(Operation System Support Facility) 操作系统支持设施
OSSL(Operation System Simulation Language) 操作系统模拟语言
OSWS(Operation System WorkStation) 操作系统工作站
OT(Output Terminal) 输出终端
OTL(On-Line Task Loader) 联机任务馈入程序

OUT(Output) 输出
out-band signaling 带外信令
out-connector 外接符号
out fade 信号渐弱,淡出
out fan 扇出
out of band 带外信号传输
out-of-band signaling 带外信令
out-of-buffers 缓冲器溢出
out-of-control 失控
out-of-date 过时的
out-of-frame alignment time 帧失调对准时间
out-of-line 超行,越线
out-of-line coding 脱机编码,外部编「码
out-of-order execution 乱序执行
out-of-order signal 无序信号,失灵信「号
out-of-paper 缺纸
out-of-process 进程外
out of ranges 超出范围
out of sequence 失序
out-of-service time 非服务时间
out-of-shape 变形
out-of-size 超出正常尺寸
out-of-step 不同步
out-of-stream method 溢流法
out-of-use 已不能使用的
out-plant system 室外系统
out-slot signaling 时隙外信号方式
outage 停机,断电
outage duration 停机期间
outage probability 停机概率
outage state 停机状态
outboard 外部的,外侧的
outboard recorder(OBR) 外部记录器
outbound 出局,出站,出网
outbound flushing 出栈队列刷新
outbound pacing 出站调步
outbound path 出端通路
outbound transport provider 出局传输提供者
outbox 发件箱,待发箱
outbuffer 输出缓冲器
outcome 结果,结局;出口;输出
outcoming signal 出局信号
outconnection (流程线)外连接
outconnector (流程线)外连接符
outdent (排版)凸出
outer 外面的,外部的

outer control limit 外控制界限
outer face 外面
outer join 外联结;外部连接
outer loop 外循环
outer macro instruction 外部宏指令
outer point method 外点法
outer product method(OPM) 外积法
outer stop 外限停止
outerplannar graph 外平面图
outflow 流出(量)
outgoing 输出,引出,外向的
outgoing access 出网访问
outgoing data 出网数据
outgoing event 外出事件
outgoing fax 外发传真
outgoing group 输出组
outgoing link 出网链路
outgoing message 出网消息
outgoing pacing 出站调步
outgoing traffic 出网通信量
outgoing trunk(OGT) 出局干线
outheader subgroup 输出首部子组
outlet 出口
outlet line 输出线
outline 轮廓;大纲
outline border 外框
outline dragging 仅显示对象外框的拖动
outline font 轮廓字形
outline input 外线输入
outline letter 外框字母;外形图符号
outline number 外形编号
outline program 摘要程序
outline symbol 分级显示符号
outline view 大纲视图
outlined font 轮廓字型
outlining 梗概的,轮廓的
Outlook Express Outlook Express 电子邮件软件(微软)
outmessage subgroup 输出消息子群
outphase 不同相,异相
outpulsing 送出地址脉冲
output 输出
output address register 输出地址寄存器
output aperture 输出孔径
output area 输出区
output assertion 输出断言
output attribute 输出属性

output bin full 输出纸匣已满
output block 输出块
output-block feedback mode 输出块反馈模式
output blocking factor 输出编块因子
output buffer 输出缓冲器
output buffer empty 输出缓冲区空
output buffer overflow 输出缓冲区溢[出
output bus 输出总线
output bus driver 输出总线驱动器
output capability 输出能力[负载量]
output capacitance 输出电容
output channel 输出通道
output characteristic 输出特性
output converter 输出转换程序
output data structure 输出数据结构
output dependence 输出相关
output device 输出设备
output document 输出文件
output enable(OE) 允许输出
output equipment 输出设备
output error rate 输出误码率
output feedback 输出反馈
output field 输出字段
output file control block 输出文件控制块
output format 输出格式
output format specifications 输出格式说明
output formatter 输出格式程序
output impedance 输出阻抗
output indicator 输出指示器
output interface 输出接口
output job queue 输出作业队列
output limit 输出限制
output limited 受输出限制的
output line 输出线路
output link 输出链路
output list 输出表
output loading factor 输出加载因数
output media 输出媒体
output medium 输出媒体
output mode 输出模式
output module(OM) 输出模块
output module valve 输出模块阀
output multiplexer 输出多路转换器
output paper tape device 输出纸带设备
output parameter address 输出参数地址
output port 输出端口
output primitive 输出原语
output priority 输出优先权
output problem 输出问题
output procedure 输出过程
output process 输出进程
output program 输出程序
output queue 输出队列
output range 输出值域,输出范围
output record 输出记录
output redirection 输出重定向
output register 输出寄存器
output register buffer 输出寄存器缓冲器
output register empty 输出寄存器空
output-restricted dequeue 输出受限双端队列
output routine 输出例程
output routine generator 输出例程产生器
output section 输出节
output selection 输出选择
output side 输出边
output signal 输出信号
output spooling subsystem 输出假脱机操作子系统
output state 输出状态
output storage 输出存储器
output stream control 输出流控制
output subsystem 输出子系统
output switch function 输出开关函数
output table 输出表
output tape sorting 输出磁带排序
output test 输出测试
output-to-output crosstalk 输出对输出串扰,远端串扰
output token 输出信标[令牌]
output tracking 输出跟踪
output transaction 输出事务处理
output transformer 输出变压器
output tray (打印机)出纸匣
output unit 输出单元
output voltage 输出电压
output work queue 输出工作队列[器
output working storage 输出工作存储
output writer 输出书写器
outscriber 输出记录机

outside border 外围框线
outside loop 外循环
outside processor 外部处理机
outside sort 外部排序
outsourcing 外包
outstanding data formatting 未完成数据格式化
outstanding frame 尚未认可帧
outward 向外的,外面的
outward dialing 向外拨号
OVD(Optical Video Disc) 视频光盘
oven chamber 恒温箱
over-charged 过充电
over-clocking 超频
over-current protection 过流保护
over-over communication 双向交互通信
over shoot amplitude 过冲幅度
over-temperature protection 过温保护
over-voltage protection 过压保护
overall 总体的,全面的
overall availability 总利用率
overall computing speed 总计算速度
overall efficiency 整体效率
overall framework 整体结构
overall loss 总损耗
overall structure 总体结构
overall test 全面测试
overall transmission time 总传输时间
overcoat 外涂层
overcompensation optical fiber 过补偿光导纤维
overcoupling 过耦合
overdivided region 过分割区域
OverDrive Processor(ODP) 超驱动处理器,加速芯片
overdue report 过期报告
overflow 溢出
overflow addressing method 溢出寻址法
overflow alarm 溢出告警
overflow area 溢出区
overflow attribute 溢出属性
overflow bucket 溢出桶
overflow chain 溢出链
overflow check 溢出校验
overflow error 溢出差错
overflow handling 溢出处理
overflow hash 溢出散列
overflow indicator 溢出指示器

overflow linking overflow technique 溢出链接溢出技术
overflow operation 溢出操作
overflow page 溢出页面
overflow position 溢出部位
overflow probability 溢出概率
overflow processing technique 溢出处理技术
overflow record 溢出记录
overflow records 溢出[超限]记录
overflow route 溢出路由
overflow signal 溢出信号;全忙信号
overflow traffic 溢出通信量
overflow trap 溢出中断,溢出陷阱
overflow/underflow-free 无上下溢出
overfrequency (对低标称时钟速度的CPU)超频
overhang (排版)突出,悬挂
overhaul 全面检修,大修
overhead 开销;内务操作
overhead assessment 总开销评价
overhead bit 开销位,附加位
overhead block 开销块,附加块
overhead code 管理码,非信息代码
overhead digit 附加数字
overhead information 内务处理信息
overhead method 内务操作方法
overhead operation 内部事务处理
overhead projection 自顶向下的投影
overhead time 开销时间,准备时间
overhead traffic 内务通信量
overlaid windows 重叠的视窗
overlap across 重叠访问,交叉存取
overlap active windows 重放活动窗口
overlap condition 重叠状态
overlap factor 重叠因子
overlap mode 重叠模式
overlap operand 重叠操作数
overlap processing 重叠处理
overlap signaling 重叠传信
overlapped data channel 重叠数据通道
overlapped execution 重叠执行
overlapped interpretation 重叠解释
overlapped operation 重叠操作
overlapped-operations buffer 重叠操作缓冲器
overlapped span of control 重叠跨区控制

overlapping bar-like patter 重叠条形图样
overlapping bridge 重叠桥道
overlapping data channel 重叠数据通
overlapping field 交叠域
overlapping sublist 重叠子表
overlapping tree 重叠树
overlay 覆盖
overlay approach 覆盖法
overlay area 覆盖区域
overlay bank （内存中的）覆盖区段；套印
overlay card 覆盖卡
overlay controller 覆盖控制程序
overlay device 覆盖设备
overlay drafting 套用绘画
overlay keyboard 覆盖板键盘
overlay linkage editor 覆盖连接编辑程序
overlay load module 覆载模块
overlay model 覆盖模型
overlay module 覆载模块
overlay planes 覆盖平面
overlay region 覆盖区域
overlay segment 覆盖段
overlay structure 覆盖结构
overlay tree 覆盖树,堆栈树
overlay value axis 覆盖数值轴
overlay windows 覆盖窗口
overload 超载,过负荷
overload alarm control 超载报警控制
overload circuit breaker 过载断路器
overload module test 超载模块测试
overload operating time 超载操作时间
overload protection 过载保护
overload rating 过载额定值,过负荷能力
overload recovery time 超载恢复时间
overload scenario 过载方案
overload simulator 超载仿真程序
overloading 重载,复载
overloading subroutine 复载子例程
overmodulation 过调制
overpaint 过着色
overprint 套印,叠印
overprogram 重复编程
overrelaxition 超松驰
override 超越,废弃；重设

override cataloged memory allocation 最优先编目存储器分配
override control 越权控制
override interrupt 最优先中断,越权中断
override precedence 超越优先地位
overrun 超限
overrun error 超限差错
oversampling 过取样
overscan 过扫描
overscrolling 滚屏过量
oversegmentation 过多分段
overshoot 过冲量
overshoot rise time 过冲时间
oversizing 扩界；超尺寸
overspeed test 超速试验
overstrike 叠印
overtime 超时
overtone absorption 过色调吸收
overtype mode 覆盖（改写）模式
overview 概述,综述
overview panel 概述画面
overvoltage interruption (OVI) 过压中断
overvoltage protection 过压保护
overwrite 覆盖写
overwrite existing child (Netware)重写现存的孩子
overwrite existing parent (Netware)重写现存的双亲
overwrite mode 覆写[改写]模式
overwriteable disk 可改写盘,可重写盘
OWE(One-Way Encryption) 单向加密
OWF(Optimum Working Frequency) 最佳工作频率
OWL OWL语言
OWL(Object Window Library) 对象视窗库
own 拥有,自有的
own code 自有代码
own process 自有进程
own variable 固有变量
own virtual space 固有虚拟空间
owned 自身拥有的
owner 拥有者
owner-draw 自画的
owner-draw button 自绘制按钮

owner file 自有文件,主文件
owner record 自有记录,主记录
owner pointer 首指针
ownership 所有权
ownership protocol algorithm 主权协议算法
oxidation 氧化
oxidation film 氧化膜
oxidation mask pattern 氧化掩膜图样
oxide 氧化物
oxide-isolated logic 氧化物隔离逻辑
oxide-isolation 氧化物绝缘[隔离]
oxide passivation 氧化物钝化
oxigenant 氧化剂
ozone 臭氧

P p

P(Pico) 皮,微微(10^{-12})
P(Power) 功率;电源
P2P(Peer to Peer) 对等(网)
P5 P6 微处理器芯片(Intel Pentium)
P6 P6 微处理器芯片(Intel Pentium Pro)
P7 P7 微处理器芯片(Intel)
P54C P54C 系列微处理器芯片(Intel)
P54CT P54CT 系列微处理器芯片(Intel)
P55C P55C 微处理器芯片(Intel)
P address P 地址
P and V operations P 操作与 V 操作
P-channel P 沟道
P-channel metal oxide semiconductor (PMOS) P 沟道金属氧化物半导体
P-channel MOS PMOS 器件
P-code(Pseudo code) P 码,伪码
P-condition P 条件
P field descriptor P 字段描述符
P format item 图像格式项
P-limited architecture P-限制体系结构
P-limited computation P-有限计算
P-machine(Pseudo machine) P-机器,虚拟机器
P=? NP question P=? NP 问题
P overflow 页面溢出
P picture(Predicted picture) 预测图像,P 图像
P-pulse 位置脉冲
p region p 型区
p+ region p+区
p-q generalized inverse p-q 广义逆

P-rating P 速率
P-system P 操作系统
P/T system P 位置/迁移系统,P/T 系统
P-tree algorithm P 树算法
P-valued logic P 值逻辑
P-well reflecting barrier P 阱反射势
PA(Packet Assembly) 信息包装配
PA(Parallel Access) 并行存取
PA(Physical Address) 物理地址
PA(Predictive Analyzer) 谓词分析程
PA(Public Address) 公共地址
PA key(Program Attention key) 程序注意键
PAB(Personal Address Book) 个人地址簿
PABX(Private Automatic Branch eXchange) 专用自动交换分机
PAC(Program Authorized Credentials) 程序特许凭证
PACE(Priority Access Control Enable) 优先访问控制
PACE(Programmable Automatic Communication Equipment) 可编程自动通信设备
pace 调步
pacing count 调步计数
pacing device 调步[定步]设备
pacing group size 调步组规模
pacing message 调步消息
pacing parameter 调步参数
pacing request 调步请求
pacing response 调步响应
pacing value 调步值

pacing window 调步窗口
PACK (Positive ACKnowledgment) 肯定回答
pack 压缩(永久性删除);组装,封装;磁盘组
PACK command 压缩命令
pack placement 紧缩布局
pack procedure 压缩过程
pack to 压缩成…
pack unit 组装部件
package 组件;软件包;封装外壳;信息包,分组
package all libraries internally 将所有库打包在作品内
package assembly 插件组装;信息包装配
package base 封装基座
package board 插件板
package body 程序包体
package card 组件卡
package count 组件数
package declaration 信息包说明
package filling factor 封装填充因素
package identifier 信息包标识符
package lead 组件引线,外壳引线
package level 组件级;封装级
package library 组件库
package lid 管壳盖板,管帽
package of subroutine 子例程集
package paralleled device 组件并行设备
package pin limitation 组件引线限制
package sealing 封装密封
package shell 组件外壳
package specification 信息包规格说明
package technique 封装技术
package terminal 组件引出线(端子)
package transfer unit 信息包传送单位
package transistor 密封式晶体管
package types 管壳类型
packaged electronic circuit 封装式电子电路
packaged program 套装程序,软件包
packaged program set 组装式程序集
packaged software 套装软件
packager (对象)包装程序

packaging 封装,组装;打包
packaging bridge 封装桥接器
packaging density 封装[组装]密度
packaging design 组装设计
packaging efficiency 组装效率
packaging level 组装级
packed 紧缩的,压缩的
packed array 紧缩数组
packed attribute 紧缩属性
packed BCD 压缩二-十进制码
packed byte 紧缩字节
packed data 被压缩数据
packed data structure 紧缩型数据结构
packed decimal number format 压缩十进制数格式
packed decimal string 压缩十进制串
packed file 紧缩文件
packed format 紧缩格式
packed format messages 紧缩格式消息
packed record 压缩记录
packed structure 紧缩结构
packed wiring 紧缩布线
packet 信息包,分组
packet A A类信息包[分组]
packet address recognition 信息包地址识别
packet addressing 信息包寻址
packet assembly/disassembly (PAD) 信息包装配/分解,分组装拆
packet assembler/disassembler (PAD) 信息包装配/分解器
packet B B类信息包[分组]
packet broadcast 信息包广播
packet burst protocol (PBP) 信息包突发协议
packet by packet layer 3 switching (PPL3) 逐包转发第三层交换技术
packet data terminal equipment (PDTE) 分组数据终端设备
packet delay 包延迟
packet disassembly 信息包解装,分组拆卸
packet error detection 信息包错误检测,分组差错检测
packet error rate 信息包差错率
packet filter 信息包过滤器,滤路器
packet filtering router 包过滤路由器

packet flow 包流,分组流
packet flow control 信息包流控制
packet format 信息包[分组]格式
packet fragmentation 包分割
packet framing 包成帧
packet gateway 信息包网关
packet handling module 信息包处理模块
packet head 信息包报头,分组标题
packet insertion rate 信息包[分组]插入率
packet interface 分组接口,信息包界面
packet interference 分组干扰
packet interleaving 信息包交错
packet layout 信息包结构,分组结构
packet lead address 信息包引导地址
packet length 信息包长度
packet length selection 信息包长度选择
packet level 信息包级,分组级
packet level error control 分组级差错控制
packet link 信息包链路
packet loss rate 信息包丢失率
packet message delay 信息包消息延迟
packet message switch 信息包消息交换,分组报文交换
packet mode 信息包方式,分组方式
packet-mode operation 信息包模式作业,分组式作业
packet mode terminal(PMT) 信息包式终端
packet multicommunication 信息包多路通信
packet multiplexing technique 信息包多路复用技术
packet network 信息包网络
packet network communication 信息包网络通信
packet network architecture 信息包传输体系结构
packet network interface 信息包网络接口
packet number 分组编号
packet priority 分组优先级
packet processing 信息包处理
packet protocol 信息包协议
packet radio 无线电分组通信
packet radio system(PRS) 分组广播系统
packet radio technique 信息包广播技术
packet rate 信息包速率
packet recovering 分组恢复
packet repeater 信息包中继器
packet retransmission interval 信息包重发间隔
packet route 信息包路由
packet routing 信息包路由选择
packet sequence number 信息包顺序号
packet sequencing 信息包定序
packet size 信息包长度,分组大小
packet switch 包交换,分组交换
Packet Switch Stream 包交换流
packet switched data network(PSDN) 分组交换数据网络
packet switched data transmission service 分组交换数据传输业务
packet-switched network(PSN) 分组交换网络
packet switching(PS) 分组交换,包交换
packet switching center(PSC) 分组交换中心
packet switching environment 分组交换环境
packet switching equipment 分组交换设备
packet switching network 分组交换网络
packet-switching network operation 分组交换网络操作
packet switching S/F computer network 分组存储转发式计算机通信网
packet switching service(PSS) 分组交换业务
packet switching technology 分组交换技术
packet system charge 信息包系统负荷
packet technology 分组交换技术
packet terminal 信息包终端
packet train 分组串
packet transmission 分组传送
packet transmission control(PC) 信息包传输控制
packet transport 信息包传送
packet transport mechanism 信息包传送机制
packet voice communication system 分组语音通信系统

packet voice simulator 分组语音仿真
packetize 打包,形成分组
packetized voice 包结构声音信息,包化语音
packing code 压缩码,紧缩码
packing density 紧束密度;存储密度
packing factor 装填系数,填充因子;存储利用系数
packing routine 压缩例程
packing sequence 装填次序
packing washer 密封垫圈
pacuit 信息包电路交换
PACUIT system PACUIT混合交换系统
PACX(Private Automatic Computer eXchange) 专用自动计算机交换设备
PAD(Packet Assembler/Disassembler) 信息包装拆器
PAD(Page Address Register) 页地址寄存器
PAD(Problem Analysis Diagram) 问题分析图
pad 填充,衬填;焊盘;焊接区
pad character 填充字符
pad library 焊接点库
padder 微调(垫整)电容器
padding 填充,装填,整垫
padding bit 填充位
padding character 填充字符
padding data 填充数据
padding with zero 附加零
paddle 摇柄,摇动台
paddle switch 宽柄开关
Pade approximant 帕德逼近式
PADLA(Programmable Asynchronous Dual Line Adapter) 可编程异步双线适配器
PAE36(Physical Address Extension) 36位寻址物理地址扩展(Intel)
PAFT(Programmable Automatic Function Tester) 可编程功能测试器
PAGE(Preview And Graphics Editing) 预览与图形编辑
page(P,PG) 页面,页
page abandoned 本页取消
page access time 页面存取时间
page address 页地址

page address register 页面地址寄存器
page address transformation 页面地址变换
page addressing 页面寻址
page advance 换页
page alignment 页面调整
page assignment table(PAT) 页分配表
page-at-a-time printer 页式打印机
page balancing 页均衡
page base address 页面基地址
page body 页体(页内正文部分)
page boundary 页边界,页界
page boundary error 页界误差
page break 分页符
page breakage 页面零头,页面碎片
page buffer 页面缓冲器
page-by-page memory protection 逐页存储保护
page change 换页
page check 页校验
page check word 页校验字
page clause 页子句
page composer 组页器
page control block(PCB) 页控制块群
page control packet(PCP) 页控制码
page controls 页控制
page copy 页拷贝
page counter 页面计数器
page data set 页数据集
page-depth control 页深度控制,版面长度控制
page description language(PDL) 页面描述语言
page device description table 页式设备描述表
page directory 页面目录
page displacement 页面换位
page down 向后翻页,向下翻页
Page Down key 向下翻页键
page editing 页面编辑
page eject 跳页,换页
page end character 页终字符
page entry 页面入口,续页入口
page exit 页面出口,续页出口
page fault 缺页故障
page fault cluster size 缺页错误群数
page fault frequency 缺页频率

page fault rate 缺页率
page file 页式文件
page fixing 页面固定
page flip 页面翻转
page footer 页面脚注
page footing 页合计栏
page format item 页格式项
page frame 页帧,表框架
page frame number 页帧编号
page frame table(PFT) 页帧表
page head 页标题
page header 页头,页标题
page header back color(PB) 页头背景色
page heading 页标题
page hierarchical memory 页面层次存储器
page-image buffer 页面图像缓冲区
page-image file 页面图像文件
page-in 页面调进
page invalid bit 页无效位
page layout 页面布局
page layout program 页面布局软件
page layout view 页面布局视图
page length field 页长字段
page locking 页面锁定
Page Maker 页面构建软件
page makeup 页面构建,整页拼版
page map address 页面变换地址
page map table 页面映像表
PAGE marker 页面标识软件
page marker 页标记
page memory system 页式内存系统
page merging 页合并
page merging print 页合并打印
page migration 页迁移
page mode memory 页式存储器
page mode RAM 页式RAM
page node 页结点
page number(PN) 页码,页号
page option 页选项
page order (打印)页顺序
page-oriented program memory 面向页的程序存储器
page-out 页面调出
page overflow condition 页溢出条件
page pointer 页指针
page pool 页槽,页池,页面共用区
page preview (打印)页面预览

page printer 页式打印机
page printing 页式打印
page proof 页面校样
page property 页面属性
page protection 页保护
page queue available 可用页队列
page range 页面范围
page reader 页式阅读机
page reclamation 页回收
page recognition 页识别
page refresh 页面刷新
page register 页面寄存器
page replacement 页面替换
page replacement strategy 页替换策略
page replacement time 页面替换时间
page scan 页面扫描
page scrolling 页面滚动
page segment 页段
page service row 页服务排
page setup 页面设置
page sharing 页面共享
page size option 页面大小选择
page slot 页线,页缝
page splitting 页面划分
page stealing 页挪用
page storage 页式存储器
page swapping 页交换,页置换
page system 页式
page table(PT, PGT) 页表
page table base register 页表基址寄存器
page table entry 页表入口;页表项
page table lookup 页表查看
page table origin 页表起始地址
page teleprinter 页式电传打字机
page transition 网页过渡
page translation exception 页转换异常
page transmission 按页发送
page turning 页调换;翻页
page type 页面类型
page up 向前翻页,向上翻页
Page Up key 向上翻页键
page use list 页面使用(情况)列表
page view terminal 页式显示终端
page virtual storage system 页式虚拟存储系统
page wait 页等候
page width 页面宽度
page-white display 页白显示

page zero 页零点
pageable dynamic area 可分页动态区
pageable link pack area(PLPA) 可分页的链集区
pageable nucleus 可分页核心程序
pageable partition 可分页的分区
pageable region 可分页区域
pageable system task 可分页系统任务
paged address 页式地址
paged-direct addressing 按页直接寻址
paged hierarchical storage 页式层次存储器
paged machine 分页式机器
paged memory management unit(PMMU) 分页内存管理单元
paged segmentation 段页式
PageMaker 页面构建排版软件(Adobe)
pager 调页程序
pager plotter 页式印刷机
pages per minute(ppm) 每分钟页数
paginal 逐页进行的
paginal translation 逐页对照翻译
paginary 逐页对照的
paginate 编页码
pagination 标页码,编页码,分页
paging 页式管理法,调页法
paging activity indexes 调页活动指数
paging algorithm 调页算法
paging device 调页设备
paging disorder 页码错乱
paging model 页面模型
paging problem 调页问题
paging rate 调页率
paging supervisor 页调度程序
paging system 分页系统
paging technique 分页技术
paging terminal 分页终端机
paint 着色
paint file format 绘图文件格式
paint-on technique 着色技术
paint program 绘图软件
paint tool 着色工具
paintbrush 画笔
painter 绘图器
painter's algorithm 画家算法
painting robot 涂漆机器人
pair 对,偶;对线

pair cable 双股电缆
pair diode 二极管对
pair loop network 双环网络
pair of complementary channels 互补通道对
pair of element 元件对
pair of module 模块对偶,模块对
pair transistor 成对晶体管
pair-wise exchange 对偶交换
paired cable 双绞电缆
paired comparison 成对比较
paired-disparity code 成对不均等性码
paired multiplier 双乘法器
paired selected ternary code 成对选择的三进制码
pairing 并列;配对
pairing function 对偶函数
pairwise independent events 两两独立事件
PAL(Phase Alternation line) 逐行倒相制
PAL(Programmable Array Logic) 可编程阵列逻辑
PAL color television PAL 制彩色电视
PAL-D PAL-D 彩色电视制式
PAL language (Paradox Application Language) Paradox 数据库应用语言
PAL-N(New PAL) 新 PAL 制
palette 调色板,调色盘
palette animation 调色板动画
Palette Manager 调色板管理器
palette shift 调色板移位
palette toolbar 调色板工具栏
palindromes 回文串
pallet 调色板;托盘
pallet mode 调色板模式
palprint analysis 掌纹分析
palm PC(PPC) 掌上型个人计算机
palmtop computer 掌上型计算机
palmtronic 手提式
PAM(Partitional Access Method) 分区存取法
PAM(Peripheral Adapter Module) 外围设备适配器模块
PAM(Pulse-Amplitude Modulation) 脉冲调幅调制
PAMD(Parallel Access Multiple Distribution) 并行存取多址分配

PAMS (Predictive Adaptive Multiple Suppression) 预测自适应多重抑制

PAN(Personal Account Number) 个人账号

pan 画面平移；镜头摇移，扫视

pan film 全色胶卷

pan head screw 平头螺钉

pan scrolling 画面(左右)翻滚

panchromatic film 全色胶片

Pandorra box 潘朵拉盒子（给软件系统添了许多麻烦的引入程序）

pane 窗格

panel 面板，控制板

panel data interface 屏面数据接口

panel definition program 屏面定义程序

panel display 平面显示器

panel dynamic response 屏面动态响应

panel interrupt mask off 面板中断屏蔽撤消

panel interrupt mask on 面板中断屏蔽有效

panel number 屏面号

panel path 平面路径

panel services 屏面服务程序

panic 紧急的，紧迫的

panic button 应急按钮

panic dump 应急转储

panic message 紧急(出错)信息

panning 摇移，摇摄全景

Panon language Panon 语言

pantograph 缩图器，缩图仪

Pantone Matching system 色匹配系统

PAP(Password Authentication Protocol) (PPP)口令认证协议

PAP(Printer Access Protocol) 打印机访问协议

paper advance mechanism 进纸机构

paper capacity (打印机纸匣)装纸容量

paper carrier 输纸装置

paper cassette 存纸匣

paper change 换纸

paper core 卷筒纸轴芯

paper curl 纸皱折

paper deflector 导纸板

paper delivery 送纸出口

paper document conveyor 文档纸稿传送器

paper driver (输送)纸驱动器

paper end stop 纸端阻档块

paper extraction 抽纸

paper feed 输纸，送纸

paper feed control 输纸控制

paper feed control electronics 输纸控制电路

paper feed fault sensing 输纸故障指示

paper feed gate 输纸门

paper feed mechanism 输纸机构

paper feed motor 输纸马达

paper feed rollers 送纸滚筒

paper feed speed 输纸速度

paper feed tray 送纸托架

paper feed unit 输纸部件

paper guide 导纸机构

paper holder 压纸辊

paper injection 纸引入

paper jam 卡纸

paper lift 纸张提升

paper-low indicator 缺纸指示

paper-low reset 缺纸复位

paper-out 缺纸，纸用完

paper-out sensor 缺纸传感器

paper platform 托纸架

paper registration 纸张对齐

paper shredder 碎纸机

paper side guide 纸侧挡板

paper size 纸张大小

paper skip 跑纸

paper slew 跳纸，超行距走纸

paper stack 纸叠

paper-supply section 供纸部分

paper support extension 纸托架扩展

paper tape 纸带

paper tape punch 纸带穿孔机

paper tape reader 纸带阅读机

paper tape sprocket 纸带中导孔

paper thickness adjustment 纸厚度调整

paper throw 超行距走纸，跑纸

paper transport 输纸器

paper transport mechanism 输纸机构

paper-white monitor 白底显示器

paperless office 无纸办公室

paperless publication 无纸出版物

paperlike interface 仿纸接口

PAR(Packet Adaptive Routing) 信息

包自适应路径选择
PAR(Page Address Register) 页地址寄存器
PAR(PARameter) 参数,参量
PAR(Positive Acknowledgment with Retransmission) 重发式肯定应答
parabola 抛物线
parabola method 抛物线法
parabolic 抛物线的
parabolic antenna 抛物面天线
parabolic distribution 抛物线分布
parabolic interpolation 抛物线内插法
parabolic interpolator 抛物线插补程序;抛物线插补器
parabolic rule 抛物线法
paraboloid 抛物面
paracomputer 并行计算机
paraconsistent logic 并行相容性逻辑
paradigm 风范,范型
Paradox Paradox 数据库管理系统(Ausa)
paradox 悖论;矛盾论点
Paradox Application Language(PAL) Paradox 应用程序语言(Ausa)
ParaGraph ParaGraph 并行化支援系统
paragraph(PAR) 段
paragraph assembly 段落组装
paragraph format 段落格式
paragraph header 段头,段首
paragraph justification 段落调整
paragraph mark 段标记
paragraph name 段名
paragraph number 段号
paragraph preview 段落预览
paragraph type 段落类型
parallax 视差
parallax angle 视差角
parallax correction 视差校正
parallel(P) 并行;并联
parallel A/D converter 并行模/数转换器
parallel abstract machine 并行抽象机
parallel access 并行存取
parallel accumulator 并行累加器
parallel action 并行作用,并行相加
parallel active tracking program 并行主动跟踪程序
parallel adder 并行加法器
parallel addition 并行加法
parallel algorithm 并行算法
parallel allocation 并行分配
parallel and pipeline processing 并行与流水线处理
parallel application 并行应用程序
parallel architecture 并行体系结构
Parallel Architecture Extended(PAX) 并行体系结构扩展
parallel arithmetic 并行算术
parallel arithmetic unit 并行算术单元
parallel array processor 并行阵列处理机
parallel artificial intelligence system 并行人工智能系统
parallel assignment algorithm 并行指派算法
parallel associative processor 并行相联处理机
parallel asynchronous computer 并行异步计算机
parallel asynchronous computer architecture 并行异步计算机体系结构
parallel backend text searcher 并行后端正文搜索器
parallel backtracking 并行后溯
parallel bi-directional bus driver 并行双向总线驱动器
parallel bit transmission 并行位传输
parallel block 并行块,并行分程序
parallel buffer 并行缓冲器
parallel bus 并行总线,并联总线
parallel by bit 按位并行
parallel by byte 按字节并行
parallel by character 按字符并行
parallel cache 并行高速缓存
parallel cascade action 并行串级动作
parallel cellular chain 并行细胞链
parallel cellular inverted list 并行单元倒排表
parallel cellular organization 并行单元组织
parallel channel 并行通道
parallel circuit 并联电路
parallel classification algorithm 并行分类算法
parallel clause 并行子句
parallel cluster system 并行群集系统

parallel clustering 并行聚类
parallel combinational circuit 并行组合电路
parallel communication 并行通信
parallel compensation 并联补偿
parallel compiler 并行编译程序
parallel computation 并行计算
parallel computation thesis 并行计算论题
parallel computation asynchronous 异步并行计算
parallel computation environment 并行计算环境
parallel computation problem 并行计算问题
parallel computer 并行计算机
parallel connection 并联
parallel context-free array 并行上下文无关阵列
parallel conversion 并行变换
parallel data allocation system 并行数据分配系统
parallel data controller 并行数据控制器
parallel data medium 并行数据媒体
parallel data path 并行数据通路
parallel data transfer 并行数据传送
parallel data transmission 并行数据传输
parallel database access 并行数据库存取
parallel debugger 并行调试程序
parallel decimal adder 并行十进制加法器
parallel decoder 并行译码器
parallel decomposition 并行分解
parallel detection 并行检测
parallel diagnosis 并行诊断
parallel digital computer 并行数字计算机
parallel distributed processing system 并行分布式处理系统
parallel dynamic interaction 并行动态交互作用
parallel edge 并行边
parallel engineering 并行工程
parallel entry 并行入口
parallel enumeration sorting 并行枚举分类法

parallel executable statement 并行执行语句
parallel execution 并行执行
parallel extended routes 并行扩展路由
parallel expansion 并行展开
parallel fault simulation 并行故障仿真
parallel fault-tolerant 并行容错
parallel feed 并行馈电
parallel feedback 并联反馈
parallel FEM 并行有限元法
parallel FFT 并行快速傅里叶变换
parallel file 并行文件
parallel filling process 并行填充过程
parallel filter bank 并行滤波器组
parallel finite state automaton 并行有限状态自动机
parallel flow 并行流程
parallel Floyd algorithm 并行弗洛伊德算法
parallel fold 并行折叠
parallel formal conversion 并行形式转换
parallel frontal solution algorithm 并行前置解算法
parallel full subtracter 并行全减器
parallel gap welding 并行间隙焊接
parallel garbage collection 并行废料收集
parallel Gauss elimination 并行高斯消除
parallel graph-coloring 并行图着色
parallel half adder 并行半加器
parallel hash algorithm 并行散列算法
parallel head disk 并行头磁盘
parallel heap 并行堆
parallel heuristic search algorithm 并行启发式搜索算法
parallel hexahedron classification 平行六面体分类法,相似比较分类法
parallel homotopy algorithm 并行同论算法
parallel image processing 并行图像处理
parallel inference machine(PIM) 并行推理机
parallel information retrieval 并行信息检索
parallel input 并行输入
parallel input port 并行输入端口

parallel input-output(PIO) 并行输入/输出
parallel input/output interface 并行输入/输出接口
parallel input-output card 并行输入/输出插卡
parallel insertion 并行插入
parallel instruction control unit 并行指令控制单元
parallel interface 并行接口
parallel iterative solver 并行迭代求解程序
parallel join algorithm 并行连接算法
parallel knowledge base machine 并行知识库机器
parallel language 并行语言
parallel library 并行程序库
parallel line 并行线路
parallel link 并行链路
parallel list processing 并行表处理
parallel logic inference 并行逻辑推理
parallel logic word 并行逻辑字
parallel loop 并行循环
parallel machine model 并行机器模型
parallel machine organization 并行机组织
parallel manner 并行方式
parallel matrix factorization 并行矩阵因子分解法
parallel memory(PM) 并行内存
parallel memory access 并行内存存取
parallel memory unit 并行内存单元
parallel merging 并行归并
parallel mesh generation algorithm 并行网格生成算法
parallel mode 并行模式
parallel model 并行模型
parallel multiplier 并行乘法器
parallel network architecture 并行网络体系结构
parallel omega network 并行 Ω 网络
parallel operation 并行作业
parallel optimization 并行优化
parallel output 并行输出
parallel-parallel logic 并行-并行逻辑
parallel parsing 并行语法分析
parallel perceptron 并行感知器
parallel permutation 并行排列
parallel perspective 并行透视
parallel pipelined processor 并行流水线处理机
parallel pivoting 并行主元选择法
parallel poll 并行询问
parallel port 并行端口「器
parallel port connector 并行端口连接
parallel port IRQ 并行端口中断请求
parallel port mode 并行端口模式
parallel prefix computation 并行前置计算
parallel primitive 并行原语
parallel printer 并行式打印机
parallel printing 并行打印
parallel procedure structure 并行过程结构
parallel processing(PP) 并行处理
parallel-processing building blocks 并行处理构件
parallel processing language 并行处理语言
parallel processing organization 并行处理组织
parallel processing system(PPS) 并行处理系统
parallel processing system evaluation board 并行处理系统评价小组
parallel processing task 并行处理任务
parallel processing types 并行处理类
parallel processor 并行处理机 「型
parallel processor operating system 并行处理机操作系统
parallel processor software 并行处理机软件
parallel processor system hardware 并行处理机系统硬件
parallel processor system software 并行处理机系统软件
parallel production system 并行产生式系统
parallel program 并行程序
parallel program model 并行程序模型
parallel program schema 并行程序模式
parallel programming environment 并行程序设计环境
parallel programming language 并行程序设计语言

parallel projection 并行投影
parallel proof 并行证明[验证]
parallel queue 并行队列
parallel random access machine (PRAM) 并行随机存取机器
parallel ray tracing 并行光线跟踪
parallel reading 并行读出
parallel real-time processing 并行实时处理
parallel recurrence 并行递归
parallel redundancy 并行冗余度
parallel redundant UPS 并联冗余不间断电源
parallel refutation 并行反演
parallel register 并行寄存器
parallel reliability system 并行可靠性系统
parallel representation 并行表示
parallel research memory 并行搜索存储器
parallel resonance 并联谐振
parallel retrieval 并行检索
parallel rewriting system 并行重写系统
parallel ring register 并行环形寄存器
parallel robot 并行机器人
parallel root-finding method 并行求根法
parallel routing 并行路由选择,并行布线法
parallel run test 并行运行测试
parallel sampling 并行取样
parallel scheduling 并行调度
parallel schema 并行模式
parallel scheme 并行实现方案
parallel search 并行检索,内容寻址
parallel sequential computer 并行时序计算机
parallel sequential computer architecture 并行时序计算机体系结构
parallel-serial 并串联,混联
parallel-serial conversion 并串行转换
parallel-serial register 并-串行寄存器
parallel session 并行对话
parallel set 并行置位
parallel shared bus 并行共享总线
parallel shift 并行移位
parallel signal 并行信号
parallel signature analysis 并行签名分析
parallel simulating computer 并行模拟计算机
parallel simulation 并行仿真
parallel sort 并行排序
parallel speedup 并行加速
parallel splitmerge 并行分解归并
parallel-structured computer 并行结构计算机
parallel sub-channel 并行子通道
parallel substitution scheme 并行置换方案
parallel switching network 并行交换网络
parallel synchronous computer 并行同步计算机
parallel symbol 并行符号
parallel syntactical analyzer 并行语法分析程序
parallel system 并行系统
parallel task spawning 并行任务派生
parallel tautology algorithm 并行同义反复算法
parallel termination 并联端接
parallel test 并行测试
parallel thinning 并行细化
parallel-to-serial converter 并行/串行变换器
parallel transfer 并行传送
parallel transmission 并行传输
parallel Turing machine 并行图灵机
parallel unification 并行合一
parallel vector operation 并行向量运算
parallel version 并列版本
Parallel Virtual Machine(PVM) 并行虚拟处理机
parallel work-flow 并行操作流
parallelepiped method 并行六面体法
parallelism 并行性,并发性
parallelism of multiprocessing 多重处理并行性
parallelization 并行化
parallelization supporting system 并行化支援系统
parallelize 并行化处理
parallelizing compiler 并行化编译程
paralyzer 并行分析程序
PARAM(PARAMeter) 参数,变量
paramagnetic material 顺磁性材料

paramagnetism 顺磁性
parameter(PAR,PARM) 参数,参量
parameter adaptation 参数适应
parameter and non-parameter classification 参数分类与非参数分类法
parameter argument 参数自变量
parameter attribute 参数属性
parameter attribute list 参数属性表
parameter-based fault diagnosis 基于参数的故障诊断
parameter block 参数块
parameter block introduction sequence 参数块引入序列
parameter block request indication 参数块申请指示
parameter bound 参数界限
parameter calculation 参数计算
parameter card 参数卡
parameter classification 参数分类法
parameter definition 参数定义
parameter delimiter 参数定界符
parameter dependent operator 参数相关算符
parameter down-converter 参数向下转换器
parameter-driven 参数驱动
parameter driver 参数驱动程序
parameter format 参数格式
parameter group identifier(PGI) 参数群标识符
parameter identification 参数标识符
parameter ignorance 参数忽略
parameter instruction 参数指令
parameter learning 参数学习
parameter length 参数长度
parameter line 参数行
parameter list 参数表
parameter management frame(PMF) 参数管理帧
parameter mode 参数模式
parameter model 参数模型
parameter name 参数名
parameter optimal control 参数优化控制
parameter optimization 参数优化
parameter packet 参数包
parameter passing mechanism 参数传递机制
parameter perturbation 参数扰动
parameter plane 参数平面
parameter position 参数位置
parameter preserving 参数保存
parameter RAM 参数存储器
parameter receive block 参数接收块
parameter segment descriptor register 参数段描述符寄存器
parameter selection mechanism 参数选择机制
parameter send block 参数发送块
parameter set 参数集
parameter specification 参数说明
parameter specifier 参数说明符
parameter spread 参数值扩展
parameter stack segment descriptor 参数栈段描述符
parameter statement 参数语句
parameter string 参数串
parameter substitution 参数替换
parameter subsystem 参数子系统
parameter table 参数表
parameter testing 参数测试,参数检查
parameter transmission 参数传输
parameter tuning 参数调整
parameter uncertainty 参数不定性
parameter user 参数用户
parameter value(PV) 参数值
parameter variation 参数变更
parameter word 参数字
parameterization 参数化
parameterize 参数化操作
parameterized decision-making 参数化决策
parameterized model 参数化模型
parameterized module 参数化模块
parameterized programming 参数化程序设计
parameterized variational principle 参数化变分法原理
parameterized view definition 参数化视图定义
parameterless procedure 无参数过程
parametric amplifier 参量放大器
parametric and non-parametric classification 参量分类法和非参量分类法
parametric classifier 参量分类器
parametric command 参数命令

parametric curve 参数曲线	parasitism 寄生现象
parametric degree 参数级	Parassit Parassist 并行化支援系统
parametric dependence 参量相关性	parbegin 并行开始
parametric descriptor 参量描述符「法	PARC(Palo Alto Research Center) PARC 研究中心
parametric differentiation 参数微分	parend 并行结束
parametric fault 参数故障	parent 双亲；上层
parametric linear programming 参数线性规划	parent alias 双亲别名
parametric method 参数法	parent-child 父-子关系
parametric optimization 参数优化	parent-child relationship 父子关系
parametric pattern router 参数模式布线算法	parent clause 父辈子句 「件
	parent dedicated file(PDF) 父专有文
parametric polymorphism 参数多形性，参数多态现象	parent directory 父目录，上级目录
parametric polynomial curve 参数多项式曲线	parent element 母体元素
	parent environment 母环境，父代环境
parametric procedure 参数过程	parent ion 母离子
parametric programming 参数规划	parent object 父对象
parametric reliability 参数可靠性「法	parent page 父页面
parametric representation 参数表示	parent population 母体
parametric signal modeling 参量信号建模 「线	parent process 父进程
	parent program 先辈程序
parametric spline curve 参数样条曲线	parent segment 父段
parametric stabilization channel 恒参信道	parent slice 母片
	parent structure 父结构
parametric subroutine 参数子例程	parent table 父表
parametric surface 参数曲面	parent-to-child mapping 父-子映射
parametric synthesis 参数合成	parent widget 上层窗口部件
parametric test 参数测试 「析	parent window 父窗口
parametric test anatomy 参数量度解	parentheses 括号
parametric variation channel 变参信	parentheses-free notation 无括号记法
parametron 变抗管，变参管 「道	parentheses matching 括号匹配
parametron shift register 变抗管	parentheses nesting 括号嵌套
paramodulation 参变调解法	parenthesis 括号，圆括号
paranotion 派生概念	parenthesis language 括号语言
paraperspective 平行透视	parenthesized 带括号的，括号括起的
paraphase amplifier 分相放大器	parenthesized expression 带括号的表达式
paraphasing 意译，释义	
ParaScope Editor ParaScope 编辑器并行化支援系统	parity 奇偶性
	parity bit 奇偶位
parasite 寄生物，寄生病毒	parity block 奇偶校验块
parasitic 寄生的，附加的	parity check 奇偶校验
parasitic capacitance 寄生电容	parity check bit 奇偶校验位
parasitic effect 寄生效应	parity check code 奇偶校验码
parasitic noise 寄生噪声	parity check matrix 奇偶校验阵列
parasitic oscillation 寄生振荡	parity check system 奇偶校验系统
parasitic solution 寄生解	parity drive 奇偶校验磁盘机
parasitic transistor 寄生晶体管	parity error 奇偶校验错误
	parity flag 奇偶标记

parity function 奇偶功能
parity generator-checker 奇偶发生检验电路
parity interrupt 奇偶性中断
parity-line circuit 奇偶线电路
parity prediction 奇偶预测
parity state 奇偶校验状态
parity track 奇偶校验磁道
parity tree 奇偶树
parity Turing machine 奇偶图灵机
park 停留区;停车,(磁头)归位
parked (磁头)归原位的
parking systems simulation model 停车系统仿真模型
parlance 专用术语;说法
parling process 分析过程
PARM(PARaMeter) 参数,参量
parse 剖析,语法分析;分列
parse line 分列线
parse network (语法)分析网络
parse tree (语法)分析树
parser (语法)分析程序
parser generator (语法)分析程序生成器
parsimonious architecture 吝啬(费用很节省的)体系结构
parsimonious transformation 吝啬变换
parsing 剖析,语法分析
parsing algorithm 语法分析算法
parsing machine 剖析机
parsing phase 剖析阶段
parsing sentence 剖析句
parsing tree 语法分析树
part 元件,部分;片段
part classification 零件分类
part classification data 零件分类数据
part detection 零件识别
part edit 片段编辑器
part fabricator 部件制作者
part failure rate 元件失效率
part family 零件族,部件系列
part group 零件组
part grouping 零件分类[分组]
part hierarchy 零件分级
part inspection 零件检验
part list 零件清单统
part measurement system 零件测量系
part orientation 零件姿态

part program 零件加工程序
part public interface 部件公共接口
part recognition 零件识别
part registration 零件对位[配准]
part set 成套零件
part setup 零件安装
partial 部分的;偏的
partial animation 半动画
partial asynchronous 部分异步
partial belief 部分置信
partial carry 部分进位
partial combinatory algebra 部分组合代数
partial commutation 部分转换
partial computability 部分可计算性
partial contents 部分内容
partial correctness 部分正确性
partial correctness proof 部分正确性证明
partial decision procedure 部分判定过程
partial dependency 部分依赖[相关]
partial derivation 部分派生[导出]
partial derivative 偏导数,偏微商
partial details 部分详细资料
partial dial tone 部分拨号音
partial dichotomy 部分二分支
partial differential equation 偏微分方程
partial directed set 部分有向集
partial directory 局部目录,部分目录
partial distribution function 部分分布函数
partial donor cell method 部分施主单元法
partial double error detecting 部分双错检测法
partial drive pulse 半选驱动脉冲
partial dump 部分转储
partial emulation 部分仿真
partial enumeration method 部分枚举法
partial evaluation 部分求值
partial expansion 部分展开
partial failure 部分失效
partial fault-tolerance 部分容错
partial feedback 部分反馈
partial fraction expansion 部分分式展开
partial full-duplex 部分全双工
partial function 部分函数

partial function semantics 部分功能语义学
partial generalization 部分归纳
partial graph 部分图
partial group 部分群
partial index 部分索引
partial interaction 部分交互作用
partial interpretation 部分解释
partial-match query 部分匹配询问
partial matching 部分匹配
partial melting 部分熔化
partial model 局部模型
partial multiple 部分复接
partial order graph 部分有序图
partial ordering 偏序,部分定序
partial ordering relation 偏序[半定序]关系
partial ordering set 偏序[部分定序]
partial packet discard 部分包丢弃[集
partial parameterization 部分参数化
partial phrase 部分短语
partial pivot 部分主元素
partial pivoting 部分选主元法
partial plan 部分平面图
partial power on 部分加电
partial preordering 偏预序关系
partial product 部分乘积
partial program 部分程序 「器
partial projection filter 部分投影滤波
partial qualified name 部分限定名
partial recognition 不完全识别 「数
partial recursive function 部分递归函
partial recursive predicate 部分递归谓词
partial register stall 寄存器部分阻塞
partial regression coefficient 偏回归系数
partial regression equation 偏回归方
partial response 部分响应 「程
partial response code 部分响应编码
partial-reversal processing 半逆向显影
partial-scan technology 部分扫描技术
partial screen transmit 局部屏幕传送
partial-seek 部分搜索 「冲
partial-select input pulse 半选输入脉
partial select output 半选输出 「冲
partial-select output pulse 半选输出脉

partial selected cell 半选单元
partial shape recognition 部分形状识别
partial simulation 部分模拟,局部仿
partial solution 部分解 「真
partial solvability 部分可解性 「索
partial state exploration 部分状态探
partial substitution 部分替换
partial sum 部分和
partial sum register 部分和寄存器
partial switching 部分切换;部分翻转
partial syntax tree 部分句法树
partial tree 部分树
partial word 部分字
partial-write operation 部分写操作
partially coherent optical processor 部分相干光处理机
partially completed tree 部分完全树
partially computable 部分可计算的
partially computable function 部分可计算函数
partially constructed syntax tree 部分构造语法树
partially decidable 部分可判定的
partially decidable problem 部分可判定问题
partially inverted file 部分倒排文件
partially ordered set 偏序集,半序集
partially ordered space 半序空间
partially ordered system 半序系
partially ordered task 半序任务
partially qualified name 部分限定名
partially self-checking circuit 局部自检电路 「题
partially solvable problem 半可解问
partially specified boundary 部分规定边界
partially symmetric function 偏对称函数
participation 参与,参加;合作
particle 质点;粒子,颗粒
particle diffraction 粒子衍射
particle in cell method 格网质点法
particle induced noise detection test 颗粒感应噪声检测
particle modeling 粒子建模,粒子模型化
particle orientation 质点定向,磁粉定

向,粒子取向
particle system 粒子系统
particular case 特定情况,特例
particular characteristic 特定性能
particular postlude 特定尾序
particular program 特定程序
particular solution 特解
particulate 粒子,颗粒
particulate disk 微粒型磁盘
particulate recording media 微粒型记录媒体
partition 分区,部分
partition access method 分区存取法
partition activity monitor 分区活动监督程序
partition allocation method 分割配置法,分区法
partition background 后台区
partition control descriptor 分区控制描述符
partition control table 分区控制表
partition data set 划分数据集
partition exchange sorting 划分交换排序
partition identifier 分区标识符
partition load 分区装载
partition map 分区图
partition method 分区法
partition number 分区编号;划分数
partition of automation 自动机分割
partition programming 分块规划
partition queue element 分区队列元素
partition save area 分区保留区
partition sequential access method 分区顺序存取法
partition specification table 分区明细表
partition table 分区表
partition test 分拆检验;分区测试
partition user 分区用户
partitionability 可划分性,可分割性
partitionable architecture 可分割体系结构
partitional 分割(开来的),分区的
partitioned access method 分区访问法
partitioned cache model 分区高速缓存模型
partitioned data organization 分区数据组织
partitioned data set 分区数据集
partitioned emulation programming extension 分区仿真程序设计扩充
partitioned file access 分区文件存取
partitioned formulation 分段公式化
partitioned hash function 分区散列函数
partitioned list 分区表
partitioned logic 分区逻辑
partitioned memory 分区存储器
partitioned mode 分区运行方式
partitioned normal form 分区范式
partitioned real-time database 分区实时数据库
partitioned representation 分区表示
partitioned segmentation 分区式分段
partitioned semantic network 分区语义网络
partitioned sequential file 分区顺序文件
partitioned specification table 分区说明表
partitioned statistical database 分区统计数据库
partitioning 分块,分割
partitioning algorithm 分割算法
partitioning approach 分割法,划分法
partitioning of matrix 矩阵分割
partitioning problem 划分问题
partitioning selection algorithm 分组选择算法
partitioning selection network 分组选择网络
partly Java driver 部分 Java 驱动程序
partly structural decision problem 部分结构化决策问题
PARTMGR 分区管理
partner 伙伴,合作者,对方
partnership concept 伙伴关系概念
parts catalog 零件目录
parts explosion 零件分解图
parts inspection robot 零件检验机器人
parts library 零件库
parts list 零件明细表
parts number 零件编号
parts palette 部件选择区
parts relationship 部件关系
parts per million(PPM) 百万分之几
PARTSET(PARTitioned data SET) 分区数据集

party-line 合用线路
party-line bus 同线总线
party-line driver 合用线路驱动器
party-line service 合用线路服务,同线业务
PAS(Program Access Specification) 程序存取规范
PAS(Protocol Analysis System) 协议分析系统
PASC(Precision Adaptive Subband Coding) 精密自适应子带编码
PASC(Precision Adaptive Subsidiary Coding) 精密自适应辅助编码
PASCAL PASCAL语言 「序
PASCAL compiler PASCAL编译程
Pascal computer system PASCAL计算机系统
PASCAL-like language 类PASCAL语言
Pascal P-Code Pascal伪码
Pascal structure Pascal(程序)结构
Pascal's triangle 帕斯卡(杨辉)三角形
PASRO(PASCAL for Robots) PASRO语言
PASS(Programming Aid Software System) 程序设计辅助软件系统
pass 通过;传递;遍
pass algorithm 传送算法
pass by address 按地址传送
pass by name 按名传送
pass by reference 按引用传送
pass by value 按值传送
pass by value-result 值-结果传送
pass counter 扫描遍数计数器
pass name 传送名
pass parameter 传递参数
pass sorting 通过排序
pass through 传递;(程序执行)通过
passage 通路;通过
passband 通频带,通带
passband channel 通带信道
passed data set 通行[交接]数据集
passing parameters 传递参数
passivation 钝化
passive 无源的,被动的
passive accommodation 被动调节
passive attach 消极攻击
passive branching 无源分支[分接头]

passive broadcast channel 无源广播信道
passive bubble generator 无源磁泡产生器
passive bus 无源总线
passive circuit 无源电路 「列
passive component array 无源元件阵
passive computed torque algorithm 被动计算的转矩算法
passive decoder 无源译码器
passive defensive programming 被动防错性程序设计
passive device 被动式设备,无源器件
passive element 无源元件
passive fault-detection 无源(不加电)故障检测
passive feedback control 从动反馈控
passive filter 无源滤波器 「制
passive focus 无源聚焦
passive grab (X协议)非活动[被动]占取
passive graphics 非活跃图形,无源图
passive hub 无源集线器 「形
passive hybrids 无源混合微电路
passive isolation 无源隔离
passive line monitor 无源线路监视器
passive matrix LCD 无源阵列液晶显示
passive memory element 无源存储元
passive network 无源网络 「件
passive object 被动对象
passive ranging 被动式测距方法
passive satellite 无源卫星
passive security 被动安全
passive signal-distribution unit 无源信号分配设备
passive simulation 被动模拟
passive star 无源星形网
passive state 被动状态
passive station 从站,副站
passive transducer 无源变换器
passive type 被动类型 「法
passive wire tapping 被动线路截收方
password(PW) 口令,密码,通行字
password aging 口令生命期
Password Authentication Protocol (PAP) 口令验证协议
password expires 口令过期

password information 口令[密码]信息
password management 口令管理
password protection 口令保护
password requestor 口令请求程序
password restriction 口令限制
password security 密码安全性
password strike-over mask 密码输入隐蔽
password uniqueness 口令惟一性
paste 粘贴
paste bookmark 粘贴书签
paste function 粘贴函数
paste picture 粘贴图片
Paste Special 选择性粘贴
paster 不干胶粘贴纸
paster scan laser printing 不干胶粘贴纸扫描激光打印
PAT(Production Acceptance Testing) 产品验收测试
PAT(Programmable Automatic Testing) 可编程自动测试
patch 修补码,补丁;临时连线
patch algorithm 修补算法
patch area 插入区
patch bay 插头安装板
patch board 插线板
patch cable 临时连接电缆
patch cord 插线,接线绳
patch formation model 修补模型
patch mapping 插入映射
patch output converter 修补输出转换程序
patch panel 插线板;配电板
patch program 修补程序
patch routine 修补例程,插入例程
patch-program plugboard 修补程序插接工具软件
patch test 分片检验
patched-grid method 修补网格法
patches 饰片,面片
patching 修补法,补丁法
patching board 接线板
patchplug 接线插头
patent 专利
patent citation 专利引证
patent information retrieval system 专利信息检索系统
patent protection 专利保护
patent right 专利权
patentee 专利人
patenting 专利登记,专利申请
path 路径,通路
path accuracy 轨迹精度
path addition algorithm 路径相加算法
path allocation 通路分配
path analysis 路径分析
path choice 路径选择
path command 路径命令
path compression 路径压缩
path computation 轨迹计算
path condition 路径条件
path conflict 路径冲突
path control 轨迹控制,通路控制
path control element(PCE) 通路控制元件
path control layer 路径控制层
path control network 路径控制网络
path control program 通路控制程序
path delay analysis program 路径延迟分析程序
path dependency 通路相关性
path desensitizing 路径脱敏
path diagram 路径图
path difference 路程差
path-down 向下路径
path expression 路径表达式
path finding with collision-free 无碰撞路径寻找方法
path generation method 通路形成法
path information unit(PIU) 路径信息单元
path length 路径长度
path loss 路径损耗
path measuring system 轨迹测量系统
path name 路径名
path name component 路径名分量
path number matrix 路径编号矩阵
path 路径,通路
path optimization 路径优化
path planning 路径[轨迹]规划
path position (对象在)路径上的位置
path predict 路径预测
path rank-ordered search 通路定序搜索
path representation 路径表示法
path rule 通路规则
path schedule compiling 路径调度编译

path search 通路搜索
path selection server （网络）路径选择服务器
path select table 路径选择表
path sensitization 通路敏化
path sensitizing test generation 路径敏化测试产生法
path setting 通路建立
path space limit 路径空间限制
path statement 路径语句
path survey 通路勘定
path switch 路径开关
path table 路径表
path testing 路径测试
path-up 向上路径
path update rate 轨迹修改速率
path way 通道
pathological 故障连接
PATHWORKS PATHWORKS软件
patience 忍耐时间
patient care system 病员监护系统
PATT (Partial Automatic Translation Technique) 部分自动翻译技术
pattern 图案,图形；结构；模板,样式；特性曲线；晶体点阵
pattern adaptive writing 模式自适应写入
pattern analysis 模式分析
pattern articulating device 图案清晰化设备
pattern character 图形字符
pattern classification 模式分类
pattern clustering 模式类聚[群集]
pattern cognition 模式识别
pattern color 模式色；图案颜色
pattern comparison inspection 模式比较检测
pattern configuration 模式配置[结构]
pattern conversion 模式转换
pattern correlation 模式相关性
pattern correspondence index 模式相符指数
pattern data representation 模式数据表示法
pattern description 模式描述
pattern description language 模式描述语言

pattern-directed inference system 模式导向的推理系统
pattern-directed invocation 模式导向调用
pattern-directed retrieval 模式导向检
pattern discrimination 模式判别 ∟索
pattern displacement 模式替代
pattern distortion 模式畸变
pattern driven subroutine 模式驱动子例程
pattern editor 图形(样式)编辑程序
pattern enumeration 模式列举
pattern error analysis 模式误差分析
pattern evaluation 模式评价
pattern extraction 模式析取
pattern fill 图案填充
pattern finding program 模式查找程序
pattern generation 模式生成
pattern grammar 模式文法
pattern handling statement 模式处理语句
pattern identification 模式标识
pattern information processing 模式信息处理
pattern information processing system (PIPS) 模式信息处理系统
pattern input language 模式输入语言
pattern input method 模式输入方法
pattern inspection system 图样检查系
pattern interpretation 图形解释 ∟统
pattern inversion technology 模式反演技术
pattern learning 模式学习法
pattern learning parser 模式学习语法分析程序
pattern library 模式库
pattern list 图样列表
pattern making 模式产生
pattern matching technique 模式匹配技术
pattern memory 图案存储器
pattern movement 模式移动
pattern noise 图像噪声
pattern operand 模式操作数
pattern operation editing sequence 模式操作编辑序列
pattern operator 模式操作数

pattern perception 模式感知
pattern playback 图像重现
pattern primitive 模式元
pattern profile 图形断面
pattern recognition 模式识别
pattern recognition device 模式识别设备
pattern recognition theory 模式识别理论
pattern refresh 图案刷新
pattern ripple 图形杂波
pattern search 模式搜索
pattern search method 模式搜索法
pattern segmentation 模式分割
pattern selection 模式选择
pattern sensitive fault 码型敏感故障；特定模式故障
pattern sensitivity 码型敏感性
pattern separation 图案分割
pattern space 模式空间
pattern specification 模式说明
pattern teletex 图形扫描方式图文电视
pattern transformation memory 码型变换存储器
pattern understand 模式理解
pattern variable 模式变量
pattern vector space 模式向量空间
patterned gray 填充灰度
PAUDIT 审计显示
pause 暂停，间歇
pause before branching 分支前暂停
pause control 间歇控制
pause input 暂停输入
pause instruction 暂停指令
pause pending 暂停搁置
pause-retry 暂停重传
pause sequence 暂停序列
pause statement 暂停语句
pause stop 暂停结束
PAX(Parallel Architecture eXtended) 并行体系结构扩展
PAX(Private Automatic eXchange) 专用自动交换机
PAX-1 并行体系结构扩展软件
pay actual computer time 支付实际机时费
pay cable network 付费电缆网络
pay cable TV 付费有线电视
pay station 投币式公用电话亭

pay television 付费电视
payback period 回收期
payload 有效荷载
payload type 净荷载类型
payment gateway 支付网关
payment method 付费方式
payment system 资金调拨系统
payments mechanism 支付机构
payoff 清算，付清
payroll 工资单
payware 付费软件
PB(Page Buffer) 页面缓冲器
PB(PetaByte) 千万亿字节，2^{50}字节
PB(PowerBuilder) PowerBuilder 数据库开发工具
PB(Print Board) 印刷电路板
PBP(Packet Burst Protocol) 信息包突发协议
PBT(Parallel Bit Transmission) 位并行传输
PBX(Private Branch eXchange) 专用小交换机
PBX attendant 专用小交换机话务员
PBX line hunting services 专用小交换机自动连选业务
PBX tie trunk 专用小交换机通信干线
PBX trunk 专用小交换机干线
PC(Personal Computer) 个人计算机
PC(Pocket Calculator) 袖珍计算器
PC(Printed Circuit) 印刷电路
PC(Program Counter) 程序计数器
PC(Programmable Controller) 可编程控制器
PC 98 PC 98规范(微软, Intel)
PC and stack profiling data 程序计数器与堆栈配置数据
PC-based router 基于PC的路由器
PC board 印刷电路板
PC board portable tester 印刷电路板袖珍测试器
PC-bus 个人计算机总线
PC card 个人计算机卡，PC卡
PC card slot PC卡插槽
PC compatibility 个人计算机的兼容性
PC compatible 个人计算机兼容的
PC color codes 个人计算机彩色码
PC display mode 个人计算机显示模式

PC DOS PC DOS 操作系统(IBM)
PC-FAX card 个人计算机-传真卡
PC-FAX system 个人计算机-传真系
PC Install PC 安装程序生成工具
PC keyboard 个人计算机键盘
PC LAN 个人计算机局域网络
PC memory card 个人计算机存储器卡,PC 机内存卡
PC memory card international association(PCMCIA) 个人计算机存储卡国际协会标准
PC memory map 个人计算机内存布局
PC-MOS/386 个人计算机多用户操作系统
PC-net PC 网
PC Network PC 局域网络
PC network PC 网络
PC Paintbrush PC 画笔软件
PC profiling data 程序计数器配置数据
PC-relative addressing 程序计数器相对寻址
PC Tools 个人计算机工具软件
PC Tools Deluxe 个人计算机工具软件包
PC/XT PC/XT 个人计算机(IBM)
PC/XT keyboard PC/XT 键盘
PCA buffer pool 主通信附属缓冲池
PCB(Page Control Block) 页面控制块
PCB(Printed Circuit Block) 印刷电路板
PCB(Process Communication Block) 进程通信块
PCB test language 印刷板测试语言
PCC(Permuted Cyclic Code) 循环置换码
PCD(PreConfigured system Definition) 预配置系统定义
PCE(Processing and Control Element) 处理控制部件
PCF(Pilot Carrier Frequency) 导频频率
PCF(Programmed Cryptographic Facility) 程控加密设备
PCG(Print Character Generator) 打印字符发生器
PCH(Program Counter High) 程序计数器高位部分

PCI(Packet/Circuit Interface) 信息包/电路方式接口
PCI(Parallel Communication Interface) 并行通信接口
PCI(Peripheral Component Interconnect) 外围部件互连,PCI 总线(Intel)
PCI(Programmable Communication Interface) 可编程通信接口
PCI(Protocol Control Information) 协议控制信息
PCI local bus(Peripheral Component Interconnect local bus) 外围部件互连局部总线,PCI 本地总线
PCL(Packet Control Layer) 信息包控制层
PCL(Parallel Communication Link) 并行通信链路
PCL(Physical Child Last) 最后物理子女
PCL(Printer Control Language) 打印机控制语言
PCL language(Process Control Language) 过程控制语言
PCL statement PCL 语句
PCM(Plug Compatible Mainframe) 插接兼容主机
PCM(Plug Compatible Manufacture) 插接兼容制造厂商
PCM(Plug Compatible Memory) 插接兼容内存
PCM(Pulse Code Modulation) 脉码调制
PCM binary code 脉冲编码调制二进制码
PCM digital reference sequence 脉冲编码调制数字参考序列
PCM-LOG(Pulse Code Modulation - Logarithmic Companded) 对数压缩扩张脉码调制
PCM multiplex equipment 脉码调制多路复用设备
PCM terminal 脉码调制终端机
PCMCIA(PC Memory Card International Association) PC 机存储卡国际协会
PCMCIA card PCMCIA 卡
PCMCIA Flash Disk PCMCIA 快擦

写盘
PCMCIA slot PCMCIA 插槽
PCMI(PhotoChromic Micro-Image) 彩色照相缩微图像
PCN(Personal Communication Network) 个人通信网
PCNE(Protocol Converter for Native X.25 Equipment) 本地 X.25 设备用协议转换器
PCONSOLE 打印控制台
PCS(Personal Communication Service) 个人通信业务
PCS(Preferred Character Set) 优选字符集
PCS(Priority Control Sequence) 优先权控制顺序
PCS(Process Communication Supervisor) 进程通信管理程序
PCS(Production Control System) 生产控制系统
PCS(Programmed Control Sequencer) 可编程控制定序器
PCT(Partition Control Table) 分区控制表
PCT(Private Communication Technology) 保密通信技术
PCTG(Programmable Channel Termination Group) 可编程通道终接组
PCU(Primary Control Unit) 主控单元
PCU(Programmable Control Unit) 可编程控制单元
PCW(Program Control Word) 程序控制字
PCX PCX 图形格式
PD(Packet Disassembly) 信息包拆卸
PD(Panel Display) 平板显示器
PD(Pattern Description) 模式描述
PD(Phase Detector) 相位检波器
PD(Plasma Display) 等离子体显示
PDA(Personal Digital Assistant) 个人数字助理(苹果)
PDA(Push Down Automaton) 下推自动机
PDC(Personal Digital Cellular) 个人数字式蜂窝移动电话
PDD(Physical Device Driver) 物理设备驱动程序
PDF(Portable Document Format) 可移植文档格式
PDH(Plesiochronous Digital Hierarchy) 准同步数字系列
PDIP(Plastic Dual-In-line Package) 双列直插式塑料封装
PDL(Page Description Language) 页面描述语言
PDL(Push Down List) 后进先出表,下推表
PDM(Pulse-Duration Modulation) 脉宽调制
PDMA(Polar Division Multiple Address) 极分多址
PDN(Physical DEvice Number) 物理设备号
PDN(Public Data Network) 公用数据网络
PDP(General Purpose Data Processor) 通用数据处理机,PDP 计算机系列(DEC)
PDP(Plasma Display Panel) 等离子体显示板
PDP(Programmed Data Processor) 可编程数据处理器,PDP 计算机
PDQ(Parallel Database Query) 并行数据库查询
PDS(Problem Descriptor System) 问题描述符系统
PDS(Public Domain Software) 公益软件
PDT(Program Description Table) 程序描述表
PDT(Programmable Data Terminal) 可编程数据终端
PDT(Push Down Transducer) 下推翻译机
PDU(Plasma Display Unit) 等离子显示器
PDU(Programmable Diagnostic Unit) 可编程诊断单元
PE(Page End character) 页终字符
PE(Parity Error) 奇偶性错误
PE(Peripheral Equipment) 外围设备
PE(Personal Editor) 个人编辑器
PE(Phase Encoding) 相位编码
PE(Picture Element) 像元,像素
PE(Processing Element) 处理单元

PE(Protocol Emulation)　协议仿真
PEACE　PEACE 专家系统
peak　尖峰，波峰
peak-and-hold　峰值保持
peak capacity　最高容量；高峰生产能力
peak current　峰值电流
peak current rating　额定峰值电流
peak data-transfer rate　峰值数据传输率
peak detection　峰值检测
peak distortion　峰值失真
peak envelope power　峰值包络功率
PEB　峰值因数
peak flux density　峰值磁通密度
peak forward voltage　正向峰值电压
peak holding circuit　峰值保持电路
peak inverse voltage　反向峰值电压
peak limiting　峰值限制
peak load　峰值负载，峰值业务量
peak magnetizing force　最大磁化力
peak megaflops　峰值每秒百万次浮点运算次数
peak noise　尖峰噪声
peak output power　峰值输出功率
peak point　峰值点
peak point current　峰值点电流
peak point voltage　峰值点电压
peak power　峰值功率
peak pulse amplitude　脉冲峰值幅度
peak-reading voltmeter　峰值电压表
peak recognition　峰点识别
peak shift　峰值漂移，峰点偏移
peak speed　峰值速度
peak-to-peak amplitude　峰-峰振幅
peak-to-valley ratio　峰谷比
peak traffic flow　高峰信流量
peak transfer rate　峰值传送速率
peak transmission rate　尖峰传输率
peak value　峰值
peak voltage　峰值电压
peaking circuit　峰化电路
PEB(Process Environment Block)　进程环境块
pecking motor　步进电动机
peculiar　特有的，特殊的
peculiar test equipment　特殊测试设备
pedestal　消隐脉冲电平；底座，基座
pedestal design　轴架结构
pedestal footprint　底脚

pedestal robot　落地式机器人
pedestal sensor　基本传感器
Peedy　Peedy 鹦鹉(微软)
PEEK　(BASIC)取数指令
peel off operator　删除运算符
peel strength　抗剥强度
peeling　剥皮，剥落
peep　窥视；隐约显现
peep table generator　窥视表生成程序
peephole mask　窥孔掩码
peephole optimization　窥孔最佳化
peer　同位体，同级，对等
peer entities　对等层实体
peer group　同级设备群，"同颗"
peer layer　对等层
peer layer communication　对等层通信
peer-to-peer file transfer　对等文件传送
peer-to-peer network　对等网络
peer-to-peer replication　对等结构复制器
peer network　对等网络
peer network software　对等网络软件
peer protocol　对等协议
peer review　对等评审
peer-to-peer communication　对等通信
peer-to-peer network　对等网络
peer view　同级评审
peg count　呼叫计数
pegging　占线计次
Peirce　非析取符号
PEL(Picture Element)　像素
pellet　小球，片状器件
pellet part　片状器件，片状元件
PEM(Performance Enhancement Module)　性能增强模块
pen annotation　书写批注，光笔批注
pen arm　笔架
pen based computer　笔式计算机
pen-based computing　笔式计算
pen-based interface　基于笔的接口
pen computer　笔操纵计算机
pen computing　笔式计算，笔操作计算
pen data　绘图笔数据
pen-down　下笔
pen-driving mechanism　笔驱动机构
pen light control　光笔控制
pen-like device　类笔设备
pen move　笔移动

pen plotter 笔式绘图仪
pen plotter emulation program 笔式绘图仪仿真程序
Pen Point 笔指引操作系统(GO)
pen scanner 笔式扫描仪
pen scribe 笔尖划线法
pen station number 笔位号
pen touch input 笔触输入
pen-up 抬笔
penalty 惩罚,损失;性能恶化
penalty approximation 性能恶化的近似估计
penalty function 罚函数,补偿函数
penalty function method 惩罚函数法
penalty parameter 罚参数
pencil 铅笔,画笔
pencil follower 笔跟踪器
pencil representation 细线表示
pending 未决的;挂起的
pending active session 未决的活动对话
pending deletion 搁置(作业)删除
pending interrupt condition 未决中断条件
pending queue 未决队列
pending read state 待决读状态
pending status 未决[待定]状态
pending write state 待决写状态
PenDOS 笔式操作系统
penetrability 可渗透性
penetrance 渗透率
penetration 渗透,突破
penetration control 穿透深度控制
penetration CRT 穿透型阴极射线管
penetration depth 穿透深度
penetration signature 渗透特征
penetration test 渗透试验
penetration testing 渗透试验操作
Pentium "奔腾"处理器(Intel)
Pentium MMX "多能奔腾"处理器(Intel)
Pentium Pro "高能奔腾"处理器(Intel)
Pentium Ⅱ 奔腾Ⅱ处理器(Intel)
Pentium Ⅲ 奔腾Ⅲ处理器(Intel)
pentravel 笔行程
penumbral 半阴影
PEP(Peak Envelope Power) 峰值包络功率
PEP(Programmable Extension Package) 可编程扩充软件包
PEP(Prototyping Evaluation and Programming) 原型评价与编程
PEPE(Parallel Element Processing Ensembler) 并行部件处理复合系统
PEPPER board PEPPER图形板
PER(Packet Error Rate) 包出错率
PER(Program Error Report) 程序错误报告
PER(Program Event Recording) 程序事件记录(IBM)
per-recipient option 预接收选项
per seat licensing 每座席许可协议
percent 百分比
percent character 百分比符号(%)
percent completed 已完成的百分比
percent decode 识别率百分率
percent defective 废品率
percent defective allowable 容许的次品百分率
percent intelligibility 可懂率百分比
percent of call lost 呼损率
percent recovery 复原百分率
percent sign 百分比符号
percent style 百分比式样
percent symbol 百分比符号
percentage 百分比
percentage modulation 调幅度百分数
percentage overflow(%OFL) 溢呼百分比
percentile life 百分比寿命
percentiles 百分位数
perception 感知
perceptron 感知器,感知单元
percolation 渗流,渗滤,净化
percolation scheduling compiler 渗透调度编译程序
perfect 完善的,完全的,理想的
perfect balance 理想均衡
perfect conductor 良导体,全导体
perfect crystal 完美晶体
perfect cube 完全立方
perfect dielectric 理想电介质
perfect duality 完全对偶性
perfect elasto-plastic deform 全弹塑性变形
perfect graph 理想图,完备图

perfect hashing 完全散列
perfect induction 完全归纳法
perfect information game 完备信息博弈
perfect matching algorithm 完美匹配算法
perfect number 完全数
Perfect Office 办公自动化套件(Corel)
perfect secrecy 理想[完善]保密
perfect shuffle 全混洗
perfect square 完全平方
perfecting 双面印刷
perfection 完备,完整,完全
perfection of instruction set 指令系统完备性
perfective maintenance 完善性维护
perforated module board 有孔模件板
perforated tape 穿孔纸带
perfectly balanced tree program 理想均衡树状程序
perfectly legal 完全合法
perfectly-random 完全随机
perforated panel 穿孔板
perforated tape 穿孔纸带
perforator 穿孔机
perform 执行,完成
perform mask discovery 执行掩码搜索
PERFORM statement 执行语句
performability 可运行性
performance 性能,特性
performance analysis 性能分析
performance attribute 性能属性
performance bottleneck 性能瓶颈
performance characteristic 性能特性
performance classification 性能分类
performance cost ratio 性能价格比
performance criteria 性能标准
performance curve 性能曲线
performance deficiency 性能缺陷
performance estimation 性能估计
performance evaluation 性能评估
performance evaluation and review technique(PERT) 性能评价与审定技术
performance group 性能组
performance guarantee 性能保证
performance measure of search algorithms 搜索算法的性能度量
performance model 性能模型

performance modeling 性能模型化
performance monitoring 性能监视器(程序)
performance objective 性能目标
performance optimization 性能优化
performance optimizer 性能优化程序
performance option 性能选择
performance period 性能周期
performance perspective 性能透视
performance prediction 性能预测
performance projection 性能设计目标
performance reference 性能标准
performance requirements 性能要求
performance scalability 性能伸缩性
performance specification 性能规格说明
performance standard 性能标准
PERFORMANCE statement (COBOL)执行语句
performance statistics 性能统计
performance synthesis 性能综合
performance test analysis 性能测试分析
performance tool 性能工具
performance trace 性能跟踪
performance transparency 性能透明
performance varification 性能验证
performance visualization 性能可视化
perigee 近地点
perimeter 周长,周边
period(P) 周期
period definition 周期性定义
period length 周期长度
period of revolution 旋转周期
period of sampling 取样周期
periodic 周期性的
periodic boundary condition 周期性边界条件
periodic component 周期分量
periodic composite 周期性组合体
periodic control 周期性控制
periodic convolution 周期卷积
periodic damping 周期性衰减(阻尼)
periodic dumping 周期性转储
periodic duty 周期工作方式
periodic error integrating controller 周期性误差积分控制器
periodic execution 周期性执行程序
periodic function 周期性函数
periodic interrupt 周期性中断

periodic job 周期性作业
periodic law 周期律
periodic maintenance 按周期进行的维修
periodic multistep method 周期性多步法
periodic porous media 周期多孔性媒体
periodic pulse train 周期性脉冲串
periodic random process 周期性随机过程
periodic regulator 周期性调节器
periodic replacement 定期更换
periodic report 定期报告
periodic sampling 周期抽样
periodic sequence 周期性序列
periodic solution 周期解
periodic state 周期性状态
periodic substructure 周期性子结构
periodic table 周期表
periodic test 定期进行的测试
periodical 定期的
periodicity 周期性
periodization 周期化
periods processing 分阶段处理
peripheral 外部设备；外围的
peripheral adapter 外围设备适配器
peripheral allocator 外设分配程序
peripheral apparatus 外部设备
peripheral assignment table 外设指派表
peripheral buffer(PB) 外围缓冲器
peripheral bus 外围总线
peripheral compatibility 外围设备兼容性
peripheral computer 外围计算机
peripheral control 外围设备控制器
peripheral control program 外围设备控制程序
peripheral control switching unit 外围设备控制交换单元
peripheral control transfers 外围控制传送
peripheral control unit(PCU) 外围控制单元
peripheral controllers(PC) 外围控制器
peripheral controls 外围控制
peripheral conversion program 外围变换程序
peripheral data bus 外设数据总线

peripheral decoding 外设译码
peripheral device 外围设备，外部设备
peripheral device controller 外围设备控制器
peripheral disk file 外部磁盘文件
peripheral driver 外围驱动器(程序)
peripheral equipment 外围设备
peripheral equipment list 外围设备列表
peripheral equipment operator 外围设备操作员
peripheral file 外设文件
Peripheral Interchange Program (PIP) 外围交换程序
peripheral interface 外围设备接口
peripheral interface adapter(PIA) 外围接口适配器
peripheral interface channel 外围接口通道
peripheral interface module 外围设备接口模块
peripheral interrupt 外围中断
peripheral-limited 受外围设备限制的
peripheral link 外围链路
peripheral LU 外围逻辑单元
peripheral manager 外围管理程序
peripheral manufacturer 外围设备制造厂家
peripheral module 外围设备模块
peripheral node 外部节点，外围结点
peripheral operation 外围操作
peripheral physical unit 外围物理单元
peripheral processor 外围处理机
peripheral processor memory 外围处理机内存
peripheral prompt 外围设备提示符
peripheral PU 外围物理单元
peripheral slots 外围设备插槽
peripheral software driver 外围软件驱动器
peripheral subsystem 外围子系统
peripheral support chip 外围支持芯片
peripheral support computer 外围支持计算机
peripheral switching unit 外围设备交换部件
peripheral system 外围系统
peripheral transfer 外围传送，外设信号传送

peripheral trunks 外围信息干线
peripheral unit fault recognition 外围单元故障识别
peripherals 外围设备
PERL(Practical Extraction and Reporting Language) (CGI 脚本编程)Perl 语言
permalloy 坡莫合金
permalloy head 坡莫合金磁头
permanent 永久性的,固定的
permanent circuit 永久性[固定]电路
permanent connection 永久性[固定]连接
permanent data call 永久数据调用
permanent data file 永久性数据文件
permanent data set 永久性数据集
permanent dynamic storage 永久动态存储器
permanent elongation 永久伸长
permanent error 固定错误[误差]
permanent failure 永久失效
permanent fault 固定故障
permanent files 永久文件
permanent fitting 永久固定
permanent magnet 永久磁铁
permanent-magnet erasing head 永磁抹除磁头
permanent magnet material 永磁性材料,恒磁材料
permanent magnetization 永磁化
permanent member 永久性成分「器
permanent memory(PM) 永久性存储
permanent-memory computer 永久记忆计算机
permanent-memory pool (Netware)永久存储池
permanent object 永久性对象
permanent page store 永久性页面存储器
permanent physical link 永久性物理链路
permanent read/write error 永久性读写错误
permanent relationship 固定关系「卷
permanent resident volume 永久驻存
permanent segment 永久段
permanent signal 固定信号
permanent state 持久状态

permanent storage 永久性存储器
permanent storage area(PSA) 永久存储区,固定存储区
permanent structure library 固定结构程序库
permanent subscriber number 永久性用户号码
permanent swap file 永久置换文件
permanent symbol 永久符号
permanent user file 固定用户文件
permanent virtual circuit(PVC) 永久虚电路
permanently resident volume 永久性常驻卷
permatron 磁控管
permeability 导磁率;透过率
permeance 磁导
perminvar 镍铁钴合金
permissible code block 许用码组
permissible error 容许误差
permissible interference 可容许干扰
permissible limit 容许限界,容许极限
permission 许可,容许;权限
permission log 许可清单
permissive 容许的
permissive matching 容错匹配
permissive timing system 容错定时制
permit "通行证","许可证"
permit packet 许可信息包
permit pool "通行证"储集站
permitted transfer 容许转送
permittivity 介电常数
permutability 可排列性,可交换性
permutable 可排列的;可置换的「引
permutated-title index 标题关键词索
permutation 排列
permutation code 置换码
permutation graph 置换图
permutation group 置换群
permutation index 循环置换标题索引
permutation matrix 置换矩阵
permutation network 置换网络
permutation of a set 集合的排列「列
permutation of multi-set 多重集的排
permutation representation 置换表示法
permutation routing 置换路由选择
permutation switching 置换开关

permutation symbol 排列符号
permutation table 排列表
permutation tree 置换树;排列树
permuted cyclic code 循环置换代码
permuted index 置换索引
perpendicular 垂直的
perpendicular head 垂直磁头
perpendicular magnetic recording 垂直磁记录
perpendicular magnetization 垂直磁化
perpendicular recording media 垂直磁记录介质
perpetual 永久的
perpetual motion 永恒运动
perseverance 持续动作
persisted current 持续电流
persisted state 持久状态,持续状态
persistence 余辉;持久性,连续性
persistence of vision 视觉暂留
persistent 持久的,持续的
persistent connection 持续性连接
persistent CSMA 坚持型 CSMA
persistent current memory cell 持续电流存储单元
persistent data 持久性数据
persistent fault 持续故障
persistent link 持续链接
persistent name server 固定名称服务器
persistent object 持续目标,永久性对象
persistent object manager 固定对象管理程序
persistent property 持续属性
persistent registration 持久性对位
persistent storage 持久型存储器
persistent type object 持久型对象
PERSON (PERsonal Simulation ONline) 个人联机仿真
Person to Person for OS/2 Warp OS/2 人际联系软件
person-to-person service 个人对个人业务
personal 个人的
Personal Address Book(PBA) 个人地址簿
personal address list 个人通讯录
personal AI computer 个人用人工智能计算机

personal analogy 亲身类推
personal appraisal 人员鉴定
personal area network 个人区域网
personal-assignment problem 人员分配问题
personal biological model 个人生物模型
personal board 专用插件
personal call 定人呼叫
personal code 个人密码
Personal Communication Network (PCN) 个人通信网
Personal Communication System(PCS) 个人通信系统
Personal Computer(PC) 个人计算机(IBM)
personal computer(PC) 个人计算机
personal computer security 个人计算机保密
personal computing 个人计算
PERSONAL CONSULTANT 个人咨询语言
personal CP/M 个人 CP/M 操作系统
personal data terminal 个人数据终端
personal decision 个人决策
personal development system 个人开发系统
Personal Digital Assistant(PDA) 个人数字助理
personal disclosure 个人泄密
personal document 个人文档
personal dynamic media 个人动态媒体
personal error 个性化误差
personal folder 个人文件夹
personal form library 个人窗体库
personal greeting 个人应答词
personal identification code 个人识别码
personal identification number(PIN) 个人识别码
personal identifier 个人标识符
Personal Information Manager(PIM) 个人信息管理程序
personal intelligent communicator(PIC) 个人智能通信器
personal interviews 面谈,直面会晤
personal investigation 人员调查
personal manufacturing system 专用制造系统
personal message store(PST) 个人消

息存储
personal module 专用模块，特制模组
Personal NetWare 个人 NetWare 软件系统
Personal OS/2 单用户 OS/2 操作系统
personal password 个人通行字
personal phonebook 个人电话簿
personal robot 个人专用机器人
personal security 人事安全
personal sequential inference machine 个人顺序推理机
Personal Service(PS) 个人服务软件
Personal System/2 个人系统计算机/2(IBM PS/2)
personal telecommunication 个人通信
personal telecommunication number (PTN) 个人电信号码
personal unblocking code(PUC) 个人解锁码
personal verification 个人验证
personal web 个人站点
Personal Web Manager (Windows)个人 Web 管理器(微软)
Personal Web Server (PWS) (Windows)个人 Web 服务器(微软)
personal workstation 个人工作站
personalistic decision theory 个性决策理论
personality cards （装有个人数据的）个人专用插件
personality module 特性组件，个性模块
personalized computing environment 个性化计算环境
personnel 全体成员；人事部门
personnel database system 人事信息数据库系统
personnel document 个人文档
personnel management software 人事管理软件
personnel record 人事记录
perspective 透视；远景，前途
perspective deep 透视深度
perspective projection 透视投影
perspective scene 透视场景
perspective transformation 透视变换
perspective view 透视图
perspectivity 透视性
persuation-support system 信念支持系统

PERT (Performance Evaluation and Review Technique) 性能评价与审定技术
PERT(Project Evaluation and Review Technique) 计划评审技术
PERT/cost 计划评审技术成本分析
PERT/CPM (PERT/Critical Path Method) 计划评审技术关键路径法
PERT diagram 计划评审技术图
PERT net PERT 网
PERT network 计划评审技术网络
PERT/time 计划评审技术时间分析
pertinency 切合性
pertinency factor 恰当因数，切合性因数
pertinent retrieval 切合检索
perturbation 扰动
perturbation analysis 扰动分析
perturbation method 摄动法
perturbation problem 扰动问题
perturbations of daily schedule 每日故障记录表
PES(Parallel Enterprise Server) 并行企业服务器(IBM S/390)
PES(Photo-Electric Scanner) 光电扫描仪
pessimistic 悲观的，不顺利的；保守的
pessimistic buffering 保守式缓冲
pessimistic design 保守设计法
pessimistic estimate 保守估计
pessimistic forward pruning 保守正向修剪法
pessimistic row buffering 保守式行缓冲
PET (Physical Equipment Table) 物理设备表
PET(Positive Electron Tomography) 正电子 X 射线断层扫描分析
PET computer (Personal Electronic Transaction computer) 个人电子事务处理计算机
peta- 表示 $10^{15}(2^{50})$ 的前缀
petabype- 千万亿字节，2^{50} 字节
Petaflops Computing 千万亿次浮点计算
Petri net 皮特里网，位置-迁移网
PEU(Port Expander Unit) 端口扩展单元
PEV(Peak Envelope Voltage) 峰值包络电压

PEX(PHIGS Extension to X) 程序员分层交互图形标准的 X 扩充标准
PEX(Private Electronic eXchange) 电子用户交换机
PF(Packet Format) 信息包[分组]格式
PF(Page Formatter) 页面格式符
PF(Parity Flag) 奇偶标志
pf(pico Farad) 皮法,微微法
PFB(PreFetch Buffer) 预取指令缓存
PFC(Positive Feedback Circuit) 正反馈电路
PFD(Position Finding Device) 定位设备
PFF(Page Fault Frequency) 缺页频率
PFFP(Programmable Front End Processor) 可编程前端处理机
PFN(Permanent File Name) 永久文件名
PGA(Pin Grid Array) 引脚格阵
PGA(Programmable Gate Array) 可编程门阵列
PGM(Path Generation Method) 路径生成法
PGN(Performance Group Number) 性能组编号
PGP(Pretty Good Privacy) 优秀密钥
PgUp/PgDn keys 向前/向后翻页键
PH(Packet Head) 信息包标题
PH(Page Heading) 页标题
phantastron 幻像延迟电路
phantom branch 幻像分支
phantom cable 幻像电缆
phantom channel 镜像信道
phantom circuit 幻像电路
phantom ROM 幻像只读存储器
phase 阶段,相位,相替
Phase Alternating Line(PAL) 相位交
phase ambiguity 相位模糊
phase/amplitude distortion 相位振幅失真
phase angle 相位角,相角
phase bandwidth 相位带宽
phase by phase 按阶段进行
phase-by-phase build-up 逐阶段建立
phase-change coefficient 相位常数
phase-change ink-jet printer 相变型喷墨打印机
phase changing rewritable optical disk 相变型可重写光盘
phase chief 阶段主管
phase class name 阶段类名称
phase compensating network 相位补偿网络
phase constant 相位常数
phase corrector 相位校正器
phase delay 相位延迟
phase detector 相位检测器
phase deviation 相位偏移
phase difference 相位差
phase diagram 相位图,相位转变图
phase difference 相位差
phase discrimination 鉴相
phase discriminator 鉴相器
phase distortion 相位失真
phase distortion coefficient 相位失真系数
phase drift 相位漂移
phase encode 相位编码
phase encoding 相位编码
phase equalization 相位均衡
phase filter 相位滤波器
phase/frequency distortion 相位频率畸变
phase/frequency response characteristic 相位频率响应特性
phase function 相位函数
phase hit 相位跳跃
phase hologram 相位全息图
phase image 相位图像
phase integral approximation 相位积分逼近法
phase inversion 相位反转,倒相
phase-inversion modulation 反相调制
phase jitter 相位抖动
phase loading entry 分阶段加载入口
phase lock 锁相
phase lock loop 锁相环
phase locked oscillator(PLO) 锁相振荡器
phase logic 阶段逻辑
phase modulation 相位调制
phase modulation recording 调相记录
phase name 可执行程序段名
phase pattern 相位模式
phase plane 相位平面

phase pre-equalization 相位预均衡
phase response characteristic 相位响应特性曲线
phase reviews 阶段评审
phase separation 相位分割,分相
phase servo-system 相位伺服系统
phase shift 相移
phase-shift discriminator 鉴相器
phase shift keying(PSK) 移相键控
phase sorting 分阶段排序
phase space 相位空间
phase splitter 分相器
phase transfer function(PTF) 相位传递函数
phase transition optical 相变型光盘
phase velocity 相速
phase voltage 相电压
phasing 定相,相位调整
phasing signal 定相信号
phenomenological coefficient 现象逻辑系数
phenomenon 现象,征兆
phenotype 表现型
PHIGS(Programmer's Hierarchical Interactive Graphics Standard) (三维图形库)程序员分层交互图形标准
PHIGS(Programmer's Hierarchical Interactive Graphics System) 程序员分层交互式图形系统
PHIGS Extension to X(PEX) PHIGS的X扩充标准
PHIGS PLUS(Programmer's Hierarchical Interactive Graphics System Plus Lumiere Und Surfaces) PHIGS(添加光照与表面效果的)扩充版本
PHM(PHoto Memory) 光存储器
Philips 飞利浦公司
philosophy 哲学;基本原理;原则
Phoenix BIOS Phoenix 基本输入/输出系统
phone 电话
Phone Blaster 声霸通信卡
phone connector 电话连接器
Phone Dialer 电话拨号程序
phone line 电话线
phone receiver 受话器
phone template matching 音素模板匹配

phoneme 音位,音素
phoneme map 音素图
phoneme recognition 音素识别器
phoneme-voice synthesizer 话音合成
phonemic information extraction 语音信息抽取
PhoneNET PhoneNET 网络
Phonepower card 电话语音处理卡
phonetic accelerator 语音加速器
phonetic code 语音码
phonetic encoding 语音编码
phonetic keyboard 语音键盘
phonetic spelling 语音拼写
phonetic symbol 语音符号
phonetic transcription 语音录制
phonetic typewriter 口授打字机
phonetically defined state 语音学定义状态
phonetics 语音学
Phong lighting 冯贝通(Phong Buituong)表面光泽计算机法
Phong shading Phong 阴影计算法
phono configurational code 音形码
phono connector 语音连接器
phonograph 摄像机
phonology 音韵学
phonon 声子;振动量子
phosphor 荧光物质,磷光物质
phosphor aging 磷光体老化
phosphor dots 磷光点
phosphor persistence 磷光保持时间
phosphorescence 磷光
photo 照相;光
photo CD 光片 CD
photo communication 光通信
photo computer 光计算机
photo-coupler 光耦合器
photo-Darlington 光达林顿器件
photo-data quantizer 光电数据量化器
photo-detector 光检测器器
photo document sensor 光电文档阅读
photo etch 光刻蚀
photo-excitation 光致激发
photo-isolator 光电隔离开关
photo-magneto effect 光磁效应
photo-masking 光掩蔽
photo-optical recorder tracker 光电记录跟踪装置

photo-pattern generation 光学掩膜生成
photo plotter 感光绘图仪
photo-realistic 真彩色照相技术
photo rendering 上光着色
photo sensor 光传感器
photocathode 光电阴极
photocell matrix 光电器件阵列
photochromic micro image 彩色缩微图像
photocomposition 照相排版
photoconduction 光电导
photoconductive film 光电导薄膜
photoconductive gain factor 光电导增益因子
photoconductive infrared sensor 红外光电导传感器
photoconductivity 光电导性
photoconductor(PT) 光电导体
photoconductor drum 光导鼓
photoconductor gap 光导缝隙
photoconverter 光电变换器
photocopier 照片复印机
photocopy 影印
photocoupler 光电耦合器
photocurrent 光电流
photodetector 光检测器
photodetector array 光检测器阵列
photodiode 光电二极管
photodirect lithography 照相平版术,光刻
photoelectric alarm 光电报警
photoelectric coded disk 光电编码盘
photoelectric detection 光电检测
photoelectric device 光电器件
photoelectric effect 光电效应
photoelectric element 光电元件
photoelectric emission 光电发射
photoelectric keyboard 光电键盘
photoelectric mark reading 光电标记读出
photoelectric mouse 光电鼠标
photoelectric reader 光电阅读器
photoelectric scanner 光电式扫描仪
photoelectric sensor 光电传感器
photoelectric sorter 光电分类仪
photoelectric tape reader(PTR) 光电纸带阅读器
photoelectron spectroscopy 光电子光谱学
photoelectronic control 光电控制
photoelectronics 光电子学
photoelement 图素,像素
photoemission 光电子发射
photoemitter 光电子发射体
photoetching 光刻
photofine 图像细化
photograph facsimile telegram 相片传真电报
photograph facsimile telegraphy 相片传真电报技术
photograph interpretation 相片判读
photographic document copying machine 照相式文档复印机
photographic imagery 摄影成像
photographic reduction dimension 照相缩小尺寸
photographic storage 照相存储器
photographic typesetter 照相排版机
photogravure 照相凹版印刷术
photointerpretive program(PIP) 图像判读程序
photolithography 光刻法;影印
photomagnetic memory 光磁存储器
photomask 光刻掩膜
photomask substrates 光刻掩模基板
photomicrography 缩微照相术
photomultiplier 光电倍增器
photon 光子
photonics 光子学
photoprint 影印;影印件
photoreader 光电阅读器
photorealism 图像真实感
photorealistic image synthetic 似真图像合成
photorealistic output 似真图像输出
photoreceptor 感光器,光电接收器件
photoresist 光致抗蚀剂,感光保持膜
photoresist developers 光致抗蚀剂显影液
photoresist developing 光刻胶显影
photoresistor 光敏电阻器
photoresists 光致抗蚀剂,光刻胶
photosensor 光电传感器
photosetting 照相排版
Photoshop Photoshop 图像处理软件(Adobe)

PhotoStyler　PhotoStyler 图像处理软件(Aldus)
photoswitch　光电开关
phototelegram service　传真电报业务
phototransistor　光晶体管
phototranslation　光电转换
phototypegraphy　光凸版印刷术
phototypesetter　照相排版机
phototypesetting　照相排版
photovoltaic cell　光生伏特电池
photovoltaic effect　光生伏特效应
phracker　电话欺诈者
phrase　短语,词组
phrase marker　短语标记
phrase searching　词组搜索
phrase speech recognition　短语识别
phrase structure　短语结构
phrase structure grammar　短语结构文法
phrase structure rule　短语结构规则
phrase table　短语表
phraseology　成语
phrasing　语法措辞;分节法
phreak　电话窃贼,电话欺诈
PHY(PHYsical layer)　物理协议子层
phylogenetic tree　系统发育树
phylogeny　语言发展研究
physical　物理的,实际的
physical access control　物理存取控制
physical access level　物理存取级
physical address　实地址,物理地址
physical address space　实地址空间,物理地址空间
physical binding　物理联编
physical block number　物理块号
physical channel　物理通道
physical child segment　物理子段
physical circuit　物理电路,实电路
physical compression　物理压缩
physical connection　物理连接
physical constraint gripper　机械约束夹持器
physical contiguity　物理接触
physical control space(PCS)　物理控制空间
physical data　物理数据
physical data base　物理数据库
physical data base record　物理数据库记录
physical data description language　物理数据描述语言
physical data independence　物理数据独立性
physical data structure　物理数据结构
physical database　物理数据库
physical design for database　数据库物理设计
physical device　实体设备,物理设备
physical device address(PDA)　物理设备地址
physical device driver(PDA)　物理设备驱动程序
physical device table　物理设备表
physical drive　物理驱动器
physical entity　物理实体
physical fault　物理故障
physical file　物理文件
physical format　物理格式
physical I/O address　物理输入/输出地址
physical I/O control system(PIOCS)　物理输入/输出控制系统
physical I/O function　物理输入输出功能
physical image　物理映像
physical interface　物理接口
physical layer　物理层,实体层
Physical Layer Medium Dependent(PMD)　物理媒体相关子层
physical link　物理链路
physical location　物理位置
physical lock　物理加锁
physical logging　物理登记,实际注册
physical main storage　物理主内存
physical map　物理映像
physical master tape　原版带　「层
Physical Medium(PM)　物理介质子
physical medium attachment sublayer(PMA sublayer)　物理媒体连接子
physical memory　物理内存　」层
physical message　物理消息[报文]
physical model　物理[实体]模型
physical module　物理模块
physical modeling　物理模型法
physical name　物理名,实体名称
physical node　物理节点

physical output device 物理输出设备
physical page 物理页面
physical paging 物理分页
physical pairing 物理配对
physical parent segment 物理父段
physical path 物理通路
physical portable 物理可移植性
physical position 物理位置
physical property measurement 物理性能测量
physical record delete 物理记录删除
physical relationship 物理关系
physical requirement 物理需求
physical resource 物理资源
physical schema 物理模式
physical sector 物理扇区
physical security 物理安全性
physical segment 物理段
physical sequence access method 物理顺序存取法
physical signaling sublayer(PLS sublayer) 物理信令子层
physical simulation 物理模拟
physical space 物理空间
physical stack 物理堆栈
physical storage 物理存储器
physical storage address 物理存储器地址
physical storage block 物理存储块
physical storage organization 实际存储器组织
physical storage table 物理存储器表
physical symbolic system 物理符号系统
physical system time 实际系统时间
physical systems simulation 物理系统模拟
physical terminal 物理终端
physical threat 物理威胁
physical timer 物理定时器
physical transient area 实际暂存区
physical twin backward pointer 物理孪生后向指针
physical twins 物理孪生员
physical unit 物理部件,实际部件
physical unit 2.1(PU 2.1) 2.1型物理单元
physical unit control point(PUCP) 物理单元控制点
physical unit services 物理单元服务
physical unit type 物理单元类型
physical volume 物理卷
physical word address 物理字地址
physical world 实体世界
physically based modeling 基于物理的造型
physically contiguous list 物理连续表
PI(Program Interrupt) 程序中断
Pi 圆周率,π
PI-clash PI 对撞,PI 碰撞
PI control 程序中断控制
PI-resolution PI 消解
PIA(Peripheral Interface Adapter) 外围设备接口适配器
PIA(Programmable Interface Adapter) 可编程接口适配器
piano-key switch 琴键开关
PIC(PICture) 图片,相片;描述
PIC clause (COBOL)描述子句
PIC file PIC(图形)文件格式
PIC(Personal Identification Code) 个人识别码
PIC(PICture) 图像,图片;格式描述
pica 12 点活字
pick 挑拣,拾取
pick-and-place robot 抓放机器人
pick aperture 拾取孔径
pick device 拾取设备
pick ID 挑拣标识符
pick identifier 挑拣标识符
pick list 选项表
Pick operating system Pick 操作系统
Pick System 匹克系统公司(美)
pick-up coil 拾取线圈
pick-up robot 抓取式机器人
pick-up tube 摄像管
picker 检出器
picking 检选,拾取
pico 皮,微微(即 10^{-12})
pico architecture 皮(微微)计算机结构
picocomputer 皮计算机
picofarad 皮法
picogram 皮克
picoinstruction interpreter 皮指令解释器
picoJava picoJava 芯片(Sun)

picon 图标化
picoprogram 皮程序
picoprogramming language 皮程序设计语言
picosecond 皮秒
PICT(PICTure) PICT(图像)文件格式
PICT file 图像文件
pictograph 象形文字
pictorial 图示的,以图形方式表示的
pictorial data representation 数据图形表示法
pictorial display 图像显示
pictorial element(PE) 图形元素
pictorial information 图像(图形)信息
pictorial query language 图像查询语言
pictorial representation 直观表示法
pictorial semantic network 图像语义网络
picture 图像,图片;格式描述
picture animation 动画
picture archiving and communication system(PACS) 图像存档与通信系统
picture attribute 图像属性
picture black 图像黑区
picture block 图像块,画区
picture box 图片框
picture building system 画面建立系统
picture bullet 图形项目符号
picture carrier 图像载波
picture channel 图像通道
picture character 对照说明符号
PICTURE clause 形象子句,描述子句
picture coding 图像编码
picture communication 图像通信
picture compiler 图像编译程序
picture composition 图像拼合
picture compression 图像压缩
picture cues 图像提示
picture data 图像数据
picture data arithmetic 算术图像数据
picture description instruction 图形描述指令
picture editing 画面编辑
picture element(pel) 像素
picture file 图形文件
picture finding 图像查找
picture formatting 图片格式安排

picture frame 图像帧
picture frequency 图像频率
picture grammar 图形描述语法
picture-in-picture 画中画
picture input device 图像输入设备
picture interpolation 图像插值
picture interpretation 图像解释,画面判读
picture inversion 图像翻白
picture line 图像扫描线
picture mask 图片掩模
picture matching 图形匹配
picture noise 图像噪声
picture object 图形对象
picture pattern understanding 图样理解
picture perception 形象感知
picture phone 电视电话
picture placeholders 图片框
Picture Power PicturePower 图像数据库
picture processing 图像处理
picture push button 图像下推按钮
picture quality evaluation 图像质量评价
picture radio button 图片单选按钮
picture recognition 图像识别
picture record 图像记录
picture registration 图像配准[对位]
picture reproduction 图片复制
picture scanner 图像扫描仪
picture segmentation 图像分段
picture signal 图像信号
picture specification 形象描述部分
picture specification character 形像描述字
picture stop 图像停止
picture structure 图形结构
PICTURE symbol 形象符号
picture synchronizing signal 图像同步信号
picture synthesis 图片合成
picture telegraphy 图像电报
picture template code 图像模板代码
picture tone 图像色调
picture tracking system 图像跟踪系统
picture transmission 图像传输
picture tube 显像管
picture width control 画面宽度控制

picture white 图像白点,图像亮区
picture white level 图像白电平
PictureMark 图像印记
picturephone 图像电话,可视电话
Picturephone Meeting Service 电视电话会议设备
PictuerTel PictureTel 公司
PID(Personal IDentification) 个人身份标识
PID(Process IDentification) 进程标识
PID(Proportional Integral and Differential controller) 比例积分与微分控制器
PID(Pseudo Interrupt Device) 伪中断设备
PID action 比例积分微分作用
PID control expert regulator 比例积分微分专家调节器
pidgin code 事务码
PIE(Program Interrupt Entry) 程序中断入口
pie chart 圆饼图
pie graph 百分率图
pie slice 扇形图
piece identification number 条标识号
piece polynomial 分段多项式
piece work 计件工作
piemeal 逐段;逐点
piemeal determination 逐段确定法
piemeal strategy 分段策略
piecewise 分段,片段
piecewise analytic function 分段解析函数
piecewise interpolation 分段插值
piecewise linear approximation 分段线性线性近似法
piecewise linear classifier 分段线性分类程序
piecewise linear discriminant function 分段线性判别函数
piecewise linear interpolation 分段线性插值
piecewise linear machine 分段线性机
piecewise linear model 分段线性模型
piecewise linear transformation 分段线性变换
piecewise parabolic method 分段抛物线法

piecewise polynomial 分段多项式
piecewise regression 分段回归
piecewise smooth coefficient 分段光滑系数
piecewise testable event 分段可测试事
piercing gripper 穿刺式夹持器 L件
piezocrystal 压电晶体
piezoeffect 压电效应
piezoelectric 压电的
piezoelectric crystal 压电晶体
piezoelectric detector 压电传感器
piezoelectric effect 压电效应
piezoelectric material 压电材料
piezoelectric modulus 压电模量
piezoelectric pressure gauge 压电式压力计
piezoelectric strain gauge 压电应变仪
piezoelectric transducer 压电式传感器
piezoelectricity 压电现象,压电效应
piezomagnetic effect 压磁效应
piezomagnetic material 压磁材料
piezopolymer 压电聚合物
piezoresistor 压敏电阻器
PIF editor (Picture Intermediate Frequency) 图像中频
PIF editor (Program Information File) 程序信息文件编辑程序
pigeonhole principle 鸽巢原理,信箱原理
piggyback board 子板,寄生板
piggyback entry 寄生进入
piggyback hardware 搭载硬件,背负硬件
piggybacking 寄生,搭载,顺手窃取
PIGS(Passive Infrared Guidance System) 无源红外制导系统
pigtail 尾光纤
pike noise 尖噪声
PIL(Picture Interpretation Language) 图像解释语言
PIL (Publishing Interchange Language) 出版交换语言,PIL语言
PIL-1 图像解释语言,PIL-1语言
pile 堆,桩;堆积
pile group settlement 堆群确定,桩群确定
pillar 导柱

Pilot Pilot 手持机
pilot 引导程序;导频
pilot bearing 导向轴承
pilot channel system 引导信道系统
pilot hole 定位孔,导孔
pilot lamp 指示灯
PILOT language PILOT 语言
pilot model 试验性模型
pilot operation 引导操作
pilot project 试验性项目
pilot signal 引导信号,测试信号
pilot system 先导测试系统;试验性系统
pilot tape 引导带
PIM(Parallel Inference Machine) 并行推理机
PIM(Personal Information Manager) 个人信息管理程序
PIN(Personal Identification Number) 个人身份识别号
PIN(Program Identification Number) 程序标识号
pin 管脚,引脚,引线
pin and socket connector 针孔型连接器
PIN assignment 个人识别号分配
pin assignment 引线[引脚]分配
pin board 插接板
pin-compatible 引脚兼容的
pin configuration 引脚配置
pin console typewrite 针式控制台打印机
pin contact 插针式触点
pin-cushion distortion 枕形失真
pin dot matrix 针点矩阵
pin-feed device 突脚馈送设备
pin-feed platen 突脚送纸滚筒
pin force 插针压力
pin grid array(PGA) 格栅阵列
pin hole 针孔
PIN issuance 个人识别号发放
pin jack 管脚插孔
pin-jointed frame 针孔连接框架
PIN mailer 个人识别号邮鉴
PIN management and security 个人识别号的管理与保密
pin map 标位图
pin packing 引线封装
pin reduction 引线精简
pin saving design 节省引线的设计(方案)

pin-socket contacts 针孔式接触对
pin summary 引脚功能一览表
pin terminal 引脚末端
PIN validation 个人身份认证
PIN verification 个人身份验证
pinboard 接插板
pinch 挤压
pinch point 挤夹区
pinch roller 压轮
pinch roller plotter 压轮式绘图仪
pinched resistor 夹心电阻,沟道电阻
pinfeed form 针孔馈送表格纸
PING(Packet INternet Groper) 因特网包(分组)探索程序
ping 强制回应
ping pong 乒乓法通信
ping pong buffer 交替缓存器
ping-pong procedure 乒乓法
ping-pong transmission 乒乓式传输,往返传输
pinhole 针孔
Pink Pink 操作系统
pinless chip 无引线芯片
pinouts 引脚外特性
pinpoint accuracy 高精确度
PIO(Parallel Input/Output) 并行输入/输出
PIOC(Programmable Input/Output Chip) 可编程输入/输出芯片
PIP(Path Independent Protocol) 与路径无关的协议,独立于路径的协议
PIP(Peripheral Interchange Program) 外围交换程序
PIP(Picture In Picture) 画中画
PIP(Problem Identification Program) 问题识别程序
pipe 管道,流水线
pipe communication mechanism 管道通信机构
pipe file 管道文件
pipe file create 管道文件创建
pipelaying 管道敷设,管线架设
pipe synchronization 管道同步
pipelinable loop processing 流水线循环处理
pipeline 流水线,管道

pipeline architecture 流水线体系结构
pipeline arithmetic 流水线运算
pipeline chaining 管道链接,流水线链
pipeline computer 流水线计算机
pipeline control 流水线控制
pipeline cycle 流水线周期
pipeline efficiency 流水线效率
pipeline element(PLE) 流水线单元
pipeline flushing time 流水线冲洗时间
pipeline interval 流水线间隔时间
pipeline iterative operation 流水线迭代运算
pipeline mode 流水线模式
pipeline multiplier chip 流水线乘法芯片
pipeline overhead time 流水线开销时间
pipeline processing 流水线处理
pipeline processor 流水线处理机
pipeline segment 流水线段
pipeline setup time 流水线建立时间
pipeline speech-recognition system 流水线音识别系统
pipeline stage 流水线阶段,流水线站
pipeline start-up time 流水线启动时间
pipeline technology 流水线技术
pipeline transparency 流水线透明性
pipeline vector processor 流水线向量处理机
pipelined multistage switch 流水线多级开关
pipelining 流水线作业
pipelining algorithm 流水线算法
piping 流水线传送
Pippin "品然"计算机(苹果)
PIQ(Parallel Instruction Queue) 并行指令队列
PIR(Passive InfraRed detector) 被动式红外传感器
piracy 非法复制
PIRL(Pattern Information RetrievaL system) 模式信息检索系统
PIRT(Precision InfraRed Tracking system) 精密红外跟踪系统
PIRV(Programmed Interrupt Request Vector) 程序中断请求向量
piston 活塞
PIT(Programmable Interval Timer) 可编程时间间隔定时器
pit 坑
pitch 孔距,间距;声调
pitch contour 行距轮廓线
pitch control 间距控制
pitch period 音调周期
pitch-row 行距
pitch selector 字距选择器
pitch synchronous analysis 基音同步分析
PIU(Path Information Unit) 路径信息单元
PIU(Peripheral Interface Unit) 外围接口部件
PIU(Programmable Interface Unit) 可编程接口设备
pivot 支点;重点,中心点
pivot element 主元素
pivot grammar 枢轴文法
pivot operation 主元素运算
pivot point 支点
pivot step 主要步骤
pivot table wizard 数据透视表向导
Pivot Table Add 添加数据透视表
Pivot Table Name 数据透视表名称
Pivot Table Starting Cell 数据透视表起始单元
pivot transformation 取主转移
pivotal line 枢轴线
pivoting 选主元
PIW(Program Interrupt Word) 程序中断字
pixel 像素,像元
pixel array 像素阵列
pixel-based algorithm 基于像素的算法
pixel graphics 像素图形
pixel image 像素映像
pixel level rendering 像素级润色
pixel linking 像素连接
pixel map 像素映像图
pixel pattern 像素图案
pixel replication 像素复制
pixel skipping 像素间取
Pixelpaint 像素着色软件
pixmap 像素映像,像素图
Pixrects Pixrects 二维图形软件包
Pixwin Pixwin 二维图形程序库(Sun)

PK(Public Key) 公开密钥
PK software PK 文件压缩软件
PKA(Public Key Algorithm) 公开密钥算法
PKUNZIP PKUNZIP 数据解压缩软件
PKZIP PKZIP 数据压缩软件
PL/1(Programming Language/1) PL/1 语言
PL/1-80 PL/1-80 语言
PL/1-FORMAC PL/1-FORMAC 语言
PL/M PL/M 语言
PL/M-plus(PL/M+) PL/M+语言
PLA(PipeLine Architecture) 流水线体系结构
PLA(Programmable Line Adapter) 可编程线路适配器
PLA(Programmable Logic Array) 可编程逻辑阵列
PLA control 可编程逻辑阵列控制
PLA control generator 可编程逻辑阵列发生器
PLA microprogramming 可编程逻辑阵列微程序设计
PLA priority encoding 可编程阵列优先级编码
place 位置;地点;放置
place information 位置信息
place value 位值
place/transition net 位置/迁移网(即 Petri net)
placeholder 占位符
placeholder object 占位符对象
placeholder record 位置保持记录
placement 布局
placement algorithm 布局算法
placement model 布局模型
placement policy 布局规则
placement strategy 置放策略
plain 明码;无格式
plain blank board 无孔空白插件板
plain bullet 简单项目符号
plain denotation 简单标志
plain module board 无孔插件板
plain language 明语;简明语言
plain text document 纯文本文件
plain value 简单值
plaintext 明语;无格式文本
PLAN(Problem Language ANalyzer) 解题语言分析程序
plan 计划,规划;平面图
plan amending 修改规划
plan execution 计划执行
plan knowledge 策略知识
plan management information system 计划管理信息系统
plan merging 方案合并
plan operator 平面操作符[运算符]
plan recognition 平面图识别
plan representation 平面图表示
PLAN series PLAN 系列网络
plan view display 平面图显示
planar 平面的,二维的
planar board 平面板
planar convex hull 平面凸壳
planar diffusion 平面扩散
planar diode 平面二极管
planar domain 平面域
planar element 平面元素
planar epitaxial transistor 平面外延晶体管
planar film 平面膜
planar flexible mechanism 平面柔性机构
planar frame 平面帧
planar graph 平面图
planar Hall effect 平面霍尔效应
planar integrated circuit 平面集成电路
planar method (制作晶体管的)平面法
planar module 平面组装插件
planar network 平面[无层次]网络
planar package 平面封装
planar passivated transistor 平面钝化晶体管
planar process 平面工艺
planar resistor technology 平面型电阻技术
planar robot 平面机器人
planar scene 平面场景
planar separator theorem 平面分隔理论
planar set 平面集
planar shape representation 平面外形表示法
planar solution 平面解
planar stress anisotropy 平面应力各向异性
planar transistor 平面三极管

planarity testing 平面性检验
planarity testing algorithm 平面性测试算法
planarization algorithm 平面化算法
plane 平面
plane curve singularity 平面曲线奇异〔性
plane elastic-plastic frame 平面弹塑性衍架
plane element hexahedral solid 平面元素实六面体
plane frame analysis 平面框架分析
plane hologram 平面全息照相
plane hybrid element 平面混合元素
plane normal 平面法线
plane-polarized wave 平面极化波
plane position indicator(PPI) 平面位置显示器
plane problem 平面问题,二维问题
plane-rotation 平面旋转
plane strain 平面应变
plane stress 平面应力
plane tree 平面树
plane vibration 平面振动
plane wave 平面波
planetary driver 行星驱动机构
planned overlay structure 计划覆盖结〔构
planned stop 计划停机
planned target 计划目标
planned time table 计划时间表
planner language 规划者语言
planning 规划,计划
planning failure 规划无效,计划失效
planning generation 规划生成,计划产生
planning island 规划岛
planning library 规划库
planning methodology 规划方法学
planning model 规划模型
planning objective 规划目标
planning paradigm 规划范例
planning philosophy 规划基本原理
planning-reacting system 规划-反应系〔统
planning sheet 规划工作表
planning software project 规划软件工〔程
planning standard 规划标准
planning system 规划系统
planning table 计划表
plant 设置

planted record 欺诈记录
plasma back etching 等离子背面腐蚀
plasma bubble display design 等离子磁泡显示设计
plasma diagnostics 等离子诊断
plasma diffusion 等离子扩散
plasma display 等离子体显示
plasma display device(PDD) 等离子体显示器
plasma equilibrium 等离子平衡
plasma panel 等离子显示屏
plasma planarization 等离子平面化
plasma polymerized film 等离子聚合物胶片
plasma-ray device 等离子射线设备
plasma sputtering 等离子溅射法
plasma stability 等离子稳定性
plastic 塑料的;可塑的
plastic card 塑料卡
plastic-clad silica fiber(PCS) 塑料包层 石英芯光纤
plastic cyclic analysis 可塑性循环分〔析
plastic device 塑封器件
plastic deformation 塑性形变
plastic design 可塑性[造型]设计
plastic encapsulation 塑料封装
plastic foam 泡沫塑料
plastic-film capacitor 塑料膜电容器
plastic leaded chip carrier(PLCC) 有引线塑料芯片载体
plastic molding 塑性模
plastic optical fiber 塑料光纤
plastic optical memory 塑盘光存储器
plastic package 塑料封装
plastic quad flat pack(PQFP) 塑料扁平方外壳
plastic strain 塑性应变
plastic torsion 塑性扭力
plastic zone 塑性区
plasticity 可塑性
plasticity model 可塑性模型
plate 阳极;极板
plate bending element 板弯曲元
plate-foundation interaction 板基相互作用
plate-like space lattice structure 类板空间网格结构
plate-shell structure 板-壳结构

plateau 平顶
plateau voltage 台阶电压
plated film disk 镀膜磁盘
plated magnetic wire 镀磁线
plated-through hole 镀通孔,金属化孔
plated wire memory 镀线存储器
plated wire storage 镀线存储器
platen 压板;压纸卷轴
platen cover 平盖板;模板罩
platen knob 滚筒旋钮
platen machine 速印机
platen press 小批量胶印机
platform 平台
Platform Computing 平台计算公司(美国)
platform ID 平台标识符
platform independence 不依赖于平台的,与平台无关的
platform integration 平台集成
platform-specific device 特定平台设备
platform-specific router 特定平台路由器
plating 电镀
plating contacts 电镀触点
plating film disk 电镀薄膜磁盘
PLATO(Programmed Logic for Automatic Teaching Operations) 自动教学的可编程逻辑
platten 压纸滚筒,字辊
platter 底板;盘片
plausibility 似真性
plausibility check 真实性检查
plausibility function 似然函数
plausibility ordering 似真排序
plausible inference 似然推理
plausible reasoning 似真推理
play 演播,播放
play back 背景播放
play backward 向后播放
play forward 向前播放
play list 演播表,播放表
play slider 演播滑动块
playback 重放,回放
playback accuracy 再现[回放]精度
playback control 重放[再现]控制
playback format 回放格式
playback head 回放头
playback robot 再现机器人
playback window 回放窗口
player 播放器;局中人
playing space 活动空间
playout 播出
PLB(Picture Level Benchmark) 图片级基准程序
PLB(Print Line Buffer) 打印行缓冲器
PLC(Programmable Logic Controller) 可编程逻辑控制器
PLD(Phase-Locked Demodulation) 锁相解调器
PLE(PipeLine Element) 流水线单元
plesiochronous 准同步
plesiochronous digital hierarchy(PDH) 准同步数字系列
plesiochronous interface 准同步接口
plex 丛,网
plex database 丛型数据库
plex entry 丛条目,网关系
plex format 丛格式
plex grammar 丛状文法
plex processing 丛处理
plex programming 丛程序设计
plex structure 丛结构,网结构
plexicoder 错综编码器
PLI(Private Line Interface) 专用线路接口
PLL(Phase Locked Loop) 锁相环路
PLM(Port Level Manager) 端口级管理程序
PLO(Phase Locked Oscillator) 锁相振荡器
plod 模压
plosive 破裂音
plot 绘图;曲线,图表
plot area 绘图区,图形区
plot chart on 绘图起始于
plot data 绘图数据
plot file 绘图文件
plot marker 绘图;多点标记
plot mode 绘图模式
plot order 绘图次序
plot pen 绘图笔
plot speed 绘图速度
plot statement 绘图语句
plot visible cells only 只按可见单元格数据绘图
plot writing head 绘图写头

plotomat 自动绘图机
plotted solution 图解
plotter 绘图仪
plotter font 绘图仪字体
plotter pen setup 绘图笔安装
plotter step size 绘图仪步长
plotting board 绘图板
plotting continuity 绘图连续性
plotting device 绘图设备
plotting hand 绘图臂
plotting head 绘图头
plotting mode 绘图模式
plotting program 绘图程序
plotting repeatability 绘图重复精度
plotting solution 图解
plotting tablet 图形输入板
PLP(Packet Level Protocol) 包(分组)级协议
PLP(Presentation Level Protocol) 表示层协议
PLP(Procedural Language Processor) 过程语言处理程序
PLPA(Pageable Link Pack Area) 可调页面链接装配区
PLS(Private Line Service) 专线业务
PLU(Primary Logical Unit) 主逻辑单元
plug 插头
Plug and Play(PnP) 即插即用
plug and play BIOS 即插即用基本输入输出系统
plug and play hardware 即插即用硬件
plug and play operating system 即插即用操作系统
Plug and Pray "即插即祈祷"(对"即插即用"的一种讥讽的说法)
plug and socket 插头和插座
plug board 插接板,配线盘
plug compatible 插接兼容的
plug compatible CPU 插接兼容的CPU
plug-compatible hardware 插接兼容硬件
plug-compatible mainframe(PCM) 插接兼容主机
plug compatible memory chip 插接兼容的存储器芯片
plug connection 插件板连接

plug connector 插件连接器
plug-in 插件
plug-in board 插接板
plug-in card 插卡
plug-in package 插入式组件
plug-in unit 插接式组件
plug on terminator 插接式终接器
plug socket 插孔,插座
plug-to-plug compatibility 插接兼容性
plug wire 插接线
plugboard 插接板
pluggable 可插接的
pluggable unit 插接件
plugged program computer 插接程序计算机
plugging chart 插接图
plural 复数的
plural number 复数
plural process 多次过程
plural relaxation factor 复数松驰因子
plurality 大多数;复数性
plus 加;加号;正数的
PLUS function 加函数
plus-minus 2I network 加减2I网络
plus range 正号区
plus sign 加号
plus zero 正零
PLV(Production-Level Video) 生产水平的视频
PM(Phase Modulation) 相位调制,调相
PM(Program Memory) 程序存储器
PMA(Preassigned Multiple Access) 预分配多路存取
PMA(Protected Memory Address) 受保护的内存地址
PMD(Physical Layer Medium Dependent) 物理媒体相关子层
PMD(Post Mortem Dump) 事后析误转储
PMD(Program Module Dictionary) 程序模块辞典
PME(Processor Memory Enhancement) 处理机内存增强
PMF(Programmable Matched Filter) 可编程匹配滤波器
PMF(Parameter Management Frame) 参数管理帧

PMG(Permanent Magnet Generator) 永磁发电机
PMG(Phase Modulation Generator) 相位调制发生器
PMI files(Protected Mode Interface files) 保护模式接口文件
PMOS(P-channel Metal Oxide Semiconductor) P沟道金属氧化物半导体
PMPO(Peak Music Power Output) 峰值音乐功率
PMR(Post-Mortem Routine) 事后析误例程
PMS(Pantone Matching System) Pantone配色系统
PMS(Permanent Magnet Speaker) 永磁扬声器
PMT(Page Mapping Table) 页面变换表
PMT(Physical Master Tape) 原版磁带
PMT(Program Master Tape) 程序主带
PMX(Packet MultipleXer) 分组多路复用
PMX(Protected Message eXchange) 受保护的消息交换
PN(Packet Number) 分组(包)编号
PN(Page Number) 页码,页面编号
PN(Pseudo-random Number) 伪随机数
PN boundary PN间界
PN junction PN结
PN junction diode PN结二极管
PN junction isolation PN结隔离
PNC(Programmed Numerical Control) 程序数字控制
pneumatic capstan 气动主动轮
pneumatic controller 气动控制器
pneumatic reel 气动带盘
pneumatic robot 气动机器人
pneumatic servo control 气动伺服控制
pneumatic tape transport 气动磁带传送
pneumatic valve 气阀
PNM(Path Number Matrix) 通路编号矩阵
PNOS(Portable Network Operating System) 可移植的网络操作系统
PnP(Plug and Play) 即插即用
PnP(Plug and Pray) "即插即祷告"

PnP BIOS(Plug and Play Basic Input / Output System) 支持即插即用的基本输入/输出系统
PNP transistor PNP型晶体管
Pnuele-Lempel-Even's algorithm PLE算法
PO(Page Out) 出页
pocket 袖珍的,小型的
pocket calculator 袖珍计算器
pocket computer 袖珍型计算机
pocket-size reel 袖珍带盘
pocketronic 袖珍式电子计算机
POGO(Program-Oriented Graphics Operation) 面向程序的图形操作
Pohlig-Hellman cipher 波利格-赫尔曼密码
POI(Program Operator Interface) 程序操作员接口
point 点,小数点;磅(=1/72英寸)
point and shoot 点击
point approximation 点近似法
point beam 点波束
point-by-point computation 逐点计算
point-by-point method 逐点法
point chain 指定字链
point chart 点图,散点图
point connectivity 点连通性
point contact 点接触
point-contact diode 点接触型二极管
point-contact transistor 点接触型晶体管
point covering number 点覆盖数
point critical graph 点临界图
point degradation 点退化
point-dependent segmentation 按点分割
point-disjoint path 点不相交通路
point estimation 点估计
point frame 点框架;点帧
point identification 点标识
point iterative method 点迭代过程
point loading 点荷载
point match method 点匹配法
point-marker 点标记符
point matrix 点阵
point matrix method 点阵法
point-mode display 点式显示
point-mode servoing 点式伺服控制
point-mode display 点式显示

point number 数据标记序号
point of failure 失效点,故障点
point-of-failure restart 故障点重新启动
point of invocation 调用点
point-of-last environment(POLE) restart 最近现场点重新启动
point of no return 不返回点
POP(Point of Presence) 出现点
point of return 返回点
point-of-sale terminal(POS) 销售点终端
point operation 点操作,点运算
point plotting technique 点绘图技术
point protection 点保护
point recognition 点识别
point sampling 点抽样
point set curve 点集曲线
point set topology 点集拓扑
point single step method 点单步法
point singularity 奇点
point size 点大小
point source light 点光源
point specifier 点阵
point spectrum 点谱,离散谱
point spread function 点分布函数
point symbol 点符号
point symmetric graph 点对称图
point-to-multipoint transmission 一点对多点传输
point-to-point 点对点
point-to-point circuit 点对点电路
point-to-point communication 点对点通信
point-to-point configuration 点对点配置
point-to-point connection 点对点连接
point-to-point control 点到点控制,逐点控制
point-to-point control system 点到点控制系统
point-to-point controlled robot 点到点控制机器人
point-to-point line 点对点线路
point-to-point link 点对点链路
point-to-point operation 点对点操作
point-to-point program 点对点程序
Point-to-Point Protocol(PPP) 点对点协议
point-to-point traffic 点对点业务量

point-to-point transmission 点对点传输
point-to-set mapping 点到集映射
point-visible polygon triangle 可见点多面三角形
pointer(P,PTR) 指示字,指针
pointer address 指针地址
pointer array 指针阵列
pointer assignment 指针赋值
pointer assignment statement 指针赋值语句
pointer attribute 指针属性
pointer-based join 基于指针的连结
pointer constant 指针常量
pointer data 指针数据
pointer declaration 指针说明
pointer expression 指针表达式
pointer field 指针字段
pointer grab (X协议)指针占取
pointer information 指针信息
pointer jumping 指针跳跃法
pointer loop 指针循环
pointer machine 指针机器
pointer manipulation 指针操作
pointer method 指针法
pointer moniker 指针别名
pointer operation 指针操作
pointer path 指针路径
pointer position 指针位置
pointer segment 指针段
pointer structure 指针结构
pointer type 指针类型
pointer type definition 指针类型定义
pointer value 指针值
pointer variable 指针变量
pointer variable qualification 指针变量限制
pointing 定位,指向
pointing accuracy 定位精度
pointing device 定位设备
pointing method 指示法
pointing metric space 无点度量空间
pointwise 逐点的
pointwise iteration 逐点迭代
Poisson 泊松
Poisson distribution 泊松分布
Poisson equation 泊松方程
Poisson probability distribution 泊松概率分布

Poisson probability function 泊松概率函数
Poisson process 泊松过程
POKE 存数,送数
POKE statement 送数语句
poke request 发送请求
poke status 发送状态
POL(Problem-Oriented Language) 面向问题的语言
POL(Procedure-Oriented Language) 面向过程的语言
POL(Pseudo Off-Line) 虚拟离线,假脱机
polar 极性的
polar capacitor 极性电容器
polar coordinate 极坐标
polar coordinate system 极坐标系统
polar crystal 极性晶体
polar decomposition 极坐标分解
polar diagram 极坐标图
polar form 极型
polar keying 极性键控
polar mode 有极性模式
polar operation 极性操作
polar orbit 极性轨道
polar plot 极坐标图
polar relay 极化继电器
polar signal 双极性信号
polar transmission 双极性传输
polar vector 极向量
polarential telegraph system 极性差动电报系统
polarity(PO) 极性
polarity coincidence correlator 极性重合相关器
polarity error detector 极性误差检测器
polarity hold 极性保持
polarity indicator 极性指示器
polarity reversal 极性反转
polarity selector(PS) 极性选择器
polarizability 极化率,极化性
polarizable medium 极性介质[媒体]
polarization 极化;偏振
polarized capacitor 极化电容器
polarized component 有极性元件
polarized filter 偏振滤镜[滤光器]
polarized light 偏振光
polarized plug 定位[有极性]插头

polarized return to zero 极化归零
polarized return-to-zero recording 极化归零记录
polarized spot 极化点
polarizer 偏振片;极化器
polarizing angle 偏振角
polarizing filter 偏振滤光镜
polarizing slot 定位槽
polarograph 极谱仪
polaroid filter 偏振滤光镜
POLE(Point Of Last Environment) 最近现场点
pole 极,极点
pole assignment algorithm 极点赋值算法
pole location 极点位置
pole placement 极性安排,极性布置
POLER (Point-Of-Last-Environment Restart) 最近现场点重新启动
police connect 警方联系
policy 策略,政策
policy improvement algorithm 策略改进算法
policy map 策略图
policy of least privilege 最少特权策略
policy space 策略空间
polish (软件)润色版本;抛光,磨光
Polish notation 波兰记法
Polish postfix 波兰后缀
Polish prefix notation 波兰前缀记法
polisher 抛光器
polishing 抛光
polishing paste 抛光膏
polite agent 斯文代理
politeness 优美性,精练性
poll 轮询
poll pattern 轮询模式
poll reject message 轮询拒收报文
poll train 探询序列
poll-type command 轮询型命令
pollable 可轮询的,可移植的
polled circuit 轮询电路
polling 轮询,探询
polling analysis 轮询分析
polling characters 轮询字符
polling circuit 轮询电路
polling cycle 轮询周期
polling delay 探询延迟

polling discipline 轮询规定
polling ID 轮询标识符
polling interrupt 轮询中断
polling interval 轮询间隔
polling list 轮询表
polling message 轮询消息
polling message format 轮询消息格式
polling method 轮询法
polling mode 轮询方式
polling operation 轮询操作
polling overhead 轮询开销
polling procedure 轮询过程
polling program 轮询程序
polling ratio 轮询比
polling scheme 轮询计划[方案]
polling sequence 轮询序列
polling system 轮询系统
polling technique 轮询技术
polling train 轮询连列表
pollutant 污染物
pollution 污染
pollution control terminal 污染控制终端机
poly-cell approach 多单元法
poly line 折线
poly-processor system 多处理机系统
polyadic operator 多重目算符
polyalphabetic cipher 多表置换密码
polyautomata 多自动机
polybinary coding 多级二进制编码
polybipolar coding 多级双极性编码
polybox 多框
polycell approach 多单元法
polycode 复码
polycomputer 多计算机,聚合计算机
polycrystal 多晶体
polycrystalline 多晶的
polycrystalling silicon device 多晶硅器件
polycrystalline structure 多晶结构
polyester 聚酯
polygamma function 多γ函数
polygon 多边形
polygon clipping 多边形裁剪
polygon fill 多边形填充
polygon mesh 多边形网孔
polygon overlay 多边形叠置
polygon pushing 多边形缩放法

polygon rasterization 多边形光栅化
polygon rendering 多边形着色
polygon tessellation 多边形镶嵌
polygonal curve 多角曲线
polygonal cylinder 多边柱体
polygonal domain 多角形域 「法
polygonal representation 多边形表示
polygonizaation 多边形化,多角形化
polygonous 多边形的,多角的
polygram 多字母
polyhedra 多面体
polyhedra region 多面体区域
polyhedral convex set 多面凸集 「策
polyhedral game 多面博弈,多面体对
polyhedron recognition 多面体识别
polylaminate 多层
polyline 折线;多叉线
polyline intersection 多线相交
polymarker 多点标记
polymer 聚合物,聚合体
polymer theology 聚合物流变学
polymeric thermoforming process 聚合物热成形工艺
polymorphic 多态的,多形的
polymorphic code 多形码
polymorphic database system 多形数据库系统
polymorphic programming language 多形编程语言
polymorphic system 多态[多形]系统
polymorphism 同式多型;多态性,多形性
polynazy 多元
polynomial 多项式
polynomial algorithm 多项式算法
polynomial code 多项式代码
polynomial complexity 多项式复杂性
polynomial cyclic code 多项式循环码
polynomial deflation 多项式降阶
polynomial equation 多项式方程 「法
polynomial extrapolation 多项式外插
polynomial factorization 多项式因式分解
polynomial function 多项式函数
polynomial generation 多项式产生
polynomial hashing 多项式散列 「法
polynomial interpolation 多项式内插
polynomial interpolating function 多

项式插值函数
polynomial interpolation 多项式插值
polynomial item algorithm 多项式时间复杂性的算法
polynomial of local best approximation 局部最佳逼近多项式
polynomial ring 多项式环
polynomial space 多项式空间
polynomial splines 多项式样条
polynomial time 多项式时间
polynomial-time algorithm 多项式时间算法
polynomial-time complex 多项式时间复杂性
polynomial-time isomorphism 多项式时间同构
polynomial-time reduction 多项式时间归约
polynomial-time simulation 多项式时间模拟
polynomial transformation 多项式变换
polynomial transformation cipher 多项式密码
polynomially equivalent problem 多项式等价问题
polyphase 多相
polyphase merging 多相合并(排序)
polyphase microinstruction 多相微指令,多步微指令
polyphase modulation 多相调制
polyphase processor 聚合处理机,多相处理机
polyphase sort 多相排序
polyphase merging sort 多相归并分类
polyphony 多音调合成
polyprocessor 聚合处理机
polysemy 多义性
polysilicon 多晶硅
polytope 多面体;可剖分空间
polyvalence 多价
polyvalent 多价的
polyvalent notation 多价表示法
polyvalent number 多价数
Polyvision Polyvision 显示器
POM(Persistent Object Manager) 永久对象管理程序
POMI(PhOtochromic Micro Image) 光致变色缩微图像

pool 池,缓冲池
pool dictionary 组合库
pool of processor 处理机池,共用处理机群组
pool of queue 共用队列区
pool of resource 资源池,共用资源
pool of task 任务池
pool queue 池队列,后备队列
pool size 池容量
pooled addresses 地址池
pooled buffer 共用缓冲器组
pooled-sample statistics 合并样本统计
pooling function 共用功能,合并功能
poor conductor 不良导体
POP(Parallel Output Platform) 并行输出平台
POP(Post Office Protocol) 邮局协议
pop 上托,退栈,弹出
POP-2 POP-2 语言
POP3 (Post Office Protocol 3)(TCP/IP)邮局协议 3
POP-11(Package for Online Programming) POP-11 语言
pop instruction 弹出[上托]指令
pop operation 上托[弹出]操作
pop-up 上托,弹出
pop-up menu 弹出菜单
pop-up program 弹出程序
pop-up window 弹出窗口
popout heading 弹出标题
popular 普及的,流行的
popular mesh generator 通用网格生成器
populate 总装
population 总体,全体
population equilibrium 总体平衡
population mean 总体均值
population model 群体模型
population moment 总体矩
population parameter space 总体参数空间
population variance 总体方差
popup definition 弹出式定义
popup text 弹出文本
popup translation 弹出式翻译
popup utility 弹出实用程序
popup window 弹出型窗口
pore 毛孔,气孔,微孔

poroelasticity 多孔弹性
porosity 多孔性
porous 多孔的
porous ceramics 多孔陶瓷
porous material 多孔材料
porous medium 多孔介质[媒体]
port 端口;移植
port access 端口存取
port address 端口地址
port conflict 端口冲突
port-contention unit 端口争用部件
port conflict 端口冲突
port controller 端口控制器
port density 端口密度
port-driven subsystem 端口驱动子系统
port expander 端口扩充部件
port grouping 端口成组
port interconnection 端口互连
port level manager 端口级管理程序
port monitor 端口监视器;端口监督程序
port multiplier 端口多路器
port name 端口名
port operation instruction 端口操作指令
port pins 端口引线
port protection device 端口保护设备
port selector 端口选择器
port sharing 端口共享
port sharing unit(PSU) 端口共享单元
port speed(PSU) 端口速度
port trunking (交换机)端口中继
port width 端口宽度
portability 可移植性
portability of program 程序移植性
portability-prediction and correction 可移植性预测与修正
portable 便携式的;可移植的
portable application software 可移植的应用软件
portable audio terminal 便携式声频终端
portable bar-code decoder 便携式条码解码器
portable command language 可移植命令语言
portable common tools environment (PCTE) 可移植通用工具环境
portable compiler 可移植的编译器

portable computer 便携式计算机
portable computer system 便携式计算机系统
portable data acquisition system 便携式数据采集系统
portable data terminal 便携式数据终端
portable debugger 可移植的调试程序
portable dictation machine 便携式口述记录机
portable disk pack 可拆卸磁盘组
portable document 可移植文档
portable document software 可移植文档软件
portable duress sensor 便携式强迫传感器
portable language 可移植语言
portable native-code package 可移植本机码程序包
Portable NetWare 可移植 NetWare 操作系统
portable operating system 可移植操作系统
portable operating system interface UNIX(POSIX) 可移植 UNIX 操作系统接口
portable program 可移植程序
portable PROM programmer 便携式 PROM 编程器
portable standard LISP(PSL) 可移植标准 LISP 语言
portable syntax 可移植语法
portable system organization 简便式系统结构
portable telephone set 便携式电话机
portable terminal 便携式终端
portable test chip 可移植测试芯片
portable toolbox (屏幕上)可移动工具箱
portable typewriter 便携式打字机
portal 网络门户
portal site 入口站点
portfolio 文件包,证券
portmapper 端口分配程序
portrait 肖像;立式结构的
portrait mode 肖像模式,竖式
portrait monitor 直立式监视器
portrait orientation 肖像式定向,竖式定向

portrait page 纵向页面
portrait sample 纵向(版面)示例
portrayal 描绘
portrayer 描绘词
POS(Point Of Sale terminal) 销售点终端
POS(Primary Operating System) 主操作系统
POS central controller 销售点中央控制器
POS system 销售点系统
POS terminal 销售点终端
pose 姿势,姿态
pose recovery 姿势恢复,姿态校正
poset 半序集
posinomial 正项式
posinomial program 正几何规划
posiode 正温度系数二极管
posistor 正温度系数热敏电阻
posit 假定;布置
posit-else logical structure 假定-否定逻辑结构
position 部位,位置
position analog unit 位置模拟设备
position code 位置代码
position contouring system 位置轮廓控制系统
position control 位置控制
position control system 位置控制系统
position coordinate 位置坐标
position-dependent code 非独立位置代码
position error 位置误差
position feedback 位置反馈
position field descriptor 位置字段描述符
position holding 位置保持 「码
position-independent code 地址无关代
position indicator 位置指示器
position information 位置信息
position invariant 位置不变的
position mark 位置标志
position pulse(P-PULSE) 位置脉冲
position read out 位置读出
position sensor 位置传感器
position sign 符号位置
position storage 位置存储器
position telemeter 位置遥测仪

position transducer 位置变换器
position transparency 位置透明
position value 位置值
position variant 位置可变的
position vector 位置向量
positional code 位置码
positional format 位置格式
positional light 定位光 「差
positional limitation tolerance 限位容
positional notation(PN) 位置记数法
positional number 位置计数
positional operand 定位操作数
positional parameter 定位参数,位置参数
positional representation 位置表示法
positional representation system 按位计数制
positioner 定位器
positioning 定位
positioning accuracy 定位精度
positioning action 定位作用
positioning board 定位板
positioning control 定位控制
positioning device 定位设备
positioning time 定位时间
positive 正向的;肯定的;正片
positive acknowledge 肯定应答
positive acknowledgement 肯定应答
positive acknowledgement with retransmission(PAR) 重发式肯定应答
positive AND gate 正"与"门
positive automata network 正向自动机网络
positive bias 正偏置
positive booster 升压器
positive carrier 正电荷载流子,空穴
positive charge 正电荷
positive clause 正子句
positive closure 正闭包
positive control 正向控制
positive controllability 正向可控制性
positive definite 正定的 「积
positive definite inner product 正定内
positive definite integral form 正定积分型
positive definite kernel 正定核
positive definite matrix 正定矩阵
positive definite operator 正定算子

positive definite quadratic form 正定二次型
positive direction 正方向
positive distortion 正畸变
positive divisor 正除数,正因子
positive electricity 正电
positive electrode 正电极,阳极
positive example 正例
positive exponent 正阶码
positive extendibility 正向可伸展性
positive feedback 正反馈
positive film 正片
positive frequency deviation 正向频移
positive-going noise 正向噪声
positive-going signal 正向信号
positive-going zero crossover 正向过零点
positive hole 正性空穴
positive image 正像
positive indication tone 肯定指示音
positive integer 正整数
positive ion 正离子
positive justification 正调整
positive logic 正逻辑
positive mask 肯定词
positive modulation 正调制
positive negative controller 正负控制器
positive nonzero integer 正非零整数
positive number 正数
positive OR gate 正"或"门
positive output 正输出
positive poll response 肯定查询响应
positive pressure filtration system 正压空气过滤系统
positive pulse 正脉冲
positive pulse stuffing 正脉冲填充
positive real matrix 正实矩阵
positive response 肯定回答
positive semidefinite matrix 正半定矩阵
positive sign 正号
positive stuffing 正向速度匹配
positive temperature coefficient 正温度系数
positive temperature coefficient ceramic (PTC) 正温度系数电子陶瓷
positive value 正值
positive vector 正向量
positive zero 正零

positron 正电子
POSIX(Portable Operating System Interface UNIX) 可移植 Unix 操作系统接口(IEEE)
POSIX standard 可移植 Unix 操作系统接口标准
possibilistic relational model 可能性关系模型
possibility 可能性,概率
possibility of trouble 故障率,事故率
possible-world semantics 可能范围语义学
POST(Point Of Sale Terminal) 销售点终端
POST(Power-On Self Test) 通电自检
post 录制,登记
post-analysis 事后分析
post assembly stage 装后阶段
post billing system 货到开单制
post code 后置代码
Post computability 波斯特可计算性
post-condition 后置条件,后续条件
post-coordinate index 后协合索引,后组式索引
post-coordination 后组式
post-coordination information retrieval language 后组信息检索语言
Post correspondence problem 波斯特对应问题
post-decrementing 后减量
post-detection combiner 检波后合成器
post-development review 开发后评议
post-dial terminal screen 拨号后终端画面
post document 邮送文档
post-edit programs 算后编辑程序
post editing 事后编辑
post equalization 后均衡
post-fault equilibrium 故障后平衡
post fix notation 后置记法,后缀表示
Post generable set 波斯特生成集
post-implementation review 实现后评议
post increment 算后增量
post-indexed 后指针
post-indexing operation 后变址操作
post-installation review 装后复查
post layout simulation 布设后模拟
Post machine 波斯特机器

post macro 算后宏
post-mortem(PM) 事后剖析
post-mortem dump(DMP) 算后析误转储
post-mortem program 算后检查程序
post mortem routine(PMR) 事后析误例程
post normalize 后规范化
post office box 邮政信箱
Post Office Protocol(POP) 邮局协议
post-peak structural behavior 后顶点结构特性
post-processing 后处理
post processor 后端处理程序;后端处理机
Post production 波斯特产生式
Post production system 波斯特产生式系统
Post program 波斯特程序
post script 后记,附言,附录
post set 后置集
post-set time 退出时间,撤退时间
Post system 波斯特系统
Post Telephone and Telegraph Administration 邮电管理局
post-transfer-loop processing 传送后环路处理
Post-Turing computability 波斯特-图灵机可计算性
Post-Turing computable function 波斯特-图灵机可算函数
Post-Turing computation 波斯特-图灵机计算
Post-Turing machine 波斯特-图灵机
Post-Turing program 波斯特-图灵机程序
Post-Turing tape 波斯特-图灵机带
post write disturbed pulse 写后干扰脉冲
postage 邮费,邮资
postage stamp problem 邮票问题
postal 邮政的
postal address reader-indexer system 邮政地址读出-索引系统
postal card 明信片
postal code 邮政编码
postal network 邮政网络
postal OCR 邮政光学字符识别
postal service 邮政业务
postamble 后同步信号
postamble block 后文块
postbyte 后字节
postcard 明信片
postcondition 后置条件
postconnect complete 后段连接完成
postedit 事后编辑,算后编辑
postedit program 算后编辑程序
posterior 后验的,后端的
posterior density 后验密度
posterior detection function 后验检测函数
posterior distribution 后验分布
posterior error bound 后验误差界限
posterior estimate 后验估计
posterior odds processing 事后成败机会处理法
posterior probability 后验概率
posteriori 后验的,凭经验的
posteriori error estimation 后验错误估计
posteriority 后置状态,滞后性
postfilter 后过滤器
postfax apparatus 信函传真机
postfix 后缀;词尾
postfix decrement operator （C语言）后缀减1运算符(－)
postfix-expression （C语言）后缀表达式
postfix form 后缀形式
postfix increment operator （C语言）后缀加1运算符(＋＋)
postfix notation 后缀表示法
postfix operator 后置算子,后缀算符
postfix Polish notation 后缀波兰表示
postfix translation 后缀转换法
postfixed point 后定点
postindexing 后变址
posting 贴出,显出,记入
posting date 投送日期
posting field 记录区域
posting machine 信函分检机
postlude 尾序部
postmaster 邮政管理器;邮政管理员
postmortem and diagnostic processor 算后检查与诊断处理程序
postmortem dump 事后析误转储
postmultiplication 自右乘运算
postmultiply 后乘,自右乘

postnormalization 后规范化,后规格
postnormalize 后规范化 匚化
postoffice 邮局
Postoffice Network List 邮局网络列表(微软)
postoptimality analysis 优化后分析
postoptimality problem 优化后问题
postorder 后根次序
postorder traverse 后序遍历
postpone 延期,推迟
postponed-jump technique 推迟转移技术
postponed result 延期结果
postposition 后置
postprior degradation modeling 后验退化建模
postprocess 后置处理
postprocessor 后处理程序,后处理机
postproduction 后期制作
postprogram 算后程序
postread 后读出;读出之后
postrun 后运行;运行之后
PostScript 页面描述语言
PostScript character operation instruction 页面描述语言字符操作指令
PostScript clip instruction 页面描述语言裁剪指令
PostScript color space PS 彩色空间
PostScript devices independence 页面描述语言的设备无关性
PostScript filter PS 语言过滤器
PostScript font library PS 字库
PostScript form 页面描述语言图案
PostScript image 页面描述语言图像
PostScript image model PS 成像模型
PostScript interpreter 页面描述语言解释程序
PostScript language 页面描述语言, PS 语言
PostScript laser printer PostScript 激光打印机 匚版
PostScript Level 1 页面描述语言第一
PostScript Level 2 页面描述语言第二版
PostScript path instruction 页面描述语言路径指令 匚机
PostScript printer 页面描述语言打印
PostScript program structure 页面描述语言程序结构
postset 后置集合
postulate 假设,假定
postulated threat 假定威胁
postulational method 假设法
postural control 姿势控制
posture 倾斜;姿态
postwrite 写入口
POT(Picture Object Table) 图片对象表
pot (数据)保留区
potential 电势,电位
potential barrier 势垒
potential difference 电位差
potential distribution 电位分布
potential-divider network 分压网络
potential drop 电压降
potential energy 位能,势能
potential fall 电位降
potential flow method 位流法
potential function 势函数,位函数
potential gradient 电位梯度
potential risk 潜在危险
potential solution tree 期望解树
potential user 潜在用户
potentiometer 电位器
POTS(Plain Old Telephone Service) 普通老式电话业务
potted package 浇灌封装
potting 灌注
pound 磅
pouring tool 泼墨工具
powder 粉末
powder pressed core 粉末压制磁芯
POWER (Performance Optimization with Enhanced RISC) 性能优化的增强型精简指令集芯片(IBM、Apple、Motorola)
POWER POWER 程序
power(F) 乘力,幂,功率
power adapter 电源适配器
power amplifier 功率放大器
power balancing 功率平衡
power board 配电板
power box 电源箱
power bus 电源总线
power cable 电力电缆
Power Challenge Power Challenge 超

级计算服务器(SGI)
power circuit breaker 电力断路器
power conditioner 电源调节器
power consumption 功率损耗
power control microcode 电源控制微码
power cord 粗电源线
power curve 功率曲线
power cut 断电
power cycling 周期性供电
power-delay product 功率时延乘积
power density 功率密度
power density spectrum 功率密度谱
power device packaging 功率器件封装
power dissipation 功率损耗,耗
power distribution unit 配电设备
power down 电源关闭,掉电
power down control 掉电控制
power down stand-by 掉电备用设备
power dump 停电,掉电
power engineering 电力工程
power exponent 幂指数
power factor 功率因数
power-fail 电源失效[故障]
power-fail and automatic restart 掉电并自动再起动
power-fail auto-restart capability 电源故障自动恢复能力
power-fail circuit 掉电处理电路
power-fail interrupt 电力不足中断
power-fail interrupt/auto-restart 电源故障中断/自动重新起动
power fail logic 掉电逻辑
power failure detection 电源故障检测
power failure interrupt 掉电中断
power-fall circuit 电源跌落电路
power frame 电源机架
power frequency deviation 电源频率偏移
power function 幂函数
power gain 功率增益
power generation system 发电系统
power ground 电源地
power group enumeration theorem 幂群计数定理
power hungry 功耗较大的
power hybrid 功率混合微电路
power indicator 电源指示器(灯)
power inteference filter 电源干扰滤波器
power level 功率电平
power leveling 功率电平调节
power line 电源线,电力线
power-line carrier 电力线载波
power line carrier communication system 电力线载波通信系统
power line interference 电力线干扰
power loss 功率损失
Power Mac 基于PowerPC的麦金塔计算机(苹果)
power management 电源管理
power management setup 电源管理设置
power model 功率模块
power modulation factor 功率调制因数
power of number 指数
power of relation 关系的幂
power-off 断电
power off condition 断电状态
power-off protection 断电保护
power on 加电,上电
power on hours 加电时数
power-on reset 加电复位
power on self test(POST) 通电自检
Power Open Power Open 操作系统(Unix)
power operation 带电操作
power optimization 功率优化
power output 电源输出,功率输出
power pack 功率单元
power plane (印刷电路板上的)电源层
power plant 发电厂
Power Platform 增强型平台
power rate 功率比
power rating 额定功率
power ratio 功率比
power recovery processing 复电处理
power rectifier 电源整流器
power reduction 功耗减小,节省电力
power requirement 电源需求
power residue method 幂剩余法
power restart 电源再起动
power save on 进入省电状态
power semiconductor 半导体功率器件
power series 幂级数
power series reduction method 幂级数缩减法

power set 幂集
power source 电源
power spectrum 功率谱
power spectrum filter 功率谱过滤器
POWER stations POWER 工作站(IBM)
power status object 电源状态对象
power supply(PS) 电源,供电
power supply ambient temperature 电源环境温度
power supply box 电源箱,配电盒
power supply cabinet 配电柜
power supply circuit 供电线路
power supply connector 电源连接器
power supply control 电源控制
power supply distribution 电源分配
power-supply fluctuation 电源波动
power supply kit 成套电源设备
power supply protection system 电源保护系统
power supply reliability 电源可靠性
power supply security 电源安全性
power supply sensitivity 电源灵敏度
power supply stand-by 电源备用
power supply surge 电源浪涌
power-supply system 电源系统,供电系统
power supply test 电源测试
power supply trace 电源跟踪
power supply unit 供电设备
power surge 电源浪涌
power switch 电源开关
power transistor 功率晶体管
power transmission 送电,输电
power turn-off 断电
power turn-on 加电,电源接通
power unit 发电机组;功率单位
power up 加电
power-up diagnostics 加电诊断
power up reset 加电复位
power user 高级用户
power warning interrupt 电源告警中断
PowerBook Powerbook 笔记本计算机
PowerBuilder Powerbuilder 数据库开发工具(PowerSoft)
PowerChute Plus PowerChute Plus 电源管理软件
powerful 功能强大的

PowerPC Power PC 微处理器(IBM, Apple, Motorola 合作研制)
PowerPoint PowerPoint 简报软件(微软)
PP(Parallel Processor) 并行处理机
PP(Peak to Peak) 峰-峰值
PP(Post Processor) 后处理机
PP(PreProcessor) 预处理机,前处理程序
P2P(Peer to Peer) 个人对个人
PP/in(Pages Per inch) 页/英寸
PPADPCM(Pitch Predictive Adaptive Differential Pulse Code Modulation) 音节预测自适应差动脉冲编码调制
PPC(Parallel Path Counter) 并行通路计数器
PPC(Peak Power Control) 峰值控制
PPC(Peer-to-Peer Communication) 对等通信
PPC(Print Position Counter) 打印位置计数器
PPCU(Parallel Processor Control Unit) 并行处理机控制部件
PPD(Plasma Panel Display) 等离子体平面显示器
PPDL(Point-to-Point Data Link) 点对点数据链路
PPG(Print Pattern Generator) 打印字模发生器
pph(pages per hour) 每小时页数
PPI(Plan Position Indication) 平面位置指示
PPI(Programmable Parallel Interface) 可编程并行接口
PPI(Programmable Peripheral Interface) 可编程外围接口
PPID(Parent Process ID number) 父进程标识号
PPL(Polymorphic Programming Language) 多用途程序设计语言
PPM(Pulse-Position Modulation) 脉冲相位调制
ppm(pages per minute) 每分钟页数
PPP(Point-to-Point Protocol) 点对点协议
PPP authentication 点对点协议认证
PPQA(Pageable Partition Queue Ele-

ment) 可分区页面队列单元
PPR(Photo Plastic Recording) 光塑记录
PPS(Parallel Processing System) 并行处理系统
PPS(Peripheral Processing System) 外围处理系统
PPS(Picture Perception System) 图像感知系统
PPS(Poly-Processor System) 多处理机系统
PPS(Pure Packet Switching) 纯包交换
PPS-R PPS-R计算机
PPSN(Public Packet Switching Network) 公用分组交换网络
PPSS(Public Packet Switching Service) 公用分组交换业务
PPT(Primary Program operator interface Task) 主程序操作员接口任务
PPU(Peripheral Processing Unit) 外围处理部件
PPX(Packet Protocol eXtension) 分组协议扩充
PQA(Protected Queue Area) 受保护队列区
PQDM(Picture Quality Distortion Measurement) 图像质量失真测量
PQE(Partition Queue Element) 分区队列元素
PQFP(Plastic Quad FlatPack) 塑料四列平面封装
PR(Pattern Recognition) 模式识别
PR(Pen Recorder) 笔式记录仪
PR(Physical Record) 物理记录
PR/SM(Processor Resource/Systems Manager) 处理机资源/系统管理器(IBM)
PRA(Packet Routing Address) 包路由选择地址
PRA(Page Replacement Algorithm) 页面替换算法
practibility 实用性,可用性
practical 实用的,可用的
practical computability 实用可计算性
practical computer 实用计算机
practical privacy 物理保密
practical test 实践测试
practical tool kit 实用成套工具
practitioner 实践者,研制人
pragma 杂注,注记;编译指示
pragmatic 语用的;实用的
pragmatic abbreviation rule 语用缩写规则
pragmatic analysis 语用分析
pragmatic reasoning 语用推理
pragmatic remark 语用注记
pragmatics 语用学
pragment 插话
PRAM(Parameter RAM) 参数存储器
PRAM(Pseudo-Random Access Memory) 伪随机存取存储器
PRB(Parameter Request Block) 参数请求块
PRBS(Pseudo-Random Binary Sequence) 伪随机二进制序列码
PRC(Primary Return code) 主返回码
PRC(Program Required Credentials) 程序使用凭证
PRCA(Propotional Rate Control Algorithm) 均衡速率控制算法
PRE(PREfix) 前缀
pre-alarm 预报警
pre-align operation 预对齐操作
pre-assembly time 预编译时间
pre-assignment 预分配
pre-bucking 预变形,预弯曲
pre-cleaning 预清洗
pre-dial terminal screen 拨号前终端屏幕画面
pre-edit 事前编辑,预编辑
pre-edit checking program 预编辑校验程序
pre-edit program 预编辑程序
pre-edit region 预编辑区域
pre-edit window 预编辑窗口
pre-edited interpreter 预编辑解释程序
pre-elaboration 预加工
pre-emphasis 预加重
pre-emphasis network 预加重网络
pre-emptive multitasking 抢占式多任务处理
pre-equalization 预均衡
pre-group 前群
pre-indexing operation 预变址操作
pre-list 预列表

pre-mix 预混合
pre-modulation 预调制
pre-network 预置网络
pre-processing 预处理
pre-programming test 预程序设计检「验
pre-run-time scheduling 预运行时间调度
pre-SNA terminal SNA网络前终端
pre-test analog 预检验模拟
pre-transfer loop processing 传送前循环处理
preallocated buffer 预分配缓冲器
preallocated control block stack 预分配控制块堆栈
preallocation 预分配
preamble 前导码;前同步信号
preamble field 前导码区
preamplification 前置放大
preamplifier 前置放大器
preanalysis 事前分析,预分析
preassembly 预汇编
preassembly time 预汇编时间
preassign 预指定,预分配,预赋值
preassigned multiple access 预分配多路访问
preassigned pattern 预定模式
preassignment 预赋值,预分配
preassignment system 预分配制
prebias 预偏置
prebind module 预结合模块,预联编模块
prebinding 预结合
prebox 前置组件
preburning 预烧,老化
precalculated 预先计算的
precaution 预防
precede 优先,先于
precedence(PREC) 优先顺序
precedence analyzer 优先分析程序
precedence class 优先类
precedence code 前置码,前缀码
precedence constraint 优先约束,优先限制
precedence designation 优先标志
precedence designator 优先标志符
precedence function 优先函数
precedence grammar 优先文法
precedence grammar parser 优先文法分析程序 「图
precedence graph 前趋图,优先次序
precedence language 优先语言
precedence level 先后次序,优先级
precedence matrix 优先矩阵
precedence message 优发信息
precedence method 优先数法
precedence order 优先次序,先后顺序
precedence parsing 优先语法分析
precedence presign 前置字符组,预示信号
precedence relation 优先关系
precedence rule 优先规则
precedence table 优先表
precedence technique 优先技术
precedence type 优先类型
precedent 先前引用的(单元格)
preceding 先前的,前面的
preceding channel 向前接续通道
preceding test step 先前测试步
precharge 预充电
precheck 预校验
precise 精确的,精密的
precise access block diagram 精确存取方框图
precise definition 精确定义
precise explication 精确分析
precise interrupt 精确中断
precise interruption 精确中断
precise report formatting 精确报表格式编排法
precision 精度
precision as displayed 以显示值为准
precision attribute 精度属性
precision comparator 精密比较器
precision device 精密器件
precision display 精度显示
precision evaluation 精度评价
precision gate 精密门电路
precision graph recorder 精密图式记录器
precision hybrids 精密混合微电路
precision instrument 精密仪器
precision iterative operation 精确迭代操作
precision measure 精密测量
precision net 精密网络
precision of format item 格式项精度

precision pattern recognition 精确模式识别
precision plotter 高精度绘图仪
precision processing 精处理
precision ratio 查准率
precision reached 达到的精度 「度
precision/recall measure 查准/检索量
precision resistor 精密电阻
precision rule 精度规则
precision selection 精度选择
precoded form 预编码形式
precompile time 预编译时间
precompiled header file 预编译标头文件
precompiler 预编译程序
precompiler program 预编译程序
precomputed 预计算的
precondition 前置条件；先决条件
precondition analysis 先决条件分析
precondition concept 前置条件概念
precondition of production rule 产生式规则的先决条件
preconditioning 预调节
preconditioning technique 预条件技术
preconfigured system definition 预配置系统定义
precoordinate index 先组式索引
precoordination 先组式
precoordination information retrieval language 先组信息检索语言
precorrection 预校正
precursor chain 前身链
precursor relation 前身关系
predebugging 预调试
predecessor 前趋
predecessor address 先行地址
predecessor block 前趋块
predecessor function 前趋函数
predecessor matrix(PM) 先趋矩阵
predecessor set 前趋集
predefined 预先定义的
predefined data type 预定义数据类型
predefined identifier 预定义标识符
predefined instruction 预定义指令
predefined operation 预定义操作
predefined operator 预定义运算符
predefined process 预定义进程
predelay 预延迟

predeposition 预淀积
predesign 预设计
predesignated user 预定用户
predesigned order 预定次序
predetermined 预置的,预定的
predetermined category 预定范畴
predetermined counter 预置计数器
predetermined value 预定值
Predicasts Data System 预测数据系统
predicate 判定;谓词
predicate-based representation 基于谓词的表示法
predicate calculus 谓词演算
predicate calculus language 谓词演算语言
predicate converter 谓词转换器
predicate function 判定函数
predicate interrupt 可预测中断
predicate language 谓词语言
predicate letter 谓词字母
predicate logic 谓词逻辑
predicate node 判定节点
predicate symbol 谓词符号
predicate transformer 谓词变换式「络
predicate-transition net 谓词转移网
predicate variable 谓词变量
predicate-weakening procedure 谓词弱化过程
predicated 预测的;断定的
predicating 断定
predication 判断,预测,推算
predicted encoding 预测编码
predicted interrupt 可预测中断
predicted method 预测法
predicted picture 预测图像,P图像
predicted value 预报值
predicting machine 预测机
prediction 预测
predictive analysis 预测分析
predictive coding 预测编码
predictive control 预测控制
predictive distribution 预测分布
predictive encoding 预测编码
predictive recognizer 预测识别算法
predictively valid 预测有效 「器
predictor 预测程序;预示变量;预测
predictor-corrector method 预测校正
predictor formula 预示公式 「法

predifined specification 预定义说明
predigestion of data 数据预加工
predistortion 预失真
preedit 预编辑
preedit check program 预编辑校验程
preedit checking program 预编辑校验程序
preediting 译前编辑
preelaboration 预加工
preemergency 应急备份
preemptible page 可抢占页面
preemptible program 可抢占程序
preemption 抢先
preemption dispatching policy 抢先调度策略
preemption service 预占式服务
preemptive 占先式,抢先式
preemptive algorithm 抢先算法
preemptive multitasking 抢先式多任务处理
preemptive priority 抢先优先权
preemptive scheduling 抢先调度
preemptive scheduling strategy 抢先调度策略
preexecution-time table 预执行时间表
preexecution-time table or array 预先执行时间表或阵列
PREF(PREFix) 前置,前缀
prefabricate 预制
preface 前言,序言
prefeasibility study 初步可行性研究
preferability condition 更可取的条件
preference 首选项;优先选择项;偏好
preference chain 优选链
preference curve 优选曲线
preference judgement 优选判断
preference pattern 首选模式
preference preordering 偏好预序关系
preference relation 偏好关系
preference reversal 偏好逆转
preference semantics 优先语义学
preference substitute 偏好互换
preferential 优先的
preferential deduction 优先演绎
preferential model 优先模型
preferential relation 择优关系
preferred 优先选择的,更合适的
preferred character set 首选字符集

preferred order 优选次序
preferred plan 优选方案
preferred server 更喜欢使用的服务器
preferred term 优先选择项
preferred virtual machine 优选虚计算机
prefetch 预取指令
prefetch microinstruction 预取微指令
prefetched operand 预取操作数
prefilter 前置滤波器
prefiltering 前置过滤,前置筛选
prefire 预烧,预点火
prefix 前置,前缀
prefix area 前缀区
prefix block 字组前缀,块前缀
prefix calculation 前束范式计算
prefix character 前缀字符
prefix closure 前缀闭包
prefix condition code 前置条件码
prefix decrement operator （C语言)前缀减1运算符
prefix detection problem 前缀检测问题
prefix expression 前缀表达式
prefix form 前缀式
prefix increment operator （C语言)前缀加1运算符
prefix label 前置标号
prefix method synchronization 词头法同步
prefix multipliers 倍数前缀[前置]
prefix notation 前缀表示法
prefix operator 前缀运算符
prefix property 前缀性质
prefix register 前缀寄存器
prefix type 前置型,前缀型
prefixed point 前定点
prefixing notation 前缀表示法
preflow 预选流
preformat 预格式化
preformatting 预格式化
preformed 预成型的,预制成的
pregenerated operating system 预生成操作系统
preheating 预热
preheating time 预热时间
preimplication routine 预蕴含例程
preindexing 前置索引
preindication 预指示
prejudge 预判断

preliminary 预备性的,初步的
preliminary analysis 初步分析
preliminary data 初始数据
preliminary definition 预先[大致]定义
preliminary design 概要[初步]设计
preliminary proposal review 预先建议检查
preliminary reading 预先读出
preliminary review 预审查
preliminary view 预览
preliminary write 预写入
preload 预加载
preloaded software 预装软件
preloaded table 预装入表
prelogical 预置逻辑的
prelude (程序)首部;序言
premastering 光盘(原版)预烧录
prematrix 前置矩阵
premise 前提
premise-conclusion pair 前提-结论对
premise-free 无前提的
premix 预混合
premodification 预修改
premodulation 预调制
premultiplication 自左乘
premultiply 自左乘
prenex-conjunctive normal form 前束合取范式
prenex-disjunctive normal form 前束析取范式
prenex form 前束形
prenex-normal form 前束范式
prenormalization 预规格化
prenormalize 预标称化
preoperation 试运行,空转
preorder 先根次序;前序
preorder thread 前序线索
preorder traverse 前序遍历
preout 前输出
prepaging 预约式页面调度
Preparata's enumeration sorting 普瑞珀塔枚举排序
preparation 预备,准备
preparation operating 预准备操作
preparatory function 预置功能
preparatory period 准备周期
prepare 制备,配制
prepare for publishing 准备发布

prepattern 预置模式
prepattern template matching 预置模式样板匹配
prepause 预暂停
preplaced line 预置线
preplanned allocation 预先计划分配
preplanned search 预先计划的搜索
preplanning 预先计划
preplay communication 预演通信
preposition group case 介词组格
prepotent 优势符号
prepress 预编辑
preprint 印前的
preprocess 预处理[加工]
preprocessed display 预处理显示
preprocessed text 预处理正文
preprocessing 预处理
preprocessing high-speed memory 预处理高速存储器
preprocessor(PP) 预处理程序,预处理器
preprocessor capabilities 预处理机功能
preprocessor procedure 预处理器程序
preprocessor statement 预处理程序语句
preprocessor time 预处理程序执行时间
preprocessor variable 预处理程序变量
preproduction 试制
preproduction prototype 生产样机[原型]
preprogrammed-control 预编程控制
preprogrammed robot 预编程机器人
preprogramming 预编程序
preread head 预读头
prerecorded data medium 预记录数据媒体
prerecorded form 预记录形式
prerecorded tracks 预记录轨道
prereduction 预精简,预简化
prerelease version 预发行版本
prerequisite 先决条件
prerequisite application 预备应用程序
prerequisite class 预备类
prerequisite list 先决条件表
prerequisite relationship 先决关系

preroll 预处理
prerun-time array 运行前数组
prerun-time table 运行前表
prescalar 预定标器
prescheduled algorithm 预调度算法
prescheme 预模式,预定方案
prescript 规定,指定,命令
prescriptive decision model 指示性决策模型
preselection 预选
preselector 预选器
presence 存在,出现
presence bit 存在位
presence detector 存在传感器
present 在场,存在;表示
present age computers 当代计算机
present page address 当前页地址
present position (对象)当前位置
present standard background system 现行标准后台系统
present status 现行[当前]状态
present value 当前值,现值
present value saving 现值即存原则
presentable binary counter 可预置值二进制计数器
presentation 显示,表达,呈现;演示文稿
presentation class 提示种类
presentation context 表示上下文
presentation control function 显示控制功能
presentation device for program 节目显现方式
presentation data 表示性数据
presentation format 表示格式
presentation function 表示功能
presentation graphics 演示图形
presentation graphics program 简报图形软件
presentation graphics routine 图形演示例程
presentation image 演示图像
presentation integration 表述集成
presentation layer 表示层
Presentation Manager 表示管理软件 (IBM)
presentation medium 呈现媒体,表示介质
presentation of monoid 类群表示

presentation protocol 表示协议
presentation renewal controls 显现更新控制
presentation service 表示服务
presentation space 表示空间
presenting 表示
preservation relation 保存关系
preserve 保存,保留
preserve convex fitting 保凸拟合
preserve directory 保存目录
preserve file attributes 保存文件属性
preserved context index system 保留上下文索引系统
preset 预置
preset automatic equalizer 预置式自动均衡器
preset checking experiment 预置检查实验
preset code 预置码
preset counter 预置计数器
preset destination mode 预置目标方式
preset experiment 预置试验
preset input line 预置输入行
preset mode 预设模式
preset parameter 预置参数
preset time 预置时间,提前时间
preset tool 预置工具
presettable I/O 可预置输入/输出
presettable I/O conditions 可预设的输入/输出条件
presetting 预置
presetting bit 预置位
preshaping 预先成形
presort 预排序,预分类
presorted list 预排序表
press bond 压力接合,压焊
press button 按钮开关
press ESC to exit 按 ESC 键退出
press key 按键
press proof 预排清样
press release 通信稿
press telegrams 新闻电报
pressure balancing 压力平衡
pressure contact 压力接触
pressure control 压力控制
pressure correction 压力校正
pressure divergence 压力偏差
pressure drop 压降

pressure fixing 加压定影
pressure head 压力头
pressure roller 压辊
pressure sensing pen 压力传感笔
pressure-sensitive 压力敏感的,压敏
pressure-sensitive paper 压敏纸
pressure-stencil 压模「版
pressure-type spirit master 加压型原
pressure welding 压接,压焊
prestaging 预登台
prestart job 预启动作用
PRESTEL 公用可视数据业务(英)
prestore 预存储
prestored microprogram 预存微程序
prestored query 预存询问
prestress design 预应力设计
prestudy 预研
presubscript 前下标
presumption 假设,想象
presumptive address 假定地址,基准地址
presumptive instruction 假定指令,原始指令
presuperscript 前上标
presupposition 预设;前提,先决条件
pretest preparation 预检验准备
pretranslation 预翻译
pretty print 整齐打印
prevailing 流行的,占优势的
prevalue 预置值
prevarication 不相关性,弥散度
prevent 预防「除
prevent automatic erase 防止自动擦
prevent of deadlock 死锁预防
preventable 可预防的
prevention of cycling 循环防止
preventive 预防性的
preventive action 预防性措施
preventive maintenance 预防性维护
preventive maintenance contracts 预防性维护合同
preventive service 预防性服务
preview 预览
preview picture 预览图片
preview switcher 预览切换器
preview table 预览表
preview zoom tool 预览缩放工具
previous 先前的,以前的,原先的

previous carry 前位进位
previous cell 前一单元格
previous column 前一列
previous environment 原先的环境
previous input state 先前输入态
previous output state 先前输出态
previous record 前记录
previous screen 上一屏幕,前页画面
previous tip 上一提示
previous version 先前的版本
previously-definited statement 原先定义的语句
previously fixed error 原先存在的固定错误
previously stored file 原先存储的文件
prewire 预连线
prewired instruction 预配指令
prewired options 预配选件
prewired program 预配程序
Prewitl mask Prewitl 掩模
prewrite compensation 写前补偿
PRF(Permanent Requirement File) 固定需求文件
PRI(Primary Rate Interface) (ISDN)基群速率接口
PRI(PRIority) 优先权,优先级
price marking 标价
pricompiler 预编译程序
primal 最初的,原始的;主要的
primal algorithm 原始算法
primal dual simplex method 原对偶单纯形法
primal environment 原始环境
primal linear programming 原始线性规划
primal map 原图「的
primary 主站;初等量;基本的,最初
primary account number 主账号
primary accumulator 主累加器
primary address code 原址代码
primary algorithm 初等算法
primary application 主站应用
primary arithmetic 算术初等项
primary attribute 主属性
primary axis 主坐标轴
primary block 基群,一次群
primary bus 主总线
primary cache 一级高速缓存

primary channel 基本通道
primary circuit 一次电路
primary cluster 一次簇
primary coating 一次涂层
primary code modulation 原代码调制
primary colors 原色
primary color signal 基色信号
primary communication attachment 基本通信附加设备支持程序
primary console 主控制台
primary control program(PCP) 主控制程序
primary copy locking 主副本锁定法
primary data 原始数据
primary data set group 基本数据集组
primary data type 基本数据类型
primary decomposition 原始分解,基本分解
primary device 主设备
primary display 一次显示
primary display sequence 主显示序列
primary distribution 原始分布
primary domain controller 主域控制器
primary dump system 基本转储系统
primary electrons 一次电子,原电子
primary element 基本元件
primary emission 一次发射
primary entry point 一次入口点
primary equipment 主设备
primary expression 初等表达式
primary failure 原始失效
primary feedback 主反馈
primary file 原始文件;主文件
primary graph 初等图
primary group 一次群,基群
primary half-session 主对话方
primary IDE interface 主 IDE 接口
primary identity 主标识项
primary impedance 初级阻抗
primary index 主下标,主索引
primary inductance 初级电感
primary information 原信息,一次信息
primary instruction pipeline 主指令流水线
primary key 主密钥,主关键字
primary key encrypting keys 主密钥加密密钥
primary key field 主关键字字段

primary key index 主关键字索引
primary knowledge base 原始知识库
primary leading 原始间距
primary letters 初等字母
primary library 主库
primary link station 主链路站
primary literature 一次文献
primary logical unit(PLU) 主逻辑部件
primary memory 主内存,主存
primary memory space 主内存空间
primary menu 主菜单
primary module 主模块
primary muldex 主复用分路器
primary operand specifier 主操作数说明符
primary operating system 主操作系统
primary operator control station 主作业员控制台
primary output 初级输出
primary paging device 主调页设备
primary partition 初始分区,主分区
primary path 主路径,主通路
primary pattern generator 主模式发生器
primary processing unit 主处理部件
primary program 主程序,基本程序
primary program operator interface task (PPT) 主程序操作员接口任务
primary rate interface(PRI) (ISDN)基群速率接口
primary rate user-network interface 基群速率用户-网络接口
primary record 主记录
primary register set 主寄存器组
primary request 主[初级]请求
primary return code 主返回码
primary route 主选[首选]路由
primary sample 一次取样
primary segment 主段
primary service area 主服务区
primary session 基本会话期
primary side 主面
primary site locking 主节点封锁法
primary space allocation 初始空间分配
primary standard data 原标准数据
primary statement 原命题
primary station 主站

primary storage 主存储器
primary subset 简单子集
primary switching center 初级[主]交换中心
primary system operator privilege class 主系统操作员特许类
primary table 主表
primary task 主任务
primary test board 主测试台
primary-to-secondary flow 主站到次站数据流
primary track 主轨,原磁道
Primary Type Library Header File 主类型库标题文件
primary unit 初等单位
primary user disk 主用户盘
primary vector 主向量
primary volume 主卷,初级卷
primary winding 初级绕组
primary window 主窗口
prime 基本的,主要的,原始的,最初
prime area 基本区域,初始区域
prime attribute 主属性
prime compatible set 本原相容集合
prime compression character 主[基本]压缩字符
prime event generation 主要事件生成
prime factor algorithm 质因子算法
prime factor fast Fourier transform 质因子快速傅里叶变换
prime fault method 主故障法
prime flow table 本原流程表
prime focus 主焦点
prime graph 素图
prime implicant 素项,质蕴含
prime index 主索引
prime information 原[未加工]信息
prime key word 主关键字
prime number 素数
prime phrase deduction 素短语归约
prime polynomial 素多项式
prime record key 主记录键
prime shift 主工作时间
prime singular cube 素奇异立方
prime sort chart 原始分类图
prime superposition 素叠加
primitive 基元;原语
primitive action 基本动作

primitive attribute 图元属性
primitive axiomatic language 原始公理语言
primitive component 原始成分
primitive connection matrix 原始连通矩阵
primitive coordinates 主坐标,本原空间
primitive cube 原始立方
primitive D-cube of failure 故障的原始 D 立方
primitive D-cube of fault 故障的原始 D 立方
primitive data item 基本数据项
primitive decision 基本判定
primitive deduction 本原演绎
primitive digraph 本原有向图
primitive domain 原始域
primitive equations of meteorology 原始气象方程组
primitive event 原始[本原]事件
primitive expression 原始表达式
primitive extraction-embedding parser 原语提取-嵌入式语法分析程序
primitive file 原始文件
primitive flow table 原始流程表
primitive for software interrupt 软件中断原语
primitive index 原始索引
primitive method 原语(描述)法
primitive modeling 图元建模,原始建
primitive name 原名
primitive network 原始网络
primitive object 原始目标;基本对象
primitive operation 基本[原始]作业
primitive polynomial 本原多项式
primitive problem 本原问题
primitive pushdown machine 原始下推(自动)机
primitive recursive function 原始递归函数
primitive recursive predicate 原始递归谓词
primitive resolution 原语分解
primitive root 原根
primitive scheduling 原语调度
primitive statement 原始命题
primitive token 原始令牌
primitive type 原语类型

primitive widget 原始窗口部件
primitives 基元
Prim's algorithm 普锐姆算法
principal 主要的,为主的
principal axis 主轴
principal component 主要分量
principal diagonal 主对角线
principal disjunctive normal form 主析取范式
principal factor method 主因子法
principal frequency 主频率
principal ideal domain 主理想域
principal maintenance period 规定的维护期
principal minor 主子式
principal path sensitization method 主通路敏化法
principal plane 主平面
principal ray 主光线
principal register group 主寄存器组
principal square submatrix 主子方阵
principal type scheme 主类型方案
principal vertex 主顶点
principle 原则,原理
principle of complementary energy 余能原理
principle of conservation 守恒原理
principle of duality 对偶性原理
principle of exclusion 排斥原理
principle of least common mechanism 最少共用机构原则
principle of least privilege 最少权限原则
principle of locality 局部性原则
principle of optimality 最优化原理
principle of secure systems 保密系统原则
principle of superposition 叠加原理
print 打印;显示
print all 全部打印
print area 打印区域
print attribution 打印属性
print barrel 打印滚筒
print bound 打印限界
print buffer 打印缓冲器
print character generator 打印字符发生器
print Chinese character recognition 印刷汉字识别
print choice 打印选择「座
print circuit connector 印刷电路板插
print client 打印客户机
print column 打印栏
print command 打印命令
print contrast ratio 印刷对比度
print control character 打印控制字符
print controller 打印控制器
print crop mark 打印剪裁标志
print cup 打印字形杯
print cycle 打印周期
print data set 打印数据集
print device 打印设备
print document 打印文档
print dump program 打印转储程序
print end 打印结束
print engine 打印机引擎
print envelope 打印信封
print file 打印文件
print format 打印格式
print function 打印函数
print gridlines 打印网格线
print group 打印组
print hammer 打印锤
print head 打印头
print head carriage 打印头滑架
print head driver 打印头驱动器
print image 打印映像;打印图像
print in black and white 以黑白方式打印
print inhibit 禁止打印
print intercept routine 打印截取例程
print interlock time 打印联锁时间
print job 打印作业
print line 打印行
print line length 打印行长度
print mechanism 打印机构
print member 打印构件
print merge 打印合并
print name 打印名称
print on first page 打印在首页上
print only 只能打印「项
print option 打印选择部件;打印任选
print optional data 打印可选数据
print order 打印次序
print out task 印出任务
print page 打印页

print pattern generator 打印字模发生器
print point 打印点
print positions(PP) 打印位置
print preview 打印预览
print quality 打印质量
print queue 打印队列
print range 打印范围
print record 打印记录
print record header 打印记录标题
printer-resident fonts 打印机驻留字体
print restore(PR) 恢复打印
print result type 打印结果类型
print routine 打印例程
print screen 打印屏幕
Print Screen key 打印屏幕键
print sequence number(PSN) 打印序列号
print server 打印机服务器
print setting 打印设置
print span 打印宽度
print speed 打印速度
print spooler 打印机假脱机程序
print spooling program 打印假脱机程序
print statement 打印语句
print station 打印站
print subroutine 打印子例程
print suppression 打印限制
print through 打印穿透
print timing dial 打印定时度盘
print title 打印标题
print to disk 打印到磁盘
print totals only 仅打印总和
print train 打印链
print transparent 透明打印
print using statement 自选格式打印语句
print value 打印值
print wheel 打印轮
print-wheel assembly 打印轮组合件
print wire 打印针
print zone 打印区域
printable area 可打印区
printable character 可打印字符
printable group 可打印栏
printable item 可打印项
PRINTCON 打印配置
printed board 印刷板

printed board assembly 印刷板组件
printed board CAD 印刷电路板计算机辅助设计
printed capacitor 印制电容器
printed character 印出字符
printed chart size 打印图表尺寸
printed circuit(PC) 印刷电路
printed-circuit assembly(PCA) 印刷电路组件
printed circuit backplane 印刷电路底板
printed-circuit board(PCBD) 印刷电路板
printed circuit card 印刷电路插件
printed circuit edge connector 印刷电路板插座
printed component 印刷元件
printed conductor 印制导线
printed contact 印制触点
printed dot 打印点
printed element 印刷元件
printed map 印刷(电路)图
printed matrix wiring 印制矩阵布线
printed text 印刷文本
printed wiring 印制导线
printer(PRN) 打印机
Printer Access Protocol 打印机访问协议
printer buffer 打印机缓冲器
printer busy 打印机忙
printer cable 打印机电缆
printer calculator 打印计算器
printer character set 打印机字符集
printer control language(PCL) 打印机控制语言
printer control logic 打印机控制逻辑
printer controller 打印控制器
printer driver 打印机驱动程序
printer emulation 打印机仿真
printer engine 打印机引擎,打印机芯
printer error 打印机出错
printer file 打印机文件
printer font 打印机字体
printer hammer 打印字锤
printer interface 打印机接口
printer limited 受打印机限制的
printer line 打印行
printer modes 打印机状态
printer operating speed 打印机工作速度

printer plotter 打印绘图机
printer port 打印机端口
printer redirection 打印机重定向
printer server 打印机服务器
printer setup 打印机设置
printer sharing 打印机共享
printer-sharing environment 打印机共享环境
printer skipping 打印机跳越
printer slew control 打印机跑纸控制
printer spacing chart 打印机空白表
printer speed 打印机速率
printer spooler 打印假脱机程序
printer terminal 打印机终端
printer terminal component 打印机终端组件
printer terminal interface 打印机终端接口
printf function (C语言)格式输出函数
printing 印刷,打印
printing calculator 打印计算器
printing data protection 打印数据保护
printing hammer 打印锤
printing head 打印头
printing key 打印键
printing method 打印方法
printing options 打印选项
printout 打印输出
prior 先前的,先验的,预先进行的
prior degradation modeling 先验退化建模
prior density 先验密度
prior error bound 预先估计误差界限
prior estimate 预先估计
prior information 先验信息
prior model 先验模型
prior probability 先验概率
priorable 可优先的
prioritization 列入优先地位
prioritize 优先化,列入优先
prioritized bus controller 优先化总线控制器
prioritized interrupt 优先中断
prioritized list 优先表
prioritized order 优先序
prioritized vector 优先向量
priority 优先权,优先级,优先数
priority adjustment 优先权调整
priority-arbitration circuit 优先权仲裁电路
priority bit 优先位
priority built-in function 内建优先权函数
priority chain 优先权链
priority change 优先权变更
priority check 优先权校验
priority circuits 优先权电路
priority communication multiplexer 优先权通信多路转换器
priority control sequence 优先控制顺序
priority control unit 优先权控制单元
priority declaration 优先权说明
priority definition 优先权定义
priority discipline 优先规定
priority encoding 优先编码
priority error dump 优先错误转储
priority facility 优先设施
priority field 优先权字段
priority indication 优先权指示
priority indicators 优先指示器
priority inheritance 优先权继承性
priority interrupt 优先中断
priority interrupt channel 优先中断通道
priority interrupt control 优先中断控制
priority interrupt control module 优先中断控制模块
priority interrupt control unit(PICU) 优先中断控制单元
priority interrupt controller(PIC) 优先中断控制器
priority interrupt function 优先权中断管理功能
priority interrupt input/output 优先中断输入/输出
priority interrupt level 优先中断级
priority interrupt module 优先中断模块
priority interrupt scheme 优先中断方案
priority interrupt system 优先中断系统
priority interrupt table 优先中断表
priority inversion 优先权反转
priority job 优先作业
priority level 优先级
priority limit 优先限制[界限]

priority list 优先权表
priority lockup 优先权闭锁
priority logic 优先逻辑
priority mode 优先权模式,优先方式
priority multiplexing 优先多路复用
priority number 优先数
priority number scheduling algorithm 优先数调度算法
priority one indication 优先数1指示
priority option 优先权任选
priority or precedence 优先或领先
priority ordered interrupts 优先排序中断
priority orderly interrupt 优先有序中断
priority parameter 优先权参数
priority performance option 优先性能选择项
priority phase 优先阶段
priority PRAM 优先并行随机存取机器
priority processing 优先处理
priority protocol 优先权协议
priority pseudo-variable 优先伪变量
priority query 优先权询问
priority queuing 优先权排队
priority register 优先权寄存器
priority resolver 优先权判决器
priority resolver logic 优先权判决逻辑
priority routine 优先例程
priority rules 优先规则
priority scheduling 优先调度
priority scheme 优先方案
priority selection 优先权选择
priority selection interrupt 优先选择中断
priority sequence 优先顺序[序列]
priority solver logic 优先权分辨逻辑
priority specification 优先权说明
priority structure 优先结构
priority switch 优先权开关
priority symbol 优先符号
priority threshold 优先阈值
priority value 优先值
priority-write strategy 优先写策略
PRISM (Parallel Reduced Instruction Set Multiprocessor) 并行精减指令系统多处理机
privacy 保密性
privacy clearance 保密许可
privacy code 保密码
privacy consideration 保密考虑
privacy key 保密键
privacy lock 保密锁
privacy problem 隐私问题
privacy procedure 保密过程
privacy protection 保密防护
privacy transformation 保密变换
private 专用的,私有的
private address space 专用地址空间
private automatic branch-exchange (PABX) 专用自动交换分机
private automatic exchange 专用自动交换机
private automatic switching system (PASS) 专用自动交换系统
private branch exchange (PBX) 专用交换机
private bus 专用总线
private channel 专用信道
private circuit 专用电路
private class member 私有类成员
private code 专用代码
Private Communication Technology (PCT) 保密通信技术
private data 专用数据
private data communication networks 专用数据通信网
private data network 专用数据网
private dedicated leased line 专门租用线
private dial port 专用拨号端口
private domain 专用区域
Private Enhanced Mail (PEM) 保密增强邮件
Private Eye "专用眼"(头盔式显示器)
private file 私人文件
private folder 私人文件夹
private franking privilege telegrams 私务免费优待电报
private initialization file 个人初始化文件
private key 私有密钥
private leased line 租用线路
private library 专用程序库
private line 专用线
private line arrangement 专线连接
private line characteristic 专用线特征

private line service 专线服务
private-line voice band 专用话音线路
private local memory 专用局部内存
private management domain(PRMD) 专营范围
private memory 专用内存
private network 专用网络
Private Network to Network Interface (PNNI) 专用网间界面
private packet-switching network 专用分组交换网络
private partition 专用分区
private process stack 专用进程堆栈
private queue 专用队列
private read-only memory 专用只读存储器
private relocatable library 专用可重定位程序库
private section 专用段
private semaphore 私有信号量
private storage 专用存储器
private switching network 专用交换网络
private telephone network 专用电话网络
private type 私有类型
private virtual network 专用虚拟网络
private volume 专用卷
privilege 特权,特许
privilege class 特许级
privilege level 特权级别
privilege of access 访问特权
privilege profile 特权提问文件
privileged 特许的
privileged access 特许存取
privileged class 特许级
privileged command 特权命令
privileged data 特权数据
privileged instruction 特权[特许]指令
privileged instruction operation 特权指令操作
privileged instruction simulation 特权指令仿真
privileged mode 特权模式
privileged module 特权模块
privileged operation exception 特权操作异常
privileged process 特权进程

privileged processor state word 特权处理机状态字
privileged profile 特权轮廓
privileged program state 特许程序状态
privileged state 特许状态
privileged task 特权任务
privileged user 特权用户
privity 默契
PRML (Partial Response Maximum Likelihood) 部分响应最大似然 (IBM)
PRN(PRiNter) 打印机
PRN(Pseudo-Random Number) 伪随机数
Pro/Engineer Pro/Engineer 软件
PRO series 预编译程序系列,PRO 系列
probabilistic 概率性的
probabilistic algorithm 概率算法
probabilistic analysis 概率分析
probabilistic approach 概率处理法
probabilistic automaton 概率自动机
probabilistic decoding 概率译码
probabilistic error estimate 概率性误差估计
probabilistic indexing 概率性索引
probabilistic logic 概率逻辑
probabilistic machine 概率机
probabilistic model 概率模型
probabilistic programming 概率规划
probabilistic reasoning 概率推理
probabilistic relaxation 概率松弛法
probabilistic Turing machine(PTM) 概率图灵机
probability 概率;可能性
probability after effect 后效概率
probability analysis 概率分析
probability-analysis compaction 概率分析精简法
probability correlation 概率相关
probability density 概率密度
probability density function 概率密度函数
probability differential 概率微分
probability distribution 概率分布
probability estimation 概率估计
probability function 概率函数
probability integral transformation 概率积分变换法

probability limit 概率极限
probability mass function 概率质量函
probability measure 概率度量
probability model 概率模型
probability of error per digit 每数字错误概率
probability of misclassification 错误分类概率
probability of successful service completion 成功服务完成概率
probability propagation 概率传播
probability proportional sampling 概率比例取样法
probability retrieval model 概率检索模型
probability state variable 概率状态变量
probability theory 概率论
probability vector 概率向量
probable 可能的,概率的
probable deviation 概率偏差
probable error(PE) 概率误差
probe 探针,探头(X.400中指具有消息等级标识但无内容的消息)
probe effect 观测影响
probe points 探针
probe scenario 探测方案
prober 探测器
probing 探测,探示
probit 概率值,概率单位
probit range 概率值范围
probit transformation 概率值变换
probit weighting coefficient 概率值加权系数
problem 问题,题目
problem analysis diagram(PAD) 问题分析图
problem analysis method(PAM) 问题分析法
problem-based abstracting 基于问题的抽象
problem-behavior graph 问题-行为图
problem board 解题板
problem class 问题类
problem complexity 问题复杂性
problem context 问题的前后关系
problem data 问题数据
problem decomposition 问题分解
problem definition 问题定义
problem-dependent description 问题相关说明
problem description 问题说明
problem determination 问题判定
problem determination aid(PDAID) 问题决定辅助软件
problem determination procedure 问题确定步骤
problem diagnosis 问题诊断
problem domain 问题领域
problem file 问题文件
problem folder 问题文件夹
problem formulation 问题形成
problem generator 作业生成器
problem identification code 问题标识码
problem input tape 问题输入带
problem language 问题语言
problem mode 问题模式,目态
problem model 问题模型
problem oriented decision support system 面向问题的决策支持系统
problem-oriented environment 面向问题的环境
problem-oriented language 面向问题的语言
problem output 问题输出
problem program 问题程序
problem reduction 问题归约[分解]
problem reduction approach 问题归约法
problem reformulation 问题重组
problem representation 问题表示
problem scope 问题范围
problem-setup computer 立题计算机
problem size 问题规模,问题大小
problem solution 问题解
problem solver 问题求解程序
problem solving 问题求解
Problem Solving Distributed Database System 问题求解分布式数据库系统
problem solving environment 问题求解环境
problem space 问题空间
problem specification language 问题说明语言
problem state 解题状态,目态
problem statement 问题语句;问题陈述
problem statement analyzer 问题陈述

分析程序
problem throughput 问题吞吐量，问题处理能力
problem time 解题时间
problematic 有问题的，可疑的；未定的
PROC(PROCedure) 过程，，工序
Proc 定制过程
PROC statement 过程语句
procedural 过程性的
procedural abstraction 过程抽象
procedural and exception test 过程异常检查
procedural attachment 过程附加段
procedural block 过程块
procedural call 过程调用
procedural cohesion 过程内聚
procedural command language 过程命令语言
procedural component 过程性成分
procedural control language 过程控制语言
procedural conveyer 过程传送程序
procedural deduction system 过程演绎系统
procedural grammar 过程文法
procedural knowledge 过程性知识
procedural knowledge representation 过程性知识表示
procedural language processing 过程语言处理
procedural markup 过程性置标
procedural model 过程模型
procedural modeling 过程式建模
procedural-oriented design technique 面向过程的设计技术
procedural parameter type 过程参数类型
procedural representation 过程表示
procedural section 过程段
procedural security 过程安全
procedural semantic model 过程语义模型
procedural strength 过程强度
procedural test 过程测试
procedural type 过程类型
procedural versus declarative 过程与说明
proceduralization 过程化

procedure(PROC) 过程
procedure abstraction principle 过程抽象原则
procedure activation 过程激励
procedure analysis 过程分析
procedure block 过程分程序
procedure body 过程体
procedure boundary 过程界
procedure branching statement 过程分支语句
procedure call 过程调用
procedure call information 过程调用信息
procedure call request 过程调用请求
procedure caller 过程调用程序
procedure chart 过程流程图
procedure command 过程命令
procedure communication 过程通信
procedure control 过程控制
procedure data area 过程数据区
procedure declaration 过程说明
procedure definition 过程定义
procedure dependence 过程相关
procedure descriptor 过程描述符
procedure designer 过程设计员
procedure deterministic 过程确定性
procedure division 过程部
procedure entry 过程入口
procedure epilogue 过程结尾
procedure execution 过程执行
procedure exit 过程出口
procedure expression 过程表示
procedure heading 过程导引
procedure identifier 过程标识符
procedure information vector table 过程信息向量表
procedure initialization 过程初始化
procedure input 过程输入
procedure interactive action 过程交互作用法
procedure interface 过程接口
procedure invocation 过程引用
procedure language 过程语言
procedure level 过程级
procedure level transformation 过程级变换
procedure library(PROCLIB) 过程库
procedure linkage 过程链接

procedure lock 过程锁定
procedure member 过程成员
procedure name parameter 过程名参数
procedure narrative 过程叙述
procedure oriented 面向过程的
procedure-oriented language 面向过程的语言
procedure-oriented method 面向过程的方法
procedure pack 过程包
procedure parameter type 过程参数类型
procedure pointer 过程指针
procedure prologue 过程开端
procedure reclamation 过程恢复
procedure recursion level 过程迭代级
procedure reference 过程引用
procedure schema 过程模式
procedure sign 过程符号
procedure start request 过程开始请求
procedure statement 过程语句
procedure step 过程步
procedure structure 过程结构
procedure subprogram 过程子程序
procedure symbol 过程符号
procedure synchronization 过程同步
procedure template tree 过程模式树
procedure value input 过程值输入
procedure value output 过程值输出
proceed 开始,进行
proceed-to-select 进行选择信号
proceed-to-select signal 开始选择信号
proceed-to-send signal 开始发送信号
proceeding 会刊
process 处理,加工;进程,组
process access group(PAG) 进程访问组
process address space 进程地址空间
process algorithmization 进程算法化
process analysis 进程分析
process assembly 过程组合
process assignment 进程分配
process attachment table 进程附加表
process automation 过程自动化
process bound 处理限制的
process box 操作框,处理框
process cancel 进程撤消
process capability 处理[加工]能力
process chart 过程图,流程图,工序图
process check 过程检验
process code 进程码
process communication 进程通信
process context 进程上下文
process context switching 进程关联交换
process control(PC) 进程控制;过程控制
process control analog modules 过程控制模拟模块
process control block(PCB) 进程控制块
process control compiler 过程控制编译器
process control computer 过程控制计算机
process control equipment 过程控制设备
process control language 过程控制语言
process control loop 过程控制环路
process control model 过程控制模型
process control software 过程控制软件
process control special module 过程控制专用模件
process control system 过程控制系统
process controller 过程控制器
process cooperation 进程合作
process cost 加工费用
process creation 进程创建
process definition language 进程定义语言
process description 进程描述
process descriptor 进程描述项
process development 工艺过程研究
process-distinguish stack 进程区分堆栈
process distinguish stack number 进程区分栈号
process dynamic recorder 进程动态记录器
process entry 进程表目
process environment 进程环境
process exception 进程异常
process exclusive 进程互斥
process flow chart 工艺流程图
process functions 过程函数
process gain 处理增益
process generation 进程生成
process header 进程标题
process header slots 进程标题块

process host 进程宿主机
process I/O segment 过程输入/输出段
process ID 进程标识
process identification number(PID) 进程标识号
process image 进程映像
process initiation 进程初启
process input/output channel 过程输入/输出通道
process integration 过程综合
process integrity 进程完整性
process interaction approach 过程交互作用法
process interface system 过程接口系统
process interrupt 进程中断
process interrupt card 过程中断卡
process interrupt signal 过程中断信号
process isolation 进程隔离
process life time 进程生存期
process limited 过程受限的
process-limited sorting 步骤限制排序
process line 加工流水线
process-local working space 进程局部工作空间
process lock 进程锁
process logic 过程逻辑
process loop testing 过程环路测试
process management 进程管理
process map 进程映像
process map controller 处理映像控制程序
process migration 进程迁徙
process mode 处理方式
process model 过程模型
process modeling 工艺模型
process module 处理模块
process monitor system(PMS) 过程监督系统
process multiplexing 进程多路转换
process name 进程名
process naming 进程命名
process number 过程号
process optimization 过程优化
process partition 进程划分
process priority 进程优先权
process privilege 进程特权
process-program entry 进程程序入口
process queue DASD 直接存取存储设备进程队列
process scheduler 进程调度程序
process scheduling 进程调度
process scheduling algorithm 进程调度算法
process simulation 过程仿真
process simulation program 工艺模拟程序
process space 进程空间
process specification 进程说明
process-specific working space 进程专用工作空间
process state 进程状态
process statement 过程语句
process status table 进程状态表
process structure 过程结构
process study 过程研究
process supervisory program 进程管理程序
process switching 进程转换
process synchronization 进程同步
process table 进程表
process text element 过程文本单元
process time 处理时间,过程时间
process to process communication 进程间通信
process to process level communication 进程级通信
process-to-process protocol 进程间协议
process tolerance assignment 进程容限分配
process trace set 过程跟踪设置
process transparency 进程透明
process tree 进程树
process uniformity 处理均匀性
process verification 工艺验证
process virtual memory 过程虚拟存储器
process working space 过程工作空间,进程临时工作存储区
processable scored card 可处理的记分卡
processing 处理,加工
processing and control element(PCE) 处理和控制单元
processing array wafer 处理阵列圆片
processing attribute 处理属性
processing capacity 处理容量,处理能力
processing center 处理中心
processing command 处理命令

processing control 处理控制
processing control parameter 处理控制参数
processing control sequence 处理控制序列
processing cycle 加工周期
processing data rate 数据处理速率
processing duty cycle 处理任务周期
processing element(PE) 处理单元
processing environment 处理环境
processing function 处理功能
processing in memory 内存中处理
processing intent 处理意图
processing interrupt 进程中断
processing item 处理项
processing limit 处理极限
processing list 处理列表
processing load 处理负荷
processing mode 处理模式
processing modularity 处理模件化
processing module 处理模块
processing operation 处理作业
processing paradigm 处理范例
processing program 处理程序
processing ratio 处理比
processing resource 处理资源
processing section 处理部分
processing sequence 处理顺序
processing service 处理业务
processing specification 加工要求
processing speed 处理速度
processing state transition 处理状态转换
processing support 处理支持
processing time 处理时间
processing unit(PU) 处理单元
processor 处理机,处理器
processor address space 处理器地址空间
processor allocation 处理机分配
processor architecture 处理机体系结构
processor array 处理器阵列
processor basic instructions 处理机基本指令
processor-bounded 受处理机限制的
processor bus 处理机总线
processor chip 处理器芯片
processor clock 处理机时钟

processor complex 处理机复合体
processor configuration 处理机配置
processor consistency 处理机一致性
processor control 处理机控制
processor-controlled instrument 处理机控制的仪器
processor controller 处理机控制器
processor-controller application 处理机控制器应用
processor cycle 处理机周期
processor cycle time 处理机周期时间
processor-dependent interrupt 与处理机有关的中断
processor-error interrupt 处理机出错中断
processor evaluation module 处理机评估模块
processor family 处理机系列
processor-independent bus 与处理器无关的总线
processor-independent interrupt 处理机无关中断
processor-independent use access 与处理机无关的用户访问
processor input interface 处理机输入接口
processor input-output channel 处理机输入/输出通道
processor interconnection 处理器互连
processor interconnection pattern 处理器互连模式
processor interface 处理机接口
processor interface module 处理机接口模块
processor interface routine 处理机接口例程
processor interrupt(PINT) 处理机中断
processor interrupt chip 处理机中断芯片
processor interrupt facility 处理机中断设施
processor limited 受处理机限制的
processor link 处理机链接
processor local storage 处理器局部存储器,处理机本地存储器
processor management 处理机管理
processor-memory configuration 处理机-内存配置

processor memory connection 处理机内存连接
processor microcode 处理机微码
processor module(PM) 处理机模块
processor multiplexing mechanism 处理机多路转换机构
processor operation 处理机操作
processor organization 处理机组织
processor output test 处理机输出检测
processor pair 处理器对
processor performance 处理机性能
processor pipeline 处理器流水线
processor register 处理机寄存器
processor scheduling 处理机调度
processor sharing 处理机共享
processor-sharing discipline 处理机共享规则
processor slice 处理机位片
processor stack pointer 处理机堆栈指针
processor state word(PSW) 处理器状态字
processor status longword(PSL) 处理机状态长字
processor status register(PSR) 处理机状态寄存器
processor status word(PSW) 处理机状态字
processor storage 处理机存储器
processor storage relocation 处理机存储器再分配
processor table 处理机表
processor time 处理机时间
processor-time efficiency 处理机时间效率
processor time-optimal solution 处理机时间优化解
processor to processor interconnect network 处理机间的互连网络
processor transfer time 处理机间传送时
processor upgrade 处理器升级
processor utilization 处理器利用率
processor verbs 处理程序动词
processor word cell 处理机字单元
Procomm Procomm 通信程序
Prodigy Information Service Prodigy 信息服务
ProDOS (Professional Disk Operating System) ProDOS 操作系统

produce 产生,发生;制造
producer 生产者;制造厂
producer-consumer problem 生产者-消费者问题
producer robot 加工机器人
producibility 生产能力
product 产品;乘积
product accumulator 乘积累加器
product and support requirements request(PSRR) 产品及支持需求申请
product assurance 产品保证
product catalog 产品目录
product cipher 乘积密码
product code 乘积码
product cost 产品成本;产品价格
product cycle 产品周期
Product data exchange specification (PDES) 产品数据交换规范
product development system 产品开发系统
product interchangeability 产品互换性
product library 产品库
product modeling language 产品建模语言,产品模型化语言
product order 产品订单
product overflow 乘积溢出
product rule 乘积规则
product service 产品服务
product space 乘积空间
product specification 产品说明书
product support 产品支持
product time 乘法运算时间
production(PROD) 产生式;产生程序
production and inventory control system 生产与库存控制系统
production automation 生产自动化
production capacity 生产能力
production control 生产控制
production cycle 生产周期
production database 生产数据库
production information control system (PICS) 生产信息控制系统
production library 产品库
production line 生产线
production master 生产底版
production model 生产模型
production optimization 生产优化[调优]

production order 生产凭单
production poll 生产性(有数据传送)查询
production position 产生式状态
production process control management system 生产过程控制管理系统
production rule 产生式规则
production rule semantic network 产生式规则语义网络
production run 生产性运行
production schedule 生产调度,生产计划安排
production simulation technique 生产仿真技术
production status 生产状态
production system 产生式系统
production system interpreter 产生式系统解释器
production time 生产时间
production tree 产生式树
production turnover 生产交付
productive man year 生产人年
productive metamember 产生式元成员
productive poll 生产性查询
productive set 产生集
productive task 生产性任务
productive time 生产时间
productivity 生产率
productivity improvement and control 生产率改进与控制
productivity measurement model 生产率度量模型
productivity tool 生产率工具
professional 专业(级)的,专业水平的
professional-degree program 专业级程序
professional developer 专业开发工具
professional edition (软件)专业版
professional feeling 专业知识
professional graphic adapter(PGA) 专业级图形适配器
professional graphic display 专业级图形显示器
professional group on electronic computers 电子计算机专业组统
professional office system 专业办公系
professional programmer 专业级程序员

professional publishing system 专业级排版系统
professional responsibility 专业职责
professional workstation 专业级工作站
Professional Write 专用文字处理软件
Professional YAM(Professional Yet another modem) YAM专业通信软件
PROFILE (PROgram overview and FILE) 程序概要和文件
profile 轮廓,剖面图;概要,简图;提问文件;配置文件
profile chart 剖面图
profile data 配置数据
profile device 仿形装置
profile editor 简介表编辑程序
profile-front minimization algorithm 前视轮廓图的最简化算法
profile meter 表面测量仪
profile name 配置文件名
profile packet 配置包,配置分组
profile projector 轮廓投影仪
profile provider 配置文件提供者
profile report 系统简要特征表
profile section (MAPI)配置节
profile subject 剖析主体
profile table (MAPI)配置表
profile tangent 纵向切线
profile terminal 仿形终端
profile testing instrument 轮廓测试仪
profile variable 仿形变量
profiling 造型,成型;作断面图;配置
profitable semi-join 有用的半连接
PROFS(PRofessional OFfice System) 专业办公系统(IBM)
PROG(PROGram) 程序
PROG function PROG函数
PROG variable 程序变量
progeny process 子进程
progmetics 语用学
program(P,PGM) 程序;计划,规划,方案;节目单
program abort 程序异常中止
program access code 程序存取代码
program access key 程序存取键
program activation vector(PAV) 程序激活矢量

program-address counter(PAC) 程序地址计数器
program address error 程序地址错误
program address register 程序地址寄存器
program addressable clock 程序可寻址时钟
program allocation and loading 程序配置与加载
program analysis 程序分析
program analysis method 程序分析方法
program analyst 程序分析员
program analyzer 程序分析器
program animation 程序动画表示
program annotation 程序注释
program architecture 程序结构
program area 程序区
program area block 程序区块
program attention key 程序注意键
program authority 程序权限
program authorization 程序审定
program authorized credentials 程序授权证书
program automatic-controller 自动控制程序
program automatic synthesis 程序自动综合
program behavior 程序功效型
program behavior model 程序功效模
program binder 联编程序
program block 程序块
program body 程序体
program break down 程序细分
program breakpoint 程序断点
program browser 程序浏览器
program buffer 程序缓冲区
program call 程序调用
program card 程序卡
program cartridge 程序盒
program cell 程序单元
program certification 程序认证
program chain 程序链
program chaining 程序链接
program channel 程序通道
program chart 程序框图
program check 程序校验
program check interruption(PCI) 程序校验中断
program checking 程序校验
program checkout 程序检验
program checkout condition 程序校验条件
program clarity 程序清晰性
program comment 程序注释
program communication block(PCB) 程序通信块
program compaction 程序压缩
program compatibility 程序兼容性
program competition multiprogramming 程序竞争式多道程序设计
program compilation 程序编译
program compiler 程序编译器
program compiling 程序编译
program complexity measure 程序复杂性度量
program component 程序成分
program composition 程序编制
program comprehensibility 程序可理解性
program connectivity 程序内连关系,程序连接性
program construction process 程序构造过程
program control 程序控制
program control data 程序控制数据
program control execution 程序控制执行
program control flow 程序控制流
program control flow analysis 程序控制流分析
program control hardware 程序控制硬件
program control information 节目控制信息
program control instruction 程序控制指令
program control structure 程序控制结构
program-control transfer 程序控制转移
program control unit(PCU) 程序控制单元
program-controlled carriage 程序控制传动装置
program-controlled channel 程序控制通道
program-controlled I/O 程序控制输

入输出
program-controlled industrial robot 程控工业机器人
program-controlled interruption（PCI）程序控制中断
program-controlled real-time clock 程控实时时钟
program-controlled sequential computer 程序控制的顺序计算机
program controller 程序控制器
program controlling element 程序控制部件
program conversion 程序变换
program copyright 程序版权
program correctness 程序正确性
program correctness proof 程序正确性证明
program counter（PC） 程序计数器
program counter address 程序计数器地址
program counter control 程序计数器控制
program counter operation 程序计数器作业
program crash 程序崩溃
program creation 程序建立
program cycle 程序循环　　「复
program damage repair 程序损坏修
program data 节目数据
program data flow analysis 程序数据流分析
program data set（PDS） 程序数据集
program data transfer 程序数据传送
program date 程序日期　　「件
program database file 程序数据库文
program debug 程序调试
program debugging 程序调试
program debugging tool 程序调试工具
program deck 程序卡片叠
program decoder 程序译码器
program decomposition 程序分解「件
program described file 程序描述的文
program derivation 程序出处，程序分支
program description document 程序说明文档
program descriptor 程序描述符

program design 程序设计　　「言
program design language 程序设计语
program design prototyping technique 程序设计原型法
program determination 程序确证「发
program development（PDP） 程序开
program development facility 程序开发工具
program development system（PDS）程序开发系统
program development time 程序开发时间
program development tool 程序开发工具
program development worksheet 程序开发工作单
program device 程序设备　　「盖
program device override 程序设备覆
program-distribution amplifier 节目分配放大器
program documentation 程序文档化，程序说明文档
program documentor 程序文档编制者
program-driven 程序驱动
program dump list 程序转储表
program economy 程序经济性
program editor 程序编辑器
program efficiency 程序效率
program electron beam 程控电子束
program element 程序单元
program emulator 程序仿真器
program end flag 程序结束标志
program end message 程序结束消息
program environment 程序环境
program equivalence problem 程序等价问题
program error 程序错误
program error control 程序错误控制
program error dump 程序错误转储
program error interrupt 程序错误中
program evaluation 程序评价　　「断
program evaluation and review technique（PERT） 计划评核技术
program event 程序事件
program event recording（PER） 程序事件记录
program exception 程序异常
program exception code（PEC） 程序异

常码 「式
program execution mode 程序执行模
program execution monitor 程序执行监控程序
program execution services 程序执行服务
program execution time 程序执行时
program-exit hub 程序出口桩 」间
program extension 程序扩展
program fault 程序错误
program fetch 程序提取
program fetch time 程序取出时间
program file 程序文件
program flexibility 程序灵活性 「序
program flow analyzer 程序流分析程
program flow diagram 程序流程图
program flowchart 程序流程图
program for numerical tool operation (PRONTO) 数控机床操作程序
program format 程序格式
program fragment 程序段
program function 程序函数
program function key 程序功能键
program-generated parameter 程序生成参数
program generation system 程序生成系统
program generator(PG) 程序生成器
program graph 程序图
program graph parallelization 程序图并行化 「简
program graph reducibility 程序图化
program graph reducibility algorithm 程序图化简算法
program group 程序组
program halt 程序停止
program header block(PHB) 程序标题块
program heading 程序首部
program hierarchy chart 程序分层结构示意图
program ID 程序标识符 「段
PROGRAM-ID paragraph 程序标识
program image 程序映像
program improvement 程序改进
program in machine code 机器码程序
program inclusion 程序包含
program indentation 程序缩进式编排

program independence 程序独立性
program independent modularity 与程序无关的模块化设计
program index control 节目索引控制
program index control information 节目索引控制信息
program index data 节目索引数据
program index data unit 节目索引数据单元
program index information 节目索引信息
program index packet 节目索引码群
program indicator code 程序指示码
program information block 程序信息块
program information file(PIF) 程序信息文件
program initialization 程序初始化
program instance 程序实例
program instruction 程序指令
program instrumentation 程序探测
program interaction 程序牵制
program interchange 程序互换
program interface 程序接口
program interrupt 程序中断
program interrupt transfers 程序中断转移
program isolation 程序隔离
program isolation lock manager 程序隔离锁定管理程序
program item icon 程序项目图标
program label 程序标号
program language type 程序语言类型
program level 程序级
program librarian 库控程序
program library 程序库
program library management 程序库管理
program life cycle 程序生命周期 「督
program limit monitoring 程序界限监
program line 程序行
program linkage 程序链结,程序连接
program linking 程序链接
program list 程序列表[清单]
program list control block(PLCB) 程序列表控制块
program listing 程序列表
program listing output 程序列表输出

program loader 程序载入器
program loading 程序加载
program loading operation 程序装入操作
program loading routine 程序加载例[程
program locality 程序局部性
program location counter 程序单元计数器
program logic 程序逻辑
program logic array 程序逻辑阵列
program logic flowchart 程序逻辑流程图
program loop 程序循环
program maintainability 程序可维护[性
program maintenance 程序维护
program maintenance expenditure 程序维护经费
program maintenance procedure 程序维护过程
program management 程序管理
program management control table (PMCT) 程序管理控制表
program manager 程序管理员
Program Manager Window 程序管理器窗口
program manipulation instruction 程序操作指令
program mapping 程序映像
program mask 程序屏蔽
program master file update 程序主文件更新
program memory(PM) 程序存储器
program mode 程序模式
program model 程序模型
program modeling 程序建模[模型化]
program modification 程序修改[改进]
program modularity 程序模块化
program module 程序模块
program module dictionary(PMD) 程序模块词典
program monitoring and diagnosis 程序监控与诊断
program mutation 程序变异
program name 程序名
program notation 程序表示法
program number 节目号
program object 程序对象

program offering 程序转售
program optimization 程序优化
program organization 程序组织
program origin 程序起始地址
program output 程序输出
program overlay 程序覆盖
program overlay capability 程序覆盖能力
program overlay structure 程序覆盖结构
program package 程序包 「果
program paging behavior 程序分页效
program paging function 程序分页功能
program parallelization 程序并行化
program parameter 程序参数
program part 程序部分
program partitioning 程序划分
program patch 程序补片;程序修补
program patching plug 程序修补插件
program path 程序路径
program performance 程序性能
program phase 程序阶段
program plagiarism 程序剽窃
program portability 程序可移植性
program post-edit 程序后编辑
program postcondition 程序后置条件
program precondition 程序前置条件
program preparation 程序准备
program preparation aids 程序准备辅[助
program preparation facilities 程序准备工具
program preprocessor 程序预处理器
program priority 程序优先级
program processor 程序处理器
program product 程序产品 「间
program production time 程序生产时
program proof 程序证明
program propagation 程序传播
program property 程序性质
program protection 程序保护
program proving 程序证明
program quality 程序质量
program range 程序范围
program read-in 程序读入
program readability 程序可读性
program reader 程序阅读器
program reconstruction algorithm 程

序重建算法
program recovery 程序恢复
program recycling 程序重循环
program reduction 程序归约[简化]
program reference 程序引用
program reference tables 程序参照表
program refinement 程序精炼
program region length register 程序区长度寄存器
program register(PR) 程序寄存器
program relative branch 程序相对转
program reliability 程序可靠性　　「移
program relocatability 程序可重定位
program relocation 程序重定位　　「性
program request block 程序请求块
program request count 程序请求计数
program requestor 程序请求器
program required credentials 程序使用凭证
program reset 程序复位
program restoration point 程序恢复点
program restriction 程序限制
program restructuring 程序重构
program retry 程序复执
program review 程序审查
program risk analysis 程序风险分析
program robustness 程序健壮性[坚固性]
program roll back 程序退回重算
program runs 程序运行
program scheduler 程序调度程序
program section name 程序节名
program sectioning 程序分节
program security 程序安全性
program segment 程序段
program segment prefix(PSP) 程序段前缀
program segment size 程序段长度
program segment table 程序段表
program segmentation 程序分段
program segmenting 程序分段
program-selected terminal 程序选择的终端
program selection 程序选择
program selector 程序选择器　　「误
program-sensitive error 程序敏感错
program-sensitive fault 程序敏感故障
program-sensitive malfunction 程序敏感失灵
program sequencing librarian 程序定序库管理程序
program sharing 程序共享
program sheet 程序纸
program similarity 程序类似性[趋同性]
program simplification 程序简化
program simulator 程序仿真程序
program size 程序长度
program source code 程序源代码 「配
program space allocation 程序空间分
program specification 程序规范 「性
program specification block(PSB) 程序说明块
program stack 程序堆栈
program state 程序状态
program statements 程序语句
program statements assembler 程序语句汇编程序
program status 程序状态　　「器
program status register 程序状态寄存
program status vector 程序状态矢量
program status word(PSW) 程序状态字
program step 程序步　　　　　「令
program stop 程序停机
program stop instruction 程序停止指
program storage 程序存储器
program storage unit(PSU) 程序存储单元
program structure 程序结构
program structure block 程序结构块
program suite 程序组,成套程序
program support 程序支持
program support library(PSL) 程序支持库
program support representative(PSR) 程序支持代表
program suspending 程序挂起
program swapping 程序对换
program switching 程序转换
program switching interrupt 程序转接中断
program syntax 程序语法　　「合
program synthesis 程序合成,程序综
program system description 程序系统描述
program system specification 程序系

统规范
program tab 程序标签
program tailoring 程序裁剪
program tape(PT) 程序带
program temporary fix 程序临时修改
program termination 程序终结
program termination processing 程序终结处理
program test 程序测试
program test system 程序测试系统
program test tape 程序测试带
program test time 程序测试时间
program tester 程序测试器
program testing 程序测验
program testing time 程序测试时间
program time 程序时间
program timer 程序定时器
program timing matrix 程序定时矩阵
program to program communication 程序间通信
program-to-program message switch 程序间消息交接
program tool 程序工具
program tracing 程序跟踪
program transferability 程序可移植
program transformation 程序变换
program translation 程序翻译
program transportability 程序可移植
program type and classification 节目类型及划分
program understanding 程序理解
program unit 程序单元
program update 程序更新
program utility routine 程序实用例程
program validation 程序确认
program validation services(PVS) 程序确认服务程序
program variable 程序变量
program vectorization 程序向量化
program verbs 程序动词
program verification 程序验证
program verification system 程序验证系统
program view 程序视图
program visualization 程序可视化
program window 程序窗口
program word 程序字
program working area 程序工作区
program writing phase 程序编码阶段
programatics 程序学
programmability 可编程性
programmable 可编程的
programmable arbiter 可编程仲裁器
programmable array logic(PAL) 可编程阵列逻辑
programmable asynchronous line adapter 可编程异步线路适配器
programmable calculating oscilloscope 可编程计算示波器
programmable calculators 可编程计算器
programmable cellular array 可编程细胞阵列
programmable character generator 可编程字符发生器
programmable clock 可编程时钟
programmable communication controller 可编程的通信控制器
programmable communication interface 可编程通信接口
programmable concentrators 可编程集中器
programmable controller 可编程控制器
programmable counter 可编程计数器
programmable data control unit 可编程数控单元
programmable data logger 可编程数据记录器
programmable data rate 可编程数据速率
programmable data selector 可编程数据选择器
programmable delay 可编程延时
programmable digital filter 可编程数字滤波器
programmable distributed control system 可编程分布式控制系统
programmable divider 可编程除法器
programmable filter 可编程滤波器
programmable frequency synthesizer 可编程频率合成器
programmable front end processor 可编程前端处理机
programmable function key 可编程功能键
programmable gate array(PGA) 可编程门阵列

programmable graph generator 可编程图形发生器
programmable image memory 可编程图像存储器
programmable index register 可编程变址寄存器
programmable input buffer 可编程输入缓冲器
programmable input-output(PIO) 可编程输入/输出器
programmable instrument 可编程仪
programmable interface 可编程接口
programmable interrupt controller (PIC) 可编程中断控制器
programmable interval 程序控制的时间间隔
programmable interval timer(PIT) 可编程时间间隔定时器
programmable linear address register 可编程线性地址寄存器
programmable logic array(PLA) 可编程逻辑阵列
programmable logic controller(PLC) 可编程逻辑控制器
programmable logical device(PLD) 可编程逻辑器件
programmable peripheral interface (PPI) 可编程外围接口
programmable point-of-sale terminal 可编程销售点终端源
programmable power supply 可编程电
programmable read-only memory (PROM) 可编程只读存储器
programmable signal processor 可编程信号处理机
programmable sound output 可编程声音输出
programmable terminal 可编程终端
programmable timer 可编程定时器
programmable workstation 可编程工作站
programmatics 程序设计学
programmed channel 程序控制通道
programmed check 程序化检验
programmed control 程序控制
programmed cryptographic facility 程序密码设施
programmed data processor(PDP) PDP 系列计算机(DEC)
programmed data transfer 程控数据传输
programmed direct control 程序直接控制
programmed dump 程控式转储
programmed dwell 程控暂停
programmed environment 编程环境
programmed function key 编程功能键
programmed guidance 程序制导
programmed halt 程序控制停机
programmed inspection 程序检验
programmed instruction 程序化教学
programmed instructions 程序设计指令;程序设计教学
programmed interrupt request vector 程序中断请求向量
programmed learning 程序教学
programmed level 编程级
programmed logic 程控逻辑
programmed marginal check 程控边际校验
programmed read-only memory 已编程只读存储器
program scheduler 程序调度程序
programmed selective dump 编程选择转储
programmed stop 程控停机
programmed switch 程控开关
programmed symbol set attribute 编程符号集属性
programmer 程序员;编程器
programmer analyst 程序分析员
programmer assistant 程序员助理;程序设计辅助工具
programmer card 编程器插件
programmer check 程序员校验
programmer control panel 程序员控制板
programmer defined identifier 程序员定义标识符
programmer defined function 程序员定义函数
programmer defined macro 程序员定义的宏指令
programmer-defined structure value 程序员定义的结构值 器
programmer/duplicator 编程器/复制

programmer expertise 程序员专业知识
programmer hierarchical interactive graphics system(PHIGS) 程序员分层交互图形系统
programmer job 程序员作业
programmer logical unit 程序员逻辑单元
programmer-named condition 程序员命名条件
programmer panel 程序员操作面板
programmer socket 编程器插座
programmer subsystem 程序员子系统
programmer tools 程序员工具
programmer unit 编程设备
programmer version 程序员版本
Programmer Workbench 程序员工作台
programmer's console diagnostic 程序员的控制台诊断例程
Programmer's Hierarchical Interactive Graphics Standard(PHIGS) 程序员分层结构的交互式图示标准
Programmer's Switch 程序员开关
programmer's workbench 程序员工作台
programming 程序设计,编程
programming accessories 程序设计附件
programming aids 编程工具
programming audit 程序设计审计
programming by prompting 受提示编程
programming compatibility 程序设计兼容性
programming control panel 编程控制面板
programming convention 程序设计约定
programming cost 程序设计成本
programming device 程控设备
programming environment 编程环境
programming flexibility 编程灵活性
programming flow diagram 程序设计流程图
programming flowchart 程序设计流程图
programming job 程序设计作业
programming language 编程语言
programming language bootstrap combined(BCPL) BCPL语言
programming language for interactive teaching(PLANIT) 交互式教学用编程语言,PLANIT语言
programming language model 编程语言模型
programming linguistics 程序设计语言学
programming logic(PL) 程序设计逻辑
programming machine 编程机
programming manager 程序设计管理者
programming methodology 程序设计方法学
programming module 程序设计模块
programming program 编译程序
programming redesign 程序重新设计
programming semantics 程序设计语义学
programming specification 程序设计规格说明
programming standards 程序设计标准
programming statement 程序设计语句
programming style 程序设计风格
programming support environment 编程支持环境
programming system 程序设计系统
programming technique 程序设计技术
programming theory 程序设计理论
programming tool 程序设计工具
programming transformation 程序转换
programming transparency 程序设计透明性
programming visualization 编程可视化
progress indicator 进程指示器
progress message 进程指示信息
progression 级数
progressive encoding 递增编码
progressive offset track 递增偏移磁道
progressive overflow 向前溢出
progressive scanning 顺序扫描
progressive stress test 递增应力试验
progressively controlled network 顺序控制网络,步进控制网络
project 投影
project file 项目计划文件
project group 工程组
Project Gutenberg 盖丁堡计划
project initiation process 项目初始化过程
project-join normal 投影-连接范式

project librarian 文档管理员
project management program 计划管理程序
project manager 工程项目管理程序
project monitoring and control process 项目监督控制过程
project name 工程名
project notebook 项目文卷
project organization 项目组织
project person 项目人员
project plan 项目计划
project platform 方案平台
Project Rescue "再生"方案
Project Settings dialog box 工程设置对话框
Project Web 项目站点
projection 投影;规划;估计
projection center 投影中心
projection copying 投影拷贝
projection function 投影函数
projection geometry 投影几何学「像
projection-join mapping 投影连接映
projection of best approximation 最佳逼近的估计
projection operation 投影运算
projection plane 投影平面
projection rule 投影学习规则
projection transformation 投影变换
projector 投影线
projects list 工程列表
PROLOG(PROgramming in LOGic) PROLOG 语言
PROLOG computer PROLOG 计算机
prologue 前序,开端程序
PROM (Programmable Read Only Memory) 可编程只读存储器
PROM blank check PROM 空白校验
PROM blaster PROM 写入器
PROM bootstrap 可编程只读存储器引导
PROM continuity test PROM 连续性测试
PROM copying PROM 复制
PROM monitor PROM 监控程序
PROM programmer PROM 编程器
PROM programming PROM 编程
PROM simulator PROM 仿真器「器
PROM UV eraser PROM 紫外线擦除

PROM verify PROM 检验
promise 承诺,约定
promoter 发起者,创办人
prompt 提示符
prompt facility 提示功能[设备]
prompt line 提示列
prompt mode 提示方式
prompting 提示
prompting output 提示输出
pronunciation 发音
proof 证明,验证
proof by contradiction 反证法,矛盾证明法
proof control 证明[验证]控制
proof finding program 证明寻找程序
proof list 验证表
proof listing 证明列表
proof of partial correctness 部分正确性证明
proof of program correctness 程序正确性证明
proof of total correctness 全正确性证
proof reading 校对 ⌊明
proof rule 证明规则
proof sample 试样
proof total 查证总数,总计验证
proof tree 证明树
proofreading system 校对系统
propagate 传播
propagated error 传播误差,延伸错误
propagating system 延伸系统
propagation 传播;传播性
propagation A/D converter 行波模/数转换器
propagation coefficient 传输系数
propagation constant 传播常数
propagation D-cube 传播 D 立方
propagation delay 传播延迟
propagation hierarchy 繁衍层次
propagation loss 传播损耗
propagation performance 传播性能
propagation rule 繁衍规则
propagation time 传播时间
propellant 推进剂
propeller 推进器
proper 固有的;常态的;特征的
proper area 固有区
proper class 真类

proper convex 正常凸函数
proper fraction 真分数
proper function 特征函数
proper grammar 适定文法
proper map 特征映射
proper name 固有名称
proper network 常态网络
proper operation 正常操作
proper prefix 真前缀
proper program 真程序
proper string 合适串
proper subclass 真子类
proper subset 真子集
proper subtraction 真减
proper tail 真尾
proper termination 正常终止
proper tree 固有树
proper value 特征值
proper vector 本征[特征]向量
properties database 特征数据库
property 特征;特性,属性
property database 特征数据库
property detector 特征检测器
property driven model(PDM) 特征驱动模型
property entity 特征实体
property frame 属性框架
property identifier 属性标识符
property inheritance 特征继承
property integrity 特征完整性
property lattice 特性格
property list 特性表,P表
property page 属性页
property page site 属性页站点
property selection 特征选择
property set 属性集
property sheet 属性表
property sort 特征排序
property table 特征[属性]表
property tag 属性标签
property type 属性类型
property value 属性值
proportional 成比例的,相称的
proportional action 比例作用
proportional band 成比例的范围
proportional coefficient 比例系数
proportional control 比例控制
proportional control action 比例控制动作
proportional font 比例字体
proportional gain 比例增益
proportional pie graph 比例圆饼图
proportional pitch 比例间距
proportional-position action 比例位置作用
proportional range 成比例的区间,线性范围
proportional sample 比例抽样
proportional space 比例间隔
proportional spacing 比例定间隔
proportional spacing mechanism 比例间隔机构
proportionally-spaced font 按比例间隔字体
proposal 建议书,提案
proposal activity 投标活动
proposed algorithm 推荐算法
proposed parameter 建议参数
proposition 命题
proposition letter 命题字母
proposition logic 命题逻辑
proposition tree 命题树
propositional algebra 命题代数
propositional attitudes 命题姿态
propositional calculus 命题演算
propositional calculus system 命题演算系统
propositional constant 命题常量
propositional dynamic logic 命题动态逻辑
propositional formula 命题公式
propositional letter 命题字母
propositional logic 命题逻辑
propositional variable 命题变量
proprietary 专用的,专有的
proprietary benchmark 专用基准程序
proprietary data 独有数据,专用数据
proprietary file format 专有文件格式
proprietary local bus 专有局部总线
proprietary program 专用程序
proprietary software 专利软件
props 道具
prosody 韵律,语音特征
prospect 视野
PROSPECTOR "预言家"专家系统
prosthetic 弥补性的

prosthetic robot 关节式机器人
protect mode 保护方式
protected check 保护性核查
protected conversation 受保护会话
protected distribution system 受保护的分布系统
protected dynamic storage 受保护动态存储器
protected field 受保护字段
protected-fields terminal 有保护字段的终端
protected file 被保护文件
proprietary file format 专用文件格式
protected files 保护文件
protected formatting 保护格式
protected key 保护键
protected information 受保护信息
protected level 保护级
protected line 受保护线路
protected load 受保护负载
protected location 受保护位置
protected mode 保护模式
protected object 受保护对象
protected queue area 保护队列区
protected resource 受保护资源
protected storage 受保护存储器
protected wireline distribution system 受保护有线分布系统
protection 保护
protection asterisk 星号保护
protection channel 保护通道
protection character 保护字符
protection code 保护码
protection domain 保护域
protection exception 保护异常
protection group 保护组
protection kernel 保护内核
protection key 保护钥
protection master 母版保护
protection pattern 保护格阵
protection philosophy 保护原则
protection ratio 保护比
protection ring 保护环
protection span 保护跨度
protection switching 保护性转换
protective grounding 保护接地
protective jacket 保护套
protective package 保护性包装

protective redundancy 保护性冗余
protector frame 保护器盘
protocol 协议,规约
protocol analyzer 协议分析器
protocol analysis 协议分析
protocol boundary 协议边界
protocol chip 协议芯片
protocol control information(PCI) 协议控制信息(ISO/OSI)
protocol conversion 协议转换
protocol converter 协议转换器
protocol data unit(PDU) 协议数据单元(ISO/OSI)
protocol emulator 协议仿真程序
protocol engineer 协议工程
protocol family 协议族,协议系列
protocol function 协议功能
protocol levels 协议层
protocol machine(PM) 协议机
protocol reference point 协议参考点
protocol specification of OSI 开放系统互连协议规格说明
protocol stack 协议栈
protocol standards 协议标准
protocol suite 成套协议
protocol synthesis 协议合成
protocol transfer 协议传输
protocol type 协议类型
protocol window 协议窗口
proton 质子
proton decay 质子衰变
proton implanted 质子注入
protonotion 原始概念
protosystem 原型系统
prototype 原型;样机
prototype boards 原型板
prototype debug 样机调试
prototype design 原型设计
prototype development system 原型开发系统
prototype expert system 专家系统原型
prototype inference system 原型推论语言,PRISM语言
prototype life cycle model 原型生存期模型
prototype method 原型法
prototype network 原型网络
prototype printed-circuit board 原型

印刷电路板
prototype revision 原型修订
prototype statement 原型语句
prototype system 原型系统
prototype unit 原型单元
prototype version 原始版本
prototyping 原型法
prototyping boards 原型开发板
prototyping kit 整套原型零件,样机成套零件
prototyping method 原型方法
prototyping technique 原型技术
prototyping tool 原型开发工具
provable 可证的
provably secure operating system (PSOS) 可验证安全操作系统
prove 证明
provide 提供
provider 供应商,提供者
provider table 提供者表
proving 验证,证明
proving correctness 正确性验证
proving program 验证程序
proving time 求证时间,验证时间
provisional 临时的,暂时的,候选的
provisional backup value (PBV) 候选返上值
proximity 邻近,附近
proximity effect 邻近效应
proximity recording 贴近记录(Maxtor)
proximity search 近似匹配搜索
proximity sensor 接近传感器
proximity zone 邻近区域
proxy 代理
proxy address 代理地址
proxy agent 委托代理
proxy ARP (proxy address resolution protocol) 代理地址转换协议
proxy attribute 代理品质 「列
proxy cache array 代理服务器缓存阵
proxy manager 代理管理程序
proxy object 代理对象
proxy server 代理服务器
proxy software 代理服务软件
PRQ(Pacing ReQuest) 调步请求
PRT(PRinTer) 打印机
PRTY(PRioriTY) 优先权,优先级

prudent 谨慎的
prudent evaluation 谨慎的估算
prune 修剪,子目录删除
pruned cell 被修剪单元
pruning 修剪
pruning implementation 修剪实现
pruning of goal tree 目标树修剪
PS(Packet Switching) 分组(包)交换
PS(Production System) 产生式系统
PS/1(Personal System/1) PS/1个人计算机(IBM)
PS/2(Personal System/2) PS/2个人计算机(IBM)
PS/2 bus PS/2总线(IBM)
PSC(Programmable Systolic Chip) 可编程脉动阵列芯片
PSDN(Packet Switched Data Network) 分组交换数据网络
PSDN(Public Switched Data Network) 公用交换数据网络
PSE(Packet Switch Equipment) 分组交换设备
PSE(Programming Support Environment) 程序设计支持环境
PSE36(Page Size Extension) 36位寻址页面长度扩展(Intel)
PSECT(Prototype SECTion) 原型段,样机部件
pseudo- 伪,假
pseudo-address 伪地址 「序
pseudo-application program 伪应用程
pseudo-arithmetic operation 伪算术运算
pseudo-Boolean algebra 伪布尔代数
pseudo-clock 假时钟
pseudo-code 伪码
pseudo-code element 伪码元素
pseudo-color 伪彩色
pseudo-comment 伪注释
pseudo compiler 伪编译
pseudo computer language 伪计算机语言
pseudo-cursor 伪光标
pseudo-cyclic code 伪循环码
pseudo-cylinder 伪柱面
pseudo-delimiter 伪正文定界符
pseudo-device driver 伪设备驱动程序
pseudo-duplexing 伪双工

pseudo-equilibrium 伪平衡
pseudo-exhaustive testing 伪穷举测试
pseudo-file address 假文件地址
pseudo-file name 伪文件名
pseudo-front-end system 伪前端系统
pseudo-host 伪主机
pseudo-instruction 伪指令
pseudo-instruction form 伪指令形式
pseudo-inverse 伪逆
pseudo-inverse filtering 伪逆过滤法
pseudo-job scheduling 伪作业调度
pseudo language 伪语言
pseudo-LU-LU session 伪逻辑单元对话
pseudo-median graph 伪中位图
pseudo-monitor cursor 伪监视器光标
pseudo-monotone function 伪单调函数
pseudo-monotone map 伪单调映射
pseudo-movement parallax 伪运动视差
pseudo-noise code 伪噪声码
pseudo-noise sequence 伪噪声序列
pseudo-object 伪对象
pseudo-offline I/O 假脱机输入输出
pseudo-offline working 假脱机工作
pseudo-operation 伪操作
pseudo-order 伪指令
pseudo page 伪页
pseudo page fault 伪页面故障
pseudo parallel program 伪并行程序
pseudo-perspective view 伪透视图
pseudo-polynomial-time algorithm 伪多项式时间算法
pseudo-random 伪随机的
pseudo-random binary sequence 伪随机二进制序列
pseudo-random code 伪随机码
pseudo-random fashion 伪随机方式
pseudo-random number (PN) 伪随机数
pseudo-random number sequence 伪随机数序列
pseudo-random sequence 伪随机序列
pseudo-random signal 伪随机信号
pseudo-random vector 伪随机向量
pseudo-reasoning 伪推理,假设推理
pseudo-reduction 伪归约
pseudo-register 伪寄存器
pseudo-scalar 伪标量

pseudo-sectoring 伪扇形扫描
pseudo-semantic tree 伪语义树
pseudo-static 伪静态的
pseudo-structure 伪结构
pseudo-terminal subsystem 模拟终端子系统
pseudo-ternary codes 伪三进制码
pseudo-ternary signal 伪三进制信号
pseudo-text 伪正文,伪文本
pseudo-timer 伪计时器
pseudo-variable 伪变量
pseudoconcave function 伪凹函数
pseudoconvex function 伪凸函数
pseudocursor 伪光标
pseudoflow 伪流程
pseudoinstruction 伪指令
pseudolanguage 伪语言
pseudolinear function 伪线性函数
pseudomachine 伪机器
pseudopaging 伪分页
pseudoprogram 伪程序
pseudorandom 伪随机性
pseudorandom binary sequence 伪随机二进制序列
pseudorandom code 伪随机代码
pseudorandom number 伪随机数
pseudorandom number sequence 伪随机数序列
pseudorandom sequence (PRS) 伪随机序列
pseudostatic RAM 伪静态随机读写存储器
pseudotransitivity 伪传递性
PSG language PSG 语言
PSI (Packet Switching Interface) 包交换接口
PSI (Personal Security Identifier) 个人保密标识符
PSI (Personal Sequential Inference machine) 个人顺序推理机
PSI system PSI 系统
PSIU (Packet Switch Interface Unit) 分组交换接口部件
PSK (Phase Shift Keying) 移相键控
PSL language PSL 语言
PSN (Packet Switching Network) 包交换网络
PSN (Packet Switching Node) 包交换

节点
PSN(Public Switched Network) 公共交换网
PSOS(Provably Secure Operating System) 可证明安全的操作系统
pSOS pSOS 操作系统
PSP(Packet Switching Processors) 包交换处理机,分组交换处理器
PSP(Process Simulation Program) 过程模拟程序
PSP(Program Segment Prefix) 程序段前缀
PSS(Packet Switching Stream) 包交换流
PSS(Product Support System) 生产支持系统(IBM)
PST(Public Segment Table) 公用段表
PSU(Packet Switching Unit) 分组交换单元
PSU(Port Sharing Unit) 端口共享部件
PSU(Program Storage Unit) 程序存储单元
PSU chip circuits 程序存储单元芯片电路
PSV(Program Status Vector) 程序状态向量
PSW(Processor Status Word) 处理机状态字
PSW(Program Status Word) 程序状态字法
psychoacoustic algorithm 心理声学算
psychological 心理学的
psychological effect 心理效应
psychological-meditative-degree 心理调节度
psychology 心理
psychophysical property of vision 视觉心理性能
psychophysics 心理物理学
psychovisual redundancy 视觉心理多余度
PSYCO PSYCO 语言
PSYNC(Processor SYNChronous) 处理机同步
PT(Page Table) 页表
PTC(Programmer Transparent Coordination Scheme) 程序员透明的协作方案
PTC thermistor 正温度系数电阻
PTDM(Probabilistic Time Division Multiple Access) 概率时分多路存取
PTI(Packet Type Identifier) 信息包方式标识符
PTN(Public Telephone Switch Network) 公共电话网
PTO(Please Turn Over) 请翻到下页,请见本页的反面
PTPFT(Peer-To-Peer File Transfer) 对等(同层)文件传送
PTPN(Peer-To-Peer Network) 对等网络
PTPS(Person-To-Person Service) 个人至个人服务
PTR(PoinTeR) 指针,指示字
PTSN(Public Telephone Switch Network) 公共电话交换网
PTT(Post Telegraph and Telephone administration) 邮电管理局元
PU(Physical Unit) 实体单元,物理单
PU 2.1(Physical Unit 2.1) 物理单元 2.1
PU-PU flow 物理单元间数据流
PU services manager 物理单元服务管理程序
public 公共的,公用的
public address system 有线广播系统
public array 公共数组
public authority 公共权限
public benchmark 通用基准程序
public carrier 公共通信
public class member 公有类成员
public data 公用数据
public data network(PDN) 公用数据网络
public data transmission service 公用数据传输服务
public dial port 公用拨号端口
PUBLIC directory 公共目录
public domain 公用范畴
public domain code 公共领域代码(有著作权,但允许用户免费使用)
public domain software 公共流通软件,公开软件
public elementary file(PEF) 公共元文件

public exchange 公共交换
public facsimile bureau 公众传真局
public facsimile station 公众传真站
public file 公共文件
public folder 公共文件夹
public interface editor 公用接口编辑程序
public key 公开密钥
public key certificate 公开密钥证书
public key cipher 公开密钥密码
public key cryptography 公开密钥加密
public-key cryptosystem 公开密钥加密系统
public key infrastructure 公开密钥基础设施
public key system 公开密钥系统
public library 公用库；公共图书馆
public message service(PMS) 公用消息服务
public microprogram 公用微程序
public network 公用网络
public note 公共标记
public operation 公共操作
public packet switching network(PPSN) 公用分组交换网络
public packet switching service(PPSS) 公用分组交换服务
public queue 公用队列
public segment(PS) 公用段
public segment table 公用段表
public switched network 公用交换网
public telegram service 公众电报业务
public telephone network 公用电话网络
public telephone service(PTS) 公用电话业务
public tool interface 公用工具接口
public utility 公用事业
public utility commission 公用事务委员会
public variable 公有变量
public videotex system 公共可视图文系统
public volume 公用档卷
publication 出版,发行；公布
publication language 出版物语言
Publish and Subscribe 发行与订户

Publisher 印刷出版软件
publishing (Web)发布
publishing directory (Web)发布目录
publishing interchange language(PIL) 出版交换语言,PIL语言
publishing standard 出版标准
puck 光标定位器
PUCP(Physical Unit Control Point) 物理单元控制点
PUD(Physical Unit Directory) 物理单元目录
pull 拉出
pull back 退回,退却
pull-down menu 下拉式菜单
pull-in time 同步引入时间
pull operation 提取运算
pull-up menu 上拉菜单
pull-up resistor 上拉电阻
pulsatance 角频率
pulsation cycle 脉动周期
pulse 脉冲
pulse advancing 脉冲提前
pulse amplifier 脉冲放大器
pulse amplitude 脉冲幅度
pulse-amplitude modulation(PAM) 脉冲振幅调制
pulse analyzer 脉冲分析器
pulse attenuator 脉冲衰减器
pulse bandwidth 脉冲带宽
pulse base 脉冲基值
pulse-broadening circuit 脉冲展宽电路
pulse channel 脉冲通道
pulse clock generator 脉冲时钟发生器
pulse code 脉冲码
pulse code modulation(PCM) 脉冲编码调制
pulse-code modulation multiplexing 脉码调制的多路复用
pulse communication 脉冲通信
pulse compression 脉冲压缩
pulse count 脉冲计数
pulse counter 脉冲计数器
pulse counting module 脉冲计数模块
pulse crowding 脉冲拥挤
pulse decay time 脉冲衰减时间
pulse decoder 脉冲解码器
pulse delay 脉冲延迟
pulse-delay binary modulation(PDBM)

脉冲延迟式二进制调制
pulse delay fall time 下降时延
pulse delay rise time 上升时延
pulse delay time 脉冲延迟时间
pulse dialing 脉冲拨号
pulse discriminator 脉冲鉴别器
pulse dispersion 脉冲扩散
pulse distance 脉冲间距
pulse distribution amplifier 脉冲分配放大器
pulse distributor 脉冲分配器
pulse drop 脉冲下降
pulse duration 脉冲持续时间,脉冲宽度
pulse duration modulation 脉冲宽度调制
pulse duty factor 脉冲占空比
pulse echo fault locator 线路故障脉冲回波测定器
pulse echo meter 脉冲回波测试器
pulse echo return loss 脉冲回波损耗
pulse emitter 脉冲发射器
pulse enable 脉冲启动,脉冲使能
pulse encoder 脉冲编码器
pulse envelope 脉冲包络
pulse equalizer 脉冲均衡器
pulse excitation 脉冲激发
pulse fall time 脉冲下降时间
pulse flatness deviation 脉冲平坦性偏差
pulse former 脉冲整形器
pulse forming circuit 脉冲形成电路
pulse frequency 脉冲频率
pulse-frequency modulation(PFM) 脉冲频率调制
pulse generator 脉冲发生器
pulse-height discriminator 脉冲鉴幅器
pulse height modulation 脉冲振幅调制
pulse height selector 脉冲幅度选择器
pulse interlacing 脉冲交错
pulse-interval modulation 脉冲间隔调制
pulse jitter 脉冲颤动
pulse length 脉冲宽度
pulse modulation(PM) 脉冲调制
pulse noise 脉冲噪声
pulse normalization 脉冲标准化
pulse pairing 脉冲成对产生现象
pulse period 脉冲周期
pulse-polarization binary modulation (PPBM) 脉冲极化二进制调制
Pulse-position modulation(PPM) 脉冲位置调制
pulse-position modulator 脉位调制器
pulse rate 脉冲速率
pulse recurrence frequency 脉冲重复频率
pulse regeneration 脉冲再生
pulse regenerator 脉冲再生器
pulse repeater 脉冲转发器
pulse repetition frequency 脉冲重复频率
pulse-repetition period 脉冲重复周期
pulse-repetition rate(PRR) 脉冲重复率
pulse reshaping 脉冲整形
pulse rise time 脉冲上升时间
pulse sampling 脉冲取样
pulse separator 脉冲分离器
pulse shape 脉冲波形
pulse shaping 脉波整形
pulse shaping circuit 脉冲整形电路
pulse shrinkage 脉冲变狭
pulse soldering 脉冲焊接
pulse source 脉冲源
pulse spacing 脉冲间隔
pulse spectrum 脉冲谱
pulse spreading 脉冲扩散
pulse stretcher(PS) 脉冲展宽器
pulse stretching 脉冲展宽
pulse string 脉冲串
pulse-swapping standardization 脉冲交换标准化
pulse-time modulation(PTM) 脉冲时间调制
pulse train 脉冲长串
pulse transformer 脉冲变压器
pulse width 脉冲宽度
pulse width discriminator 脉冲宽度鉴别器
pulse width encoding 脉冲宽度编码
pulse width modulation 脉冲宽度调制
pulser 脉冲发生器
pulsive noise 脉冲性噪声
PUMA(Programmable Universal Micro Accelerator) 可编程通用微加速器
pump 泵
PUMP(Parts Usage Maintenance Pro-

gram) 零部件使用维护程序
pumping lemma 泵引理
punch 穿孔机
punch card 穿孔卡
punch tape 穿孔纸带
punched card format 穿孔卡格式
punck 手持光标
punctuation 标示,标点
punctuation bits 标点位,标长位
punctuation mark 标点符号
punctuation symbol 标点符号
puncture test 击穿[耐压]试验
puncture voltage 击穿电压
puppet 芭比玩偶
puppet animation 木偶动画
Purdue real-time BASIC Purdue 实时 BASIC 语言
pure 纯的
pure binary 纯二进位
pure binary numeration system 纯二进数制
pure birth process 纯增加过程
pure code 纯码
pure conflict game 纯冲突对策
pure dead process 纯消灭过程
pure demand paging 纯请求式调页
pure delay 纯延迟
pure generator 纯产生器
pure hiding strategy 纯隐藏策略
pure integer programming 纯整数规划
pure Java application 纯 Java 应用程序
pure Java driver 纯 Java 驱动程序
pure literal rule 纯文字[纯句节]规则
pure machine-aided translation 纯机器辅助翻译
pure machine translation 纯机器翻译
pure multi-path frame network 纯多路径框架网络
pure procedure 纯过程
pure resistance 纯电阻
pure time-delay factor 纯时延因子
pure tone 纯音
PURGE 清除
purge 彻底清除
purge data 净化数据
purge date 清除日期
purging 清除

purging system 净化系统
purification 净化,提纯
purpose 目的,效果,用途
purpose-directed analogy 目的导向类比
purposiveness 目的性
pursuer 追击者
pursuit-evasion problem 跟踪-逃避问题
pursuit game 追击对策
pursuit tracking 追逐跟踪
push 推
push-button 按钮开关
push-button array 按钮开关阵
push-button dialing 按键式拨号
push-button reset 按钮复位
push contact 按钮触点
push-down 下推
push-down automaton(PDA) 下推自动机
push-down list 下推表
push-down memory 下推存储器
push-down nesting 下推嵌套
push-down queue 下推队列法
push-down stack 下推堆栈
push-down transducer 下推翻译机
push-down symbol 下推符号
push-down transducer 下推转录程序
push-off strength 推离力强度
push on 推进,进栈
push operation 下推操作
push-pull amplifier 推挽放大器
push-up list 上推[先进先出]表
push-up queue 上推队列
push-up storage 上推[先进先出]存储器
pushable module 可压入模块
put 放置,存放
put-away 存储,存放
put-back 回放,返回原地
put instruction 放置指令
put predicate 输出谓词
put procedure 送出过程
put signal 放置信号
put statement 放置语句,送出语句
putaway 存储
putc macro 输出字符宏指令
putchar macro 输出字符宏指令
PUTPROP function 置特性值函数
puts function 字符持续输出函数
puzzle 难题,迷语

PVC(Permanent Virtual Circuit) 永久虚电路
PVGA(Paradise VGA) PVGA 显示
PVI(Primitive VTAM Interface) VTAM 基本接口
PVI(Programmable Video Interface) 可编程视频接口
PVN(Private Voiceband Network) 专用音频网络
PVT(Public Volume Table) 公用卷表
PW(PassWord) 口令,通行字
PW(Program Word) 程序字
PWB/UNIX Unix 程序员的工作台
PWC(Pulse Width Coder) 脉宽编码器
PWD(Pulse-Width Discriminator) 脉宽鉴别器
PWM(Personal Web Manager) 个人 Web 管理程序
PWM(Pulse-Width Modulator) 脉宽调制器
PWM controller IC 脉宽调制控制器集成电路
PWS(Personal Web Server) 个人 Web 服务器(微软)
Px64 (64kb/s ISDN)Px64 标准
pyroelectric effect 热电效应
pyramid 金字塔
pyramid algorithm 金字塔算法

Q q

Q(Quality factor) 品质因数
Q&A "问与答"
Q-character 特征字符
Q demodulator Q 信号解调器
Q-FAX(Quick Facsimile) 快速传真
Q output Q 输出
Q signal Q 信号
Q-switch Q 开关
Q-switched laser Q 开关激光器
Q-switching Q 切换
Q test Q 测试
Q-unsatisfiability Q 不可满足性
QA(Quality Assurance) 质量保证
QAM(Quadrature Amplitude Modulation) 正交调幅
QB(Quasi-Bidirectional) 准双向的
QBE(Query By Example) 实例查询语言
QBF QBF 格式查询接口程序
QBIC(Query By Image Content) 按图像内容查询(IBM)
QBS(Query By Screen) 屏幕查询
QC(Quartz Crystal) 石英晶体
QCB(Queue Control Block) 队列控制块
QCB extension 队列控制块扩充区
QCIF(Quarter Common source Intermediate Format) (视频)1/4 公共源媒体格式
QE(descriptor Queue Element) 描述符队列元素
QE(Queue Empty) 队列空
QED 本文编辑程序
QF(Queue Full) 队列满
QF(Quick Format) 快速格式化
QFP(Quad Flat Package) 方形扁平封装
QI(Quality Index) 质量指数
QIC(Quarter-Inch Cartridge) 1/4 英寸盒带
QIC(Working Group for Quarter-Inch Cartridge Drive Compatibility) 1/4 英寸盒带兼容性工作组
QIL(Quad In-Line) 四列直插式
QL(Query Language) 查询语言
QLISP QLISP 语言
QM(Queuing Message) 排队信息
QM-1 QM-1 计算机
QoS(Quality of Service) 服务质量
QPM(Quantized Phase Modulation) 量化相位调制
QPPM(Quantized Pulse Position Modulation) 量化脉位调制
QPSK(Quaternary Phase Shift Ke-

ying) 四相位相移键控
QR algorithm   QR算法
QSAM (Queued Sequential Access Method)   队列顺序存取法
QSS(Quasi-Stable State)   准[暂]稳态
QTAM (Queued Telecommunications Access Method)   排队远程通信访问法
quad   四芯线组；四边形；四面体
quad-bus transceiver   四总线收发器
quad cable   四芯电缆
quad clock driver   四端时钟驱动器
quad density   四倍密度
quad-in-line   四列直插
quad-in-line package   四列直插式封装
quad-issue processor   四出口处理器
quad speed drive   四倍速驱动器
quad split   四线组跳组
quad straight joint   四线组直接连接
quad tree   四叉树
quad word   四倍长字
quadded cable   扭绞四芯电缆
Quadra   Quadra 计算机
quadra-phase   四相制
quadraflop   四态电路
quadrand   象限；直角扇面
quadrantal symmetry   象限对称
quadraphonic   四声道立体声
quadratic   二次的
quadratic convergence   二次收敛
quadratic curve   二次曲线
quadratic dual problem   二次对偶问题
quadratic equation   二次方程式
quadratic factor algorithm   劈因子法
quadratic fix   二次拟合
quadratic form   二次型
quadratic function   二次函数
quadratic interpolation   二次插值法
quadratic minimization problem   二次极小化问题
quadratic performance index   二次型性能指标
quadratic programming   二次规划
quadratic quotient search   二次寻商法
quadratic rehash method   二次再散列法
quadratic root   平方根   ⌐法
quadratic search   二次搜索
quadratic sum   平方和

quadratic surface   二次曲面
quadratic variational problem   二次变分问题
quadrature   正交
quadrature amplifier   正交放大器
quadrature amplitude modulation (QAM)   正交幅度调制
quadrature component   正交分量
quadrature crosstalk   正交串音
quadrature encoding   正交编码
quadrature information correlator   正交信息相关器
quadrature modulation   正交调制
quadrature phase shift keying (QPSK)   正交相移键控
quadrature reactance   正交电抗
quadrature transform method   正交变换方式
quadrature transformer   正交变压器
quadriphase shift keying   四相移键控
quadrilateral(quad)   四边形；四面体
quadrilateral mesh   四边形网孔
quadruple   四元组
quadruple address   四地址
quadruple display   四重显示
quadruple form   四元组形式   ⌐器
quadruple-length register   四倍长寄存
quadruple notation   四元组表示法
quadruple operator   四元组算符
quadruple register   四倍长寄存器
quadrupler   四倍乘器
quadtrees   四元树   ⌐定
qualification(QUAL)   鉴定,验证；限
qualification locator   定位限定
qualification testing   鉴定测试
qualified call   限定调用
qualified data name   限定数据名
qualified expression   限定表达式
qualified global name   限定全程名
qualified logical link control   限定逻辑链路控制
qualified name   限定名
qualified name vector   限定名向量
qualified programmer   合格程序员
qualified reference   限定引用
qualified relation   限定关系
qualified segment search argument   限定段查找变元

qualifier 限定词,限制符
qualifying bit 限定位
qualifying connective 限定联结
qualitative algebraic reasoning 定性代数推理
qualitative data 定性数据
qualitative model 定性模型
qualitative evaluation 定性评估
qualitative reasoning 定性推理
quality 质量
quality assurance(QA) 质量保证
quality control 质量控制
quality control system 质量控制系统
quality diagnostic 质量诊断程序
quality engineering 质量工程
quality factor 品质因数
quality index of channel 通道质量指「数
quality of service(QoS) 服务质量,业务质量「制
quality of service control 服务质量控
quality of service maintenance 服务质量维护
quality of service management 服务质量管理
quality of service monitoring 服务质量监视
quality of service negotiation 服务质量协商
quality of service renegotiation 服务质量重协商
quantified system analysis 定量系统分析
quantification 量化
quantification symbol 量化符号
quantified analogy 定量类推
quantified Boolean formula problem 量化布尔公式问题
quantified statement 量化命题
quantifier 量词
quantifier-free conjunctive normal form 量词无关的合取范式
quantitative 定量的
quantitative analysis 定量分析
quantitative evaluation techniques 定量评估技术
quantitative theory 定量理论
quantity 量,数量
quantization 量化

quantization distortion 量化失真
quantization effect 量化效应
quantization error 量化误差
quantization law 量化律
quantization level 量化电平
quantization noise 量化噪声
quantization resolution 量化分辨率
quantization uncertainty 量化不确定性,量化误差
quantization value 量化值
quantize 量化
quantized computer 量化计算机
quantized feedback 量子化反馈
quantized interval 量化区间
quantized pulse modulation 量化脉冲调制
quantized signal 量化信号
quantized symbol 量化符号
quantized value 量化值
quantizer 量化器
quantizer noise 量化器噪声
quantizing distortion 量化失真
quantizing error 量化误差
quantizing interval 量化间隔,量化阶
quantizing noise 量化噪声
Quantum (硬盘生产厂商)昆腾公司
quantum 时限;量子,量阶
quantum clock 量子钟
quantum cryptography 量子密码学
quantum efficiency 量子效率
quantum electronics 量子电子学
quantum noise 量子噪声
quantum number 量子数
quantum statistics 量子统计学
quantum theory 量子理论
quantum transmission 量子传输
quarantine service 隔离服务
quark 夸克(X协议中定义名称、类或类型的整数) 「件
Quark Xpress Quark Xpress排版软
quarter-inch cartridge(QIC) 1/4英寸盒带
Quarter-Inch Cartridge Drive Standard (QIC) 1/4英寸盒带驱动器标准组织
quartet 半字节
quartic 四次的
quartz 水晶,石英

quartz clock 石英钟
quartz crystal 石英晶体
quartz-crystal clock 石英晶体钟
quartz-crystal filter 石英晶体滤波器
quartz delay line 石英延迟线
quartz delay-line memory 石英玻璃延迟线存储器
quartz oscillator 石英晶体振荡器
quartz resonator 石英谐振器
quasi-analog signal 准模拟信号
quasi-associated mode 准直联模式
quasi-associated operation mode 准直联操作模式
quasi-associated signaling 准直联信令
quasi-bidirectional 准双向的
quasi-conductor 准导电体
quasi-cycling signal 准周期性信号
quasi-dynamic robot 准动态机器人
quasi-horizontal microinstruction 准水平微指令
quasi-impulsive noise 准脉冲性噪声
quasi instruction 准指令,伪指令
quasi-instruction form 准指令形式
quasi-language 准语言,拟语言
quasi-linear equation 准[拟]线性方
quasi-linear feedback control system 准线性反馈控制系统
quasi-linearization 拟线性化
quasi-optical waves 准光波
quasi order relation 拟序关系
quasi-parallel processing 准并行处理,拟并行处理
quasi-random call 准随机呼叫
quasi-random code generator 准随机代码发生器
quasi-real time simulation 准实时仿真
quasi-smooth terrain 准平坦地形
quasi-stable state 准稳态
quasi-static 准静态的
quasi-synchronous 准同步的
quasi-uniform distribution 拟均匀分
quasimonotone function 拟单调函数
quasiprojective scheme 拟射影概型
quasivariable 准变量
quaternary 四进制的
quaternary notation 四进制记数法
quaternary phase-shift keying 四相相移键控

quaternary signal 四元信号
quaternary signaling 四元信号传输
Quattro 电子数据表格软件(Borland)
Quebec-Actualize 魁北克新闻(加拿大)
QUEL language QUEL语言
quench 淬灭,淬熄
quench pulse 淬灭脉冲,置"0"脉冲
QUERY 数据库查询子系统
query 查询
query and report processor 查询与报告处理程序
query answering system 查询应答系
query buffer 查询缓冲器
query by example(QBE) 按例查询
query complexity 查询复杂性
query decomposition 查询分解
query enhancement 查询扩充
query evaluation algorithm 询问求值算法
query form 查询窗体[表单]
query interactive processor 查询交互处理器
query key value 查询键值
query language 查询语言
query mapping 查询映像
query modification 查询修改
query mutant state 查询变异状态
query normalization 查询规范化
query optimization 查询优化
query optimizer 查询优化程序
query option 查询选项
query processing 查询处理
query restriction 查询限制
query script 查询底稿
query set 查询组
query set size control 查询组规模控
query similarity 查询相似性
query stacking 查询堆栈
query station 查询站
query time 查询时间
Quest Quest语言
QUEST(Query Evaluation and Search Technique) 查询评价和查找技术
Questel "魁斯特"主机(法国)
question answering system 问题回答系统
question file 问题文件

question logical formulation 提问逻辑
question mark 问号　　　　　└式
question vector 提问向量
queue 队列,排队
queue-based share 基于队列的共享
queue control 队列控制　　　　┌块
queue control block(QCB) 队列控制
queue data set 队列数据集
queue disciplines 队列规则
queue-driven task 队列驱动任务
queue element 队列元素
queue empty 队列空
queue front 队列前端
queue full 队列满
queue head 队列头
queue head pointer 队列头指针
queue indicator 队列指示器
queue length 队列长度
queue link word 队列链接字
queue linkage entry 队列连接入口
queue management 队列管理
queue name 队列名
queue pointer 队列指针
queue full 队列满
queue priority 排队优先权
queue register 排队寄存器
queue request 队列请求
queue search 队列检索
queue size 队列大小
queue tail 队列尾
queue tail pointer 排队尾指针
queue traffic 排队通信量
queued access 队列存取
queued access method(QAM) 排队存取法
queued communication interface 队列通信接口
queued content addressed memory 排队型内容寻址内存
queued for connection 队列等候连接
queued for logon 队列注册
queued indexed sequential access method (QISAM) 队列索引按序存取法
queued logon request 队列注册请求
queued printing services 排队打印业务
queued sequential access method (QSAM) 排队顺序存取法
queued session 队列对话
queued telecommunication access method(QTAM) 队列远程通信存取方
queuing 队列,排队　　　　　　└法
queuing analysis 排队分析
queuing delay 排队延迟
queuing delay time 排队延迟时间
queuing discipline 排队规则
queuing list 排队表
queuing mechanism 排队机构
queuing message 排队消息
queuing model 排队模型
queuing problem 排队问题
queuing process 排队进程
queuing register 排队寄存器
queuing theory 排队论
queuing theory problem 排队论问题
queuing time 排队时间
quibinary code 5-2码
quick access 快速存取,快速访问
quick-access memory 快速存取内存
quick-access storage 快速存取存储器
quick action relay 速动继电器
Quick Assembler 快速汇编程序
Quick BASIC Quick BASIC 语言(微软)
quick boot 快速自举
quick break 快断路
quick break fuse 速断保险丝
quick break switch 速断开关
Quick C Quick C 语言编译程序(微软)
quick cell 快速单元
quick cell facility 快速单元工具
quick change real-time(QCRT) 快速切换实时操作
quick closedown 快速停机,快速停发
quick connect 快速接通
quick convert terminal 易转换终端
quick disconnect 快速拆线
quick disconnector 快速分离器
quick draw graphics system 快速绘图系统
quick editor 快速编辑程序
quick erase 快速清除
Quick Law System(QLS) 快速检索法律系统
quick look and checkout system 粗查

询校验系统
quick-make 快速接通
quick make and break contact 快速通断接触
quick-make switch 快速接通开关
quick mask 快速蒙版
Quick Panel 快速操作面板
Quick PASCAL Quick PASCAL语言
quick power on self test 快速加电自检
quick preview 快速预览
quick printer 快速打印机
quick reaction 快速反应
quick recovery 快速恢复
quick relocation and link(QRL) 快速重定位与链接
quick response 快速应答,快速响应
Quick Silver Quick Silver 程序
quick sort 快速排序
quick start 快速启动
quick switching 快速转换,快速切换
quick text editor 快速文本编辑程序
QUICKDRAW 快速绘图系统
QuickDraw QuickDraw 图形显示系统(苹果)
Quicken Quichen 支票管理软件
Quickfile 快速文件管理
quicksort 快速排序法
QuickTask 快速事务命令
QuickTime Quicktime 多媒体软件(苹果)
QuickTime for Windows QuickTime的 Windows 版本
QUICKTRAN 快速 FORTRAN 语言(IBM)
quiesce 禁止,静默
quiesce-at-end-of-chain indicator(QEC) 链结束时静止指示符
quiesce communication 停顿通信
quiesce-completed indicator 静止指示符
quiesce protocol 停止协议,停顿协议
quiescent 停顿,静止
quiescent carrier modulation 抑制载波调制
quiescent carrier transmission 抑制载波传输
quiescent condition 静止状态
quiescent current 静态电流
quiescent operation 静态操作
quiescent period 间歇期间
quiescent point 静点
quiescent terminal 静止终端
quiescing 停顿,停止
quiet 静止的;无噪声的;单调的
quiet area 静区
quiet automatic gain control 无噪声自动增益控制
quiet error 静态错误
quiet recording mode 静态记录模式
quiet tuning 无噪声调谐
quinary 五进制
quinary code 五进制码
quinary notation 五进制记数法
Quine's method 奎因法
quintic curve 五次曲线
quintuple form 五元组形式
quintuplicate 五倍的,五重的
quit 退出,结束
quiz 测验
QUM(QUadrature Modulation) 正交调制
quota 限量,份额
quotation 引证,引用
quotation mark 引号
quote 引号;引证
quote character 引号字符
quote mark 引号
Quote Printable(QP) (MIME 标准下的)电子邮件编码规则
quote symbol 引号
quoted string 引用串,引证串
quotient 商
quotient counter 商计数器
quotient-difference algorithm 商差算法
quotient field 商域
quotient group 商群
quotient-multiplier register 商数乘数寄存器
quotient ring 商环
quotient set 商集
quotient space 商空间
quotient topology 商拓扑
QUP(QUadra-Phase) 四相制
QUS(QUery Station) 查询台(站点)
QUSM(QUeued Sequential Access Method) 排队按序存取法
QW(Quadruple Word) 四倍长字

QWA(Queue Work Area) 队列工作区
QWB(Queue Work Block) 队列工作块
QWERT arrangement 键盘 QWERT 布局方式
QWERT keyboard QWERT 键盘

R r

R(Radius) 半径
R(Read) 读
R(Resistance) 电阻
r-ary function r 元函词
r-ary predicate r 位谓词
R;BASE R;BASE 数据库
r-perfect hypergraph r 完备超图
r-rank clique r 秩集团
R/W(Read/Write) 读/写
R1 R1 系统
R1-SOAR R1-SOAR 专家系统
R/W head(Read/Write head) 读/写头
RA(Random Access) 随机存取
rabbit "兔子"程序
Rabin's public-key cryptosystem 拉宾公开密钥加密系统
Rabin signature 拉宾签名
RACE(Research into Advanced Communication in Europe) 欧洲高级通信技术研究与开发计划
RACE(Results Analysis, Computation and Evaluation) 结果分析、计算与评估
race 竞争,竞态
race condition 竞争情况,电路竞态
race hazard 竞争冒险
race problem 竞争问题
raceway 电缆管道,走线槽
RACF(Resource Access Control Facility) (MVS)资源访问控制程序
racing 竞态
rack 机架,机柜
rack earth 机架地
rack-mount computer 架装计算机
rack-mount extender 架装扩展器
rack mounted 架装的
rack mounted server 架装服务器
RAD(Rapid Access Disk) 快速存取磁盘
RAD(Rapid Application Development) 快速应用程序开发
rad 弧度
radar 雷达
radar-aided tracking computer 辅助雷达跟踪计算机
radar command guidance 雷达指令制导
radar computer simulator 雷达计算机仿真器
radar data processing 雷达数据处理
radar information command system 雷达信息指挥系统
RADIAL RADIAL 语言
radial basis interpolation 径向基插值法
radial component 径向分量
radial search 径向搜索
radial servo 径向伺服
radial transfer 径向传送
radian 弧度
radian frequency 角频率
radiance of surface 表面发光强度
radiant efficiency 辐射效率
radiant energy 辐射能量
radiant flux 辐射通量
radiant intensity of a source 光源的发光强度
radiated emission 辐射发射
radiating fin 散热叶片
radiating flange 散热片
radiation 辐射
radiation damage 辐射损伤
radiation loss 辐射损耗
radiation measurement 辐射测量
radiator 辐射体
radical 部首,偏旁
radical encode method 字根编码法
radical life cycle 自由的生命周期法

radio astronomy 射电天文学
radio autocontrol 无线电自动控制
radio broadcasting 无线电广播
radio button 单选按钮,虚按钮
radio channel 无线电通道
radio command guidance system 无线电指令制导系统
radio common channel 无线电公用通道
radio communication electric warfare 无线电通信对抗
radio communication network 无线电通信网络
Radio Corporation of American(RCA) 美国无线电公司
radio data link 无线电数据链路
radio direction finder 无线电测向器
radio frequency(RF) 射频
radio frequency interference(RFI) 射频干扰
radio group 单选按钮组
radio interference 无线电干扰
radio link 无线电链路
radio mobile communication 无线电移动通信
radio position finding 无线电定位
radio relay station 无线电中继站
radio remote control 无线电遥控
radio repeater 无线电转发器
radio wave 无线电波
radioactivity 放射性
radioguidance 无线电制导
radiometer 辐射计
radiometric transformation 辐射变换
radiophoto 无线电传真
radiosity 辐射度,辐射通量密度
radius 半径
radix 数基,基数
radix base 数基
radix complement 基数补码,补码
radix conversion 基数变换
radix-minus-one complement 反码
radix notation 基数记数法
radix number 基数数
radix numeration system 基数记数系统
radix point 基数点,小数点
radix scale 基数标度
radix sort 基数排序
RADSL(Rate Adaptive Digital Subscriber Link) 速率自适应数字用户线
ragged 未对齐的
ragged-left alignment 左边未对齐
ragged margin 未对齐边界
ragged right 右边未对齐
ragged text (版面)未对齐的文本
RAID(Redundant Arrays of Inexpensive Drives) 廉价磁盘冗余阵列
RAIL RAIL语言
RAIR(Remote Access Immediate Response) 远程访问立即应答
raise of exception 异常的引发
raised character 凸起字符
raised cosine pulse 升余弦脉冲
raised cosine wave 升余弦波
raised floor 活动地板
raised statement 引发语句
RAL(Rapid Access Loop) 快速存取环路
RAM(Random Access Memory) 随机存取存储器
RAM cache RAM高速缓存器
RAM card RAM卡,随机存取记忆卡
RAM chip RAM芯片
RAM cram RAM塞满
RAM diagnostic program RAM诊断程序
RAM disk RAM盘
RAM dump RAM转储
RAM enable RAM使能,RAM允许
RAM interface 随机存取存储器接口
RAM latched output RAM锁存输出
RAM loader RAM装载程序
RAM mail box RAM邮箱,RAM信箱区
RAM memory expansion RAM内存扩充
RAM refresh RAM刷新
RAM refresh clock RAM刷新时钟
RAM refresh frequency RAM刷新频率
RAM refresh time interval RAM刷新时间间隔
RAM resident RAM驻留
RAMAC(Random Access Method of Accounting and Control) RAMAC计算机

Rambus DRAM 内存总线动态存储器
RAMDAC(Random Access Memory Digital to Analog Converter) 随机存取存储器数/模转换器,RAMDAC芯片
RAMDRIVE.SYS RAM盘管理程序
ramification 分歧,分支
ramp 鳄鱼夹
ramp response 斜波响应
ramp response time 斜波响应时间
ramp signal 斜坡信号
ramp type A/D converter 斜坡型模/数转换器
RAND(Research ANd Development Corp) 研究与开发公司,兰德公司
Rand Intelligent Terminal-Agent(RITA) 兰德智能终端代理系统
RAND Object-oriented Simulation System(ROSS) 面向对象的仿真语言
random 随机的,不规则的
random access(RA) 随机访问
random access auxiliary storage 随机存取辅助存储器
random access card equipment(RACE) 随机存取卡式装置
random access computer 随机存取计算机
random access control unit(RAC) 随机存取控制单元
random access device(RAD) 随机存取装置
random access discrete address(RADA) 随机存取离散寻址
random access disk file bank 随机存取磁盘文件组
random access file 随机存取文件
random access I/O routine 随机存取输入/输出例行程序
random access input/output 随机存取输入/输出
random access machine(RAM) 随机存取机器
random access memory(RAM) 随机存取存储器 「理
random access processing 随机存取处
random access programming 随机存取程序设计 「件
random-access software 随机存取软

random-access sort 随机存取排序
random-access sorter 随机存取排序程序 「器
random-access storage 随机存取存储
random access time 随机存取时间
random bit-stream signaling 随机位流发信
random call 随机调用,随机呼叫
random cipher 随机密码
random counter 随机计数器
random data perturbation 随机数据扰
random distribution 随机分布 └动
random disturbance 随机干扰
random dot pattern 随机点模式
random entry 随机询问
random error 随机差错
random error-correcting ability 随机差错校正能力
random error-correcting convolutional code 随机纠错卷积码
random event 随机事件
random factor 随机因素
random failure 随机失效[故障]
random fault 随机性故障
random file 随机文件
random file key 随机文件键
random fractal 随机分形
random function 随机函数
random load 随机荷载
random logic 随机逻辑
random logic design 随机逻辑设计
random logic device 随机逻辑装置
random logic testing 随机逻辑测试
random multiple access 随机多路访问
random noise 随机噪声
random noise digital simulation 随机噪声数字仿真
random number 随机数
random number generator 随机数发生器
random number program 随机数产生程序
random number sequence 随机数序列
random packet length 随机包长度
random page replacement 随机页替换
random path 随机通路
random permutation 随机排列[置换]
random perturbation optimization 随

机扰动优化
random process 随机过程
random processing 随机处理
random pulse sequence 随机脉冲序列
random reduction 随机归约
random replacement 随机替换
random rounding 随机舍入
random sample queries 随机抽样查询
random sampling 随机抽样
random scan 随机扫描
random schedule 随机调度
random searching 随机检索
random selection 随机选择
random sequence 随机顺序,随机时序
random-sequential access 随机顺序存取
random signal 随机信号
random system 随机系统
random test generation 随机测试产生法
random testing 随机测试
random testing method 随机测试方法
random topology 随机拓扑
random traffic 随机通信量,随机话务量
random-uniform number 均匀分布随机数
random variable 随机变量
random variation 随机变动
random vector 随机向量
random walk 随机游动
random walk method 随机游动法
random walk routing 随机漫步路由选择
randomization 随机化
randomize scheme 随机规划
randomized algorithm 随机算法
randomized decision function 随机决策函数
randomized non-return-to-zero-change on one(R-NZRI) 随机逢"1"变化不归零制
randomized routing 随机路由选择
randomizer 随机数产生器
randomizing 随机化
randomly distributed data 随机分布数据
randomly to any path 随机选择任意路径
randomly to unused path 随机选择不重复路径
randomly traceable graph 随机可溯图
randomness 随机性,偶发性
range 值域;量程
range analysis 值域分析,量程分析
range check 范围校验,区域检查
range constraint 范围约束
range expression 范围表达式
range format 范围格式
range index 范围索引
range limit 范围限制
range name 范围名称
range of balanced error 平衡误差范围
range of DO DO 语句域,DO 循环域
range variable 范围变量,区域变量
rank 排序,等级;秩
rank analysis 秩分析
rank statistics 秩统计量
ranked matching 排列匹配
rapid access 快速存取
rapid access loop 快速存取环路
rapid access management information system(RAMIS) 快速存取信息管理系统
rapid access memory 快速存取内存
rapid access recording 快速存取记录
rapid access storage 快速存取存储器
rapid application development(RAD) 快速应用程序开发
rapid application development system (RAD system) 快速应用程序开发系统
rapid application development tools (RAD tools) 快速应用程序开发工具
rapid information technique for evaluation 快速信息评估技术
rapid memory 快速内存
rapid processing system 快速处理系统
rapid prototyping 快速原型法
rapid prototyping method 快速原型设计法
rapid thermal annealing(RTA) 快速热退火
raplot 等点绘图法
RAQ (Reservation and Acknowledgment Queue) 保留与确认队列
RARE(Reseaux Associes pour la Re-

cherche Europeenne) 欧洲学术研究网络协会
RAS(Reliability Availability Serviceability) 可靠性,有效性和可服务性,RAS指标
RAS(Remote Access Service) 远程访问服务
RAS(Row Address Strobe) 行地址选通
RAS user(Remote Access Service user) 远程访问服务用户
raster 光栅
raster count 光栅计数
raster display 光栅显示
raster distortion 光栅失真
raster font 光栅字体
raster file 光栅文件
raster graphics 光栅制图法
raster grid 光栅网格
raster image processor(RIP) 光栅图像处理器
raster pattern generator 光栅模式发生器
raster pattern storage 光栅模式存储器
raster plotter 光栅绘图仪
raster scan 光栅扫描
raster timing 光栅定时
raster unit 光栅单位
rasterization of vectors 向量光栅化
rat's nest (简单描述印刷电路版图的)鼠窝图
ratchet 棘爪
ratchet wheel 棘轮
rate adaptive digital subscriber link(RADSL) 速率自适应数字用户线
rate-based flow control 基于速率的流控制
rate control 速率控制
rate signal 比率信号
rated continuous working voltage 额定连续工作电压
rated output 额定输出
rated speed 额定速率[速度]
rated voltage 额定电压
rating 额定值
ratio call congestion 呼损率
ratio control 比例控制
ratio controller 比例控制器

ratio of gate-to-pin 门引脚比
rational approximation 有理逼近
rational B-splines curve 有理B样条曲线
rational expression 有理表达式
rational interpolation 有理插值
rational number 有理数
rave 咆哮
raw copy 原始副本
raw data 原始数据
raw footage 原始容量
raw material case 原材料角色
raw mode 原始模式
raw read data 原始读出数据
ray casting 射线造型法,视线投射法
ray tracer 光线跟踪程序
ray tracing algorithm 光线跟踪算法
ray tracing rendering 光线跟踪润色法
ray tracing shading technique 光线跟踪阴影设置技术
Rayleigh distribution 瑞利分布
Rayleigh scattering 瑞利散射
RBOC(Regional Bell Operating Company) 区域性贝尔公司
RCA connector RCA连接器
RCAM(Remote Computer communication Access Method) 远程计算机通信存取法
RCB(Resource Control Block) 资源控制块
RCN(Remote Computer Network) 远程计算机网络
RCONSOLE(Remode CONSOLE) 遥控台
RCT(Resource Control Table) 资源控制表
RCT(Routing Control Task) 路由控制任务
RD(ReaD) 读
RD(Receive Data) 接收数据
RDB(Relational Data Base) 关系型数据库
Rdb(Relational database/VMS) 关系型数据库
RDBMS(Relational DataBase Management System) 关系型数据库管理系统

RDBP (Relational Data Base Processor) 关系数据库处理机
RDC (Rand Development Corporation) 兰德发展公司
RDC (Remote Diagnostic Center) 远程诊疗中心
RDL (Relational Database Language) 关系数据库语言
RDOS (Real-time Disk Operating System) 实时磁盘操作系统
RDRAM (Rambus Dynamic Random Access Memory) 内存总线动态随机读写存储器
RDS (Remote Data Service) 远程数据服务
re-encipher to master key 主密钥再加密
re-entrant reusable routine 可重入再用的例行程序
re-order 重排列；再订货
reachability 可达性
reachability relation 可达关系
reachable 可达的
reachable point 可达点
reachable set 可达集
reachable state 可达状态
reaction control 反应控制
reaction mode 反应模式
reaction time 反应时间
reactive learning environment 反应式学习环境
reactive mode 反应模式
reactance 电抗
read 读；理解；代语
read access 阅读存取
read address counter 读地址计数器
read-after-write (RAW) 写后读
read-after-write check 写后读校验
read after write verify 写后读验证
read-ahead (Unix)提前读出
read-ahead queue 读前队列，读前区
read amplifier 读出放大器
read-around number 读出次数
read authority 读出授权
read-back check 回读校验
read-back signal 回读信号
read backward 反读
read buffer 读缓冲器
read bus 读出总线

read channel initialize 读通道起始
read check 读出检查
read conflict 读冲突
read controls 读控件
read cycle time 阅读周期时间
read data strobe 读数据选通
read enable 读出使能，读出允许
read error 阅读错误
read error rate 读出误码率
read-eval-print loop 读-求值-印出循环
read event 读事件
read flag 读标记[标志]
read forward 正向读出
read gap scatter 读出缝隙离散
read gap skew 读出磁头缝隙扭斜
read-gather/write-scatter 集中读分散写
read head 读头
read in 读入
read-in counter 读入计数器
read-in mode 读入模式
read in program 读入程序
read inhibit 读禁止
read interface unit 读接口单元
read-mainly memory (RMM) 主读内存
read-modify-write 读出-修正-写入
read mostly memory (RMM) 可改写的只读存储器
read noise 读噪声
read notation 读通知[告示]
read only 只读
read-only attribute 只读属性
read-only flag 只读标志
read-only memory (ROM) 只读存储器
read-only optical disk 只读式光盘
read-only register 只读寄存器
read-only storage 只读存储器
read-out 读出
read-out device 读出装置
read-out equipment 读出设备
read-out error 读出错误
read-out gate 读出门
read-out information 读出信息
read-out time 读出时间
read-out unit 读出装置
read output signal 读出信号
read path 阅读路径
read permission 读许可
read predicate 读谓词

read primitive 读入原语
read printer 读打印机
read-process-write 读-处理-写
read protection 读出防护
read pulse 读出脉冲
read rate 读出速度
read receipt 读取收据
read recovery 读恢复
read release 读释放
read report 读取报告[报表]
read request 读请求
read response 读响应
read reverse 反向读带
read right 阅读权限
read-scatter 分散读
read screen 读屏幕
read sector command 读扇区命令
read-side 读出边,读出侧
read signal 读信号
read skew 读扭斜
read start time 起读时间
READ statement 读语句
read time 读出时间
read-to-read crosstalk 读间串音,读间串扰
read verify 读出校验
read-while-write 边读边写
read with incandescent 白炽光(扫描)阅读
read with infrared 红外光(扫描)阅读
read with visible LED 发光二极管光源(扫描)阅读
read-write association 读-写相关
read/write channels 读写通道
read/write check 读写校验
read/write check indicator 读写校验指示器
read/write compatible head 读写兼用磁头
read/write counter 读写计数器
read-write cycle 读写循环
read/write cycle time 读写周期
read/write/erase 读写抹除
read/write/erase head assembly 读写抹除磁头组合件
read/write execute 读/写执行
read/write expandable memory 读/写可扩充内存
read/write head 读/写头
read write initialize 起始读写
read write memory(RWM) 读写存储器
read write memory module 读写存储器模块
read/write scatter 散布读写,分散读写
read/write volatility 读/写的依电性
read/write waiting time 读/写等待时间
readability 可读性
readability testing 可读性试验
readable 可读的
readable character 可读字符
reader 阅读机,阅读器;阅读程序
Reader-Copier 阅读复印机
reader/interpreter 读取/解释程序
reader light 阅读器指示灯
reader-printer 阅读打印机
readers/writers problem 读者/写者问题
reading 读
reading-access time 读数存取时间
reading accuracy 读出精确度
reading and writing amplifier circuit 读写放大电路
reading beam 读出(电子或光)束
reading brush 读取刷
reading head 读头
reading mechanism 读取机构
reading rate 读出率,阅读速度
reading station 读取站
reading task 阅读任务
readme file 自我说明文件
ready(RDY) 就绪
ready condition 就绪状态
ready for data signal 数据传输就绪信号
ready for next message 准备好接收下一消息
ready for receiving 接收就绪
ready for sending 发送就绪
ready light 就绪指示灯
ready line 就绪线
ready list 就绪表
ready list of process 进程就绪序列
ready mode 就绪模式
ready queue 就绪队列
ready-read card 可读卡片
ready-record 就绪记录
ready signal 就绪信号
ready state 就绪状态

ready state of process 进程就绪状态
ready status word 就绪状态字
real address 实地址
real address area 实地址区
real address space 实地址空间
real arithmetic 实数运算
real axis 实轴
real circuit 实际电路
real component 实数分量;有功分量
real constant 实常数
real data type 实数类型
real end open system 末端开放实系统
real image 实像
real line 实线
real literal 实文字,实直接量
real mode 实模式
real module 实模块
real number 实数
real open system 开放实际系统
real page number 实页数
real partition 实分割,实区划分
real ratio(time) 实时比
real storage 实际存储器
real storage manager(RSM) 实际存储器管理程序
real storage page table 实际存储页表
real system 实际系统
real time 实时
real-time adaptive control 实时自适应控制
real-time address 实时地址
real-time addressing 实时寻址
real-time animation 实时动画
real-time application 实时应用
real-time BASIC 实时BASIC
real-time batch monitor 实时批处理监督程序
real-time batch processing 实时批处理
real-time bit mapping(RTBM) 实时位映射
real time channel 实时通道
real-time clock(RTC) 实时时钟
real-time clock diagnostic 实时时钟诊断例程
real-time clock interrupt 实时时钟中断
real-time clock-interrupt operation 实时时钟中断操作
real-time clock log 实时时钟记录

real-time clock module 实时时钟模块
real-time clock pins 实时时钟引脚
real-time clock routine 实时时钟例程
real-time clock time-sharing 实时时钟分时
real-time communication executive 实时通信执行程序
real-time communication processing 实时通信处理
real-time communication system 实时通信系统
real-time computer 实时计算机
real-time computing complex(RTCC) 实时计算复合体
real-time concurrency operation 实时并发操作
real-time control 实时控制
real-time control expert system 实时控制专家系统
real-time control input/output 实时控制输入/输出
real-time control routine 实时控制例程
real-time control system 实时控制系统
real-time data 实时数据
real-time data base manager 实时数据库管理程序
real-time data base system 实时数据库系统
real-time data processing 实时数据处理
real-time data reduction 实时数据精简
real-time data system 实时数据系统
real-time data transmission 实时数据传输
real-time debug 实时调试
real-time debug routine 实时调试程序
real-time delay 实时延迟
real-time device 实时设备
real-time digital simulation 实时数字仿真
real-time disc operating system 实时磁盘操作系统
real-time executive(RTX) 实时执行程序
real-time executive routine 实时执行例程
real-time executive system 实时执行系统

real-time graphic system 实时绘图系统
real-time guard mode 实时保护模式
real-time I/O control system 实时输入/输出控制系统
real-time information retrieval system 实时信息检索系统
real-time information system 实时信息系统
real-time input 实时输入
real-time input/output 实时输入/输出
real-time interactive 实时交互
real-time interface 实时接口
real time language 实时语言
real-time link 实时链路
real-time management system 实时管理系统
real-time mode 实时模式
real-time monitor 实时监督程序
real-time multicomputing 实时多重计算
real-time multitasking executive 实时多任务执行程序
real-time on-line operation 实时联机操作
Real-time on-line Simulated operation 实时联机仿真作业
real-time operating system 实时操作系统
real-time operation 实时操作
real-time operation mode 实时作业模式
real-time option board 实时选件板
real-time output 实时输出
real-time penetration reaction 实时渗透反应
real-time procedural language(RTPL) 实时过程语言
real-time processing 实时处理
real-time processing communication 实时通信处理
real-time processing management 实时处理管理
real time product(RTP) 实时控制机
real-time program 实时程序
real-time programming 实时程序设计
real-time programming system 实时程序设计系统
real-time ratio 实时比
real-time recording 实时记录
real-time remote inquiry 实时远程查询
real-time replication 实时复制器
real-time resource-sharing executive 实时资源共享执行程序
real-time simulation 实时仿真
real-time simulation operation 实时联机仿真操作
real-time software 实时软件
real-time system 实时系统
real-time system executive 实时系统执行程序
real-time task processing 实时事务处理
real-time transmission 实时传输
real-time transport protocol(RTP) 实时传输协议
real-time trend panel 实时趋势画面
Real-Time Video(RTV) 实时视频
real-time working 实时工作
real-time working ratio 实时工作比
real type 实型
real variable 实变量
real world computing(RWC) 真实世界计算
real-world problem 现实世界问题
realistic communication 临场感通信
Realistic Display Mixer(RDM) 真实显示混合器
reality built for 2 persons 双人幻真系统
Realizer Realizer程序
realm 领域
realm currency indicator 领域现行指示符
realm data item 领域数据项
realm description entry 领域描述体
realtime 实时
realtime compression 实时压缩
realtime conferencing 实时会议
realtime input 实时输入
realtime operation 实时操作
realtime output 实时输出
realtime processing software 实时处理软件
realtime reaction 实时反应
rear end 后端
rear-end compaction 后端压缩
rear end truncation 后端截断
rear view 后视镜
rearrange 重新排列,重新整理

rearrangeable switching network 可重排交换网络
rearrangement 重排
rearward communication system 后向通信系统
reasonability 合理性
reasonable test 合理性测试
reasonableness check 合理性校验
reasonableness test 合理测试
reasoning 推理
reasoning by analogy 模拟推理 「理
reasoning by circumscription 范围推
reassembly 重汇编；重装配
reassign 重赋值
reblock 重组块
reboot 重自举
rebound 弹回，回跳
rebuild 重构，重建
Rebus language Rebus 语言
recalculate 重算
recalculation method 重算方法
recalculation order 重算顺序
recalibrate 重校
recall 复检；二次呼叫
recall factor 复检系数，查全因子
recall-fallout plot 查全率错检率曲线
recall ratio 复检比，查全率
recall response signal 重呼叫应答信号
recall signal 二次呼叫信号
recapitulation 摘要表
recast 重计算，重作
receipt 收据，回执
receipt communication method 回执通信法
receipt signal 回执信号
receive 接收
receive-after transmit time delay 发送后接收时延
receive buffer 接收缓冲器
receive buffer chain 接收缓冲器链
receive clock pulse 接收时钟脉冲
receive data enable 接收数据使能
receive data service request 接收数据服务请求
receive folder 接收文件夹，收件夹
receive interruption 接收中断
receive not ready 接收未就绪 「帧
receive not ready frame 接收未就绪

receive only(RO) 仅收，只接收
receive-only monitor 只收监视器
receive only printer 仅收打印机
receive-only service 仅收服务
receive only terminal(RO terminal) 只收接收终端
receive packet miscellaneous error 接收包混杂错误
receive packet overflow count 接收包溢出个数
receive pair 接收线对
receive port 接收端口
receive processor 接收处理机
receive ready 接收就绪
receive/send keyboard set 键盘式收发装置
receive time-out 接收超时
receive timing(RT) 接收定时
received data 接收数据
received data circuit 数据接收电路
received data lead 接收数据头标
received data present 接收数据出现
received frame 接收帧
received line signal detector 接收线路信号检测器
received noise power 接收噪声功率
received signal level 接收信号电平
receiver(RX) 接收机
receiver card 接收电路板
receiver gating 接收机选通
receiver holding register 接收保持寄存器
receiver initiated 接收者发起
receiver isolation 接收机隔离
receiver latch enable 接收锁定允许
receiver location loss 接收机位置损失
receiver pair 接收线对
receiver queue 接收机队列
receiver register 接收机寄存器
receiver signal element timing 接收信号元定时
receiver threshold 接收机定限，接收阈值
receiver transmitter 收发两用机
receiver/transmitter communication controller 接收/发送通信控制器
receiving 接收
receiving-end crossfire 收端串扰

receiving item 接收项
receiving margin 接收边际
receiving perforator 接收穿孔机
receiving signal conversion equipment 接收信号变换设备
recent pages 最近访问过的页面
recently added file 最近增加的文件
recently used directory 最近使用过的目录
receptacle 插座,插孔
reception congestion 接收阻塞
reception node 接收节点
reception poor 接收不良
reception sampling plan 验收抽样计「划
receptor 接收器,感受器
recharging mode 再充电状态
recheck 复核
recipient 接受者,收件人
recipient list 收件人列表
recipient table (MAPI)收件人表
reciprocal 互逆的,可逆的
reciprocal base 互逆基,对偶基「型
reciprocal bilinear form 互逆双线性
reciprocal coefficient 互逆系数
reciprocal equation 倒数方程
reciprocal iteration algorithm 逆迭代算法
reciprocal kernel 逆核
reciprocal polynomial 互易多项式
reciprocal table 倒数表
reciprocating motion 往复运动
reciprocator 倒数器
reciprocity 互反性
reciprocator 倒数器
recirculating loop 重环路,循环圈
recirculating loop memory 再循环回路内存
recirculating memory 再循环存储器
recirculating network 再循环网络
recirculating register 循环寄存器
reclaimer 回收程序
RECNO 当前记录号 「号
RECNUM(RECord NUMber) 记
recognition 识别
recognition accuracy 识别准确度
recognition algorithm 识别算法
recognition device 识别设备
recognition gate 识别门

recognition logic 识别逻辑
recognition of handwritten character 手写字符识别
recognition of virus 病毒识别
recognition rule 识别规则
recognition time 识别时间
recognizable character 可识别字符
recognizable pattern 可识别模式[图案]
recognize-act cycle 识别动作周期
recognized language 识别语言
recombining 合流 「准
recommended standard (EIA)推荐标
recompaction 重新紧凑法
recompile 重新编译
recompression 再压缩
recomputing 重算
reconcile 协调
reconciliation 一致,和谐;调和
reconciliation procedure 调解过程
reconciliation protocol 调和协议
reconditional-carrier reception 重置载波接收法
reconfigurable binary tree 可重构二叉树
reconfigurable bus system 可重构总线系统
reconfigurable distributed data 可重构分布式数据 「境
reconfigurable environment 可重构环
reconfigurable front-end processor 可重构前端处理机
reconfigurable mesh 可重构网络
reconfigurable multiprocessor 可重构多处理机
reconfigurable system 可重构系统
reconfiguration 重新配置
reconfiguration algorithm 重构算法
reconfiguration classification 重构分类
reconfiguration console 重构控制台
reconfiguration ladder diagram 重构梯形图
reconfiguration scheme 重构方案
reconfiguration waveform 重构波形
reconnect 重新连接
reconstructed database 重构数据库
reconstruction 重构

reconstruction conjecture 重构猜想
reconstruction procedure 重构过程
reconstruction sample 重构样本
reconsult predicate 修正谓词
reconvergent fan-out 再汇聚扇出
record 记录
record addition 记录追加
record aggregate 记录聚合
record and replay 记录与重放
record area 记录区
record-based perturbation 基于记录的扰动
record-based system 以记录为基础的系统
record block 记录块
record blocking 记录编块
record carrier 记录载体
record check time 记录校验时间
record class 记录类型
record code 记录代码
record communication facility 记录通信设施
record compaction 记录压缩
record compression & decompression 记录压缩与解压缩
record control block 记录控制块
record control program 记录控制程序
record control schedule 记录控制调度
record count 记录计数
record counting 记录数统计
record definition field(RDF) 记录定义域
record deletion 记录删除
record density 记录密度
record description 记录描述
record description entry 记录描述体
record detail 详细记录
record field 记录字段
record file 记录文件
record format 记录格式
record gap 记录间隙
record group 记录群,记录组
record head 记录头
record header 记录首标
record heading 记录首标
record identify number 记录标识号
record instance 记录样例
record interface 记录接口
record key 记录键
record layout 记录布置
record length indicator 记录长度指示符
record level 记录电平
record level rule 记录级规则
record lock 记录封锁
record locking 记录锁定
record management 记录管理
record management service(RMS) 记录管理服务
record management system 记录管理系统
record mark 记录标记
record medium 记录媒体
record mouse 记录鼠标动作
record name 记录名
record new macro 录制新宏
record number 记录编号
record-oriented data base management program 面向记录的数据库管理程序
record oriented input/output 面向记录的输入输出
record-oriented transmission 面向记录的传输
record overflow 记录溢出
record payload protection 记录有效负载保护
record placement mode 记录存放方式
record playback 记录重放
record pointer 记录指针
record position 记录位置
record ready 记录就绪
record reference 记录引用
record replacement 记录替换
record retention schedule 记录留存调度表
record retrieval 记录检索
record selection expression 记录选择表达式
record separator(RS) 记录分隔符
record separator character 记录分隔字符
record sheet 记录纸
record slot 记录存储槽
record sorting 记录排序[分类]
record source 记录源
record spanning 记录跨距
record storage mark 记录存储标示

record strip 记录条,带状记录
record structure 记录结构
record traffic 记录通信量
record transport 记录传送器
record type 记录类型
record update 记录更新
recorded program 录放节目
recorded spot 记录点,记录位置
recorded tape 录音[录像]带;记录带
recorded value 记录值
recorded voice announcement 录音广播
recorder 记录器
recording area 记录区
recording channel 记录通道[线
recording characteristic 录音特性曲线
recording density 记录密度
recording disc 记录盘
recording head 记录头
recording line frequency 记录行频率
recording line rate 记录行速率
recording medium 记录媒体
recording method 记录方法
recording noise 记录噪声
recording offset angle 记录偏角
recording paper 记录纸
recording phase （刻录机）记录阶段
recording-playback head 记录回放头
recording-reproducing head 记录复制磁头,录放头
recording signal 记录信号
recording speed 记录（录制）速度
recording spot 记录点
recording stylus 记录触针
recording surface 记录表面
recording trunk 记录中继线
records per track 记录数/轨道
records retention schedule 记录保留一览表
records series 记录序列
recordset type 记录集类型
recover 恢复 [束
recoverable ABEND 可恢复的异常结
recoverable error 可恢复错误
recoverable file 可恢复文件
recoverable read error rate 可恢复读错误率
recoverable synchronization 可恢复的同步

recovered audio 恢复的音频
recovered signal 复原信号
recovery 恢复,复原;收回
recovery block 恢复块
recovery control 恢复控制
recovery file 恢复文件
recovery from fallback 降级运行恢复
recovery information set 恢复信息组
recovery interrupt 恢复中断
recovery library 恢复库
recovery line 恢复线
recovery log 恢复登记
recovery management support(RMS) 恢复管理支援程序
recovery mechanism 恢复机制
recovery point 恢复点
recovery procedures 恢复过程
recovery process 恢复进程
recovery program 恢复程序
recovery routine 恢复例程
recovery termination manager 恢复终止管理程序
recovery time 恢复[校正]时间
recreatable data base 可重建数据库
rectangular 矩形
rectangular array 矩形阵列
rectangular connector 矩形连接器
rectangular coordinate system 直角坐标系
rectangular distribution 矩形分布
rectangular hysteresis loop 矩形磁滞回线
rectangular mesh 矩形网格
rectangular pulse(RECTP) 矩形脉冲
rectangular rule 矩形法则
rectangular wave 矩形波
rectangular window 直方窗口
rectifier(RECT) 整流器
rectilinear coordinate robot 直线坐标机器人
rectilinear scan 直线扫描
recto 奇数页
recurrence code 再现码,迭代码
recurrence event 循环事件 [式
recurrence formula 迭代公式,递推公
recurrence relation 迭代关系,递推关系
recurrence relation for orthogonal poly-

nomials 正交多项式的递推公式
recurrence system 迭代系统
recurrent net 链形网
recurrent neural network 链形神经网
recurrent state 回归态,循环状态
recurrent transmission code 再现传输码
recursion 递归,循环
recursion analysis 递归分析
recursion instruction 递归指令,循环指令
recursion length 递归长度
recursion procedure 递归过程
recursion programming 递归程序设计
recursion routine 递归例程
recursive 递归的,回归的
recursive algorithm 递归算法
recursive control algorithm 递归控制算法
recursive data structure 递归数据结构
recursive definition 递归定义
recursive estimation 递归估计
recursive fashion 递归方式
recursive filtering 递归过滤
recursive game 递归对策
recursive grammar 递归文法
recursive invocation 递归调用
recursive least square processing 递归最小二乘方处理法
recursive linear hashing 递归线性散列
recursive list processing 递归表处理
recursive macro 递归宏功能
recursive macro call 递归宏调用
recursive median filter 递归中值滤波
recursive parallelism 递归并行性
recursive parameter identification 递归参数识别
recursive pattern matcher 递归模式匹配程序
recursive procedure 递归过程
recursive process 递归处理
recursive programming 递归程序设计
recursive routine 递归例程
recursive schema 递归模式
recursive selection algorithm 递归选择算法
recursive set 递归集
recursive subroutine 递归子例程
recursive subroutine method 递归子例程法
recursive topology 递归拓扑
recursive vector instruction 递归向量指令
recursive vector reduction 递归向量化简
recursively-defined array 递归定义阵列
recursively-defined sequence 递归定义序列
recursively enumerable set 递归可枚举集
recursiveness problem 递归性问题
recycle bin 回收站
recycle process 再循环过程,回收处理
recycling 再循环
recycling of programs 程序再循环
recycling programs 再循环程序
red 红色
red area 红色区域
red-black concept 红-黑概念
red/black engineering 红/黑工程
red/black interface 红/黑接口
red-black tree 红黑树
red book 红皮书
red circuit 红色线路
Red Hat 红帽子(Linux 软件公司)
red language 红色语言
red signal 红色信号
red tape 红带
red-tape operation 红带作业,内务操作
red unit 红色单元
redaction 编修,编校
RedBook audio 红皮书音频标准
redefine 重定义
redesign 重新设计
redesign phase 再设计阶段
redex 可约表达式
redial 重拨
redial after timing out 超时
redirected call 改向呼叫
redirected call indicator 改向呼叫指示符
redirected-to-new address signal 请求改向新地址信号
redirect output 改向输出,重定向输出
redirection 重定向,改向
redirection address 改向地址
redirection operator 重定向操作符

redirector 重定向程序
redivide 再划分
redistributable file 可重分发文件
redlining 划红线,标异
Redo 重复(执行)
Redraw 重绘
reduce 精简,简化;归约;还原
Reduce language Reduce语言
reduced carrier transmission 抑制载波传输
reduced flow table 缩减流程表
reduced gradient method 简化梯度法
reduced grammar 归约文法
reduced instruction count computer 精简指令计数计算机
reduced instruction set 精简指令系统
reduced instruction set computer(RISC) 精简指令系统计算机
reduced-order model 降阶模型
reduced sampling inspection 缩减抽样检查
reduced set of residues 剩余简化集
reduced space 退化空间,既约空间
reducer 减压器
reducibility 可约性
reducible graph 可约图形
reducible matrix 可约[可简化]矩阵
reducible operator 可约算子
reducible polynomial 可约多项式
reducible representation 可约表示
reducing 还原,简化,简约
reduction 缩减,简化;归约
β-reduction β归约
reduction factor 缩减因数
reduction machine 归约机
reduction planing 简约规划法
reduction ratio 缩减率
reduction relation 归约关系
reduction routing algorithm 归约路由选择算法
reduction rule 简约规则
redundance bit 冗余位
redundancy 冗余度,冗余
redundancy bit 冗余位
redundancy character 冗余字符
redundancy check 冗余校验
redundancy check bit 冗余校验位
redundancy check character 冗余校验字符
redundancy checking 冗余校验
redundancy computer system 冗余计算机系统
redundancy computers system for space shuttle 航天器用冗余计算机系统
redundancy loop map 冗余环图
redundancy of knowledge 知识的冗余
redundancy testing 冗余测试
redundancy unit 冗余单元
redundant 冗余的
redundant arrays of inexpensive drives (RAID) 廉价驱动器冗余阵列
redundant bit 冗余位
redundant check 冗余校验
redundant code 冗余码
redundant combination 冗余组合
redundant digit 冗余数字
redundant fault 冗余故障
redundant information 冗余信息
redundant n-ary signal 冗余的n元信
redundant permutation 重复排列
redundant phase recording 冗余调相记录法
redundant power supply 备用电源
redundant processing 冗余处理
redundant programming 冗余程序设计法
redundant state 冗余状态
redundant subexpression 冗余子表达式
redundant system 冗余系统
redundant term 冗余项
REDY(REaDY) 就绪
Reed-Muller circuit 李德-米勒电路
reed relay 簧片继电器
Reed Solomon code RS码
reel 卷盘
reel number 卷带号码
reel servo 盘卷伺服机构
reel-to-reel tape transport 带盘驱动式磁带机
reencipher from master key 来自主密钥的再加密
reengineering 二次工程化
reenterable 可重入的,可再入的
reenterable load module 可重入装载模块
reenterable routine 可重入例程

reenterable subroutine 可重入子例程
reentrance 重入
reentrancy 重入
reentrant 可重入的,可再入的
reentrant call 可重入调用
reentrant code 可重入码
reentrant code generation 重入码生成
reentrant program 可重入程序
reentrant reusable routine 可重入再用例程
reentry point 重入点
reentry system 重入系统
REF(REFerence) 参考,引用,基准
reference 参考;引用;基准
reference address 基准地址
reference analysis 引用分析
reference architecture 参考体系结构
reference axis 参考轴,基准线
reference bit 参考位,访问位
reference block 参考块 「组
reference burst 参考脉冲串,参考位
reference class 参考类
reference clock 参考时钟,基准时钟
reference configuration (ISDN)参考配置
reference copy 参考副本
reference counter 参考[基准]计数器
reference database 参考数据库 「序
reference debugging aids 调试辅助程
reference designator 参考标志符
reference edge 参考[基准]边 「移
reference excursion 参考游移,参考偏
reference format 基准[参考]格式
reference frame 参照帧
reference frequency 参考频率
reference grid 参考网格线
reference input 参考[基准]输入 「件
reference input element 参考输入元
reference input signal 参考输入信号
reference instruction 参考指令
reference key 参考键
reference level 参考电平
reference listing 参考列表
reference mark 参考标志
reference modulation 参考调制
reference monitor 基准监察
reference monitor concept 基准监控原则

reference node 参考节点
reference number 参考[基准]号码
reference parameter 引用参数
reference pattern 参考模式
reference personal identification number 基准个人识别号
reference pilot 参考导频
reference PIN 基准个人识别号 「点
reference point (ISDN)参考点,参照
reference power supply 参考[基准]电源
reference program table 参考程序表
reference relation 参照关系
reference retrieval 引文检索
reference scan 参考扫描
reference signal 基准信号
reference speech power 基准语音功率
reference stream 参考流,引用流
reference supply 参考[基准]电源
reference surface 参考[基准]面
reference surface center 基准面中心
reference system 参考系统;参照系
reference table 参考表
reference tape 参考带,基准带
reference time 参考时间
reference transmission level point 传输电平参考点
reference transparency 引用透明性
reference variable 参考变量
reference vector 参考向量
reference voltage 参考[基准]电压
reference volume 基准音量
reference wave 参考波
referential integrity 引用完整性
referential integrity constraints 参考完整性约束
refile 转接,接力传送
refile message 转接消息
refinement 提纯,求精
refinement criterion 提纯判据,求精准则
refinement step 求精步
refinement strategy 提纯策略
refit 改装,重新装配
reflectance 反射能力,反射率
reflectance ink 反光墨水
reflectance ratio 反射比,反射率
reflected binary code 反射二进制码

reflected binary unit distance code 反射二进制单位间距码
reflected code 反射码
reflected factor 反射系数
reflected wave 反射波
reflection 反射
reflection angle 反射角
reflection coefficient 反射系数
reflection factor 反射因子,反射系数
reflection gain 反射增益
reflection law 反射定律
reflection loss 反射损耗
reflection mapping 反射映射
reflection point 反射点
reflective mark 反射标记
reflective marker 反射标志
reflective scan 反射扫描
reflective sensor 反射型传感器
reflective spot 反射点
reflective star-coupler 反射式星形耦合器
reflector 反射器
reflex action in the robot 机器人的反射作用
reflexive 自反
reflexive closure 自反闭包
reflexive inverse 自反逆
reflexive relation 自反关系
reflexivity 自反律
refolder 重折叠器
reformat 重新格式化
reformatting 重定格式化;重格式化
reformulation rule 重组规则
refracted wave 折射波
refraction 折射
refractive index 折射率
refractive index gradient 折射率梯度
reframing time 复帧[帧定位恢复]时间
refresh 刷新
refresh all 全部刷新
refresh buffer 刷新缓冲器
refresh clock 刷新时钟
refresh cycle 刷新周期
refresh grant 刷新许可
refresh interval 刷新间隔
refresh local file list 刷新本地文件列表
refresh memory 刷新存储器
refresh overhead time 刷新开销时间

refresh operation 刷新操作
refresh-RAM 刷新随机存取存储器
refresh rate 刷新速率
refresh request 刷新请求
refresh scan 刷新扫描
refresh testing 刷新测试
refreshable 可刷新的
refreshed-picture display 刷新式画面显示
refreshing 刷新
refrigerant 致冷剂
refrigeration 致冷
refutation 反驳
refutation process 反驳过程,反演过程
refutation tree 反驳树,反演树
regenerate 再生,重写
regenerate cycle 再生周期
regeneration 再生,更新
regeneration buffer 再生缓冲器
regeneration link 再生链路
regeneration period 再生周期
regeneration rate 再生速率
regenerative connection 再生连接
regenerative feedback 再生反馈
regenerative link 再生链
regenerative memory 再生存储器
regenerative read 再生阅读
regenerative repeater 再生转发器
regenerator 再生器
region 区域
region clustering 区域聚集
region control task (RCT) 区域控制任务
region-dependent segmentation 按区域分割
region description 区域描述
region fill 区域填充
region growing 区域生长
region job pack area (RJPA) 区域作业包装区
region list 区域表
region merging 区域合并
region of absolute stability 绝对稳定区域
region-position code 区位码
region segmentation 区域分割
region size 区域大小
region splitting 区域分割

regional address 区域地址
regional center(RC) 区域中心
regional identity code 区域标识码
regional network measurement center 区域网络测量中心
regional office 地区局
regional processing center 地区处理中心
register 寄存器
register address field 寄存器地址字段
register addressable 寄存器可寻址的
register addressing 寄存器寻址
register array 寄存器阵列
register capacity 寄存器容量
register check 寄存器校验
register dump 寄存器转储
register file 寄存器文件
register insertion 寄存器插入
register insertion ring 寄存器插入环
register length 寄存器长度
register level compatibility 寄存器级兼容
register level simulation 寄存器级仿真
register memory 暂存内存
register mode 寄存器模式
register output 寄存器输出
register pair 寄存器对
register parallel transfer 寄存器并行传送
register pointer 寄存器指针
register select 寄存器选择
register-select multiplexer 寄存器选择多工器
register selection 寄存器选择
register serial transfer 寄存器串行传送
register set 寄存器组
register to register 寄存器至寄存器
register transfer 暂存转移
register transfer language(RTL) 寄存器转移语言
register transfer level simulation 寄存器级模拟
register transfer microprogramming language 寄存器转移微程序设计语言
register transfer simulation 寄存器传送仿真
registered trademark 注册商标
registration 登录;对齐

registration mark 对版标记;对准标志
registration of layout design protection 布线图设计保护的登记
registry 注册表
registry provider 登录服务供应商
regrade 再分级,再分类
regression analysis 回归分析
regression inference 回归推理
regression reasoning 回归推理
regular binary 正规二进制
regular expression 正则表达式
regular expression matching problem 正则表达式匹配问题
regular file 正规文件
regular grammar(RG) 正规文法
regular index 常规索引
regular language 正规语言,正则语言
regular matrix 正则矩阵
regular network 正规网络
regular non-linear recursion 正则非线性递归
regular processor network 正规处理机网络
regular set 正规集,正则集
regular shape 规则形状
regular splitting 正则分解
regular transaction 常规事务
regular tree grammar 正则树文法
regular tree language 正则树语言
regulation(REG) 调整,调节;规则
regulation factor 稳压系数
rehashing 重散列
rehost 换主机
REI(REturn Instruction) 返回指令
reimbursed time 补偿时间
reindex 重新索引
reinfection 重新感染,再传染
reinforce 加强
reinforcement learning system 强化学习系统
reinitialization 重新初始化
reinstallation 重新安装
reinversion 重反演
reject 拒绝
reject character 拒识字符
reject frame 拒收帧
reject rate 否决率,拒绝率

reject region 否决区,拒绝区
rejection 否决,拒斥
rejection gate "或非"门
rejuvenate 复初,复原
rekey 重定密钥
REL(Rapidly Extensible Language) 可快速扩充语言
Rel(Recorder element) 记录元素
related file 相关文件
related request 相关情求
related term 相关词
relation 关系;关系式
relation algebra 关系代数
relation broken 关系解除
relation calculus 关系演算
relation character 关系字符
relation condition 关系条件
relation constraint 关系约束
relation identifier 关系标识符
relation integrity 关系完整性
relation model 关系模型
relation net 关系网
relation record 关系记录
relation schema 关系模式
relation type 关系类型
relational algebra 关系代数
relational break-point 关系断点
relational calculus 关系演算
relational character 关系字符
relational checking 关系校验
relational complete language 关系完备语言
relational completeness 关系完备性
relational data base machine(RDBM) 关系数据库机
relational data base management system (RDBMS) 关系数据库管理系统
relational database 关系数据库
relational database management 关系数据库管理
relational database schema 关系数据库模式
relational expression 关系表达式
Relational Extenders 关系数据库扩展器
relational file 关系文件
relational graph 相关图
relational memory 相关存储器
relational model 关系模型

relational operator 关系算子[操作符]
relational spreadsheet 关系型表格
relational structure 关系结构
relational symbols 关系符号
relational system 关系系统
relationship 关系
relationship frame 关系框架
relative 相对的
relative address 相对地址
relative address label 相对地址标号
relative addressing 相对寻址
relative addressing mode 相对寻址模式
relative articulation 相对清晰度
relative buffer utilization 缓冲器相对利用率
relative byte address(RBA) 相对字节地址
relative cell addressing 相对单元格寻址
relative character 相对字符
relative code 相对代码
relative coding 相对编码
relative command 相对命令
relative coordinate 相对坐标
relative coordinate data 相对坐标数据
relative data 相对数据
relative database 相对数据库
relative delay 相对时延
relative departure 相对偏离
relative efficiency 相对效率
relative end position 相对终结位置
relative entropy 相对熵
relative error 相对误差
relative file 相对文件
relative file organization 相对文件组织
relative frequency 相对频率
relative generation number 相对世代号
relative harmonic content 相对谐波含量
relative humidity 相对湿度
relative identifier 相对标识符
relative key 相对键
relative level 相对电平
relative line number 相对线路号码
relative loader 相对装入程序
relative magnitude 相对值,相对幅度大小
relative maximum 相对最大值
relative minimum 相对最小值

relative moniker 相对别名
relative move 相对移动
relative order 相对命令
relative organization 相对组织
relative origin 相对原始地址
relative path name 相对路径名
relative phase telegraphy 相对相位电报
relative pointing device 相对定位设备
relative positioning 相对定位法
relative program 相对程序
relative record data set 相对记录数据集
relative record file 相对记录文件
relative redundancy 相对冗余度
relative redundancy of source 源的相对冗余度
relative sequential access method (RSAM) 相对顺序访问法
relative stability 相对稳定性
relative table size control 相对表尺寸控制
relative time clock(RTC) 相对时钟
relative track address 相对磁道地址
relative transmission level 相对传输电平
relative vector 相对向量
relatively prime 互素，互质
relativity of knowledge 知识的相对性
relaxation 松弛法
relaxation factor 松弛因子
relaxation oscillator 弛张振荡器
relaxation parameter 松弛参数
relaxation procedure 松弛过程
relaxor 弛张振荡器
relay 继电器；中继
relay amplifier 中继放大器
relay center 转接中心
relay communication 中继通信
relay communication method 中继通信方法
relay computer 转接计算机；继电器式计算机
relay contacts 继电器接点
relay driver 继电器驱动器
Relay Gold Relay Gold 通信软件
relay group 继电器组
relay host 转发主机
relay interface 中继接口
relay logic 继电器逻辑

relay open system 中继开放系统
relay pilot 转发引导[中继传输]指令
relay selector 继电器式选择器
relay station 中继站
relay switch 继电器开关
relay system 中继系统
relay transaction 转接交易
relaying 中继，转发
relaying envelope 中继包封
release 释放；复原；版次
release alarm 释放告警
release command 释放命令
release connection 断接，连接释放
release guard 释放保护
release-guard signal 释放保护信号
release node 释放节点
release note 版本注释
release number 版次号码
release read 释放读取
release statement 释放语句
release time 复位时间，释放时间
release time and date 释放时间和日期
release token 释放权标(令牌)
relevance 关联性，相关性
relevance feedback 关联性反馈
relevance matrix 关联矩阵
relevance ratio 检出率
relevance tree 相关树
relevant backtracking 相关回溯
relevant character 关联字符
relevant document 关联文档
relevant failure 关联失效
relevant word list 相关词表
reliability(R) 可靠性
reliability assessment 可靠性评价
reliability assignment 可靠性分配
reliability assurance test 可靠性保证测试
reliability block diagram 可靠性方块图
reliability certification 可靠性认证
reliability compliance test 可靠性符合试验
reliability design 可靠性设计
reliability determination test 可靠性确定试验
reliability distribution 可靠性分配
reliability engineering 可靠性工程
reliability estimation 可靠性估计

reliability evaluation 可靠性评估
reliability function 可靠性函数
reliability graph 可靠性图
reliability growth 可靠性增长
reliability improvement factor 可靠性改善系数
reliability index 可靠性指标
reliability level 可靠性等级
reliability logic 可靠性逻辑
reliability mathematics 可靠性数学
reliability model 可靠性模型
reliability model of software 软件可靠性模型
reliability of transducer 转换器可靠「性
reliability optimization 可靠性最优化
reliability policy 可靠性策略
reliability prediction 可靠性预测
reliability principle 可靠性原理
reliability rate 可靠度
reliability software 软件可靠性
reliability sampling 可靠性抽样
reliability statistics 可靠性统计
reliability test 可靠性试验
reliability testing 可靠性测试
reliability trial 可靠性试验
reliable datagram protocol(RSP) 可靠数据报协议
reliable stream protocol(RSP) 可靠流协议
reliable transfer service element(RTSE) 可靠传输服务元素
relinquish 撤回,放弃,停止
reloadable control store 可再馈入控制存储器
relocatability 重定位性,浮动性
relocatability attribute 浮动属性
relocatable 可重定位的
relocatable address 可重定位地址
relocatable assembler 可重定位汇编程序
relocatable code 可重定位码
relocatable code addressing mode 可重定位码寻址模式
relocatable coding 可重定位编码
relocatable emulator 可重定位仿真器
relocatable entry address 可重定位入口地址
relocatable expression 可重定位表式

relocatable form 可重定位形式
relocatable input/output 可重定位输入/输出
relocatable library 可重定位程序库
relocatable-library module 可重定位程序库模块
relocatable linking loader 可重定位链接装配程序
relocatable macroassembler 可重定位宏汇编程序
relocatable module 可重定位模块
relocatable partitioned storage management 可重定位分区存储管理
relocatable program 可重定位程序,浮动程序
relocatable program loader 可重定位程序装配程序
relocatable routine 可重定位例程
relocatable sequence 浮动序列 「程
relocatable subroutine 可重定位子例
relocatable symbolic address 浮动符号地址
relocatable term 可重定位项
relocate 重定位,浮动
relocate hardware 重定位硬件
relocating assembler 重定位汇编程序
relocating linking loader 重定位链接装配程序
relocating loader 重定位装配程序
relocating object loader 重定位目标装配程序
relocation 重定位,浮动
relocation address 浮动地址
relocation binary program 重定位机器码程序 「典
relocation dictionary(RLD) 重定位字
relocation factor 重定位因数
relocation interrupt 重定位中断
relocation pack 重定位包装
relocation-processor storage 重定位处理机存储器
relocation register 重定位寄存器
relog file 重登录文件
REM(REMark) 附注,注释
REM statement 注释语句
REM(REMote) 远程的,遥控的
remainder(REM,RMDR) 余数,余项
remainder term for interpolation formu-

1a 插值公式的余项
remaining time 剩余时间
remanence 剩磁
remanent flux 剩余磁通
remanent magnetization 剩磁
remapping 重映像,重变换
remark(REM) 附注,注记;重标记,改标(一种以次充好的商业欺骗行为)
remark CPU 改标处理器
remark memory bank 改标内存条
remarks column 备注栏
remedial feedback 修正式反馈
remedial maintenance 补救维护,出错维修
remembrance 备忘录
Remes algorithm 里米兹算法
remeshing 重分网格
reminder 提醒信号;提示项
remirror 重镜像
remodulation 重调制
REMOTE 远程访问
remote 远程的,远距离的;遥控
remote access 远程存取[访问]
remote access computing system 远程访问计算系统
remote access data processing 远程存取数据处理
remote access information 远程存取信息
remote access service 远程访问控制
remote access service user 远程访问控制用户
remote access software 远程访问软件
remote-access storage and retrieval 远程存取存储与检索
remote area terminal(RAT) 远程终端
remote assistance 远程支持
remote automatic telemetry equipment 自动遥测装置
Remote Automation 远程自动化
remote axis admittance 运动轴导装置
remote backup 远程备份
remote batch 远程批处理法
remote batch access 远程批量存取
remote batch computing 远程整批计算
remote batch entry(RBE) 远程批量输入
remote batch facility 远程批量设施
remote batch module(RBM) 远程批处理模块
remote batch processing 远程批处理
remote batch system(RBS) 远程批处理系统
remote batch terminal(RBT) 远程批处理终端
remote batch terminal application 远程批处理终端应用
remote batch terminal emulator(RBTE) 远程批处理终端仿真程序
remote batch terminal system 远程批处理终端系统
remote BIOS redirection 远程BIOS重定向
remote boot 远程自举[引导]
remote boot file 远程引导文件
remote boot service 远程自举服务
remote calculator 远程计算器
remote center compliance(RCC) 远程定心装置
remote collaboration system 远程协作系统
remote command submission 远程命令提交
remote communications concentrator(RCC) 远程通信集线器
remote computer(RC) 远程计算机
remote computer pool(RCP) 远程计算机池
remote computing(RC) 远程计算
remote computing service(RCS) 远程计算服务
remote computing system(RCS) 远程计算系统
remote computing system completeness errors 远程计算系统完整性错误
remote computing system concentrator 远程计算系统集中器
remote computing system consistency error 远程计算系统一致性错误
remote computing system error detection 远程计算系统错误检查
remote computing system exchange 远程计算系统交换机
remote computing system execution er-

ror 远程计算系统执行错误
remote computing system language 远程计算系统语言
remote computing system log 远程计算系统运行记录
remote computing system monitor 远程计算系统监督程序
remote concentrator 远程集中器
remote connection 远程联结
remote console(RECON) 远程控制台
remote console system(RECON) 遥控台系统
remote control(RC) 远程控制,遥控
remote control adapter(RCA) 遥控适配器
remote control board 远程控制台
remote control channel(RMCC) 遥控通道
remote control coder 遥控编码器
remote control command 远程控制命令
remote control equipment(RCE) 遥控设备
remote control file 远程控制文件
remote control language 远程控制语言
remote control monitoring system 遥控监测系统
remote control panel(RCP) 遥控板
remote control program 远程控制程序
remote control signals 遥控信号
remote control software 远程控制软件
remote control switch 遥控开关
remote control system(RCS) 遥控系统
remote control unit(RCU) 遥控单元,遥控器
remote controlled vehicle(RCV) 遥控运载工具
remote controller 远程控制器,遥控器
remote copy 远程复制
remote data acquisition subsystem 远程数据采集子系统
remote data base access(RCBA) 远程数据库存取
remote-data base access service 远程数据库存取服务
Remote Data base Access Service Protocol(RDASP) 远程数据库访问服务协议
remote data collection(RDC) 远程数据收集
remote data concentrator(RDC) 远程数据集中器
remote data processing(RDP) 远程数据处理
Remote Data Service(RDS) 远程数据服务
remote data station 远程数据站
remote data terminal 远程数据终端
remote data transmitter(RDT) 远程数据发送机
remote debugging 远程调试
remote device 远程装置
remote diagnostic center(RDC) 远程诊断中心
remote digital loopback test 远程数字回绕式测试
remote display 远程显示器
remote display unit 远程显示单元
remote echo 远程回应
remote enable(REN) 远距允许,远地使能
remote entry service(RES) 远程输入服务
remote entry unit(REU) 远程进入单元
remote equipment 远程设备
remote error sensing 远程误差检测
remote Ethermail 远程以太网电子邮件
remote exchange(RX) 远程交换机
remote file access(RCF) 远程文件存取
remote file access monitor(RFCM) 远程文件存取监督例程
remote file service(RFS) 远程文件服务
remote format specification 远程格式说明
remote global computer access service(RGCAS) 远程全球计算机存取业务
Remote Graphics Instruction Set(REGIS) 远程图形指令集
remote graphics processor(RGP) 远程图形处理例程
remote host 远程主机

remote identifier 远程标识符
remote information management system (RIMS) 远程信息管理系统
remote information query system (RIQS) 远程信息查询系统
remote information system(RIS) 远程信息系统
remote input/output controller 远程输入/输出控制器
remote inquiry 远程查询
remote inquiry-answer 远程查询回答
remote inquiry unit 远程查询单元
remote intelligent terminal 远程智能终端
remote job entry(RJE) 远程作业输入
remote job entry executive(RJEX) 远程作业登录执行例程
remote job entry mode 远程作业登录模式
remote job entry protocol(RJEP) 远程作业输入协议
remote job entry terminals(RJET) 远程作业登录终端
remote job output(RJO) 远程作业输出
remote job processor(RJP) 远程作业处理例程
remote job service(RJS) 远程作业服务
remote line adapter(RLA) 远程线路适配器
Remote Login 远程登录
remote loop adapter 远程环路适配器
remote maintenance switch 远程维护开关
remote management 远程管理
remote master data circuit-terminal equipment 远程主数据电路终端设备
remote measurement 遥测
remote message input/output 远程消息输入/输出
remote message processing 远程消息处理
remote method invocation(RMI) 远程方法调用
remote mode 远程模式
remote modem self-test 远程调制解调器自测
remote multiplexer 远程多路转换器
remote network(RNET) 远程网络
remote network access controller 远程网络访问控制器
remote network control 远程网络控制
remote network monitoring service 远程网络监控服务
remote object 远程对象
remote object class definition 远程对象类定义
remote-operation display 远程作业显示器
remote oriented simulation system (ROSS) 远程导向仿真系统
remote packet concentrator 远程分组集中器
remote performance monitor 远程性能监视器
remote polling 远程轮询
remote position control 远距位置控制
remote power-off 遥控断电
remote power-on 远程加电
remote printing 远程打印
remote procedure call(RPC) 远过程调用
remote program loader 远程程序装入器
remote programming 远程程序设计
remote real-time terminal 远程实时终端
remote record access 远程记录存取
remote request number 远程请求数
remote reset 远程复位
remote resource 远程资源
remote resource access capability 远程资源访问能力
remote sensing 遥感
remote sensing digital image 遥感数字图像
remote sensing digital image processing system 遥感数字图像处理系统
remote sensing image interpretation 遥感图像解释
remote server 远程服务器
remote shell 远程命令解释程序
remote site 远地
remote slave display 远程从属显示器
remote software 远程软件
remote spooling communication subsystem(RSCS) 远程假脱机通信子系

统
remote station 远程站点
remote subset 远程子站
remote system 远程系统
remote teaching 远程示教
remote terminal(RT) 远程终端
remote terminal access method 远程终端存取法
remote terminal emulator 远距终端仿真程序
remote-terminal processing 远程终端处理
remote terminal type 远程终端类型
remote testing 远程测试
remote transaction program 远程事务处理程序
remote transfer point 远程传送点
remote user 远程用户
remote visualization system 远程可视化系统
remote wakeup 远程唤醒
remote work station 远程工作站
remotely accessed resource-sharing computer system 远程访问资源共享计算机系统
remotely controlled robot with manned platform 带载人平台的远程控制机器人
remotely sensed data 遥感数据
RemotePoint 遥控光标
removability 可更换性
removable cartridge disk 可更换盒式盘
removable direct access storage 可装卸的直接存取存储器
removable disk unit 可移动式磁盘机
removable hard disk 可移动硬盘
removable mass storage 移动式海量存储器
removable patch panel 活动排题板,活动插线板
removable plugboard 移动插头板
removable storage media 移动式存储媒体
removal class 移去类别
removal of virus 病毒消除
remove 搬移,移动
REMOVE DOS 移除DOS
remove empty tag 移除空标签
remove frame 移除框架
remove redundant nested tag 移除多余的嵌套标签
REMS(Registered Equipment Management System) 注册设备管理系统
REN(Remote ENable) 远程使能
REN(RENming) 重命名,更名
rename 更名,重命名
rename inhibit 更名禁止
rename_namespace attribute 命名空间更名属性
rename variable 更改变量名
render 再现,表演;润色,着色
rendering 着色,润色
rendering attribute 润色属性
rendering pipeline 润色流水线
rendering rate 着色速率
rendering simulator 着色仿真程序
Renderman interface Renderman接口
rendezvous 会合,内聚;集合点
rendezvous element 聚集元素
rendezvous method 对接法
RENDIR(REName DIRectory) 目录更名
renewal 更新
renewal corrective maintenance 更新校正维护
renewal process 更新过程
rental system 租用系统;租赁制
renumbering 重编号
reorder 重组,重排序
reorganization of knowledge base 知识库重组
reorganization of the interconnection network 互连网络重组
reorientation 重取向
reorigin 再定位原点
repacking 重组,改组
repagination 重编页码,重新分页
repaint 重绘,重画
repair cycle 检修周期
repair delay time 检修延迟时间
repair time 检修时间
repairability 可修复性
repairable data base 可修复数据库
repairing circuit 自检修电路
repay time 回访时间
repeat 重复

repeat-action key 重复作用键
repeat call 重复呼叫
repeat counter 重复次数计数器
repeat filter 重复过滤器
repeat key 重复键
repeat operator 重复运算子
repeat predicate 重复谓词
repeat request 重复请求
REPEAT statement 重复语句
repeat test 重复测试
repeat transmission system 重复传输系统
repeat-until 重复直到语句
repeatability 重现性,重复性
repeatability error 重复性错误
repeatability measure 重复性量度
repeatable 可重复的
repeatable read 可重复读
repeated attempt 重复尝试
repeated hyperlinks 重复超链接
repeated optical link 中继光链路
repeated selection sort 重复选择排序
repeater 中继器,转发器
repeater coil 增音器线圈,增音线圈
repeater distribution frame 中继配线
repeater station 增音站,中继站 └架
repeating field 重复字段
repeating group 重复组
repeating key 重复键
repeating label 重复标记
repeats per minute 每分钟重复数
repertorier 栈单
repertory 栈单,指令集
repertory dialer 栈单拨号器,号码表拨号器
repetition factor 重复因子
repetition instruction 重复指令
repetition rate 重复频率
repetitive addressing 重复寻址
repetitive analog computer 重复模拟计算机
repetitive construction 重复构造
repetitive operation 重复操作
repetitive specification 重复规范说明
repetitive strain injury(RSI) 手部职业病
repetitive unit 重复单位[单元]
replace 替换,代换,置换

replace current subtotals 替换当前分类汇总
replace existing categories 替换现有分类
replace bullets only 只替换项目符号
replaceable parameter 可替换参数
replaceable unit 可替换部件
replacement 替换,代换
replacement algorithm 替换算法
replacement character 替换字符
replacement in strings 串替换
replacement policy 替换策略
replacement problem 替换问题
replacement rule 置换规则
replacement strategy 替换策略
replacement theory 替换论
replanning 重新规划
replay 重播;回放
replenishment 补充
replica master 复现主控器
replica reproduction 复制品,副本
replicate 复制 「关
replicate/transfer switch 复制转移开
replicated database system 复制数据库系统
replication (批量)复制,复制器技术
replication factor 重复因子
replication tool 复制工具
replication transparency 复制透明性
replicator 重复符
reply 回答,答复
reply message 回答消息,应答报文
report 报告,报表
report band 报表带区
report clause 报表子句 「栏
report control toolbar 报表控制工具
report delay 报告延迟
report description(RD) 报表描述
report detail band 报表细节带区
report file 报表文件
report footer band 报表注脚带区
report footing 报表注脚
report form 报表窗体
report format 报表格式
report generation 制表,报表生成
report generation parameters 制表参
report generator 报表生成程序 └数
report group 报表栏,报表组

report header band 报表标头带区
report heading 报表头
report interval 报表间隔时间
report name 报表名
report program 报表程序
report program generator(RPG) 报表程序生成器
report program generator language 报表编制程序语言
report section 报表节
report wizard 报表向导
report write control system(RWCS) 报表书写控制系统
report write logical record 报告书写逻辑记录
report writer 报表输出程序
reporting file 报表文件
reporting net 报告网络
reporting period 报表周期
reporting time interval 报告时间间隔
reporter 制表程序
reposition 再定位
repository 系统信息中心库,知识库
repost 重寄
represent 表示,表现,代表
representation-language-language(RLL) 表示语言的语言,RLL 语言
representation of knowledge 知识表示,知识表达
representation of knowledge organization 知识组织表示
representation specification 表示法规范
representative calculating operation 代表性计算操作
representative calculating time 代表性计算时间
representative computing time 代表性运算时间
representative element 代表元素
representative graph 代表图
representative sampling 代表性抽样
representative simulation 代表性仿真
representative value 代表值,典型值
reproduce 复制
reproduce head 再生磁头
reproducer 复制机;复制程序
reproducibility 复制性,重现性
reproducible 可再现的

reproducing head 复制磁头
reproducing unit 复制装置
reproduction code 复制码
reproduction ratio 重现率
reproduction replica 复制品,复制副本
reproduction speed 重现速率
reprogrammable associative ROM 可重编程的结合只读存储器
reprogrammable ROM(REROM) 可重编程的只读存储器
repudiation 否认,拒绝
REQ(REQuest) 请求
request 请求
request block 请求块,请求分组
request channel 请求通道
request denied frame(RDF) 请求拒绝帧
request element 请求元件
request for buffer space 请求缓冲器空间
Request For Comment(RFC) 征求意见文件
request for information 请求信息
request for next message(RFNM) 请求下一报文
request for proposal(RFP) 投标请求书
request for service message 请求服务消息
request foreground program 请求前台程序
request/grant logic 请求/同意逻辑
request header 请求标题
request next character 请求下个字符
request ID 请求标识符
request on line 请求联机
request operator's control panel 请求操作员控制面板
request-oriented information management system 面向需求的信息管理系统
request parameter list(RPL) 请求参数表
request pending light 请求待处理灯
request primitive 请求原语
request-repeat signal 请求重复信号
request-repeat system 请求重复系统
request-repeat system by interference detection 干扰侦察请求重复系统

request repeat system with error detecting code 带检错码的请求重传系统
request-response 请求响应
request/response header 请求/应答标题
request-response unit(UR) 请求响应单元
request-send circuit 请求发送电路
request service initiation 请求服务起始
request signal 请求信号
request slip 请求滑移
request stacking 申请堆栈
request stringing 请求串
request time 请求时间
request timeout 请求超时
request to send(RS,RTS) 请求发送
request to send circuit 请求发送电路
request to send signal 请求发送信号
request unit 请求单元
request words for input/output 输入/输出请求字
requester 请求程序
requesting process 请求过程
required 需求的,不可缺少的
required hyphen 所需连字符
required input 需求输入
required list 请求表
required page break 请求的页中止
required page end character 请求页结束字符
required parameter 所需参数
required space 所需空间;不可省略空格
requirement 需求
requirement analysis 需求分析
requirement analysis tool 需求分析工具
requirement definition 需求定义
requirement definition phase 需求定义阶段
requirement description language 需求描述语言
requirement engineering 需求工程
requirement specification 需求说明
requirement specification language 需求规格说明语言
requirement statement language(RSL) 需求陈述语言
requirement verification 需求验证
requisition 正式请求

rereading 重读
rerouting 重选路由
rerun 重新运行
rerun mode 重运行模式
rerun point 重运行点
rerun routine 重运行例程
rerun time 重新运行时间
resampling 重抽样
rescale 重定比例
rescue dump 挽救转储
rescue point 救援点
research networks 研究型网络
research open systems for Europe (ROSE) 欧洲研究开放系统
RESEDA RESEDA专家系统
ResEdit(Resource Edit) 源编辑
reselection 重选
reservation 预约,预留
reserve 保留
reserve clause 保留子句
reserved area 保留区
reserved bandwidth 保留带宽
reserved field 保留字段
reserved file type 保留文件类型
reserved memory 保留内存
reserved name 保留名
reserved operand 保留操作数
reserved page option 保留页面任选项
reserved unit 保留单元
reserved volume 保留卷
reserved word 保留字
reset 复位
reset button 复位按钮
reset collision 重设冲突,重置冲突
reset condition 复位条件
reset confirmation packet 复位确认包
reset control logic 复位控制逻辑
reset enable 复位允许
reset gate 复位门
reset inhibit 复位禁止
reset input 复位输入
reset key 复位键
reset line 复位线
reset packet 重设信息包
reset procedure 复位过程
reset pulse 复位脉冲
reset rate 重设率,复位率
RESET ROUTER 重定位路由器

reset-set(RS) 复位-置位
reset-set-toggle(RST) 复位-置位转换
reset switch 复位开关
reset terminal 复位端
reset time 复位时间
reset-to-n 复位到n,重设于n
resettable data base 可重置数据库
reshaping 整形
reshaping signal 整形信号
residence system 常驻系统
residence volume system 常驻卷系统
resident 驻留,常驻;驻留程序
resident assembler 驻留式汇编程序
resident compiler 常驻编译程序
resident control program 常驻控制程
resident disc operating system 常驻磁盘操作系统
resident executive 常驻执行程序
resident executive program 常驻管理程序
resident font 常驻字体
resident macroassembler 常驻宏汇编程序
resident module 驻留模块,常驻模块
resident monitor 驻存监察器
resident name 驻留用名
resident operating system 常驻操作系
resident program 常驻程序
resident routine 驻存例程
resident segment 常驻段
resident set limit 驻存集限制
resident shared-page index 驻存共享页索引
resident software 常驻软件
resident supervisor 驻存监督程序
resident task 常驻任务
residual control 后效控制,余迹控制
residual error 剩余误差,残留错误
residual error rate(RER) 剩余差错率
residual-error ratio 剩余差错比
residual intelligibility 剩余可懂度
residual magnetism 剩磁
residual mean 平均剩余,平均残差
residual modulation 剩余调制
residual noise 剩余噪声
residual risk 剩余风险
residual vector 残向量
residue 剩余,残数;残余物
residue check 余数校验
residue class 剩余类
residue code 剩余码
residue problem 剩余问题
residue system 余数系统
resist 抗蚀剂
resist film 抗蚀膜
resistance 电阻
resistance attenuator 电阻衰减器
resistance divider 电阻分压器
resistive touch screen 电阻式触摸屏
resistivity 电阻率
resistivity isolation 电阻性隔离
resistivity rings 电阻率环
resistor 电阻器,电阻
resistor-diode logical 电阻器-二极管逻辑电路
resistor matrix 电阻矩阵
resistor-transistor logic(RTL) 电阻晶体管逻辑电路
resize 调整尺寸
resize handle 尺寸调整柄
resize pointer 尺寸调整指针
resoftware engineering 再造软件工程
resolution 分辨率,清晰度
resolution error 分辨率误差
resolution factor 分解因子
resolution method 消解法,归结法
resolution mode 分辨率模式
resolution principle 归结[消解]原理
resolution proof graph 消解证明图
resolution proof tree 消解证明树,归结证明树
resolution ratio 分解比
resolution refutation 归结反驳
resolution-refutation graph 归结反驳图,消解反驳图
resolution theorem proving 归结定理证明
resolution time 分辨时间
resolvable 可解析的
resolve 解决,解答
resolved recipient 已辨识收件人
resolvent 消解式,归结式
resolvent matrix 预解矩阵
resolvent operator 预解算子
resolver 分解器
resolving power 分辨能力

resolving time 分解时间
resonance 谐振;共鸣
resonant cavity 谐振腔,空腔谐振器
resonant circuit 谐振电路
resonant frequency 谐振频率
resource 资源
resource access control facility(RACF) 资源存取控制设施
resource allocation 资源分配
resource allocation and multiple project scheduling(RAMPS) 资源分配与多项目调度
resource allocation control tool 资源分配控制工具
resource allocation frame(RAF) 资源分配帧
resource assignment table(RDT) 资源分配表
resource attribute 资源属性
resource-based access control 基于资源的访问控制
resource-bounded Kolmogorov complexity 资源限制科莫洛夫复杂性
resource class 资源类
resource compiler(RC) 源编译程序
resource component 资源成分
resource control block(RCB) 资源控制块
resource data(RDF) 资源数据
resource data file(RDF) 资源数据文件
resource deallocation 资源分配取消
resource-definition file 资源定义文件
resource definition table(RDT) 资源定义表
resource dispenser 资源分配器
resource file(RDF) 资源文件
resource fork 资源派生
resource group class 资源组类
resource group profile 资源组轮廓文件
resource handler 资源处理器
resource heap 资源堆
resource hierarchy 资源层次
resource ID 资源标识符
resource identification table(RSID) 资源识别表
Resource Interchange File Format(RIFF) 资源交换文件格式
resource label 资源标志

resource level 资源级
resource lockout 资源封锁
resource manage 资源管理
resource management agent(RMA) 资源管理机构
resource manager 资源管理程序
resource name 资源名
resource notebook 资源登录簿
resource number 资源编号
resource object 资源对象
resource pool 资源池
resource protection 资源保护
resource queue 资源队列
resource redundancy 资源冗余
resource registration 资源登记
resource release 资源释放
resource request table 资源请求表
resource reservation protocol(RSVP) 资源保留协议
resource scheduling 资源调度
resource script file 资源脚本文件
resource security 资源安全性
resource sequence number 资源序号
resource sharing 资源共享
resource-sharing computer system 资源共享计算机系统
resource-sharing control 资源共享控制
resource-sharing multiprocessor 资源共享多处理机
resource-sharing time-sharing system 资源共享分时系统
resource status collector 资源状态收集器
resource starved node 资源缺乏网点
resource subnet 资源子网
resource take-over 资源接管
resource type 资源类型
resource utilization factor 资源利用系数
resource utilization graph 资源利用图形
resource utilization monitor 资源利用监察例程
resource utilization time 资源利用时间
resource vector table(RVT) 资源向量表
resource view 资源视图
RESP(RESPonse) 响应,回答
respond opportunity 响应时机

respond output 响应输出
responder 响应站
responder module 应答模块
response 响应,应答
response analysis program 响应分析程序
response assembly 响应组合
response curve 响应曲线
response duration 响应时间
response frame 响应帧
response header 响应标题
response indicator 响应指示器
response message 响应消息
response mode 响应模式,答复方式
response primitive 响应原语
response ratio 响应比,响应率
response register 应答寄存器
response service message 响应服务消息
response speed 响应速度
response threshold 响应门限
response time 响应时间
response-time monitor 响应时间监督程序
response to request service message 响应请求服务消息
response type 响应类型
response vector 响应向量
response window 响应窗口
responsibility 责任
restart 重始,再启动
restart address 重始[再启动]地址
restart and recovery technique 重始与恢复技术
restart call 重启动调用
restart checkpoint 重启动检验点
restart condition 重始条件
restart-confirmation packet 重启动确认分组
restart each entry 每次输入时重启动
restart from flag 自标志处重启动
restart-indication packet 重启动指示分组
restart instruction 重始指令,再启动指令
restart interrupt 再起动中断
restart key 重始键,再启动键
restart number 重算数
restart point 重始点,重新起动点

restart-point-of-last-environment 上一环境点重始
restart procedure 再启动过程
restart routine 重始例程
restart sorting 重始排序
restartable job 可重启动作业
restore 恢复,复原,再存入,再生
restore button 恢复按钮
restore command 恢复命令
restore image 恢复图像
restore icon 恢复图标
restore session 恢复对话
RESTORE statement 恢复语句
restore video 恢复屏幕
restored polar signal 还原极性信号
restorer pulse 重定脉冲
restorer-pulse generator 复原脉冲产生器
restricted 受限制的
restricted area 限定区域
restricted edge emitting diode(REED) 受限边发射二极管
restricted function 受限功能
restricted fuzzy automaton 受限模糊自动机
restricted language 受限语言
restricted master programming 约束主规划
restricted problem 受限问题,约束问题
restricted-use volume 限制使用卷
restricted variable length code 限定变长编码
restriction 限制,限定
restructure 重构
restructuring program 重构程序
result 结果
result address 结果地址
result-based perturbation 基于结果的扰动
result cell 结果单元
result element 结果元
result error 结果误差
result field 结果字段
result flow 结果流
result identifier 结果标识符
result packet 结果包
result register 结果寄存器
result set 结果集合

result sharing 结果共享
result status 结果状态
result string 结果串
resultant fault 综合故障
resultant field 合成场
resultant output listing 合成输出列表
resultant string 合成串;结果串
resultless 无结果的
resume 重新继续,重新开始
resume broken download 断点续传下载
resync 再同步
resync tolerance value 再同步宽容值
resynchronization 再同步
RET program RET 计划
retail terminal system 零售终端系统
retailer 零售机
retained data 保留数据
retained segment 保留段
retardation 推迟;减速
retarded system 性能落后的系统
retention class 保留类别
retention cycle 保存周期
retention period 保持期间,保存期
retentivity 剩磁,顽磁性
retest 重复测试
reticles 初缩掩膜版
reticular structure 网状结构
retiming 重定时
retina character reader(DCR) 网膜字符读出机
retirement phase 退役阶段
RETMA(Radio, Electronics, Television Manufacturers Association) 无线电、电子、电视制造商协会(现在是 EIA)
retrace 回扫迹
retrace time 回扫时间
retract predicate 撤消谓词
retractable erase head 可伸缩擦除磁头
retraction method 撤消法
retransmission 重传,重发
retransmission ACK/NAK 重发确认/否定
retrievable information 可检索信息
retrieval 取出,检索
retrieval characteristic 检索特征
retrieval code 检索码
retrieval command language 检索命令语言
retrieval coordinate 组配检索
retrieval efficiency ratio 检索效率比
retrieval mark 检索标记
retrieval ordering 检索定序
retrieval performance 检索性能
retrieval usage mode 检索使用模式
retrieve 检索
retrofit 修整,改进,更新
retrofit testing 修整测试
retrograde path equation 后退方程
retrogression principle 退步原理
retrospective conversion 追溯转换
retrospective search(RS) 追溯查寻法
retrospective verbalization 回溯性词语表达方法
retry 重试,重发
retry capability 重试能力
retry counter 重试次数计数器
retry parameter 重试参数
retry point 重试点
return(RET) 返回
return address 返回地址
return address register 返回地址寄存器
return attribute 返回属性
return character 返回字符,回车字符
return clause 返回子句
return code 返回码
return code register 返回码寄存器
return from dead 死而复生
return from subroutine 从子例程返回
return instruction 返回指令
return key 回车键
return loss 回波损耗
return message 返回消息
return on carry 有进位则返回
return on noncarry 无进位则返回
return on nonzero 非零则返回
return on positive 为正则返回
return path 返回路径
return point 返回点
return point sorting 转回点排序
return pointer 返回指针
return receipt 回执
return signal 返回信号
return stack 返回栈
return statement 返回语句
return-to-bias(RB) 归偏,归偏制

return to bias recording 归偏制记录
return-to-reference recording 归基准记录法
return to zero(RZ) 归零
return to zero binary code 归零二进制码
return to zero code 归零码
return to zero method 归零法
return to zero mode 归零模式
return to zero recording 归零记录
return to zero space 归零空位
returned value 返回值
returning spring 还原弹簧
reusability 可复用性,可重用性
reusability method 可重用性方法
reusable 可重用的,可再用的
reusable architecture 可重用结构
reusable data set 可重用数据集「队
reusable disk queuing 可重用磁盘列
reusable file 可重用文件
reusable module 可重用模块
reusable program 可重用程序
reusable resource 可重用资源
reusable routine 可重用例程
reusable script 可重用脚本
reusable software 可重用软件
revalidation 重新确认
reverse 反向,反转「器
reverse acting controller 反作用控制
Reverse Address Resolution Protocol(RARP) 反向地址解析协议
reverse assembler 反汇编程序
reverse break 逆向断开「轮
reverse capstan 反向绞盘,倒转主动
reverse channel 反向通道
reverse charge 反向付费
reverse clipping 反向削波
reverse code dictionary 反码字典
reverse convex program 反向凸规划
reverse current relay 逆流继电器
reverse digit sorting method 反向数字排序法
reverse direction flow 逆向流程
reverse engineering 逆向工程
reverse find 反向查找
reverse image 反转图像
reverse index 倒排索引
reverse inference 逆推理

reverse inference induction knowledge acquisition 逆推理归纳知识获取
reverse interrupt 反向中断
reverse leading 反向引导
reverse line-feed 逆向换行
reverse order 逆序
reverse pointer 反向指针
reverse Polish notation(RPN) 逆波兰表示法「机
reverse printout typewriter 双向打字
reverse read 反向阅读,反读
reverse relay 逆流继电器
reverse scan 逆向扫描
reverse search 逆向搜索
reverse signal 反向信号
reverse software engineering 逆向软件工程
reverse solenoid 反向螺线管
reverse video 反视像,反相显示
reversed polish notation 逆波兰表示
reverser sign 正负号变换器
reversible 可逆的,双向的
reversible coding 可逆[双向]编码
reversible counter 可逆[双向]计数器
reversible operation 可换向操作
reversible permeability 可逆导磁率
reversible transducer 可逆换能器
revert 回复
revert statement 回复语句
review and approval 检查和批准
review button 检查按钮
review status 检查状态
reviewer 审查者
revisable-form text(RFT) 可修订形式的文本
revise 修订,校正
revised flow 修正流
revised report 修订报告
revised simplex method 修正单纯形法
revision 修正,订正
revision control system(RCS) 可视控制系统
revision level 修订级
revision number 版本修正号
REVOKE 撤消,取消
revoke all 全部撤消
revolutions per inch 每英寸走刀(主轴)转数

revolutions per minute 每分钟转数
revolutions per minute indicator 每分钟转数指示器
revolver 快转区,快速存取磁道
revolver track 快速存取磁道
REW(REWind) 反绕,倒带
rewind(REW) 回卷,倒带,反绕
rewind time 倒带[反绕]时间
rewiring 重接线,重布线
reworking 返工
rewritable 可重写的
rewritable optical disc 可重写光盘
rewrite 重写
rewrite dual gap head 重写双隙磁头
rewrite procedure 重写过程
rewrite statement 重写语句
rewriting proving method 重写证明法
rewriting rule 重写规则
REXX(Restructured Extended eXecutor) 重组延伸执行器,REXX 语言
rezero operation 归零操作
RF(Radio Frequency) 射频,无线电频率
RF bandwidth 射频带宽
RF modulation 射频调制
RF shielding 射频屏蔽层
RFA(Remote File Access) 远程文件访问
RFC(Request For Change) 请求更改
RFC(Request For Comment) 征求意见文件,RFC 文件
RFD(Request For Discussion) 请求讨论
RFI(Radio Frequency Interference) 射频干扰
RFID(Radio Frequency Identification) 射频标识(卡)
RFP(Request For Proposal) 投标请求书
RFR(Real Frame Replacement) 实帧替换厂率
RFR(Reject Failure Rate) 拒收故障
RFS(Remote File Service) 远程文件服务(协议)
RFS(Remote File Sharing) 远程文件共享
RFSK/FH (Random Frequency Shift Keying/Frequency Hopping) 随机频移键控跳频
RFT(Revisable-Form Text) 可修订形式的文本
RG-58 RG-58 电缆
RG-59 RG-59 电缆
RG-62 RG-62 电缆
RGB(Red, Green, Blue) 红、绿、蓝(彩色显示中的三基色)
RGB monitor RGB 监视器
Rhapsody "狂想曲"操作系统(苹果)
rheostat 变阻器,电阻盒
rhombic 斜方形的,菱形的
rhombus box 菱形框,条件判断框
RI(Radio Interface) 无线电接口
RI(Ring Indicate) 振铃指示
RIA(Robot Institute of America) 美国机器人学会
RIB(Resource Information Block) 资源信息块
rib site 主脉站点
ribbon 色带;带状电缆;光纤带
ribbon cable 扁平电缆,带状电缆
ribbon guide 色带导向器
ribbon inter-connection 互连条
ribbon reverse control 色带反绕控制
ribbon wire 带状导线
Rice encode(RE) 赖斯编码
rich e-mail 增强式电子邮件
rich text format(RTF) 多功能文本格式
RIF(Remote InterFace) 远程接口
RIFF(Resource Interchange File Format) 资源交换文件格式
RIFF chunk 资源交换文件格式块
RIFF compound file RIFF 复合文件
RIGHTS 权限
right 权限
right-adjusted data 右靠[向右调节]数据
right-aligned 右对齐的
right angle adapter 直角配接器
right angle edge connector 直角边连接器
right click 右击
right hand intent 右侧缩进
right hand side 右手边,右侧的
right justify 右整版,向右对齐
right-linear grammar 右线性语法

right-linear recursion 右线性递归
right margin 右缘,右界
right most bit 最右位
right most derivation 最右派生
right nibble 右尼,右半字节
right scale integration 适当规模集成电路
right-sentential form 右句型
right shift 右移
right shift instruction 右移位指令
right-sided system 右侧系统
right-through control 直通[全权]控制
right truncation 右修剪,右截断
rightmost character 最右字符
rightmost derivation 最右派生
rightmost node 最右节点
rightmost symbol 最右符号
rightsizing 规模优化,适当规模,适型化
RightWriter 文法检查程序
rigid disk 硬磁盘
rigid disk drive 刚性磁盘驱动器
RIM(Resource Interface Module) 资源接口模块
rimming light 环晕光
RIMP(Remote Input Message Processor) 远程输入消息处理机
ring 环,圈
ring attaching device 环形网附接设备
ring back tone 回铃音
ring bracket 环界
ring buffers 环式缓冲器
ring bus 环形总线
ring code 环形码
ring connection 环形连接
ring control scheme 环形网控制模式
ring counter 环形计数器
ring data structure 环形数据结构
ring down signaling 响铃发信
ring error monitor 环错误监控程序
ring file 环形文件
ring forward signal 前向呼叫[重呼]信号
ring head 环形磁头
ring in(RI) 环入
ring index pointer 循环索引指示器
ring indicator 振铃指示器
ring interface(RI) 环接口
ring interface adapter(RIA) 环形接口适配器
ring interface processor(RIP) 环式接口处理机
ring latency 环潜在时间
Ring Management(RMT) 环管理
ring modulator 环形调制器
ring network 环形网络
ring network node 环形网络节点
ring network structure 环式网络结构
ring of integers 整数环
ring out(RO) 环出
ring register 环式寄存器
ring shift left 循环左移位
ring shift right 循环右移位
ring stack 环式栈
ring sum 环和
ring switched computer network 环形交换计算机网络
ring type element 环形元件
ring wiring concentrator 环接线集中器
Ringdoc Ringdoc 数据库
ringer 电铃,振铃器
ringing circuit 振铃电路
ringing set 振铃装置
rinse 清洗,冲刷
RIO(Relocatable Input/Output) 可重定位输入/输出
RIP(Raster Image Processor) 光栅图像处理器
RIP(Routing Information Protocol) (Unix)路径信息协议
rip up 剥去,剥离
ripple 涟波;波纹,脉动
ripple adder 行波式加法器
ripple counter 行波计数器
ripple effect 涟波效应
ripple factor 纹波系数
ripple group delay 涟波群时延,行波组时延
ripple-through carry 行波传送进位
ripple-through effect 涟漪效应
ripple voltage 脉动电压
RISC(Reduction Instruction Set Computer) 精简指令系统计算机
RISC architecture 精简指令系统体系结构
RISC System/6000 RS/6000 计算机(IBM)

rise-fall delay 上升下降延迟
rise time 上升时间
risk 风险
risk analysis 风险分析
risk assessment 风险估计
risk average 风险均值
risk decision 风险性决策
risk index 风险指数
risk management 风险管理
RITA RITA语言
Rivest-Shamir-Adleman(RSA) RSA密码体制
RJ(ReJect processor) 拒收处理程序
RJ-11 RJ-11连接器
RJ-12 RJ-12连接器
RJ-45 RJ-45连接器
RL(ReLocatable) 可重定位的
RLC(Remote Line Concentrator) 远程线路集中器
RLC(Run Length Encoding) 游程长度编码方式
RLD(Relocation Dictionary) 重定位词典
RLE(Run Length Encoding) 游程长度编码
RLIB(Relocatable Library) 可重定位程序库
RLL(Relocating Linking Loader) 可重定位连接馈入例程
RLL(Run Length Limited) 游程长度受限码
RLL RLL语言
RLL interface 游程长度受限码接口
RLM(Resident Load module) 驻存装入模块
rlogin (Unix)远程登录
RM(Routing Matrix) 路由选择矩阵
rm(remove) 删除
RMA(Resource Management Agent) 资源管理机构(DG)
RMI(Remote Method Invocation) 远程方法调用
rmdir(remove directory) 删除目录
rmgroup(remove) 删除新闻组
RMPI(Remote Memory Port Interface) 远程存储器端口接口
RMS(Resource Management System) 资源管理系统
RMS(Root Mean Square) 均方根
RMS error averaged over an image array 图像阵列平均均方根误差
RMU(Resource Management Unit) 资源管理单元
RMX(Real-time Multitasking Executive) 实时多任务执行程序(Intel)
rn rn新闻阅读器
RNA(Request Node Address) 请求节点地址
RNRZ(Random Not Return-to-Zero) 随机不归零制
RNRZ1(Randomized Non-Return-to-zero change on One) 随机不归零按1变化
RNZ(Return on No Zero) 非零值返回
RO(Receive Only) 只收
RO terminal 只读终端
Robert gradient 罗伯特梯度
robocancel 自动删除
robot 机器人
robot calibration 机器人校准
robot capability 机器人能力
robot engineering 机器人工程学
robot for fixed program 固定程序机器人
robot for poor environment 恶劣环境机器人
robot for repeat memory 记忆重复机器人,存储再生机器人
robot for test and inspection 试验和检查机器人
robot for variable program 可变程序机器人
robot problem 机器人问题
robot problem solving 机器人问题求「解
robot problem-solving system 机器人问题求解系统
robot programming language 机器人编程语言
robot revolution 机器人革命
robot sense 机器人感觉
robot series 机器人系列
robot vision system 机器人视觉系统
robot with sense organ 带感觉器官的机器人
robot with tactile sensing 带触觉的机

器人
robotic artificial intelligence 机器人的人工智能
robotics 机器人学,自动仪器学
robotization 机器人化
robotology 机器人学
robots arm 机器人臂
robust coding scheme 健壮的编码方案
robust control 健壮控制
robust decentralized control 坚固的分散控制
robustness 健壮性,坚固性
Rock Ridge file system (HSFS)洛克瑞德文件系统
Rockwell International Corp. 洛克威尔国际公司
rod 棒,杆
rofl(rolling on the floor laughing) 捧腹大笑
Roger 同意,知道了
rogue fiber 光缆窃听装置
Roland Moreno Technology(RMT) Roland Moreno 技术公司
role 任务,角色
role consistency 作用一致性
role indicator 作用[角色]指示符
Role Playing Game(RPG) 角色扮演游戏
role pragmatics 作用语用学
roll 卷动
roll-back 转返,回退;重算,重新运行
roll-back entry point 重算入口点
roll-back point 重算点,转返点
roll-back segment 转返段
roll back snapshot 转返抽点记录
roll-back snapshot system 抽点重新运行系统
roll-back system 转返系统
roll-call polling 重呼轮询
roll-down 下卷
roll forward 前卷
roll-in 转入
roll-in/roll-out 转入转出
roll microfilm 卷轴式缩微胶片
roll-out 转出
roll paper 卷轴纸
roll screen 滚动屏幕
roll-up 上卷

rollback 重算,返回
roller (打印机)墨辊
roller coating 墨辊涂层
rolling 滚动,卷动
rolling code 滚动码
rolling mode 滚动模式
rollover 同时按键;翻转
rollover effect 翻转效果
rollover indexing 翻转索引
ROM(Read Only Memory) 只读存储器
ROM address register ROM 地址寄存器
ROM BIOS(Read Only Memory Basic Input/Output System) ROM 基本输入/输出系统
ROM BIOS swapping ROM BIOS 对换
ROM bootstrap ROM 启动程序
ROM bus interface(TTL) ROM 总线接口(晶体管-晶体管逻辑)
ROM card ROM 卡
ROM-oriented architecture 面向 ROM 体系结构
ROM simulator ROM 仿真器
ROM terminal ROM 终端
ROMable ROM 使能的
Roman numeral 罗马数字
roof filter 防干扰过滤器
room temperature 室温
root 根
root agent 根代理
root branch 根分支
root compiler 根编译程序
root device 根设备
root directory 根目录
root disk 根盘(Sun)
root field 根域
root file system 根文件系统
root-finding 求根
root-folder 根文件夹
root locus method 根轨迹法
root mean square(RMS) 均方根值,(电压/电流)有效值
root mean square error 均方根误差
root-mean-square question 均方根提问
root name 主文件名,根名
root node 根节点,根结点
root object 根目标
root of tree 树根

root-relative path 根相对路径
root segment 根段
root-squaring method 平方根法
root storage object 根存储器对象
root test 根检验
root user name 根用户名(Sun)
root window (X协议)根窗口
rooted directed graph 有根有向图
rooted graph 有根图
rooted tree 有根树
rooting 求根
ROP(Receive Only Printer) 仅收打印机
ROS(Real-time Operating System) 实时操作系统
ROS(Resident Operating System) 驻存操作系统
ROSE(Remote Operations Service Element) (PRC协议)远程操作服务单元(ISO/OSI)
ROSE(Retrieval by On-line SEarch) 联机检索
ROSIE ROSIE系统
ROSIE language ROSIE语言
ROSS(Rand Object-oriented Simulation System) 兰德面向对象仿真语言
ROSS language 面向对象仿真语言
ROT-13 ROT-13加密方案
rotary dial 旋转拨号盘
rotary head 旋转磁头
rotary positioner 旋转定位机构
rotary switch 旋转开关
rotate 回转,旋转
rotate instruction 旋转指令
rotate/shift operation 回转/移位运算
rotated term 回转检索词,轮排检索词
rotated type 旋转字形
rotating cylinder printer 旋转柱式打印机
rotating drum image scanning digitizer 旋转鼓形图像扫描数字化仪
rotating head 旋转磁头
rotating magnetic storage 旋转磁存储器
rotation 旋转,转动
rotation delay 旋转延迟
rotation group 旋转群
rotation of binary tree 三叉树的旋转
rotation tool 旋转工具

rotation transformation 旋转变换
rotational delay 旋转延迟
rotational position sensing(RPS) 旋转位置传感
rotational time 旋转时间
rotator 转子;轮转程序
rotator schedule 轮转程序调度
rote knowledge acquisition 注入式知识获取
rote learning 机械式学习
Roth's D-algorithm 罗斯D算法
rotor 转子
rough calculation 概算
rough cut 粗剪
rough draft 草图,略图,示意图
rough estimate 粗略估计
rough exit 粗暴退出
rough sketch 草图
rough translation 粗译文
rough tuning 粗调谐
round 舍去
round-down 下舍,向下舍入
round-off 舍入
round off error 舍入误差
round robin 循环(共享)
round-robin algorithm 循环算法
round-robin scheduling 轮转法调度
round trip delay time 往返延时
round trip propagation time 往返传播时间
round trip time 往返时间
round-up 上舍入,尾数进入
rounded 舍入,环绕
rounded analysis 全面分析
rounded interval arithmetic 舍入区间运算
rounded system 完整的体系
rounding 舍入,四舍五入
rounding bit 舍入位
rounding error 舍入误差
route 路由
route caching 路由高速缓存
route-control digits 路由控制数字
route dialing 路由拨号
route diversity system 路由分集制
route extension 路由扩展
route flip-flop 路由倒换
route matrix 路由矩阵

route-once, switch many "一次路由，多次交换"
route optimization 路由最佳化
route planning 路由规划
route restriction 路由限制
route search packet 路由搜索信息包
route segment 路由段
route selection 路由选择
route sheet 路线表
route weight 路由权重
Router 布线程序
router 路由器
router group 路由器群
router tracking screen 路由跟踪屏幕
Routh theorem 庐斯定理
routine 例程,例行程序
routine analyzer 例程分析器
routine check 例程校验
routine extremity 带端处理例程
routine editor 例程编辑器
routine interface 例程接口
routine library 例程库
routine loading 例程加载
routine maintenance 例行维护
routine name 例程名
routine package 程序包,例行程序包
routine select 例程选择
routine test 例程测试;例行测试
routing 路由选择;布线 「序
routing accelerator 路由选择加速程
routing affinity 路由选择亲合性
routing algorithm 路由选择算法
routing approach 路由选择法
routing area compaction 布线区压缩
routing bridge 路由桥
routing by destination 按目的地选择路由
routing by key 按关键字选择路由
routing chart 路由选择表
routing code 路由选择码
routing control 路由选择控制
routing criterion 路由选择准则
routing diagram 路由说明图
routing directory 路由目录
routing domain 路由选择域
routing emulation 游动仿真
routing expression 路由表达式
Routing Header (Ipv6)路由选择包头
routing indicator 路由选择指示符
routing information 路由选择信息
Routing Information Protocol(RIP) 路由信息协议
routing key 路由选择键
routing key table 路由选择关键字表
routing list 路由表
routing logic 路由选择逻辑
routing page 路由选择页面
routing problem 寻径问题,走线问题
routing protocol 路由选择协议
routing queue 路由选择队列
routing strategy 路由选择策略
routing table 路径选择表
Routing Table Maintenance Protocol (RTMP) 路径表管理协议
ROW(Remote Output Writer) 远程输出记录程序
row 行,排
row adaptive transmission 行自适应传送
row address 行地址
row address strobe(RAS) 行地址选通信号
row buffering 行缓冲
row canonical form 行规范形式
row column header 行号列标
row control box 行控制框
row counter 行计数器
row displacement 行位移
row drive wire 行驱动线
row head 行头
row height 行高
row input cell 按行输入单元格
row iteration 行迭代
row major order 行主次序
row order 行次序
row parity 行奇偶性
row pitch 行距
row pivoting 行主元法
row rank 行秩
row replacement 行替换
row scanning 行扫描
row selection 行选择
row vector 行向量
row-wise recalculation 行主重算
rowset 行集
RP(Reject Protocol) 拒收协议

RP(Request Packet) 请求信息包
RPB(Restart Parameter Block) 重始参数块
RPC(Remote Packet Concentrator) 远程信息包集线器
RPC(Remote Procedure Call) 远过程调用
RPCNET(REEL Project Computer NETwork) REEL方案计算机网络
RPCNET(Resource sharing Packet Communication NETwork) 资源共享分组交换通信网
RPG(Role Playing Game) 角色扮演游戏
RPG(Report Program Generator) 报表程序生成器
RPG language RPG语言
RPG11 compiler RPG11编译程序
RPH(Request Parameter Header) 请求参数头标
RPH(Request Processing Header) 请求处理头标
RPH(Revolutions Per Hour) 转数/小时
RPI(Rows Per Inch) 行/英寸
RPM(Repeat Per Minute) 重复次数/分钟
RPM(Revolution Per Minute) 回转数/分钟
RPM(Rotations Per Minute) 转数/分钟
RPmm(Rows Per mm) 每毫米行数
RPQ(Request for Price Quotation) 报价请求书
RPRINTER 远程打印机
RPRN(Return Primary Resource Name) 返回主资源名
RPS(Revolutions Per Second) 每秒转数
RPS/EDX(Real-time Programming System / Event-Driven Executive) 实时程序设计系统/事件驱动执行程序
RPSM(Resource Planning and Scheduling Method) 资源计划与调度法
RPT(Records Per Track) 每磁道记录数
RPT(Remote PrinT) 远程打印机
RPY(RePlY) 回答,应答
RQ(ReQuest) 请求
RQE(Reply Queue Element) 回答队列元素
RQE(Request Queue Element) 请求队列元素
RQI(ReQuest for Initialization) 初始化请求
RR(Running Reverse) 反转
RR 轮转调度
RRN(Remote Request Number) 远程请求号
RRT(Resource Request Table) 资源请求表 「准
RS(Recommended Standard) 推荐标
RS(Routing Selector) 路由选择器
RS-232 compatible controller RS232C通用控制器
RS-232 interface RS-323接口
RS-232-C standard RS-232-C标准
RS-269 RS269标准
RS-334 RS334标准
RS-357 RS357标准
RS-362 RS362标准
RS-366 RS366标准
RS-404 RS404标准
RS-410 RS-410标准
RS-422 RS-422标准
RS-422A RS-422A标准
RS-423 RS-423标准
RS-449 RS-449标准
RS-485 RS-485标准
RS-530 RS-530标准
RS/6000 RS/6000计算机(IBM)
RSA(Random Sequential Automation) 随机顺序自动机
RSA(Rivest-Shamir-Adleman) RSA公开密钥密码系统
RSAM(Relative Sequential Access Method) 相对顺序存取法
RSI(Repetitive Strain Injury) 重复性疲劳损伤
RSI(Right Scale Integration) 适当规模集成电路
RSL(Relocatable Subroutine Library) 可重定位子例程库
RSM(Resource Setup Manager) 资源

配置管理程序
RST(ReSTart) 重始,再启动
RSTS/E RSTS/E 操作系统(DEC)
RSU(Reconfigurable Storage Unit) 可重配置的存储单元
RSUP(Route Set-Up Packet) 路径设置分组
RSVP(Remote Spooling Vector Processor) 远程假脱机向量处理程序
RSW(Resource Status Word) 资源状态字
RSX(Real-time resource Sharing eXecutive) 实时资源共享执行程序
RSX(Resource Sharing eXecutive) 资源共享执行程序
RSX-11(Resource Sharing eXtension-PDP-11) 资源共享扩展系统,RSX-11 操作系统(DEC)
RT(Real Time) 实时
RT-11 operating system RT-11 操作系统
RT workstation RT 工作站(IBM)
RTC(Real-Time Clock) 实时时钟
RTC(Real-Time Control) 实时控制
RTCC(Real-Time Computer Complex) 实时计算复合体
RTDMA(Random Time Division Multiple Access) 随机时分多路存取
RTE(Real Time Event) 实时事件
RTF(Rich Text Format) 多功能文本格式
RTFM(Read The Flaming Manual) 抢救,"抢读烧着的手册"
RTFM(Read The Fucking Manual) 请读各类手册
RTI(Real Time Interface) 实时接口
RTI(ReTurn from Interrupt) 自中断返回指令 「库
RTL(Run Time Library) 运行时间
RTM(Real The Manual) 请读手册
RTMOS(Real Time Multiprogramming Operating System) 实时多道作业操作系统
RTMP(Routing Table Maintenance Protocol) 路由表管理协议
RTOS(Real-Time Operating System) 实时操作系统
RTPC(Real-Time Processing Communication) 实时处理通信
RTS/CTS(Request-To-Send/Clear-To Send) 请求发送/清除发送
RTSE(Reliable Transfer Service Element) 可靠传输服务元(ISO/OSI)
RTU(Remote Terminal Unit) 远程终端单元
RTU(right to use) 有权使用(Sun 软件许可)
RTU real time microsupercomputer RTU 实时微巨型计算机
RTX(Real Time eXecutive) 实时执行程序
RTZ(Return To Zero) 归零
RU(aRe yoU ···?) 你是谁?(符号)
RU(Request Unit) 请求单元
RU(Response Unit) 响应单元
RU chain 链式请求单元
rub-out character 擦除[抹掉]字符
rubber 擦除工具,橡皮
rubber-band outline 橡皮筋式轮廓
rubber-banding 橡皮筋式画线法
rubber stamp 橡皮图章
rubout key 擦除键
RUBRIC(RUle-Based Retrieval of Information by Computer) 基于规则的计算机信息检索系统
rudiment 基本原理
rudimentary relation 基本关系
rugged computer 加固计算机
ruggedized computer 加固型计算机
ruggedized packaging 加固组装
rule 规则,法则
rule base 规则库
rule-based deduction system 基于规则的演绎系统
rule-based expert system 基于规则的专家系统
rule-based method 基于规则的方法
rule-based problem reduction 基于规则的问题归约
rule-based program 基于规则的程序
rule-based system 基于规则的系统
rule clause 规则子句
rule cluster 规则簇
rule connection graph 规则连接图
rule driven design 规则驱动设计

rule editor 规则编辑程序
rule group 规则组
rule interpreter 规则解释程序
rule-like principle 似规则原理
rule-like representation 类规则表示
rule list 规则表
rule match 规则匹配
rule model 规则模型
rule-oriented system 面向规则的系统
rule set 规则集
RULE WRITER 规则书写系统
RULEGEN system RULEGEN系统
RULEMASTER RULEMASTER专家系统工具
RULEMOD RULEMOD专家系统
ruler 标尺
ruler line 标尺线
rules 规则；尺度线
ruling English 定规英语，准确英语
run 运行
run around 躲闪
run book 运行手册[说明书]
run chart 运行流程图
run code 运行码
run cost 运行成本
run diagram 运行图
run duration 运行期间
run end point 运动端点
run engineering 运行工程学
run history 运行历史
run indicator 运行指示器
run length coding 游程长度编码
run length encoding(RLE) 游程长度编码
run-length-limited code(RLLC) 游程长度受限码
run level (SunOS)运行级
run list 运行表
run locator 运行定位例程
run mode 运行模式
run on top of 在…之上运行
run-out tolerance 跳动公差，摆差
run-out field of bubble 磁泡形成场
run phase 运行阶段
run schedule 运行调度，运行预定计划表
run stream 运行流
run switch 运行开关

run-time 运行时间
run-time diagnosis 运行时诊断
run-time library(RTL) 运行时间库
run-time parameter 运行时间参数
run-time property 运行时刻属性
run-time reduction ratio 运行时间减少比
run-time routines 运行时间例程
run-time version 运行版本
run-to-run totals 运行-运行总数
run under 在…之下运行
run unit 运行单元
run-unit currency 运行单位当前值
runaway 失控，超出控制范围
Rung-Kutta method 龙格-库塔法
Runge phenomenon 龙格现象
runnable process 可运行进程
running accumulator 运行[后进先出]累加器
running check 运行校验
running object table(ROT) 运行对象表
running force system 动力系统
running open 空转
running state 运行状态
running state of process 进程执行状态
running time 运行时间
runtime error 运行期间错误
runtime library 运行时间库
runtime method determination 运行时间方法确定
runtime procedure library 运行过程库
runtime version 运行期间版本
rush hours 高峰时间
Russian parallel ETOL system 俄罗斯并行ETOL系统
Russian parallel grammar 俄罗斯并行文法
RVA(Relative Virtual Address) 相对虚地址
RVC(Restricted Variability Codes) 受限可变性编码
RVLC (Restricted Variable Length Codes) 受限可变长度编码
RVT (Recovery management Vector Table) 恢复管理向量表
RVT(Resource Vector Table) 资源向量表
RWC(Real World Computing) 真实

世界计算
RWCP(Real World Computing Partnership) 新信息处理发展机构
RWI(Radio-Wire Interface) 有-无线接口
RWI(Reset Window Indicator) 重设窗口指示符
RX(Remote eXchange) 远程交换机

RXD(Receive Data) 接收数据
RZ(Return-to-Zero) 归零制
RZ recording 归零记录
RZL(Return-to-Zero Level) 归零电平
RZM(Return-to-Zero Mark) 归零标记
RZP(Polarized Return-to-Zero) 极化归零

S s

s(second) 秒;第二
S(Siemen) 西门子(电导的国际标准单位)
S(Source) 源
S(South pole) S极,南(磁)极
S.1 S.1语言
S-50 Bus S-50总线
S-100 Bus S-100总线
S/360(System/360) IBM系统/360计算机
S/370(System/370) IBM系统/370计算机
S/390(System/390) IBM系统/390计算机
S3 chip S3(显示)芯片
S3 Inc. (Sight,Sound,Speed) S3公司
S3 Texture Compression S3纹理压缩技术
S3 ViRGE(S3 Video and Rendering Graphics Engine) S3视频与润色图形引擎
s-a-0 fault 固定"0"错误
s-a-1 fault 固定"1"错误
S-correction (CRT显示器的)S校正
S-disk 系统盘
S-expression S表达式
S-grammar S语法,S文法
S-language S语言
S-memory 系统内存,S存储器
S-MFSK(Slow-hopped M-ary Frequency Shift Keying) 慢跳M次频移键控
S-mode 系统模式
S-mode records S形记录
S/N(Signal-to-Noise ratio) 信噪比

S/O(Send Only) 只发送
S-P(Serial to Parallel) 串行到并行
S-path(Single path) 单通路
S-register(Storage Register) S寄存器
S/S(Source/Sink) 信源/信宿
S/S(Spooler/Scheduler) 假脱机程序/调度程序
S/S(Start/Stop) 启动/停止
S-SNOBOL(Structured SNOBOL) 结构化SNOBOL语言
S-video(Separation video) 分离视频(端子)
SA(System Administrator) 系统管理员
SA(System Analyst) 系统分析员
SAA(Systems Application Architecture) 系统应用体系结构(IBM)
SAB(Session Awareness Block) 对话感知块
SAB(Stack Access Block) 堆栈存取块
SAB(System Advisory Board) 系统咨询部
Saber LAN Workstation Saber局域网工作站
Sabermetrician "预言家"
Sabor Sabor机器人
sabotage 破坏
SABRE SABRE数据库机
SAC(Semi-Automatic Coding) 半自动编码
SAC(Sequential Advanced Control) 顺序先行控制
SAC(Service Access Controller) (Unix)服务访问控制程序

SAC(Storage Access Channel) 存储器访问通道
SAD(Streams Administrative Driver) 流式管理驱动程序
SAD(System Allocation Document) 系统分配文档
saddle 管托，支管架
saddle node 鞍结点
saddle point 鞍点
saddle point criteria 鞍点准则
saddle point game 鞍点对策
saddle point method 鞍点法
SADF(System Analysis and Design Facility) 系统分析与设计程序
SADMP(Stand-Alone Dump Program) 独立转储程序
SADP (System Architecture Design Package) 系统体系结构设计软件包
SAF(Service Access Facility) (SunOS)服务访问设施(协议)
SAE(Shaft Angle Encoder) 轴角编码器
SAF(Store-And-Forward) 存储转发
SAF(System Authorization Facility) 系统认可设施
SAFE(System Architecture For Expansion) 可扩充系统体系结构(IBM)
safe 安全的
safe address register 安全地址寄存器
safe area 安全区域
safe concurrency control model 安全并发控制模型
safe expression 安全表达式
safe format 安全格式化
SAFE II(System for Advanced Financial Environment Interactive Interface) 高级金融环境交互接口系统
safe length 安全长度
safe net 安全网
safe ordering 安全排序法
safe prediction 安全预测
safe prime 安全素数
safe shutdown 安全停机
safe situation 安全状况
safe state 安全状态
safeguard 保护，防护
safeguarding statement 防护[保护]语句
safeness 安全性
safenet 安全网
safety 安全的，安全性的
safety assessment 安全性鉴定书
safety circuit 安全[保安]电路
safety code 安全代码
safety communication 安全通信
safety cut-out 安全断电器
safety data network system(SDNS) 安全数据数据网络系统
safety extra-low voltage circuit 安全特低压电路
safety factor 安全系数
Safety First Network Bank(SFNB) 安全第一网络银行
safety management module 安全管理模块
safety mechanism 安全机构
safety message 安全消息，安全报文
safety of data processing equipment 数据处理设备安全
safety plan 安全计划
safety policy 安全策略
safety property 安全性
safety stock 安全库存
safety strategy 安全策略
safety switch 安全开关
safety test 安全测试
safety traffic 安全通信量
safety verification 安全性检验
sag 跌落，下陷
SAFF(Store And Forward Facsimile) 存储转发式传真
SAG(Standard Address Generator) 标准地址发生器
SAG(Syntax Analyzer Generator) 语法分析生成器
SAIL (Stanford Artificial Intelligence Language) 斯坦福人工智能语言，世纪 SAIL 语言
SAILS(Software Adaptable Integrated Logic System) 软件自适应综合逻辑系统
SAIM (System Analysis and Integration Model) 系统分析与综合模型
SAINT(Symbolic Automatic INTegrator) 符号自动积分程序

SAL(Structured Assembly Language) 结构化汇编语言
Salami technique （计算机金融犯罪）意大利香肠术
Salary accounting 薪金记账
Sales & Business Reservations done Electronically(SABRE) 联机飞机订票系统
sales engineer 销售工程师
sales mode 销售模式
sales order processing 订单处理
sales quota 销售分配额[份额]
sales transaction 销售交易[事务]
salesman's portable computer terminal 推销员便携式计算机终端
salesman problem 推销员问题
salesmanship 推销术
SALT (Symbolic Algebraic Language Translator) 符号代数语言翻译程序
salient feature 突出特征
salt-spray test 盐雾试验
salvage 挽救,救助;恢复
salvage from deleted directory 从被删除目录中恢复选项
salvage option 恢复选项
salvage value 可挽救价值
salvageable files 可挽救文件
SAM(Scientific Accelerator Module) 科学计算加速模块
SAM(Self-Address Memory) 自寻址存储器
SAM(Semantic Analyzing Machine) 语义分析机
SAM(Sequential Access Method) 顺序存取法
SAM(Standard Assembly Module) 标准组装模块
SAM(Symantec Antivirus for Macintosh) SAM 抗病毒程序
SAM(System Activity Monitor) 系统活动监视器
SAM(System Availability Model) 系统可用性模型
SAM(System Analysis Module) 系统分析模块
SAM* SAM*模型
same application 同一应用程序
same area clause 同域子句
same body chain 同体链
same body relation 同体关系
same domain LU-LU session 同域逻辑部件对话
same phase 同相
same priority 相同优先权,同级优先
same record area 相同记录区
same size 相同尺寸
same way 同路
SAMIS(Structural Analysis and Matrix Interpretation System) 结构分析与矩阵解释系统
samizdaf （因特网上的）非官方信息系统
SAMM(Systematic Activity Modeling Method) 系统活动建模法
Sammie Sammie 模拟语言
Samon （荷兰）萨蒙（数据管理机构）
SAMPLE (Single-Assignment Mathematical Programming LanguagE) 单赋值数学程序设计语言
sample 样值;样本;实例
sample and hold 取样与保持
sample and hold circuit 取样保持电路
sample average 样本均值
sample central moment 样本中心矩
sample change compaction 样值变更精简
sample chart 示例图表
sample configuration 样本配置
sample controller 取样控制器
sample correlation coefficient 样本相关系数
sample covariance 样本协方差
sample data control 取样数据控制
sample decile 样本十分位数
sample delay 取样延迟
sample design 样本设计
sample dispersion 样本离差
sample distribution 样本分布
sample error 样本误差
sample evaluation method 抽样鉴定法
sample fractile 样本分位数
sample-hold circuit 取样保持电路
sample hold serial D/A converter 取样保持串行数/模转换器
sample hold switch 取样保持开关
sample input 样值输入

sample interactive task 取样交互式任务
sample interval 抽样时间间隔
sample job stream 样本作业流
sample linker directive 样本连接程序指令
sample mean 样本平均值
sample mean estimator 样本均值估算器
sample mechanism 取样机构
sample median 样本中位数
sample moment 样本矩
sample number 样本数
sample output 样本输出
sample percentiles 样本百分位数
sample program 示例程序
sample program listing sequence 取样程序列表序列
sample protocol 抽样[采样]协议
sample quartiles 样本四分位数
sample query procedure 示例式询问过程
sample range 样本范围
sample rate 抽样率;抽样速率
sample reduction 取样简化;样本精简
sample session 示例式对话
sample session editing 示例式对话编辑方法
sample set 样本集合
sample size 样本容量,样本量大小
sample space 样本空间
sample standard deviation 样本标准差
sample time 抽样时间
sample time aperture 抽样时间孔径
sample tree 样本树
sample variance 样本方差
sample wafer 样本圆片
sampled data 抽样数据
sampled data control 抽样数据控制
sampled-data measurement 样本数据量度
sampled-data system 取样数据系统
sampled image quality measure 取样图像质量度量
sampled regulating 抽样式调节
sampler 取样器
sampler chip 取样器芯片
sampling 抽样,取样,采样
sampling cell 抽样单元
sampling distribution 取样分布

sampling error 抽样误差
sampling frequency 抽样频率
sampling gate 抽样门
sampling grid size 取样格点大小
sampling inspection 抽样检验
sampling interval 抽样时间间隔,取样区间
sampling life test 抽样寿命试验
sampling mechanism 取样机构
sampling network 抽样[取样]网络
sampling noise 抽样噪声
sampling normal distribution 抽样正态分布
sampling oscilloscope 取样示波器
sampling period 抽样周期
sampling point 抽样点
sampling rate 抽样速率;抽样比率
sampling scheme 抽样方案
sampling scheme with replacement 有返回抽样方案
sampling scheme without replacement 无返回抽样方案
sampling signal 抽样[取样]信号
sampling survey method 抽样调查法
sampling synthesizer 抽样合成器
sampling theorem 抽样定理
sampling unit 取样单元
sampling window 取样窗口
SAN(Storage Access Network) 存储访问网络
sand-blast 喷砂,砂磨
sandwich digit 中间位
sandwich plate 夹层板
sandwich tape 夹层磁带
sandwich type element 夹层结构元件
sanitization 消磁
SANS(Stand-Alone Network System) 独立网络系统
sans serif 无衬线字体
SANTAK corp. 山特公司(不间断电源)
SAP(Server Advertising Protocol) 服务器广告协议
SAP(Service Access Point) 服务访问点(ISO)
SAP(Service Advertising Protocol) 服务广告协议
SAP(Secondary Audio Program) 辅

SAP(Simulation Analysis Program) 助音频程序
SAP(Simulation Analysis Program) 仿真分析程序
SAP(Symbolic Address Program) 符号地址程序
sapphire 蓝宝石
sapphire substrate 蓝宝石衬底
SAR(Safe Address Register) 安全地址寄存器
SAR(Segment Address Register) 段地址寄存器
SAR(Source Address Register) 源地址寄存器
SAS(Self-Adaptive System) 自适应系统
SAS(Single Attached Station) 单连通站点
SAS(Statistical Analysis System) 统计分析系统
SASD(Single-Access Single-Distribution) 单存取单分配
SAT(Subscriber Access Terminal) 用户存取终端
SAT(Swap Allocation Table) 交换分配表
SAT(Synchronous/Asynchronous Transmitter) 同步/异步发送器
SAT(System Analysis Table) 系统分析表
sat routing 饱和路径选择
SATAN(Security Administrator Tool for Analyzing Networks) 网络分析安全管理工具
Satcom "萨特康姆"卫星
satellite 卫星
satellite access 卫星访问信道
satellite address 卫星地址
satellite attitude 卫星姿态
satellite beacon 卫星信标
satellite bus 卫星总线
satellite business 卫星业务
Satellite Business System(SBS) 卫星商业系统
satellite channel 卫星信道
satellite communication 卫星通信
satellite communication controller 卫星通信控制器
satellite communication system 卫星通信系统
satellite communication topology 卫星通信拓扑
satellite computer 卫星计算机
satellite computer compatibility 卫星计算机兼容性
satellite computer network 卫星计算机网络
satellite computer terminal 卫星计算机终端
satellite data collection system 卫星数据采集系统
satellite droplet 卫星墨滴
satellite earth station 卫星地面站
satellite earth terminal 卫星地面终端
satellite eclipse 卫星蚀
satellite graphic job processor(SGJP) 卫星图形作业处理器
satellite ground station 卫星陆基站
satellite hop-time 卫星传送时延
satellite information 附属信息
satellite inspector 卫星监视器 「机
satellite minicomputer 卫星小型计算
satellite navigation computer 卫星导航计算机
satellite processor 卫星处理机
satellite recovery 卫星回收
satellite relay system 卫星转发系统
satellite repeater 卫星中继器
satellite spot beam separation 卫星点波束分离
satellite station 卫星站
satellite switching 卫星转换系统 「络
satellite XTEN network 卫星全球网
SATF(Shortest Access Time First) 最短存取时间最先
saticon 硒砷碲管
satisfaction 满意,满足
satisfaction proof 满意证明
satisfiability 可满足性
satisfiability problem 可满足性问题
satisfiable 可满足的
satisfiable combination 可满足的组合
satisficing 满意决策制定
satisfiers 满意因素
Satstream 卫星流
saturable reactor 饱和电抗器
saturate 饱和

saturated color 饱和色
saturated cut 饱和切割
saturated edge 饱和边界
saturated logic 饱和逻辑
saturated path 饱和通路,饱和路径
saturated porous medium 饱和多孔媒体
saturated reactor regulated AC power supply 磁饱和交流稳压电源
saturated submodel 饱和子模型
saturating integrator 饱和积分器
saturation 饱和
saturation area 饱和区
saturation arithmetic 饱和算法
saturation computing 饱和式运算
saturation flux density 饱和磁通密度
saturation jamming 饱和阻塞
saturation magnetic recording 饱和磁记录
saturation magnetization 饱和磁化
saturation noise 饱和噪声
saturation point 饱和点
saturation region 饱和区
saturation resistance 饱和电阻
saturation routing 饱和路由选择
saturation signaling 饱和信令
saturation testing 饱和试验
saturation threshold 饱和阈值[门限]
saturation zone 饱和区
SAU(Smallest Addressable Unit) 最小可寻址单元
SAU(Subscriber Access Unit) 用户存取单元
SAV(SAVed File) 副本[已存]文件
save 保存,存入
save all 全部保存
save application 保存应用程序
save area 保留区
save as 另存为
save command 存入命令
save copy as 另存副本
save data with table layout 数据与数据透视表一起保存
save file 副本文件
save filtered packet 保存经过滤的包
save format 保存格式
save image 保存图像
save instruction 保存指令
save key 保存密钥
save memory 保护内存
save new application library 保存新应用程序库
save palette 保存调色板
save preference 保存个性选项
save register 保存寄存器
save scheme 保存方案
save search as 保存搜索条件为
save sent message 保存已发送消息
save settings 保存设定值
save settings on exit 退出时保存设定值
SAVE statement 保存语句
save workspace 保存工作区
saved area 保留区
saved search 已保存搜索条件
saving space 节省空间
saving time 保存时间;节省时间
SAVOIR SAVOIR语言
SAVT(Secondary Address Vector Table) 辅助地址向量表
SAW(Secondary Activation Word) 辅助动作字
SAW(Stop-And-Wait) 停机和等待
SAW(Surface Acoustic Wave screen) 表面声波式触摸屏
saw blade defect 切片刀痕
SAWDL(Surface Acoustic Wave Delay Line) 声表面波延迟线
SAWF(Surface Acoustic Wave Filter) 声表面波滤波器
sawtooth generator 锯齿波发生器
sawtooth pulse 锯齿脉冲
sawtooth wave 锯齿波
say (FoxBASE中的)显示命令
SB(Secondary Buffer) 二级缓存
SB(Signaling Bit) 信令位
SB(Sound Blaster) 声霸卡(Creative)
SB(SuBtract) 减
SBA(Shared Batch Area) 共享批处理区
SBA(Support Bus Adapter) 支持总线适配器
SBACKUP 系统备份
SBASIC language SBASIC语言
SBC(Single Board Computer) 单板计算机
SBC(Single Byte Correction) 单字节

校正
SBD(Schottky Barrier Diode) 肖特基势垒二极管
SBI(Single Byte Interleaved) 单字节交错存取
SBI(Speaker Box Interface) 音箱接口(Sun)
SBI(Storage Bus In) 存储器总线输入
SBI(Synchronous Backplane Interconnect) 同步底板互连(DEC公司)
SBI(System Bus Interface) 系统总线接口
SBK(Developer Kit for Sound Blaster Series) 声霸系列开发工具包(Creative)
SBL(Structure Building Language) 结构汇编语言
SBP(Single Board Processor) 单板处理机
SBR(Segment Base Register) 段基址寄存器
SBS(Sensor-Based System) 基于传感器的系统
SBS(Shared Bus System) 共享总线系统
SBS(Silicon Bidirectional Switch) 双向硅开关
SBSO(Small Business Small Office) 小业务/小办公室群体
SBU(Station Buffer Unit) 工作站缓冲单元
SBus (SPARC 工作站)SBus(32位)总线
SBus bridge SBus 桥
SBus expansion card SBus 扩充卡
SBus master SBus 主控器
SBus slave SBus 从属装置
SC(SeCtor address) 扇区地址
SC(Self-Check) 自校验,自检验
SC(Slave Clock) 从属时钟,副时钟
SC(Software Certification) 软件认证
SC(Switching Center) 交换中心
SC-1(SubCommittee 1) 第一分会
SCA(Sequence Control Area) 时序控制区
SCA(Sequential Classification Algorithm) 顺序分类算法
SCA(Synchronous Communications Adapter) 同步通信适配器
scalability 规模可伸缩性
scalable 可缩放的,规模可改变的
scalable coherent interface 可缩放相关接口
scalable font 可缩放字模
scalable share memory multiprocessing(SSMP) 可伸缩共享内存多处理系统
scalable parallel processing(SPP) 可伸缩并行处理
scalable structure 可伸缩性结构
scalable typeface 可缩放字体
scalar 数量,标量;阶跃量;增减器;定标器;换算器
scalar access 标量[纯量]存取
scalar assignment 标量赋值「式
scalar autonomous mode 标量自主模
scalar chain principle 梯形链原则
scalar computation 标量计算
scalar computer 标量计算机
scalar constant 标量常数
scalar data 标量数据
scalar data flow analysis 标量数据流分析
scalar data type 标量数据类型
scalar date 标量日期
scalar enumerated type 标量枚举类型
scalar expression 标量表达式
scalar function 标量函数
scalar item 标量项
scalar matrix 标量矩阵
scalar multiplication 标量乘法运算
scalar pipeline 标量流水线
scalar predictor 标量预测器
scalar processing 标量处理
scalar product 标量积,内积
scalar quantity 纯量,标量
scalar register 标量寄存器
scalar result 标量结果
scalar singular diffusion problem 标量奇异性扩散问题
scalar type 标量类型
scalar type identifier 标量类型标识符
scalar variable 标量变量
scale 标度;规模;刻度;标尺
scale change 尺寸变化;标度变化
scale coefficient 标度系数,比例因子

scale control 标度[比例]控制
scale coordinate system 缩放坐标系
scale detection 标度检测
scale-down 按比例缩小
scale-down MOS 按比例缩小的 MOS
scale factor 比例系数,标度因子
scale factor check 比例因子校验「符
scale factor designator 比例因子指示
scale factor register 比例因子寄存器
scale height 工作区高度
scale label 标尺刻度
scale left 工作区左边界
scale line 刻度线
scale mark 刻度线,分度标记
scale mode 量度模式
scale model 比例模型 「器
scale modifier 标度修正量;标度修正
scale operation 比例运算,定标操作
scale plate 刻度板
scale space 标度空间
scale simulation 比例模拟[仿真]
scale to fit page 缩放到页面大小
scale top 工作区顶边界
scale-up 按比例放大
scale value 标度值,刻度值
scale width 工作区宽度 「面
scaled-down coplane 按比例缩小共平
scaled-integer lattice algorithm 比例整数网格算法
scaler 定标器;计数器;换算器
scaling 定标,换算,比例缩放;剥落
scaling algorithm 定标算法
scaling attribute 定标属性
scaling circuit 定标计数电路
scaling-down 按比例缩小
scaling factor 换算因数,比例因数
scaling function 定标函数;换算功能
scaling instruction 定标指令
scaling law 换算律
scaling method 比例法
scaling position 小数点位置
scaling principle 成比例缩小原则
scaling transformation 标度变换
scaling-up 按比例放大
SCAM (Synchronous Communications Access Method) 同步通信存取方法
scan 扫描
scan abort 扫描异常终止,扫描失败

scan address 扫描地址
scan address generator 扫描地址发生器
scan algorithm 扫描算法
scan area 扫描区域
scan backwards 反向扫描
scan band 扫描带
scan code 扫描码
scan command 扫描命令
scan command word 扫描命令字
scan control register 扫描控制寄存器
scan control unit 扫描控制单元
scan conversion 扫描变换 「序
scan conversion program 扫描转换程
scan converter 扫描变换器
scan depth 扫描景深
scan digitizer 扫描数字化仪
scan element 扫描元素
scan for new device 新设备扫描
scan forward 正向扫描
scan frequency 扫描频率
scan head 扫描头
scan-in 扫描输入
scan limit 扫描极限量,扫描界限
scan line 扫描线
scan-line algorithm 扫描线算法
Scan Maker 扫描生成器
scan material 扫描材料
scan mode 扫描模式
scan-out 扫描输出,扫出
scan path 扫描路径
scan pattern 扫描模式
scan period 扫描周期
scan pickup unit 扫描拾取部件
scan plotter 扫描绘图仪
scan pointer 扫描指针
scan rate 扫描速率
scan reset 扫描复位
scan resolution 扫描分辨率
scan-round 循环扫描
scan selector 扫描选择器
scan size 扫描尺寸
scan speed 扫描速度
scan test 扫描检测
scan width 扫描宽度
ScanDisk 磁盘扫描程序(微软) 「数
scanf function (C语言)格式输入函
scanned character 被扫描字符
scanned document 被扫描文件

scanned symbol 被扫描符号
scanner 扫描仪,扫描器;扫描程序
scanner encoder 扫描编码器
scanner resolution 扫描仪分辨率
scanner selection 扫描程序选择
scanner selector 扫描选择器
scanner test 扫描仪测试
scanner types 扫描仪类型
scanner with enhanced parallel port 带增强型并行端口的扫描仪
scanning 扫描
scanning accuracy 扫描精度
scanning algorithm 扫描算法
scanning area 扫描区域
scanning beam 扫描波束[电子束]
scanning circuit 扫描电路
scanning control 扫描控制
scanning controller 扫描控制器
scanning density 扫描密度
scanning direction 扫描方向
scanning distortion 扫描失真
scanning field 扫描区域,扫描场
scanning head 扫描头
scanning interval 扫描间隔
scanning limits 扫描极限;扫描界限
scanning line 扫描线
scanning line frequency 扫描线频率
scanning line period 扫描线周期
scanning line rate 扫描线速率
scanning linearity 扫描线性度
scanning log file 扫描注册文件
scanning machine 扫描机器
scanning pass 扫描遍
scanning period 扫描周期
scanning pitch 扫描线距
scanning pointer 扫描指针
scanning rate 扫描速率
scanning search 扫描搜索
scanning selector 扫描选择器
scanning shift 扫描位移
scanning speed 扫描速度
scanning spot 扫描光点
scanning transverse 扫描横移
scanning unit 扫描部件
scanning yoke 扫描线圈
scant 不足,缺乏
ScanWizard 扫描向导(软件)
scarf 嵌接

scarf joint 嵌接;楔面接头
scary 嵌接处
scatter 散射;散布
scatter-context grammar 散射文法
scatter diagram 散布式曲线图,散点[图
scatter format 散布格式
scatter gap 散布间隙,分散间隙
scatter/gather 分散/集中
scatter load 分散载入,分散装入
scatter loading 分散载入
scatter matrix 散布矩阵
scatter plot 散布式绘图法
scatter proofs 分散校样
scatter propagation 散射传播
scatter read 分散读入
scatter-read/gather-write 分散读入/集中写入
scatter read-write 分散读写
scatter table 散布表,分散表
scatter transfer 分散传送
scatter write 分散写
scattered data point 分散数据点
scattered seeds 杂散籽晶
scattering 散射,散布
scattering center 散射中心
scattering coefficient 散射系数
scattering loss 散射损失
scavenger 清除程序
scavenging 剩余检索,残余拾拾 「块
SCB(SCSI Control Block) SCSI 控制
SCB(Session Control Block) 对话控制块
　　　　　　　　　　　　　　　「块
SCB(Stack Control Block) 堆栈控制
SCB(Stream Control Block) 流控制块
SCB(Subscriber Control Block) 用户控制块
SCC(Satellite Communication Controller) 卫星通信控制器
SCC(Single Chip Computer) 单片计算机
SCC(Sound Control Computer) 声控计算机
SCC(Synchronous Communication Controller) 同步通信控制器
SCC(System Communication Controller) 系统通信控制器
SCCS(Source Code Control System)

源码控制系统
SCCS history file 源码控制系统历史文件
SCCU(Single Channel Control Unit) 单通道控制部件
SCCW(Swap Channel Command Work area) 交换通道命令工作区
SCD(SPARC Compliance Definition) 按 SPARC 规范定义
SCDE(Software Common Development Environment) 软件公用开发环境
SCE(Single Cycle Execute) 单周期执行
scenario 情况说明；方案；脚本
scenario analysis 情况[场景]分析
scenario-based design 基于场景的设计
scenario manager 方案管理器
scenario pivottable 数据透视表式方案
scenario specialist 全局专ँ程序
scenario testing 场景测试,情节测试
scene 景区,场景,场面；实况
scene analysis 景物分析
scene border 景物边界
scene change 场景变换
scene description 景物描述
scene domain 景物区域
scene interpretation 景物判读[解释]
scene matching 场景匹配
scene recognition 场景识别
scene representation 景物表示法
scene segmentation 景物分割
scene synthesis 场景合成
scene understanding 景物理解
scenic analysis 场景分析
SCERT(System and Computer Evaluation and Review Technique) 系统和计算机评价与鉴定技术
SCERT Ⅱ(System and Computers Evaluation and Review Technique) 系统与计算机评审技术
SCH(SCHeduler) 调度程序
SCH(Seizures per Circuit per Hour) 电路小时占用
SCHDELAY(SCHeduled DELAY) 预排时延
schedulability 可调度性
schedulable 可调度的
schedule(SCH) 调度；图表,目录；清单
schedule and scheduler 调度与调度程序
schedule job 预定作业,调度作业,工序
schedule loop iteration 调度循环迭代
schedule status pre-processor(SSPP) 调度状态预处理器
schedule table 调度表
scheduled 预先安排的,有计划的
scheduled circuits 预安排线路
scheduled down time 预定停机时间
scheduled engineering time 预安排工程时间
scheduled event 预安排[预定]事件
scheduled fault detection 预定故障检测
scheduled job 预排作业
scheduled maintenance 预定计划维修,例行维修
scheduled maintenance time 预定维修时间,例行维修时间
scheduled operating time 预定操作时间
scheduled operation 预排作业
scheduled output 预定输出,例行输出
scheduled plan 进度计划,预定计划
scheduled start time 预定开始时间
scheduler(SCH) 调度程序；日程安排程序
scheduler module 调度模块
scheduler program 调度程序
scheduler proposed-queue 调度程序申请队列
scheduler waiting queue 调度程序等待队列
scheduler work area(SWA) 调度程序工作区
scheduler work area data set(SWADS) 调度程序工作数据集
scheduling 调度；日程安排
scheduling algorithm 调度算法
scheduling discipline 调度规则
scheduling graph 调度图
scheduling information pool 调度信息池
scheduling intent 调度意图
scheduling management display 调度管理显示
scheduling mode 调度方式
scheduling model 调度模型
scheduling monitor computer 调度监控计算机
scheduling of resources 资源调度

scheduling operation 调度作业
scheduling policy 调度策略
scheduling priority 调度优先权
scheduling problem 调度问题
scheduling process 调度处理
scheduling queue 调度队列
scheduling resource 调度资源
scheduling rule 调度规则
scheduling strategy 调度策略
scheduling support 调度支持
scheduling system sequential 调度系统顺序
scheduling theory 调度理论
scheduling vector 调度向量
schema 模式;概要;简图
schema abstraction 模式抽象
schema acquisition 模式采集
schema category 模式种类
schema chart 模式图
schema data description entry 模式数据定义项
schema data description language 模式数据描述语言
schema declaration 模式说明
schema decomposition 模式分解
schema description 模式描述
schema entry 模式项目
schema evolution 模式演变
schema expression 模式表示
schema instance 模式实例
schema integration architecture 模式综合结构
schema mapping 模式映像
schema name 模式名
Schema Representation Language 模式表达语言
schema reformatting 模式重定格式
schema restructuring 模式重构
schema update 模式更新
schema view 规划视图
schema virtualization 模式虚拟化
schematic 原理图,示意图,简图
schematic circuit 原理电路
schematic design 原理设计
schematic diagram 原理图,简图
schematic entry 原理图输入
schematic library 电路原理图库
schematic simulation 概念性模拟

schematic theory 图解理论
scheme 方案,计划;图,图解;分类表
SCHIB (SubCHannel Information Block) 子通道信息块
SCHID(SubCHannel IDentification) 子通道标识符
SCHM(Set CHannel Monitor Instruction) 置通道监控指令
Schmitt trigger 施密特触发器
Schottky barrier 肖特基势垒
Schottky barrier diode 肖特基势垒二极管
Schottky field effect transistor 肖特基场效应晶体管
SchottkyI2L 肖特基集成注入逻辑电路
Schottky transistor logic(STL) 肖特基晶体管逻辑
Schottky transistor-transistor logic(STTL) 肖特基晶体管-晶体管逻辑电路
Schottky TTL memory 肖特基 TTL 存储器
SCI(Scalable Coherence Interface) 规模可扩展的计算机连接界面
SCI (System Configuration Information) 系统配置信息
SCI(System Control Interface) 系统控制界面
SCI Search 科学引文索引检索
SciAn SciAn 软件包
SCIB(Search Compressed Index Block) 搜索压缩索引块
SCIB(Selective Channel Input Bus) 选择通道输入总线
SCID(System Call Interrupt Decoder) 系统调用中断译码器
Science and Technology Information System(STIS) 科技信息系统
science citation index(SCI) 科学引文索引
science information service 科学信息服务
science-oriented 面向科学的
scientific accelerator module(SAM) 科学加速器模块
scientific and engineering calculation 科学与工程计算
scientific and technical information 科

学技术信息
scientific assist firmware 科学计算辅助固件
scientific calculation 科学计算
scientific calculator 科学计算器
scientific community 科学团体
scientific computer 科学用计算机
scientific computing 科学计算
scientific data center 科学数据中心
scientific data processing 科学数据处理
scientific database 科学数据库
scientific language 科学计算语言
scientific library 科学计算程序库
scientific notation 科学计数法
scientific program 科学计算程序
scientific programmable calculator 科学可编程计算器
scientific sampling 科学抽样
scientific subroutine package 科学子程序包
scientific visualization 科学可视化
SCIL(System Core Image Library) 系统核心映像库
scintillation 目标快速移动;(接收电磁波场强)起伏
scintillation material 闪光材料
SCIP(System Control Interface Package) 系统控制接口软件包
SCIRT(System Control In Real Time) 实时系统控制
scissoring 修剪,切除,剪裁
SCK(Set ClocK) 时钟设置
SCL(SCaLe) 刻度,标尺,规模,标度
SCL(Select Code Least) 选择码最低有效位
SCL(Semi-Custom Logic) 半定制逻辑
SCN(Satellite Control Network) 卫星控制网络
SCN(Self-Checking Number) 自校验号
SCO(Santa Cruz Operation, Inc.) SCO公司
SCO Global Access SCO 全程存取,SCO 全局访问
SCO Open Desktop SCO 开放式桌面系统
SCO Open Server Enterprise SCO 开放式服务器软件

SCO UNIX System V SCO UNIX 操作系统第五版
SCO VP/ix SCO VP/ix 程序
SCO XENIX System V SCO XENIX 操作系统第五版
SCOAP(Sandia Controllability / Observability Analysis Program) SCOAP 程序
scope 显示器;物镜;作用域,辖域
scope attribute 作用域属性
scope delimiter 作用域定界符
scope link 作用域链接
scope note 范围注释
scope of a condition prefix 条件前缀作用域
scope of a declaration 说明作用域
scope of a name 名称作用域
scope of a variable 变量作用域
scope of an external name 外部名字作用域
scope of an object 对象作用域
scope of an operator 操作数作用域
scope of automatic 自动作用域
scope of command facility 命令设备作用域
scope of control of a module 模块控制范围
scope of declaration 说明作用域
scope of effect 有效范围
scope of identifier 标识符作用域
scope of quantifier 量词辖域
scope of recovery 恢复作用域
scope of symbolic name 符号名作用域
scope unit 作用域单位
scoping rule 作用域规则
scoptopic vision 暗视觉
score 成绩,得分,分数
scoring 计分
SCP(Service Control Point) 服务控制点
SCP(SunLink Communications Processor) SunLink 通信处理器(Sun)
SCP(Supervisory Control Program) 监督控制程序
SCP(Symbolic Conversion Program) 符号转换程序
SCP(System Control Program) 系统控制程序

SCR(Silicon-Controlled Rectifier) 可控硅整流器
SCR(Software Change Report) 软件更改报告
SCR(Store Control Register) 存储控制寄存器
SCR(System Change Request) 系统更改请求
SCR regulated circuit 可控硅稳压电路
scramble 倒频,扰频,置乱
scramble binary 乱码二进制
scramble network 不规则[杂混]网络
scramble pattern 不规则[乱码]模式
scramble rule 置乱规则
scramble system 不规则系统
scramble time 插用时间,零星时间
scrambled 保密的,乱码加密的;杂乱
scrambled order 杂乱次序 的
scrambled speech 扰频(加密)语言
scrambler 置乱器,扰码器
scrambling 置乱,加密;不规则性
scrambling and unscrambling network 播散与收集网络
scrap 剪贴片;碎片
Scrapbook 剪贴簿
scratch 擦除;划痕,擦伤;临时的
scratch command 清内存命令
scratch data cartridge 临时数据带
scratch disk 暂用盘,无可用数据盘
scratch diskette 暂存盘
scratch edition 暂用版本
scratch file 临时文件;废文件
scratch memory 暂时存储器
scratch memory location 暂时存储器单元
scratch pack 暂存盘组
scratch pad 暂存区;便笺
scratch pad addressing 便笺式寻址法
scratch pad memory 草稿存储器
scratch pad storage 草稿存储器
scratch pad test channel 中间结果测试通道
scratch tape 暂用磁带
scratch volume 暂用卷
scratch workspace 暂用工作区
scratching 损伤,擦伤,刻痕,擦除
screen 屏幕;筛选;屏栅
screen address 屏幕地址

screen attribute byte 屏幕属性字节
screen blanking 屏幕清空
screen buffer 屏幕缓冲器
screen capacity 屏幕容量
screen capture 屏幕捕获[抓图]
screen context printing 屏幕内容打印
screen coordinate 屏幕坐标 统
screen coordinate system 屏幕坐标系
screen copy 屏幕拷贝,屏面复制
screen cursor 屏幕光标
screen cut and paste 屏幕剪切与粘贴
screen design aid 屏幕设计辅助程序
screen-door translucency 纱门式半透
screen dump 屏幕转储 明
screen editor 屏幕编辑程序
screen element 屏幕元件
screen enhancement character 屏幕增强字符
screen exchange 屏幕切换
screen file 屏幕[软拷贝]文件
screen flicker 屏幕闪动
screen font 屏幕字形
screen form file 屏幕格式文件
screen format 屏幕格式
screen generator 屏幕生成程序
screen grabber 屏幕抓图程序
screen image 屏幕图像
screen layout 屏幕布局
screen load 屏幕画面加载
screen lock 画面锁定
screen mode 屏幕模式
screen open 屏幕画面开启
screen overlay 屏幕覆盖,屏面重叠
screen position 显示屏位置 体
screen-printed conductor 丝网印制导
screen printing 屏幕打印;丝网印刷
screen reader 屏幕内容阅读程序
screen resolution 屏幕分辨率
screen saver 屏幕保护程序 序
screen saver utility 屏幕保护实用程
screen size 屏幕尺寸
screen space 屏幕空间
screen status area 屏幕状态区
screen status register 屏幕状态寄存器
screen tension test equipment 网膜张力测试
screen test 筛选测试
screen tone 屏幕色调

screen width 屏幕宽度
screenfull 满屏
screening 筛选;屏蔽,遮蔽;丝网印刷
screenload 全屏承载
SreenReader "屏幕阅读"浏览器(IBM)
screw 螺丝钉
screw plug 螺旋塞
screwdriver 螺丝刀
scribe 划片,划线
scribe projection 划线投影
scribing plotting display 笔绘显示设备
script 过程;稿本,脚本,底稿
script alias 脚本别名
script command 脚本命令
script-driven simulation 原稿驱动模拟
script editor 脚本编辑程序
script engine 脚本引擎
script event 原型事件
script file 底稿[脚本]文件
script graphics tablet 手迹图形输入板
script handwriting 手写体
script intensity 原本对比度
script knowledge representation 脚本知识表示
script language 脚本语言
script library 脚本库
script manager 脚本管理程序
script reader 手写体阅读器
script representation 脚本表示
scripted computer aided instruction 剧本式计算机辅助教学
scripting 底稿编制
scroll 滚屏,卷动,卷轴
scroll area 滚屏区域
scroll arrow 滚屏箭头
scroll bar 滚动条
scroll box 滚动框
scroll buffer 滚动缓冲区
scroll down 下滚,向下卷动
scroll file 滚动文件
scroll forward 向前滚动
scroll frozen 滚屏冻结
scroll key 滚动控制键
scroll lock 滚屏锁定;滚屏锁定键
scroll lock key 滚屏锁定键
scroll mode 滚动模式
scroll mode terminal 上卷式终端
scroll off 滚屏停止
scroll ribbon 卷动色带
scroll text box 滚动文本框
scroll text buffer 滚动文本缓冲区
scroll timing 滚屏定时;卷移定时
scroll window 卷动窗口
scroll up 上滚,向上卷动
scrollable field 可滚动区域
scrollable list 可滚动列表
scrolling 滚屏
scrolling down 向下滚屏,向下翻滚
scrolling up 向上滚屏,向上翻滚
scrubbing 擦洗,清除
scrubbing action 擦除作用
SCS(Single-Channel Simplex) 单通道单工
SCS(Stripe Card Standard) 条形卡标准
SCS code points(SNA Character String code points) SNA 字符串编码点
SCSI(Small Computer System Interface) 小型计算机系统接口
SCSI-1 SCSI-1 接口标准
SCSI-2 SCSI-2 接口标准
SCSI-3 SCSI-3 接口标准
SCSI bus SCSI 总线
SCSI chain SCSI 链
SCSI device SCSI 设备
SCSI ID SCSI 标识符
SCSI Interface Connector SCSI 接口连接器
SCSI terminator SCSI 端接器
SCSI tray SCSI 盘(Sun)
SCT(Special Character Table) 专用字符表,特殊字符表
SCU(Sequence Control Unit) 顺序控制器
SCU(Synchronous Control Unit) 同步控制器
scuzzym SCSI 的读音
SCVT(Secondary Communication Vector Table) 辅助通信向量表
SCW(Segment Control Word) 段控制字
SD(Send Data) 发送数据
SD(Single Density) 单密度
SDA(Synchronous Data Adapter) 同步数据适配器
SDA(System Dump Analyzer) 系统

转储分析程序
SDA(System Dynamic Analyzer) 系统动态分析程序
SDAP(System Development Analysis Program) 系统开发分析程序
SDAT(Symbolic Device Allocation Table) 符号设备分配表
SDB(Segment Descriptor Block) 段描述符块
sdb(symbolic debugger) (Unix)符号调试程序
SDC(Serial Data Controller) 串行数据控制器
SDD(System Development Division) 系统开发部(IBM)
SDDI(Serial Digital Data Internet) 串行数字数据互联网(Sony)
SDDL(Schema Data Description Language) 模式数据描述语言
SDDL(Software Design Description Language) 软件设计描述语言
SDDM(Source Distributed Data Manager) (AS/400)源分布式数据管理程序
SDDTTG(Stored Data Definition and Translation Task Group) 存储数据定义与翻译任务组
SDE(Software Development Environment) 软件开发环境
SDE(Standard Data Element) 标准数据单元
SDF(Screen Definition Facility) 屏幕画面定义程序
SDF(Syntax Diagram Form) 语法图形式
SDF(System Definition File) 系统定义文件
SDH(Synchronous Digital Hierarchy) 同步数字系列
SDI(Scanned Data In) 扫描数据输入
SDI(Selective Dissemination of Information) 定题信息提供
SDI(Standard Data Interface) 标准数据接口
SDI(Switching Device Interface) 交换设备接口
SDIO(Serial Digital Input/Output) 串行数字输入/输出
SDIU(Subscriber's Digital Interface Unit) 用户数字接口设备
SDK(System Design Kit) 系统设计成套工具(软件);系统设计套件(硬件)
SDK(System Development Kit) 系统开发成套工具
SDL(Functional Specification and Description Language) 功能规范和描述语言(CCITT)
SDL(Structural Description Language) 结构描述语言
SDL(System Directory List) 系统目录表
SDLC(Software Development Life Cycle) 软件开发生命周期
SDLC(Synchronous Data Link Control) 同步数据链路控制规程
SDLC frame 同步数据链路控制帧
SDLC link SDLC链路
SDM 1.0(System Development Multitasking release 1.0) 系统开发多任务基准程序1.0版本
SDM(Selective Dissemination of Microfiche) 缩微平片的定题服务
SDM(Semiconductor Disc Memory) 半导体盘存储器
SDMA(Sequence Division Multiple Access) 顺序分配多路存取
SDMA(Space-Division Multiple Access) 空间分割多路存取
SDMA/SS-TDMA(Space Division Multiple Access/Space craft Switched-Time Division Multiple Access) 空分多路存取/卫星转接时分多路存取
SDN(Switched Digital Network) 交换数字网络
SDN(Synchronous Digital Transmission Network) 同步数字传输网
SDP(Synchronous Distributed Processor) 同步分布式处理机
SDPS(Signal Data Processing System) 信号数据处理系统
SDPS(Signature Data Processing System) 签字数据处理系统
SDR(System Definition Record) 系统定义记录
SDRAM(Synchronous DRAM) 同步

动态存储器
SDS(Servo Drive System) 伺服驱动系统
SDS(Shared Data Set) 共享数据集
SDS(Software Design Specification) 软件设计规范
SDS(Software Development System) 软件开发系统
SDS(System Dynamics Simulator) 系统动态仿真器
SDSL(Super Data Subscriber Loop) 高速数字用户环路
SDSS(Software Development Support System) 软件开发支持系统
SDT(Serial Data Transmission) 串行数据传送
SDT(Start-Data-Traffic) 启动数据传送
SDTV(Standard Digital TV) 标准数字电视
SDU(Service Data Unit) 服务数据单元
SDU(Signal Distribution Unit) 信号分配单元
SDU(Spectrum Display Unit) 频谱(光谱)显示部件
SDU(Synchronous Data Unit) 同步数据单元
SDV(Switched Digital Video access) 交换式数字视频进入
SDW(Segment Descriptor Word) 段描述字
SE(Sign Extended) 符号扩充的
SE(Software Engineering) 软件工程
SE(Stack Empty) 堆栈空
SE(Synchronous Ethernet) 同步以太网
SE(System Engineering) 系统工程
SE(System Extension) 系统扩充
SEA(System Effectiveness Analyzer) 系统效能分析程序
Seagate Technology International 希捷国际科技公司(硬盘生产厂家)
seal 绝缘,密封
seal-impression verification 印记验证
seal test 密封性试验
seal washer 密封垫圈
sealant 密封胶,密封剂
sealed cap 密封帽,密封盖
sealed disk drive 密封式磁盘驱动器
sealer 密封器;密封层

seam 裂缝,接缝
seam tracking system 裂缝跟踪系统
seamless connection 无缝连接
seamless integration 无缝集成
seamless model 无缝模型
search 搜索,查找
search algorithm 搜索[检索]算法
search and kill 搜索与删除
search and replace 搜索与替换
search area 搜索区域
search argument 检索自变量
search backward 向后搜索
search capability 检索能力
search chain 搜索链,查找链
search clue 查找线索
search command 检索[查找]命令
search complete 查找完成
search count 查找计数
search criteria 检索判据,搜索条件
search cycle 搜索周期
search direction 查找方向
search engine 搜索引擎
search expression 搜索表达式
search field 检索字段
search finding 搜索求解
search for 搜索指定对象
search for application 搜索应用程序
search for help 搜索帮助信息
search firm 人才搜寻公司
search function 检索功能;搜索函数
search game AND/OR tree 搜索博弈"与或"树
search graph 查找图,搜索图
search heuristics 搜索试探法
search hints 搜索提示
search immediately 立即开始查找
search index 查找索引
search interface 检索界面
search key 检索键,搜索关键字
search length 检索[查找]长度
search list 搜索表,查找列表
search mask 搜索屏蔽
search memory 搜索[相联]存储器
search method 检索方法
search model 搜索模型
search only 只搜索
search operation 搜索操作
search path 搜索路径

search pattern 搜索模式
search performance 检索性能
search procedure 查找过程
search pruning 搜索修剪
search-read function 寻读函数
search receiver 搜索接收机
search-result folder 搜索结果文件夹
search routine 检索例程;定位检测程序
search rule 搜索规则
search space 搜索空间
SEARCH statement 查找语句
search strategy 搜索策略
search string 搜索字符串
search terms 查寻项目
search theory 检索理论
search time 搜索时间
search trajectory 搜索轨迹
search tree 搜索树
search-verification process 搜索-校验过程
search word 检索字
searchable information 可供查找信息
searchable physics information notes (SPIN) 可检索物理信息文献
searcher 搜索程序
searching 搜索;仔细的,严格的
searching algorithm 搜索算法
searching architecture 搜索用系统结构
searching directory tree 搜索目录树
searching examination 严格考核
searching storage 检索[相联]存储器
SeaShield 硬盘屏蔽技术(Seagate)
seasoning 陈化,老化
seat reservation system 座位预订系统
sec(second) 秒
Sec.(Section) 节,段
SEC(Single-Entry Single-Exit Computer) 单入口单出口计算机
SEC(Single Error Correction) 单错校正
SEC(Switching-Equipment-Congestion signal) 交换设备阻塞信号
SEC-BED-DED(Single Error Correction-Byte Error Detection-Double Error Detecting code) 单纠错-字节错误检测-双错误检测码
SEC-DED(Single Error Correcting and Double Error Detecting) 单错校正-双错检测
SEC-PDED(Single Error Correcting and Partial Double Error Detecting) 单错校正和部分双错检测
SECAM(Séquential Couleur á Mémoire) 顺序传送彩色与存储体制,SECAM电视体制
secant method 割线法
SECD(Self-regulating Error-correcting Coder-Decoder) 自调节纠错编译码器
SECDED code 单错校正双错检测码
second 秒;第二的
second addition time 第二次加法时间
second approximation 二次近似
second boundary-value problem 第二类边值问题
second breakdown 二次击穿
second byte 第二字节
second category axis 第二分类轴
second choice route 第二选用路由
second computer age 第二计算机代
second data multiplexer 二次数据多路复用器
second generation 第二代
second generation computer 第二代计算机
second generation data model 第二代数据模型
second generation operating system 第二代操作系统
second largest entry 次最大项
second-level address 二级地址
second-level addressing 二级寻址
second level cache 二级高速缓存
second level definition 二级定义
second level directory 第二级目录
second level interrupt 二级中断
second level message 第二级信息
second level of packaging 第二级组装;二级装配
second level outcome 二级[辅助]结果
second level predicate 第二层次谓词
second level stack 二级堆栈
second-level statement 第二级语句
second level storage 第二级存储器
second mean-value theorem 第二中值定理

second normal form 第二范式
second operand 第二操作数
second-order 二阶的,二次的
second-order closure 二次闭包
second-order difference 二次差分
second order differential equation 二阶微分方程
second-order logic 二阶逻辑
second-order noncorresponding control 二阶无差控制
second-order phase-locked loop 二阶锁相环
second-order polynomial 二阶多项式
second-order predicate calculus 二阶谓词演算
second-order singularity 二阶奇异性
second-order stochastic process 二阶随机过程
second order subroutine 二级子例程
second-order system 二阶系统
second recursion theorem 第二递归定「理
second-person virtual reality 二人虚拟现实
second place 第二位的
second predicate calculus 二阶谓词演「算
second quantization 二次量化
second source 第二来源
secondary 次级的;下级的;第二位的
secondary activation word 辅助激励字
secondary address vector table 二级[辅助]地址向量表
secondary application 辅助应用
secondary application block(SAB) 辅助应用块
secondary attribute 辅助属性
secondary axis 辅助轴,次坐标轴
secondary buffer 辅助缓冲区
secondary calibration 二级校准
secondary cache 二级高速缓存
secondary channel 辅助信道
secondary cluster 二次簇
secondary coating 二次涂覆
secondary coil 次级线圈
secondary color 混合色,调和色
secondary computer 辅助[从]计算机
secondary console 副控制台
secondary constraint 次要约束

secondary control point 辅助控制点
secondary data 辅助数据
secondary data channel 辅助数据通道
secondary destination 第二接收点[信宿]
secondary device 辅助设备
secondary dump system 辅助转储系统
secondary entry point 二次入口点
secondary failure 诱发故障,二次故障
secondary file 辅助文件
secondary function 二级功能;辅助功「能
secondary half-session 辅助对接端
secondary impact ionization 二次碰撞电离
secondary index 辅助索引
secondary input port 辅助输入端口
secondary interface 次级接口,二级接口
secondary iteration 第二迭代,副迭代
secondary key 辅助关键字;次密钥
secondary key encrypting keys 二级关键码密钥,辅助关键保密键码
secondary key field 辅助关键码字段
secondary key retrieval 辅助关键字检索
secondary lattice group 二次网络群
secondary line 辅助[次要]线路
secondary link station 辅助链路站
secondary logical unit(SLU) 辅助逻辑部件
secondary logic unit key 辅助逻辑单元关键字
secondary memory 辅助[二级]存储器
secondary multiplex 二次复用
secondary network support 辅助网络支持
secondary operator control station 副操作控制站
secondary optimization problem 次最优问题「置
secondary paging device 辅助分页装
secondary partition 辅助分区
secondary program 辅助程序
secondary prompt (Unix)辅助提示符
secondary register set 辅助寄存器组
secondary routes 次要[辅助]路由
secondary row 辅助行

secondary segment 辅助分段
secondary selection sorting 二次选择排序
secondary side 次面
secondary space allocation 辅助空间分配
secondary station 副站,从站
secondary status 辅助状态,从状态
secondary storage 辅助存储器
secondary switching center 二级转接中心
secondary task 辅助任务
secondary user 二级用户
secondary vector 二次向量
secondary winding 次级绕组
secondary window 二级窗口,辅助窗口
seconds 秒数
seconds until timeout 超时秒数
secrecy classification 密级
secret 保密的,秘密的
secret communication 保密通信
secret document 保密文档
secret language 密语
secret language telegrams 密语电报
secret reproduction 保密复制
secret sharing system 保密共享系统
Secret Store 安全存储
section 段,节;扇区;剖视
section bit 区段位
section break 分节符
section-by-section 逐节进行的
section debugging 分节排错
section header 节头,节标题
section layout 分节布局
section name 节名
section number 节号,节编号
section paper 方格纸
section start 节开始
section system 剖面系统,剖面图
section termination 段终端
section text 节文本
section to 分成章节
sectional assembly 分节汇编 「局
sectional center 区域中心;分区中心
sectional testing 分段测试
sectional view 横断面
sectionalization 分段
sectionalized 分节的

sectioning 分节,分段;分区缩微摄影
sectioning search 分割搜索
sector 扇区;区,段
sector address 扇区地址
sector associative buffer storage 区联缓存
sector buffer 扇面缓冲器
sector chaining 扇区链接 「器
sector counter 扇区计数器;区段计数
sector entry 扇区项
sector hole 扇区孔
sector index hole 扇区索引孔
sector interleave 扇区交错
sector label 扇区标号
sector map 扇区安排
sector mark 扇区标记
sector number 扇区编号
sector pulse 扇区(标识)脉冲
sector queue 扇区队列
sector ring 扇区环
sector scan 扇区扫描
sector servo 扇区伺服
sector transducer 扇区转换器
sectored file 分区[分段]文件
SecuDe SecuDe 安全软件包
secular equation 特征方程
secure 安全,保密
secure archival storage system 安全档案存储系统
secure automatic data information exchange 保密型自动数据信息系统
secure communication 安全通信,保密通信
secure configuration management 安全配置管理
SECURE CONSOLE 安全控制台
Secure Electronic Payment Protocol (SEPP) 安全通信电子结算协议
Secure Electronic Transaction (SET) 安全电子交易
secure failure set 安全故障集
secure filter 安全过滤器
Secure HyperText Transport Protocol (SHTTP) 安全超文本传输协议
secure line 安全[保密]线路
secure logon facility 安全登录机制
secure model 安全模型
secure module 安全模块

secure operating system 安全操作系统
secure property 安全属性
secure protocol 安全协议
secure query function 安全查询功能
secure schedule program 安全调度程序
Secure Socket Layer(SSL) 安全套接层(Netscape)
secure state 安全状态
secure system 安全系统
secure traffic 安全通信量；保密通信业务量
Secure Transaction Channel(STC) 安全事务通道
Secure Transaction Technology(STT) 安全事务处理技术
secure transmission 安全传输
secure voice 保密语音
secure voice cord board 保密话音转接
secure working area 安全工作区
SecurID 安全识别卡
securities trading 证券交易
security 安全性，保密性
security algorithm 安全性算法
security and integrity 安全性与完整性
security arrangements 安全措施
security audit 安全审计
security audit trail 保密检查跟踪
security awareness program 安全识别程序
security axiom 安全性公理
security class 安全类
security clearance 安全许可
security code 密码，安全码
security coefficient 安全系数
security console 安全控制台
security console logs 安全控制台记录
security constraint 安全性约束
security critical mechanism 安全判别机制
security custodian 安全员
security definition language 安全定义语言
security dump 安全转储
security feasibility study 安全可行性研究
security features 防护件，防护设备
security fence 安全性防护

security filter 安全过滤器[程序]
Security First Network Bank 安全第一网络银行(美)
security flaw 安全性缺陷
security flow analysis 保密(信息)流分析
security guard robot 保安机器人
security incident 安全事故
security inspection 安全检查
security interrogation sequence 安全询问序列
security isolation 安全隔离
security kernel 安全中心，保密核心
security kernel approach 安全内核法
security kernel interface 安全核心接口
security keylock 安全键锁
security label 安全标记
security level 安全级
security life 保密期限
security maintenance 安全维护
security management 安全管理
security management information database 安全管理信息数据库
security measures 保密措施
security mechanism 安全机制
security model 安全模型
security modem 安全调制解调器
security number 安全号
security of user file 用户文件安全性
security officer 安全官员
security optical fiber 安全光纤
security package 安全封装
security perimeter 安全防线
security policy 安全策略
security profile 安全框架
security protection 安全保护
security proving 安全证明
security-relevant event 与安全有关的事件
security restore 安全恢复
security safeguards 安全防护
security server 安全服务器
security software 安全软件
security specifications 保密规程
security system architecture 安全系统体系结构
security test and evaluation 安全检测与评估

security testing 保密测试
security threats 保密威胁
security violation 违反安全
SED(Software Engineering Development) 软件工程开发
sed(stream editor) 流编辑命令
SEDED(Single Error and Double Erasure Detecting) 单错与双清除检测
SEE(Software Engineering Environment) 软件工程环境
see also 另见…
see folder 查看文件夹
see predicate 读操作谓词
see-saw circuit 推挽电路 「器
see through HMD 合成图像头戴显示
see through plate 彩色板
seed 籽数;气籽
seed crystal 籽晶
seed value 种籽值
seeding 种籽形成
seeing predicate 查询输入流谓词
seek 查找,搜索,检索
seek area 查找区域,搜索区域
seek arm 查找臂,存取臂
seek error 寻道错误
seek key 检索关键字
seek offset 寻道偏移量
seek only time 纯查找(寻道)时间
seek ordering 寻道时间,查找时间
seek retry 重新寻道
seek time 查找时间,搜索时间;寻道时间
seeking 查找,寻找;故障检查
seen predicate 停止读谓词
seepage 泄露,渗漏
seepage flow 渗流
seesaw repeater 交互转换中继器
SEF(Software Engineering Facility) 软件工程设施
SEF(Standard External File) 标准外部文件
SEG(SEGment) 段,程序段
SEG(Sequence of Events Generator) 事件序列产生程序
segment 段;图块;切分成份
segment address 段地址
segment addressing 段寻址
segment attribute 段属性;图块属性

segment base 段基址,段起始地址
segment body 段体
segment buffer 段缓冲器
segment call 段调用
segment classification 段分类
segment control bit 段控制位
segment decoder 分段译码器
segment descriptor 段描述符
segment designation 段标识 「器
segment display 分段显示;笔划显示
segment entry save register 段入口保存寄存器
segment fault 段出错,段故障
segment hard core module 分段硬核心模块
segment identification 段标识
segment invalid bit 段无效位
segment-level sharing 段级共享
segment limit clause 段限定子句
segment limits origin 段限界始址
segment mapping table(SMT) 段映像
segment mark 段标记 「表
segment matching 分段匹配 「法
segment merging algorithm 段合并算
segment mode 分段模式
segment name 段名
segment number 段号
segment occurrence 段事件
segment overlay 段覆盖
segment phrase 段短语
segment pointer 段指针
segment prefix 段前缀
segment register 段寄存器
segment search argument 段搜索变元
segment sharing 段共享
segment size 段长度
segment structure 段结构
segment table(SGT) 段表
segment table address 段表地址
segment table base register(STBR) 段表基址寄存器
segment table entry(STE) 段表目
segment table length 段表长度
segment table length register(STLR) 段表长度寄存器
segment table look-aside buffer 段表后备缓冲器
segment table look-up 段表查阅

segment table origin(STO)　段表起始地址
segment time unit　分段时间单位
segment transformation　图块转换
segment translation　段移送
segment translation exception　段转换异常
segment type　段类型
segmentation　分段法
segmentation algorithm　分段算法
segmentation and reassembly sublayer (SAR)　装拆子层
segmentation fault　分段错误
segmentation facility　分段程序
segmentation hardware　分段式硬件
segmentation module　程序分段模块
segmentation of BIUs　基本信息单元分段
segmentation of words　词的切分
segmentation overlays　段覆盖
segmentation paging mode　分段编页方式
segmentation register table(SRT)　分段寄存器表
segmentation scheduling　段式调度
segmentation strategy　分段策略
segmented address space　分段地址空间
segmented addressing architecture　分段寻址结构
segmented and demand-paged storage management　分段及按需分页式存储管理
segmented dictionary　分段词典
segmented encoding law　折线编码规则
segmented image database　分段图像数据库
segmented memory system　分段式存储系统
segmented mode　分段模式
segmented program　分段程序
segmented storage management　分段存储器管理
segmented virtual display file　分段虚拟显示文件
segmenting　分段
segmenting size　分段大小
segmenting unit　分段单元
SEGNO(SEGment Number)　段号

segregation　分离；分凝法
segregation coefficient　分离[偏析]系数
segregation constant　分凝常数
segregation of duties　责任分离[放]
SEGREL(SEGment RELease)　段释
SEGTBL(SEGment TaBLe)　段表
SEGWT(SEGment load and WaiT)　段加载并等待
SEI(Software Engineering Institute)　(美国国防部在卡内基-梅隆大学办的)软件工程研究所
seismic pattern recognition　地震模式识别
seize　占机，占线
seizing signal　占机信号
seizure　占用，占线
seizure condition　占用[占线]状态
seizures per circuit per hour(SCH)　电路小时占用
SEL(System Event Log)　系统事件日志(Intel)
select　选择
select address output signal　选择地址输出信号
select all　全选
select articles　选择文章
select base address　选定基地址
select bit　选择位
select chart　选择图表
select chart type　选择图表类型
select circuit　选择电路
SELECT clause　选择子句
select column　选择列(栏)
select command　选择命令
select current directory　选择当前目录
select current region　选择当前区域
select data source　选择数据源
select DMA channel　选定 DMA 通道
select document to add　选择加入的文档
select drive　选择驱动器
select-error　选择差错
select file　选定文件
select frequency　选择频率
select function　选择功能
select group　选定组
select help topic　选择帮助主题
select in signal　选择输入信号
select line　选择线；选择行

select object 选定对象
select order 选择命令
select out signal 选出信号
select page separator 选择分页符
select plot area 选择绘图区域
select plus routine 选"+"号例程
select port 选定端口
select printer 选定打印机
select receive frequency 选择接收频率
select sheet 选定工作表
select special 特殊选择
select standby 选择备用(设备或部件)
select switch 选择开关
select table 选定表格
select transmit frequency 选择发送频率
select unit 选择部件
select visible cell 选定可见单元格区域
selectability 选择能力
selectable 可选择的
selectable-length word 可选择长度字
selectable unit 可选择单元
selectavision 选播电视
selected 被选中的,被选定的
selected address 被选中地址
selected area 被选区
selected axis 已选定坐标轴
selected bit 被选中位
selected category labels 选定分类标志
selected chart area 选定图表区域
selected chart title 选定图表标题
selected down bar 选定倒置条状图
selected error bar 选定误差线
selected gridline 选定网格线
selected force-out 被选强制输出
selected function group 选定函数组
selected gridline 选中网格线
selected high-low line 选定高-低线
selected job queue 被选中作业队列
selected legend entry 选定图例项
selected length field 长度选择字段
selected master file tape 被选主文件带
selected mode 选定模式
selected object 选定对象
selected parameter 选定参数
selected plot area 选定绘图区
selected popup color 选定快显色
selected slot 选定插槽

selected trendline 选定趋势线
selected up bar 选定正向条状图
selected wall 选定背景墙
selecting data 选择数据
selecting mode 选择模式
selecting operation 选择操作
selecting priority 选择优先权
selecting robot 精选机器人
selection 选择;选址
selection acknowledgement output 选择证实输出
selection addressing 选择寻址
selection bar 选择条
selection calling system 选择呼叫系统
selection character 选择字符
selection check 选择检查
selection component 选择成份
selection control 选择控制
selection cursor 选择光标
selection data 选择数据
selection diversity 选择分集
selection handle 选择控制柄
selection identity 选择标识码
selection input 选择输入
selection marquee 选择蒙版
selection path 选择通路
selection plugboard 选择插件板
selection pointer 选择指针
selection position 选择位置
selection priority 选择优先级
selection ratio 选择比,选择率
selection-replacement approach 选择替代法
selection-replacement technique 选择替换技术
selection scheme 选择方案
selection signal 选择信号
selection signal code 选择信号码
selection sort 选择排序
selection stage 选择级
selection state of cell 单元选择状态
selection time 选择时间
selection type 选择类型
selection wire 选择线
selective 选择性的
selective abstract 选择性抽取
selective accounting 选择性记账
selective addressing 选择寻址

selective area recovery 选择性区域恢
selective assembly 选择汇编 [复
selective calling 选择呼叫
selective casing routine 事例选择例程
selective channel 选择通道
selective clock stretching 选择性时钟展宽
selective combiner 选择组合器
selective construct 选择构造
selective cryptographic session 选择密码对话
selective diffusion 选择性扩散
selective display 选择显示
selective dissemination of information (SDI) 定题信息提供
selective diversity combining 选择性分集合并
selective dump 选择转储
selective epitaxial growth 选择性外延生长
selective erase 选择性擦除
selective fading 选择性衰落 [护
selective field protection 选择字段保
selective flooding routing 有选择的洪泛式路由选择
selective generalization rule 选择性概括规则
selective index 有选择下标
selective induction 选择性归纳
selective induction learning 选择性归纳学习
selective interference 选择性干扰
selective listing 选择列表
selective preemption 选择性抢占
selective printing 选择性打印
selective prompting 选择性提示
selective reject 拒选
selective reject command 拒选命令
selective repeat 选择性重发
selective ringing 选择性振铃
selective rule 选择性规则
selective scaling 选择性定标
selective sequence calculator 选择序列计算机
selective sequential 顺序选择
selective-serial update 顺序选择更新
selective shrinking 选择性收缩
selective statement 选择语句

selective stroke linkage method 选择性笔划连接法
selective substitution grammar 选择性替换文法 [选
selective top-down 自顶向下选择, 顺
selective trace 选择性跟踪
selective track 选择磁道
selective transmission 选择性传输
selective updating 选择性更新
selective visibility 选择性可见度
selective wait 选择性等待
selective weighting procedure 选择性加权过程
selectivity 选择性
selectivity factor 选择性因子
selector 选择器; 选线器
selector bus 选择器共用线
selector circuit 选择器电路
selector channel 选择通道
selector mode 选择方式
selector pen 选择笔 [号
selector pen attention 选择笔注意信
selector pen detector 选择笔检测
selectron 选数管
selenium(Se) 硒
selenium rectifier 硒整流器
self-acting 自作用的
self-actualization 自我调节
self-adapting 自适应
self-adapting algorithm for numerical integration 自适应数值积分算法
self-adapting communication 自适应通信
self-adapting computer 自适应计算机
self-adapting mesh 自适应网络
self-adapting production cell 自适应生产单元
self-adapting program 自适应程序
self-adapting report generator 自适应报表生成程序
self-adaptive control 自适应控制
self-adaptive interface 自适应接口
self-adaptive system 自适应系统
self-address memory 自寻址存储器
self-adjointness 自伴性, 自共轭性
self-adjusting automaton 自调节自动机
self-aligned 自动调准的, 自对准的

self anti-dual function 非自对偶函数
self assembler 自汇编程序
self-assessment 自我评价
self-authentication 自行鉴别
self-balanced 自平衡的
self-bias 自偏压
self-booting 自启动
self calibration 自校准
self-care 自看管的
self-check 自校验
self-checking arbiter 自校验仲裁器
self-checking circuit 自校验电路
self-checking code 自检验码
self checking computers modelers 自检计算机模块
self-checking number 自校验数
self-checking redundant structure 自校验冗余结构
self checking sequential machines 自校验时序机
self-checking synchronous sequential computer 自校验同步时序计算机
self-cleaning cleaner 自清洗清洁器
self-clocking 自供时钟;自同步
self-compensation 自补偿
self-compiling compiler 自编译编译程序
self-compiling language 自编译语言
self-complementary graph 自补图
self-complementing code 自补码
self-complementing counter 自补计数器
self-complementing digraph 自补有向图
self-complementing graph 自补有向图
self-configuring operating system 自构操作系统
self conjugate 自共轭
self-consistent 自相容的,自相一致的
self-contained 自含的,齐备的
self-contained control 独立完备控制
self contained data base 自含式数据库
self contained data manipulation language 自含式数据操纵语言
self contained environment 完备环境
self-contained hardware unit 自备的硬件设备
self-contained language 自含式语言
self-contained loop 自封闭循环

self-contained mobile robot 独立移动机器人
self-contained processor 整装处理机
self-contained program loader 自备式软件装入程序
self-contained system 自含式系统
self-control access 自控制访问
self-converse digraph 自逆有向图
self-cooling 自然冷却
self-correct 自校正
self-correcting code 自校正码
self-coupling 自耦合
self-debugger 自调试程序
self decode 自解码,自译码
self decoding readout 自解码读出
self-defining character 自定义字符
self-defining data 自定义数据
self defining data expression 自定义数据表示
self-defining delimiter 自定义分界符
self-defining function 自定义函数
self-defining key 自定义键
self-defining name 自定义名
self-defining term 自定义项
self-defining value 自定义值
self delimiting description 自定界描述
self delimiting Kolmogorov complexity 自定界科莫洛夫复杂性
self delimiting Turing machine 自定界图灵机
self-demagnetization 自去磁,自然退磁
self-demarcating code 自定界码
self-determination 自确定
self-diagnostic 自诊断
self-diagnostic alarm panel 自诊断报警画面
self-diagnostic feature 自诊断特性
self-diagnostic program 自诊断程序
self-documenting code 自成文档的编码
self-documenting program 自编文档程序
self-dual function 自对偶函数
self-duality 自对偶性
self editor 自编辑程序
self-embedding grammar 自嵌入文法
self-embedding inference 自嵌入推理
self-embedding termination 自嵌入端

接

self-enclosed 自闭合的
self-equilibration 自平衡
self-erasure 自抹除
self-evident code 自显码
self-excitation oscillation 自激振荡
self-excitation oscillator 自激振荡器
self-explanatory 自解释的
self-extensible language 自扩充语言
self-extensible software package 自扩充软件包
self-extracting 自展,自解压缩
self-extracting setup 自展安装
self-fitting 自拟合
self-focusing optical fiber 自聚焦光纤
self-government finite automaton 自治有限自动机
self-healing 自修复,自行恢复
self imaging 自成像
self-implicating structure 自蕴含结构
self-imposed alias 自动加入的别名
self-improvement 自改进,自完善
self-improving teaching system 自完善教学系统
self-indexed file 自索引文件
self inductance 自感
self induction 自感应
self-initialize 自初始化
self-initializing test sequence 自置初值测试序列
self-installability 自安装能力
self-instructed carry 自动进位
self-isolating resistor 自隔离电阻器
self-knowledge 自省知识
self-latching relay 自锁式继电器
self-learn 自学习
self-learning 自学习功能
self-learning machine 自学习机器
self-learning system 自学习系统
self left recursion 自左递归
self loading head assembly 自加载磁头组件
self-loading program 自装载程序
self-lock mechanism 自锁机制
self-locking property 自锁特性
self-loop 自循环
self-magnetic flux 自感磁通量
self-metric approach 自度量方法

self-modification 自修改
self-modification program 自修正程序
self-monitoring 自监督
self-monitoring system 自监督系统
self-operated controller 自操作控制器
self-optimizing 自优化
self-optimizing communication 最佳自适应通信
self-optimizing control 自优化控制
self-optimizing control system 自优化控制系统
self organization controller 自组织控制器
self-organized learning 自组织学习
self-organizing computer (SOC) 自组织计算机
self organizing file 自组织文件
self-organizing machine (SOM) 自组织机器
self-organizing neural network 自组织神经网络
self-organizing routing method 自组织路由选择法
self-organizing system 自组织系统
self-orthogonal code 自正交码
self-orthogonalizing algorithm 自正交化算法
self-oscillating regime 自振荡状态
self-paced instruction 自调节式教学
self-paced instructional tool 自调节式教学工具
self-paced training 自调节式训练
self-phasing code 自同相码
self-planning 自规划
self-positioning 自定位
self programming 自编程
self programming computer 自编程序计算机
self-protecting 自保护
self-purging redundancy 自清除冗余
self reconfigurable structure 可自重组结构
self reconfigurating parallel algorithm 自重组并行算法
self-recovery 自恢复
self-reference 自引用
self-referential relation 自引用关系
self-referential structure 自参照结构

self-referential system 自引用系统
self-reflective program 自反程序
self-refresh 自刷新
self-refreshed dynamic memory 自刷新的动态存储器
self-registered program 自注册程序
self-registration 自行注册；自对准
self-regulating 自调节，自调整
self-relative addressing 自相对寻址
self-relocation 自重定位
self-repairing 自修复
self-repairing fault-tolerant system 自修复容错系统
self-representation 自表达
self-reproducing 自再生
self-reproducing automaton 自再生自动机
self-reproducing robot 自再生机器人
self-reset 自复位
self-resetting loop 自复位循环
self-restoring loop 自恢复循环
self-routing 自选路由；自动布线
self-routing shuffle-exchange 自选路由混洗交换
self-scaling 自定标
self-scheduling 自调度
self-scheduling scheme 自调度方案
self-shift display 自移位显示
self-similar solution 自相似解，自型解
self-similarity 自相似性
self-sorting 自排序
self-stabilization 自稳定
self-standing system 自独立系统
self-starting explicit architecture 自启动显式架构
self-steering 自驾驭
self-supervisor 自管理程序
self-synchronizing 自同步
self-synchronous sequence cipher 自同步序列密码
self test 自测试
self test page （打印）自检页面
self-testing capability 自测试能力
self-testing circuit 自测试电路
self-testing embedded parity 自检嵌入奇偶位
self-timed data writing 自定时数据写入
self-timing 自定时，自同步

self-training environment 自训练环境
self-translator 自翻译程序
self-triggered program 自触发程序，
self-tuning controller 自调谐控制器
self-validating code 自确认码
self-ventilation 自行通风
self-virtualizing machine 自虚拟机
self-walking scanner 自走式扫描仪
selsyn 自动同步电机
selsyn motor 自同步马达
SEM(Sample Evaluation Method) 取样鉴定法
SEM(Scanning Electron Microscope) 扫描电子显微镜
SEM(Silicon-target Electronic Multiplexer) 硅靶电子倍增摄像管
semanteme 语意元素，语义
semantic 语义学；语义
semantic action 语义作用
semantic ambiguity 语义二义性
semantic ambiguous 语义含糊，二义性
semantic analysis 语义分析
semantic analyzer 语义分析程序
semantic attribute 语义属性
semantic binary relationship model 语义二元关系模型
semantic check 语义检查
semantic clash 语义不合
semantic compatibility 语义兼容性
semantic complexity 语义复杂性
semantic component 语义成分
semantic consistency 语义一致性
semantic constraint 语义限制(约束)
semantic convention 语义约定
semantic correctness 语义正确性
semantic correlation(SEMCOR) 语义相关
semantic data independence 语义数据独立性
semantic data model 语义数据模型
semantic database integrity 语义数据库完整性
semantic definition 语义定义
semantic description 语义说明
semantic disintegrity 语义不完整性
semantic domain 语义域
semantic equation 语义方程
semantic equivalence 语义等价

semantic error 语义错误
semantic evaluation 语义评价
semantic extension 语义扩充
semantic function 语义函数
semantic gap 语义间隙
semantic grammar 语义文法
semantic indexing 语义索引
semantic information 语义信息
semantic integrity 语义完整性
semantic interpretation 语义解释
semantic line finder 语义行寻找程序
semantic lock 语义锁定　　　「法
semantic logic notation 语义逻辑表示
semantic matching 语义匹配
semantic matrix 语义矩阵
semantic meaning 语义意义
semantic memory 语义存储器
semantic metalanguage 语义元语言
semantic navigation 语义导航
semantic net 语义网络
semantic network 语义网络
semantic notation 语义表示法
semantic-oriented language 面向语义的语言
semantic paradox 语义悖论
semantic predicate 语义谓词
semantic preference 语义个性选择
semantic primitive 语义元,语义原语
semantic procedure 语义过程
semantic processing 语义处理
semantic query optimization 语义查询优化
semantic reasoning 语义推理
semantic relation data model 语义关系数据模型
semantic representation language 语义表示语言　　　「结
semantic resolution 语义消解,语义归
semantic routine call 语义例程调用
semantic stack 语义堆栈
semantic stack configuration 语义堆栈配置,语义堆栈构形
semantic stack element 语义堆栈元素
semantic structure analysis 语义结构分析
semantic symbol 语义符号　　「示
semantic transfer schema 语义转移图
semantic transparency 语义透明性

semantic tree 语义树
semantics 语义学
semantics translator 语义翻译程序
semaphore 信号量
semaphore primitive 信号量原语
semaphore queue management 信号量排队管理
semaphore signaling 旗语信号表示
semaphore word 信号量字
semasiology 语义学
semeiology 符号学;症状学
sememe 语义要素
semi-analytical finite element 半分析有限元
semi-asynchronous message-passing 半异步消息传递
semi-automatic programming 半自动编程
semi-automatic retrieval 半自动检索
semi-autonomous multiprocessor 半独立多处理机
semi-closed shop 半封闭式计算站
semi-colloid 半胶体
semi-compiled 半编译
semi-compiled program 半编译程序
semi-computable predicate 半可计算谓词
semi-conditional grammar 半条件文
semi-conductor 半导体　　　「法
semi-continuous channel 半连续信道
semi-custom 半定制
semi-custom integrated circuit 半定制集成电路
semi-decidability 半可判定性
semi-decidable 半可判定的　　「近
semi-discrete approximation 半离散逼
semi-discretization 半离散化
semi-dominator 半支配顶点
semi-distributed hardware system 半分布式硬件系统
semi-duplex 半双工
semi-electronic switch 半电子开关
semi-electronic switching system 半电子交换系统
semi-empirical equation 半经验方程
semi-exact solution method 半精确解题法
semi-explicit 半显式的

semi-fixed length record 半定长记录
semi-formal domain 半形式域
semi-fuzzy classification 半模糊分类
semi-graphics 半图形表示法
semi-graphical method 半图解法
semi-group method 半群法
semi-heavy loading 半重负荷
semi-implicit scheme 半隐式图
semi-increment 半增量
semi-infinite 半无限的
semi-infinite integral 半无限积分「带
semi-infinite storage tape 半无限存储
semi-insulating poly silicon (SIPOS) 半绝缘多晶硅
semi-insulating substrate 半绝缘衬底
semi-integrated type 半集成类型
semi-intelligent process planning 半智能过程规划
semi-iterative method 半迭代法
semi-join selectivity 半连接选择性
semi-lattice 半格点
semi-logarithmic coordinate paper 半对数坐标纸
semi-Markov chain 半马尔可夫链
semi-natural language 半自然语言
semi-numerical analysis 半数值分析
semi-open shop 半开放式计算站
semi-orbit 半轨道
semi-parabolic 半抛物线
semi-parallel processing 半并行处理
semi-permanent connection 半永久性连接
semi-physical simulation 半物理模拟
semi-predicate function 半谓词函数
semi-private circuit 半专用线路
semi-random access 半随机存取
semi-realtime 半实时
semi-realtime processing 半实时处理
semi-result 半结果
semi-stochastic 半随机的
semi-synchronous model 半同步模型
semi-threshold logic 半阈值逻辑
semi-Thue grammar 半图厄文法
semi-Thue system 半图厄系统
semi-vocoder 半声码器
semi-weak key 半弱密钥
semiaddition 半加法
semiautomatic 半自动的

semiautomatic message-switching 半自动报文交换
semiautomatic relay system 半自动中继系统
semicolon 分号
semicompiler 半编译程序
semicomputable 半可计算的 「词
semicomputable predicate 半可计算谓
semicomputable set 半可计算集
semicomputer 准计算机
semiconductive ceramic 半导电陶瓷
semiconductive glass 半导电玻璃
semiconductive 半导电的
semiconductor 半导体
semiconductor active memory 半导体有源存储器
semiconductor bipolar processor 双极型半导体处理器
semiconductor channel 半导体沟道
semiconductor chip 半导体芯片
semiconductor chip bonding 半导体芯片焊接
semiconductor diffusion 半导体扩散
semiconductor diode 半导体二极管
semiconductor disk 半导体盘 「备
semiconductor disk device 半导体盘设
semiconductor donor 半导体施主
semiconductor dopant 半导体掺杂剂
semiconductor dual in-line package 半导体双列直插式组件
semiconductor energy gap 半导体能隙
semiconductor film 半导体薄膜
semiconductor function block 半导体功能块
semiconductor hole 半导体空穴
semiconductor integrated optics 半导体集成光学
semiconductor junction 半导体结
semiconductor laser 半导体激光器
semiconductor memory 半导体存储器
semiconductor RAM 半导体随机读写存储器
semiconductor storage module 半导体存储器模块
semicontinuous function 半连续函数
semicustom chip 半定制芯片
semicut set 半割集
semicycle 半圆

semidefinite operator 半定算子
semidefinite quadratic form 半定二次「型
semideformable material 半可变形材「料
semiduplex 半双工
semiflexible board 半柔性印刷线路板
semigraphical method 半图解法
semigroup 半群
semihyper simple set 半超简单集
semijoin 半联结
semilinear 半线性的
semilinear bounded language 半线性限界语言
semilocal convergence 半局部收敛性
semimetal 半金属
seminar 讲座,讨论会
seminorm 半范数
seminumerical algorithm 半数值算法
semiotics 符号学
semipath 半通路
semiperiod 半周期
semipermanent data 半永久数据
semipermanent electronics storage 半固定电子存储器
semipermanent store 半永久存储
semirecursive set 半递归集
semirigid cable 半硬性电缆
semirigid joint 半刚性接合
semisinusoidal 半正弦的
semiskilled operator 半熟练操作员
semisolid 半固态的
semistate model 半状态模型
semistatic memory 半静态存储器
semistructured message 半结构消息
semiwalk robot 半行走机器人
senary 六进制的
SEND 发送
send 发送,送出
send after text 置于文字之后
send-and-forget (搜索代理)派出即忘
send back 回送
send behind text 置于文字之后
send binary file 发送二进制文件
send binder 发送活页夹
send data condition 发送数据条件
send filter 发送滤波器
send garbage octet 发送无意义字节数
send in error 误发
send mail as attachment 以附件方式发送邮件
send network message 发送网络消息
send note 发送便笺
send only(SO) 只发送
send-only service 只发送服务
send pacing 发送调步
send packet miscellaneous error 发送包混杂错误
send packet retry count 发送包重试次「数
send packet too big count 发送包过大次数
send-request circuit 请求发送电路
send sequence number 发送序列号
send state variable 发送状态变量
send statement 发送语句
send to back 后置;置于后面「人
sender 发送器;送话器;发送者,发件
sender attachment delay 发送器接通延迟
sender initiated(SI) 派生者发起
sender initiated negotiation 发送器启动的协商
sender/receiver buffers 发送器/接收器缓冲
sender/receiver terminals 发送器/接收器终端
sending 发送
sending acknowledgement 发送确认
sending buffer 发送缓冲器
sending-end crossfire 发送端串扰
sending field 发送字段
sending filter 发送滤波器
sending item 发送项
sending node 发送节点
sending processor 发送处理机
sending signal 发送信号
sending station 发送站
Sendmail 邮件传送程序
SENET(Slotted ENvelope NETwork) 时间片分割法网络
senior 高级的,资深的
senior programmer 高级程序员
senior system analyst 高级[资深]系统分析员
seniority 高位数
seniority logic 高位逻辑
sense 感测,读出
sense amplifier 感测[读出]放大器

sense analysis 读出分析
sense and control lines 感测控制线
sense bit 感测位,读出位
sense byte 读出字节
sense circuit 读出电路
sense control block 读出控制块
sense data 感测数据
sense-digit line 数字读出线
sense information 读出信息
sense latch 检测闩锁
sense light 感测指示灯,读出灯
sense line 感测线,读出线
sense order 读出指令
sense recovery time 读出恢复时间
sense response 检测响应
sense signal 感测信号
sense station 阅读站
sense status byte 检测状态字节
sense switch 传感开关
sense winding 读出绕组
sensibility 灵敏性
sensible information processing 可感测信息处理
sensing 检测,感知,读出
sensing element 感测[传感]元件
sensing head 读出头
sensing hole 读出孔,检测孔
sensing line 检测线,读出线
sensing pin 读出引脚;感测探头
sensing signal 读出信号
sensing station 读出位置
sensing winding 读出绕组
sensistor 正温度系数热敏电阻器
sensitive 敏感的,灵敏的
sensitive application 敏感应用
sensitive data 敏感数据
sensitive information 敏感信息
sensitive printer 感光型打印机
sensitive relay 灵敏继电器
sensitive segment 感知片段
sensitive software 敏感软件
sensitive statistic 敏感统计量
sensitive systems 敏感系统
sensitivity 灵敏度;敏感性
sensitivity adjustment 灵敏度调节
sensitivity assessment 敏感性评价
sensitivity 灵敏度;敏感性
sensitivity calculation method 灵敏度计算法
sensitivity computation 灵敏度计算
sensitivity curve 灵敏度曲线
sensitivity function 灵敏度函数
sensitivity level 灵敏度级别
sensitivity optimization 灵敏度优化
sensitivity-time control 灵敏度时间控制
sensitization 敏化;致敏
sensitized block 敏化块
sensitized function value 敏化函数值
sensitized material 敏化材料
sensitized medium 敏感媒质
sensitizer 激活剂,敏化剂
sensitizing 敏化法
sensitometer 感光计;曝光表
sensor 传感器
sensor array 传感器阵列
sensor-based computer 基于传感器的计算机
sensor-based system 基于传感器的系统
sensor card 传感器卡
sensor control system 传感器控制系统
sensor data processing 传感器数据处理
sensor data record(SDR) 传感器数据记录
sensor detectability 传感器可检测性
sensor devices 传感器设备
sensor-driven signal 传感器驱动的信号
sensor element 传感器元素
sensor glove 传感手套
sensor model 传感器模型
sensor scan 传感器扫描
sensor simulator unit 传感器仿真单元
sensorless manipulator 无传感器机械手
sensory 感知的;灵敏的
sensory capability 感知能力
sensory control 传感控制
sensory controlled robot 感觉控制机器人
sensory feedback 传感反馈
sensory hierarchy 传感层次
sensory imagery 感觉表像
sensory pathway 感测途径;读出通路
Sent Items folder 已发送项目文件夹
sent mail 已发送邮件
sentence 语句;句子
sentence articulation 句子清晰度

sentence by sentence execution 逐句执行
sentence by sentence syntactic analysis 逐句语法分析
sentence case 句首字母大写
sentence delimiter 句子分界符
sentence error probability 语句差错概率
sentence intelligibility 句子可懂度
sentence key 语句键,句子键
sentence length 语句[句子]长度
sentence pattern 句型
sentence structure 语句[句子]结构
sentence synthesizing program 句子合成程序
sentence understanding 句子理解
sentential calculus 句子演算
sentential form 语句形式,句型
sentential shape 句子形状
sentinel 哨兵,标志
separability 可分离性
separable 可分离的,可分开的
separable codes 可分离码
separable kernel 可分离核
separable library 可分离程序库
separable programming 可分离程序设计
separable recursion 可分离递归
separable sequence 可分序列
separable transition diagram 可分迁移图
separate 分离,分开,分隔
separate and mediate 分隔和调停
separate assembly 分别汇编
separate bus 分离总线
separate channel signaling 独立信道信令
separate code 分离码
separate common channel signaling system 独立公共信道信令
separate compilation 分头编译
separate controlled integrator 独立控制积分器
separate cylinder 分离柱面
separate executive operating system 分开执行式操作系统
separate library 分离程序库
separate overflow area 分离溢出区
separate partition option 分离分区选项
separate semantic specification 分离语义说明
separate text with 文本分隔符
separated 分离的,各自独立的
separated clock 分离时钟
separated code 分离码
separated data 分离数据
separated face 分离面
separated graphics 分离图形学
separated region 分隔区域
separating character 分隔字符
separating 分隔,分离
separating hyperplane 分离超平面
separating keyword 分隔关键字
separating plane 分离平面
separation 间隔;分离
separation character 分隔符
separation mark 分隔标志
separation of duties or function 忙闲度或功能间隔
separation of privilege 特权分离
separation principle 分离原理
separation theorem 分离定理
separative sign 分隔符号
separator 分界符,分隔符
septenary 七进制的
septet 七位,七位的字节
septum 隔片,隔膜
SEQ(SEQuencer) 序列发生器,定序器
SEQUEL (Structured English QUEry Language) 结构式英语查询语言
SEQUEL/2 结构式英语查询语言第二版
SEQUELINK SEQUELINK 中间件
sequence 序列,顺序;定序
sequence alternator 序列变换器
sequence breakpoint 序列断点
sequence by merging 合并排序
sequence calling 顺序调用
sequence chart 顺序图,定序图
sequence check 顺序检验
sequence checking routine 顺序校验例程
sequence circuit 时序电路
sequence cipher 序列密码
sequence code 顺序码,序列码
sequence computer 时序计算机
sequence concatenation 序列并置

sequence construct 顺序结构
sequence control 顺序控制
sequence control counter 顺序控制计数器
sequence control register 顺序控制寄存器
sequence control structure 顺序控制结构
sequence controlled computer 顺序控制计算机
sequence controller 顺序控制器
sequence criterion 排序准则
sequence error 顺序错误
sequence field 顺序字段
sequence frame 顺序帧
sequence generator 序列发生器
sequence in time 按时间顺序
sequence independence 与顺序无关的
sequence length 序列长度
sequence monitor 顺序监督程序
sequence number 序号
sequence of control 控制顺序
sequence-operated lock 按序操作锁
sequence packing 顺序压缩(打包)
sequence power on 顺序加电
sequence register 顺序寄存器
sequence robot 顺序控制机器人
sequence separator 顺序分隔符
sequence set 顺序集
sequence sorting key 排序键
sequence timer 时序脉冲发生器
sequence token 顺序令牌
sequenced 有序的
sequenced acknowledge 按序确认
sequenced chain 有序链
sequenced frames 有序帧
Sequenced Packet Exchange(SPX) 顺序分组交换协议
sequencer 定序器;音序器
sequencer program 定序程序
sequencing 定序
sequencing by merging 合并定序「制
sequencing control 顺序控制,时序控
sequencing criteria 排序准则
sequencing indicator 排序指示码
sequencing key 排序关键码
sequencing merging 排序合并
sequencing time 排序时间,定序时间
sequencing token 排序令牌
sequencing unit 定序单元
sequency 序数
sequential 顺序的,依次的
sequential access 顺序存取,顺序访问
sequential access method 顺序存取法
sequential access storage 顺序存取存储器
sequential addressing 按序编址
sequential advanced control 顺序超前控制
sequential aggregation 按序聚合「块
sequential alarm module 顺序报警模
sequential algorithm 按序算法
sequential allocation 顺序分配
sequential batch processing 顺序成批处理
sequential carry 按序进位
sequential circuit 时序电路 「试
sequential circuit testing 时序电路测
sequential cohesion 顺序内聚
sequential collating 顺序对并
sequential coloring algorithm 依次着色算法
sequential complexity 时序复杂性
sequential computer 顺序计算机
sequential connection 顺序连接
sequential control 顺序控制
sequential control mechanism 时序控制机构
sequential data bit 顺序数据位
sequential data set 顺序数据集
sequential decision problem 顺序判定问题
sequential dependence 顺序相互依赖
sequential dependent segment 顺序相关段
sequential element 时序元件
sequential encoding 顺序编码
sequential events recorder 顺序事件记录器
sequential execution 顺序执行
sequential fault diagnosis 顺序故障诊断
sequential fault diagnostic 按序故障诊断
sequential field 顺序字段
sequential file 顺序文件

sequential file organization 顺序文件组织
sequential file rollback 顺序文件重算
sequential file sort 顺序文件排序
sequential file structure 顺序文件结构
sequential filtering 序列滤波
sequential fuzzy language 时序模糊语言
sequential garbage collection 时序式废料收集
sequential hazard 时序冒险
sequential hierarchy 时序层次
sequential index 顺序索引
sequential inference machine 顺序推理机
sequential interpretation 顺序解释
sequential interval timer 顺序间隔定时器
sequential logic 时序逻辑
sequential logic control 时序逻辑控制
sequential logic element 时序逻辑元件
sequential machine 时序机
sequential machine model 串行机器模型
sequential mapping 顺序映射
sequential marked graph 时序标记图
sequential memory location 顺序存储单元
sequential merging 顺序合并法
sequential method 顺序法
sequential microprogramming 时序微程序设计
sequential mode 时序模式
sequential network 时序网络
sequential operation 顺序操作
sequential operator 顺序运算器
sequential organization 顺序组织
sequential parsing scheme 顺序剖析方案
sequential pattern recognition 顺序模式识别
sequential pipeline 顺序流水线
sequential processing 顺序处理
sequential programming language 串行编程语言
sequential propagation 顺序传播
sequential queue 顺序排队
sequential record access mode 顺序记录存取方式
sequential redundant access 顺序冗余访问
sequential sampling 顺序取样
sequential scanning 顺序扫描
sequential scheduling system 顺序调度系统
sequential search 顺序检索
sequential selection 顺序选择
sequential simplex method 顺序单纯形法
sequential-stacked job control 顺序堆栈作业控制
sequential stochastic programming 顺序随机程序设计
sequential structure 顺序结构
sequential switcher 时序开关,时序转换器
sequential system 时序系统
sequential testing 按序检测
sequential thining algorithm 顺序细化算法
sequential time delay 顺序时延
sequential T-fault-diagnosable T 故障顺序可诊断的
sequential timer 顺序定时器
sequential topology 顺序拓扑
sequential transducer 时序变换器
sequential transmission 顺序传送
sequential unconstrained minimization technique 序列无约束最优化技术
sequentialization 顺序化
serial(SER) 串行的,串联的
serial access 串行存取
serial access memory 串行存取内存
serial access storage 串行存取存储器
serial-access system 串行存取系统
serial accumulator 串行累加器
serial adder 串行加法器
serial algorithm 串行算法
serial arithmetic operation 串行算术运算
serial batch system 串行批处理系统
serial binary adder 串行二进制加法器
serial bit transmission 位串行传输
serial bus protocol 串行总线协议
serial-by-bit 按位串行
serial-by-character 按字符串行
serial carry 串行进位

serial CCD memory 串行电荷耦合元件存储器
serial chaining control 串行链接控制
serial clause 串行子句
serial clock receive 串行时钟接收
serial communication link 串行通信链路
serial communication interface 串行通信接口
serial comparator 串行比较器
serial complexity 串行复杂性
serial computing 串行运算
serial control 串行控制
serial copy management system(SCMS) 串行拷贝管理系统
serial counter 串行计数器
serial cryptographic device 串行加密设备
serial data 串行数据
serial data controller 串行数据控制器
serial data handshaking 串行数据交换
serial data input 串行数据输入
serial data link 串行数据链路
serial data stream 串行数据流
serial data transmission 串行数据传送
serial decomposition 串行分解
serial diagnosis 串行诊断
serial digit operation 串行数字运算
serial digital adder 串行数字加法器
serial digital decoder 串行数字译码器
serial distributed decision support system 串行分布式决策支持系统
serial entry 串行输入
serial feedback A/D converter 串行反馈模数转换器
serial feeding 串行馈送
serial file 串行文件, 顺序文件
serial file processing 串行文件处理
serial flow 串行信息流
serial full adder 串行全加器
serial full subtracter 串行全减器
serial half adder 串行半加器
serial I/O 串行输入/输出
serial in 串行输入
serial inference computer 串行推理计算机
serial input 串行输入
serial input-output(SIO) 串行输入/输出
serial input-output controller 串行输入/输出控制器
serial input/output interface 串行输入/输出接口
serial insertion 串行插入
serial interface 串行接口
Serial-Line Internet Protocol(SLIP) 串行线路因特网协议
serial logic 串行逻辑
serial loop 串联环路
serial memory 串行存储器
serial mouse 串行鼠标器
serial multiple detecting 串行多重检测
serial multiplier 串行乘法器
serial number 序列号, 顺序号
serial numbering 顺序编号
serial operation 串行操作
serial organization 顺序组织
serial output(SO) 串行输出
serial overhead 串行开销
serial packet controller 串行分组控制器
serial-parallel 串-并行
serial-parallel A/D converter 串并联模/数转换器
serial-parallel converter 串并行转换器
serial-parallel conversion 串并行转换
serial parallel register 串并行寄存器
serial peripheral interface 串行外设接口
serial poll 串行查询
serial polling 串行轮询
serial port 串行端口
serial port connector 串行端口连接器
serial printer 串行打印机
serial processing 串行处理
serial program 串行程序
serial receive control signal 串行接收控制信号
serial reusable routine 串行可重用例程
serial scheduling 串行调度
serial search 顺序查找
serial shadow register 串行映像寄存器
serial shift register 串行移位寄存器
serial signaling rate 串行信令速率
serial sort 串行排序, 串行分类
Serial Storage Architecture(SSA) 串行存储体系结构

serial synchronous hunt mode 串行同步寻线模式
serial transfer 串行传送
serial transmission 串行传输
serial type adder 串行加法器
serial type of task 串行任务
serial use buffer 串行用户缓冲器
serializability 可串行性
serializable 可串行化的
serialization 串行化,顺序化
serialized job processor 串行作业处理程序
serialized scheduling 串行调度
serially-connected beam 串行连接梁
serially reusable load module 串行可重用装入模块
serially reusable routine 可连续重用例程
series 串联,级数,序;系列
series architecture 系列体系结构
series assignment algorithm 串行分配算法
series circuit 串联电路
series distribution 系列分布
series excitation 串联激励
series in 系列产生在…
series lines 系列线
series loss 串行损耗
series machine 系列机
series mode 串接模式
series mode interference 串模干扰
series mode rejection 串模抑制
series modulation 串联调制
series motor 串激电动机
series name 序列名
series number 序列号
series order 系列次序
series parallel contact network 串并联触点网络
series parallel control 串并行控制
series parallel network 串并联网络
series resonance 串联谐振
series solution 级数解
series termination 串联端接
series transmission 串行传输
Series X Recommendation X 序列建议
serif (字母上用于装饰的)衬线
serious 严重的
serious error condition 严重错误条件
serration 锯齿状突起
server 服务器;服务(程序)模块
Server Administration 服务器管理
server alias 服务器别名
server application 服务器应用程序
server-based application 基于服务器的应用程序
server browser 服务器浏览程序
Server Certificate 服务器认证
server cluster 服务器群集
server component 服务器组件
server consolidation 服务器整合
server disconnect 服务器连接断开
server engine 服务引擎
server grab (X 协议)服务器占取
Server Hello 服务器问候
Server Hello Done 服务器问候结束
Server Key Exchange 服务器密钥交换
Server Memory Statistics (Netware)服务器内存统计
Server Message Block(SMB) 服务器消息块
server monitoring 服务器监视
server name remark 服务器名称注释
server node 服务器节点
server process 服务器进程
server root 服务器根目录
Server Side Include(SSI) 服务器端嵌入
Server Side Include command 服务器端嵌入命令
Server Side Include object 服务器端嵌入对象
Server Side Include page(SSIP) 服务器端嵌入页面
server-side image maps 服务器端映像布局
server system 服务器系统
server type 服务器类型
server viewer 服务器查看程序
service 服务,业务
service ability 服务能力
service access point(SAP) 服务存取点
service advertising protocol 服务广告协议
service advises 业务公电

service aid 服务工具,维修辅助手段
service area 服务区
service bit 服务位,辅助位
service bits 业务比特
service book 服务手册
service bureau 服务局
service center 服务中心
service character 业务字符
service circuit 服务线路,业务电路
service class 服务等级
service code 辅助码
service code prefix 业务代码前缀
Service Control Point(SCP) 服务控制点
service conversation 业务对话
service definition of OSI 开放系统互连服务定义
service dependability 服务可靠性
service digits 服务位
service director 服务指导程序
service document 业务文档
service efficiency 服务效率
service engineer (维修)服务工程师
service engineering 服务工程
service facility 服务设施
service frequency 工作频率
service grade 服务质量等级
service identification 业务标识码
service indicator 服务指示符
service information 服务信息
service inspection 业务检查
service instruction 服务规范
service interface 服务接口
service interrupt 服务中断
service interworking 业务交互工作
service level update 服务等级修改
service life 使用寿命
service log 服务记录
Service Management System(SMS) 服务管理系统
service manager 业务管理者
service manual 工作[维护]手册
service message 服务消息,公务报文
service mode 服务模式
service monitor 服务监督程序
service observation 业务观察
service operability performance 业务可操作性能
service operational data(SOD) 业务运行数据
service order table 服务顺序表
service pack 服务包,补丁程序
service package 服务信息包
service point (维修)服务点
service primitive 服务原语
service probability 服务概率
service procedure 服务过程
service processor unit(SPU) 服务处理器单元
service program 服务程序
service protection 业务保护
service provider 服务供应商
service provider interface(SPI) 服务供应商界面
service quality 服务质量
service queue 服务队列
service rate 服务率
service reliability performance 业务可靠性能
service representative privilege class 服务代表特许级
service request interrupts 服务请求中断
service routine 服务例程
service seeking 查询服务
service-seeking pause 查询服务暂停
service signal 服务信号
service specification 服务规范
service speed 服务速度
service state 服务状态
service test 维护测试
service time 服务时间
service type 服务类
service virtual machine 服务虚拟机
serviceability 可维修性,可服务性
serviceability level indicator processing 可服务性级别指示处理
serviceability ratio 可服务时间比
serviceable 可用的
serviceable time 可服务时间
servicer 服务器,服务程序
servicing time 维护时间,服务时间
servo 伺服,随动
servo action 伺服作用
servo amplifier 伺服放大器
servo-analog computer 伺服模拟计算机
servo channel 伺服信道
servo control 伺服控制

servo control level 伺服控制级
servo control system 伺服控制系统
servo-controlled robot 伺服控制机器人
servo-controlled search 伺服控制检索
servo drive 伺服驱动「器
servo-driven positioner 伺服驱动定位
servo field 伺服区域;伺服字段
servo function generator 伺服函数发生器
servo gear 伺服齿轮
servo head 伺服磁头
servo integrator 伺服积分器
servo link 伺服链,伺服传动装置
servo loop 伺服环路
servo mark 伺服标志
servo-mechanism 伺服机构,随动机构
servo-motor 伺服马达,伺服电机
servo-multiplier 伺服乘法器
servo noise 伺服噪声
servo-offset 伺服偏置
servo oscillation 伺服[随动]振荡
servo positional rate 伺服定位速率
servo-positioning 伺服定位
servo repeater 伺服中继器
servo-resolver 伺服式分解器
servo sector 伺服扇区
servo stability 伺服稳定性
servo surface 伺服面
servo system 伺服[随动]系统
servo system integral control 伺服系统积分控制
servo track 伺服磁道
servo-type function generator 伺服式函数发生器
servo-type operational element 伺服式运算部件
servocomponent 伺服部件
servodisk 伺服磁盘
servodyne 伺服系统动力传动
servohead 伺服磁头
servointegrator 伺服积分器
servolag 伺服延迟
servomechanism 伺服机构
servonoise 伺服噪声
servoresolver 伺服分解器
servosurface encoding 伺服盘面编码
servovalve 伺服阀

SESS (Semi-Electronic Switching System) 半电子交换方式
session 对话,会话,对话期
session activation 会话发起
session activation request 对话激活请求
session address space 对话地址空间
session authorization check 对话授权检验
session awareness block (SAB) 对话认知块
session command 对话命令
session control 对话控制,会话控制
session connection synchronization 对话连接同步
session control block 对话控制块
session control protocol 对话控制协议
session count 对话计数
session cryptographic key 对话保密关键字
session cryptography seed 对话保密种籽数
session deactivation 对话撤消
session deactivation request 会话撤消请求
session end 对话端
session establishment 对话建立
session-establishment macro instruction 对话建立宏指令
session-establishment request 对话建立请求
session handle 对话句柄
session handler 对话处理程序
session hold 对话保持
session indicator 对话指示符
session information block (SIB) 对话信息块
session initiation request 对话初始化请求
session key 对话密钥
session layer 对话层,会话层
session level pacing 对话级调步
session limit 对话限量
session local protocol 对话本地协议
session management protocol (SMP) 会话管理协议
session manager 对话管理程序
session memory pool 对话存储池
session network service 会话网络服务

session pacing 对话调步
session parameter 对话参数
session partner 对话伙伴
session pointer (MAPI)会话指针
session presentation service 对话表示服务
session protocol 对话协议
session seed 对话初始值
session sequence identifier 对话顺序标识符
session sequence number 对话顺序号
session server 对话服务器
session service 对话服务
session structure 会话结构
session synchronization 对话通步
session termination 对话终止
session termination request 对话终止请求
session time-out 对话超时
session type 对话类型
sessionc indicator SESSIONC指示符
set 集合,集;置位;设置
set and subset 集合与子集
set as default chart 设置为默认图表
set associative buffer storage 成组相联缓存器
set associative mapping 成组相联映射
set asynchronous response mode 成组异步响应方式
set attribute 集合(系)属性
set-based data 基于集合的数据
set bit 设置位
set breakpoint 设置断点
set cell 设置单元格
set clause 集合子句
set clock 设置时钟
set covering 系覆盖,系覆盖
set criteria 设置条件
set currency 系当前值
set database 设置数据库
set description entry 系描述体
set difference 集合差,差集
set element 集合元素
set entry 集合项,系项
set expression 集合表达式
set font 设置字体
SET function 置值函数
set grid 设置网格线

set grouping 集分群
set identification 集合标识
set index instruction 设置变址指令
set language 集合语言
set inhibit 置位禁止
set intersection 集合交会
set language 集合语言
set location mode 系定位模式
set membership 系成员
set merging 集合归并
set-miss 设置错误
set mode 系实现方式
set name 集合名
set occurrence 系值,集值
set occurrence selection 系值选择
set of automorphism 自同构集
set of data 数据集
set of elementary event 基本事件集
set of fields 字段组
set of instructions 指令集[组]
set of integer 整数集
set of language 语言集
set of maximal edges 极大边集
set of node 节点集
set of nonnegative integer 非负整数集
set of pulse 脉冲组
set-of-support strategy 支持集策略
set of symbol 符号集
set of WFF 合式公式集合
set of well-formed formula 合式公式集合
set-off 断开,断流
set operator 集合运算符
set option parameters 设置选择参数
set order 系序
set ordering criteria 系定序标准
set oriented language 集合型语言
set owner 系主
set page break 设置分页线
set point 设定点
set point computer control system (SPCC) 计算机定点控制系统
set point control 调整点控制
set pointer 系指针
set preference 设置个性选项
set preferred 设置首选项
set print area 设置打印区
set print titles 设置打印标题

set process quotas 设置进程配额
set program mask 设置程序屏蔽
set program status word 程序状态字
set prompt 设置提示符
set pulse 置位脉冲,置"1"脉冲
set recorder 设置记录区域
set save option 设置保存选项
set representation 集合表示法
set screw 拧紧螺丝钉
set salvage options(Netware) 设置恢复选项
set selection 系值选择
set size 设置尺寸
set statement 设置语句,置标语句
set strobe time 设置选通时间
set symbol 置位符号
set system algebra 集系代数
set terminal 置位端
set theoretical language 集合论语言
set theory 集合论
set thread context 设置线程上下文
set time counter 设置时间计数器
set to zero 置"0",清"0"
set-top-box 顶置盒
set type 集合类型
set type currency indicator 系类型当前指示符
set type definition 集合类型定义
set union 集合并
set up 建立,安装
set up application 安装应用程序
set-up diagram 准备工作图,设置图
set-up linked list 链表的建立
set up printer 设置打印机
set-up procedure 准备[建立]过程
set-up register 建立寄存器
set-up service 准备服务
set-up time 建立时间
set up user information 设置用户信息
set-valued mapping 设定值映射
set width 活字宽度,字体宽度
sets attribute 赋值属性
setting 设置
setting breakpoint condition 置位断点条件
setting page 设置页面
setting position 装配位置;调整位置
setting pulse 置位脉冲

setting time 置位[建立]时间
setting view 设置视图
settle 稳定,完成
settlement 结算;确定;解决
settling time 稳定时间
setup 建立,安装
setup code 初始化代码
setup diagram 配置图,安排图
setup parameters 设置参数
setup script 安装过程
setup time 建立时间
setup windows 设置窗口
setup wizard 安装向导
SEU(Source Entry Utility) 源输入实用程序
SEV(Subjectively Expected Value) 主观期望值
SEVAS(SEcure Voice Access System) 安全的话音存储系统
seven-channel paper tape 七轨纸带
Seven Dwarfs 七个小矮人(六十年代称呼除 IBM 以外的七家计算机公司)
seven track tape 七轨磁带
seven-segment display 七段显示
several-for-one 多对一
severe environment memory system 恶劣环境存储系统
severe error 严重(非致命的)错误
severity code 严格代码
severity of sampling 抽样严格度
sex changer 变性连接器,阴阳连接器
sexadecimal 十六进制的
sexadecimal notation 十六进制记数法
sexangle 六角形
sextet 六位,六位字节
SF(Sign Flag) 符号标志
SF(Soft Fail) 软失效
SF(Stack Full) 堆栈满
SFB(SCSI Function Block) SCSI 功能块
SFB(Spool File Block) 假脱机文件块
SFC(Sectored File Controller) 扇区文件控制器
SFG(Signal Flow Graph) 信号流图
SFL(Substrate Feed Logic) 衬底馈电逻辑
SFL(Symbolic Flowchart Language)

符号流程图语言
SFNB(Security First Network Bank) 安全第一网络银行
S. G.(Standard Gauge) 标准线径规
SG(Sensor Glove) 传感手套
SG(Super Group) 超群
SG(Symbol Generator) 符号发生器
SGC(Super Group Connector) 超群连接器
SGDF(Super Group Distribution Frame) 超群配线架
SGE(Standard Graphic Element) 标准图形元
SGI(Silicon Graphics Inc.) SGI公司
SGI Challenge Challenge网络服务器
SGI Indigo Indigo工作站
SGI Indy Indy工作站
SGI Onyx Onyx图形计算机
SGI Power Challenge Power Challenge服务器
SGIS(System Graphical Interface Software) 系统与图形界面软件
SGL(System Generation Language) 系统生成语言
SGML(Standard Generalized Markup Language) 标准通用标记语言(ISO,1986)
SGMP(Simple Gateway Monitoring Protocol) 简单网关监控协议
SGP(Screen Generator Program) 屏幕生成程序
SGP(Statistics Generation Program) 统计生成程序
sh(shell) (Unix)命令解释程序
shade 阴影,色调;底纹;罩,帽
shade graphing 阴影图解法
shade page table 阴影页表
shaded area 阴影(加底纹)区域
shaded curve surface 浓淡曲面
shaded letter 加阴影字符
shaded picture 阴影图,灰度图
shading 浓淡处理,寄生信号,黑斑
shading compensation 浓淡补偿
shadow 映像,影像;阴影
shadow area 静区,盲区;阴影区
shadow BIOS 映像BIOS
shadow DRAM feature 映像动态存储器特性
shadow factor 阴影系数
shadow file 影子文件(Sun)
shadow graphing 阴影图解,投影成图
shadow mask 荫罩板
shadow mask color CRT 荫罩式彩色显像管
shadow memory 影像内存
shadow page table 投影页表
shadow price 预示价格
shadow printing 阴影印刷
shadow RAM 映像存储器,影像内存
shadow resource 影像[影子]资源
shadow ROM 影像只读存储器
shadow table 影像表
shadowed 带阴影的
shadowing 遮蔽法;加阴影
shaft 轴
shaft angle encoder 轴角编码器
shaft encoder 轴角编码器
shaft position digitizer 轴角数字转换
shaft position encoder 轴位编码器
shaft recorder 轴记录器
shake-down period 试用期
shaker-sort program 筛选分类程序
shallow 浅的,薄的
shallow binding 浅层结合
shallow channel 浅沟道
shallow diffusion 浅扩散
shallow grooved-isolation 浅槽隔离
shallow search procedure 浅搜索过程
shallow shell element 浅层[壳层]单
Shannon 香农
Shannon black box 香农未知框
Shannon equation 香农方程
Shannon formula 香农公式
Shannon ideal code 香农理想码
Shannon limit 香农极限
Shannon page table 香农页表
shannon's five criteria 香农五准则
Shannon's theorem 香农定理
shape 形状,造型
shape anisotropy 形状各向异性
shape approximation system 形状近似系统
shape averaging 形状均匀化
shape classification 开头分类
shape code 形状代码
shape coding 形状编码

shape controls 形状控件
shape decomposition 形状分解
shape deformation 形状变形
shape description 形状描述
shape descriptor 形状描述符
shape discrimination operator 形状鉴别算子
shape extraction 形状特征抽取
shape factor 形状因子
shape feature abstraction 形状特征抽象
shape fill 形状填充
shape fitting 形状拟合
shape-from-texture algorithm 从纹理中恢复形状算法
shape function 形状函数
shape library 图形库
shape modification 形状修正
shape optimum design 形状最佳设计
shape parameter 形状参数
shape preserving spline 形状保持样条
shape recognition 形状识别
shape restoration 形状恢复
shape segmentation 形状分割
shape sensitivity analysis 形状敏感性分析
shape similarity 形状相似性
shape smoothing 形状光滑
shape symmetry 形状对称
shape table 形状描述表
shape toggle 半角/全角切换
shape tool 形状工具
shape transform 形状变换
shaped-character printer 定型字符打印机
shaped pulse 已整形脉冲
shaper 整形器
shaping 整形
shaping circuit 整形电路
shaping network 整形网络
shaping pulse 整形脉冲
shaping signal 整形信号
sharable object 可共享对象
sharable routine 可共享例程
SHARE(Society of Help to Avoid Redundant Efforts) 用户科技共享协会
share 共享,共用
share base 共享库
share directory 共享目录

share file 共享文件
share limit 共享极限,共用极限
share load 分摊负载
share operating system 共享操作系统
shareable 可共享的
shareable device 可共享设备
shareable global area 可共享全局区域
shareable image 可共享映像
shared 共享的
shared access path 共享存取路径
shared batch area 共享成批存储区
shared border 共享边框
shared-bus multiprocessor 共用总线多处理机
shared-bus system 共用总线系统
shared-cache memory 共享高速缓存
shared central memory 共享中央内存
shared class 共享类
shared-common data 共享公用数据
shared-contingency computer center 共享应急计算中心
shared control 共享控制
shared control unit 共享控制单元
shared DASD option 共享直接存取存储器初始化程序选择
shared data bank 共享数据块
shared data base 共享数据库
shared data environment 共享数据环境
shared data set 共享数据集
shared data set integrity 共享数据集完整性
shared data space 共享数据空间
shared device 共享设备
shared directory 共享目录
shared disk 共享磁盘
shared disk structure(SD) 共享磁盘结构
shared environment 共享环境
shared electron bond 共价键
shared everything structure(SE) 完全共享结构
shared-executive system 共享执行系统
shared file 共享文件
shared file system 共享文件系统
shared firmware 共享固件
shared folder 共享文件夹
shared font store 共享字模库
shared fixture 共用固定插座,共用夹具

shared index data base 共享索引数据库
shared instruction 共享指令
shared line 共用线,合用线
shared lock 共用锁,共享锁
shared logic 共享逻辑
shared logic system 共享逻辑系统
shared logic word processing equipment 共享逻辑文字处理设备
shared main memory 共享主内存
shared main storage multiprocessing 共享主内存多重处理
shared memory 共享内存
shared memory architecture 共享内存体系结构
shared memory computer control system 内存共享计算机控制系统
shared memory hyper-parallel computer 共享内存型超并行计算机
shared memory structure(SM) 共享内存结构
shared memory table 共享存储表
shared multi-port memory 共享多端口内存
shared name 共享名
shared near neighbor 共享近邻
shared network resource 共享网络资源
shared node 共享节点
shared nothing structure(SN) 无共享资源结构
shared object 共享对象
shared page table 共用页面表
shared partition 共享分区
shared path 共享通路,共用路径
shared peripheral 共享外围设备
shared printer 共享打印机
shared processor 共用处理机
shared property 共享属性
shared queue 共享队列
shared read-only system residence disk 共享只读系统驻留盘
shared register 共享寄存器
shared resource 共享资源
Shared Resource Manager 共享资源管理系统
shared routine 共享例程
shared run-time library 共享运行时间库
shared segment 共享段

shared sensor 共享传感器
shared-service line 共用线
shared session 共享对话期
shared software 共享软件
shared spooling 共用假脱机
shared storage 共享存储器
shared structure 共享结构
shared subchannel 共享子通道
shared system 共享系统
shared task address space 共享任务地址空间
shared task set 共享任务集
shared-time control action 分时控制作用
shared track 共享轨,共享道
shared variable set 共用变量集
shared virtual area(SVA) 共享虚拟区
shared virtual memory 共享虚拟存储器
shared virtual memory space 共享虚拟存储空间
shared virtual memory system 共享虚拟存储器系统
shared working space 共享工作空间
sharename 共享名
sharer 共享者
shareware 试用软件,共享软件
sharing 共享,共用
sharing data set 共享数据集
sharing logical link 共享逻辑链路
sharing multiprocessing 共享多重处理
sharing of duplicate equipment 多重设备共用
sharing option 共享选项
sharing resource 共享资源
sharing script libraries 共享脚本库
sharing subchannel 共享子通道
sharp clear printing 清晰整洁打印
sharp edge 陡沿,陡峭边沿
sharp image 清晰影像,锐化图像
sharp step 陡阶跃
sharpen edges 锐化边缘
sharpening 锐化
sharpness 锐度;清晰度
sharpness screen 高清晰度显示屏
sharing technique by differentiation 微分锐化技术

SHB(Second Harmonic Band) 二次谐波频带
shear 修剪,扭曲
shear deformation 剪切变形
shear scaling factor 剪切比例因子
shear strength 剪切强度
sheath 外皮
sheet 打印纸;图表,表格;薄层
sheet conductance 薄层电导
sheet detector 供纸检测器
sheet dielectric 片状电介质
sheet feeder 输纸器
sheet film 页式胶片
sheet glass 平板玻璃
sheet metal forming process 金属板成型工艺
sheet microfilm 页式缩微胶片
sheet option 工作表选项
sheet paper 页式纸
sheet resistance 薄层电阻
sheet resistivity 薄层电阻率
sheet sample 工作表示例
sheet tag 工作表标签
Sheffer 非合取
Sheffer stroke gate "与非"门
shelf 货架;层,格
shelf aging 搁置老化
shelf label 货架标签
shelf life 储藏期限,保存寿命
shelf storage 备用存储器
shelfware 搁置件
shell 外壳,命令解释程序;原子壳层
shell account 外壳计账
shell command 外壳命令
shell document 外壳文档
shell language 外壳语言,作业控制语言
shell out 出壳
shell procedure (Unix)命令解释过程
shell process 外壳进程
shell program 外壳程序
shell prompt 外壳提示符
shell script 外壳脚本,外壳底稿
Shell sort 希尔排序法
shell structure 壳层结构
shell variable (Unix)外壳变量
shell viruses 外壳型病毒
shellscripts 外壳脚本程序
Sherwood algorithm 舍伍德算法

shield 屏蔽
shield line 屏蔽线
shield twisted pair(STP) 屏蔽双绞线
shielded cable 屏蔽电缆
shielded enclosure 屏蔽室
shielded joint 屏蔽接头
shielded line 屏蔽线
shielded pair 屏蔽线对
shielded room 屏蔽室
shielding 屏蔽
shielding box 屏蔽盒,屏蔽箱
shielding case 屏蔽罩
shielding wire 屏蔽线
shift(SHF) 移动,移位;转换,转义
shift action 移位动作
shift arithmetically 算术移位
shift cells left 单元格左移
shift cells up 单元格上移
shift chain 移位链
shift character 换档字符
shift circuit 移位电路
shift clicking 换档加单击
shift control 移位控制
shift control counter 移位控制计数器
shift counter 移位计数器
shift divisor 移位除数
shift down 向下移位
shift down modem 下调制解调器
shift end 移位结束
shift folding 移位折叠
shift forward 前移
shift in(SI) 移入,换入
shift-in character 移入字符
shift instruction 移位指令
SHIFT key 换档键
shift keying 移位键控
shift left 左移
shift left arithmetic 算术左移
shift left logical 逻辑左移
shift left long 向左长移位
shift left operator 左移运算符
shift lock 移位锁定;换档锁
shift locker 移位锁定器
shift locking character 移位锁定字符
shift matrix 移位矩阵
shift microoperation 移位微操作
shift motion 移位行程
shift network 移位网络

shift of origin 原点移位
shift operator 移位算子
shift order 移位指令
shift out(SO) 移出,换出
shift out character(SO) 移出字符
shift pulse 移位脉冲
shift-reduce parser 移位归约分析程「序
shift register 移位寄存器
shift-register memory 移位寄存器式内存
shift reverse 移位反向
shift right 右移
shift right arithmetic 算述右移
shift right double 双倍右移
shift right logical 逻辑右移
shift right operator 右移运算符
shift signal 移位信号
shift stack 移位堆栈
shift up 向高位移位 「码
shifted alphabet cipher 移位字母表密
shifted diagonal test 对角线移动测试
shifter 移位器;移带器
shifting 移位
shifting counter 移位计数器
shifting function 移位操作
shifting register 移位寄存器
shifting sort 上推分类法
SHISAM(Simple Hierarchical Indexed Sequential Access Method) 简单层次索引顺序访问法
SHL(Shift Left) 左移
SHLD(SHieLD) 屏蔽
SHM(SHared Memory) 共享内存
SHM+ SHM+模型
shock 冲击,震动,电击
shock absorber 减震器,振动吸收器
shock decay 冲击波衰变
shock fitting 激波拟合
shock front 激波阵面
shock interaction 激波相交
shock isolation system 减震系统
shock isolator 减震器
shock mount 防震支架
shock proof 防震的
shock pulse 冲击脉冲
shock response spectrum 冲击响应谱
shock sensor 冲击传感器
shock strength 冲击强度

shock test 冲击试验
shock wave 冲击波
Shockly diode 肖克莱二极管
Shockwave 动态网页技术(Macromedia)
shoe 滑轨
shoot 拍摄
shooting algorithm 打靶算法
shooting method 打靶法
shooting script 分镜头剧本
shop 计算站
shop floor production model 车间生产模型
Shore hardness 肖尔硬度
short-access storage 快速存取存储器
short address 短地址
short block 短块
short block encipherment 短分组加密
short branch 短转移
short break 瞬间中断
short card 短卡
short channel effect 短沟道效应
short channel MOS transistor 短沟道MOS晶体管
short-circuit evaluation 短路估算
short circuit fault 短路故障
short-circuit impedance 短路阻抗
short-circuit protection 短路保护
short citation 短引文
short code dialing 短码拨号
short-cut calculation 简捷计算
short-cut menu 快捷菜单
short-cut method 简捷法
short-cut multiplication 简捷乘法
short cutting 简化
short cycle 短周期
short cyclic code 缩短循环码
short data message 短数据报文
short date format 短日期格式
short distance transmission 短距离传
short duration failure 短暂失效 「输
short duration repair 短期修理
short element 短单元
short Fire code 缩短 Fire 码
short floating point number 短浮点数
short frame data 短帧数据
short haul communication 短程通信
short haul modem 短程调制解调器

short-hold mode 短暂保持方式
short instruction format 短指令格式
short line elements 短线元素
short line seeking 短行查找
short message 短报文,短消息
short noise 散射噪声
short number 短数
short offset addressing 短偏移量寻址
short operation 短操作
short period fading 短周期衰落
short pointer 短指针
short range modem 短程调制解调器
short run equilibrium state 短运行平衡状态
short sign-on 简化开始
short stack 短堆栈
short-term buffering 短暂缓冲
short-term entry identifier 短期项目标识符
short-term ionospheric forecast 短期电离层预报 「储
short-term memory 短期记忆;短期存
short-term predication 短期预测
short-term schedule 短期调度
short-term schedule and medium-term schedule 短期调度与中期调度
short-term scheduling 短期调度
short-term security 短期保密
short-term storage 短期存储
short-time constant 短时间恒定量
short time diffusion 短时间扩散
short time statistics 短期统计特性
short transaction traffic 短事务业务
short trouble 短暂故障 「量
short type 短类型
short vector 短向量
short wavelength semiconductor laser 短波长半导体激光器
short word 短字
shortage 短缺
shortcut 简化的,快捷的
shortcut bar 快捷工具栏
shortcut key 快捷键
shortcut menu 快捷菜单
shorten symbol 短缩符号
shortened block codes 缩短分组码
shortest access time first 最短访问时间优先

shortest job first(SJF) 最短作业优先法
shortest latency time first 最短执行时间优先
shortest Manhattan path 最短曼哈顿路径
shortest path 最短路径
shortest path algorithm 最短路径算法
shortest path routing 最短路径选择
shortest path problem 最短路径问题
shortest processing time first policy 最短处理时间优先策略
shortest queue routing 最短队列路由选择
shortest-remaining time first algorithm 最短停留时间算法,最短剩余时间算法
shortest seek time first 最短查找时间优先
shortest spanning subtree 最小生成树
shortest word 最短字
shortest word length encode 最短字长编码
shotgun microphone 鸟枪式麦克风
shotgunning 鸟枪法
shorthand 简写,速记
shorthand code 速记码
shorthand notation 速记符号 「序
shorthand preprocessor 速记预加工程
shorthand recognition 速记识别
shoulder 肩部
shoulder point 肩点
shoulder tap "肩接",肩式分接头
show 展示,显示
show all 显示全部
show auditing toolbar 显示审核工具
show countdown 显示倒数计秒 L栏
show detail 显示细节
show guide 显示辅助线
show in context 在上下文中显示
show in task bar 在任务栏中显示
show label 显示标志
show level 显示层次
show pages 分页显示
show palette 显示调色板
show scroll bar 显示滚动条
show through 透视
show time remaining 显示剩余时间

show toolbar 显示工具栏
show tooltip 显示工具按钮提示
show topics 显示主题
shredder 碎纸机
shrink 收缩,压缩
shrink to fit 收缩至适当大小
shrink working set 收缩工作集
shrink-wrap license 紧包装许可
shrink wrapped software 缩卷软件
shrinking and thinning 收缩与细化
shrinking subgraph 收缩子图
SHSAM (Simple Hierarchical Sequential Access Method) 简单层次顺序访问法
shuffle 正移,混洗
shuffle automaton 混洗自动机
shuffle-exchange interconnection 混洗交换互连
shuffle-exchange network 混洗交换网
shuffle grammar 混洗文法
shuffle interconnection 混洗互连
shufflenet multihop network 混洗网多跳站网络
shunt 分路
shunt circuit 并联电路;分路
shunt compensation 并联补偿
shunt feed 并联馈电
shunt feedback 并联反馈
shunt loss 并联损耗
shunt resistance 分流电阻　　「偿
shunt-series compensation 串并联补
shunted condenser 旁路电容器
shut-down 运行停止,停机
shut off 关闭,切断
shutdown 停止运行,停机
shutoff sequence(SO) 切断定序
shutter 快门,遮挡板
shutting down 正在关机
shuttle-pulse test 断续脉冲试验
SI(Serial Interface) 串行接口
SI(Shift In) 移入
SI(Single Instruction) 单指令
SI(Soft Interrupt) 软中断
SIAM (System Integrated Access Method) 系统综合访问法
SIB(Session Information Block) 对话信息块
sibling 兄弟,同属,(树上)同级结点

SIC (Structural Influence Coefficient) 结构影响系数
SIC(Synchronous Idle Character) 同步空转字符
SICS (Secondary Infrared Calibration System) 二次红外校准系统
SID (Segmented Image Database) 分段图像数据库
SID(Sequence Information Data) 顺序信息数据　　　　　　　　「据
SID(Serial Input Data) 串行输入数
SID (Software Interface Definition) 软件接口定义
SID (Source Image Distortion) 源像失真
SID (Standard Instrument Departure) 仪器标准偏差
SID (Symbolic Instruction Debugger) 符号指令调试程序　　　　「识
SID(System IDentification) 系统标
sidac 双向触发器件
side 面,边
side armature 边衔铁
side-by-side column 并排文字栏
side-by-side dual control system 并列双控制系统
side-by-side listing 并排列表
side circuit 实线电路,侧电路
side circuit loading coil 实线电路加感线圈
side crosstalk 侧音串扰
side effect 副作用
side erase 侧边擦除
side erase head 侧边擦除磁头
side frequency 边频,旁频
side information 辅助[补充]信息
side lay 侧面定位设备
side lay adjuster 侧边定位调节器
side plate 侧板
side select signal 面选择信号
side-shielded 侧面屏蔽的
side stable relay 侧稳继电器
side tray 侧边纸匣
side view 侧视图
side wall 侧壁
sideband 边带
sideband carrier 边带载波　　　「平
sideband reference level 边带参考电

sideband-suppressed carrier transmission 边带抑制载波传输
sideband transmission 边带传输
sidebar 边注
sidegating 侧向选通
Sidekick 辅助程序
Sidekick plus Sidekick ＋实用软件
sidetone 侧音
sideways diffusion 侧向扩散
sideways sum 横行和,数字迭加和
SIE(Standard Interface Equipment) 标准接口设备
siemens(S) 姆欧,西门子
SIEMENS 西门子公司
sieve method 筛法
Sieve of Eratosthenes Eratosthenes 筛法基准程序
SIF(Source Input Format) 信源输入格式
SIF(Status Information Frame) 状态信息帧
SIF(Step-Index Fiber) 梯度光纤「件
SIF(System Image File) 系统映像文
sift-out modular redundancy (SMR) 筛模冗余
SIFT system (Software Implement Fault-Tolerant system) 软件实现容错的系统
sifting 筛选
SIG(Special Interest Group) 专业组
sight 视线;视野
sight check 目测
sight hole 窥视孔
sighted robot 有视觉的机器人
sighted sensor 有视觉的传感器
sighting 观察
sigma-delta oversampling 总和-增量(Σ-Δ)过采样
sigma memory 求合存储器
sigma modulation 总和[Σ]调制
SIGN 求符号运算
sign(S) 符号
sign and currency symbol character 数值符号与货币符号字符
sign binary digit 符号二进制数字
sign bit 符号位,正负号位
sign changer 符号变换器
sign changing amplifier 符号变换放大器
sign character 符号字符
sign check 符号校验
sign check indicator 符号检验指示器
sign clause 符号子句
sign code 符号代码
sign comparator 符号比较器
sign condition 符号条件
sign-controlled circuit 符号控制电路
sign digit 符号数字
sign extension 符号扩展
sign field 符号域,符号字段
sign flag 正负号标志,符号标志
sign flip-flop 符号触发器
sign frame 符号框架
sign function 符号函数
sign in 注册
sign inversion 符号反转
sign magnitude 符号数值
sign-magnitude representation 符号数值表示法
sign of operation 运算符号
sign-off 结束指令
sign-on 开始指令,开始
sign-on screen 启动屏幕
sign-out 退出
sign pattern 符号样式
sign picture character 符号描述字符
sign position 符号位置
sign propagation 符号传播
sign pulse 符号脉冲
sign reverser 符号变换器
sign symbol 正负符号
signal(SIG) 信号
signal abstraction 信号抽象
signal acquisition 信号获取
signal adapter 信号适配器
signal alarm 信号告警
signal amplification 信号放大
signal amplitude 信号幅度
signal analyze frequency range 信号分析频率范围
signal attenuation 信号衰减
signal attribute 信号属性
signal averaging 信号平均法
signal bias 信号偏置
signal broadcast multiaccess channel 信号广播多路存取信道

signal carrier FM recording 载波信号调频记录法
signal center 信号中心
signal channel 信号通道
signal characteristics 信号特性
signal charge 信号负荷
signal combining 信号组合
signal comparator 信号比较器
signal conditioner 信号调节器
signal conditioning 信号波形加工
signal contrast 信号对比度
signal conversion 信号转换
signal conversion equipment 信号转换设备
signal converter 信号转换器
signal correction form 信号校正法
signal correlation 信号相关
signal cover 信号覆盖范围
signal current 信号流
signal damping 信号阻尼
signal decomposition 信号分解
signal delay 信号延迟
signal delay time 信号延迟时间
signal dependent noise 信号相关噪声
signal design 信号设计
signal detection 信号检测
signal detector 信号检测器
signal distance 信号距离
signal distortion 信号失真
signal distributor(SD) 信号分配器
signal disturb 信号干扰
signal document interface(SDI) 单文档界面
signal element 信号元
signal enabling 信号使能
signal encrypt system 信号加密系统
signal estimation algorithm 信号估计算法
signal extraction 信号抽取
signal fading badly 信号严重衰落
signal feedback 信号反馈
signal filter 信号滤波器
signal filtering 信号滤波
signal flow graph 信号流图
signal frequency shift 信号频率偏移
signal generator 信号发生器
signal ground 信号地
signal handling equipment 信号处理设备
signal highlighting 信号加亮
signal identification 信号标识
signal imitation 信号模拟
signal independent intermittent fault 信号独立间歇故障
signal inhibiting 信号抑制
signal injector 信号注入器
signal input 信号输入
signal input interrupt 信号输入中断
signal integration 信号积累
signal interpolation 信号插值
signal interpretation 信号解释
signal lamp 信号灯
signal lead 信号引脚,信号引线
signal leading edge 信号前沿
signal-level 信号电平
signal line 信号线
signal message 信号消息
signal-muting switch 无噪声开关
signal network 信号网络
signal node 信号节点
signal/noise ratio 信噪比
signal normalization 信号标准化
signal notation 信号记法
signal optimal reconstruction 信号最佳重建
signal output current 信号输出电流
signal panel 信号显示面板
signal parameter analyzer 信号参数分析器
signal pattern 信号样式
signal plane (印刷电路板)信号层
signal plate 信号板
signal-plus-noise to noise ratio 信号加噪声与噪声之比
signal power 信号功率
signal preprocessing 信号预处理
signal preservation 信号保存
signal processing 信号处理
signal processing of infrared system 红外线系统的信号处理
signal processing of multi-channel system 多通道系统的信号处理
signal processor 信号处理器
signal propagation 信号传输
signal quality 信号质量
signal quality detector 信号质量检出

signal quantization 信号量化
signal race 信号竞赛
signal rate 信号速率
signal reading 信号读出
signal reading control 信号读出控制
signal reconstruction 信号重建,信号再现
signal recording 信号记录
signal regeneration 信号再生
signal reshaping 信号整形
signal restoration 信号恢复
signal routine 信号路由选择
signal sample 信号样值
signal sampling 信号抽样,信号取样
signal scanner 信号扫描器
signal selector 信号选择器
signal sequence 信号时序
signal shaping network 信号整形网络
signal smoothing 信号平滑
signal source bearing estimation 信号源方位估算
signal space 信号间隔
signal standardization 信号标准化
signal statement 信号语句
signal strength 信号强度
signal swing 信号摆幅
signal synthesis 信号合成
signal to crosstalk ratio 信号串扰比
signal to noise ratio(S/N, SNR) 信噪比
signal tracing 信号跟踪
signal trailing edge 信号后沿
signal train 信号序列
signal transfer point(STP) 信号传送点
signal transformation 信号变换
signal transition 信号过渡
signal unit 信号单位
signal unit indicator 信号单元指示符
signal wavefront 信号波前
signaling 信令,信号方式
signaling data link 信令数据链路
signaling exchange 信令交换
signaling filter 信令滤波器
signaling in band 带内振铃[发信号]
signaling indicator 信令指示器
signaling information 信令信息
signaling information content 信令信息量
signaling information field 信令信息字段
signaling interworking 信令互通
signaling link 信令链路
signaling link blocking 信号链路阻塞
signaling link code 信号链路码
signaling link error monitoring 信号链路差错监测
signaling link failure 信号链路故障
signaling link group 信号链路群
signaling link restoration 信令链路恢复
signaling link selection field 信令链路选择字段
signaling link set 信令链路集合
signaling link unblocking 信号链路阻塞消除
signaling message 信令消息
signaling message discrimination 信令消息鉴别
signaling message distribution 信令消息分配
signaling message handling functions 信令消息处理功能
signaling message routing 信令消息路由选择
signaling network 信令网络
signaling network management signals 信令网络管理信号
signaling out of band 带外振铃[发信号]
signaling path 信令通路
signaling point 信令点
signaling power 信令功率
signaling rate 信令传输速率
signaling rate indicator 信令速率指示器
signaling rate transparency 信令速率透明性
signaling route 信令路由
signaling route set 信令路由集合
signaling route-set-test procedure 信令路由集合测试程序
signaling routing 信令路由选择
signaling system 信令系统
signaling time slot 信令时隙
signaling unit 信令单元,振铃器
signaling vocabulary 信号词汇表
signature 签名;特征;标记图
signature analysis 特征[笔迹]分析
signature analyzer 特征分析器

signature block 签名块
signature check 签字校验,笔迹检验
signature data processing system 签名数据鉴别系统
signature file 签名文件
signature function 签名功能
signature identification 特征标识
signature image system 笔迹映像系统
signature recognition 签字[笔迹]识别
signature table 签名表
signature testing 签字测试
signature verification 签名验证
signatured instruction stream 有特征标民的指令流
signed 有符号的,带符号的
signed binary 带符号的二进制数
signed binary arithmetic 带符号的二进数运算
signed decimal number 带符号十进制数
signed digit number system 带符号记数系统
signed exponent 带符号指数
signed field 带符号字段
signed integer 带符号整数
signed magnitude 带符号量值
signed packed decimal 带符号压缩十进制数
significance 有效位,有效值
significance bit 有效位
significance digit 有效数字
significance exception 有效位异常
significance indicator 有效指示符
significance interrupt 有效中断
significant 重要的;有效的;有意义的
significant allocation 有效分配
significant backlog 大量积压
significant character 有效字符
significant condition 有效状态,有效条件
significant condition number 有效状态数
significant digit 有效数字
significant-digit arithmetic 有效数字运算
significant digits 有效数字
significant figure 有效图表,有效符号
significant instant 有效瞬间,有效时
significant instants 有效瞬时 [刻
significant instants of a digital signal 数字信号的有效瞬间
significant interval 有效时间间隔
significant interval theoretical duration 理论有效时间间隔
significant part 有效数字部分
signification 正式通知;词义,含义
signification starter 有效初始值
significative 有意义的,有效的
signify 符号化
signless integer 无符号整数
SIL(Save Image Library) 保存映像库
silastic 硅橡胶
silence 寂静;禁止,抑制
silence interval 寂静区间
silence zone 寂静区,抑制区
silent boundary 静止边界
silent period 静寂时间
silent speed 无声速度
silent zone 静区
silex 石英玻璃
silhouette edge 轮廓边
silhouette mask method 轮廓屏蔽法
SILI(Suppress Incorrect Length Indicator) 取消错误长度指示符
silica 硅胶,二氧化硅
silica cladded fiber 石英包层光纤
silica colloidal polishing 二氧化硅胶体抛光
silica fiber 石英光纤
silica gel 硅胶
silica glass 石英玻璃
silica graded fiber 石英渐变型光纤
silicide film 硅化物薄膜
silicide resistor 硅化物电阻
silicon 硅
silicon alloy 硅合金
silicon anodization 硅阳极氧化
silicon assembler 硅片汇编程序
silicon associative memory machine 硅联想记忆机
silicon bilateral switch 硅双通道开关
silicon block 硅堆
silicon carbide 碳化硅
silicon chip 硅片 [统
silicon compilation system 硅编辑系
silicon compiler 硅编译器
silicon controlled rectifier(SCR) 可控

硅整流器
silicon controlled switch(SCS) 可控硅开关
silicon crystal 硅晶体
silicon die 硅片
silicon diode 硅二极管
silicon dioxide 二氧化硅
silicon dioxide layer 二氧化硅膜
silicon disk 硅盘
silicon doping 硅掺杂
silicon epitaxial planar transistor 硅外延平面晶体管
silicon foundry 硅加工厂
silicon gate 硅栅
Silicon Graphics Inc.(SGI) SGI公司（美国）
silicon image sensor 硅图像传感器
silicon micromachining 硅微加工
silicon monolithic circuit 硅单片电路
silicon nitride ceramics 氮化硅陶瓷
silicon nitride passivation 氮化硅钝化
silicon on sapphire(SOS) 蓝宝石硅片
silicon oxide 氧化硅
silicon pellet 小硅片
silicon photo transistor 硅光电池
silicon photoelectric diode 硅光电二极管
silicon rectifier 硅整流器
silicon rectifying cell 硅整流元件
silicon-rich deposition 富硅沉积
silicon slice 硅片
silicon software 硅软件；固化软件
silicon solar cell 硅太阳能电池
silicon substrate 硅衬底
silicon tip 硅接点
silicon unijunction transistor 硅单结晶体管
Silicon Valley 硅谷（美）
silicon variable capacitor 硅可变电容器
silicon wafer 硅圆片
silicone 硅有机树脂，硅酮
silicone grease 硅脂
silicone protective material 硅保护材料
silicone rubber 硅橡胶
siliconizing 硅化处理，扩散渗硅
silk covered wire 丝包线
silk paper 薄纸
silk screen 丝网
silk screen printing method 丝网印制电路法，丝网漏印法
silly group 傻瓜组
silo memory 竖井式存储器
silver 银
silver-mica capacitor 银云母电容器
silver migration 银迁移
silver solder 银焊料
silver zinc storage battery 银锌蓄电池
SIM(Sequential Inference Machine) 顺序推理机
SIM(Set Interrupt Maskable) 置可屏蔽中断
SIM(Society for Information Management) 信息管理团体
SIM(Subscriber Identification Memory card) 用户识别卡
SIM(Synchronous Interface Module) 同步接口模块
SIMAN language SIMAN语言
SIMD(Single Instruction stream Multi Data stream) 单指令流多数据流
SIMD architecture 单指令流多数据流体系结构
SIMD computer 单指令流多数据流计算机
SIMDAG model SIMDAG模型
similar 相似的
similar binary trees 相似二叉树
similar character recognition 相似字符识别
similar geometry 相似几何
similar part 相似件
similar representation 相似表示
similar to search 相似检索
similarity 相似性
similarity-based learning 基于相似性的学习
similarity criterion 相似性判据
similarity distance 相似性距离
similarity function 相似性功能
similarity level 相似性水平
similarity measure 相似性测度
similarity parameter 相似性参数
similarity reduction 相似精简
similarity-rule estimation method 相似性规则估算法
similarity solution 相似解

similarity transformation 相似性转换
SIML(SImulation Language) 仿真语言
SIMM(Single In-line Memory Module) 单列直插式内存模块
SIMNET SIMNET 虚拟现实系统
SIMO(Single Input-Multiple Output) 单输入多输出
Simon decision model 西蒙决策模型
SIMPL (Single Identify Micro-Programming Language) 单标识微程序设计语言
SIMPLE (SImulation Programming LanguagE) 仿真程序设计语言
simple 简单的
simple access path 简单存取路径
simple arithmetic expression 简单算术表达式
simple assignment form 简单赋值形式
simple assignment statement 简单赋值语句
simple attributive classification 简单属性分类
simple Boolean expression 简单布尔表达式
simple buffering 简单缓冲法
simple chain 简单链
simple combo 简单组合框
simple command 简单命令
simple common subexpression 简单公用子表达式
simple condition 简单条件
simple cooperative symmetric 简单协作对称的
simple declaration 简单说明
simple designational expression 简单命名表达式
simple deterministic language 简单确定性语言
simple dichotomy 简单二分支
simple discontinuity 简单间断
simple disjunctive decomposition 简单析取分解
simple event 简单事件,单纯事件
simple expression 简单表达式
simple fan-in argument 简单扇入变元
simple file manipulation 简单文件处理
simple formal parameter 简单形式参数
simple gate 简单门
simple generic algorithm(SGA) 简单遗传算法
simple grammar 简单文法
simple graph display 简单图形显示器
simple graphical partition 简单图划分
simple grid method 简单网格法
simple group 单群
simple insertion character 简单插入字符
simple interrupt 简单中断
simple language 简单语言
simple list text chart 简单文字列表
simple logic element 简单逻辑元件
simple macro-call 简单宏调用
simple macro-scheme 简单宏方案
Simple Mail Transfer Protocol(SMTP) 简单邮件传送协议
simple majority function 简单多数决定函数
simple mapping 简单映像
simple mixed strategy precedence grammar 简单混合策略优先文法
simple multipoint circuit 简单多端电路
simple name 简单名
simple net 简单网
Simple Network Management Protocol (SNMP) 简单网络管理协议
simple object 简单对象
simple one-way chain 简单单向链
simple output format translator 简单输出格式翻译程序
simple parameter 简单参数
simple parameter argument 简单参数自变量
simple path name 简单路径名
simple phrase 简单短语
simple plex structure 简单丛结构
simple post-fix translation 简单后缀翻译
simple precedence grammar 简单优先文法
simple precedence relation 简单优先关系
simple priority method 简单优先法
simple program structure 简单程序结构

simple proposition 简单命题
simple pushdown automaton 简单下推自动机
simple random sampling 简单随机取样
simple recursion 简单递归
simple relational query language 简单关系查询语言
simple repeatable robot 简单重复式机器人
simple right-linear grammar 简单右线性文法
simple serial 简单串行
simple set 单纯集合,简单集合
simple stack 简单堆栈
simple statement 简单语句
simple straight-line procedure 简单直线式过程
simple straight-forward instruction 简单顺序执行指令
simple string processor 简单串处理程序
simple structure 简单结构
simple substitution cipher 简单代替密码
simple transmission 单向传输,单工传输
simple type 简单类型
simple variable 简单变量
Simple Wide Area Information Server (SWAIS) 简单广域信息服务器
simplest unifier 最简一致置换
simplex 单工通信;单纯形法
simplex algorithm 单纯形算法
simplex channel 单工通道
simplex circuit 单工线路
simplex/duplex modem 单工/双工调制解调器
simplex/duplex terminals 单工/双工终端
simplex fixture 单工件夹具
simplex line 单工线路
simplex link 单工链路
simplex method 单纯形法
simplex mode 单工模式
simplex multiplier 单纯形因子
simplex radiotelegraph procedure 单工无线电报过程
simplex remote communication 单工远程通信
simplex script font 简化手写体

simplex signaling 单工信令
simplex table 单纯形表
simplex transmission 单工传输
simplexed circuit 单工化电路
simplicity 简明性
simplification 简化
simplified 简化的
simplified Chinese character 简化汉字
simplified covering table 简化覆盖表
simplified discrete method 简化离散法
simplified hardware block diagram 简化硬件框图
simplified logic diagram 简化逻辑图
simplified message processing simulation 简化消息处理仿真
simplified real-time monitor 简化实时监视器
simply connected 单连通的
simply connected component 单连通成份
simply homomorphic 单同态
Simply Interactive PC (SIPC) 简单交互式个人计算机
simply linked list 简单链表
simply ordered set 全序集
simply-supported plate 简支板
simply table 单纯形表
Simpson formula 辛普森公式
Simpson's rule 辛普森法则
SIMULA 模拟语言,SIMULA 语言
SIMULA-67 模拟语言 67
simulate 模拟,仿真
simulated 模拟的,仿真的
simulated attention 模拟关注,模拟注意
simulated data 模拟数据
simulated data reduction program 模拟数据精简程序
simulated input condition 模拟输入条件
simulated logon 模拟注册,仿真登记
simulated machine indexing 模拟机器索引编排
simulated network analysis program 模拟网络分析程序
simulated normal color image 模拟真彩色图像
simulated normal color image processing 模拟真彩色图像处理

simulated performance 模拟性能
simulated program 仿真程序
simulated real-time on-line operation 模拟实时联机操作
simulated remote station 模拟远程站
simulated routine 仿真例程
simulating computer 仿真计算机
simulation 仿真,模拟
simulation accelerator 模拟加速器
simulation algorithm 仿真算法
simulation control subsystem 模拟控制子系统
simulation cycle 模拟周期
simulation device 仿真设备
simulation equipment 模拟设备
simulation examination 模拟检验,仿真实验
simulation executive 模拟运行
simulation game 模拟对策
simulation input devices 模拟输入设备
simulation interface 仿真界面
simulation language 模拟语言
Simulation Language 67 模拟语言 67
simulation lemma 模拟引理
simulation manipulation 模拟操纵
simulation metamodel 模拟元模型
simulation methodology 模拟方法学
simulation model 仿真模型
simulation monitoring 仿真监控
simulation of logic array 逻辑阵列模拟
simulation of simplicity 简单性模拟
simulation operation 仿真运算
simulation organization 模拟组织结构
simulation oriented language(SOL) 模拟定向语言
simulation package 模拟软件包
simulation performance 模拟性能
simulation procedure 仿真过程
simulation program 仿真程序
simulation programming 模拟编程
simulation programming language(SPL) 模拟程序设计语言
simulation pulse transmission 模拟脉冲传输
simulation report 仿真报告
simulation scriptor 模拟语言;模拟事件
simulation software 仿真软件
simulation software technology 仿真软件技术
simulation software unity 仿真软件一体化
simulation strategy 仿真策略
simulation study 模拟研究
simulation supervisory program 模拟监督程序
simulation technique 仿真技术
simulation thread 模拟线程
simulation training 模拟培训
simulation visualizing 仿真可视化
simulation wire list 模拟布线表
simulator(SIM) 仿真器;仿真程序
simulator debug 模拟程序调试
simulator debug utility 模拟程序调试实用程序
simulator load 仿真器负载
simulator program 模拟器程序
simulator prototype development 模拟原型机研制,仿真样机开发
simulator routine 模拟器程序
simulator software program 模拟器软件程序
simultaneity 同时性,同时操作
simultaneous 同时的,并行的
simultaneous access 同时存取
simultaneous acquisition 同时采集,同时获取
simultaneous binding 同时联编
simultaneous bus operation 同时操作
simultaneous carry 同时进位
simultaneous communication 同时通信,双向通信
simultaneous computer 并行计算机
simultaneous connection 同时连接
simultaneous contrast 同时对比度
simultaneous control 同时控制
simultaneous differential equation 联立微分方程组
simultaneous displacement 同时位移
simultaneous equation 联立方程
simultaneous error 同时出错
simultaneous failure tolerance 同时容错
simultaneous I/O bus interface 并行输入/输出总线接口
simultaneous input/output 同时输入输出
simultaneous iteration 同时迭代

simultaneous linear algebraic equation 联立线性代数方程
simultaneous mode 同时处理模式
simultaneous multiplier 同时乘法器
simultaneous operation 并行作业
simultaneous-operation computer 并行操作计算机
simultaneous operation scanner selector 同时作业扫描选择器
simultaneous operation subchannel 同时操作子通道
simultaneous peripheral operation on-line(spool) 假脱机,外围设备联机并行操作
simultaneous processing 同时处理
simultaneous processing operation system(SIPROS) 并行处理操作系统
simultaneous recursion 联列递归「代
simultaneous row iteration 同时行迭
simultaneous scan 同时扫描
simultaneous statistical inference 同时统计推理
simultaneous throughput 同时吞吐量
simultaneous transmission 同时传输
simultaneous voice/data 话音/数据同
simultaneous working 同时处理 「传
SIN(Security Information Network) 安全信息网络
SIN(SINe) 正弦 「器
SIN(Symbolic INtegrator) 符号积分
sine function 正弦函数
sine series 正弦级数
sine transform 正弦变换
sine wave 正弦波
Singapore Federation of Computer Industry(SFCI) 新加坡电脑工业协会
Singer Co. network Singer 公司网络
singing 振鸣音,蜂音
singing margin 振鸣边际
single 单个的,单独的
single access station(SAS) 单连接站
single access user 单访问用户 「点
single accumulator system 单累加器系统
single action line 单作用线
single action mechanical system 单作用机构

single action trunk 单向中继线
single address 单地址
single-address code 单地址码
single-address instruction 单地址指令
single-address message 单地址信息
single address order code 单地址指令码
single address trunk 单地址业务量
single agent approach 单模块法
single argument routine 单变元例程
single-arm plotter 单臂式绘图仪
single arrow link 单箭头链接 「言
single assignment language 单赋值语
single assignment rule 单赋值规则
single bit buffer 单比特缓冲器
single bit generator 单比特发生器
single bit image 单比特图像
single board computer(SBC) 单板计算机
single board computer controller 单板机控制器
single board microcomputer 单板微型计算机
single branch fault 单分支错误
single-buffered input 单缓冲输入
single bundle cable 单束光缆 「构
single bus architecture 单总线体系结
single-bus operation 单总线操作
single-bus system 单总线系统
single byte correction 单字节校正
single-cable system 单电缆制
single call 单次呼叫
single capstan mode 单主动轮模式
single capstan tape drive 单主动轮磁带机
single carry 单一进位
single chain 单链
single channel 单信道
single-channel amplitude analyzer 单通道幅度分析器
single channel communication 单信道通信
single channel error 单通道错误
single channel magnetic head 单通道磁头
single channel per-carrier PCM multiple-access demanded assignment equipment(SPADE) 单路单载波脉

冲编码调制多址按需分配设备
single channel routing 单通道路由选
single-channel simplex 单路单工 择
single-channel single-bundle cable 单信道单束光缆
single-channel single-fiber cable 单信道单根光纤光缆
single character delimiter 单字符定界符
single character identifier 单字符标识
single character recognition 单字符识别
single-chip adapter 单片适配器
single-chip IR-CCD 单片式红外电荷耦合器件
single-chip microcomputer 单片微计算机
single chip microprocessor 单片微处理器
single chip modem 单芯片调制解调器
single-chip power supply 单片电源
single chip processor 单片处理机
single chip system 单芯片系统
single chip system configuration 单芯片系统配置
single chip system I/O hardware 单片系统输入/输出硬件
single circuit 单工线路,单电路
single-clad board 单面敷箔板
single closing quote 右单引号
single command 单一指令
single comment 单注释
single-concept learning 单一概念学习
single conductor cable 单导线电缆
single contiguous allocation 单接近配置
Single Copy Object Store (SCOS) 单一拷贝对象存储
single crystal 单晶
single current/double current converter 单双流转换器
single current method 单电流法
single current signaling 单流信令
single current transmission 单电流传
single-cycle key 单循环键 输
single data stream 单数据流
single declaration 单一说明
single defruit 单异步回波过滤
single-degree of freedom system 单自由度系统

single density 单密度
single density encoding 单密度编码
single-die-per-package 单片组件
single domain 单畴;单域
single-domain network 单控网络,单畴网络
single domain particle 单畴粒子
single driver 单驱动器
single edge positioning 单边定位
single end user 单端用户
single-ended control 单端控制
single-ended list 单端列表 步
single-ended synchronization 单端同
single entry 单输入,单入口
single entry-single exit computer 单入口单出口计算机
single error 单个错误
single error correcting/double error detecting code (SEC/DEC) 单错校正双错检测码
single-factor 单因子
single-fault diagnosis 单一错误诊断
single fiber 单纤
single-fiber cable 单纤光缆
single fiber jacket 单纤维套层
single-fiber light-guide 单纤光波导
single font 单字体
single frequency duplex 单频双工 扰
single frequency interference 单频干
single-frequency signal 单频信号
single-frequency signaling 单频信令
single ground 单接地
single group link 单群链路 真
single harmonic distortion 单谐波失
single heterostructure laser 单异质结构激光器
single hop 单跳
single host 单主机
single identifier 单标识符
single in-line memory module (SIMM) 单列直插式内存组件
single-in-line module 单列直插式模块
single in-line package (SIP) 单列直插式组件 址
single indirect addressing 单重间接寻
single input-single output system 单输入单输出系统

single instruction execution time 单指令执行时间
single instruction-multiple data stream organization 单指令多数据流结构
single instruction-multiple data stream system(SIMD) 单指令多数据流系统
single instruction-single data stream system(SISD) 单指令单数据流系统
single instruction stream 单指令流
single item 单项
single job 单作业
single key stroke 单击键
single large expensive disk(SLED) 单个大容量昂贵硬盘
single layer 单层次,单层
single layer board 单层板
single layer routing problem （印刷电路板上)单层布线问题
single length 单长度,单字长
single length arithmetic 单倍长运算
single length number 单倍长数
single length real value 单倍长实值
single length register 单倍长寄存器
single lens 单镜头
single level address 一级地址
single level encoding microinstruction 一级编码微指令
single level memory 一级内存
single level network 单级网络
single level weighting function 单级加权函数
single line border 单线边框
single line box 单线框
single line diagram 单线图
single line interrupt 单线中断
single line of reasoning 单线推理
single line repeater 单线中继器
single line subscriber 单线用户
single link 单链路
single link flexible robot 单链灵活机器人
single link list 单链接表
single lock manager 单锁管理程序
single login 单一登录
single loop 单循环;单回路
single-loop control system 单回路控制系统

single machine cycle 单机器周期
single magnetic head 单体磁头
single message mode 单消息模式
single message rate timing 单消息速率定时
single-mode connector 单模连接器
single-mode coupler 单模耦合器
single-mode dispersion-shifted fiber 单模色散移频光纤
single mode fiber 单模光纤
single-mode launching 单模入射
single mode optical fiber 单模光纤
single modem 单片调制解调器
single module structure 单模块结构
single network management protocol 单一网络管理协议
single network node 单网络节点
single node 单一节点,单独结点
single node network 单节点网络
single noun 单名词
single office exchange 单局交换
single opening quote 左单引号
single operand 单操作数
single operand addressing 单操作数寻址
single operand instruction 单操作数指令
single operation 半双工操作
single optical fiber 单根光纤
single order 一阶的
single output switch function 单输出开关函数
single packet message 单分组报文
single particle effect 单粒子效应
single partition 单一分区
single pass 单遍,单次遍历
single-pass assembler 单遍汇编程序
single-pass compiler 单遍编译程序
single-pass program 单遍程序,一遍程序
single-pass scanner 单遍扫描仪
single-pass translation 单遍翻译
single-path storage director 单路径存储导向器
single phase 单相的
single phase clock 单相时钟
single phase clock generator 单相时钟脉冲发生器

single-phase full bridge rectifier 单相全波桥式整流器
single phase merging 单步归并
single pixel position 单像素位置
single place shift 单个空间移位
single-point ground 单点接地
single-point integrator 单点积分器
Single Point VisiNet 单点可视网络
single polarity 单极性
single polarity pulse 单极性脉冲
single polarization optical fiber 单极化光纤
single pole double throw 单刀双掷开关
single pole multiple throw 单刀多掷开关
single pole single throw 单刀单掷开关
single-precedence message 单前导报
single-precision 单精度
single precision arithmetic 单精度运算
single-precision floating-point data format 单精度浮点数据格式
single-precision floating-point format 单精度浮点格式
single-precision integer 单精度整数
single pressure maintained mechanical system 单压力保持机构
single-process server 单进程服务器
single processor system 单处理机系统
single program initiator(SPI) 单程序启动程序
single program operation 单道程序作业
single program statement 单一程序语句
single protocol layer 单协议层
single pulse device 单脉冲设备
single pulse generator 单脉冲发生器
single purpose computer 单一用途计算机,专用计算机
single query 单次查询
single quick access report 单个快速访问报告
single quote mark 单引号
single rack mounting 单机架装配
single radical character 独体字
single rail 单轨
single record chain 单记录链
single recording medium word processing equipment 单记录媒体文字处理设备
single region execution 单区域执行
single ring 单环
single row router 单行布线器
single sampling inspection 单次抽样检验
single segment environment 单段环境
single segment mode 单段模式
single selection 单一选择
single semantic interpretation 单语义解释
single server 单一服务器
single server model 单服务器模型
single server queue 单一服务队列
single session 单次会话
single setup 单步设置
single-sheet feeding 单页输纸
single shot 单触发;单步执行
single-shot circuit 单触发电路
single-shot computer 单步运算计算机
single-shot logic block 单脉冲逻辑块
single-shot multivibrator 单稳多谐振荡器
single shot operation 单步操作
single side(SS) 单面
single side abrupt junction 单边突变结
single side access head 单面读写头
single side rank test 单边秩检验
single sideband broadcast 单边带广播
single-sideband modulation 单边带调制
single-sideband transmission 单边带传输
single-sideband voice 单边带话音
single sided board 单面板
single sided copying 单面复制
single sided diskette 单面磁盘
single sided-double density diskette 单面双密度磁盘
single sided minidiskette 单面小型软盘
single sided printed board 单面印刷电路板
single sided printed circuit 单面印刷电路
single sided single density diskette 单面单密度磁盘
single sign-on(SSO) 单一登录
single-signal receiver 单信号接收器

single-simplex communication 单工通信
single site database system 单一地域数据库系统
single-slope ADC 单斜率模数转换器
single solution relation 单解关系
single source of knowledge 单知识源
single space 单间隔,单空格
single span beam 单跨梁
single speed CD-ROM 单速只读光盘驱动器
single stage 单级,单步骤
single stage interconnection network 单级互连网络
single stage interconnection network feature 单级互连网络特性
single stage joint 单级关节
single step 单步,单步执行
single-step debugging 单步调试
single step method 单步法
single-step mode 单步模式
single-step mode diagnosis 单步式诊断
single-step operation 单步作业
single step process 单步处理
single step run 单步运行
single step switch 单步开关
single stimulus rating(SSR) 单一激励评定法
single storage word 单存储字
single-stream batch processing 单流批处理
single structure 单体结构
single stuck at fault model 单固定故障
single sweep 单次扫描
single system 单一系统
single system bus 单一系统总线
single system image(SSI) 单一系统映像
single table cipher 单表密码
single tape Turing machine 单带图灵机
single task 单一事务
single term expression 单项表达式
single terminal entry 单终端机进入
single thread 单线程
single thread application program 单线程应用程序
single thread processing 单线程处理
single-threaded control 单线程控制
single threading 单线程,单线索

single-throw circuit breaker 单掷电路断电器
single throw switch 单掷开关
single time-shared system 单一分时系统
single track 单磁道,单轨
single transaction access 单事务访问
single transition time 单次转换时间
single turn film head 单匝薄膜磁头
single upper case letter 单个大写字母
single-use plan 单用途计划
single user driver module 单用户驱动程序模块
single user facility 单用户设施
single-user mode 单用户模式
single user operating system 单用户操作系统
single user system 单用户系统
single value function 单值函数
single valued current D/A decoder 单值电流数/模译码器
single-valued property 单值属性
single verb 单动词
single vertical key 单垂直键
single virtual storage 单虚拟存储器
single volume data set 单卷数据集
single volume file 单卷文件
single wafer 单圆片
single-wire line 单线式线路
single-word instruction 单字指令
single-word instruction format 单字指令格式
single-word external data bus(SX) 单字外部数据总线
singleton 惟一的,单个的;单元素
singleton cycle 单元素环
singleton sequence 单元素序列
singleton set 单元素集合
singleton substitution 单一替换
singular cover 奇异覆盖
singular cube 奇异立方
singular integral equation 奇异积分方程
singular operator 奇异算子
singular perturbation 奇异摄动
singular ordinal 奇异序数
singular plane 奇异平面
singular point 奇异点
singular predicate 单谓词
singular proposition 奇异命题

singular root 奇异根
singular set 奇异系
singular solution 奇异解
singular value 奇异值
singular value decomposition (SVD) 奇异值分解
singular vector 奇异向量
singular vertex 奇异顶点
singularity 奇点,奇异点;奇异性
singularity-separating method 奇异性分隔法
sink 槽,信宿;沟道;吸收;散热片
sink current 吸收电流
sink node 汇节点
sink tree 收点树,汇集树
sink user 接收用户
sink vertices 汇点,收点
sink virtual machine 信宿虚拟机
sinter 烧结,热压结
sinusoid 正弦曲线;正弦波
sinusoid function 正弦函数
sinusoid impulse 正弦脉冲
sinusoidal 正弦的
sinusoidal oscillator 正弦振荡器
sinusoidal signal 正弦信号
sinusoidal voltage 正弦电压
SIO(Serial Input/Output) 串行输入/输出
SIO interface 串行接口
SIP(Satellite Information Processor) 卫星信息处理机
SIP(Scheduling Information Pool) 调度信息池
SIP(Single In-line Package) 单列直插式组件
SIPC(Simple Interactive PC) 简单交互个人计算机
SIPE(System Internal Performance Evaluation) 系统内部性能评估
siphon recorder 虹吸记录器
siphoning 虹吸法
SIPO(System Installation Productivity Option) 系统安装辅助选件
SIR (Selective Information Retrieval) 定题信息检索
SIR (Semantic Information Retriever) 语义信息检索程序
Sirch robot Sirch 机器人

SIRR (Software Interrupt Request Register) 软件中断请求寄存器
SIS(Scientific Instruction Set) 科学指令集
SIS(Simulation Interface System) 仿真接口系统
SISD (Single Instruction stream and Single Data stream) 单指令流单数据流
SIT (Silicon Intensified Target) 硅靶增强视像管
SIT(Smart Interactive Terminal) 智能交互式终端
SIT (System Initialization Table) 系统初始化表
SITA high level network 国际航空通信学会高级网络
site 位置,地点,网站,站点
site address 站点地址
site administrator 现场管理员
site assignment 区域分配
site code 位置代码
site data processing system 现场数据处理系统
site error 地点错误,位置误差
site failure 现场失效
site-independent mode 地点无关方式
site license 场地许可证;网站许可
site list 网站列表
site map 站点布局图
site operation people 现场操作人员
site operator 网点操作员
site polling 区段轮询,组轮询
site recovery 现场恢复
site selection 位置选择
site service account 站点服务账号
site summary 站点总览
site visitor 站点[网站]访问者
situation-action pair 情景-动作对
situation analysis 状态分析;情势分析
situation-based representation 基于情景表示法
situation console 状态控制台
situation design theory 情势设计理论
situation display 状态显示;位置显示
situation theory of leadership 情势领导理论
situational argument 情势自变量

six-axis system 六轴系统
six-bit byte 6位字节
six-bit code 六单位制电码
six DOF 六自由度
SIXEL language SIXEL语言
sixteen-bit microcomputer 16位微型计算机
sixteen-sheet 16开纸
size 长度,大小,尺寸
size box 缩放格
size clause 长度子句
size error 长度误差
size error condition 长度错误条件
size error phrase 长度错误短语
size field 长度字段
size latch 长度锁存器
size of code 代码量
size of input 输入规模
size of memory 内存容量
size phrase 长度短语
size select 尺寸选择
sized with window 随窗口大小调整
sizing 改变尺寸;评价,分级
sizing button 改变尺寸按钮
sizing cursor 改变光标大小
sizing grid 改变网格大小
SJF(Shortest Job First) 最短作业优先法
SJP(Stacked Job Processing) 栈存作业处理
SJQ(Selected Job Queue) 被选作业队列
SKD(Systems Knock Down) 大散件
skeletal 骨架的,轮廓的
skeletal code 骨架代码,结构码
skeletal coding 骨架编码
skeletal knowledge engineering language 骨架型知识工程语言
skeletal planning technique 骨架规划技术
skeletal query 提纲式询问法
skeletal representation 骨架表示法
skeletal system 骨架系统
skeleton 骨架,轮廓
skeleton code 骨架码
skeleton diagram 方块图,骨架图
skeleton instruction 骨架[轮廓]指令
skeleton of parse tree 语法分析树骨架
skeleton table 骨架表,宏指令表
skeptical 怀疑的,不相信的
Sketchpad 草图画板;草图,略图
skew 歪斜的,偏离的;非对称的
skew boundary condition 扭曲边界条件
skew buffer 斜移缓冲器
skew correction 扭曲校正
skew curvilinear coordinate 非对称曲线坐标
skew distortion 偏斜失真
skew error 扭斜错误
skew failure 错位故障
skew Hermite matrix 反埃尔米特矩阵
skew line 斜线
skew pulse 歪斜脉冲
skew ray 不交轴光线
skew scheme 斜移方案
skew symmetric 反对称的
skew symmetric operator 反对称算子
skew symmetric tensor 反对称张量
skewed connection routing 斜扭连接布线
skewed joint 斜扭连接
skewed overload 错位超限;非均衡超载
skewed storage 交错存储器
skewing 扭曲,斜移
skewing distance 斜移距离
skewing scheme 斜移模式
skewness 偏斜度
skill analysis 技能分析
skill refinement 技能求精
skilled programmer 熟练程序员
skin 外皮,表皮
skin depth 趋肤深度
skin effect 趋肤效应,集肤效应
Skinner hand Skinner机械手
skinny client 小客户机
skip(SK) 跳越,跳转
skip after 后跳
skip backward 向后跳转,快退
skip before 前跳
skip blank 忽略空白
skip bus 跨越总线
skip capability 跳越能力
skip chain 跳转链
skip code 跨越码,跳转码
skip displacement 跳越位移量

skip distance 跳转距离
skip factor 省略因子,跳越因子
skip fading 跳越衰落,越程衰落
skip field 空字段
skip flag 跳转标志
skip format item 跨越格式项
skip forward 向前跳越,快进
skip instruction 跳越指令
skip key 跳越键
skip on condition 条件跳跃
skip option 跳跃任选
skip over 越过,跨过
skip philosophy 跳跃方法
skip sampling 跳跃抽样
skip sequential access 跳跃顺序存取
skip spill method 跳跃溢出法
skip symbol 跳跃符,空符号
skip tabling 跳跃制表
skip tape 跳越带
skip test 跳越测试
skip testing 跳越测试
skip zone 跳越区域
skipped file 被忽略的文件
skipping 跳行
Skolem function 斯柯伦函词
Skolem normal form 斯柯伦范式
Skolem standard form 斯柯伦标准形
Skolem's constant 斯科伦常数
Skolemization 斯柯伦化
sky wave 天波
Skylab 太空实验室　　　　　　「线
SL(SDLC Line) 同步数据链路控制
SL(Simulation Language) 模拟语言
SL(SLeep time) 休眠时间
SL(Source Language) 源语言
SL(Source Library) 源程序库
slab 板,片,晶体片
slab serif 有粗截线的西文字体
slack 松驰的,空闲的
slack byte 备用字节,空字节
slack variable 松驰变量
SLAM(Simulation Language for Analogue Modeling) 模拟建模的仿真语言
slant 斜拉
slant angle 斜度,倾斜角
slant distance 斜距,倾斜距离
slant matrix 斜矩阵

slant transform 斜变换
slanted abstract 倾向性摘要
SLAP(Symbolic Language Assembly Program) 符号语言汇编程序
slash 斜线,斜杠
slash mark 斜线标志
slash sheet 斜线表
Slater conditions 斯雷特条件
slave 从属的
slave application 从属应用
slave computer 从计算机
slave cycle 从属周期;受控周期
slave driver 副驱动器,从驱动器
slave emulator 从属仿真程序
slave interface 从接口
slave/master relationship 从/主关系
slave microcomputer 从属微计算机
slave microcomputer architecture 从属微计算机体系结构
slave mode 从属模式
slave operation 从动操作
slave peripheral processor control 从属外围处理机控制
slave prefix area 从属前缀区
slave process 从属进程
slave processor 从处理器
slave program activity monitor 从属程序活性监督程序
slave program compatibility 从属程序兼容性
slave program prefix 从属程序前缀
slave register set 从寄存器组
slave relation 从属关系
slave segment 从属片段
slave server 从服务器
slave station 从站,副站
slave stream 辅助流
slave stream handler 辅助流管理器
slave support processor 从属支持处理
slave synchronization 从属同步　　「机
slave system 从属系统
slave system/terminal 从系统/终端机
slave terminal 从终端
slave timing system 从定时系统
slave unit 从属设备
SLC(Secured Logon Coordinator) 安全注册协调程序　　　　　　　「路
SLC(Subscriber Line Circuit) 用户线

SLCM(Software Life Cycle Model) 软件生命周期模型
SLD(Simplified Logic Diagram) 简化逻辑图
SLD(SoLiD) 固态的,固体的
SLD(SuperLuminescent Diode) 高亮度发光二极管
SLDRAM (Synchronous Linking DRAM) 同步链接动态随机存取存储器
SLED(Single Large Expensive Disk) 单体大容量昂贵硬盘
sleek 磨光,修光
sleep 睡眠,休止
sleep mode 休止模式;休眠状态
sleep pattern 睡眠模式
sleep queue 休眠队列
sleeping process 休眠进程
sleeping sickness 嗜眠病
sleeve 套筒,套管
sleeve bearing 滑动轴承
sleeve splicer 松套管连接器
slew 超行距走纸
slew rate 转换速率
slewing 转换,换向,改变
slewing rate 转换速率
SLG(Secondary Lattice Group) 二次网络群
SLI(Service-Level Indicator) 服务级指示符
SLI(Synchronous Line Interface) 同步线路接口
SLIB(Source LIBrary) 源程序库「库
SLIB(Subroutine LIBrarian) 子例程
SLICE(System LIfe Cycle Estimation) 系统生命周期估计
slice 位片;时间片;片段
slice architecture 位片式体系结构
slice architecture microcomputer 位片式微型计算机
slice memory 片式内存
slice memory interface 片式内存接口
slice pipeline system 位片式流水线系
slice processor 位片式处理器 「统
slice system 位片式系统
slicer 削波器,限幅器
slicing 划分法
slicing criterion 分片判据

slicing time 划分时间片
slide 滑臂;幻灯片
slide changer 幻灯片切换器
slide control menu 幻灯片控制菜单
slide-in chassis 插入式抽屉
slide linkage 滑轨连接
slide multiplier 滑臂式乘法器
slide pad 浮动块,滑动块
slide projector 幻灯片投影仪
slide rule 滑尺,计算尺
slide setting entry device 滑动定位输入装置
slide show 幻灯片式演示
slide switch 滑动开关
slide sync recorder 幻灯同步录音机
slide wire potentiometer 滑线电位器
slider 滑块
slider bearing 滑动轴承 「构
slider-crank mechanism 滑块曲柄机
slider layout 滑块外观
slider pitch axis 滑块俯仰轴
sliding pin 滑动销轴
sliding window 滑动窗口 「议
sliding window protocol 滑动窗口协
sliding window size 滑动窗口尺寸
SLIM (Single-Layer Interconnection Medium) 单层互连媒体
SLIM (Software LIfe cycle Management) 软件生命周期管理
SLIP(Serial Line Internet Protocol) 串行线路网际协议
SLIP (Serviceability Level Indicator Processing) 可服务性级指示处理
SLIP(Symmetric List Interpretive Program) 对称表解释程序
slip 滑移,滑动
SLIP connection SLIP(协议)连接
SLIP emulator SLIP(协议)仿真程序
slip friction 滑动摩擦
slip joint 滑动接头
SLIP/PPP(Serial Line Internet Protocol/Point to Point Protocol) 串行线路网际协议/点对点协议
slip ring 滑环,集流环
slip scan 转差扫描
SLIST (NetWare)服务器列表
slit disk 裂缝盘
slit-divided scan 分割式扫描仪

slit scan 开缝扫描
slit width 缝隙宽度
sliver 存储条
SLL(Shift Left Long) 长左移
SLL(Shift Left single Logical) 逻辑单左移
SLM(Subscriber Loop Multiplexer) 用户环路多路复用器
SLM(Synchronous Line Multiplexer) 同步线路多路复用器
slope 斜率,倾斜度
slope adaptive delta modulator 斜率自适应增量调制
slope compensation 斜率补偿
slope equalizer 斜率均衡器
slope filter 斜率滤波器
slope keypoint compaction 关键点斜率数据压缩
slope overload 斜率过载
slope tolerance 斜率容限
Sloped Roman 斜罗马字体
SLOR(Successive Line Over-Relaxation) 逐行超松弛
SLOT(Scheduler LOok-up Table) 调度程序查看表
slot 槽;隙,缝
Slot 1 1型主板插槽规范(Intel)
Slot 2 2型主板插槽规范(Intel)
slot duration 时间片,时间槽
slot frequency 隙缝频率
slot group 槽群
slot name 槽名
slot number 槽号
slot sorting 页槽排序
slot time 时隙
slot value 槽值
slotted ALOHA 分时片 ALOHA 系统
slotted envelope network 时间片分割法网络
slotted non-persistent CSMA 时间片非坚持型 CSMA
slotted protocol 时间片协议
slotted ring network 时间片分隔环形网
slotted ring protocol 时间片分隔环协议
slotting 开槽
slow access 慢存取
slow back 慢返回
slow clock ratio 慢时钟速率

slow death 慢损坏
slow execution 慢速执行
slow filter 慢速滤波器
slow link 慢速连接
slow mail 慢速邮递
slow memory 低速内存
slow motion 慢动作
slow-pages 慢速(下载时间较长)网页
slow-poll list 慢轮询列表
slow-release relay 缓释继电器
slow scan 慢扫描
slow scan TV 慢扫描电视
slow start (TCP/IP 中的)慢速启动(算法)
slow storage 低速存储器
slow time scale 慢速时比,慢时标
slowdown 降速,延迟
SLP(Self-Loading Program) 自载入程序
SLP(SLew Paper) 超距走纸,跑纸
SLR(Services Level Reporting) 服务级别报告
SLR(Storage Limits Register) 存储界限寄存器
SLR(System Length Register) 系统长度寄存器
SLR(1) method SLR(1)分析法
SLR method(syntax left-right method) 自左向右语法分析法
SLS(Speed limiting Switch) 限速开关
SLSI(Super Large Scale Integrated circuit) 超大规模集成电路
SLT(Section List Table) 段目录表
SLT(Segment Load Table) 段装入表
SLT(System Linkage Table) 系统连接表
SLTF(Shortest Latency Time First) 最短执行时间优先
SLU(Secondary Logic Unit) 辅助逻辑部件
SLU(Source Library Update) 源库更新
slug 金属插销
sluggish network (结构变更)不灵活网络
SM(Secondary Menu) 二级菜单
SM(Servo Motor) 伺服马达
SM(SiMulator) 仿真程序
SMA(Structured Markov Algorithm)

结构化马尔可夫算法
SMAC(Scene Matching Area Correlation) 场景匹配区域相关
small-area network 小区域网络
small business computer 小型商用计算机
small capitals 小型大写字体
small caps 小型大写字体
small card release processing 小插件防松脱处理
small class 小类
small computer system interface(SCSI) 小型计算机系统接口,SCSI接口
small earth terminal 小型地面终端
small face 小号字面
small font 小字体 「管
small geometry transistor 小尺寸晶体
small kernel operating system 小内核操作系统
small language 小语言
small memory mode 小内存模式
small process 小进程
small routine 小例程 「成
small scale integration(SSI) 小规模集
small signal 小信号
small signal analysis 小信号分析
small signal equivalent circuit 小信号等效电路
small signal parameter 小信号参数
small signal status 小信号状态
small size computer 小尺寸计算机
small size loop 小循环,短循环
small strain plasticity problem 微小应变塑性问题
small vibration 小振动
smaller than 小于
smallest addressable unit 最小可编址单元
smallest alphabet 最小字母表
Smalltalk Smalltalk 语言(IBM)
Smalltalk V Smalltalk V 语言(IBM)
SMART(System for the Mechanical Analysis and Retrieval of Text) 文本检索与机器分析系统
SMART(System Monitoring And ReporT system) 系统监督和报告系
smart 灵巧的,机智的 「统
smart architecture 灵巧结构

Smart card 灵巧卡,智能卡
smart console 智能控制台
smart dot-matrix printer 灵巧点阵打印机
smart editing terminal 智能编辑终端
smart front end 灵活前端
smart hub 智能集线器
smart install program 智能安装程序
smart instrument 智能仪表
smart interactive terminal 智能会话终端
smart linkage 智能连接
smart machine 灵巧型机器
smart mobile access 智能化移动访问
smart modem 智能调制解调器
smart multiplexer 智能多路复用器
smart point processing 灵巧点处理
smart pointer declarations 智能指针声明
smart-pointer implementation 智能指针实现
smart-power IC 智能功率集成电路
smart power switch 智能电源开关
smart quote 花引号
smart recompilation 智能化再编译
smart sensor 灵巧传感器
smart terminal 智能终端
smart terminal characteristics 智能终端特性
smart tool 灵巧工具,智能工具
SmartBay (驱动器)灵巧托架(AST)
Smartcom Smartcom 通信程序(Hayes)
Smartdrive Smartdrive 磁盘管理程序
SmartKey SmartKey 键盘管理程序
SmartPoint 灵巧指点器(AST)
SmartWare SmartWare 软件包(Informix)
Smartwork Smartwork 印刷电路板图设计软件
SMC(Surface-Mounted Components) 表面安装器件
SMD(Standard storage MoDule) 标准存储器模块
SMD(Storage Module Device) 存储器模块设备
SMD(Storage Module Drive) 存储模块驱动电路

SMD(System Monitor Display) 系统监控显示器

SMDS (Switched Multimegabit Data Services) 交换式兆级容量数据服务

smear 拖影,浸润

smeared-out boundary 模糊边界

SMF(Standard Message Format) 标准消息格式

SMF(System Monitoring Facility) 系统监督程序(IBM)

SMG(Super Master Group) 超主群

SMG(RTL Screen ManaGement procedures) 运行时间库屏幕管理程序

SMGDF(Super Master Group Distributing Frame) 超主配线架

SMH(Stream Manager Help) 流管理帮助

SMI(Shared Memory Interface) 共享主存接口

SMI(Structure of Management Information) 管理信息结构

SMI(System Memory Interface) 系统内存接口

SMIB(Single Machine Infinite Bus) 单机无限总线

SMIL(Synchronous Multimedia Interchange Language) 同步多媒体集成语言

smileys (网上对话用的)表情符号组

SMIS (Spectrum-Matching Imaging System) 频谱匹配映像系统

SMLC(Synchronous Multi-Line Controller) 多路同步控制器

SMM(Shared Multiport Memory) 共享多端口内存

SMM(System Management Monitor) 系统管理监督程序

SMN(Switched Message Network) 报文交换网络

smoke 烟雾

smoke detector 烟尘检测器

smoke test 烟雾试验

smooth 平滑,修匀

smooth contact 平滑接触

smooth curve 平滑曲线,光滑曲线

smooth edge 平滑边缘

smooth filter 平滑滤波器

smooth filtering 平滑滤波

smooth line 平滑线

smooth optimization 平滑优化

smooth reshuffling algorithm 平滑重混洗算法

smooth sequence 光滑序列

smooth shading 平滑阴影

smooth solution 修匀解,平滑解

smooth traffic 平滑业务量

smooth transition 平稳过渡

smoothed binary image 平滑二值图像

smoothed data 平滑数据

smoother 平滑滤波器

smoothest approximation 最光滑逼近

smoothing 修匀,平滑

smoothing factor 平滑系数

smoothing filter 平滑滤波器

smoothing formula 修匀公式,平滑公式

smoothing function 磨光函数

smoothing problem 平滑问题,修匀问题

smoothing process 平滑处理

smooth shading 平滑阴影建立

smoothing solution 修匀解

smoothing splines 磨光样条

smoothing style 修匀风格,求同存异风格

smoothing width 磨光宽度

SMP(Service Management Point) 业务管理点

SMP(Simple Management Protocol) 简单管理协议

SMP(Sybase Migration Program) Sybase 转移计划

SMP(Symmetric MultiProcessing) 对称多机处理

SMPHD(SaMPle and HolD subroutine) 取样与保持子例程

SMPTE(Society for Motion Picture and TV Engineers) 电影及电视工程师协会

SMPTE time code SMPTE 时间码

SMS(Service Management System) 服务管理系统

SMS(Short Message Service) 短消息服务

SMS(Systems Management Server) 系统管理服务器(微软)

SMT(Station ManagemenT) 站管理

SMT(Surface Mount Technology) 表

面安装技术
SMT(System Management Tool) 系统管理工具
SMTP(Simple Mail Transfer Protocol) 简单邮件传送协议
smudge 拭抹;污渍,污染
smudge resistance 抗污染力
smudge tool 拭抹工具
SN(Sequence Number) 顺序号
SN(Signal to Noise ratio) 信噪比
SN(Stack Number) 栈号
SNA(Systems Network Architecture) 系统网络体系结构(IBM)
SNA distribution services(SNADS) SNA 分布式服务
SNA gateway SNA 网关
SNA network SNA 网络
SNA node SNA 节点
SNA station SNA 站
SNA terminal SNA 终端
SNADS(SNA Distribution Services) SNA 分布式服务
snaf 报表纸屑,打印纸边条
snail mail 蜗牛邮件(常规投送邮件)
snake-like manipulator 蛇形操纵器
SNANI(System Network Architecture Network Interconnection) 系统网络体系结构网络互连
SNAP(Semantic Network Array Processor) 语义网络阵列处理机
SNAP(System Network Architecture Program) 系统网络体系结构程序
snap 抽点;抓取
snap-action contacts 快动作触点
snap-action switch 快动作开关
snap-off diode 阶跃二极管
snap-on pointing device 揿扣式定位设备
snap out 排出,放出,流出
snap to center 锁定到中心
snap to grid 对齐网格线
snap varactor 阶跃变容二极管
SNAPS(Standard Network Access Protocol Specification) 标准网络存取协议说明
snapshot 快照;快速转储
snapshot copy 快速拷贝
snapshot debug 抽点查错
snapshot dump 抽点转储
snapshot program 抽点打印程序
snapshot roll-back system 快速转返系统
snapshot routine 抽点打印例程
snapshot statistics 瞬态统计
snapshot trace program 抽点跟踪程序
snapshots 快照,抽点打印
snatch 获取,提取
SNBU(Switched Network BackUp) 交换网络备份
SNDL(Switched Network Data Link) 交换网络数据链路
sneak current 寄生电流
sneak path 潜通路
sneaker net 人工传递网络
Snell's law 斯涅尔定律
SNF(Sequence Number Field) 序号字段
SNF(Silicon Nitride Film) 氮化硅薄膜
SNG(Stabilization Network Group) 稳定网络群
SNI(Sequence-Number Indicator) 序号指示符
SNI(SNA Network Interconnection) SNA 网络互连
sniffer "嗅查"程序
SNMP(Simple Network Management Protocol) (TCP/IP)简单网络管理协议
SNMP agent 简单网络管理协议代理
SNOBOL(StriNg Oriented symBOlic Language) 面向串的符号语言
SNOBOL language 字符串处理语言,SNOBOL 语言
SNOBOL strings SNOBOL 字符串
snooping 窥探
snooping protocol 窥探协议
snow 雪花(干扰)
SNP(SigN-on Program) 起始程序
SNP(Synchronous Network Processor) 同步网络处理机
SNV(Switch Network View) 交换网络视图
SO(Send Only) 只发送
SO(Serial Output) 串行输出
SO(Shift Out) 移出
SO(Sneak Out) 渐隐,淡出

SO(Static Object) 静态对象
SOA(Start Of Address) 起始地址
soak 吸收,掺入
soak time 保温时间;吸收时间
SOAP (Symbolic Optimal Assembly Program) 符号优化汇编程序
SOB(Start Of Block) 块开始
Sobel nonlinear mask 索贝尔非线性模板
SOC(Self-Organizing Control) 自组织控制
SOC(System On Chip) 系统集成
SOC(System Operation Console) 系统操作控制台
social assessment 社会评价
social decision process 社会决策过程
social interface 社会化界面
social model 社会模型
social science data 社会科学数据
Social Security Card 社会安全卡
social security number(SSN) 社会安全号
Society for Computer Medicine(SCM) 计算机医学学会
Society for Computer Simulation(SCS) 计算机模拟学会
Society for Industrial and Applied Mathematics(SIAM) 工业与应用数学学会
Society for Information Display(SID) 信息显示学会
Society for Management Information Systems(SMIS) 管理信息系统协会
Society for Wang Applications and Programs(SWAP) 王安计算机应用与程序协会
Society of Certified Data Processors (SCDP) 合格数据处理工作者协会
Society of Computer Simulation(SCS) 计算机仿真学会
Society of Data Processing Machine Operators and Programmers(DPMOAP) 数据处理机操作员和程序员协会
Society of Motion Picture and Television Engineers(SMPTE) 运动图像与电视工程师协会
sociological abstracts(SOCABS) 社会学文摘

sociology 社会学
socket 插座,插孔;套接字;套接口
socket 7 (321脚)微处理器插座7型
socket 370 (370脚)微处理器插座
socket adapter 插座适配器
socket compatibility 接插兼容性
socket connector 接插件
socket contact 插座接触;插座触点
socket flash memory 插卡式快擦写存储器
socket library 接口程序库
socket pair 套接字对
socket screw 沉孔螺钉
socket service 插接服务
socket strips 插座板
socket under test 被试插座
socketable user interface 可插入用户接口
SOCRATE SOCRATE数据库
Socratic argument 苏格拉底论证
Socratic tutoring method 苏格拉底教导法
SOF(Start Of Format) 格式开始
SOF(Start Of Frame) 帧开始
soft 软的,软件的
soft adder 软加法器
soft automation 软自动化
soft bomb 软件炸弹
soft boot 软自举
soft breakdown 软击穿
soft bug 软件错误,软件故障
soft cell boundaries 软单元边界
soft check 软件校验
soft clone 软克隆
soft copy 软拷贝
soft core 软核
soft decision decoding 软判决译码
soft display processor 软显示字处理
soft error 软错误
soft error rate 软错误率
soft fail 软失效
soft failure 软故障
soft failure run 软失效运行
soft fault 软故障
soft feeling 软接触
soft font 软字模
soft font panel 软面板
soft format 软格式

soft gripper 软夹具,软夹持器
soft hyphen 软连字符
soft inference and problem solving 柔性推理与问题求解
soft information processing 柔性信息处理
soft interrupt 软中断
soft interrupt communication 软中断通信
soft interrupt mechanism 软中断机构
soft interrupt number 软中断号
soft interrupt process mode 软中断处理模式
soft interrupt signal 软中断信号
soft interrupt transmit 软中断发送
soft junction 软结
soft key 自定义键;软键
soft key terminal 软关键字终端
soft keyboard 软键盘
soft landing head 软着陆磁头
soft macro 软宏元
soft magnetic material 软磁性材料
soft maintenance 软维护;软件维护
soft object 软目标
soft package 软封装,软包装
soft page break 软分页
soft panel 软面板
soft patch 软配接;软修补
soft position 软位置
soft real-time response 软实时响应
soft recognition and understanding 柔性识别与理解
soft reset 软复位
soft resource 软资源
soft return 软回车
soft science 软科学
soft sector 软扇区
soft sector format 软扇区格式
soft sector formatting 软扇区格式化
soft sector treatment 软扇区处理
soft sectored disk 软扇区磁盘
soft sectored formatting 软扇区格式
soft sectoring 软扇区划分
soft self-excitation 软自激
soft software 软软件
soft solder 软焊料
soft space 软空格
soft start 软启动

soft stop 软停机
Soft-Switch 软交换软件
soft wait 软等待
soft wired system 软连接系统
softclone software 软兼容软件
softening temperature 软化温度
softly fail 软化故障
softpanel structure 软面板结构
Softstrip Softstrip 扫描仪
software 软件
software acceptance testing 软件验收测试
software activity 软件活动
software aided multifont input (SWAMI) 软件辅助的多字体输入
software alteration 软件修改
software analysis tool 软件分析工具
software application 软件应用
software architecture 软件体系结构
software associative memory 软件相关内存
software assurance 软件保险
software audit 软件审计
software availability 软件可用率
software base 软件库
software breadboard 软件试验板,软件面包板
software bug 软件错误
software bus 软件总线
software capability 软件效能
Software Carousel 软件"宴会"
software category 软件种类,软件类
software center 软件中心
software certification 软件认证
software change 软件更改
software change control 软件更改控
software change management report 软件更改管理报告
software change request 软件更改请
software character generator 软件字符发生器
software check sum 软件校验和
software check sum word 软件校验和
software clock 软件时钟
software combining 软件组合
software command language 软件命令语言
software compatibility 软件兼容性

software compatible 软件兼容的
software complexity 软件复杂性
software component 软件成份
software component description library 软件成份描述库
software composing 软件合成
software configuration 软件配置
software configuration baseline 软件配置基线
software configuration management 软件配置管理
software consideration 软件设计考虑
software context 软件上下文,软件关联
software controls 软件控制
software convention 软件约定
software conversion 软件转换
software copyright protection 软件版权保护
software cost 软件成本
software costing 软件成本估计
software costing tool 软件计费工具
software crash 软件崩溃
software crisis 软件危机
software cross assembler 软件交叉汇编程序
software cross-product 软件交叉产品
software cryptography 软件加密
software cursor 软件光标
software database document 软件数据库文档
software debouncing 软件消抖动法
software debugging aids 软件调试工具
software defect 软件缺陷
software definition 软件定义
software dependability 软件可靠性
software design 软件设计
software design aids 软件设计辅助程序
software design approach 软件设计手段
software design document 软件设计文件
software design engineering 软件设计工程
software design generation 软件设计代
software design language 软件设计语言
software design maintenance 软件设计维护
software design methodology 软件设计方法学
software design procedure 软件设计过程
software design tool 软件设计工具
software detection 软件检测
software development 软件开发
software development aid 软件开发工具
software development board 软件开发组
software development cycle 软件开发周期
software development environment 软件开发环境
software development estimate 软件开发估算
software development facility 软件开发设施
software development kit (SDK) 软件开发工具包
software development kit tools 软件开发成套工具
software development library 软件开发库
software development lifecycle 软件开发生命周期
software development management planning 软件开发管理计划
software development management policy 软件开发管理策略
software development notebook 软件开发笔记
software development plan 软件开发计划
software development process 软件开发过程
software development productivity 软件开发效率
software development support system 软件开发支持系统
software development system 软件开发系统
software development tool 软件开发工具
software diagnostic instruction 软件诊断指令
software disaster 软件灾难
software distribution 软件发布
software document 软件文档

software documentation 软件文档编制
software driver 软件驱动程序
software education 软件教育
software efficiency 软件有效性
software emulation 软件模拟,软件仿真
software emulator 软件仿真程序
software encrypting 软件加密法
software end-of-file 软件文件结束
software engineer 软件工程师
software engineering 软件工程
software engineering economics 软件工程经济学
software engineering environment 软件工程环境
software engineering method 软件工程方法
software engineering methodology 软件工程方法学
software engineering project 软件工程项目
software engineering project management 软件工程项目管理
software engineering psychology 软件工程心理学
software engineering standard 软件工程标准
software engineering standardization 软件工程标准化
software engineering support environment 软件工程支持环境
software enhancement 软件增强
software environment 软件环境
software error 软件错误
software error classification 软件错误分类
software error effect analysis 软件错误影响分析
software error interrupt 软件错误中断
software evaluation and development modules 软件评价与开发模块
software experience data 软件经验数据
software factory 软件工厂
software failure 软件失效,软件故障
software failure rate 软件失效率
software fault 软件故障
software fault-tolerance strategy 软件容错策略
software feature 软件特性

software fix 软件修复
software flexibility 软件灵活性
software flow chart 软件流程图
software for display 显示软件
software function 软件功能
software generalization 软件通用化
software generation system 软件生成系统
software guide 软件指南,软件手册
software house 软件公司
software IC 软集成块
software implementation language 软件实现语言
software implemented sharing virtual memory 软件实现的共享虚拟存储器
software industry 软件产业
software innovation 软件更新
software inspection 软件检验
software integrated testing 软件综合测试
software integrity 软件完整性
software interface 软件接口
software interface definition 软件接口定义
software interrupt 软件中断
software interrupt process mode presetting 软中断处理方式预置
software interrupt queue 软件中断队列
software interruption 软件中断
software inventory 软件清单
software kernel 软件内核
software kit 软件配套
software layer 软件层
software legislation 软件立法
software library 软件库
software license 软件许可证
software life cycle 软件生命周期
software lifetime 软件寿命
software linguistics 软件语言学
software look-aside buffer 软件后备缓存
software maintainability 软件可维护性
software maintenance 软件维护
Software Maintenance Assn. (SMA) 软件维护协会
software maintenance tool 软件维护工具
software management 软件管理

software malfunction 软件故障
software manual testing 软件人工测试
software manufacturing tool 软件生产工具
software mapping 软件映射
software masking 软件屏蔽
software measurement 软件测试
software method 软件方法
software methodology 软件方法学
software metrics 软件度量
software model 软件模型
software modifiability 软件可修改性
software modification 软件修改
software modularity 软件模块化
software module 软件模块
software module specification 软件模块说明
software monitor 软件监督程序
software multiplexing 软件多路复用
software manufacturing tool 软件生产工具
software market 软件市场
software measurement tool 软件测量工具
software modularity 软件模块化程序
software modularization 软件模块化
software module specification 软件模块说明
software network component 网络软件成份
software network design 软件网络设计
software network design component 软件网络设计成份
software object 软件对象
software optimization 软件优化
software or computer numerical control 软件或计算机数字控制
software origin 软件原点
software overhead 软件开销
software package 软件包
software parallelism 软件并行性
software performance 软件性能
software piracy 软件侵权,软件盗版
software platform 软件平台
software polling 软件轮询
software portability 软件可移植性
software priority 软件优先权
software priority interrupt 软件优先权中断
software probe 软件监视程序
software problem report 软件问题报告
software procedure 软件编制过程
software process control block 软件进程控制块
software product 软件产品
software product long life technique 软件产品长寿技术
software product package 软件成品包
software production environment 软件生产环境
software productivity 软件生产率
software program 软件程序
software project 软件项目
software project estimation 软件项目估算
software project management 软件项目管理
software protecting 软件保护
software prototyping 软件原型法
software prototyping system 软件原型法系统
software psychology 软件心理学
software publisher 软件发行者
Software Publisher Association(SPA) 软件出版协会
software qualification testing 软件合格性测试
software quality 软件质量
software quality assurance 软件质量保证
software quality management process 软件质量管理过程
software quality metrics 软件质量度量
software readability 软件可读性
software reconfiguration 软件重构
software recording facility 软件记录设备
software redundancy 软件冗余
software release 软件版本
software release identifier 软件版本标识符
software reliability 软件可靠性
software repository 软件储藏库
software requirement 软件需求
software requirement analysis 软件需求分析

software requirement document 软件需求文档
software requirement engineering 软件需求定义技术
software requirement specification 软件需求说明书
software resource 软件资源
software resource utilization 软件资源利用率
software responsiveness 软件响应能力
software reusability 软件可重用性
software reuse 软件重用
software review 软件评审
software reverse engineering 软件逆向工程
software risk management 软件风险驾驭
software robustness 软件健壮性
software science 软件科学
software sealed-in 软件密封
software security 软件安全性
software simulation 软件仿真
software simulator 软件仿真器
software simulator test 软件模拟测试
software sneak analysis 软件潜行分析
software specification 软件说明书,软件规范
software spending 软件花费
software stack 软件堆栈
software stack register 软件堆栈寄存器
software standard 软件标准
software standardization 软件标准化
software strategy 软件策略
software structure 软件结构
software study 软件研究
software suite 套装软件
software supplier 软件供应商
software support environment 软件支持环境
software support service 软件支持服务
software support system 软件支持系统
software support tool 软件支持工具
software synthesis 软件合成
software system 软件系统
software system testing 软件系统测试
software technique 软件技术
software test 软件测试

software test environment 软件测试环境
software test set 软件测试程序集
software test strategy 软件测试策略
software test tool kit 软件测试工具集
software testing methodology 软件测试方法
software timer 软件定时器
software tool 软件工具
software tool box 软件工具箱
software toolkit 软件工具箱
software trace 软件跟踪
software trace mode 软件跟踪方式
software transportability 软件可移植性
software transportation 软件移植
software trap 软件陷阱
software understandability 软件可理解性
software unit testing 软件单元测试
software update 软件更新
software upgrade 软件升级
software usability 软件可用性
software user's manual 软件用户手册
software validation testing 软件确认测试
software vendor 软件供应者
software version 软件版本
software visualization tool 软件可视化工具
software workbench performance 软件工作台性能
SOH (Start Of Heading character) 标题起始符
SOHO (Small Office/Home Office) 小型办公室/家庭办公室
SOJ (Small Outline J lead) 小外廓J形引脚元件
SOL (Simulation Oriented Language) 面向仿真的语言
SOL (System Oriented Language) 面向系统的语言
SOL (System Output Language) 系统输出语言
Solar16 索拉小型计算机(法)
solar battery 太阳能电池
solar cell 太阳能电池单元
Solaris Solaris 操作系统(Sun)
Solaris 2.0 Solaris 操作系统 2.0 版

Solaris for SPARC　Solaris 操作系统 SPARC 版本
Solaris for x86 2.1　Solaris 操作系统 x86 版本
solder　焊料,焊锡;焊接
solder bridge　焊桥
solder cream　焊锡膏
solder connection　焊接
solder cup　焊锡坑
solder eye　焊眼,焊孔
solder glasses　焊料玻璃
solder joint fatigue　焊接疲劳
solder leveling　焊剂均匀化
solder mask ink　阻焊印料
solder mask　阻焊掩膜
solder paste　焊锡膏
solder plating printed circuit　涂敷焊料的印刷电路
solder reflow soldering　回流锡焊
solder resistor　阻焊剂
solder side　焊接面
solder sucker　吸锡器
solderability　可焊性
soldered joint　焊接点
soldering　焊锡;焊接
soldering flux　焊剂
soldering iron　烙铁
soldering iron reflow　电烙铁再流
soldering materials　焊接材料
soldering paste　焊剂,焊膏,焊糊
soldering resistance　耐焊性
soldering terminal　焊片,接线柱
solderless　无焊的
solderless connection　无焊连接
solderless connector　无焊连接器
solderless joint　无焊连接　「接
solderless wrapped connection　无焊绕
sole user　单一用户,独占用户
solenoid　螺线管
solicit operation　征求操作
solicit request　请求,征求
solicited message　请求消息,征求消息
solicited operation　请求操作
solid　固体的;原色的;实心的
solid area　实心区
solid arrow　实线箭头
solid border　实线边框
solid circuit　固体电路

solid color　单色,纯色
solid conductor　实芯导线
solid dielectric laser　固态介质激光器
solid error　固定性错误
solid failure　固定失效
solid geometry　立体几何学
solid image　固体成像
solid ink jet printer　喷蜡式打印机
solid line　实线
solid logic　固态逻辑
solid mapping　实体映像
solid metal mask　固态金属掩膜
solid model　实体模型
solid modeling　实体造型,实物建模
solid modeling system　实体模型系统
solid object　实体,复合体
solid offsetting　体偏移
solid section　实心截面
solid sharing model　实体共享模型
solid state　固态
solid-state camera　固态摄像机
solid-state circuit　固体电路
solid state component　固态元件
solid state computer　固态计算机
solid state computer system　固态计算机系统
solid state device　固态元器件
solid state disk　固态盘
solid state display　固体显示器
solid state electronics　固体电子学
solid state laser　固体激光器　「块
solid state magnetic modules　固态磁模
solid state memory　固态存储器
solid state relay(SSR)　固体继电器
solid state sensor　固体传感器
solid state software　固化软件
solid texture　固体纹理
solid ultra-sonic delay line　固态超声延迟线
solid visualization　实体显示
solidifying　固化,凝固
solidly grounding　固定接地
solitary　单元的,惟一的
soliton laser　孤子激光器
solubility　可溶性;可解性
soluble　可溶的;可解的
soluble flux　可溶焊剂　「法
soluble quotient algorithm　可解商算

solution 解法；溶液
solution approach 解题步骤(方法)
solution check 答案校验，解答校验
solution error 解题误差
solution graph 解图
solution maximum time 最长解题时间
solution of nonlinear equations 非线性方程求解
solution package 解题软件包
solution path 解路径
solution repetitive frequency 解题重复频率
solution space 解空间
solution strategy 求解策略
solution tree 解树
solution vector 解向量
solvable 可解答的，可解释的
solvable group 可解组
solve-labeling procedure 可解标记过程
solved node 可解节点
solver 解算机
solving algebraic equations 代数方程式求解
solving ordinary differential equations 常微分方程求解
solving partial differential equations 偏微分方程求解
solving the problem of impact 命中问题求解
solving visibility problem 可视化问题求解
SOM(System Object Model) 系统对象模型
somatic data 人体数据
somatic sensation 体态感觉
somatic sensation television game 体感电视游戏
some line 匹配线
SONET (Synchronous Optical NETwork) 光纤同步网络
son field 子字段
son file 子文件
son node 子节点，子结点
son process 子进程
son vertex 子顶点
sonagraph 声谱图
sonar 声纳
sonar imaging 声纳成像

SONET (Synchronous Optical NETwork) 异步光纤网标准
sonic delay line 超声波延迟线
sonic film memory 声薄膜存储器
sonic pen 声笔
SOP(Screen-Oriented Program) 面向屏幕的程序
SOPHIE SOPHIE 教学系统
sophisticated robot 高级机器人
sophisticated vocabulary 复杂词汇
SOR(Start Of Record) 记录开始
SOR(Start Of Reel) 磁带开始
SOR(Successive Over-Relaxation) 逐次超松弛
SORT 排序命令，分类命令
sort 排序，分类
sort algorithm 排序算法
sort and merge generator 分类归并生成程序
sort application 排序应用，分类应用
sort ascending 升序
sort balance 平衡分类
sort blocking factor 编块因数
sort-by-date 按日期排序
sort-by-insertion method 插入排序法
sort-by-name 按名称排序
sort-by-priority 按优先权排序
sort-by-size 按大小排序
sort-by-type 按类型排序
sort criteria 排序条件，排序准则
sort descending 降序排序
sort field 排序字段
sort file 排序文件
sort file description entry 分类文件描述体
SORT function 排序函数
sort generator 排序生成程序
sort hierarchy 分类层次
sort in ascending order 按升序排序
sort in descending order 按降序排序
sort input file 排序输入文件
sort key 排序键
sort/merge generator 排序合并生成程序
sort/merge package 分类归并程序包
sort/merge program 分类合并程序
sort needle 排序指针
sort order 排序次序

sort package 排序软件包
sort parameter 排序参数
sort pass 排序遍历
sort phase 排序阶段
sort program 排序程序
sort tree structure 分类树结构
sort utility 排序实用程序
sort warning 排序报警
sorted algebra 类别代数
sorted array 已分类数组
sorted deduction 分类演绎
sorted file 已排序文件
sorted list 分类表
sorted set order 排序的系序
sorted table 排序表
sorter 排序程序；排序器，分类机
sorter-comparator 排序比较器
sorter-reader 排序-阅读器
sorting 排序，分类
sorting and merging 排序合并
sorting and search operation 排序和检索操作
sorting by insertion 插入排序
sorting comparison pairs 排序比较对
sorting device 排序设备
sorting field 排序字段
sorting input tape 排序输入带
sorting item 排序项
sorting key 排序键
sorting machine 分类机
sorting network 分类网络
sorting output tape 排序输出带
sorting parameter 分类参数
sorting phase 排序阶段
sorting program 分类程序
sorting representation 排序表示法
sorting restart 排序重始
sorting rewind time 排序倒带时间
sorting routing 排序例程
sorting routing generator 排序例程生成器
sorting scratch tape 排序暂用磁带
sorting sequencing criteria 排序定序准则
sorting sequencing key 排序定序关键
sorting string 分类串
sorting tree structure 排序树形结构
sorting work tape 排序工作带

SOS(Share Operating System) 共享操作系统
SOS chip 蓝宝石硅片
SOSIC(Silicon-On-Sapphire Integrated Circuit) 硅蓝宝石集成电路
sound analyzer 声谱分析仪
sound articulation 单音清晰度
sound attenuation 声音衰减
sound bandwidth 声音带宽
sound bearing medium 声传播介质
Sound Blaster 声霸卡(Creative)
sound board 音效卡，声卡
sound buffer 声音缓冲器
sound card 声卡
sound carrier 伴音载波
sound channel 伴音通道；音频信道
sound compression 声音压缩
sound controlled computer 声控计算机
sound controlled switch 声控开关
sound device preference 声音设备首选项
sound driver 声音驱动程序
sound effect designer 音响效果设计师
sound effect library 音响效果库
sound file 声音文件
sound generator 声音发生器
sound head 录音头
sound hood 隔音罩
sound import 声音输入
sound-in-sync 声内同步
sound intensity 声强
sound intermediate 传声介质
sound level 声级
sound level meter 声级计
sound notification 声音通知
sound power level 声能级
sound pressure 声压
sound pressure level 声压级
sound program circuit 声音节目电路
sound program circuit section 声音节目电路段
sound ranging 声波测距
sound recognition system 声音识别系统
Sound Recorder 录音机
sound reflection coefficient 声反射系数
sound source 音源
sound spectrograph 语图仪
sound spectrum 声谱

sound strip 伴音剥离
sound synthesizer 声音合成器
sound takeoff 伴音信号检出
sound track 声道,声轨
sound velocity 声速
sound wave 声波
sounder 发声器;声码器
soundness 坚实性
sounds like 同音
source 源;源极
source address 源地址
source address field 源地址字段
source address instruction 源地址指令
source area 源区
source area block 源区数据块
source block 源块
source book 源卷
source bus 源总线
source card 源卡片
source case 源角色
source clause 源子句
source code 源代码
source code compatibility 源码兼容性
source code conversion 源码转换
source-code instruction 源码指令
source code library 源代码库
source code viruses 源码病毒
source computer 源计算机
source contact 源接点,源极接点
source control 源控制
source converter 源转换程序
source-coupler loss 光源耦合器损耗
source-coupling efficiency 光源耦合效率
source current 源电流
source data 源数据
source data acquisition 源数据采集
source data automation 源数据自动化
source data automation equipment 源数据自动化设备
source data card 源数据卡
source data capture 源数据获取
source data collection 源数据采集
source data entry 源数据入口;源数据项目
source data structure 源数据结构
source database 源数据库
source-destination instruction 源-目的地指令,无操作数指令

source detected interference 源检测干扰
source directory 源目录
source drive 源驱动器
source disk 源磁盘
source diskette 源软盘
source document 源文档
source edit utility option 源编辑实用程序选项
source editor 源编辑程序
source electrode 源极
source encoding 信源编码
source entropy 源熵
source-fiber coupling 光源-光纤耦合
source field 源域
source file 源文件
source file editor 源文件编辑程序
source format profile 源格式框架
source frame 源帧
source function 源函数
source host 源主机
source identifier 源标识符
source image 源映像
source impedance 源阻抗
source IP address spoolfing attack 源IP地址欺骗式攻击
source information 源信息
source item 源项
source key 源键
source language 源语言
source language construct 源语言构造
source language debugging 源语言调试
source language instruction 源语言指令
source language level 源语言级
source language specification 源语言规范
source language symbol 源语言符号
source language translation 源语言翻译
source level interactive debugger 源码级交互调试程序
source library 源程序库
source license 源码许可证
source list 源码列表,源程序清单
source machine 源机器
source macro definition 源宏定义
source map 源映像
source member 源成员

source module 源模块
source module library 源模块库
source node 源节点
source of infrared radiation 红外辐射源
source operand register 源操作数寄存器
source optimization 源码优化
source packet 源信息包
source preparation 源准备
source procedure 源过程
source program 源程序
source program character 源程序字符
source program form 源程序形态
source program library 源程序库
source program maintenance on-line 源程序联机维护程序
source program pointer 源程序指示字
source program symbol 源程序符号
source program variable 源程序变量
source program word 源程序字
source record 源记录
source recording 原始记录
source reel 源磁带卷
source region 源区;源极区域
source register 源寄存器
source route 源路径
Source Route Algorithm 源路由算法
source route bridge 源路由桥接器
source route transparent bridge 源路由透明桥接器
source routine 源例程
source routing 源路由选择
source routing bridge 源路由选择网桥
source schema 源模式
source script property 源脚本属性
source segment 源段
source/sink relationship 信源/信宿关系
source socket 源套接字
source statement comment field 源语句注释字段
source statement library(SSL) 源语句库
source station 源站
source string 源串
source subnet address 源子网地址
source subschema 源子模式
source suppression method 抑源法
source table 源表
source tape cross-assembler 源带交叉汇编程序

source tape preparation 源带准备程序
source terminal 源终端;源极接线端
source text 源程序文本
source time 源时间
source-to-fiber coupler power 光源-光纤耦合功率
source-to-fiber loss 光源-光纤耦合损耗
source-to-destination path 源到目标间路径
source update 源更新
source user 信源用户
source utility 源应用程序
source vertices 源点
source virtual machine 源虚拟机
source voltage 源电压
source window 源窗口
source word 源字
source word location 源字位置
source worksheet 源工作底稿,源表格
source zone 源区
south bridge (芯片组)南桥
south geo-magnetic pole 南地磁极
south pole 南极,S极
Southern Pacific Communications Company(SPCC) 南太平洋通信公司
SP(Serial Port) 串行端口
SP(Shift Pulse) 移位脉冲
SP(Single Precision) 单精度
SP(Single Processor) 单处理器
SP(SPace character) 空格字符
SP(Stack Pointer) 堆栈指针
SP(Start Point) 起始点
SP(SubPool) 子池
SPA(Scratch Pad Area) 暂存区域
SPA(Software Publishers Assn.) 软件发行者协会
space 空间;空白,空格;空号;间隔
space after 后间隔
space allocation 空间分配
space attenuation 空间衰减
space attribute 空间属性
space bar 空格键,空格杆
space between 间距
space bit 空白位
space character 空白字符
space charge 空间电荷
space charge debauching 空间电荷散焦

space charge density 空间电荷密度
space charge layer 空间电荷层
space charge wave 空间电荷波
space clustering 空间聚集,空间聚类
space code 空格代码
space-coherent light 空间相干光
space complexity 空间复杂性
space condition 空白状态
space constructable function 可构造空间函数
space coordinate 空间坐标
space curve 空间曲线
space descriptor 空间描述符
space directory 空目录
space distribution 空间分布
space diversity 空间分集
space diversity reception 空间分集接收
space division 空间分割
space-division multiple-access (SDMA) 空分多址连接
space-division multiplexing 空分多路复用
space-division switching 空间分割交换
space effect 空间效应
space encoding 空间编码
space environment 太空环境
space expand key 空格扩充键
space feed 输格,空格馈送
space file 空白文件
space filling 填空
space frame 空间构架
space-hold 空号保持
space invariant 空间不变的
space jam 空间拥塞
space key 空格键
space lattice 空间点阵,空间晶格
space level 空间级
space-like 类空白的
space list 空表
space manager 空间管理程序
space mark 空号;间隔标记
space on right 右边空白,右间隔
space optical communication 空间光通信
space-optimal encoding 空间优化编码
space optimization 空间优化
space-oriented 面向空间的
space out 加宽间距

space permeability 空间导磁率
space phase 空间相位
space pointer 空间指针
space record 空记录
space redundancy 空间冗余
space representation 空间表示法
space required 所需空间
space saver 空间节省符号
space segment 空间部分
space service 空间业务
space-sharing 空间共享
space simulator 空间模拟器
space state 空号状态
space station 空间站
space suppression 空格抑制,停止走纸
space symbol 空格符号
space telemetering 空间遥测
space-time diagram 时间-空间示意图
space-time measure model 空间-时间测量模型
space-time processing 时空处理
space-time product 空间时间积
space-time relationship 空间-时间关系
space-time representation 空间-时间表示
space-to-mark transition 空号-传号转换
space tracking 空间追踪
space variant 位置可变的
space versus time trade-off 时间-空间折衷
spaceball 空间球
spacer 衬垫,衬套,衬片
spacing 空号,空格,间距
spacing bias 空号偏畸
spacing chart 空白表格
spacing condition 空号状态;空白状态
spacing end distortion 空号脉冲后沿失真
spacing interval 空号间隔
spacing pulse 空号脉冲
SPADE (Single-channel-per-carrier Pulse-code-modulation multiple-Access Demand-assignment Equipment) 单信道载波脉冲编码调制多路复用设备按需分配系统
spaghetti code (带有太多 GOTO 语句的)无头绪码
SPAM(SPool file Allocation Manager)

假脱机文件分配管理程序
spam 滥言
span 幅度,变化范围;跨距
span line 跨接线路
span of control 控制范围
spanned record 越界记录
spanning set 生成集合
spanning space 生成空间
spanning subgraph 生成子图
spanning supergraph 生成超图
spanning tree 生成树
spanning tree algorithm 生成树算法
spanning value 跨越值
SPARC(Scalable Performance ARChitecture) 规模可缩放体系结构(Sun)
SPARC chip 规模可缩放处理器体系结构芯片(Sun)
SPARC station SPARC工作站(Sun)
SPARCprinter SPARC视频影像打印机
spare 备用的,备份的
spare area 备用区
spare bit 备用位
spare block 备用信息块
spare channel 备用通道
spare decoder 备用译码器
spare head 备用头
spare line 备用线路
spare memory cell 备用存储单元
spare part 备用部件
spare processor 备用处理器
spare track 备用磁道
spare wire 备用线
spark 火花
spark gap 火花间隙
sparking voltage 跳火电压
sparklies 噪声点
sparse addressing 稀疏编址
sparse array 稀疏阵列,稀疏数组
sparse data representation 稀疏数据表示
sparse Gaussian elimination 稀疏高斯消去法
sparse graph 稀疏图
sparse index 稀疏索引
sparse lambda-matrix 稀疏λ矩阵
sparse language 稀疏语言
sparse linear equation package 稀疏线性方程组
sparse matrix 稀疏矩阵
sparse orthogonal factorization 稀疏正交因子化
sparse set 稀疏集
sparse solution 稀疏解
sparse symmetric system 稀疏对称系统
sparse vector 稀疏向量
sparse vector instruction 稀疏向量指令
spatial 空间的
spatial averaging 空间平均值
spatial clustering 空间群集
spatial coordinates 空间坐标
spatial correlation 空间相关
spatial data 空间数据
spatial digitizer 空间数字化仪
spatial discretization 空间离散化
spatial distribution 空间分布
spatial domain 空间域
spatial domain method 空域法
spatial encoder 空间编码器
spatial filter 空间滤波器
spatial filtering 空间域滤波
spatial frequency domain 空间频域
spatial graph 空间图,立体图
spatial image 空间图像
spatial index 空间索引
spatial isotropy 空间各向异性
spatial join 空间连接
spatial locality 空间局部性
spatial masking 空间屏蔽
spatial matched filter 空间匹配滤波器
spatial object 空间目标
spatial parameter 空间空间参数
spatial pattern randomness 空间模式随机性
spatial relationship 空间关系
spatial representation 空间表示
spatial warping 空间扭曲
spatially invariant system 空间不变系统
spawn 分散;产生
spawner (Unix)进程生成程序
spawning tree 产生树,分散树
SPDIF(Sony/Philips Digital Interface Format) 索尼/菲利浦数字接口格式
Speakeasy Speakeasy语言
speaker 扬声器;讲者
speaker circuit 扬声器电路;业务电路

speaker connector 扬声器连接器
speaker-dependent 与讲话者有关的
speaker-dependent recognition system 与讲话者有关的识别系统
speaker-dependent speech recognition 特定人语音识别
speaker-dependent system 与发音者有关的系统
speaker identification 讲话者识别
speaker identify 讲话人识别
speaker impedance 扬声器阻抗
speaker-independent 与讲话者无关的
speaker-independent recognition system 与讲话者无关的识别系统
speaker-independent speech recognition 非特定人语音识别
speaker-independent system 与发音者无关的系统
speaker recognition system 发音人识别系统
speaker verification 讲话者证实
SPEC (Speech Predictive Encoding Communication system) 语音预测编码通信系统
SPEC(System Performance Evaluation Cooperative) 系统性能测试合作体
SPEC(System Performance Evaluation Committee) 系统性能评定委员会
spec 说明书
SPEC 1.0 基准测试程序集 1.0 版本
SPEC float SPEC 浮点数
SPEC integer SPEC 定点数
SPEC mark SPEC 数
SPEC organization 系统性能测试合作体组织
SPEC ratio SPEC 率
SPEC reference time SPEC 参考时间
special 专用的,特殊的
special add 特殊加法,双精度加法
special analog computer 专用模拟计算机
special analog system 专用模拟系统
special assembly 专项组合
special attribute 特殊属性
special buffering procedure 专用缓冲过程
special cable 专用电缆,特殊电缆
special character 特殊字符

special character combination 特殊字符组合,专用字符组合
special character table 专用符号表,特殊符号表
special circuit 专用线路
special clock transmit 专用时钟发送
special delimiter 专用定界符
special effect 特殊效果
special entity 特设机构;特殊实体
special feature 特殊功能
special file 特殊文件
special finite element 特殊有限元
special flag 专用标记
special form 特殊形式
special front-end unit 专用前端部件
special function 特殊函数,专用函数
special function generator 特殊函数发生器
special-grade access line 特别等级存取线
special hardware 专用硬件,特殊硬件
special I/O interface device 专用输入/输出接口器件
special index analyzer 专用索引分析器
special information 特殊信息
special information tone 特种通知音
special insertion 专用嵌入
special instruction repertoire 专用指令系统
special interest group(SIG) 专题组
special keyboard 专用键盘
special keyboard device 专用键盘设备
special logic 专用逻辑,特殊逻辑
special logic record 专用逻辑记录
special module testing 专用模块测试法
special multigrid method 专用多网格法
special name 专用名
special names paragraph 专用名段
special net theory 狭义网络理论
special operation exception 专用操作异常
special operator 特殊操作数,特殊算符
special optical cable 专用光缆
special parallel voice-recognition 专用并行声音识别
special priority 特别优先权
special provision 特别规定

special purpose 专用的,特殊用途的
special purpose chip 专用芯片
special-purpose computer 专用计算机
special-purpose intelligent terminals 专用智能终端
special-purpose language 特殊语言,专用语言
special-purpose logic 专用逻辑
special purpose memory 专用内存
special purpose module board 专用模件板
special purpose packet 专用信息包
special-purpose routing indicator 专用路由指示符
special-purpose terminal 专用终端
special purpose translator 专用翻译程序
special register(SR) 专用寄存器
special ROM 专用只读存储器
special service 特殊业务
special sign 特别记号,专用记号
special solution 特解
special symbol 特殊符号,专用符号
special terminal 专用终端
special time 特定时间
special token 专用令牌
special volume 专用卷
special volume file 专用卷文件
specialist 专家
specialization 专业化,专门化
specialized application language 专用语言
specialized common carrier(SCC) 专业化通信公司
specialized data processing 专业化数据处理
specialized hardware 专用硬件
specialized processing 特别化处理,专业化处理
specialized software 专用软件
specific 特定的,特别的,具体的
specific address 特定地址
specific addressed location 特定寻址位置
specific addressing 具体编址
specific agreement 特别协定
specific application program 特殊应用程序
specific application service element (SASE) 特定应用服务元素
specific code 特定码
specific coding 特定编码
specific command 特定命令
specific field 专用字段
specific interface 专用接口
specific intermittent fault 特定间歇故障
specific language 特定语言
specific mode 专用模式,专用方式
specific object model 特定目标模型
specific physical space 专用物理空间
specific polling 专用轮询
specific printer 特定打印机
specific program 专用程序
specific record type 特定记录类型
specific request 特殊请求
specific routine 专用例程
specific speed 特有速度
specific symbol 专用符号
specific volume request 专用卷请求
specification 规范,说明,规格
specification analyzer 说明分析程序
specification and description language (SDL) 功能说明和描述语言,SDL语言
specification code 详细代码
specification consistency 规格一致性
specification file 规格说明文件
specification format 规范格式
specification granularity 规格说明的详细程度
specification language 规范语言
specification macro 说明性宏
specification part 说明部分
specification readability 规范可读性
specification sheet 规格表
specification statement 说明语句
specification subprogram 区分子程序
specification system 规范说明系统
specification technique 说明技术
specification tool 说明工具,规范工具
specification tree 规范树
specificator 说明符
specificity 专指性,特殊性
specified 指定的,特定的
specified file format 指定的文件格式
specified input 指定输入
specified window 指定的窗口

specifier 说明符,区分符
specify 指定,规定,确定
specify feature 规定功能
specify task asynchronous exit(STAE) 指定任务异步出口
specify text 指定文本
specimen 样品,样本
speck 斑点
speckle 小斑点
speckle effect 斑纹效应
speckle image procession 斑点图像处理
speckle noise 斑点噪声
speckle pattern 斑纹图案
speckling 形成斑点
SPECmark(Systems Performance Evaluation Cooperative mark) 系统性能评价协作标记
spectator 旁观者
spectra 光谱;频谱
spectra data 光谱数据
spectral 光谱的,频谱的
spectral absorption coefficient 光谱吸收系数
spectral analyzer 光(频)谱分析仪
spectral bandwidth 光谱带宽
spectral character 光谱特性
spectral color 谱色
spectral condition number 谱条件数
spectral decomposition 谱分解
spectral density 谱密度
spectral domain 谱域
spectral filtering 光谱过滤
spectral function 谱函数
spectral highlight 光谱最强处
spectral irradiance 光谱辐射度
spectral mapping 谱变换
spectral norm 谱范数
spectral preconditioning 频谱预调节
spectral property 频谱特性
spectral radiant intensity 频谱辐射强度
spectral radius 谱半径
spectral reflectivity 光谱反射率
spectral representation 谱表示
spectral response 频谱响应,光谱响应
spectral signature testing 谱特征检验
spectral window 谱窗
spectrometer 分光计
spectrophotometer 分光光度计
spectroscope 分光镜
spectroscopic plate 分光板
spectroscopy 光谱学,频谱学
spectrum 频谱
spectrum analysis 频谱分析
spectrum analyzer 频谱分析仪
spectrum-envelope of voice 语音频谱包络
spectrum line 谱线
spectrum map 频谱图
spectrum measurement 频谱测量
spectrum scrambling 频谱不规则性
spectrum sensitivity 频谱灵敏度
spectrum signature 频谱特性
specular highlight 镜面反射光
specular reflection 镜面反射
specular surface 镜面
specular transmission 镜面传输
speculative 推测性的,预测性的
speculative branching 推测分支
speculative execution 推测执行
speech 讲话;话音
speech act 语音行为
speech amplifier 话音放大器
speech analysis 语言分析
speech band 语音频带
speech channel 语音通道
speech chip 语音芯片
speech coder 语音编码器
speech coding 语音编码
speech communication 语音通信
speech compression 语言压缩
speech converter 语言转换器
speech database 语音数据库
speech decoder 语音解码器
speech decoding 语音译码
speech demonstrator 语音示教器
speech digit signaling 语音数字信令
speech digital signal processing 语音数字信号处理
speech digitization 语音数字化
speech encoding 话音编码
speech equalizer 语音均衡器
speech feature extraction 语音特征抽取
speech information processing 语音信息处理
speech input 语音输入
speech input equipment 语音输入设备

speech input/output device 语音输入/输出设备
speech interference level 语音干扰电平
speech interpolation 语言内插法
speech inverter 话音转换器
speech level 话音电平
speech linear predictive coding 语音线性预测编码方式
speech memory 话音存储器
speech model 语音模型
speech modulation 语音调制
speech noise 语音噪声
speech output 语言输出
speech packet 语音信息包
speech path controller 语路控制器
speech pattern matching 语音模式匹配
speech perception 语音感知
speech power 语言功率
speech predictive encoding communication system(SPEC) 话音预测编码通信系统
speech processing 语音处理
speech quality 话音质量
speech recognition 话音识别
speech recognition procedure 语音识别过程
speech recognition system 语音识别系统
speech scrambler 语音置乱器
speech segmentation 语音分段
speech signal processing 语音信号处理
speech spectral representation 语音频谱表示法
speech subband coding 语音子频带编码方式
speech synthesis 语音合成
speech synthesis data capture 语音合成数据获取
speech synthesizer 语音合成器
speech-to-text 语音到文本
speech translation system 语音翻译系统
speech understanding 语音理解
speech waveform coder 语音波形编码器
speed 速度
speed buffer 速度缓冲器
speed calling 快速呼叫
speed change control 速度变化控制
speed coding 快速编码

speed control 速度控制
speed controller 速度控制器
speed dial 快速拨号
speed drive 速率传动
speed driver 速率传动设备
speed limiting device 限速设备
speed of answer index 应答速度指数
speed of light 光速
speed of response 响应速度
speed of sound 声速
speed regulator 调速器
speed test cassette 速度测试盒式磁带
speed tolerant recording 速度容限记录
speed-up capacitor 加速电容
speed-up loop 加速回路
speed-up ratio 加速比
Speedikon Speedikon建筑设计软件
speedup of pipeline 流水线加速比
spell check 拼写检查
spell checker 拼写检查程序
spelling 拼写方法,拼法
spelling checker 拼写检验程序
spelling correction procedure 拼写改正程序
spelling error 拼法错误
spelling graph 拼法图
spelling table 拼法表
spelling variation 拼法变化,拼法差别
SPERT(Schedule Performance Evaluation and Review Technique) 调度性能评审技术
sphere 球体,球面;区域,范围
spherical console typewriter 球形控制台打字机
spherical coordinate 球坐标
spherical coordinate robot 球面坐标机器人
spherical resolver 球坐标分解器
spherical type head 球形打印头
spherical typewriter 球形打印机
spherize 球面化
SPI(Serial Peripheral Interface) 串行外设接口
SPICE(Sales Point Information Computing Equipment) 销售点信息计算设备
SPICE benchmark SPICE基准程序
spice2g6 spice2g6基准程序

Spider (因特网)搜索蜘蛛
spider bonding 辐射形接合
spider web 蜘蛛网
spider-web antenna 蛛网天线
spike 尖峰信号
spike potential 峰值电位
spike pulse 尖峰脉冲
spike-over shoot 上冲
spill 漏出,漏失;溢出
spill backup volume 溢出备份卷
spill tag 漏标
spill volume 溢出卷
spillover route 附加路由,溢出路由
spillway 溢洪道
spin 自旋,旋转,螺旋
spin block 旋转块
spin box 轮转框
spin flip laser 自旋反转激光器
spin lock 螺旋锁
spin relaxation data 自旋松驰数据
spin stabilization 自旋稳定
spin style 旋转样式
spindle 模块;主轴,心轴
spindle hole 主轴孔
spindle motor 主轴马达
spinner 微调控制项
spiral 螺旋式的
spiral delay line 螺旋延迟线
spiral four cable 螺旋扭绞四芯电缆
spiral model 螺旋模型
spiral parity checking transmission code 螺旋式奇偶校验传输码
spiral scanning 螺旋式扫描
spiral storage 螺旋式存储器
SPIRIT (Sales Processing Interactive Real-time Inventory Technique) 交互式实时销售处理报表技术
SPK (Storage Protection Key) 存储保护键
SPL (Service Priority List) 服务优先级表
SPL (Simulation Programming Language) 仿真程序设计语言
SPL (Source Program Library) 源程序库
SPL (Structured Programming Language) 结构化程序设计语言
SPL (Symbolic Programming Language) 符号编程语言
splice 连接;接头
splice program 接合程序
splicer (线路断头)接合器
splicing 接合
splicing block 拼接块
splicing loss 接头损耗
splicing tape 粘接带
spline 样条
spline approximation of least squares 样条最小二乘法逼近
spline-based recognition 基于样条的识别
spline curve 样条曲线
spline finite strip method 样条有限带法
spline fit 样条拟合
spline function 样条函数
spline interpolation 样条插值
spline matrix 样条矩阵
spline space 样条空间
spline subdivision 样条子划分
spline surface 样条曲面
spline value 样条值
splines 样条函数
split 划分,拆分
split array 数组拆分
split bar 划分条
split-browse display 分割浏览显示
split catalog 分类目录,分划目录
split cell 拆分单元格
split conductor cable 分股电缆
split cycle transfer 分离式传输
split cylinder mode 分离柱面模式
split display 分屏显示
split-edit display 分屏编辑显示
split field 分栏
split fountain 分色墨斗法
split frame video recording 分帧视频记录
split gear 拼合齿轮
split graph 划分图
split image 拆分图像
split instruction 分指令
split-join model 拼接模型
split keyboarding 分离式键盘控制
split keyword 分离关键字
split knowledge 分离知识
split memory 分裂记忆,分离存储

split pair 串绕
split plot 分裂画面
split screen 屏幕划分,多窗口屏幕
split site 分离场所
split step spectral method 分步频谱法
split stream 流分裂
split system 分离系统
split table 拆分表
split winding transfer circuit 抽头绕组传送电路
split word operation 字划分操作
splitter 分路器,分束器
splitting 划分,分割
splitting of matrix 矩阵的划分
splitting physical block 可划分物理块
splitting plane 分割面
splitting scheme 划分方案
splitting technique 划分方法
splitting-word operation 分字操作
SPM(Scratch Pad Memory) 便笺内存
SPM(Software Productivity Metrics) 软件生产率度量
SPM(Source Program Maintenance) 源程序维护
SPN(Switched Public Network) 公用交换网络
spoiler 答案,谜底
spoken language 口语
sponge layer 海绵层
sponge tool (图像处理软件)海绵工具
spontaneous 自发的
spontaneous emission 自发辐射
spontaneous generation of lookahead 先自发生成
spontaneous inquiry 自发询问
spontaneous output 自发输出
spontaneous speech 自发语言
SPOOF(Structure and Parity-Observing Output Function) 结构与奇偶性观察输出功能
spoofing 电子欺骗
SPOOL(Shared-Peripheral Operations On Line) 假脱机操作,共享外设联机操作
SPOOL(Simultaneous Peripheral Operation On-Line) 假脱机操作,外围设备联机并行操作

spool 装带;带卷;轴;假脱机操作
spool access support 假脱机存取支持
spool configuration 假脱机配置
spool data set 假脱机数据集
spool file 假脱机文件
spool file class 假脱机文件级
spool file flag 假脱机文件标识
spool intercept buffer 假脱机截取缓冲器
spool job 假脱机作业
spool management 假脱机管理
spool partition 假脱机分区
spool queue 假脱机队列
spool spindle 卷盘轴
spool writer 假脱机输出程序「制
spooled input control 假脱机输入控
spooled listed output 假脱机列表输出
spooler 后台打印程序,假脱机管理程序「池
spooler memory pool 假脱机程序存储
spooling 假脱机操作,联机并行外围设备操作
spooling area 假脱机存储区
spooling device 联机并行外围操作设备,假脱机设备
spooling operator privilege class 假脱机操作员特权级别
spooling priority 假脱机操作优先权
spooling system 假脱机系统
sporadic fault 散乱故障,间发性故障
spot 斑点;地点,点焊
spot beam 点波束
spot carbon 分区炭化
spot color 复合点彩色
spot function 复合点功能
spot gluing 点粘接
spot jammer 选择干扰机
spot jamming 选择性干扰
spot light 聚光灯
spot mark 记号
spot noise 点噪声,特定频率噪声
spot recovery 现场恢复
spot saving 现场保护
spot scanner 点扫描仪
spot size 光点大小
spot speed 点扫描速率
spot welding 点焊
SPP(Sequenced Packet Protocol) 顺

序信息包协议

SPP(Special Purpose Processor) 专用处理机

SPP(Speech Processing Peripheral) 语音处理外围设备

SPP(Standard Parallel Port) 标准并行端口

spray 喷射,喷涂,溅射,喷雾
spray coating 喷涂
spray nozzle 喷嘴
spray plotter 喷墨式绘图机
spray tube 喷管
spray wiring 喷涂布线
sprayed coating 喷涂层
sprayer 喷雾器
spraying 喷雾,喷涂
spraying process 金属喷涂法
spread 扩散;弥散度,偏离度
spread angle 扩展角
spread effect 波及效果
spread footing 扩展底座
spread function 扩展函数
spread option 匀布选项
spread sheet compiler 电子表格编译程序
spread-spectrum 扩展频谱
spread-spectrum code-sequence generator 扩频序列码发生器
spread-spectrum multiple-access(SSMA) 扩频多址存取
spreading activation 链锁激活
spreading lens 发散透镜
spreading ray model 扩散光线模型
spreading resistance 扩散电阻
spreadsheet 电子数据表格
spreadsheet program 电子表格程序
spring 弹簧;有弹性的
spring contact 簧片接触
spring loaded pop-up 弹出型窗口
spring pad 弹簧垫
spring searching algorithm 弹性搜索算法
spring washer 弹簧垫圈
springy column 弹性列
SPRINT(Selective PRINTing) 选择打印
sprite 子画面,单色画面
sprite code 单色画面代码
sprite control 子画面控制
sprite number 子画面编号
sprite pattern 单色画面模式
sprite size 子画面尺寸
sprocket 链轮
sprocket bit 定位位
sprocket channel 定位信道
sprocket feed 链轮输纸
sprocket holes 齿孔,输送孔
sprocket pulse 中导脉冲
sprocket track 输送道,馈送道
SPS(Stored Program System) 存储程序系统
SPS(String Processing System) 字符串处理系统
SPS(Structured PostScript) 结构化页面描述语言
SPSS(Statistical Package for the Social Sciences) 社会科学统计软件包
SPST(Single Pole Single Throw) 单刀单掷开关
SPT(Shared Page Table) 共享页表
SPT(Start Print) 启动打印
SPT(System Page Table) 系统页表
SPU(Slave Processing Unit) 从属处理机
SPU(System Processing Unit) 系统处理单元
spur 支线
spurious 寄生的,假的,乱真的;杂散
spurious capacitance 寄生电容,杂散电容
spurious coupling 寄生耦合,杂散耦合
spurious impedance 寄生阻抗
spurious interrupt 假中断
spurious modulation 寄生调制
spurious noise 寄生噪声
spurious oscillation 寄生振荡
spurious output 乱真输出
spurious pulse 假脉冲,寄生脉冲
spurious reflection 寄生反射
spurious root 寄生根
spurious signal 寄生信号,乱真信号
spurt signaling 突发呼叫,突发信令
sputter 溅射,喷射
sputtered film disk 溅射薄膜磁盘
sputtering 溅射
SPX(Sequenced Packet eXchange) 顺

序分组交换协议
SPX(Set PrefiX)　置前缀
spy predicate　侦探谓词
SQA(Software Quality Assurance)　软件质量保证
SQA(System Queue Area)　系统排队区
SQA Suite　SQA Suite 成套测试软件
SQE(Signal Quality Error)　信号质量错误
SQL(Structured Query Language)　结构化查询语言
SQL Access Group(SAG)　结构化查询语言访问组
SQL * Calc　SQL * Calc 接口软件
SQL * Design Directory(SDD)　结构查询语言设计字典
SQL/DS(SQL/Data System)　结构查询语言/数据系统(IBM)
SQL editor　结构查询语言编辑程序
SQL engine　结构查询语言驱动程序
SQL * Forms　SQL * Forms 接口软件
SQL language　结构查询语言,SQL 语言
SQL-like language　类结构查询语言
SQL * Menu　结构查询语言菜单程序
SQL * plus　SQL * Plus 接口软件
SQL series　SQL 系列
SQL Server　结构查询语言服务系统
SQL * Star　SQL * Star 数据库管理系统
SQR(SQuaR)　平方
SQR function　平方函数
SQRT function　平方根函数
SQS(Stochastic Queuing System)　随机排队系统
square　平方;正方形
square brackets　方括号
square chip carrier　正方形芯片载体
square error averaged over an image array　图像阵列的均方误差
square error pattern　平方误差模式
SQUARE language　SQUARE 语言
square-law characteristic　平方律特性
square law envelope detector　平方律包络检波器
square law function generator　平方律函数发生器

square-loop core　矩形磁滞回线磁芯
square matrix　方阵
square mesh　正方网格
square parenthesis　方括号
square pixel　方形像素
square pulse　矩形脉冲
square root　平方根
square root function　平方根函数「法
square-rooting algorithm　求平方根算
square wave　矩形波,方波
squared error averaged over a image array　图像阵列均方误差
squeal　尖叫,吱吱声
squeegee　胶辊
squeeze　挤压,紧排
squeeze out　排出,压出,渲染
squeeze zoom　缩小推进
squeezed file　紧排文件
squeezeout ink　排出油墨
squeezing parameter　挤压参数
SR(Shift Register)　移位寄存器
SR(Stack Register)　堆栈寄存器
SR(Status Register)　状态寄存器
SRAM(Static Random Access Memory)　静态随机读写存储器
SRAM(Synchronous RAM)　同步存储器
SRB(Service Request Block)　服务请求块
SRCNET　科学与工程研究协会网络
SRI(Stack Reference Indicator)　堆栈引用指示符
SRL(Shift Right single Logical)　单逻辑右移
SRM(Shift Register Memory)　移位寄存器存储器
SRM(Short Range Modem)　近程调制解调器
SRM(Storage Resource Management System)　存储资源管理系统
SRP(System Recovery Program)　系统恢复程序
SRPI(Server Requester Programming Interface)　服务器请求者程序设计接口
SRQ(Send/Receive Queue)　发送/接收队列
SRQ(Service ReQuest)　服务请求

SRR(Software Requirement Review) 软件需求评审
SRS(Software Requirement Specification) 软件需求规范
SS(Single Step) 单步
SS(Source Statement) 源语句
SS(Stack Segment) 堆栈段
SS(Start Sentinel) 起始标记
SS/SD(Single Surface/Single Density) 单面/单密度
SSA(Serial Storage Architecture) 串行存储体系结构(IBM)
SSAP(Session Service Access Point) 对话服务访问点
SSB(Single SideBand) 单边带
SSB(SubScriber-Busy signal) 用户忙信号
SSB-AM(Single-SideBand Amplitude Modulation) 单边带调幅
SSB-SC transmission(Single-SideBand Suppressed-Carrier transmission) 载波抑制单边带传输
SSC(Subsystem Support Chip) 子系统支持芯片
SSC(Super-Smart Card) 超级智能卡
SSCF(System Services Control Facility) 系统服务控制设施
SSCH(Start SubCHannel instruction) (SNA)启动子通道命令
SSCP(System Service Control Point) 系统服务控制点
SSCP backup 系统服务控制点后备
SSCP domain 系统服务控制域
SSCP ID 系统服务控制点标识
SSCP-LU(System Services Control Point and the Logical Unit) 系统服务控制点和逻辑设备
SSCP-LU session(System Service Control Point-Logical Unit session) 系统服务控制点与逻辑设备间的对话
SSCP major node (VTAM)系统服务控制大节点
SSCP services 系统服务控制点服务
SSCP-PU session(System Service Control Point-Practical Unit session) 系统服务控制点与实际设备间的对话
SSCP rerouting (SNA)系统服务控制点重新路由选择
SSCP-SSCP session 系统服务控制点之间对话
SSDB(Software Support Data Base) 软件支持数据库
SSDU(Session Service Data Unit) 会话服务数据单位
SSE(Stream SIMD Extension) 数据流单指令多数据扩展指令集(Intel)
SSES(Software Specification and Evaluation System) 软件说明与评价系统
SSI(Send Service Information) 发送服务信息 「人
SSI(Server Side Include) 服务器端嵌
SSI(Single System Image) 单一系统映像
SSI(Small-Scale Integration) 小规模集成
SSI(Synchronous System Interface) 同步系统接口
SSID(SubSystem IDentification) 子系统标识
SSIE Current Research(Simthsonian Science Information Exchange current research) SSIE信息中心当前研究信息
SSL(Secure Socket layer) (TCP/IP)安全套接层
SSL(Software Specification Language) 软件规格说明语言
SSL(Super Speed Logic circuit) 超高速逻辑电路
SSL(System Specification Language) 系统规格说明语言
SSL handshake protocol 安全套接层握手协议
SSL record protocol 安全套接层记录协议
SSM(Synchronous Stream Manager) 同步流管理器
SSMA(Spread-Spectrum Multiple Access) 扩展频谱多路存取 「号
SSN(Segment Stack Number) 段栈
SSN(Social Security Number) 社会安全号
SSO(Single Sign-On) 单一登录(Novell)

SSP(Screen Saver Program) 屏幕保护程序
SSR(Static Shift Register) 静态移位寄存器
SSR(Subschema Set Reference table) 子模式系引用表
SSR(System Status Register) 系统状态寄存器
SST(System Scheduler Table) 系统调度程序表
SSTDMA(Satellite Switched Time-Division Multiple Access) 卫星转接时分多路存取
SSU(System Services Unit) 系统服务器
SSVT(SubSystem Vector Table) 子系统向量表
SSW(Silicon SoftWare) 硅软件
SSX(Small System eXecutive) 小系统执行程序
ST(Smart Terminal) 智能终端
ST(Software Tools) 软件工具
ST(StarT signal) 启动信号
ST Computer ST电脑系统及服务有限公司(新加坡)
ST computer ST计算机
ST412 (磁盘驱动器)ST412接口
ST506 (磁盘驱动器)ST506接口
ST506 RLL interface ST506游程长度受限接口
stability 稳定性
stability analysis 稳定性分析
stability criterion 稳定判据
stability factor 稳定系数
stability index 稳定性指数
stability margin 稳定边际
stability number of a hypergraph 超图的稳固数
stability of channel 通道稳定性
stability of digital filter 数字滤波器的稳定性
stability of similarity transformation 相似变换的稳定性
stability point 稳定点
stability property 稳定性质
stability region 稳定区
stability robustness 稳定健壮性
stabilization 稳定化

stabilization network 稳定网络
stabilization time 稳定时间
stabilized current supply 稳流电源
stabilized local oscillator 稳定本机振荡器
stabilized master oscillator 稳定的主振荡器
stabilized voltage supply 稳压电源
stabilizer 稳定电路
stabilizing feedback 稳定反馈
stabistor 稳压二极管
stable 稳定的,稳态的
stable and unstable system 稳定和不稳定系统
stable boundary condition 稳定边界条件
stable circuit 稳定电路
stable control 稳定控制
stable equilibrium 稳定平衡
stable equilibrium path 稳定平衡路径
stable group 稳定群
stable law 稳定律
stable marriage problem 稳定结合问题
stable matrix 稳定矩阵
stable model 稳定模型
stable oscillation 稳定振荡
stable scheme 稳定方案
stable set of a hypergraph 超图的稳固子集
stable solution 稳态解
stable sort 稳定排序
stable state 稳定状态
stable zone 稳定区
stack 堆栈,栈
stack access block 堆栈存取块
stack address 堆栈地址
stack addressing 堆栈编址
stack algorithm 堆栈算法
stack allocation 堆栈分配
stack architecture 堆栈体系结构
stack area 堆栈区
stack automaton 栈自动机
stack bottom 堆栈底
stack bucket algorithm 堆栈桶式算法
stack capability 堆栈容量
stack cell 栈单元
stack column graph 堆叠式直条图
stack combination 堆栈组合
stack contents 堆栈内容

stack control block 堆栈控制块
stack deletion 堆栈删除
stack distance 堆栈长度;栈距
stack dump 堆栈转储
stack element 堆栈元素
stack empty 堆栈空
stack facility 堆栈设施
stack filter 栈过滤器
stack frame 堆栈结构,栈帧
stack full 堆栈满
stack hardware 堆栈硬件
stack head 栈顶
stack implementation 栈实现
stack indicator 堆栈指示器
stack insertion 堆栈插入
stack instruction 栈指令
stack instruction type 堆栈指令类型
stack interrupt 堆栈中断
stack-job processing 堆栈作业处理
stack level 堆栈深度
stack limit register 堆栈限界寄存器
stack machine 堆栈机器
stack management discipline 栈管理规则
stack manipulation 堆栈操作
stack marker 堆栈标志
stack mechanism 堆栈机构
stack number 栈号
stack of document 文件堆栈
stack operation 堆栈作业
stack operation instruction 栈操作指令
stack operator 堆栈算符
stack option 堆栈选择区
stack organization 堆栈组织
stack order 堆栈指令
stack-oriented register 面向堆栈的寄存器
stack overflow 堆栈溢出
stack overflow interrupt 堆栈溢出中断
stack page 栈页面
stack permutation 栈排列
stack pointer 堆栈指针
stack pointer address 堆栈指针地址
stack pointer operation 堆栈指针操作
stack pointer register 堆栈指针寄存器
stack pop-up 堆栈上托,堆栈弹出
stack push-down 堆栈下推,堆栈推入

stack reduction 堆栈精简,栈归约
stack register 堆栈寄存器
stack replacement 栈替换
stack representation 堆栈表示法
stack retention discipline 栈保存规则
stack scan 堆栈扫描
stack segment 堆栈段
stack sequence 栈序列
stack-state-control machine 堆栈-状态-控制机器
stack string 堆栈串
stack symbol 堆栈符号
stack symbol table 堆栈符号表
stack top 栈顶
stack top location 栈顶单元
stack transform 栈变换
stack tree 堆栈树
stack type 堆栈类型
stack underflow interrupt 堆栈下溢中断
stack unwinding 堆栈解退
stack-up 层叠
stack vector 堆栈向量
stack virtual memory 堆栈虚拟存储器
stackable hub 堆叠式集线器
stacked column chart 堆积柱形图
stacked-gate avalanche-injection MOS 叠栅器件
stacked-gate avalanche injection type MOS memory (SAMOS memory) 叠栅雪崩注入 MOS 内存
stacked-gate structure 叠栅结构
stacked goal 堆栈目标
stacked graph 叠式图表
stacked integrated circuit 层叠集成电路
stacked interrupt 堆栈式中断
stacked job 堆栈作业
stacked job processing 堆栈式作业处理
stacked multiprocessor 堆叠多元处理器
stacked optical disk(SOD) 光盘堆
stacked solar cells 叠层太阳电池
stacked wafer module 叠片组件
stacker 堆卡箱
stacking 堆垛,层积
stacking order 堆叠顺序
STACKS 栈帧设置
STAE(Set Task Abnormal Exits) 置任务异常出口

STAE(Set Task Asynchronous Exit) 置任务异步出口
STAE(Specify Task Asynchronous Exit) 特定任务异步出口
staff 本部门人员;五线谱
staff size 人员规模
stage 级;登台
stage interface simulator 级间接口模拟器
stage space 阶段空间,站空间
staged circuit switching 分级电路交换
staged scanning 隔行扫描
staged search strategy 分阶段搜索策略
stagger 参差,摆差
staggered circuits 参差调谐电路
staggered-contact connector 错列接触件连接器
staggered input network 交叉输入网络
staggered mesh 交叉网格
staging 登台
staging adapter 进级适配器,登台适配器
staging disk 梯级磁盘
staging driver 登台驱动器
staging drive group 登台驱动器组
staging effective data rate 数据有效登台率
staging error 登台错误
staging hierarchy 分级体系结构
staging library 分级库
staging memory 分级存储器
staging pack 登台磁盘组
stagnant module 不动模型
stagnant part 不动部分
stagnation flow 滞流
STAI(SubTask Abend Intercept) 子任务异常终止
stain 着色
staining technique 染色法
stainless steel 不锈钢
stair stepping 阶梯效应
staircase generator 阶梯波发生器
staircase iteration 阶梯迭代
staircase signal 阶梯信号
staircasing 阶梯状的
stale line 失效链
stale NFS file handle 失效 NFS 文件句柄

stamp 冲压
stamp coupling 特征耦合
stamp floating 固化浮动
stamp problem 邮票问题
stamper 压模
stamping 冲压片
stand-alone 单独的,独立的
stand-alone capability 独立运行能力
stand-alone computer 独立计算机
stand-alone concentrator 独立线路集中器
stand-alone data-processing system 独立数据处理系统
stand-alone display 独立显示器
stand-alone emulator 独立仿真程序
stand-alone entry 独立项目
stand-alone executive 独立执行程序
stand-alone function 独立函数
stand-alone intelligent terminal 独立智能终端
stand-alone interface 独立接口
stand-alone interactive terminal 独立交互终端
stand-alone logon 独立登录
stand-alone machine 独立作业机器
stand-alone microcomputer system 独立微型计算机系统
stand-alone modem 外接式调制解调器
stand-alone network system 独立网络系统
stand-alone object 独立对象
stand-alone package 独立包
stand alone point of sale terminal 独立销售点终端
stand-alone printer 独立打印机
stand-alone procedure 独立过程
stand-alone program 独立程序
stand-alone shell 独立命令解释程序
stand-alone software aids 独立软件辅助程序
stand-alone system 单机系统,独立系统
stand-alone terminal 独立终端
stand-alone terminal component 独立终端部件
stand-alone utility 单机应用
stand-alone word-processing equipment 独立字处理设备
stand-by 备用,辅助(凡 standby)

standalone 独立的,单独的(见 stand-alone)
standard 标准
standard activity limit 标准活动极限
standard analyzer 标准分析程序
standard application library 标准应用程序库
standard assembly module 标准组装模块
standard atmosphere 标准大气层
standard background system 标准后台系统
standard blank 标准间隔
standard block 标准块
standard burst 标准位串
standard bus system 标准总线系统
standard byte I/O bus 标准字节输入/输出总线
standard candle 标准烛光
standard card enclosure 标准卡片盒
standard cell 标准单元;标准电池
standard character 标准字符
standard circuit simulator 标准电路仿真程序
standard classification list 标准分类表
standard CMOS setup 标准 CMOS 设置
standard code for information interchange 信息交换标准代码
standard color 标准色
standard column width 标准列宽
standard communication link 标准通信链路
standard communication protocol 标准通信协议
standard communication subsystem 标准通信子系统
standard compiler default 标准编译程序默认选项
standard component 标准元件
standard conforming program 标准相容程序
standard contents table 标准内容表
standard context 标准上下文
standard control logic structure 标准控制逻辑结构
standard converter 标准转换器
standard coordinate 标准坐标

standard data exchange 标准数据交换
standard data format 标准数据格式
standard data interchange 标准数据交换
standard data interface 标准数据接口
standard data set 标准数据集
standard declaration 标准说明「法
standard deduction method 标准演绎
standard default 标准默认选项
standard deviation 标准偏差
standard deviation in population 总体标准偏差
standard disk pack 标准盘组「式
standard display format 标准显示格
standard distortion 标准畸变
standard distribution list 标准分配表
standard electronic module program 标准电子模块化程序
standard electronic package 标准电子组件
standard enforcer 标准强制实施程序
standard error 标准误差
standard error recover procedure 标准误差校正过程
standard external file 标准外部文件
standard fiber module 标准光纤模组
standard file 标准文件
standard fixed-length record 标准定长记录
standard flowchart symbol 标准流程图符号
standard font 标准字体
standard form 标准形式
standard format 标准格式
standard FORTRAN 标准 FORTRAN 语言
standard function 标准函数
Standard Generalized Markup Language (SGML) 标准通用标记语言
standard grammar 标准文法
standard graph 标准图形
standard handler 标准处理程序
standard hardware interface program 标准硬件接口程序
standard I/O interface 标准输入输出接口
standard identifier 标准标识符
standard input device 标准输入设备

standard input file 标准输入文件
standard input/output interface 标准输入/输出接口
standard instruction set 标准指令集
standard interface adapter 标准接口适配器
standard interrupts 标准中断
standard job model 标准作业模型
standard key 标准键
standard label(SL) 标准标号
standard language 标准语言
standard language symbol 标准语言符号
standard layout 标准布局
standard length 标准长度
standard library 标准库
standard line format 标准行格式
standard lookup 标准查看方式
standard macro 标准宏
standard master terminal 标准主终端
standard mathematics function 标准数学函数
standard memory interface 标准内存接口
standard memory location 标准存储单元
standard memory unit 标准内存单元
standard mode 标准模式
standard modular interface 标准模块接口
standard modular system 标准模块系统
standard modular system card 标准模块系统插件卡
standard multigrid method 标准多网格法
standard multimedia device controls 标准多媒体设备控制
standard NCCF mode 标准网络通信控制设施方式,标准 NCCF 方式
standard network architecture 标准网络体系结构
standard noise temperature 标准噪声温度
standard normal deviate 标准正态偏离
standard normalized form 标准规格化形式
standard notation 标准记数法
standard objects 标准对象
standard operating procedure (SOP) 标准操作过程
standard operation 标准运算
standard operator 标准算符
standard option 标准选件
standard output device 标准输出设备
standard package 标准组件;标准信息包
standard package protocol 标准信息包协议
standard palette 标准调色盘
standard parameter passing 标准参数传递
standard pattern 标准模式,标准样式
standard peripherals 标准外围设备
standard postlude 标准尾
standard precision 标准精度
standard prelude 标准序
standard print file 标准打印文件
standard priority 标准优先权
standard procedure 标准过程
standard processing mode 标准处理模式
standard profile selection 标准轮廓选择
standard program 标准程序
standard program method 标准程序法
standard RAM 标准随机存取存储器
standard read/write memory 标准读写存储器
standard reduction 标准归约
standard reference surface 标准盘面
standard report generator 标准报表生成程序
standard segment 标准段
standard serial program 标准串行程序
standard session protocol 标准对话协议
standard setup 标准设置
standard source 标准光源;标准信号源
standard subroutine 标准子例程
standard subset 标准子集合
standard symbol list 标准符号表
standard system action 标准系统操作
standard system program 标准系统程序
standard system scanner 标准系统扫描程序
standard tape 标准磁带
standard test 标准测试
standard test-tone power 标准音测试

功率
standard text file 标准文本文件
standard tool kit 标准工具箱
standard tooling 标准工艺装备
standard type 标准类型
standard UNIX kernel 标准 UNIX 内 「核
standard vector high-level language 标准向量高级语言
standard virtual machine 标准虚拟机
standard warranty 标准保修
standard width 标准宽度
standardization 标准化,规格化
standardization pulse 标准脉冲
standardize 标准化,规格化
standardized benchmark 标准化基准测试程序
standardized documentation 标准化文档编制
standardized normal distribution 标准化正态分布
standardized option 标准化选择
standardized program 标准化程序
standardized random variable 标准化随机变量
standardized synthetic module 标准化合成模块
standardizing mail gateway 标准化邮件网关
standardizing number 标准化数
standardizing order 标准化指令
standby 待命,备用
standby application 备用,待用
standby block 备用块
standby channel 备用信道
standby circuit 备用电路
standby computer 备用计算机
standby current 维持电流
standby equipment 备用设备
standby facility 备用设备
standby maintenance 辅助维护,例行维护
standby mode 备用模式
standby power 维持功率;备用电源
standby power system(SPS) 备用电源系统
standby-ready-acknowledgement signal 备用链路就绪证实信号 「号
standby-ready signal 备用链路就绪信

standby redundancy 备用冗余
standby register 备用寄存器
standby replacement redundancy 备用替换冗余
standby replacement redundancy system 备用替换冗余系统
standby system 备用系统
standby time 备用时间
standby time-out 备用超时
standby unattended time 闲置时间
Stanford University Network(SUN) SUN 公司(美)
standing instruction 现行指令 「位
standing-on-nines carry 逢九跳跃进
standing wave 驻波
standoff 孤立,低消
star 星形
Star AR3240 Star AR3240 打印机
star architecture 星形体系结构
star configuration 星形配置
star connect 星形连接
star coupler 星形耦合器
Star CR3240 Star CR3240 打印机
star expansion 星形展开
star graph mapping 星形图映射 「图
star interconnection graph 星形互连
star mode distributed programming 星形分布式程序设计
star network 星形网络
star program 星级程序,高质量程序
star topology 星形拓扑
STARCOS STARCOS 智能 IC 卡
StarLAN 星形局域网
starlet-architecture 小星形结构
STARN STARN 计算机
start 启动,起动,起点
start at 起始于
start bit 启始位,起始位
start button 启动按钮
start delay 启动延迟
start delimiter 启始分界符
start dialing signal 启拨信号,请发码信号,R1 信号
start distance 启动距离
start element 启始码元,起始信号元
start formula 初始值公式
start from 起始于
start I/O instruction 启动输入/输出

命令

start input-output 启动输入/输出
start key 起始关键字;启动键
start knob 启动按钮
start logging 开始登录
start message 起始报文
start new column 开始新列
start node 起始节点
start of block(SOB) 数据块开始
start of chain 链起始
start of format(SOF) 格式开始
start of format control 格式控制开始
start-of-header(SOH) 标题起始符
start of heading 标题开始
start-of-heading character(SOH) 标题起始符
start-of message(SOM) 消息开始码
start-of message indicator 消息开始指示符
start of page 页始
start of pulsing signal 脉冲起始信号
start of text character(STX) 正文开始字符
start of track controller 磁道起始控制器
start option 起始任选项
start page number 起始页号
start-pending 初始搁置
start-recording signal 记录开始信号
start search 开始搜索
start signal 起始信号
start significance 起始有效位
start state 起始状态
start-stop 起止式
start-stop apparatus 起止式设备
start-stop character 起止字符
start-stop distortion 起止失真
start-stop envelope 起止信号封包
start-stop equipment 起止式设备
start-stop margin 起止失真容限
start-stop modulation 起止式调制
start-stop multivibrator 单稳态多谐振荡器
start-stop restitution 起止式解调
start-stop signal 起停式信号
start-stop signal generator 起止式信号发生器
start-stop supervisor 起止管理程序
start-stop synchronization 起止式同步
start-stop time 起停时间
start-stop transmission 起止式传输
start-stop zone 起停区
start switch 启动开关
start symbol 起始符号
start time 启动时间
start-up 启动,起动
start up directory 启动目录
start-up disk 启动盘
start-up procedure 启动过程
start-up protocol 启动协议
start-up screen 启动屏幕
start value 起始值,初始值
started 已启动的
starter formula 初始值公式
starting address 起始地址
starting algorithm 起步算法
starting autosave 开始自动保存
starting frame delimiter 起始帧定界符
starting location 开始位置
starting point 起始点
starting pulse 启动脉冲
starting signal 启动信号
starting slope 起点斜率
starting solution 初始解
starting time 启动时间
starting torque 启动转矩
starting value 初值
starting vector 起始向量
startup application 启动应用程序
STARTUP. CMD 启动命令文件
startup disk 启动盘
startup option 初始选项
startup position 启动后初始位置
startup ROM 启动只读存储器
starvation 饥饿
starvation-free solution 满意方案
state 状态
state analyzer 状态分析程序
state approach 状态逼近
state assignment 状态赋值,状态分配
state box 状态框
state code 状态码
state component 状态分量
state control 状态控制
state control register 状态控制寄存器
state description scheme 状态描述模

式
state diagram 状态图
state equation 状态方程
state equivalence table 状态等价表
state estimation algorithm 状态估计算法
state event 状态事件
state feedback decoupling 状态反馈去耦
state grammar 状态文法
state graph 状态图
state indicator 状态指示符
state machine 状态机
state matching condition 状态匹配条件
state matrix 状态矩阵
state matrix method 状态矩阵法
state minimizing 状态极小化
state observability 状态可观测性
state of knowledge 知识状态
state of rest 休止状态
state of the art 最新技术水平
state of the art component 目前最新元件
state of the art technology 当前最新技术
state of value 值状态
state probability 状态概率
state procedure 状态过程
state queue 状态队列
state recognition 状态识别
state reduction 状态简化
state register 状态寄存器
state restoration 状态复原
state simulator 状态仿真程序
state space 状态空间
state space construction 状态空间构建
state space searching 状态空间搜索
state stack 状态堆栈
state symbol 状态符号
state table 状态表
state table analysis 状态表分析
state transition algorithm 状态转换算法
state transition diagram 状态迁移图
state transition matrix 状态转移矩阵
state transition table 状态转换表
state variable 状态变量
state vector 状态向量
stated set 陈述集
statement 语句;陈述;命题

statement algebra 命题代数
statement body 语句体
statement calculus 命题演算
statement classification 语句分类
statement error diagnostics 语句错误诊断
statement function 语句函数
statement function name 语句函数名
statement function reference 语句函数引用
statement identifier 语句标识符
statement interlude 语句中间段
statement label 语句标号
statement label array 语句标号数组
statement label assignment statement 语句标号赋值语句
statement label constant 语句标号常量
statement label data 语句标号数据
statement label expressing 语句标号表达式
statement label identifier 语句标号标识符
statement label variable 语句标号变量
statement law 命题法则
statement logic 命题逻辑
statement minimal slice 最少语句片
statement mix 语句混合体
statement number 语句编号
statement number column 语句编号列
statement of control 控制语句
statement option 语句可选项
statement part 语句部分
statement prelude 语句序
statement rearrangement 语句重排
statement renumber 语句重编号
statement-response pair 陈述-响应对
statement separator 语句分隔符
statement sequence number 语句序列号
statement substitution 语句替换
statement substitution 语句部分替换
statement terminator 语句结束符
statement verb 语句动词
static 静态的,不变的
static allocation 静态内存分配,静态定位
static analysis 静态分析
static analysis tool 静态分析工具
static analyzer 静态分析程序

static architecture 静态体系结构
static array 静态数组
static attribute 静态属性
static binding 静态结合,静态绑定
static bipolar memory 静态双极内存
static block structure 静态分程序结构
static branch instruction 静态转移命令
static buffer 静态缓冲器
static buffer allocation 静态缓冲器分配
static buffering 静态缓冲
static cell 静态单元
static characteristic 静态特性
static check 静态检验
static color 静态颜色
static constant 静态常数
static control 静态控制
static convergence 静态会聚
static data area 静态数据区
static data item 静态数据项
static data stream computer 静态数据流计算机
static data structure 静态数据结构
static declaration 静态说明
static display 静态显示
static display image 静态显示图像
static dump 静态转储
static electricity 静电
static equilibrium analysis 静态平衡分析
static error 静态误差,静态错误
static evaluation 静态评估
static evaluation value 静态求值
static expression 静态表达式
static file 静态文件
static filtering 静态筛选
static gain 静态增益
static handling 静态处理
static hazard 静态冒险
static home page 静态主页
static image coding 静态图像编码
static image communication 静态图像通信
static index 静态索引
static induction 静态归纳法
static input characteristic 静态输入特性
static interconnection network 静态连接网络
static link 静态链
static link library 静态链接库
static linking 静态链接
static load 静态负载
static load balancing 静态负载平衡
static magnetic cell 静态磁性单元
static mapping 静态映射
static mathematics model 静态数学模型
static memory 静态内存
static memory card 静态内存卡
static memory cell 静态内存单元
static memory interface 静态内存接口
static mode check 静态方式检查
static model 静态模型
static modulation 静态调制
static MOS circuit 静态 MOS 电路
static MOS RAM 静态 MOS 随机存取存储器
static multifunctional pipeline 静态多功能流水线
static network 静态网络
static object 静态对象
static parameter 静态参数
static parallelization 静态并行化
static physical model 静态物理模型
static pipeline 静态流水线
static pressure flying head 静压浮动磁头
static print out 静态打印
static priority 静态优先权
static problem 静态问题
static property measurement 静态性能量度
static protection 静态保护
static RAM(SRAM) 静态 RAM
static read/write memory 静态读写存储器
static redundancy 静态冗余
static redundancy system 静态冗余系统
static refresh 静态刷新
static register 静态寄存器
static relocation 静态重定位
static reset 静态复位
static resource 静态资源
static route 静态路由
static scheduling 静态调度
static schema 静态模式

static scheme　静态方案
static scope check　静态作用域检验
static screen　静电屏蔽
static segment attribute　静态图块属性
static semantic　静态语义
static semantic analysis　静态语义分析
static semantic rule　静态语义规则
static set　静态集
static shape control　静态形状控制
static shift register　静态移位寄存器
static single assignment(SSA)　静态单一赋值
static skew　静态扭斜
static stimulus tester　静态刺激因素测试仪
static storage　静态存储器
static storage allocation　静态存储器分配
static storage cell　静态存储单元
static store　静态存储
static table　静态表
static table searching　静态表检索
static test　静态测试
static test pattern sequence　静态测试模式序列
static text　静态文本
static topology　静态布局,静态结构
static tree table　静态树表
static turtle　静态龟标
static type checking　静态类型检查
static variable　静态变量
static video　静态视频图像信号
statically determinate structure　静态确定结构
statically indeterminate structure　静态不确定结构
staticize　静止化
staticizer　串并行数据转换器
station　站,台
station arrangement　站布局
station buffer unit　站缓冲单元
station clock　站时钟
station cluster　站群集器
station code　站代码,局代码
station control block(SCB)　站控制块
station deactivation　站停止活动
station error detection　站差错检测
station failure　站失灵

station-keeping satellite　位置保持卫星
station lock　站锁定
Station Management(SMT)　站管理
station master log　站主登录
station monitor　工作站监测程序
station name　工作站名称
station restriction　站点限制
station selection code　站选择码
station-to-station service　站到站业务
stationary channel　平稳信道
stationary continuous wave　平稳连续波
stationary domain　固定域
stationary flow　平稳流
stationary free boundary problem　固定自由边界问题
stationary fuzzy process　平稳模糊过程
stationary Gaussian process　平稳高斯过程
stationary information source　稳定信息源
stationary iterative method　定常迭代法
stationary language　平稳语言
stationary message source　稳定消息源
stationary paper carrier　静态输纸器
stationary point　平稳点
stationary process　平稳过程
stationary random function　平稳随机函数
stationary random process　平稳随机过程
stationary satellite　静止卫星
stationary state　平稳状态
stationary state probability distribution　定态概率分布
stationary stochastic sequence　平稳随机序列
stationary value　稳态值
stationary wave　驻波
stationary white noise ground　平稳白噪声背景
stationary work-load　平稳工作负荷
statistical　统计的;统计变异性
statistical analysis　统计分析
Statistical Analysis System(SAS)　统计分析系统
statistical arbitration　统计判优法
statistical burst-correction　统计突发纠正

statistical calculation 统计计算
statistical characterization 统计特征
statistical computer 统计计算机
statistical correlation 统计相关
statistical data base 统计数据库
statistical data recorder(SDR) 统计数据记录器
statistical decision method 统计判定法
statistical decision theory 统计判定论
statistical dependence 统计相关
statistical design 统计设计
statistical differencing 统计差值法
statistical distribution 统计分布
statistical equalizer 统计均衡器
statistical error 统计误差
statistical estimator 统计估算程序
statistical expectation 统计期望
statistical failure model 统计失效模型
statistical hypothesis 统计假设
statistical inference 统计推理
statistical interpretive language(STIL) 统计解释语言
statistical library 统计程序库
statistical linearization 统计线性化
statistical machine 统计机
statistical mask 统计模板
statistical method 统计方法
statistical model 统计模型
statistical multiplexer 统计式多路转换器
statistical multiplexing 统计式多路复用
statistical parameter 统计参数
statistical pattern recognition 统计模式识别
statistical phenomena 统计现象
statistical quality control 统计质量控制
statistical reception 统计接收
statistical reasoning 统计推理
statistical reduction 统计归约
statistical sample 统计样本
statistical simulation 统计仿真
statistical software 统计软件
statistical survey database 统计调查数据库
statistical test 统计测试
statistical test model 统计测试模型
statistical time-division multiplexing 统计式时分多路复用
statistical tolerance limit 统计容差极限
statistical validity 统计真实性
statistical variance 统计方差
statistics 统计学
statistics file 统计文件
stator 定子;定片
status 状态
status area 状态区
status attribute 状态属性
status available 状态有效
status bar 状态栏
status bar text 状态栏说明文字
status bit 状态位
status bit handshaking 状态位联络
status channel 状态通道
status code 状态码
status display 状态显示
status field 状态字段
status flag 状态标志
status indicator 状态指示符
status information 状态信息
status information frame(SIF) 状态信息帧
status input instruction 状态输入指令
status line 状态行
status map 状态图
status of processor 处理机状态
status parameter 状态参数
status poll 状态轮询
status queue 状态队列
status register 状态寄存器
status report frame(SRF) 状态报告帧
status routine 状态例程
status save area 状态保护区
status scan 状态扫描
status signaling 状态信令
status strobe 状态选通
status switching 状态转换
status switching instruction 状态切换指令
status word 状态字
status word program 状态字程序
status word register 状态字寄存器
stay on top 保持在前面
STB(STroBe) 选通
STD bus 工业控制总线标准
STDA(StreetTalk Directory Protocol)

StreetTalk 目录协议
stderr (Unix)标准误差
stdin (Unix)标准输入
STDM(Statistical Time Division Multiplexing) 统计时分复用
stdout (Unix)标准输出
STE(Serviceability level indication processing Time sharing option Element) 可服务性级别标志处理分时选项元素
STE(Subscriber Terminal Equipment) 客户终端设备
STE bus STE 总线
steady 稳定的,恒稳的
steady current 稳定电流
steady load 恒稳负载
steady signal 稳定信号
steady-state 稳定状态
steady state characteristic 稳态特性
steady state condition 稳态条件
steady state deviation 稳态偏差
steady state error 稳态误差
steady state hazard 稳态冒险
steady state optimization 稳态优化
steady state output 稳态输出
steady state signal 稳态信号
steady state solution 稳态解
stealing cycle 窃用周期
Steelman language requirement "钢人"语言要求
steep pulse 陡前沿脉冲
steepest ascent 最陡上升
steepest descent method 最快下降法
steepness 陡度
steepness of pulse edge 脉冲边沿陡度
steerability 可操纵性
steerable 可操纵的,可控制的
steering 操纵,控制;导引
steering command 导引命令
steering order 导引指令
steering signal 导引信号
Steiner minimal tree 斯坦纳最小树
Steiner tree 斯坦纳树,最小连接树
Steiner vertex 斯坦纳顶点
stencil 模板,漏印板
stencil bit 特征位
stencil film 漏印薄膜
stencil master 漏印原版

stencil plate 模板
STEP(Safeguard Test and Evaluation Program) 安全测试和评价程序
STEP(Specification Technology Evaluation Program) 规范技术评价程序
STEP(STandard for the Exchange and Presentation of product model date) 产品模型数据的表达和交换标准
step 步;步长
step and repeat camera 分步重复照相机
step-and-repeat equipment 分步光刻机
step and repeat process 分步重复处理工艺
step backward 步退
step-by-step carry 逐位进位
step-by-step control 步进式控制
step-by-step operation 步进操作;单步操作
step-by-step simulation 步进仿真
step-by-step switch 步进开关
step-by-step system 步进制系统
step change 阶跃变化
step control 分级控制
step counter 步进计数器;操作步计数器
step divide 步进式除法
step-down 步降,步降,逐级下降
step expression 步长表达式
step forward 步进
step function 阶跃函数
step in 向内步进
step-index fiber 阶跃折射率光纤
step-index profile 阶跃折射率分布
step invariance 阶跃不变性
step logic 步进逻辑
step macro 单步执行宏
step multiplier 步进式乘法器
step multiply 步进式乘法
step out 失步;向外步进
step parameter 步长参数
step pulse 阶跃脉冲
step rate 步进速率
step-recovery diode 阶跃恢复二极管
step refinement program 逐步求精程序
step response 阶跃响应
step restart 作业步再启动
step-servo motor 步进伺服电机
step signal 阶跃信号

step size 步长
step-size change 步长改变
step stress test 级增应力试验
step-switch converter 步进式转换器
step-temperature-stress testing 步进式升温加电试验
step through 单步通过
step tracking 单步跟踪
step type multimode fiber 阶跃型多模光纤
step-up 上升,升压
step value 步长值
step waveform 阶跃波形
step width 步宽,步长
stepped addressing 步进式寻址
stepped start-stop transmission system 分步起-止式传输系统
stepper 步进控制器
steppers 分步光刻机
stepper motor 步进电机,步进马达
stepper motor control 步进电机控制
stepping 步进
stepping motor 步进电机
stepping register 步进寄存器
stepping technique 步进法
stepping through code 单步执行代码
stepwise 逐步的,步进的
stepwise debugging 逐步调试
stepwise refinement 逐步求精法
stepwise regression 逐步回归「法
stepwise subdivided method 逐步对分
steradian 立体角单位
stereo 立体声;立体的,立体感觉的
stereo image representation 立体图像表示法
stereo-lithography 立体成形术
stereogram 立体图
stereomapping 立体映射
stereoscope 立体视镜
stereopsis 立体观察
stereoscopic 立体的,体视的
stereoscopic effect 立体效果
stereoscopic picture 立体图像
stereovision 立体视觉
sterilization 消毒
sterilize 消毒
sterilizer 消毒程序
sticker 磁带头/尾标记

sticking 趋稳性,坚持性
stickup initial 突显的段首
Sticky key 粘滞键
sticky mode 粘滞模式
stiff 刚性的,非弹性的「题
stiff initial value problem 刚性初值问
stiffness matrix 刚度矩阵
still file 静态文件
still frame 静止帧
still image 静态图像
still-image coding 静态图像编码
still optimizable loop 尚可优化循环
still-picture broadcasting(SPB) 电视静止图像广播「缩
still picture compression 静止图像压
still video 静态视频图像
still video capture adapter 静态视频图像捕获卡
stimulated emission 受激发射
stimulation 激励
stimulating signal 激励信号
stimulator 激励器
stimulus-response table 激励响应表
stitch bond 点焊
stitch bonding 针脚式接合法
stitching image 缝合图像,拼接图像
STK(STacK) 堆栈
STL(Schottky Transistor Logic) 肖特基晶体管逻辑
STLP(Secure Transport Layer Protocol) 传输层安全协议
STM(Synchronous Transfer Mode) 同步传输模式
STMPX(Statistical Time-Division MultiPleXer) 统计时分多路转换器
STN(STatioN) 站,工作站
STNT(Switched Telephone Network Interface) 交换电话网络接口
stochastic 随机的
stochastic adaptive optimization 随机自适应优化
stochastic approximation 随机逼近
stochastic augmented transition network 随机增广转移网络
stochastic automaton 随机自动机
stochastic behavior 随机特性
stochastic bottleneck 随机瓶颈
stochastic complexity 随机复杂性

stochastic context-free grammar 随机上下文无关文法
stochastic control model 随机控制模型
stochastic controllability 随机可控性
stochastic convergence 随机收敛
stochastic decision process 随机决策过程
stochastic deformation model 随机变形模型
stochastic dependence 随机相关性
stochastic dynamic programming 随机动态规划
stochastic error-correction 随机纠错
stochastic estimator 随机估计量
stochastic filter 随机过滤器
stochastic finite element method 随机有限元法
stochastic finite-state language 随机有限状态语言
stochastic game 随机博弈,随机对策
stochastic grammar 随机文法
stochastic high-level Petri nets (SHLPN) 随机高级 Petri 网
stochastic incentive problem 随机诱因问题
stochastic independent model 随机独立模型
stochastic indexed production 随机索引产生式
stochastic iteration algorithm 随机迭代算法
stochastic learning automaton 随机学习自动机
stochastic loading 随机加载
stochastic mapping 随机映射
stochastic marked graph 随机标识图
stochastic maximum principle 随机极大值原理
stochastic model 随机模型
stochastic multivariable system 随机多变量系统
stochastic neural net 随机神经网络
stochastic noise 随机噪声
stochastic optimal control 随机调优控制
stochastic optimization 随机优化
stochastic Petri nets(SPN) 随机 Petri 网
stochastic process 随机过程
stochastic programming 随机规划

stochastic pushdown automaton 随机下推自动机
stochastic relation 随机关系
stochastic relaxation 随机松驰
stochastic retrieval 随机检索
stochastic search pattern 随机搜索模式
stochastic shortest route 随机最短路由
stochastic simulation 随机模拟
stochastic stability 随机稳定性
stochastic syntax analyzer 随机语法分析程序
stochastic transition matrix 随机转移矩阵
stochastic Turing machine(STM) 随机图灵机
stochastic variable 随机变量
stock 库存;股票
stock control utility 库存控制应用程序
stone 微粒,小粒子
STOP 停机命令
stop 停止,停机
stop-and wait 停止等待
stop-and-wait ARQ 等待式反馈重传纠错
stop and wait protocol 停止等待协议
stop bit 停止位
stop button 停止按钮
stop calculation 停止计算
stop character 停止字符
stop code 停止码
stop cylinder press 停辊压力
stop distance 停转距离
stop element 停止码元
stop instruction 停机指令
stop key 停止键
stop list 停止列表;非引用词表
stop logging 停止登录
stop loop 中止循环
stop macro 停止宏
stop notice 停机通知
stop order 停机命令
stop page 停用页
stop pulse 停止脉冲
stop record 停止录制
stop recording signal 停止记录信号
stop signal 停止信号
stop statement 停止语句
stop time 停止时间

stop value 终止值
stop word 无用词,除外词
stopped job 被停止作业
stopped state 停机状态
stopper 停机地址
stopping criteria 停机判据
stopping signal 停止信号
storability 可存储性
storable value 可存储值
storage 存储器
storage access 存储器存取
storage access conflict 存储器存取冲突
storage access network(SAN) 存储访问网络
storage access width 存储器存取宽度
storage address display light 存储器地址显示灯
storage addressing error 存储器寻址错误
storage administration 存储器管理
storage administration scheme 存储器管理方案
storage allocation 存储器分配
storage allocation algorithm 存储器分配算法
storage allocation location 存储器分配单元
storage allocation of compiler 编译程序的存储器分配
storage allocation routine 存储器分配例程
storage allocator 存储器分配程序
storage area 存储区域
storage bit 存储位
storage block 存储块
storage bounds checking 存储边界检验
storage buffer 存储器缓冲器
storage capacity 存储容量
storage capacity unit 存储容量单位
storage card 存储器插卡
storage cell 存储单元
storage center 存储中心
storage channel 存储器通道
storage charge 存储电荷
storage chip 存储芯片
storage class 存储类
storage compaction 存储压缩
storage component 存储部件

storage contents 存储内容
storage control unit 存储器控制单元
storage controller definition record (SCDR) 内存控制器定义记录
storage cycle 存储周期
storage cycle time 存储周期时间
storage data 存储数据
storage data transfer rate 存储数据传送速度
storage decoder 存储译码器
storage density 存储密度
storage descriptor 存储描述符
storage device 存储设备
storage dump 存储转储
storage element 存储元件
storage exchange 存储器内容交换
storage facility 存储设备
storage file segment 存储文件段
storage fill 存储器填充
storage flip-flop 存储触发器
storage format 存储格式
storage fragmentation 存储碎片
storage head 存储头
storage hierarchy 分级存储体系
storage hole 存储孔
storage image 存储器映像
storage indicator 存储指示器
storage interference 存储冲突,存储干扰
storage interleaving 存储器交叉存取
storage key 存储键
storage keyboard 存储键盘
storage layout 存储器布局
storage level 存储级
storage level representation 存储级的表示法
storage life 存储寿命
storage limit register(SLR) 存储器界限寄存器
storage link pointer 存储器链指针
storage list 存储器列表
storage load module 存储器载入模块
storage location 存储位置,存储单元
storage location selection 存储器地址选择
storage management 存储器管理
storage management service 内存管理服务

storage management strategy 内存管理策略
storage map 存储图
storage mapping 存储器分布
storage mark 存储标记
storage medium 存储媒体
storage modification machine 存储修改机器
storage module 存储模块
storage module device(SMD) 存储器模块装置
storage module drive interface 存储器模块驱动接口
storage normalizer 存储归一化器
storage operation 存储器操作
storage organization 存储器组织
storage oscilloscope 存储示波器
storage output 存储器输出
storage overlay 存储覆盖
storage overlay area 存储覆盖区
storage parity 存储器奇偶校验
storage pattern 存储模式
storage plate 存储板
storage pool 存储池
storage print program 存储打印程序
storage processor 存储器处理机
storage protection 存储器保护
storage protection key 存储保护键
storage queue 存储队列
storage reconfiguration 存储器重配置
storage recovery 存储恢复
storage redundancy 存储冗余
storage region 存储区
storage register 存储寄存器
storage resolver 存储分解器
storage resource 存储器资源
storage ring FEL 存储环自由电子激光器
storage rule 存储规则
storage sampling oscilloscope 存储取样示波器
storage scheme 存储方案
storage selection circuit 存储器选择电路
storage-sharing architecture 共享存储器体系结构
storage site 存储位置
storage site assignment 存储位置指定
storage slice 存储片
storage space 存储空间
storage space-time product 存储时-空乘积
storage stack 存储堆栈
storage state 存储器状态
storage structure 存储器结构
storage swapping 存储交换
storage switch 存储器开关,存储器切换
storage system 存储器系统
storage system IOPro 存储系统输入输出处理
storage tab setting 存储制表置位
storage table 存储表
storage tape 存储带
storage technology 存储技术
storage temperature 存储温度
storage time 存储时间
storage tube 存储管
storage unit 存储单元
storage utilization 存储器利用率
storage volatility 存储器易失性
storage volume 存储卷
storage within the network 网上存储器
storage writing speed 存储器写入速度
storatron 存储管
store 存储,保存
store access controller 存储存取控制器
store access cycle 存储访问周期
store access time 存储器取数时间
store accumulator 存储累加器
store-and-forward 存储转发法
store-and-forward data transmission 存储转发式数据传输
store-and-forward message switching center 存储转发消息交换中心
store-and-forward mode 存储转发方式
store-and-forward network 存储转发网络
store-and-forward packet 存储转发信息包
store-and-forward replication 存储转发复制器
store-and-forward switching 存储转发式交换
store-and-forward switching center 存储转发交换中心
store block 存储块

store controller 存储控制器
store controller data 存储控制器数据
store cycle time 内存周期时间
store drive circuit 存储器驱动电路
STORE function 存储函数
store instruction 存储指令
store interface link 存储器接口链接
stored life 存储寿命
store location 存储单元
store logic panel 存储逻辑面板
store loop 存储回路
store loop driver 存储回路驱动器
store macro 保存宏
store management 存储管理
store protection 存储保护
store shuffling 存储混洗
store support procedure 存储支援程序
store-through cache 经高速缓冲器存储
store violation 存储违规
stored carry 存储进位
stored clause 存储子句
stored data description language 存储数据描述语言
stored format instruction 存储格式指令
stored logic array 存储逻辑阵列
stored logic computer 存储逻辑计算机
stored logic control 存储逻辑控制
stored matrix 存储矩阵
stored paragraph 已存段
stored procedure application 存储过程应用程序
stored program computer 存储程序计算机
stored program concept 存储程序概念
stored-program control 存储程序控制
stored program controlled electronic telephone switching system 存储程序控制电子电话交换机
stored program monitor 存储程序监视器
stored record 存储记录
stored reference test 存储参考测试
stored response testing 存储响应测试
stored routine 存储例程
storing device 存储设备
storing hybrids 存储混合微电路
storyboard 记事板,场记板
storyboarding 记事板制作

stowed name 复合名
STP(Stereoscopic Television) 立体电视
STP(System Termination Program) 系统终止程序
STR(Segment Table Register) 段表寄存器
STR(STatus Register) 状态寄存器
stradle erase head 跨立式抹除磁头
straggler message 离散消息
straight beam 直射束;平行光束
straight binary 直接二进制
straight binary code 直接二进制码
straight-forward network 直通网络
straight-forward routine 简明程序
straight insertion sorting 直接插入排序
straight line block 直线式程序块
straight line code 直线式程序,无转移代码
straight line coding 直接式编程方法
straight line process 直线进程
straight merge sort program 直接合并分类程序
straight platen 平面字辊
straight selection sorting 直接选择排序
straightforward 直接的,简单的,无分支转移的
strain 应变,形变
strain-bias 应变偏置
strain-displacement relation 应变位移关系
strain gauge 应变仪
strain relief clamp 电缆紧固卡子
strain-softening material 应变软化材料
strain space formulation 应变位移关系
strand 导线束
strap 跨接,短接
strapping table 短接表
strategic computer program 战略计算机计划
strategic decision 战略性决策
Strategic Defense Initiation(SDI) 战略防御倡议计划
strategic information 战略信息
strategic layer 战略层
strategic military communication system 战略军用通信系统
strategic planning 战略计划

strategy 策略,战略
strategy-independent restructuring 与策略无关的重构法
strategy-oriented restructuring 面向策略的重构法
stratification 层次化;成层法
stratified 分层的,层化的
stratified indexing and retrieval 分层索引与检索
stratified language 分层语言,排元语
stratified polymorphism 分层多形性
stratified sampling 分层取样
Stratus Stratus 容错计算机
stray 杂散的,寄生的
stray capacitance 杂散电容,寄生电容
stray current 寄生电流
stray electron 杂散电子
stray field 杂散场
stray inductance 寄生电感
stray loss 杂散损耗
stray parameter 杂散参数
stray pointer 迷失指针
stray radiation 杂散辐射
streak 拖尾;条纹
streak image 拖尾图像
streak reduction 减少条纹(拖尾)
stream 流,数据流
stream access 流式存取
stream attribute 数据流属性
stream bit transmission 位流传输
stream cartridge tape drive 数据盒式磁带机
stream cipher 流式密码
stream computing 流式计算
stream connector 流连接器
stream control block 流控制块
stream data transmission 流式数据传
stream encryption 数据流加密
Stream end 流尾端
stream handler 流处理器
stream handler command(SHC) 流处理器命令
Stream head 流首端
stream line 流线
stream manager 流管理器
stream manager helper 流管理器帮助
stream object 流对象
stream option 流选择项

stream-oriented file 流式文件
stream-oriented input/output 流式输入/输出
stream-oriented transmission 流式传
stream parallelism 流并行性
stream processing mechanism 流处理机制
stream programming interface(SPI) 流编程接口
stream protocol 流协议
stream protocol control block(SPCB) 流协议控制块
stream routing 流路由选择
stream socket 流套接口
stream transmission 流式传输
streamer 流式磁带机
streaming data procedure(SDP) 流式数据过程
streaming data protocol 流式数据协
streaming output 流式输出
streaming tape drive 流式磁带机
Streamline Streamline 程序(Adobe).
Streamline 流线型的
STREAMS (Unix)STREAMS 体系结构
STREAMS-based pipe 基于 STREAMS 的管道
street address matching system(SAMS) 街道地址匹配系统
StreetTalk StreetTalk 全局命名服务(Banyan)
strength 强度
strength-member optical cable 加固芯光缆
strength-of operation 运算强度
strength optimization 强度优化
strength reduction 强度削减
strength reduction pass 强度削减扫描
strength reduction processor 强度削减处理程序
stress 应力
stress analysis 应力分析
stress anisotropy 应力各向异性
stress-free 无应力
stress testing 应力测试;强化测试
stressless 无应力的
stretch 拉伸,伸展
stretch circuit 展宽电路

stretch mode 伸展模式
stretch-surface recording 延展表面记录方式
stretch to window 拉伸到满窗口
strict language 严格语言
stretching 拉伸,伸展,扩展,展开
stretching function 扩展函数
stria 擦痕;条纹
strict 严格的
strict deterministic grammar 严格确定性文法
strict digraph 严格有向图
strict local maximum 严格局部极大[值]
strict root condition 严格根条件
strict sequential order 严格时序
strict upper bound 严格上界
strictly fuzzy convex set 强模糊凸集
strictly unilateral digraph 严格单侧有向图
strictly weak digraph 严格弱有向图
strictness 严格性
stride 跨距
strike 划掉,删除
strike control 击打控制
strikeout 划掉;(在文字中间)加删除[线]
strikethrough 划掉;加删除线
striking 打印锤
Strim 100 Strim 100 计算机辅助设计软件
string 字符串;串操作命令
string array 字符串阵列
string assignment 串赋值
string attribute 串属性
string break 串截断
string built-in function 串内建函数
string command 串命令
string comparison 字符串比较
string concatenation 串连接,串并置
string constant 串常数
string control byte 串控制字节
string data 串式数据
string denotation 串标志
string editing 串编辑
string encoding 串编码
string expression 串表达式
string format item 字符串格式项
string formula 字串公式
string frame 串帧

string grammar and high dimensional grammar 串文法和高维文法
string item 串项
string length 串长度
string list 串列表
string manipulation 串操作
string matching 字符串匹配
string matching with d differences d项差异的字符串匹配
string of bit 位串
string of character 字符串
string operator 串运算符
string option 串选项
string pattern matching 串模式匹配
string pointer 串指针
string processing 串处理
string processing language 串处理语[言]
string processing system (SPS) 串处理系统
string quotes 串引号
string reduction 串归约
string reduction computer 串归约计算[机]
string reduction machine 串归约机
string resource 字符串资源
string searching algorithm 字符串搜索算法
string sort 串排序
string sorting 串排序,串分类
string space 字符串空间
string statement 字符串处理语句
string storage representation 字符串存储表示法
string symbol 串符号
string table 串表
string too long 字符串太长
string type 串类型
string-valued expression 串值表达式
string variable 字符串变量
strip 条,片,带;剥离
strip code 条形码
strip line 带状线
strip mapping 带状映射
strip record 条纹记录
strip width 条纹宽度
strip transmission line 带状传输线
stripe set 带区集
striping 横线;盘组
stripline 带状线

stripline connector 带状线接插件
stripper 剥线器
stripping 剥皮；去膜
STRIPS STRIPS(机器人求解)系统
STROBE STROBE语言
strobe 选通
strobe lamp 闪光灯
strobe pulse 选通脉冲
strobe release time 选通释放时间
strobe signal 选通信号
strobing gate 选通门
stroke 笔划，线段；击键
stroke analysis 笔划分析
stroke center line 笔划中线
stroke character generator 笔划字符发生器
stroke counting 笔划数
stroke device 笔划记录设备
stroke display 笔划显示
stroke edge 笔划边缘
stroke edge irregularity 笔划边缘不规则性
stroke encoding 笔划编码
stroke extraction 笔划提取；往返行程
stroke font object 笔划字体对象
stroke generator 笔划发生器
stroke linkage rule 笔划连接规则
stroke order 笔划顺序
stroke pattern 笔划模式
stroke position stability 笔划位置稳定性
stroke press 笔划力度
stroke recognition 笔划识别
stroke segmentation 笔划分段
stroke set 笔划集
stroke weight 笔划轻重
stroke width 笔划宽度
strong 强的
strong consistency 强一致性
strong convergence 强收敛
strong coupling 强耦合
strong definition 强定义
strong extremum 强极值
strong independence number 强独立数
strong interaction 强相互作用
strong intersymbol dependence 码间强相关性
strong lock 强锁定

strong n-coloring 强 n-着色
strong reference 强引用
strong stability 强稳定性
strong stability number 强稳固数
strong type 强类型
strong type checking 强类型检查
strong type concept 强类型概念
strong type language 强类型语言
strong typing 强类型化
strongest element 最强元素
strongly chromatic number 强着色数
strongly connected component algorithm 强连通支算法
strongly connected digraph 强连通有向图
strongly connected region 强连通域
strongly connected sequential machine 强连接时序机
strongly consistent program 强相容规划
strongly convex problem 强凸问题
strongly implicit procedure 强隐性过程
strongly NP-complete problem 强 NP 完全问题
strongly stable set 强稳固集
STRUC(STRUCture) 结构
struct 结构，结构体
structural analysis 结构分析
structural approach to pattern recognition 模式识别结构法
structural compound index 结构复合索引
structural damping model 结构阻尼模型
structural decision problem 结构化决策问题
structural decision tree 结构判定树
structural dependence 结构相关性
structural description 结构描述
structural design criterion 结构设计准则
structural diagram 结构图
structural dynamic response 结构动态响应
structural dynamics 结构动力学
structural element 结构元素
structural equivalence 按结构等价
structural frame design 结构框架设计
structural graph-oriented digital simula-

tion 面向结构图的数字仿真
structural identification 结构标识
structural idex structure 结构化索引结构
structural induction 结构归纳法
structural information 结构信息
structural instability 结构不稳定性
structural integrity checking 结构完整性检验
structural membrane 结构薄膜
structural mode control system 结构化控制系统
structural modeling system 结构化建模系统
structural network analysis program 结构网络分析程序
structural nonlinear 结构非线性
structural operational semantics 结构式操作语义学
structural optimization design 结构优化设计
structural pattern recognition 结构模式识别
structural performance 结构性能
structural property 结构特性
structural reanalysis 结构再分析
structural redundancy 结构冗余
structural refinement 结构精炼
structural response 结构响应
structural state model 结构状态模型
structural statistical simulation 结构统计仿真
structural variation 结构变分
structural vibration analysis 结构振动分析
structural weight optimization program 结构加权优化程序
structure 结构
structure analysis method 结构分析法
structure animation 结构动画制作
structure array 结构数组,结构阵列
structure assignment 结构赋值
structure assignment statement 结构赋值语句
structure attribute 结构属性
structure building language 构造语言
structure category 结构目录
structure chart 结构图
structure component 结构成分
structure composition 结构综合
structure constant identifier 结构常量标识符
structure dash 结构冲突
structure declaration 结构说明
structure decomposition 结构分解
structure definition 结构定义
structure description 结构描述
structure design 结构设计
structure design specification 结构设计规格说明书
structure diagram(SD) 结构图
structure discrimination 结构判别
structure display 结构显示
structure editor 结构编辑程序
structure element 结构元素
structure expression 结构表达式
structure factor 结构因子,构造因数
structure field 结构域
structure flowcharts 结构流程图
structure-free name management 无结构名字管理
structure function paradigm 结构函数范例
structure grammar 结构文法
structure idealization 结构理想化
structure initialization 结构初始化
structure length 结构长度
structure level number 结构层数
structure matrix 结构矩阵
structure member 结构构件
structure member operator 结构成员运算符
structure modeling 结构建模
structure modify 结构修改
structure name 结构名
structure node 结构节点
structure of arrays 数组结构
structure operation 结构操作
structure option 结构选择项
structure page 结构页面
structure pattern recognition 结构模式识别
structure pointer operator 结构指针运算符
structure prediction 结构预测
structure-preserved error-correcting tree

automaton 结构保持误差校正树状自动机
structure qualification 结构限定
structure reference 结构引用
structure representation 结构表示法
structure restoration 结构复原
structure retrieval 结构检索
structure schema 结构模式
structure sharing 结构共享
structure specification 结构说明
structure specify descriptor 结构说明描述符
structure stability 结构稳定性
structure storage allocation 结构存储器分配
structure symbol 结构符号
structure synthesis 结构合成
structure table 结构表
structure tag 结构标记
structure tree 结构树
structure type 结构类型
structured analysis and design technique(SADT) 结构分析设计技术
structured approach 结构法
structured assembler 结构化汇编程序
structured chart 结构化图表
structured coding 结构化编码
structured data 结构化数据
structured data model 结构数据模型
structured decision 结构化决策
structured descriptor 结构化描述符
structured design 结构化设计
structured design phase 结构设计阶段
structured documentation 结构化文档编制
structured editing 结构编辑
structured editor 结构编辑程序
Structured English Query Language(SEQUEL) 结构化英语查询语言,SEQUEL语言
structured extraction 结构化抽取
structured gate array 结构化门阵列
structured graphics 结构化图形
structured hardware design 结构化硬件设计
structured index 结构化索引
structured induction 结构归纳法
structured knowledge engineering 结构化知识工程
structured language 结构化语言
structured layout 结构化布局
structured logic editor 结构化逻辑编辑器
structured loop control 结构循环控制
structured macro cross assemble 结构化宏交叉汇编
structured matching 结构化匹配
structured message passing 结构化消息传递
structured microprogram 结构化微程序
structured multiprocessor system 结构化多处理机系统
structured object 结构化对象
structured object representation 结构化对象表示法
structured object representing 结构化对象表示
structured operating system 结构化操作系统 「统
structured paging system 结构分页系
structured parallel computing 结构化并行计算
structured program 结构化程序
structured programming 结构化程序设计
Structured Query Language(SQL) 结构查询语言
structured representation 结构化表示
structured segment matching 结构化分段匹配
structured specification 结构化说明
structured statement 结构语句
structured system analysis 结构化系统分析
structured system design 结构化系统设计
structured system implementation 结构化系统实现
structured type 构造类型
structured variable 结构变量
structured walk-through 结构化走查
structured wiring 结构化布线
structuring data design 结构数据设计
structuring document 结构化文档
structuring element 结构化元素

structuring module 结构化模块
STTL(Schottky Transistor-Transistor Logic) 肖特基TTL电路
stty(set terminal type) (Unix)设置终端类型
STU(Streaming Tape Unit) 流式磁带机
stub 占位程序,承接软件;抽头
stub card 存根卡片
stub development 占位程序开发
stub manager 占位程序管理器
stub network 存根[承接]网络
stuck-at fault 固定型故障
stuck-at-one fault 固定为"1"的故障
stuck-at-zero fault 固定为"0"的故障
stuck-open fault 固定开路型故障
stuck sender 维持发送器
student model 学生模型
student-problem score table 学生问题分数表
STUDENT system 学生系统
stuffable digit time slot 可填充数字时隙
stuffer 填充项;填充器
stuffing 填充项;填充材料
stuffing character 填充字符
stuffing digit 填充数字
stuffing rate 填充率
stuffing ratio 填充比率
stuffing service digit 填充服务数字
stunt box 特技箱,阻打器
stuttering clock 结巴时钟
STW(Shiyan Tongxin Weixing) 实验通信卫星
STX(Start of TeXt character) 文本开始字符
STX/ETX(Start of TeXt and End of TeXt) 报文开始与结束
style 风格,式样
style definition dialog box 样式定义对话框
style definition list 样式定义列表
Style Manager 式样管理器
style name 式样名
style sheet 格式底稿,式样表单
style variability 风格可变性
stylized font 特殊风格字体
stylus 指示笔;触针
stylus density 记录针密度
stylus pen 记录笔;触针
stylus printer 针式打印机
SU(Switch User) 切换当前用户环境
SU/ST(Single-User/Single Task) 单用户/单任务
SUB(SUBtraction) 减法操作
Subactivity 子活动
subaddress 分地址
suballocated file 子分配文件
suballocation 子分配
subalphabet 部分字母表
subapplication 子应用程序
subarchitectural interface 分体系结构接口
subarea (SNA)子域,子区
subarea address 子域地址
subarea ID 子域标识符
subarea link 子域链路
subarea node 子域节点
subarea physical unit(PU) 子域物理单元
subassembly 组件,部件
subband 子频带
subblock 子块;划分子块
subbox 小格子
subcarrier 副载波
subcarrier frequency modulation 副载波频率调制
subcarrier oscillator 副载波振荡器
subcase 子情况
subcategory 子种类
subchannel 子通道,子信道
subchannel interface 子通道接口
subchassis 副底盘
subchunk 子块
subclass 子类
subclassing 继承
subclone 亚克隆
subcode 子代码
subcommand 子命令
subcompiler 子编译程序
subcomponent 子分量
subconfiguration 子格局
subconsistent 次相容的
subcontrol station 分控制站
subcovering 子覆盖
subcritical 亚临界的
subcycle 子循环

subdatabase 子数据库
subdirectory 子目录
subdivision 子部分
subdispatch queue 区域调度排队
subdomain 子区域,子域
subedge connector 片状插座
subentry 分入口;次索引项
subentry address 分入口地址
subenvironment 子环境
subevaluation 子求值
subexpression 子表达式
subfamily 子系列,子族
subfield 子字段,子域
subfield code 子字段代码
subfield definition 子字段定义
subfile 子文件
subfile definition 子文件定义
subfile system 子文件系统
subfolder 子文件夹
subformula 子公式
subframe 子帧
subfunction 子函数
subgeneration 子代
subgoal 子目标
subgoal deduction 子目标演绎
subgoal induction 子目标归纳
subgoal node 子目标节点
subgradient 子梯度
subgraph 子图
subgraph homeomorphism problem 子图同胚问题
subgroup 子群,子组
subhost 副机,从机
subhypergraph 子超图
subindex 子索引
subinterval 子区间
subitem 子项,部分项
subject 主体,主动实体;主题
subject authority list 主题规范表
subject copy 主件副本
subject drift 主题偏离
subject heading 主题标目
subject matter of patent protection 专利保护的客体
subject of entry 主体项,项的主体
subject program 源程序
subject selector 主题选择器
subject tree 主题树

subjective assessment of TV picture quality 电视图像质量主观评价
subjective fidelity criteria 主观保真度标准
subjob 子作业
subjunction gate 禁止门
subkey 子密钥
sublanguage 子语言
sublattice 子格,亚点阵
sublayer 子层
sublevel 子级,子层
sublibrary 子库
sublimation 升华,精炼化
subline 辅助线
sublink 子链路
sublist 子列表
sublock 子锁
sublogic 子逻辑
subloop 子环路,子回路
submarining 潜没
submask bit 子屏蔽位
submenu 子菜单
submethod 子方法
submicron 亚微米
submilliwatt circuit 亚毫瓦电路
subminiaturization 超小型化
submission 提交
submission envelope 提交包封
submit state 提交状态
submodular phase 子模块可执行程序
submonitor 子监督程序
subnanosecond 亚毫微秒
subnet 子网
subnet address 子网编址
subnet mask 子网掩码
subnet number 子网编号
subnet routing 子网寻址
subnetwork 子网络
subnetwork access protocol (SNAP) 子网存取协议
subnetwork failure 子网失效
subnode 子节点
subobject 子对象,子目标
suboptimal filter 次最优滤波器
suboptimization 次优化
subordinate 属体
subpage 子页
subpage frame 子页框

subpanel 副面板,辅助面板
subparameter 子参数
subpicture 子图
subplan 子规划
subpool 子池
subpool queue 子池队列
subpool segment 子池段
subport 子端口
subproblem 子问题
subproblem graph 子问题图
subproblem tree 子问题树
subprocess 子进程
subprogram 子程序
subprogram reference 子程序引用
subprogram statement 子程序语句
subqueue 子队列
subregion 子区域
SUBRG(SUBscript RanGe) 下标范围
subroutine 子例程
subroutine address stack 子例程地址堆栈
subroutine call 子例程调用
subroutine call instruction 子例程调用指令
subroutine data area 子例程数据区
subroutine entry address 子例程入口地址
subroutine for special use 专用子例程
subroutine instruction 子例程指令
subroutine library 子例程库
subroutine name 子例程名
subroutine nesting 子例程嵌套
subroutine package 子例程包
subroutine parameter 子例程参数
subroutine reentry 子例程重入
subroutine reference 子例程引用
subroutine return 子例程返回
subroutine statement 子例程语句
subroutine storage 子例程存储器
subroutine subprogram 子例程的辅程序
subroutine table 子例程表
subroutine test 子例程检验
subroutinization 子例程化
subsampling 二次取样;(从样品中再抽取的)子样品
subschema 子模式
subschema description entry 子模式描述体

subschema entry 子模式体
subschema name 子模式名
subschema section 子模式节
subscribe 预约,加入
subscriber 用户,订户
subscriber access terminal 用户访问终端
subscriber-busy signal 用户占线信号,忙音
subscriber call charge meter 用户呼叫计费表
subscriber calling rate 用户呼叫率
subscriber channel in a multiplexed DTE/DCE interface 多路复用DTE/DCE接口的用户信道
subscriber identification 用户标识
subscriber interface 用户接口
subscriber line 用户线
subscriber line busy 用户线占线
subscriber line out of order 用户线失效信号
subscriber line PE 用户线路图像元素
subscriber line signaling 用户线信令
subscriber loop 用户回路
subscriber number 用户号码
subscriber optical loop 用户光纤环路
subscriber or terminal category PE 用户或终端类别图像元素
subscriber response unit 用户应答器
subscriber's facsimile station 用户传真机
subscriber's line 用户专用线路
subscriber's loop 用户回路
subscriber set 用户设备
subscriber stage 用户级
subscriber terminal 用户终端
subscriber traffic rate 用户业务率
subscriber trunk dialing 用户中继线拨号
subscript 下标,脚注
subscript bound 下标界
subscript character 下标字符
subscript depth 下标深度
subscript expression 下标表达式
subscript list 下标列表
subscript name 下标名
subscript operator 下标算子
subscript out of bound 下标越界

subscript pair 下标偶
subscript position 下标位置
subscript qualified name 下标限定名
subscript quantity 下标量
subscript range 下标范围
subscript reference 下标引用
subscript statement 下标语句
subscript value 下标值
subscript variable address 下标变量地「址
subscripted data-name 下标数据名
subscripted variable 带下标变量
subscripting 带下标的
subscription 登录,注册
subsegment 子段
subsequence 子序列
subsequence counter 子序列计数器
subsequence table 子序列表
subsequent 后续的,相继的
subsequent address message(SAM) 后续地址消息
subsequent counter 子序列计数器「域
subsequent parameter field 后续参数
subsequent signal unit(SSU) 后续信号单元
subsequent start up 相继启动
subset 子集;子设备
subset closure 子集闭包
subset construction 子集构造
subset language 子集语言
subset of array 数组子集
subsetting 子集构造
subsidence 下沉,凹陷
subsidiary 辅助的,附加的
subsidiary condition 辅助条件
subsidiary field of one bit 一位附属字
subsidiary file 附属文件 「段
subsidiary goal 附属目标
subsidiary overflow table 附加溢出表
subsidiary pointer 附属指示字,附属指针
subsidiary table 附属表
subsidiary wire 辅助线,附加线
subsidiary word 附加字
subspace 子空间
subspace iteration 子空间迭代
SUBST(SUBSTitute) 代入,替换
substantive input 直接输入
substep 分步,子步

substitutability 可代换性,可置换性
substitute 替换,置换
substitute character(SUB) 替换字符
substitute mode 替换模式,置换方式
substitute table 替换表
substituted font 替代字体
substitution 置换,替代
substitution box 替换框
substitution cipher 代替密码
substitution error 替换错误
substitution instance 置换实例
substitution list 代换表,替换表
substitution permutation network 代入置换网络
substitution principle 代换原理
substitution variable 置换变量
substrate 基底,衬底
substrate feed logic(SFL) 衬底馈电逻辑
substrate interconnection 衬底互连
substring 子串
substring expression 子串表达式
substring reference 子串引用
substring variable 子串变量
substructure 子结构
substructure condensation 子结构缩合作用
substructure synthesis method 子结构合成法
subsubstitution 子代换
subsumed clause 被包含子句
subsumption 归类,包含
subsumption principle 包孕原理
subsystem 子系统
subsystem communication 子系统通信
subsystem component 子系统部件
subsystem controller 子系统控制器
subsystem controller definition record (SCDR) 子系统控制器定义记录
subsystem definition 子系统定义
subsystem definition statement 子系统定义语句
subsystem description 子系统描述
subsystem failure 子系统故障
subsystem generation 子系统生成
subsystem identification 子系统标识
subsystem information retrieval facility 子系统信息检索设施

subsystem interface 子系统接口
subsystem library(SLIB) 子系统库
subsystem maintenance 子系统维护
subsystem support services 子系统支援服务程序
subtable 子表
subtabulation 子表制作
subtask 子任务
subtask control block(SCB) 子任务控制块
subtask initiator 子任务初始化程序
subtasking 子任务分配
subtelephone frequency 亚音频
subterm 子项
subthreshold region 亚阈区
subtitle 副标题
subtotal 小计,分类汇总
subtrace 部分追踪
subtrace fault 部分跟踪故障
subtrace list 部分跟踪列表
subtract 减
subtract time 减法运算时间
subtract with borrow 带借位减
subtracter 减法器;减数
subtraction 减法
subtraction circuit 减法电路
subtraction with serial operation 串行减法
subtractive mixture 减色混合
subtractive primaries 相减基色,相减原色
subtractive process 腐蚀法,消去法
subtractor 减法器
subtrahend(SBHD) 减数
subtree 子树
subtree order 子树次序
subtype 子类型
subunit 子单元
subvalue 子值
subvoice channel 亚音频信道
subvoice-grade channel 亚音频级信道
subwidget 子窗口部件
success audit 成功审核
success ratio 成功率
successful block transfer 成功的信息块传送
successful call 成功呼叫
successful disengagement 成功脱离,成功释放
succession 逐次性,继承性
successive 逐次的,相继的
successive approximation 逐次逼近法
successive approximation A/D converter 逐次逼近模/数转换器
successive approximation A/D with software 软件实现的逐次逼近模/数转换器
successive carry 顺序进位
successive character 相继字符
successive displacement method 逐次位移法
successive node 后继节点
successive overrelaxation 逐次超松弛
successive projective 逐次投影
successive refinement 逐步求精
successive substitution 逐次代换法
successive value 逐次值
successor 后继
successor address 后继地址
successor block 后继块
successor instruction 后继指令
successor listing 邻接顺序法
successor matrix 后继矩阵
successor node 后继节点
successor tree 后继状态树
sudden death 突然死亡
sudden failure 突然失效
sudden ionospheric disturbance 电离层突然骚扰
sufficient condition 充分条件
sufficient estimation 充分估计
sufficient sequence 完全序列
sufficient set 充分集
suffix 后缀,词尾
suffix array 后缀阵列
suffix-free grammar 后缀无关文法
suffix notation 后缀表示法
suffix operator 后缀算符
suffix partition 后缀划分
suffix tree 后缀树
suffix truncation 截尾,后缀截去
suggested design 建议设计方案
suggested protocol 建议规程
suitability 适合性
suitable parallel structure 适量并行结构
suitcase 附属软件箱

suite 成套程序
SuiteSpot SuiteSpot 群件(Netscape)
sum 和数;求和
sum accumulator 求和累加器
sum check 累加和检验
sum check digit 累加和校验数字
sum clause 求和子句
sum digit 和数位
sum module-two 模 2 和
sum module-n 模 N 和
sum operand 求和操作数
sum of product form "与或"式
sum out gate 和数输出门
sum output 和数输出
sum pulse 求和脉冲
sum readout 和数读出
sum rule 求和规则
sum storage 和数内存
sum string 合串
summand 被加数
summarization 摘要,概述,总结
summarize 摘要,汇总
summarizing instruction 汇总指令
summary 摘要,概要,总结
summary below data 汇总结果在数据下方
summary cell 累加和单元格
summary counter 累加计数器
summary design 概要设计
summary info 摘要信息
summary journal 累计日志
summary list 汇总列表
summary record 累计记录
summary recorder 总结记录器
summary report 简明报告,汇总报表
summary table 汇总表
summary tag-along sort 沿用标志累加分类
summation 求和,累计
summation check 和数校验
summation cipher 求和密码
summation instruction 求和指令
summation sign 累加符号
summator 加法器,求和器
summed current 总和电流
summer 加法器,求和器
summing amplifier 求和放大器
summing circuit 加法电路

summing integrator 求和积分器
summing junction 求和连接器
summing point 求和点,相加点
summing unit 加法单元
Summit Summit 计算机
SUN(Stanford University Network) SUN 公司(美)
SUN Microsystems Company SUN 微系统公司
sun outage 日致中断
sun sensor 太阳能传感器
SUN workstation SUN 工作站
SunDisk SunDisk 公司
SunGKS library Sun 图形核心系统库
SunINGRES system INGRES 数据库 Sun 版本
sunken 凹下
sunlight battery 太阳电池
sunlight-viewable display 日光下可视显示器
SunOS Sun(Unix)操作系统
Sunpics Sunpics 公司
SunScreen Sun 过滤器
SUNSITE(SUN Software Information and Technology Exchange) SUN 软件信息与技术交换
Sunspot 太阳黑子
super-class 超类
super clean room 超净室
super database tool package 超级数据库工具包
super floppy 超级软盘
super impose 重叠,叠加
super-large-scale integration (SLSI) 超大规模集成
super-large-scale integrated circuit(SLSI) 超大规模集成电路
super mass capacity transmission 超大容量传输
super master group 超主群
super miniature disk 超小型磁盘
super network server 超级网络服务器
super parallel machine 超级并行机
super set 超集
supper structure 上层结构
super vertex 超顶点
super video graphics array(SVGA) 超级视频图形阵列

SUPERB (SUPrenum parallelizER Bonn) SUPERB 并行化支援系统（波恩大学）
superbar 上划线
superblock 超块
SuperCalc SuperCalc 表格软件（Sorcim）
superchip 超级芯片
superchip RAM 高密度芯片随机存取存储器
superclass 超类
supercombinator 超组合子
supercompaction 超级压缩
supercompilation 超级编译
supercomputer 超级计算机
supercomputer architecture 巨型机体系结构
supercomputing 超级计算
superconducting 超导性的
superconducting cell 超导单元「机
superconducting computer 超导计算
superconducting computer device 超导计算机元件 「线
superconducting delay line 超导延迟
superconducting device 超导器件
superconducting memory 超导存储器
superconducting quantum interface device 超导量子接口设备
superconductive material 超导材料
superconductive tunnel effect 超导隧道效应
superconductivity 超导性 「器
superconductivity memory 超导存储
superconductor 超导体
superconsistent 超相容的
superconvergence 超收敛性
supercritical 超临界的
SuperDrive 超级驱动器（苹果）
superencryption 超级保密
SuperFAT (OS/2)超级文件分配表
superfiche 超缩微平片
superfluous 冗余的,多余的
superfluous rule 冗余规则
superfluous term 冗余项
supergroup 超群
supergroup distribution frame (SGDF) 超群分配机构（配线架）
supergroup link 超群链路
supergroup section 超群段
supergroup translating equipment 超群转换设备
superheat 过热
superhigh frequency(SHF) 超高频
superhigh speed computer 超高速计算
superimpose 重叠,叠放 「机
superimposed circuit 重叠电路
superinjection 超注入
superior 主体
SuperKey 超键
superluminescent diode 高亮度发光二极管
supermachine 巨型计算机
supermarket subsystem definition record 超级市场子系统定义记录
supermastergroup 超主群
supermastergroup link 超主群链路
supermastergroup section 超主群段
supermemory gradient method 超存储梯度法 「机
supermicro computer 超级微型计算
superminifloppy disk 超小型软盘
supermode laser 超模激光器
supernetwork media 超网络媒体
supernode 超节点
superpacket 复合信息包
SuperPaint SuperPaint 绘图软件
superpipeline 超级流水线
superpipelined computer 超级流水线计算机
superpipelined superscalar computer 超级流水线超标量计算机
superpipelining 超级流水线处理
superpipelining processor 超级流水线处理器
superplane 超平面
superplastic sheet forming 超塑性板料成形
superposed circuit 叠加电路
superposed ringing 叠加振铃
superposition 叠加
superposition display 叠加显示
superposition theorem 叠加定理
superposition of signal 信号叠加
superposition principle 叠加原理
superpotential 过电压
superrefraction 超折射

superresolution restoration 超分辨率恢复
supersaturated 过饱和的
superscalar 超级标量
superscalar architecture 超标量体系结构
superscalar computer 超标量计算机
superscalar processor 超级标量处理器
superscript 上标
superscript character(SPS) 上标字符
superscript height 上标高度
superserver 超级服务器
superset 超集
supersonic delay-line 超声延迟线
supersonic detector 超声检测器
supersonic flow 超声速流
SuperSparc Module 超级Sparc模块(Sun)
superstable method 超稳定法
SuperStation 超级台
supersystem 超级系统
supertext 超文本
supertwist nematic LCD 超扭曲向列型液晶显示器
superuser 超级用户
supervised classification 监督分类法
supervised learning 监督学习
supervising program 监督程序
supervising system 管理系统,监控系
supervision 监视;管理
supervisor 监督例程,监控程序
supervisor call(SVC) 监督例程调用,访管
supervisor call instruction(SVC) 监督例程调用指令,访管指令
supervisor call interrupt 监督程序调用中断
supervisor call interruption 监督器调用中断,访管中断
supervisor console 监控台
supervisor interrupt 监督例程中断,访管中断
supervisor lock 管理程序锁定
supervisor mode 管理状态,管态
supervisor mode and problem mode 监督模式与问题模式,管态与目态
supervisor option 管理员选项
supervisor overlay 管理覆盖程序
supervisor position 监视位置
supervisor process 管理进程
supervisor-privileged instruction 管理特权指令
supervisor processor 管理处理机
supervisor queue area 管理程序队列
supervisor request block 管理程序请求程序块
supervisor resident area 管理程序驻留区
supervisor state 管理状态,管态
supervisor status 监督模式,管态
supervisory 监督,监控
supervisory channel 监控通道
supervisory computer control system(SCC) 计算机监督控制系统
supervisory communication 监督通信
supervisory computer 监督计算机
supervisory console 监督控制台
supervisory control 监督控制
supervisory control computer(SCC) 监督控制计算机
supervisory control desk 控制台
supervisory control program 监督程序
supervisory control signals 管理控制信号
supervisory control system 监督控制系统
supervisory frame 监控帧
supervisory instruction 监督指令
supervisory keyboard 管理键盘
supervisory mode 管理模式,管态
supervisory printer 监控打印机
supervisory processor 监控处理机
supervisory program 管理程序,监控程序
supervisory program simulation 管理程序模拟
supervisory routine 监督例程
supervisory sequence 管理序列
supervisory service 管理服务
supervisory signal 监控信号
supervisory system 监督系统
supervisory tones 监控音调
SuperVoice SuperVoice通信管理软件
superworkstation 超级工作站
Superzapping 超级干预程序
Suppl. (Supplement) 补遗;补码

supplement file 增补文件
supplementary ground electrode 补充接地电极
supplementary information 附加信息
supplementary maintenance 补充维护
supplementary maintenance time 补充维修时间
supplementary storage 辅助存储器
supplementary subroutine 辅助子例程
supplementary telephone service 附加电话业务
supply 电源;供给
supply bay 配电架
supply line 电源线
supply main 供电干线
supply power 电源
supply-roll 供纸轴;供带盘
supply voltage 电源电压
supply voltage indicator 电源电压指示器
support 支持
support chip 支持芯片,配套芯片
support circuit 配套电路
support environment 支援环境
support hardware 支援硬件
support object 支持对象
support personnel 保障人员
support processor 支援处理器
support program 支持程序
support software 支持软件
support software package 支援软件包
support system 支持系统
supportability 可支援性
supporting file 支持文件
supporting hyperplane 支撑超平面
SUPPR(SUPPRess) 抑制,取消
suppress 抑制,消除
suppress column heading 不输出列标题
suppress endnote 取消尾注
suppress footnote 消除脚注
suppress form feed 取消进纸
suppress index order 取消索引序列
suppress line number 不输出行号
suppress zero 消零
suppressed carrier transmission system 抑制载波传输系统
suppressed clock pulse-length modulation 抑制时钟脉宽调制
suppressible character frame 可抑制字符帧
suppressing exception 消去异常
suppression 抑制,取消
suppression character 抑制字符
suppression circuit 抑制电路
suppressor 抑制器
SUPRA SUPRA 数据库(Cincom)
Suprenum Suprenum 并行巨型机
SurePoint SurePoint 销售点终端(IBM)
surface 表面,外表
surface acoustic wave delay line 声表面波延迟线
surface-acoustic-wave filter 声表面波滤波器
surface analysis 表面分析
surface barrier 表面势垒
surface channel 表面沟道
surface charge transistor 表面电荷晶体管
surface clearness 表面清洁度
surface coating 表面喷涂
surface contact hole 表面接触孔
surface contamination 表面污染
surface defect 表面缺陷
surface diffusion 表面扩散
surface element 面积元素
surface feature 表面特性
surface fitting 表面拟合
surface imperfection 表面缺陷
surface leakage 表面泄漏
surface lifetime 表面寿命
surface machining 表面加工
surface mobility 表面迁移率
surface model 曲面模型
surface modeling 曲面建模,曲面造型
surface mount component(SMC) 表面安装元件
surface-mount package(SMP) 表面安装外壳
surface mounting technology 表面安装技术
surface normal 曲面法线
surface passivation 表面钝化
surface photoelectric effect 表面光电效应
surface plasmon resonance 表面胞间

谐振
surface recombination 表面复合
surface recording 表面记录
surface rendering 表面润色；面绘制
surface representation 曲面表示法
surface resistivity 表面电阻率
surface scan 表面扫描
surface scattering 地面散射
surface servo 表面伺服
surface solid modeling 曲面实体建模
surface speed 表面速度
surface structure 表层结构
surface tension 表面张力
surface test 表面测试
surface texture 表面纹理
surface trapping 表面俘获，表面吸收
surface treatment 表面处理
surface treatment of magnetic layer 磁层表面处理
surface wave 表面波，地波
surface wave touchscreen 表面波触摸屏
surfing （网上）冲浪
surge 浪涌
surge current 浪涌电流
surge protector 浪涌保护器
surge resistance 浪涌电阻
surge suppressor 浪涌抑制器
surge voltage 浪涌电压
surge withstand resistance 抗浪涌电阻
surplus variable 过剩变量
surrounding block 外层分程序
surrounding loop 外层循环
surrounding procedure 外层过程
surveillance 监视
survey 检查，调查；测量；综述
survey article 综述文章
surveying engineering 勘测工程
survivability 存活率；残存性；耐久性
survival function 残存函数，存活率函数
survival probability 生存概率
susceptibility 磁化系数，磁化率
susceptibility to failure 故障敏化
susceptible 敏感的
suspend 挂起，暂停
suspend execution 暂停执行
suspend lock 悬锁，挂锁
suspend mode 挂起模式
suspend primitive 挂起原语

suspend time-out 挂起超时
suspendable 可挂起的，可暂停的
suspended call 挂起呼叫，暂停呼叫
suspended primitive 挂起原语
suspended process 挂起处理
suspended state 挂起状态，中止状态
suspension 挂起，中止，暂停
suspension time 挂起时间
sustained fault 持续故障
sustained oscillation 持续振荡
sustaining voltage 持续电压
SVA(Shared Virtual Area) 共享虚存
SVC(SuperVisor Call instruction) 访管调用指令
SVC(Swap Virtual Chain) 交换虚链
SVC(Switched Virtual Call) 交换虚呼叫
SVC(Switched Virtual Circuit) 交换式虚电路
SVC 76 error recording interface SVC出错记录接口
SVC interruption 访管中断
SVC routine 管理程序调用例程
SVD(Simultaneous Voice/Data) 声音/数据同时传输
SVG(Scalable Vector Graphics) 可缩放矢量图形
SVGA(Super Video Graphics Array) 超级视频图形阵列
SVID(System V Interface Definition) (UNIX)系统 V 接口定义
SVN(Switching Virtual Networking) 交换式虚拟连网
SVR4(System V Release 4 operating system) SVR4 操作系统(AT&T)
SVRB(SuperVisor call Request Block) 访管请求块
SVS(Single Virtual Storage system) 单一虚拟存储系统
SVS(Single Virtual System) 单虚系统
SVT(System Vector Table) 系统向量表
SW(ShareWare) 共享软件
SW(SWitch) 开关，交换
SWA(System Work Area) 系统工作区
SWAP(SWitching Assembly Program) 转换汇编程序
swap 调换，对换，交换

swap allocation unit 对换分配单元
swap area 交换区
swap byte 交换字节
swap channel 交换通道
swap data set control block 交换数据集控制块
swap file 交换文件
swap floppy disk 交换活动盘
swap gate 交换门
swap high-low bytes 高低字节对换
swap-in 换进,调入
swap list 对换表
swap memory 对换内存
swap mode 对换模式
swap network 交换网络
swap-out 调出,换出
swap server 交换服务器
swap set migration 对换集迁移
swap space 对换空间
swap status 交换状态
swap table 对换表
swap time 对换时间
swap volume 对换卷
swappable 可对换的,可调换的
swapper 调换器
swapping 交换,对换
swapping buffer 交换缓冲区
swapping priority 交换优先权
swapping set 对换集
SWB(Scheduler Work Block) 调度程序工作块
SWB(SoftWare Bus) 软件总线
sweep 扫描,掠过
sweep amplifier 扫描放大器
sweep circuits 扫描电路
sweep object 扫描对象
sweep phase 扫描阶段
sweep ray tracing 扫描射线跟踪
sweep record 扫描记录
sweep speed 扫描速度
sweeping beam 扫描射束
sweeping receiver 扫描接收机
sweeping scheme 扫描方案
sweetening 精选;"加甜料"
Sweettea "甜茶"(Apple 与东芝合作开发的多媒体设备系列产品的通称)
SWG(Standard Wire Gauge) 标准线径规范

SWI(SoftWare Interrupt) 软件中断
SWI(SWitch Interlock) 开关互锁
SWIFT(Society for Worldwide Interbank Financial Telecommunication) 世界银行间财经远程通信协会
SWIFT(System for Worldwide Interbank Funds Transfer) 世界性银行财务远程通信协会
swim 游动,浮动
swing 摆动;漂移
swinging arm head-positioning actuator 摆臂式磁头定位驱动器
swirls 漩涡
switch 开关;替换项;转移;翻转
switch and search capability 切换与查询能力
switch board 开关板,配电盘
switch buffer 开关缓冲器
switch chain 开关链
switch character(SW) 开关字符
switch change test 开关变换测试
switch code 转换代码
switch combination 开关组合
switch connection 交换连接
switch control computer 交换控制计算机
switch control statement 转移控制语句
switch debouncing 开关抖动消除法
switch driver 开关驱动器
switch element 开关元件
switch engine 交换引擎
switch filter 开关滤波器
switch function 开关函数
switch gap 开关间隙
switch identifier 开关标识符
switch indicator 开关指示符
switch information vector table 开关信息向量表
switch insertion 开关插入,手工插入
switch instruction 开关指令,交换指令
switch leakage current 开关漏电流
switch level simulation 开关级仿真
switch list 开关表
switch matrix 开关矩阵
switch message 开关消息
switch module 交换模块
switch network 开关网络

switch noise 开关噪声
switch-off 开关断开
switch offset voltage 开关残余电压
switch-on 接通;接向
switch order 开关指令
switch over 开关切换,转接
switch panel 配电板
switch parameter 转移参数,开关参
switch point 转换点,开关点
switch register(SR) 开关寄存器
switch setting 开关设定
switch statement 开关语句
switch-status condition 开关状态条件
switch stepping 开关步进转换
switch storage 开关存储器
switch stream 交换流
Switch Stream-1 交换数据网 1 型（英）
Switch Stream-2 交换数据网 2 型（英）
switch testing 开关测试
switch theory 开关理论
switch-timing error 开关定时误差
switch to alert view 切换至告警视图
switch train 开关序列
switch transmission 交换传输
switch tree 开关树
switch value 开关值
Switchboard 交换板
switchboard panel 配电板
switched block 开关部件,交换部件
switched circuit 交换电路
switched communication line 交换通信线路
switched communication network 转接式通信网
switched connection 交换连接
switched data transmission service 交换数据传输业务
switched diversity 交换分集
switched input value 开关输入值
switched line 交换线路
switched major node 交换主节点「网
switched message network 信息交换
switched message reformatting 交换消息再生
Switched Multimegabit Data Services (SMDS) 交换式多兆位数据服务

switched network 交换网络 「份
switched network backup 交换网络备
switched operational amplifier 开关运算放大器
switched output value 开关输出值
switched SNA major node 交换式系统网络体系结构大节点(IBM)
switched star 交换式星形网
switched telecommunication network 交换式远程通信网
switched time-division multiple-access 转接时分多址连接
switched transit country 交换转接国
switched telephone network 交换电话网络
switched virtual circuit(SVC) 交换式虚电路
switcher 转换开关
switching 开关,切换
switching algebra 开关代数
switching and message distribution center 转接及信息分发中心
switching and processing center(SPC) 交换与处理中心
switching application 交换应用
switching capacitor 开关电容
switching center 转接中心,交换中心
switching characteristic 开关特性
switching circuit 交换电路,开关电路
switching coefficient 交换系数,开关系数
switching computer 转接计算机
switching computer ports 转接计算机出入口
switching congestion 交换拥挤,转接拥挤
switching control character 开关控制字符
switching declaration 开关说明
switching delay 开关延迟,转换延迟
switching device 交换装置
switching diode 交换二极管
switching distribution 转接分配
switching element 开关元件
switching equipment 交换设备
switching equipment congestion signal 交换设备拥塞信号
switching equipment irregularities 交

换设备事故
switching error 转换错误
switching exchange 交换机,交换台
switching function 开关函数
switching group 交换群;开关组
switching matrix 开关矩阵,交换矩阵
switching mechanism 开关机构
switching module PE 交换模块图像元素
switching network 交换网络
switching node 交换节点,转接节点
switching off 开关断开
switching on 开关接通
switching pad 交换衰减器
switching path 交换通路,转接通路
switching path PE 交换路径图像元素
switching point 交换点
switching power supply 开关电源
switching processor 交换处理机
switching process time 交换时间
switching regulator 开关式稳压器
switching release 交换释放
switching space 交换空间
switching spike 开关尖峰
switching stage 交换级,开关级
switching station 切换站
switching system 交换系统
switching theory 开关理论
switching tie 交换枢纽
switching time 开关时间
switching transient 开关瞬态
switching transistor 开关晶体管
switching trunk 交换中继线
switching unit 交换单元
switching variable 开关变量
switching waveform 开关波形
switchover 转接
switchpoint 转移点,开关点
switchtail ring counter 倒环式计数器
SWS(Shift-Word Substituting) 移位字替换
Sybase Sybase数据库管理系统
Sybase Migration Program(SMP) Sybase转移计划
SyGate 代理服务器软件(SyberGen)
syllabary ordering 音节次序
syllabic companding 音节压缩扩张
syllabic compander 音节压缩扩张器

syllable 音节,拍节;拼音
syllable-based recognition 基于音节的识别
syllable chart 音节表
syllable code 拼音码
syllable dependent 音节相关
syllable hyphen character 字节连字符号
syllable independent 音节不相关
syllabus 提纲
syllogism 三段论
symbiont 共生例程,共存程序,协同程序
symbiont control 共生例程控制
symbiont control input output 共存程序控制的输入/输出
symbiont manager 共生例程管理
symbiont operation 共存程序操作
symbionts 共生体,共存程序
symbiosis 共生体;协作
symbol 记号,符号,标号
symbol address 符号地址
symbol atom 符号原子
symbol base 符号基
symbol bit 符号位
symbol class 符号类
symbol code 符号码
symbol coding 符号化编码
symbol concatenation 符号并置
symbol convention 符号应用惯例
symbol cross-reference table 符号交叉参考表
symbol definition table 符号定义表
symbol description 符号说明
symbol dictionary 符号字典
symbol editing 符号编辑
symbol error rate 符号差错率
symbol expression 符号表达式
symbol expression definition 符号表达式定义
symbol handling 符号处理
symbol input 符号输入
symbol instruction 符号指令
symbol language 符号语言
symbol level 符号级
symbol library 符号库
symbol list organization 符号表结构
symbol manipulating 符号处理

symbol manipulating language 符号处理语言
symbol manipulation 符号处理
symbol name syntax 符号名语法
symbol pair 符号对
symbol parameter 符号参数
symbol placement 符号位置
symbol plot 符号图像
symbol point 符号点
symbol printing mechanism 符号印刷机构
symbol processing language 符号处理语言
symbol queue 符号队列
symbol rank 符号排列位置
symbol rate 符号速率
symbol recognition 符号识别
symbol request 符号请求
symbol segmentation algorithm 符号分段算法
symbol sequence 符号顺序,符号序列
symbol set 符号集
symbol string 符号串
symbol string manipulation 字符串处理
symbol substitution 符号替换
symbol synchronization 符号同步
symbol table 符号表
symbol table abstraction 符号表抽象化
symbol table algorithm 符号表算法
symbol table construction 符号表构造
symbol table control 符号表控制
symbol table dump 符号表转储
symbol table element 符号表元素
symbol table entry 符号表项目
symbol table routine 符号表例程
symbol toggle 中英文符号切换
symbol token 符号信标
symbol trace 符号跟踪
symbol type 符号类型
symbol variable 符号变量
symbolic 符号的,符号化的
symbolic address 符号地址
symbolic addressing 符号编址
symbolic assembler 符号汇编程序
symbolic assembly 符号汇编
symbolic assembly language 符号汇编语言
symbolic assembly language format 符号汇编语言格式
symbolic assembly language listing 符号汇编语言列表
symbolic assembly system 符号汇编系统
symbolic automatic integrator(SAINT) 自动积分程序符号
symbolic calculus 符号演算
symbolic character 符号字符
symbolic chunk 符号组块
symbolic cluster 符号聚类
symbolic code 符号码
symbolic coding 符号编码
symbolic coding format 符号编码格式
symbolic conceptual clustering 符号概念聚类
symbolic concordance program 符号索引程序
symbolic constant 符号常量
symbolic constraint satisfaction 符号约束补偿
symbolic conversion program 符号转换程序
symbolic cross assembler 符号交叉汇编程序
symbolic data set 符号数据集
symbolic debugger 符号调试程序
symbolic debugging 符号调试
symbolic debugging program 符号调试程序
symbolic definition statement 符号定义语句
symbolic destination name 符号目标名
symbolic device name 符号设备名
symbolic dump 符号转储
symbolic editor 符号编辑程序
symbolic entry name 符号项目名
symbolic equivalent 符号等价
symbolic error correcting code 符号纠错码
symbolic evaluation 符号求值
symbolic execution 符号执行
symbolic expression 符号表达式
symbolic field 符号栏,符号字段
symbolic file 符号文件
symbolic function 符号函数
symbolic generation name 符号生成名
symbolic I/O assignment 符号输入/输出分派

symbolic I/O referencing 符号输入/输出引用
symbolic identifier 符号标识符
symbolic image description 符号图像描述
symbolic inference 符号推理
symbolic input language 符号输入语言
symbolic input/output referencing 符号输入/输出引用
symbolic instruction 符号指令
symbolic integrator 符号积分器
symbolic interpretation 符号解释
symbolic key 符号键
symbolic language 符号语言
symbolic language programming 符号语言编程
symbolic layout and compact 符号布设与压缩
symbolic library 符号库
symbolic link object 符号链接对象
symbolic logic 符号逻辑
symbolic look-up 符号查找
symbolic machine 符号机器
symbolic machine code 符号机器码
symbolic macroassembler 符号宏汇编程序
symbolic manipulation 符号处理
symbolic matching 符号匹配
symbolic math system 符号数学系统
symbolic method 符号法
symbolic microprogram 符号微程序
symbolic name 符号名称
symbolic notation 符号记法
symbolic number 符号数值
symbolic offset name 符号偏移量名
symbolic operation code 符号操作码
symbolic optimal assembly program 符号优化汇编程序
symbolic page label 符号页标记
symbolic parameter 符号参数
symbolic pattern matching 符号模式匹配
symbolic placeholder 符号占位符
symbolic pointer 符号指针
symbolic program 符号程序,符统
symbolic program system 符号程序系
symbolic programming 符号程序设计
symbolic propagation 符号传播

symbolic rank 符号位置,符号序列号
symbolic reference 符号引用
symbolic representation 符号表示
symbolic reasoning 符号推理
symbolic simplification 符号简化
symbolic stream 符号流
symbolic string 符号串
symbolic structure 符号结构
symbolic table entry 符号表项
symbolic terminal name 符号终端名
symbolic text editor 符号文本编辑程序
symbolic transformation 符号变换
symbolic unit 符号单元
symbolic unit table 符号单元表
symbolic variable 符号变量
symbolic variable definition 符号变量定义
symbolic variable definition instruction 符号变量定义指令
symbolic virtual address 符号虚地址
symbolically 用符号表示
symbolism 符号化
symbology 符号体系,符号表示
SYMBUG(SYMbolic deBUGger) 符号调试程序
SYMDEB 符号调试实用程序
symmetric 对称的
symmetric application 对称应用(程序)
symmetric axis 对称轴
symmetric binary B-tree 对称二叉B树
symmetric binary channel 二进制对称信道
symmetric binary code 对称二进制码
symmetric channel 对称通道,对称信道
symmetric closure 对称闭包
symmetric configuration 对称配置
symmetric cooperative game 对称合作对策
symmetric cryptology 对称密码制
symmetric cryptosystem 对称密码体
symmetric-difference gate 对称差门,异或门
symmetric-difference set 对称差集
symmetric digital subscriber link(SDSL) 对称数字用户线
symmetric digraph 对称有向图

symmetric eigenvalue problem 对称本征值问题
symmetric fast Fourier transformation 对称傅里叶变换
symmetric fiber 对称光纤
symmetric flow 对称流
symmetric function 对称函数
symmetric I/O unit 对称输入/输出装置
symmetric kernel 对称核
symmetric key system 对称密钥体制
symmetric linear programming 对称线性规划
symmetric linked list 对称链表
symmetric list processor 对称列表处理程序
symmetric load 对称负荷
symmetric matrix 对称矩阵
symmetric multiprocessing 对称多道处理
symmetric multiprocessor 对称式多处理机
symmetric operating system 对称式操作系统
symmetric processor 对称处理机
symmetric quadratic form 对称二次型
symmetric relation 对称关系
symmetric self-electro-optic-effect-device 对称自光电效应器件
symmetric storage configurations 对称存储器配置
symmetric successive overrelaxation 对称逐次超松驰
symmetric surveillance protocol 对称监视协议
symmetric system 对称系统
symmetric triple-diagonal matric 对称三角矩阵
symmetric Turing machine 对称图灵机
symmetric varistor 对称型压敏电阻器
symmetric video compression 对称视频压缩
symmetrical 对称的
symmetrical binary code 对称二进制码
symmetrical cable 对称电缆
symmetrical cable carrier telephone 对称电缆载波电话

symmetrical channel 对称信道
symmetrical circuit 对称回路,对称线路
symmetrical coding 对称编码方式
symmetrical I/O unit 对称输入/输出单元
symmetrical junction 对称结
symmetrical kernel 对称内核
symmetrical multiprocessing 对称多道处理
symmetrical network 对称网络
symmetrical pair cable 对称成对电缆
symmetrical pattern 对称模式
symmetrical return-to-zero waveform 对称回零波形
symmetrical transformation 对称变换
symmetry 对称性
symmetry breaking 对称性破缺
symmetry exploitation 对称性使用
symmetry of instruction operation 指令操作对称性
symmetry set 对称集
symmetry transformation strategy 对称性变换策略
Symphony "交响曲"软件包(Lotus)
symposium 论坛;论文集
symptom 故障现象,症状,迹象
SYN(SYNchronous code) 同步码
SYN character 同步字符
SYN code 同步码
SYN idle code 空转同步码
SYN register 同步寄存器
SYN synchronous idle SYN 同步空闲字符
synapse 突触
synaptic learning circuit 突触学习电路
synaptic weight 突触权值
SYNC(SYNChronize) 同步
sync 同步;同步操作
sync bit 同步位
sync byte 同步字节
sync character 同步字符
sync generator 同步信号发生器
sync level 同步电平
sync point 同步点
SyncBurst Cache 同步突发高速缓存
SYNCH(SYNchronization CHaracter) 同步字符
synch 同步信号

synch signal 同步信号
synchro 同步电机
synchro-counter 同步计数器
synchro-digital converter 同步机-数字转换器
synchro-duplexing 同步双工
synchro or resolver/digital angle converter 同步机或分解器数字轴角转换器
synchro or resolver/digital sine/cosine converter 同步机或分解器数字正弦余弦转换器
synchro to digital converter 同步机数字转换器
synchromesh 同步配合
synchronic distance 同步距离
synchronism 同时性,同步性
synchronization(SYNC) 同步
synchronization acquisition time 同步收集时间
synchronization action 同步动作
synchronization adjust 同步调整
synchronization architecture 同步体系结构
synchronization bit 同步位
synchronization circuit 同步电路
synchronization confine 同步限制
synchronization constrain 同步约束
synchronization correction signal 同步修正信号
synchronization delay 同步时延
synchronization hardware 同步硬件
synchronization information 同步信息
synchronization interface 同步接口
synchronization line 同步线路
synchronization link 同步链路
synchronization mechanism 同步机制
synchronization node 同步节点
synchronization of task 任务同步
synchronization operation 同步操作
synchronization pattern 同步模式
synchronization point 同步点
synchronization point serial number 同步点序列号
synchronization primitive 同步原语
synchronization protocol 同步协议
synchronization pulse 同步脉冲
synchronization scenario 同步化动作顺序,同步化脚本
synchronization scheme 同步方案
synchronization sequence 同步顺序,同步序列
synchronization signal 同步信号
synchronization skeleton 同步骨架
synchronization system 同步系统
synchronization tree 同步树
synchronization variable 同步变量
synchronize 同步化
synchronized clock 被同步时钟
synchronized algorithm 同步算法
synchronized network 同步式网络
synchronized non-return-to-zero change on one(SNR ZI) 同步逢"1"变化不归零制
synchronized process 同步进程
synchronized switching equipment 同步交换设备
synchronizer 同步装置
synchronizing 同步化
synchronizing buffer 同步缓冲器
synchronizing buffers queue 同步缓冲器队列
synchronizing clock 同步时钟
synchronizing cycle 同步周期
synchronizing impulse 同步脉冲
synchronizing message request 同步消息请求
synchronizing microprocessor 同步微处理机
synchronizing network 同步网络
synchronizing pilot 同步导频
synchronizing pulse 同步脉冲
synchronizing sequence 同步序列
synchronizing sequential circuit 同步时序电路
synchronizing signal 同步信号
synchronous 同步的
synchronous algorithm 同步算法
synchronous bus 同步总线
synchronous cache 同步高速缓存器
synchronous character 同步字符
synchronous circuit 同步电路
synchronous clock 同步时钟
synchronous clock operation 同步时钟作业
synchronous communication 同步通信

synchronous communication character format 同步通信字符格式
synchronous communication interface 同步通信接口
synchronous communication satellite 同步通信卫星
synchronous communication system 同步通信系统
synchronous computation 同步计算
synchronous computer 同步计算机
synchronous control 同步控制
synchronous converter 同步转换器
synchronous correction 同步修正
synchronous counter 同步计数器
synchronous cryptooperation 同步加密
synchronous data link control(SDLC) 同步数据链路控制
synchronous data message block 同步数据消息块
synchronous data network 同步数据网
synchronous data transfer 同步数据传送
synchronous data transmission 同步数据传输
synchronous data transmission channel 同步数据传输通道
synchronous demodulation 同步解调
synchronous device 同步设备
synchronous digital computer 同步数字计算机
Synchronous Digital Hierarchy(SDH) 同步数字系列
synchronous digital transmission network 同步数字传输网络
synchronous DRAM(SDRAM) 同步动态存储器
synchronous earth satellite 同步地球卫星
synchronous execution 同步执行程序
synchronous flow 同步流
synchronous height 同步高度
synchronous hypercube 同步超立方结构
synchronous idle(SYN) 同步空闲信号
synchronous idle character 同步空闲字符
synchronous input 同步输入
synchronous line control 同步线路控制

synchronous line modem 同步线路调制解调器
synchronous logic 同步逻辑
synchronous machine 同步机
synchronous machinesynchro-control 同步机械控制
synchronous margin 同步失真容限
synchronous modem 同步调制解调器
synchronous multiprocess communication 同步多进程通信
synchronous network 同步网络
synchronous operation 同步操作
Synchronous Optical Network(SONET) 光纤同步网,同步光网络
synchronous orbit 同步轨道
synchronous parallel algorithm 同步并行算法
synchronous protocol 同步协议
synchronous preprocessor 同步预处理
synchronous processor 同步处理器
synchronous pulse 同步脉冲
synchronous radar bombing 同步雷达轰炸
synchronous RAM(SRAM) 同步内存,同步存储器
synchronous receiver 同步接收机
synchronous receiver margin 同步接收机的容限
synchronous record operation 同步记录操作
synchronous refresh 同步刷新
synchronous replication 同步复制
synchronous request 同步请求
synchronous satellite 同步卫星
synchronous separator 同步分离器
synchronous sequence 同步序列
synchronous sequence cipher 同步序列密码
synchronous sequential circuit 同步时序电路
synchronous sequential system 同步时序系统
synchronous serial data adapter 同步串行数据适配器
synchronous serial data communication 同步串行数据通信
synchronous serial transmission 同步串行传输

synchronous shift register 同步移位寄存器
synchronous signal character 同步控制字符
synchronous signaling 同步信号传输
synchronous signals 同步信号
synchronous speed 同步速度
synchronous system 同步系统;同步体
synchronous terminal 同步终端机
synchronous time division multiplexer (STDM) 同步时分多路复用器
synchronous timer 同步定时器
synchronous tracking computer 同步跟踪计算机
synchronous transfer 同步传送
synchronous transmission 同步传输
synchronous transmission device 同步传动装置
synchronous transmitter receiver(STR) 同步收发机
Synchronous Transport Module(STM) 同步传输模块
synchronous working 同步工作,同步作业
synchronous tree 同步树
synclink DRAM 同步链动态 RAM
syncopated code 中略码
syncpulse 同步脉冲
syndetic 互连;交互关系
syndetic catalog 交互目录
syndrome 并发位,伴随式
syndrome code 症状码
syndrome decoding algorithm 并发位译码算法
syndrome test 症兆测试
synergetic 协同的
synergic 合作性的,协同的
synergistic 协同的,协作的
synonym 同义词
synonym chain 同义词链
synonymity 同义项
synonymous physical unit 同义物理单元
synoptic 摘要,提要
SYNR(SYNchronous Read) 同步读
syntactic analyzer 语法分析程序
syntactic analysis 语法分析
syntactic analysis phase 语法分析阶段
syntactic approach to pattern recognition 语法模式识别法
syntactic chart 语法图
syntactic correction 语法校正
syntactic definition 语法定义
syntactic description 语法描述
syntactic distance 语法距离
syntactic element 语法元素
syntactic entity 语法实体
syntactic errors 语法错误
syntactic item 语法项
syntactic mark 语法标记
syntactic matching 语法匹配
syntactic metalanguage 语法元语言
syntactic model 语法模型
syntactic parser 语法分析程序
syntactic pattern recognition 语法模式识别
syntactic picture parsing 语法图形分析
syntactic processing 语法处理
syntactic query optimization 语法查询优化
syntactic recognition 语法识别
syntactic reduction 语法归约
syntactic representation 语法表示
syntactic rule 语法规则
syntactic-semantic mechanism 语法语义机制
syntactic singularity detector 语法奇异性检测程序
syntactic source 语法源
syntactic specification 语法功能描述
syntactic stack 语法栈
syntactic structure 语法结构
syntactic token 语法标记
syntactic treatment 语法处理
syntactic tree 语法树
syntactic variable 语法变量
syntactical 语法的
syntactical predicate 语法谓词
syntax 语法
syntax analysis 语法分析
syntax analysis phase 语法分析阶段
syntax analyzer 语法分析程序
syntax box 语法框
syntax chart 语法图
syntax check 语法检验
syntax checker 语法检验程序

syntax constructor 语法构造程序
syntax definition 语法定义
syntax description 语法描述
syntax diagram 语法图
syntax diagram form(SDF) 语法图格式
syntax-directed compiler 面向语法的编译程序
syntax-directed editor 面向语法的编辑器
syntax-directed recognition algorithm 面向语法的识别算法
syntax domain 语法域
syntax driven parser 语法驱动分析程序
syntax driven interpreter 语法驱动解释程序
syntax error 语法错误
syntax format 语法格式
syntax graph 语法图
syntax language 语法语言
syntax node 语法节点
syntax-oriented compiler 面向语法的编译程序
syntax-oriented recognition algorithm 面向语法的识别算法
syntax-oriented translator 面向语法的翻译程序
syntax parser 语法分析器
syntax parsing 语法分析
syntax rule 语法规则
syntax recognizer 语法识别例程
syntax rules 语法规则
syntax-semantic tradeoff 语法-语义权衡
syntax test program 语法检查程序
syntax transducer 语法转换程序
syntax tree 语法树
synthesis 合成,综合
synthesis database 综合数据库
synthesis of the object program 目标程序合成
synthesis rule 合成规则
synthesized attribute 综合属性
synthesized image 合成图像
synthesized signal generator 合成信号发生器
synthesizer (多媒体)合成器
synthesizer bank 合成器组
synthesizer emulation 合成器仿真

synthetic address 合成地址
synthetic benchmarks 人为合成基准程序
synthetic display 合成显示
synthetic dynamic display 综合动态显示
synthetic grammar 合成文法
synthetic image 合成图像
synthetic instruction 合成指令
synthetic job parameter 综合作业参数
synthetic language 合成语言,人工语言
synthetic program method 合成程序法
synthetic reasoning 综合推理
synthetic test program 综合检测程序
synthetic voice 合成语音
synthetic workload 合成工作负载
SYNW(SYNchronous Write) 同步写
SYS(SYStems) 系统,体制
SYS.COM 系统转移
SYS volume 系统卷
SYSCILM(SYStem Core Image Library Maintenance Program) 系统核心图像库维护程序
SYSCON(SYStem CONtrol) 系统控制
SYSDEF(SYStem DEFinition) 系统定义
SYSGEN(SYStem GEneration) 系统生成
SYSIN(SYStem INput) 系统输入
SYSINFO Tool 系统信息工具
SYSLIB(SYStem LIBrary) 系统库
SYSLIB(SYStem relocatable LIBrary) 系统浮动程序库
SYSLIB(SYStem Subroutine LIBrary) 系统子例程库
SYSLOG(SYSstem LOG) 系统登录
SYSMON(SYStem MONitor) 系统监督程序
SYSOUT(SYStem OUTput) 系统输出
Sysplex Timer Sysplex 定时器
SYSREQ(SYStem REQuest) 系统请求
SYSREQ key(SYStem REQuest key) 系统请求键
SYSRESET(SYStem RESET) 系统重设
system 系统;体制
System/3 系统/3 计算机(IBM)
System 7 系统 7 操作系统(苹果)

System/32　系统/32 计算机(IBM)
System/34　系统/34 计算机(IBM)
System/36　系统/36 计算机(IBM)
System/38　系统/38(IBM)
System/88　系统/88 容错计算机(IBM)
System/360　系统/360 计算机(IBM)
System/370　系统/370 计算机(IBM)
System/390　System /390 计算机(IBM)

system accuracy model　系统精度模型
system action command　系统处理命令
system activity　系统活动, 系统运行
system activity measurement facility　系统活动测量装置
system activity monitor　系统活动监督程序
system adaptation　系统适应性
system administration　系统管理
system administrator　系统管理员
system adaptation　系统适应性
system alert sound　系统告警声
system algorithm　系统算法
system allocation document　系统分配文档
system analysis　系统分析
system analysis manager　系统分析主管
system analyst　系统分析员
system analyst privilege class　系统特许级分析员
system and computers evaluation and review technique(SCERT)　系统和计算机鉴定与评论技术
system and procedure analyst(SPA)　系统与程序分析员
system and procedure association　系统与程序协会
system and support software　系统与支持软件
system allocation process　系统分配过程
system application　系统应用
system approach　系统方式, 系统分析法
system arbiter　系统仲裁器
system architecture　系统体系结构
system area　系统区
system assembly　系统装配
system assisted linkage　系统辅助连接

system audit　系统监督
system authentication key　系统鉴别关键字
system availability　系统利用率
system availability information point　系统可用性信息点
system back-up　系统备份
system balancing　系统平衡
system behavior　系统功效
system behavior model　系统功效模型
system BIOS　系统基本输入/输出系统
system BIOS cacheable　系统基本输入/输出系统高速缓存化
system blocking signal　系统阻塞信号
system board　系统板
system bootstrap routine　系统引导程序
system bottleneck problem　系统瓶颈问题
system boundary　系统边界
system builder　系统构造程序
system buffer　系统缓冲区
system bus　系统总线
system bus interface logic　系统总线接口逻辑
system bus loading　系统总线荷载
system bus width　系统总线宽度
system call　系统调用
system call interrupt　系统调用中断
system capacity　系统容量
system centerline　系统略图
system chart　系统流程图, 系统框图
system check　系统检验
system check model　系统检验模型
system check module　系统检验模块
system checkout　系统检验
system checkpoint　系统检验点
system clear button　系统清除按钮
system clock　系统时钟
system clock control　系统时钟控制
system code　系统代码
system color　系统颜色
system command　系统命令
system command executive　系统命令执行程序
system command interpretation　系统命令解释
system command interpreter　系统命令

令解释程序
System Commander 系统命令程序
system commands 系统命令
system communication 系统通信
system communication interface 系统通信接口
system communication locations 系统通信单元
system communication modems 系统通信调制解调器
system communication processing 系统通信处理
system communication table 系统通信表
system compatibility 系统兼容性
system complexity 系统复杂性
system components 系统组件
system composite environment 系统合成环境
system composite level 系统合成级
system concept 系统概念
system configuration 系统配置
system console 系统控制台
system consolidation 系统强化
system constants 系统常数
system constraint 系统约束
system construction 系统构造
system consultant 系统顾问
system contention analysis 系统冲突分析
system control 系统控制
system control area 系统控制区
system control block 系统控制块
system control block base register 系统控制块基寄存器
system control facility 系统控制设施
system control file 系统控制文件
system control panel 系统控制面板
system control program 系统控制程序
system control programming(SCP) 系统控制程序设计器
system control register 系统控制寄存器
system control signal 系统控制信号
system control signal unit 系统控制信号单元
system control station 系统控制站
system controllability 系统可控性
system controller 系统控制器

system controller and bus driver 系统控制与总线驱动器
system convention 系统常规选项
system conversion 系统更换
system coordination document 系统协调文档
system core image library maintenance 系统核心映像库维护
system crash 系统崩溃
system damage 系统损坏
system data address 系统数据地址
system data address space 系统地址空间
system data analyzer 系统数据分析程序
system data bus 系统数据总线
system data set 系统数据集
system date 系统日期
system deadlock 系统死锁
system debug 系统调试
system decomposition 系统分解
system default 系统默认值
system default parameter 系统默认参数
system defined category 系统定义范畴
system definition 系统定义
system definition information 系统定义信息
system definition record 系统定义记录
system degradation 系统性能降低,系统退化
system description language(SYSL) 系统描述语言
system description maintenance 系统现状的保存
system design 系统规划,系统设计
system design aids 系统规划工具
system design criteria 系统规划标准
system design problem 系统设计问题
system design simulator 系统设计仿真器
system designer 系统设计师
system deterioration 系统恶化
system development 系统开发
System Development Corporation(SDC) 系统开发公司
system development cycle 系统开发周期
system development journal 系统开发日志
system development methodology 系统

开发方法学
system device 系统设备
system device swap file 系统设备交换文件
system device table 系统设备表
system diagnostic 系统诊断
system diagnostics 系统诊断程序
system diagram 系统框图
system directory 系统目录
system directory list 系统目录清单
system disk 系统盘
system dispatch queue 系统调度队列
system dispatching 系统配送
system documentation 系统文档处理
system down 系统故障
system down time 系统故障时间
system dump 系统转储
system dynamic memory 系统动态存储器
system dynamic simulation 系统动力学仿真
system dynamics 系统动态学
system effective data rate 系统有效数据传送速率
system effectiveness 系统效能
system element 系统元件
system engineer 系统工程师
system engineering 系统工程 「具
system engineering tools 系统工程工
system environment recording 系统环境记录
system environment simulation 系统环境仿真
system error 系统误差
system error detection 系统故障检测
system error detection and feedback 系统误差检测及反馈
system error record editing program (SEREP) 系统故障记录编辑程序
system error recovery 系统错后复原
system evaluation 系统评价
system evolution 系统演变
system exclusive 系统排它性
system expansion 系统扩充
system failure 系统故障,系统失效
system fault tolerance 系统容错
system feasibility 系统可行性
system feature 系统特性

system file assignment 系统文件分配
system firmware 系统固件
system flexibility 系统灵活性
system flowchart 系统流程图
system folder 系统文件夹
system font 系统字体
system for information on gray literature in Europe 欧洲灰色文献信息系统
system for worldwide interbank funds transfer (SWIFT) 世界性银行财务远程通信协会
system format 系统格式
system framework 系统框架
system gain 系统增益 「成
system generation (SYSGEN) 系统生
system generation macrolanguage 系统生成宏语言
system group 系统组
system guidance 系统制导
system halt 系统停止运行
system handbook 系统手册
system hardware 系统硬件
system hierarchy 系统层次结构
system history 系统运行历史
system hold status 系统保持状态
system ID 系统标识符
system identification problem 系统识别问题
system identification register 系统标识寄存器
system image 系统映像
system image buffer 系统映像缓冲器
system image preservation 系统映像保存
system implementation 系统实现
system improvement 系统改进 「间
system improvement time 系统改进时
system info 系统信息
system initialization 系统初始化
system initiation 系统初始化
system initiated scratch function 系统初始化暂存功能
system input 系统输入
system input device 系统输入设备
system input file 系统输入文件
system input source 系统输入源
system input unit (SYSIN) 系统输入

单元
system inspect 系统审查
system installation 系统安装
system instruction address space 系统指令地址空间
system integration 系统集成
system integrity 系统完整性
system interconnection 系统互连
system interface 系统接口
system interface adapter 系统接口适配器
system interface board 系统接口板
system interface card 系统接口卡
system interface design 系统接口设计
system interface module 系统接口模块
system internal name 系统内部名
system interrupt 系统中断
system interrupt request 系统中断请求
system interval 系统时间间隔
system invoke 系统调用
system job queue 系统作业队列
system job status information 系统作业状态信息
system journal 系统运行日志
system junction module 系统连接模块
system kernel 系统核心,系统内核
system key 系统保护键
system language 系统语言
system layout 系统布局
system length register 系统长度寄存器
system level 系统级
system level simulation 系统级仿真
system librarian 系统管理员
system library 系统库
system life cycle 系统生命周期
system link library 系统连接程序库
system linkage segment descriptor 系统连接段描述符
system list 系统列表
system literal 系统文字
system loader 系统载入程序
system lock 系统封锁
system log(SYSLOG) 系统日志
system log file 系统日志文件
system logger 系统日志记录程序
system logical resource 系统逻辑资源
system macro 系统宏

system macro definition 系统宏定义
system macro instruction 系统宏指令
system maintenance 系统维护
system maintenance journal 系统维护日志
system management 系统管理
system management facilities(SMF) 系统管理功能
system management elementary file(SMEF) 系统管理元文件
system management monitor 系统管理监督程序
system management server 系统管理服务器
system manager 系统主管人
system manual 系统手册
system map 系统图
system mask 系统屏蔽
system mask register 系统屏蔽寄存器
system master catalog 系统主目录
system matrix 系数矩阵
system memory map 系统内存布局
system message field 系统消息字段
system mistake 系统错误
system mode 系统模式,管态
system mode instruction 管态指令
system model 系统模型
system modularity 系统模块性
System Module Information (Netware)系统模块信息
system modeling 系统建模
system monitor 系统监督程序
system multiplex 系统多工
system name table 系统名表
system noise 系统噪声
system nucleus 系统核心
system object model(SOM) 系统对象模型
system of notation 记数制
system of records 记录系统
System On a Chip 整合型单芯片系统(IBM)
system on chip(SOC) 系统集成
System on Silicon 芯片系统
system online test system 系统联机测试系统
system operation 系统作业
system operating time 系统操作时间

system operator 系统操作员
system operator station 系统操作员站
system optimization 系统优化
system ordinary life operation 系统常规寿命操作
system organization 系统组织
system-oriented computer 面向系统的计算机
system-oriented hardware 面向系统的硬件
system output device 系统输出设备
system output unit 系统输出单元
system output writer 系统输出程序
system overhead 系统总开销
system overhead information 系统附加信息
system pack 系统磁盘组
system page table(SPT) 系统页表
system palette 系统调色板
system parameter record 系统参数记录
system parameter table(SPT) 系统参数表
system partition 系统分区
system patch file 系统修补文件
system performance 系统性能
system performance monitor 系统性能监督程序
system planner 系统计划者
system pool 系统公用区,系统池
system power supply 系统电源
system preparation routine 系统准备例程
system preservation utility 系统映像保存实用程序
system printer 系统打印机
system privileged slave program 系统特许从属程序
system procedure library 系统过程库
system process 系统进程
system product interpreter 系统产品解释程序
system production time 系统生产时间
system productivity 系统生产率
system profile 系统轮廓文件
system program 系统程序
system program error 系统程序错误
system program loader 系统程序装载器

system programmed operators 系统程序操作
system programmer 系统程序员
system programmer privilege class 系统程序员特许级
system programming 系统程序设计
system project planning 系统项目规划
system prompt 系统提示符
system protection 系统保护
system prototype 系统原型(样机)
system queue area(SQA) 系统队列区
system quiescence 系统停转
System R System R 关系数据库(IBM)
system realization 系统实现
system reconfiguration 系统重配置
system recorder file 系统记录文件
system recovery 系统恢复能力
system refresh 系统刷新
system region 系统区域
system registry 系统注册
system reliability 系统可靠性
system relocatable library 系统可重定位程序库
system repairability 系统可修复性
system requirement 系统需求
system reset 系统复位键
system reset clear key 系统复位清除
system reset key 系统复位键
system reset pad 系统复位按钮
system residence 系统驻留区域
system residence volume 系统常驻卷
system resident 系统驻留
system resident file 系统驻留文件
system resident volume 系统驻留卷
system resource management 系统资源管理
system resource operator privilege class 系统资源操作员特许级
system resources manager(SRM) 系统资源管理程序
system response 系统响应
system response field 系统响应域
system restart 系统再启动
system restoration 系统恢复
system roll-back 系统重算
system root 系统根目录
system run-time library 系统运行时

间库
system saboteur 系统故意破坏者
system saturation 系统饱和
system schedule 系统调度
system scheduled checkpoint 系统调度检验点
system scheduler 系统调度程序
system scheduler table 系统调度表
system security 系统安全性
system segment 系统程序段
system self-testing 系统自测
system service 系统服务
system service control point (SNA)系统服务控制点
system service request 系统服务请求
system services 系统服务程序
system services interface functions 系统服务接口函数
system sequential scheduling 系统顺序调度
system service programs 系统服务程
system services control point(SSCP) 系统服务控制点
system shutdown 系统关闭
system simplification 系统简化
system simulation 系统仿真
system slave process 系统从属进程
system slowdown 系统减速
system software 系统软件
system software component 系统软件成份
system software types 系统软件类型
system solver program 系统求解程序
system space 系统空间
system specification 系统说明书
system stability 系统稳定性
system stack 系统堆栈
system state object 系统状态对象
system standard 系统标准
system start option 系统启动选项
system start-up 系统启动
system state table 系统状态表
system statistics 系统统计
system status display 系统状态显示
system status interrogation 系统状况询问
system storage capacity 系统存储器容量

system structural analysis 系统结构分析
system study 系统研究
system subcomponents 系统子组件
system subroutines 系统子例程
system supervisor 系统监督程序
system support 系统支持
system support device 系统支持设备
system support program 系统后援程
system swap block 系统交换块
system symbol 系统符号
system symbolic address name 系统符号地址名
system synthesis 系统综合,系统合成
system tailoring 系统裁剪
system tape 系统带
system task 系统任务
system task save area 系统任务保存
system task set 系统任务集
system task set table 系统任务集表
system terminal 系统终端
system test 系统测试,系统检验
system test time 系统测试时间
system tester 系统测试仪
system testing time 系统测试时间
system timer 系统定时器
system timer task 系统定时任务
system trace 系统跟踪
system transfer function 系统传递函
system trap 系统陷阱
system unit 系统部件
system update 系统更新
system user 系统用户
system utility device 系统应用设备
system utility program 系统应用程序
system utility program support 系统应用程序支援
system utilization logger 系统利用率记录程序
System V 系统 V(Unix)操作系统 (AT&T)
System V Interface Definition(SVID) 系统 V 接口规范(AT&T)
system variable 系统变量
system variable symbol 系统变量符号
system variable table 系统变量表
system view 系统视图
system virtual address 系统虚地址

system virtual space 系统虚拟空间
system volume 系统卷
system with one degree of freedom 单自由度系统
system with several degrees of freedom 多自由度系统
system work area 系统工作区
system work stack 系统工作堆栈
systematic analysis 系统分析
systematic code 系统码
systematic cross connection 系统交叉连接
systematic design discipline 系统设计规则
systematic deviation 系统偏差
systematic error 系统误差
systematic grammar 系统文法
systematic inaccuracy 系统不准确性
systematic noise 系统性噪声
systematic occurrence 有次序出现
systematic overrelaxation 系统超松弛
systematic proof method 系统证明法
systematic sampling scheme 系统抽样方案
systematic tree 系统树
systematicness 系统性,规则性
Systems Application Architecture (SAA) 系统应用程序体系结构(IBM)
systems architecture 系统体系结构
Systems Management Server(SMS) 系统管理服务器(微软)
Systems Network Architecture(SNA) 系统网络体系结构(IBM)
systems with individual tokens 独立令牌系统
SYSTIME 系统时间
systolic algorithm 脉动算法
systolic array architecture 脉动阵列体系结构
systolic-like method 类脉动方法
systolic scheduling 脉动调动方法
systolic trellis automaton 脉动框架自动机
systolization 脉动化
systolizing compiler 脉动化编译程序

T t

T(True) 真
T1 T1 服务等级(1.544 Mb/s)
T2 T2 服务等级(6.312 Mb/s)
T3 T3 服务等级(44.736 Mb/s)
T4 T4 服务等级(274.176 Mb/s)
T-carrier T 载波系统(AT&T)
T-complete net 事件完备化网,T 完备化网
T-connector T 型连接器
T-disk 暂存盘
T. H. E. Multiprogramming T. H. E. 多道程序系统
t-out-of-s diagnosable S 中取 t 可诊断的
T-PROLOG T-PROLOG 仿真系统
TA(Terminal Adapter) (ISDN)终端适配器
TA service 转账业务
TAB(Tab-Automated Bonded) 自动接合薄片(东芝)
TAB(TABulate) 制表
tab 标记;制表键;卡片系统
tab character 制表字符
TAB command 制表命令,标记命令
tab delimited 制表符定界的
tab group 制表组
tab index 制表键响应顺序
tab key 制表键
tab interval 制表间隔
tab leader 制表前导字符
tab sequential 列表顺序
tab stop 制表位
tabbing 制表;跨栏
table 表,表格
table access 表存取
table address 表地址
table alias 表别名
table autoformat 表格自动套用格式
table base register 表格基址寄存器

table block 表块
table buffering 表缓冲
table compression 表压缩
table constructor 表格构造程序
table description 表式说明，表描述
table directory 表目录
table-driven simulation 表格驱动仿真
table-driven technique 表格驱动法
table element 表元素
table element reference 表元素引用
table field 表栏，表域
table file 表格文件
table fragmentation 表存储碎片
table function 表函数
table gridlines 表格框线
table handling 表处理
table header 表头
table indicator 表指示符
table language 表格语言
table layout form 表布局形式
table look-at 直接查表
table look-up 查表
table look-up instruction 查表指令
table look-up program 查表程序
table of contents 目录表，内容表
table operation 表格操作
table organization 表组织，表结构
table-oriented database management program 面向表格的数据库管理程序
table pack 表组合
table property 表属性
table reference character 表引用字符
table restriction 表限制，表保密
table search 表检索
table segment 表段
table segmenting 表分段
table simulator 制表仿真程序；算表程序
table size 表尺寸，表大小
table skeleton 表轮廓，表格填写单
table sort 表排序
table space 表空间
table structure 表结构
table technique 列表技术
table transform 表变换
table utility 制表实用程序
table view 表格视图

table wizard 表向导
table word-processing equipment 台式文字处理设备
Tables Manager/1(TM/1) 表格管理软件
tables pack 数表压缩
tablespace 表空间
tablet 图形输入板
tablet digitizer 平板式数字化仪
tablet menu 数字化仪菜单
taboo frequency 禁忌频率
taboo term 禁忌词
tabular display 列表显示
tabular form 列表形式，表格
tabular gray-scale 查表灰度
tabular interpretive program 列表翻译程序
tabular language 列表语言
tabular representation 表格表示法
tabular systems-oriented language 制表系统结构语言
tabulate 制表
tabulated data 列表数据
tabulating space 制表间隔
tabulation 制表
tabulation character 制表控制符
tabulation sequential format 制表顺序格式
tabulator 制表机，制表员；制表程序
tabulator clear key 制表机构清除键
tabulator gang clear key 制表机构群清除键
tabulator key 制表键
tabulator language 制表语言
tabulator mechanism 制表机构
tabulator set key 制表机置位键
tabulator stop 制表定位器
TAC(Telenet Access Controller) 电信网络存取控制器
tackogram 转速图
tackometer 测速计，转速计
tackosensor 速度传感器
tacit knowledge 默认知识
tactical computer 战术计算机
tactical decision 战术决策
tactical digital information link(TAIL) 战术数字信息链路
tactical planning 战术计划

tactile 触觉
tactile feedback 触觉反馈
tactile keyboard 触摸式键盘
tactile sensor 触敏传感器
tactual vocoder 触觉声码器
Tad "小灵通"计算机
tag 标记,标签
tag all 全部选定
tag along sort 按标签排序
tag bus type 特征总线字节
tag check 特征检查
tag converting unit 标签变换器
tag default option 标签默认选项
tag delete 标签删除
tag end 末端
tag field 标记域
tag file 标记文件
tag format 标签格式
Tag Image File format(TIF) 标记图像文件格式
tag list 特征表
tag mark 标签符号
tag none 不选定
tag number list 标记号码表
tag path 标签路径,标记通路
tag reader 特征读出器
tag sequence 标记次序
tag set 标记集合
tag slot 标记存储槽
tag sort 标签排序
tag sorting 标签排序
tag special option 标签特定选项
tag switching 标记交换
tag system 特征系统
tag-value compilation(TVC) 标记值编排
Tagged Image File Format(TIFF) 标签式图像文件格式
tagged keys 标识密钥
tagged word 标签字,标记字
tagging reader 特征阅读器,标签阅读器
TAIE (Terminal Attention Interrupt Element) 终端引起注意中断元素
tail 尾标,结束符
tail frame 尾帧
tail link 尾连接
tail pointer 尾指针

tail optical fiber 尾光纤
tail pointer 尾指针
tail recursive 尾递归
tail symbol 尾部符号
tailing 拖尾
tailor 裁剪,剪辑
tailor-made algorithm 专用算法
tailorable option 可剪辑选项
tailored configuration 特定配置
take back 取回
take care 照看
take down connection 拆线
take in 接收,包括
take off 起飞;发射
take over 取代;接过
take ownership 取得所有权
take-up reel 收带盘
take-up roll 收纸轴
take-up spool 收带轴
takedown 卸下
takedown time 卸下时间
TALIB TALIB专家系统
Taligent Taligent公司(美)
Talisman Talisman计划(微软)
talk 对话,通话
talk address 通话地址
talk device number 对话设备号
talk key 通话控制键
talk off 对话关闭
talk on 对话开启
talker 发送者,讲者
talker echo 发话者回声
talker-independent system 非特定说话者语音理解系统
talker/listener 讲者/听者
talking printer 声控打印机
tally 计数
tally down 减1
tally light 记录指示灯
tally register 计数寄存器
tally set 标签集
tally up 加1
tamper-proof database 防篡改数据库
tamper-resistant module 防捣毁模块
TAN 正切函数
TANDEM 16 TANDEM 16计算机
tandem 串接,级联
tandem center 汇接中心

tandem central office 汇接局
Tandem Computer Inc. Tandem 计算机公司(美)
tandem connection 级联
tandem control 串行控制
tandem data circuit 级联数字电路
tandem exchange 汇接局,中继交换机
tandem link 串行链路
Tandem nonstop system Tandem 不停机系统
tandem office 汇接局,中继局
tandem processors 级联处理器
tandem routing 直通联络编路
tandem selector 汇接选择器
tandem switch 汇接交换机
tandem system 串级系统
tandem trunk 汇接中继线
Tandy Corp. Tandy 公司(美)
Tandy high-intensity optical recorder (THOR) Tandy 高强度光记录器
tangent 正切
tangential approximation method 切线逼近法
tangential coupling 切向耦合
tangent plane 切平面
tangent point 切线点
tangent vector 正切向量
tangible benefit 有形效益
Tango Tango 绘图软件(Accel)
Tango-PCB Tango 印刷电路板图设计软件包
Tango schematic Tango 原理图设计软件包
Tanimoto's expression 塔尼莫托表达式
tank circuit 振荡回路
tantamount 等值的,同义的
TAP(Terminal Access Processor) 终端存取处理机
tap 分接头,抽头
tape 带,磁带,纸带
tape alternation 换带,带交替
tape automatic bonding(TAB) 带式自动焊接
tape backup 磁带备份
tape beginning control 带始控制
tape beginning marker 带始标志
tape bin 快速取数磁带机
tape block 磁带信息块

tape bootstrap routine 磁带引导例程
tape bound 受带限制的
tape cable 带状电缆
tape cartridge 盒式磁带
tape character 带字符
tape check character 带校验字符
tape code 带码
tape comparator 带比较器
tape control unit 带控制装置
tape-controlled carriage 带控输纸机
tape deck 走带机构
tape dialer 磁带拨号器
tape drive(TD) 磁带机;纸带机
tape drive controller 带驱动控制器
tape dump 磁带转储
tape editor 带编辑程序
tape erasure 带清除
tape error 带错误
tape feed 带馈送
tape file 带文件
tape from card conversion 卡片磁带变换
tape handling option routines(THOR) 带处理选择程序
tape input 带输入
tape label 带标号,带标记
tape leader 带首
tape library 带程序库
tape light 带指示灯
tape limited 受带限制的
tape limited operation 受带限制的操作
tape load key 磁带加载键
tape load point 磁带起始工作点
tape mark(TM) 带标
tape operating system(TOS) 磁带操作系统
tape-oriented system 面向磁带的计算机系统
tape perforator 纸带穿孔机
tape plotting system 磁带绘图系统
tape printer 带式打印机
tape punch 纸带穿孔机
tape record region 磁带记录区
tape recorder 磁带记录器
tape recording density 磁带记录密度
tape reel 磁带卷
tape reflection marker 磁带反射标记

tape rewind 倒带,反绕
tape skew 磁带扭斜
tape skip 带跳越
tape-skip restore 磁带跳越复原
tape sort 带排序
tape sort and collate program 带排序与整理程序
tape speed 带速
tape speed variation 带速变化
tape square 带方格
tape standalone dump/restore 磁带独立转储/恢复程序
tape storage 磁带存储器
tape switching 磁带交换
tape synchronizer 磁带同步器
tape trailer 带尾
tape unit 磁带机
tape unit servo system 磁带机伺服系统
tape volume 带卷
tapered n-best forward pruning 锥形n最佳正向修剪
tapered quantization 锥形量化
tapered search 锥形搜索
TAPI (Telephony Applications Program Interface) 电话应用程序接口
tapping of circuit 线路窃听
taps 分接点
tar(tape archive) (Unix)磁带存档文件
tar file (Unix)磁带存储文件
tar format (Unix)磁带存档格式
tar program (Unix)磁带存档程序
Targa(TAG) (图像显示)Targa格式
Targa Electronic System Inc. Targa电子系统公司(加拿大)
target 目标
target abort 目标中止
target acquisition 目标捕获
target angle 目标角
target approach chart 进入目标图
target area 目标区域
target attribute 目标属性
target rearing 目标方位
target block 目标程序块
target cache 目标高速缓存
target characteristic identification 目标特征识别
target code 目标代码
target component 目标要素

target computer 目标计算机
target coverage 目标覆盖
target data model 目标数据模型
target data set 目标数据集
target data structure 目标数据结构
target directory 目标目录
target designation 目标命名
target directory 目标目录
target discrimination 目标识别,目标辨认
target disk 目标盘,目的盘
target distance 目标距离
target domain 目标域
target drive 目标驱动器
target file 目标文件
target graph 目标图
target image tracking 目标图像跟踪
target language 目标语言
target level 目标级
target line 目标行
target machine 目标机
target noise 目标噪声
target path 目标路径
target pattern 目标样式
target phase 目标阶段
target position finding 目标位置寻求
target process 目标进程
target processor 目标处理机
target program 目标程序
target recognition 目标识别
target routine 目标例程
target screen 目标屏
target seeker 目标搜寻器,寻的装置
target segment 目标段
target signature 目标特征
Target Token Rotation Time(TTRT) 目标令牌循环时间
target track 目标磁道
target travel 目标运动
target value 目标值
target variable 目标变量
target view 目标视图
target zone 目标区
targeting browser 目标浏览器
targeting links 目标链接[链路]
tariff 费率,计价率
TASI(Time Assignment Speech Interpolation) 时间分配语音插空技术

task 事务,任务
task abnormal exit routine 任务异常出口例程
task activation 任务活化,任务激活
task adaptive partitioning 事务自适应划分
task allocation 事务分布,任务分布
task appendage routine 任务附属例程
task attribute 任务属性
task body 任务体
task builder 任务建立程序
task call 任务调用
task check point 任务检查点
task code word 任务代码字
task concurrent processing 任务并行处理
task configuration 任务配置
task control block(TCB) 任务控制块
task control table 任务控制表
task creation 任务创建
task data sheet 任务数据表
task declaration 任务说明
task decomposition 任务分解
task definition table 任务定义表
task dependency 任务相关性
task-dependent option 任务相关选项
task descriptor 任务描述符
task dialog 任务对话框
task dispatcher 任务分配程序
task domain 任务域
task dump 事务转储
task error exit routine 任务出错退出例程
task execution area 任务执行区域
task flow char 任务流程图
task graph description language 任务图描述语言
task group resource 任务组资源
task I/O table(TIOT) 任务输入/输出表
task identification 任务标识符
task immigration 任务迁移
task input queue(TIQ) 任务输入队列
task interrupt control 任务中断控制
task layer 任务层
task level controller 任务级控制器
task level programming language 任务级编程语言
task level queuing model 任务级排队模型
task library 任务库,事务库
task list 事务列表
task macro 任务宏
task management 事务管理,任务管理
task manager 任务管理器
task mapping 任务映像
task migration 任务迁移
task model 事务模型,任务模型
task modeling 任务建模
task name 事务名称,任务名
task nest 任务嵌套
task number 任务号
task object 任务目标
task option 任务选项
task-oriented image database 面向事务图像数据库
task pipeline 任务流水线
task precedence graph 任务优先图
task priority dispatching 任务优先级分配
task processing 任务处理
task processing management system 任务处理管理系统
task processing transparency 事务处理透明
task queue 任务队列
task quit 任务退出
task ready queue 任务就绪队列
task reassignment 任务重指定
task request block 任务请求块
task retry routine 任务重执例程
task run online 任务联机运行
task scheduler 任务调度程序
task-scheduling priorities 任务调度优先权
task selection 任务选择
task server 事务服务器
task set 事务组,任务集
task set control block(TSCB) 任务集控制块
task set installation 任务集配置
task set library 任务集库
task set load module 任务集装入模块
task set reference table(TSRT) 任务组参考表

task-sharing 任务分担
task shuffling 任务混洗
task space augmentation 任务空间强「化
task specification 任务规格说明
task start 事务启动,任务启动
task state 任务状态
task supervisor 任务管理程序
task suspension 事务挂起
task swapping 任务交换
task switch 事务转换,任务转移
task symbol 任务标号
task system work stack 任务系统工作栈
task switching 任务切换　　　　「块
task table control block 任务表控制
task-task communication 任务间通信
task termination 任务终结
task tree partitioning 任务树划分
task type 任务类型
task unit 任务单元　　　　　　「栈
task user work stack 任务用户工作堆
task variable 任务变量
task views 任务视图
task virtual storage 任务虚拟存储器
task work stack descriptor(TWSD) 任务堆栈描述符
tasking 任务分配
tasking protocol 任务分配协议
tautological consequence 真值推论
tautological equivalence 真值等价
tautological implication 真值蕴含
tautology 重言式,永真式
tautology rule 重言式规则,同语反复规则
Tax-Cut 纳税专家系统
taxis system 归类系统,分类系统
TAXMAN 纳税人专家系统
taxology 分类学
taxon 类名,分类单元,分类群
taxonomic 分类的,归类的
taxonomic description 归类描述
taxonomic organization 分类组织
Taylor algorithm 泰勒算法
Taylor-series method 泰勒级数法
TB(TeraByte) 太字节,2^{40}字节
Tb(Terabit) 太位,万亿位,2^{40}位
TBDF(Ttrans-Border Data Flow) 过境数据流

Tbit(Terabit) 太位,万亿位
Tbits/sec(Terabits per second) 每秒太位
Tbps(Terabits per second) 每秒太位,每秒万亿位
TBps(TeraBytes per second) 每秒太字节,每秒万亿字节
Tbyte(terabyte) 太字节,2^{40}字节
TC(Technical Committee) 技术委员会
TC(Terminal Concentrator) 终端集线器
TC(Terminal Controller) 终端控制器
TC(Transmission Convergence) 传输聚合子层
TC 11 TC 11 委员会(IFIP)
TC 20000 TC 2000 并行计算机(BBN)
TC 68/SC2 TC 68/SC2 委员会(ISO)
TC 97/SC17/WG4 TC 97/SC17/WG4 工作小组(ISO)
TC 97/SC20 TC 97/SC20 委员会(ISO)
TCAM (TeleCommunications Access Method) 远程通信访问法(IBM)
TCAM control task(TCT) TCAM 控制任务(IBM)
TCAM destination address field (TCAF) TCAM 目标地址栏(IBM)
TCAM network address TCAM 网络地址(IBM)
TCAM origin address field(TOAF) TCAM 初始地址栏(IBM)　「块
TCB(Task Control Block) 任务控制
TCB(Trusted Computing Base) 可信计算基
TCC (Transmission Control Characters) 传输控制字符
TCK(TraCK) 磁道,轨道
TCK(TraCKing) 跟踪,追踪
TCL (Transaction Control Language) 事务处理语言
TCM(Thermal Conduction Module) 热传导模块
TCM(Time Compression Multiplex) 时间压缩多路传输

TCM(Trellis-Coded Modulation/ Viterbi Decoding)　Trellis 编码调制/Viterbi 解码
TCP/IP(Transmission Control Protocol/Internet Protocol)　传输控制协议/网间协议
TCP/IP for OS/2　用于 OS/2 的 TCP/IP
TCP/IP network layer　TCP/IP 网络层
TCP/IP transmission layer　传输控制协议/网际协议传输层
TCP/IP utility　TCP/IP 实用程序
TCS(Trusted Computer System)　可信计算机系统
TCSE(Technical Committee on Software Engineering)　软件工程技术委员会
TCT(Task Control Table)　任务控制表
TCU(Timing Control Unit)　定时控制器
TD(Track Density)　磁道密度
TDCC(Transparent Data Communication Code)　透明数据通信码
TDMA(Time Division Multiple Access)　时分多路存取
TDMC(Time Division Multiplexed Channel)　时分多路转换信道
TDR(Transmit Data Register)　发送数据寄存器
TDS(Transaction Driven System)　事务驱动系统
TE(Terminal Emulation)　终端仿真
TE(Terminal Equipment)　(ISDN)终端设备
TE1(Terminal Equipment type 1)　一类终端设备
TE2(Terminal Equipment type 2)　二类终端设备
TE(Text Editor)　文本编辑程序
teaching by showing　示教
teaching expert system　教学专家系统
teaching interface　示教界面
teaching machine　教学机
teaching pendant　示教盒
teaching program　教学程序
TEAM(Terminology Evaluation and Acquisition Method)　技术评价与获取方法
team　队,组
team computing　成组计算,组合计算
team design　集体设计
team operation　集体协同工作
tear-off menu　移走菜单;撕下菜单
TechNet CD　技术网络信息支持(微软)
technetronic era　电子技术时代
technical & office protocol(TOP)　技术与办公协议
technical article　技术性论文
technical data　技术数据
technical decision　技术决策
technical delay time　技术延迟时间
technical document author　技术文件编者
technical feasibility study　技术可行性研究
technical lemma　技术引理
technical objective document　技术测验文档
technical order　技术规程
technical proposal　技术方案,技术建议
technical safeguard　技术防护措施
technical security　技术安全性
technical support　技术支持
technical vulnerability　技术弱点,技术脆弱性
technique　技术,方法
technique flowcharts　技术流程图
technocentrism　技术中心论者
technocracy　专家管理
technological attack　技术攻击
technological data bank　工艺数据库
technological documentation　工艺文件
technological efficiency of design of part　零件结构工艺性
technological efficiency of design of product　产品结构工艺性
technological efficiency of production　生产工艺性
technological efficiency of use　使用技术效率
technological management　工艺管理
technological preparation of production　生产工艺准备

technological selection 工艺选择
technological transfer 技术转让
technology 技术,工艺
technology assessment 技术评价
technology breakthrough 技术突破
technology definition file(TDF) 技术定义文件
technology development cycle 技术开发周期
technology outlook 技术展望
technology utilization 工艺应用
TECNET(Tokyo Experimental Computer NETwork) 东京大学试验性计算机网络
TEIRESIAS TEIRESIAS专家系统工具
Tektronix Tektronix(打印机)公司(美)
Telcon 泰尔康通信网络系统(Univac)
teleautograph 传真电报
telebanking 远程银行业务
telecenter 远程计算中心
TELECOM(TELECOMmunication) 远程通信
telecommunication 远程通信
telecommunication access method (TCAM) 远程通信访问法(IBM)
telecommunication administration 电信管理局
telecommunication and automated information system security 远程通信和自动信息系统安全
telecommunication conference 长途通信会议
telecommunication control unit 远程通信控制器 「备
telecommunication equipment 电信设
telecommunication facility 远程通信设施
telecommunication laser 远程通信激光器
telecommunication line 远程通信线路
telecommunication link 远程通信链路
Telecommunication Management Network(TMN) 电信管理网络(CCITT0
telecommunication network(TelNet) 远程通信网络(协议)

telecommunication security 通信安全
telecommunication service 远程通信业务
telecommunication system 远程通信系统
telecommunication traffic(Teletraffic) 电信业务量
telecommuting 在家上班,电信办公
telecomputing 远程计算
telecoms 电信
teleconferencing 远程会议
teleconferencing network 远程会议网
telecontroller 远程控制器,遥控器
telecopier 远程复印机
telecopying 远程拷贝
teledata 远程数据业务
telefax 远程传真机
telefile 远程文件系统
telegraph(TG) 电报
telegraph channel 电报信道
telegraph code 电报码
telegraph grade channel 电报级信道
telegraph signal 电报信号
telegraphy 电报
teleinformatic services 远程信息服务
teleinformatics 远程信息传输
telelearning system 远程学习系统
telemail 远程邮政
telemanagement 远程管理
telematic network 远程信息处理网络
telematic service 远程信息处理业务
telematics 远程信息技术
telematique 计算机通信
telemedicine 远程医学
telemeter 遥测仪
telemetering 遥测
telemetry 遥测学
telemetry command 遥测指令 「站
telemetry command station 遥测指令
telemetry parameter 遥测参数
telemetry system 遥测系统
TELENET TELENET网
Teleoperator 遥控操作器
teleordering 远程订购
Telepack 远程信道
telephone call 电话呼叫
telephone channel 电话信道
telephone circuit 电话电路

telephone communication unit 电话通信设备
telephone coupler 电话耦合器
telephone data set 电话数传机
telephone dialer 电话拨号器
telephone exchange 电话交换机
telephone frequency 电话频率
telephone instrument 电话设备
telephone line data set 电话线路数据传输设备
telephone message 电话通信
telephone network 电话网络
telephone set 电话机
telephone switching 电话交换
telephone transducer 电话转换器
telephone trunk 电话中继线
telephone user part 电话用户分系统
telephones on transport systems 运输系统使用的电话
telephony 电话学
Telephony Applications Program Interface(TAPI) 电话应用程序界面(微软)
Telephony Service API(TSAPI) 电话服务应用程序界面(AT&T)
telephotography 传真电报术
telepionter 远程指示符
telepresence 远地出席
teleprinter 电传打字机
teleprinter interface 电传打字机接口
teleprocessing 远程处理
teleprocessing monitor 远程处理监控程序
teleprocessing network 远程处理网络
teleprocessing online test executive(TOTE) 远程处理联机测试执行程序
teleprocessing security 远程处理安全
teleprocessing system 远程信息处理系统
teleprocessing terminal 远程处理终端
teleprompter 电子提示器
teleputer 通信计算机
telereference 远程咨询
telerobotics 远程机器人操纵技术
telescreen 远程电视屏幕
telescope 望远镜
Teleset 芬兰的可视数据系统
teleshopping 远地购物
telesoftware 远程软件
Telesystems questel 远程检索系统
teletex 智能用户电报
teletex call 用户电报呼叫
teletex character repertoire 用户电报字符集
teletex control function repertoire 用户电报控制功能集
teletex terminal 用户电报终端
teletext 图文电视,电视文字广播
teletext data-line 图文电视数据行
teletext service 电视文字广播服务
teletraffic 长途业务量
teletraffic theory 长途业务量理论
Teletrust 远程可信交易系统
teletype mode 电传打字机模式
teletypewriter(TTY) 电传打字机
teletypewriter automatic send/receive unit 电传打字机自动收发器
teletypewriter communication 电传机通信
teletypewriter grade 电传级线路
television 电视
television circuit 电视电路
television control center 电视控制中心
television demodulator 电视解调器
television monitor 电视监视器
television projector 电视投影仪
television receiver 电视接收机
television scan 电视扫描
television system 电视体制
television tubes 电视显像管
television typewriter(TVT) 电视电传打字机
teleworker 远程工作人员
teleworking 远程办公
telewriter 传真电报机
telewriting 电传书写
TELEX(TELegraph EXchange) 用户电报,电传电报
telex(TEX) 用户电报
Telidon Telidon电视显示系统(加拿大)
TELNET(TELecommunication NETwork) 远程通信网络(Sprint)
Telnet Telnet虚拟终端协议
Telnet function 远程终端功能

Telnet protocol 远程登录网络协议
Telpak 宽带通信业务(AT&T)
Telpak private line service 宽频带专线通信业务(AT&T)
Telpak voice-grade line 宽频带通信中的话音级线路(AT&T)
Telstar Telstar通信卫星(美)
temp 临时
temp file 临时文件
temperature 温度
temperature behavior 温度特性
temperature coefficient 温度系数
temperature compensation 温度补偿
temperature controller 温度控制器
temperature cycling test 温度循环试验
temperature dependence 温度依赖性
temperature difference 温差
temperature distribution 温度分布
temperature drift coefficient 温度漂移系数
temperature gradient 温度梯度
temperature-non-operating 非运行温度
temperature-operating 运行温度
temperature regulator 温度调节器
temperature relay 温度继电器
temperature response 温度响应
temperature sensitive liquid crystal material 温敏液晶材料
temperature sensor 温度传感器
temperature stability 温度稳定性
temperature to frequency converter 温度-频率转换器
temperature variation 温度变化
TEMPEST 防电磁泄射技术(NSA)
TEMPEST control zone 电磁辐射泄露控制范围
TEMPEST proofing 电磁辐射泄露检验
template 模板,样板
template algorithm 模板算法
template class 模板类
template detector 模板检测器
template generator 模板生成器
template identifier 模板标识符
template macro 模板宏
template matching 模板匹配
template specializations 模板说明

tempo setting 节拍设置
temporal cohesion 时间内聚
temporal constraint 时态约束
temporal diagnosis 瞬时诊断,短时间诊断
temporal domain 时间域
temporal estimation 时间估计
temporal event 瞬时事件
temporal interval 时态区间,时间间隔
temporal join 瞬时连接
temporal locality 时间局部性
temporal logic 瞬态逻辑,时序逻辑
temporal model 时序模型
temporal reasoning 时序推理
temporal redundancy 瞬时冗余
temporal relation constraint 时间关系约束
temporal representation 时序表示法
temporal semantics 时态语义学
temporal uncertainty 时序不确定性
temporal window 瞬时窗口
temporally-coherent light 时间相干光
temporary 临时的,临时性的
temporary area 临时区
temporary assignment 临时分配
temporary connection 暂时连接
temporary data set 临时数据集
temporary disk 临时磁盘
temporary fault 暂时性故障
temporary file 临时文件
temporary library 临时库
temporary license transfer 临时转换特许
temporary memory 临时存储器
temporary pointer variable 临时指针变量
temporary program file 临时程序文件
temporary read/write error 临时读写错误
temporary realm 临时领域
temporary register 临时寄存器,暂存器
temporary relationship 临时关系
temporary storage 临时存储器
temporary storage area 临时存储区
temporary storage location 临时存储单元
temporary storage table 临时存储表
temporary suspension 暂时挂起

temporary swap file 临时置换文件
temporary text delay(TTD) 文本临时延迟符
temporary variable 临时变量
temporary working space 临时工作空间
TEMR(TEMporary Register) 临时寄存器
ten-key pad 十进位按键
ten's complement 十的补码
tenancy 租用,占据
tenancy condition 占据条件
tenant 占据者
tender 投标
TENET 德克萨斯大学计算机网
tense analyzer 时态分析程序
tense logic 时态逻辑
tensile strength 抗张力强度
tension 张力
tension arm 张力臂
tensor 张量
tensor algebra 张量代数
tensor of stress 应力张量
tensor product 张量积
tensor spline 张量样条
tensor viscosity 张量粘滞性
tentation data 试验性数据
tentative control strategy 试探性控制策略
tentative inductive assertion 试验性归纳断言
tera(T) 太,兆兆,万亿,2^{40}
terabyte(TB) 太字节,2^{40}字节
term 项;检索词,术语
λ-term λ项
term clustering 检索词聚类
term compression 检索词压缩
term frequency 检索词频率
term language 项语言
term unification 术语统一化
term vector 检索词向量
terminal 终端,终端机
terminal access 终端存取,终端访问
terminal access controller(TAC) 终端存取控制器
terminal address 终端地址
terminal and host interface processor 终端机与主机的接口处理机
terminal architecture 终端体系结构

terminal area 终端区域;焊接盘
terminal automatic identification 终端自动识别
terminal block 接线盒
terminal box 接线端子板
terminal called 终端已叫出
terminal cluster 终端群集
terminal column 末列
terminal component 终端部件
terminal configuration facility(TCF) 终端配置设施
terminal control block(TCB) 终端控制块
terminal control system(TCS) 终端控制系统
terminal control unit(TCU) 终端控制器
terminal controller 终端控制器
terminal controller functions 终端控制器功能
terminal cursor 终端光标
terminal data processing 终端数据处理
terminal device 终端设备
terminal device interface 终端设备接口
terminal digit posting 终端数字记入
terminal display language(TDL) 终端显示语言
terminal display mode 终端显示方式
terminal distributed system 终端分布系统
terminal echo suppressor 终端回声抑制器
terminal edit operation 终端编辑操作
terminal emulation 终端仿真
terminal end-to-end-control 终端机的端端控制
terminal-engaged signal 终端占线信号
terminal entry 终端输入;终端入口;终端表项目
terminal environment block(TEB) 终端环境块
terminal equipment 终端设备
terminal equipment type 1(TE1) 一类终端设备
terminal equipment type 2(TE2) 二类终端设备
terminal fanout 终端扇出

terminal font 终端字体
terminal handler 终端处理器
terminal hardware 终端硬件
terminal I/O wait 终端输入/输出等待
terminal identification 终端标识
terminal image 终端图像
terminal impedance 端阻抗
terminal input buffer 终端输入缓冲器
terminal input/output task(TIOT) 终端输入/输出任务
terminal installation 终端安装
terminal installation for data transmission 数据传输终端安装
terminal interchanger 终端交换器
terminal interface 终端接口
terminal interface message processor (TIP) 终端接口消息处理机
terminal interface processor(TIP) 终端接口处理机
terminal interface subsystem 终端接口子系统
terminal international center(TIC) 终端国际中心
terminal international exchange 终端国际局
terminal job 终端作业
terminal job identification(TJID) 终端作业标识
terminal key 终端密钥
terminal keyboard 终端机键盘
terminal layout 终端布局
terminal light pen system 终端光笔系统
terminal loop adapter 终端回路适配器
terminal mode 终端方式
terminal/modem interface 终端调制解调器接口
terminal/modern interface operation 终端机与调制解调器间的接口操作
terminal module 终端模块
terminal monitor program(TMP) 终端监督程序
terminal multiplexing and control 终端多路转换和控制
terminal node(TN) 终端节点;目标节点,终止节点
terminal office 终端局
terminal operating mode 终端工作方式
terminal-oriented network 面向终端的网络
terminal pad 端接焊盘
terminal paging 终端分页
terminal port 终端端口
terminal port name 终端端口名
terminal preference 终端首选项
terminal printer 终端打印机
terminal processor 终端处理器
terminal protocol 终端协议
terminal queue 终端队列
terminal quiescence 终止静默
terminal reliability 终端可靠性
terminal repeater 终端中继器
terminal response mode 终端响应方式
terminal room 终端室
terminal screen manager 终端屏幕管理程序
terminal security 终端安全措施
terminal security features 终端安全特性
terminal self-testing 终端自测试
terminal server 终端服务程序
terminal session 终端对话期
terminal simulation 终端仿真
terminal snapshot 终止瞬像
terminal source editor 终端源编辑程序
terminal state 终止状态
terminal statement 终止语句
terminal station 终端设备;终点站
terminal status blocks(TSB) 终端状态块
terminal string 终结串
terminal strip 接线条,端子板
terminal suffix 终结后缀
terminal support 终端支持
terminal symbol 终端符号;终止符
terminal table 终端表
terminal-table entry 终端表目
terminal task processing 终端任务处理
terminal traffic 终端业务量
terminal transaction facility(TTF) 终端事件处理程序
terminal transmission interface 终端传输接口
terminal transparency 终端透明性
terminal trunk 终接中继线
terminal type 终端类型
terminal unit 终端设备
terminal user 终端用户

terminal user language 终端用户语言
terminal value 终值
terminal versatility 终端通用性
terminal view 端视图
terminate 终止
terminate and stay resident program (TSR) 终止驻留程序
terminate load 终止负载
terminate parameter 终止参数
terminate statement 终止语句
terminated attribute 终止属性
terminated line 端接线
terminated task 已终止任务
terminating 终止,终结
terminating adapter 终接适配器
terminating chain 终止链
terminating circuit 终接电路
terminating error 端接错误
terminating office 终端局
terminating packet 终结信息包
terminating production 终结产生式
terminating queue 终结队列
terminating symbol 终止符号
terminating traffic 终端业务量
termination 终端,终止
termination character 终止字符
termination condition 终止条件
termination efficiency test 终端效率试验
termination interrupt 结束中断
termination job processing 终止作业处理
termination message 终止信息
termination of a block 分程序终结
termination of a session 对话终止
termination of a task 任务终结
termination phase 终止阶段
termination point 端接点,端头
termination procedure 终止过程
termination proof 终止性证明
termination queue overflow 终止队列溢出
termination record 终结记录
termination routine 终止例程
termination statement 终结语句
termination table 终端接线表;终止表
termination voltage 端接电压
terminator 终止程序;终端匹配器;端子

terminator/initiator 停启程序
terminological data bank 术语数据库
terminological knowledge representation 术语知识表示法
terminological reasoning 术语推理
terminology bank 术语库
terminus 光纤终端组件
Termium Termium 翻译系统
ternary 三进制的;三态的
ternary code 三进制代码
ternary incremental representation 三进制增量表示法
ternary model 三值模型
ternary neuron 三元神经图
ternary notation 三进制记数法
ternary signal 三态信号
ternary tree 三元树
terrestrial interface equipment 地面接口设备
terrestrial link 陆上链路
terrestrial TV 地面电视
terrestrial system 地面通信系统
terrestrial telemetric station 地面遥测站
tertiary device 第三设备
tessellate 镶嵌成棋盘格状的
tessellation automaton 棋盘格形自动机
test 测试,检验
test access 测试通路
test access point 测试入口点
test and verification tool 测试和验证工具
test and verify program 测试与检验程序
test bed 测试床,测试台
test board 测试板
test call indicator 测试呼叫指示符
test call of type 1 1类测试呼叫
test call of type 2 2类测试呼叫
test call of type 3 3类测试呼叫
test card 测试卡
test case 检验实例
test channel 测试通道
test chart 测试图
test chip 测试芯片
test completeness 测试完整性
test complexity 测试复杂性
test condition 测试条件
test console 测试控制台

test cover 测试覆盖
test criteria 测试标准,检测判据
test data 测试数据
test driver 测试驱动程序
test environment 测试环境
test equipment calibration services 测试仪器校准服务
test event 测试事件
test example 测试实例
test example design 测试实例设计
test executive 测试执行程序
test fixtures 测试夹具
test for ambiguity 二义性检验
test for blanks 消隐测试
test generation 测试生成
test generator 测试码生成程序
test indicator 测试指示器
test initialization 测试初始化
test interconnection line 测试互连线
test interface 测试接口
test interval 测试时间间隔
test invalidation 测试无效
test item 测试项目
test joint 测试连接
test lead 测试引线,检测引线
test library 测试(例程)库
test log 测试日志
test logic 测试逻辑
test loop 测试回路
test macro 测试宏
test matrix 试验矩阵
test model 测试模型
test module 测试模块
test numeric 数值测试
test ok 测试正常
test overflow condition 测试溢出条件
test pack 测试组件
test page 测试页面
test path 测试路径
test pattern 测试模式
test pattern generator 测试码模式发生器
test period 测试期间
test phase 测试阶段
test plan 测试计划
test plate 测试板,试验板
test point 测试点
test probe 测试探针

test problem 测试题目
test program 测试程序
test program package 测试程序包
test program system 测试程序系统
test repeatability 测试可重复性
test replacement 测试替换方案
test report 测试报告
test request message(TRM) 测试请求消息
test requirement 测试要求
test response 测试响应
test routine 测试例程
test run 试运行
test script 测试脚本
test section 测试段
test selector 测试选择器
test sequence 测试顺序
test set 测试集
test signal characteristic 测试信号特性
test skip 测试跳步
test specification 测试技术要求
test standard 测试标准
test step 测试步
test subroutine 测试子例程
test suite 测试组,成套测试
test system of logic device 逻辑部件测试系统
test table 测试表
test task 测试任务
test terminal 测试终端
test time 测试时间,检验时间
test tone 测试音
test tool 测试工具
test validity 测试有效性
testability 可测试性
testability design 易测性设计
testability of software 软件可测试性
testing 测试,检测
testing and scoring system(TASS) 测验与记分系统
testing chain 测试链
testing consistency 测试相容性
testing efficiency 测试效率
testing envelope 测试包络
testing environment 测试环境
testing head 检测磁头
testing nominative 测试额定值
testing phase (刻录机)测试阶段

testing predicate 测试谓词
testing sequence 测试顺序
testing services 测试服务
testing time 检测时间
testing tools 测试工具
testing vector 测试向量
tetrad 四位组
tetrahedron 四面体
TeX TeX 排版语言
Texas Instrument Graphics Architecture (TIGA) 德克萨斯仪器公司图形体系结构
Texas Instruments, Inc.(TI) 德克萨斯仪器公司(美)
texel(texture element) 纹理元素
text 文本,正文
text area 文本区,正文区
text attribute 文本属性
text based 基于文本的
text-based graphics 基于文本的图形
text block 文字块
text border 文字边框
text box 文本框
text box builder 文本框生成器
text buffer 文本缓冲器;正文缓存器
text chart 文字图表
text compaction 文本紧缩,正文紧排
text compression 文本压缩;正文压缩
text delimiter 文本定界符
text editing 文本编辑
text editing buttons 文本编辑按钮
text editor 文本编辑程序
text enhancement 正文增强
text field 文本字段;文本区域
text file 文本文件
text flow 文本流
text font 正文字体
text formatter 文本格式化程序
text formatting system(TFS) 文本格式编辑系统
text function 文本功能
text input mode 文本输入格式
text justification 正文对齐
text justifier 正文整版程序
text left justified 文本左对齐
text library 文本库
text line 正文行
text link 文本链接

text mode 文本模式
text module 文本模块
text move 文本移动,文本搬移
text name 正文名
text note 文本附注
text only 纯文本
text orientation 文本定向
text part 正文部分
text processing 文本处理
text processing networks 文本处理网络
text processing system 文本处理系统
text read-processor 文本阅读处理器
text recognition 文本识别
text replacement 文本替换
text retrieval 正文检索
text retrieval system 文本检索系统
text revision 文本修订
text right justified 文本右对齐
text scanning 文本扫描
text segment 正文段
text sequence 文本顺序
text size 文本篇幅大小
text string 正文串
text string search 正文串搜索
text suppression 文本删除
text-to-speech conversion program 文本到声音转换程序
text tool 文本工具
text transparency 文本透明性
text truncate 正文截断
text understanding 篇章理解,文本理解
text word 正文字,文本字
text wrap 正文围绕
textbox anchor 文本框锚点
TextEdit 文本编辑软件
textmerge option 文本合并选项
Textpert 文本阅读识别软件
textual character 文本符号,正文符号
textual edit 文本编辑
texture 纹理
texture analysis 纹理分析,结构分析
texture coding 纹理编码
texture discrimination 纹理判别
texture mapping 纹理匹配,纹理映射
texture memory 纹理存储器
texture segmentation 纹理分段
texture substrate 网纹衬底
TFS(Translucent File Service) 半透

明文件服务
TFT(Thin Film Transistor) 薄膜晶体管
TFT LCD(Thin Film Transistor LCD) 薄膜晶体管液晶显示器
TFTP(Trivial File Transfer Protocol)(TCP/IP)次要文件传送协议
TG(Task Group) 任务组
TGA(Targa) TGA图像文件格式
TH(Transmission Header) 传输标题
The White House 白宫节点(美)
theft of computer service 计算机窃用
thematic mapper 专题测绘仪
theme 主题
theorem proving 定理证明
theoretical duration significant interval 理论有效时间间隔
theoretical privacy 理论保密「率
theoretical resolving power 理论分辨
theoretical value 理论值
theoretically secure 理论上安全的
theory-driven learning method 理论驱动学习法
theory of algorithm 算法理论
theory of program correction 程序正确性理论
thermal characteristic 热特性
thermal chuck 热卡盘
thermal coefficient of expansion 热膨胀系数「块
thermal conduction module 热传导模
thermal contact resistance 接触热阻
thermal control 热控制
thermal convection 热对流
thermal cut-out 热断路器
thermal design 热设计
thermal design of PCB 印刷电路板的热设计
thermal diffusion mechanism 热扩散机理
thermal dissipation 热耗散
thermal dry sublimation 热升华
thermal dye diffusion 热染料扩散
thermal endurance 热持续时间
thermal equilibrium state 热平衡状态
thermal equivalent 热当量
thermal expansion 热膨胀
thermal fatigue 热疲劳
thermal imaging system 热成像系统
thermal insulator 隔热体
thermal mismatch 热失配
thermal noise 热噪声
thermal printer 热敏打印机
thermal printing technique 感热式印刷技术
thermal radiation 热辐射
thermal resistance 热阻
thermal runaway 热损坏,热击穿
thermal sensitive paper 热敏纸
thermal shift 热漂移
thermal shock test 热冲击试验
thermal tail 热尾效应
thermal time constant 热时间常数
thermal transfer 热转印
thermal warning 热报警
thermal wax transfer 热蜡转印
thermionic emission 热电子发射
thermistor 热敏电阻器
thermo-electric effect 热电效应
thermocompression bonding 热压键合
thermocouple 热电偶
thermocouple fitting 热电偶拟合
thermocouple linearization 热电偶线性化
thermoelectric effect 热电效应
thermoforming process 加热成形工艺
thermography 热敏复印法
thermomagnetic writing 热磁写入
thermoplastic 热塑性
thermostat 控温器
thermostated bath 恒温槽
thermostatic switch 恒温开关
thesaurus 词库,主题词表
thesaurus construction 主题词表构成
thesaurus management system(TMS) 主题词管理系统
thick 粗的,厚的
thick border 粗边框
thick Ethernet 粗缆以太网
thick film 厚膜
thick film circuit 厚膜电路「路
thick film hybrid circuit 厚膜混合电
thick film materials 厚膜材料
thick film screen printing equipment 厚膜丝网印刷设备
thick underline 粗下划线

thickness 厚度
thickness measurement equipment 厚度测量仪
thicknet 粗缆网络,10BASE5 网络
Thiele algorithm 赛利算法
thimble printer 套筒式打印机
thin 细的,薄的,瘦的
Thin Client notebook 瘦客户笔记本计算机(IBM)
thin client 瘦客户机
thin Ethernet 细缆以太网
thin film 薄膜
thin film circuit 薄膜电路
thin film conductors 薄膜导体
thin film electroluminescent display device 薄膜型电致发光显示器件
thin film head 薄膜磁头
thin film hybrid integrated circuit 薄膜混合集成电路
thin film integrated circuit 薄膜集成电路
thin film laser 薄膜激光器
thin film laser element 薄膜激光元件
thin film magnetic head 薄膜磁头
thin film magnetic modules 薄膜磁性组件
thin film magnetoresistive head 薄膜磁阻磁头
thin film materials 薄膜材料
thin film memory 薄膜存储器
thin film microelectronics 薄膜微电子技术
thin film microelectronics 薄膜微电子
thin-film optical modulator 薄膜光学调制器
thin-film optical multiplexes 薄膜光多路复用器
thin-film optical switch 薄膜光开关
thin-film optical waveguide 薄膜光波
thin film photocell 薄膜光电池
thin film resistors 薄膜电阻
thin film solar cell 薄膜太阳能电池
thin film storage 薄膜存储器
thin film superconductor 薄膜超导体
thin film supertwist nematic LCD (FSTN LCD) 薄膜式超级扭曲向列型液晶显示器
thin film technology 薄膜技术
thin film transistor 薄膜晶体管
thin film transistor display(TFT) 薄膜晶体管显示屏
thin film transistor display device 薄膜晶体管显示器
thin film transistor LCD(TFT LCD) 薄膜晶体管液晶显示器
thin gate epitaxial GaAs MESFET 薄栅外延砷化镓金属氧化物场效应管
thin line 细线
thin list 薄表
thin membrane 薄膜
thin route master station 稀路由主站
thin window display 窄窗口显示器
thin wire 细线条
thinning 细线化
think bank 思想库
think group 智囊团
think time 判断时间,思考时间
thinking behavior 思维行为
thinking machine 思维机器
thinking science 思维科学
thinnet 细缆网络,10BASE2 网络
third generation computer 第三代计算机
third-generation language 第三代语言
third-generation Web site 第三代网站
third-level addressing 三阶寻址
third-level storage 第三级存储器
third normal form 第三范式
third-party database 第三方数据库
third-party vendor 第三方供应者
thisform 本表单
Thistle machine Thistle 机器(卡内基-梅隆大学)
Thomas Legislative Information on the Internet 网际网络上的 Thomas 立法信息网络节点
Thompson algorithm 托马森算法
THOR (Tandy High-intensity Optical Recorder) Tandy 高强度光记录器
thrashing 系统颠簸
thread 线程
thread binary tree 穿线二叉树
thread context 线程描述表
thread control block(TCB) 线索控制
thread object 线程对象
thread of control 控制线串

thread scheduling 线程调度
thread status 线程状态
thread structure 穿线结构
threaded code 串线编码法,线索编码
threaded file 链式文件,线索文件
threaded newsreader 线索专题阅读器
threaded tree 线索树
threading 线索化
threat 威胁
threat agent 威胁因素
threat analysis 威胁分析
threat monitoring 威胁监视
threat team 威胁小组
three address 三地址
three-address code 三地址码
three-address instruction 三地址指令
three-condition cable code 三态电报
three-condition coding 三态编码［码
three-dimension display 三维显示
three dimensional array 三维阵列,三维数组
three dimensional computer graphics 三维计算机图形
three dimensional graphics 三维图形技术
three-dimensional integrated circuits 三维集成电路
three dimensional interconnection 三维互连
three dimensional model 三维模型
three-dimensional spreadsheet 三维电子数据表格
three-input adder 三输入端加法器
three-layer architecture 三层体系结构
three-layer construction logic circuit 三层结构逻辑电路
three-length recording 三倍长度记录
three-level addressing 三级寻址
three-level subroutine 三级子例程
three party conference 三方会话
three party services 三方业务
three-plus-one address instruction 三加一地址指令
three point perspective 三点透视
three-port network 三端口网络
three-position modulation(3PM) 三单元调制

three-set space diversity 三重空间分集
three-state gate 三态门
three-tier architecture 三层结构
three-tiered diagram 三级图表
three tracks head 三轨磁头
three-value simulation 三值仿真
three-way calling 三路呼叫
three-way-handshake 三方握手联络
threshold 阈值,门限
threshold control 阈值控制
threshold decoder 阈值译码器
threshold effect 阈效应
threshold element 阈元件
threshold extension demodulator 阈值扩展解调器
threshold function 阈函数
threshold gate 阈值门
threshold Jacobi method 阈雅克比法
threshold learning process 阈值学习过程
threshold logic circuit(TLC) 阈值逻辑电路
threshold quantity 阈量
threshold value 阈值
threshold voltage 阈[门限]电压
thresholding 阈值处理
throttling 调速
through capacity 通过能力
through connection 直通连接
through group 直通群
through-group connection point 直通基群连接点
through-group equipment 直通群设备
through-hole mounting 通孔安装
through line 直通线
through-mastergroup connection point 直通主群连接点
through path 直通路径
through-rate 通过速率
through supergroup 直通超群
through-supergroup connection point 直通超群连接点
through-supergroup equipment 直通超群设备
through-supermastergroup connection point 直通超主群连接点
throughput 吞吐量
throughput analysis 吞吐量分析

throughput capacity 吞吐能力
throughput class negotiation 吞吐量级别协商
throughput delay 贯通延迟
throughput efficiency 吞吐效率
throughput of pipeline 流水线吞吐量
throughput rate 吞吐速率
throughput time 通过时间,解题时间
throw-away character 废弃字符
throw-away compiling 撤开编译,废弃编译
THRU(Through) 穿过,通过
THT(Token Holding Time) 令牌持有时间
Thue system 图厄系统
thumbnail 略图
thumbwheel 拇指旋轮
Thunder Thunder 编程系统
thunk 形式实在替换程序
TI(Terminal Interface) 终端接口
TI(Texas Instruments) 德克萨斯仪器公司
tick mark 计时标志
tick tick 滴答声
ticket vendor 自动售票机
ticking 标记,加小标记
tictactoc 井字棋
TIDAL (Transportable Integrated Design Automation Language) 可移植综合设计自动化语言
tie 孔距
tie line 专用线路
tie point 约束点
tie station 转接局
tie trunk 连接中继线
tiebreaker 仲裁器
tier 等级
TIF(Tag Image File format) 标签式图像文件格式
TIF(Terminal Independent Format) 与终端无关的格式
TIFF(Tagged Image File Format) 标记图像文件格式
TIGA (Texas Instruments Graphics Architecture) 德克萨斯仪器公司图形体系结构
Tiger Tiger 视频服务软件
tiger team (计算机安全)核查小组

tight 紧密的,紧凑的
tight alignment 精密调整
tight consistency 紧凑一致性
tight constraint 紧约束
tightly coupled 紧耦合
tightly coupled group 紧耦合工作组
tightly-coupled multiprocessor 紧耦合多处理机
tightly-coupled parallel computer 紧耦合并行计算机
tightly-coupled system 紧耦合系统
tilde 波浪号(～)
tile 平铺显示法,并列式开窗口
tiled 并排的,平铺式的
tiled window 瓷砖型视窗,平铺式窗口
tilling 铺砌,平铺
tilt angle 倾角
timbre 音质
TIME 时间显示
time abstraction 时间抽象
time and space requirements 时间和空间要求
time advancing algorithm 时间超前算法
time-assignment speech interpolation (TASI) 时分话音插入法
time base control 时基控制
time base corrector 时基校正器
time base error 时基误差
time base generator 时基发生器 「器
time-based replication 时间调度复制
time behavior simulation 时间变化特性模拟
time between failures 故障间隔时间
time bomb 时间炸弹
time case 时间角色,时间格
time cell 时间单元
time chart 时间图表
time clock 定时时钟
time code 定时码
time-coherent light 时间相干光
time comparator 时间比较器
time-complexity 时间复杂性
time component 时间分量 「码
time compression coding 时间压缩编
time congest ratio 时间拥塞率
time congestion 时间拥塞

time consistent busy hour　时间一致忙
time constant　时间常数
time constructable function　可构造时间函数
time conversion chart　时间变换表
time correlation system　时间相关系统
time cost　时间成本,时间代价
time-critical application　优先考虑时间因素的应用程序
time-delay circuit　延时电路
time delay distortion　延时失真
time dependent error　时间相关错误
time-dependent password　时间相关通行字
time dimension　时间维
time discretization　时间离散化
time discriminator　时间鉴别器
time displacement error　时间偏移错
time display　时间显示
time diversity　时间分集法
time-divided channel　时分信道
time divided network　时分网络
time division　时间分割
time-division data link　时分数据链路
time division exchange　时分交换
time division highway　时分制公共信道
time-division multiple access (TDMA)　时分多址存取;时分多重访问
time-division multiplex (TDM)　时分多路复用
time-division multiplex communication system　时分多路通信系统
time-division multiplex equipment　时分多路复用设备
time division multiplex telegraph equipment　时分多路电报设备
time-division multiplexing (TDM)　时分多路复用
time division multiplexing system　时分多路传输系统
time division switch　时分转换开关
time division switching　时分交换
time-division switching system　时分交换系统
time-domain analysis　时域分析
time-domain equalizer　时域均衡器
time-domain filter　时域滤波器
time-domain measurement　时域测量

time-domain multiple access system (TDMA)　时域多重访问系统
time-domain reflectometer　时域反射测试仪
time-domain specification　时域特性
time drift　时间漂移
time driven　时间驱动
time driven multimedia object　时间驱动多媒体对象
time duration　持续时间
time element scrambler　时间单元倒频器
time factor　时间因素
time filter　时间滤波器
time frame　时间帧,时间范围
time forecasting method　时间预测方法
time gate　定时门
time gauge (TG)　定时计
time guard band　时间保护带
time history file　时间历程文件
time hopping　时间跳动,计时起伏
time index　时间索引
time interleaving　时间交错差
time interval error (TIE)　时间间隔误差
time invariant operation　时间不变性运算
time jitter　时间跳动,计时起伏
time keeping system　时间记录系统
time lag　时滞作用
time level　时间段,时间级
time limit　时间限制
time loss　时间损耗
time-mapping asynchronous simulation　时间映射异步仿真
time margin　时间边际,时间余量
time mark generator　时标发生器
time measurement　时间测量
time model　时间模型
time modulation　时间调制
time-of-day (TOD) clock　日历钟,日时钟
time of file (TOF)　文件交付处理时间
time of filing　归档时间
time-of recovery　恢复时间
time optimal control algorithm　时间优化控制算法
time out　超时,时间超限
time-out control　超时控制
time-out interrupt　超时中断

time overhead 时间总开销
time overlapping 时间重迭
time-parameter 时间参数
time-polarity-control coding 时间极性控制编码
time preassign 时间预分配
time prediction 时间预测
time proportioning controller 时间比例控制器
time-pulse distributor 时钟脉冲分配器
time-pulse generator 时间脉冲发生器
time quantum 时间量子
time-quantum method 时间量子法
time-quantized control of synchronization 时间量化同步控制
time recovery 定时恢复
time redundancy 时间冗余
time register 时间寄存器
time relay 时间继电器
time restriction 时间限制
time response 时间响应
time reversal invariance 时间反演不变性
time scale 时标
time scale factor 时标因子
time schedule controller 时间表控制器
time separator 时间分隔符
time sequence 时序
time series techniques 时间序列技术
time server 时间服务器
time service 时间服务
time share 分时,时间共享
time-shared bus 分时总线
time-shared computer 分时计算机
time shared control 分时控制
time shared network 分时网络
time-shared or common bus 分时或共用总线
time-shared system 分时系统
time sharing(TS) 分时
time sharing accounting 分时记账
time sharing allocation of hardware resources 硬件资源的时间分配
time sharing allocator 分时分配程序
time sharing computer 分时计算机
time sharing control task(TSC) 分时控制任务
time-sharing deferred batch mode 分时延期批量处理模式
time sharing driver 分时驱动程序
time sharing dynamic allocator 分时动态分配程序
time sharing graceful degradation 分时从容退化,分时弱化故障
time sharing incremental compiler 分时递增编译程序
time sharing input QCB(TSID) 分时输入队增控制块
time-sharing interchange 分时交换
time sharing interface area 分时接口区域
time sharing interface program 分时接口程序
time sharing interface terminal 分时接口终端
time sharing interrupt capability 分时中断能力
time sharing job control block(TJB) 分时工作控制块
time-sharing monitor system 分时监督系统
time sharing multiplexer channel 分时多路转接器信道
time sharing operating system 分时操作系统
time-sharing option 分时选择
time sharing priority 分时优先权
time sharing program monitor system 分时程序监督系统
time-sharing quantum 分时量子「式
time-sharing ready mode 分时就绪模
time sharing running modes 分时运行模式
time-sharing scheduler system 分时调度程序系统
time sharing scheduling rules 分时调度规则
time-sharing system(TSS) 分时系统
time-sharing system command 分时系统命令
time-sharing system reliability 分时系统可靠性
time-sharing system subcomponent 分时系统子成分
time-sharing time-quantum method 定量分时法

time-sharing user modes 分时用户方式
time-sharing waiting mode 分时等待模式
time slice 时间片
time-slice multitasking 时间片多任务
time slicing 时间片划分法
time slot 时隙
time slot interchange 时隙互换
time slot sequence integrity 时隙序列完整性
time-space trade-off 时间空间折衷
time spread code 时间展宽码
time-spreading process 时间展宽过程
time stamp 时间戳,时间标记
time step monitoring algorithm 时间节拍监控算法
time stepping finite element method 时间步有限元法
time switch 时间接线器
time synchronization 时间同步
time system 定时系统
time table 时间表
time-to-digital conversion 时间-数字转换
time to failure 无故障工作时间
time to first failure 首次无故障工作时间
time to live 生存时间
time tolerance 时间容差
time trade-off 时间折衷
time transparency 时间透明性
time utilization 时间利用
time-varying data 时变数据
time window protocol 时间窗口协议
timecode 时间代码
timed backup 定时备份
timed event graph 时控事件图
timed preemption 定时抢占
timed task 定时任务
Timed Token Protocol(TTP) 定时令牌协议
Timed Token Rotation Protocol(TTRP) 定时令牌循环协议
timeline （视频、动画编辑）流程线
timeline panel 流程线窗口
timeout 超时
timer(T) 计时器,定时器

timer interrupt 定时器中断
timer initiation facility 计时器初始化设施
timer request 计时器请求
timer request element 计时器请求单元
timer response 计时器响应
timer supervision （OS/VS2）计时器管理程序
times 次数
timesharing 分时的
TimeSlips Ⅲ TimeSlips Ⅲ记时程序
timestamp 时间戳
timetable scheduling algorithm 时间表调度算法
TIMIC(Time Interval Modulation Information Coding) 时间间隔调制信息编码
timing algorithm 定时算法
timing and control circuit 定时与控制电路,时控电路
timing calibration device 时标校正设备
timing channel 定时通道
timing clock 定时时钟
timing control 定时控制
timing device(TD) 计时设备
timing diagram 时序图
timing error 定时错误,同步错误
timing estimation 定时估算
timing extraction 定时抽取
timing inquiry control 定时查询控制
timing jitter 定时信号抖动
timing mark check 时标检验
timing meter 计时器,定时表
timing model 定时模型
timing network 定时网络
timing out 定时时间已过,超时
timing pulse 定时脉冲
timing pulse distributor 定时脉冲分配器
timing pulse generator 定时脉冲发生器
timing recalculation 定时重算
timing recovery 定时恢复
timing reference signal 定时参考信号
timing sampling 定时取样
timing sequence 时标序列
timing signal 定时信号,时标信号
timing signal generator 定时信号发生器
timing simulation 定时仿真

timing system 定时系统;同步系统
timing track 同步磁道;同步跟踪
timing tracking accuracy 定时跟踪精度
timing verification 定时校验
TIMP (Terminal Interface Message Processor) 终端接口信息处理机
Tin-Lead for plating 镀锡铅
Tin-Nickel for plating 镀锡镍
TINET (Transparent Intelligent Network) 透明智能网络
TINMAN "锡人"要求
tinning 镀锡
Tiny BASIC 微型BASIC语言
Tiny C 微型C语言
tiny fragment attack 极小数据段攻击
tiny loop 小循环
tiny model 小模式
TIP (Terminal Interface message Processor) 终端接口消息处理机
TIP (Terminal Interface Package) 终端接口程序包
tip 提示;技巧;端头
tip help 提示性帮助
tip node 端结点
tip of the day 日积月累
tip side 接头端,触点端
tip wizard box 操作向导框
TIP/TOP(Tape InPut / Tape OutPut) 带输入输出
title 标题
title band 标题带区
title bar 标题条
title option 标题选项
title placeholder 标题占位符
TLI (Transport Level Interface) (Unix)传输层接口
TLIST 置信权限列表
TLM (Time Linearization Method) 时间线性化法
TM/1(Tables Manager/1) 表格管理程序/1
TMR(Triple Modular Redundancy) 三重模块冗余
TMR/single modular system 三模冗余/单模工作系统
TN(Transport Network) 传输网络
TOC(Table Of Contents) 内容表
TOCTTOU(Time Of Check To Time Of Use) problems 查看时间对使用时间问题
TOD(Time Of Day) 日历时间「钟
TODC(Time-Of-Day Clock) 日历时
Toeplitz structure 托易普利兹结构
TOF(Top Of Form) 页开始
toggle 触发器,双迭态元件
toggle case 大小写转换
toggle flip flop 翻转触发器,T触发器
toggle key 转换键
toggle switch 转换开关
token 记号,标记;权标,信标,令牌
token bus 令牌总线
token bus access control 令牌总线访问控制
token bus network 令牌总线型网络
token-driven algorithm 令牌驱动算法
token frame 令牌帧
token holding time(THT) 令牌持有时间
token lost 令牌丢失
token matching 令牌匹配
token name 令牌名
token passing protocol 令牌传递协议
token pool 令牌池
token queue 令牌队列
token replacement 令牌置换
token restoration algorithm 令牌恢复算法
token ring 令牌环
Token Ring network 令牌环网络(IBM)
token ring network 令牌环网络
token rotation time(TRT) 令牌循环时间
token transaction 令牌事务处理
TokenTalk 令牌对话软件
Tokyo Shibaura Electric Co. (TOSHIBA) 东芝公司(日)
tolerability 可容许性
tolerable delay 可容许延迟
tolerable error rate 可容许差错率
tolerance 容差,公差
tolerance analysis 容差分析
tolerance design 容错设计
tolerance interval 容许区间
tolerance processing 容错处理
toll 长途电话

toll center 长途电话中心局
toll-free number 免费电话号码
toll hierarchy 长途电话分级结构
toll line release 长途线路释放
toll network 长途通信网络
toll office 长途电话局
toll service 长途通信服务
toll switching trunk 长途交换中继线
tomcatv tomcatv 基准程序
tomographic image 断层分析图像
tomography 层析成像
tone 信号音,音调;色调
tone alternator 音调振荡器
tone-burst generator 突发单音发生器
tone control 音调控制
tone-control aperture 色调控制孔
tone control circuit 音调控制电路
tone curves 色调曲线
tone dialing 按键式拨号,音频拨号
tone illustration 带色调图
tone image 灰度图像
tone line 色调线
tone on hold 保持音
tone recognition 音调识别
tone separation 音调(色调)分离
toner 着色剂,碳粉,墨粉
toner cartridge 墨粉盒
toner hopper 墨粉盒,碳粉盒
toner low 墨粉不足
toner mark 色剂标记
toner offset 色剂偏移
toner reservoir 调色剂存储器
tones transmission 音调传输
toning control 色调控制
toning system 显影系统
tool 工具
tool bar 工具栏
tool-based programming environment 基于工具的程序设计环境
tool box 工具箱
tool builder 工具建造者
tool for knowledge engineering 知识工程工具
tool function 工具函数
tool integration 工具集成
tool interface 工具接口
tool kit 工具箱
tool lock button 工具锁定按钮
tool manager 工具管理程序
tool mode 工具方式
tool palette 工具盘
tool path 工具轨迹
tool position compensation 刀具位置补偿
tool set 工具组
tool system 工具系统
tool tip text 工具提示信息
toolbar 工具条,工具栏
toolbox 工具箱
tooling 工艺装备
toolkit 工具箱
toolset 成套工具
TOP(Technical & Office Protocol) 技术与办公室协议
top align 顶端对齐
top border 顶端边框
top clause 顶层子句
top document 顶层文档
top-down approach 自顶向下分析法
top-down design 自顶向下设计
top-down development 自顶向下研制法
top-down error correcting 自顶向下纠错法
top-down error recovery 自顶向下差错恢复
top-down estimation 自顶向下估算
top-down fast-back parser 自顶向下快速回退分析算法
top-down goal-oriented analysis procedure 自顶向下的面向目标分析过程
top-down logic 自顶向下逻辑
top-down machine 自顶向下机器
top-down method 自顶向下法
top-down parsing 自顶向下语法分析
top-down partitioning rule 自顶向下划分规则
top-down program refinement 自顶向下程序求精
top-down programming 自顶向下程序设计
top-down reasoning 自顶向下推理
top-down refinement 自顶向下求精法
top-down strategy 自顶向下策略
top-down structuring design 自顶向下的结构化设计

top-down syntax analysis 自顶向下语法分析
top-down testing 自顶向下测试
top-down understanding 自顶向下理解
top element 栈顶元素
top entry 顶端插入
top environment 顶层环境
top-level domain 最高层域
top-level environment 顶层环境
top-level folder 顶层文件夹
top-level function call 顶层函数调用
top-level goal 最高层目标
top-level monitor 顶层监督程序
top-level response 顶层响应
top-level specification 顶层说明
top-level structure 顶层结构
top-level window 顶层窗口
top-loading 自顶装入的
top margin 顶边距
top-most element 最顶层元素
top node 顶端节点
top of file(TOF) 文件头
top of form 页头
top of page 页眉
top of stack pointer 栈顶指针
top operand 栈顶运算对象
top operator 栈顶运算符
top-rank retrieval 顶端排队检索
top row 顶行,首行
top secret classification 绝密级
top speed 最高速度
top stack location 栈顶单元
top term 主题词
top-to-bottom 自顶向下
top view 顶视图
Topic 证券数据库系统
TOPIC(Teletext Output of Price Information by Computer) 计算机价格信息电视数据输出
topic 主题;细目
topic drift 论题转移
topic group 论题小组
topic sentence 课题句子
TOPICS(Total On-line Program and Information Control System) 一体化联机程序与信息控制系统
topless end extension 无顶端扩展
topmost 最顶层的,最高的

topographic map 地形图,拓扑图
topological optimization 拓扑优化
topological problem in parallel searching 并行搜索的拓扑问题
topological sorting 拓扑排序
topological variation 拓扑差异
topologically integrated geographic encoding and referencing system(TIGER) 拓扑学综合地理编码参照系统
topology 布局技术,拓扑学
topology design of network 网络拓扑设计问题
topology of networks 网络拓扑
TOPS(Transparent OPerating System) 透明操作系统(Sun)
TOPS TOPS操作系统(DEC)
TOPVIEW TOPVIEW视窗环境(IBM)
torn-off tab 可拖下选项表
torque 转矩
torque amplifier 转矩放大器
torque sensor 转矩传感器
torsion 扭力;转矩;挠率
torsional loading 转矩加载
TOS(Tape Operating System) 磁带操作系统
total 数,总计
total allowance for machining 加工总余量
total architecture 总体结构
total backup 整盘备份,完整备份
total bypass 全旁路
total channel noise 总信道噪声
total check 累加校验
total chromatic dispersion 总色散
total composite error 总合成误差
total consumption set 总消费集
total correctness 完全正确性;总和正确性
total cost 总成本,总开支
total counter 总量计数器
total demand 总需求
total departure 总偏差,总偏离度
total distributed control system 全分布式控制系统
total divisor 全因子
total dump 全部转储

total emissivity 全发射度
total error 总误差
total failure 全失效,完全失败
total function 全函数
total graphic library 全图形库
total harmonic distortion(THD) 总谐波失真
total information system 总体型信息系统
total inspection 总数检验
total internal reflection 全内反射
total life cycle time 整个生命周期时间
total management system 总体管理系统
total memory 总共内存空间
total numerical control 总体数字控制
total ordering relation 全序关系
total packet received 已接收包总数
total packet sent 已发送包总数
total performance 总性能
total predicate 全谓词
total preventive maintenance 预防性维护总时间
total quality control(TQC) 全面质量管理
total recursive function 全递归函数
total regression curve 总回归曲线
total resource 总资源
total scanning line length 总扫描线长度
total server work memory 服务器工作内存总数
total solution 完整解决方案
total solution time 总求解时间
total space 总空间
total state 全状态
total system 全系统
total traffic 总通信量
totality problem 完全性问题
totally additive 完全可加性
totally centralized network 完全集中式网络
totally decentralized network 完全分散式网络
totally optimal plan 整体最优方案
totally ordered set 全有序集合
totally self-checking circuit 全自检电路
totally self-checking sequential machine 全自检时序机
totally self-testing circuit 全自检电路
totally symmetric function 全对称函数
touch 触摸
touch area 触摸区
touch-call 按键式呼叫
touch input system 触摸输入系统
touch pad 触摸板
touch screen 触摸屏
touch screen converter 触摸屏转换器
touch screen terminal 触摸屏终端
touch-sensitive display 触感显示器
touch-sensitive membrane keyboard 触敏膜片键盘
touch-sensitive software 触敏软件
touch sensitive switch 接触敏感开关
touch tablet 触摸式图形输入板
touch-tone data service 按键式数据服务
touch typing 盲打
Touchstone Touchstone 计算机(Intel)
touchtone dial 按钮音拨号盘
tournament method 锦标赛法
tournament sort 联赛排序
tournament table 赛程表
toward peak performance(TPP) 接近峰值性能
tower case 立式机箱,塔式机箱
Towers 阵列盘
toy 玩具
toy computer 玩具计算机
toy database 小型数据库
TP(Time Parallel) 时间平行
TP(Transaction Processing) 事务处理
TP(Twisted Pair cable) 双绞线电缆
TP monitor (Transaction Processing monitor) 任务处理监视程序
TP0(Transport Protocol class 0) 传输协议类 0(ISO/OSI,简单类)
TP4(Transport Protocol class 4) 传输协议类 4(ISO/OSI,差错检测与恢复类)
TPD(Time Pulse Decoder) 定时脉冲译码器
TPG(Timing Pulse Generator) 定时脉冲发生器
TPI(Transport Provider Interface) 传输供应商界面
tpi(tracks per inch) 每英寸道数
TPIOS(Telecommunication Process In-

put/Output System) 远程通信处理输入输出系统
TR(Terminal Ready) 终端机准备好
Trace Trace 长指令计算机(Multiflow)
trace 跟踪;亮迹
trace analysis 跟踪分析
trace control 跟踪控制
trace debug 跟踪调试程序
trace diagnostic program 跟踪诊断程序
trace exception 跟踪异常
trace flow 跟踪流程
trace handler 跟踪处理程序
trace interrupt 跟踪中断
trace packet 跟踪信息包
trace program 跟踪程序
trace range 跟踪范围
trace relay 历史重放
trace routine 跟踪例程
trace set 迹集合
trace simulation 轨迹仿真
trace statement 跟踪语句
trace table 跟踪表
traceability 可跟踪性
tracer 跟踪程序
TraceRoute 路由跟踪程序
tracing facility 跟踪设施
tracing loop pass 跟踪循环遍
tracing routine 跟踪例程
track 磁道,轨道
track advance 进轨
track and hold unit 跟踪保持设备
track ball 轨迹球,跟踪球
track buffering 磁道缓冲
track calibration 磁道校准
track center-to-center spacing 磁道中心距
track change control 磁道交换控制器
track current address register 磁道当前地址寄存器
track density 磁道密度
track distortion 磁道畸变
track fitting 轨道拟合
track following feedback control 磁道跟踪反馈控制
track following servo system 磁道跟踪伺服系统
track format 磁道格式
track group 磁道组
track hold 磁道保持,磁道占用
track hole 输纸孔
track identifier 磁道标识符
track index 磁道索引
track label 轨道标号
track layout 磁道布局
track mark 轨道标记
track off 跟踪关闭
track offset 磁道偏差,轨道偏移量
track on 跟踪开始
track overflow 磁道溢出
track pitch 磁道间距
track predication 跟踪预报
track protection 磁道保护
track recording density 磁道记录密度
track recovery 磁道恢复
track reverse 退轨
track select 磁道选择
track spacing 磁道间距
track time remaining 曲目剩余时间
trackability 可跟踪能力
trackball 跟踪球
tracker 跟踪器
tracking 跟踪
tracking A/D converter 跟踪式模/数转换器
tracking condition 跟踪条件,轨迹条件
tracking control system 轨迹控制系统
tracking cross 跟踪十字光标
tracking display system 跟踪显示系统
tracking mark 跟踪标志
tracking mouse movement 跟踪鼠标移动
tracking network 跟踪网络
tracking object 跟踪目标
tracking preprocessor 跟踪预处理机
tracking range 跟踪范围
tracking speed 跟踪速度
tracking symbol 跟踪符
trackpad 轨迹板
tracks per inch 每英寸道数目
TrackWrite keyboard 可收缩键盘(IBM)
tractable problem 易处理的问题
tractor feed 履带牵引输纸
tractor feeder 牵引输纸器
tractor holes 牵引输纸孔

tractors 牵引器
trade-off 折衷,权衡
trade-off decision 折衷判定
trade-off evaluation system 折衷评定系统
trade-off process 权衡过程
trade-off relation 折衷关系
trademark 商标
TradeNet 贸易网络(新加坡)
traditional Chinese 繁体字
traditional debugging 传统调试法
traditional decision support system (TDSS) 传统决策支持系统
traffic 通信量,业务量
traffic analysis 通信量分析
traffic bifurcation routing 分散通信量路由选择
traffic capacity 通信容量
traffic-carrying device 业务传输设备
traffic class 通信量分类
traffic congestion 流量拥挤
traffic control program 流通控制程序
traffic coordinator 通信量控制器
traffic cover 通信量覆盖范围
traffic diagram 通信量图表
traffic distribution 通信量分配
traffic flow security 通信流安全
traffic information 业务信息
traffic intensity 业务量强度
traffic item 业务项
traffic load 业务负荷
traffic matrix 业务量矩阵
traffic model 业务模型
traffic network 业务网络
traffic node 通信节点
traffic offered 流入业务量
traffic performance 业务量性能
traffic rate control 通信量控制
traffic relation 业务关系
traffic requirement matrix 流量需求矩阵
traffic routing 业务量路由选择
traffic service position system 业务服务座席系统
traffic shaping 传输流量整形
traffic statistics 通信量统计
traffic stream 业务流
traffic usage recorder(TUR) 业务使用记录器
traffic volume 业务量
trafficability performance 业务量性「能
Traffix Traffix网管软件(3Com)
trail 轨迹;指针
trailer 尾部,报尾
trailer block 附随信息组
trailer encapsulation 尾部压缩
trailer field 尾部字段
trailer gap 尾间隙
trailer label 尾标
trailer page 结束页
trailer record 尾部记录
trailer statement 结束语句
trailing blank 尾随空白
trailing decision 尾部判定
trailing edge 后沿
trailing end 结尾
trailing flag 结束标志
trailing parameter 后缀参数
trailing zero 尾随零
train 列,串;训练
train type printer 列车式打印机
trainable pattern classifier 可训练模式分类器
training 训练
training mode 训练模式
training pattern 训练模式
training pattern classifier system 训练模式分类器系统
training process 训练过程
training samples 训练样本
training set 训练集
training statistics 训练统计
trajectory 轨迹
trajectory control 轨迹控制
trajectory decomposition 轨迹分解
trajectory generation 轨迹生成
TRAN(TRANsmit) 发送,传送
transacted access mode 交易访问模式
transacted mode 交易[事务处理]模式
transaction 交易,事务;事务处理
transaction analysis 事务分析,交易分析
transaction application driver 事务处理应用驱动程序
transaction area 编目区

transaction backout 事务复原
transaction-based routing 基于事务的路由选择
transaction code 事务处理码
transaction command security 事务命令安全性
transaction context object 事务上下文相关对象
transaction control table 事务控制表
transaction data 事务数据集
transaction data set record block 事务数据集记录块
transaction detail record 事务细节记
transaction display 事务显示
transaction-driven system 事项驱动系统
transaction execution flow 事务处理执行流
transaction file 事务文件
transaction interface package(TIP) 事务接口软件包
transaction journal 事务处理日志,交易日志
transaction key 事务密钥
transaction key set 事项密钥组
transaction library 事务处理库
transaction load balancing 事务处理负荷均衡
transaction log 事项记录,事务处理日志
transaction model 事务处理模型
transaction modeling 事项建模
transaction network service 事务处理网络服务
transaction number 事项号
transaction-office information system (TOIS) 事务型办公信息系统
transaction-oriented application 面向事务的应用程序
transaction-oriented message control system 面向事务的消息控制系统
transaction-oriented system 面向事务的系统
transaction processing 事务处理
transaction processing language 事务处理语言
transaction processing per second 每秒事务处理

transaction processing system 事务处理系统
transaction program 事务处理程序
transaction record 事务记录 「部
transaction record header 事务记录首
transaction record number 事务记录号 「动
transaction restart 事务处理重新启
transaction scheduling 事务处理调度
transaction selection menu 事务处理选择表
Transaction Server Core Components 事务服务器核心组件
Transaction Server object 事务服务器对象
transaction services 事项处理服务
transaction tape 事务处理带 「量
transaction throughput 事务处理吞吐
transaction tracking system(TTS) 异动[事务处理]跟踪系统
transaction videotex 事务可视图文
transaction wait for graph 事务处理等待图表 「区
transaction work area 事务处理工作
transactional application 事务型应用程序
transborder data flow 越境数据流通
transceiver 收发器,收发信机
transceiving equipment 收发设备
transcoding 代码转换
transcribe 转录
transcriber 信息转换器
transcription 转录,转换
transcription break 符号分解
transcription machine 转录机
transducer 换能器;传感器;翻译机
transducer translating unit 换能转换
transfer 传送,转移 「器
transfer ability 移植能力
transfer address 转移地址
transfer algorithm 转移算法
transfer-allowed procedure 转换允许过程
transfer buffering 转送缓冲
transfer card 控制转移卡片
transfer channel 转接信道
transfer characteristic 转移特性,传输特性

transfer check 转移检验
transfer circuit 传送电路
transfer control 转移控制
transfer count 传送计数
transfer delay 传送延迟
transfer function 传递函数,传输函数
transfer gain 传输增益
transfer instruction 转移指令
transfer key 传送键
transfer matrix 转移矩阵
transfer medium 转移媒体
transfer network 转移网络
transfer of control 控制转移
transfer operation 传送操作
transfer option 传输选项
transfer phase 传送阶段
transfer process 转移进程
transfer-prohibited procedure 禁止转接程序
transfer-prohibited signal 禁止转接信号
transfer rate 传送速率
transfer request signal 传送请求信号
transfer sequence 转移序列
transfer statement 控制转移语句
transfer station 转移站,转印装置
transfer speed 传送速度
transfer statement 转移语句
transfer syntax 传送语法
transfer table 转移表
transfer time 转移时间
transfer tree 转移树
transfer vector 转移向量
transfinite 无限的;超限的
transfinite element method 超限元法
transfinite incompleteness 超限不完全性
transfinite interpolation 超限插值
transform 变换
transform centering 对中变换
transform coding 变换编码
transform decoding 变换解码
transform diagram 变换图
transform identity 恒等变换
transform object 变换对象
transform operator 变换运算符
transform pair 变换对
transform statement 变换语句
transformation(T) 变换

transformation algorithm 变换算法
transformation coefficient 变换系数
transformation definition language (TDL) 变换定义语言
transformation equation 变换方程
transformation group 变换群
transformation library 变换库
transformation matrix 变换矩阵
transformation pipeline 变换流水线
transformation rule 变换规则
transformation strategy 变换策略
transformational grammar 转换语法,变换语法
transformational semantics 变换语义
transformer 变压器
transformer core 变压器铁心
transforming tree 变换树
transient 过渡的,瞬变的
transient analysis 瞬态分析,过渡过程分析
transient analyzer 瞬态分析器
transient area 暂存区,过渡区
transient area control table(TACT) 暂驻存储区控制表
transient area descriptor(TAD) 暂驻存储区描述符
transient behavior 暂态特性;瞬时行
transient command 瞬时命令
transient condition 瞬态条件
transient control executive area 暂时控制执行区
transient data 瞬态数据
transient data control 瞬时数据控制
transient delay time 瞬变延迟时间
transient directory 暂用目录
transient distortion 过渡失真
transient disturbance 瞬时干扰,瞬态扰动
transient error 瞬态误差,瞬时错误
transient failure 瞬时失效
transient fault 瞬时故障
transient hazard 瞬时危险
transient image 瞬时图像
transient library 暂用库
transient member 瞬时成分
transient memory 暂用存储器
transient model 暂态模型
transient overshoot 瞬时过冲

transient performance 瞬时性能
transient phase 瞬变阶段,过渡阶段
transient program 暂用程序,非常驻程序
transient program area 暂用程序区
transient program table(TPT) 暂用程序表
transient protection 瞬态保护
transient recorder 瞬变记录器
transient response 瞬态响应
transient routine 暂用例程,过渡例程
transient signal detection 瞬时信号检测
transient solution 瞬态解
transient stability 瞬时稳定性
transient state 瞬态,暂态
transient stress concentration 瞬时应力集中
transient suppress 瞬态抑制
transient temperature distribution 瞬时温度分布
transient uncycle 瞬变非周期
transient upset 瞬时扰动
transient voltage protection 瞬时电压保护
transient waveform analysis 瞬时波形分析
transinformation content 传送信息量
transinformation rate 传送信息率
transistor 晶体管
Transistor Sizing System 晶体管版图设计专家系统
transistor-transistor logic(TTL) 晶体管-晶体管逻辑电路
transit 转接,过渡
transit center 转接中心
transit country 转接国
transit error 过渡性错误
transit exchange 转接局
transit model 转移模型
transit network 中继网,过渡网
transit network identification 转接网络标识
transit share 过境分摊额
transit through-connect signal 转接直通连接信号
transit time 转接时间
transit traffic 转接业务量
transition 变迁,过渡,切换

transition assertion 变迁断言
transition closure 传递闭包
transition coding 变换编码,变迁编码
transition count 跳变计数
transition description 转移描述
transition deviation 转换误差
transition diagram 转换图
transition effect 过渡效果
transition fiber 过渡光纤
transition function 转移函数
transition graph 转换图
transition matrix 转移矩阵
transition modeling 过渡造型
transition network 转移网络
transition network grammar 转移网络文法
transition-oriented state representation 面向迁移的状态表示法
transition point 过渡点,状态转换点
transition region 过渡区
transition state 过渡状态
transition table 转换表
transition time 过渡时间,渡越时间
transition transformation 平移变换
transitive closure 传递闭包
transitive dependency 传递相关性
transitive reduction 传递归约
transitively orientable graph 传递可定向图
transitivity 传递律;传递性
translate 翻译;平移
translated axis line 平移轴线
translated channel 转换信道
translated line 平移线
translating algorithm 翻译算法
translating program 翻译程序
translating routine 翻译例程
translating time 翻译时间
translation 转换,翻译
translation bridge 翻译桥接器
translation buffer 转换缓冲器
translation cipher 转换密码,单表密码
translation control block 转换控制块
translation cycle 翻译周期,转换周期
translation environment 翻译环境
translation exception 转换规则例外
translation filter 转换过滤器
translation grammar 翻译文法

translation instance 翻译实例
translation lookaside buffer(TLB) 翻译后援缓冲器
translation model 转换模型
translation phase 转换阶段
translation paradigm 翻译风格
translation process 转换过程
translation quality 翻译质量
translation rule 转换规则
translation schema 翻译模式
translation specification exception 转换描述异常
translation table 转换表
translation table entry 转换表项目
translation time 翻译时间
translation tool 翻译工具
translation transformation 平移变换
translator 翻译程序；翻译机
translator package 翻译程序组
TransLISP Plus TransLISP＋语言
transliteration 音译；直译
transliteration table 直译对照表
translucent 半透明的
translucent screen 半透明荧光屏
transmission 传输，传送
transmission adapter(TA,XA) 传输适配器
transmission band 传输频带
transmission block 传送块
transmission block number(TBN) 传输块序号
transmission buffer 传输缓存
transmission category 传输范畴
transmission channel 传输信道
transmission characteristics 传输特性
transmission code 传输码
transmission code violation 传输码破坏
transmission coefficient 传输系数
transmission control 传输控制
transmission control character 传输控制字符
transmission control element(TCE) 传输控制元件
transmission control flag(TF) 传输控制标志
transmission control layer 传输控制层
transmission control protocol(TCP) 传输控制协议
transmission control unit(TCU) 传输控制器
transmission convergence (TC) (ATM)传输聚合子层
transmission cycle 传输周期
transmission delay 传输延迟
transmission deviations 传输偏差
transmission distortion 传输失真
transmission efficiency 传输效率
transmission equipment 传输设备
transmission error control 传输错误控制
transmission extension 传输扩展
transmission facility 传输设施
transmission frame 传输帧
transmission gain 传输增益
transmission group 传输群
transmission header(TH) 传输标题
transmission interface 传输接口
transmission interface converter 传输接口转换
transmission interruption 传输中断
transmission level 传输电平
transmission level point(TLP) 传输电平点
transmission limit 传输极限
transmission line 传输线
transmission link 传输链路
transmission loss 传输损耗
transmission medium 传输媒体
transmission message unit(TMU) 传输信息单元
transmission mode 传输方式
transmission network 传输网络
transmission objectives 传输指标
transmission packet 发送信息包
transmission pad character 传输填充字符
transmission path 传输路径
transmission path delay 传输路径延迟
transmission performance 传输性能
transmission preprocessor 传输预处理机
transmission priority 传输优先级
transmission quality 传输质量
transmission queue 发送队列
transmission reference point 传输参考点
transmission retry 传输重试

transmission route 传输路由
transmission service profile 传输服务配置文件
transmission signal 传输信号
transmission speed 传输速度
transmission subsystem 传输子系统
transmission system code 传输系统码
transmission time 传输时间
transmission-utilization ratio 传输利用率
transmission window 传输窗口
transmissive scanning 透光扫描
transmit 发送,传送
transmit buffer 发送缓冲器
transmit buffer chain 发送缓冲器链
transmit buffer ready 发送缓冲器就绪
transmit control block 发送控制块
transmit copy line 发送拷贝线
transmit data register 发送数据寄存器
transmit data set 传输数据集
transmit filter 发送滤波器,发送过滤程序
transmit flow control 发送流控制
transmit format generator 发送格式产生器
transmit interrupt 发送中断
transmit leg 发送边
transmit mode 发送方式
transmit once 一次性传输
transmit pair 发送线对
transmit port 发送端口
transmittable property 可传送属性
transmittance 透射率,传递系数
transmitted information 发送信息
transmitter 发送器,发射机
transmitter card 发送器插件
transmitter-receiver serial/parallel module 串并行发收器
transmitter register 发送寄存器
transmitter start code (TSC) 发送设备启动码
transmitting branch 发信支路
transmitting channel 发送信道
transmultiplexer 多路信号变换器
transmultiplexer channel 多路变换器信道
transnational data flow 跨越国界的数据流
transonic 超音速的
TRANSPAC TRANSPAC公用数据网
transparency 透明性
transparency media adapter 透射器
transparency mode 透明方式
transparency processing 透明处理
transparent 透明的
transparent access mechanism 透明访问机制
transparent bridge 透明网桥
transparent code 透明代码
transparent control statement 透明控制语句
transparent data 透明数据
transparent data communication code 透明数据通信码
transparent data transfer phase 透明数据传递阶段
transparent file system sharing 透明文件系统共享
transparent information 透明信息
transparent interconnection 透明互连
transparent interface 透明接口
transparent media adapter (TMA) 透射媒体适配器
transparent mode 透明方式
transparent network 透明网络
transparent original 透明原件
transparent paging 透明分页法
transparent recovery 透明恢复
transparent refresh 透明刷新
transparent scheme 透明方案
transparent text mode 透明电文方式
transparent transmission 透明传输
transparentness 透明性,透明
transponder 脉冲转发器
transport 传送;走带机构
transport delay 传输延迟
transport device 传输设备
transport endpoint 传输终止点
transport interface 传输接口
transport layer 传输层
Transport-Neutral Encapsulation Format (TNEF) 传输不确定封装格式
transport object 传输对象
transport protocol 传输协议
transport provider 传输供应商[提供

者]
transport station 传送站
transport user 传输用户
transportable 可移动的,可移植的
transportable communication equipment 移动式通信设备
transportable computer 可移动计算机
transportable compiler 可移植编译程序
transportable interpreter 可移植解释程序
transportable link terminal 可移动链路终端
transportation 传输;转送;迁移
transportation vehicle 运输车辆
transpose 转置
transpose matrix 转置矩阵
transposed file 转置文件
transposition 置换,换位
transposition cipher 换位密码,移位密码
transposition relation 置换关系
transputer(TRANSistor comPUTER) 群联计算机
transversal equalizer 横向均衡器
transversal filter 横向滤波器
transversal number 横截数
transversal of a hypergraph 超图的横截集
transverse 横向的;横线
transverse check 横向校验
transverse cross-section 横截面
transverse judder 横向位移
transverse magnetic recording 横向磁记录方式
transverse mode noise 横模噪声
transverse parity check 横向奇偶校验
transverse recording 横向记录方式
transverse redundancy check(TRC) 横向冗余校验
transverse scanning 横向扫描 「像
transverse sectional image 横切面图
transverse shear deformation 横向剪切变形
trap 俘获;陷阱
trap address 陷阱地址
trap/break point 断点俘获 「体
trap community (Netware)陷阱共同

trap condition 自陷条件
trap door 陷门
trap effect 陷阱效应
trap enable 允许自陷,允许俘获
trap flag 陷阱标志
trap interruption 自陷中断
trap mask 陷阱屏蔽
trap pending 自陷挂起
trap word 陷阱字
trapdoor 陷门,活动天窗
trapdoor function 陷门函数
trapdoor one-way function 陷门单向函数
trapezoid rule 梯形法
trapezoidal filter 梯形滤波器
trapezoidal highpass filter 梯形高通滤波器
trapezoidal integration 梯形积分
trapezoidal lowpass filter 梯形低通滤波器
trapezoidal network resistance 梯形网络电阻
trapezoidal quadrature rule 梯形求面积法则
trapezoidal response 梯形响应
trapped instruction 设陷指令
trapping 俘获,设陷阱
trapping class mark 俘获类标志
trapping mechanism 设陷机构
trapping mode 俘获方式,设陷阱模式
trash (MacOS)废纸篓
trash can 垃圾箱
trashware 废件
travel 行程;移动;传播
travel indicator 行程指示器
travel mechanism 移动机构
travel seller problem 旅行商问题
travel time 传播时间
travelling salesman problem 货郎问题
travelling-wave A/D converter 行波模/数转换器
Traverstar Travelstar 硬盘驱动器(IBM)
travesability 可遍历性
traversal 遍历
traversal type 遍历类型
traverse 遍历;横过
traverse of tree 树的遍历

tray 托架,托盘
tray delivery mechanism 托架传送机构
treat as equal 同等处理
treatment effect 处理效果
treble 高音
tree 树
tree adjunct grammar 树形修饰文法
tree analysis code 树形分析代码
tree architecture 树结构
tree automaton 树自动机
tree balance 树平衡
tree branch 树枝
tree classifier 树分类器
tree commit 树接合法
tree compaction algorithm 树紧致算法
tree construction function 树构造函数
tree copy 树复制
tree decomposition 树分解
tree degree 树的度
tree depth 树的深度
tree directory 树形目录
tree domain 树域
tree embedding 树嵌入
tree entry 树登录项
tree erasing 树抹除
tree form language 树形语言
tree function 树形函数
tree generation algorithm 树生成算法
tree grammar 树文法
tree graph 树图
tree height 树的高度
tree heuristic 树启发式
tree hierarchy 树形层次
tree identity 树恒等式
tree index 树形索引
tree insertion 树插入
tree intermediate language 树形中间语法
tree labeling algorithm 树标号设置算法
tree language 树语言
tree leaf 树叶
tree level 树的层
tree locking protocol 树封锁协议
tree linear order 树线性次序
tree machine 树型机器
tree matching 树匹配
tree name 树名
tree network 树形网络
tree node 树结点
tree optimization 树优化
tree pruning 树修剪
tree reduction 树精简
tree representation 树形表示法
tree root 树根
tree saturation 树饱和
tree scheduling 树调度
tree schema 树模式
tree searching algorithm 树搜索算法
tree selection sorting 树选择排序
tree simplification 树简化
tree sorting 树排序
tree string structure 树形串结构
tree structure 树结构
tree structure database machine 树结构数据库机
tree-structured directory 树形结构目录
tree structured system 树形结构系统
tree terminal node 树末端结点,树叶
tree traversal 树的遍历
tree topology 树形拓扑
tree type 树类型
tree view 树视图
tree-walk information collecting 攀树式信息收集
tree worktape 树型工作带
treelike version model 树状版本模型
trellis 网格;框架;格状
trellis architecture 网格结构
trellis-coded modulation 梳状编码调制
trellis coding 梳状编码,格栅编码
trellis coding modulation 梳状编码调制
trellis diagram 格子图
tremolo 颤音
trend 趋势
trend detector 趋势探测器
trend line 趋势线
trend prediction 趋势预测
tri-bit encoding 三位编码
tri-state logic(TSL) 三态逻辑电路
tri-state output buffer 三态输出缓冲器
triac 三端双向可控硅器件
triad 三元组
triagonal matrix 三对角矩阵
trial 试探,尝试
trial-and-error search 试凑法搜索
trial divisor 试用除数

trial run 试验性运行
triangle 三角形的
triangular array 三角形阵列
triangular decomposition 三角分解
triangular domain 三角域
triangular matrix 三角矩阵
triangular net 三角形网络
triarray 三角阵列处理
tribit 三位
tribit encoding 三位编码
tributary channel 辅助信道
tributary circuit 分支电路
tributary DTE 从属数据终端设备
tributary station 从属站,分站
tributary trunk 从干线
trichromatic 三原色,三基色
trick 技巧
tridimensional 三维的
tries limit 尝试限次
trigger 触发器
trigger action 触发动作,来回翻转动作
trigger circuit 触发电路
trigger delay 触发延迟
trigger event 触发事件
trigger level 触发电平
trigger pair 触发对,双稳态触发器
trigger point 触发点
trigger pulse 触发脉冲
trigger signal 触发信号
trigger staring system 触发启动系统
triggered rule 被触发的规则
triggered time 触发时间
triggering circuit 触发电路
trigonometric polynomial 三角多项式
trigonometry 三角学
trigram 三字母组
Trilevel Cache (Pentium Ⅲ)三级高速缓存(Intel)
trillion 太,万亿,10^{12}(美);10^{18}(英)
trim 剪裁,截尾
trim fields 剪裁字段
trim line 外形线
trim mark 微调标志
trimmer potentiometer 微调电位器
trimming 切边
Trinitron 单枪三束彩色显像管(SONY)
trio 三元闭合语言类

trip button 解扣按钮
trip computer 行程计算机
trip count 行程计数
trip key 解扣键
trip magnet 解扣电磁铁
trip protection circuit 断开式保护电路
trip signal 解扣信号,断开信号
triple 三重的;三元组
triple address 三地址
triple bus architecture 三总线结构
triple click (鼠标)三连击
triple diversity 三重分集
triple form 三元组形式
triple interleaved parity 三重插入奇偶校验
triple-length register 三倍长寄存器
triple-length working 三倍长工作
triple modular redundancy 三重模块冗余
triple-precision 三倍精度
triple-precision number 三倍精度数
triple triple modular redundancy system 三重三模冗余系统
triple register 三倍长寄存器
triplet 三元组
tristate gate 三态门
tristimulus values 三色值,三激励值
trit 三进制数字
trivial 普通的,平凡的,直接的
trivial digraph 平凡有向图
Trivial File Transfer Protocol (TFTP) 次要文件传输协议
trivial problem discriminator 不重要问题鉴别程序
trivial response 普通响应
trivial solution 平凡解
trivial subgroup 平凡子群
trivial uncertainty vector 平凡不定态向量
Trojan horse 特洛伊木马
Trojan horse direct release 特洛伊木马直接释放
Trojan horse leakage 特洛伊木马泄漏
Trojan horse scenario 特洛伊木马方案
trombone(loop) connection 环路连接
TRON(The Realtime Operating System Nucleus) 实时操作系统内核

tropical language 转义语言
troposphere 对流层
troposphere scatter communication 对流层散射通信
trouble 故障
trouble analysis 故障分析
trouble chart 故障图
trouble finder 故障寻迹器
trouble-free personal computing 无忧计算,无故障计算
trouble indicator 故障指示器
trouble-location problem 故障定位问题
trouble shoot 故障寻找
trouble unit 故障单元
TRT(Token Rotation Time) 令牌循环时间
true 真,实
true add 原码加
True BASIC True BASIC 语言
true binary notation 二进制原码表示法
true code 实代码
true color 真彩色
true concurrency 真并发
true dependence 真依赖,真相关
true exit 真退出;真出口
true form 原码形式
true optimal path 实际最佳路径
true proposition 真命题
true random search 真随机搜索
true run list 真运行表
true symbol 真符号
true time 实时
true-time operation 实时操作
true value 真值
true video on demand(TVOD) 真点播电视
TrueImage 真实影像语言(微软,苹果)
truespeech 原声
TrueType TrueType 字形(微软,苹果)
trumpet newsreader 传播专题论坛阅读器
truncate 截断
truncated binary exponential backoff algorithm 截断的二进制指数回退算法
truncated bit 截去位

truncated distribution 截断分布
truncated domain 截断域
truncated median filter 截尾式中值滤波器
truncated packet 截尾分组
truncation error 截断误差
truncation specification 截断规定
trunk 干线,中继线
trunk circuit 中继线路
trunk coupling unit 干线耦合单元
trunk encryption device 中继加密设备
trunk group multiplexer 中继群多路复用器
trunk hunting 中继寻号,自动选中继线
trunk junction 中继连接线
trunk line 中继线路
trunk loop 中继线环路
trunk order 中继线序
trunk PE 长途电话图像元素
trunk prefix 长途字冠
trunk seized condition 长途电路占用状态
trunk selector 中继线选择器
trunk switch 中继转接,长途交换
trust 委托;信任
trust relationship 委托关系
trusted 可信的;受委托的
trusted computer system 可信计算机系统
trusted computing base(TCB) 可信计算基
trusted domain 受托域
trusted filter 可信过滤器
trusted function 可信功能
trusted functionality 可信功能度
trusted identification forwarding 可信识别发送
trusted path 可信通道
trusted process 可信进程,受托进程
trusted products 可信产品
trusted share access 可信共享访问
trusted software 可信软件
trusted subject 受托主题
trusted system 可信系统
trustee 托管者,置信者
trustee directory assignment 托管者目录指派

trustee file assignment 托管者文件指派
trustee right granted 准许的托管者权限
truth 真值；"真"
truth clause 真值子句
truth function 真值函数
truth maintenance 真值维持
truth maintenance system 真值维护系统
truth set 真值集
truth table 真值表
truth table generator 真值表生成程序
truth value 真值
try again 重试
TS(Temporary Storage) 临时存储器
TSAP(Transport Service Access Point) 传输服务访问点
TSC(Totally Self-Check) 全面自检
TSC(Transmitter Start Code) 发送开始码
TSD(Touch Sensitive Display) 触摸显示
TSDU(Transport Service Data Unit) 传输服务数据单元
TSF(Through Supergroup Filter) 直通超群滤波器
TSK(Time Shift Keying) 时移键控
TSL(Trouble Shooting Loop) 故障查找回路
TSO(Time Sharing Option) 分时操作选项，分时选择
TSO command language 分时选择命令语言
TSO/VTAM(Time Sharing Option for the Virtual Tele communication Access Method) 分时选择/虚拟远程通信存取法
TSP(Traffic Service Position) 服务席座
TSR(Terminate and Stay Resident) 终止驻留程序
TSR interface(Terminate and Stay Resident interface) 终止驻留程序界面
TSS(Time-Sharing System) 分时系统
TSS Network 分时系统计算机网
TTL(Transistor-Transistor Logic) 晶体管-晶体管逻辑电路
TTL compatibility TTL兼容性
TTM(Transparent Text Mode) 透明文本方式
TTRP(Timed Token Rotation Protocol) 定时令牌循环协议
TTRT(Target Token Rotation Time) 目标令牌循环时间
TTS(Transaction Tracking System) 事务处理追踪系统
TTY(Tele TYpewriter) 电传打字机
TTY controller 电传打字机控制器
tty driver 电传打字机驱动程序
TTY protocol 电传打字机协议
tub curve 浴盆曲线
tube 管，真空管；石英管
tucking up 修整
Tukey window 图基窗函数
tumbler 滚筒；反转机构
tumbling 滚动，转动
tunability 可协调性
tunable 可协调的
tunable laser 可调谐激光器
tunable network parameter 可调网络参数
tune 色彩，色调；调谐
tuned circuit 调谐电路
tuner 调谐器
tuning 调谐；调整
tuning effect 隧道效应
tuning fork 校速音叉
tuning fork contact 音叉式触点簧片
tunnel (VPN)隧道
tunnel diode 隧道二极管
tunnel erase head 隧道擦除磁头
tunnel exchanger 隧道交换机
tunnel initializer 隧道开通器
tunnel junction 隧道结
tunnel terminator 隧道终止器
tunneling 隧道技术
tuple 元组
tuple calculus 元组演算
tuple identifier(TID) 元组标识符
tuple length 元组长度
tuple space 元组空间
tuple variable 元组变量
turbo 加速
Turbo C Turbo C语言(Borland)
Turbo C++ Turbo C++语言(Borland)
Turbo channel 快速信道(DEC)

Turbo Mouse Turbo 鼠标器
Turbo Pascal Turbo Pascal 语言(Borland)
Turbo-Prolog Turbo-Prolog 语言 (Borland)
Turbo Vision Turbo Vision 系统 (Borland)
turbulator 湍流器
turbulence 湍流
Turing computability 图灵可计算性
Turing control 图灵控制
Turing degree 图灵级
Turing machine 图灵机
Turing reduction 图灵归约
Turing tape 图灵带
Turing test 图灵测试
Turing's thesis 图灵论题
turn 转折
turn key system 交钥匙系统
turn-off 断开
turn-off decay time 关断下降时间
turn-on 接通
turn-on over shoot 接通过冲
turn-on response 接通响应
turn-on time 接通时间
turnaround 转向,换向
turnaround document 周转文件
turnaround sequence 转向序列
turnaround system 周转系统
turnaround time 周转时间;转向时间
turning conjunction into disjunction rule 转换合取式为析取式的规则
turnkey 总控键,总控开关
turnkey console 总控制台
turnkey system 承包系统
turtle 海龟,龟标
turtle geometry 海龟几何
turtle graphics 龟图,龟标制图
tutorial 使用说明书;指导,辅导
tutorial courseware 指导型课件
tutorial disk 教学盘
tutorial lights 指示灯
tutorial message 指导信息
tutorial program 辅导程序
tutorial rule 辅导规则
tutorial sample 辅导样板 「块
tutoring strategy module 教学策略模
TV(TeleVision) 电视

TV add-on 电视机附加件
TV camera pickup tube 电视摄像管
TV card 电视卡
TV conference 电视会议
TV optical-fiber link 电视光纤线路
TV terminal 电视终端
TV tuner 电视选台器
TVGA(Trident Video Graphics Array) TVGA 显示格式
TVOD(True Video On Demand) 真点播电视
TWAIN(Toolkit Without An Interesting Name) TWAIN(扫描仪)标准
tweak 修整,细调
tweaking 细调
tweening 中间计算;插空技术
twice-around-the-spanning-tree algorithm "沿生成树走两次"算法
twice skew transformation 二次扭斜变换
twig 枝,杈
twin 孪生的,成双的
twin cable 双电缆
twin channel 双通道
twin check 双重校验
twin contact 双触点
twin lead 平行馈线
twin pointer 孪生指针
twin port 双端口 「输
twin-sideband transmission 双边带传
twinaxial cable 双轴电缆
twinned binary 孪生二进制
twip 缇(1 twip = 1/15 pixel)
twist 扭曲,扭转
twist-on connector 扭转接通连接器
twist strength 扭曲强度
twisted numatic LCD(TN LCD) 扭曲向列型液晶显示器
twisted pair 双绞线
twisted pair cable(TT) 双绞线电缆
two action line 双向传输线
two-address code 双地址码
two-address instruction 双地址指令
two bit wide slice 二位芯片
two-channel switch 双信道开关 「器
two-channel synthesizer 双通道合成
two chip microprocessor 二片式微处理机

two-dimension display 二维显示
two-dimension run length encoding 二维行程编码
two-dimension systolic array 二维脉动阵列
two-dimension wormhole grid structure 二维蛀孔式网格结构
two-dimensional array 二维数组，二维阵列
two-dimensional model 二维模型
two-dimensional table 二维表
two-dimensional Turing machine 二维图灵机
two element field 二元域
two-end device 双端设备
two-independent sideband carrier 双独立边带载波
two independent-sideband transmission 双独立边带传输「制
two-key cryptosystem 双密钥加密体
two-key rollover 双键翻转
two-key system 双密钥体制
two-layer architecture 双层结构
two-level address 二级地址
two-level addressing 二级寻址
two-level encoding microinstruction 二级编码微指令
two-level grammar 二级文法
two level microprogram control 二级微程序控制
two-level optical signal 双电平光信号
two-level subroutine 二级子例程
two-level system 双能级系统
two-out-of-five code 五中选二码
two-phase commit protocol 两步认可协议「序
two-pass assembler 二遍扫描汇编程
two-person game 双人博弈，二员对策
two-phase commit 两阶段提交
two-phase locking 双相封锁
two-piece printed circuit connector 二件式印刷电路板插件
two-pilot regulation 双导频调整
two-plus-one address instruction 二加一地址指令
two-point perspective 二点透视
two-port network 双端口网络
two-redundant code 二冗余码

two's complement 二进制补码
two's complementer 求补器
two scale 二进制记数法
two-scale notation 二进制记数法
two-sided diskette 双面软盘
two-sided double-density diskette 双面倍密度软磁盘
two-sided error 双侧错误
two-sided printing 双面打印
two-sided single-density diskette 双面单密度软磁盘
two-sided system 双侧系统
two-sorted logic 二类逻辑
two-state picture 二态图
two-state system 双态系统
two-state variable 二态变量
two step commitment protocol 二步确认协议
two-step read 两步读出
two-tier architecture 两层结构
two-tone image 双色图像
two-tone keying 双音调制，双音键控
two value logic 二值逻辑
two-valued variable 二值变量
two-way alternate communication 双向交替通信
two-way alternate operation 双向交替操作
two-way associative cache 两路相联超高速缓存
two-way deterministic finite automaton (2DFA) 双向确定型有限自动机
two-way finite automaton 双向有限自动机
two-way infinite tape 双向无限带
two-way logical relationship 双向逻辑联系
two-way merge sorting 双路归并排序
two-way printing 双向打印
two-way push-down automaton 双向下推自动机
two-way repeater 双向中继器
two-way ring 双向环
two-way simplex 双向单工
two-way simultaneous communication 双向同时通信
two-way simultaneous interaction 双向同时交互作用

two-way switch 双路开关
two-way tape 双向带
two-way trunk 双工中继线
two-wire channel 二线信道
two-wire circuit 双线线路
two-wire connection 双线连接
two-wire full duplex 双线全双工
two-wire link 双线链路
two-wire switching 二线制交换
TWS(Translator Writing System) 翻译程序书写系统
TWSO(Two-Way Simultaneous Operation) 双向同时工作
TX(TeleX) 用户电报
TYMNET TYMNET 商用分组交换网络
type 打印字符,活字;类型
type 0 grammar 0 型文法
type 0 language 0 型语言
type 1 batch 第一类批处理
type 1 grammar 1 型文法
type 1 language 1 型语言
type 1 programming 第一类程序
type 2 batch 第二类批处理
type 2 grammar 2 型文法
type 2 language 2 型语言
type 2 programming 第二类程序
type 3 grammar 3 型文法
type 3 language 3 型语言
type 3 programming 第三类程序
type 4 programming 第四类程序
type 1~9 cable 1~9 类电缆
type ahead 之前打入
type ahead buffer 超前键入缓冲器
type ahead capability 超前键入能力
type assignment 类型赋值
type association 类型结合
type attribute 类型属性
type ball printer 球型打印机
type box 字盒
type carrier 字模托架
type checking 类型检查
type compatibility 类型兼容
type concept 类型概念
type conflict 类型冲突
type consistency 类型相容性
type conversion 类型转换
type declaration 类型说明

type definition 类型定义
type equivalence 类型等价
type face 字样
type font 字体,字形
type hammer 打印锤
type impression control 打印压力控制
type inference algorithm 类型推理算法
type mark 类型标记
type mismatch 类型不匹配
type name 类型名
type object 类型对象
type-out key respond 打印输出键响应
type over 改写
type P transmultiplexer P 型多路复用转换器
type page number 键入页码
type parameter 类型参数
type plate 字模板
type posture 字模形态
type procedure 类型过程
type S transmultiplexer S 型多路复用转换器
type safe 类型安全
type script 打印底稿
type set 类型集合
type size 字形尺寸,字体大小
type statement 类型语句
type structure 类型结构
type style 字样
type theory 类型理论
type wheel 打印轮
typeface 字体,字样
typeless 无类型
typeless entity 无类型实体
typeless intrinsic function 无类型内在函数
typeless language 无类型语言
typematic 击键的
typeover 打印覆盖;打印插入
typesetting 制版,排版
typewriter 打字机
typical algorithm benchmarks 典型算法基准程序
typical element 典型元素
typical installation 典型安装
typical problem 典型问题
typical procedure 典型工艺规程
typical technology 典型工艺

typing 键入
typing in 输入,打入
typing position 打字位置
typing speed 打字速度

typography 版面构思技巧
TYPOUT(TYPewriter OUTput routine) 打字输出程序

U u

U(Ultra) 超,特别
U format 无编号格式,U 格式
U-frame 未编号帧
U-mode records 不定长方式记录
U. S. Robotics (调制解调器)USR 公司
UA(User Agent) 用户代理
UA(User Area) 用户区
UART(Universal Asynchronous Receiver Transmitter) 通用异步接收器/发送器
UART controller UART 控制器
UART functions UART 功能
UART simulator UART 仿真器
UB(Unidirectional Bus) 单向总线
UBA(UNIBUS Adapter) 单总线适配器
UBC(Universal Buffer Controller) 通用缓冲器控制器
UBF(User BuFfer) 用户缓冲器
UBI(UNIBUS Interconnect) 单总线互连
UC-DOS UC-DOS 汉字操作系统(希望)
UCB(Universal Character Buffer) 通用字符缓冲器 「表
UCL(Update Control List) 更新控制
UCSD(Universal Controller-System Bus) 通用控制器系统总线
UCSD(Universal Communications Switching Device) 通用通信转接装置
UCSD P-system UCSD-P 操作系统(加里福尼亚大学) 「表
UCT(User Control Table) 用户控制
UCW(Unit Control Word) 设备控制字
UDA(Universal Data Access) 全局数据存取,统一数据访问(微软)

UDF(Universal disk form) 通用磁盘(光盘)格式
UDF(User Defined Function) 用户定义函数
UDLC(Universal Data Link Control) 通用数据链路控制
UDP(User Datagram Protocol) 用户数据报协议
UDR(USART Data Register) 通用同步/异步接收/发送器数据寄存器
UFD(User File Directory) 用户文件目录
UFI(User Friendly Interface) 用户友好界面
UFO(User Files On-line) 用户文件联机
UFS(Universal Financial System) 通用财务系统
UFS(UNIX file system) (SunOS) UNIX 文件系统
UGII UGII 辅助设计软件(麦道)
UGT(User Group Table) 用户群表
UHF(UltraHigh Frequency) 超高频
UHL(User header Label) 用户首部标签
UHP(Universal Host Processor) 通用主处理机
UHR(Ultra-High Resolution) 超高分辨率
UI(Unnumbered Information frame) 未编号信息帧
UI(User Interface) 用户界面,用户接口
UL(User Layer) 用户层
ULA(Uniform-Ladder Algorithm) 均匀梯形算法 「块
ULB(Usable Logic Block) 可用逻辑
ULC(Universal Logic Circuit) 通用

逻辑电路
ULD(Universal Language Definition) 通用语言定义
ULD(Universal Language Description) 通用语言描述
ULF(Ultra-Low Frequency) 超低频
ULSI(Ultra Large Scale Integration) 超大规模集成电路
ultimate 极限的,最终的
ultimate boundedness 终极有界性
ultimate capacity 极限容量
ultimate sequence 最终序列
ultimate sink 终端(末级)散热器
ultimate tensile strength 极限抗拉强度
ultimately controlled variable 终极控制变量
Ultimedia Ultimedia 计算机(IBM)
Ultra ATA/66 66MB/s IDE 硬盘标准
ultra clean technology 超净技术 └准
Ultra DMA/33 33MB/s IDE 硬盘标准
ultra-fast computer 超高速计算机
ultra-high frequency(UHF) 超高频
ultra high-speed D/A converter 超高速数/模转换器
ultra high-speed ECL hybrid D/A converter 超高速 ECL 混合数/模转换器
ultra high-speed multiplying D/A converter 超高速乘法数/模转换器
ultra high-speed track-and-hold amplifier 超高速跟踪保持放大器
ultra large scale integration(ULSI) 特大规模集成电路
ultra LSI 超大规模集成电路
ultra sonic wave 超声波
ultraclean room 超净室
ultrafast computer 超高速计算机
ultrafiche 超缩微胶片
ultrafiltration 超细过滤
Ultra Enterprise 超级企业服务器(Sun)
ultrahigh frequency(UHF) 超高频
ultraJava 超级 Java 芯片(Sun)
ultralight computer 超轻型计算机
ultraprecision display 超高精度显示器

ultrasonic 超声的,超声波
ultrasonic bonding 超声键合
ultrasonic camera 超声照相机
ultrasonic cleaning 超声清洗
ultrasonic converter 超声波换能器
ultrasonic delay line 超声延迟线
ultrasonic delay line memory 超声波延迟线存储器
ultrasonic diagnosis apparatus 超声波诊断机
ultrasonic equipment 超声设备
ultrasonic fatigue 超声疲劳
ultrasonic flaw detection 超声探伤
ultrasonic holograph 超声全息术
ultrasonic imaging system 超声成像系统
ultrasonic inspection and measurement 超声检测
ultrasonic machining 超声波加工
ultrasonic memory 超声存储器
ultrasonic pen pointer 超声波指示笔
ultrasonic power converter 超声波换能器
ultrasonic power supply 超声波源
ultrasonic sensor 超声传感器
ultrasonic soldering 超声波焊接
ultrasonic transducer 超声换能器
ultrasonic vision 超声视觉
ultrasonic wave 超声波
ultrasonic wave computer tomography(UCT) 超声波计算机断层摄影
ultrasonogram 声像图
ultrasound 超声
ultrasound tomography 超声断层成像
ultraviolet 紫外线 「的
ultraviolet erasable 可用紫外线擦除
ultraviolet erasable PROM 紫外线可擦除可编程只读存储器
ultraviolet erasing 紫外线擦除
ultraviolet light 紫外光
ultraviolet light erasing 紫外线灯擦除
ultraviolet ray 紫外线
ULTRIX ULTRIX 操作系统(DEC)
UMA (Universal Memory Architecture) 统一内存体系结构
UMA(Upper Memory Area) 高端内存区域,上位内存区域
UMB(Upper Memory Block) 上位内

存块,上端内存块
umbral 文档标题,文件标题
UMC(Unibus MicroChannel) 单总线微通道
UMD(Ultrasonic Motion Detector) 超声波探测仪
UMOS(U series MOnitor System) U系列监视器系统(富士通)
UMR(UNIBUS Memory Register) 单总线存储寄存器
UMS(Universal Memory System) 通用存储器系统(Intel)
UMS(Universal Multiprogramming System) 通用多道程序作业系统(Intel)
UN(User Name) 用户名
UMS(Universal Memory System) 通用存储器系统(Intel)
unable to open log file 无法打开登录文件
unacceptable event 不可接受事件
unacknowledged 未确认的
unacknowledged data 未确认数据
unacknowledged frame 未确认帧「器
unaddressable storage 不可寻址存储
unallocated logical storage 非分配的逻辑存储器
unallocated number signal 未分配号码信号
unallocated physical storage 非分配的实际存储器
unallowable character 未允许字符
unallowable code 未允许码
unallowable code check 非法码校验
unallowable combination check 非法组合检验
unallowable command check 非法命令检验
unallowable digit 非法数字
unallowable instruction check 非法指令校验
unallowable instruction correction 非法指令校正
unallowable instruction digit 禁用指令数字
unambiguity 无歧义性
unambiguous grammar 无歧义文法
unambiguous Turing machine(UTM) 无歧义图灵机
unanchored mode 非锚定模式
unanticipated request 非先行请求
unary arithmetic operation 一元算术运算 「符
unary Boolean operator 一元布尔运算
unary expression 一元表达式
unary message 一元消息符
unary minus operator 一目减法运算
unary operation 一元运算 「符
unary operator 一元算子,一目运算
unary plus operator 一元加法运算符
unary predicate calculus 单谓词演算
unary subquery 一元子查询
unary variety 一元簇
unasserted 未证实的
unassignable 非赋值的,未赋值的
unassignable node 非赋值节点
unassignable primary input 非赋值初始输入
unassigned real address area 未分配实地址区 「置
unassigned storage site 非赋值存储位
unattended automatic exchange 无人值守自动交换
unattended communication 无人照看通信
unattended installation 无提示安装
unattended mode 无人值守方式
unattended operation 自动操作
unattended stand-by time 非值守备用时间
unattended time 无人照管时间
unattended trail printer 无人照管跟踪打印机
unauthorized access 非授权存取
unauthorized operation 未经核准作业
unauthorized use 未授权应用
unavailability 不可用性
unavailability time 不可用时间
unavailable 不可用的
unavoidable 不可撤消的
unbalanced class of procedure 非平衡型过程
unbalanced data link 非平衡数据链路
unbalanced error 不平衡误差
unbalanced line 不平衡线路 「序
unbalanced merge sort 非平衡归并排

unbalanced modulator 不平衡调制器
unbalanced network 不平衡网络
unbalanced tree 不平衡树
UNBIND(UNBIND session) 终止会话
UNBINDF(UNBIND Failure) 终止会话失败
unblank 开启,增辉
unblind 非封闭
unblocked 非成块的
unblocked record 未成块记录
unblocking 块合并
unblocking-acknowledgement signal 阻塞消除证实信号
unblocking signal 阻塞消除信号
unbound control mode 无约束控制方式
unbound domain 无界域
unbounded-buffer problem 无界缓冲区问题
unbounded task set load module 无界任务组装入模块
unbounded universal quantifier 无界全称量词
unbounded wave 无限制波
unbuffered attribute 无缓冲属性
unbuffered input 无缓冲输入
unbuffered option 无缓冲任选
unbundled program 非附随程序
unbending software 非附随软件
UNC(Universal Naming Convention) 统一命名约定
uncatalog 未编目,未列入目录
UNCC(United Nations Computing Center) 联合国计算中心
UNCDRP(UNiversal CarD Read-in Program) 通用卡片读入程序
uncertain 不确定的
uncertain decision 不确定决策
uncertain inference 不确定性推理
uncertain knowledge 不确定知识
uncertain region 不确定区
uncertain symbol PE 不确定符号图像元素
uncertainty 不确定性
uncertainty relation 不定关系
unchecked symbol 未检验符号
unclamp (夹具)松开
unclassified 未分类的
unclocked 无时钟

unclosed 非封闭的
uncoded 未编码的,非编码的
uncommitted logic array 独立逻辑阵列
uncommitted order 未承诺的订单
uncommitted storage list 自由存储区表
uncompressed 未压缩的
uncompleted task 未完成的任务
uncompression 解压缩
unconditional branch 无条件转移
unconditional branch instruction 无条件分枝指令
unconditional capture 无条件俘获
unconditional control transfer instruction 无条件转移控制指令
unconditional force 无条件强制
unconditional formatting 无条件格式化
unconditional GO TO statement 无条件转向语句
unconditional jump command 无条件转移命令
unconditional jump debug 无条件转移调试
unconditional Kolmogorov complexity 无条件科莫洛夫复杂性
unconditional stability 无条件稳定性
unconditional statement 无条件语句
unconditional transfer 无条件转移
unconnected graph 非连通图
unconnected trim curve 未连接的裁剪曲线
unconstrained array 无约束数组
unconstrained minimization 无约束极小化
unconstrained model 无约束模型
unconstrained optimization 无约束优化
unconstrained problems 无约束问题
uncontinuity 不连续性
uncontrolled not ready signal 不受控未准备好信号
uncontrolled slip 不受控滑码
uncooperative environment 不协调环境
uncorrectable error 不可校正的错误
uncorrectable error detecting 不可校正错误测定
uncorrelated error 不相关错误
uncorrelated function 不相关函数
uncorrelated variable 不相关变量
uncountable 不可数的

uncover 取消覆盖
uncovered 未覆盖的
uncovered symbol 未被公认的符号
undamped natural mode of vibration 固有模式
undamped oscillation 无阻尼振荡
undecidable 不可判定的
undeclared identifier 未说明标识符
undefined 未定义的,未定界的
undefined data 未定义数据
undefined file 未定义文件
undefined format 未定义格式
undefined length record 不定长记录
undefined OP code 未定义操作代码
undefined record 未定义记录
undefined statement label 未定义语句标号
undefined symbol 未定义符号
undefined variable 未定义变量
undelayed pulse 无延迟脉冲
undelete 删除恢复
undelete command 删除恢复命令
undelete utility 删除恢复实用程序
under line 下划线
under run 欠载运行
under shoot 下冲负尖峰
under-the-cover modem 内置式调制解调器
under voltage 欠压
under voltage release 欠压断路
undercapacity 非满载容量
undercolor separation 原色彩分离法
undercompensated optical fiber 欠补偿光纤
undercompensation 欠补偿
undercoupling 欠耦合,耦合不足
undercritical 亚临界的
undercut 侧蚀
underdamping 欠阻尼
underdeterminant 子行列式
underestimation 低估,估计不足
underexposure 曝光不足
underfloor raceway 地板下电缆信道
underflow 下溢
underflow characteristics 下溢特性
underflow exception 下溢异常
underflow indicator 下溢指示器
underframe 底架,底框

underfrequency 频率过低
underlap 脱节;欠重叠;图像变窄
underline 下划线
underline mark 下划线记号
underlined character 加下划线字符
underlined letter 加下划线字母
underlit 照明不足
underload 欠载,轻负载
underload service system 轻载服务系统
underlying carrier 基础载波
underlying characteristic grammar 基础表征文法
underlying database 基础数据库
underlying property 基本性质
undermodulation 欠调制
underoxide diffusion 横向扩散
underpan 底盘
underpass 下穿交叉
underplate 底座,底板
underpopulation 未装满元件
underproof 低于标准
underpunch 下部穿孔
undersampling 欠抽样,采样不足
underscore 下划线
undershoot 下冲,负尖峰
undersizing 尺寸减小,图形缩小
underspeed 速度不足
understandability 可理解性
understanding connected speech 理解连贯话音
underswing 幅度不足
undertake 承担
undervoltage 欠压
underwater acoustics hydroacoustics 水声学
underwater robot 水下机器人
Underwriter's Laboratories(UL) 安特鲁特实验室
undesirable facility 不理想设备
undesired signal 不希望有的信号
undetectable 不可检测的
undetected branch 未检分支
undetected error rate 漏检故障率
undetected failure time 漏检故障时间
undetected fault 未检故障
undetermined model 待定模型
undirected action 不定向活动
undirected graph 无向图

UNDIS(UN Documentation Information System) 联合国文献信息系统
undiscovered 未被发现的
undistorted output 无失真输出
undistorted transmission 无失真传输
undisturbed read out 无扰动读出
undisturbed zero output 无扰动零输出
undo 取消,还原,撤消
undo depth 撤消深度,撤消层次数
undo last 撤消上一次操作
undo typing 撤消键入
undocking 移动;出坞
undocumented 未形成文献的
undulate 波动,起伏
unedited 未编辑过的
unencrypted 未加密的
unequal 不相等的
unequivalence interrupt 不等价中断
unerase 恢复删除
UNESCO(United Nations Educational, Scientific & Cultural Organization) 联合国教科文组织
unessential 非本质的
unevaluated 不计算的
unevaluated operand 不计算的操作数
uneven 不均匀的,非均衡的
uneven data usage 非均衡数据应用
uneven length code 不等长电码
unexcited 未激励的
unexecuted statement 非执行语句
unexpected 意外的,非期望的
unexpected file format 不正常文件格式
unexpected halt 意外停机
unexpected symbol 意外符号
unfailing 无失效的,可靠的,不间断的
unfaithful random reduction (UR-reduction) 不确切随机归约
unfavorable 不利的
unfeasible 不能实行的
unfitting 不适合的
unfiltered packet 未级过滤的包
unfixed fault 不固定故障
unfold 展开
unforeseeable fault 不可预见故障
unformat utility 格式化恢复实用程序
unformatted capacity 未格式化容量
unformatted diskette 未格式化磁盘

unformatted display 未格式化显示
unformatted image 无格式图像
unformatted media 无格式媒体
unformatted read 无格式读
unformatted record 无格式记录
unformatted request 非格式化请求
unformatted system service(USS) 无格式系统服务
unformatted text file 无格式文本文件
unformatted write 无格式写
unfreeze 解冻
unground 不磨的,未磨过的
ungroup 取消对象组,解散组合
unguarded interval 无保护间隔
unguyed 未加固的,非连结的
unhadled exception 无法处理的异常
unhide 取消隐藏
unhide sheet 取消表单隐藏
unhide workbook 取消工作簿隐藏
UNI(User-to-Network Interface) 用户-网络接口
uniaxial anisotropy 单轴各向异性
uniaxial crystal 单轴晶体
uniaxial magnetic anisotropy 单轴磁各向异性
UNIBUS(UNIversal BUS) 通用总线
Unibus Unibus 总线
unibus 单总线
unibus architecture 单总线体系结构
unibus timing 单总线定时
UNIC(United Nations Information Center) 联合国信息中心
unicast 单播,一对一传播
unicast packet 单播包
unichannel 单通道
unichassis 单层底板
Unicode 统一字符编码
unicomputer 单计算机
unicontrol 单一控制
UNICOS (用于 Cray 机的 Unix)操作系统
unidimensional 一维的
unidirectional bus 单向总线
unidirectional circuit 单向电路
unidirectional connection 单向连接
unidirectional element 单向元件
unidirectional flow of information 单向信息流

unidirectional microphone 单向麦克
unidirectional pulse 单向脉冲 风
unidirectional pulse train 单向脉冲链
unidirectional transducer 单向换能器
unidirectional transmission 单向传输
Uniface Uniface 公司
unification 一致化
unification algorithm 通代算法
unification rule 统一规则
unification set 一致集合
unified database language 统一数据库语言
unified file format 统一文件格式
unfied network 一体化网络
unified system development 统一系统开发
unifier 一致置换,通代符
uniflow 单向流
uniform 均匀,一致
uniform approximation 一致近似法
uniform array-based microcomputer 基于均匀阵列的微型计算机
uniform baseline offset 统一基线位移
uniform bound 一致界
uniform channel 均匀信道
uniform command language 统一命令语言
uniform commercial code(UCC) 统一商业码 列
uniform computing array 均匀计算阵
uniform continuity 一致连续
uniform convergence 一致收敛
uniform data transfer 统一数据传送
uniform distribution 均匀分布
uniform encoding 均匀编码 则
uniform evaluation rule 一致计算规
uniform field 均匀场
uniform file 均匀文件
uniform function 单值函数
uniform game tree 统一博奕树
uniform geometry technique 规则形状技术
uniform hashing 均匀散列
uniform hypergraph 匀称超图
uniform interconnected cellular automaton 一致互连细胞自动机
uniform interface 一致接口
uniform line 均匀线

uniform magnetization 均匀磁化强度
uniform measure 一致度量
uniform norm 一致模,统一范数
uniform quantization 均匀量化
uniform quantizing 均匀量化
uniform random number 均匀随机数
uniform recurrence 均匀递归
uniform referencing 均匀参照
Uniform Resource Locator(URL) 统一资源定位器
uniform rotation 一致转动,均匀转动
uniform sampling 均匀取样
uniform stability 一致稳定
uniformity 均匀性,一致性
uniformization 单值化
uniformly distributed load 均匀分布的负载
UniForum Unix 论坛
unifunction pipeline 单功能流水线
unifunctional circuit 单功能电路
unifunctional pipeline 单功能流水线
UNIFY UNIFY 数据库
unify 合并
unifying composition 一致置换合成,通代合成
unifying model 一致化模型
unijunction transistor(UJT) 单结晶体管,双基极二极管
unilateral conductivity 单向传导
unilateral connected digraph 单侧连通有向图,单向连通图
unilateral constrain 单向约束
unilateral continuity 单向连续性
unilateral control 单向控制
unilateral element 单向元件
unilateral gate 单向门
unilateral limit 单侧极限
unilateral network 单向网络
unilateral signal flow 单向信号流
unilateral switch 单向开关
unilateral synchronization system 单向同步系统
unimicroprocessor 单微处理机
UNIMOD(UNIversal MODule) 通用模块
unimodal distribution 单峰分布
unimodal function 单峰函数
unimodality 单峰性

unimodular 单模的;单组件的
unimodular matrix 单模矩阵
unimodular property 单模特性
unimodule 单模块的
uninformed graph search 无启发图搜「索
uninitialized object 未初始化对象
uninitialized state 未初始化状态
uninitialized variable 未初始化变量
uninked ribbon 无油墨色带
uninstall 卸载
uninstallation 卸载
unintelligent terminal 非智能终端
uninterpreted 未解释的,无解释的
uninterruptible power supply (UPS) 不间断电源
union 联合,合并
union catalogue 联合目录
union compatible 可求并的
union gate "或"门
union ideal 理想合并
union list 期刊联合目录
union of set 集合并集
union of subinterval 子区间的和
UNION operation 联合操作 「元
union operator 合并操作符,联合运算
union set 并集
union tag 联合标记
unipath 惟一通路,单通路
unipolar 单极的,单极性
unipolar input 单极性输入
unipolar signal 单极性信号 「理
uniprocessing (UP) 单级处理,单机处
uniprocessing system 单处理系统
uniprocessor 单处理器
uniprocessor configuration 单处理器配置
uniprocessor operating 单处理器操作
uniprocessor system 单处理机系统
uniprogrammed system 单道程序系统
uniprogramming 单道程序设计
unique 惟一的,单一的,独一无二的
unique address 惟一地址
unique alternate key 惟一替换键
unique factorization theorem 惟一析因定理
unique file 惟一文件
unique handle 惟一控制柄
unique identifier 惟一标识符

unique index 惟一索引
unique inevitability grammar 可惟一逆转文法
unique index snapshot 惟一初始瞬像
unique information prompt 惟一信息提示
unique load module 惟一装入模块
unique select slave 惟一选择从属
unique solution 惟一解
unique user name 惟一用户名
unique variable 惟一变量 「图
uniquely colorable graph 惟一可着色
uniquely decodable code 惟一可译码
uniqueness 惟一性
uniqueness of name 名字的惟一性
unirecord 单记录
unirecord block 单记录块
uniselector 单动作选择器
uniset 单体机
uniset console 单体机控制台
UNISIST (UNIversal System for Information in Science and Technology) 通用科技信息系统
unisolvent function 惟一可解函数
Unisys 优利公司,Unisys公司(美)
UNIT (Universal Numerical Interchange Terminal) 通用数字交换终端
unit 装置,单元
unit address 单元地址,设备地址
unit affinity 单元相似
unit analysis 单元分析
unit area 单位面积;单面积
unit backspace character 单位退格符
unit class 部件类型
unit construction computer 单元结构式计算机
unit control 部件控制,单元控制
unit control block 单元控制块 「息
unit control information 单元控制信
unit control word 单元控制字
unit development folder 单元研制表
unit diagnostics 单元诊断程序
unit disparity binary code 单位差异二进制码
unit distance code 单位距离码
unit element 单位码元
unit factor clause 单元因子子句

unit gap 单位间隔
unit impulse 单位脉冲,单位冲击
unit impulse signal 单位脉冲信号
unit interval 单位间隔
unit length 单位长度
unit load 单位荷载
unit matrix 单位矩阵
unit number 单元号
unit of operation 操作单位
UNIT PACKAGE 单元汇编语言
unit record 单元记录
unit record device 单位记录装置
unit record equipment 单元记录装置
unit record principle 单元记录法
unit record system 单元记录系统
unit replacement 单元替换,部件更换
unit resolution 单元归结
unit response function 单位响应函数
unit rule 单元规则
unit run time 部件运行时间
unit sample 单位取样
unit separator 单元分隔符
unit slop signal 单位斜坡信号
unit space 单元空间
unit status information 单元状态信息
unit-step response 单位阶跃响应
unit step signal 单位阶跃信号
unit string 单字符串
unit synchronizer 单元同步器
unit test 单元测试
unit time 单位时间
unit time step 单位时间步
unit under test 被测部件
unit vector 单位向量
unitary clause 单子句
unitary code 单位码
unitary matrix 单位矩阵,酉矩阵
unitary transformation 酉变换,单位变换
uniterm 单元词;单一项目
uniterm system 单元名词系统,单项系统
uniterming 单项选择
unitized construction 组合式结构
unitor "或"门
unity 单一,合一,整体
unity gain inverter 单位增益反相器
unity gain small signal response 小信号单位增益响应

UNIVAC (UNIVersal Automatic Computer) 通用自动计算机,UNIVAC 计算机
universal 通用的,普遍的,广义的
universal access 通用存取,通用访问
universal address 通用地址,统一地址
universal algorithm 通用算法
universal approximation 广义近似
universal asynchronous receiver transmitter (UART) 通用异步收发器
universal black box 通用黑匣子
universal buffer-controller 通用缓冲控制器
universal character 通用字符
universal character set 通用字符集
Universal Client 通用客户机,全能客户机(Netscape)
universal closure 全称闭包
universal coding 通用编码方法
universal command 通用命令
universal computer 通用计算机
universal constant 通用常数,全称常
universal controller 通用控制器
universal conversion 全称转换
universal copyright convention (UCC) 世界版权公约
universal data access (UDA) 全局数据存取,统一数据访问
universal database access system 通用数据库访问系统
universal data link control (UDLC) 通用数据链路控制规程
universal decimal classification (UDC) 通用十进制分类法
universal default 通用默认值
universal digital computer 通用数字计算机
universal digital interface 通用数字接
universal disk format (UDF) 通用磁盘(光盘)格式
universal document reader 通用文档阅读器
universal electron microscope 通用电子显微镜
universal emulator 通用仿真器
universal fixturing 通用夹具
universal floppy reader 通用软盘阅读

universal function 通用[广义]函数
universal global symbol 通用全局符号
universal grammar 通用文法
universal gripper 通用夹持器 「图
universal implication graph 通用隐含
universal instance assumption 通用实例假设
universal instruction set 通用指令集
universal interconnection device 通用互连设备
universal interrupt controller 通用中断控制器
universal job control language 通用作业控制语言
universal key 通用键,多用途键
universal keyboard 通用键盘
universal language 通用语言
universal logic element 通用逻辑元件
universal lower bound 全下界
universal machine 通用机
universal meter 万用表
Universal Mobile Telecommunication System(UMTS) 通用移动通信系统(欧洲共同体)
universal modular tree 通用模块树
universal motor 通用电动机,通用马达
universal naming convention(UNC) 通用命名约定
universal naming protocol 通用命名协议
universal network 通用网络
universal peripheral interface chip 通用外围接口芯片
Universal Personal Telecommunication(UPT) 通用个人通信
universal port 通用端口
universal product code(UPC) 通用产品码
universal program 通用程序
universal PROM programmer 通用PROM编程器
universal property 通用性质
universal proposition 全称命题
universal quantified variable 全称量词化变元
universal quantifier 全称量词
universal relation assumption 泛关系假设
universal relation database system 泛关系数据库系统
universal relation schema assumption (URSA) 泛关系模式假定
universal relation theory 泛关系理论
universal robot 通用机器人
universal schema 泛模式
Universal Serial Bus(USB) 通用串行总线
universal set 全集
universal simulator 通用仿真程序
universal small keyboard 通用小键盘
universal specialization 全称消去
universal synchronous asynchronous receiver transmitter(USART) 通用同步异步接收发送器
universal synchronous receiver transmitter(USRT) 通用同步接收发送器
Universal Synthesizer Interface(USI) 通用合成器接口
universal terminal 通用终端
universal tooling 通用工艺设备
universal tree domain 全树域
universal Turing machine 通用图灵机
universal unification 泛合一
universality 通用性
universalization 全称泛化
universally quantified variable 全称量词化变元
universe 全域,总体
universe address 全域地址
universe network 总体网络
universe set 全域
universe time 世界时
uniwafer 单圆片
Unix Unix操作系统(贝尔实验室)
Unix 1 BSD 柏克莱软件版本Unix第一版
Unix 2 BSD 柏克莱Unix第二版
Unix 3 BSD 柏克莱Unix第三版(1979年) 「本
Unix 32V Unix操作系统32V分时版
Unix 4 BSD 柏克莱Unix第四版(1979年)
Unix 4.2 BSD 柏克莱Unix第4.2版(1983年)
Unix 4.3 BSD 柏克莱Unix第4.3版

(1986年)
Unix 4.3 BSD Release 2　柏克莱 Unix 第 4.3 版第二次修改
Unix client　Unix 客户
UNIX International　Unix 国际组织
UNIX MIPS　Unix MIPS 基准程序
Unix shell　Unix 命令解释程序
Unix Support Group(USG)　Unix 支持小组(AT&T)
Unix SVR 4.0ES　Unix 操作系统 SVR 4.0 增强安全性版本(AT&T,1991 年)
Unix SVR 4.0MP　Unix 操作系统 SVR 4.0 多处理机版本(AT&T,1991 年)
Unix System Development Lab(USL)　Unix 系统开发实验室(AT&T)
Unix System V Release 3(SVR 3)　Unix 操作系统第 3 版(AT&T,1991 年)
Unix System V Release 4.2(SRV 4.2)　Unix 操作系统 4.2 版本(AT&T,1992 年)
Unix System Version Release 4 Desk Top(**Unix SVR4 DT**)　Unix 操作系统第四版桌上型(美国 Unix 系统开发实验室,1992)
UNIX to UNIX copy program(UUCP)　UNIX 到 UNIX 拷贝程序
Unix V.1　Unix 操作系统 V.1 版本(贝尔实验室,1969 年)
Unix V.6　Unix 操作系统 V.6 版本(贝尔实验室,1976 年)
Unix V.7　Unix 操作系统 V.7 版本(贝尔实验室,1978 年)
UnixWare　UnixWare 操作系统(Univel)
UnixWare AS　应用服务型 UnixWare 操作系统(Novell)
UnixWare PE　个人计算机 UnixWare 操作系统(Novell)
unjustified　未对齐的
unjustified text　未对齐文本
unknown　未知的
unknown-algorithm attack　未知算法攻击法
unknown character　未识别字符
unknown number　未知数
unknown object　未知对象;未知物体
unknown parameter　未知参数
unknown periodic component　未知周期分量
unknown pulse　未知脉冲
unknown quantity　未知量
unknown state　未知状态
unlabelled basic statement　无标号基本语句
unlabelled common block　无标号公用程序块
unlabelled compound statement　无标号复合语句
unlicensed usage　未授权使用
unlimited architecture　无限体系结构
unlimited computation　无限计算
unlink　拆散,解链接
unlinked file　未链接的文件
unlisted pattern　未列出的图案
unload　去载,卸载
unloaded　无负载的,空载的
unloading foreground job　卸载前台作业
unlock　开锁,开启
unlock anchor　开启锁定点,解锁锚点
unlock statement　启封[开锁]语句
unlocked resource　解锁[未锁]资源
unmagnetized region　未磁化区
unmanned factory　无人值守工厂,自动化工厂
unmanned machining　无人机械加工
unmanned machining cell　无人加工单元
unmanned machining system　无人加工系统
unmapped address space　非变换地址空间
unmapped conversation　未映射对话
unmapped physical storage　未映射物理存储器
unmapped system　非映射系统
unmark　去标记,无标志
unmark editable region　无标记可编辑区域
unmarked area　未标志区
unmarked list node　无标记列表节点
unmarked nonterminal　无标记非终结符

unmarshaling 未配置的
unmask 无屏蔽,中止屏蔽
unmatch 未匹配,失配
unmatched record 失配记录「表
unmoderated mailing list 非仲裁邮递
unmodified instruction 非修改指令
unmodulated 未调制的
unmount 拆下,卸下
unmovable data set 不可移数据集
unnamed 无命名的
unnested version 非嵌套形式
unnormalized number 非规格化数
unnumbered commands 未编号命令
unnumbered frames 无编号帧
unnumbered responses 无编号应答
unoptimizable 非优化的
unordered file 无序文件
unordered list 无序列表
unordered symbol 无序标号
unordered table 无序表
unpack 非紧缩,压缩恢复;拆开
unpack procedure 压缩恢复过程
unpacked decimal 非压缩十进制
unpacked format 非压缩格式
unpacket 拆包
unpaired rank test 非成对,秩检验
unpopular 不流行的,不普及的
unpopulated board 空插孔电路板
unpredictable event 不可预测事件
unpredictable result 不可预测的结果
unpredictable table size 不可预知表长度
unprintable 不可打印的,非打印的
unprinted dot 非印出点
unprotect 解保护,去保护
unprotect document 撤消文档保护
unprotect sheet 撤消表单保护
unprotected dynamic memory 未保护的动态存储器
unprotected field 非保护域
unprotected link 非保护链路
unqualified call 未限定调用
unreachable code 不可达码,执行不到的代码
unreachable nonterminal 不可达的非终结符
unreachable position 盲点,盲位
unreadable signal 无法读出的信号

unrealistic 无真实感的
unreasonable 不合理的,无理的
unrecognizable character 无法识别的字符
unrecognized format 无法识别格式
unrecognized keyword 无法识别的关键字
unrecognized phrase 无法识别的词组
unrecoverable ABEND 不可恢复的异常终止
unrecoverable application error (UAE) 无法恢复的应用程序错误
unrecoverable error 不可恢复错误
unrecoverable parity error 不可恢复的奇偶校验错误
unreduced matrix 不可约矩阵
unreducible expression 不可约表达式
unreferenced field 未引用字段,未参考字段
unregistered software 未注册软件
unreliable data or knowledge 不可靠数据或知识
unreliable link 不可靠链路
unreliable process 不可靠进程
unrepeatable operation 不可重复操作
unresolved 未解决的
unresolved recipient 未辨识接收者
unrestricted 无约束的
unrestricted grammar 不受限文法
unrestricted random sampling 无限制随机采样
unrestricted variable 无约束变量
unrooted tree 无根树
unrounded 不舍入的
unsafe file 不安全文件
unsafe region 不安全区
unsafe reset 不安全复位
unsafe situation 不安全状况
unsatisfiability 不可满足性
unsatisfiable 不可满足的
unsaturated 非饱和的
unsaturated logic circuit 非饱和逻辑电路
unsaturated path 非饱和路径
unsave 恢复
UNSCC (United Nations Standard Coordinating Committee) 联合国标准协调委员会

unscheduled maintenance time 非预定维修时间,计划外维护时间
unscreened twisted pair(UTP) 非屏蔽双绞线
unscrew 卸螺钉
unsegmented external file 未分段外部文件
unserviceable 不可使用的
unset 复位,置零,清除
unshaped region 非阴影区,空白区
unshared control unit 非共用控制器
unshared structure 非共享结构
unsharp image 模糊影像,钝化图像
unsharp mask 钝化掩模
unshielded cable(UTP) 无屏蔽电缆
unshielded magneto-resistive head 无屏蔽磁阻磁头
unshielded twisted pair(UTP) 无屏蔽双绞线
unshift 不换档
unshift-on-space 不印字间隔
unshuffle 反混洗,逆混洗
unshuffle interconnection 反移[反混洗]互连
unsigned 无符号的
unsigned integer 无符号整数
unsigned number 无符号数
unsolicited message 非请求消息传送
unslotted protocol 非分片协议
unsolder 焊开
unsolicited key-in 非请求型键入
unsolicited message 非请求型信息
unsolvability 不可解性
unsolvable labeling procedure 不可解标识过程
unsolvable node 不可解节点
unsolvable problem 不可解问题
unsorted table 未整理表,未排序表
unspecified bit rate(UBR) 不确定位速率
unspecified bound 未说明边界
unstable equilibrium 不稳定平衡
unstable servo 不稳定伺服
unstable state 非稳态
unstationary random process 非平稳随机过程
unsteady state 不稳状态
unstratified language 非成层语言,非排元语言
unstring statement 拆串语句
unstructured data item 非结构数据项
unstructured database 非结构化数据库
unstructured decision 非结构化决策
unsubscribe 退出,注销
unsubscripted variable 无下标变量
unsubscripted variable name 无下标变量名
unsuccessful call 不成功呼叫
unsuccessful execution 不成功执行
unsuccessful search 不成功查找
unsuitable value 不适合的值 「类
unsupervised classification 无监督分
unsupervised learning 无监督学习
unsupported bitmap type 不支持的位图类型
unsuppressible literal 不可抑制文字
unsymmetric matrix 不对称矩阵
untended automatic exchange 无人照管自动交换
until all paths used 直到所有路径被使用
until click 直到单击鼠标
until keypress 直到按键
until true 直到条件为真
untitled 无标题的
untitled document 无标题文档
unusable samples 无用取样
unused bit 未用位
unused code 非法代码
unused combination 未用组合
unused command 未使用命令
unused command check 非法命令校验
unused memory 未使用内存
unused name 未用名
unused storage location 未用存储单元
unused themes 未使用的主题
unused time 关机时间,设备未用时间
unused word 未用字
unverified hyperlink 未验证的超链接
unvoiced sound 清音
unwanted signal 非期望[干扰]信号
unwanted string 非期望的字符串
unwind 展开,循环展开
unwind call stack 展开调用堆栈
UP(UniProcessor) 单处理机

UP(Unit Processor) 单元处理机
up arrow 向上箭头
up-down bar 涨跌柱图
up/down counter 可逆计数器
up grade 升级
up level 高电平
up link 上行链路
up path 上行路径
up shift 换上档字符
up-side-down mounting （集成电路芯片)倒装法
up station 上端局
up stream 上游
up stream failure indication 上游故障指示器
up stroke 上行程
up time 可作业时间,正常工作时间
up-to-date information 最新信息
up-to-date style 现代式的,最新式样
UPB(UPper Bound) 上界,上限
UPC(Universal Product Code) 通用商品码　　　　　　　　　　「码
UPC bar-code 通用商品条码,UPC 条
UPC-A bar-code UPC-A 条码
UPC-E bar-code UPC-E 条码
updatable 可更新的,可修改的
updatable microfiche 可更改的缩微胶片
updatable object 可更新对象
update 更改,更新
update all 全部更新
UPDATE attribute 修正属性
update authority 更新权限
update control list 更新控制表
update current page 更新当前页面
update cursor 更新光标
update cycle 更新周期
update data 更新数据　　　　「量
update displayed variable 更新显示变
update existing conponents 升级已有的版本
update field 更新域
update file 更新文件
update generation 更新世代
update graph 修改图
update intent 更新意向
update install 重新安装
update mark 更新标志

update note 更新注释　　　　　「案
update numbering scheme 更新编号方
update plus 添加升级
update right 更新权
update run 更新运行
update script 更新脚本
update transaction 更改事务处理
update usage mode 更改使用状态
updated attribute 更新属性
updated collision count 更新碰撞计数
updated parameter 更新参数
updater 更新程序
updating and file maintenance 更改和文件维护
updating links 更新链接
UPE(UNIBUS Parity Error) 单总线奇偶错
upgradable computer 可升级计算机
upgrade 升级,更新
UPI(Universal Peripheral Interface) 通用外围接口
UPL (Universal Programming Language) 通用程序设计语言
uplink 上行链路
upload 上传,向上装入
upper arm 上臂
upper binding 上层联编,上层绑定
upper bound 上界
upper bound expression 上界表达式
upper CASE 上位计算机辅助软件工
upper case 大写　　　　　　　　「程
upper case letter 大写字母
upper CASE tools 上游 CASE 工具
upper cut-off frequency 上限截止频
upper dead center 上死点　　　　「率
upper dimension bound 上维界　「阵
upper Hessenberg matrix 上海森堡矩
upper layer protocol (Ipv6)上层协议
upper level switching center 高层交换中心
upper limit register 上界寄存器
upper memory area(UMA) 上位内存区域,高端存储区
upper memory block(UMB) 上位内存块
upper operation temperature 作业温度上限
upper print line 上部打印线

upper range 上界
upper real-time simulation 超实时仿真
upper-side band 上边带
upper state 可用状态
upper state symbol 上态符号
upper stream 上游
upper tray （打印机）上纸匣
upper triangular matrix 上三角矩阵
UPS(Uninterruptable Power Supply) 不间断供电电源
UPS(Uninterrupted Power System) 不间断电源系统
UPS(Universal Processing System) 通用处理系统
UPS monitor 不间断电源系统监视器
upset 翻转，倒转
upset exposure mechanism 翻转曝光机理
upside-down 倒置
upsize 向上适化
upsizing 向上规模优化；升迁
upstop 上止机构
upstream 上游
upstream weight technique 上游加权技术
UPT(Universal Personal Telecommunication) 通用个人通信 「表
UPT(User Process Table) 用户进程
UPT(User Profile Table) 用户配置文件表
uptime 正常工作时间
UPU(User Protocol Unit) 用户协议单元
upward capability 向上兼容性，升级能力
upward communication 向上通信，向上信息交换
upward compatibility 向上兼容
upward compatible 向上兼容
upward multiplexing 向上多路转接
upward reference 向上引用
URA(User Requirement Analysis) 用户需求分析
URL(Uniform Resource Locator) 统一资源定位器［地址］
URL mapping 统一资源地址映射
USA(Universal Synchronous Asynchronous) 通用同步/异步 「真
usability 可用性
usable direction 可用方向
usable samples 可用取样
usable scanning line length 可用扫描线长度
USAC(United States Army Computer system) 美国军用计算机系统
USAGE(USer Application GEnerator) 用户应用生成程序
usage 用法
usage clause 用法子句
usage counter 使用计数器
usage license 使用特许
usage mode 用法模式
usage summary 用法摘要
USAH(Unshared Subchannel Attachment Handler) 非共享子信道连接处理器
USAM(Unique Sequential Access Method) 惟一顺序存取方法
USAR(User Security Authorization Record) 用户安全保密授权记录
USART(Universal Synchronous / Asynchronous Receiver / Transmitter) 通用同步/异步收发器
USART communication interface USART 通信接口
USB(Universal Serial Bus) 通用串行总线
USB Implementers Forum 通用串行总线实施者论坛
USC(User Service Center) 用户服务中心
USCB(Universal Character Set Buffer) 通用字符集缓冲区
USDS(User Attribute Data Set) 用户属性数据集
use 打开数据库
use attribute 使用属性
use authority 使用授权
USE BEFORE REPORTING statement 报表前使用语句
use bit 使用位
use clause 使用子句
use joint 联合使用
use mask color 使用屏蔽色 「息
use overhead information 用户附加信
use point 使用点

use prefix 使用前缀 「句
USE statement 使用(打开数据库)语
used area 占用区
used cluster 已用簇数
used entries 已用表目
used space 已用空间
useful life 使用寿命,有效寿命
useful throughout 有用吞吐量
useful life 使用寿命,有效寿命
USENET USENET 新闻网
USENET News USENET 电子新闻
USENET newsgroup USENET 新闻组
USENET site USENET 网点
USER(User System EvaluatoR) 用户系统评价程序
user(U) 用户,使用者
user accessible graphics subroutine 用户可访问的图形子例程
user accessible register 用户可访问寄存器
user account 用户账号,用户登录号
user accounting 用户记账
user action frame 用户动作帧
user address list 用户地址表
user agent(UA) 用户代理 「络
user-application network 用户应用网
user area(UA) 用户区
user assigned alias 用户赋予的别名
user attribute 用户属性 「集
user attribute data set 用户属性数据
user attribute file 用户属性文件
user authentication 用户身份验证
user authorization file 用户特许文件
user block handling routine 用户块处理例程
user break point 用户断点
user browser 用户浏览程序
user buffer 用户缓冲器
user catalog 用户目录
user centricity 用户中心性
user class indicator 用户类别指示符
user class service 用户类服务
user code 用户代码
user command 用户命令
user communication interface 用户通信接口
user concept 用户概念

user contact hour 与用户接触的时间
user controlled searching 用户控制检
user coordinate 用户坐标 「索
user created library 用户创建程序库
user data 用户数据
user data segment 用户数据段
user data space 用户数据空间
user datagram protocol(UDP) 用户数据报协议
user date 用户日期
user default 用户默认的 「数
user definable function 用户可定义函
user definable key 用户可定义键
user-defined 用户定义的,用户规定的
user defined attribute 用户自定义属性
User-Defined AutoFormats 用户定义自动套用格式
user-defined characters 用户定义字符
user-defined class 用户自定义类
user-defined data stream 用户自定义数据流
user-defined data type 用户自定义数据类型
user-defined format 用户自定义格式
user-defined function 用户自定义函数
user-defined function key 用户自定义功能键
user-defined message 用户定义消息
user-defined subsystem 用户定义子系统
user defined type 用户定义类型
user-defined word 用户定义字
user designed command 用户设计的命令
user-determined form 用户决定形式
user disk 用户盘
user document 用户文档
user-driven system 用户驱动系统
user element(UE) 用户元素
user entry time 用户进入时间
user environment profile 用户环境配置文件
user environment test packet 用户环境测试包
user exit 用户出口
user exit queue 用户出口队列

user exit routine 用户出口例程
user facility 用户服务设施
user file 用户文件
user file directory 用户文件目录
user flag 用户标志
user friendly 对用户友好的
user friendly database system 用户友好数据库系统
user friendly development system 用户友好的开发系统
user friendly interface 用户友好界面
user friendly system 用户友好系统
user generated assembly program 用户生成的汇编程序
user group 用户组,用户群
user guide 用户指南
user handbook 用户手册
user hold status 用户保留态
user hotline 用户热线
user ID 用户标识
user identification 用户标识
user identification code(UIC) 用户标识码
user identifier 用户标识符
user information bit 用户信息位
user information block 用户信息块
user information throughput 用户信息吞吐量
user input area 用户输入区
user instruction space 用户指令空间
user interest profile 用户需求概述
user interface(UI) 用户界面,用户接口
user interface development tool 用户界面开发工具
user interface management system (UIMS) 用户界面管理系统
user interface management system for X windows(UIMX) 用于 X 窗口的用户界面管理系统
user interface model 用户界面模型
user interface toolbox 用户界面工具箱
user interrupt service routine 用户中断服务例程
user intervention 用户干预
user involvement 用户参与的
user job 用户作业

user journal 用户日志
user key 用户关键字
user label 用户标号
user language 用户语言
User Language 1(UL/1) UL/1 语言
user level protocol 用户级协议
user level security 用户级安全性
user level thread model 用户级线程模型
user library 用户库
user line 用户线路
user log off 用户注销
user log on 用户登记,用户注册
user loop 用户环路,用户回路
user main storage map 用户主存分配
user manager 用户管理器 「图
user manual 用户手册
user map 用户图,用户映像
user master catalog 用户主目录
user memory 用户内存
user memory map 用户存储映射图
user message table 用户消息表
user microprogrammability 用户可微程序设计性
user microprogrammable computer 用户可编微程序计算机
user microprogrammer 用户微程序编制器;用户微程序设计员
user microprogramming 用户微程序设计
user mode 用户模式,用户态
user model 用户模型
user modeling 用户建模
user name 用户名
user-named procedure 用户命名过程
user network interface 用户网络接口
user node 用户节点[结点]
user number 用户代号,用户号
user object 用户对象
user operated table 用户操作表
user option 用户任选项
user-oriented 面向用户的
user-oriented database management system 面向用户的数据库管理系统
user-oriented job control language 面向用户的作业控制语言 「言
user-oriented language 面向用户的语
user overlay 用户覆盖
user own coding 用户固有编码

user packet channel 用户信息包通道
user participation 用户共享,用户参与
user partition 用户区
user performance 用户性能
user pointer 用户指针
user preference 用户偏爱性
user privileges 用户特许级
user process interface 用户进程界面
user profile 用户轮廓[工作环境设置文件]
user profile table 用户概述表,用户简要特征表
user program 用户程序
user program area 用户程序区
user program error 用户程序错误
user program list 用户程序清单
user program size 用户程序大小
user program structure 用户程序结构
user program verification facility 用户程序校验设施
user-programmable 用户可编程的
user programmable keys 用户可编程键
user programmed gain 用户程序定义的增益
user programming 用户编程
user prompts 用户提示
user protocol conversion 用户协议转换
user rating 用户额定值
user record 用户记录
user relevant 用户相关资料
user requirement 用户需求
user right 用户权力
user segment 用户段
user selectable configuration 用户可选配置
user/server computing mode 客户/服务器计算模式
user service class 用户服务类别
user session 用户对话[会晤]
user side 用户端
user signal 用户信号
user space 用户空间
user specification file 用户描述[说明]文件
user stack 用户堆栈
user stack pointer 用户堆栈指针
user state 用户状态

user status table 用户状态表
user structure 用户结构
user subnet 用户子网
user supervisor 用户监督程序
user supplied directive 用户提供的指令
user survey 用户调查
user/system interaction 用户与系统交互作用
user table 用户表
user task scheduling 用户任务调度
user task set 用户任务集
user terminal 用户终端
user time 用户时间
user time-sharing 用户分时
user train 用户训练
user transaction processing routine 用户事务处理例程
user transient program 用户过渡程序
user transparent 用户透明的
user trap address 用户陷阱地址
user validation 用户合法性
user version 用户文本
user view 用户视图
user virtual address space 用户虚拟地址空间
user volume 用户卷
user word 用户词汇
user working area(UWA) 用户工作区
user writer 用户写入程序
user's file directory 用户文件目录
user's set 用户设备
UserControl 用户控件
USERDEF 用户定义
USERID(USER IDentification) 用户标识
userinfo 用户信息
userkit 用户工具箱
userlist 用户列表
username 用户名
USI(Universal Software Interface) 用户软件界面
USL(Unix System Laboratories, Inc.) Unix 系统实验室
USM(Unsharp masking) 除锐化掩蔽
USO(Unix Software Operation) Unix 软件操作分部
USOA(Uniform Systems of Accounts) 统一账目系统

USOC(Universal Service Order Code) 通用服务指令码
USP(User Stack Pointer) 用户堆栈指针
USRT(Universal Synchronous Receiver-Transmitter) 通用同步接收器/发送器
USSG(United States Standard Gauge) 美国标准线规
UT(Universal Time) 世界时间
UT(User Terminal) 用户终端
UTI(Unconditional Transfer Instruction) 无条件转移指令
utilities 实用事务程序
utility 实用程序;实用性
utility control console 作业控制台
utility device list 使用设备表
utility debug 实用调试程序
utility facilities program(UFP) 实用功能程序
utility functions 实用功能
utility graph 应用图
utility logger system 实用登录系统
utility model 实用模型
utility package 实用程序包
utility program 实用程序
utility programmer 实用程序设计者
utility ratio 实用率,应用率
utility routine 实用例程
utility software 实用软件
utility subroutine library 实用子例程库
utility system 实用系统
utility time 实用时间
utilization logger system 运行登录系统
utilized bandwidth 实际使用带宽
utilized bandwidth ratio 使用带宽比
UTL(User Task List) 用户任务表
UTP(Unshielded Twisted Pair) 非屏蔽双绞线
UU(Ultimate User) 最终用户
UUCP(Unix to Unix Copy Program) UNIX 间复制程序
uudecode(Unix to Unix decode) Unix 间解码
uuencode(Unix to Unix encode) Unix 间编码
UUNET(Unix to Unix NETwork) Unix 间网络
UV(Ultra Violet) 紫外线
UVC UVC 视频处理板
uvicon 紫外二次电子导电管
UVL(User Volume Label) 用户卷标
UVPROM(UltraViolet Programmable Read-Only Memory) 紫外线可编程只读存储器
UWA(User Working Area) 用户工作区

V v

V.1 国际电话电报咨询委员会(CCITT)的 V.1 标准(与符号表有关的规定,以下皆同)
V.2 电话线路数据传输的功率电平
V.3 国际 5 号电码
V.4 公用电信网上数据传输用 5 号电码的信号结构
V.5 公用电信交换网上同步数据传输速率的标准化
V.6 租用电话线上同步数据传输速率的标准化
V.7 电信网上进行数据通信的用词定义
V.10 与数据通信用集成电路设备通用的不平衡双流式交换电路的电气特性
V.11 与数据通信用集成电路设备通用的平衡双流式交换电路的电气特性
V.15 数据传输用的声耦合
V.17 三类传真的调制标准,数据传输速率可达 14.4 kb/s
V.19 采用电话信号频率的并行数据传输调制解调器
V.20 公用交换电信网络中通用的标准化并行数据传输调制解调器
V.21 公用交换电信网络上用的标准

化 300b/s 调制解调器
- **V.22** 公用交换电信网络或租用线上标准化 600/1200b/s 全双工调制解调器
- **V.22 bis** 公用交换电信网络或租用线上标准化 2400b/s 双工调制解调器标准,在拨号电话线上的传输速率为 600/1200 b/s
- **V.23** 公用交换电信网络拨号线路上用的标准化 600b/s,1200b/s 调制解调器
- **V.24** DTE(数据终端设备)与 DCE(数据线路端接设备)互连定义的一种标准电气接口,相当于由美国 EIA(电子工业协会)定义的 RS-232 标准
- **V.25** 公用电话交换网上自动呼叫应答设备,包括人工连接呼叫,禁止使用回声抑制器
- **V.25 bis** 拨号线并行接口的自动通话、应答系统标准,有三种模式:异步模式、面向字符的同步模式和面向位的同步模式
- **V.26** 四线制租用线路上用 2400b/s 调制解调器的标准
- **V.26 bis** 公用交换电信网络上用 2400b/s,1200b/s 调制解调器的标准
- **V.27** 租用线路上用 4800b/s 调制解调器连接人工均衡器的标准
- **V.27 bis** 租用线路上用的 4800b/s,2400b/s 调制解调器连接自动均衡器的标准
- **V.27 tec** 公用交换电信网络上用的 4800b/s,2400b/s 调制解调器的标准,可用于三类传真
- **V.28** 不平衡双流交换电路的电气特性
- **V.29** 租用线路上用的 9600b/s 调制解调器,已被采纳作为三类传真通信标准
- **V.32** 在租用线路上使用 9600b/s 调制解调器的标准,带有回音消除措施,可以为每个波特编 4 个数据位,还带有出错检查功能
- **V.32 bis** 在租用线路上把 V.32 扩展成 7200,12000,14400b/s 的调制解调器标准
- **V.32 terbo** AT&T 等公司假想的一个标准,用来支持 19200 b/s 的调制解调器传输
- **V.33** 按时分多路复用传输方式共一条四线租用线路的 12000 b/s 和 14400 b/s 的调制解调器标准
- **V.34** 用于 28800 b/s 调制解调器的标准
- **V.35** 用 60~108kHz 基群电路上速率高于 72Kb/s 的同步数据传输
- **V.36** 用 60~108kHz 基群电路的同步数据传输调制解调器
- **V.40** 用于机电式设备的差错指示
- **V.41** 与代码无关的控制系统
- **V.42** 用于检错的标准,使用 LAP-M 作为主检错协议
- **V.42 bis** 用于检错的标准,在 V.42 的基础上增加了英国电信公司的 Lempel-Ziv 数据压缩技术,压缩比可达 3.5~1
- **V.50** 数据传输质量的限制标准
- **V.51** 用于数据传输的电话电路维护的组织
- **V.52** 数据传输误码率测量设备的畸变性
- **V.53** 用于数据传输的话路维护限制范围
- **V.54** 调制解调器的环路测试设备标准
- **V.55** 话路脉冲噪声量度仪器规格
- **V.56** 话路使用的调制解调器的比较测试
- **V.57** 高速码的广范围测试仪器
- **V.110** 在综合服务数字网(ISDN)中使用同步或异步串行接口的 DTE 标准
- **V.120** 在 ISDN 中采用一个协议封装终端时如何支持使用同步或异步串行接口的 DTE 标准
- **V. fast** Hayes 和 Rockwell 公司为 28800 b/s 调制解调器提出的一种假想标准,后来发展成为 V.34 标
- **V-format** V 形记录格式
- **V-MOS transistor** VMOS 晶体管,纵向沟道金属氧化物半导体晶体管
- **V-resolution** V 消解,V 归结
- **V shell** 可视外壳程序
- **VA**(Virtual Address) 虚地址

VA（VisualAge） 可视编程环境（IBM）
VAB(Voice Answer Back) 语音应答
VAC(Value Added Carrier) 增值载波
VAC(Video Amplifier Channel) 视频放大器通道
vacancy 空位,空格点
vacancy defect 空位缺陷
vacant 空余的,空闲的
vacant channel 空余信道
vacated cell 腾空单元
vaccine 疫苗
vaccine program 疫苗程序
vacuum absorbing tape buffer 真空吸带缓冲器
vacuum accessories 真空辅助设备
vacuum capstan mode 真空主动轮模
vacuum chuck 真空吸盘 「式
vacuum deposition 真空淀积
vacuum guide 真空导向装置
vacuum range 真空范围
vacuum servo 真空伺服机构
vacuum switch 真空开关
vacuum tube 真空管
vacuum vapor deposition method 真空蒸发沉积法
VADR(Virtual ADdRess) 虚地址
VAL VAL语言
VALC(VALue Call) 值调用 「值
VALDEFD(VALue DEFineD) 规定
Valdocs (VALuable DOCuments) Valdocs文字处理软件
valence band 价带
valence band edge 价带顶
valence bond 共价键
valence electron 价电子
Valiant's merge-sorting 威林特归并排序法
Valiant's randomized parallel algorithm for routing 威林特并行随机路由选择算法
valid 有效的
valid address 有效[合法]地址
valid bit 有效位
valid code 有效代码
valid combination 有效组合 「用
valid exclusive reference 有效互斥引

valid formula 有效公式,逻辑有效式
valid FORTRAN statement 有效FORTRAN语句
valid function 有效函数
valid input domain 有效输入范围
valid memory access 有效存储器访问
valid memory address 有效内存地址
valid operation 有效操作
valid parity check 有效奇偶校验
valid prefix property 有效前缀特性
valid request 有效请求
valid user virtual address space 有效用户虚拟地址空间
validate(VDT) 确认,证实
validated program 已经验证的程序
validation 确认,证实 「畴
validation category 确认目录,证实范
validation checking 有效性检验
validation error 合法性错误
validation suite 验证程序组
validation task 确认任务
validity 确实性,有效性
validity check(VC) 有效性检验
validity checker 有效性检验程序
validity checking 有效性检验 「址
validity memory address 有效内存地
validity problem 永真问题
valley current 谷值电流
valley point 谷值点
valuation 赋值
valuator device 标量设备
value(VAL) 值,数值
value-added carrier 增值载波通信
value-added common carrier 增值公用载波通信 「络
value-added network(VAN) 增值网
value-added process 增值过程
value-added processor 增值处理机
value added reseller(VAR) 增值销售
value-added service 增值服务 「商
value analysis(VA) 价值分析
value call 值调用
value cell 值单元
value clause 赋初值子句
value judgment 价值判断
value link program 值连接程序
value nomenclature 数值命名法
value numbering 值编号法

value of information 信息值
value out of range 数值超出范围
value output module 数值输出模块
value parameter 值参数
value parameter expected 期望值参数
value part 值部分
value pointer 数值指针
value representation 值表示
value-result parameter 值-结果参数
value-returning procedure 有返回值过程
value separator 值分隔符
value set 值集
value shading 数值层析图
value substitution 值替换
value tag 值特征
value trace 值跟踪
value type 数值类型
valve 电子管；阀
valve amplifier 电子管放大器
Van Duren ARQ system 范·杜伦自动反馈重发系统
VAN(Value Added Network) 增值网络
VAN gateway 增值网关
Vandermonde's identity 范德蒙恒等式
VANDL/1 VANDL/1语言
vanilla 原型
vanishing line 没影线
vanishing point 灭点，消失点
vanishing trace 消迹
VAP (VASM subtask monitor Program) 虚存取方法子任务监控程序
VAP(Videotex Access Point) 可视图文接入点子任务监控程序
vapor deposition 汽相淀积
vapor epitaxy 汽相外延
vapor phase growth type 汽相生长型
vapor phase reflow 汽相再流
vaporware 雾汽软件，朦胧件（曾宣布上市却最终不了了之的软件产品）
VAR(Value Added Reseller) 增值销售商
varactor 变容二极管
varactor diode 变容二极管
varactor tuning 变容二极管调谐
variability 可变性
variable(V, VAR) 变量

variable abbreviated dialing 可变缩位拨号
variable address 可变地址
variable architecture processor 可变体系结构处理机
variable area(VA) 可变区域
variable bias 可变偏置
variable binary scalar 可变二进制计数器
variable bit rate(VBR) 可变比特率
variable block(VB) 可变块
variable block format 可变块格式
variable capacitance diode 变容二极管
variable class 变量类
variable connector 可变连接符
variable control block area(VCBA) 可变控制块区
variable cycle 可变周期
variable-cycle operation 可变周期作业
variable data 可变数据
variable declaration 变量说明
variable declaration section 变量说明部分
variable definition 变量定义
variable error 可变错误
variable expression 变量表达式
variable field 可变字段
variable field length 可变栏字段]长
variable field storage 可变字段存储器
variable field store 可变字段存储
variable format 可变格式
variable-format message 可变格式消息
variable frequency 可变频率
variable function 可变函数
variable function generator 可变函数发生器
variable gain 可变增益
variable gain amplifier 可变增益放大器
variable hue sound recording 变调录音
variable identifier 变量标识符
variable information 可变信息
variable information processing(VIP) 可变信息处理
variable label 可变标号
variable length(VLN) 可变长度
variable-length addressing 可变长寻

址
variable-length bit field 可变长度位字段
variable-length block 可变长块
variable-length code 可变长代码
variable-length code set 变长代码集
variable-length coding 可变长度编码
variable-length data 可变长数据项
variable-length data item 可变长数据
variable length data package 变长数据包
variable length descriptor 可变长度描述符
variable-length field 可变长字段
variable-length instruction 可变长度指令
variable length instruction format 可变长度指令格式
variable length instruction set 变长指令系统
variable-length record 变长记录
variable-length record file 可变长记录文件
variable-length record format 可变长记录格式
variable-length record sorting 变长记录排序
variable-length record system 变长记录系统
variable length string 变长字符串
variable-length table 可变长表
variable-length token 可变长令牌
variable-length vector 可变长向量
variable-length word 变长字
variable logic 可变逻辑
variable master clock 可变主时钟
variable memory 可变存储器
variable micrologic 可变微程序控制逻辑
variable multiplier 变量乘法器
variable name 变量名
variable node 可变结点
variable occurrence data item 可变重复次数数据项
variable parameter 变量参数
variable partitioning 可变分区
variable phase 可变相位
variable point 可变小数点

variable point numeral 可变小数点数
variable-point representation 可变小数点记数法
variable-point representation system 可变小数点记数体制「统
variable-point system 可变小数点系
variable-pointer list 可变指针表
variable precision coding compaction 可变精度压缩编码
variable radix 可变基数
variable range 可变范围
variable rate adaptive multiplexing 可变速率自适应多路复用
variable reference 变量引用
variable renumbering 可变长编号
variable reluctance 可变磁阻「式
variable scanning method 可变扫描方
variable scope 变量作用域
variable size item 可变长度数据项
variable size record 可变长度记录
variable size virtual memory unit 可变大小虚拟存储器
variable slope delta modulation 可变斜率增量调制
variable space 变量空间
variable space font 可变空间字体
variable-spacing encryption 可变间隔加密
variable speech control(VSC) 可变语音速率控制
variable-speed drive 变速传动机构
variable-speed gear 变速齿轮
variable speed control 变速控制「器
variable speed modem 变速调制解调
variable step size 可变步长
variable structure computer 可变结构计算机
variable symbol 变量符号
variable table 变表
variable text 可变文本
variable threshold logic 可变阈值逻辑
variable threshold logic circuit(VTL) 可变阈值逻辑电路
variable time scale 可变时标
variable-tolerance-band compaction 变容许度压缩
variable with fixed-length control record format 带固定长度控制块的可变

记录格式
variable word 可变字
variable word length(VWL) 可变字「长
variable word length computer 可变字长计算机
variance 方差
variance analysis 方差分析
variance matrix 方差矩阵
variance mismatch 方差失配
variance reduction 方差精简
variant 变种,变体,变异的
variant Chinese character 异体汉字
variant field 变体字段,变体域
variant part 变体部分
variant record 变体记录
variation 偏差,变化
variation monitors 偏差监视器
variation of function 函数的变分
variational approximation 变分近似
variational calculus 变分法 「法
variational inequality 变分不等式
variational problem 变分问题
variational solution 变分解
variode 变容二极管
variohm 可变电阻器
variplotter 可变幅面绘图仪
variset 可变框架结构
varistor 变阻体,压敏电阻
varistructure 可变结构
varistructured array 可变结构阵列
varistructured system 可变结构系统
varnished wire 漆包线
vary by category 依分类变化
vary off line 变为脱机
vary on line 变为联机
VAT(Virtual Address Table) 虚拟地址表
VAT(Virtual Address Translator) 虚拟地址翻译程序
VAX VAX 计算机系列(DEC,以下皆同)
VAX-11 Record Management Services (VAX-11 RMS) VAX-11 记录管理服务
VAX-11/780 VAX-11/780 计算机
VAX 6200 VAX 6200 计算机系列
VAX 6300 VAX 6300 计算机系列
VAX 6400 VAX 6400 计算机系列
VAX 8200/8300 VAX 8200/8300 系列计算机
VAX 8800 VAX 8800 计算机系列
VAX 9000 VAX 9000 计算机系列
VAX drawer VAX 绘图软件
VAX SQL(VAX Structural Query Language) VAX 结构查询语言
VAX station 2000 VAX 2000 工作站
VAX station 3100 VAX 3100 工作站
VAX station 3520/3540 VAX 3520/3540 工作站
VAX station 8000 VAX 8000 工作站
VAX structural query language (VAX SQL) VAX 结构查询语言
VAX unit of performance (VUP) VAX 性能单位
VAX/VMS VAX/VMS 操作系统
VAX/VMS V5.0 VAX/VMS 5.0 版
VAXcluster VAX 计算机簇 「本
VAXELN VAXELN 操作环境
VAXmate VAXmate 计算机
VB(Visual Basic) 可视 Basic 语言(微软)
VB(Voice Band) 音频频带
VB script(Visual Basic script) 可视 Basic 脚本语言
VBA(Visual Basic for Application) 可视 Basic 语言应用程序版本(微软)
VBE(VGA BIOS Extensions) VGA 基本输入/输出系统扩展
VBN(Virtual Block Number) 虚块号
VBP(Virtual Block Processing) 虚块处理
VBPPL(VBP Parameter List) 虚块处理参数表
VBScript(Visual Basic Scripting Edition) 可视 Basic 脚本编辑语言
VBW(Video BandWidth) 视频带宽
VC(Validity Check) 有效性校验
VC(Versatility Code) 多用途码,通用码
VC(Video Cipher) 视频加密系统
VC(Video Conference) 电视会议
VC(Virtual Call) 虚调用
VC(Visual C) 可视 C 语言(微软)
VCA(Voice Connecting Arrangement) 话音连接设备

VCAS (Video Coorperate Application Service) 视频协作应用服务
VCB (Volume Control Block) 卷控制
VCC (Video Conversion Card) 视频转换卡
Vcc 电源电压
VCD (Video Compact Disc) 视盘
VCH (Virtual Channel Handler) 虚通道处理程序
VCI (Video Color Interface) 视频彩色接口
VCI (Virtual Channel Identifier) 虚通道标识符
VCL (Visual Component Library) 可视组件库
VCM (Voice Coil Motor) 音圈电机
VCM (Volume Control Manager) 卷控制管理程序
VCN (Video Coorperate on Network) 网上视频协作
VCP (Video Compress Processor) 视频压缩处理器
VCP (Virtual Channel Identifier) 虚通道标识符
VCP (Virtual Circuit control Program) 虚电路控制程序
VCP (Volume Control Program) 卷控制程序
VCPI (Virtual Control Program Interface) 虚拟控制程序接口
VCR (Video Cassette Recorder) 视频磁带录像机
VCS (Video Computer System) 视频计算机系统
VDC space (Virtual Device Coordinates space) 虚拟设备坐标空间
VDC transformation matrix 虚拟设备坐标转换矩阵
VDCP (Video Data Collection Program) 视频数据采集程序
VDD (Virtual Device Driver) 虚拟设备驱动程序
VDDL (Virtual Data Description Language) 虚拟数据描述语言
VDDP (Video Digital Data Processing) 虚拟数字数据处理
VDE (Video Display Editor) 视频显示编辑器
VDH (Virtual Device Helper) 虚拟设备帮助程序
VDI (Video Display Input) 视频显示输入
VDI (Virtual Device Interface) 虚拟设备接口
Vdisk (Virtual disk) 虚拟盘
VDL (Variable Delay Line) 可变延迟
VDL (Vienna Definition Language) 维也纳定义语言，VDL 语言
VDM (Video Display Metafile) 视频显示元文件
VDMA (Variable Destination Multiple Access) 可变地址多路存取
VDP (Video Display Processor) 视频显示处理器
VDS (Virtual DMA Services) 虚拟直接存储器访问服务
VDS (Visual Docking Simulator) 目视对接仿真器
VDSL (Very high Digital Subscriber Link) 极高速数字用户线
VDT (Video Dial Tone) 视频拨号机
VDT (Video Display Terminal) 视频显示终端
VDT radiation 视频显示终端辐射
VDU (Video Display Unit) 视频显示单元
vector (V) 向量，矢量
vector addition 向量加法
vector address 向量地址
vector admittance 向量[矢量]导纳
vector algebra 矢量代数
vector algorithm 向量算法
vector arithmetic 向量运算
vector-based graphics 基于向量的图
vector cache 向量高速缓存
vector compiler 向量编译器
vector computation 向量计算
vector computer 向量计算机
vector convergence 向量收敛
vector conversion jump 向量转换跳越
vector coprocessor 向量协处理器
vector descriptor 向量描述符
vector diagram 向量[矢量]图
vector display 向量显示
vector element 向量元素
vector expression 向量表达式

vector facility 向量设施	vector pipeline processor 向量流水线处理机
vector feed rate 向量进给率	vector priority 向量优先权
vector field 矢量场	vector power 向量功率
vector floating-point data 向量浮点数据	vector power factor 向量功率因数
vector font 向量字形	vector process language 向量处理语言
vector format 向量格式	vector process mode 向量处理模式
vector function 向量函数	vector processing 向量处理
vector function unit 向量功能部件	vector processor 向量处理机
vector generation 向量生成	vector product 向量积
vector generator(VG) 向量产生器	vector quantity 向量,矢量
vector graphics 向量[矢量]图形	vector quantization 向量量化
vector-graphic movie 矢量图形动画	vector random function 向量随机函数
vector hardware instruction 向量硬件指令	vector ratio 向量比,矢量比
vector identification 向量标识	vector reduction method 向量归约法
vector inner-product 向量内积,向量点积	vector refresh 向量再生
	vector refresh display 向量再生显示
vector instruction controller(VIC) 向量指令控制器	vector register 向量寄存器
vector instruction description 向量指令描述	vector representation 向量表示法
	vector retrieval model 向量检索模型
vector instruction set 向量指令系统	vector rule 向量规则
vector length register 向量长度寄存器	vector scan 向量扫描
vector loop 向量循环	vector space 向量空间
vector machine 向量机,向量计算机	vector speed 向量速度
vector machine model 向量机模型	vector spline 向量样条
vector mask register 向量屏蔽寄存器	vector storage 向量存储器
vector merge 向量归并	vector structure 向量结构
vector method 向量法	vector sum 向量和
vector mode 向量运算模式	vector summation 向量求和
vector mode data 向量型数据	vector supercomputer 向量巨型计算机
vector mode display 向量式显示	vector supercomputer architecture 向量巨型机体系结构
vector-mode graphic display 向量型图形显示	vector table 向量表
vector multiplication 向量乘法	vector to raster conversion 向量到光栅转换
vector node 向量节点	vector transfer 向量转移,矢量传送
vector norms 向量范数	vector transfer table 向量转移表,矢量传递表
vector operand 向量操作数	
vector operation 向量运算	vector type 向量类型
vector optimization 向量优化	vector variable 向量变量
vector-oriented 面向向量的,向量性	vectored interrupt 向量中断
vector parallel processor 向量并行处理机	vectored interrupt system 向量中断系统
	vectored priority interrupts 向量优先权中断
vector parameter 向量参数	
vector parameter file 向量参数文件	vectored restart 向量重始
vector performance 向量性能	vectoring 转向,定向
vector pipeline 向量流水线	vectorizable serial computation 向量化串行计算

vectorization 向量化,矢量化
vectorization procedure 向量化过程
vectorization ratio 向量化比例
vectorized congruential method 向量同余法
vectorized priority interrupt 向量优先中断
vectorizer 向量化程序
vectorizing compilers 向量化编译器
vectors per second(VPS) 每秒向量数
vectorscope 矢量显示器
VECTRAN VECTRAN语言,向量化FORTRAN语言
VED(Voice EDitor) 话音编辑程序
Veitch chart 维奇图
Veitch diagram 维奇图
velocimeter 测速仪
velocity 速度
velocity correction 速度校正
velocity correction circuit 速度校正电路
velocity error 速度误差
velocity factor 速度因子
velocity limiting control action 速率限制控制作用
velocity-limiting servo 速度限制伺服
velocity of light 光速
velocity of propagation 传播速率
velocity of sound 声速
velocity pickup 速度传感器
velocity saturation 速度饱和
velocity servo 速度伺服积分器
velocity shaped canceler 速度型补偿器
velocity transducer 速度传感器
velocity variation 速度调制,变速
velodyne 伺服积分器
vendor 销售商
vendor specific drivers 售主特定驱动程序
Venn diagram 维恩图,文氏图
vent 孔,通风孔
ventilate 通风
ventilation device 通风设备
ventilation louver 通风百叶窗
ventilator 排风扇,通风机
Ventura Publisher Ventura排版软件
verb 动词
verb group case 动词组角色

verb phrase 动词短语
verb processor 动词处理程序
verbal 口头的,语言的
verbal communication 语言通信
verge 边界,边缘
verifiable secure operating system 检验可靠的操作系统
verification 验证,检验
verification and validation 验证与确
verification expression 验证表达式
verification mode 验证模式
verification program 验证程序
verification setting 验证设置
verification tool 验证工具
verification trunk 验证干线
verifier 检验器;校对员
verify 验证,检验
verify after restore 还原后检验
verify error 检验误差
verify hyperlink 检验超链接
verify unit 检验设备
verifying unit 校验设备
Vernam enciphering Vernam加密法
vernier 微调器,光标,游标
vernier auto tracker 微调自动跟踪
vernier caliper 游标卡尺
vernier control 游标调节
vernitel 精确数据传送设备
Veronica(Very Easy Rodent Oriented Net-wide Index to Computerized Archies)(Gopher) 极简易面向"啮齿动物"的环网索引计算机化搜索工具(内华达大学)
VersaCAD VersaCAD软件
Versatec Versatec静电印刷机
versatile 多用途的,多功能的,易变的
versatile message transaction protocol (VMTP) 通用消息事务协议
versatility 多功能性,多面性
VersaVision VersaVision液晶显示器
version 版本
version control 版本控制
version description document 版本说明文档
version dependency 版本相关性,版本依赖性
version ID 版本标识号
version management 版本管理

version management strategy 版本管理策略
version number 版本号
version server 版本服务器
version space 解释空间
version time stamped database 版本时间标记数据库
version up 版本更新,版本升级
verso 偶数页
VERSO database machine VERSO数据库计算机
vertex 顶点
vertex adjacency graph 顶点邻接图
vertex connectivity algorithm 顶点连通算法
vertex cover problem 顶点覆盖问题
vertex distance 顶点距离
vertex enumeration 顶点枚举
vertex graph 顶点图
vertex independence number of a hypergraph 超图的点独立数
vertex plate 顶点匹配板
vertex ranking algorithm 顶点排列算法
vertex separator 顶点分隔符
vertex transitive graph 顶点迁移图
vertical 垂直的,纵向的
vertical alignment 垂直对齐
vertical amplification 垂直放大
vertical amplifier 垂直放大器
vertical-amplitude controls 垂直幅度控制
vertical application 特定对象应用软件
vertical axis 垂直轴
vertical blanking 垂直消隐
vertical blanking interval(VBI) 垂直消隐时间
vertical blanking pulse 垂直消隐脉冲
vertical Bloch line(VBL) 垂直布洛赫线
vertical cabinet 立式机箱
vertical centering 垂直居中
vertical centering control 垂直中心控制
vertical check 垂直校验
vertical convergence 垂直会聚
vertical convergence control 垂直会聚控制
vertical definition 垂直清晰度
vertical deflecting coil 垂直偏转线圈
vertical deflecting plates 垂直偏转电极
vertical deflection electrodes 垂直偏转电极
vertical deflection oscillator 垂直偏转振荡器
vertical display 垂直[纵向]显示
vertical display height 垂直显示高度
vertical distribution 纵向分布
vertical drive 垂直驱动
vertical dynamic convergence 垂直动态会聚
vertical field-effect transistor(VFET) 垂直场效应晶体管
vertical field-strength diagram 垂直场强图
vertical film head 垂直薄膜磁头
vertical format 纵向格式
vertical format control character(VFCC) 垂直格式控制字符
vertical format unit(VFU) 垂直格式单元
vertical-frequency response 垂直频率响应
vertical hold control 垂直同步控制
vertical hold control circuit 垂直同步控制电路
vertical integration 纵向一体化
vertical interval 垂直间隔
vertical interval reference(VIR) 垂直扫描时基
vertical justification 垂直调整,垂直对齐
vertical-lateral recording 垂直横向录音
vertical linearity control 垂直线性控制,帧线性调节
vertical magnetic recording 垂直磁记录
vertical magnetic recording head 垂直磁记录头
vertical market program 特殊行业软件
vertical metal oxide semiconductor technology 垂直金属氧化物半导体工艺
vertical microinstruction 垂直微指令
vertical microprogramming 垂直微程序设计
vertical migration 垂直迁移
vertical MOS(VMOS) 垂直金属氧化物半导体

vertical oscillator 垂直[场]振荡器
vertical-output stage 垂直[帧]输出级
vertical parity check 垂直奇偶校验
vertical partitioning 纵向划分
vertical pointer 纵向指针
vertical polarization 垂直极化
vertical polarized wave 垂直极化波
vertical positions 垂直[纵向]位置
vertical processor 垂直处理器
vertical-raster count 垂直光栅计数
vertical recording 垂直记录方式
vertical redundancy 垂直冗余
vertical-redundancy check(VRC) 垂直冗余校验
vertical refresh rate 垂直刷新速率
vertical resolution 垂直分辨率[清晰度]
vertical retrace 垂直回扫
vertical scrolling 纵向滚动
vertical services 纵向服务
vertical slope 纵向斜率
vertical spacing 垂直[纵向]间距
vertical stress distribution 纵向应力分布
vertical sweep 垂直扫描
vertical-sync pulses 垂直同步脉冲,帧同步脉冲
vertical-sync signal 垂直同步信号
vertical synchronizing pulse 垂直同步脉冲
vertical tab control(VT) 纵向增表控制
vertical table 纵向表
vertical tabulation(VT) 纵向制表
vertical tabulation character(VT) 纵向制表字符
vertical tabulator key 纵向制表键
vertical timebase 垂直扫描时基
vertical text 垂直文本
vertical text orientation 垂直文本取向
vertical validate height 垂直[纵向]有效高度
vertical vibration 垂直振动
vertical wraparound 纵向环绕
vertically-polarized electromagnetic wave 垂直极化电磁波
very high digital subscriber link(VDSL) 极高速数字用户线
very high frequency(VHF) 特高频,甚高频
very high frequency oscillator 特高频振荡器
very high frequency tuner 特高频调谐器
very high level language(VHL) 甚高级语言
very high speed integrated circuit hardware description language(VHDL) 超高速集成电路硬件描述语言
very large database(VLDB) 特大型数据库
very large memory(VLDB) 特大型内存
very large scale integration(VLSI) 特大规模集成电路
very long instruction word computer (VLIW) 超长指令字计算机
very low frequency(VLF) 甚低频
very low frequency emission 甚低频辐射
very small aperture terminal(VSAT) 甚小口径天线卫星终端站
VESA (Video Electronics Standard Assn.) 视频电子标准协会
VESA bus VESA 总线
vesicular film 小泡状膜
VESS(Visual Environment Simulation System) 目视环境仿真系统
vestigial sideband(VSB) 残留边带
vestigial sideband filter 残留边带滤波器
vestigial sideband modulation(VSM) 残留边带调制
vestigial sideband transmission 残留边带传输
vestigial sideband transmission system 残留边带传输系统
vestigial sideband transmitter 残留边带发射机
vest-pocket calculator 袖珍计算器
VF(Vertical File) 直列文件
VF(Voice Frequency) 音频
VFC(Vertical Format Control) 垂直格式控制
VFC(Voice Frequency Channel) 音频通道
VFC(Voltage Frequency Converter) 电压频率转换器

VFD(Voice Frequency Dialing) 音频拨号
VFC(Voice Frequency Generator) 音频产生器
VFM(Virtual File Manager) 虚拟文件管理程序
VFO(Variable Frequency Oscillator) 可变频率振荡器
VFO(Voice Frequency Oscillator) 音频振荡器
VFP(Visual FoxPro) 可视 FoxPro 数据库(微软)
VFS(Virtual File System) 虚拟文件系统
VFT(Voice Frequency Transmission) 音频传输
VGA(Video Graphics Array) (显示适配器)视频图形阵列
VGA HC(VGA HiColor) VGA HC 格式
VH(Valid Halfword) 有效半字
VHD(Video High-density Disc) 高密度视盘(JVC)
VHDL(Very high speed integrated circuit Hardware Description Language) 超高速集成电路硬件描述语言
VHF(Very High Frequency) 甚高频
VHF link 甚高频链路
VHF omnidirectional communication 甚高频全向无线电通信
VHF omnidirectional range station 甚高频全向无线电信标台
VHLL(Very High-Level Language) 超高级语言
VHS(Video Home System) VHS 录像机格式(松下)
VHSIC(Very High Speed Integrated Circuits) 超高速集成电路
VI(Volume Indicator) 音量指示器
vi vi 编辑器,Unix 文本编辑程序
Vi collision Vi 冲突
VIA(Versatile Interface Adapter) 通用接口适配器
Via Via 中间件(Moda)
via 通孔
via contact hole 通路接触孔
via hole 通路孔,辅助孔
via minimization algorithm 通路极小化算法
via net loss(VNL) 通路净损耗
via pin 通路引线
via resistance 通路电阻
via spacing rule 通路空白规则
viability 生存能力
VIAS (Voice Intelligibility Analysis System) 语音可懂度分析系统
VIAS(Voice Interference Analysis Set) 语音干扰分析装置
ViaVoice ViaVoice 语音输入软件(IBM)
vibrating system 振荡系统
vibration 振动
vibration analysis 振动分析
vibration control system 振动控制系
vibration damper 振动抑制器
vibration equation 振动方程
vibration fatigue test 振动疲劳试验
vibration-free tables 减振桌
vibration isolator 减震器
vibration meter 测振仪
vibration noise 振动干扰
vibration table 振动台
vibration test 振动试验
vibration transducer 振动传感器
vibrator 振动器;振荡器
VIC (Variable Instruction Computer) 可变指令计算机
VIC(Virtual Interaction Controller) 虚拟交互控制器
VICAM(Virtual Integrated Communications Access Method) 虚拟综合通信访问法
VICAR (Video Image Communication And Retrieval) 视频图像通信与检索
vicon 视频图符
victim emitter 干扰发射机
victim frequency 干扰频率
VID(Video Image Display) 视频图像显示器
VID(Voltage Identification Definition) 电压标识定义
Video-1 Video-1 编码
video adapter 视频适配卡
video amplifier(VA) 视频信号放大器

video amplitude 视频振幅
video and cassette personal computer 带电视和卡式磁带的个人计算机
video attribute 显示属性
video bandwidth 视频带宽
video black 视频黑场
Video Blaster 视霸卡(Creative)
video board 视频显示板
video buffer 视频缓冲区
video cable 视频电缆
Video-Call Video-Call 交互式视频平台
video camera 视频摄像机
video camera digitizer 电视摄像机数字化仪
video capture card 视频捕获卡
video carrier 视频载波
video cassette 盒式录像磁带
video cassette journal 盒式录像带杂志
video cassette recorder 盒式磁带录像机
video channel 视频信道
video chip 视频芯片
video circuit 视频电路
video clip 视频剪图
video codec 视频编/解码器
video collect 视频收集
video communication network 视频通信网络
video compression 视频压缩
video computer system(VCS) 视频计算机系统
video conferencing 电视会议
video confidence head 视频置信头
video controller 视频控制器
video data 视频数据
video data digital processing 视频数据数字处理
video data integrator 视频数据积分器
video data interrogator 视频数据询答器
video data terminal 视频数据终端
video decompressor 视频解压卡
video detector 视频检波器
video dial tone(VDT) 视频拨号机构
video digitizer 视频数字化器
video disc 视盘,影碟
video disc player 视盘播放机
video discriminator 视频鉴频器

video disk computer system 视盘计算机系统
video disk recorder 视盘记录设备
video disk system 视盘系统
video display 视频显示器
video display adapter 视频显示适配器
video display board 视频显示板
video display card 视频显示卡
video display controller 视频显示控制器
video display metafile(VDM) 视频显示元文件
video display page 视频显示页
video display processor 视频显示处理器
video display system 视频显示系统
video display terminal(VDT) 视频显示终端
video display tube 视频显示管
video display unit(VDU) 视频显示单元
video documentation 视频文档建立
video done 视频播放完毕
video driver 视频驱动程序
video editor 视频编辑程序
video education 电视教育
Video Electronics Standards Association(VESA) 视频电子标准协会
video encoder 视频解码器
video file 视频文件,可视文件
video filter 视频滤波器
Video for Windows Windows 视频
video frame store 视频画面存储
video frequency 视频
video-frequency amplifier 视频放大器
video-frequency channel 视频通道
video gain control 视频增益控制
video game 视频游戏机
video generation unit(VGU) 视频发生单元
video generator 视频发生器
video gram 视频节目成品
video-graph printer 视频信号印刷器
video graphics 视频图形
video graphics array(VGA) 视频图形阵列
video graphics board 视频图形板
video image 视频图像
video information exchange window 视频信息交换窗口

video integration	视频集成化
video integrator	视频积分器
video interface	视频接口
video mapping	视频映像
video masking	视频屏蔽
video matrix terminal	视频矩阵终端
video memory	视频存储器
video mixer	视频混合器
video mode	视频模式
video module	可视模块
video monitor	视频监视器
video network	视频网络
video on demand(VOD)	点播电视
video optical detector	视频光学检波器
video optical source	视频光源
video overlay card	视频叠加卡
video palette	视频调色板
video patsearch	可视专利检索
video phone	可视电话
video picture	视频图像
video plane	视频平面
video player	电视放像机
video printer	视频图像打印机
video processor	视频处理机
video programming	视频图像处理程序设计
video programming interface(VPI)	视频编程接口
video pulse	视频脉冲
Video Pump	视频泵
video quality	视频质量
video quantizer	视频量化器
video RAM(VRAM)	视频随机存取存储器
video receiver	视频信号接收机
video record rate	视频录制速率
video record frame duration	视频录制帧时间
video recorder	录像机
video recording	录像,视频记录
video replay	电视节目重放
video scaling	视频缩放
video scan	视频扫描
video scan management	视频扫描管理
video-scan optical character reader	视频扫描光学字符阅读机
video segment	视频片段
video server	视频服务器
video signal	视频信号
video signal standards	视频信号标准
video society	电视化社会
video source select	视频源选择
video speed A/D converter	视频速度模数转换器
video standard	视频标准
video stretching	视频频谱展宽
video structure	视频图像结构
video tape	录像带
video tape recorder	磁带录像机
video tape replay	录像磁带重放机
video teleconferencing	视频远程会议
video telephone	电视电话
video telephone set	可视电话机
video terminal(VT)	视频终端
video terminal paging	视频终端分页
video tracking system	视频跟踪系统
video transmitting power	视频发射功率
video trunk	视频干线,视频中继线
video tuner	视频调谐器
video unit files	视频单元文件
video waveform	视频信号波形
video window	视频窗口
videocast	电视广播
videodisc	视盘
videodisc microprocessor	视盘微处理器
videodisk	视盘
videognosis	视频诊断
videogram	录像制成品
videograph	视频印像机
videographic display	视频图形显示
videography	视频电报
videophone	可视电话
VideoPlace	VideoPlace 虚拟现实系统
videoscan	视频扫描
VideoShare	视频共享卡
videotape	录像带
videotape recording(VTR)	磁带录像
videotape replay	录像磁带重放机
videotex	可视图文
videotex adapter	可视图文适配器
videotex center	可视数据检索中心
videotex information service	可视图文信息服务
videotex networks	可视数据检索网络
videotex system	可视数据检索系统

videotext 可视数据
vidicon 视像管,光导摄像管
vidicon camera 光导摄像管
Viditel Viditel 图文电视系统(荷兰)
Vidon Vidon 图文电视系统(加拿大)
VIDS(Virtual Image Display System) 虚图像显示系统
Vienna Definition Language(VDL) 维也纳定义语言
Vienna development method(VDM) 维也纳开发方法
VIEW(Video Information Exchange Window) 视频信息交换窗口
VIEW(Virtual Interactive Environment Workstation) 虚拟交互环境工作站
view 视图,视窗
view backup log 查看备份记录
view classification 视图分类
view definition 视图定义
view designer 视图设计程序
view endnote 查看尾注
view error log 查看错误记录
view field 视图区域
view footnote 查看脚注
view integration 意图综合
view integration process 意图综合过程
view manager 视图管理器
view mapping 视图映像
view menu 视图菜单
view mode 打印时的观察方式
view model 视觉模型
view modeling 意图模型化;视觉建模
view modeling approach 意图模型法
view modeling technique 意图模型技术
view parameter 视图参数
view plane 视平面,投影平面
view plane distance 投影平面距离
view plane normal 投影平面法线
view point 视觉点,视见点,观察点
view port 视窗,视见区
view procedure 察看过程
view reference point 视见参考点
view restructuring 意图重构
view specification 视图说明
view surface 视图输出面
view text file 查看文本文件
view transformation 视图变换,取景变换
view transformation matrix 视图变换矩阵
view update 视图更新
view volume 视见约束体
view wizard 视图向导
viewdata 可视数据
viewer 阅读器,取景器
viewfinder 取景器
viewing area 视区
viewing frustum 视锥,视见平截头体
viewing pipeline 视见流水线
viewing pyramid 观察空间,视锥
viewing screen 视屏
viewing storage tube 可视存储管
viewing time 观察时间
viewing transformation 视觉变换
viewphone 可视电话,图像电话
viewpoint invariance 观察点不变性
viewport 取景框
viewscreen 观察屏幕
VIG(Video Image Generator) 视频图像发生器
vignetting 渐晕
Villari effect 维拉利效应
VIM(Vendor Independent Message interface) 与供应者无关的消息接口
VINES(VIrtual NEtworking System) 虚拟网络系统,VINES 网络操作系统(Banyan)
vinyl resin 烯基树脂,乙烯基树脂
VIO(Video Input/Output) 视频输入/输出
VIO(Virtual I/O) 虚输入/输出
VIOC(Variable Input-Output Code) 可变输入/输出码
violation 破坏,违规
violet 紫色
VIP(Vector Information Processor) 向量信息处理机
VIP(Versatile Information Processor) 通用信息处理器
VIP(Visual Image Processor) 可视图像处理器
VIP(Voice Information Processor) 语音信息处理器
virgin 空白的,未使用过的

virgin coil 空白带卷
virgin medium 未启用媒体
virgin paper-tape coil 无孔纸带卷
virtual(V) 虚的,虚拟的
virtual 8086 mode 虚拟8086模式
virtual access method 虚拟存取法
virtual address(VA) 虚地址
virtual address space 虚地址空间
virtual address translation 虚地址转换
virtual addressing 虚拟寻址
virtual addressing mechanism 虚寻址机构
virtual agent 虚拟代理
virtual algorithm 虚拟算法
virtual array 虚阵列
virtual auxiliary memory 虚拟辅助存储器
virtual bank 虚拟存储块
virtual base class 虚基类
virtual basic terminal 基本虚终端
virtual bidirectional relationship 虚拟双向关系
virtual bit map 虚位图
virtual block multiplexer mode 虚拟块多路复用方式
virtual button 虚按钮
virtual cache 虚拟高速缓存
virtual call 虚调用;虚呼叫
virtual call capability 虚呼叫能力
virtual call circuit 虚呼叫电路
virtual call control 虚呼叫控制
virtual call facility 虚呼叫设施
virtual call mode 虚呼叫模式
virtual call network 虚呼叫网络
virtual call service 虚呼叫服务
virtual carrier 虚载频
virtual channel 虚拟信道
virtual channel identifier(VCI) 虚通道标识符
virtual channel logic 虚信道逻辑
virtual channel network 虚信道网络
virtual circuit(VC) 虚电路
virtual circuit control program 虚电路控制程序
virtual circuit number 虚电路编号
virtual circuit pacing 虚电路调步
virtual circuit service 虚电路服务
virtual common memory 虚拟公用存储器
virtual community 虚拟团体
virtual computer 虚计算机
virtual computing system 虚计算系统
virtual connection 虚连接
virtual console 虚拟控制台
virtual console function 虚控制台功能
virtual console spooling 虚拟控制台假脱机操作
virtual control program interface(VCPI) 虚拟控制程序接口
virtual coordinate system 虚拟坐标系
virtual copy 虚拷贝
virtual CPU time 虚拟CPU时间
virtual cut through 虚拟直通
virtual cycle 虚拟循环
virtual data circuit 虚数据电路
virtual data connection 虚数据连接
virtual data-item 虚数据项
virtual datagram 虚数据报
virtual-datagram transport network 虚数据包传送网络
virtual decision value 虚判定值
virtual declaration 虚说明
virtual derived data item 虚导出数据项
virtual device 虚设备
Virtual Device Driver(VxD) 虚拟设备驱动程序
virtual device interface(VDI) 虚拟设备接口
virtual directory 虚拟目录
virtual disc 虚拟光驱
virtual disc system 虚拟盘系统
virtual disk(VDISK) 虚拟盘
virtual disk initialization program 虚拟盘初始化程序
virtual disk system 虚拟盘系统
virtual DMA services 虚直接存储器存取服务
virtual document 虚拟文档
Virtual DOS Machine(VDM) 虚拟DOS机器
virtual drive 虚拟驱动器
virtual earth 虚地
virtual enterprise 虚拟企业
virtual enterprise network(VEN) 虚拟企业网
virtual enterprise on network 网络上

的虚拟企业
virtual environment 虚拟环境
virtual factory(VF) 虚拟工厂
virtual field 虚拟字段
virtual file 虚文件
virtual file protocol 虚文件协议
virtual floppy 虚拟软盘
virtual form terminal 表格虚终端
virtual graphic terminal 图形虚终端
virtual ground 虚地
virtual hashing 虚拟散列法
virtual host storage(VHS) 虚主机存「储
virtual hybrid terminal 混合虚终端
virtual hypercube 虚拟超立方体
virtual I/O device 虚拟输入/输出设
virtual image 虚拟映像,映像 「备
virtual image buffer 虚拟影像缓冲区
virtual image terminal 图像虚终端
virtual integration 虚拟集成
Virtual Interactive Environment Workstation(VIEW) 虚拟交互环境工作站(NASA)
virtual job 虚拟作业
virtual key code 虚拟键码
virtual LAN 虚拟局域网
virtual link packet switching 虚拟链路分组交换
virtual machine 虚拟机
virtual machine concept 虚机概念
virtual machine control block 虚机控制块
virtual machine identifier 虚机标识符
virtual machine interface 虚拟机接口
virtual machine kernel 虚机核心
Virtual Machine Management(VMM) 虚拟机管理器(微软)
virtual machine specification 虚拟机器规范,虚拟运行环境标准
virtual machine/system product(VM/SP) 虚拟机操作系统,VM/SP操作系统(IBM)
virtual machine technique 虚拟机器技术
virtual manipulator 虚拟操纵器
virtual meeting 虚拟会议
virtual memory 虚拟存储器
virtual memory address 虚拟存储器地址
virtual memory computer 虚拟存储器计算机
virtual memory concept 虚拟存储器概念 「施
virtual memory facility 虚拟存储器设
virtual memory hardware 虚拟存储硬件
virtual memory machine 虚拟存储器计算机
virtual memory management 虚拟存储器管理
virtual memory mechanism 虚存机构
virtual memory operating system 虚拟存储器操作系统
virtual memory page swap 虚拟存储器页面对换
virtual memory pointer 虚存指针「栈
virtual memory stack 虚拟存储器堆
virtual memory strategy 虚拟存储器策略
virtual memory structure 虚拟存储器结构 「统
virtual memory system 虚拟存储器系
virtual memory technique 虚存技术
virtual message template 虚拟消息模
virtual method 虚拟方法 「板
virtual method table(VMT) 虚拟方法表
virtual mode 虚拟模式
virtual model 虚拟模型
virtual monitor 虚拟显示器
virtual networking 虚拟组网能力
virtual networking system(VINES) 虚拟网络系统
virtual operating system 虚拟操作系统
virtual page 虚页
virtual page number(VPN) 虚页号
virtual parameter 虚参数
virtual partition 虚分区
virtual path 虚路径
virtual path identifier(VPI) 虚路径标示符
virtual peripheral 虚拟外围设备
virtual printer 虚拟打印机
virtual private network(VPN) 虚拟专用网
virtual processing 虚拟处理
virtual processing time 虚处理时间

virtual processor 虚处理机
virtual processor complex(VPC) 虚拟处理器复合
virtual processor ratio 虚处理器比率
virtual prototype 虚样机;虚拟原型
virtual pushbutton 虚按钮
virtual real mode 虚拟实模式
virtual reality 虚拟现实
Virtual Reality Modeling Language (VRML) 虚拟现实造型语言
virtual region 虚区域
virtual route 虚路由
virtual route pacing request(VRPRQ) 虚路由调步请求
virtual route pacing response(VRPRS) 虚路由调步响应
virtual row 虚行
virtual screen 虚屏
virtual segment 虚段
virtual segment structure 虚段结构
virtual server 虚拟服务器
virtual space 虚空间
virtual spooling device 虚拟假脱机设备
virtual stack 虚拟堆栈
virtual storage 虚存储器
virtual storage access method(VSAM) 虚存储访问法
virtual studio system(VSS) 虚拟演播室系统
virtual system 虚系统
virtual telecommunication access method (VTAM) 虚拟远程通信访问法
virtual terminal 虚终端
virtual terminal environment 虚拟终端环境
virtual terminal network 虚终端网络
virtual terminal protocol 虚终端协议
virtual terminal standard 虚终端标准
virtual token passing 虚拟令牌传送
virtual volume 虚拟卷
virtual window 虚拟窗口
virtual workstation 虚拟工作站
virtualization 虚拟化
virus 病毒
virus analysis 病毒分析
virus attack 病毒攻击
virus breeding 病毒繁殖
virus carrier 病毒载体

virus family 病毒家族
virus filter(VF) 病毒过滤器
virus hiding mechanism 病毒隐蔽机制
virus immunity 病毒免疫
virus infection 病毒感染
virus isolation 病毒隔离
virus marker 病毒标志
virus model 病毒模型
virus mutation 病毒变种
virus precaution 病毒预防
virus replication 病毒复制
virus self-encryption 病毒自加密
virus spread 病毒扩散,病毒蔓延
virus structure 病毒结构
virus trigger condition 病毒触发条件
virus warning 病毒告警
ViruSafe 病毒安全疫苗
virusafe 抗病毒程序
VIS(Vector Instruction Set) 向量指令系统
VIS(Video Information System) 视频信息系统
VIS(Visual Instruction Set) 可视化指令集(Sun)
VIS(Voice Information Service) 话音信息服务
VISCA(VIdeo System Control Architecture) 视频系统控制体系结构
viscosity 粘滞性
visibility 可见性,能见度
visibility factor 能见度系数
visibility point 可见点,能见点
visible 可见的,直观的
visible cell 可见单元格
visible class 可视类
visible file 可见文件
visible light 可见光
visible page 可视页面
visible ray 可见光线
visible record 直观记录
visible search 直视检索
visible spectrum 可见光谱
visible speech 可视语言,可见语言
VisiCalc VisiCalc 电子表格软件
VISION(computer VISION system) 计算机视觉系统
vision 视觉
vision analyzer 视觉分析器

vision computing 视觉计算
vision information 视觉信息
vision mixer 图像混合器
vision model 视觉模型
vision optical system 视觉光学系统
vision robot 视觉机器人
vision sensor 视觉传感器
Vista (Visual Information for Satellite Telemetry Analysis) 卫星遥测可视信息分析系统
visual 直观的,可视的,形象的
visual alignment 目视调准
Visual Basic(VB) 可视 Basic 语言(微软)
Visual Basic for Application (VBA) 可视 Basic 语言应用程序版本(微软)
visual behavior 视觉行为
visual body signal 目视机体信号
Visual Café Java 开发工具(Symantec)
visual carrier 图像载波
visual cell 视细胞
visual check 目视检查
visual class 可视类
visual code 可视代码
visual communication 视觉通信
visual component 可视组件
visual component library(VCL) 可视组件
visual component manager 可视部件管理器
visual computing 可视计算
visual continuity 视觉连续性
visual control 视觉[直观]控制
visual data acquisition 视觉数据获取
visual design tool 视件设计工具
visual display 直观显示[台
visual display console 视觉显示控制
visual display interface 视觉显示接口
visual display microprocessor controller 直观显微处理机控制器
visual display terminal 视觉显示终端
visual display terminal capability 直观显示终端能力
visual display unit(VDU) 视觉显示单元
Visual Edge 视觉接口卡

visual edit 可视化编辑
visual editing terminal 可视编辑终端
visual editor 可视编辑程序
visual effect 可视效果
visual ergonomics 视觉工效学
visual error representation 直观错误表示法
visual fatigue 视觉疲劳
visual feedback 视觉反馈
visual field 视野
Visual FoxPro 可视化 FoxPro 数据库(微软)
visual illusion 幻觉,幻影
visual image 可视图像
visual inference 直觉推理,形象化推理
Visual Information Retrieval DataBlade 可见信息查询数据刀片(Informix)
visual inquiry 可见查询
visual inquiry display terminal 视觉查询显示终端
visual inquiry station 可视查询站
visual inspection 目测
Visual Instruction Set(VIS) 可视化指令集(Sun)
visual interface 可视界面
Visual J++ 可视化 Java 语言(微软)
visual language 可视语言
visual learning 直观学习
visual operation console 可视操作台
visual part 可视部件
visual range 可视区域
visual readout 可视读出,可见读出
visual recognition 直观识别,目视识别[器
visual scanner 可视扫描器,显像扫描
visual sensing system 视觉传感系统
visual sensor 视觉传感器
visual signal 可视信号
visual spectrum 可见光谱,可视频谱
visual supervisory control 目视监督控制
visual terminal 视觉终端,直观终端设备
visual terminal type 直观终端类型
visual test 直观检查,目视检查

visual thinking 形象思维
visual tracking 目视跟踪
VisualAge 可视化编程环境(IBM)
VisualAge Database for Oracle 支持 Oracle 的可视化数据库编程环境(IBM)
VisualAge Distributed 支持分布式运算的可视化编程环境(IBM)
VisualAge Java Java 语言可视化编程环境(IBM)
VisualAge Organizer 可视化编程环境组织程序(IBM)
VisualAge Professional Server 可视化编程环境专业服务器(IBM)
VisualAge Quick Start 可视化编程环境快速启动程序(IBM)
VisualAge Report 可视化编程环境报表程序(IBM)
VisualAge Standard 可视化编程环境标准(IBM)
visualization 显像,目视,可视化计算
visualization paradigm 可视化范例
visualizing system 可视化系统
VITAL(VHDL Initiative Toward ASIC Libraries) 推动 VHDL 的 ASIC 库初始协会
vivid reasoning 明确推理
VL bus VESA 局部总线 「段
VLF(Variable Length Field) 变长字
VLF(Very Low Frequency) 甚低频
VLIW(Very Long Instruction Word) 超长指令字
VLM(Very Large Memory) 特大型内存
VLM(Virtual Loadable Module) 虚拟加载模块
VLP 密纹视盘系统
VLS(Virtual Linkage Subsystem) 虚连接子系统
VLSI(Very Large Scale Integration) 特大规模集成电路
VLSI architecture design principles VLSI 体系结构设计规则
VLSI model of computation 特大规模集成电路计算模型
VLSI parallel algorithm 特大规模集成电路并行算法
VLTP(Variable Length Text Processor) 变长文本处理程序
VM(Video Mail) 视频邮件
VM/370(Virtual Machine System/370) 虚机系统/370(IBM)
VM/386 VM/386 操作系统
VM/AS(Virtual Machine/Application System) 虚机应用系统(IBM,以下皆同)
VM/CMS(Virtual Machine / Conversational Monitor System) 虚机/会话监督系统
VM/DM(Virtual Machine/Directory Maintenance) 虚机目录维护
VM/ESA(Virtual Machine/Enterprise System Architecture) 虚机企业系统体系结构
VM/IFS(Virtual Machine/Interactive File Sharing) 虚机交互式文件共享
VM/SE(Virtual Machine/System Extended) 虚机扩充系统
VM/SP(Virtual Machine/System Produce) 虚机系统产品
VMAPS(Virtual Memory Array Processing System) 虚拟存储器阵列处理系统
VMC(Vertical Micro-Code) 垂直微码
VMCB(Virtual Machine Control Block) 虚机控制块
VME(Virtual Machine Environment) 虚拟计算机环境
VME bus(VersaModule Eurocard bus) VME 总线(Motorola)
VME system bus VME 系统总线
VMM(Virtual Machine Management) 虚拟机管理器(微软)
VMM(Virtual Machine Monitor) 虚拟机监控程序
VMM(Virtual Memory Management) 虚拟存储管理程序(IBM)
VMOS(Virtual Memory Operating System) 虚拟存储器操作系统
VMPE(Virtual Memory Performance Enhancement) 虚存性能增强
VMS(Virtual Machine System) 虚机系统
VMS(Virtual Memory System) 虚拟

存储器系统,VMS 操作系统
VMS(Voice Mailbox Service) 语音信箱业务
VMT(Virtual Method Table) 虚拟方法表
VMTP(Virtual Message Transaction Protocol) 虚拟消息交易协议
VN(Virtual Network) 虚拟网络
VNOD(Video Near On Demand) 准电播电视
VOC(Video Overlay Card) 视频叠加卡
vocabulary 词汇表
vocabulary file utility 词汇表文件公用程序
vocabulary of speech recognition system 语音识别系统词汇表
vocoder 声码器
VOD(Video ON Demand) 点播电视
voice 声音
voice activation 声音激活
voice adapter 声音适配器
voice answer-back device 声音应答设备
voice band 音频带
voice band line 音频线路,话路
voice call sign 话音呼叫
voice channel 音频信道
voice coder 语音编码器
voice coil 音圈
voice cord board 音频塞绳接插板
voice data entry 语音数据输入
voice/data integration 语音/数据集成
voice data service 语音数据服务
voice data signal 语音数据信号
voice detector 语音检测器
voice development system 语音开发系统
voice digitization 语音数字化
voice/document delivery system 语音/文档传递系统
voice encoder 声音编码器
voice exchange 话音交换机
voice file server 语音文件服务器
voice frequency band 话音频带
voice frequency carrier telegraph 音频载波电报
voice frequency channel 话音信道
voice frequency telegraph 音频电报
voice frequency truncation 音频截取
voice grade 音频级,话音级
voice-grade channel 音频信道
voice grade line 音频级线路
voice guard 声音防护
voice input system 语音输入系统
voice intelligibility 话音可懂度
voice limiter 声音限幅器
voice mail 声音邮件
voice mail service 语音邮件服务
voice message storage system 语音消息存储系统
voice messaging 声音消息传送器
voice modem 带语音功能的调制解调器
voice motor 音圈电机
voice network 话音网络
voice notes 声音注释
voice-operated coder 语音处理编码器,声码器
voice-operated device 声控设备
voice operation demonstrator 声控演示装置
voice output chip 语音输出芯片
voice output chip with vocabulary encoded 带编码词汇表的语音输出芯片
voice-output scanner 语言输出扫描器
voice over 话外音
voice packet communication 语音分组通信
voice quality synthesizer 音质合成器
voice recognition 声音识别
Voice Relay 声中继
voice response 声音应答
voice response device 声音响应设备
voice response output unit 声音响应输出单元
voice response system 语音应答系统
voice service 话音业务
voice signal 语音信号
voice slot 语音时间片
voice store and forward 声音存储转发
voice switching 语音交换
voice synthesis 语音合成
voice synthesizer 语音合成器
voice terminal 语音终端
voice traffic 语音信息量
voice unit 音量单位
voice waveform digitization 话音波形数字化

voicegram 声音报
VOICES(Voice-Operated Identification Computer Entry System) 音控识别计算机输入系统
VoiceType VoiceType 声控软件 (IBM)
void 空白点,脱墨点
void collapse 空隙故障
void function 空函数
void item 空白项
void relation 空关系
void set 空集
void transaction log 无效事务日志
void value 空值,没有值
VOK(Verify OK) 验证成功
volatibility test 易失性测试
volatile 挥发的,易失的
volatile circular file 易变循环文件
volatile dynamic storage 易失性动态存储器
volatile file 易失文件
volatile key 易失项
volatile memory 易失性存储器
volatile objects 不稳定对象(常指网站上经常被改动的对象)
volatile storage 易失性存储装置
volatility 易失性
volatility of file 文件变动性
volatility of memory 存储器易失性
volatility of storage 存储器易失性
VOLID(VOLume IDentifier) 卷标识
VOLINFO (NetWare)卷信息 「符
volt 伏特
volt-amperes(VA) 伏安
voltage comparator 电压比较器
voltage comparison encoding 电压比较编码
voltage control 电压控制
voltage control circuit 电压控制电路
voltage control oscillator 压控振荡器
voltage-controlled current source 电压控制电流源
voltage-controlled voltage source 电压控制电压源 「性
voltage-current characteristic 伏安特
voltage dependent capacitance 随电压变化的电容
voltage digitizer 电压数字化器

voltage divider 分压器
voltage doubler 倍压器
voltage doubler rectifier 倍压整流器
voltage drift 电压漂移
voltage drop 电压降
voltage fluctuation 电压波动
voltage follower circuit 电压跟随电路
voltage gain 电压增益
voltage instability 电压不稳定性
voltage jump 电压跳跃
voltage level 电压电平
voltage-offset amplifier 电压补偿放大器
voltage pen pointer 电压式指示笔
voltage pulse 电压脉冲
voltage rating 额定电压 「管
voltage reference diode 电压基准二极
voltage reference element 电压基准元件
voltage regulation diode 稳压二极管
voltage regulator 稳压器,调压器
voltage-selected switch 电压选择开关
voltage spike 电压尖脉冲
voltage stabilizer 稳压器
voltage swing 电压摆幅
voltage to digit converter 电压数字转换器
voltage to frequency converter 电压频率转换器
voltmeter 伏特表,电压表
volume 卷;音量;体积
volume assignment table 卷分配表
volume charge density 体电荷密度
volume compressor 音量压缩器
volume control 音量控制
volume definition table 卷定义表
volume directory 卷目录
volume distribution 卷分布
volume effect semiconductor device 体效应半导体器件
volume end label 卷尾标号
volume formatter 卷格式化程序
volume group 卷组
volume header label 卷首标号
volume index 卷索引 「字
volume indicator 音量指示器;卷指示
volume initialize 卷初始化
volume label 卷标号

volume level 音量级,音量电平
volume model 体模型,体素模型
volume maintenance 卷维护
volume mark 卷标记
volume options 卷选项
volume positioning 卷定位
volume production 批量[成批]生产
volume rendering 体绘制,体润色
volume resistance 体电阻
volume resistivity 体电阻率
volume root directory 卷根目录
volume security 卷安全性
volume serial number 卷序号
volume set 卷集
volume space in use 使用的卷空间
volume space limit 卷空间限制
volume table of contents 卷目录表
volume test 巨量数据试验;卷测试
volume trailer labile 卷尾标
volume unit 音量单位
volumetric efficiency 组装效率 「断
voluntary interrupt 自行中断,自发中
von Neumann architecture 冯·诺依曼体系结构
von Neumann bottleneck 冯·诺依曼瓶颈
von Neumann computer 冯·诺依曼计算机
von Neumann condition 冯·诺依曼条件 「法
von Neumann method 冯·诺依曼方
Von Wijngaarden grammar(VW-grammar) 冯·韦京加登文法
vortex 涡流
vortex element 涡旋元素
vortex point 涡流点
vortex sheet 涡流图表
vortex telecommunication access method 涡流式远程访问通信
VOS(Virtual Operating System) 虚拟操作系统
vote 表决,投票
voted multi-processor computer 表决多处理器计算机
voter 表决器
voter-comparator switch 表决比较器开关
voting element 表决元件

voting model 表决[投票]模型
voting system 表决系统
vowels 元音
voxel 体素,三维像素
voxel architecture 体素结构
voxel block transfer 体素块传输
voxel data 体素数据
voxel field 体素场
voxel index 体素索引
voxel map engine 体素映像引擎
voxel model filtering 体素模型滤波
voxel record 体素记录
voxel spanning 体素生成
voxel tessellating 体素装饰
voxmap 体素图
VP(Vector Processor) 向量处理机
VP(Virtual Processor) 虚拟处理机
VP 2000 VP2000 计算机
VP/ix VP/ix 操作系统
VP-Planner Plus VP-Planner＋报表软件
VP ratio(Virtual Processor ratio) 虚处理器比率
VPAM (Virtual Partitioned Access Method) 虚拟分区存取法
VPE(Vector Processing Element) 向量处理部件
VPL research Inc VPL 探索公司(虚拟现实设备)
VPM(Virtual Processor Monitor) 虚拟处理机监督程序
VPN(Virtual Page Number) 虚页号
VPN(Virtual Private Network) 虚拟专用网
VPP(Vector Pipeline Processor) 向量流水线处理机
VPS(Vector Processing System) 向量处理系统 「数
VPS(Vectors Per Second) 每秒向量
VPT(Virtual Packet Terminal) 虚拟分组终端
VR(Virtual Reality) 虚拟现实
VR(Virtual Route) 虚拟路由
VR(Visible Record) 可视记录
VR pacing 虚拟路由调步
VRAM(Video RAM) 视频 RAM
VRC(Vertical Redundancy Check) 垂直冗余校验

VREPAIR (NetWare)卷修复
VRID(Virtual Route IDentification) 虚路由标识
VRN(Virtual Route Number) 虚路由号
VRU(Voice Response Unit) 话音应答装置
VRX(Virtual Resource eXecutive) 虚资源执行程序
VS(Virtual System) 虚系统
VSA(Visual Scene Analysis) 可视场景分析
VSAM(Virtual Storage Access Method) 虚拟存储访问法(IBM)
VSAT(Very Small Aperture Terminal) 甚小口径终端
VSAT center earth station 甚小口径天线卫星数据通信系统中央地球站
VSAT earth small station 甚小口径天线卫星数据通信系统小型地面站
VSAT network structure VSAT 网络结构
VSAT satellite data communication VSAT 卫星数据通信
VSAT satellite data communication network VSAT 卫星数据通信网
VSAT space segment SAT 空间段
VSAT system 甚小口径天线卫星数据通信系统
VSAT userface board VSAT 用户接口板
VSB(Vestigial SideBand) 残留边带
VSB modulation 残留边带调制
VSB transmission system 残留边带传输系统
VSC(Virtual Subscriber Computer) 虚拟用户计算机
VSC(Visualization in Scientific Computing) 科学计算可视化
VSE(Vector Symbol Editor utility) 向量符号编辑实用程序
VSE(Disk Operating System/Virtual Storage Extended) VSE 操作系统(IBM)

VSI(Virtual Storage Interrupt) 虚拟存储器中断
VSM(Vestigial Sideband Modulation) 残留边带调制
VSM(Virtual Storage Manager) 虚拟存储器管理程序
VSM(Visual Switch Management) 可视交换机管理(Cisco)
VSN(Volume Serial Number) 卷序号
VSS(Video Storage System) 视频存储器系统
VSS(Virtual Studio System) 虚拟演播室系统
VSS(Virtual Support Subsystem) 虚支持子系统
VSYNC(Vertical SYNChronous) 垂直同步
VT(Video Terminal) 视频终端
VT(Virtual Terminal) 虚拟终端
VT(Voice Telegraph) 音频电报
VT-100 VT-100 终端
VTA(Virtual Terminal Agent) 虚拟终端代理
VTAM (Virtual Telecommunications Access Method) 虚拟远程访问法(IBM)
VTP(Virtual Terminal Protocol) 虚拟终端协议
VTS(Virtual Terminal System) 虚拟终端系统
VU(Voice Unit) 音量单位
vulnerability 脆弱性
vulnerable 脆弱的,易损坏的
vulnerable network (经不起攻击的)脆弱网络
VUP (VAX Unit of Performance) VAX 性能单位(DEC)
VWL(Variable Word Length) 可变字长
VWS(Voice Warning System) 声音告警系统
VxD(Virtual Device Driver) 虚拟设备驱动程序(微软)
VZ(Virtual Zero) 虚零

W w

W(Watt) 瓦,瓦特
W+(Weakly positive) 略正,弱正
W-(Weakly negative) 略负,弱负
W(Write) 写
W3C(World Wide Web Consortium) 万维网协会
W/M(Words Per Minute) 每分钟字数
W/R(Write/Read) 写/读
W-shaped breadboard W形面包板
W-type-fiber W型光纤
WA(Word Address) 字地址
WACS(Wide-Area Computing Service) 广域计算业务
WADS(Wide Area Data Service) 广域数据服务
WADS(Wide Area Dial Service) 广域拨号服务
wafer 圆片
wafer cutting machine 圆片切割机
wafer fabrication 圆片加工
wafer grinding 圆片研磨
wafer level 圆片级
wafer level integration 圆片级集成
wafer matrix 圆片矩阵
wafer package 圆片组件
wafer reclamation 圆片再生
wafer-scale integration 圆片规模集成
wafering 切片
WAIS(Wide Area Information Server) 广域信息服务器
WAIS(Wide Area Information Service) 广域信息服务系统
wait 等待条件,等候
wait acknowledge(WAK) 等候认可,等待肯定应答
wait before transmit positive acknowledgement(WACK) 发送肯定应答信号前等待
wait character 等候字符
wait character logic 等候字符逻辑
wait condition 等待条件
wait cursor 等待光标
wait for interrupt 等待中断
wait I/O processing 等待输入输出处理
wait instruction timing 等待指令时序
wait list 等待表
wait loop 等待循环
wait macro 等待宏指令
wait-on-user-defined event (WOUDE) 等待用户定义事件
wait state 等待状态
wait statement 等待语句
wait time 等候时间,等待时间
wait time limit 等待时间限制
wait timeout period 等待超时周期
wait until done 等待到完成
waiting 等候,等待
waiting allowed facility 等待允许服务
waiting facilities 等候设施
waiting lines 候队,排队
waiting list 等候表
waiting loop 等待循环
waiting period 等待周期
waiting-queue channel 等候排队信道
waiting state 等待状态
waiting system 等候系统,延迟系统
waiting time 等待时间
wake 激活,唤醒
Wake-on-LAN 网络唤醒
wake-up character 唤醒字符
wakeup primitive 唤醒原语
wake-up switch 唤醒开关
wake-up waiting 唤醒等待
walk 图路径
walk random 随机漫步,随机波动
walk through 预排工作,走查
walk through method 预排工作法
walkie-talkie 步话机
walking "1" and "0" 走步"1"和"0"
walking pattern 行走模式
walking robot 行走机器人
wall 畸壁;背景
wall capacitor 壁电容
wall effect 壁效应
wall mounted 壁装式的

wall of computer case 计算机壁板
wall paper 墙纸;背景
wall receptacle 墙上插座
Wallace add tree 华莱士加法树
Wallis nonlinear mask 沃利斯非线性掩模
Walsh-Hadamard transformation 沃尔什-哈达马德变换
Walsh transform 沃尔什变换
WAN(Wide Area Network) 广域网络
WAND(Wide Area Network Distribution) 广域网分发(系统)
wand 条形码读入器
wand reader 条形码读入器
wanding 读条码
Wang Labs(Wang Laboratories Inc.) 王安公司
Wang net 王安网
Wangnet 王安网络
WAP(Wireless Application Protocol) 无线应用协议
warble 颤音
WARCAT (Workload And Resources Correlation Analysis Technology) 工作负荷与信源相关分析技术
ward 守护
Wardialing 自动连续拨号软件
ware 制成品
warehouse automation 仓库自动化
warehouse problem 库存问题
warf 竞争,冲突
warfare 竞争现象
warm boot 热自举,热启动
warm key point 热关键点
warm link 热链接
warm restart 热态重启动
warm standby 热备份
warm start 热启动
warm-up period 加热期
warm-up time 加热时间
Warnier-Orr diagram 沃尼尔-奥尔图
warning 报警,告警
warning character 报警字符
warning circuit 告警电路
warning condition 报警条件
warning device 报警装置
warning facilities 报警设备

warning mark 告警标志
warning message 告警消息
warning net 预警网络
warning plane 预警飞机
warning sign 告警标志[符号]
warning tone 警告音
warning whistle 警告哨音
WARP WARP并行处理器(卡内基-梅隆大学)
Warp Warp操作系统(IBM)
warranty 保修
warranty period 保修期
Warren's algorithm 华伦算法
Washall's algorithm 瓦歇尔算法
washer 垫圈;衬垫,垫片
waste 废物,废品,废料
waste instruction 空指令
waste operation 空操作
wastebasket 废纸篓
watch 监视
watch point 监视点
WatchDog 看门狗(加密装置)
watchdog 监视程序,监视器
watchdog box 监控盒,监护匣
watchdog circuit 监视电路
watchdog software 监视软件
watchdog subsystem 监视器子系统
watchdog timer(WDT) 监视时钟
WatchMan 看门人
water-jug problem 水和罐的问题
water mark magnetics 水印磁条
waterfall model 瀑布模型
waterprint 水印
WATS(Wide Area Telecommunication / telephone Service) 广域电信电话服务
WATS(Wide Area Telephone Service) 广域电话服务
WATS(Wide Area Transmission System) 广域传输系统
Watson code 沃森编码
watt 瓦特(功率单位)
watt-hour 瓦特小时
watt-hour efficiency 瓦特/小时效率
watt loss 功率损耗,功耗
wattage rating 额定功率
Wave 波语言,Wave机器人语言
wave 波;波形

wave amplitude 波幅
wave analyzer 波形分析器
wave band 波段
wave digital filter 波形数字滤波器
wave division multiplex(WDM) 波分多路复用
wave equation 波动方程
wave file 波形文件
wave form 波形
wave front 波阵面,波前
wave function 波动函数
wave gait 波形步法
wave guide 波导
wave impedance 波阻抗
wave in mux 波形输入静音
wave interference 电波干扰
wave mode 波模式
wave node 波节
wave number 驻波数
wave output volume level 波形输出音量电平
wave shape 波形
wave shaping circuit 波形整修电路
wave-soldering 波峰焊
wave source 波源
wave table 波形表
wave table card 波表卡
wave table synthesis 波表合成
wave theory 波动说
wave trap 陷波器
waveform 波形
waveform analyzer 波形分析仪
waveform corrector 波形校正器
waveform digitalization 波形数字化
waveform distortion 波形失真
waveform generator 波形产生器
waveform recording method 波形记录法
waveform segment 波形段
Wavefront 三维幻彩真实世界
wavefront 波前,波阵面
wavefront algorithm 波阵面算法,波前算法
wavefront array 波前阵列
wavefront array architecture 波前阵列体系结构
wavefront method 波前法
waveguide 波导
WaveLAN 无线局域网产品(朗讯)

wavelength 波长
wavelength division multiplexing 波分多工法
wavelength multiplexing 波长多路复用
wavelet 子波,小波
wavelet expression 小波表达式
wavelet function 小波函数
wavelet packet 小波包
wavelet transformation 小波变换
wavelet tree 小波树
waveshape 波形
waveshaping 波形整形
way-operated circuit 分路操作电路,方向转接线路
way sort 线路分类
way station 中途站
Wb(Weber) 韦伯(磁通单位)
WBE(Write-Black Engine) 写黑机芯
WBEM(Web-Based Enterprise Management) 基于 Web 的企业管理
WC(World Coordinates) 世界坐标
WCDMA (Wireless Code Division Multi-Addressing) 无线码分多址
WD(Write Data) 写数据
WDC-A(World Data Center-A) 世界数据中心 A(华盛顿)
WDC-B(World Data Center-B) 世界数据中心 B(莫斯科)
WDL (Windows Driver Library) Windows 驱动程序库
WDL(Wireless Data Link) 无线数据链路
WDM(Wave Division Multiplex) 波分多路复用
WDM(Win32 Driver Model) Win32 驱动模式
WE(Write-Enable) 写允许,写使能
weak and strong problem-solving methods 问题求解的弱方法和强方法
weak bit 弱位
weak consistency 弱一致性,弱顺序
weak convergence 弱收敛
weak coupling 弱耦合
weak definition 弱定义
weak equality 弱相等
weak external reference(WXTRN) 弱外部引用
weak generalized inverse 弱广义逆

weak interference 弱干扰
weak key 弱密钥
weak Lagrange expression 弱拉格朗日表达式
weak lock 弱锁定
weak mutation 弱变异方法「法
weak precedence grammar 弱居先文
weak precedence parser 弱居先文法分析程序
weak reference 弱引用,弱参考
weak stability 弱稳定性
weak transitive closure 弱传递闭包
weaked connected graph 弱连通图
weaken consistency 弱化一致性
weaker bound 较弱边界
weakest environment 最弱环境
weakest liberal precondition(WLP) 最弱富足前置条件
weakest-link theory 最薄弱环节理论
weakest precondition(WP) 最弱前置条件
weakly-connected directional graph 弱连通有向图
weakly connected graph 弱连通图
weakly invertibility 弱可逆性
weakness of computer system 计算机系统的脆弱性
wear 磨损
wear history 磨损曲线
wear model 磨损模型
wear-out 磨损,消耗
wear-out characteristic 磨损特性;衰老特性
wear-out failure 磨损故障,磨损失效
wear-out failure period 耗损故障周期
wear process 磨损过程
wear resistance 耐磨性
wear resistance tape head 耐磨磁带读写头
wearable PC 可佩戴个人计算机(IBM)
weather analysis 气象分析
weather center(WECEN) 气象中心
weather chart facsimile apparatus 气象图传真装置
weather computer 气象计算机
weather facsimile network 气象传真通信网络

weather massage switching system 气象信息交换系统
weather prediction 气象预报
weather satellite data 气象卫星数据
Web 万维网,环球网
web 卷筒纸印刷;网膜;散热片(现已与 Web 混用)
Web Access Kit 网上访问工具(IBM)
web address Web 网址
web-based management(WBM) 基于 web 的网管
web browser 万维网浏览器
web class web 类
web client 万维网客户机
web cookies 网上"甜饼"(安全防护软件)
Web-EDI(Web Electronic Data Interchange) 万维网电子数据交换,网上无纸贸易
Web DataBlade 网上数据刀片(Informix)
web grammar 网文法
web host 万维网主机
web index 万维网索引
web page 网页
web publishing wizard 网上发布向导
Web Printsmart 万维网智能打印(HP)
Web Robot 万维网机器人(自动搜索程序)
web server 万维网服务器
web site 万维网点
web surfing 网络冲浪
Web walking 网上漫游
Web Wanderer 万维网漫游搜索程序
Webclass designer web 类设计器
WebDB(Web DataBase) 数据库开发系统(Oracle)
Weber(Wb,W) 韦伯
WebFORCE Internet Gateway WebFORCE 因特网网关(SGI)
webmaster 网站管理员
WebIndex 万维网索引系统
Webmaster 网络设计管理者
webportal 网络门户
WebServer Web 服务器
Websheet 网上表格
WebSphere 环球 Web 服务系统

(IBM)
WebTone 网音(Sun)
WebTV 网上电视
webware 网件
webweaver 网络建设者
webzine(web magazine) 网络杂志
wedge 楔
wedge approximation 楔形逼近法
wedge contact 楔形接点
weed 抛弃,剔除;废物
weed out 注销,淘汰
weekday 工作日
weekly-planner 每周计划设计程序
WEF(Working Elementary File) 工作元文件
Weibull distribution 维泊尔分布
Weierstrass first approximation theorem 维尔斯特拉斯第一逼近定理
Weierstrass second approximation theorem 维尔斯特拉斯第二逼近定理
weight 权数,位权
weight-balanced multiway tree 平衡加权多元树
weight-bit code 加权位代码
weight coefficient 加权系数
weight data transmitter 加权数据发送器
weight encoder 加权编码器
weight function 加权函数,权函数
weight spanning tree 加权生成树
weight sum 加权和
weight vector 权向量
weighted 4 bit code 加权的四位代码
weighted-area masks 加权区域掩码
weighted average 加权平均
weighted average utility 加权平均利用率
weighted balanced tree 加权平衡树
weighted bidirectional search 加权双向查找
weighted check list 加权校验表
weighted code 加权码
weighted concept 加权概念
weighted current D/A converter 加权电流数/模转换器
weighted directed graph 加权有向图
weighted entropy 加权熵
weighted external path length 加权外通路长度
weighted factor method 加权因子法
weighted generalized inverse 加权广义逆
weighted graph 加权图
weighted least squares 加权最小二乘法
weighted likelihood ratio 加权似然比
weighted logic reasoning 加权逻辑推理
weighted longest common subsequence 加权最长共同子序
weighted matching algorithm 加权匹配算法
weighted means 加权平均值
weighted median filter 加权中值滤波
weighted metric 加权度量
weighted minimum variance 加权极小均方差
weighted moving average 加权移动平均
weighted optimization 加权优化
weighted path length 加权路径长度
weighted push-down language 加权下推语言
weighted rank filter 加权序过滤器
weighted-resister D/A converter 加权电阻数/模转换器
weighted residual method 加权余量法
weighted substring search 加权子串搜索
weighted sum 加权和
weighted term logic 检索词加权逻辑
weighted threshold disjunction 加权阈值析取
weighted transformation 加权变换
weighted turnaround time 加权周转时间
weighted value 权值
weighted voting algorithm 加权表决算法
weighting 加权,权重
weighting function 加权函数,权函数
weighting function method 权函数法
weighting network 加权网络
Weitek coprocessor Weitek 协处理器
welcome page 欢迎页面
weld 熔接,焊接
weldability 可焊性
weldable 可焊的
welder 焊接装置

welding flux 助焊剂,焊料
welding robot 焊接机器人
well 井
well-behaved intermittent fault 良性间歇故障
well-behaved net 良性网络
well-behaved program 良性程序
well-conditioned 良态,好条件
well-defined function 良定函数,严格定义的函数
well-defined support structure 定义完善的支持结构
well-documented software tool 文档齐全的软件工具
well-formed formula(WFF) 合适公式,合式公式
well-formed formula of predicate calculus 谓词演算的合式公式
well-formed net 合式网络
well-formed program 构造良好的程序
well-formed propositional formula 命题合式公式
well-formed string 合式串
well-formed transaction 合式交易
well-founded set 整序集,良基集
well-known architecture 良好的体系结构
well-known port 知名端口
well-ordered set 良序集
well-ordering principle 良序原则
well-posed problem 适定问题
well-structured programming language 结构良好的程序设计语言
Wellfleet Wellfleet 公司
Westinghouse Electric Corporation (WEC) 威斯汀豪斯电气公司,西屋电气公司
wet 浸润
wet process development 湿法显影
wetzel 强对比像素
WFC(Windows Foundation Class) Windows 基本类库
WFF(Well Formed Formula) 合适公式
WFL(Work Flow Language) 工作流语言
WFM(Wave Form Monitor) 波形监视器
WFW(Windows For Workgroups) 工作组视窗(微软,Windows 3.11)
WG(Wire Gauge) 线规
WGN(White Gaussian Noise) 白高斯噪声
WHCA(White House Communication Agency) (美国)白宫通信管理
What in analysis 假设分析
Whatis 这是什么?(关键字查询)
Wheatstone bridge 惠斯登电桥
when-determinate 时间确定型
where-determinate 地点确定型
Whestone benchmark test program 惠斯通基准测试程序
while 当,条件循环
while loop 当循环
while schema while 模式
while statement WHILE 语句,当语句
whirl 旋转
Whirlwind computer 旋风型计算机
whirly bird 直升飞机(形容工作噪声很大的硬盘的俚语)
whisker 晶须;螺旋
whisker contact 点接触
whistle 哨声
White Board 白板
White Book (VCD 标准)白皮书(Sony、Philips 等,1994 年)
white box method 白箱法
white box testing 白盒测试法
white Gaussian noise 高斯白噪声
white light 白光
white line recognition 空白行识别
white noise 白噪声
white out 不透明
white page 白页
white plague 白斑
white residue 无用剩余
white space count program 白空间计数程序
white space skid 空白区跳过
whitening transform 白化变换
Whitney head 惠特尼磁头
Whittaker-Shannon sampling theorem 维特克-香农抽样定理
who-are-you(WRU) 询问,谁?
whois 是谁?(用户信息查找程序)

whole course tracing 全程跟踪
whole-number solution 全数解法
whole page 整页
Whr(Watt-hour) 瓦特小时
WHSS(White House Signal Support) 白宫通信支援
WHT(Wireless Handheld Terminal) 无线手持终端
wide 宽,宽广
wide-angle sensor(WAS) 广角传感器
wide application system adapter (WASAR) 广泛应用系统适配器
wide area data service 广域数据服务
Wide Area Information Service(WAIS) 广域信息服务
wide area network 广域网络
wide area telecommunication service (WATS) 广域远程通信业务
wide band 宽带
wide-band amplifier 宽带放大器
wide-band antenna 宽带天线
wide-band channel 宽带信道
wide-band data set 宽带数据传输设备
wide line character 粗体字符
wide shot 广角摄影
wideband communication system 宽带通信系统
wideband data transmission system 宽带数据传输系统
wideband modem 宽带调制解调器
widening 拓展,展宽
widening alter 展宽变换
widget 窗口小部件,饰件
widget class 饰件类
widget class hierarchy 饰件类层次
widget instance 饰件实例
widget set 饰件集
widow line 短行,不足行
width 宽度
width coding 宽度编码
width control 宽度控制
width value 宽度值
Wiener filter 维纳过滤器
Wijngaarden grammar 维恩加登文法
wild-card 通配卡;通配符
wild-character 通配字符(*,?)
willful intercept 故意截收

Win32 Win32 规范(微软)
WinBench WinBench 基准测试程序
Winchester 温彻斯特技术
Winchester disk 温彻斯特磁盘
Winchester disk drive 温彻斯特磁盘驱动器
Winchester disk technology 温彻斯特磁盘技术
Winchester head 温彻斯特磁头
Winchester suspension 温彻斯特悬挂机构
wind 绕,卷绕
wind-tunnel computer 风洞计算机
winder 绕线机
winding 绕组,线圈
winding pitch 线圈节距
window 窗口
window background 窗口背景
window-based interface 基于窗口的界面
window border 窗口边框
window clipping 窗口截割[剪取]
window close 窗口关闭
window concept 窗口概念
window coordinates 窗口坐标
window corner 窗角
window definition block status word 窗口定义块状态字
window edge 窗口边界
window environment 窗口环境
window gravity (X协议中)窗口重力
window frame 窗口外框
window icon 窗口图标
window layout 窗口轮廓[外观]
window machine 窗口机
window management 窗口管理
window management software 窗口管理软件
window manager 窗口管理程序
window menu 窗口菜单
window menu button 窗口菜单按钮
window operation 窗口操作
window option 窗口选项
window pacing 窗口调步
window popup 窗口弹出
window preview 窗口预览
window raster 窗口光栅
window server 窗口服务器

window signal 窗信号,触发脉冲信号
window size 窗口尺寸
window system 窗口系统,视窗系统
window system kernel 窗口系统核心
window text 窗口正文
window title 窗口标题
window-to-viewport mapping 窗口到视见区映射
window toolbox 窗口工具箱
window/viewport transformation 窗口视见区变换
window width 窗口宽度
window workspace 窗口工作空间
window Xmodem 窗口式 Xmodem
windowed pattern primitive 窗口模式原语
windowing 开窗口
windowing environment 窗口环境
windowing flow control 窗口法流量控制
windowing function 开窗功能
windowing schema 开窗口方案
windowing transformation 窗口变换
Windows Windows 操作系统软件(微软,以下皆同)
Windows 95 Windows 95 操作系统
Windows 98 Windows 98 操作系统
Windows 386 enhanced mode Windows 386 增强模式
Windows 2000 Windows 2000 操作系统
Windows accelerator Windows 加速器程序
Windows application Windows 应用程序
Windows applications group Windows 应用程序组
Windows cardfile Windows 卡片文件
Windows CE(Windows Consumer Electronics) Windows 消费者电子产品(操作系统,1996 年)
Windows client Windows 客户
Windows clipboard 剪贴板
Windows command line Windows 命令行
Windows desktop Windows 工作台
Windows dialog box Windows 对话框
windows environment 视窗环境,窗口环境
Windows for Pen Computing 笔式计算视窗软件
Windows For Workgroups(WFW) 工作组视窗
Windows Help Windows 联机求助
Windows Internet Name Server(WINS) Windows 互联网络命名服务器
Windows list box Windows 列表框
Windows Me Windows Me 操作系统
Windows message window Windows 信息窗口
Windows Metafile(WMF) Windows 元文件
Windows NT 新技术(网络)版本 Windows
Windows NT Server Windows NT 服务器版本
Windows NT Workstation Windows NT 工作站版本
Windows operation mode Windows 操作模式
windows overlay 窗口重叠
Windows platform 视窗平台 「序
windows program 视窗程序,窗口程
Windows RAM(WRAM) 视窗内存
Windows real mode Windows 实模式
Windows recorder Windows 记录器
Windows running environment Windows 运行环境
Windows Sockets API Windows 套接字应用程序界面
Windows standard mode Windows 标准模式
windows switch 窗口切换
Windows text box Windows 文本框
Windows Tutorial Windows 教程
Windows utilities Windows 实用程序
Windows XP Windows XP 操作系统(微软)
WINDS(Weather Information Network and Display System) 气象信息网络与显示系统
wing panel 翼板
WINGZ WINGZ 电子表格
WinJet WinJet 仿真器
wink-off 关闭闪烁
wink signal 闪烁信号

WinMark WinMark 评分
Winograd algorithm 维诺格兰算法
Winograd-Fourier transform algorithm (WFTA) 维诺格兰-付里叶变换算法
WinPad WinPad 操作系统
WINS(Windows Internet Name Service) Windows 互联网络命名服务
Winsock(Windows sockets) Windows 套接口
Winstone 基准测试程序
Wintel Wintel 平台(Windows+Intel)
Wintif(Windows-Motif) Windows 外观的 Motif
WinZip WinZip 压缩工具
WIP(Work In Process) 处理过程中的作业
wipe 擦除；划变
wipe down （画面）向下擦除
wipe left （画面）自左向右擦除
wipe out 擦去,擦除
wipe right （画面）自右向左擦除
wipe up （画面）向上擦除
wiper 滑臂；刮片；弧刷
wiper switch 滑动开关
wiping 摩擦接触
wiping action 擦拭作用
wiping contact 摩擦式触点
WIPO(World Intellectual Property Organization) 世界知识产权组织
WIR(Weekly Intelligence Report) 每周信息报告
WIRDS(Weather Information Remoting and Display System) 气象数据遥测和显示系统
wire 导线
wire-AND 线"与"
wire-ANDing 线"与"连接
wire board 接线板
wire bonding 引线键合
wire cable 线缆
wire chart 布线图
wire communication 有线通信
wire contact relay 线接触型继电器
wire delay 线延迟
wire fault 连线故障

wire file 成串文件
wire frame 线框,全帧显示方式
wire-frame graphics 线框图形
wire frame modeling 线框造型
wire frame representation 线框表示法
wire gauge 线规
wire guide （针式打印机）针导管
wire-guided cart 电感制导车
wire-in check 布线核对
wire jumper 跳线,跨接线
wire lapping 导线重叠法装配
wire layout 连线布局
wire length 连线长度
wire list 连线表,接线表
wire matrix 点阵
wire matrix printer 点阵针式打印机
wire memory 磁线存储器
wire modeling 线框建模
wire net 连线网络,线网
wire net list 线网表
wire-OR 线"或"
wire photo 有线传真
wire printer 针式打印机
wire program computer 连线程序计算机
wire service 在线服务
wire sharing system 线路共用系统
wire shift register(WSR) 磁线移位寄存器
wire speed routing 线速路由选择
wire tag 线标记,线路标签
wire tip 针头；线端
wire tip profile 画线端头外形
wire-type acoustic delay line 线形声延迟线
wire-wound resistor 线绕电阻
wire wrap 绕接
wire wrap assembly 绕接装配
wire-wrap connection 绕线连接,绕接
wire wrap module 绕接模件
wire wrap tool 绕接工具
wired AND 线"与"
wired back 布线背面
wired logic control 布线逻辑控制
wired OR 线"或"
wired program computer(WPC) 布线程序计算机
wired remote control 有线遥控

wired-screen storage 编线网存储器
wireframe model 线框模型
wireframe modeling 线框建模
wireless data link 无线数据链路
wireless keyboard 无绳键盘
wireless microphone 无线话筒
wireless prepaid 无线预付
wireless terminal 无线终端机
wireless transport service 无线传输服务
wireless voice-activated dialing 无线话音激活拨号
wireline modem 有线调制解调器
wiretapping 线路窃听,线路截收
wirewound rheostat 线绕变阻器
wiring capacitance 引线电容
wiring closet 布线室
wiring concentrator 布线集线器
wiring diagram 布线图
wiring elementary 布线原理图
wiring error 接线错误,布线错误
wiring grid 布线网格
wiring layout 接线图,布线图
wiring material 布线材料
wiring pattern 布线图案
wiring problem 布线问题
wiring system 布线系统
wiring topology 接线布局
wiring track 布线轨道
Wirth-Weber precedence relation 沃斯-韦伯优先关系
WITH statement 限定语句,WITH语句
Wizard 向导程序
WL(Wave Length) 波长
WL(Wired Logic) 布线逻辑
WLAN(Wireless Local Area network) 无线局域网
WLL(Wireless Local Loop) 无线本地环路
WLM(Work Load Manager) 工作负荷管理程序
WMF(Windows Metafile Format) Windows元文件格式
WO(Wipe Out) 清除
Wolfe duality problem 沃尔夫对偶问题
WOODENMAN "木人"语言计划
Word 文字处理软件(微软)
word 字,单词
word access time 字存取时间

word accumulator 字累加器
word address 字地址
word address format 字地址格式
word address register 字地址寄存器
word addressable 按字寻址的
word addressing 字编址;字寻址
word and byte addressing 字与字节混合编址
word arithmetic 字运算
word-around 字环绕,字绕回
word association 字联想,词联想
word boundary 字边界
word break character 断字符
word capacity 字长,字容量
word cell 字单元
word character 单字字符
word/character frequency techniques 字/字符频度技术
word clock 字时钟
word code 字代码
word compaction algorithm 字紧缩算法
word computer 字计算机
word concatenation 字连接
word count 字计数
word count register 字计数寄存器
word counter 字计数器
word cycle 字周期
word decoder 字译码器
word delimiter 字定界符
word dictionary 字典
word direction 字方向
word display 字符显示
word error probability 错字概率
word family 词族
word for word translation 逐字[词]翻译
word format 字格式
word frequency 字频率
word frequency index 字[词]频索引
word gap 字间隔,字距
word generator 字发生器
word index 字[词]索引
word instruction 字指令
word key 字键
word length 字长
word length emulation 字长仿真
word length mismatch 字长失配
word list 词表
word locality 字位置

word locator 字定位器
word mark 字标志
word memory 字存储器
word modules 字模块
word order 词序,字序
word organized memory 字组织存储器
word organized storage 字组织存储器
word oriented 面向字的
word-oriented machine 面向字的机器
word-oriented scientific instruction 科学用单词式指令
word-oriented serial access file 面向字的串行存取文件
word-oriented storage 面向字的存储器
word parallel arithmetic operation 字并行运算操作
word pattern 字模式
word period 字周期
word problem of semi-Thue system 半图厄系统的判字问题
word problem system type-0 grammar 0型文法判字问题系统
word processing 文字处理
word processing and office equipment 文字处理和办公设备
word processing capability 文字处理能力
word processing equipment 文字处理设备
word processing program 文字处理软件
Word Processing Society(WPS) 文字处理协会
word processor 文字处理器
word recognition 字码识别
word redundancy 字冗余
word root 词根
word search instruction 字搜索指令
word segment 词划分,词分割
word segmentation unit 分词单位
word select memory 字选存储器
word select register 字选寄存器
word separator 字分隔符
word serial 字串行
word serial associative processor 字串行相联处理机
word size 字长
word size bus 字长总线
word space 字空间

word state 字状态
word stem 词干
word stock 字库
word terminal(WT) 字终端机
word time 字时间
word-time rate 字时间率
word transfer instruction 字传送指令
word underscore character(WUC) 字下划线字符
word variable-length 变长字
word with variable length 可变字长
word wrap 字绕回,整字换行
word wraparound 字环绕,字返转
WordPerfect 文字处理软件(Corel)
WordPro 文字处理软件(Lotus)
words per minute(WPM) 每分钟字数
words per second(WPS) 每秒钟字数
wordspacing 字间隔调整
Wordstar WordStar 文字处理软件
work analysis program 工作分析程序
work area 工作区
work assembly 工作汇集
work assignment procedure(WAP) 工作安排过程
work breakdown structure(WBS) 任务分解构造
work breaking structure chart 工作分解结构图
work center 工作中心
work content 工作量
work coordinate 工作坐标
work cycle 工作周期
work data file 工作数据文件
work data sets 工作数据集
work disk 工作盘
work distribution chart 工作分配图
work factor 工作因子
work file 工作文件
work load 工作负荷
work load characterization 工作负荷特性表示法
work load manager 工作负荷管理程序
work measurement 工作量度
work output queue 作业输出队列
work period 工作周期
work piece 加工工件
work process schedule 工作过程调度
work queue 工作排队

work queue directory(WKQDR) 工作队列目录
work queue entry 工作排队条目
work sampling 工作取样
work screen 工作屏幕
work session 工作对话
work simplification program(WSP) 工作简化程序
work slice 工作时间片
work space 工作空间
work space register 工作空间寄存器
work specification 工作规范
work stack 工作堆栈
work station 工作站
work status analysis 工况分析
work storage 工作存储器
work storage address register(WSAR) 工作存储器地址寄存器
work table 工作台
work tape 工作磁带
work unit 工作单元
work volume 工作卷
workable microprocessor 可工作的微处理机
workable program 可工作程序
workflow application 工作流应用程序
workflow approach 工作流法
workflow computing 工作流计算
workflow database 工作流数据库
workflow enabling 工作流启动
workflow initiating 工作流初始化
workflow processor 工作流处理器
workflow report 工作流报表
workflow software 工作流软件
workflow structure 工作流结构
workflow trigger 工作流触发程序
workgroup computing 工作组计算
workgroup hub 工作组集线器
workgroup productivity software 工作组效率软件
workgroup switches 工作组交换机
workgroups 工作组,工作群
workhorse 骨干,主力
working area 中间结果存储区
working at home 家庭办公
working backward method 倒推法
working cell 工作单元,临时单元
working code 工作码

working condition 工作状态
working current 工作电流
working data file 工作数据文件
working database 工作数据库
working directory 工作目录
working display 工作显示
Working Draft 工作草案
working drawing 加工图
working efficiency 工作效率
working elementary file(WEF) 工作元文件
working envelope 工作包络
working equipment 工作设备
working file 工作文件
working frequency 工作频率
working group standards(WGS) 工作组标准
working life 工作寿命
working memory 工作存储器
working memory area 工作存储区
working off-line 脱机工作
working on-line 联机工作
working page 工作页面
working point 工作点
working position 工作位置
working process 工作进程
working program 工作程序
working range 工作范围
working reference plane 工作基准面
working register 工作寄存器
working routine 工作例程
working set 工作集
working set dispatcher 工作集分派程序
working set storage management 工作集存储器管理
working set swapper 工作集调换程序
working set swapping 工作集对换
working set theory of program behavior 程序行为的工作集理论
working space 工作空间,暂存空间
working space control table 工作空间控制表
working space number assignment 暂存区编号
working space register 工作区寄存器
working space structure 工作空间结构
working storage 工作存储器
working storage section 工作存储节

working tape 工作带
working temperature 工作温度
working temperature range 工作温度范围
working together 协同工作
working version 工作版本
working voltage 工作电压
working volume optimization 工作空间优化
workload(WL) 工作负荷,工作负载
workload control file(WCF) 工作负荷控制文件
workpiece 工件;加工作业
workplace 工作场所
Workplace operating system Workplace 操作系统(IBM)
Workplace Shell Workplace 命令解释程序(IBM)
worksheet 工作表
worksheet style 工作表样式
worksheet window 工作表视窗
workshop 专题讨论会
workspace 工作空间,工作区
workspace background 工作区背景
workspace manager 工作区管理器
workspace menu 工作区菜单
workspace object 工作区对象
workspace switch 工作区开关
workstation 工作站
workstation attribute 工作站属性
workstation cluster 工作站群集
workstation controller 工作站控制器
workstation mapping 工作站映射
workstation message queue 工作站消息队列
workstation resource 工作站资源「换
workstation transformation 工作站变
workstation user profile 工作站用户简表
workstation utility(WSU) 工作站实用程序
workstation viewport 工作站视区
workstation window 工作站窗口
world 全体;世界
World Administration Radio Conference(WARC) 世界无线电管理会议
world coordinates 世界坐标,全局坐标

World Meteorological Organization(WMO) 世界气象组织
world mode 世界方式
world numbering plan(WNP) 世界编号计划
World Patents Index(WPI) 世界专利索引
world subdivision 场景划分
world time zone 世界时区
world weather watch(WWW) 世界气象监测网络
World Wide Web(WWW) 万维网
World Wide Web Consortium(W3C) 万维网联盟
world-zone number 世界区域编号
WORLDCOM(WORLD COMmunications Inc) 世界通信有限公司
WorldMail 电子邮件服务器软件(Qualcomm)
WorldMark WorldMark 计算机(NCR)
worldwide network 全球通信网
worldwide satellite communication network 全球卫星通信网络
WORM(Write Once Read Many) 一次写入多次读出
Worm 蠕虫
Worm program 蠕虫程序
Worm virus 蠕虫病毒
wormhole routing 虫孔路径选择法
WORSE(WORd SElection) 字选择
worst case 最坏情况,最坏条件
worst-case amplitude-derivation pattern 最坏幅度偏移模式
worst-case analysis 最坏情况分析
worst-case bound 最坏情况边界
worst-case circuit analysis 最坏情况电路分析「性
worst-case complexity 最坏情况复杂
worst-case design 最坏情况设计
worst case difference 最坏情况差异
worst-case loop 最坏情况循环
worst-case measure 最坏情况度量
worst-case noise 最坏情况噪声
worst-case noise pattern 最坏情况噪声模式
worst-case peak-shift pattern 最坏峰值漂移模式

worst case performance 最坏情况性能
worst-case time behavior 最坏情况时间特性
worst-fit 最差分配法
worst-fit strategy 最不适合策略
worst pattern of stored information 信息存储的最坏模式
worst peak-shift pattern 最坏峰值位移模式
worst status check 最坏状态检验
WOSA(Windows Open Services Architecture) Windows开放服务系统体系结构
Wosac (Worldwide synchronization of atomic clocks) 世界同步原子钟
WOUDE (Wait-On-User-Defined Event) 等待用户定义事件
woven-fiber optics 编织纤维光学
wow and flutter 抖晃,颤动和抖动
WP(Word Processor) 文字处理机
WP(Workspace Pointer) 工作区指针
WPI(World Patent Index) 世界专利索引 「数
WPM(Words Per Minute) 每分钟字
WPS (Windows Printing System) Windows打印系统
WPS(Word Processing System) 文字处理系统(金山) 「数
WPS(Words Per Second) 每秒钟字
WPS 97 文字处理软件(金山,1997年)
WPS 2000 文字处理软件(金山,1999年)
WR(WRite) 写
WRAM(Windows RAM) 视窗内存
WRAM System(Wide-range Recording And Monitoring System) 广域记录与监视系统
wrap 弯曲,翘曲
wrap-around 返转,环绕式处理
wrap-around error 缠绕误差
wrap-around memory 环绕存储器
wrap-around storage 环绕存储器
wrap-around type 环绕类型
wrap capability 绕回能力,回接能力
wrap count 轮询计数
wrap prompt 换行提示符

wrap test 轮回测试
wrap text 文字换行
wrap title 标题换行
wrap word 自动换行
wrapage 卷曲,翘曲
wraparound 环绕,回绕,环绕式处理
wraparound computing 环绕式计算
wrappable 可自动换行的
wrapped connection 绕接法
wrapper class (C语言)传接类
wrapping 环绕,绕接
wrapup 收卷装置
wrapup procedure 收卷过程
WRC(Workstation Resource Center) 工作站资源中心
WREN WREN系列硬盘驱动器(CDC)
wrench 扳手
wrist 机械腕;手腕
wrist socket 腕座
writability 可写性,易写性
writable character 可写字符
writable character generation module (WCGM) 可写字符生成模块
writable control memory 可写控制存储器
writable control storage(WCS) 可写控制存储器
writable control storage firmware 可写控制存储器固件
writable control storage programming 可写控制存储器编程 「器
writable control store 可写控制存储
writable diagnostic control store 可写诊断控制存储器
writable information 可写信息
write(WR) 写,写入
write access key 写存取键
write access type 写存取类型
write address counter 写地址计数器
write addressing 写寻址
write after read 读后写
write allocate 写定位,写分配
write back 写回
write back cache 回写式高速缓存
write-black engine 写字机
write break point 写入断点
write buffer 写缓冲器

write bus 写总线
write cache 写盘高速缓存
write clock pulse 写时钟脉冲
write conflict 写冲突
write control 写控制
write control character 写控制字符
write control character reset 写控制字符复位
write count register 写计数寄存器
write current 写电流
write current down 写电流减小
write cycle 写周期
write cycle time 写周期时间
write data 写数据
write down 记下,记录
write drive winding 写驱动绕组
write driver 写驱动器
write enable 写使能,写允许
write enable ring 写保护环
write font 写字体
write forward 正向写入
write gap scatter 写入间隙离散
write gap skew 写入间隙扭斜
write gate 写选通门
write gating 写选通
write head 写磁头
write head stack 写磁头组
write in 写入
write in cache 写入高速缓冲器
write inhibit 写禁止
write-inhibit ring 禁写环
write instruction 写指令
write interval 写间隔
write-into memory port 写入存储器端口
write into ROM 写入只读存储器
write key 写关键字
write key field 写关键字字段
write latency 写等待时间
write line 写入行
write line command 写入行命令
write lockout 写封锁
write magnetic tape 写入磁带
write-once optical disk 一次性写入光盘
write-once read-many(WORM) 一次写入多次读出
write only 仅写,只写
write-only memory 只写存储器

write operation 写入操作
write out 写出
write pen register 光笔记录寄存器
write permit ring 允写环
write precompensation 写预补偿
write protect 写保护
write protect error 写保护错误
write-protect label 写保护标记
write protect notch 写保护缺口
write protect signal 写保护信号
write protect tab 写保护贴片
write protection 写保护
write protection ring 写保护环
write pulse 写脉冲
write rate 写速率
write read head 读写头
write recovery time 写入恢复时间
write ring 写环
write signal 写入信号
write skew (磁头)写入扭斜
write statement 写语句
write tape mark 写磁带标记
write through 写直达
write through cache 直写式高速缓存
write time 写时间
write-to-operator(WTO) 写给操作员
write-to-operator with reply(WTOR) 写给操作员的回答
write-to-read crossfeed 写读串扰
write-up 写完
write-while-read 同时读写
write winding 写入绕组
write-write association 写-写相关
writer 记录器;输出程序
writing circuit 写电路
writing gun 写入电子枪
writing machine 书写机
writing phase 编写阶段;写入阶段
writing position 写入位置
writing rate 写速率
writing speed 写速度
writing tablet 数据输入板
writing task 写任务
writing-while-reading 同时读写式
written form of order 指令的书写形式
written-out program 输出程序,写出程序
written PROM 已写 PROM

written record 已写记录
wrong 故障,错误
wrong disk 坏盘
wrong response 错误响应
WRT(WRiTe) 写,写入
WRY(Who-Are-You) 询问字符,谁
WS(Work Station) 工作站
WSI(Wafer Scale Integration) 圆片级集成
WSP(Work Simplification Program) 工作简化程序
WST(Word Synchronizing Track) 字同步轨道
WST(World Service Television) 世界服务电视(网)
WSUPDATE (NetWare)工作站更新
WSUPGRD (NetWare)工作站升级
WSUS(Wang System Users Society) 王安系统用户协会
WT(WaiT) 等候,等待
WT(Walk Through) 预排,预演
Wt(Watt) 瓦特
WT(WeighT) 权,加权;重量
WT(Word Terminal) 字终端

WTS(Windows Terminal Server) Windows 终端服务器
WTS(Wireless Transport Service) 无线传输服务
WUF(Where Used File) (询问字符)哪里使用的文件
WWW(World Wide Wait) 干等网(对因特网的一种讥讽称呼)
WWW(World Wide Waste) 白费网(对因特网的一种讥讽称呼)
WWW(World Wide Web) 万维网
WWW(World Wide Worry) 干着急网(对因特网的一种讥讽称呼)
WWW Network(World Weather Watch Network) 世界气象监测网络
WXmodem(Window Xmodem) 视窗Xmodem 协议
wye junction Y 形[星形]连接
wye rectifier circuit Y 型[星形]整流电路
WYSIWYG(What You See Is What You Get) 所见即所得
WYSIWYW(What You See Is What You Write) 所见即所印

X x

X(X axis) X 坐标,X 轴
X(eXchange) 交换;交换机
X.1 数据通信公用数据网络(以下简称公用网)中的国际用户服务等级
X.2 公用网中的国际用户设备
X.3 公用网中的限定信息包收集器/分离器(PAD)
X.4 公用网中传输数据的国际字母表第五号编码信号的一般结构
X.20 公用网中起止式传输服务的数据终端装置和数据线路端接装置之间的接口
X.20 bis 公用网中起止式传输服务的数据终端装置和数据线路端接装置之间 V 系列建议的相容接口
X.21 公用网中为同步运行的数据终端装置和数据电路端接装置之间的相容接口

X.21 bis 公用网中的数据终端装置与同步 V 系增的调制解调器对接
X.22 数据通信用户等级为 3～6 的复接数据终端装置和数据线路端接装置之间接口
X.24 公用网中的数据终端装置和数据线路端接装置之间的交换线路定义明细表
X.25 公用网中使用包交换操作方式的数据终端装置和数据线路端接装置之间的接口的推荐标准,1976 年首次公布
X.26 数据通信中具有数据通信领域内集成电路装置的不平衡双流交换线路的电气特性
X.27 数据通信中,具有数据通信领域内集成电路装置的平衡双流交换线路的电气特性

X.28 数据通信中,在同一国家内的公用网上,可存取包装配/拆卸装置的数据终端装置/数据线路端接装置接口的推荐标准,1972年提出

X.29 数据通信中,以信息包形式传输的数据终端装置与包装配/拆卸装置之间控制信息和用户数据的交换规程的推荐标准,1977年提出

X.30 数据通信中,按国际第五号字母表的基本型页式打印机的标准化

X.31 数据通信中,按传输的观点,采用根据国际第五号字母表的200波特起止式数据终端时,数据终端装置和数据线路端接装置之间交换点的特性

X.32 数据通信中,按国际第五号字母表的200波特起止式机用的应答装置

X.33 数据通信中,按国际第五号字母表,为测量起止式机容限用的国际文本标准化

X.40 数据通信移频调制传输系统的标准化,由主群频率分割以扩充电报和数据信道容量

X.50 数据通信各同步数据网络间国际接口多路复用方案的基本参数

X.50 bis 数据通信中,用户信号速率为48kb/s的各同步数据网络间国际接口传输方案的基本参数

X.51 数据通信中,采用10个二进制位包络线结构的各同步数据网络间国际接口多路复用方案的基本参数

X.51 bis 数据通信中,采用10个二进制位包络线结构,用户信号速率为48kb/s的各同步数据网络间国际接口传输方案的基本参数

X.52 数据通信中,不等时信号构成用户同步载体信号的编码方法

X.53 数据通信中,64kb/s国际多路通信链路的信道编号

X.54 数据通信中,64kb/s国际多路通信链路的信道分配

X.60 数据通信同步数据应用的数据用户部分公用信道信号发送

X.61 数据通信中,七号信令数据用户部分

X.70 数据通信中,不等时数据网络间国际通信线路起止式服务的终端和转接控制信号发送系统

X.71 数据通信同步数据网络间国际通信线路上分散终端和转接控制信号发送系统

X.75 数据通信包交换网络间国际通信线路上的终端和转接呼叫控制规程和数据传送系统的推荐标准,又称为X.25网关

X.80 数据通信互换信号发送系统交换数据服务交互工作

X.87 公用网中实现国际用户装置和网络设施的原则和规程

X.92 数据通信公用同步数据网络的假设参考连接法

X.93 数据通信包交换数据传输服务的假设参考连接法

X.95 公用网的网络参数

X.96 公用网中的呼叫进行信号

X.110 数据通信中,同类型交换公用网的国际公用数据服务路径选择原则

X.121 公用网的国际编号计划

X.130 数据通信公用同步网(线路转换)中,呼叫建立与拆线次数的暂定目标

X.132 数据通信交换公用网中国际数据通信服务等级的暂定目标

X.150 数据通信中,X.21协议和X.21协议副页接合的情况下,公用网数据终端装置和数据线路端接装置的测试回路

X.180 数据通信中,国际闭路用户群的管理方案

X.200 数据通信中,开放系统互连(OSI)参考模型各层次服务常规定义的推荐标准,以文档形式加以说明

X.400 国际电子邮件分布系统中,消息如何通过网络传递的推荐标准

X.500 在全球目录系统中查找电子邮件用户的推荐标准,其作用类似于一个世界各国的电话号码本,与X.400一起作用

X.nn X.nn建议CCITT关于数字装置和使用数字信号的公用网连接问题的一个系列推荐标准,另外一个系列推荐标准是V.nn系列

X3 美国国家标准协会(ANSI)下属的计算机与信息处理委员会

X3. 美国国家标准协会(ANSI)关于计算机与信息处理标准的命名法
X3.1 ANSI 关于数据传输的同步信号发送速率的标准。以下皆同
X3.3 流程图符号及其在信息处理中的应用的标准
X3.4 磁墨水字符识别的印字规格的标准
X3.5 磁墨水识别的银行支票规格的标准
X3.6 信息交换用穿孔带代码的标准
X3.9 Fortran FORTRAN 语言
X3.11 信息处理通用纸卡片的规「格
X3.14 信息交换用记录磁带的标准
X3.15 按位串行数据传输时信息交换用 ASCII 码的位排序的标准
X3.16 以 ASCII 码进行按位串行数据通信的字符结构和字符奇偶检测的标准
X3.17 光学字符识别的字符组和印出质量的标准
X3.18 信息交换用一英寸穿孔纸带的标准
X3.19 信息交换用十六分之一英寸穿孔纸带的标准
X3.20 信息交换用一英寸穿孔纸带卷带盘的标准
X3.21 信息交换用十二列穿孔卡的矩形孔的标准
X3.22 信息交换用记录磁带的标准
X3.23 COBOL 程序设计语言的标准
X3.24 串行数据传输用数据处理终端设备和同步数据通信设备之间接界的信号质量的标准
X3.25 以 ASCII 码进行按位并行数据通信的字符结构和字符奇偶检测的标准
X3.26 Hollerith 穿孔卡代码的标准
X3.27 信息交换用磁带标号和文件结构的标准
X3.28 美国国家信息交换标准码(ASCII)的通信控制字符在专用数据通信网络中的使用方法的标准
X3.29 未穿孔的油绝缘穿孔纸带的规格的标准
X3.30 信息交换用日历日期和顺序日期中控制字符的图形表示法的标准
X3.31 信息交换用美国各州的识别码结构的标准
X3.32 美国国家信息交换标准码(ASCII)中控制字符的图形表示法的标准
X3.34 信息交换用穿孔带交换卷筒的标准
X3.36 数据终端装置与数据通信装置间的同步高速数据信号发送速率的标准
X3.37 APT 程序设计语言的标准
X3.38 信息交换用美国各州(包括伦比亚特区)的识别的标准
X3.39 信息交换用记录磁带(记录密度为 1600CPI)的标准
X3.40 信息交换用记录磁带(9 磁道,NRZI 制式,记录密度为 200CPI 或 800CPI)的标准
X3.41 美国国家信息交换标准码(ASCII)的 7 位编码字符组的代码扩充技术的标准
X3.42 信息交换用字符串中的数值表示法的标准「准
X3.43 信息用本地时间表示法的标
X3.44 数据通信系统性能判定的标
X3.45 手写字符组的标准「准
X3.46 未记录的六磁盘组一般特性、物理特性和磁特性的标准
X3.47 信息交换用美国各州已命名的居民区和有关实体的识别符号结构的标准
X3.48 信息交换用盒式磁带(宽度为 0.15 英寸,记录密度 800CPI)的标准「准
X3.49 光学字符识别用字符组的标
X3.50 美国常用单位制、国际单位制和行将用于有限字符组系统中其他单位制的表示的标准
X3.51 信息交换用世界时,地区时差和美国时区基准的表示法的标准
X3.52 未记录单个卡式磁盘(正面装)的一般要求、物理要求和磁性要求的标准
X3.53 PL/1 程序设计语言的标准
X3.54 信息交换用记录磁带(记录密度为 6250CPI,群码记录)的标准
X3.55 信息交换用未记录卡式磁带(4 磁道,宽度 0.25 英寸,记录密度

1600BPI,相位编码)的标准
X3.56 信息交换用已记录卡式磁带(4磁道,宽度0.25英寸,记录密度1600BPI,相位编码)的标准
X3.57 在数据通信系统控制中采用美国国家信息交换标准码的信息交换报头格式编辑结构的标准
X3.58 未记录11盘组的一般要求、物理要求和磁性要求的标准
X3.59 信息交换用盒式磁带(宽度为0.15英寸)的标准
X3.60 程序设计语言"最小BASIC"的标准
X3.61 信息交换用地理位置表示的标准
X3.62 光学字符识别系统用纸的标准
X3.63 未记录的12磁盘组的推荐标准
X3.64 用于ANSII的附加控制器的标准
X3.66 先进数据通信控制过程(AD-CCP)的标准
X3.67 输入/输出信道接口的推荐标准
X3.68 功率控制接口的推荐标准
X3.69 公用数据网络的通用接口DTE/DCE的推荐标准
X3.70 代表主要地理政治区域划分的推荐标准
X3.71 单盒式磁带(顶端装入)的推荐标准
X3.72 四分之一英寸并行记录盒式磁带的推荐标准
X3.73 单面软磁盘的推荐标准
X3.74 程序设计语言PL/1的通用子集的推荐标准
X3.75 磁带子系统操作规划的推荐标准
X3.76 单盒式磁盘(顶端装入)的推荐标准
X3.77 信息封装选择字符的推荐标准
X3.78 垂直滑架定位字符的推荐标准
X3.79 系统性能量度的推荐标准
X3.80 盒式软磁盘驱动器及其主控制器之间接口的推荐标准
X3.81 回转的大容量存储系统操作规则的推荐标准
X3.82 单面单密度的未格式化5.25英寸软磁盘的推荐标准
X3.83 按照ISO2375由美国草拟的ISO注册手续的推荐标准
X3.84 未格式化的12磁盘组的推荐标准
X3.85 1.5英寸磁带互换和自装入的推荐标准
X3.86 光学字符识别非读出墨水的推荐标准
X3.87 一种信息交换数据描述文件的推荐标准
X3.89 未记录单面双密度盒磁盘的推荐标准
X3A1 光学字符识别委员会(ANSI,以下皆同)
X3A7 磁墨水字符识别委员会
X3B1 磁带委员会
X3B2 打孔媒体委员会
X3B3 打孔卡片委员会
X3B5 盒式、卡式磁带委员会
X3B6 仪器磁带委员会
X3B7 可互换磁盘媒体委员会
X3B8 可互换软磁盘媒体委员会
X3J1 PL/1语言委员会
X3J2 BASIC语言委员会
X3J3 FORTRAN语言委员会
X3J4 COBOL语言委员会
X3J7 APT语言委员会
X3J8 ALGOL语言委员会
X3J9 PASCAL语言委员会
X3J11 C语言委员会
X3K1 规划文件编制委员会
X3K2 流程图委员会
X3K5 术语和词汇委员会
X3K6 网络规划管理委员会
X3L2 字符代码委员会
X3L5 标号委员会
X3L8 数据元素表示委员会
X3S3 数据通信委员会
X3T9 输入/输出标准委员会
X4 办公用计算机和供应品委员会
X10.4 X Window 10.4版本
X11/AT X Window 11/AT版本
X11R3 X Window 11R3版本
X11R4 X Window 11R4版本
X11R5 X Window 11R5版本
X-60Tr system X-60Tr系统

X86 CPU X86 系列 CPU(兼容 8086 指令系统的 CPU 产品,如 Intel 486,Pentium,AMD K5,K6 等)
X address X 地址,水平地址
X architecture X 架构(IBM 关于多种成熟技术集成应用的构想)
X axis X 轴,横轴
X axis amplifier X 轴放大器
X axis input X 轴输入
X-band X 波段
X-band Communications Transponder (XCT) X 波段通信应答机
X-band radar X 波段雷达
X-bar X 芯片
X-based desktop 基于 X 窗口的桌面管理程序
X-based graphic-user interface 基于 X 的图形用户接口
X button 关闭按钮
X client X 客户
X Consortium X 集团
X cut X 切割
X-datum line X-基准线
X deflection 水平偏转
X deflection angle 水平偏转角度
X deflection sensitivity 水平偏转灵敏度
X direction 横轴方向
X edit descriptor X 编辑描述符
X environment X 环境
X-extent 窗口宽度
X fusion 多业务(通信、计算机等)融合
X guide X 形波导
X-height X 高度
X index register X 变址寄存器
X-intercept X 截距
X multiscreen workstation X 多屏工作站
X network transparency X 网络透明性
X-off 关闭发送器
X-on 打开发送器
X/OPEN X/OPEN 组织
X-particle X 粒子
X. PC X. PC 协议
X Portable Character Set X 可移植字符集
X protocol X 协议
X-ray X 射线
X-ray diffraction X 射线衍射法
X-ray machine X 光机
X-ray tube X 射线管
X-series of recommendation of CCITT 国际电报电话咨询委员会的 X 系列建议
X Server X 服务器
X-Stream X 数据流
X-System X 系统
X Terminal X 终端
X Toolkit X 工具箱
X-tree X 树
X Vision X Vision 窗口软件
X window X 窗口系统
X window environment X 窗口环境
X window structure X 窗口结构
X-Y coordinate CRT display X-Y 坐标阴极射线管显示器
X-Y plotter X-Y 绘图仪,平面绘图机
X-Y plotter control unit 平板绘图机控制装置
X-Y recorder 平板记录器
X-Y scanner 平板扫描仪
X-Y table X-Y 工作台
XA(Cross-Assembler) 交叉汇编程序
XA(Transmission Adapter) 传输适配器
Xanadu Xanadu 计划
Xbase Xbase 语言
XBM(eXtended Basic Mode) 扩充基本方式
XCH(exchange) 交换,交换机
XCMD(eXternal CoManD) 外部命令
XCON XCON 专家系统
XCOPY (DOS)XCOPY 命令
XCS(Xerox Computer Services) XEROX 计算机服务
XCU(Crosspoint Control Unit) 交叉点控制单元
XCU(Transmission Control Unit) 传输控制单元
XD(eXecute with Delay) 延迟执行
XDOS XDOS 翻译器
XDR(Extended Dynamic Range) 扩展动态范围(三星)
XDSL(Any Digital Subscriber Link) 任何数字用户线
XENIX XENIX 操作系统(微软)
XENIX boot XENIX 引导程序

XENIX kernel XINEX 内核
XENIX operating system XENIX 操作系统
XENIX partition XENIX 分区
XENIX prompt XENIX 提示符
XENIX root XENIX 根
XENIX swap area XENIX 交换区
xenon 氙
xenon arc lamp 氙弧灯
xenon flash 氙闪光灯
xenon flash lamp 氙闪光灯
xenon lamp 氙灯
Xeon 至强处理器(Intel)
xerocopy 静电复印
xerographic printer 静电打印机
xerography 静电复印
Xerox 施乐公司(美)
xerox 静电复印机
Xerox computer services 施乐计算机业务
Xerox Data System(XDS) 施乐数据管理系统
Xerox Network Service(XNS) 施乐网络服务
Xerox Telecommunications Network(XTEN) 施工乐远程通信网络
Xerox Venture Publisher Xerox 标准桌面印刷系统
xeroxing 静电复印
XFC(eXtended Function Code) 扩充功能码
XFCN(eXternal FunCtioN) 外部函数
XGA(eXtended Graphics Array) 扩充图形阵列显示标准(IBM)
XGML XGML 文本处理软件
XIC(Transmission Interface Converter) 传输接口转换器
XID(eXchange IDentification) 交换标识，交换标志
XID frame XID 帧
Xing MPEG Player Xing MPEG 解压缩软件
XIO(eXecute Input/Output) 执行输入/输出指令
XIT(eXtra Input Terminal) 附加输入终端
XL(eXecution Language) 执行语言

Xlib Xlib 程序库
XLISP XLISP 语言
XLL(eXtensible Linking Language) 可扩展链接语言
XLT(Transaction List Table) 交易列表
XM(eXpanded Memory) 扩充内存
XMAEM(eXtended Memory Adapter EMulation) 扩展内存适配板模拟
Xmass-tree sorting 圣诞树排序
XMI XMI 总线
XML(eXtensible Markup Language) 可扩展标记语言
Xmod(eXperimental module) 试验性模块
Xmodem Xmodem 协议
Xmodem-CRC Xmodem-CRC 协议
XMOS(high-speed metal oxid semiconductor) 高速金属氧化物半导体
XMS(eXtended Memory Specification) 扩展内存规范
XMS memory XMS 内存
XN(eXecution Node) 执行节点
XNOR(eXclusive NOR) 异或非
XNOR gate 异或非门
XNS/ITP(Xerox Network System/Internet TransPort) 施乐网络系统/网际传送
XNT(Transmit) 传输，发送
XODIAC XODIAC 网络管理系统
Xodiac system Xodiac 系统
XON/XOFF handshaking XON/XOFF 联络
XON/XOFF protocol XON/XOFF 协议
XOR 异或运算
XOR matrix(XORM) 异或阵列
XPERT XPERT 软件工具
XPL XPL 语言
XPLAN(eXPLANation) 解释，说明
XPN(eXternal Priority Number) 外部优先权号
XPSW (eXternal Processor Status Word) 外部处理机状态字
XPT(crosspoint) 交叉点
XPT(eXternal Page Table) 外部页表
XR(eXternal Reset) 外部复位
XR(indeX Register) 索引寄存器

XREF(Cross-reference) 交叉参考
XS-3(eXcess three) 余三码
XS-3 code 余三码
XSEL XSEL 专家系统
XSL(eXtensible Style Language) 可扩展式样语言
XSP(eXtanded Set Processor) 扩充指令集处理器
xStream DSP （彩色激光打印机）x 流数字信号处理技术(TI)
XT(Cross Talk) 串扰,串音
XT(eXecute Time) 执行时间
XTAL(Crystal) 晶体
xterm X终端仿真窗口程序
xterm window X终端仿真窗口
XTR(Transmitter) 发送器,发信机
XTRAN(Experimental Translator) 实验性翻译程序
Xtree Xtree 系统程序
XTSI(eXtended Task Status Index) 扩展任务状态索引
Xview Xview 工具箱
XVT(eXpanded Virtual Toolbox) 可扩展的虚工具箱
XXX(International Urgency Signal) 国际紧急信号
XY-cut crystal XY 切割晶体
XY loading XY 载入
XY plotter XY 绘图仪
XY recorder XY 坐标记录仪
XY switch XY 接线器,XY 开关
XY switching system XY 交换系统
xylography 木刻版印刷术

Y y

Y 导纳
Y address 垂直地址,Y 地址
Y axis Y 轴,纵坐标
Y axis amplifier Y 轴放大器
Y axis input Y 轴输入
Y-bar Y 芯片
Y/C 亮度/色度信号
Y channel 垂直通道,Y 通道
Y-connection Y 型连接,星形连接
Y cut Y 切割
Y direction 纵轴方向,Y 轴方向
Y-extent 窗口高度
Y index register Y 索引[Y 变址]寄存器
Y network Y 形网络,星形网络
Y-plate 垂直偏转板
Y select input Y 选择输入
Y signal Y 信号,亮度信号
Y2K(Year 2000) 2000 年问题（到 2000 年时因过去用 2 位数表示日期带来的问题）
yacc(yet another compiler compiler) 编译程序的编译程序
Yahoo （因特网搜索引擎）Yahoo 网站(美)
YAI (You And I) YAI 病毒
yard 码;工场,堆放场
yard automatic control system(YACS) 工厂自动控制系统
yaw 回转角
yaw angle 回转角
YEC(Youngest Empty Cell) 最近期空闲单元
Yellow Book 黄皮书
Yellow Page 黄页(因特网商业目录)
Yellow Page service 黄页(电话号码目录)服务
YES/MVS YES/MVS 专家系统
yes or no test 是否[Yes 或 No]测试
yield 合格率;合格品;屈服
yield condition 屈服条件
yield enhancement 成品率提高
yield formula 成品率公式
yield gradient 成品率梯度
yield improvement 成品率改进
yield load(YL) 屈服点荷载
yield map 成品率图
yield point 屈服点;接点;击穿点
yield strength 屈服强度
yield stress 屈服应力
YL(Yield Load) 屈服点荷载

YMCK(Yellow,Magenta,Cyan,Black) 黄紫青黑色系统,YMCK 色系统
YMD(Year/Month/Day) "年/月/日"格式
Ymodem Ymodem 文件传输协议
yoke 磁头组;偏转线圈;磁轭
yon clipping pane 远(后)裁剪平面
yon pane 远平面,后平面
youngest empty cell(YEC) 最近期空闲单元
YP(Yield Point) 屈服点;拐点;击穿点
Yttrium-iron garnet(YIG) 钇铁石榴石
Yttrium system (低轨道卫星通信)钇系统(Motorola)
YUV PAL 彩色电视制式使用的彩色分量格式(Y 代表亮度分量,U,V 分别代表色差分量)
YY/MM/DD(Year/Month/Day) 年/月/日

Z z

Z(impedance) 阻抗
Z-1 Z-1 型计算机
Z-3 Z-3 型计算机
Z-80 development system Z80 开发系统
Z-80 microprocessor Z80 微处理器(Zilog)
Z-8000 microprocessor Z8000 微处理器
Z-80000 microprocessor Z80000 微处理器
Z.100 国际电信联盟(以下皆同)关于功能规格和描述语言的建议
Z.200 CCITT 高级语言(CHILL)
Z.301 CCITT 人机语言介绍
Z.302 描述 MML 语法的对话过程的元语言
Z.311 语法和对话过程的介绍
Z.312 基本格式安排
Z.314 字符集和基本元素
Z.315 输入命令语言语法的规定
Z.316 输出命令语言语法的规定
Z.317 人机对话过程
Z.323 人机交互动作
Z.331 人机接口规定介绍
Z.332 人机接口规定方法论-一般工作过程
Z.333 人机接口规定方法论-工具和方法
Z.334 用户管理
Z.335 路由选择管理
Z.336 话务测量管理
Z.337 网络操作管理
Z.341 术语汇编
Z address Z 地址
Z-axis Z 轴
Z-axis amplifier Z 轴放大器,调辉放大器
Z-buffer Z 缓冲器
Z-buffer algorithm Z 缓冲算法
z-clipping 深度剪裁
Z-bit 零位,空位
Z code Z 编码,Z 密语
Z-disk Z 盘
Z-height Z[小写字母字体的 Z]高度
Z-order 窗口叠放顺序
Z-SUB 零减法指令
Z time Z 时
Z transform Z 变换
zap 擦除,清除
zapf Dingbats Zapf 图形符号集
zatacode 坐标码
zatacoding 重叠编码
ZAW(Zero Administration for Windows) 零管理 Windows 技术
ZB(Zero Beat) 零拍,零差拍
ZBR(Zone Bit Recording) 区位记录法
ZD(Zone Description) 存储区说明
Zener breakdown 齐纳击穿
Zener current 齐纳电流
Zener diode 齐纳[稳压]二极管
Zener effect 齐纳效应
Zener impedance 齐纳阻抗
Zener voltage 齐纳电压

Zener voltage temperature coefficient 齐纳电压温度系数
ZENGIN system 日本全国银行通汇系统
zero 零
zero access 零存取,立即访问
zero access addition 零存取加法
zero access memory 立即访问存储器
zero access storage(ZAS) 立即存取存储器
zero accident(ZA) 无事故的,无意外
zero address 零地址,无地址
zero address code 零地址代码
zero-address computer 零地址计算机
zero address instruction(ZAI) 无地址指令
zero address instruction format 零地址指令格式
zero address order 零地址指令
zero adjust 调零,零位调整
zero adjusted 调整到零的,零点调整
zero adjustment 零位[零点]调整
Zero Administration for Windows (ZAW) 零管理 Windows 技术(微软)
zero and add(AD) 清零与相加指令
zero balance 零平衡
zero beat 零拍,零差拍
zero bias 零偏压,零偏置
zero bit 零位
zero blanking 消零
zero branch 零转移,零分枝
zero byte 零字节
zero center 零位中心,汇接局
zero charge 零电荷
zero check circuit 零校验电路
zero check routine 零校验程序
zero circuit 零电路,零线路
Zero Committed Information Rate(0CIR) 零承诺信息速率
zero complement 补码
zero compression 零压缩,消零
zero condition 零状态;零条件
zero control current residual voltage 零控制电流残留电压
zero correction 零位校正
zero count interrupt 零计数中断,数零中断

zero-cross detection 零点[过零]检测
zero-cross detector 过零点检测器
zero cross signal 过零信号
zero cross switch circuit 过零翻转电路
zero crossing detection 过零检波
zero-crossing detector 过零检测器
zero crossover 零交叉,过零
zero destination address 零目标地址
zero-detection circuit 零点检测电路
zero-detection operation 零点检测操作
zero dimension set 零维集合
zero disparity binary code 零不均等二进制码
zero-disparity code 不均零码
zero-division 零除法
zero drift 零点漂移
zero drift error 零点漂移误差
zero element 零元素;零单元
zero elimination 消零
zero energy entropy 零能熵
zero-entropy source 零熵源
zero error 零误差
zero-error reference 零误差基准
zero extended 零扩充,零扩展
zero field residual voltage 零磁场残留电压
zero field residual voltage temperature drift 零磁场残留电压温度漂移
zero fill 零填充
zero flag 零标记,零标志
zero-force connector 无插拔力接插件
zero frame 零帧
zero free region 无零点区域
zero game 零博弈
zero-gate-voltage drain current 零栅电压漏电流
zero gravity 零重力,失重
zero hold 零保持
zero input 零输入
zero insertion 零插入
zero kill 零消除,消零
zero-knowledge proof 零知识证明
zero label 零标号
zero-length buffer 零长度缓冲器
zero-length string 零长度字符串
zero level 零电平;零级
zero-level address 零级地址

zero-level addressing 零级寻址
zero level comma 零层逗号
zero-level transmission reference point 零电平传输参考点
zero marker 零标记符
zero mask 零屏蔽
zero-match gate "或非"门
zero matrix 零矩阵
zero memory channel 零记忆信道
zero-minus call 零减呼叫,零负呼叫
zero modulation(ZM) 调零,零调制
zero offset 零位偏差;零点补偿
zero operator 零运算元,零算符
zero-order hold 零阶[零级]保持
zero-page addressing 零页寻址,零页面访问
zero page instruction 零页面指令
zero-phase current transformer 零相变流器
zero-phase-shift 零相移
zero-phase-shift filter 零相移滤波器
zero-place function 零位函词
zero-place predicate 零位谓词
zero-plus call 零正呼叫
zero point 零点
zero point error 零点误差
zero potential 零电位,零电势
zero power level 零功率电平
zero proof 零证明法,零检查
zero properties for orthogonal polynomial 正交多项式的零点性质
zero reader 零位读出器
zero redundancy memory 无冗余内存
zero relative level 零相对电平
zero repeat factor 零重复因子
zero replacement editing 零置换编辑
zero reset 零复位,零位复位
zero ring 零环,零循环
zero scan 零扫描
zero sequence 零序列
zero shift 零移位
zero signal zone 零信号区
zero-slot LAN 不占扩充槽的局域网络
zero state 零状态
zero status 零状态
zero status flag 零状态标记[标志]
zero-sum game 零和博弈
zero-sum two-person game 二人零和博弈
zero suppress 零抑制,消零
zero suppression 消零,零抑制
zero-suppression character 消零字符
zero synchronization 零点同步化,原点同步;零对准
zero transfer function 零传输函数
zero transmission level reference point 零传输电平参考点
zero valued base 零值底,底数零值
zero valued exponent 零值指数
zero vector 零向量,零矢量
zero wait accessing 零等待存取
zero wait state 零等待状态
zero wander 零点漂移
zero word 零字
zeroes 零点
zerography 静电印刷术
zeroing 置零;调零,零位调整
zeroing block of storage 置零存储块
zeroize 填零,补零,零填充
ZFS(Zone Field Selection) 区段选择
ZGP(Please Give Priority) 请给予优先权
ZI(Zero Input) 零输入
ZIF(Zero Insertion Force) 零插拔力
ZIF socket 零插拔力插座
Ziff-Davis Ziff-Davis出版公司
zigzag 锯齿形的,折叠的,盘旋的
zigzag paper 折叠式打印纸
Zilog Zilog公司(微处理器)
zinc 锌
zinc oxide 氧化锌
ZIP(Zone Information Protocol) 区域信息协议
zip code 邮政区域码(美国,5位)
Zip Drive Zip驱动器(Iomega)
Zipf law 齐夫定律
ZipFolders ZipFolders文件压缩工具
Zipped file (Zip格式)压缩文件
Zmodem Zmodem协议
ZO(Zero Output) 零输出
ZOC(Zone Operation Control) 区域操作控制
zoetrope 活动画片
zombie process 僵进程
zonal sampling 区域抽样[采样]
zone 区段,区域

zone bit 区段位,区域位,标志位	zoned sign 区位式符号
zone bit recording(ZBR) 区位记录技术,准等线密度技术	zoning 区域制,分区制
zone boundary 区域边界	Zoo 自由软件压缩程序
zone center 电话区域交换中心	zoom 图像缩放;图形变化比
zone composition 分区组成系统	zoom blimp 变焦距隔音罩
zone coverage 区域覆盖	zoom box 伸缩框
zone curve 距限曲线	zoom control 缩放控制,显示比例
zone digit 区段数字;分区数字	zoom down 镜头移远,图像缩小
zone distance 区间距离	zoom drive 变焦距驱动器
zone division 区域划分	zoom factor 缩放系数
zone indicator 区域指示器	zoom finder 变焦距取景器
zone leveling 区域平均法	zoom icon 最小化的图标
zone metering system 分区计量法,按区统计制	zoom in 镜头移近,图像放大
	zoom lens 调焦[变焦距]镜头
zone of action 作用区	zoom out 镜头移远,图像缩小
zone of ambiguity 不定区,模糊区	zoom out option 缩放选项
zone of authority 授权区	zoom page width 满页宽缩放
zone of saturation 饱和区	Zoom Smart Scaling Technology 智能化比例缩放技术(HP)
zone of silence 静区	
zone position indicator(ZPI) 分区位置指示符	zoom table 速查表
	zoom to fit in window 缩放到满窗口大小
zone-setting 区域设置	
zone station 地区电话局	zoom tool 缩放工具
zone switching center (电话)区域交换中心	zoom up 镜头移近,图像放大
	zoomed port video(ZPV) 变焦通道视频
zone system 区域制,分区制	zoomer lens 可变焦距透镜
zone time(ZT) 区域时间,分区时间	zooming 渐进定标;图像缩放
zone tracking(ZT) 区段跟踪	ZPI(Zone Position Indicator) 分区位置指示符
zone width 分区[区段]宽度	
zoned decimal 区段式十进制数	ZS(Zero Suppression) 零抑制,消零
zoned decimal number format 分区十进制数格式	ZT(Zone Time) 分区时间,区域时间
	Zulu time 格林威治时间
zoned field 区位字段	Zuse 楚泽德国科学家(1910~1995),1938年发明了世界上第一台机电式数字计算机
zoned format 分区[区段]格式	